Worldmark
Encyclopedia of
Cultures and
Daily Life

Worldmark
Encyclopedia of
Cultures and
Daily Life

VOLUME 4 Asia & Oceania
Second Edition

Editors

Timothy L. Gall and Jeneen Hobby

GALE
CENGAGE Learning™

Detroit • New York • San Francisco • New Haven, Conn • Waterville, Maine • London

GALE
CENGAGE Learning™

Worldmark Encyclopedia of Cultures and Daily Life, Second Edition

Editors: Timothy L. Gall and Jeneen Hobby

Product Management: Julia Furtaw and Carol Nagel

Manufacturing: Rita Wimberley

Gale
27500 Drake Rd.
Farmington Hills, MI 48331-3535

ISBN 978-1-4144-4882-4 (set)
ISBN 978-1-4144-4883-1 (vol. 1)
ISBN 978-1-4144-4890-9 (vol. 2)
ISBN 978-1-4144-4891-6 (vol. 3)
ISBN 978-1-4144-4892-3 (vol. 4)
ISBN 978-1-4144-6430-5 (vol. 5)

ISSN 0196-2809

© 2009 Gale, Cengage Learning

For product information and technology assistance, contact us at Gale Customer Support, 1-800-877-4253.
For permission to use material from this text or product, submit all requests online at www.cengage.com/permissions.
Further permissions questions can be emailed to permissionrequest@cengage.com

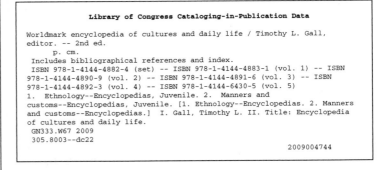

Library of Congress Cataloging-in-Publication Data

Worldmark encyclopedia of cultures and daily life / Timothy L. Gall, editor. -- 2nd ed.
        p. cm.
  Includes bibliographical references and index.
  ISBN 978-1-4144-4882-4 (set) -- ISBN 978-1-4144-4883-1 (vol. 1) -- ISBN 978-1-4144-4890-9 (vol. 2) -- ISBN 978-1-4144-4891-6 (vol. 3) -- ISBN 978-1-4144-4892-3 (vol. 4) -- ISBN 978-1-4144-6430-5 (vol. 5)
1. Ethnology--Encyclopedias, Juvenile. 2. Manners and customs--Encyclopedias, Juvenile. [1. Ethnology--Encyclopedias. 2. Manners and customs--Encyclopedias.] I. Gall, Timothy L. II. Title: Encyclopedia of cultures and daily life.
  GN333.W67 2009
  305.8003--dc22
                                        2009004744

This title is also available as an e-book.
ISBN: 978-1-4144-4893-0
Contact your Gale sales representative for ordering information.

Printed in the United States of America
1 2 3 4 5 6 7 13 12 11 10 09

CONTENTS

Contributors vii
Country Index xi
Preface xxi

For entries on the Acehnese through Kuwaitis *see* Vol. 3

Kyrgyz 543
Lao 548
Lebanese 553
Lepchas 559
Li 564
Lingayats 567
Ma'dan (Marsh Arabs) 571
Madurese 575
Malays in Indonesia 580
Malaysian Chinese 585
Malaysian Indians 590
Malaysian Malays 595
Man (Manchus) 602
Manggarai 606
Mangyan (Hanuno'o group) 610
Manuvu' (Upland Bagobo) 615
Maori 619
Maranao 623
Marāthas 627
Maronites 632
Melanesians 635
Melpa 639
Miao in china 642
Micronesians 647
Minahasans 650
Minangkabau 654
Minas 659
Mongols in China 664
Mons 669
Moro 673
Motu 679
Mountain Mon-Khmer groups 682
Mundas 688
Muslims in South Asia 693
Naga 699
Naxi 705
Negrito (Pinatubo Aeta group) 710
Nepālis 714
New Caledonians 721
New Zealanders 724
Newars 729
Ngaju Dayak 733
Niasans 738
Nicobarese 742

Ni-Vanuatu 747
Omanis 750
Orang Asli 756
Oraons 760
Oriya 766
Pakistanis 770
Palestinians 777
Pamiri 785
Parsis 789
Pashtun 795
Penan 799
Polynesians 803
Punjabis 807
Qataris 813
Rājasthānis 818
Rajputs 825
Rakhines 832
Rohingyas 836
Sa'dan Toraja 840
Samoans 844
Santals 848
Sasak 854
Saudis 859
Shans 866
Sherpas 871
Sikhs 877
Sindhis 882
Sinhalese 888
South Koreans 893
Sri Lankans 898
Sumbanese 903
Sumbawans 908
Sundanese 911
Syrian Christians in India 916
Syrians 920
Tagbanua 926
Tahitians 930
Taiwan Indigenous Peoples 934
Tajiks 940
Tamils 946
Tao 951
Tausug 957
T'boli 962
Thai 966
Tibetans 972
Timorese 977
Todas 981
Tongans 986
Traditional Orthodox Jews 990
Tujia 995

Turkmens 998
Turks 1004
Uighurs 1010
Uzbeks 1014
Veddas 1020
Vietnamese 1025
Vietnamese Highlanders 1032
Yao 1039

Yazidis 1043
Yemenis 1046
Yi. 1052
Zhuang. 1056

Glossary. 1061
Subject Index. 1073

STAFF

Editors: Timothy L. Gall and Jeneen Hobby

Senior Editors: Daniel M. Lucas

Associate Editors: Susan Bevan Gall, Caitlin Corrigan, Karen Ellicott, Alexander Barnes

Copy Editors: Deborah Baron, Janet Fenn, Mary Anne Klasen, Patricia M. Mote, Deborah Ring, Kathy Soltis, Rosalie Wieder

Typesetting and Graphics: Brian Rajewski, Daniel Mehling

Data Input: Janis K. Long, Maggie Lyall, Cheryl Montagna, Tajana G. Roehl, Karen Seyboldt, Kira Silverbird

Proofreaders: Deborah Baron, Janet Fenn

Editorial Assistants: Katie Baron, Jennifer A. Spencer, Daniel K. Updegraff

ADVISORS

CATHY BOND. Librarian, Conestoga Senior High School, Berwyn, Pennsylvania.

MARION CANNON. Librarian, Winter Park High School, Winter Park, Florida.

KELLY JONS. Librarian, Shaker Heights High School, Shaker Heights, Ohio.

JOHN RANAHAN. High School Teacher, International School, Manila, Philippines.

NANCY NIEMAN. Middle School Teacher, Delta Middle School, Muncie, Indiana.

VOLUME INTRODUCTIONS

RHOADS MURPHEY. Emeritus Professor of History, University of Michigan.

JAMES L. NEWMAN. Professor, Department of Geography, Maxwell School of Citizenship and Public Affairs, Syracuse University.

ARNOLD STRICKON. Professor Emeritus, Department of Anthropology, University of Wisconsin.

ROGER WILLIAMS WESCOTT. Emeritus Professor of Anthropology and Linguistics, Drew University.

CONTRIBUTORS AND REVIEWERS

ANDREW J. ABALAHIN. Assistant Professor of History, San Diego State University.

JAMAL ABDULLAH. Doctoral candidate, Department of City and Regional Planning, Cornell University.

SANA ABED-KOTOB. Editor, Middle East Institute.

MAMOUD ABOUD. Charge d'Affaires, a.i., Embassy of the Federal and Islamic Republic of the Comoros.

JUDY ALLEN. BISHINIK Editor, Choctaw Nation of Oklahoma.

THERESA ALT. Independent Researcher, Ithaca, New York

IS EXCELLENCY DENIS G. ANTOINE. Ambassador to the United States, Embassy of Grenada.

LESLEY ANN ASHBAUGH. Instructor, Sociology, Seattle University.

HASHEM ATALLAH. Translator, Editor, Teacher; Fairfax, Virginia.

HECTOR AZEVES. Cultural Attaché, Embassy of Uruguay.

VICTORIA J. BAKER. Associate Professor of Anthropology, Anthropology (Collegium of Comparative Cultures), Eckerd College.

POLINE BALA. Lecturer, Universiti Malaysia Sarawak.

MARJORIE MANDELSTAM BALZER. Research Professor; Coordinator, Social, Regional, and Ethnic Studies Sociology, and Center for Eurasian, Russian, and East European Studies, Social, Regional, and Ethnic Studies Sociology, and Center for Eurasian, Russian, and East European Studies, Georgetown University.

JOSHUA BARKER. Doctoral candidate, Department of Anthropology, Cornell University.

IGOR BARSEGIAN. Department of Sociology, George Washington University.

IRAJ BASHIRI. Professor of Central Asian Studies, Department of Slavic and Central Asian Languages and Literatures, University of Minnesota.

DAN F. BAUER. Department of Anthropology, Lafayette College.

JOYCE BEAR. Historic Preservation Officer, Muscogee Nation of Oklahoma.

SVETLANA BELAIA. Byelorussian-American Cultural Center, Strongsville, Ohio.

HIS EXCELLENCY DR. COURTNEY BLACKMAN. Ambassador to the United States, Embassy of Barbados.

BETTY BLAIR. Executive Editor, Azerbaijan International.

ARVIDS BLODNIEKS. Director, Latvian Institute, American Latvian Association in the USA.

ARASH BORMANSHINOV. University of Maryland, College Park.

HARRIET I. BRADY. Cultural Anthropologist (Pyramid Lake Paiute Tribe), Native Studies Program, Pyramid Lake High School.

MARTIN BROKENLEG. Professor of Sociology, Department of Sociology, Augustana College.

REV. RAYMOND A. BUCKO, S.J. Assistant Professor of Anthropology, LeMoyne College.

ANNA BERGLUND. Doctoral Candidate, Ecole des Hautes Etudes en Sciences Sociales.

VIRGINIA CLAIRE BREEDLOVE. Doctoral Candidate, Johns Hopkins University.

WAYLES BROWNE. Associate Professor of Linguistics, Cornell University

JOHN W. BURTON. Department of Anthropology, Connecticut College.

DINEANE BUTTRAM. University of North Carolina-Chapel Hill.

RICARDO CABALLERO. Counselor, Embassy of Paraguay.

CHRISTINA CARPADIS. Researcher/Writer, Cleveland, Ohio.

SALVADOR GARCIA CASTANEDA. Department of Spanish and Portuguese, The Ohio State University.

SUSANA CAVALLO. Graduate Program Director and Professor of Spanish, Department of Modern Languages and Literatures, Loyola University, Chicago.

BRIAN P. CAZA. Doctoral candidate, Political Science, University of Chicago.

VAN CHRISTO. President and Executive Director, Frosina Foundation, Boston.

YURI A. CHUMAKOV. Graduate Student, Department of Sociology, University of Notre Dame.

J. COLARUSSO. Professor of Anthropology, McMaster University.

FRANCESCA COLECCHIA. Modern Language Department, Duquesne University.

JUSTIN CORFIELD. Department of History, Geelong Grammar School.

DIANNE K. DAEG DE MOTT. Researcher/Writer, Tucson, Arizona.

CATHARIN DALPINO. Department of Asian Studies, Georgetown University

MICHAEL DE JONGH. Professor, Department of Anthropology, University of South Africa.

GEORGI DERLUGUIAN. Senior Fellow, Ph.D., U. S. Institute of Peace.

CHRISTINE DRAKE. Department of Political Science and Geography, Old Dominion University.

ARTURO DUARTE. Guatemalan Mission to the OAS.

CALEB DUBE. Department of Anthropology, Northwestern University.

BRIAN DU TOIT. Professor, Department of Anthropology, University of Florida.

LEAH ERMARTH. Worldspace Foundation, Washington, DC.

NANCY J. FAIRLEY. Associate Professor of Anthropology, Department of Anthropology/Sociology, Davidson College.

GREGORY A. FINNEGAN, Ph.D. Tozzer Library, Harvard University.

ALLEN J. FRANK, Ph.D.

DAVID P. GAMBLE. Professor Emeritus, Department of Anthropology, San Francisco State University.

FREDERICK GAMST. Professor Emeritus, Department of Anthropology, University of Massachusetts, Harbor Campus.

PAULA GARB. Associate Director of Global Peace and Conflict Studies and Adjunct Professor of Social Ecology, University of California, Irvine.

HAROLD GASKI. Associate Professor of Sami Literature, School of Languages and Literature, University of Tromsø.

STEPHEN J. GENDZIER.

FLORENCE GERDEL.

ANTHONY P. GLASCOCK. Professor of Anthropology; Department of Anthropology, Psychology, and Sociology; Drexel University.

LUIS GONZALEZ. Researcher/Writer, River Edge, New Jersey.

JENNIFER GRAHAM. Researcher/Writer, Sydney, Australia.

MARIE-CÉCILE GROELSEMA. Doctoral candidate, Comparative Literature, Indiana University.

ROBERT GROELSEMA. MPIA and doctoral candidate, Political Science, Indiana University.

MARIA GROSZ-NGATÉ. Visiting Assistant Professor, Department of Anthropology, Northwestern University.

ELLEN GRUENBAUM. Professor, School of Social Sciences, California State University, Fresno.

N. THOMAS HAKANSSON. University of Kentucky.

ROBERT HALASZ. Researcher/Writer, New York, New York.

MARC HANREZ. Professor, Department of French and Italian, University of Wisconsin-Madison.

ANWAR UL HAQ. Central Asian Studies Department, Indiana University.

LIAM HARTE. Department of Philosophy, Loyola University, Chicago.

FR. VASILE HATEGAN. Author, Romanian Culture in America.

BRUCE HEILMAN. Doctoral candidate, Department of Political Science, Indiana University.

JIM HENRY. Researcher/Writer, Cleveland, Ohio.

BARRY HEWLETT. Department of Anthropology, Washington State University.

SUSAN F. HIRSCH. Department of Anthropology, Wesleyan University.

MARIDA HOLLOS. Department of Anthropology, Brown University.

HALYNA HOLUBEC. Researcher/Writer, Cleveland, Ohio.

YVONNE HOOSAVA. Legal Researcher and Cultural Preservation Officer, Hopi Tribal Council.

HUIQIN HUANG, Ph.D. Center for East Asia Studies, University of Montreal.

MARCEL IONESCU-HEROIU. Teaching Assistant, Cornell University

ASAFA JALATA. Assistant Professor of Sociology and African and African American Studies, Department of Sociology, The University of Tennessee, Knoxville.

STEPHEN F. JONES. Russian Department, Mount Holyoke College.

THOMAS JOVANOVSKI, PH.D. Lorain County Community College.

A. KEN JULES. Minister Plenipotentiary and Deputy Head of Mission, Embassy of St. Kitts and Nevis.

GENEROSA KAGARUKI-KAKOTI. Economist, Department of Urban and Rural Planning, College of Lands and Architectural Studies, Dar es Salaam, Tanzania.

EZEKIEL KALIPENI. Department of Geography, University of Illinois at Urbana-Champaign.

DON KAVANAUGH. Program Director, Lake of the Woods Ojibwa Cultural Centre.

SUSAN M. KENYON. Associate Professor of Anthropology, Department of History and Anthropology, Butler University.

ALLA GOLOVINA KHADKA. PhD Candidate, University of Pittsburgh

MARIA GROSZ-NGATÉ. Visiting Associate Director of the African Studies Program, Indiana University.

ADEL ISKANDAR. Center for Contemporary Arab Studies, Georgetown University

ASAFA JALATA. Professor of Sociology, The University of Tennessee, Knoxville.

THOMAS JOVANOVSKI, Ph.D. Lorain County Community College.

EZEKIEL KALIPENI. Associate Professor of Geography, University of Illinois at Urbana-Champaign.

SUSAN M. KENYON. Associate Professor of Anthropology, Butler University.

WELILE KHUZWAYO. Department of Anthropology, University of South Africa.

PHILIP L. KILBRIDE. Professor of Anthropology, Mary Hale Chase Chair in the Social Sciences, Department of Anthropology, Bryn Mawr College.

RICHARD O. KISIARA. Doctoral candidate, Department of Anthropology, Washington University in St. Louis.

SARAH KLUMP. Center for Eurasian, Russian and East European Studies, Edmund A. Walsh School of Foreign Service, Georgetown University .

KAREN KNOWLES. Permanent Mission of Antigua and Barbuda to the United Nations.

MELISSA KERR. Eurasian, Russian, and East European Studies, Georgetown University.

IGOR KRUPNIK. Research Anthropologist, Department of Anthropology, Smithsonian Institution.

LEELO LASS. Secretary, Embassy of Estonia.

ROBERT LAUNAY. Professor, Department of Anthropology, Northwestern University.

BENJAMIN LAZARUS. Eurasian, Russian, and East European Studies, Georgetown University.

CHARLES LEBLANC. Professor and Director, Center for East Asia Studies, University of Montreal.

RONALD LEE. Author, Goddam Gypsy, An Autobiographical Novel.

PHILIP E. LEIS. Professor and Chair, Department of Anthropology, Brown University.

MARIA JUKIC LESKUR. Croatian Consulate, Cleveland, Ohio.

RICHARD A. LOBBAN, JR. Professor of Anthropology and African Studies, Department of Anthropology, Rhode Island College.

DERYCK O. LODRICK. Visiting Scholar, Center for South Asian Studies, University of California, Berkeley.

NEIL LURSSEN. Intro Communications Inc.

GREGORIO C. MARTIN. Modern Language Department, Duquesne University.

HOWARD J. MARTIN. Independent scholar.

HEITOR MARTINS. Professor, Department of Spanish and Portuguese, Indiana University.

ADELINE MASQUELIER. Assistant Professor, Department of Anthropology, Tulane University.

DOLINA MILLAR.

EDITH MIRANTE. Project Maje.

ROBERT W. MONTGOMERY, Ph.D. Indiana University.

THOMAS D. MORIN. Associate Professor of Hispanic Studies, Department of Modern and Classical Literatures and Languages, University of Rhode Island.

CHARLES MORRILL. Doctoral candidate, Indiana University.

CAROL A. MORTLAND. Crate's Point.

FRANCIS A. MOYER. Director, North Carolina Japan Center, North Carolina State University.

MARIE C. MOYER.

NYAGA MWANIKI. Assistant Professor, Department of Anthropology and Sociology, Western Carolina University.

KENNETH NILSON. Celtic Studies Department, Harvard University.

MARTIN NJOROGE. PhD. SRF/UPenn Postdoctoral Fellow, Graduate School of Education, University of Pennsylvania.

JANE E. ORMROD. Graduate Student, History, University of Chicago.

JUANITA PAHDOPONY. Carl Perkins Program Director, Comanche Tribe of Oklahoma.

TINO PALOTTA. Syracuse University.

ROHAYATI PASENG.

PATRICIA PITCHON. Researcher/Writer, London, England.

STEPHANIE PLATZ. Program Officer, Program on Peace and International Cooperation, The John D. and Catherine T. MacArthur Foundation.

MIHAELA POIATA. Graduate Student, School of Journalism and Mass Communication, University of North Carolina at Chapel Hill.

MANSAH PRAH. Dean, Faculty of Social Sciences, University of Cape Coast, Ghana.

LEOPOLDINA PRUT-PREGELJ. Author, Historical Dictionary of Slovenia.

J. RACKAUSKAS. Director, Lithuanian Research and Studies Center, Chicago.

J. RAKOVICH. Byelorussian-American Cultural Center, Strongsville, Ohio.

HANTA V. RALAY. Promotions, Inc., Montgomery Village, Maryland.

SUSAN J. RASMUSSEN. Associate Professor, Department of Anthropology, University of Houston.

RONALD REMINICK. Associate Professor of Anthropology, Cleveland State University.

BRUCE D. ROBERTS. Associate Professor of Anthropology, Department of Anthropology & Earth Science, Minnesota State University, Moorhead.

LAUREL L. ROSE. Philosophy Department, Carnegie-Mellon University.

ROBERT ROTENBERG. Professor of Anthropology, International Studies Program, DePaul University.

CAROLINE SAHLEY, Ph.D. Researcher/Writer, Cleveland, Ohio.

VERONICA SALLES-REESE. Associate Professor, Department of Spanish and Portuguese, Georgetown University.

MAIRA SARYBAEVA. Kazakh-American Studies Center, University of Kentucky.

DEBRA L. SCHINDLER. Institute of Arctic Studies, Dartmouth College.

KYOKO SELDEN, Ph.D. Department of Asian Studies, Cornell University.

ELIZABETH SERLEMITSOS. Chief Advisor, National AIDS Council, Zambia.

ENAYATULLAH SHAHRANI. Central Asian Studies Department, Indiana University.

ROBERT SHANAFELT. Department of Sociology & Anthropology, Georgia Southern University.

TUULIKKI SINKS. Teaching Specialist for Finnish, Department of German, Scandinavian, and Dutch, University of Minnesota.

JAN SJÅVIK. Professor, Scandinavian Studies, University of Washington.

MAGDA SOBALVARRO. Press and Cultural Affairs Director, Embassy of Nicaragua.

PAMELA SODHY. History Department, Georgetown University

MICHAEL STAINTON. Researcher, Joint Center for Asia Pacific Studies, York University.

RIANA STEYN. Department of Anthropology, University of South Africa.

PAUL STOLLER. Professor, Department of Anthropology, West Chester University.

CRAIG STRASHOFER. Researcher/Writer, Cleveland, Ohio.

SANDRA B. STRAUBHAAR. Assistant Professor, Nordic Studies, Department of Germanic and Slavic Languages, Brigham Young University.

DAVID STRAUB. Masters Program in Central Eurasian Studies, Indiana University.

VUM SON SUANTAK. Author, Zo History.

MURAT TAISHIBAEV. Kazakh-American Studies Center, University of Kentucky.

CHRISTOPHER C. TAYLOR. Associate Professor, Anthropology Department, University of Alabama, Birmingham.

FATIMA TLISOVA. Kennedy School at Harvard.

EDDIE TSO. Office of Language and Culture, Navajo Division of Education.

DAVID TYSON. Foreign Broadcast Information Service, Washington, D.C.

NICOLAAS G. W. UNLANDT. Assistant Professor of French, Department of French and Italian, Brigham Young University.

GORDON URQUHART. Professor, Department of Economics and Business, Cornell College.

CHRISTOPHER J. VAN VUUREN. Associate Professor, Department of Anthropology, University of South Africa.

DALIA VENTURA-ALCALAY. Journalist, London, England.

CATHERINE VEREECKE. Assistant Director, Center for African Studies, University of Florida.

CAMILA VERGARA. Journalist, New York.

KORA BATTIG VON WITTLESBACH. Department of Romance Studies at Cornell.

GREGORY T. WALKER. Associate Director, Office of International Affairs, Duquesne University.

GERHARD WEISS. Department of German, Scandinavian, and Dutch, University of Minnesota.

PATSY WEST. Director, The Seminole/Miccosukee Photographic Archive.

WALTER WHIPPLE. Associate Professor of Polish, Germanic and Slavic Languages, Brigham Young University.

ROSALIE WIEDER. Researcher/Writer, Cleveland, Ohio.

JEFFREY WILLIAMS. Professor and Chair, Department of Sociology, Anthropology, & Social Work, Texas Tech University.

KOSTAS YIAVIS. Lecturer in Modern Greek, Cornell University.

GUANG-HONG YU. Associate Research Fellow, Institute of Ethnology, Academia Sinica.

RUSSELL ZANCA. Associate Professor of Anthropology, Northeastern Illinois University.

COUNTRY INDEX

AFGHANISTAN

Afghanis—*Asia & Oceania* 3:16
Balūchī—*Asia & Oceania* 3:97
Brahui—*Asia & Oceania* 3:151
Hazaras—*Asia & Oceania* 3:311
Pashtun—*Asia & Oceania* 4:795
Turkmens—*Asia & Oceania* 4:998
Uzbeks—*Asia & Oceania* 4:1014

ALBANIA

Albanians—*Europe* 5:23
Vlachs—*Europe* 5:514

ALGERIA

Algerians—*Africa* 1:23
Berbers—*Africa* 1:78
Tuaregs—*Africa* 1:548

AMERICAN SAMOA

Samoans—*Asia & Oceania* 4:844

ANDORRA

Andorrans—*Europe* 5:46

ANGOLA

Angolans—*Africa* 1:35
Bakongo—*Africa* 1:51

ANTIGUA AND BARBUDA

Antiguans and Barbudans—*Americas* 2:54

ARGENTINA

Argentines—*Americas* 2:62
Galicians—*Europe* 5:200
Mapuches—*Americas* 2:345

ARMENIA

Armenians—*Europe* 5:50
Kurds—*Asia & Oceania* 3:518
Peoples of the Caucasus—*Europe* 5:373
Yazidis—*Asia & Oceania* 4:1043

AUSTRALIA

Anglo Australians—*Asia & Oceania* 3:49
Australian Aborigines—*Asia & Oceania* 3:66
Roma—*Europe* 5:394

AUSTRIA

Austrians—*Europe* 5:55
Slovenes—*Europe* 5:459
Tyrolese—*Europe* 5:495

AZERBAIJAN

Armenians—*Europe* 5:50
Azerbaijanis—*Asia & Oceania* 3:70
Kurds—*Asia & Oceania* 3:518
People of Dagestan—*Europe* 5:367
Peoples of the Caucasus—*Europe* 5:373

BAHAMAS

Bahamians—*Americas* 2:84

BAHRAIN

Bahrainis—*Asia & Oceania* 3:76
Bedu—*Asia & Oceania* 3:122

BANGLADESH

Banglādeshīs—*Asia & Oceania* 3:102
Bengālīs—*Asia & Oceania* 3:127
Chakmas—*Asia & Oceania* 3:185
Chin—*Asia & Oceania* 3:202
Hindus—*Asia & Oceania* 3:319
Muslims—*Asia & Oceania* 4:693
Santals—*Asia & Oceania* 4:848

BARBADOS

Barbadians—*Americas* 2:89

BELARUS

Belarusans—*Europe* 5:70

BELGIUM

Belgians—*Europe* 5:77
Flemish—*Europe* 5:187
Walloons—*Europe* 5:517

BELIZE

Belizeans—*Americas* 2:94
Garifuna—*Americas* 2:226
Maya—*Americas* 2:355

BENIN

Beninese—*Africa* 1:73
Ewe—*Africa* 1:217
Fulani—*Africa* 1:222
Jola—*Africa* 1:299
Songhay—*Africa* 1:501
Yoruba—*Africa* 1:593

BHUTAN

Bhutanese—*Asia & Oceania* 3:137
Bhutia—*Asia & Oceania* 3:142
Buddhists—*Asia & Oceania* 3:163
Hindus—*Asia & Oceania* 3:319

Lepchas—*Asia & Oceania* 4:559
Muslims—*Asia & Oceania* 4:693

BOLIVIA

Aymara—*Americas* 2:79
Bolivians—*Americas* 2:98
Quechua—*Americas* 2:462

BOSNIA

Bosnians—*Europe* 5:81
Croats—*Europe* 5:135

BOTSWANA

San—*Africa* 1:463

BRAZIL

African Brazilians—*Americas* 2:16
Asháninka—*Americas* 2:70
Brazilians—*Americas* 2:103
Guaranis—*Americas* 2:245
Kayapos—*Americas* 2:327
Tenetehara—*Americas* 2:507
Xavante—*Americas* 2:543

BRUNEI

Bruneians—*Asia & Oceania* 3:155

BULGARIA

Armenians—*Europe* 5:50
Bulgarians—*Europe* 5:91
Vlachs—*Europe* 5:514

BURKINA FASO

Burkinabe—*Africa* 1:85
Dyula—*Africa* 1:167
Fulani—*Africa* 1:222
Mossi—*Africa* 1:395
Tuaregs—*Africa* 1:548

BURMA. SEE MYANMAR

BURUNDI

Burundians—*Africa* 1:90
Hutu—*Africa* 1:277
Tutsi—*Africa* 1:562

CAMBODIA

Cham—*Asia & Oceania* 3:191
Khmer—*Asia & Oceania* 3:495
Mountain Mon-Khmer—*Asia & Oceania* 4:682

CAMEROON

Cameroonians—*Africa* 1:95
Fulani—*Africa* 1:222

CANADA

Amish—*Americas* 2:48
Canadians—*Americas* 2:116
Dakota and Lakota—*Americas* 2:179

French Canadians—*Americas* 2:217
Inuit—*Americas* 2:296
Iroquois—*Americas* 2:304
Native North Americans—*Americas* 2:384
Ojibwa—*Americas* 2:412
Traditional-Orthodox Jews—*Asia & Oceania* 4:990

CAPE VERDE

Cape Verdeans—*Africa* 1:101

CENTRAL AFRICAN REPUBLIC

Aka—*Africa* 1:17
Azande—*Africa* 1:40
Central Africans—*Africa* 1:105

CEYLON *SEE* SRI LANKA

CHAD

Fulani—*Africa* 1:222
Chadians—*Africa* 1:111

CHILE

Aymara—*Americas* 2:79
Chileans—*Americas* 2:124
Mapuches—*Americas* 2:345

CHINA

Bai—*Asia & Oceania* 3:82
Buyi—*Asia & Oceania* 3:181
Chinese National Minorities—*Asia & Oceania* 3:208
Dai—*Asia & Oceania* 3:217
Derong—*Asia & Oceania* 3:225
Dong—*Asia & Oceania* 3:228
Ewenki—*Asia & Oceania* 3:241
Gaoshan—*Asia & Oceania* 3:260
Hakka—*Asia & Oceania* 3:297
Han—*Asia & Oceania* 3:302
Hani—*Asia & Oceania* 3:307
Hmong—*Asia & Oceania* 3:327
Hui—*Asia & Oceania* 3:332
Kachins—*Asia & Oceania* 3:442
Kashmiris—*Asia & Oceania* 3:472
Kazakh Chinese—*Asia & Oceania* 3:479
Korean Chinese—*Asia & Oceania* 3:514
Kyrgyz—*Asia & Oceania* 4:543
Li—*Asia & Oceania* 4:564
Man (Manchus)—*Asia & Oceania* 4:602
Miao—*Asia & Oceania* 4:642
Mongols—*Asia & Oceania* 3:664
Naxi—*Asia & Oceania* 4:705
Shans—*Asia & Oceania* 4:866
Tibetans—*Asia & Oceania* 4:972
Tujia—*Asia & Oceania* 4:995
Tuvans—*Europe* 5:489
Uighurs—*Asia & Oceania* 4:1010
Uzbeks—*Asia & Oceania* 4:1014
Yao—*Asia & Oceania* 4:1039
Yi—*Asia & Oceania* 4:1052
Zhuang—*Asia & Oceania* 4:1056

COLOMBIA

Colombians—*Americas* 2:139
Guajiros—*Americas* 2:241
Páez—*Americas* 2:418
Vaupés—*Americas* 2:530

COMOROS

Comorians—*Africa* 1:134

CONGO, DEMOCRATIC REPUBLIC OF THE

Azande—*Africa* 1:40
Bakongo—*Africa* 1:51
Congolese (Zairians)—*Africa* 1:144
Efe and Mbuti—*Africa* 1:171
Tutsi—*Africa* 1:562
Twa—*Africa* 1:568

CONGO, REPUBLIC OF

Aka—*Africa* 1:17
Bakongo—*Africa* 1:51
Congolese—*Africa* 1:139
Twa—*Africa* 1:568

COSTA RICA

Costa Ricans—*Americas* 2:149

CÔTE D'IVOIRE (IVORY COAST)

Dyula—*Africa* 1:167
Ivoirians—*Africa* 1:294
Malinke—*Africa* 1:375
Mossi—*Africa* 1:395

CROATIA

Croats—*Europe* 5:135

CUBA

Cubans—*Americas* 2:170

CYPRUS

Greek Cypriots—*Asia & Oceania* 3:276

CZECH REPUBLIC

Czechs—*Europe* 5:143

DENMARK

Danes—*Europe* 5:147
Frisians—*Europe* 5:196

DJIBOUT

Djiboutians—*Africa* 1:162

DOMINICA

Dominicans (Dominica)—*Americas* 2:190

DOMINICAN REPUBLIC

Dominicans (Dominican Republic)—*Americas* 2:195

EAST TIMOR

Timorese—*Asia & Oceania* 4:977

ECUADOR

Ecuadorans—*Americas* 2:203
Jivaro—*Americas* 2:323
Quechua—*Americas* 2:462

EGYPT

Bedu—*Asia & Oceania* 3:122
Coptic Christians—*Africa* 1:149
Egyptians—*Africa* 1:177

EL SALVADOR

Maya—*Americas* 2:355
Salvadorans—*Americas* 2:481

EQUATORIAL GUINEA

Equatorial Guineans—*Africa* 1:198

ERITREA

Tigray—*Africa* 1:536
Eritreans—*Africa* 1:203

ESTONIA

Estonians—*Europe* 5:163

ETHIOPIA

Amhara—*Africa* 1:30
Ethiopians—*Africa* 1:210
Fulani—*Africa* 1:222
Nuer—*Africa* 1:431
Oromos—*Africa* 1:449
Tigray—*Africa* 1:536

FIJI

Banias—*Asia & Oceania* 3:108
Fijians—*Asia & Oceania* 3:245
Indo-Fijians—*Asia & Oceania* 3:369

FINLAND

Finns—*Europe* 5:182
Sami—*Europe* 5:430

FRANCE

Armenians—*Europe* 5:50
Basques—*Europe* 5:65
Bretons—*Europe* 5:87
French—*Europe* 5:191

FRENCH GUIANA

French Guianans—*Americas* 2:222

GABON

Gabonese—*Africa* 1:227

GAMBIA, THE

Gambians—*Africa* 1:233
Malinke—*Africa* 1:375

GEORGIA

Abkhazians—*Europe* 5:15
Adjarians—*Europe* 5:19
Armenians—*Europe* 5:50
Georgians—*Europe* 5:205
Karachai—*Europe* 5:250
Ossetians—*Europe* 5:361
People of Dagestan—*Europe* 5:367
Peoples of the Caucasus—*Europe* 5:373

GERMANY

Frisians—*Europe* 5:196
Germans—*Europe* 5:214
Kurds—*Asia & Oceania* 3:518

GHANA

Dyula—*Africa* 1:167
Ewe—*Africa* 1:217
Ghanaians—*Africa* 1:240
Jola—*Africa* 1:299

GREECE

Albanians—*Europe* 5:23
Greeks—*Europe* 5:221
Vlachs—*Europe* 5:514

GRENADA

Grenadians—*Americas* 2:237

GUAM

Micronesians—*Asia & Oceania* 4:647

GUATEMALA

Garifuna—*Americas* 2:226
Guatemalans—*Americas* 2:250
Maya—*Americas* 2:355

GUINEA

Fulani—*Africa* 1:222
Guineans—*Africa* 1:257
Malinke—*Africa* 1:375

GUINEA BISSAU

Malinke—*Africa* 1:375

GUYANA

Guyanans—*Americas* 2:255
Hindus of Guyana—*Americas* 2:276

HAITI

Haitians—*Americas* 2:262

HONDURAS

Garifuna—*Americas* 2:226
Hondurans—*Americas* 2:282
Maya—*Americas* 2:355
Miskito—*Americas* 2:373
Sumu—*Americas* 2:497

HUNGARY

Hungarians—*Europe* 5:225
Slovenes—*Europe* 5:459
Vlachs—*Europe* 5:514

ICELAND

Icelanders—*Europe* 5:229

INDIA

Ahirs—*Asia & Oceania* 3:24
Andamanese—*Asia & Oceania* 3:40
Andhras—*Asia & Oceania* 3:44
Anglo-Indians—*Asia & Oceania* 3:54
Assamese—*Asia & Oceania* 3:62
Banias—*Asia & Oceania* 3:108
Bengālīs—*Asia & Oceania* 3:127
Bhils—*Asia & Oceania* 3:131
Bhutia—*Asia & Oceania* 3:142
Brahmans—*Asia & Oceania* 3:146
Buddhists—*Asia & Oceania* 3:163
Chakmas—*Asia & Oceania* 3:185
Chamars—*Asia & Oceania* 3:197
Chin—*Asia & Oceania* 3:202
Goans—*Asia & Oceania* 3:265
Gonds—*Asia & Oceania* 3:270
Gujaratis—*Asia & Oceania* 3:284
Hindus—*Asia & Oceania* 3:319
Jains—*Asia & Oceania* 3:404
Jats—*Asia & Oceania* 3:418
Jews of Cochin—*Asia & Oceania* 3:431
Kachins—*Asia & Oceania* 3:442
Kashmiris—*Asia & Oceania* 3:472
Khasi—*Asia & Oceania* 3:491
Kolis—*Asia & Oceania* 3:502
Kols—*Asia & Oceania* 3:506
Konds—*Asia & Oceania* 3:510
Lingayats—*Asia & Oceania* 4:567
Marathas—*Asia & Oceania* 4:627
Minas—*Asia & Oceania* 4:659
Mundas—*Asia & Oceania* 4:688
Muslims—*Asia & Oceania* 4:693
Naga—*Asia & Oceania* 4:699
Nicobarese—*Asia & Oceania* 4:742
Oraons—*Asia & Oceania* 4:760
Oriya—*Asia & Oceania* 4:766
Punjabis—*Asia & Oceania* 4:807
Rājasthānis—*Asia & Oceania* 4:818
Rajputs—*Asia & Oceania* 4:825
Roma—*Europe* 5:394
Santals—*Asia & Oceania* 4:848
Shans—*Asia & Oceania* 4:866
Sikhs—*Asia & Oceania* 4:877
Syrian Christians—*Asia & Oceania* 4:916
Tamils—*Asia & Oceania* 4:946
Tibetans—*Asia & Oceania* 4:964
Todas—*Asia & Oceania* 4:981
People of India—*Asia & Oceania* 3:360

INDONESIA

Acehnese—*Asia & Oceania* 3:11

Ambonese—*Asia & Oceania* 3:35
Asmat—*Asia & Oceania* 3:58
Bajau—*Asia & Oceania* 3:86
Balinese—*Asia & Oceania* 3:90
Banjarese—*Asia & Oceania* 3:112
Batak—*Asia & Oceania* 3:117
Bugis—*Asia & Oceania* 3:169
Dani—*Asia & Oceania* 3:221
Indonesians—*Asia & Oceania* 3:371
Javanese—*Asia & Oceania* 3:423
Madurese—*Asia & Oceania* 4:575
Makassarese—*Asia & Oceania* 3:169
Malays—*Asia & Oceania* 4:580
Mandarese—*Asia & Oceania* 3:169
Manggarai—*Asia & Oceania* 4:606
Minahasans—*Asia & Oceania* 4:650
Minangkabau—*Asia & Oceania* 4:654
Ngaju Dayak—*Asia & Oceania* 4:733
Niasans—*Asia & Oceania* 4:738
Sa'dan Toraja—*Asia & Oceania* 4:840
Sasak—*Asia & Oceania* 4:854
Sumbanese—*Asia & Oceania* 4:903
Sumbawans—*Asia & Oceania* 4:908
Sundanese—*Asia & Oceania* 4:911

IRAN

Azerbaijanis—*Asia & Oceania* 3:70
Balūchī—*Asia & Oceania* 3:97
Brahui—*Asia & Oceania* 3:151
Iranians—*Asia & Oceania* 3:382
Kurds—*Asia & Oceania* 3:518
Turkmens—*Asia & Oceania* 4:998

IRAQ

Bedu—*Asia & Oceania* 3:122
Iraqis—*Asia & Oceania* 3:390
Kurds—*Asia & Oceania* 3:518
Ma'dan—*Asia & Oceania* 4:571
Yazidis—*Asia & Oceania* 4:1043

IRELAND

Irish—*Europe* 5:234

ISRAEL

Bedu—*Asia & Oceania* 3:122
Circassians—*Europe* 5:130
Druze—*Asia & Oceania* 3:232
Israelis—*Asia & Oceania* 3:397
Palestinians—*Asia & Oceania* 4:777
Traditional-Orthodox Jews—*Asia & Oceania* 4:990

ITALY

Italians—*Europe* 5:238
Slovenes—*Europe* 5:459
Tyrolese—*Europe* 5:495

IVORY COAST *SEE* CÔTE D'IVOIRE

JAMAICA

Jamaicans—*Americas* 2:314

JAPAN

Ainu—*Asia & Oceania* 3:27
Japanese—*Asia & Oceania* 3:409

JORDAN

Bedu—*Asia & Oceania* 3:122
Circassians—*Europe* 5:130
Druze—*Asia & Oceania* 3:232
Jordanians—*Asia & Oceania* 3:436

KAZAKHSTAN

Karakalpaks—*Asia & Oceania* 3:460
Kazaks—*Asia & Oceania* 3:482

KENYA

Embu—*Africa* 1:185
Gikuyu—*Africa* 1:248
Gusii—*Africa* 1:267
Kalenjin—*Africa* 1:304
Keiyo—*Africa* 1:316
Kenyans—*Africa* 1:321
Luhya—*Africa* 1:337
Luo—*Africa* 1:342
Maasai—*Africa* 1:350
Oromos—*Africa* 1:449
Swahili—*Africa* 1:519

KIRIBATI

Micronesians—*Asia & Oceania* 4:647

KOREA, REPUBLIC OF

South Koreans—*Asia & Oceania* 4:893

KOSOVO

Kosovars—*Europe* 5:265

KUWAIT

Bedu—*Asia & Oceania* 3:122
Kuwaitis—*Asia & Oceania* 3:523

KYRGYZSTAN

Kazakh Chinese—*Asia & Oceania* 3:479
Kyrgyz—*Asia & Oceania* 4:543

LAOS

Hmong—*Asia & Oceania* 3:327
Kammu—*Asia & Oceania* 3:455
Lao—*Asia & Oceania* 4:548
Miao—*Asia & Oceania* 4:642
Shans—*Asia & Oceania* 4:866

LATVIA

Latvians—*Europe* 5:270

LEBANON

Bedu—*Asia & Oceania* 3:122
Druze—*Asia & Oceania* 3:232
Kurds—*Asia & Oceania* 3:518
Maronites—*Asia & Oceania* 4:632
Lebanese—*Asia & Oceania* 4:553

LESOTHO
Sotho—*Africa* 1:506

LIBERIA
Malinke—*Africa* 1:375

LIBYA
Berbers—*Africa* 1:78
Libyans—*Africa* 1:329
Tuaregs—*Africa* 1:548

LIECHTENSTEIN
Liechtensteiners—*Europe* 5:276

LITHUANIA
Lithuanians—*Europe* 5:280

LUXEMBOURG
Luxembourgers—*Europe* 5:287

MACEDONIA
Albanians—*Europe* 5:23
Macedonians—*Europe* 5:291
Vlachs—*Europe* 5:514

MADAGASCAR
Malagasy—*Africa* 1:355

MALAWI
Chewa—*Africa* 1:123

MALAYSIA
Banias—*Asia & Oceania* 3:108
Hakka—*Asia & Oceania* 3:297
Iban—*Asia & Oceania* 3:340
Kadazan—*Asia & Oceania* 3:446
Kelabit—*Asia & Oceania* 3:487
Malaysian Chinese—*Asia & Oceania* 4:585
Malaysian Indians—*Asia & Oceania* 4:590
Malaysian Malays—*Asia & Oceania* 4:595
Orang Asli—*Asia & Oceania* 4:756
Penan—*Asia & Oceania* 4:799

MALDIVES
Maldivians—*Africa* 1:364

MALI
Bamana—*Africa* 1:56
Dyula—*Africa* 1:167
Fulani—*Africa* 1:222
Malians—*Africa* 1:371
Malinke—*Africa* 1:375
Songhay—*Africa* 1:501
Tuaregs—*Africa* 1:548

MALTA
Maltese—*Europe* 5:298

MARSHALL ISLANDS
Micronesians—*Asia & Oceania* 4:647

MAURITANIA
Berbers—*Africa* 1:78
Mauritanians—*Africa* 1:382

MEXICO
Maya—*Americas* 2:355
Mexicans—*Americas* 2:367

MICRONESIA
Micronesians—*Asia & Oceania* 4:647

MOLDOVA
Moldovans—*Europe* 5:312
Vlachs—*Europe* 5:514

MONACO
Monégasques—*Europe* 5:318

MONGOLIA
Ewenki—*Asia & Oceania* 3:241
Kalmyks—*Europe* 5:243
Mongols in China—*Asia & Oceania* 4:664
Tuvans—*Europe* 5:489

MONTENEGRO
Albanians—*Europe* 5:23
Montenegrins—*Europe* 5:324

MOROCCO
Berbers—*Africa* 1:78
Moroccans—*Africa* 1:388

MOZAMBIQUE
Chewa—*Africa* 1:123
Mozambicans—*Africa* 1:404
Swahili—*Africa* 1:519

MYANMAR
Buddhists—*Asia & Oceania* 3:163
Burman—*Asia & Oceania* 3:174
Chakmas—*Asia & Oceania* 3:185
Chin—*Asia & Oceania* 3:202
Kachins—*Asia & Oceania* 3:442
Karens—*Asia & Oceania* 3:467
Miao—*Asia & Oceania* 4:642
Mons—*Asia & Oceania* 4:669
Rakhines—*Asia & Oceania* 4:832
Rohingyas—*Asia & Oceania* 4:836
Shans—*Asia & Oceania* 4:866

NAMIBIA
Namibians—*Africa* 1:409
San—*Africa* 1:463

NAURU
Micronesians—*Asia & Oceania* 4:647

NEPAL

Brahmans—*Asia & Oceania* 3:146
Buddhists—*Asia & Oceania* 3:163
Gurungs—*Asia & Oceania* 3:291
Hindus—*Asia & Oceania* 3:319
Lepchas—*Asia & Oceania* 4:559
Muslims—*Asia & Oceania* 4:693
Nepalis—*Asia & Oceania* 4:714
Newars—*Asia & Oceania* 4:729
Sherpas—*Asia & Oceania* 4:871

NETHERLANDS

Frisians—*Europe* 5:196
Netherlanders—*Europe* 5:346

NEW CALDONIA

New Caledonians—*Asia & Oceania* 4:721

NEW ZEALAND

Maori—*Asia & Oceania* 4:619
New Zealanders—*Asia & Oceania* 4:724
Polynesians—*Asia & Oceania* 4:803
Roma—*Europe* 5:394

NICARAGUA

Garifuna—*Americas* 2:226
Miskito—*Americas* 2:373
Nicaraguans—*Americas* 2:402
Sumu—*Americas* 2:497

NIGER

Fulani—*Africa* 1:222
Hausa—*Africa* 1:272
Nigeriens—*Africa* 1:425
Songhay—*Africa* 1:501
Tuaregs—*Africa* 1:548

NIGERIA

Fulani—*Africa* 1:222
Hausa—*Africa* 1:272
Igbo—*Africa* 1:282
Ijo—*Africa* 1:289
Nigerians—*Africa* 1:420
Yoruba—*Africa* 1:593

NORWAY

Norwegians—*Europe* 5:358
Sami—*Europe* 5:430

OMAN

Balūchī—*Asia & Oceania* 3:97
Bedu—*Asia & Oceania* 3:122
Omanis—*Asia & Oceania* 4:750

PAKISTAN

Balūchī—*Asia & Oceania* 3:97
Brahui—*Asia & Oceania* 3:151
Hindus—*Asia & Oceania* 3:319
Jats—*Asia & Oceania* 3:418
Kashmiris—*Asia & Oceania* 3:472
Muslims—*Asia & Oceania* 4:693
Pakistanis—*Asia & Oceania* 4:770
Parsis—*Asia & Oceania* 4:789
Pashtun—*Asia & Oceania* 4:795
Punjabis—*Asia & Oceania* 4:807
Sindhis—*Asia & Oceania* 4:882

PANAMA

Cuna—*Americas* 2:175
Panamanians—*Americas* 2:432

PAPUA NEW GUINEA

Iatmul—*Asia & Oceania* 3:336
Melanesians—*Asia & Oceania* 4:635
Melpa—*Asia & Oceania* 4:639
Motu—*Asia & Oceania* 4:679

PARAGUAY

Guaranis—*Americas* 2:245
Mennonites of Paraguay—*Americas* 2:360
Paraguayans—*Americas* 2:437

PERU

Amahuacas—*Americas* 2:25
Asháninka—*Americas* 2:70
Aymara—*Americas* 2:79
Jivaro—*Americas* 2:323
Matsigenka—*Americas* 2:349
Peruvians—*Americas* 2:447
Quechua—*Americas* 2:462

PHILIPPINES

Filipinos—*Asia & Oceania* 3:249
Hiligaynon—*Asia & Oceania* 3:315
Ifugao—*Asia & Oceania* 3:345
Ilocanos—*Asia & Oceania* 3:351
Ilongot—*Asia & Oceania* 3:355
Kalinga—*Asia & Oceania* 3:450
Mangyan—*Asia & Oceania* 4:610
Manuvu'—*Asia & Oceania* 4:615
Maranao—*Asia & Oceania* 4:623
Moro—*Asia & Oceania* 4:673
Negrito—*Asia & Oceania* 4:710
Tagbanua—*Asia & Oceania* 4:926
Tausug—*Asia & Oceania* 4:957
T'boli—*Asia & Oceania* 4:962

POLAND

Poles—*Europe* 5:384
Roma—*Europe* 5:394

PORTUGAL

Portuguese—*Europe* 5:390

PUERTO RICO

Puerto Ricans—*Americas* 2:458

QATAR

Qataris—*Asia & Oceania* 4:813

ROMANIA

Roma—*Europe* 5:394
Romanians—*Europe* 5:404
Vlachs—*Europe* 5:514

RUSSIA

Altays—*Europe* 5:37
Bashkirs—*Europe* 5:61
Buriats—*Europe* 5:96
Chechens—*Europe* 5:111
Chukchi—*Europe* 5:118
Chuvash—*Europe* 5:123
Circassians—*Europe* 5:130
Dolgany—*Europe* 5:152
Evenki—*Europe* 5:170
Evens—*Europe* 5:176
Inuit—*Americas* 2:296
Kalmyks—*Europe* 5:243
Karachai—*Europe* 5:250
Karakalpaks—*Asia & Oceania* 3:460
Khakass—*Europe* 5:255
Koriak—*Europe* 5:259
Maris—*Europe* 5:308
Mordvins—*Europe* 5:330
Nanais—*Europe* 5:334
Nentsy—*Europe* 5:341
Nivkhs—*Europe* 5:351
Ossetians—*Europe* 5:361
People of Dagestan—*Europe* 5:367
Peoples of the Caucasus—*Europe* 5:373
Russians—*Europe* 5:413
Sakha—*Europe* 5:424
Sami—*Europe* 5:430
Tatars—*Europe* 5:483
Turkmens—*Asia & Oceania* 4:998
Tuvans—*Europe* 5:489
Udmurts—*Europe* 5:501

RWANDA

Hutu—*Africa* 1:277
Rwandans—*Africa* 1:456
Tutsi—*Africa* 1:562
Twa—*Africa* 1:568

ST. KITTS AND NEVIS

Kittitians and Nevisians—*Americas* 2:331

ST. LUCIA

St. Lucians—*Americas* 2:470

ST. VINCENT AND THE GRENADINES

Garifuna—*Americas* 2:226
St. Vincentians—*Americas* 2:475

SAMOA

Samoans—*Asia & Oceania* 4:844

SAN MARINO

Sammarinese—*Europe* 5:435

SÃO TOMÉ

São Toméans—*Africa* 1:469

SAUDI ARABIA

Bedu—*Asia & Oceania* 3:122
Saudis—*Asia & Oceania* 4:859

SENEGAL

Fulani—*Africa* 1:222
Malinke—*Africa* 1:375
Senegalese—*Africa* 1:473
Wolof—*Africa* 1:582

SERBIA

Albanians—*Europe* 5:23
Kosovars—*Europe* 5:265
Serbs—*Europe* 5:443
Vlachs—*Europe* 5:514

SEYCHELLES

Seychellois—*Africa* 1:479

SIERRA LEONE

Creoles of Sierra Leone—*Africa* 1:154
Malinke—*Africa* 1:375

SINGAPORE

Banias—*Asia & Oceania* 3:108
Hakka—*Asia & Oceania* 3:297

SLOVAKIA

Slovaks—*Europe* 5:452

SLOVENIA

Slovenes—*Europe* 5:459

SOLOMON ISLANDS

Melanesians—*Asia & Oceania* 4:635

SOMALIA

Oromos—*Africa* 1:449
Somalis—*Africa* 1:495
Swahili—*Africa* 1:519

SOUTH AFRICA

Afrikaners—*Africa* 1:12
Colored People of South Africa—*Africa* 1:129
The English in South Africa—*Africa* 1:193
Karretijie People—*Africa* 1:310
Ndebele—*Africa* 1:415
Roma—*Europe* 5:394
San—*Africa* 1:463
Sotho—*Africa* 1:506
Xhosa—*Africa* 1:587
Zulu—*Africa* 1:612

SPAIN

Andalusians—*Europe* 5:42
Basques—*Europe* 5:65

Castilians—*Europe* 5:102
Catalans—*Europe* 5:106
Galicians—*Europe* 5:200
Roma—*Europe* 5:394
Spaniards—*Europe* 5:467

SRI LANKA

Buddhists—*Asia & Oceania* 3:163
Hindus—*Asia & Oceania* 3:319
Muslims—*Asia & Oceania* 4:693
Sinhalese—*Asia & Oceania* 4:888
Sri Lankans—*Asia & Oceania* 4:898
Tamils—*Asia & Oceania* 4:946
Veddas—*Asia & Oceania* 4:1020

SUDAN

Azande—*Africa* 1:40
Dinka—*Africa* 1:158
Fulani—*Africa* 1:222
Nuer—*Africa* 1:431
Shilluk—*Africa* 1:490
Sudanese—*Africa* 1:512

SURINAME

Surinamese—*Americas* 2:501

SWAZILAND

Swazis—*Africa* 1:525

SWEDEN

Sami—*Europe* 5:430
Swedes—*Europe* 5:472

SWITZERLAND

Swiss—*Europe* 5:477

SYRIA

'Alawis—*Asia & Oceania* 3:32
Bedu—*Asia & Oceania* 3:122
Circassians—*Europe* 5:130
Druze—*Asia & Oceania* 3:232
Kurds—*Asia & Oceania* 3:518
Syrians—*Asia & Oceania* 4:920
Syrian Christians—*Asia & Oceania* 4:916
Yazidis—*Asia & Oceania* 4:1043

TAHITI

Tahitians—*Asia & Oceania* 4:930

TAIWAN

Gaoshan—*Asia & Oceania* 3:260
Hakka—*Asia & Oceania* 3:297
Han—*Asia & Oceania* 3:302
Taiwan Indigenous Peoples—*Asia & Oceania* 4:934

TAJIKISTAN

Pamiri—*Asia & Oceania* 4:785
Tajiks—*Asia & Oceania* 4:940

TANZANIA

Chagga—*Africa* 1:117
Luo—*Africa* 1:342
Maasai—*Africa* 1:350
Nyamwezi—*Africa* 1:439
Shambaa—*Africa* 1:485
Swahili—*Africa* 1:519
Tanzanians—*Africa* 1:530

THAILAND

Hmong—*Asia & Oceania* 3:327
Kachins—*Asia & Oceania* 3:442
Karens—*Asia & Oceania* 3:467
Lao—*Asia & Oceania* 4:548
Miao—*Asia & Oceania* 4:642
Shans—*Asia & Oceania* 4:866
Tao—*Asia & Oceania* 4:951
Thai—*Asia & Oceania* 4:966

TOGO

Ewe—*Africa* 1:217
Jola—*Africa* 1:299
Yoruba—*Africa* 1:593

TONGA

Polynesians—*Asia & Oceania* 4:803
Tongans—*Asia & Oceania* 4:986

TRINIDAD AND TOBAGO

Garifuna—*Americas* 2:226
Trinidadians and Tobagonians—*Americas* 2:516

TUNISIA

Berbers—*Africa* 1:78
Tunisians—*Africa* 1:553

TURKEY

Adjarians—*Europe* 5:19
Circassians—*Europe* 5:130
Kurds—*Asia & Oceania* 3:518
Turks—*Asia & Oceania* 4:1004

TURKMENISTAN

Balūchī—*Asia & Oceania* 3:97
Karakalpaks—*Asia & Oceania* 3:460
Kazakh Chinese—*Asia & Oceania* 3:479
Turkmens—*Asia & Oceania* 4:998

UGANDA

Baganda—*Africa* 1:44
Banyankole—*Africa* 1:61
Twa—*Africa* 1:568
Ugandans—*Africa* 1:574

UKRAINE

Ukrainians—*Europe* 5:505
Vlachs—*Europe* 5:514

UNITED ARAB EMIRATES (UAE)

Emirians—*Asia & Oceania* 3:236

UNITED KINGDOM

English—*Europe* 5:157
Irish—*Europe* 5:234
Scots—*Europe* 5:438
Welsh—*Europe* 5:521

UNITED STATES OF AMERICA

African Americans—*Americas* 2:11
Aleuts—*Americas* 2:20
Americans—*Americas* 2:38
Amish—*Americas* 2:48
Arab Americans—*Americas* 2:59
Armenian Americans—*Americas* 2:67
Asian Indian Americans—*Americas* 2:75
Cajuns—*Americas* 2:109
Cambodian Americans—*Americas* 2:113
Central Americans in the US—*Americas* 2:122
Chinese Americans—*Americas* 2:130
Choctaw—*Americas* 2:134
Circassians—*Europe* 5:130
Comanches—*Americas* 2:144
Creeks—*Americas* 2:154
Creoles of Louisiana—*Americas* 2:161
Cuban Americans—*Americas* 2:166
Dakota and Lakota—*Americas* 2:179
Dominican Americans—*Americas* 2:187
Dutch Americans—*Americas* 2:200
English Americans—*Americas* 2:207
Filipino Americans—*Americas* 2:211
French Americans—*Americas* 2:214
French Canadians—*Americas* 2:217
Garifuna—*Americas* 2:226
German Americans—*Americas* 2:230
Greek Americans—*Americas* 2:233
Haitian Americans—*Americas* 2:259
Hawaiians—*Americas* 2:271
Hmong Americans—*Americas* 2:279
Hopi—*Americas* 2:287
Hungarian Americans—*Americas* 2:292
Inuit—*Americas* 2:296
Irish Americans—*Americas* 2:300
Iroquois—*Americas* 2:304
Italian Americans—*Americas* 2:310
Japanese Americans—*Americas* 2:317
Jewish Americans—*Americas* 2:320
Korean Americans—*Americas* 2:335
Laotian Americans—*Americas* 2:339
Lebanese Americans—*Americas* 2:342
Mexican Americans—*Americas* 2:364
Miccosukees—*Americas* 2:488
Mormons—*Americas* 2:378
Native North Americans—*Americas* 2:384
Navajos—*Americas* 2:397
Norwegian Americans—*Americas* 2:408
Ojibwa—*Americas* 2:412
Paiutes—*Americas* 2:424
Polish Americans—*Americas* 2:453
Puerto Rican Americans—*Americas* 2:456

Russian Americans—*Americas* 2:467
Scottish Americans—*Americas* 2:485
Seminoles—*Americas* 2:488
Sudanese Americans—*Americas* 2:495
Swedish Americans—*Americas* 2:505
Tlingit—*Americas* 2:512
Ukrainian Americans—*Americas* 2:522
Vietnamese Americans—*Americas* 2:539

URUGUAY

Uruguayans—*Americas* 2:525

UZBEKISTAN

Karakalpaks—*Asia & Oceania* 3:460
Uzbeks—*Asia & Oceania* 4:1014

VANUATU

Melanesians—*Asia & Oceania* 4:635
Ni-Vanuatu—*Asia & Oceania* 4:747

VENEZUELA

Guajiros—*Americas* 2:241
Pemon—*Americas* 2:442
Venezuelans—*Americas* 2:535

VIET NAM

Cham—*Asia & Oceania* 3:191
Hmong—*Asia & Oceania* 3:327
Miao—*Asia & Oceania* 4:642
Shans—*Asia & Oceania* 4:866
Vietnamese—*Asia & Oceania* 4:1025
Vietnamese Highlanders—*Asia & Oceania* 4:1025

YEMEN

Bedu—*Asia & Oceania* 3:122
Yemenis—*Asia & Oceania* 4:1046

ZAIRE. SEE CONGO, DEM. REP. OF THE

ZAMBIA

Bemba—*Africa* 1:68
Chewa—*Africa* 1:123
Tonga—*Africa* 1:543
Twa—*Africa* 1:568
Zambians—*Africa* 1:600

ZIMBABWE

Zimbabweans—*Africa* 1:606

PREFACE

The *Worldmark Encyclopedia of Cultures and Daily Life, Second Edition,* contains over 500 articles exploring the ways of life of peoples of the world. Arranged in five volumes by geographic regions—*Africa, Americas, Asia & Oceania* (two volumes), and *Europe*—the volumes of this encyclopedia parallel the organization of its sister set, the *Worldmark Encyclopedia of the Nations.* Whereas the primary purpose of *Nations* is to provide information on the world's nation states, this encyclopedia focuses on the traditions, living conditions, and personalities of many of the world's culture groups. Entries emphasize how people live today, rather than how they lived in the past.

Defining groups for inclusion was not an easy task. Cultural identity can be shaped by such factors as geography, nationality, ethnicity, race, language, and religion. Many people, in fact, legitimately belong in two or more classifications, each as valid as the other. For example, the citizens of the United States all share traits that make them distinctly American. However, few would deny the need for separate articles on Native Americans or African Americans. Even the category Native American denies the individuality of separate tribes like the Navajo and Paiute. Consequently, this encyclopedia contains an article on the Americans as well as separate articles on the Native Americans and the Navajo. Closely related articles such as these are cross-referenced to each other to help provide a more complete picture of the group being profiled. Included in this encyclopedia are articles on groups as large as the Han of China, with over one billion members, and as small as the Jews of Cochin, with only a few dozen members. Unfortunately, although the vast majority of the world's peoples are represented in this encyclopedia, time and space constraints prevented many important groups from being included in the first edition. Twenty-three new groups have been added to this second edition, and the editors look forward to including many more culture groups in future editions of this work.

New entries include in Americas: Sudanese Americans ("Lost Boys"); in Africa: Afar, Berbers, Ewe, Guineas of Guinea Bissau, Jola, Maldivians, San (Bushmen), Sao Tomeans, and Twa; in Asia and Oceania: Brunei, Coptic Christians, Kashmiris, Moro, Rajasthanis, and Timorese; and in Europe: Alsatians, Kosovars, Maltese, Montenegrins, Serbs, Tyrolese, and Vlachs.

Over 175 contributors and reviewers participated in the creation of this encyclopedia. Drawn from universities, consulates, and the press, their in-depth knowledge and first-hand experience of the profiled groups added significantly to the content of the articles. A complete listing of the contributors and reviewers together with their affiliations appears in the front of each volume.

ORGANIZATION

Each volume begins with an introduction that traces the cultural developments of the region from prehistoric times to the present. Following the introduction are articles devoted to the peoples of the region. Within each volume the articles are arranged alphabetically. A comprehensive table cross referencing the articles by country follows the table of contents to each volume.

The individual articles are of two types. The vast majority follow a standard 20-heading outline explained in more detail below. This structure allows for easy comparison of the articles and enhances the accessibility of the information. A smaller number do not follow the 20-heading format, but rather present simply an overview of the group. This structure is used when the primary purpose of an article is to supplement a fully rubriced article appearing elsewhere in the set.

Whenever appropriate, articles begin with the **pronunciation** of the group's name, a listing of **alternate names** by which the group is known, the group's **location** in the world, its **population,** the **languages** spoken, the **religions** practiced, and a listing of **related articles** in the five volumes of this encyclopedia. Most articles are illustrated with a map showing the primary location of the group and photographs of the people being profiled. The twenty standard headings by which most articles are organized are presented below.

INTRODUCTION: A description of the group's historical origins provides a useful background for understanding its contemporary affairs. Information relating to migration helps explain how the group arrived at its present location. Political conditions and governmental structure(s) that typically affect members of the profiled ethnic group are also discussed.

LOCATION AND HOMELAND: The population size of the group is listed. This information may include official census data from various countries and/or estimates. Information on the size of a group's population located outside the traditional homeland may also be included, especially for certain groups with large diaspora populations. A description of the homeland includes information on location, topography, and climate.

LANGUAGE: Each article lists the name(s) of the primary language(s) spoken by members. Descriptions of linguistic origins, grammar, and similarities to other languages may also be included. Examples of common words, phrases, and proverbs are listed for many of the profiled groups, and some include examples of common personal names and forms of address.

FOLKLORE: Common themes, settings, and characters in the profiled group's traditional oral and/or literary mythology are highlighted. Many entries include a short excerpt or synopsis of one of the group's most noteworthy myths, fables, or legends. Some entries describe the accomplishments of famous heroes and heroines or other prominent historical figures.

RELIGION: The origins of traditional religious beliefs are profiled. Contemporary religious beliefs, customs, and practices are also discussed. Some groups may be closely associated with one particular faith (especially if religious and ethnic identification are interlinked), while others may have members of diverse faiths.

MAJOR HOLIDAYS: Celebrations and commemorations typically recognized by the group's members are described. These holidays commonly fall into two categories: secular and religious. Secular holidays often include an independence day and/or other days of observance recognizing important dates in history that affected the group as a whole. Religious holidays are typically the same as those honored by other peoples of the same faith. Some secular and religious holidays are linked to the lunar cycle or to the change of seasons. Some articles describe unique customs practiced by members of the group on certain holidays.

RITES OF PASSAGE: Formal and informal episodic events that mark an individual's procession through the stages of life are profiled. These events typically involve rituals, ceremonies, observances, and procedures associated with birth, childhood, the coming of age, adulthood, and death. The impact of twenty-first century communications and global media on customs are addressed here.

INTERPERSONAL RELATIONS: Information on greetings, body language, gestures, visiting customs, and dating practices is included. The extent of formality to which members of a certain ethnic group treat others is also addressed, as some groups may adhere to customs governing interpersonal relationships more/less strictly than others.

LIVING CONDITIONS: General health conditions typical of the group's members are cited. Such information includes life expectancy, the prevalence of various diseases, and access to medical care. Information on urbanization, housing, and access to utilities is also included. Transportation methods typically utilized by the group's members are also discussed.

FAMILY LIFE: The size and composition of the family unit is profiled. Gender roles common to the group are also discussed, including the division of rights and responsibilities relegated to male and female group members. The roles that children, adults, and the elderly have within the group as a whole may also be addressed.

CLOTHING: Many entries include descriptive information (size, shape, color, fabric, etc.) regarding traditional clothing (or a national costume), and indicate the frequency of its use in contemporary life. A description of clothing typically worn in the present is also provided, especially if traditional clothing is no longer the usual form of dress. Distinctions between formal, informal, and work clothes are made in many articles, along with clothing differences between men, women, and children.

FOOD: Descriptions of items commonly consumed by members of the group are listed. The frequency and occasion for meals is also described, as are any unique customs regarding eating and drinking, special utensils and furniture, and the role of food and beverages in ritual ceremonies. Many entries include a sample recipe for a favorite dish.

EDUCATION: The structure of formal education in the country or countries of residence is discussed, including information on primary, secondary, and higher education. For some groups, the role of informal education is also highlighted. Some articles may include information regarding the relevance and importance of education among the group as a whole, along with parental expectations for children. In addition, literacy levels are described where appropriate.

CULTURAL HERITAGE: Since many groups express their sense of identity through art, music, literature, and dance, a description of prominent styles is included. Some articles also cite the contributions of famous individual artists, writers, and musicians.

WORK: The type of labor that typically engages members of the profiled group is discussed. For some groups, the formal wage economy is the primary source of earnings, but for other groups, informal agriculture or trade may be the usual way to earn a living. Working conditions are also highlighted.

SPORTS: Popular sports that children and adults play are listed, as are typical spectator sports. Some articles include a description and/or rules to a unique type of sport or game.

ENTERTAINMENT AND RECREATION: Listed activities that people enjoy in their spare time may include carrying out either structured pastimes (such as public musical and dance performances) or informal get-togethers (such as meeting for conversation). The role of popular culture, movies, theater, and television in everyday life is also discussed.

FOLK ARTS, CRAFTS, AND HOBBIES: Entries describe arts and crafts commonly fabricated according to traditional methods, materials, and style. Such objects may often have a functional utility for everyday tasks.

SOCIAL PROBLEMS: Internal and external issues that confront members of the profiled group are described. Such concerns often deal with fundamental problems like war, famine, disease, and poverty. A lack of human rights, civil rights, and political freedom may also adversely affect a group as a whole. Other problems may include crime, unemployment, substance abuse, and domestic violence.

GENDER ISSUES: New to this edition is a section focusing on women's issues including cultural attitudes, discrimination, status, health, sexual issues, education, and work and employment. Some discussion on the group's attitudes toward homosexuality may be included in this section, where relevant.

BIBLIOGRAPHY: References cited include works used to compile the article, as well as benchmark publications often recognized as authoritative by scholars. Citations for materials published in foreign languages are frequently listed when there are few existing sources available in English.

A glossary of terms and a comprehensive index appears at the end of each volume.

ACKNOWLEDGMENTS

The editors express appreciation to the members of the Cengage Gale staff who were involved in a number of ways at various stages of development of the *Worldmark Encyclopedia of Cultures and Daily Life, Second Edition:* Christine Nasso, Barbara Beach, and Leah Knight, who helped the initial concept of the work take form; and Larry Baker and Allison McNeill, who supported the editorial development of the profiles for the first edition. Carol Nagel and Ellen McGeagh were instrumental in the planning and scheduling of the second edition of this work. Anne Marie Hacht selected the photo illustrations and provided valuable review of the entries. Marybeth Trimper,

Evi Seoud, and Shanna Heilveil oversaw the printing and binding process.

In addition, the editors acknowledge with warm gratitude the contributions of the staff of Eastword Publications—Debby Baron, Dan Lucas, Brian Rajewski, Kira Silverbird, Maggie Lyall, Karen Seyboldt, Tajana G. Roehl, Janet Fenn, Cheryl Montagna, Jeneen Hobby, Dan Mehling, Karen Ellicott, Alexander Barnes, and Elizabeth Gall—who managed interactions with contributors; edited, organized, reviewed, and indexed the articles; and turned the manuscripts into the illustrated typeset pages of these five volumes.

SUGGESTIONS ARE WELCOME: Maintenance of a work the size and scope of *Worldmark Encyclopedia of Cultures and Daily Life, Second Edition, is a daunting undertaking; we appreciate any suggestions that* will enhance future editions. Please send comments to:

Editor
*Worldmark Encyclopedia
of Cultures and Daily Life*
Cengage Gale
27500 Drake Rd
Farmington Hills, MI 48331-3535

KYRGYZ

PRONUNCIATION: KIR-ghiz
LOCATION: Kyrgyzstan; China
POPULATION: 5.3 million
LANGUAGES: Kyrgyz; Russian; English
RELIGION: Islam (Sunni Muslim)

¹ INTRODUCTION

Tracing the origins and history of the Kyrgyz people is difficult because, until recently, they used no written language. Therefore, much of what is known about the early Kyrgyz is based on archeological discoveries and oral stories passed down over the generations. The Kyrgyz people were nomads throughout much of their history, initially living in the region of south-central Russia between the Yenesei River and Lake Baikal about 2,000 years ago. The ancestors of the modern Kyrgyz were probably not Turks at all, but either Yeniseyans (ancestors of the modern Kets) or South Samoyedic peoples, and they exhibited European-like features (such as fair skin, green eyes, and red hair). During the 6th through 9th centuries, the Kyrgyz mixed with the various invading Mongol and Turkic tribes. At some time between the 12th and 16th centuries, they settled in the Tien Shan Mountains.

During the era of Mongol rule, the Kyrgyz were loosely governed until the Kokand Khanate lost control in about 1850. At that time, imperial Russia was expanding its control in Central Asia by moving Russian colonists into the area. The Russians finally gained control over the Kyrgyz in 1876. The new Russian settlers staked claims on the most fertile land, and the nomadic Kyrgyz were given minimal attention by the Russian government. In 1916, ethnic Kyrgyz inhabitants revolted against this practice, but the rebellion was crushed by Russian forces.

After the Russian Revolution of 1917, the area inhabited by the Kyrgyz was made part of Soviet Turkistan. In 1921, its status changed by becoming part of the Turkistan Autonomous Soviet Socialist Republic. In 1924, the region was split away from the Turkistan ASSR and assigned as an autonomous area *(oblast)* within the Russian Soviet Federated Socialist Republic (RSFSR). In 1924, the region became the Kirghiz Autonomous Soviet Socialist Republic of the RSFSR. In 1936, the territory finally became a full-fledged republic of the USSR.

During the Soviet era, from 1917 to 1991, the way of life for the Kyrgyz people as residents of the Kirghiz Soviet Socialist Republic (KSSR) changed significantly. Forced collectivization of farming quickly ended nomadic life. Mechanization, irrigation, and mining were introduced, but many Kyrgyz wanted to keep farming or raising livestock. As a result, the Kyrgyz became ethnic minorities within the industrial and urban areas of the KSSR. The economic and political restructuring that occurred in the Soviet Union during the late 1980s under Soviet leader Gorbachev never made it to the KSSR. In 1990, ethnic tensions along the border with Uzbekistan resulted in 200-400 deaths. The chaos created by that event caused the ruling Kyrgyz Communist Party (KCP) to lose any credibility that it had with the people. During the attempted Soviet coup of August 1991 in Moscow, there was a similar coup taking place in the KSSR. When the attempted coup failed, the KCP voted itself out of existence. When the Soviet Union dissolved in 1991, the KSSR became independent Kyrgyzstan.

Since 1991, Kyrgyzstan has been led by an elected president and parliamentary form of government. The government has concentrated on elevating the status of Kyrgyz culture in Kyrgyzstan without alienating persons of other ethnic backgrounds. Unlike in some of the other former Soviet republics, a citizen of Kyrgyzstan does not need to be Kyrgyz. In 2005 Kyrgyzstan experienced its "Tulip Revolution," which resulted in the mainly peaceful ouster of the former president, Askar Akayev and the parliament elected during his rule. Today it is somewhat politically stable, but faces a very dissatisfied population because of its very poor economy.

² LOCATION AND HOMELAND

There are approximately 5.3 million Kyrgyz living throughout the former Soviet Union, with about 88% of them in Kyrgyzstan. Ethnic Kyrgyz constitute slightly more than half of the population of Kyrgyzstan. There are also about 80,000 Kyrgyz living in the Sinkiang-Uygur Autonomous Region of China and a few tens of thousands in Afghanistan.

Kyrgyzstan is located in Central Asia along the western range of the Tien Shan Mountains. This area was known as the Kirghiz Soviet Socialist Republic during the Soviet era. The boundaries with neighboring countries (Kazakhstan, China, Tajikistan, and Uzbekistan) run along mountain ranges, and about 85% of Kyrgyzstan itself is mountainous. In the southwest, the Fergana River Valley is the largest expanse of lowlands in the country. The only other lowland areas are in the north, along the Chu and Talas valleys. Most of the lowland area occupied by Kyrgyz people is arid, receiving less than seven inches of rainfall per year. Although the climate is dry where the land is cultivated, mountain lakes and streams provide ample water through irrigation.

The largest mountain lake, Issyk-Kul, is located high in the mountains of eastern Kyrgyzstan, and many Kyrgyz fishing villages are located around the edge of the lake.

³ LANGUAGE

Most Kyrgyz people speak the Kyrgyz language, which is a distinct Turkic language with Mongolian influences. The Kyrgyz language is a member of the Nogai group of the Kypchak division of the Turkic branch of Ural-Altaic languages. Until 1926 the Kyrgyz and Kazak languages were considered as one. The Kyrgyz literary language was therefore heavily shaped by Kazak, with some Mongolian influences in the vocabulary. Although the Kyrgyz language is spoken in the home, most Kyrgyz also speak Russian, which is the language of business and commerce. English is the third language of communication. The Kyrgyz government had begun a program to gradually switch over to the Kyrgyz language for all state institutions and educational establishments by 1998, but this has been delayed because of its impracticality. The written language originally used Arabic script, but the Roman alphabet was introduced after World War I. The written Kyrgyz language was formally organized in 1923 and was modeled after the northern dialects. In 1940, Stalin forced all Central Asian republics to switch to the Cyrillic alphabet (which is used by the Russian language). Since independence, there has been discussion of switching back to the Roman alphabet.

The Kyrgyz people have many proverbs and sayings related to horses, such as: "A horse is a man's wind." Some proverbs deal specifically with pacers. Two examples of such are: "Don't let your horse run beside a pacer" and "If you have only one day left to live, you should spend half of it riding a pacer."

4 FOLKLORE

The telling of traditional oral tales dates back about 1,000 years among the Kyrgyz people. One of the most famous epics tells the saga of *Manas*, the father of the Kyrgyz people, his son Semetey, and his grandson Seytek. The entire poem is about a million lines long is (twice as long as the *Iliad* and the *Odyssey* combined) can take up to three weeks to recite, and went unwritten until the 1920s. Here is a translated example of some of the epic's verse: "The mighty Manas resembles a tower built of silver. His snow-white steed Ak-Kula carries him swiftly over the mountain tops. The horse looks like a bird hovering over the sharp peaks of mountains." In the epic, the 40 Kyrgyz tribes strive for freedom and unity. Under the leadership of Manas, the people, who were the slaves of various tribes, are gathered as a nation. Manas is believed to be interred at a small mausoleum near the town of Talas, in western Kyrgyzstan near the border with Kazakhstan. Throughout the 1990s and into the 2000s, the *Manaschi* (reciters of the Manas) have made tours with Central Asian artistic groups all over the world, including many performances in the United States.

5 RELIGION

Horses figured prominently in the traditional spiritual beliefs of the early Kyrgyz. It was believed that a horse carried the spirit of a dead person to a higher spiritual world. Most Kyrgyz today are Sunni Muslims, but many ancient shamanist and animist traditions persist.

Since the 8th century, Islam has been the dominant religion in the Fergana Valley. By the 10th and 11th centuries, the Kyrgyz had built many beautiful mosques and mausoleums in that region. During the 13th and 14th centuries, however, the development of Islam among the Kyrgyz slowed considerably, due to the conquest by the Mongols. Islam extended to the nomads of the northern regions over the next few centuries at first by force, but later through Islamic missionaries. Therefore, Islam did not gain a strong presence among all the Kyrgyz until the 19th century.

The Kyrgyz are generally more secular in daily life than some of the other Islamic peoples of Central Asia. This is probably because the religion was only firmly established in some areas of the country in the last century. Kyrgyzstan also has a large proportion of non-Muslims, and the government is not oriented toward incorporating any religion into the political structure. Outside Islamic influences from the Middle East and South Asia have featured in the creation of some radical Muslim movements in Kyrgyzstan, especially in the Osh and Jalalabad provinces, located in the southern part of Kyrgyzstan—its Ferghana valley region. Some of these mainly younger people are part of the Hizb-ut-Tahrir radical international movement. They wish to establish a theocratic government throughout the entire Muslim world. Overall, radical or extremist Islam is not a major threat to Kyrgyz sovereignty at the moment.

6 MAJOR HOLIDAYS

New Year's Day (January 1) and Christmas (January 7) are official holidays in Kyrgyzstan. Holidays with their origins to the Soviet era include Women's Holiday (March 8), International Day of Solidarity Among Workers (May 1), and the Day of Victory over Fascism (May 9). The vernal equinox (around March 21) is called *Nooruz* and is an important holiday among the Kyrgyz people as it marks the start of the Muslim new year. *Kurban Ait* (Remembrance Day, June 13) and Independence Day (August 31) are also official Kyrgyzstan holidays. Generally speaking, people do tend to celebrate religious holidays, especially the Muslim days of remembrance more now than during the Soviet period.

7 RITES OF PASSAGE

Kyrgyz rites of passage are similar to those of other Turkic-influenced peoples of Central Asia. Large birthday parties with many friends and relatives are important social occasions, and these feasts often last five or six hours. Celebrations are held for a birth, for a baby's 40th day of life, for the first day of school, and for graduations. A wedding serves to honor the married couple and assemble together an extended family or clan. In the past, arranged marriages were common, and a dowry payment was expected upon betrothal.

8 INTERPERSONAL RELATIONS

Kyrgyz people typically greet one another with handshakes or hugs if they are women, and then proceed to ask a series of questions about one another's lives. Male-female relations among the Kyrgyz are far less formal and rigid than, say, among the Uzbeks or Tajiks. Men and women eat together and share many work burdens together. Like many other peoples of Central Asia, the Kyrgyz are very hospitable, although more reserved and low-key than the Uzbeks or Tajiks. If you were invited to have tea in Kyrgyz *yurta*, you would not feel yourself quite the focus of attention as would be true in the case of an Uzbek village home. Kyrgyz often honor their guests by serving them a cooked sheep's head.

9 LIVING CONDITIONS

The traditional Kyrgyz home is a *yurta*—a round, felt-covered structure built upon a collapsible wooden frame. Most Kyrgyz today live in individual permanent homes, but about 40,000 Kyrgyzstani citizens still live in *yurtas*. The arched opening of a *yurta* is called the *tundruk*. The flag of the Republic of Kyrgyzstan features a *tundruk*.

One legacy of the Soviet era is a chronic lack of urban housing in Kyrgyzstan. In the late 1980s, housing space was equivalent to 12 sq m (129 sq ft) per person.

Irregular service with public transportation occurs frequently. In Bishkek, for example, evening bus service is erratic. There are a sufficient number of taxis in the city, but people looking for a ride will often stop a private car and pay the driver because it is cheaper than using a taxi.

Since the mid- to late-1990s, it has become increasingly common to find shanty-town type dwellings in major cities, such as Bishkek and Osh, because poverty has caused many people to take up urban residence in hopes of making a more prosperous life.

10 FAMILY LIFE

Women in Kyrgyz society still perform the bulk of household chores, but there is far more egalitarianism practiced between the sexes among the Kyrgyz than among nearby peoples such as the Uzbeks or Tajiks. The Kyrgyz and Kazaks are very similar in this regard. Women hold all manner of professional jobs and are encouraged to be professionals as well as mothers. Both forms of polygamy are legal in Kyrgyzstan, and the custom is not limited to ethnic Kyrgyz but is practiced by ethnic Russians and other residents in Kyrgyzstan. Polygyny (one man having multiple wives) is most common, and a husband must financially provide each wife with her own separate household as well as provide for all the children each wife bears. In order for a woman to have multiple husbands (polyandry), she must have substantial wealth or influence.

Kyrgyz families are large, with an average of four to six children, although they are slightly smaller in the capital city of Bishkek. In the countryside, it is common for three generations to live together in a patrilocal residence, which means that a married woman moves in with her husband's family). Thus, 10 to 12 people may share a home during the cold months and a yurt when the people go to the *zhailovs* (summer pastures) with their animals in the summer. Genealogical knowledge is very important to the Kyrgyz, and some older people are able to recount their ancestors stretching back as far as seven generations or two centuries.

A Kyrgyz girl in traditional attire offers tourists snacks near Bishkek, Kyrgyzstan. (AP Images/Xinhua, Wei Zhongjie)

11 CLOTHING

One of Kyrgyzstan's oldest cities, Osh, was once an important trading point along the historic Silk Roads—the ancient overland trade route of commerce between China and the Middle East. Osh is the center of Kyrgyzstan's silk industry.

Traditional everyday clothes were made of wool, felt, and fur. Ornate silks were, and still are, used for special occasions and ceremonies. Since the Soviet era, cotton denim and other fabrics have become popular for everyday wear. Headgear figures prominently in Kyrgyz culture, although during the Soviet era women were prohibited from wearing their large traditional hats, which were a symbol of Kyrgyz culture. There is also a traditional hat proudly worn by men as a symbol of Kyrgyz culture, the *ak-kalpak* ("white hat"). This is a dome-shaped white felt hat with a black brim, black piping, abstract curved stitching, and a black tassel on top. The basic design of the *ak-kalpak* has been the same for generations.

12 FOOD

Because many Kyrgyz live in areas with little precipitation, the variety of crops grown depends on irrigation from the mountains. Sugar beets and cereal grains are the main crops. Livestock is an important source of food, with sheep, goats, cattle, and horses most common. Pigs, bees, and rabbits are also raised in the uplands.

Examples of traditional Kyrgyz fare include *manti* (mutton dumplings), *irikat* (a type of pasta salad made with noodles, carrots, and radishes), and *koumiss* (fermented mare's milk). A great Kyrgyz delicacy reserved especially for guests is a combination plate of fresh sliced sheep liver and slices of sheep tail fat. It is often boiled and salted and tastes far more delicious than it sounds. At the breakfast table, one often finds bountiful amounts of yogurt, heavy cream, butter, and wonderful honey along with bread and tea. Dairy products are an essential part of Kyrgyz life.

Along with traditional cooking, the Kyrgyz also enjoy Russian, Korean, Ukrainian, German, and Chinese cuisine. The dishes of both local and European cooking dominate the menus in Bishkek's restaurants and cafés.

13 EDUCATION

For the most part, Kyrgyz people have poor native language proficiency except in the remote *auls* (villages). Kyrgyzstan has been heavily Russified, and most high school and university instruction is in Russian. Although this is slowly beginning to change, rural Kyrgyz are often ill-equipped to compete at the national level on university entrance exams. The whole educational system requires overhauling. Parents tend to favor a broad educational development for their children, but it is impossible for many parents to send their children to universities and technical schools because education has become privatized and the costs are prohibitively expensive. Today, along with the Kazakhs, more and more Kyrgyz speak competent English than people in any of the other Central Asian countries. This is partly due to American influence and teaching in Kyrgyzstan as well as the people's own desire to add English as a part of their international focus, especially as a means toward increasing one's chances in the professional world.

14 CULTURAL HERITAGE

The *kyiak* and *komuz* are traditional musical instruments used by the Kyrgyz. The *kyiak* resembles a violin and is played with a bow but has only two strings. The three-stringed *komuz* is the favorite folk instrument among the Kyrgyz and is played by strumming. The Kyrgyz have several titles of honor that are given to various musical performers. A *jïrchïï* is a singer-poet, whereas an *akin* is a professional poet and musician-composer. The *jïrchïï* is primarily a performer of known music, while the *akin* is a composer who plays original compositions as well as traditional music. A special performer called a *manaschï* performs the famous saga of Manas. There are also several types of Kyrgyz songs, such as *maktoo* (eulogies), *sanat* and *nasiyat* (songs with a moral), and *kordoo* (social protest tunes).

15 WORK

Work hours vary depending on the type of business and state institution. As a rule, people work between seven and eight hours a day. Most often work runs from 8:00 am to 5:00 pm, with lunch taken sometime between noon and 2:00 pm. Mills and factories operate on a relay system, with shifts set up by the management. Retail shops are usually open from 7:00 am to 8:00 pm, with an afternoon lunch period. Department stores, book stores, and other shops usually open according to state institution hours. Bazaars are open from 6:00 am until 7:00 or 8:00 pm.

16 SPORTS

Equestrian sports are very popular among the Kyrgyz. Racing and wrestling on horseback are especially enjoyed. Wrestling on horseback for a goat's carcass, called *ulak tartysh* or *kok boru*, is a common game among the Kyrgyz. (*Kok boru* means "gray wolf"). The game may have its origin in ancient times, when herds of cattle grazed in the steppes and mountains and were exposed to the threat of attack by wolves. Shepherds would chase after a wolf on horseback and beat it with sticks and whips and then try to snatch the dead carcass away from each other for fun. *Kok boru* was later replaced with *ulak tartysh*, played with a goat's carcass on a field measuring 300 meters by 150 meters (about 328 yards by 164 yards). The opposite ends of the field are the two goals. A goat's carcass, usually weighing 30 to 40 kilograms (66–88 pounds), is placed in the center of the field. Each game lasts 15 minutes, and the object is to seize the goat's carcass while on horseback and get it to the goal of the other team. Players are allowed to pick up the carcass from any place within the limits of the field, take it from opponents, pass or toss it to teammates, carry it on the horse's side, or suspend it between the horse's legs. Players are not allowed to ram other horses, take an opponent's horse by the bridle or remove its reins, whip another's horse, or talk with the opponent.

Falconry (the sport of hunting with trained falcons) while on horseback is another part of Kyrgyz culture that has been practiced for centuries. In addition to falcons, sakers and golden eagles are also trained for the sport. *Jumby atmai* is a game that involves shooting at a target while galloping on horseback. *Tyin enmei* is a contest to pick up coins from the ground while riding at full speed on horseback.

17 ENTERTAINMENT AND RECREATION

Bishkek has large parks, public gardens, shady avenues, and botanical gardens enjoyed by people traveling on foot. Opera, ballet, and national folklore groups are also popular forms of entertainment. The most popular form of relaxation for city dwellers is to spend a weekend in a country cottage. Tens of thousands of these cottages are located on the outskirts of Bishkek, the capital. In recent years, Bishkek and other cities have added many taverns, restaurants, and casinos, so city life has become nocturnally raucous, and part of these businesses cater to the tastes of expatriates from China, Europe, and the United States.

18 FOLK ART, CRAFTS, AND HOBBIES

The Kyrgyz are best known for crafting utensils, clothes, equipment and other items used in everyday life and making them beautiful. Many articles are made of felt: carpets (*shirdak* and *alakiyiz*), bags for keeping dishes (*alk-kup),* and woven patterned strips of carpet sewn together into bags or rugs (*bashtyk).* Ornate leather dishes called *keter* are also made.

19 SOCIAL PROBLEMS

After years of life under the Soviet system of central planning and socialism, the transition to a market-oriented economy is a difficult undertaking for the Kyrgyz. The poor service and uninspired work ethic that were results of the Soviet era will take a long time to change. Alcoholism and public drunkenness are now a visible social problem, partly because of rising unemployment. Even though Kyrgyzstan was supposed to have developed a large tourism industry, its development has been slow and not very lucrative; getting to Kyrgyzstan remains difficult and expensive.

From 2000–2005, Kyrgyzstan's economy stagnated and allegations of sizable political corruption brought down the government that had been in power since 1991. The much heralded "Tulip Revolution" did little to improve the politics or economics of the country, and since then the population has only become more disgruntled as most people become more impoverished. This has raised crime rate in urban areas and led to a more oppressive political environment than was true of the 1990s. The new government is perceived to be weak in the face of more powerful Central Asian states, such as Kazakhstan and Uzbekistan. Close to one million Kyrgyz now seek at least temporary housing and employment abroad to help bolster their household budgets, and this has led to very trying conditions for many families. With the exception of Kazakhstan, labor migration is the social problem as well as "social solution" story to emerge from contemporary Central Asia.

20 GENDER ISSUES

Along with the Kazakhs, the Kyrgyz long have featured a high degree of gender equity. Many scholars attribute this to their pastoral nomadic heritage. While there naturally is a division of labor between the sexes, many men and women do many things together, such as yurt erection and packing up as well as cooperative milking and food production activities. Men consider women to be their literal fellow travelers (*yoldash*) rather than simply the "wife" or the "mother of their kids." When it comes to education, Kyrgyz girls long have been seen almost as the equal of boys, but again with the exception that boys will be seen favorably to pursue higher education and advanced professional degrees. However, this is definitely not the rule in all families.

Since the early 2000s, gender issues have changed because of the increase in bride kidnapping, which is more and more common among the Kyrgyz, Karakalpaks, and Kazakhs. This relieves pressures on young men to make a bride wealth payment or *qalym*, just as it obviates the need for in-law arrangements in the first place, but it puts young women in a terrible position because they rarely can exercise their own free will once kidnapped. However, divorces often ensue shortly after these unhappy marriages take place. Still, it is a kind of traditional social institution that shows up as one very unfair aspect of gender relations.

Moreover, labor migration is changing the nature of gender relations as many men and women now work abroad to try and increase family wealth. While it provides young women with opportunities and a kind of freedom, it puts great pressure on mothers and wives who sometimes go abroad despite the disapproval they face from other family members, including husbands. Labor migration, generally speaking, puts huge pressure and stress on people willing to take what they consider to be a crucial step in making a better life for themselves and their families.

21 BIBLIOGRAPHY

Allworth, Edward, ed. *Central Asia: 130 Years of Russian Dominance, A Historical Overview.* Durham, NC: Duke University Press, 1994.

Burghart, Daniel L., and Theresa Sabonis-Helf, eds. *In the Tracks of Tamerlane: Central Asia's Path to the 21st Century.* Washington, D.C.: Center For Technology and National Security Policy, National Defense University, 2004.

Cagatay, Ergun. "Kyrgyzstan: A First Look." *Aramco World.* (Houston: Aramco Services Company) 46, no. 4 (1995): 10–21.

Hughes, James, Gwendolyn Sasse, eds. *Ethnicity and Territory in the Former Soviet Union: Regions in Conflict.* London: Frank Cass, 2002.

Khan, Aisha. *A Historical Atlas of Kyrgyzstan.* 1st ed. New York: Rosen Pub. Group, 2004.

Kyrgyzstan: Heartland of Central Asia. Hong Kong: Odyssey, 2004.

Pomfret, Richard W. T. *The Central Asian Economies since Independence.* Princeton: Princeton University Press, 2006.

Ro'i, Yaacov. *Democracy and Pluralism in Muslim Eurasia.* London: Frank Cass, 2004.

Tolstov, S. P., ed. *Narody Srednei Azii i Kazakhstana I* The Peoples of Central Asia and Kazakhstan, Vol. I). Moscow: Izdatel'stvo Akademii Nauk, 1962.

—by R. Zanca

LAO

PRONUNCIATION: LAH-OO
LOCATION: Laos; Thailand
POPULATION: About 23 million
LANGUAGE: Lao
RELIGION: Theravada Buddhism; animism
RELATED ARTICLES: Vol. 3: Kammu

¹ INTRODUCTION

The Lao originated in southern China and moved southward into present-day Laos, forming a kingdom in the Mekong River valley in the 14th century and pushing the earlier inhabitants of the area, the Kammu, into more mountainous areas. After three centuries, however, disputes over succession to the throne and foreign invasions split the country into three rival kingdoms in the north, center, and south. Caught between the growing power of the Siamese and the Vietnamese, the Lao lost power and territory so that most Lao people now live in Thailand (formerly Siam).

Laos was colonized by the French in the 1890s and treated as the hinterland to their colonies in Vietnam. The French preferred to work with the Vietnamese and used many of them as officials in Laos. Laos was unified after World War II and achieved independence within the French Union in 1949 and full independence in 1953. However, regional divisions were replaced by political ones. The Lao were divided into three factions: a right-wing group backed by the United States; Thailand, a neutralist group; and a Communist group backed by Vietnam, the Soviet Union, and China. After a devastating civil war fought with heavy American bombing on behalf of the right, and with Vietnamese troops on behalf of the left, the Communist Pathet Lao (Lao Nation) took control of the country in 1975, abolished the monarchy, and established the Lao People's Democratic Republic (LPDR). In the political, economic, and social upheavals that followed, about 10% of the population fled as refugees, draining the country of skilled and educated people. Although the aging Lao leadership maintains one-party control and continues to assert Communist ideology, it has loosened social and economic controls and now invites foreign investment and tourism.

² LOCATION AND HOMELAND

Laos is a small landlocked country in Southeast Asia bordering on Thailand, Myanmar (Burma), China, Vietnam, and Cambodia. Laos has an area of about 236,800 sq km (91,400 sq mi), roughly the size of Idaho. It runs about 1,126 km (700 mi) from N to s and averages about 240–320 km (150–200 mi) across. The country is extremely mountainous, with only about 4% of the land suitable for farming. Different ethnic groups tend to be located at different altitudes. It has a tropical monsoon climate, and most people engage in subsistence rice agriculture. The Lao (usually referred to as "lowland Lao") make up two-thirds of the population, or somewhat over 3 million of the population of 4.8 million. They occupy the most desirable land in the river valleys and live clustered along the Mekong River across from northeast Thailand, most of whose people are Lao, and in the southern plateau. The Lao of northeast Thailand, together with Lao groups in northern Thailand, represent one-third of the whole population of Thailand, or about 20 million people—many times the number of Lao in Laos itself. The Mekong River has always been a cultural bridge, not a barrier. However, the Thai government has tried hard to assimilate the "northeast Thai" (it never uses the term "Lao") to central Thai culture and language, a process that is occurring rapidly through education, mass media, and greater geographic mobility. Both the Lao and the Thai belong to the Tai linguistic group, have related languages, and share many cultural features. The two cultures have distinctive features, however, and the Thai have tended to consider themselves superior to the Lao.

After the Communists seized power in Laos in 1975, about 360,000 refugees left the country. Refugees were predominantly Lao, but included many Hmong and smaller numbers of other minority groups. Many of the French-speaking elite went to France, but most Lao came to the United States and live scattered across the country, although southern California is a favorite location because of the warmer climate. Canada and Australia also took thousands of Lao refugees, and thousands of others stayed illegally in Thailand, blending in with the Lao population of northeast Thailand.

³ LANGUAGE

Lao belongs to the Tai family of languages and is related to Thai, but Lao has its own alphabet and numbers. Many words have Sanskrit and Pali roots, especially terms relating to religion, royalty, and government. Most Lao words have one syllable and the grammar is very easy. However, Lao is difficult for Westerners to speak because it is a tonal language. There are six tones, and words that sound similar to a Western ear may be very different depending on the tone. For example, the word *ma* in mid tone means come; *ma* in a high tone means horse; and *ma* in a rising tone means dog.

Lao is written from left to right, but no space is left between words, only between phrases or sentences. You have to know where one word ends and the next word starts. Vowels can appear before, after, above, or below the consonants they go with, or in various combinations thereof. Relatively few people, probably only just over two million people, can read Lao. While the Lao in Thailand speak Lao, their education is in Thai, so they are literate in that language.

Girls are often given names of flowers or gems, while boys might be given names that suggest strength. However, many have simple names like Daeng (red) or Dam (black), or might be called by nicknames like Ling (monkey). Family names were made compulsory in 1943 but aren't as important as first names. The phone book is alphabetized by first names, and a man named Sitha Sisana would be addressed as Mr. Sitha.

Some common expressions are: *sabai dee* (greeting), *la kon* (goodbye); *khob jai* (thank you); *kin khaw* (eat—literally, eat rice, the most important food); *bo pen nyang* (it doesn't matter, never mind, it's nothing).

⁴ FOLKLORE

A Lao legend explains the origins of the Lao and Kammu, the original inhabitants of the land:

> Once upon a time three chiefs settled the earth and began rice farming with their water buffalo. After a few years the water buffalo died, and from his nostrils grew a creeping plant that bore three gourds that grew to enor-

mous size. Hearing a loud noise from inside the gourds, one of the chiefs took a red hot iron and pierced each gourd. Crowds of men came squeezing out of the narrow openings. The chief then used a chisel to carve out new openings for the men. This is the origin of the different people in Laos. The Kammu, a dark skinned people who wore their hair in chignons, came out the holes made with the red hot iron; and the Lao, a lighter skinned people who wore their hair short, came out the openings made by the chisel.

Lao proverbs give us an idea of their cultural attitudes.

To judge an elephant, look at its tail;
To judge a girl, look at her mother.

If you love your cow, tie it up;
If you love your child, beat him.
(In fact, the Lao are very indulgent towards their children, but they like to threaten them with this proverb.)

Flee from the elephant and meet the tiger;
Flee from the tiger and meet a crocodile.
(Their version of "out of the frying pan into the fire.")

When the water level falls, the ants eat the fish;
When the water level rises, the fish eat the ants.

When the buffalo fight, it is the grass that suffers.

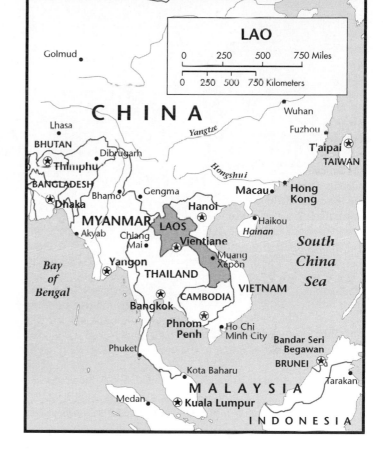

⁵ RELIGION

The first Lao king, Fa Ngum, made Buddhism the state religion in the 14th century, and almost all Lao are Theravada Buddhists. Buddha is regarded as a great teacher—not a god, a creator, or a savior. He taught that suffering is caused by desire, anger, and illusion. Each person is responsible for his own salvation. A person's karma, the balance of good and bad deeds, will affect this life and future reincarnations.

When the Communists took over in 1975, they did not dare do away with something so central to Lao identity as Buddhism. Rather, they continued state control of the Buddhist hierarchy and tried to manipulate religion for political purposes. Many monks fled as refugees or disrobed rather than promote government policies. In recent years government controls have eased and there has been a revival of Buddhism. This revival is due not only to changes in government policy but also to the infusion of funds from foreign tourists—primarily Thais who share the Buddhist religion—for the restoration of Buddhist temples.

Animism, a belief in spirits, co-exists with Buddhism for the Lao. Ancestor spirits, the local guardian spirits of each village, are appealed to at the beginning of the agricultural year for successful crops. These spirits should also be informed of major changes in a person's life—sickness, a move, a marriage. The Lao believe the body contains 32 spirits, and illness can result if a spirit leaves the body. A *baci* ceremony is held to call the spirits back to the body in order to cure illness, to protect someone about to make a major life change, or to bring health, happiness, and prosperity. A beautifully decorated tray filled with ritual offerings is presented to the spirits. Cotton strings are tied around the wrists of the person who is sick or who is being honored, and blessings are recited when the strings are tied.

⁶ MAJOR HOLIDAYS

The most important Lao holiday is Songkarn, the Lao New Year, which is celebrated April 13–15. After several months of drought, the first rains of the year begin in April, bringing the start of the agricultural year. Water is poured over Buddha images and elders as a blessing. After this is done very decorously, Songkarn turns into one big water fight, with water splashed on everyone in sight. Since the temperature is over 32°C (90°F) at that time of year, the water feels good. People try to return to their home villages for Songkarn to visit friends and relatives and to join in the fun.

The Rocket Festival is a popular traditional Lao holiday, although not an official holiday. It is celebrated on Wisakha Bucha, the day celebrating the birth, enlightenment, and death of Buddha; but the Rocket Festival is based on a fertility rite that predates Buddhism in the area. Village men build bamboo rockets packed with gunpowder, and villages compete to see whose rocket can fly the highest. The men hold boat races on the rivers, and the village women hold folk dance contests. This holiday is based on a lunar calendar and falls sometime in May.

Independence Day on July 19 celebrates the granting of autonomy, or independence, within the French Union in 1949.

National Day on December 2 celebrates the proclamation of the Lao People's Democratic Republic in 1975, a one-party Communist state.

Lao women pray at Pha That Luang during the Wai Thatluang festival in Vientiane, Laos. Hundred of thousands of Laotians visit Vientiane to pay homage to a Buddha relic they believe is kept inside a pagoda. (AP Images/David Longstreath)

The That Luang Festival occurs on the day of the full moon in the twelfth lunar month and celebrates the most sacred Buddhist monument in Laos.

7 RITES OF PASSAGE

The main rite of passage for a Lao man is ordination as a Buddhist monk. In the past most Lao men spent at least one three-month period of Buddhist Lent as a monk, learning about religion, chanting Pali texts, and practicing self-control and meditation. The man to be ordained reenacts the life of Prince Gautama, who renounced the world and became Buddha, the Enlightened One. He is dressed in finery and escorted with pomp to the monastery, where his head and eyebrows are shaved. Then, he changes into a simple robe, renounces the world, and takes his vows as a monk. There is no set period for ordination, so a monk can disrobe and return to lay life at any time. Fewer men become ordained today and often for shorter periods, but it is believed that a man gains maturity by doing so, and women consider it desirable for a male. There is no ordination for women.

8 INTERPERSONAL RELATIONS

The Lao tend to be warm, personable, friendly, and have a nice sense of humor. They enjoy having people around and are quick to invite people to share a meal or sit and talk for a bit. They try to avoid confrontation and appreciate a person with self-control.

It is considered improper for men and women to touch in public. However, if men hold hands with each other or women hold hands with other women, it is considered friendly, and there are no sexual connotations.

In the past both the spoken language and body language showed relative social position, with the inferior person bowing to the superior person, but the Communist government insisted on more egalitarian relations, at least overtly. Still, a Buddhist will prostrate himself and bow his head to the floor three times in front of a Buddha image or a monk as a sign of respect.

9 LIVING CONDITIONS

Laos is one of the poorest countries in the world with an estimated per capita income in 1996 of $325, or the equivalent United States purchasing power of $2,071 per person. The population is overwhelmingly rural with 85% depending on agriculture, mostly subsistence rice cultivation. The Lao are largely engaged in wet rice agriculture, depending on seasonal rains to flood their fields.

Water buffalo are used to plow, and agricultural practices have changed little over the centuries. Mechanization in the form of water pumps and small tractors is just beginning.

Rural homes are built on stilts to avoid flooding. They are made of wood or bamboo, often with walls of bamboo matting and roofs of thatch or corrugated tin. Lao houses generally have little or no furniture. One sits and eats on the floor and sleeps on a mat on the floor. Village houses are built close together, and farmers walk to their fields outside the village. There are no secrets in a small village, and gossip is a potent weapon to keep people in line.

Villages rarely have electricity or running water. Laos has great potential for hydroelectric power and currently exports electricity to Thailand. But the Lao buy electricity back from the Thai for their cities across the Mekong River from northeast Thailand, as Laos has no national power grid.

There are few roads, and some of these are impassable quagmires in the rainy season. Much transportation is by boat along the rivers. Ox carts are still common.

Health facilities are limited. Malaria, dysentery, malnutrition, and parasites are major problems. In Laos there is one doctor for every 23,000 people (compared to one per every 3,000 people in Vietnam and one per every 300 people in the United States). Life expectancy is about 50 for men and 53 for women in the country. The Lao undoubtedly do better than minority populations, as they are more likely to live in or near the cities or along transportation routes, and they continue to favor themselves at the expense of minorities. In addition, the construction of a bridge across the Mekong, linking the Lao capital Vientiane to the northeastern Thai city of Nongkhai, gives urban Lao access to the Thai medical system, which is decidedly superior to Laos.

10 FAMILY LIFE

Lao families are close and children are welcome. The LPDR government had banned birth control devices until fairly recently, but few people have access to birth control services. Women have many children but there is high infant and child mortality.

There is no dating, but groups of young men in the village go from house to house in the evening to call on families with young women and engage in banter with them and their parents. Traditionally, the young man is expected to pay a bride-price and move in with the wife's family on marriage. When the next daughter marries, the couple might set up housekeeping on their own with help from the wife's parents. Ultimately, the youngest daughter is left to take care of the parents and inherit the family home and remaining farm plot.

Women are responsible for much heavy work—hauling water for the household and pounding the rice in big mortars of hollowed out logs to husk it where rice mills aren't available. The men plow and deal with draft animals, while women tend to be responsible for pigs and poultry and vegetable gardens. The animals usually live under the house. Everyone, including the children, helps with transplanting and harvesting rice.

Children rarely have toys but enjoy catching fish, frogs, insects, etc., to supplement the family diet. Boys are skillful with slingshots and blowguns in bagging small birds. Young girls help with child care and often carry a younger sibling astride a hip while they play with their friends.

11 CLOTHING

When the Communist government came to power in 1975, it tried to ban blue jeans, calling them bourgeois Western decadence. It even tried to do away with the *sin*, the traditional sarong-like women's lower garment, but the government soon had to back down. The sin is a very practical garment—one size fits all. It is a tube of cloth folded with a pleat to fit the waist and secured with a belt or a tuck in the waist. Worn above the breasts, it makes a modest garment for bathing in public at the stream or well, necessary as few village homes have bathrooms. A dry garment is slipped over the wet garment that is then dropped without any loss of modesty. Lao women continue to wear the sin, sometimes adapted into a skirt, with a blouse. On special occasions women wear handwoven silk sin with beautiful tie-dyed patterns and a colorful woven and embroidered strip added to the hem.

Lao men wear shirt and pants, but bathe and relax around the house in a *phakhawma*, a length of cloth about 1.8 m (6 ft) long and 76 cm (30 in) wide that can be worn as a skirt-like garment or wrapped into shorts. Little children often go naked or wear only a shirt. It is common for people to go barefoot or wear rubber sandals. In the cities, of course, Western dress is common.

12 FOOD

The Lao love to eat. Their staple food is sticky rice, also known as glutinous rice or sweet rice. The rice must be soaked for several hours before being steamed in a basket over a pot of boiling water. It is then put in another basket that serves as a serving dish or lunch pail. Sticky rice is eaten with the fingers, so one doesn't need dishes or silverware. One takes a bit of rice from the basket and shapes it into a small ball and dips it into the serving dish for whatever other food is offered, most likely a hot sauce of chilies, garlic, fish sauce, and lime. The Lao have two categories of food—rice and "with rice." Foods other than rice are limited and serve more as condiments, something to add flavor, so they tend to be very hot or very salty so that one will eat a lot of rice with them.

Dried salty beef is a favorite dish if meat is available. Beef is sliced thin and liberally doused with fish sauce (a salty liquid made from salt and fish) or salt and placed on a tray to dry in the sun to preserve it. You can deep-fry the meat to cook it and drive out most of the moisture. If the meat is very, very salty, you can eat a lot of sticky rice with it.

Papaya salad is a common dish. Shred a green papaya (lacking that, shredded cabbage or rutabaga, sliced green beans, or grated carrots can substitute). Pound two or three cloves of garlic with two or three fresh, small, hot Thai chilies in a mortar. Gradually add about 3 cups of shredded vegetables and a few cherry tomatoes and pound together. Add fresh lime and fish sauce (or salt) to taste and a teaspoon of sugar. Lao salad is hot, sour, salty, and sweet all at once. Serve with lots of sticky rice.

13 EDUCATION

Literacy in Laos is estimated at 45%. The Lao are much more likely to be literate than minority peoples, and men are more likely to be literate than women. The LPDR government is the first to make a serious effort to extend education beyond the Lao areas to minorities. However, with the loss of about 90% of its most educated population as refugees, education has perhaps been set back a generation, and already low standards have declined further. Universal primary education has been declared a goal by several leaders but remains elusive. Many village schools have only one or two grades and little in the way of books, paper, or school supplies. Teachers are paid little and often infrequently, so they often have to farm or hold a second job to support their families. School sessions, therefore, tend to be sporadic.

There are five years of primary school, but probably only half of primary school children finish fifth grade. This is followed by three years of lower secondary school and three years of upper secondary school. Secondary schools are few in number and located in cities and provincial capitals. One must pass a test to enter secondary school. School uniforms and supplies are too expensive, the distance to schools too great, and village education too rudimentary for many village children to continue their education. There are a few colleges and technical institutes in Vientiane, the capital.

In the early days of the LPDR, teenagers from "bad" family backgrounds, as defined by the Communists (children of officials from the old regime or of shopkeepers), were often denied entrance to secondary education. Some teens fled the country on their own, risking shooting or drowning as they swam the Mekong River to Thailand. They were hoping to be resettled abroad and have a chance to continue their education.

Private schools have been allowed and are preferred to public schools by parents who can afford school fees. Lack of financial resources and trained teachers remains a problem for Laos. The government has cobbled together a basic university system—the National University of Laos—formed by consolidating teacher training colleges. This university has attracted foreign assistance and attempts to keep pace with Laos's economic reform program. Because of its proximity to Laos and the linguistic similarities, Thailand is a popular venue for overseas study, along with Vietnam, which has provided scholarships for Lao students since 1975.

14 CULTURAL HERITAGE

The most distinctive Lao instrument is the *khaen*. According to a popular saying, those who eat sticky rice, live in dwellings mounted on piles, and listen to the music of the khaen are Lao. The khaen is a collection of bamboo pipes of different lengths, each with a small hole for fingering and a metal reed, preferably of silver, all attached to a mouthpiece. There are 6-hole, 14-hole, and 16-hole instruments. A khaen musician accompanies a *mohlam* performance, a traditional Lao entertainment that usually involves two singers, a man and a woman, and offers courting poetry, suggestive repartee, and dance. The songs and poetry represent oral literature passed on to performers by their teachers. Relatively few have been written down. Ability to add witty and rhyming repartee on the spot is valued. Males and females never touch in Lao dance.

A great work of Lao literature is *Sin Xay,* an epic poem. Sin Xay (he who triumphs through his merits), the hero, is rejected by his father, the king. He sets out to rescue his aunt, the beautiful Sumontha, from a giant who has carried her off. After many trials and combat with giants, demons, monstrous beasts, and magical beings, plus treacherous attacks by six half- brothers, Sin Xay rescues his aunt and reunites her with her brother, Sin Xay's father. The king regrets his previous rejection of Sin Xay and now recognizes his nobility of character.

15 WORK

The vast majority of people are engaged in agriculture, especially subsistence rice farming on small family plots. Children help with farm chores from an early age, and most are engaged full-time in farming after leaving primary school. There is little industry. With the New Economic Mechanism, a loosening of controls by the LPDR government, some people have gone into business and there is increasing interest in developing tourism and handicraft. Major foreign investment in Laos—in mining and hydroelectric power—does not lend itself to widespread job creation. The Lao predominate in the government bureaucracy.

16 SPORTS

Few Lao have time for sports, but those that do enjoy soccer, volleyball, and *takraw,* a Southeast Asian sport that involves keeping a rattan ball in the air without touching it with the hands. The feet and head are used as in soccer. Nevertheless, with its increasing participation in the international community, Laos aspires to participate in international and regional sporting competitions and receives some assistance from neighboring countries for this purpose.

17 ENTERTAINMENT AND RECREATION

The biggest entertainment for the Lao in Laos, especially in the cities, is tuning in to Thai radio and television stations from across the Mekong River. However, with the advent of Star TV, which is relatively inexpensive, many urban Lao have access to television programs beyond the region. Even some Buddhist temples in Vientiane have satellite dishes on their rooftops. The Lao government worries that Lao language and culture is being corrupted by the popularity of these programs and that youth are learning the wrong values from the commercialism of Thailand. Mass media in Laos are under tight Communist party control and tend toward heavy-handed propaganda. They have nowhere near the influence of Thai mass media on the Lao. In Thailand itself, mass media are spreading Thai language and culture to Lao-speaking areas.

18 FOLK ART, CRAFTS, AND HOBBIES

The Lao are becoming increasingly better known for their exquisite hand-woven textiles in cotton and silk with intricate tie-dyed designs. Basketry is another Lao specialty.

19 SOCIAL PROBLEMS

Discrimination by the Lao against the minority groups that make up one-third of the population of Laos remains a problem. In Thailand, on the other hand, the central Thai feel superior to the Lao of the Northeast. Human rights are an issue as the LPDR government will not tolerate criticism of the one-party Communist control. Disaffection is widespread with the aging ideologues who hold power and an increasingly corrupt bureaucracy and military. The youth seem particularly disaffected and attracted to the alternate vision of society offered by Thai television. Even the Communist leadership of Laos is now calling for a return to Buddhist values, and leaders of the early Communist regime that took power after 1975 are often cremated in high-profile Buddhist ceremonies. Poverty and lack of health and education will continue to hamper development and make life difficult, especially in the rural areas.

Although the Lao monarchy was abolished, the government is increasingly aware that it lingers on as a social institution, albeit a lost one. Many urban Lao express admiration for the Thai monarchy and visits by members of the Thai royal family—especially the king—draw a great deal of attention. To counter this, the government has attempted to revive interest in Laos's ancient monarchs—particularly the kings of the Lan Xuan era—with new monuments and celebrations.

20 GENDER ISSUES

The Lao constitution forbids discrimination on the basis of gender, but social dynamics and tradition, particularly in some of the poorer ethnic groups, often place women at a disadvantage. Although rape meets with strong disapproval from both society and the law, spousal battery is widespread. Nevertheless, Laos has a higher proportion of women in positions of authority in government, education, and commerce—than in neighboring Vietnam or Cambodia. Several factors may account for this. Laos is highly donor-dependent, and Western aid agencies tend to emphasize income generation and leadership training for women. In addition, women tend to dominate handicraft and textile production, which attract foreign investment and the tourist trade, giving them an advantage in the commercial sector.

On the other side of the coin, Laos is increasingly plagued by trafficking of women, particularly into Thailand. The eradication of opium production has left some areas with resulting deficits in income and the short-term response has been to sell or otherwise push women into prostitution. In addition, the influx of foreign business—particularly Chinese investment—and new infrastructure projects (especially new transnational roads) have unfortunately provided new markets for trafficking.

21 BIBLIOGRAPHY

De Berval, Rene. *Kingdom of Laos.* Saigon: France-Asie, 1959.

Hayashi, Yukio. *Practical Buddhism among the Thai-Lao: Religion in the Making of a Region.* Kyoto: Kyoto University Press, 2003.

Mansfield, Stephen. *Lao Hill Tribes: Traditions and Patterns of Existence.* New York: Oxford University Press, 2000.

Savada, Andrea Matles, ed. *Laos: A Country Study.* Washington, D.C.: Library of Congress, 1995

Stuart-Fox, Martin. *Buddhist Kingdom, Marxist State: The Making of Modern Laos.* Bangkok: White Lotus, 1996.

Wayupha Thotsa. *Lao Folktales.* Westport, Conn: Libraries Unlimited, 2008.

—revised by C. Dalpino

LEBANESE

PRONUNCIATION: leb-un-EEZ
LOCATION: Lebanon
POPULATION: 3,971,941 (2008 estimate)
LANGUAGE: Arabic (official), French, English, Armenian
RELIGION: Muslim 59.7%, Christian 39%, other 1.3%

1 INTRODUCTION

Lebanon is a small country on the east coast of the Mediterranean Sea. Throughout its history, Lebanon has been the stage for conflicts between city-states, world powers, and local tribespeople. Located in what is known as the Fertile Crescent (a curved band of green, fertile lands along the eastern Mediterranean coast, bordered by the Arabian and African deserts) and at the juncture of three continents—Africa, Asia, and Europe—Lebanon is a valuable and highly desired territory.

Historically, Lebanon has been known as the home of the Phoenicians. The Phoenicians were Semitic traders whose maritime culture flourished in the Fertile Crescent for more than 2,000 years (c.2700–450 BC). Lebanon's mountains also served as a refuge for Christians during the early years of Christianity. During the Crusades, Christian warriors established strongholds in the mountains. One area, known as Mount Lebanon, continued to be a Maronite Christian enclave within the Ottoman Empire, which ruled much of the Middle East from the 16th century until the end of World War I.

After World War I, Britain and France divided the Middle East between them. Mount Lebanon and several surrounding areas became known as Greater Lebanon and was organized as a French protectorate. The rest of the Fertile Crescent became known as Syria and fell under British control. Although Lebanon became a republic in 1926, French troops remained in the country until 1946. At the time, Christians made up a slight majority of the population, but other religious groups also had a strong presence. In an effort to make sure that all of the major religious groups had representation, a power-sharing arrangement was established for the Lebanese government. The president was to be a Maronite Christian, the prime minister a Sunni Muslim, and the president of parliament a Shia Muslim. All religious groups were to receive representation in the National Assembly according to their numbers. In many ways, this power-sharing arrangement created the tensions that culminated in the long and brutal civil war that Lebanon endured from 1975 to 1990.

Tensions between religious groups began in 1932 when Christians refused to acknowledge the results of a census that showed Christians holding a majority but significant numbers of Muslim Lebanese. Then, Palestinians who were pushed out of present-day Israel with the formation of the Jewish state in 1948 began settling in Lebanon. By 1967, more than 500,000 Palestinians lived in the country. Many Muslim and Christian Lebanese protested the arrival of Palestinians and accused Israel of trying to displace the native Lebanese populations with Palestinians who had long lived in Israel.

Civil war erupted in 1975, and Syrian troops entered Lebanon in 1976, largely to protect Christian interests. A cease-fire that year maintained partial peace until 1982, when Israel invaded Lebanon and occupied the area south of Beirut. During

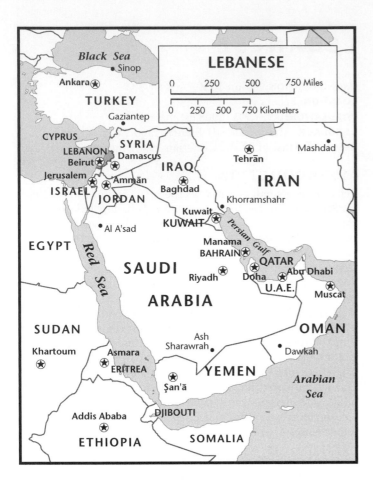

a siege of Beirut, a multinational peacekeeping force (MNF) evacuated members of the Palestine Liberation Organization (PLO) from the city. The MNF remained in Lebanon until 1984. Then, civil war broke out again, and continued until 1990. Elections were put on hold, although a Maronite leader, Michel Aoun, took control of the government in 1988 and dissolved the parliament. Muslim groups aligned against Aoun, defeated his troops in 1990, and forced him into exile in Paris, where he remained until 2005.

Aoun's departure from Lebanon allowed for a peace treaty to be signed. The Taif Accord reorganized Lebanon's government so that representation in the parliament was divided equally between Christians and Muslims. It also left intact the dictate that the president of Lebanon be a Maronite Christian, the prime minister a Sunni Muslim, and the speaker of parliament a Shi'ah Muslim. Fighting ceased in 1990. At that point, it was estimated that 100,000 Lebanese had been killed, 100,000 were permanently maimed, and nearly 1 million had been forced to leave their homes to settle abroad.

Efforts to rebuild Lebanon's economy and restore political stability to the country have preoccupied the country through the 1990s and the early years of the 21st century. Syria formally withdrew its troops in 2005 and Israel pulled out in 2006. Lebanon, however, remains vulnerable to attack from both countries, as of 2008. It also has been a target of violence by militant groups fighting for Palestinian rights.

² LOCATION AND HOMELAND

Lebanon is a tiny country, with an area of only a little more than 10,400 sq km (4,000 sq mi)—about the size of the state of Connecticut. It lies on the east coast of the Mediterranean Sea, north of Israel, south of Turkey, south and west of Syria, and southeast of Cyprus. Although it is only about 200 km (124 mi) from north to south and averages only 50 km (30 mi) east to west, Lebanon has two mountain ranges (Mount Lebanon and Anti-Lebanon), a coastal strip, an inland plain, dozens of rivers (the two major ones being the al-Assi and the al-Litani), and four lakes. Lebanon was famous in previous times for its cedars, but due to centuries of cutting and herds of goats eating the seedlings, less than 5% of its land contains the trees. Those that remain are now protected.

The rainy season lasts from mid-November through March, with very heavy rains at times causing flooding due to poor drainage. Summers on the coast are hot and humid; the mountains are somewhat cooler and breezier. Plant and animal life is quite varied because of the diverse terrain. Because Lebanon is located at the juncture of Europe, Asia, and Africa, it is home to species from all three zones. The most important cultivated crops are citrus fruits, apples, grapes, potatoes, sugar cane, tomatoes, wheat, vegetables, tobacco, oats, and olives. The biggest cash crop in the Beqa'a valley is hashish, which is illegal.

The human population of Lebanon is as varied as its terrain. So many different peoples have lived in and traveled through the land of Lebanon over its turbulent history that the current population contains quite a mix of cultures. In 2008, the population of Lebanon was just under 4 million. Most Lebanese (95%) are Arab, and about 58% of the population consists of Muslims of various sects. The rest are Christian, also of various sects. The vast majority (85%) of Lebanese are urban dwellers, with about one-third of the population living in the Beirut area. Beirut has a population of approximately 1.5 million. The three next largest cities are Tripoli (population 210,000), Zahle (60,000), and Sidon (50,000). The Bekaa Valley still contains many rural villages.

³ LANGUAGE

The first language spoken in the area that is now Lebanon was Canaanite. Since then, the common languages have been, in succession, Aramaic, Greek, Latin, Arabic, and French during the French mandate years. Upon independence, Arabic became the official language, but many Lebanese also speak English, and some still consider French to be the more "sophisticated" language. Armenians who live in Lebanon speak Arabic as well as Armenian and Turkish. It is not uncommon for Lebanese to speak three or more languages fluently.

"Hello" in Arabic is *"marhaba"* or *"ahlan,"* to which one replies, *"marhabtayn"* or *"ahlayn."* Other common greetings are *"As-salam alaykum"* ("Peace be with you"), with the reply of *"Walaykum as-salam"* ("and to you peace"). *"Ma'assalama"* means "Goodbye." "Thank you" is *"Shukran,"* and "You're welcome" is *"Afwan."* "Yes" is *"na'am"* and "no" is *"la'a."* The numbers one to ten in Arabic are: *wahad, itnin, talata, arba'a, khamsa, sitta, saba'a, tamania, tisa'a,* and *ashara.*

⁴ FOLKLORE

One of the most popular characters in Arab folklore is Jeha the Fool, who figures in many stories, from teaching tales to purely humorous anecdotes. Also popular are the real-life lovers,

Ablah and Antar. Antar was a 6th century Arab who was born a slave but became a heroic warrior. He was also a poet (poetry is considered the highest art in Arab culture). Antar fell in love with Ablah, the daughter of the chief, and she fell in love with him; but, of course, a slave could not marry the chief's daughter. Eventually, after many tragic and star-crossed struggles, Antar was given his freedom, and he and Ablah married.

Other Lebanese folktales that Westerners usually do not associate with Lebanon are the story of the Greek hero Adonis and the Christian legend of Saint George and the Dragon. In Greek mythology, Adonis was a handsome young man loved by Aphrodite, the goddess of love and beauty. Adonis was later killed by a wild boar. The story of Adonis takes place at Byblos, in Lebanon. Also Saint George, who later became the patron saint of England, lived in Lebanon and fought the famous sea-dragon at the mouth of a river near Beirut. Most likely, the Christian Crusaders brought Saint George's tale back with them to the West.

The Lebanese are very fond of proverbs and can quote one for almost any situation. Proverbs usually teach a lesson or give a nugget of wisdom in just a few words, such as, "Better blind eyes than a closed mind," and "The one who took the donkey up to the roof should be the one who brings it down."

⁵ RELIGION

The original inhabitants of the land now called Lebanon were worshipers of the fertility goddess known as Asherah, Astarte, or Anat. Christianity arrived during the Byzantine Roman era (AD 4–636), and its followers in Lebanon have since become divided into a variety of sects including Maronite, Roman Catholic, Greek Catholic, Greek Orthodox, Armenian Catholic, Armenian Orthodox, and Protestant. The Islamic revolution of the 7th century ad took hold in the land of Lebanon as in other Arab countries. Muslims are now divided into Sunnis, several types of Shi'ites (including Ismaeli), and Sufis (Muslim mystics). Other religious sects in Lebanon include the Alawis and Druze, as well as the Baha'is. A total of 17 religious sects are recognized in Lebanon today.

The Lebanese government practices a system called "confessionalism" in which it keeps a record of every citizen's religious affiliation. A person may belong to any religion, but each person *must* belong to one. No Lebanese can be religiously unaffiliated. As of 2008, about six out of 10 Lebanese were Muslim, and about three out of 10 were Christian. Because seats in the government are based on religious representation, the number of followers each faith commands is of significance. When the 1932 census was taken, Christians were in the majority, so they were given greater representation (and, therefore, authority) in the government. Now that it is becoming apparent that Muslims are the majority, they are demanding more representation. In 1995, Lebanon conducted its first census in more than 20 years.

⁶ MAJOR HOLIDAYS

The Lebanese love a good party, so they all celebrate all of the holy days—both Christian (including Greek Orthodox who have different dates for the festivals than other Christians) and Muslim—plus a couple of secular public holidays. Islam uses a lunar calendar, so Muslim holidays occur on a different date of the Gregorian calendar each year. The major Muslim holidays are *Ramadan*, the ninth month of the Muslim year, dur-

ing which Muhammad received his first revelations, celebrated by complete fasting from dawn until dusk each day of the entire month; *Ayd Al-Fitr*, the end of Ramadan, a three-day festival; *Ayd Al-Adha*, a feast at the end of the *Hadj* (the pilgrimage month to Mecca); the First of *Muharram*, the Muslim New Year; *Ashura*, a Shi'ite commemoration and day of mourning, and the prophet Muhammad's birthday.

The Christian holiday of Easter is also movable. Being calculated on a lunar basis, it always occurs sometime during March or early April. Two Easters are celebrated in Lebanon: the Greek Orthodox date and the date for the rest of the Christian population. Other Christian holidays are: New Year's Day (January 1); St. Maroun's Day (the patron saint of Maronite Christians, February 9); the Day of the Ascension (May 15); the Feast of the Assumption (August 15); and Christmas and Boxing Day (December 25 and 26). Three secular public holidays in Lebanon are: Labor Day (May 1); Martyr's Day, which honors patriots killed by the Turks during World War I (May 6); and Independence Day (November 22).

The Christian New Year's Day (January 1) is celebrated in Beirut by shooting tracer bullets out over the Mediterranean Sea. Since tracer bullets are multicolored, they look like fireworks but are much louder. It is also customary to go "strolling" along the coast road in one's car after midnight on New Year's. Such "strolling" is a Lebanese tradition for almost any festival.

Both Muslim and Christian children play a game with colored (hard-boiled) eggs at Easter time. One child taps the tip of his or her egg against the tip of another child's egg. One shell will crack; the other will not. The child whose egg stays intact while cracking everyone else's eggs wins the game. The children then eat their eggs. On Lebanese television, films that re-enact the crucifixion and resurrection of Jesus are played throughout Easter weekend, interspersed with live coverage (by satellite) of the Pope's festivities in Rome.

⁷ RITES OF PASSAGE

Most Lebanese mark major life events, such as birth, marriage, and death, within the Islamic or Christian religious traditions. Regardless of religion, Lebanese parents celebrate the birth of a child by cooking meghli (a spiced rice pudding, topped with nuts and coconut). The family serves the sweet dish to visitors who come to the household to congratulate the family. At birth, it is common to bring gifts of clothing and gold for the new baby. Boys born to Muslim and Druze families are circumcised at the hospital just after the birth. Christian babies are dressed in white and baptized. A major event for a Christian child (usually before age nine) is First Communion.

Lebanese in cities typically date, but families in rural areas continue to arrange marriages. Lebanese men place a great deal of importance on being financially independent and often wait until their late twenties or early thirties to marry. Women, however, marry in their early twenties. Christian weddings generally take place in churches and Muslims are wed before a cleric and two witnesses. Lebanese of all faiths celebrate weddings with a first dance between the bride and groom, a belly dancing performance, and a dinner buffet. The bride and groom, however, cut the wedding cake and have a toast before the meal.

Funeral rituals for the deceased vary by religion. Muslims typically bury the deceased before sunset on the day that the person has died. Christians often wait several days. Followers of both religions set aside the fortieth day after the death for prayer and an offering of condolences to the family of the deceased.

8 INTERPERSONAL RELATIONS

Most Lebanese people are very hospitable, generous, and polite, although Arab politeness sometimes means saying what one thinks the other person wants to hear. Most Lebanese will greet each other with handshakes and will inquire about a person's family and health. Formal titles, such as "Dr." or "professor" are used when appropriate.

The Lebanese lifestyle is relaxed, but by no means lazy. The Lebanese are typically entrepreneurs; men and women have a "get ahead" attitude and lots of ambition to go with it. Opinions are strongly held and fiercely defended with vigorous gestures in heated discussions. At the market, the same vigor is used to haggle prices, something the average Lebanese is quite good at. The same attitude prevails on the road, where there are few (if any) traffic signals or stop signs, and drivers simply "get ahead" as they need to. Fortunately, the Lebanese do not generally drive at high speeds, so few accidents occur. Pedestrians also cross the road whenever and wherever they choose, leaving it to drivers to stop for them.

Traditional Arab hospitality reigns in Lebanon, where hosts provide feasts for their guests and then smoke the *nargile* after dinner. The *nargile* is a pipe in which Persian tobacco called *tumbak* is filtered through water before being inhaled, like a hookah or "hubble-bubble" pipe. Smoking from a *nargile* varies as a fad, but smoking in general remains a strong constant. Visits are not planned in advance but rather happen spontaneously, usually between the hours of 4:00 and 8:00 pm. An Arab will never ask personal questions, as that is considered rude. However, exactly what is considered personal in Lebanese culture varies somewhat from in Western culture. For example, asking how much rent someone pays is not normally considered a personal question but asking about a marital dispute is. A person is expected to say what he or she wishes without being asked. Lebanese are very affectionate with friends and family, touching each other often, holding hands, and men even kiss each other on the cheeks.

9 LIVING CONDITIONS

Lebanon has been rebuilding its economic infrastructure by borrowing heavily from banks. The rebuilding effort has drawn many Lebanese to cities such as Beirut, Tripoli, and Sidon, where educational and employment opportunities abound. Most of those who live in cities reside in apartments in concrete buildings. Free standing houses are rare. Electricity remains unreliable, and water often is scarce. Many families have access to water for only a few hours per day, so they pump enough for their daily needs into rooftop storage tanks. Although most Lebanese have migrated to cities, the people remain proud of their village heritage. Some families still own a dwelling in their ancestral village and will use it for vacationing and other activities. Rural homes generally are much larger than the urban apartments, with rooms for hosting guests, living areas, and bedrooms.

Even though Lebanon is covered by an extensive system of roadways, most of which are in fair condition, traffic is highly congested in major cities and along popular travel routes (such as the coast road or roads heading to mountain resorts on weekends). Buses and taxis are the primary means of public transport. Lebanon's rail system became unusable during the war and still has not been rebuilt.

Health care in Lebanon is modern and fairly accessible. Although public facilities exist, those who can afford to pay for higher quality care in private clinics generally do so. Malaria is prevalent but native Lebanese have generally built up a resistance to it, so it is not a serious problem for them; only visitors have difficulty with it. In addition, water shortages often mean that not all water is drinkable. As a result, most families have two water systems. One contains water that has been chlorinated and is safe to drink, and the other contains untreated water. The average life expectancy for Lebanese men is 71 years, which has increased from 65 years in the mid-1990s; for Lebanese women, the average life expectancy is 76 years, compared with 70 years in the mid-1990s.

10 FAMILY LIFE

Strong family ties are the rule in Lebanon. Most businesses are family-owned and run, and the revenue sent back by family members working abroad has kept the Lebanese economy afloat during the difficult war years. That revenue reached $5.5 billion in 2007 and has increased steadily each year, according to the World Bank. City dwellers in Lebanon have a fairly Western lifestyle, although with a very high cost of living. Most city families are small, averaging two children each. Children are cherished in Arab families and are treated well. Most children live with their parents until they get married, and it is not unusual for more than one generation to live in the same household. Cousins are considered to be as close as brothers and sisters, and children grow up understanding that if they do not show respect for their elders, they will be disciplined.

Mothers play an important role in caring for home and family. Although many women work outside of the home, that work often is done out of necessity rather than choice. Lebanon also contains many class distinctions, which limit opportunities for advancement to the wealthier. In the past, Maronite Christians were the most privileged class, but other Christian and Muslim groups have gained more economic power and social status in recent years.

Rural families generally live on small family farms and have many more children—usually between 10 and 15—to provide help with the farm work. Farmhouses are made of stone or concrete with tile floors, have only a few necessary pieces of furniture and use a small wood-burning or kerosene stove for heat in the winter. Most rural houses have running water. The social center of rural life is the *foorn*, the village bakery where the women bake their loaves of bread. Women on the farms have a very busy life; they do all the cooking, cleaning, and laundry (in old-fashioned washtubs, with no electric dryers), plus they work in the fields when needed. Men work in the fields.

11 CLOTHING

Western-style fashions are popular in Lebanon's cities. Urban women are very fashion-conscious and want to wear the latest styles from the West. More traditional clothes are still worn in some villages. Women wear long dresses for and men wear black pants and jackets. Men's pants are full and baggy from the waist to the knee and tightly fitted from the knee to the ankle. Their jackets have fancy, brightly colored, embroidered trim. Traditionally, Lebanese men wore a short, rounded, cone-shaped brown felt hat, which some older rural men continue to wear. Most modern Lebanese men, however, have traded it in for a *keffiya*, the common Arab headscarf.

¹² FOOD

Lunch is the big meal in Lebanon, and almost everything is eaten with bread. Two types of unleavened Lebanese bread are *khub,* which resembles pita bread, and *marqouq*, which is paper thin. Lebanese do not eat fish and dairy in the same meal, and restaurants do not serve sweets. The usual dessert in a Lebanese restaurant is *fawakeh*, a huge bowl of whatever fresh fruit is in season. *Mezze* are widespread in the Middle East, including Lebanon; the closest Western equivalent is appetizers, though this hardly does them justice. Often a whole meal is made of mezze, which really just means any food served in small portions. Dinners are not served in set courses as in the West, but rather are put out all at once on the table for people to pick and choose from as they wish. *Kibbeh* (or *kibbe*) is the "national dish" of Lebanon—a concoction made of either lamb or beef and cracked wheat (bulghur, or *birghol*), of which there are as many variations as there are Lebanese cooks.

Lebanese pantries generally stock allspice, anise, Arabic coffee, cracked wheat, chickpeas, cinnamon, cloves, coriander, cumin, various dried beans, grape leaves (which are served stuffed with various things, such as rice or meat), *laban* (home-made yogurt), lentils, mint, nutmeg, olive oil, orange blossom water, oregano, parsley, pine nuts, pistachios, ghee (clarified butter), rice, rose water, sesame seeds, and tahini (sesame paste). These are the most common ingredients in Lebanese cooking.

Wine has been made in Lebanon for thousands of years. A unique Lebanese alcoholic creation is *arak*, a colorless, 100%-alcohol beverage flavored with anise. (Anise seed is used quite a bit in Lebanese cooking; it has a licorice-like flavor.) *Arak* turns white when diluted with water, which is how it is served; the Lebanese call it "lion's milk." The other popular beverages are coffee served very thick, tea with lots of sugar and no milk, and local spring water from the mountains, which the Lebanese drink from special spouted decanters (pouring it into their mouths from a short distance away—a skill which must be developed).

¹³ EDUCATION

Lebanon's educational system is still undergoing reconstruction following the civil war. Education is highly valued in Lebanon, so parents send their children to private schools when they can afford to do so. Schools usually teach a combination of Lebanese, French, and U.S. curricula, and all children are required to attend at least eight years of school. Lebanon's literacy rate was 87.4% in 2003, a significant improvement from 75% in the mid-1990s. Children are strongly encouraged to prepare for college, and Lebanon has six major universities and several technical institutions.

¹⁴ CULTURAL HERITAGE

Lebanon was known as a center for Arabic culture before the civil war. The country is slowly regaining that reputation. Each year, international artists gather at the Baalbek International Festival (popularized by the Lebanese superstar Fairuz), at the ruins of Roman temples in the Bekaa Valley.

Lebanon also has long been known for its high-quality book publishing, and a flourishing film industry produces high-quality films. There is some serious dramatic theater, but most of the energy in the last two to three decades has gone into a folk art and music and dance revival that began in the late 1960s. The national folk dance of Lebanon is the *debki*, a line dance in which people hold hands and step and stamp to the beat of a small drum called a *derbekki*. Classical belly dancing also plays an important role at weddings, and instrumental music is experiencing a revival. Lebanese craftsmen also are known for their glassmaking, weaving, pottery, embroidery, and brass and copper work. Many authors write in French, English, and Arabic, and celebrate a coming together of cultures through a form of poetry known as *zajal*, in which several poets sing in an improvised dialogue.

¹⁵ WORK

Lebanon traditionally has had a higher proportion of skilled labor than other Arab countries, but the civil war caused many of those skilled workers to seek better opportunities abroad. Those who have remained in the country often have difficulty finding work that is equal to their skills. The Lebanese economy relies on services, but agriculture and industry are important contributors, as well.

Many educated Lebanese do not take their government seriously. Government workers, as a result, tend to keep erratic hours. Remittances from Lebanese abroad contribute substantially to the economy, but the country's long-term progress depends on whether it is able to attain long-term political stability. Post-war rebuilding also has widened the economic divide between Lebanon's rich and poor. A strong middle class has yet to emerge.

¹⁶ SPORTS

Sports are taken very seriously by the Lebanese. The war made it difficult to pursue organized or professional sports in recent years, but soccer, basketball, and volleyball are popular. Horseback riding was popular before the war closed the clubs, and horse-racing still occurs in the Beirut hippodrome. Cross-country running, particularly in the mountains, and the martial arts are widely practiced. Skiing, rock-climbing, and caving are also enjoyed in the mountains. Many Lebanese go swimming and fishing in the lakes, rivers, or visit beaches along the Mediterranean coast.

¹⁷ ENTERTAINMENT AND RECREATION

Lebanon has numerous television stations, and television is a more common media source than newspapers. Some of the television stations devote their time completely to Christian programming, while others emphasize Muslim programming or offer a mix. Lebanese cinemas tend to show violent and/or sexy American and European films, although Lebanon itself also has a vital filmmaking industry. Dramatic theater, particularly comedies that poke fun at government leaders and Lebanese society is popular, as are nightclubs and pubs. At home, besides watching television, Lebanese enjoy playing board games (especially *Monopoly*), chess, checkers, card games, and backgammon, which is called *tawleh* (translating literally as "table"). The national pastime in Lebanon, however, is talking.

A Lebanese police officer patrols as customers sit at a sidewalk café on Hamra street Beirut, Lebanon. Hamra Street fills with people rediscovering its cafés, bars, and restaurants. (AP Images/Hussein Malla)

18 FOLK ART, CRAFTS, AND HOBBIES

Traditional Lebanese crafts include basketry, carpet-weaving, ceramics and pottery, copper and metalworking, embroidery, glass-blowing, and gold- and silver-smithing. Lebanon is also known for its finely crafted church bells. Wine-making can also be considered an art, dating back for thousands of years in Lebanon.

19 SOCIAL PROBLEMS

Lebanon's civil war caused widespread destruction and a huge social upheaval. It will take several decades for the country to recover from its effects. At least 120,000 people were killed and 300,000 wounded in the fighting, most of them civilians. Another 800,000 or so left the country, mostly the wealthy and well-educated. As many as 1,200,000 Lebanese—almost half the population—had to move from their homes and neighborhoods during the war. Those who remain face a future of high unemployment and a widening gap between the very rich and the poor.

Unrest in the Middle East continues to leave Lebanon vulnerable to attack, even with the end of the civil war. A 2006 eruption of violence between Israeli troops and Hizbullah militants in Lebanon offers ample evidence of the outside threats

that face Lebanon. Although most Lebanese Christians and Muslims maintain cordial relations with each other, some hostility from the war still lingers. Each religion maintains a separate court system under Lebanese law to handle matters of marriage, divorce, and inheritance, and marriage between persons of different religions is strictly forbidden.

Lebanon also faces the question of how to handle Palestinian refugees who fled Israel in 1967. Several hundred thousand refugees still reside in decaying and overcrowded camps in Lebanon, and many of them have lived without adequate healthcare, education, housing, or opportunities for employment for their entire lives. The Lebanese government restricts Palestinians from seeking economic and social aid. In addition to the long-time Palestinian refugee community, Lebanon now faces growing numbers of Iraqis fleeing their war-torn country.

20 GENDER ISSUES

Lebanese laws and court systems do little to help women. As a result, women face widespread discrimination in both public and private life. Lebanese laws allow for each religion to have a separate court system to handle matters of marriage, divorce, and inheritance. Frequently, the religious customs fail to protect women from domestic violence. The human rights organization Amnesty International reported in its 2008 Human Rights Watch report that female domestic workers who had migrated from other countries also face violence in Lebanese households. At least six female migrant workers died in 2007 under suspicious circumstances, according to Amnesty International.

²¹ BIBLIOGRAPHY

Amnesty International. *Amnesty International Report 2008: State of the World's Human Rights.* http://thereport.amnesty.org/eng/Homepage (October 26, 2008).

Aziz, Barbara Nimri. "Life Links Arab Muslims and Christians." In *National Catholic Reporter* 31, no. 31 (2 June 1995): 14.

Background Note: Lebanon. United States Department of State, http://www.state.gov/r/pa/ei/bgn/35833.htm (October 25, 2008).

Keen, Lynda. *Guide to Lebanon.* Old Saybrook, CT: The Globe Pequot Press, 1995.

Lebanon. CultureGrams: World Edition. Ann Arbor, Mich.: ProQuest LLC, 2008.

"Lebanon's remittance inflow reaches $5.5 billion in 2007," *The Daily Star,* August 22, 2008, http://www.dailystar.com.lb/article.asp?edition_id=1&categ_id=3&article_id=95259 (October 26, 2008).

Marston, Elsa. *Lebanon: New Light in an Ancient Land.* New York: Dillon Press, 1994.

St. Elias Church Ladies Guild. *Cuisine of the Fertile Crescent.* Leawood, KS: Circulation Service, 1993.

—revised by H. Gupta-Carlson

LEPCHAS

PRONUNCIATION: LEP-chuhz
ALTERNATE NAMES: Rong
LOCATION: Nepal; Bhutan (Mt. Kanchenjunga in the Eastern Himalayas)
POPULATION: 75,000 (estimate)
LANGUAGE: Lepcha; Nepali
RELIGION: Animism and Buddhism

¹ INTRODUCTION

Lepchas are the original inhabitants of Sikkim, formerly an independent kingdom situated in the Himalayas between Nepal and Bhutan. *Lepcha* is the name given to this group by their Nepali neighbors and is interpreted by some as a derogatory word meaning "nonsense talkers." The Lepchas call themselves *Rong.*

The Lepchas are of Mongoloid stock, and some anthropologists trace their origins to Mongolia or Tibet. However, the people themselves have no traditions of past migrations and place the home of their ancestors (Mayel) near Mt. Kanchenjunga. The early history of the Lepchas is obscure, their isolation no doubt limiting contacts with the outside world. The Bhutias began moving into the region from Tibet in the 14th century AD. Sometime before the beginning of the 17th century, Sikkim became subject to Tibet. Internal upheavals in Tibet early in the 17th century led to three "Red Hat" lamas (monks) fleeing to Sikkim, where they converted the population to Buddhism and created a Sikkimese Tibetan king. For the next three centuries, the Lepchas of Sikkim were dominated by the Bhutias, the Nepalese, and later the British. In 1950, although it remained independent under its ruling *chogyal* (king), Sikkim became a protectorate of India. Following a plebiscite in which Hindu immigrants from India made the difference in the voting, Sikkim became the twenty-second state of the Indian union in 1975.

² LOCATION AND HOMELAND

Lepchas occupy the southern and eastern slopes of Mt. Kanchenjunga, in the eastern Himalayas, and parts of neighboring western Bhutan and of Nepal. Population estimates for the Lepcha vary wildly. Some sources claim a total Lepcha population of around 50,000, while others see 85,000 in western Bhutan alone. Given the fact that the Lepchas are known as the "Vanishing Tribe," 50,000 to 75,000 seems a reasonable estimate for the current Lepcha population. The region Lepchas inhabit varies in elevation from 230 m (750 ft) in the Sikkim basin to the summit of Kanchenjunga at 8,586 m (28,168 ft) above sea level. The land has been dissected by the River Tista (Tîsta) and its tributaries into a jumble of steep-sided valleys separated by precipitous hills that rise northwards to the majestic peaks of the Himalayas.

Most settlements and cultivated land lie between 1,070 m and 2,285 m (3,500–7,500 ft) above the hot, steamy river valleys. Above this zone, fields give way to forests and mountain pastures. Mean temperatures range from 4.4°c to 30°c (40°F–86°F). Rain is almost continuous from June to September, with snow lying on the ground throughout the year above 2,440 m (8,000 ft).

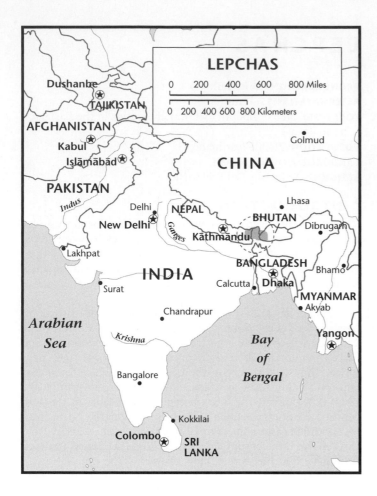

home and sending them down to the mundane world. There, Fudong-thing and Nuzong Nyu were blessed with children and became the ancestors of the Lepcha people.

⁵ RELIGION

Animism survives today side-by-side with Buddhism in Lepcha society. The older Mun religion, named after the *mun* or male priest, focuses on appeasing or warding off evil spirits *(moong)* who bring sickness and misfortune upon people. The spirits are appeased by the sacrifice of animals, or by the direct intervention of the priest or one of the lesser religious practitioners among the Lepchas. The Lepchas acknowledge the existence of various deities and benevolent spirits, but rarely make regular offerings to them.

Overlying the beliefs and practices of Mun are the formal structures of lamaistic Buddhism. It is said that Buddhism was introduced to the region from Tibet around 1641, with the first monasteries founded towards the end of the 17th century. While the Lepchas have accepted certain aspects of Tibetan Buddhism (e.g., the ritual, the mythology, and the hierarchy of lamas), concepts such as asceticism and individual responsibility for one's spiritual welfare are totally alien to them. For the common person, the mun is of far greater importance in daily religious life than is the lama. (*Lama* is a Tibetan word; the Lepcha term for a lama is *yook-mun,* literally, "honored Mun.") However, the ceremonies of the two religions are usually performed simultaneously. Some writers have gone so far as to describe the Lepcha religion as "animistic Buddhism."

A small number of Lepchas have converted to Christianity.

⁶ MAJOR HOLIDAYS

Most Mun ceremonies are performed for the benefit of individuals or households, although some important events are communal celebrations. The Cherim ceremony is held twice a year to keep the Lepchas free of illness. Both muns and lamas perform various rituals, which include offerings to the devils and the gods, and animal sacrifice. Buddhist lamas have to visit the monastery twice a month for festivals held in honor of Guru Rimpoche (the monk Padmasambhava who introduced Buddhism into Tibet) and the god Kanchenjunga. The feasts accompanying these celebrations may last up to 36 hours. The lamas also observe regular calendrical festivals such as the exorcism of the quarrel demon or the three-day *Boom koor.*

⁷ RITES OF PASSAGE

During the later months of pregnancy, Lepchas take certain ritual precautions for the safe delivery of the baby. This includes various taboos as well as sacrificing chickens to appease Sor moong, the demon who causes miscarriages. The Lepchas believe that on the third day after its birth, a baby is visited by a fairy who writes out its future on its forehead. At this time an animal, preferably an ox, but failing that, a pig or a goat, is sacrificed to mark the birth of a male, though not a female. A horoscope is cast by a *mun* (male priest) or *bonthing* (female priest), and the child is given a temporary name, often the day of the week on which it was born. The "sacred name" of the infant is recorded in the horoscope but never used. Names are unimportant to the Lepchas, and one may grow up with a variety of nicknames or pet names that are liable to change from time to time.

³ LANGUAGE

The Lepcha language, known as *Rongring* to the Lepchas, is classified as a Tibeto-Burman tongue. It is placed by some in the Naga group of this language family. Rongring is written in an alphabet that was derived from a Tibetan script by King Chador of Sikkim sometime at the end of the 17th or beginning of the 18th centuries. The purpose of this was apparently to enable the Lepchas to read the Buddhist scriptures. Today, few Lepchas speak the language or are familiar with the Lepcha script. Most Lepchas, instead, speak and write Nepali.

⁴ FOLKLORE

The Lepcha myth of origin tells that Itbu-mu, the Mother-Creator, made the earth and the heavens and all that they contained. She shaped the mountains and the lakes and the animals that inhabit the earth. Last of all, she took pure snow from the top of Mt. Kanchenjunga, shaped it into a human form, and infused it with life. This first man was known as Fudong-thing. Perceiving his state of loneliness, the goddess took marrow from his bones and created a partner for him, a woman called Nuzong Nyu. The first two humans lived in Ne Mayel Kyong, the ancestral home of the Lepchas that supposedly lies in an inaccessible valley near Kanchenjunga. Though commanded by Itbu-mu to live as brother and sister, the two commenced having sexual relations. The offspring of this forbidden union were devils and evil spirits that plague the Lepchas even today. When the gods discovered the transgression, they punished the offenders by casting them out of their idyllic

Two Lepcha women stir large pots of potatoes in a village in Sikkim, India. (© Earl and Nazima Kowall/Corbis)

Until a child is old enough to walk, it is carried in a cloth tied to the back of the mother or another adult. Children are treated as "little adults" and expected to behave accordingly. At the age of about four, a child is given a plate, a cup, a set of clothes, and a small haversack to carry objects just like an adult. Life is somewhat difficult and dull for adolescents. Boys farm or hunt with their fathers, while girls share the household chores with their mothers.

For the Lepchas, death is terrifying. All funeral rituals are performed to get rid of the dead and to ensure that they do not return as evil spirits. At the time of death, a lama is consulted to determine what spirits caused the death, how they should be appeased, and what means of disposal of the body should be followed. Ordinary women and men are usually buried, lamas and nuns are cremated, and children are placed in a river. Animal sacrifice and purification ceremonies are performed as deemed necessary. Both muns and lamas are called on to conduct the funeral rites, the former usually outside the house and the latter in the house. The body is then taken to the burial ground where it is placed in a grave, invariably facing north. Following the disposal of the corpse, the *sanglion* ritual or "speeding of the soul" is performed. This is an expensive ceremony involving a feast, distribution of gifts, animal sacrifice, and reading from the scriptures.

8 INTERPERSONAL RELATIONS

Lepchas are identified by many who have had dealings with them as a gentle, unselfish people, who are extremely shy in their dealings with strangers. They are peaceful in nature, and every effort is made to prevent or stop personal quarrels, which are seen as unsocial behavior. Casual visitors to a Lepcha house are always presented with refreshment. Gift-giving forms an important part of daily life. A guest attending a feast takes a gift with her or him, and also departs with a gift (usually uncooked meat). Any visitor takes a gift for the host, and in turn is given a gift when he or she leaves. Children are taught from an early age that it is good manners when receiving a gift from an elder to accept it with joined hands.

9 LIVING CONDITIONS

Lepcha villages consist of up to 15 or 20 houses, scattered across a hillside or in a forest. One writer notes that it is possible to walk through a village without ever knowing it is there. A Lepcha dwelling *(li)* is rectangular in plan, with a circular or rectangular roof made from straw. The floor is made of wood, raised 1 m or so (3 or 4 ft) above the ground, with the space underneath used to keep domestic animals. Walls are built of thatch covered by clay. The entire structure is built without nails or screws. A house typically contains three rooms: a bedroom, guest room, and kitchen/store room. Furnishings may include low wooden stools, or built-in wooden benches padded for comfort. Water is drawn from streams, waterfalls, or natural reservoirs.

Most villages have a *gompa* or place for Buddhist worship, and Buddhist prayer flags fluttering in the mountain breezes are a common sight in villages throughout the region. Villag es are linked by mountain tracks, rather than roads, and the people are adept at crossing the hills and carrying loads over tracks that are often too steep even for mules.

10 FAMILY LIFE

Lepchas are divided into patrilineal clans known as *ptso.* There is no ban on marriage within the same clan, although the rules of incest clearly define the closeness of the blood relationship acceptable between spouses. Uncles play an important role in matchmaking and the negotiations preceding a wedding. Marriages are arranged by the parents, and usually occur when the boy is around 16 and the girl 14 years of age. Following the betrothal ceremony, the boy is allowed to remain in the girl's house and little attention is paid if she conceives during this period. The actual wedding takes place anytime from a few days to several months later, on an auspicious day of the month. Both muns and lamas are required to officiate at the marriage ceremony, which is accompanied by the presenting of gifts to the bride's family, feasting, and other rituals. The bride returns to live with her husband's family. Divorce or separation is very rare and when it occurs is usually for incompatibility or the refusal of the wife to work properly.

11 CLOTHING

The original dress of both Lepcha men and women consists of knee-length drawers and an undershirt or bodice, over which a long piece of striped material is worn like a cloak. This coarse, homewoven outer garment is fastened at the shoulder by a brooch and is belted at the waist by a sash. The sash of ordinary people is usually red or purple, while that of lamas is yellow. The Lepcha hat *(thaktop)* is loaf-shaped and made of leaves attached to a bamboo frame and decorated with a feather. Men traditionally always carried a long knife slung from the belt in a bamboo scabbard.

Women adorn themselves with a variety of ornaments—silver hoops or rings in the ears; necklaces made from gold, silver, semiprecious stones, or even silver coins; and charm boxes and small idols. Today, many Lepchas, especially women, have given up their indigenous dress in favor of Tibetan-style clothes.

12 FOOD

The Lepcha day begins at dawn with a substantial meal of cold rice and any leftover meat or other food from the previous evening's meal. This is taken with Tibetan-style tea (served with salt and butter). Popped corn or cold rice may be carried to the fields for snacks during the day, but the next full meal is taken in the evening when the family returns to the house. The evening meal is invariably accompanied by *chi,* beer made from millet or other grains. Rice is the staple food, though wheat or maize may be eaten if rice is not available. Buckwheat is ground into flour and baked into cakes. Lepchas, despite their Buddhist religion, are nonvegetarians and eat the meat of both domesticated and wild animals. They supplement their diet with vegetables and a variety of forest produce such as wild yams. Lepcha dishes are less spicy than Nepali or Indian food.

13 EDUCATION

Levels of literacy among the Lepchas vary according to location, but generally are low. Few speak, let alone read, Rongring. Demands that the language be introduced into the curriculum have been met with deaf ears by the government of Sikkim. As a consequence, the Lepcha language has all but disappeared. Children are taught Nepali in the schools, and this is the language in which both children and adults conduct their daily affairs. Lepchas favor formal education for both boys and girls, with literacy rates in the Indian state of Sikkim standing at c. 65% (2001), though again, women, with rates of 58.6%, lag far behind men, of whom over 72% are literate. In Sikkim, almost three-quarter of children between the ages of five and fourteen attend school (72.8%), but the discrepancy between male and female becomes very clear at the level of higher education. By contrast, in Nepal literacy varies between 44% for men and 34% for women (2001). Although specific data as regards literacy is not available for Bhutan, one suspects that, with an overall literacy rate of 44% for women in Bhutan, literacy for Lepcha women in Bhutan is closer to the value for Nepal than for Sikkim.

14 CULTURAL HERITAGE

Music and dance, as well as oral traditions of myth, legend, and folk songs, form an integral part of Lepcha culture. Instruments such as drums, bamboo flutes, and various stringed instruments are used to accompany songs *(vam)* and dances at various social and ceremonial occasions. Love songs are popular, while other songs focus on themes such as marriage, agriculture, and war. Lepcha dances *(lok)* fall into six categories: nature dances, war dances, agricultural dances, dances on historical themes, the mystic *yaba* dances, and dances presenting incidents from Lepcha mythology.

15 WORK

Though originally hunters and gatherers, Lepchas are now primarily engaged in farming and rearing livestock. Their principal food crop is rice, with other cereals and vegetables also grown for consumption. Millet is cultivated for making beer, not for eating. Cardamom is the most important cash crop and an important export of the region. Cattle, goats, pigs, and chickens are raised, as much for ritual sacrifice as for their food value.

16 SPORTS

Lepcha children have no toys and do not participate in any organized games. Older boys amuse themselves by snaring small birds and imitating bird calls, or by making and playing bamboo flutes. Adults usually do not engage in organized or spectator sports, although in towns like Darjiling they have access to sports facilities.

17 ENTERTAINMENT AND RECREATION

Although festivals and folk traditions remain a major source of entertainment for the Lepchas, radio, television, and the movies have all had their impact on Lepcha life. It is not uncommon to find the walls of Lepcha houses decorated with photographs of Hindi and Western movie stars, with Bruce Lee being among the most popular.

18 FOLK ART, CRAFTS, AND HOBBIES

Although Lepchas are skilled in activities such as basketry, weaving, spinning, and carpentry, there are no distinctive arts or crafts that can be identified specifically with the Lepcha community.

19 SOCIAL PROBLEMS

Lepchas are classed as a Scheduled Tribe under the Indian constitution. However, largely as a result of their small numbers and the cultural dominance of the Bhutias and Nepalese, they are clearly in danger of losing their cultural identity. The Lepchas' position as an ethnic minority would become even more tenuous should Nepalese demands for a "Gurkhaland" in the region of Darjiling ever succeed. Some Lepchas see conversions to Christianity as a threat to the traditional character of the community. It is, however, the loss of the Lepcha language—combined with intermarriage and assimilation with the local Nepalese population—that is the most serious threat to the continued survival of traditional Lepcha culture in the eastern Himalayas.

This is further threatened by development projects such as the Tista Valley hydroelectric project Stage V at Dzonghu. All three 170-megawatt power stations involved were commissioned in early 2008, but numerous concerns were expressed during the planning and development stage of the project. Not only have local Lepcha communities lost agricultural land that has been submerged, though one argument put forward for the project was that it was designed to use only 67.75 hectares of land, the project also brought along with it a large number of laborers who were seen to have the potential for an irreversible negative impact on the Lepcha communities residing in the area. It was feared that the influx of large number of laborers would affect the culture and way of life of the community, and cause a "sense of deprivation and loss of ethnic identity" resulting in "dilution of [Lepcha] social customs and practices" and affect the availability of labor for work on the Lepchas' remaining fields. The presence of a large number of people in an area that was earlier sparsely populated, it was also feared, might also result in health problems and outbreak of diseases, including those that may not have occurred in the past within the community. However, the environmental clearance letter that allowed the project to move forward stipulates that the labor camps should be located outside the Lepcha settlements and that when the project is completed, the labor force must not be allowed to settle anywhere in Sikkim. The conditions laid down are easier to put on paper than enforce and may not go very far in protecting local tribal communities from the influx of a large population of migrant workers for a several years. Problems that have occurred in the area since the project commenced include a considerable increase in STDs among the local population as well as the creation of illegal housing on forest lands. Local Lepchas, members of ACT (Affected Citizens of Teesta) went on a hunger strike to protest the Tista Project, which, when complete, envisages 26 dams along the Tista River in Sikkim and is part of a broader government development plan that affects the entire north-east.

This problem is not unique to the Lepchas, but is faced by tribals all across the subcontinent—development projects that threaten to damage what is, in many cases, a fragile ecosystem and disrupt a traditional way of life. It is of special significance, however, in the case of the Lepchas because of the relative small numbers of the community, whose way of life is already under threat. Once traditional Lepcha society is destroyed, it is gone forever and will never be revived. Most Lepchas in Sik-

kim see an uncaring central government in Delhi that places its own developmental needs ahead of the needs and desires of its citizens.

In Bhutan, the threat to Lepchas comes from a different quarter. After centuries of protecting local cultures by limiting contact with the outside world, the Bhutanese government has allowed satellite television to enter the country, and is also trying to encourage tourism, thus exposing its people to Western influences. Experience has shown that wherever the Western way of life comes into contact with more "primitive" cultures, the latter soon lose their character and adopt Western ways.

As minority groups in all three countries in which they live, the Lepcha lack any serious political representation. In Sikkim, they do share 12 seats in the state assembly with the Bhutia, but in general they lack any political voice—this seems to be the fate of minority ethnic groups everywhere. The recent political changes in Nepal and the dominance of the Bhutias in Bhutan, combined with the Lepchas relatively small numbers, leave them out in the political cold.

20 GENDER ISSUES

Even though Lepcha society is patriarchal and patrilineal, women are accorded a degree of respect that is the hallmark of tribal societies in the sub-continent. Marriages are arranged by families and marriage customs are strongly influenced by Tibetan practices, but divorce is very rare. This is possibly because Lepchas are highly tolerant of one another's sexual activities, and they feel very little jealousy toward each other. When disputes arise because of an extra-marital liaison to which one partner objects, the causes are blamed on the uncontrollable temperaments of individuals. However, when adultery occurs discretely, the aggrieved spouse will generally not pay attention; only if it is practiced openly and flagrantly will the other spouse appeal to the elected leader of the village.

Lepcha agricultural tasks are not sexually segregated, fathers play an important role in the care of children, the Lepcha give great emphasis to the role of the female in their conceptions of origin, and female deities occupy center stage in Lepcha mythology.

Yet, poverty, involvement in traditional economic activities (i.e. subsistence agriculture), and lack of access to education remain issues facing Lepcha women, who follow a way of life that is disappearing rapidly under the pressures of contact with the outside world.

21 BIBLIOGRAPHY

Bhasin, Veena. *Ecology, Culture, and Change: Tribals of Sikkim Himalayas.* New Delhi: Inter-India Publications, 1989.

Chattopadhyay. Tapan. *Lepchas and Their Heritage.* Delhi: B. R. Publishing Corporation, 1990.

Gorer, Geoffrey. *Himalayan Village: An Account of the Lepchas of Sikkim.* 2nd ed. New York: Basic Books, 1967.

Roy, D. C. *Dynamics of Social Formation among the Lepchas.* New Delhi: Akansha Publishing House, 2005.

Schwerzel, Jeffrey. *The Lapcha of Nepal.* Kathmandu: Udaya Books, 2000.

Thakur, R. N. *Himalayan Lepchas.* New Delhi: Archives Publishers, Distributors, 1988.

—by D. O. Lodrick

LI

PRONUNCIATION: LEE
ALTERNATE NAMES: Ha, Gei, Zun, Moi-Fau, and Shai
LOCATION: China (primarily Hainan Island province)
POPULATION: 1.2 million
LANGUAGE: Li
RELIGION: Ancestor worship
RELATED ARTICLES: Vol. 3: China and Her National Minorities

¹INTRODUCTION

The ancestors of the Li were included in the ancient "Luoyue," the general term for the minorities in southern China during the Western Han Dynasty (206 bc–ad 8). The name of Li, however, appeared in the ancient historical documents at the end of the Tang Dynasty (618–907) and has remained unchanged since the Song (960–1279). The Li continuously paid tribute to the imperial dynasties. Entering the Li's districts rather early, the Chinese developed marketplaces and towns. The development increased significantly under the imperial Tang (618–907), which became interested in trading with countries in the south by way of Hainan Island. At that time, 5 districts and 22 counties were set up. Since the Yuan Dynasty (1271–1368), Li headmen were appointed to rule their people by the imperial government. In the following centuries, the economic development of the Li districts was on par with their Chinese neighbors. They planted "double-harvest rice," made use of iron farm implements invented by the Chinese, and even learned to set up and operate bamboo-tube waterwheels for irrigation. Country fair trade at regular intervals flourished for centuries. Exports to the Chinese mainland represented an important part of the Li economy; among the main items exported were a local brand of oxen, coconut, and areca. Yet, oppression from the feudal government and native officials was so intense as to arouse quite a few uprisings of the Li in the last centuries. In contrast to the Li farmers, who adopted Chinese methods of agriculture in most Li districts, the rest of the population still lived in abject poverty. A primitive co-cultivation system, *hemu,* had been prevalent in these areas. A piece of land was owned and co-cultivated by several families bound by ties of blood and led by a senior member, the *hemu* "head." After the payment of common expenses and the reward for the *hemu,* the crops were divided equally.

²LOCATION AND HOMELAND

Li population was 1.2 million in 2000. They live in Hainan Province, dwell together with the Chinese, Miao (Hmong), and Hui in Baoting, Ledong, Dongfang, Qiongzhong, Baisha, Wanning, and Danxian counties. Hainan Island is located in the subtropics and boasts abundant rainfall and rich soil. In some areas, the hot climate yields three crops of rice annually. Corn, sweet potato, and cassava can be planted all year round. Coconut, pineapple, mango, cocoa, coffee, rubber, and areca abound in Hainan.

³LANGUAGE

Li language belongs to the Sino-Tibetan family, Zhuang-Dong group, Li Branch. There are five dialects. An alphabetical system of writing based on Latin was created in 1957. The self-given names of the Li include Ha, Gei, Zun, Moi-Fau, and Shai. Shai has been most popular; however, most now use the term Li, a traditional Chinese given name.

⁴FOLKLORE

The Li myth of origins is closely linked to the culture of pumpkins and to the history of the flood. A long, long time ago, so the story goes, there were two brothers. Both of their wives were heavy with child for three years already. One day, a white-headed old man advised them to plant a pumpkin in front of the door in order to hasten childbirth. The brothers followed his advice. Subsequently both wives gave birth to a child. The elder brother had a son, the younger a daughter. The pumpkin continued to grow year after year. Then the flood came. The brothers were barely able to put their children inside the huge pumpkin in time to save them from the flood. When they got out of the pumpkin, the flood had already receded, but all the other people had drowned. They made a double-deck bed for the brother and sister. Before long, the sister got pregnant. The god in Heaven angrily cleaved a stone into two and struck a tree down to the ground, saying: "Any brother and sister who marry will be condemned to death." Thereafter, the brother and sister lived separately. The sister bore a fleshy lump, which was cut into three by the brother. One piece was enclosed in a piece of hemp cloth, put on a board, then driven by the current of the Nandu River. Ten months later, it became a Chinese child. That is why the ancestors of the Chinese wore clothing made of hemp. The second piece was wrapped in four smaller pieces of cloth, put on a leaf of a herbaceous plant, and left to drift about on the Wanqian River. Ten months later, it became a Miao child. That is why the Miao women's skirts are made of four pieces of cloth. The last piece was bound up in linen, put on a leaf of coconut, and sent adrift along the Changhua River. Ten months later, it became a Li child. That is why Li women wear linen. After the brother and sister gave birth to the Han, the Miao, and the Li in Hainan Island they became the local gods of the land.

⁵RELIGION

Ancestor worship and belief in ghosts and gods are widespread among the Li. They pay special attention to witchcraft. Witchcraft may cause great harm in the guise of disease or even death. A man practicing witchcraft is called *jingtai,* and a woman *jingpo.* There are two kinds of ancestor spirits, one evil and the other good. The good ensure safety and prosperity, while the evil bring about misfortune. On the death of a senior person, a grand funeral with all the trappings of ancestor worship will be held. Whoever falls sick must invite the shaman, *daogong,* or shamaness, *niangmu,* to exorcise the ghost; the shamans are also adept in divination and play a role of intermediary with the ghosts and gods. The Li have a number of taboos. For example, it is not auspicious to point one's head toward the door in one's sleep, because that is the position of the body of the dead before a funeral. If a guest lies in that direction, the host will be most unhappy.

⁶MAJOR HOLIDAYS

The Li celebrate the Spring Festival from the last day of the old lunar year to January 15 (Western calendar, between January 21 and March 7). The dinner party on the eve of the lunar New Year is the occasion for the whole family to reunite. Songs of New Year greetings will be sung. On the first and second of lunar January (Western calendar, between January 21 and February 21), the men of a village organize a group hunt. Half of the kill belongs to the hunter who first hits an animal in the hunt. The rest is divided among the villagers. A pregnant woman may have two portions. A traveler who happens to be in the village will also have his share.

⁷RITES OF PASSAGE

Elaborate funeral rites among the Li are related, as mentioned before, to ancestor worship. People announce a death by firing a shot. In areas bordering on Chinese settlements, the Li practice geomancy (divination by means of geographic features) for location of the tomb. In areas of *hemu*, the coffin is buried underground at a common burial ground. No tumulus or gravestone is set up, nor are there sacrificial offerings or grave sweeping after burial. However, after the funeral the family should receive guests with beef or pork. On the occasion of funerals, family members are allowed to drink and eat as usual, except for rice, which is then taboo. They bury the dead hastily. In general, if a person dies in the morning, the burial will take place in the afternoon; if death occurs in the afternoon, the deceased will be buried the following morning. Because of belief in the "Five Element Theory," burial is never held at noon, lest it lead to disaster. After the date when a person passed away, every twelfth day is celebrated as a commemoration; on "commemorative days" family members are not allowed to work in the field. Such observances last for as long as three years after the death occurred.

⁸INTERPERSONAL RELATIONS

If a guest calls in, the host will serve him areca; if the guest is not accustomed to areca, he should explain to the host. It would be a very impolite behavior simply to refuse.

Formerly, there was a dating custom called *fangliao*. Reaching adulthood, girls would go in groups to chop wood in the mountain; they carried the wood back to the outskirts of the village or to their family house. Helped by their parents, they built up a house (or an adjacent room) called *liaofang*, where the girls stayed every night from then on. A young man would sing or blow an instrument to express his affection to the girl. If they found each other congenial, a token showing his affection would be given to her. The young man would then be received by the girl in the fangliao house or room. The fangliao relation did not always lead to marriage. The illegitimate child often born from the fangliao relation was not discriminated against by the Li people. Today, the fangliao custom is waning and is practiced only in remote Li villages. The vast majority of Li youngsters choose more modern ways of social intercourse.

⁹LIVING CONDITIONS

In rural areas Li houses are built in the shape of a short-domed cylinder. The frame is laid out with bamboo or wood and is covered with a thatched roof. The walls are built with bamboo poles or branches of trees covered with mud. The floor is made of bamboo or rattan, about 20 inches above the ground. Some of their houses are two-story, provided with a gable roof. People live upstairs, the ground floor serving for livestock and storage. In urban areas, Li houses are the same as the Chinese.

The cities in Hainan Island are modernized. Highways are well developed. A railway makes a circuit around the island.

An integrated bus system links the main towns and villages on the island. Haikou (the capital, in the north) and Sanxia (main tourist resort, in the south) boast fully-equipped international airports.

¹⁰FAMILY LIFE

Most families in a village are of the same surname. The family is patrilineal and small. Reaching adulthood, the son or daughter moves to the fangliao room beside the house or in the common house. As soon as they marry, they cook separately from their parents. Since the women do a lot of fieldwork with the men, they have a rather high position in their family. According to traditional custom, women mediated conflicts in or among the villages. Even in cases of armed fighting among villages, women intervened in the dispute and helped negotiate a settlement.

¹¹CLOTHING

In mountainous areas, men wear a kerchief over the head, an edge-to-edge buttonless linen top and, instead of pants or shorts, two pieces of linen front and back below the waist (as a skirt). Fewer and fewer men still wear this traditional garment, the majority having adopted Chinese-style dress. Women wear an embroidered kerchief on the head, an edge-to-edge buttonless trimmed top with underwear, and a tight straight skirt woven with multicolored cotton threads and adorned with figures and designs. Some of their straight white skirts may reach down to the ankles. Almost all women like to wear earrings—

sometimes a wide and heavy array—as well as bracelets and necklaces. Tattoos also serve as feminine ornaments. Some women have designs tattooed on their faces, others over their hands, feet, neck, and chest. The designs vary in different areas, ranging from rather simple figures to very intricate ones. A growing number of Li women now wear Chinese clothes and ornamentation. Urban Li women are not different in outward appearance from those of other nationalities. The men are not tattooed, but they like to wear earrings.

[12] FOOD

Rice, corn, and yams are the staple foods of the Li. They eat three meals a day. Pottery is used for rice cooking. Meat is roasted or preserved in salt with ground rice and edible wild herbs. Vegetables are rare. Men have a passion for hunting, and meat is an important source of dietary protein. Men like drinking and smoking, while women are fond of chewing areca. The eating habits of the urban Li are the same as those of the Chinese.

[13] EDUCATION

Nearly 1,000 primary schools have been set up in Li areas. Over 90% of children reaching school age are enrolled. Besides formal schooling, literary classes, reading groups, and cultural rooms in the villages contribute to the elimination of illiteracy. Middle school students and college students are quite common. Their cultural and educational level is higher than average for the minorities, but it is still below average for the whole country.

[14] CULTURAL HERITAGE

The Li are well known for their natural talent for singing. In fact, folk songs are their principal means of expressing their emotions. Lyrics spontaneously flow from their mouths when they are touched by feelings. Folk songs may be performed as solos, as antiphonal singing, in unison, or in chorus. There are quite a few traditional musical instruments. The "Mouth Bow" is made of a thin piece of bamboo or copper, which is played by flicking the fingers. There are at least four kinds of vertical bamboo flutes particular to the Li, one of which is played by nose-blowing. The Li also have a wide array of dances accompanied by music and song, the most popular being the "Cutting Firewood Dance," the "Rice Husking Dance," and the "Double Sword Dance," all of which are colorful and have a rich flavor of life.

Li literature is mainly oral and includes lengthy epics handed down through many generations, all praising their heroes and founders; among the most popular are "Brave God of Unusual Strength," "Legend of the Five-Finger Mountain," and "Brother's Constellation."

[15] WORK

The Li mainly engage in rice planting, gathering, and hunting to complement their main economic activity. Li women excel in weaving textiles, especially silk cotton. Early in the Song Dynasty (1127–1279), Li brocade was already famous and was sought after by the Chinese. Tradition has it that the legendary expert of textiles, Lady Huang Daopo, lived in Li areas for 46 years. She dedicated herself to the improvement of textiles. Li women benefited considerably from her teaching.

[16] SPORTS

"Bamboo Dancing" is very popular among the Li. People sit on the ground in two rows, face to face, in pairs. Each pair holds two bamboo sticks by the ends. They rhythmically separate the bamboos and bring them back together. The dancers, following the rhythm, must jump in and out of the gap before the bamboo sticks are brought back together, or the foot will be caught between the bamboos; it is then almost impossible for the dancer to find his rhythm again and his feet get caught at almost every beat. The competition is open to all participants, young and old, and always attracts large crowds.

"Shooting a buffalo's leg" is another traditional sport. Each village selects a good archer. The buffalo leg is hung beneath a tree, about 30 m (100 ft) away from the shooters. Whoever hits the leg is allowed to take it back to his village and share it with the villagers.

[17] ENTERTAINMENT AND RECREATION

Although available, movies and television are not yet popularized among the rural Li. Their entertainment and recreation gravitate toward singing and dancing. In urban areas, however, a wide array of recreation and entertainment is available. Beach activities, especially on the southern shores of the island, have recently begun to attract more and more Li youngsters.

[18] FOLK ART, CRAFTS, AND HOBBIES

Li brocade is an important craft. Ornaments made of silver and animal bones have a unique style. Some women wear a few earrings in different patterns and also bracelets in different styles.

[19] SOCIAL PROBLEMS

Since Hainan Province is now the largest special economic zone of China, the social economy has developed rapidly in an integrated way. The current problem among the rural Li is the intense conflict between their traditional agricultural and rural culture and the modern industrial urban culture. The process of modernization seems inevitable, but there is no way to ensure a smooth and peaceful transition between traditional and modern values.

[20] GENDER ISSUES

The Chinese constitution states that women have equal rights with men in all areas of life, and most legislation is gender neutral. Li women, in traditional household, have a relatively high position. Women were the traditional mediators of community conflicts. As the Li become more urbanized, this tradition is changing somewhat, with men taking stronger roles.

China has strict family planning laws. It is illegal for women to marry before 20 years of age (22 for men), and it is illegal for single women to give birth. Though minority populations were previously exempt from family planning regulations, policy has changed in recent years to limit minority population growth. Today, urban minority couples may have two children while rural couples may have three or four.

[21] BIBLIOGRAPHY

Chiao, Chien, Nicholas Tapp, and Kam-yin Ho, ed. "Special Issue on Ethnic Groups in China." *New Asia Bulletin* no 8 (1989).

Dreyer, June Teufel. *China's Forty Millions*. Cambridge: Harvard University Press, 1976.

Eberhard, Wolfram. *China's Minorities: Yesterday and Today*. Belmont: Wadsworth Publishing Company, 1982.

Gustafsson, Bjorn A., Shi, Li, and Sicular, Terry, eds. *Inequality and Public Policy in China*. New York: Cambridge University Press, 2008.

Heberer, Thomas. *China and Its National Minorities: Autonomy or Assimilation?* Armonk, NY: M. E. Sharpe, 1989.

Lebar, Frank, et al. *Ethnic Groups of Mainland Southeast Asia*. New Haven: Human Relations Area Files Press, 1964.

Lemoine, Jacques. "Les Li de Haïnan." In *Ethnologie régionale II* (Encyclopédie de la Pléiade). Paris: Gallimard, 1978.

Ma Yin, ed. *China's Minority Nationalities*. Beijing: Foreign Languages Press, 1989.

Ramsey, S. Robert. *The Languages of China*. Princeton: Princeton University Press, 1987.

Schafer, Edward H. *The Shore of Pearls*. Berkeley: University of California Press, 1970.

———. *The Vermilion Bird: T'ang Images of the South*. Berkeley: University of California Press, 1967.

Shin, Leo Kwok-yueh. *The Making of the Chinese State: Ethnicity and Expansion on the Ming Borderlands*. New York: Cambridge University Press, 2006.

Wiens, Harold J. *Han Chinese Expansion in South China*. New Haven: The Shoestring Press, 1967.

—by C. LeBlanc

LINGAYATS

PRONUNCIATION: lin-GAH-yuhts
ALTERNATE NAMES: Virashaivas
LOCATION: India (Karnataka state)
POPULATION: 15 million (estimate)
LANGUAGE: Kannada
RELIGION: Lingayat
RELATED ARTICLES: Vol. 3: People of India

1 INTRODUCTION

Lingayats are members of a religious sect in India that dates from the 12th century ad. The name is derived from linga and ayta and means "the people who bear the linga (phallic symbol)." This is a literal description, as members of the sect wear a small stone phallus somewhere on their body. Men carry it in a silver box suspended on a thread or scarf around the neck, while women wear it on a neck-string under their clothes. The linga is the symbol of the god Shiva, and Lingayats are also called Virashaivas because of their passionate devotion to this deity.

The Lingayat movement began as a revolt against Brahmanical Hinduism. It is based on the teachings of Basava (c. 1125–c. 1170), who lived in Kalyana, a small town in central India in what is now northern Karnataka State. A Brahman himself, Basava (also Basavana) rejected the supremacy of Brahman priests, ritualism, concepts of ritual pollution, caste, and many other features of contemporary Hindu society and religion. He preached instead a populist message of equality, fraternity, and individuality. Basava's teachings spread through the region, where they became deeply entrenched among the local population. Even today, over 800 years later, Lingayats form a significant element in Karnataka culture and society.

2 LOCATION AND HOMELAND

Lingayats are distributed throughout Karnataka, with their greatest concentrations in the northern regions. Census returns in 2001 indicated that around 20% of the state's population were Lingayats (estimates made early in the 20th century place the percentage of Lingayats between 14% and 20% of the population). Assuming this proportion did not change much by 2008, the number of Lingayats in Karnataka would be close to 12 million. With Lingayats in Maharashtra numbering several million and several hundred thousand in Tamil Nadu and Andhra Pradesh, a current estimate of around 15 million people is reasonable. In the Lingayat heartland, as many as 67% of the people follow the religion. Small Lingayat communities are also found in the states of Goa, Kerala, Madhya Pradesh and West Bengal. A few Lingayat families are to be found among Indian immigrants in the United States and Canada.

The cultural heartland of the Lingayats is located in the interior of the Deccan Plateau. In the north of the region lie the hills and escarpments of the southern edge of the Maharashtra plateaus. These soon give way southwards to the lower lands of the middle valley of the Krishna River and its tributaries (the Bhima and the Tungabhadra). Further south, the terrain begins to rise towards the Mysore Plateau. The western margins of the region are defined by the Western Ghats, but there is no clear physical boundary on the east. Elevations of the plateaus

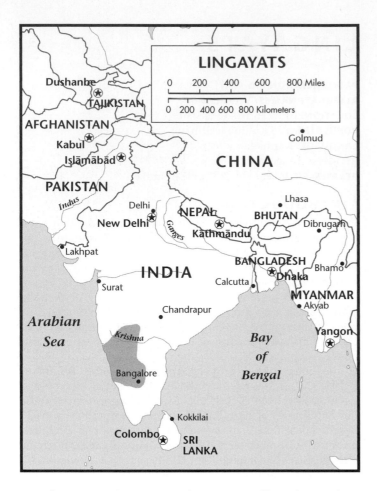

LINGAYATS

0   200   400   600   800 Miles

0   200   400   600   800 Kilometers

vary from around 455–760 m (1,500–2,500 ft) in the north to over 1,100 m (3,600 ft) in the south. Climate is of the tropical monsoon type. Mean monthly temperatures at Bellary in eastern Karnataka vary from 23°C (73.4°F) in winter to 33°C (91.4°F) in summer. Annual rainfall averages between 40 cm and 80 cm (16–31 in) throughout the entire region, except for the extreme western areas. Areas not under cultivation carry a poor scrub cover or open deciduous or thorn forest, except for a narrow belt of evergreens in the more humid west.

³ LANGUAGE

Lingayats fully identify with Kannada, which may be seen as the language of Lingayat culture. Basava, the founder of the sect, specifically set out his teachings in Kannada rather than in Sanskrit so that he could reach the common people. The boundaries of Karnataka State (called Mysore at the time) were redrawn in 1953 and 1956 to unite the Kannada-speaking peoples in a single administrative division. Kannada is one of the four major languages of the Dravidian language family. It is related to the other Dravidian tongues of South India (Tamil, Telugu, and Malayalam) but is written in its own script.

⁴ FOLKLORE

Basava, the founder of the Lingayat movement, and the other saint-mystics (e.g., Basava's nephew, Cennabasava; and Allama Prabhu) who helped spread its teachings are enshrined in the lore of the sect. Their own sayings and legendary accounts of their lives have entered the folk idiom of the Kannada people. The imagery and ideas presented in these works provide in-

teresting contrasts between Lingayat beliefs and those of the Brahmanical tradition. The crow, for instance, is a messenger of death in Brahmanical Hinduism. Many Hindus feed crows as part of their death rites, believing they are ancestors returned from the dead. In Lingayat culture, by contrast, the crow is an auspicious symbol of fellowship and sociability, known for its deep commitment to its community.

⁵ RELIGION

The Lingayats do not label themselves as Hindu. Their beliefs have been drawn from Tamil Shaivism and other Indian sources, but they have evolved a uniquely Lingayat character. Their doctrines represent a sweeping departure from those of orthodox Hinduism. Lingayats revere the *Vedas* (the sacred texts of Hinduism) but they do not accept the Brahmans' authority to interpret them. They reject the caste system and proclaim all wearers of the linga to be equal. They do not believe in rebirth and, consequently, have abandoned the doctrine of *karma* (the principle that actions in one life determine the nature of subsequent incarnations). Lingayats recognize the spiritual power (*śakti*) of Shiva; they worship him as the only god and do not recognize the other deities of Hinduism. In modern practice, however, Lingayats have taken to worshiping many gods in addition to Shiva. The doctrines and ideals of Lingayat religion and society are set out in the eight supportive systems (ashta-varna), the five principles of conduct (pañcha-âchâra), and the six-stage path (sat-sthala).

The Lingayat guru (spiritual leader) and jangama (priest) exert a considerable influence in the community. Priests, who can be male or female, officiate at life-cycle rituals. Some are also itinerant healers and astrologers, administering to the needs of the local people. Lingayats have their own temples, and their monasteries (matha) are flourishing centers of religious culture and education. Pilgrimages are undertaken to places such as Kalyan and Ulive, which are held sacred because of their association with Basava and other Lingayat saints.

⁶ MAJOR HOLIDAYS

Lingayats celebrate the birthdays of their saints, that of Basava being of particular importance. Two religious processions reported to be unique to the Lingayats are Nandi-kodu (Nandi's horn) and Vyasantol (Vyas' hand). Nandi is the sacred bull of Shiva, and the story goes that Nandi once lost a horn in a fight with a demon. His followers found the horn and triumphantly paraded it around. Lingayats follow the custom of carrying Nandi's horn (a long bamboo pole on which two brass bulls are fixed) through the streets in procession. On another occasion, a cloth hand is made and tied to Nandi's horn and paraded in the streets. This represents the hand of Vyas, reputed to be the author of the Purânas. In addition to their own celebrations, Lingayats also observe Hindu festivals such as Holi, Divali, and Ugadi (New Year's Day).

⁷ RITES OF PASSAGE

After birth, the family guru ties a linga around the neck of the newborn child, smears the child with ashes, and places on the child a garland of rudra beads (seeds of the tree *Elaeocarpus ganitrus*). These are said to be the tears of Shiva. The guru recites a prayer to Shiva in the baby's ear. The priest is sent for, and when she or he arrives, her or his feet are washed by the child's parents. The water is poured over the linga tied to the baby, who is then presented to Shiva by the priest. The priest is fed, and a small portion of food from the priest's dish is placed in the baby's mouth (this ceremony is known as *prasâd,* i.e., sacred offering). These rituals involve each of the elements in the eight supportive systems and symbols of the Lingayat religion (guru, linga, ashes, rudra beads, prayer, priest, the water that washed the priest's feet, and sacred offerings). Even today, the marks on the forehead (usually in white lime rather than ashes), the strings of rudra beads, and the linga around the neck serve to identify a follower of the Lingayat faith.

Death for the Lingayats is a cause of gladness because the dead person has exchanged the cares of this life for the joys of Shiva's heaven *(kailaś).* The body is bathed and laid out in the home. A priest reads passages from the Lingayat scriptures to help the soul in its flight to heaven. A feast is thrown for *jangams* (priests), and they are given money and clothes. The body is then placed on a gaily decorated chair and carried in procession to the grave. Lingayats always bury their dead, with the corpse seated cross-legged in the grave. Funeral rites end when the mourners return home and take purifying baths.

8 INTERPERSONAL RELATIONS

Lingayats conform to the customs of their local communities in their interpersonal relationships. Villagers meet in the streets, at tea shops, and at the *panchâyat* (village council) building to gossip and exchange news. Available leisure time is closely tied to the agricultural cycle.

9 LIVING CONDITIONS

Lingayat dwellings reflect regional house-types and rural settlement patterns. Northern Karnataka is an area where North Indian and South Indian patterns meet, with the shapeless, nucleated villages of Maharashtra giving way to the compact, square settlements—often with a tributary hamlet—found in southern areas. Houses are typically built of mud and stone, though cement is becoming more common. The house of a well-to-do Lingayat farmer typically has a roofed veranda in the front, built on a raised platform. This is used for resting and entertaining visitors. A doorway, with carved figures of Basava, leads into the living quarters, which include the kitchen, a room set aside for worship, and stalls for cattle. Hay, cow dung for fuel, and other goods are stored behind the house. Furnishings reflect the occupation, taste, and resources of the occupants.

10 FAMILY LIFE

Although Basava preached against caste and proclaimed all persons equal, the Lingayats have a complex system of social stratification that functions very much like a caste system. Women have a higher status than in traditional Hindu society. They exercise equal religious authority with men in household rites and festive ceremonies. In village communities, however, women still tend to occupy a subservient role. Considerable emphasis is placed on having male children, who are seen as essential for security in old age and salvation in the life to come.

The extended family is common in rural areas, but urban Lingayats tend towards the nuclear family. Marriages are arranged, though marriage practices are becoming much less restrictive among Lingayats with the spread of education. Residence is patrilocal (i.e., the bride and groom become part of the father's household) in rural areas, but newlyweds in urban areas often set up independent households. Divorce is uncommon. Widow remarriage is permitted.

11 CLOTHING

Apart from the ishta-linga ("personal" linga) worn around the neck, Lingayat dress resembles that of the region where the community lives. Thus, in central Karnataka a Lingayat farmer wears the *dhoti* (Indian loincloth), a long, collarless shirt, and a turban. He may throw a shoulder cloth across one shoulder. Women wear a bodice and *sâri,* with the upper end passed across the front of the body and draped over the head. Ornaments include a variety of necklaces, nose rings, earrings, bangles, and anklets. The wealthy prefer gold, while the poorer classes wear silver. Men, also, are fond of jewelry. In urban areas, men tend to follow the trend of wearing Western-style shirts, pants, and jackets.

12 FOOD

Lingayats are strict vegetarians, their staple food being *roti* (flat breads) made from millet, eaten with pulses, vegetables, chilies, onion, garlic, and condiments. Wheat, maize (corn), and rice also form part of the diet, as do milk, curds, and *ghî* (clarified butter). The use of alcohol, tobacco, and drugs such as opium is forbidden. Although theoretically an egalitarian sect, Lingayats have dining restrictions similar to those found among Hindus. For instance, members of the higher castes from which the jangams (priests) and leading merchants come do not eat with lower-ranked Lingayats who are primarily from various artisan groups. In the past, if a Maratha, a Muslim, or anyone not wearing the linga came into one's house and saw food, it would have to be thrown away.

13 EDUCATION

Education and literacy levels vary considerably among the Lingayats depending to a considerable extent on where they live. Literacy provides access to the professions, and thus the Lingayats appear to be well represented in law in Bombay compared to Lingayats in Karnataka. In a rural context, however, the typical attitude towards formal education among Lingayats is one of indifference or resistance. Although the Indian Constitution makes provision for free and compulsory education—from ages 6 to 14, attendance at school is low. Children, especially in a rural setting, are seen as much more valuable in helping support the family than in learning to read, write, and do arithmetic. A recent study in two villages in northern Karnataka (Dharwar District) dominated by Lingayats showed extremely low literacy rates (30.2% and 25.7% for the two villages, with the rates for women being 18.5% and 12.9%). This is in contrast to the overall literacy rates in Karnaatka, reported as 67.4% by the 2001 Census of India (76.29% for males and 57.45% for females). Lingayat monasteries, such as the Manvi Monastery in Belgaum, play an important role in modern education. Found in towns, both large and small, across Karnataka, the monasteries run schools and colleges and have provided many poor people with free board and lodging in urban centers to help them acquire an education and better themselves.

14 CULTURAL HERITAGE

Lingayats have a literary tradition that dates back to the 12th century AD. Their sacred literature includes the short lyrical sayings *(vāchanas)* of Basava, as well as the poetry and devotional hymns of over 200 writers. Of particular note is the fact that these are in the Kannada language rather than in Sanskrit and are accessible to the common people without reliance on Brahmanical interpretation. Lingayat literature is thus an important element in the regional culture of Karnataka. Several important Lingayat writers, such as Basava himself, writing in Kannada, have made important contributions to Karnataka culture, while Karnataka folk culture, in turn, forms part of the environment in which Lingayats live and work.

15 WORK

Lingayats are involved in a wide range of activities. Many are farmers, living in villages and leading lives not too different from other agriculturalists in northern Karnataka. Others provide the services on which the agricultural economy depends, such as carpentry, blacksmithing, leatherworking, and oil-pressing. Lingayats with the necessary educational background are also represented in government service and the professions, as teachers, doctors, lawyers, and professors. In urban areas in Karnataka, Lingayats dominate small trade, commerce, and the textile industry.

16 SPORTS

There are no games or spectator sports associated specifically with the Lingayat faith.

17 ENTERTAINMENT AND RECREATION

Lingayats have access to the same entertainment and recreational facilities as the general population of Karnataka. In villages, much of their enjoyment is derived from traditional pastimes (e.g., wrestling, bull-chasing, and folk-singing) associated with periodic fairs, festivals, and folk culture. In urban areas, television, movies, and modern sports activities are also available.

18 FOLK ART, CRAFTS, AND HOBBIES

There are no specific arts, crafts, or hobbies identified with the Lingayats. Lingayats share in the broader currents of folk traditions in Karnataka.

19 SOCIAL PROBLEMS

Lingayats face many of the problems of the general population of northern Karnataka. In rural areas, there are some Lingayats who have to deal with low living standards, poverty, and debt. Many, however, own land, and Lingayat villages are an integral element in the rural landscape of northern Karnataka. The Lingayat movement originated as a reaction against feudal Brahmanical society and rejected many aspects of traditional Hinduism. Lingayats do not wear the sacred thread and, even though they reject the caste system, they have a social stratification system that is akin to caste and, to all intents and purposes, are placed in the Shudra *varna* by Hindus. Although they have reacquired some aspects of the Hindu religion (a process for which there are many historical precedents), the Lingayats preserve a distinct identity in central India. Their commitment to populist ideals stands in direct contrast to the rigid hierarchy of traditional Hindu society. This has helped Lingayats modernize and in many ways achieve a status as one of the more progressive religious communities in modern India.

Despite rejecting the Hindu caste system of India, Lingayats have emerged as the dominant caste in many areas of Karnataka. Not only that, but they have managed to obtain political power and representation by getting themselves classified as an OBC (Other Backward Class) in Karnataka and thus gaining the benefits of this status (Lingayats, along with the Vokkaliga, another group classed as an OBC, have cornered the lion's share of seats reserved for the Scheduled Castes and OBCs). It does not matter how wealthy or educated one is, if one is classed as belonging to an OBC, one is entitled to apply for a reserved seat. On 30 May 2008 a Lingayat (B. S. Yeddyurappa) was sworn in as Chief Minister of Karnataka State. Lingayats formed a major voting bloc that put Yeddyurappa's party, the Bharatiya Janata Party (BJP), in power.

20 GENDER ISSUES

Lingayat religious ideology encompasses the principles of individuality, equality and fellowship and rejects inequalities based on gender, class or occupation. Therefore, Lingayat women do not occupy the subordinate role in which they tend to placed in Brahmanical society. Women exercise equal religious authority with men in household rites and festive ceremonies, and can even become priests. Lingayats traditionally do not favor child marriage and widow remarriage is allowed, although divorce is uncommon. In village communities, however, women still tend to occupy a subservient role, with considerable emphasis being placed on bearing male children, who are seen as essential for security in old age and salvation in the life to come. It is not uncommon for a Lingayat woman to wear a gold fertility necklace as a charm for obtaining a son, the necklace having thirty pendants, each with symbolic meaning connected to fertility.

Lingayats follow the Hindu law of inheritance and succession, but if a family does not have a son, a woman can inherit from her mother, whether gold, money or land. If a woman does not have a son, she tends not to adopt a male, as is the custom among Hindus, and passes on her wealth to her daughter.

Given their lack of commitment to Hindu principles of caste, Lingayat women tend to be in the forefront of modernization. However, in rural areas, they are still subject to poverty, low living standards, illiteracy, debt and lack of access to educational facilities—in fact, they suffer from the same problems as low caste Hindus.

21 BIBLIOGRAPHY

Chekki, D. A. *Religion and Social System of the Virasaiva Community.* Westport, CT: Greenwood Press, 1997.

Ishwaran, K. *Speaking of Basava: Lingayat Religion and Culture in South Asia.* Boulder, CO: Westview Press, 1992.

———. *Religion and Society Among the Lingayats of South India.* Leiden: E. J. Brill, 1983.

Michael, R, Blake. *The Origins of Vīraúaiva Sect : A Typological Analysis of Ritual and Associated Patterns in the Úūnyasampâdane.* Delhi: Motilal Banarsidass, 1992.

Yaravintelimath, C. R., trans. *Vacanas of Women Saints.* Bangalore: Basava Samithi, 2006.

—by D. O. Lodrick

MA'DAN (MARSH ARABS)

PRONUNCIATION: mah-DAHN
ALTERNATE NAMES: Marsh Arabs
LOCATION: Iraq (marshes at the junction of the Tigris and Euphrates rivers)
POPULATION: Fewer than 20,000 (2003 estimate)
LANGUAGE: Arabic
RELIGION: Islam (Shia Muslim)

1 INTRODUCTION

The Ma'dan, or Marsh Arabs, is a distinct group of people who originally inhabited the marshy area at the junction of the Tigris and Euphrates rivers in Iraq before the marshes were destroyed by irrigation projects developed by the Iraqi government. A seminomadic tribal people, the Ma'dan once lived in reed huts built on floating islands of reeds, and made their living by herding water buffalo, fishing, and hunting wild boars and waterfowl. Their houses were elaborately woven with Gothic-like arches made of bundles of reeds tied together at the top. This same kind of house had been built since the 4th millennium BC.

The term, Ma'dan, means "dweller of the plains." The tribal form of the Ma'dan took shape during the 17th century AD. Ma'dan culture is based on the culture of the Bedu (or bedouin, *see Bedu*) nomads of the desert, adapted for life on the watery marshes. Until the late 20th century, the Ma'dan way of life had changed little in thousands of years. However, the Ma'dan people encountered prejudice from other Arabs, and beginning in the 1970s, the marshes they had inhabited for 5,000 years were slowly destroyed for political and economic reasons by the Iraqi government. The waters of the Tigris and Euphrates were diverted in order to irrigate lands converted to agriculture and, after the 1991 Gulf War, Iraqi leader Saddam Hussein systematically drained the waters as a form of punishment for the Shia Muslims who opposed his regime.

The U.S. led invasion in 2003 removed Saddam from power and efforts to restore the marshes are underway. However, the damage done to the Ma'dan way of life in the 1990s is expected to take several decades to repair. In addition, the marshes have become extremely dangerous to inhabit as fighting among rebel groups in Iraq has intensified and moves the country toward civil war. In 2008, the marshes in a war-torn Iraq were used as a hiding area for criminals and rebels opposing the provisional Iraqi government installed by U.S. occupation forces. Many Ma'dan are believed to have joined insurgent movements in Iraq. Some are followers of the Iraqi Hizbullah organization, while others belong to Moqtada al-Sadr's movement and wield control in provincial areas under the provisional government organized by U.S. forces occupying Iraq.

2 LOCATION AND HOMELAND

The marshes where the Ma'dan once lived were created by the annual floods of the Tigris and Euphrates rivers. The marshes covered about 15,540 sq km (6,000 sq mi) and were divided into three parts: the Eastern Marshes east of the Tigris, the Central Marshes west of the Tigris and north of the Euphrates, and the Southern Marshes south of the Euphrates and west of the Shatt al Arab (the river formed by the union of the Tigris and Euphrates). Melting snow on the mountains of Iran and Turkey would cause the waters to rise on the rivers and in the marshes. The annual flood on the Tigris River typically reached its height in May. On the Euphrates River the floods peaked in June. From June on, both rivers would begin to fall, reaching their lowest levels in September and October. The water levels then would begin to rise slightly in November, increasing gradually throughout the winter.

The marshes were covered with rushes and reeds. Qasab, a kind of giant grass that looks like bamboo, covered most of the land and grew as tall as 7.6 m (25 ft). Natural islands, some floating and some anchored, dotted the waters, and the marshes were alive with wildlife, including turtles, frogs, various waterfowl, wild boars, and hordes of mosquitoes in the summer. Eagles were a common sight, soaring in the skies above the marshes. Summers were hot and humid; in the winter, the water was icy and the winds were cold. A strong wind, called the "forty days' wind," blew throughout the month of June. Some historians believe the marshes were the Garden of Eden from the Bible.

In the 1970s, the Iraqi government began to expand irrigation projects that disrupted the natural flow of water into the marshes. The efforts were continued more aggressively after the 1991 Gulf War, partly to punish Shia rebels who had risen against Saddam Hussein. By 2003, the marshes had become a desert, villages of Ma'dan had been attacked and burnt, and the water was reportedly poisoned. Most Ma'dan today are believed to live in lower income Shia communities in Baghdad or have emigrated to Iran, with a few thousand believed to have returned to their traditional homeland. Those Ma'dan who have returned to the marshes lack clean drinking water, sanitation, health care, and nutrition.

Some human rights experts have estimated that the Ma'dan population in 2003 was less than 20,000, compared with 500,000 in the 1950s.

3 LANGUAGE

The Ma'dan speak a form of Arabic that is generally considered a "lower" form by other Arabic speakers. Arabic, spoken by 422 million people worldwide, has many distinct dialects, so that people living as few as 500 km (about 300 mi) apart may not be able to understand one another. The written form of Arabic is called Classical Arabic, or, for today's literature and press, Modern Standard Arabic. It is the same for all literate Arabs, regardless of how different their spoken dialects are. Arabic is written from right to left in a unique alphabet that makes no distinction between capital and lower-case letters. It is not necessary for the letters to be written in a straight line, as English letters must be. Punctuation rules are also quite different from those of English.

"Hello" in Arabic is *marhaba* or *ahlan,* to which one replies, *marhabtayn* or *ahlayn.* Other common greetings are *As-salam 'alaykum,* "Peace be with you," with the reply of *Wa 'alaykum as-salam,* "and to you peace." *Ma'assalama* means "Goodbye." "Thank you" is *Shukran,* and "You're welcome" is *'Afwan;* "yes" is *na'am* and "no" is *la'a.* The numbers one to ten in Arabic are *wahad, ithnayn, thalatha, arba'a, khamsa, sitta, saba'a, thamanya, tisa'a,* and *ashara.*

Arab names consist of their first name, their father's name, and their paternal grandfather's name. Women do not take their husband's name when they marry but rather keep their father's family name as a sign of respect for their family of origin. Many Ma'dan have rather unusual names, especially for Muslims. The names Chilaib ("little dog"), Bakur ("sow"), and Khanzir ("pig") are common, even though Muslims consider those animals unclean. Other names include Jahaish ("little donkey"), Jaraizi ("little rat"), Wawi ("jackal"), Dhauba ("hyena"), Kausaj ("shark"), and even Barur ("dung"). Ma'dan often give unattractive names to children to ward off the evil eye, particularly to sons whose brothers died in infancy.

⁴ FOLKLORE

The traditional Ma'dan believed in *jinn,* bad spirits who could take the form of humans or other animals. Unique to Ma'dan folklore are two marsh monsters: the *anfish,* a giant serpent with hairy skin, and the *afa,* a giant serpent with legs. Both were said to live somewhere in the heart of the marshes, and both were deadly.

The Ma'dan also believed in a place called Hufaidh, an island of paradise located in the southwest part of the marshes, although no one knows exactly where. According to legends, the jinn could hide the island from human sight. On this island were palaces, palm trees, pomegranate orchards, and huge water buffalo. It was believed that anyone who saw Hufaidh was bewitched, and no one would be able to understand the person's words afterward.

⁵ RELIGION

Today, most Ma'dan are Shia Muslims, although they are not strict about following Muslim practices, such as praying five times a day facing Mecca. Karbala and Najaf are the Ma'dan's holy cities: Husain was killed and is buried in Karbala, and Ali the Saint's tomb is in Najaf.

⁶ MAJOR HOLIDAYS

Most Ma'dan observe Islamic holidays, such as Ramadan, Id al-Adha, and Id al-Fitr, which are based on a lunar calendar and thus fall on slightly different days every year. Most Ma'dan wish to make a pilgrimage to the city of Meshed, where the shrine of the eighth imam, Ali ar Ridha, is located. Anyone who makes this pilgrimage is given the title of *Zair.* Few Ma'dan have the economic resources to make the traditional Islamic pilgrimage to Mecca.

⁷ RITES OF PASSAGE

Ma'dan boys are traditionally circumcised at puberty, but many boys refuse because of the frequent occurrence of infection afterward.

After a death, some Ma'dan dye their turbans dark blue to signify mourning. Others put mud on their heads and clothes.

⁸ INTERPERSONAL RELATIONS

Ma'dan follow the traditional Arab code of honor, but with somewhat less dedication than other Arabs. Hospitality is considered a point of honor, and the Ma'dan welcome all guests and provide food and housing without expecting or accepting any payment. It is considered an insult even to thank a host for a meal, let alone pay for it, because it implies that the host is not considered generous enough to simply offer a meal (or bed, or other hospitality) to a guest. A host also never helps to carry a guest's belongings out of the house (although he or she will help to carry them in) because that would imply that the host wanted the guest to leave.

⁹ LIVING CONDITIONS

Before the destruction of the marshes, the Ma'dan marsh villages consisted of houses built of reeds, with reed mats covering the floors. These houses were built on artificial islands created by enclosing an area in the water, large enough for the house and a yard in front, with a fence of reeds about 6 m (about 20 ft) high. Reeds and rushes were packed inside of this fence. Then, when the stack of reeds and rushes reached above the level of the water, the original fence reeds were broken and laid across the stack. More rushes were piled on top and packed down tightly. The house was then built on this foundation. This type of house was called a *kibasha.* A more permanent site was produced when mud from the floor of the marsh was used to cover the foundation. The mud was then covered with more layers of rushes. This more permanent type of house was called a *dibin.* If the family that built a dibin left it unoccupied for more than a year, they lost their right to it and anyone could take possession of it. Shops within the village were marked by a white cloth fastened like a flag to a reed stuck into the roof of the building.

Traditional Ma'dan marsh houses had no electricity heat, running water, or indoor plumbing. Water was drawn from the marshes around the home. The Ma'dan did not build latrines. People simply squatted among the rushes, or over the side of a canoe, to urinate or defecate. In spite of this lack of sanitary conditions, the Ma'dan were a remarkably healthy people and experienced few occurrences of dysentery or cholera.

Food consisted of the wild boars and birds hunted with the gun, as well as crops, such as rice, that could be grown in the marshes. Personal possessions included a few water buffalo, a gun, some blankets and cooking utensils, and a reed canoe coated with bitumen (tar).

Within the marsh village, there was almost always a guest house, or a *mudhif.* The mudhif was usually owned by the village sheikh, or leader, and was often built on a grander scale than the simpler huts of the villagers, although the basic design was the same. No visitor was ever refused hospitality and, as in villagers' homes, no payment was accepted for lodging and meals in the mudhif.

All transportation in and around the marsh village was by canoe, either paddled or, more often, punted with a long reed. Called *mashuf,* the canoes were made of reeds covered with bitumen (tar). Children four or five years of age had their own mashuf and could pilot them skillfully. The Ma'dan created "roads" in the marshes by driving water buffalo through the reeds when the water was low to make a track. As the water rose, the track was kept open by the coming and going of the mashuf.

Unfortunately, these traditional marsh villages were destroyed as the marshes were drained by the government. Most of the Ma'dan who have migrated to Iraqi cities or to Iran now live in more urban dwellings. Some have converted their marsh lifestyle to a more conventional form of agriculture and rural living. A few thousand Ma'dan are believed to have returned to the marshes since 2003. However, many Ma'dan seem to have

Ma'dan children play in water canals that still are left in what is now mostly dry land in Qurnah, southern Iraq. Saddam Hussein diverted water away from this area, drying up the heart of the Fertile Crescent. (AP Images/Elizabeth Dalziel)

no wish to return because of the difficulty of the traditional lifestyle.

10 FAMILY LIFE

The traditional Ma'dan way of life was organized as a tribal society made up of various groups of families who shared a common lineage, with each family group headed by a sheikh (leader). Marriages were arranged by parents, although a couple had some choice in the matter. Paternal first cousins had the first claim to a young woman for their bride. Another who wished to marry her must have her paternal first cousin's father's agreement to give up his son's right to her. In traditional Ma'dan homes, men and women did not eat together and all meals were conducted in silence. All talking was done before and after the meal, never during it. Men and women were generally segregated in public life as well, although young children would play together.

Today, very little is known about the family life of the Ma'dan since their displacement from the marshes. It will take time for the marshes to recover and to learn whether or not the Ma'dan traditional way of life will be restored.

11 CLOTHING

Traditionally, men wore a long, thin shirt that reached to their calves or ankles. In the winter, they sometimes wore a jacket over it. They also wore the traditional Arab head cloth, usually without a rope to hold it in place (they simply tie it around the head). All grown men had short mustaches. Women wore dark robes that covered the entire body. Ma'dan women were generally not veiled, although they did cover the head with a long cloth or shawl. Only children wore colorful clothes; adults always wore plain light or dark clothes. Men usually wore white and women wore black.

Since their displacement from traditional marsh villages, it is not clear whether most Ma'dan prefer the traditional garments of their culture, or if they, perhaps, have fully adopted the styles popular in their new home towns.

12 FOOD

The traditional staple foods were fish and curdled water-buffalo milk. Some Ma'dan also grew rice. Bread was cooked over a fire on round clay platters. Today, Ma'dan diets are most likely linked to what foods are available in their new home towns.

13 EDUCATION

There were no schools in the marshes. While most Ma'dan parents wanted their children to have the advantages of a modern education, not all could afford to send them to the schools in the surrounding cities and towns. At the town and city schools, Ma'dan children were taught that their life in the marshes was primitive and backward, and some became become discontent at home. Many ended up living marginal lives in the cities and towns, too well educated to be satisfied within the marshes, yet not well enough educated in the ways of town life to be successful there. These prejudices against the Ma'dan way of life have prompted many of the now displaced Ma'dan to integrate more fully with the Arab traditions, including those of formal education, that flourish in the areas to which they have located.

¹⁴ CULTURAL HERITAGE

Ma'dan culture was been largely inherited from the Bedu (or bedouin—*see* **Bedu**). A traditional dance of the Ma'dan is known as the *hausa*. It is a type of war dance performed by men in which they dance in a circle holding their rifles over their heads and firing them.

¹⁵ WORK

In the marsh villages, Ma'dan traditionally supported themselves by fishing and by hunting wild boars and birds. They also kept small herds of water buffalo, which they used for milk. Some Ma'dan also grew rice. Fish were traditionally caught with a five-pronged spear thrown from the bow of a canoe. A more modern method was to stun them with poisoned bait, usually shrimp, laced with datura (a member of the nightshade family) that would be tossed onto the surface of the water. Only professional fishers, referred to as *berbera,* used nets. In the traditional marsh villages, collecting the grass used as fodder for the water buffalo was a constant chore, usually assigned to young boys. Weaving reed mats for sale in the surrounding towns was a common source of extra income for the Ma'dan.

¹⁶ SPORTS

In the marsh villages, hunting was both a necessity for survival and a favorite sport among the Ma'dan.

¹⁷ ENTERTAINMENT AND RECREATION

The Ma'dan love to sing and dance and often entertain each other in this way. They also play a game called *mahaibis,* or "hunt the ring." The players divide into two teams. The team that has the ring sits in a row with their hands under a cloak. One member of the other team stands in front of them and tries to guess who has the ring and in which hand. The game often ends in noisy disputes and accusations of cheating.

¹⁸ FOLK ART, CRAFTS, AND HOBBIES

The most common crafts among the traditional Ma'dan are the building and repairing of canoes, the weaving of reed mats, and blacksmithing. Ma'dan blacksmiths make fishing spears, reed splitters, sickles, and nails for the canoes. Some of the Ma'dan weave cloth. They make woolen cloth that both men and women use for cloaks.

¹⁹ SOCIAL PROBLEMS

The Ma'dan historically have been despised by other Arabs and suffered much abuse in the course of their history. The marshes are a perfect place to hide out, so soldiers and criminals are constantly invading the Ma'dan's territory. During the Iran-Iraq war (1980–88), many Ma'dan were driven out of their homes, their few possessions were stolen, and their water buffalo were slaughtered for food by the armies. These practices continued through the 1990s, and much of the Ma'dan way of life has disappeared.

Most Ma'dan are believed to live in lower income Shia communities in Baghdad or have emigrated to Iran, with a few thousand believed to have returned to their traditional homeland. Those Ma'dan who have returned to the marshes lack clean drinking water, sanitation, health care, and nutrition.

²⁰ GENDER ISSUES

The displacement of the Ma'dan from their homeland in the marshes has caused the traditional tribal structure to deteriorate. Little is known about the conditions of Ma'dan women. Nearly 4.2 million Iraqis have fled the war-torn country and an additional 2.2 million have left homelands within the country for cities and urban areas. The Ma'dan are among this group of displaced individuals and, until the situation in Iraq can be stabilized, the survival of both Ma'dan men and women is highly at risk.

Sex roles in many Arab cultures are clearly defined: women manage the household while men tend to affairs outside of the home.

²¹ BIBLIOGRAPHY

Docherty, J. P. *Iraq.* New York: Chelsea House, 1988.

Fulanain [pseud.]. *The Marsh Arab, Haji Rikkan.* Philadelphia, Penn.: J. B. Lippincott Co., 1928.

Hammer, Joshua. "Return to the Marsh: The Effort to Restore the Marsh Arabs' Traditional Way of Life—Virtually Eradicated by Saddam Hussein—Faces New Threats," *Smithsonian* 37:7 (October 2006), 46-56.

"Iraq: Millions in Flight: The Iraq Refugee Crisis." *Amnesty International* 24 September 2007. http://www.amnesty.org/en/library/asset/MDE14/041/2007/en/dom-MDE140412007en.html (5 August 2008).

Norton, Andre. "New Evidence Shows Marshlands Draining Away," *The Middle East* No. 227 (October 1993), 22-24.

Thesiger, Wilfred. *The Marsh Arabs.* New York: E. P. Dutton & Co., 1964.

Santora, Marc. "Marsh Arabs Cling to Memories of a Culture Nearly Destroyed by Hussein," *The New York Times* April 28, 2003, A10.

—revised by H. Gupta-Carlson

MADURESE

PRONUNCIATION: MAHD-oo-reez
LOCATION: Indonesia (islands of Madura and Java)
POPULATION: 6.8 million (2000)
LANGUAGE: Madurese
RELIGION: Islam
RELATED ARTICLES: Vol. 3: Indonesians; Javanese

¹INTRODUCTION

Despite their ancestral island's proximity to Java (at the closest point, only a short ferry ride from the great Javanese port of Surabaya), the Madurese, Indonesia's fourth-largest ethnolinguistic group, have maintained an identity distinct from their neighbors. Although itself of little economic value, Madura's strategic location guarding the approaches to the deltas of Java's greatest rivers, the Brantas and the Bengawan Solo, ensured an intimate involvement in Javanese history. As early as the 15th century, the kingdom of Arosbaya, a vassal of the east Javanese Majapahit court, united Madura's petty states. Arosbaya adopted Islam in 1528; in later years, a reputation for greater devotion and stricter practice to this religion would set the Madurese apart from the Javanese.

In 1624, Sultan Agung of the central Javanese kingdom of Mataram conquered Madura, which by then had fragmented into five principalities. Forty-eight years later, the Madurese prince Trunojoyo returned the favor by revolting against Mataram, getting as far as destroying the latter's capital with the help of Makassarese mercenaries. However, the Dutch East India Company put an end to his venture, eventually overseeing a division of the island into two principalities, the western one placed under the Cakraningrat dynasty.

In 1743, eastern Madura passed from the suzerainty of Mataram into the control of the Dutch East India Company. Well into the 19th century, the Madurese rulers served as virtually independent allies of the Dutch; the last portion of the island to come under direct Dutch rule did so in 1885. While the Dutch never subjected the arid island to the Forced Cultivation System, the Madurese rulers contributed to Dutch imperialism by enlisting from among their subjects recruits for Dutch armies fighting elsewhere in the archipelago.

Under direct colonial rule, Madura's welfare continued to decline. A 1918 report indicated that the economy was poor and famine was widespread, and a heavy tax burden compounded these difficulties. In response, the colonial government established a special fund for Madura relief, maintaining it until 1937. Madura suffered under the Japanese occupation of 1942–45 with peculiar severity. The returning Dutch attempted to establish a client state on Madura, but this was integrated into the Indonesian republic in 1950.

In comparison to many other regions of the country, Madura has continued to suffer from economic stagnation, forcing many Madurese to migrate off-island (for the 1997–2001 Madurese-Dayak conflicts in Kalimantan that killed many Madurese transmigrants and displaced many more, see the article entitled **Ngaju Dayak**). There is some evidence that a certain percentage of the younger generation of Madurese resident in East Java are switching over to the Javanese language as their primary language. Other trends affecting Madurese tradi-

tional culture include: modernization, which has brought the lifestyle of well-to-do urban Madurese into conformity with the Jakartan national model; and Islamic reformism, which seeks to bring Madurese life in general into line with orthodox (often Middle Eastern rather than indigenized) Muslim standards. A bridge connecting Surabaya and Bangkalan on Madura is nearing completion (as of 2008) that will accelerate the integration of Madura's western tip into the Surabaya metropolitan area; already only a short ferry ride away, Bangkalan city has been evolving into a commuter suburb and alternate location for industrial and service firms for Indonesia's second largest city (population, approximately 3 million).

²LOCATION AND HOMELAND

In contrast to much of neighboring Java, the island of Madura offers few areas suitable for the irrigation essential to wet-rice cultivation. Besides depending on rainfall, Madurese farmers must contend with the soil's high calcium content (the island has long been a major source of lime). Because of such limits on agricultural productivity, the island has often failed to sustain its population, many of whom have migrated to the opposite coast of East Java and beyond in search of a livelihood. After the wars of the 17th and 18th centuries decimated the native population of East Java, Madurese (along with Central Javanese) were brought in to repopulate large stretches of it. Already by 1930, there were more Madurese on Java than on Madura itself (2.5 million versus 2 million, respectively). According to the 2000 census, Madurese numbered 6.8 million. 2005 figures put the population of the island of Madura itself at 3.5 million. In many regencies along the north coast of East Java, Madurese are the numerically dominant ethnic group; they constitute 18% of the province's overall population (Javanese are 79%). In addition, Madurese have settled in many of the cities of Java, as well as in transmigrant communities on other islands.

³LANGUAGE

Although closely related to the fellow Austronesian tongues of the Javanese and Sundanese, the Madurese language is far from mutually intelligible with them. It is itself divided into three major dialects, centered respectively from east to west on Bangkalan, Pamekasan, and Sumenep. The language's traditional script, a version of the Javanese, is now in decline in the face of competition from the Latin alphabet used for Bahasa Indonesia. Like Javanese, Madurese possesses three language levels, ranging from the informal (named *Enja'-iya* after the words for "Yes" and "No"), to the polite (*Enghi-enten*), to the highly deferential (*Enghi-bhunten*).

⁴FOLKLORE

See the article entitled **Indonesians**.

⁵RELIGION

First introduced with the conversion of the petty kingdom of Arosbaya in 1528, Islam is central to Madurese life. Indeed, the Madurese as a group pride themselves on adhering to the tenets of Muslim orthodoxy (such as the five daily prayers) more strictly than the Javanese, many of whom practice rituals and profess beliefs more compatible with an earlier animist and Hindu-Buddhist heritage. *Pesantren*, Muslim religious schools

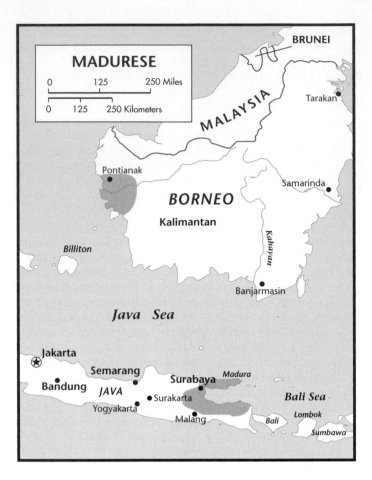

[see **Indonesians**], and *tarekat,* Muslim mystical brotherhoods, enjoy a special prominence. *Kyai,* religious scholars, often combine the role of reformist with that of traditional healer.

Nonetheless, the Madurese retain belief in the power of ancestral beings, ghosts, and other spirits who have the power to harm or help humans. Offerings and ritual feasts are prepared for these supernatural beings to ensure village welfare and a bountiful harvest, to celebrate important Islamic festivals, and to obtain success in upcoming business trips or bull races. Ritual feasts, or *kenduri,* that correspond to the Javanese *slametan* and center on huge cones of rice, are dedicated both to Allah and the ancestors. Only men partake in the feast itself, although a man always takes a portion of the dishes home for his wife and children. Other types of ceremonies include rites requesting rain and honoring the spirits of springs and wells (held annually, with *ojhung),* and those honoring sacred swords *(kris)* or spears, a type of chanting called *gumbek* accompanies weapon veneration.

⁶MAJOR HOLIDAYS

See the article entitled **Indonesians**.

⁷RITES OF PASSAGE

Important ritual celebrations mark the following life passages: the seventh month of pregnancy, an infant's first contact with the earth (several months after birth), a boy's circumcision, a girl's first menstruation, and the funeral and subsequent commemorative ceremonies. As in other Muslim cultures of Indonesia, a circumcision procedure may also be performed on girls, ranging from token rubbing of the clitoris to excision in some cases, often combined with their first ear-piercing.

Wedding customs resemble those of the east Javanese, differing for the most part only in terminology. In a first step known as *nyalabar* or *ngembang nyamplong,* the boy or man's family sounds out the possibility of marriage with a prospective girl's or woman's family. Next, the male's family formally asks *(narabas pagar)* whether the female has already been promised to another. If not, the male's parents request the female's hand by offering her food and presents (which for the rich will include jewelry and batik fabric). The engagement is confirmed when the female's family agrees *(balee pagar).* After this, the male's family delivers *(lamaran, saseraan)* the bride-price to the female's side; according to tradition, cattle are an indispensable part of the goods to be handed over. Only now can the formal wedding ceremony *(akad nikah),* conducted by a Muslim religious official, take place.

⁸INTERPERSONAL RELATIONS

In Madura's old principalities, aristocratic lineage provided a small part of the population with claims to deference and obedience from non-aristocrats. In more recent times, position in the colonial and later national bureaucracy has offered similar status. Concentrated in the towns, this highest class of nobles and civil servants patterns its lifestyle on the Javanese *priyayi* elite [see **Javanese**] (although, in accordance with the general Madurese religious orientation, focusing far less on unorthodox forms of mysticism). Similarly, modern well-to-do townspeople follow the lead of the Jakartan middle and upper classes. Far more significant in the perception of the rural population is the elevation above the "ordinary people" *(golongan biasa)* of the "children of the *kyai*" *(golongan bhindara,* including religious scholars, their students *[santre],* village religious officials *(modin),* and others well-versed in Islam *[orang alem]).* In addition to these religious elite, the group to whom "ordinary people" traditionally owed respect included various village authorities: the *kelebun* or village head; the *carek* or village clerk; and the *apel* or neighborhood (subvillage) head.

The Javanese and Sundanese have long applied certain stereotypes to their Madurese neighbors, which Dutch colonial and Indonesian national governments, academia, and popular media have adopted and perpetuated. These stereotypes portray the Madurese as more energetic and less constrained by etiquette than the Javanese or Sundanese and as more hot-tempered and quick to take offense and exact revenge; for this purpose, all Madurese men are said to carry a weapon, either a kris, a *celurit* [sickle], a *calo'* or *wadung* [machete], or a crowbar. On the "positive" side, the Madurese are appreciated as hardworking, particularly in the manual jobs left to them by other ethnic groups.

What can be said without exaggeration is that Madurese prize their personal honor. For instance, a man will not go to a party to which he has not been explicitly invited. In working his fields, a man will not ask the assistance of anyone outside his immediate family. Men will not cooperate with each other before fixing the precise division of labor and terms of compensation. They prefer to use go-betweens in conducting negotiations and will have these go-betweens witness any exchange of money. This sense of personal dignity may account for the aloofness many villagers display towards foreigners (isolation also breeds a certain wariness).

Madurese refugees arrive in Kamul, Indonesia. The Madurese were fleeing violence in Borneo after Indigenous Dayaks rampaged the area killing nearly 500 people in early 2001. (AP Images/Charles Dharapak)

An important feature of Madurese life is the *aresan,* a regular gathering in which one of the attendants wins by lot the contents of a pot to which all the others have contributed—eventually, previous winners being excluded one after one, every member of the aresan association will have his or her turn to receive the pot. Women often have their own aresan clubs, called *diba'.*

⁹LIVING CONDITIONS

The average of the 2005 Human Development Indices (combining measures of income, health, and education) for the four regencies of Madura was 59.25, far below that for Indonesia as a whole (69.6) and East Java as a whole (68.5). In Pamekasan regency, GDP per capita stood at US$2,065, less than a third of East Java's as a whole (US$7,046), and Sampang regency's Human Poverty Index was 38.3, almost twice that of East Java's as a whole (21.7). Sampang's level of infant mortality (2000 figures) was 89.55 deaths per 1,000 live births, almost twice East Java's as a whole (47.69) and four times that in Jakarta.

The classification of traditional houses distinguishes between houses consisting of a single room *(slodoran* or *malang are)* and those with more than one room *(sedanan).* Furthermore, traditional houses differ according to roof type: a *gadrim* with a two-ridge roof; a *sekodan* with four central pillars supporting the roof; and a *pacenanan* where the gables pro-

jecting from the two ends of the roof are carved in the shape of serpents, a style of Chinese inspiration. Traditional houses are windowless and oriented either north–south or in the direction of the rising sun.

Influences from outside Madurese tradition include the addition of a porch in front for sleeping and a porch in back for sitting and relaxing. Each household has a room or detached structure for praying. In the 1990s, modern utilities were much less common than on Madura than elsewhere in East Java: only 3.5% of households had access to hygienic water, and 15.8% to electricity.

Villages are laid out in no distinct pattern, houses being clustered together in the middle of fields. In upland areas, one type of village, the *kampong meji,* consists of the houses of 20 families related back to five generations. In Sumenep, another type of settlement, the *tanean lunjeng,* consists of five houses facing a common center and inhabited by kin related back to the third generation. Ownership of land in Madura is individual, although some village land falls under communal possession and is used to support the village headman and his aides.

¹⁰FAMILY LIFE

For the Madurese, the distinction between kin *(bhala)* and all other people *(oreng)* is a paramount one. Kinship is bilateral, including both paternal and maternal sides, although noble titles pass exclusively through the male line. Marriage between cousins, which preserves the purity of the lineage, is the preferred match. Solidarity between kin is expressed in one type of extended family, the *koren,* in which the descendants (up to 10 households) of a common great-grandfather occupy a single compound.

Under ideal circumstances, a newly married couple establishes its own household at once; if this is not possible, it is also common for the couple to live with the bride's parents first. According to custom, one of a family's daughters, along with her husband and children, remains in her childhood house to take care of her parents in their old age. Madurese marriages are reputed to end less frequently in divorce than those among the neighboring Javanese and Sundanese.

A family's honor rests heavily on the respectability of its women, something which the family's men will fight to defend. A corollary of this is that men may harass women traveling without male kin escorting them (such as foreign female tourists).

In the old kingdoms, although a woman could not occupy the throne, she could exercise de facto supreme power as the mother or guardian of the heir, particularly if she herself were the daughter of a former ruler.

¹¹CLOTHING

Women wear a *kebaya* (long-sleeved blouse) and a sarong extending below the knees, along with bracelets and anklets *(bingel).* Men's traditional clothing, generally of dark-colored fabric, consists of: a distinctive headdress *(destar);* an undershirt with horizontal stripes, often red and white; a long-sleeved, collarless overshirt; trousers that end just below the knees; and a wide sash tied around the waist.

¹²FOOD

Boiled rice mixed with ground maize is the primary food, supplemented by dried salted fish or side dishes of dried meat and vegetables, all accompanied by chili sauces. Meals are washed down with water or tea (since colonial times, prohibitions have been placed on indulgence in *tuak,* palm wine).

Specialties of the island of Madura include *perkedel jagung* (shrimp and corn fritters), *la'ang* (the regional beverage), *blaken* (fish paste sold in old handmade jars), yam taffy, and the fruits guava and *salak* (the latter has a dark brown, scaly skin; white, sourish fruit; and a large pit). Famous outside the home island are Madurese chicken dishes, *soto* (a type of soup), and *sate* (barbecued skewers of goat meat, dipped in a mixture of sweet soy sauce and chili before being eaten).

¹³EDUCATION

The level of literacy on Madura is low by Indonesian national standards. The average of 2005 figures for literacy for its four regencies stood at 76.19%, considerably lower than that of East Java as a whole (85.84%). One out three people in Sampang was illiterate, a greater proportion than in Papua province where 28.42% was illiterate. According to 1990s figures, elementary school attendance on Madura was at 88.2%, lower than that in southern East Java (whose Madurese-speaking population is not large). *See also* the article entitled **Indonesians.**

¹⁴CULTURAL HERITAGE

With plots also taken from the Ramayana and Mahabharata epics, *wayang topeng* resembles the Javanese shadow play in that a single narrator (who is also director and musical conductor) performs all the speaking parts, but it replaces the puppets with masked dancers or actors. Wayang topeng has come to be regarded as the consummate symbol of Madurese culture, despite the fact that it has declined in popularity. Much more vital is *loddrok,* an earthier dramatic genre in which the actors are unmasked, speak their own parts, and sing Madurese-language songs *(kejhung);* it often replaces wayang topeng as an adjunct to village ceremonies. Yet another type of popular theater is *drama* which combines "Islamic" (Arab-Persian) stories with Indian dance numbers; the performances include women and professional transvestites, and admission is charged.

The Madurese have *gamelan* (percussion) orchestras similar to those of the Javanese, although the instruments are more frequently of iron rather than expensive bronze, and the sole singer is often a female impersonator rather than a woman. Gamelan accompany wayang topeng, loddrok, and *tayub* (in which a single female performer dances for a male audience and invites individual men to dance with her). Another, highly sophisticated performing art is *mamaca* or *macapat,* in which one person sings Javanese-language poetic texts while a second translates them into Madurese for the listeners; it is still heard in the old palaces and at village ceremonies and *aresan* meetings.

Many village occasions, such as the various bull contests, are accompanied by the *kenong telo* ensemble (including a drum; one large, vertically hanging gong; two differing sets of smaller, horizontally lying gongs; a rattle of metal plates on a string; and, most characteristically, the *saronen,* a high-pitched oboe). Substitutes for the kenong telo ensemble are the *bak beng* (bamboo instruments) and the *ngik-ngok* (a violin and modified brass instruments). On Ramadan nights, village youths stroll about striking wooden slit-gongs *(tuk-tuk or tong-tong).*

Stricter adherents of Islam strongly disapprove of traditional music forms, associating them with "idolatrous" rituals, such as the veneration of *bhuju',* sacred tombs, or with the "morally corrupt" wayang topeng or loddrok. On the other hand, a number of genres exist whose greater "respectability" derives from clear Middle Eastern origins. The *haddrah* is a type of male group singing that incorporates Madurese songs and martial arts moves. In mosques, men also perform *samman,* which arrived from Yemen via Aceh in 1902; they dance in formation while chanting with dramatic waves of intensity.

¹⁵WORK

On Madura, the dominant crops are nonirrigated, such as maize. The island is also famous for its fruits and for medicinal plants. In recent years, tobacco has become a prime cash crop; Madura contains one-fifth of Indonesia's land planted with tobacco. Traditional exports included lime and salt (from sea water evaporated in pools on the long, sun-scorched beaches). Given the often meager returns from farming, livestock-raising is essential to the Madurese. Goats, horses, water buffalo, and cattle are raised, with cattle as the major export. Fishing is also very important. Madurese outrigger boats with triangular sails do an active business in shipping, particularly of timber from Kalimantan to Surabaya factories.

Many Madurese work as migrant laborers, working seasonally on East Java's plantations. Many also go far afield to conduct petty commerce, for example, in cattle, tobacco, fruits, and coconut palm sugar. In East Java's cities, others make roof tiles, shovel sand, pedal *becak* pedicabs, work in harbors, or sell Madurese specialties, such as *soto* or *sate* on the street. Some of Madura's excess labor is being absorbed by factories in Bangkalan, which is being developed as an annex to the Surabayan industrial area.

16 SPORTS

Penca' silat (an Indonesian martial art) is practiced in clubs and for competitions (women participate only as amateurs). One sport, now played in secret, is *ojhung,* in which men duel with rattan sticks. Training homing pigeons is also a popular pastime.

During the dry season (September–October), but also at other times for tourists, bull races *(kerapan sapi)* are held. Only village leaders and other rich peasants can afford to maintain a bull-racing team (a skilled jockey, bull-masseurs, and other personnel, not to mention the animals themselves, which are of the best breed and, unlike draught oxen, are pastured everyday). Elaborately carved wooden yokes, painted in bright red and gold, and other racing equipment are often passed down as family heirlooms. Winning a bull race, especially the island championship, is an intensely coveted honor. Competitors resort to spying or black magic to gain an advantage over opponents, while a full contingent of police is present at the races to suppress any outbreaks of violence.

On the days leading up to a race, specialists feed the bulls a special diet of fresh grass, eggs, coffee, and herbal potions. On the preceding night, the racing team holds an all-night vigil accompanied by continual *gamelan* music. Before the race itself, the *tari pecut* is danced, representing the steps in caring for racing bulls. The race itself involves pairs of bulls drawing sleds and jockeys down a 100-m (328-ft) or more racecourse at as much as 36 km (22 mi) per hour.

17 ENTERTAINMENT AND RECREATION

Such reading as takes place is of religious works, such as the Qur'an, sung poetry texts, comic books, and booklets of legends (a source for *drama* plots). In comparison with their urban counterparts, rural people listen more frequently to the radio (regional and national music, especially *dangdut* and *pop Indonesia*) and to cassettes of *con-locon* (clown) acts. Villagers watch television at the village head's house or at a *warung* food stall and see movies in outdoor cinemas and traditional performances sponsored by richer fellow villagers.

18 FOLK ART, CRAFTS, AND HOBBIES

Woodcarving is highly developed, as seen in bull-racing gear and in locally made furniture (beds, screens, chests, cupboards, and cake-keepers showing Chinese and European influence). Madurese batik cloth is in rich, bold reds, red-brown, and indigo and has designs depicting winged serpents, sharks, airborne houses with fish tails, and other fantastical sea animals. It is also customary for women to wear large silver bracelets; black-coral bracelets are another regional specialty, believed to prevent illness and cure rheumatism.

19 SOCIAL PROBLEMS

See the article entitled **Indonesians**.

20 GENDER ISSUES

The average Gender-Related Development Index for Madura's four regencies (2002 figures) is 46.43, dramatically lower than that for East Java as a whole (56.3). Gender Empowerment Measures (reflecting women's participation and power in political and economic life relative to men's) for the four regencies average to 35.9, lower by an even greater proportion than 54.9 for both East Java as a whole and for Indonesia as a whole.

21 BIBLIOGRAPHY

Badan Pusat Statistik: *Statistik Indonesia*. http://demografi. bps.go.id (November 9, 2008).

Bouvier, Hélène. "Diversity, Strategy, and Function in East Madurese Performing Arts." In *Across Madura Strait*, edited by Kees van Dijk, Huub de Jonge, and Elly Touwen Bouwsma. Leiden: KITLV, 1995.

Dalton, Bill. *Indonesia Handbook*. Chico, CA: Moon Publications, 1991.

Jonge, Huub de. "Stereotypes of the Madurese." In *Across Madura Strait,* edited by Kees van Dijk, Huub de Jonge, and Elly Touwen-Bouwsma. Lieden: KITLV, 1995.

Jonge, Nico de, ed. *Indonesia in Focus: Ancient Traditions—Modern Times*. Meppel: Edu'Actief, 1988.

LeBar, Frank M., ed. *Ethnic Groups of Insular Southeast Asia*. Vol. 1, *Indonesia, Andaman Islands, and Madagascar*. New Haven, CT: Human Relations Area Files Press, 1972.

Rosantini, Triana. "Madura, Suku Bangsa." In *Ensiklopedi Nasional Indonesia*, Vol. 10. Jakarta: Cipta Adi Pustaka, 1990.

—revised by A. J. Abalahin

MALAYS IN INDONESIA

PRONUNCIATION: muh-LAYZ or MAY-layz
LOCATION: Indonesia (Sumatra and its eastern offshore islands; Borneo coast [also outside Indonesia on the Malay Peninsula])
POPULATION: 7 million on Sumatra (2000 census). Another estimate runs to over 13 million; the combined total of Malays living in Indonesia, Malaysia, Thailand, Brunei, and Singapore may be over 25 million.
LANGUAGE: Malay
RELIGION: Islam
RELATED ARTICLES: Vol. 3: Indonesians; Vol. 4: Malaysian Chinese; Malaysian Indians; Malaysian Malays

¹INTRODUCTION

One possible origin for the term "Malay" (melayu) may be a Dravidian (south Indian) expression mala ur, "hill people." It is ironic, therefore, that it should come to refer to a maritime people with a sophisticated urban Islamic tradition (highlanders throughout the archipelago are considered most tenacious in their paganism). Of course, popular usage in English extends Malay's scope to include all the indigenous inhabitants of Indonesia (other Papuans), Malaysia, and the Philippines, who share, at the very least, Austronesian languages and Southern Mongoloid physical features. This article will focus on the specific ethnic group in western Indonesia known as "Malay."

Malays have identified, and to a great extent still do identify, more with the diverse small regions (once independent sultanates) to which they are native than with a broader "Malay" ethnicity. For centuries in the archipelago, converting to Islam was known as "masuk melayu," literally "entering Malayness." Thus, being "Malay" meant sharing in a cosmopolitan culture including as its key ingredients Islam and the maritime lingua franca called bahasa Melayu; common ancestry was not the decisive factor, as individual Malays might count Batak, Kubu, Javanese, Bugis, and others (as well as Arabs, Indians, Siamese, and Chinese) among their forebears.

According to the latest scholarship, around the time of Christ the ancestors of the Malays and other closely related groups began migrating from Kalimantan to the Sumatra coast, where they absorbed or displaced fellow Austronesian peoples who had settled there centuries before (forerunners of, among others, the Batak). In the early centuries AD, Malay seafarers played the role of the first intermediaries between China on the one hand and India and the Mediterranean on the other. Sumatra itself was famous as Suvarnadvipa (the "Gold Island") and as the source of camphor and other exotic items. As early as the 5th century, various Sumatran port-kingdoms enjoyed relations with China.

By the late 7th century, one of these states came to overshadow all others and would establish the tradition around which a Malay identity would grow. Centered near the present-day city of Palembang in south Sumatra, the kingdom of Srivijaya dominated the Straits of Malacca region until its decline in the 11th century (partly due to a devastating attack from the south Indian Chola state). In its heyday, Srivijaya was legendary as a center of international trade and of Buddhism.

After shifting to the rival state of Malayu (modern Jambi), leadership of the Malay world came to rest in Malacca on the west coast of the Malay peninsula, founded by a refugee prince from Palembang in 1400. Like Srivijaya, Malacca controlled traffic through the Straits and promoted a universal religion, though it was Islam which it, most successfully, propagated. Meanwhile, Palembang itself became first an enclave of Chinese pirates and then the home of a highly Javanized version of Malay culture.

The Portuguese capture of Malacca in 1509 encouraged the rise throughout the region of small sultanates, often founded by Bugis, Minangkabau, and Arab adventurers, and prospering on the pepper trade until the mid-17th century (first linguistically non-Malay Aceh and then Riau-Johor inherited Malacca's leadership of the Malay world to a certain extent) . In the 18th century, Dutch, British, and even French maritime power began to limit the freedom of the Malay states. In the early 19th century, British and Dutch colonialism split the Malay world into Malayan and a Sumatran halves, a division with cultural consequences that persist to this day despite renewed post-colonial interchange and participation in a common regional economy centered on Singapore, the present-day successor of Srivijaya and Malacca.

Along the east coast of Sumatra by the late 19th century, a flourishing plantation economy (tobacco and rubber) developed under Dutch rule, the product of collaboration between European capitalists and Malay sultans—and thousands upon thousands of Chinese and Javanese coolies. This region experienced considerable upheaval during the Indonesian struggle for independence, which included violence against the native aristocracy, one victim of which was prince Amir Hamzah, the greatest poet in Bahasa Indonesia in the 1930s and 1940s. Since that time, Sumatra's east coast and adjacent islands have experienced rapid development, fueled by oil and tin wealth as well as proximity to Singapore and Malaysia.

²LOCATION AND HOMELAND

According to the 2000 census, Malays (self-identifying as such) were Indonesia's third largest ethnic group, constituting 3.4% of the population and numbering almost 7 million. Indonesia's Malays lived primarily on Sumatra in the provinces of North Sumatra (east coast), Riau (islands and mainland, where they equaled 38% of the population according to the 2000 census), Jambi (38%), South Sumatra (31%), Bangka-Belitung (72%), and Bengkulu; the interior of these provinces is largely inhabited by non-Malays, such as the Kubu and the Rejang. In the coastal regions, non-Malays are also numerous, especially Javanese transmigrants. Figures from the 1990s estimated the number there to be as high as 13 million, obviously based on different criteria than the 2000 census.

In addition, Malays inhabit the Malay Peninsula as well as communities along the Borneo coast (Indonesian Kalimantan, Malaysian Sarawak and Sabah, and Brunei). Half of Malaysia's 2006 population of 26.6 million, or about 13.3 million, was Malay, while Pattani and three other provinces in southern Thailand were over 80% Malay. A 1998 estimate put the number of speakers of the Pattani Malay dialect at 3.1 million.

³LANGUAGE

Malay is most closely related to Minangkabau, Iban (the "Sea Dayak" of Borneo), and Acehnese, less closely to Sundanese,

MALAYS in INDONESIA

0   250   500 Miles
0   250   500 Kilometers

South China Sea

MALAYSIA

BRUNEI

Natuna
Besar

Medan

SINGAPORE

MALAYSIA

Nias

SUMATRA   Bangka   BORNEO

Kepulauan
Mentawai

Billiton   Kalimantan

Palembang

Java Sea

Jakarta

Semarang   Surabaya

Bandung   Madura
                         Bali Sea

JAVA   Bali
              Lombok

INDIAN OCEAN

Madurese, and Javanese. It is spoken in several divergent dialects; the dialect of Riau-Johor, considered a direct legacy of the Malacca sultanate, is esteemed as the "purest" or "finest" Malay and has become the basis of the official languages of Indonesia, Malaysia, Brunei, and (after English and Mandarin Chinese) of Singapore. The Malay spoken in Sumatra differs from that of Malaya in employing Dutch rather than English loanwords, and it lacks the Javanese and other influences characteristic of the Malay spoken in Jakarta and the cities of Java that is so influential on modern colloquial and written Indonesian.

Long before European colonialism, one could make oneself understood throughout maritime southeast Asia, and as far away as ports in south China and Persia, in Malay. In its own right and as a vehicle for Sanskrit, Arabic, and Portuguese loanwords, Malay has had a profound impact on languages throughout Indonesia and the Philippines.

⁴FOLKLORE

Though weaker today under the pressure of modernist Islam, belief in spirits is still widespread. Every spot has its *penunggu* (guardian spirit), *hantu* (ghost), or *jembalang* (gnome). Penunggu inhabit graves, houses, or trees, and protect a village from other "outsider" spirits; they manifest themselves as a *harimau tengkis,* a tiger with one short leg. *Puako* (spirits) occupy specific places, such as river mouths, deep spots in streams, or certain parts of the sea; they may appear in animal form as a white crocodile, a snake, or a *gajah meno* (an aquatic elephant).

Upon entering a spirit's "territory," one asks permission of the spirit, saying *"Tabek datuk nenek, cucu menumpang lalu"* (literally, "Hello, honored grandparent, your grandchild is passing through"). Offending spirits cause illness (referred to as *ketegow [ketegoran],* a "warning"). One asks pardon through making an *ancak,* a basket full of offerings (eggs, turmeric rice, grilled chicken, cigarettes, etc.— as the spirit has requested through a *bomo*); one places this in a tree (for a forest spirit) or floats it on the water (for a water spirit). More orthodox Muslims distinguish *jin* (good spirits) from *setan* (devils), and instead of uttering *"Tabik"* declare in Arabic, *"A'uu zubi'llahi nibasy syaitoni rrajim"* ("I am under the protection of Allah from cursed devils").

The power of magic is widely recognized. Amulets (*azimat*) are worn, such as a piece of iron (*tangkal*) hung from a necklace or wristband (children) or worn as a hairpin (women). Weapons, thrones, and banyan trees, and individuals, such as sultans or *ulama* (religious scholars), possess mystical power. For instance, a curse will befall those disloyal to the sultan; only confessing the disloyalty to the sultan and begging him for forgiveness will lift the curse. People ask the aid of the spirits of powerful individuals, visiting their graves and vowing to sacrifice a goat or chicken upon realization of the wish.

⁵RELIGION

Islam has been integral to the Malay identity since at least the 14th century, if not as early as the 12th; as such it enters into every aspect of the culture [*see* **Malaysian Malays**]. Although it is regarded as virtual "idolatry," *bomo* (shamans) are still known to invoke the Hindu Batara Guru and other figures, not as gods but as powerful supernatural beings.

The chanting of Islamic texts, such as the Quran and the *Barzanji* (tales of the life of Muhammad), often accompanied by the playing of tambourines (*rebana, berdah,* or *k[er]ompang*), accompanies ceremonies, such as circumcisions and weddings. At seven years of age, children begin to learn how to read the Quran, mastering the proper pronunciation, emphasis, rhythm, and tone; however, they usually do not understand what they are reading word for word. This is a prized skill, and especially expert readers compete in regional and national contests (*Mushabaqah Tiliwatil Qur'an*) that are televised with "pre-game/intermission shows" of folk dances of an "Islamic spirit" (*bernafaskan Islam*).

⁶MAJOR HOLIDAYS

See the article entitled **Indonesians**.

⁷RITES OF PASSAGE

To ensure a successful delivery, a ceremony (*tolak due* in Riau, *nuak* in Jambi) is held in the seventh month of the pregnancy. As soon as the child is born, prayers are said over it (*azan* for a boy and *qamat* for a girl; a drop of honey is dabbed on the girl's tongue, so she will grow up with a personality sweet in its virtue). The placenta is wrapped in a white cloth, placed in a small basket, and buried in the backyard. Some days later, a name-giving ceremony occurs, including the child's first haircut and the sacrifice of two goats for a boy and one goat for a girl. At three months of age, the child is made to step on the earth for the first time in a *turun tanah* ceremony (for girls, the first ear-piercing precedes this). As their passage to adulthood, boys undergo circumcision (*sunat rasul* or *khitanan*) after learning the skills of reciting the complete Quran, performing *silat* (martial arts), and dancing the *zapin*.

Getting married involves the following steps. The young man's side (parents usually do the choosing) makes an initial inquiry into the availability of the young woman. If the woman's side signals its openness to an offer, the man's family sends its *sesepuh*, the most senior kinsman and his wife, to deliver the proposal; they bring betel-chewing paraphernalia and use poetic language. The next step is for the man's kin to present the agreed-upon wedding goods to the woman's house. As a sign of the formalization of the engagement, the palms and soles of the betrothed are reddened with henna *(inai)*.

In the evening, the *akad nikah* (Islamic wedding ceremony) is held, led by an *ulama;* an odd number (3–11) of relatives line up to bless the couple with a dab of a special flour mixture. On the next afternoon, a procession takes the groom to the bride's house to the playing of *rebana* and the performing of *silat*. The bride's kin greet the groom's group by showering them with yellow-dyed raw rice; the two sides go back and forth declaiming *pantun* (structured poems) to each other. Once on the ceremonial dais *(pelaminan),* the couple enacts a ritual of mutual feeding *(suap-menyuap);* in Riau, they must refuse to eat food from each other's hands as a sign of self-respect. Later, the couple bows before their parents and asks for their blessing. With this, the wedding feast can begin.

Funerals follow the general Islamic form [*see* **Indonesians**]. Post-funeral prayers *(tahlil)* are held for three days after the burial and on the seventh, twentieth, fortieth, and hundredth day after the death.

8 INTERPERSONAL RELATIONS

Originally, a village was composed of people of the same lineage *(suku),* but, as outsiders have come to settle there, the bond of a common living place has taken precedence over lineage ties. These communities are small, such that everyone knows each other well and works together in daily activities, e.g., helps each other in emergencies or in holding each other's major celebrations. Villagers are careful to "weigh" each other's feelings *(timbang rasa)* and appeal to the *imam* or *penghulu* to resolve conflicts quickly. Each individual's internal sense of shame (self-respect, or personal and familial face), rather than external coercion, maintains social harmony. A person endeavors to avoid being marked as a person "who does not know custom," i.e., who offends by appearance, word, and action.

Community leadership includes a *penghulu,* a village head, now selected according to government regulations from among the heads of the various suku. An *imam* serves as the head of the mosque; leader of Qur'an recitation and religious education; authority in matters of marriage, divorce, and inheritance; and collector of the tithe *(zakat).* A *datuk* is a suku head who has become a territorial chief with power over other suku heads.

Since Indonesian independence, social relations have been democratized, with personality, position, and material situation carrying more weight than hereditary rank alone. In the kingdom of Siak (Riau mainland), society was traditionally divided into four classes: the sultan (or *raja*) and his consorts; descendants of the present or former rajas: the "good people" *(orang baik-baik),* the heads of prominent suku; and commoners. Using Javanese terms, such as *priyayi* (aristocrat), Palembang society distinguished the following upper strata: the

Raden (men)/*Raden Ayu* (women), descendants of royal consorts; *Mas Agus/Mas Ayu*, descendants of royal concubines; *Kemas/Nyimas,* descendants of (perhaps less-favored) royal concubines; and *Ki[ai]agus/Nyiayu,* the *ulama* or religious scholars.

9 LIVING CONDITIONS

Houses are raised on posts, and their walls are made of wooden planks, their roofs of dried leaves or shingles; the exact plan differs from region to region. In Riau, two kinds are known: the *rumah melintang* or *rumah bubungan Melayu*, with a rectangular plan and a long ridgepole; and the *rumah limas*, with a square plan and a short ridgepole (the four sides of the roof slant towards the top). In the front, often at a lower level then the floor of the main part of the house, is a *selaso*, a veranda that may be enclosed with a low wall of sago palm latticework. A kitchen structure stands behind the main house, connected to it by an intervening chamber *(telo).*

Aristocratic houses in Jambi and Palembang are basically similar but divide into several specialized chambers. At the front of the house is the *jogan*, a veranda where the family relaxes. From front to back, the rooms of a Jambi house have the following respective functions: an area for receiving male guests; the sleeping area for family's older boys; a room for newlyweds; the sleeping room for the family's older girls; and an area for receiving female guests. The interior of a Palembang house divides into sleeping areas for: young male kin who come to help with celebrations; middle-age guests; and older and highly respected guests. The kitchen is at the back. Houses built on stilts over the water are a common sight, for instance, along Palembang's Musi River or at Medan's Belawan port.

In 2005, the provinces with substantial Malay populations had higher Human Development Indices (combining measures of income, health, and education) than Indonesia's national score of 69.6: Riau's, the third highest in the country (after Jakarta and North Sulawesi) was 73.6, the Riau Islands' 72.2, Jambi's 71, Bangka-Belitung 70.7, and South Sumatra's 70.2 (all higher than Java's provinces and Bali). GDP's per capita (even subtracting income from petroleum and natural gas from GDP, important for Riau, Jambi, and South Sumatra) are very high by national standards: US$29,348 for the Riau Islands, US$6,982 for Jambi, US$7,774 for South Sumatra, US$12,234 for Bangka-Belitung, and US$17,264 for Riau. Infant mortality rates (2002), however, were not particularly low: 47.66 deaths per 1,000 live births in Riau (islands and mainland) and 52.66 in each of the other three provinces (cf. 35.72 in Bali and 43.69 in Central Java).

10 FAMILY LIFE

The nuclear family *(kelamin)* is the basic unit of Malay society, consisting of a husband, a wife, and their unmarried children. Polygamy is permissible under Islam (up to four wives) but it is rare. Newlyweds may live for a time with the bride's parents before establishing their own house nearby. While in the parents' house, the couple obeys the father and contributes their labor or earnings to the larger household. Kinship is reckoned on both the mother's and father's sides, though the male line transmits noble titles. The inhabitants of a village or of neighboring villages may belong to a single clan *(suku),* but these connections have generally lost importance for Malays.

Terms of address distinguish birth order among siblings. In Riau, these are: *long* (from *sulung*, the first-born); *ngah* (*tengah*, second); *cik* (*kecik*, third or fourth); *cu* or *ucu* (*bungsu*, the youngest); even an only child is specified, as *nggal* (*tunggal*, single). These terms also apply to siblings of grandparents (*datuk*) and of parents (*ayah/bapak*, father; and *emak*, mother); thus, the eldest granduncle (or grand-aunt) is called *tuk long*, the second-oldest uncle *yah nguh* or *pak ngah*, and the youngest aunt *mak cu*. In Palembang, the terminology differs: *kakcak* is the eldest sibling; *kakcek*, the second-born; *kakcik*, third and younger. Uncles (*mamang*) and aunts (*bibi*) are specified as *mangcak, mangcek, mangcik, bicak, bicek,* and *bicik*.

Although interactions between elder and younger kin should not be stiff, respect for the former must be palpable; relations between in-laws tend, however, to be rather formal. On the major religious holidays, one pays visits to one's elders and (for the nobility) those kin of higher-ranking lineages. One should always seek the guidance of one's parents; otherwise, one earns a reputation for arrogance. During ritual celebrations, a son-in-law must show his submission to his parents-in-law by obeying any command, however great or small.

11 CLOTHING

For everyday use, men wear pants and a long-sleeved shirt (*baju kurung*, sometimes with a high collar, in which case it is called *cekak musang* or *teluk belanga*); over the pants, with or without the *baju* tucked in, a cloth can be tied around the waist, extending down to the knee. Nowadays men wear a *peci* cap instead of the traditional turban-like headcloth, and Arab-style sandals.

Women wear a long *kebaya* or *baju kurung*, a sarong, a veil, and slippers (or go barefoot). Although Indian fabrics were once popular, now sarongs are made of plaid cloth in Bugis (Sulawesi), Trengganu (Malaya), and Samarinda (Kalimantan) patterns.

Ceremonial clothing for women differs only in the materials: sarongs of silk, decorated with motifs (such as flowers) in gold thread or gold leaf; and baju of satin. Men's attire is similar, though the predominant color is black; an additional cloth worn over one side of the torso (*kain samping*) must be of a color contrasting with the other pieces (to wear clothes all of one color, especially yellow, is the privilege of royalty). In addition, men wear a headdress, the style depending on rank, and shoes or sandals.

12 FOOD

Rice is the heart of the meal, accompanied by fish, vegetables, and *sambal* (chili sauce). The fish may be stewed with coconut milk, chili, and spices to make a curry, or boiled with chili and tamarind or most simply coked with salt and garlic; it may also be fried or grilled. Vegetables (amaranth, eggplant, string beans, and squash) are boiled with *terasi* (shrimp paste) or salt fish for flavor. The ubiquitous condiment is *sambal terasi*, red or green chili ground with salt and mixed with roasted terasi and tamarind or some other souring agent. Breakfast consists of boiled cassava or sweet potato, eaten with grated coconut and sugar or salt fish and sambal.

Foods for special occasions include *lempok* and *emping* [*see* **Banjarese** *dodol* and *amping*] as well as *wajik*, black sticky rice cooked with coconut milk or palm sugar until dry, then cut into parallelogram shapes. *Asidah* is wheat flour mixed with

water, spices, and sugar, cooked until thick, formed into flower or *candi* (Hindu temple) shapes, and finally bathed in cooking oil and sprinkled with fried garlic. *Roti canai* is Indian-style fried flat bread, eaten with meat or chicken curries. *Nasi minyak* resembles Indian *biryani* rice.

The food of Medan is particularly rich in Indian- and Arab-influenced dishes that use dried seeds and aromatic spices, e.g., the not-very-pungent yet rich goat curries, *gulai kumah* and *gulai bagar*. Specialties of Palembang include: *empek empek*, fish dumplings (sometimes stuffed with egg), served with a spicy sauce of chili, garlic, dried shrimp, palm sugar, soy sauce, and vinegar; and the local *kerupuk* (fried tapioca crackers flavored with seafood and spices), renowned because of its higher-than-average proportion of fish or shrimp. Palembang drinks include ginger tea, fruit juices, and *air rebusan kumis kucing* (literally, "water boiled with a cat's whiskers"), a diuretic.

13 EDUCATION

In 2005, the level of literacy for provinces with substantial Malay populations was high by Indonesian national standards, standing at 94.54% for Jambi, 95.44% for Bangka-Belitung, 95.63% for South Sumatra, 95.97% for the Riau Islands, and 97.76% for Riau (cf. 87.41% for Central Java and 78.79 for West Nusa Tenggara). (*See also* the article entitled **Indonesians**.)

14 CULTURAL HERITAGE

As with other aspects of Malay culture, musical traditions reflect ties to the Middle East and Islamized India. The *rebana* (tambourine) is a prominent instrument; a group of rebana players usually accompany various forms of chanting and dancing. In addition, there is a tradition of popular song (*lagu Melayu*) inspired by Arab and Indian models; in a modernized version (*orkes*, "orchestra"), influenced by Indian film music and employing Western instruments, such as the saxophone and accordion, lagu Melayu became the basis of the nationally popular *dangdut* [*see* **Indonesians**].

Malays perform numerous folk dances, the function of many of which is to greet guests. Traditional celebrations include *joget* (also called *ronggeng*); the original form begins with a single female singer-dancer (or several) performing in front of a group of men; if a man wants to dance with a woman, he must pay—this has evolved into a couple dance for young people. Another dance form accompanying rite of passage celebrations is *zapin*, a pair or pairs (formerly only men but nowadays also women and male-female couples) dancing to the accompaniment of the *gambus* (an Arab lute-like instrument), two-headed drums (*marwas*, plural *marawis*), and sometimes violins or accordions. Also popular is *zikir*, in which the performers combine unison chanting of praise to Allah with dynamic arm movements while seated. Until the mid-20th century, several forms of sung theater, some highly eclectic (combining Malay, Javanese, Indian, Middle Eastern, Indian, and Western influences) were popular in the Malay world: *mak yong, mendu, bangsawan,* and *stamboel*.

While the writings of Hindu-Buddhist Srivijaya have been lost, victims of the tropical climate, the rich literature of the later Islamic courtly tradition has been transmitted down to our time, in manuscripts that have been copied and recopied (and reworked) over the generations. These include verse chronicles of a semi-legendary character, such as the *Hikayat Raja-Raja Pasai*, the *Sejarah Melayu*, the *Hikayat Hang Tuah*, and the *Tuhfat al-Nafis*. The last great center of classical Malay literary production was the Riau island of Penyengat in the 19th century. The majority of Malays has, however, until very recently been illiterate; memorizing and improvising rhymed poetry in the short *pantun* and *syair* forms is still a common skill.

[15] WORK

Living in a region dominated by thick forests and swamplands, Indonesia's Malays have traditionally depended more on the sea than on the land for their livelihood, either as fishers or as traders. In the limited areas where it is feasible, they have also practiced wet-rice as well as swidden (shifting-cultivation) farming. Since the 19th century, the region has become known for plantation crops in high world demand such as tobacco and rubber, as well as for petroleum and tin (the latter has been mined since ancient times). The huge work force required by these enterprises has not for the most part been derived from the local Malays, but rather from Chinese and Javanese immigrants.

[16] SPORTS

Malays have long practiced their own form of martial art, called *silat*; it is characterized by graceful arm movements (reminiscent of kung fu or t'ai chi) that lend themselves easily to performance as dance.

[17] ENTERTAINMENT AND RECREATION

Spinning tops (*gasing*) is a popular pastime among males of all ages. A game begins with five or six players spinning their tops simultaneously; the player whose top stops spinning first becomes the lowest "slave," the next one to fall becomes the next higher "slave," and so on until the last, who is then named "king." In the next stage, only a player and the next-higher-ranking player spin their tops at a time; the lower-ranking attempts to strike his superior's top with his own, in which case the former gets promoted and the latter demoted.

See also the article entitled **Indonesians**.

[18] FOLK ART, CRAFTS, AND HOBBIES

The most developed crafts are woodcarving (motifs decorate a house's pillars and walls) and weaving *songket* (cloth into which dense designs have been woven with gold thread).

[19] SOCIAL PROBLEMS

One of the provinces with a substantial Malay population, Riau (including the now separate province of the Riau Islands) was among the provinces experiencing the highest occurrence of collective violence in Indonesia between 1990 and 2004: 100 people died in 165 incidents (cf. West Java with over 11 times the population but only 5 times the number of incidents). Most of the incidents involved intra-village brawling, often provoked by land-grabbing; a few were instances of vigilantes exercising "popular justice." One anomalous incident was the major riot that broke out due to a gambling dispute in the town of Selat Panjang in 2001: many Chinese houses were burned, 16 Chinese were killed, and hundreds of Chinese fled to a nearby island; except for this case, all anti-Chinese violence in Indonesia between 1990 and 2004 was confined to 1997–1998 (*see also* the article entitled **Indonesians**).

[20] GENDER ISSUES

In 2002, despite very high GDP's per capita, the provinces with substantial Malay populations had lower Gender-Related Development Indices (combining measures of women's health, education, and income relative to men's) than Indonesia's national score of 59.2: Bangka-Belitung was 59.2, Riau's 56.9, South Sumatra's 55.5 and Jambi's 53.3 (all lower than North Sulawesi, Bali, Central Java, and Central Kalimantan). Gender Empowerment Measures (reflecting women's participation and power in political and economic life relative to men's) were quite low by national standards: 46.8 for Jambi, 40.4 for Riau, and 38.9 for Bangka-Belitung—only South Sumatra's, 56.9, was higher than the national GEM (54.6).

[21] BIBLIOGRAPHY

Badan Pusat Statistik: Statistik Indonesia. http://demografi. bps.go.id (November 9, 2008).

LeBar, Frank M., ed. *Ethnic Groups of Insular Southeast Asia*. Vol. 1, *Indonesia, Andaman Islands, and Madagascar*. New Haven, CT: Human Relations Area Files Press, 1972.

Oey, Eric M. *Sumatra: Island of Adventure*. Longwood, IL: Passport Books, 1991.

Profil Propinsi Republik Indonesia, Vols. 6, *Jambi*. Jakarta: Yayasan Bhakti Wawasan Nusantara, 1992.

Profil Propinsi Republik Indonesia, Vol. 18, *Riau*. Jakarta: Yayasan Bhakti Wawasan Nusantara, 1992.

Profil Propinsi Republik Indonesia, Vol. 24, *Sumatra Selatan*. Jakarta: Yayasan Bhakti Wawasan Nusantara, 1992.

Project for the Inventorization and Documentation of Regional Cultures. *Permainan Rakyat Daerah Sumatra Selatan* [Folk Games of South Sumatra]. Jakarta: Department of Education and Culture, 1983.

Project for the Study and Recording of Regional Cultures. *Adat Istiadat Daerah Riau* [Customs of Riau]. Jakarta: Department of Education and Culture, 1978.

———. *Adat Istiadat Daerah Sumatra Selatan* [Customs of South Sumatra]. Jakarta: Department of Education and Culture, 1978.

Santoso, Budhi, ed. *Indonesia Indah, Buku ke-2: Bangsa Indonesia*. Jakarta: Yayasan Harapan Kita, 1992. Varshney, Ashutosh, Rizal Panggabean, and Mohammad Zulfan Tadjoeddin. "Patterns of Collective Violence in Indonesia (1990-2004)." Jakarta: United Nations Support Facility for Indonesian Recovery, 2004. http://www.conflictrecovery. org/bin/Patterns_of_collective_violence_July04.pdf.

Yampolsky, Philip. *Music of Indonesia 11, Melayu Music of Sumatra and the Riau Islands: Zapin, Mak Yong, Mendu, Ronggeng*, Liner Notes. Smithsonian Folkways, 1996.

—revised by A. J. Abalahin

MALAYSIAN CHINESE

PRONUNCIATION: muh-LAY-zhun chigh-NEEZ
LOCATION: Malaysia
POPULATION: 5.4 million (in 2000)
LANGUAGE: Malay; Chinese; Tamil; English
RELIGION: Buddhism; Islam; Christianity
RELATED ARTICLES: Vol. 3: China and Her National Minorities

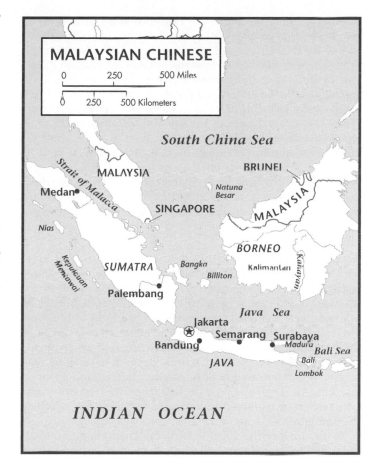

¹INTRODUCTION

Ethnically known as Orang Cina or Kaum Cina in Malaysia, the Malaysian Chinese are the descendants of Chinese who arrived between the 14th and mid-20th centuries. The first wave of Chinese emigrants in the 14th century were mostly merchants, who were partly attracted to the economic potential of the country and partly fleeing from the persecution of the Ching government of Chung Kuok (China). The latter waves were mostly poverty-stricken peasants who hoped for a better livelihood for themselves and their families.

It was only in the 19th century, particularly after the 1820s, that a great number of Chinese migrated to Malaya. This was due to colonial occupation, which caused rapid economic and land development in the region. This development included the opening up of large tracts of land, which created opportunities for mercantile expansion, which in turn attracted emigrants from China. Most of these emigrants were from rural villages and small towns of the southeastern provinces of Fujian and Gaungdong. Upon arrival in Malaya many worked as indentured laborers known as coolies.

²LOCATION AND HOMELAND

In 2000 it was estimated that there were about 5.4 million Chinese in Malaysia, making up 30% of the entire population. The Malaysian Chinese are made up of eight dialect groups which include Hokkien, Hakka, Cantonese, Teochew, Mandarin, Hainanese, Min Bei, and Foochow.

DIALECT	POPULATION
Hokkien	1,848,211
Hakka	1,679,027
Cantonese	1,355,541
Teochew	974,573
Mandarin	958,467
Hainanese	380,781
Min Bei	373,337
Foochow	249,413

Most Malaysian Chinese live in urban areas, dominating the commercial and business areas of the country. A large number also live in areas called *kampung baru* (new villages). These "new villages" were set up by the government during the Communist insurgency in the 1940s and 1950s in order to keep the Chinese community from getting involved with any subversive movements by the Communists against the government.

Nowadays, the Chinese form the majority of the population in almost all cities and towns throughout Malaysia such as Georgetown, Ipoh, Kuala Lumpur, Kuching, Petaling Jaya, and Klang. Most of them are found on the west coast of Peninsular Malaysia, the most urbanized part of the country, as well as in the major cities and towns of Sabah and Sarawak.

³LANGUAGE

Even though Malay is the national and official language of Malaysia, Chinese, Tamil, and English are also widely spoken. Mandarin is taught in Chinese schools in Malaysia (along with Malay and English). Since most of their ancestors were from southern China, Malaysian Chinese speak Cantonese, Hokkien, and Hakka dialects, which are very similar to each other. Other dialects include Teochiu, Hainanese, Hokchiu, and Hinghwa. With this many Chinese in Malaysia are trilingual, speaking and writing in Malay, English, and at least one of the Chinese dialects.

A Chinese name consists of three parts: the family name, the generation name, and the personal name. In contrast with the Western manner of putting the Christian name first, the middle name second, and the surname last, the Chinese put the family name first, the generation name next, and the personal name last. An example of a Chinese name is Foo Sing Choong. However, there a few Chinese names that consist of only two parts; for example, Chin Peng. In either case, the first part is the family name. Western-educated or Christian Chinese usually add a Christian name to their names. As a result, some of their names consist of four parts; for example, Alex Goh Cheng Leong.

⁴FOLKLORE

The Chinese have many folk tales and myths. Some of these myths and tales reveal their view of the world, such as their myth of the creation of the universe and the origin of humankind. According to this myth, heaven and earth were created by *Pan'gu,* the origin man. The existence of humans is made possible by the complementary nature of two opposites: heaven and earth, or *yang* and *yin.* Besides that, the harmony of three—heaven, earth, and humans—makes the fixation of the four cardinal directions possible. Once these four directions are defined, life forms and inanimate objects are derived from the five basic elements of *wuxing:* water, fire, wood, metal, and earth. The ethereal force of the sun and the moon is required to regulate these elements in harmony. It is the true harnessing of elements, and forces of nature, that enables humankind to flourish to the eight polar points, which are only limited by the boundaries of the nine heavens and the 10 hells. The birth of the Chinese cosmos, and with it the subsequent idea and formulation of the soul, are based on this elementary arithmetic.

⁵RELIGION

A small percentage (9.6%) of Chinese in Malaysia are Christian, while most are Buddhist and Taoist. Some, (0.7%), have converted to Islam through marriages with Malay Muslims. Although Buddhism originated in India, and early Malays in Malaysia were Buddhist, the Buddhism practiced in Malaysia today was brought by the Chinese who migrated to Malaysia in the 19th and early 20th centuries. Once in a new environment, the immigrants adopted a practical approach to religion, embracing pragmatic aspects of Buddhism, Taoism, and ancestor worship. Although the religion was rooted in Chinese tradition, once transplanted it was adapted to the current needs of the immigrants.

By the turn of the 20th century, Buddhist temples in Malaysia had increased in number to cater to the moral needs of the population. Most of these temples today promote a "folk version" of Buddhism, peopled by a multitude of gods and goddesses. These temples are concerned with putting forward the views of special Buddhist scriptures, which are connected with an individual's salvation. Special problems and requests may be brought before the deities by presenting them with joss sticks, flowers, or fruits. Devotees at Chinese temples usually burn incense to give thanks and to ask for blessings. There are times when wealthy persons may bequeath some of their estate for the upkeep of an old temple or the endowment of a new one. This will help ensure the donor's blessings in the afterlife and perpetuates her or his descendants' prosperity.

⁶MAJOR HOLIDAYS

The Chinese New Year begins on the first day of the lunar calendar and falls anywhere between January 21 and February 19. It is one of the major holidays in Malaysia when schools and offices are closed for two days. The celebrations may go on for 30 days, starting two weeks before New Year's Eve. It is the most joyous time for the Chinese, a time of new beginning. It is celebrated with feasts, fun, gambling, lion dances, lighting of firecrackers, and "Open House" [*see* **Malays**]. Friends and relatives visit each other to eat, drink, and wish each other good luck and prosperity during the "Open House." This is usually done on the first, second, and fourth days of the celebration.

Besides being a time for family reunions, Chinese New Year is a time when one's debts are paid up, new clothes and shoes are worn, the entire house is cleaned and renewed, and old arguments are forgotten and peace is restored between family and friends. It is also a time to pay one's respects to the elders and to worship the gods and ancestors. Children pay respect to their elders and are given *ang pows* ("red packets") containing money. Various festivities go on until the 15th day, *chap go mei,* at which the time Chinese New Year officially ends. The family will get together again for another reunion dinner. On this day, many unmarried women used to throw oranges into the sea or rivers as prayers to get a good husband. However, this is becoming a very rare practice among the Chinese community today. Besides Chinese-based holidays, Malaysian Chinese also consider other Festivals of Malaysia as major holidays. The list includes New Year's Day, Hari Raya Puasa or Hari Raya Aidil Fitri (end of Ramadan), Thaipusam (celebrated by Hindus on the 10th month of the Hindu calendar), Chinese New Year (celebrated over 15 days beginning on the first day of Chinese Lunar Calendar), Wesak Day, Gawai Dayak (harvest festival), Deepavali, and Christmas.

⁷RITES OF PASSAGE

In the past, women gave birth at home with the help of a midwife, whereas today the majority of women give birth in hospitals with the help of a gynecologist. During her confinement, a young mother is prohibited from eating "cold" food such as fruits. Instead, she is encouraged to eat "warm" food, particularly *kachang ma,* a chicken soup stewed in distilled rice-wine and herbs.

The most important occasion on the birth of a baby is the "first-month" celebration. Friends and relatives are invited to celebrate the occasion. A variety of food is served in abundance, and hard-boiled eggs with red-stained shells are distributed. Gifts are given to the baby during this occasion. However, this celebration is only of great importance for the first son and the first daughter. Subsequent children will have some ritual celebration, but not the elaborate affair accorded to the first-born. In the past, at this celebration, the child's hair was ritually cut off and kept in a jar along with the dried umbilical cord. This was ritually used to stop fights between the child and his or her other siblings.

During their childhood, Chinese children are expected to help their parents at work. Many boys can be found helping their parents in the shops or working on the farms, while girls help their mothers with household chores or take care of younger siblings.

Unlike the Malays and Indians, the Malaysian Chinese do not have a tradition of puberty rituals. Even though dating was never part of their cultural tradition, it is becoming a common practice among the Chinese community in Malaysia. The young people are influenced by practices they see on television, in movies, and in the magazines and novels they read. A Chinese girl starts dating when she is 17 or 18 years old and gets married at least by the age of 24, while a boy would be a few years older. A married man and woman are automatically considered adults and are expected to act accordingly. Since Malaysia does not operate on a welfare system, the children of elderly parents are expected to take care of them until they pass away.

Death among the Chinese is marked by lengthy, colorful, and traditional ceremonies. A departed relative is sent off by his or her relatives with full ceremonial honors, partly to prevent the deceased from coming back to haunt them, and partly to "save face," that is, to prevent people from talking negatively about the ceremony. Therefore, death is sometimes an expensive affair that can run into thousands of dollars. Funerals are

A Malaysian Chinese father with his baby visits a shop for colorful Chinese New Year decorations. For decades, Chinese in Malaysia have silently endured government policies giving the country's majority ethnic Malays preference in education and politics. (AP Images/Howe GOH, File)

sometimes held at home in large open spaces, or in funeral parlors.

The body of a deceased person is ceremonially washed, usually by the eldest son, before being dressed in an odd number of suits of clothing and laid in a coffin. This is followed by an elaborate ritual observation. It is important that the coffin is placed in a prominent position in the house, surrounded by the deceased's favorite possessions and refreshments. Candles are kept burning throughout the period so that the spirit of the deceased can view the surroundings. Offerings, incense, and paper money may be burnt close by. The coffin is never left unattended throughout this period. Relatives are expected to donate money for the occasion in odd denominations of RM10, RM30, or RM50, and never in multiples of RM20.

On the morning of the funeral, mourners come together for one last gathering. Sometimes stilt-dancers may perform before the coffin is taken to the graveyard. The funeral procession leaves the house at a predetermined time, often 2:00 PM. The hearse, usually a truck, is driven slowly from the house. The chief mourner and other relatives of the deceased follow the hearse on foot. Immediate members of the family dress up in shapeless garments of unbleached calico, indigo, or black cotton. Colorful attire and jewelry are unsuitable even for friends who come to visit. This procession is preceded by trucks carrying banners and wreaths of condolence from associations or sympathizers, the local drums and gongs ensemble, and sometimes also by one or more brass bands. Therefore, a funeral procession can sometimes be heard from quite a distance. Funeral processions of prominent Chinese can be very elaborate and may last a long time.

After the funeral, the family continues to mourn the deceased by wearing black patches or black armbands with their somber clothes. Prayers are read every evening by Buddhist monks until the seventh day after the death. On a set day, the family visits the graveyard bringing a grand house, a car, some temple money, servants, a TV set, and a video player, all made from paper, to be burned at the graveyard for the deceased to receive and use in the other world. Usually the family is in mourning for 100 days.

8 INTERPERSONAL RELATIONS

The Chinese normally greet each other with "Have you eaten your fill?" or "Have you taken your food?" The response is always "Yes, thank you," even if one is starving. This greeting is similar to the Western "How are you?" "Fine, thank you." In business a polite Chinese will say, "Is your business prosperous?" The response will be, "My business is moderate."

Unlike the Malays and Indians, shaking hands as a form of greeting between a man and a woman is acceptable among the Chinese. Chinese men often greet each other with a friendly pat on the arm, while hugging or kissing is prohibited except in a close relationship.

Even though the Chinese do not have religious restrictions about wearing shoes in homes, it is considered inconsiderate to wear shoes in the house. This is because they may mar or soil the floor. Chinese usually entertain their guests in the living room and seldom show the entire house, particularly the bedrooms. Even family members do not enter each other's rooms without permission. It is proper to bring gifts such as fruit, sweets, or cakes on the third and fourth visit. However, gifts should always be given in an even number, as this is a sign of happiness and good luck.

A Chinese girl does not date until she is about 17 or 18 years old, and a boy would be a few years older. Even though it is not part of their tradition, dating as understood in the West is becoming very common among the Chinese, as compared to the Malay Muslims. One of the reasons is that most Chinese live in urban areas that make them more liberal.

9 LIVING CONDITIONS

The Malaysian Chinese populate most of the urban areas in the country. This is because most of them are traders and businesspeople who are very much involved in the commercial and professional sectors. In fact, they are considered the richest ethnic group in Malaysia, possessing 40.9% of Malaysia's total wealth.

Many Chinese in urban areas live in shop houses: the second floor is the living quarter, while the first floor is for business. In recent years an increasing number live in housing estates or suburban areas. They either live in condominiums, bungalows, and/or terrace houses. This is also due to the establishment of "new villages" at the fringes of urban areas in the 1940s and 1950s, which forced many rural Chinese to be relocated to urban areas.

Since the standard of living in Malaysia has increased tremendously during the past decade due to an economic boom, most Malaysian homes have consumer items such as cars, a television set, a VCR, and a refrigerator. This is particularly true among the Chinese who are economically better-off than the other ethnic groups. They have easy access to better sanitation, electricity, water supply, and efficient public transportation. Nonetheless, Chinese who live in rural areas do not have access to these basic amenities. They are still burning kerosene for light, and depending on wells and rivers for water.

10 FAMILY LIFE

Marriage and raising a family are vital elements in the life of a Chinese. A basic Chinese household unit includes a husband, a wife, and their children. Since Chinese are expected to take care of close relatives, sometimes a household may include extended members of the family, such as grandparents, aunts, and uncles. Among the upper- and middle-class households, the unit may include a live-in servant or nanny who looks after the young children. A middle-class couple usually has two or three children, while lower-class families have more children.

Female members of a family are expected to know how to cook, clean the house, and take care of elder relatives. However, nowadays many Chinese women have professions that keep them away from their homes; therefore, they have to hire maids to take care of household chores. A husband's main responsibility is to provide shelter and financial support for his family.

Chinese families usually keep dogs and/or cats as pets. Dogs are partly kept to guard homes from burglaries. Sometimes parrots and other "singing birds" are kept as well. These birds are kept for their beautiful sounds and their ability to talk, and also for bird competitions.

11 CLOTHING

Cheongsam, a tight-fitting, high-collared, slit-skirted dress, is the traditional Chinese women's dress, while *yi fu* is the traditional Chinese men's dress. However, most Malaysian Chinese nowadays wear ordinary Western clothes, such as t-shirts, pants, skirts, jeans, dresses, shorts, blouses, etc. The color red is considered lucky by Chinese, and they never wear black except to funerals, although nowadays some youngsters dress in deep black at New Year's celebrations. Also, some elderly Chinese women, especially if they are widows, wear black silk clothes for weddings and other ritual occasions. Older men, particularly the "shop houses Chinese" men, often wear long baggy shorts and tank tops.

12 FOOD

The Chinese saying, "Anything that walks with its back to the sky can be eaten," shows that eating and drinking are their favorite pastimes and that they have a way to prepare and make tasty every edible object. Their staple foods include rice and a variety of noodles. While rice is usually eaten with meat and vegetables cooked in various ways, noodles are often prepared in broth or stir-fried. Noodles are usually eaten for breakfast, while rice is eaten for lunch and dinner. Most of these foods can be easily obtained from food stalls and cart vendors selling foods by the roadsides.

The Chinese consider certain foods as "cooling" or "heating." Heating foods such as chocolate, granola, and most meats make the body feel too hot, too full, and uncomfortable. These foods also cause certain illnesses such as sore throats. While cooling foods are the opposite of heating foods, they can also cause or aggravate illnesses such as colds and coughs. Watermelon, tea, and yogurt are a few examples of cooling foods and are not supposed to be taken on cool days.

Unlike the Malays and Indians, the Chinese eat their food with chopsticks. The Chinese observe certain taboos and manners when eating with chopsticks. Chopsticks are not to be rested on the dinner plate or rice bowl; rather, they are to be placed on a rest stand or a bone plate. Sticking a chopstick in a rice bowl is considered a bad omen as it signifies death, pointing with chopsticks and waving them in the air is considered bad manners.

One Chinese traditional food is *Yee Sang*. It is basically raw fish served with salad and is usually eaten on the third or fourth day of the Chinese New Year's celebration. Yee Sang may consist of several types of finely shredded vegetables, colorfully placed in small portions and mixed with different condiments and a few flakes of raw fish.

13 EDUCATION

Malaysia's literacy rate is about 92%. This is because primary and secondary schools are mandatory in Malaysia, which means children from the ages of 6 to 15 have to attend school. The Chinese are noted to be high achievers in education. This is partly due to their tradition that emphasizes education above everything else.

When the Chinese arrived in Malaysia, they brought along with them their schools. The first Chinese school in Malaysia was set up in 1815, and today there are about 1,300 fully and partially government-assisted Chinese primary schools which form an integral part of the Malaysian education system (salaries of teachers in these schools are paid by the government while the upkeep of school buildings and facilities is funded through donations by local communities). Most Chinese parents send their children to Chinese or English primary schools. In 2004, 90% (600,000) of all Malaysian Chinese schoolchildren were enrolled in Chinese schools. It is important to note that the Chinese schools are not solely for the Chinese, but are open to other communities in Malaysia. For instance in 1994 it was estimated that a total of about 32,000 non-Chinese students attended Chinese primary schools.

By the time a Chinese child is 4 or 5 years old, she or he is sent to kindergarten. At age 6, the child continues on to primary school. After the age of 12, some of these children will transfer to Malay and English high schools, while the others remain in Chinese medium secondary schools. However, they are all required to master the national language, Malay, since the national examinations for students at the age of 15 and 18 are conducted in Malay. Outstanding students in the examinations are allowed to go to Form Six or directly into the university. Due to a limited number of universities in Malaysia, many of these students go to universities in the United States, United Kingdom, Australia, and New Zealand.

Parents expect their children to do very well in school and will do whatever is necessary to ensure that their children are able to receive an education. Having said that, it is estimated that about 25% Chinese students usually dropout from school before reaching 18 years old. Many of these leave school to become apprentice as plumber, mechanic, builder, and running family or personal enterprise.

¹⁴CULTURAL HERITAGE

When the Chinese came to Malaysia, they brought their dance, music, and literature with them. However, due to Malaysia's multiracial society, most ethnic groups in Malaysia, including the Chinese, have adopted or assimilated each other's culture. Today, the Malaysian Chinese do not only speak the Chinese language, eat Chinese food, wear Chinese clothes, and appreciate Chinese classical songs, but they also eat Malay, Indian, and Western food, wear other clothes, and enjoy the music of other communities. Nonetheless, the Malaysian Chinese still keep their many traditional celebrations, which form a large part of Chinese cultural heritage in Malaysia. These celebrations include the Lantern festival, the Dragon Boat festival, the Tomb festival, the Hungry Ghost festival, and the Moon Cake festival.

Chinese traditional music and dance are usually aired and performed during festivities such as the Chinese New Year or when there is a funeral. One of their most popular dances is the Lion Dance, which is usually performed during the Chinese New Year's celebration. Literature such as *The Eight Immortals*, *The Monkey God*, and *Na Cha the Dragon Slayer* are ancient children's stories which are as popular in Malaysia as Mickey Mouse is in the United States.

¹⁵WORK

Initially the Chinese came to Malaya as traders, shopkeepers, planters, and miners. They worked in tin mines and opened up plantations of pepper, rubber, gambier, coconut, and sugar. But today most Malaysian Chinese are prominent professionals and businesspeople. As a result they make up of the majority middle and upper income classes in Malaysia's multiethnic society. They are economically more progressive—dominating the Malaysian economy—resulting in an economic imbalance between races. This imbalance led to race riots on 13 May 1969. In order to rectify this economic imbalance, particularly between the Malays and Chinese, the New Economic Policy (NEP) was formulated by the government with the twin-pronged objectives of eradicating poverty and restructuring society. This increased the Malays' share of the economic pie by 20% during the period of 1970 to 1990, and the Chinese managed to advance from 28% to 45% over the same period.

¹⁶SPORTS

Like most other ethnic groups in Malaysia, the Chinese have become acquainted with sports such as soccer, volleyball, basketball, swimming, ping pong, badminton, tennis, squash, etc. Three of the most popular spectator sports among the Chinese are soccer (known as "football"), basketball, and badminton. Some of the top national athletes, both men and women, who represent the country in international competitions or events are Chinese.

¹⁷ENTERTAINMENT AND RECREATION

Since most Chinese live in urban areas, their forms of entertainment and recreation are very similar to those of residents in suburban or city areas in the US and UK. They attend movies, watch television and videos, listen to radio and music (on cassettes and compact discs). They watch Western, Chinese and Malay movies, and listen to recordings of both local and imported traditional and modern music, which are available at local music stores. This includes Western, Chinese, Malay, and Indian music. Besides watching movies and listening to music, gambling with *mahjong*, a game similar to playing cards except that it is played with tiles, is a popular form of entertainment among the elderly Chinese.

¹⁸FOLK ART, CRAFTS, AND HOBBIES

The Malaysian Chinese both in Peninsular Malaysia and Borneo are fine potters. They produce clay vessels, jars, vases, tall narrow jars wired as standard lamps, round containers with and without lids, ashtrays, plates, mugs, etc.

¹⁹SOCIAL PROBLEMS

Due to the existence of the Internal Security Act (ISA) in Malaysia, the country has received plenty of criticism from human-rights activists in the West. The Act provides for detention without trial for individuals deemed detrimental to the harmony of the nation. Many prominent Chinese leaders have been detained under the Act since its enactment in 1950s.

Even though Islam is the official religion of Malaysia, and Malay is the national language, the basic rights of the Malaysian Chinese to practice their faith, speak their dialects, and keep their traditions and cultures are virtually secured by the constitution.

There is a high rate of school dropouts before the age of 18. The situation has created major concern since there is a tendency among dropouts to also engage in illicit trades and related activities.

²⁰GENDER ISSUES

Traditionally, female members of a family are expected to know how to cook, clean the house, and take care of elder relatives. However, nowadays gender roles in domestic realms have changed as a result of women's increased labor force participation. There is a more relaxed attitude in gender issues which can be gauged by the different roles husband and wife play in their duties to one another.

²¹BIBLIOGRAPHY

Beng, Tan Teik. *Beliefs and Practices among Malaysian Buddhists*. Kuala Lumpur, Malaysia: Buddhist Missionary Society, 1988.

Craig, JoAnn. *Culture Shock! What Not to Do in Malaysia and Singapore, How and Why Not to Do It*. Times Books, 1979.

Jin, Kok Hu. "Malaysian Chinese Folk Religion: With Special Reference to Weizhen Gong in Kuala Lumpur." In *Chinese Beliefs and Practices in Southeast Asia*, edited by Cheu Hock Tong. Malaysia: Pelanduk Publications, 1993.

Malaysia Department of Statistics. *Population and Housing Census of Malaysia 2000*. Kuala Lumpur: Department of Statistics Malaysia, 2001.

Sik, Lin Liong. *The Malaysian Chinese: Towards Vision 2020*. Selangor, Malaysia: Pelanduk Publications Sdn.Bhd., 1995.

—by P. Bala

MALAYSIAN INDIANS

PRONUNCIATION: muh-LAY-zhun IN-dee-uhns
ALTERNATE NAMES: Tamils
POPULATION: 1.8 million (2004)
LOCATION: Malaysia
LANGUAGE: Tamil; Malay; Chinese; other ethnic Indian languages
RELIGION: Hindu (majority); Sikh; Buddhist; Muslim; Christian
RELATED ARTICLES: Vol. 3: People of India; Vol. 4: Malaysian Malays; Tamils

¹INTRODUCTION

Indian traders came to Malaya as early as the 14th century. Through trading, they introduced Islam to the locals, particularly to the Malays. This was also done by marrying into the various royal families, consequently achieving positions of great influence. It was only in the latter half of the 19th century that an influx of Indian immigrants came to Malaya, due to its rapid economic development. The largest annual flow into Malaya occurred during the period of 1911–30, when more than 90,000 persons landed each year. They were recruited and solicited by the British, mostly as indentured laborers to work on rubber plantations. A large number of clerical workers were also brought in from Ceylon, while a number of professionals, doctors, and teachers were brought in from India, particularly after World War I. Almost every Indian ethnic subgroup is represented in Malaysia. This includes the Tamils, Gujaratis, Malayalis, Punjabi, Sindhis, Pathans, Telegus, Kannarese, and the Sri Lankan Tamil and Singhalese. They came from many parts of India and belonged to different faiths. Nevertheless, Malaysian Indians are mostly Tamils, forming 87.6 per cent of the population in Malaysia.

INDIAN ETHNIC SUBGROUPS IN MALAYSIA (2000)

Group	Population	%
Indian Tamil	1,396,480	87.6
Malayali	35,809	2.3
Telugu	38,993	2.4
Sikh	33,231	2.1
Punjabi	23,147	1.5
Other Indian	41,477	2.6
Pakistani	11,313	0.7
Bangladeshi	2,951	0.2
Sri Lankan Tamil	8,735	0.5
Singhalese	1,641	0.1
Total	1,593,77	100

Source: R. Rajakrishnan and Manimaran Subramaniam 'The Indians: Classification, origins and social organization,' IN Hood Salleh (ed.) *The Encyclopedia of Malaysia, Peoples and Tradtions.* Kuala Lumpur: Editions Didier Millet, 2006 (pg.59)

Even though the number and power of the Indians in Malaysia are far inferior to those of the Malays and Chinese, they are well represented in Malaysia's political arena. The Malaysian Indian Congress (MIC) plays an important role as a vehicle of political representation among the Indian Malaysians. It represents the Indians in the interethnic grouping of political parties called the Alliance. It was brought in as the third partner of the Alliance after the elections of 1964.

²LOCATION AND HOMELAND

Since most Malaysian Indians were brought in by the British government to work as laborers on the plantations, most of them live in the major plantation states of Selangor, Negri Sembilan, and Johor, with spillover in other states, such as Kedah, Perak, Penang, and Pahang. Even today, plantations still provide employment for most of the Indian population. Gradual urbanization, however, continues among Indians, as with other Malaysians, with many drifting from plantation areas to neighboring cities and towns. This rural-urban migration has increased since the 1980s as a result of a shift in plantation agriculture from rubber to the less labor-intensive oil palm. This is also due to improved education and industrialization. The latter has generated employment opportunities in urban areas. All of this has led to a decrease in the rural population from 65% in 1970 to 30% in 2000.

³LANGUAGE

Besides being able to read, write, and speak in their mother tongue of Tamil, or other Indian languages, almost every Malaysian Indian is also able to speak and write Malay. A large number are able to speak and read Chinese characters as well.

Unlike Western names, the Malaysian Indians do not have surnames. Their names consist of two parts: their given name, and their father's name, with "s/o" ("son of") or "d/o" (daughter of) to append the father's name. For example, Dorai, the son of Sivam s/o Ramesh, is not Dorai Ramesh, but Dorai s/o Sivam. The same principle applies to a daughter's name, except that upon marriage she has to take her husband's name. Therefore, Dorai's wife, Suseela, will be known as Mrs. Dorai or Madam Suseela. There are times when the initial of the father's name is placed in front of a person's given name. For instance, Ramesh s/o Arul will be known as A. Ramesh, "A" being the initial of the father's name, while Ramesh is the person's given name.

While the more traditional families will name a son after a Hindu god and a daughter after a Hindu goddess, the Christian Indians, such as the Thomian Christians in Malaysia, have biblical surnames like Abraham, John, Samuel, or Jacob that are perpetuated in the family. There are others who adopted Portuguese names, such as Rozario, DeSilva, and Santamaria, as family surnames. These are descendents of Indians from Ceylon, Goa, and Malacca, which were colonies of Portugal.

⁴FOLKLORE

The Malaysian Indians have many folk tales and myths that are closely related to their majority religion, Hinduism. One of their legends is the story behind the celebration of the Festival of Lights, or Deepavali, as a celebration of Nagarasuran's death. Nagarasuran was a Hindu tyrant and an extremely cruel king. As a result, his people appealed to Lord Krishna to remove him from the kingdom. Lord Krishna favored their appeal by having Nagarasuran defeated and fatally wounded in a battle. However, before his death, Nagarasuran repented from his cruelty and begged Lord Krishna for forgiveness. He also asked for a favor from Lord Krishna, that is, to let his people celebrate his death instead of weeping for him. Lord Krishna granted his request by letting them celebrate the Festival of Lights, the Deepavali.

Malaysian ethnic Indians take part in a hunger strike to protest alleged discrimination against the minorities in Port Klang, Malaysia. (AP Images/Lai Seng Sin)

⁵RELIGION

Indian Malaysians are of different faiths. However, most of them are Hindu, while others are Sikh, Buddhist, Muslim, and Christian. For most Indian Malaysians, the Hindu religion is a way of life. They believe in the ultimate reality, which appears in many forms and for different purposes such as for life, creation, energy, and protection. They also believe in reincarnation that one's life and actions will determine one's next life and that the actions of one's previous life have determined one's present life. Since the spiritual goal of a person is to reach a state of perfection and enlightenment, she or he is given an opportunity to make up for any harmful deeds during her or his previous existence by being reborn.

Malaysian Indians have a deep faith, which is woven into their everyday lives. An Indian mother offers prayers and burns incense at the family altar every morning before the sun is up. This is done to greet her god and the new day. She may perform the same ritual at sunset, too.

Friday is a special day for Hindus in Malaysia. This is the day the Malaysian Indians flock to temples to offer prayers. At the temple, they make several different kinds of offerings. One of these offerings is the "banana" offering or "half-coconut" offering. This is done by giving a donation of 30 cents for a banana or 80 cents for half a coconut and by writing their name on a small slip of paper that will be read out loud by the priests during their formal prayers. After the formal prayers, the devotees are given holy ash to put on their foreheads and betel nuts that can be chewed by the older folks or placed on the altar at home. The blessed banana or coconut is then taken home, either to be eaten or to be placed on the family altar. If the offerings are not eaten, they will not be thrown away, even after they have become rotten. Instead, they will be placed under a tree or into a river.

⁶MAJOR HOLIDAYS

Two of the Malaysian Indians' major holidays are the Deepavali and Thaipusam. The Deepavali is known as the Festival of Lights and is usually celebrated in October. The exact day of the celebration is, however, determined by astrologers. It is largely a day for family reunions and also a time for non-Hindu friends to come visit during the Open House.

While Deepavali is a family celebration, Thaipusam is a very public celebration and takes place in late January or early February. It is a festival connected with penance, atonement, and thanksgiving for favors granted by the gods. It is dedicated to Lord Murugan, a god personifying the virtues of courage, youth, power, and endurance. At this festival, a person who had received answers to prayers will reciprocate by doing some

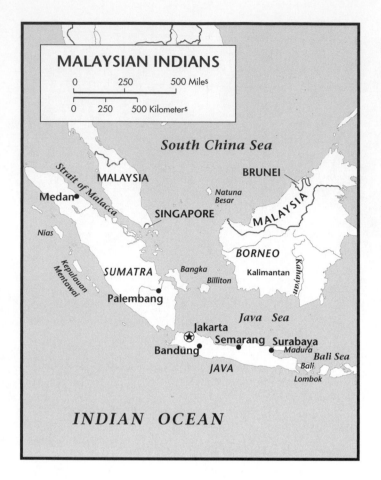

MALAYSIAN INDIANS

0   250   500 Miles

0   250   500 Kilometers

South China Sea

MALAYSIA

BRUNEI

Medan•

Natuna Besar

SINGAPORE

MALAYSIA

Nias

BORNEO

Kepulauan Mentawai

SUMATRA

Bangka

Kalimantan

Billiton

Kahayan

Palembang

Java Sea

Jakarta

⊛   Semarang   Surabaya

Bandung   *Madura*

JAVA   *Bali*   *Bali Sea*

Lombok

INDIAN OCEAN

sort of penance to show his or her gratitude. This act of gratitude is usually accomplished by carrying a *kavadi* on his or her shoulder on the procession day. Although a *kavadi* can be any form of offering to the gods, it is usually a large semicircular object, almost like half of a bicycle wheel, which is carried on the shoulder. Metal hooks and spikes are attached to the kavadi, which are fastened onto the devotee's skin.

Thousands of Hindus take part in the Thaipusam procession, which usually takes place at the Batu Caves in the State of Selangor. As a result, it enhances the social identity of the community and reinforces the spirit of "communitas." It is on this day that every Indian is equal in the sight of every other Indian. Women have equal status with men, lower castes have equal status with higher castes, and there is no distinction made between individuals.

⁷RITES OF PASSAGE

An Indian couple always hopes for sons, as only sons can perform certain rites during the father's funeral. A mother and her child are considered unclean and in a state of danger for 28 days after the birth of the child. Therefore, many restrictions are placed on the mother throughout this period. The child's birth is celebrated on the twenty-eighth day, with friends and relatives invited to the celebration. The child is dressed up in fancy clothes and jewelry for the occasion. A child will be named on this day by placing the child on the father's lap, or on the lap of some relative, while his or her name is whispered gently into his or her ears. From then on, the child will be known and called by that name.

Like many other communities in Malaysia, the Malaysian Indians increasingly observe their birthdays in the Western way. Some Indians have puberty rituals, particularly for their daughters. The Ceylonese Tamils have a ritual called *Chamati Chadanja,* which is usually carried out at the time of the girl's first menses, though it may be done just before the girl marries. This ceremony is usually held on an odd-numbered date, i.e, the seventh, ninth, or eleventh day of the month. Unlike the girls, Indian boys do not normally go through puberty rituals or circumcision.

Marriage in the Indian community is seen as sacred and eternal, lasting through life and even after. An Indian girl is expected to be married between the ages of 22 to 23, while a boy usually marries between the ages of 25 to 28. Even though young Indians have more freedom to choose their life partners than in the past, arranged marriages are still widely practiced among Malaysian Indians. Normally, two related families would arrange a marriage between their children. However, an Indian boy can only marry his father's sister's daughter or his mother's brother's daughter, but not his father's brother's daughter or his mother's sister's daughter. It is preferable to marry a girl of the same class, caste, and community.

A marriage is arranged by calling a priest from each side of the family to compare the horoscopes of the prospective bride and groom. If all is well, then the marriage is agreed upon. Once a match is made, the dowry is settled. It is important to note, however, that a marriage proposal usually comes from the girl's side. This is because, by tradition, a female has to provide a male with a dowry. The amount of the dowry depends on the eligibility (in terms of affluence and profession) of the young man.

There are certain marriage symbols used by Indian women once they are married. While South Indian women wear *pottu,* a red dot on the forehead, and *thali,* a necklace tied by their husband around their necks at the wedding, North Indian women wear bangles on their arms and red streaks on the parting of their hair.

The sixtieth birthday is the landmark age for an Indian gentleman. A celebration is held to pray for his longevity and good health. Malaysian Indians believe that when a person dies, the soul leaves the vicinity of the house only on the sixteenth or fortieth day, if the soul is very attached to his or her family. In respect for the soul, an oil lamp is left burning in the home day and night throughout that period. Although the soul may linger for a longer period, the body of the deceased is usually removed from the house within 12 hours. While most adults are cremated, children are not. When a woman's husband dies, she has to remove the thali from her neck and wipe off the pottu from her forehead. This symbolizes the end of her married life.

⁸INTERPERSONAL RELATIONS

Traditionally, handshaking as a form of greeting is not widely used by the Malaysian Indians. Their usual form of greeting is to put the palms together in the prayer position and raise the hands to chest level in front of their face, with their head slightly bowed. However, today handshaking is an acceptable form of greeting, though it is best to let an Indian woman extend her hand first for a handshake.

When entering an Indian home, it is customary to remove one's shoes, unless told otherwise. Shoes are never to be worn in kitchen and prayer areas. The right hand should be used for any social purposes, such as to give and receive items. It is considered polite to bow slightly when passing in front of people, saying, "Excuse me, please."

Conversations between members of the opposite sex are normally kept to a minimum. Coarse jokes and sex talk are not to be spoken in the presence of any woman. Even though dating has never been part of their culture, it is becoming a common practice among young Malaysian Indians. They are partly influenced by mass media—television, magazines, novels, etc. It is also a result of young Indians mixing more freely with their friends in schools and universities.

9 LIVING CONDITIONS

Among Malaysia's Indians, there is a clear distinction between the urban middle class and the rural poor. While Malaysian Indians in urban areas have easy access to a better standard of living, the Malaysian Indians on the plantations have to cope with a lower living standard. Many children on the plantations do not receive proper nutrition before being sent off to school in the morning. Many families could not afford to buy even the basic necessities for their children's education, such as uniforms, shoes, notebooks, pencils, etc.

Unlike most other industries in the country, the plantation industry has built houses to accommodate its workers. This is because the plantations are usually located far from inhabited centers. Most plantation workers are currently living in "line-site" houses. There are two types of line-site house: the wooden barracks and the raised brick cottage. The wooden barracks are old and are arranged usually in rows of five. The walls are made of planks, and the roof is usually made of aluminum. Each dwelling in a row occupies an area of roughly 3 m by 6 m (10 ft by 19 ft), and is about 3 m (10 ft) high. It has a small veranda, a living room, a bedroom measuring roughly 3 m by 2.5 m (10 ft by 8 ft), and a tiny kitchen of 1 m by 2 m (3 ft by 6 ft). The raised brick cottages have a covered floor of roughly 5 m by 6 m (17 ft by 20 ft) and consist of two living quarters inhabited by different families. The two quarters are partitioned by a brick wall, but share a common tile roof. Each quarter has a living room, two bedrooms, a kitchen, a toilet, and a bath.

Unlike the urban areas, basic amenities, such as water, sanitation, and electricity in the plantations, are seriously below legal standards. The plantations get their water supply either by water piped to each house, stand-pipes shared by a few families, well or pond water, a river, or through the JKR (Department of Public Works) water supply. While some plantations are provided with electricity by an estate generator, others obtain electricity by running their own generators, and others use gas or oil lamps.

10 FAMILY LIFE

Like many communities in Malaysia, the Malaysian Indian families are organized in relation to nuclear family units. It is through the family unit that values, culture, and religion are imparted to younger generations. Many of these nuclear families, however, are linked together into extended families. Family size among Malaysian Indians varies according to standards of living, education level, and location. There are households in the plantations that contain as many as 9, 10, 11, or even 12 family members. Living conditions for most people are crowded, but all members of the household benefit from the mutual support of parents, children, and grandchildren living under the same roof.

Malaysian Indian women in some ways are still highly conservative. This is mainly because of a strong emphasis on male line descent and a patrilineal system. The father is ranked highest in the hierarchy of authority. He commands the family. Although the mother's position is respected, she is expected to be subservient to all of the males in the family.

11 CLOTHING

A *sari*, the traditional dress of an Indian woman, is a flowing silk or cotton wrapped dress worn over a short, tight-fitting, elbow-length-sleeved blouse. An Indian girl usually starts wearing a sari when she turns 13 years old. While Indian women wear a sari, Indian men wear a *dhoti*, a wrapped white skirt worn either with or without a shirt or white tunic.

Besides the sari, a Hindu Indian woman may wear a *pottu* (dot) on her forehead. A pottu can be worn in one of three traditional colors: red, yellow or black. These colors have certain significance among Indian women. While red is worn by married women, black is traditionally worn by unmarried women. However, red and yellow can also be used simply as an auspicious color. While these two colors are thought to have a calming effect when put on the forehead after prayers, black is used to counteract the effect of the evil eye. A black dot is able to protect a girl from harm by repelling evil influences, particularly when a young girl receives too many compliments.

Except during festivities and other celebrations, it is very common to see Malaysian Indian women dressed in blouses, jeans, skirts, dresses, or shorts. Malaysian Indian men commonly wear pants, shirts, shorts, and tee-shirts. Even the color of the pottu on the forehead is worn simply to match the color of women's attire these days, regardless of their marital status.

12 FOOD

As in most Asian communities, rice is the staple food of the Malaysian Indians. Breads, such as *chapati* (a thin, flat, unleavened wholemeal bread), *naan* (leavened white bread), *puri* (a deep-fried wholemeal bread), and *rothi paratha* (a flaky wholemeal bread), are also staple foods among the Malaysian Indians. While these breads are usually eaten with hot curry gravy, rice is eaten with curries, sauces, vegetables, and other dishes. Since most Indians are Hindu, they tend to be vegetarian. Their foods are usually cooked in coconut milk or yogurt and are seasoned with hot peppers and spices, thus making them very spicy. They normally add colors to their food by adding chili powder for red, curry powder for brown, and turmeric for yellow. This helps enhance the appearance of their food. They also have a variety of snacks. These snacks include *vadai*, deep-fried cakes made with ground lentils, green chilies, and ginger; *muruku*, crispy and crunchy pretzels; *pakhora*, mixed vegetable fritters; and *samosa*, deep fried pastries containing meat, onion, and spices.

Like the Malays, the Tamils traditionally use the fingers of the right hand for eating. A popular traditional style of dining among the Malaysian Indians is by eating off banana leaves. A variety of curries, vegetables, and sauces are placed around a pile of rice on the banana leaves. Even the dessert after the main meal is served on the same banana leaf. The banana leaf is folded in half after the meal, to indicate that one has finished one's meal. Sometimes, foods are served on a *thali*, a metal tray with several small matching bowls for food. This is particularly true in traditional Indian homes. All the food, including the desserts, is served at the same time, with the rice or bread placed in the center of the tray.

¹³EDUCATION

The Indian community is the poorest of the three major communities in Peninsular Malaysia. Because of this, Malaysian Indian youth have relatively low rates of enrollment in schools. Their enrollment rates in both urban and rural areas are lower than those among Malays and Chinese. Furthermore, in comparison with the Malays and Chinese, more Indian youths drop out of school due to low motivation. As a result, the position of the Malaysian Indians in reference to education is comparatively poor in Malaysia.

However, the government has taken impressive measures to uplift the standard of education among the Indian community in Malaysia. Since it is mandatory for Malaysians to attend schools between the ages of 6 and 15, the government has made an effort to build primary and secondary schools on the plantations across the country. After the age of 15, youths are encouraged to attend vocational or technical colleges and other institutions of higher learning. They can obtain loans and scholarship programs from the government, the NUPW (National Union of Plantation Workers), and the MIC (Malaysian Indian Congress). An increasing number of Malaysian Indian parents see education as a means for their children to gain better employment than plantation work. Through and increased emphasis on education, many young adult Malaysian Indians are now working as professionals, managers, and clerical staff in all sectors of modern economy.

¹⁴CULTURAL HERITAGE

Malaysian Indians' dance, music, and literature revolve around their religion, Hinduism. Their dances are greatly influenced by the two great Indian poetic epics, the *Ramayana* and *Mahabhrata*. These two epics do not only influence Indian dances and music, but also the Malays' dance and theater performances, such as the *wayang kulit* and *makyong* (*see* **Malaysian Malays**).

Since most Malaysian Indians are Hindu, the Vedas (Hindu scriptures) play an important role in the community. They are ancient writings that explain the mystery of life. They contain some simple parables, which are easily understood by the common people, but which can also be read and understood at the highest levels of abstract philosophy.

¹⁵WORK

Even though the majority of Malaysian Indians work on plantations as laborers, there are many who are doctors, lawyers, trade unionists, police and army personnel, small shopkeepers, teachers, etc. Basically, they are found in every strata of the society class structure. As traders, they usually sell textiles, perfumes, and jewelry. Many are successful professionals, traders, and businesspeople. At the other end of the scale, however, the Indian laborers on the rubber estates are among the poorest Malaysians.

¹⁶SPORTS

Like among many other ethnic groups in Malaysia, sports such as soccer, rugby, basketball, badminton, and cricket are becoming very popular among the Malaysian Indians in rural and urban areas. The most popular spectator sport is soccer (known as football in Malaysia), particularly among the youth. Both on the plantations and in the cities, it is not unusual to see Indian youths and adults get together to play soccer on any open field.

¹⁷ENTERTAINMENT AND RECREATION

Forms of entertainment among the Malaysian Indians depend greatly on where they live. Those who live in urban areas have the same forms of entertainment that people have in suburban areas in the United States and the United Kingdom. They have easy access to movies and theater, while those who live on the plantations do not have the same privileges. In urban areas, the Malaysian Indians do not only attend Indian movies and theaters, but also have access to Chinese and Malay movies and theater. They also have access to video arcades, parks, etc., which are popular places for recreation among the youth. Televisions, radios, compact discs, and cassettes players are common forms of entertainment in Malaysian Indian homes in urban areas. Some homes on the plantations do have television sets and video players as forms of entertainment. This is, of course, only true in homes that have access to electricity.

¹⁸FOLK ART, CRAFTS, AND HOBBIES

Like most parts of their cultural heritage, Malaysian Indian arts and crafts are closely related to Hinduism. Their fine art and carvings can be seen in stone carvings and terra-cotta sculptures, inset tile work, and other colorful details in their temples across Malaysia. Their painters have also produced hundreds of paintings (or, in recent times, colored prints) of gods and goddesses. These paintings are usually for devotional use in home shrines.

¹⁹SOCIAL PROBLEMS

The persistent poverty and political powerlessness of rural Indians in Malaysia is one of the country's best-known and most-severe social problems. Even though the plantation industry is a major source of income for Malaysia, low wages and poor working conditions for its plantation laborers have caused the Indians to be one of the poorest communities in Peninsular Malaysia. Most of them, like their contract-laborer ancestors, are rubber workers, though some are now small farmers. Poor budgeting and excessive drinking seem to aggravate the problem of low incomes and savings among the Indian poor. Furthermore, features such as low self-respect, apathy, poor parental responsibility, and weak community cooperation seem to reinforce one another and worsen the economic hardship faced by the Malaysian Indians.

²⁰GENDER ISSUES

The strong emphasis on the patrilineal system among the Indians shapes gender issues and relations in the community. Women usually do not sit with the men at any function. In some homes, the wife does not even sit down when male guests are present. In some cases a wife is not to call her husband by name nor openly object to his decisions and ideas. This is particularly true in many traditional homes. A wife may serve the guests, but otherwise she will stay in the kitchen or in some other part of the house. A wife usually stays at home, except for the occasional shopping trip to the department stores. However, these traditional values are changing with modernization, educational opportunities, and equal rights of women. In the plantations, women tap rubber and weed alongside men and receive wages at identical rates.

[21] BIBLIOGRAPHY

Arasaratnam, Sinnappah. *Indians in Malaysia and Singapore.* Kuala Lumpur: Oxford University Press, 1979.

Craig, JoAnn. *Culture Shock: What Not to Do in Malaysia and Singapore, How and Why Not to Do It.* Times Books International, 1979.

R, Rajakrishnan and Manimaran Subramaniam, "The Indians: Classification, origins and social organization," IN Hood Salleh (ed.) *The Encyclopedia of Malaysia, Peoples and Traditions.* Kuala Lumpur: Editions Didier Millet, 2006 (pg.59).

Ramachandran, Selvakumaran. *Indian Plantation Labour in Malaysia.* Kuala Lumpur: S. Abdul Majeed and Co., 1994.

Tan, Raelene. *Indian and Malay Etiquette: A Matter of Course.* Landmark Books Pte. Ltd., 1992.

Weibe, Paul D., and S. Mariappen. *Indian Malaysians: The View from the Plantation.* Manohar Publications, 1978.

—by P. Bala

MALAYSIAN MALAYS

PRONUNCIATION: muh-LAY-zhun MAY-layz
LOCATION: Malaysia
POPULATION: 12,893,600 (2004)
LANGUAGE: Malay; Chinese; Tamil and other Indian languages; tribal languages; English
RELIGION: Islam

[1] INTRODUCTION

Malay is a self referent term used by the people of the Malay Archipelago who have occupied the region since Prehistoric era. They are comprised of various ethnic, linguistic, and cultural variations, but all are speakers of the Austronesian group of languages. In Malaysia today, the term Malay is defined by the federal constitution to specify one who is Muslim and practicing Malay culture. The Malay comprise the largest group of indigenous peoples (bumiputera) and constitute 53% of the country's population. Although a homogenous group, differences exist between Malay subgroups in terms of territorial location, adat (customary) practices, lineage, and the kinship system. Examples of these subgroups are the Javanese, Bugis, Minangkabau, and several other groups who are descendants of interisland migrants of the Malay Archipelago who have settled in the peninsula since the early Malay kingdom.

One of the Malays' foremost successes in the early years in Malaya was the founding of Malacca Sultanate. It thrived in the 15th century as a popular trading port where traders from East (China) and West (India, Middle East, and Europe) met to trade commodities such as spices. Unfortunately, in 1511 Malacca was conquered by the Portuguese. It was then taken over by the Dutch in 1641, and in 1811 it was handed over to the British. The British, from Malacca, gradually expanded their influence to the rest of Malaya. By 1919 the entire Malay Peninsula had been brought under the British administrative system. They eventually occupied Sabah and Sarawak on the island of Borneo by the late 19th century.

The 11 Malay states in the Malay Peninsula only gained independence from the British on 31 August, 1957. In 1963, the Malay Peninsula joined Singapore and Sabah and Sarawak on Borneo Island to form the Federation of Malaysia. However, Singapore left the federation two years later. Currently, Malaysia is made up of 12 states and a federal territory. Sultans rule nine of the states, and three are ruled by governors. While each state government is headed by a chief minister and the state Cabinet members, the Malaysian government is headed by the prime minister and his Cabinet ministers. Malaysia practices a constitutional monarchy similar to what is practiced in England. Unlike in Britain, however, the king is chosen as the head of state by nine Sultans once every five years. Elections are also called every five years to elect members of the parliament, which include the prime minister and his Cabinet ministers; and the state assemblies, which include the chief minister and the state Cabinet. Usually the leader of the victorious party in an election becomes the prime minister or the chief minister.

Malaysia has been ruled continuously since independence by a coalition of political parties—the National Fronts—representing various ethnic groups. This coalition includes the United Malays National Organization (UMNO), representing

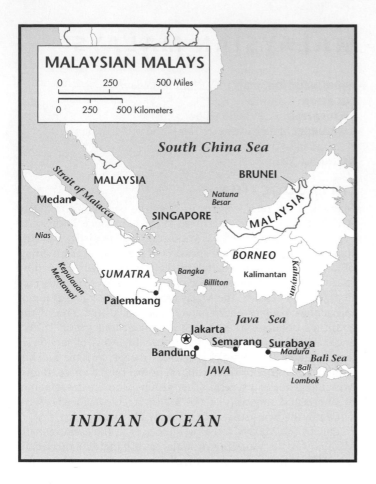

MALAYSIAN MALAYS

0   250   500 Miles
0   250   500 Kilometers

South China Sea

Strait of Malacca

MALAYSIA

Medan

Nias

SINGAPORE

BRUNEI

Natuna
Besar

MALAYSIA

Kepulauan
Mentawai

SUMATRA

Bangka

Billiton

BORNEO

Kalimantan

Kahayan

Palembang

Java Sea

Jakarta

Semarang   Surabaya

Bandung   Madura

JAVA   Bali Sea

Bali

Lombok

INDIAN OCEAN

the Malays; the Malaysian Chinese Association (MCA), representing the Chinese; and the Malaysian Indian Congress (MIC), representing the Indians; along with a few other political parties representing other ethnic groups in Sabah and Sarawak. The Malays, making up about 53% of the country's population, have the most representatives in the parliament and state assemblies. Other than the Communist insurgency in 1948 through 1960, and the communal riot between the Chinese and the Malays on 13 May, 1969, Malaysia has been a calm and peaceful country.

²LOCATION AND HOMELAND

Malaysia consists of Peninsular Malaysia, which includes the states of Penang, Perlis, Kedah, Pahang, Kelantan, Terengganu, Perak, Selangor, Negri Sembilan, Malacca, and Johor; the federal territories of Kuala Lumpur and Labuan; and Sabah and Sarawak, which are situated on the island of Borneo. Malaysia has a land area of 329,758 sq km (127,320 sq mi), making it slightly larger than the U.S. State of New Mexico. More than half of its land area is covered with tropical rain forests. Unfortunately, large areas of these rain forests are being depleted by logging. Malaysia's climate is monsoon tropical with an average annual rainfall of about 240 cm (95 in). It is warm, sunny and humid throughout the year with temperatures ranging from 23° to 31°c (73° to 88°f).

The Malays are found in all 13 states of Malaysia. While most Malays live in traditional villages, an increasing number of them have moved to cities, especially since 1970. Malaysia is a multiracial country with a population of over 25 million

people in 2004. Its multiethnic society consists of more than 70 ethnic groups. In Peninsular Malaysia there are four main groups: Malays, Chinese, Indians, and Orang Asli. Others include Eurasians, Chinese Peranakan, Chitties, Nepalese, and Sino-natives. In Sarawak, besides the Chinese and Malays, there are Iban, Bidayuh, Melanau, and the Orang Ulu groups, which include the Kelabit, Lun Bawang, Kayan, Kenyah, Kajang, Bisaya, Penan, Sekapan, Lahanan, Punan Bah, Seping, Bemali, Beketan, Berawan, Buket, Lisum, Punan Busang, Saban, Sihan, Tabun, Tring, Tagal, Tanjong, Kanowit, and Tatau. In Sabah there are Bajau, Murut, Suluk, Iranum, Tidong, Belabak, Bonggi, Kagayan, Ubian, Orang Sungai, and many others. Also included in this ethnic diversity in Malaysia are the Cocos Islanders, Thais, Myanmars, Indonesians, Filipinos, Japanese, Koreans, and Europeans. The Bumiputera, "sons of the soil" who include Malays and various ethnic groups in Sabah and Sarawak, make up 58% of the population. The Chinese account for about 30% of the total population and the Indians account for about 10%. Despite their linguistic, religious, and cultural differences, these ethnic groups live in harmony with one another.

POPULATION OF MALAYSIA 2004

Malays	12,893,600
Chinese	6,074,700
Other Bumiputera	2,808,100
Indians	1,806,800
Other Malaysians	304,400
Non-Malaysian Citizens	1,693,800
Total	25,581,400

Source: Hood Salleh, 'Introduction' In Hood Salleh (ed.) The Encyclopedia of Malaysia, Peoples and Tradtions. Kuala Lumpur: Editions Didier Millet, 2006 (pg.59)

³LANGUAGE

The Malays speak Malay, the Malaysian national language. The language belongs to the Malayo-Polynesian language family. Since Malay is Malaysia's national language, it is widely understood by the other ethnic groups, though other languages such as Chinese, Tamil and other Indian languages, and numerous tribal languages are spoken widely too. Malay as the first language, and English as the second language, are taught in almost every school throughout Malaysia.

Although the Malay language is widely spoken in Malaysia, dialects vary between the states. Generally, words are pronounced the way they are spelled, thus it is a very easy language to learn. Malay also borrows heavily from Sanskrit, Portuguese, Persian, Arabic, and English.

Malay names are basically Arabic names, since Malays are Muslim. Malay names do not have surnames. Instead, a name consists of the person's given name, followed by *bin* (son of) or *binti* (daughter of) and the father's first or full name. For example, Helmy, the son of Ismail Nik Dali, would be Helmy bin Ismail or Helmy bin Ismail Nik Dali. The same principle applies to a woman's name, except that her given name is followed by *binti*. Some common women's names are Fatimah, Lattifah, Zaiton, Aminah, and Zaleha while some common men's names are Ahmad, Sulaiman, Jamalludin, Zakaria, and Ismail.

A couple looks at share prices at a private stock market gallery in Kuala Lumpur, Malaysia. (AP Images/Andy Wong)

⁴FOLKLORE

Traditionally, the Malays had a number of folk tales and myths, especially those associated with the Hindu belief that was prevalent before the coming of Islam in the 16th century. Even as late as the 1970s, some of these folk tales were evident in the Malay Muslim society. However, with Islamic revivalism in the late 1970s and the migration of many Malays to urban areas around the same time, these folk tales and myths were gradually abandoned, since they stand in conflict with Islam.

The Malays regard Hang Tuah from the old Malacca sultanate as their traditional hero. He was noted to be a courageous warrior who fought the Siamese attacks on Malacca, and also a symbol of loyalty. His loyalty to the throne was proved when he killed his best friend, Hang Jebat, who rebelled against his sultan.

Another famous folk tale is about Mahsuri, a princess from the island of Langkawai who was wrongly accused of adultery and was executed. Upon her death, Mahsuri spilled white blood and cursed the whole island for seven generations.

⁵RELIGION

In the past, the Malays, like most other ethnic groups in Malaysia, were animists. They believed in the power of natural order. Trees, rivers, and caves were homes to penunggu (the vital force residing in a particular location) and the existence of se-

mangat (the vital force in all living things). To respect these spirits, annual rites were performed during foods were offered to them. Important figures like Shamans, ritual specialists (*pawang*), and medicine men (*bomoh*) were the mediators between the spirit world and people. These animistic beliefs and practices have decreased among the Malays, largely because most Malays in Malaysia are now Muslim. This is because the Malaysia Constitution decrees that all Malays are born Muslim. Even though Islam is the official religion of Malaysia, other religions such as Buddism, Hinduism, Christianity, and Confucianism are given freedom to be practiced. Islam's influence on the Malays goes back to the late 15th century when a sultan of Malacca was converted to Islam. Islam at that time was mostly spread by traders from India and the Middle East.

Malays are devout but tolerant Muslims. Most, especially the elderly and those in villages, pray five times a day, fast in the month of Ramadan, and perform the pilgrimage to Mecca. Muslims believe in only one God, Allah, and in Muhammad as his last messenger. While the basic beliefs are similar to those of Muslims in the Middle East, some Malay culture and Hindu influence has blended with the practices of Islam in Malaysia.

⁶MAJOR HOLIDAYS

Being a multiethnic society, there are various religious and secular holidays celebrated in Malaysia. There are three different New Year's celebrations and holidays: Muslim New Year, Christian (Roman) New Year, and the Chinese New Year. The Malaysians celebrate other religious holidays such as *Hari Raya Aidilfitri* (Id ul-Fitr) and *Aidil Adha* (Id ul-Adha) for the Muslims, *Wesak Day* for Buddhists, *Deepavali* for Hindus, and Christmas for Christians. Both government and private offices are closed on these days. All Malaysians also celebrate Independence Day, which falls on August 31, during which large-scale parades are held in cities throughout Malaysia.

Hari Raya Aidilfitri is a celebration to mark the end of the fasting month (Ramadan). Its celebration includes a two-day official holiday for all Malaysians. This is a time for joy and happiness after an exhausting month of fasting. It involves a lot of eating and a variety of special foods are prepared for the occasion. This is also a time for family reunions where children who are working in the cities visit their parents. It is also an occasion where relatives, friends, and acquaintances are invited for a visit during the Open House. The Open House is a time and day that is set aside for a person to invite her or his relatives, friends, and acquaintances to the Hari Raya celebration. Special food and drinks are prepared and served to the visitors. Hari Raya Aidilfitri provides an opportunity for Muslims to ask for forgiveness for all wrongs done the previous year.

While Hari Raya Aidilfitri marks the end of the fasting month, Hari Raya Aidil Adha commemorates the pilgrimage of Muslims to Mecca and is celebrated the same way as Aidilfitri, albeit on a smaller scale.

⁷RITES OF PASSAGE

There are some important rites of passage in traditional Malay society. After birth, a baby and a mother are in a confinement period *(dalam pantang)* of 44 days. Two common ceremonies during the infant years are *naik buaian*, a ceremony to introduce the baby to his or her cradle; *bercukur jambul*, an event when a seven-day-old boy's head is shaved to "cleanse" him; and bertindik telinga (ear-piercing) for a baby girl.

One very important rite of passage for a Malay male is the circumcision ceremony. It is an elaborate event where relatives and villagers are invited to share the occasion. Circumcisions are performed on boys when they reach puberty between the ages of 7 and 12. Circumcisions are performed on girls when they are still infants, but the event is not as elaborate as that for boys. Traditionally, or even today in the villages, the circumcision was performed with a knife by a *mudim*, a person who specializes in performing circumcision ceremonies. A boy is carried around his house to the accompaniment of traditional *kompang* (small drum) music and is then seated on a banana tree trunk where the circumcision is performed. Usually it would take about two to three weeks for the wound to be healed. Unlike the traditional method, circumcisions in urban areas are now performed by physicians in hospitals, and the ceremonies are not as elaborate as those of traditional circumcisions.

Marriage is perhaps the biggest event in a Malay person's life. Although close family friends still arrange marriages, the couple involved must give their full consent. A boy is expected to be married when he reaches the age of 25 to 28, while a girl is a few years younger. Once a couple agrees to get married, a certain amount of preparation has to be done by both families.

In the villages, wedding feasts are usually attended by all the villagers, including friends and relatives. A wedding is usually a two-day affair; on the first day it is held at the bride's home, and the following day at the groom's house. Friends, relatives, and villagers normally help with the preparation. At about noon, the groom and his entourage arrive at the bride's house with a group of kompang musicians. A *bersanding* ceremony, which is open to the public, is held in which the bridal couple sit on a raised dais *(pelamin)*. Two attendants (equivalent to the bridesmaid and best man) stand next to the bridal couple to attend to their needs. The same ceremony will be held again at night for family members, close friends, and relatives. At this ceremony, the couple receives blessings from their parents and relatives. This is done through the scattering of scented leaves and scented flower petals *(bunga rampai)* onto the open palms of the bride and groom. A similar feast and ceremony is repeated at the groom's house on the second day. Nowadays among the affluent in Malay society, weddings are held in hotels or large community halls.

Death is a very somber and religious affair in a Malay community. Visitors are expected to show respect to the dead and his or her family by dressing appropriately. The time between a death and the funeral is very minimal, since Islam requires the deceased to be buried as soon as possible. Before burial, the body of the deceased is placed in the center of the living room to give everyone a chance to offer prayers and pay their last respects. The deceased is then wrapped in white cloth and carried to the graveyard to be buried. The normal mourning period is 100 days, although special prayers are held only on the first three nights, on the seventh day, the fortieth day, and on the hundredth day.

⁸INTERPERSONAL RELATIONS

The common Malaysian Malay greeting when meeting friends in public is, "Where are you going?" The answer is, "For a stroll" or "Nowhere of importance." However, many urban Malays greet each other with "How are you?"(Apa khabar?)

Shaking hands is the most common way of greeting among Malays, but with some restrictions. It is not customary for men and women to shake hands with each other. Ideally, a Malay woman can only shake hands with a man if she covers her hand with a cloth. A Malay man normally greets another man with a handshake without grasping the hands. He offers both hands to touch lightly the other man's outstretched hands, then brings his hands to his breast, meaning "I greet you from my heart." This is done with both hands to show respect to older people. A Malay woman may use a similar form when greeting another woman.

While pointing at a place, object, or a person with the right forefinger is considered rude among the Malays, pointing with the thumb of the right hand by folding the four fingers into the palm is considered polite. It is also considered polite to bend over slightly from the waist, extend the right hand in front of you, touch the right wrist with the fingers of the left hand, then say "May I please pass," when crossing in front of another person.

Upon arrival at a Malay home, shoes must be removed before entering, for religious purposes. Shoes are considered "unclean" and may soil the living room floor, making it unsuitable for prayers (Muslims pray on a mat laid out on the floor). When

A fisherman loads fish into a container at Kudat Fishing village in Sabah, Malaysia. The rising demand for reef fish from Hong Kong and China has caused the population of the fish to plummet throughout Asia. (AP Images/Vincent Thian)

visiting relatives or friends, it is appropriate to bring food or fruit as gifts.

Public displays of affection between people of the opposite sex are discouraged, even between husbands and wives. This is particularly true among conservative Malay Muslims. In the villages, one can only visit one's lover's house when the parents are around. Unlike in the villages, Malay dating practices in urban areas are quite similar to those in the United States.

⁹LIVING CONDITIONS

During the 1990s, the standard of living in Malaysia increased tremendously because of an economic boom. Between 1990 and 2002, Malaysia made remarkable progress in eradicating poverty. The number of poor households decreased by 25.6%. This spectacular success was credited to the New Economic Policy (NEP), which aims to reduce the economic gap between different communities in the country and has uplifted the quality of life for all Malaysians. The per capita income increased from RM775 in 1957 to RM7,000 in 1992, and from RM15,819 in 2004 to almost RM22,345 in 2007. Strong economic growth

has reduced the unemployment rate to 4%, a figure considered to signify full employment. Malaysia is now rated as an upper-middle-income country. Much of the infrastructure and many of the services found in developed countries are now common in Malaysia, particularly in urban areas.

Historically, the Chinese dominated the urban areas. However, in the 1970s, many Malays migrated from the *kampungs* (villages) to urban areas, resulting in a better ethnic balance of city residents. In 2000 slightly more than 62% of Malaysia's population lived in urban areas, compared to 51% in 1991 and 34% in 1980. Meanwhile the rural population decreased from 66% of total population in 1980 to 39% in 2000. Both in the urban and rural areas, the kampung is the center of Malay life. It is a tightly knit community united by ties of kinship, marriage, or neighborliness, where consensus, compromise, and traditional values reign supreme.

The Malays in urban areas possess consumer items such as cars, television sets, VCRs, and refrigerators. They have access to good, economical, and well-maintained public transportation, such as express buses, trains, and light-rail transits. They also have access to higher standards of basic amenities such as water supply, sanitation, and electricity in comparison to those who live in the villages. In the villages, some Malays still have to rely on kerosene for light, and wells and rivers for water supply.

¹⁰FAMILY LIFE

The Malays regard marriage and raising a family (keluarga) as the most important aspects of life. The family is an autonomous unit in which the husband-father is the head. The unit promotes responsibility to family, friends, and the community takes precedence over the accumulation of profit and material goods. The average family size of urban Malays is smaller in than that of Malays in rural areas. This is partly because of the nature of professions and occupations, which keep them away from their families. In the past, it was quite common for a couple to have more than six children. Today, the average number of children is four.

In Malaysia, where the welfare system is almost nonexistent except for extreme cases, e.g., extreme poverty or disability, the extended family is still a vital unit of society. Family members are expected to care for each other, particularly those who are poor, sick, and old. Children are expected to look after their parents.

Cats, fish, and sometimes singing birds are reared as pets by Malay families. Dogs are considered "unclean" by Muslims and, therefore, are not usually kept as pets by Malays in Malaysia.

¹¹CLOTHING

Traditional Malay dress for men and women is based on a simple rectangle of batik cloth, wrapped and worn as a skirt. However, the style of wrapping is different for men and women. The women wear the skirt with a long blouse, while the men go shirtless but wear a tied headcloth.

Nowadays, since Malays are Muslim, they have a strict dress code. The women's customary dress covers the whole body, except for their face, hands, and feet. They usually dress in the *baju kurung,* a long-sleeved, loose blouse worn over an ankle-length skirt, and they cover their heads with a scarf as a sign of humility and modesty. A married woman may often wear a *baju kebaya,* a close-fitting lace blouse over an ankle-length skirt. While Malay women wear baju krung or baju kebaya, Malay men wear *baju Melayu,* long-sleeved shirts over an ankle-length *sarong* or pants. A Malay man who has made a pilgrimage to Mecca usually wears a white skull-cap, and a woman who has made the pilgrimage wears a white scarf.

Some Malays dress in Western-style clothing. However, they are discouraged from wearing shorts, miniskirts, or strapless or sleeveless tops. This is particularly true for Malay women.

¹²FOOD

Rice is the Malaysians' staple food and is eaten at least once a day. Malays eat rice with fish or meat curry and vegetables cooked in various ways. It is absolutely forbidden for Muslims to eat pork in any form as it is considered unclean. Muslims, for religious reasons, are also prohibited from eating any meat that has not been slaughtered by a Muslim.

Malays usually eat with their fingers. Therefore, hands are always washed before and after meals. This is done by using the *kendi,* a water vessel that is either put on the table or passed around from person to person. While meals are always eaten with the right fingers, the serving spoons provided for all the dishes can only be used with the left hand. The left hand is also used for passing dishes of food and for holding a glass.

One of the Malays' popular breakfasts is *nasi lemak,* rice cooked in coconut milk and served with hot and spicy *sambal* (shrimp or anchovy paste), fish, eggs and vegetables.

¹³EDUCATION

Malaysia has a literacy rate of 92%. It is mandatory for all Malaysians to attend school until the age of 15. Therefore, many Malaysians have gone to school at least up to Form Three, which is equivalent to the ninth grade in the United States. Because of greater educational opportunities under New Economic Policy, the number of Malays that have obtained degrees from local and foreign universities has increased over the last 30 years. Many of them were sent on government scholarships and loans to universities in the United States, United Kingdom, Australia, New Zealand, and Japan.

Since education is seen as a means to raise a family's reputation, parents always encourage and expect their children to do well in school. They will do whatever is necessary to ensure that their children are able to receive a formal education.

¹⁴CULTURAL HERITAGE

Traditional Malay music is normally aired during special occasions such as the grand annual festival of Hari Raya, wedding celebrations *(bersanding),* and *makan selamat* or *kenduri* (thanksgiving meal). One of their most popular musical ensembles played during such occasions is the *gamelan.* It is an instrumental ensemble or orchestra containing drums, xylophones, metallophones, tuned gongs, and bamboo flutes. An ensemble can be small or large, and its music can cover a wide range of styles, from slow and stately, to sad and haunting, to lively and cheerful. It is played either as an instrumental ensemble purely for listening, or as an accompaniment to dance.

Traditional Malay dances are sometimes performed on festive occasions, accompanied by the gamelan. These dances are usually ensemble dances for men only, for women only, and for men and women together. This includes dances such as *Kuda Kepang* (a trance dance), *joget* (a courtship dance), *ghazal* (a

dance based on Middle Eastern music that is performed by young women for the enjoyment of sultans and other members of the royal houses), and *mak yong* (a dance-drama performed by actors and actresses in imitation of heroic tales of sultans and princesses of olden times). Unfortunately, traditional dance is something of a dying art among the Malays in Malaysia. Nevertheless, a number of young choreographers have attempted to revive these dances in order to create Malay modern dances.

Unlike most indigenous people in Malaysia, the Malays have a good collection of literature written about their community going back to the 16th century. The oldest of these literatures is *Sejarah Melayu* (Malay Chronicle), a history of the kingdoms of the Malay Peninsula, with an emphasis on Malacca. Other works include *Hikayat Hang Tuah* (Hang Tuah's Life Story) and *Hikayat Abdullah* (Abdullah's Life Story). These works describe the old Malay society.

¹⁵WORK

Traditionally, the Malays dominated government and agriculture, while playing a relatively small role in commerce and industry. In the rural areas they were likely to be farmers, tending vegetable farms or small holdings of rubber or oil-palm trees. Others were fishers. Since the late 1970s, however, many Malays have migrated to the cities upon completing high school and college in search of jobs in the manufacturing and service sectors. This is a result of direct government economic policies that aim to encourage Malay involvement in business at various professional levels. Consequently, they are often civil servants, laborers, transport workers, or industrial workers. Many also have risen to the national elite, holding high-level posts in the government and military. Many others are holding posts in institutions and corporations like MARA, PERNAS, PETRONAS and HICOM, which have been set up to establish opportunities for the Malays in employment, business, capital accumulation and corporate participation.

¹⁶SPORTS

A large number of Malaysian populations regularly take part, as players or spectators, in both Western and traditional Malay sports and games. One of the Malays' popular native games is *sepaktkraw,* or kickball. It is played with a round ball made of rattan that must be kept in the air as it is kicked around or across a net (like volleyball played with the feet) by a group of players standing in a circle. A point is lost whenever the ball touches the ground.

The most popular spectator sport among Malaysians is soccer, known as football in Malaysia. The country has an annual semiprofessional soccer league, involving a team from each state in Malaysia plus Brunei. This league attracts large crowds for matches in major cities. In addition to that, there are other soccer leagues played at the regional level, and even in the smallest town. It is a common sight everywhere in Malaysia to see youngsters and adults flocking to the soccer fields either to play or to watch a soccer game.

Another popular sport among the Malays is badminton. In fact, badminton is a national passion in Malaysia, where top Malaysian players are usually among the contenders for world badminton championships. Other Western sports such as volleyball, field hockey, basketball, rugby, squash, and cricket are played not only by the Malays, but also by all the other ethnic groups in Malaysia. These sports are played both for casual recreation and in organized competitions.

¹⁷ENTERTAINMENT AND RECREATION

There is a vast difference between the forms of entertainment and recreation in rural and urban areas in Malaysia. The Malays in rural areas still relish the traditional music such as *gamelan* (musical ensemble), *kompang* (small drums), *serunai* (flute) and others; traditional dances; and traditional pastimes such as kite-flying and *gasing* (spinning tops). Kite-flying is particularly popular among people in coastal villages. Kites are flown mainly as recreation, but sometimes competitions are organized to see who can fly their kites the highest. Spinning tops is a popular pastime, particularly in Kelantan and Trengganu. These tops are made of wood and can spin for hours. The person whose top spins the longest wins.

Unlike rural Malays, in urban areas the Malays watch Western (Hollywood), Hindi, and Chinese movies and theater, besides watching Malay movies that are locally produced. Besides movies and theater, other forms of entertainment and recreation, found in urban areas in the United States can be found in Malaysia's urban areas as well. Malaysia has three basic television channels, which are monitored by the government.

¹⁸FOLK ART, CRAFTS, AND HOBBIES

The Malays of Malaysia have various folk arts and crafts. One of their most exotic folk arts is the *wayang kulit,* a traditional shadow-puppet show. These puppets are made of water-buffalo hide, stiffened by a central spine of buffalo horn, and they have movable arms manipulated by a *dalang,* the puppeteer, with thin rods. The puppets are seen only as shadows cast by an oil lamp upon a screen of stretched-cotton cloth. The dalang both recites the narrative of the play, and speaks the parts of each character. The show is usually accompanied by a small *gamelan* (musical ensemble).

Malays are renowned for their refined and delicate woodcarvings. These artistic carvings can be seen on their fishing boats and house panels and walls. In the past, the Malays were dependent on the sea for their food and livelihood. Boats were built for fishing and for long sea journeys. These boats were decorated and carved with ornamental embellishments not solely for elegance, but also to fulfill the Malays' aesthetic needs and to equip the boats with spiritual power. Traditional Malay houses have rich decorations and carvings, primarily as decorative pieces on doors, windows, and wall panels.

The weaving of *kain songket* is another fine handicraft made by the Malays. It is made from yarn, formerly silk but now usually cotton, and is woven using a shaft treadle loom made from wood. The loom is about 2.5 m (8 ft) long, and 1.5 m (5 ft) high. The making of kain songket involves seven long and complicated stages. These stages are the preparation of the yarn (spooling), warping process, winding of the warp thread on the warping board, inserting the warp thread through the reed, making string loops for the long wooden rods called heddles, making the songket pattern, and weaving.

¹⁹SOCIAL PROBLEMS

Even though Malaysia is a democratic country, it still retains its Internal Security Act (ISA), which provides for detention without trial for individuals deemed detrimental to the harmony of the nation. Therefore, Malaysia has received criticisms from human-rights activists for its political actions against individuals who were alleged to be a threat to Malaysia's racial and religious harmony. Other than the ISA, Malaysians basic human and civil rights are virtually secured by the constitution. Women are allowed to vote, work, and hold high positions in the professional field.

Since Islam forbids its followers from drinking alcohol, alcoholism is not a major problem among the Malays.

²⁰GENDER ISSUES

As in most countries, there are more males than females in Malaysia. There is a ratio of 103 men for 100 women of the total population. There are equal opportunities for education and professional careers for men and women in Malaysia. As a result, there are a number of women who hold high positions in professional fields. Nonetheless, certain aspects of the traditions that govern relations between men and women are still maintained among the Malays. For instance, women must sit apart from the men in the main portion of the mosque, and are not allowed to mix casually with men or to eat with them. Women give deference and respect to their husbands, and love and compassion to their children. On the other hand, a Malay husband plays as much of a role in rearing his children as does his wife.

²¹BIBLIOGRAPHY

Craig, JoAnn. *Culture Shock: What Not to Do in Malaysia and Singapore, How and Why Not to Do It.* Times Books International, 1979.

Hood Salleh, 'Introduction' In Hood Salleh (ed.) *The Encyclopedia of Malaysia, Peoples and Tradtions.* Kuala Lumpur: Editions Didier Millet, 2006 (pg. 100 -101).

Husaini, Siti Zaharah Abang Haji. "Kain Songket and Selayah." In *Sarawak Cultural Legacy: A Living Tradition,* edited by Lucas Chin and Valerie Mashman. Kuching, Malaysia: Society Atelier Sarawak, 1991.

Ibrahim, Odita. "Traditional Malay Woodcarving." *In Sarawak Cultural Legacy: A Living Tradition,* edited by Lucas Chin and Valerie Mashman. Kuching, Malaysia: Society Atelier Sarawak, 1991.

Major, John S. *The Land and People of Malaysia and Brunei.* HarperCollins Publishers, 1991.

Tan, Raalene. *Indian and Malay Etiquette: A Matter of Course.* Singapore: Landmark Book Pte Ltd., 1992.

—by P. Bala

MAN (MANCHUS)

PRONUNCIATION: man-CHOOZ
ALTERNATE NAMES: Jurchens, Manzhou, Manchus
LOCATION: China
POPULATION: 10.68 million
LANGUAGE: Chinese, Manchu
RELIGION: Some shamanism
RELATED ARTICLES: Vol. 3: China and Her National Minorities

¹INTRODUCTION

Dwelling mainly in northeast China, the Man, better known as the Manchus, have a long history. In addition to their direct relation with the Jurchens, their historical origins may be traced back to the Mohe of the Sui (581–618) and Tang (618–907) dynasties, to the Wuji of the Han (206 BC–AD 220) and, more remotely, to the Sushen of the Zhou (c. 12th century–256 BC). Ancient Chinese books began to record the name Jurchens as early as the Five Dynasties (907–960). In the beginning of the 12th century, led by headman Aguda of the Wanyan tribe, the Jurchens established the Jin Dynasty (1115–1234). Before long, they destroyed the Kingdom of Liao (916–1125) and the Northern Song Dynasty (960–1127) and threatened the Southern Song (1127–1279). A great number of the Jurchens came to the Central Plains (the middle and lower reaches of the Yellow River), but they were gradually absorbed into Chinese culture over a long period of time. Following the destruction of the Jin Dynasty, the Jurchens themselves were conquered by the Yuan Dynasty (1271–1368) and later on ruled by the Ming (1368–1644). Since the 15th century, the headmen of various tribes of Jurchens were appointed by the central government. In the 16th century, a hero of the Jurchens, Nurhachi (1559–1626), unified all the tribes by military force. He built up an organization that integrated military function, government administration, and production management, providing a sound basis for the later establishment and consolidation of the Qing Dynasty (1644–1911). His eighth son succeeded to the throne. In 1635, he changed the name of his nationality to Manzhou (origin of the Western term "Manchu"). The name was simplified to Man in 1911, at the end of the last dynasty of China.

²LOCATION AND HOMELAND

The Mans are scattered all over China. The largest concentration is found in Liaoning Province. Smaller communities live in Jilin, Heilongjiang, Hebei, Inner Mongolia, Xinjiang, Gansu, and Shandong provinces or regions, as well as in Beijing, Tianjin, Chengdu, Xi'an, and Guangzhou cities. This wide distribution is related to the dominant position of the Mans in the Qing Dynasty. During the dynasty's 250 years or so, Mans holding important positions lived in different parts of China, and many members of their families took root and remained there. The Man population was 10.68 million in 2000, second only to the Zhuang among the minorities.

³LANGUAGE

Their language is classified as belonging to the Altaic family, Manchu-Tungusic group, Manchu branch. It has withered since the end of the 18th century and is used only among a limited number of the Mans in a few counties of Heilongjiang.

The written language was created on the basis of the Mongolian writing system and was used extensively under the Qing Dynasty. Now, almost all of the Mans use Chinese characters.

⁴FOLKLORE

A large part of the rich Man corpus of mythology revolves around ancestors. According to one myth, three fairy maidens descended to take a bath in Tianchi (Heavenly Lake) of the Changbai Mountains. The youngest of them ate a small red fruit carried by a golden bird in its bill. She got pregnant and bore a boy who could speak right after birth. She gave him the surname of Aixinjueluo (the surname of emperors of the Qing Dynasty). When he had grown up, she told him the story of his birth and then ascended to Heaven. Drifting down the streams, the young man arrived at a place where three clans fought fiercely with each other. Taking advantage of his status, he stopped their fight and was selected to be their headman. This place was the hometown of the Jurchens, which means "the root of Man."

Another myth concerns their god and a hero. It was said that the Man god Abukainduli was very powerful. The rosy clouds were his breath, and the twinkling stars were the droplets from his cough. Unfortunately, he was so lazy that the northern lands froze in a world of snow and ice most of the year. Following an epic combat, the god defeated a demon and flattened him under the weight of a mountain. Not to be outdone, the demon transformed himself into a large elm, which obstructed the head of the river and it dried up. Unwilling to die of thirst, the tribe living there had to offer children in sacrifice to the demon. A young man, Mudan, met the god Abukainduli after innumerable hardships. The god gave him an axe and told him that he should chop down the elm by striking it 81 times with the axe and that Mudan himself would turn into a rock after doing so. To deliver his clan from evil and misery, Mudan lifted the axe and chopped fiercely at the elm. Every nine chops, he suffered a disaster. After the eighty-first chop, the demon fell, and Mudan was transformed into a mountain. At the same time, a vast amount of water sprang from the ground and flowed toward the north. Since then, people have called the river after the name of the hero, Mudan.

⁵RELIGION

The traditional beliefs of the Mans are rooted in Shamanism. According to the Mans, a shaman means "a wildly dancing man capable of magical feats." The shaman's duty is to help women bear children, to cure illness, and to shield them from misfortune. Dancing in a trance is the usual way to cure the diseased. This is done by a professional shaman; each village only employs one. He has a variety of props: a shaman's hat, clothes, shoes, drum, stick, and sword. When he performs, he wears his special hat, on which hang many long strips of multicolored cloths so that his face and even his whole head is covered. Several copper plates cover his back and the front of his chest. He wears a long skirt and a waistband with small copper bells hung on it. Muttering incantations, he beats a drum while dancing. If the diseased recovers, the family should redeem the vow made beforehand to the gods; if not, the shaman will say, "You did not come with a true heart." If a family wishes to have a son, the shaman is invited to pray to the god called Fuolifuoduorhanximama. Another shaman is responsible for sacrificial offerings on religious festivals or when a major event occurs.

Shamanism still exists in traditional Man villages but has disappeared from cities a long time ago.

6 MAJOR HOLIDAYS

The Chinese Spring Festival (lunar calendar; Western calendar, between January 21 and February 20) is a major holiday for the Mans. They put on the door red, yellow, blue, or white banners, indicating their "bannerman" status among the "Eight Banners." Some of their festivals are related to their sacrificial offerings. For example, every family offers sacrifice (usually a black male pig) to their ancestors in autumn. There is a *kang* (a heatable brick bed) in their house. The kang on the west side is the best place to lay offerings to their ancestors. Before the butchery, the butcher should sharpen his knife on that kang. Three pieces of cooked pork are put in front of their ancestors' memorial tablets. A box containing their family tree is placed on a small, short legged table near the kang. The family members kowtow, one after another, in proper order according to their position in the family hierarchy. Then, the invited shaman begins his dance, asking for protection and blessing for the family. The next day, the family will offer a sacrifice to Heaven. Again, a black pig is killed. The internal organs and neck bone are hung on an outdoor post. If the flesh is all eaten by crows, it is a lucky sign. The pork is chopped and cooked with millet. Relatives, friends, neighbors, and even passers-by are invited to take a bowl of gruel. Three days later, the leftovers, if any, should be buried. The bones are also buried at the foot of the post.

7 RITES OF PASSAGE

In order to obtain the gods' blessings, a small bow and arrow is hung at the gate when a boy is born. The ancestors of the Mans were good at archery, and a bow and arrows were always worn by men in outdoor activities. When a girl was born, three cloth bands, each 1.5 in wide, were tied outside her swaddling clothes. This was regarded as beneficial to horsemanship in the future. For this reason a strip of cloth is still hung when a girl is born. Habitually, they make the baby lie on its back and put a pillow padded with millet under the back of the baby's head. The flattened back of the head is regarded as pretty.

In the eyes of the Mans, the north kang is for senior persons and the western one is reserved for the ancestors. Therefore, nobody is allowed to die on it. The coffin is brought in and carried out through the window instead of through the door. The funeral must be held on an odd-numbered day, because a funeral on an even-numbered day would mean that two people have died. Before the funeral, a post is erected in the courtyard. A long narrow flag made of red and black pieces of cloth is hung on it. During the funeral, relatives and friends scramble to take pieces of the flag, which they will use to make clothes for their children. The clothes are believed to protect the children from evil and nightmares. After the funerary ceremony, the deceased is buried in the ground.

8 INTERPERSONAL RELATIONS

Since it is common knowledge that the west kang is reserved for the ancestors, guests avoid sitting there while visiting. Otherwise, guests are warmly welcomed in a Man home.

When the bride-to-be visits for the first time, a small heart-shaped bag for carrying money and odds and ends is usually offered as a token of love. Actually, it is a combination of two

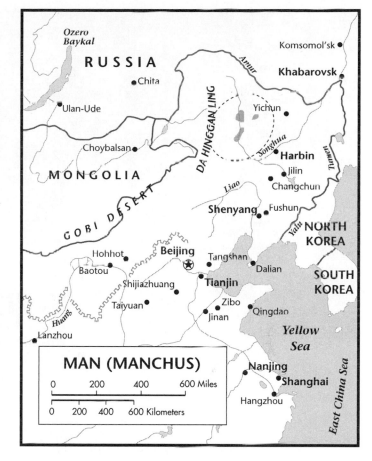

MAN (MANCHUS)

0   200   400   600 Miles

0   200   400   600 Kilometers

bags exactly of the same size and figures. The girl would keep one half and give the other half to her boyfriend.

9 LIVING CONDITIONS

There is usually a screen wall facing the gate, inside a traditional Man courtyard, where a post is erected for sacrificial offerings. The house is made of wood and adobes. The central room opens to the south. The room in the west part of the house is usually the bedroom, in which the north, west, and south sides are provided with kang. The parents and the senior persons (if any) sleep on the north kang, the children on the south kang. The inside of the kang is connected with the cooking stove and is always warm in winter.

10 FAMILY LIFE

The Man family is patrilineal. A house of three or more generations is not uncommon. The Mans have great esteem for their elders. The position of men and women is more or less equal in the family. Men engage in farming. Although women also work in the fields, they usually spend most of their time doing household chores. The family is monogamous. Arranged marriage is prevalent. When young people reach 16 or 17, they are allowed to be engaged. The matchmaker, representing the male side, usually visits the female side three times before getting an answer. Each time she pays a visit, a bottle of wine is presented. As the saying goes: "Just to ask: Is it all right? Is worth three bottles of wine!" If it is all right, the parents of the girl will ask for betrothal gifts (pigs, wine, money, clothes, ornaments),

Manchu women wear traditional Manchu dress during a festival in Fushun, China. (AP Images/Xinhua, Zhang Yanhui)

which will belong to the girl. On the wedding day, the bride is carried to the groom's house on a bridal sedan chair.

¹¹CLOTHING

In the past, men's clothing was adapted to the requirements of horsemanship and marksmanship. They shaved the fore part of their hair and combed the latter part into a braid hung on the back. The tight cuffs of the sleeves, the long vents on both sides of the robe, the waistband, the boots, and their long trousers were all designed to facilitate fighting in a cold climate. Women's costumes include a long robe (*cheongsam*), a wooden pad about 2.5 inches high placed under the middle part of the sole, and a flat bun hung behind the neck. These customs intended to stress the nobility of Man women. Except for long robes for both sexes, the other stylized clothes are not worn today. The robes, however, were prevalent in the first half of the 20th century. Then, they gradually disappeared. But, women's robes are still worn on festive occasions, although they are quite different from the originals. Today, Man clothing is not much different from the Chinese.

¹²FOOD

The Mans like to eat millet and glutinous millet. "Cooked mutton held in the hand" is absolutely necessary on the Spring Festival. Mutton is chopped in big pieces with bone and half-

cooked with a little salt. The piece is held with the hand while eating. Sometimes a knife is needed. The most famous light refreshment is *saqima*, a kind of candied fritter. It is made by mixing flour with eggs, cutting the paste into noodles, and frying. It is then taken out, covered with syrup, and stirred. It is finally put into a wooden frame, pressed, cut into squares, and served.

¹³EDUCATION

Because of the need to train large numbers of young people (mainly men) to serve as officials during the Man Qing Dynasty, the Mans have traditionally had a relatively high level of literacy. Even more important for the development of education in the recent past is the advanced urbanization of the Man people. As a result, their educational and cultural level is higher than the average for the whole country and even exceeds the average for the whole world. In China, they are second to the Koreans.

¹⁴CULTURAL HERITAGE

One of the main traditional art forms of the Mans is dancing. A traditional choreography entitled "Hunting Dance" needs actors with a strong physique. Half of them wear leopard skin, ride on horseback, and pursue and attack prop-animals. The

Man songs are accompanied by a vertical bamboo flute and a drum. The rest of the actors dress as tigers and leopards.

A form of dance still popular in northeast China developed from an ancient wedding ceremony dance; it is still performed during festivals. Both men and women, host and guests, take turns dancing. The dancing movements are simple but quite vigorous.

The Octagon Drum Opera is a traditional Man adaptation of Peking opera. The tune and melody and the musical instruments accompanying the narrative are comparable to the styles used in Tianjin, Tangshan, Beijing, and Shenyang cities. The octagon drum is the leading instrument used by the actors.

Some artists and writers of great achievement and reputation are Man, including the famous writer Lao She, the master of comic dialogue Hou Baolin, and the outstanding actor of Peking Opera, Cheng Yanqiu.

[15] WORK

In the remote past, the ancestors of the Mans were hunters. Later, under Chinese influence, they turned to agriculture. In the modern era, especially since late 19th century, former Manchuria became the most important base of heavy industry in China and a very large part of the Man population became workers, technicians, and managers in large factories. This has remained so. Heavy metals, coal, hydropower, agriculture, forestry, and stock raising are the main industrial and economic resources of the Mans.

[16] SPORTS

Ice skating has a long history for the Man people and is linked with their Nordic habitat. Centuries ago, Man warriors tied filed animal bones under their boots to march on ice. Later, they exchanged the bones for iron bars inlaid in the sole. Still later, an iron sheath was fitted on a board, which was then tied beneath the boot. In the 19th century, skating was part of the military training of the "Eight Banners" army. Today, Man people still take advantage of the long, cold winter in northeast China to go skating on rivers and lakes or in skating rinks. Some Man skaters are renowned internationally.

[17] ENTERTAINMENT AND RECREATION

For urban Mans, watching television is a daily entertainment in the evenings. They go to the movies once or twice a month. Beijing opera, chess, gardening, pet birds, storytelling, comic dialogues, and "clapper talks" are favorite pastimes of the aged and middle-aged persons. Youngsters like dancing, popular songs, and karaoke. Recreational activities are not different in the rural areas; however, access to television programs and movies is more restricted and the style of dancing and popular songs is different.

[18] FOLK ART, CRAFTS, AND HOBBIES

The Mans excel in jade sculpture, bone carving, clay and dough figurines, and snuff-bottle interior painting. They are also world-renowned for their ice carving and sculptures and have won many international competitions.

[19] SOCIAL PROBLEMS

Urban Mans have one of the highest economic levels in China, but they have lost much of their cultural identity. Because of the long and cold winters, rural areas remain economically undeveloped but have preserved many of their traditional ways.

[20] GENDER ISSUES

The Chinese constitution states that women have equal rights with men in all areas of life, and most legislation is gender neutral. However, there are continued reports of discrimination, sexual harassment, wage discrepancies, and other gender related problems. The gap in educational level between women and men is narrowing with women making up 47.1% of college students in 2005, but only 32.6% of doctoral students.

China has strict family planning laws. It is illegal for women to marry before 20 years of age (22 for men), and it is illegal for single women to give birth. The Family Planning Bureau can require women to take periodic pregnancy tests and enforce laws that often leave women with no real options other than abortion or sterilization. Though minority populations were previously exempt from family planning regulations, policy has changed in recent years to limit minority population growth. Today, urban minority couples may have two children while rural couples may have three or four.

Prostitution and the sex trade is a significant problem in China involving between 1.7 and 5 million women. It involved organized crime, businessmen, the police, and government workers, so prosecution against prostitution has limited success. In 2002, the nation removed homosexuality from its official list of mental illnesses, and though it is still a taboo topic, homosexuality is increasingly accepted, especially in large, international cities.

[21] BIBLIOGRAPHY

Chiao, Chien, Nicholas Tapp, and Kum-yin Ho, ed. "Special Issue on Ethnic Groups in China." *New Asia Bulletin,* no. 8, 1989.

Dreyer, June Teufel. *China's Forty Millions.* Cambridge: Harvard University Press, 1976.

Eberhard, Wolfram. *China's Minorities: Yesterday and Today.* Belmont: Wadsworth Publishing Company, 1982.

Gustafsson, Bjorn A., Shi, Li, and Sicular, Terry, eds. *Inequality and Public Policy in China.* New York: Cambridge University Press, 2008.

Heberer, Thomas. *China and Its National Minorities: Autonomy or Assimilation?* Armonk, NY: M. E. Sharpe, 1989.

Lebar, Frank, et al. *Ethnic Groups of Mainland Southeast Asia.* New Haven: Human Relations Area Files Press, 1964.

Lemoine, Jacques. "Les Mandchou." In *Ethnologie régionale II* (Encyclopédie de la Pléiade). Paris: Gallimard, 1978.

Ma Yin, ed. *China's Minority Nationalities.* Beijing: Foreign Languages Press, 1989.

Ramsey, S. Robert. *The Languages of China.* Princeton: Princeton University Press, 1987.

Rigger, Shelley. "Voices of Manchu Identity." In *Cultural Encounters on China's Ethnic Frontiers,* edited by Stevan Harrell, 186–214. Seattle: University of Washington Press, 1994.

Shin, Leo Kwok-yueh. *The Making of the Chinese State: Ethnicity and Expansion on the Ming Borderlands.* New York: Cambridge University Press, 2006.

—by C. Le Blanc

MANGGARAI

PRONUNCIATION: mahng-GAH-rai
LOCATION: Indonesia (island of Flores)
POPULATION: 575,000 (2000)
LANGUAGE: Manggarai; Bahasa Indonesia
RELIGION: Roman Catholic majority; traditional animism
RELATED ARTICLES: Vol. 3: Indonesians

¹INTRODUCTION

The Manggarai are the largest ethnic group on Flores, an island whose Catholic majority sets it apart from the rest of Indonesia. Chinese documents record trade for the sandalwood of neighboring Timor as early as the 12th century. Flores itself is mentioned in a 14th century Javanese poem, the "Nagarakrtagama." The Portuguese founded a fort at Solor in 1566 and a mission school at Larantuka in 1570, both far to the west of the Manggarai lands. Minangkabau immigrants had probably already made some Muslim converts along the coast. In 1666, the Makassarese attempted unsuccessfully to conquer the southern Manggarai coast. From the 17th century on, the sultanate of Bima in eastern Sumbawa dominated the northwest coast of the Manggarai region, organizing villages into *dalu* (regions) and *glarang* (lineages) and establishing the head of the Tolo dalu as *raja* (king) of the Manggarai. Early accounts reported that the native kingdom of Cibal existed in the interior.

After the Tambora eruption of 1815 weakened Bima, the Manggarai with Dutch aid, were able to drive out the Bimanese, who gave up their last claims only in 1929. In 1859, the Dutch bought the last of the Portuguese claims to the island on the condition that Catholicism would not be threatened. Dutch Jesuits followed in 1862, converting thousands, particularly from the leading families. In 1913, the Society of the Holy Word (SVD) succeeded the Jesuits in this territory and focused on education. Meanwhile, formal colonization by the Dutch commenced in 1907. In 1917, Catholic missionary activity among the Manggarai began in earnest; the strategy stressed similarities between traditional beliefs and the new religion, as well as tolerating indigenous dance and other customs. In 1930, under the advice of the Catholic hierarchy, a Dutch-educated Catholic Manggarai, Alexander Baruk, was appointed as the "first king" of the Manggarai.

In the late 1950s and early 1960s, Dutch and German Catholic organizations sponsored a "Flores-Timor" development plan. The Roman Catholic Church cooperated with the New Order government's development plans. Nusa Tenggara Timur province, of which Flores is a part, remains one of the poorest regions in the country, largely due to the limitations the dry climate imposes on agriculture.

²LOCATION AND HOMELAND

The mountainous island of Flores is part of the Lesser Sunda chain that stretches from Bali in the west to Timor in the east. Inhabiting the western third of the island, the Manggarai are the largest single ethnic group, numbering 575,000 (8% of the population of East Nusa Tenggara province in 2000—Flores as a whole was estimated to have 1.6 million people in 2003). Among them, Malay-Mongoloid physical features appear with fewer Melanesian/Papuan traits than among peoples farther east on the island. The Ngada people to the immediate east show many similarities to the Manggarai, while the more distant Endenese, Sikkanese, and Solorese show much less resemblance. On the west coast of the Manggarai region, long-standing Bajau and Bugis fishing communities exist; Bimanese farmers also pass through to sell produce.

The volcanic origin of the soil and relatively abundant rainfall favor agriculture in the Manggarai region over other parts of Flores. However, recent deforestation has led to erosion and the drying up of streams.

³LANGUAGE

The languages of Flores, like most of Indonesia's, belong to the Austronesian family, specifically to the Central Malayo-Polynesian sub-branch that includes most of the languages of the archipelago east of Sulawesi and western Sumbawa. The Manggarai language is mutually unintelligible with that of the peoples farther east on the island; in fact, it has more in common with the languages of Bima and Sumba. There are three major dialects, the Western, Central, and Eastern, as well as a number of minor ones. Most Manggarai cannot understand the type of language employed in ritual. Bahasa Indonesia is the language of education, administration, and the Catholic church, but village people prefer to speak Manggarai among themselves. In some coastal regions, the Bugis *lontara'* script was known.

⁴FOLKLORE

Ghost stories are numerous. Many folktales focus on Mori Karaeng, the supreme being. Some describe how he created the earth, humanity, the spirit world, animals, and plants like maize and rice. Others tell how he caused wind and earthquakes, punished the moon with an eclipse and the *jin* (evil spirits) with thunder. Yet, others recount how he handled those who transgressed against custom, murdered, committed incest, defied parents, and neglected rituals. Still more show him teaching humans how to weave or make palm wine.

⁵RELIGION

The island of Flores as a whole is 85% Catholic, an anomaly in the world's largest Muslim country. Earlier in this century, however, Catholicism, most firmly based in Larantuka and Ende far to the east, dominated only the eastern part of the Manggarai region. Islam was strong in the west due to the influence of the Bima sultanate and the presence of Bugis and Bajau communities. The central Manggarai lands adhered to the traditional animist religion. In recent years, this pattern has changed, with Catholics now the majority throughout the region. The Catholic religion has even become an identity marker in relation to Muslim outsiders, which now include Javanese bureaucrats and merchants in the towns.

In churches, schools, and shrines, Catholicism has transformed the landscape. On Sunday mornings, families on their way to and from Mass fill the streets, church bells ringing overhead. Rosaries, crucifixes, and other religious objects are displayed in homes, shops, and vehicles and are sold in stores alongside consumer goods. On Flores, the Catholic Church works closely with the government and supports its development plans. Townspeople have a lifestyle informed by a Catholic outlook, while rural people tend to incorporate the new religion into their traditional life.

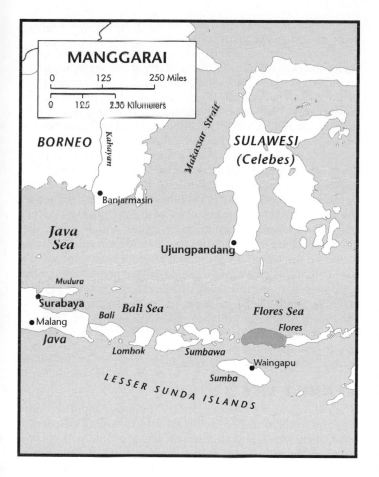

MANGGARAI

0   125   250 Miles

0   125   250 Kilometers

BORNEO

Kahayan

Makassar Strait

SULAWESI
(Celebes)

Banjarmasin

Java Sea

Ujungpandang

Madura

Surabaya

Bali   *Bali Sea*   *Flores Sea*

Malang   Flores

Java   *Flores*

Lombok   Sumbawa

Waingapu

Sumba

LESSER SUNDA ISLANDS

In addition to Mori Karaeng, the traditional religion recognizes several classes of spirits. *Empo* or *andung* are ancestral spirits who inhabit the environs of the village and who are invoked in life-cycle ceremonies. The *darat* or *ata pelesina* ("people of the other world") are spirits of nature (forests, rivers, springs). Among these, the *naga tana* guard the soil while the *ngara tana* watch gardens, fields, and the crops themselves. Evil spirits are known by the originally Islamic terms *jin* or *setan*. Wooden altars in the shape of traditional houses are erected in gardens.

Leading rituals is a priest, the *ata mbeko* (male or female). One acquires this role not through heredity but through learning by assisting an experienced *ata mbeko*. He or she performs or guides life-cycle rites in the home, as well as public ceremonies, such as the inauguration of a village hall or those for the fertility of the soil. The ata mbeko also provide *dukun* services, such as healing, predicting a person's future, or giving amulets or holy water for people to use against their enemies. Clan members return to their ancestral villages to participate in major ceremonies, which may include ritualized whip fights.

⁶MAJOR HOLIDAYS

In addition to national holidays [see **Indonesians**], Catholic feasts are an important part of the cycle of the year.

⁷RITES OF PASSAGE

A *jambat* ceremony, involving the offering of young betel nuts and a chicken with no black feathers, is held in the sixth month of pregnancy. A *tenda* rite is held if a mother and her daughter-in-law are pregnant at the same time.

Most marriages today result from courtship or dating. The man's family applies (*cangkang*) for the hand of the woman. The girl's family asks for a high bride-price (*paca*), which includes water buffalo and horses, but they will also give a large gift to the boy's family.

Frequently, parents seek their child's ideal partner in the mother's brother's daughter, a type of marriage called *tungku*, which does not require a large bride-price because of the already existing informal relationship between the families. In the past, one family would by custom take wives from a particular family, while that family in turn would take wives from a third family; relations between "wife-taking" families (*anak rona*) and "wife-giving" (*anak wina*) families would be formal, expressing status distinctions.

Elopement (*roko*) is a common alternative if a young man cannot or will not pay the bride-price, or if the young woman's family does not consent to the match. Both sides can also agree to the elopement beforehand in order to save the face of the man's family if the bride-price is too high. The man's family makes a marriage application after the "abduction," waiting until the girl's family's anger has subsided to ask forgiveness. The woman's family goes through the formality of stating a high bride-price even though their daughter is already living with her new husband and his family.

After finalizing the amount of the bride-price, the woman's family hosts a feast where they charge the man's family twice the value of what the latter has consumed. An elder inspects the liver of a sacrificed pig to learn the ancestor's opinion of the match.

In lieu of a bride-price, the groom may do service for the bride's family for a specified time. After living with the bride's family for five days (ending with the *wega mio* ceremony), the new couple moves in with the groom's family. A man may marry the widow of a deceased brother without paying a bride-price. Aristocrats used to practice polygyny, but this is now banned under Catholicism.

Burial and mourning rituals are complex. Tradition required that bodies be buried with their limbs drawn close to the body. However, a coffin now replaces the former mat. A wake is held for three nights and includes gambling. The person is buried in his or her home village. The burial is held at night because in the other world everything is opposite; thus, night here is day there, and dishes and glasses for the use of the dead are broken because they will be whole in the other world.

At first, the deceased's spirit (*ase-kae de weki*) roams around the house, especially by where it slept when alive, and then it occupies the well, big trees, house posts, or nearby crossroads (during this period, it can help its kin if they are in danger). Five days after the death, the family holds the *kelas* ritual, sacrificing animals. With this, the spirit becomes a *poti'*, who is released from this world and leaves for the other world; there it lives with Mori Karaeng and intercedes for the descendants with him.

⁸INTERPERSONAL RELATIONS

Manggarai society still preserves traces of the traditional political order. The Manggarai people used to be divided among 39 *dalu*, small regions, most of which were subordinate to either Reo or Patta, the two halves of the Cibal kingdom. Each dalu was dominated by a single *wa'u,* whose members considered themselves aristocrats. The head of the dalu was a *kraeng* (from the Makassarese word for "king"), and other prominent leaders were *sangaji.* The dalu encompassed several often unrelated *glarang,* lineages that were autonomous from the dalu in matters of land rights (including rights to hunting and fishing grounds). The glarang had a *tu'a tenu,* a hereditary specialist on the customary laws on land tenure, who distributed lands to lineage members to use; he was usually from a different family from the lineage head. Each glarang was in turn composed of *beo* (villages).

Members of the dominant lineages within dalu and glarang territories formed the *kraeng* (aristocratic class). The *ata leke* were the ordinary people: artisans, peasants, and laborers; these commoners controlled small tracts between the lands of aristocrats. Before the Dutch abolished the practice, war captives, debtors, and exiles could become slaves, which were also bought from foreign traders. The stigma of slave descent is still felt today. However, the sharpest distinction today is between townspeople and villagers.

In the past, warfare was endemic; warriors in rattan war helmets and feathered war cloaks fought with spears, knives, and shields. Through marriage, aristocratic clans formed alliances, regarding all other dalu as enemies. Before battle, warriors splattered their swords with the blood of a sacrificed pig, goat, or chicken and marched around the village center.

Among the Manggarai, adolescents of the opposite sex can associate freely, chatting at wells or dancing at feasts.

⁹LIVING CONDITIONS

Raised on 1-m (3-ft) stilts, the traditional house has a circular floor plan. Made of bundles of rice straw, the conical roof rises from the edge of the floor (i.e., there are no walls as such) to a center post that may be as high as 6 m (20 ft). Inside, a corridor separates the rooms, four to five on either side. The space immediately under the roof is the place for spirits, and heirlooms and food are stored there. The middle space is for human living. The space under the house is for storing tools and keeping animals (pigs, goats, sheep, and chickens). Before Dutch regulations early in the 20th century placed the maximum occupancy to three families, these houses could contain as many as 200 people.

Traditional houses are rare, as Manggarai now prefer houses with walls, modeled on those of other regions of Indonesia; a zinc roof has become a status symbol.

Until the Dutch began pushing for settlement in the plains, villages used to be built on hilltops for defense. In a pattern that can still be seen in modern settlements, a village had three parts: a front *(pa'ang),* a middle *(beo),* and a back *(ngaung).* Formerly, each section of a house had a sacred spot, a pile of big stones where guardian spirits could descend. Still today, the center of each village has a *kota,* a pile of large stones arranged in a step-pyramid with a table of flat stones on the top. A great banyan tree shades the kota. In front of the kota stands a sacred village hall called *mbaru gendang* (after the large sacred drum inside). Bamboo stockades 2 to 3 m (6.5–10 ft) high once encircled hilltop villages, now replaced by a dense barrier of thorny bushes (but modern villages at the foot of hills lack stockades altogether).

For occupation during the cultivation of swidden (shifting cultivation) fields, small houses called *sekang* are built. A cluster of these may become a new village if it acquires a kota, a banyan, and an mbaru gendang.

Townspeople with office jobs can afford consumer goods and dinners in restaurants, particularly at the beginning of the month right after salaries are paid. Rural people are generally well-fed but low on cash. When they take their produce to the town market, they may treat themselves to a meal from a food stall, indulge in small-time gambling, and buy cigarettes and bread or candies to take home to relatives.

The Manggarai regency has a Human Development Index (combining measures of income, health, and education) of 65.2 (2005 score), somewhat higher than that of East Nusa Tenggara province as a whole (63.6) but well below that of Indonesia as a whole (69.6). The regency's GDP per capita is us$2,174, the second lowest in East Nusa Tenggara, which in turn has the second lowest in Indonesia (cf. us$9,784 for West Sumatra, us$8,360 for North Sulawesi, and us$6,293 for Central Java, and us$3,427 for East Nusa Tenggara as a whole. GDP figures do not include income from petroleum and natural gas production, negligible in any case for these provinces). In 2000, the rate of infant mortality stood at 55.65 deaths per 1,000 live birth, only slightly lower than the rate for the province as a whole (56.65), comparable to much more developed provinces such as South Sulawesi and West Java.

¹⁰FAMILY LIFE

The *cak kilo* is the nuclear family. The most important unit, however, is the extended family, the *kilo,* including the parents' sons, their wives, and children. A group of kilo with a common patrilineal ancestor five to six generations back is a *panga;* often panga that shrink due to death will enter into other larger panga. In the past, the panga was responsible for mourning rites, the cremation of ancestral remains, and the raising of stone pillars to honor ancestral spirits, but now it serves only to give its members a surname. The *wa'u,* a unit larger still than the panga, has lost its functions by now but used to have animal totems and hold rituals that were taboo for outsiders' participation.

Kinship terminology exhibits some peculiarities. *Empo* refers to both grandparents and grandchildren. A father, his brother, and the mother's sister's husband are all *ema.* The mother, her sister, and the father's brother's wife are all *ende. Inang* is for the father's sister and the mother's brother's wife while *amang* is for the mother's brother and the father's sister's husband. *Weta* applies to a sister, a father's brother's daughter, and a mother's sister's daughter. *Kae* applies to an elder brother, a father's brother's son, and a mother's sister's son. *Kesah* refers to a father's sister's son and a mother's brother's son. The same word, *wina,* applies to a mother's brother's daughter and to a wife, while *rona* refers both to a father's sister's son and to a husband.

The terminology expresses the patrilineal bias of the kinship system, as when the term for father applies to the father's brother but not to the mother's brother. Moreover, a man who marries a sister of the father, thus taking a wife from the same family as the father, is also called father *(ema).*

¹¹CLOTHING

Traditional women's upper-body clothing resembles the Bugis-Makassar baju bodo, a blouse with wide, short sleeves. A rural woman now wears a sarong and a blouse or tee-shirt. A rural man wears a headcloth, short pants under a sarong, and a machete tied to his waist. Both sexes wear rubber thongs or go barefoot. Going into town, male villagers may carry a *peci* (the national brimless cap of black velvet) with a colorful piece of Manggarai cloth added, a cloth bag for tobacco or betel nut, and occasionally a carved cane. Female villagers wear skirts rather than sarongs into town and carry a handkerchief.

Teenagers wear jeans and tee-shirts, boys adding baseball caps and running shoes. Because of the cost and perhaps out of greater conservatism, rural teenage girls are less likely to wear jeans. Village teenagers dress traditionally at home but adopt modern clothes for visits to town. Townspeople dress like other urban Indonesians.

12 FOOD

Roasted whole or made into cakes or porridge, maize is the staple food, eaten with vegetable side dishes. Rice and chicken or pig meat is reserved for special occasions. Ceremonies also require the consumption of great quantities of palm wine. Several decades ago, betel chewing was very popular (though it is much less so now).

13 EDUCATION

In 2005, the level of literacy stood at 85.95% in Manggarai regency, slightly higher than that for East Nusa Tenggara as a whole but somewhat low for Indonesia, though comparable to more developed provinces with higher population densities and high numbers of poor, such as South Sulawesi, Bali, and East Java (*see also* the article entitled **Indonesians**).

14 CULTURAL HERITAGE

Oral literature consists of poetry (*renge* and *tudak),* requests to the gods for prosperity. This poetry forms part of nighttime rituals. An *ata molor tudak,* a storyteller, or the *tu'a tenu* of the *glarang* recite folktales.

15 WORK

Slash-and-burn agriculture is the major occupation. Fire is used to clear land, and the partially burned trunks are piled up to form borders between fields. Farmers cooperate in clearing land and divide the cleared land according to an agreement. Traditionally, fields were arranged radiating from a center (creating a spider-web-like pattern); these *lingko randang* fields are rare now. The main crops are maize and rice.

In 1918, the Dutch brought Balinese prisoners to establish wet-rice fields; years later, they sent Manggarai to study wet-rice techniques in Bima. The valleys around Ruteng constitute Flores' largest wet-rice area (swidden, or shifting-cultivation, is still the dominant form of farming on the island as a whole).

The Manggarai region is also one of the country's largest coffee areas (grown on permanent hillside farms and in house gardens). The export of oranges, jackfruit, *salak,* cacao, and cashews is just beginning to grow.

Water buffalo are status symbols, slaughtered for consumption at customary ceremonies. Horses are kept for transport and traction and constitute part of the bride-price. Water buffalo and horses are pastured on village common land and kept in a village pen. Alternately, horses are left to roam free in the surrounding grasslands to be caught when needed and later released. Pigs, goats, sheep, and chickens roam about the house yard by day and are kept under the house at night. Livestock export is another young industry.

Many young Manggarai men work in the towns for cash to be sent back to their families in the village.

16 SPORTS

Caci are whip fights that accompany ceremonies, but are now also performed to entertain tourists. The whip is of water buffalo hide, as is the shield (the latter can also be of bamboo rods). The whip leaves large scars that are attractive to women. Every young man has a fighting name, e.g., "Wild Boar," "Rearing Horse," "Naughty Rooster," or "Gone Around the World and Have Yet to be Bested."

Cockfighting with intense gambling accompanies many rituals. Despite an official ban, local police do not interfere.

Soccer is the most popular modern sport. The Catholic diocese divides Manggarai into four parts, each of which fields a team for a diocesan tournament.

17 ENTERTAINMENT AND RECREATION

See the article entitled **Indonesians**.

18 FOLK ART, CRAFTS, AND HOBBIES

Ikat (tie-dyed) cloth is produced for family use. Basketry is highly developed: typical pieces are hats and betel- and tobacco-chew holders. For these, young palm leaves are split into fine fibers, dried, and dyed with store-bought colors, often green, red, and yellow.

19 SOCIAL PROBLEMS

See the article entitled **Indonesians**.

20 GENDER ISSUES

The Gender-Related Development Index (combining measures of women's health, education, and income relative to men's) for Manggarai regency (2002 score) is 59.9, slightly above Indonesia's national GDI of 59.2 and significantly above that of East Nusa Tenggara as a whole (56.3). The residency's average Gender Empowerment Measure (reflecting women's participation and power in political and economic life relative to men's), however, is 33.33, far lower than the national GEM of 54.6 and the provincial GEM of 46.2).

21 BIBLIOGRAPHY

Badan Pusat Statistik: Data Statistik Indonesia. http://demografi.bps.go.id (November 9, 2008).

Johnston, Lois. "Social Order in an Indonesian Bus Terminal: Ruteng, Manggarai." Thesis, University of Calgary, 1993.

Harsrinuksmo, Bambang. "Adat Perkawinan" [Wedding Customs]. In *Ensiklopedi Nasional Indonesia (ENI),* vol. 1. Jakarta: Cipta Adi Pustaka, 1988.

Harsrinuksmo, Bambang, and Prijanti Pakan. "Adat dan Tata Cara Penguburan" [Customs and Protocols for Burials]. In *ENI,* Vol. 1, (1988).

Koentjaraningrat. "Kebudayaan Flores." In *Manusia dan Kebudayaan di Indonesia* [Man and Culture in Indonesia], edited by Koentjaraningrat. Jakarta: Djambatan, 1975.

LeBar, Frank M., ed. *Ethnic Groups of Insular Southeast Asia.* Vol. 1, *Indonesia, Andaman Islands, and Madagascar.* New Haven, CT: Human Relations Area Files Press, 1972.

Melalatoa, M. Junus. "Manggarai, Suku Bangsa." In *ENI*, vol. 10. (1990).

Muller, Kal. *East of Bali: From Lombok to Timor.* Berkeley: Periplus, 1991.

—revised by A. J. Abalahin

MANGYAN (HANUNO'O GROUP)

PRONUNCIATION: mahng-YAHN (hah-noo-NO-oh)
LOCATION: Philippines (island of Mindoro)
POPULATION: 7,000-13,000 (2000)
LANGUAGE: Hanuno'o
RELIGION: Traditional animism; some Catholicism
RELATED ARTICLES: Vol. 3: Filipinos

[1] INTRODUCTION

The Hanuno'o are the best known of the various groups called "Mangyan" living in the interior of the island of Mindoro. To an even greater extent than other such outsider-given names, "Mangyan" covers a wide range of meanings. In the Tagalog, Bikol, and Visayan languages of the central Philippines, the term combines the ideas of "savage," "mountaineer," and "pagan Negro," apparently once referring to Negritos rather than to Mangyan, who physically do not differ from lowland Filipinos. The word even came to mean "servant" or "debt-slave," much as, among the Tausug, captive slaves in general were called *bisaya*. In the usage of most Mindoro highlanders themselves, "Mangyan" equals "a person," a fellow "tribesperson," or "pagan." The exception is the Buhid who use it only to refer to other highland peoples and not to themselves. The Hanuno'o, on the other hand, insist that they are the "authentic" Mangyan (*hanuno'o* means "true" in their language).

Mindoro presents one of the great anomalies of Philippine history. Whereas Cebu, Panay, and, above all, Manila retained and increased their regional importance under Spanish colonial rule, Minodoro lost its pre-Hispanic prominence. Finding mention in Chinese accounts of the 13th century, the island was the first place in the Philippines to enter the historical record under the name Mait (Ma-yi in modern Mandarin pronunciation). To exchange for beeswax, musk, sandalwood, kapok, and the leather of the *tamaraw* (a wild and smaller version of the water buffalo), Chinese traders brought porcelain, metal, cloth, and silver coin; the Mait people themselves carried these goods to other islands and returned with the products the Chinese desired. Shaded by umbrellas, the Southeast Asian emblem of royalty, the chiefs of the coastal towns were powerful enough to deter pirate attacks, to exact customs duties from the Chinese traders, and to vouch for their own people, whom the Chinese regarded as "trustworthy."

Based on Panay and groping towards Manila, the Spanish first came to Mindoro in 1570. They called the coastal people "Moros," noting their connections with Muslim Brunei, which they would discover the Tagalogs farther north also enjoyed. The coastal towns were defended by moats, 4.25 m (14 ft) thick walls, and culverins (small cannons). Their inhabitants were rich in gold and savvy enough to present the greedy Spaniards with fake gold pieces that deceived even the most expert. In addition, the Spaniards also recorded that "Chichimecos" inhabited the interior. This was originally an Aztec term for the nomadic bands who lived far to the north of the Valley of Mexico; here it would generally be applied to Negritos. This is a reversal of the transfer of terminology that named the Aztecs and other American natives *indios*, "Indians." This distinction between sophisticated coast-dwellers and "primitive" interior peoples would widen through the coming centuries.

Because of its strategic position between Luzon, Panay, and Palawan, coastal Mindoro became a battleground between the Spanish and their Muslim enemies from the far south. From the 17th to the early 19th century, the Muslims controlled the entire west coast of the island, using it as a base from which to conduct piracy and slave-raids throughout Spanish Christian territory. The Spanish themselves attempted with only limited success to extend their control over the rest of the island, exacting tribute, gathering the natives into compact settlements (*reducciónes*), and establishing missions. The end result of this conflict was the Spanish evacuation of much of the coastal population to the more securely held province of Batangas on Luzon and the withdrawal to the interior of the rest whom slavers had not taken.

By the 19th century, the island that had been the Philippines' first recorded window to the outer world gained a reputation as a wild, mysterious, and inhospitable land. When Christian lowlanders (Tagalogs and Hiligaynon) began to settle the coasts, they looked on the natives as alien heathens ripe for exploitation. For a machete, Christians could demand rice crops from Mangyan in payment; Christian men would enter into sexual liaisons with Mangyan women, only to abandon them. The American colonial regime deepened the division by labeling the Mangyan as inferior to other Filipinos and designating Indian-style reservations for them. However, as many Filipinos pointed out, American interest in the Mangyan was inseparable from their desire to exploit the island's resources. Settling the coasts and penetrating the interior, Christian Filipinos have continued to exert pressure on the Mangyan.

The Mangyan response has been to seclude themselves even further and to avoid entering into any "reciprocal" relations with lowlanders, which they have long learned end up one-sided. They even distrust hierarchy among themselves, preferring egalitarian social structures. These characteristics have left them less able to assert their political rights in the manner that Cordillera and Muslim peoples have done in gaining a measure of autonomy. As the American regime in the end abandoned the policy of isolating the Mangyan, the Filipino government has favored simple integration, which would ultimately end the Mangyan existence as separate peoples. For instance, the Iraya of the northern highlands have been settled by the government in towns and have become wage laborers for Christians.

Although they are the only Mangyan group that traditionally maintained trade relations with lowlanders, re-trading the goods to the other groups, the Hanuno'o still keep to themselves, an all-the-more-striking feat since they live rather close to Hiligaynon settlements. Whereas other groups (particularly to the north), who are hunter-gatherers that grow root-crops only intermittently, may indeed be descended from the Spaniards' Chichimecos, the Hanuno'o, who not only grow dry-rice, weave cloth, make pottery, and forge metal but also possess a script, probably lived on the coast in earlier times. Many elements of their present culture correspond to those of pre-Christian Visayan culture as described by Spanish writers.

Some Hanuno'o have begun to integrate with wider Filipino society with the assistance of Antoon Postma, a Dutch Catholic priest who began work in 1958. Having failed to attract Hanuno'o to settle near lowland schools, he established a

school-clinic-chapel complex in the mountains. The Hanuno'o living around it have even begun to elect their own leaders (rather than deferring simply to age and experience), a move that will allow them to participate in Filipino politics.

²LOCATION AND HOMELAND

The Hanuno'o live inland from the southernmost tip of Mindoro. In the 1970s, the Hanuno'o numbered 6,000 out of a total of 20–30,000 Mangyan, already a minority on an island inhabited by 300,000 Tagalog and Visayan settlers. One 2000 estimate numbers the Hanuno'o 13,000. According to the 2000 census, 7,702 identified themselves as Hanuno'o in Oriental Mindoro province, 19,001 there identified themselves as simply "Mangyan," and 13,899 in Occidental Mindoro province identified themselves as "Mangyan." The other groups include, on the one hand, the Buhid and Batangan of the southern highlands, who with the Hanuno'o form a group linguistically close to Visayan and, on the other, the Iraya, Alangan, and Tadyawan, who speak languages more similar to Tagalog. In 2000, the Mangyan were proportionately an even smaller minority on their ancestral island; its total population surpassed 1 million.

³LANGUAGE

The Mangyan groups speak mutually unintelligible languages. The Hanuno'o language is similar to the Visayan tongues of the central Philippines. Along with the neighboring Buhid and the Tagbanua of central Palawan (*see* **Tagbanua**), they still use the script, ultimately of Indian origin, that was employed by the

Tagalogs and other Filipino peoples at the time of the Spanish conquest. Incised into lengths of bamboo, this script is used to write messages and courtship verse; only recently has it been used for any other purpose, namely, in election materials.

⁴FOLKLORE

See the following section on religion.

⁵RELIGION

The Hanuno'o recognize certain named deities of creation, but these play only a minor role in everyday life. Ordinarily more significant to them are nature spirits living in mountains, rocks, the forest, etc., who all can be transformed into *labang*, evil spirits who can attack a person's soul, causing illness or death. Benign spirits (such as ancestors) may allow their evil fellows to do harm to humans who have violated custom.

Each person has three *karaduwa* (souls), a good one located to the right of the chest, a neutral one in the center, and an evil one to the left. The center-soul keeps both sides in balance. If the left soul gains the upper hand, the person may lie, steal, or kill. If the right soul fails to return to the body temporarily, this causes illness; if it leaves permanently, death occurs. *Kalag* are guardian spirits, the ghosts of the recently deceased or the souls of the living who have supernatural powers, such as becoming invisible or making others invisible.

Part-time specialists, such as masseurs, herbalists, and mediums *(balyanan),* perform curing rituals. The balyanan send their spirit familiars to combat evil spirits or extract harmful objects from a victim's body. The spirit familiars reside in stones that the balyanan carefully guard. Mediums also wave leaves or other plant parts over the patient's body. Balyanan are present at ceremonies for deceased kinfolk, area spirits, and swidden (shifting-cultivation) fields, especially for rice. Spirit offerings consist of cooked rice, pig's blood, and prepared betel chew, but spirits especially appreciate glass trade-beads.

⁶MAJOR HOLIDAYS

See the sections entitled "Religion" and "Rites of Passage" in this article.

⁷RITES OF PASSAGE

Hanuno'o marry by mutual agreement of the two partners' families; the man must provide some form of bride-service to his in-laws. In contrast to non-Mangyan groups, there is no bride-price, formal ceremony, or exchange of goods between the sides. Elopement is an alternative.

For a year after death, the right soul remains in the underworld, neither dead nor alive. The left soul remains with the body, however, and may bring misfortune to surviving kin. During the first year, the body is buried with its head turned towards the west, so the face will get sunlight. After a year, the bones are exhumed *(kutkutan)* and bundled in two blankets, with two ends tied together to make the "head," while the other two make the "arms." The relatives feed, talk to, and dance with the bones at a large, expensive socioreligious festival called a *panludan,* now also called by the Hispano-Visayan term, *punsiyon.* This is an occasion for merry-making, courting, singing, and dancing. Not being able to use the former house of the deceased, the relatives build a ritual house; upon entering the ritual house, they beat each other with branches

A pregnant Mangyan tribeswoman with her daughter. (AFP/Getty Images)

to drive away the center- and left-souls of the deceased. During 24 hours of chanting, a priestly exhumation specialist *(panugkutkutan)* reconstructs the bleached bones in the form of a person and puts clothing on the "body."

Afterwards, the bones are cleaned, and certain valuables are placed in a cave niche with the remains of other relatives. The three souls become one and go towards *agsalim,* the spiritual world, situated on Mt. Aliwliwan. Before passing on to agsalim, the unified soul must pass through a checkpoint where a woman judges the soul. One's deeds, character, relations, and debts are believed to continue unchanged into afterlife. If the soul is good, the woman teaches it the way to Aliwliwan. If the soul is bad, the woman keeps silent and a big man with seven dogs appears and drives the soul into a boiling pond. These beliefs reflect the influence of Buddhism.

⁸INTERPERSONAL RELATIONS

The Hanuno'o live in autonomous, named settlements largely corresponding to a kin-group. Society is egalitarian with some prestige accorded to age and special skills, such as weaving, smithing, spirit mediation. Individuals and families possess wealth in the form of ritual glass beads, bronze gongs, porcelain jars, and cattle, but accumulated property does not give rise to social differentiation. The eldest member of a kinship group acts as a caretaker or consultant. Disputes are settled by the eldest relatives of the disputing parties. Some cases are resolved by ordeal by hot water. Penalties take the form of fines in glass beads. Although the closest relatives of a murder victim will avenge the death, the Hanuno'o, like other Mangyan groups, have no recent tradition of warfare; their response to attack by outsiders (such as Moro slavers) has been evasion.

At *panludan* funerary feasts, young men and women engage in a highly stylized pattern of courtship involving the exchange of love songs (*ambahan*). The boy starts and the girl answers, both aiming to choose the wittiest or most appropriate verse.

9 LIVING CONDITIONS

Villages are semipermanent, traditionally autonomous, and consist of five to six single-family houses (50–60 persons maximum). They are generally built on valley slopes or hill spurs overlooking a water source. The sites are identified by a geographical landmark, and the settlement itself by the name of its eldest resident. Settlements within an hour's easy walking distance form a "local area" to which a person maintains a lifelong affiliation and ethnocentric attachment, no matter where he or she moves.

Houses are raised on piles, sturdily constructed of wood or bamboo, and roofed with thatch. They include a veranda that may connect to the verandas of other houses, linking several in a chain. Granaries resemble houses but are smaller and lack a veranda. Some Hanuno'o live in tree houses for protection.

Average family income in the MIMAROPA region (Mindoro, Masbate, Romblon, and Palawan islands) amounted to 109,000 pesos (US$2,137) in 2006, the second lowest in the country (above the Autonomous Region in Muslim Mindanao), cf. the national average of P173,000, the National Capital Region's P311,000, and those of the neighboring regions, Southern Tagalog, P198,000, and the Western Visayas, P130,000.

In Oriental Mindoro province, the proportion of houses with a roof of galvanized iron/aluminum increased from 27% in 1990 to 52% in 2000, with a roof of grass or palm thatch from 67.1% in 1990 to 40.7% in 2000. Houses with outer walls of concrete, brick, or stone reached 27% in 2000 and with wooden outer walls 16.2%; the proportion of houses with outer walls of grass or palm thatch remained high, 33.9% in 2000, though substantially down from the 1990 figure of 54.4%.

10 FAMILY LIFE

A family consists of a man, his wife or wives, and their unmarried offspring. This may be extended to form a local family group with married daughters, and their families usually live in adjacent houses. Such a group always respects its oldest male member. A single family may move away from the settlement but will always set up its residence near the kin of either the husband or wife.

The Hanuno'o use the body as a metaphor for the extended family, whose members cannot intermarry without infringing the incest taboo and who do *arawatan*, i.e., aid each other in farming. The husband is equated with the right breast, the wife with the left. The right upper arm represents the husband's siblings, and the left represents the wife's. The forearms are the cousins of the respective spouses, the hands are the second cousins, and the spaces between the thumb and forefinger are the third cousins. The right neck-cheek area signifies the father

and the left symbolizes the mother, while the top of the head indicates the grandparents and all the ancestors. The two sides of the abdomen represent the husband's and wife's siblings, the right thigh represents the children, the left thigh symbolizes the nephews and nieces, the knees are the grandchildren, and the lower legs are great-grandchildren and all other descendants. This imagery parallels the terminology in other Filipino and Indonesian languages, such as the Hiligaynon *apo sa tuhod*, "grandchild at the knee" or great-grandchild; *apo sa umang-umang*, "grandchild at the thumb" or great-great-grandchild; and *apo sa ingay-ingay*, "grandchild at the smallest toe" or great-great-great-grandchild.

As most people marry within their locality, they often have to wed cousins; this is permissible after performing a cleansing ritual. At first, most couples settle with the wife's family, moving on only later. A set of brothers is allowed to marry a set of sisters, and a widow or widower is encouraged to marry the sibling of the deceased spouse.

11 CLOTHING

Hanuno'o are noted for long hair, men as well as women. They weave and dye (indigo) their own clothing, which consists of short shirts and short sarongs.

12 FOOD

Rice is the food of prestige and ritual importance, but half of all calories in the Hanuno'o diet comes from bananas and tubers (sweet potatoes, yams, and taro). Most animal protein comes from fishing, less from game or livestock.

13 EDUCATION

With the exception of those attracted by Father Postma, the Dutch Catholic priest who established a school-clinic-chapel complex in the highlands, Hanuno'o avoid modern schools to a greater extent than do other minority groups.

14 CULTURAL HERITAGE

Large repertoires of verse (*ambahan*) are incised on bamboo strips. Consisting of seven syllables with rhyming endings, these highly metaphorical verses are in an archaic poetical language that is quite distant from everyday speech. An integral part of courtship, they are chanted with or without the accompaniment of guitars, jaw harps, nose flutes, and *git-git*, a locally produced small wooden fiddle with strings of human hair. One example translates: "The honey-eater bird,/Not yet having left the nest,/A blinking trembler,/Began to be tempted/ By a pretty dear,/In the *ulang* bushes of the *cogon* meadow." Another goes: "Though I love your body,/I love not to intrude on two./If one accompany a married woman/Who shall obey his wink,/His head shall have a nightmare/Up there in the mountains."

Another mood is expressed in an *urukay* song of the neighboring Buhid: "Like a tree overgrown with branches and leaves,/My mind is full of turmoil./Though loaded with pain and grief,/My dreams continually seek for an end,/Let it be known that I am on my way./Perchance you'll catch up with me."

15 WORK

The Hanuno'o rely on swidden agriculture. To ensure the success of their efforts, they employ not only astronomical lore, augury, and dream interpretation but also extensive pragmatic knowledge of soil types, crop rotation, erosion, and a knowledge of plants more precise than a Western botanist's. They recognize 1,625 mutually exclusive plant forms in 890 categories, of which 600 are edible, 406 are medicinal, and the rest have no use but are classified in order to complete their understanding of an ordered environment. By contrast, Western botanists distinguish only 1,100 plant species.

The Hanuno'o practice intercropping—before harvesting one species, they plant another. In this way, they grow maize, rice, beans, sugarcane, bananas, and papayas. They do not acknowledge permanent ownership of land but rather usufruct, the rights of those tilling it at any given time; fallow land may be reopened by another party. Individuals do own trees, spears, and beads, while families own heirloom gongs and porcelain.

For consumption at ritual feasts, the Hanuno'o keep pigs, chickens, and humped cattle (the last are also used as draft animals). Using spears, traps, poisoned arrows, dogs, and formerly fire-surrounds involving 50 or more men, they hunt wild pig, deer, monkeys, and in the past *tamaraw* (small, wild water buffalo). They also catch fish and crustaceans.

The Hanuno'o make occasional trips to the lowlands to trade their surplus rice, maize, bananas, cacao, and tobacco for salt, metal (scrap, needles, kettles), ritually important glass beads (also the standard of value in the south Mindoro pagan interior), red cloth, Moro gongs, and Chinese porcelain (for ancestral offerings). They trade these goods obtained from lowlanders to the neighboring Buhid, their fellow highlanders, for clay cooking pots.

16 SPORTS

See the article entitled **Filipinos.**

17 ENTERTAINMENT AND RECREATION

Because of their isolation, Hanuno'o have less access to modern entertainment forms than other "minority" groups.

18 FOLK ART, CRAFTS, AND HOBBIES

Using double-piston bellows, men forge knives and other articles from scrap metal obtained through trade with lowlanders. Women plant, pick, gin, and weave cotton into clothing and blankets and also grow indigo for dyeing. Basketry is highly developed, using red-dyed rattan and displaying fine geometrical designs.

19 SOCIAL PROBLEMS

See the article entitled **Filipinos.**

20 GENDER ISSUES

According to the 2000 census, among the Hanuno'o, men and women are nearly equal in number (50.2% vs. 49.8%). In the Oriental Mindoro population as a whole, more women had a college undergraduate education or higher and received academic degrees than men by a substantial margin; elementary school completion, a measure likely more relevant to the Hanuno'o, was lower for girls than for boys; 52.6% of elementary school graduates were male while only 51.5% of the population was male.

21 BIBLIOGRAPHY

Gordon, Raymond G., ed. *Ethnologue: Languages of the World,* 15th edition. Dallas, TX: SIL International, 2005. http://www.ethnologue.com/ (November 16, 2008)

Kikuchi, Yasushi. *Mindoro Highlanders: The Life of Swidden Agriculturalists.* Quezon City: New Day Publishers, 1984.

LeBar, Frank M., ed. *Ethnic Groups of Insular Southeast Asia.* Vol. 2, *The Philippines and Formosa.* New Haven, CT: Human Relations Area Files Press, 1972.

Lopez, Violeta P. *The Mangyans of Mindoro: An Ethnohistory.* Quezon City: University of Philippines Press, 1976.

Mayuga, Sylvia, and Alfred Yuson. *Philippines.* Hong Kong: APA Productions, 1987.

National Statistics Office: Government of the Philippines. http://www.census.gov.ph (November 16, 2008).

—revised by A. Abalahin

MANUVU' (UPLAND BAGOBO)

PRONUNCIATION: man-NOH bo
ALTERNATE NAMES: Bagobo
LOCATION: Philippines (island of Mindanao)
POPULATION: About 30,000
LANGUAGE: Manuvu'/Bagobo
RELIGION: Indigenous beliefs
RELATED ARTICLES: Vol. 3: Filipinos

¹INTRODUCTION

The Manuvu' are one of the many Mindanao groups to whom Visayans, Spanish, and Moros apply the name *Bagobo* (anthropologists specify the Manuvu' as the "Upland Bagobo"). The term is a contraction of *bago*, "new," and *obo*, "man." Originally, the term Bagobo referred to the peoples of coastal southwestern Mindanao who converted to Islam. However, its scope was extended to include unconverted hill tribes such as the Manuvu', whose name means "native people." They are themselves not a homogeneous group, displaying dialectal differences and occupational and artistic specializations.

The Manuvu' *Tuwaang* epic locates their origin in the valley of the Kuaman river (a tributary of the Pulangi). This region's present population speaks a dialect that Manuvu' can understand, and who are otherwise culturally similar. Little Islamic influence (or, rather, the culture of the Islamized lowlanders such as the Maguindanao) can be found in Manuvu' culture. In the 19th century, Moro warriors struck into the uplands, compelling the Manuvu' to ally with their traditional enemies, the Matigsalug, in order to mount a resistance. At the same time, by the middle of that century, external trade was making an impact on Manuvu' life. The Manuvu' received woven clothing from the coastal Attaw in exchange for boar and deer meat. The Attaw also delivered gongs, horses, and water buffalo to the Manuvu' who in turn "reexported" them to the Matigsalug in exchange for long-bladed knives. Another lucrative business for the Manuvu' was the sale of Matigsalug slaves to the Attaw.

Seeking to end the warfare endemic to the region, the American colonial administration (fully imposed on Mindanao only in the 1910s) discouraged the Manuvu' from carrying arms. The Manuvu' gradually abandoned ambush weapons such as the blowgun and the bow and arrow; only individuals willing to pay a special tax were issued with licenses to carry the *palihumas* long-blades (after World War II, one still brought a spear on trips but otherwise left spears stacked in the house). Having adopted the crops from Japanese and American planters, the Attaw introduced abaca and coffee to the Manuvu', many of whom came to rely on them, especially after World War II. During that war, hoping to flush out Filipino guerrillas taking refuge among the Manuvu', the Japanese built the first roads into the uplands. In later years, on these roads and those cut by logging companies, Visayan settlers poured in, displacing Manuvu' from more and more of their ancestral lands.

²LOCATION AND HOMELAND

The Manuvu' (population estimated at about 30,000) inhabit an extensive region between the Pulangi and Davao rivers in central Mindanao (southern Bukidnon, northeast Cotabato, and northwest Davao provinces). This territory begins as rugged, mountainous terrain in the east, then flattens into gentler slopes and wider valleys towards the west. Although the soil in the western valleys is more suitable for rice, the Manuvu' prefer the eastern hillsides where swidden (shifting-cultivation) farming strains the back less.

³LANGUAGE

The Manuvu'/Bagobo language belongs to the Manobo subgroup of the Southern Philippine branch of the Austronesian family; as such, its closest relatives are other indigenous languages of Mindanao.

Relatives select a name for a child that refers to natural phenomena or memorable events accompanying the birth (e.g., an earthquake or a visitor's arrival); physical peculiarities of the child; or persons known to the relatives personally or by reputation (including Christians such as the Filipino president). Manuvu' do not have surnames, adding their father's name for further identification if necessary.

⁴FOLKLORE

Consisting of 100 sung episodes, the *Tuwaang* epic recounts the adventures of the hero of that name. Tuwaang is a *bahani'*, one of whose marks of distinction is the possession of 200 wives. The epic provides the Manuvu' with their mythology as well as behavioral ideals, such as the characteristics of the proper leader; Manuvu' even see in it predictions of the future, e.g., airplanes are believed to have been prefigured in the *sinalimba* boat that carries Tuwaang and his followers into heaven. The Manuvu' believe there is a creature in the mountains named the busao/buso that eats their children.

⁵RELIGION

According to Manuvu' belief, there are two parallel universes, one good and the other bad, each divided into a skyworld, an earthworld, and an underworld. While the bad universe is only vaguely delineated, the good universe's skyworld consists of nine layers, at the topmost of which resides Manama, the supreme deity. Manama is little involved in earthly affairs, although eventually he will take the souls of the good from the underworld to live with him. Lesser gods (*diwata'* and anitu) inhabit the lower layers of the skyworld. Some lesser gods are those to which a hunter prays before setting off on the chase: Timbaong, god of animals; Mahumanay, goddess of the mountains; and Tahamaling, goddess of the forest. Another is Anit, the deity who punishes incest and inflicts deformities on those who mock dogs, cats, and frogs.

Household heads, artisans, and hunters make offerings to ensure the success of their endeavors. The most common religious specialist is the *walian,* who leads agricultural and healing rituals. More prestigious is the *tumanuron,* who enjoys curative and predictive powers through the patronage of an *anitu.* Most revered of all is the *pohohana',* a diviner who can perform rainmaking and other miracles. *Datus* (chiefs) very often function also as ritual leaders.

⁶MAJOR HOLIDAYS

There are no holidays as such, but there are regularly held ritual celebrations.

⁷RITES OF PASSAGE

Nowadays regarded as too painful, tattooing and tooth filing no longer mark the transition to adulthood for boys and girls. Boys, however, still undergo circumcision.

In a young person's life, marriage is the most important rite of passage. The family of the groom is required to pay the bride's family a dowry, which may take years to accumulate. Before the bride-price negotiations, the sides reconstruct their genealogies in order to check whether the union might be incestuous. Once incest is ruled out, the boy's family sends an intermediary to negotiate the bride-price. This consists of the *panamung,* goods for the girl's parents and kin, plus the *pantun,* goods for the girl herself. She makes a great show of refusing the proposal, often holding out for a bigger *pantun*—if the boy's kin can't afford it, they have to withdraw.

The wedding celebration opens with the groom's parents presenting a spear to the bride's parents, an act to propitiate Dohanganna Karang, the god of marriage, so that the couple will prosper. The groom's parents then hand over a gong set and a *palihuma'* blade to the bride's parents to appease Kayag and Pamua', gods who will guarantee the success of the couple's farm work. Following is a tedious assessment of each item of the bride-price. After this is a ceremony in which the bride and groom simultaneously feed each other lumps of rice with chicken. Brothers or uncles then perform the rite of knocking the bride's and groom's heads together. Finally, relatives give the couple advice on how to have a happy marriage.

Tree burial was once common, but now the deceased's relatives leave the body in his or her house, then abandon the house. In abaca- and coffee-growing areas, burial is now in the house yard with a thatch hut raised over it (which the relatives leave to rot).

⁸INTERPERSONAL RELATIONS

Traditional Manuvu' society knew no social classes because the obligation to contribute to the bridewealth and blood money needed by kinfolk prevented individuals' permanent accumulation of wealth. Moreover, the status of slave, acquired through being captured in a raid, was hardly a permanent one, being little more than a prelude to being married into the captor's village.

Nor was there any authority above the village chief or *datu;* larger villages would even have three or more *datu,* none of which was superior to the others. The *datu's* role is to arbitrate disputes within the community and to represent it in dealings with other communities. A *datu* must possess *goro',* the charisma that wins people's trust and obedience. More concretely, he must be skilled in negotiating, expert in customary law *(batassan),* and have wealth (rice, maize, cloth, gongs, blades, water buffalo, and horses) enough to provide hospitality to his followers who come calling and to underwrite the penalties they may incur. *Datus* train their sons to succeed them, but any individual fulfilling the above criteria can win the status. Since World War II, the threat posed by loggers and Visayan settlers has led the Manuvu' for the first time to recognize a single *datu* as spokesman for their entire ethnic group.

Preserving honor is of paramount concern. Even teasing *(sollog)* can lead to conflict and is permissible only among children and old people; parents can tease younger children but cannot tease adolescents. Feuds arise most often from verbal insults and disputes over bride-wealth. Datus judge cases that

conflicting parties themselves cannot settle. He determines which side must compensate which side and by how much (even paying first what the fined party cannot immediately cover) and, in the most serious cases, holds a *pagkitan* (the sharing of ceremonial food by both sides) in his house. In the endemic feuding before World War II, villages sent raiding parties or commissioned a *bahani',* an independent warrior (and such companions as he might recruit), to exact revenge. Feuds could be concluded with a *pakang,* a peace-making ritual, in which a slave was killed to make the sides "even" in deaths.

⁹LIVING CONDITIONS

Houses are raised on piles and have windowless walls of bark and a roof of bamboo, grass, or bark. Parents, children up to eight years old, and guests sleep on the *lantawan,* a raised portion of the floor. Unmarried daughters, however, occupy a separate bedroom, the *sinavong,* while boys and unmarried men sleep on boards suspended from and close to the ceiling. An extension may be added for a married daughter. Rice is stored in granaries, which are also raised structures but smaller than houses.

In more violent times, settlements grouped two or three tree houses linked by bamboo bridges. In the mountainous east, villages consist of a few widely scattered ground houses on hill spurs or on the edge of deep ravines; house floors are 6–8 m (20–26 ft) off the ground, beyond the reach of a spear-thrust from below.

Such settlements are impermanent, moving with the opening of new swidden fields (though within a fixed territory). In the broader valleys of the west, permanent villages of as many as 100 families living in low houses is the norm.

¹⁰FAMILY LIFE

In raising bride-wealth or blood-money or forming a vengeance-taking party, an individual can rely on the assistance of kin from both paternal and maternal sides.

Strict enforcement of incest taboos (the deity Anit punishes perpetrators and their kin, e.g., by petrifaction) means that persons marry outside their village of birth, as fellow villagers are nearly always kin. Initially, a new husband lives in his in-laws' house before establishing his own—still within his wife's village. Surrounded by his wife's people, a husband is in effect a hostage, ensuring no feuding breaks out between the two kin groups. In such a position, a husband can never become too dominating a partner (he makes the decisions outside the home, such as for farming, while the wife makes decisions inside the home).

If one spouse dies, a same-sex cousin substitutes, preserving the intergroup relations established by the original union. A few men who can afford it take additional wives to demonstrate their sexual prowess, gain political influence, or even to provide the first wife (who must approve beforehand in any case) with assistance in her work. Either spouse can initiate a divorce by issuing a formal complaint (of infidelity, insult, abuse, nonsupport, etc.) to the datu for his judgment.

Manuvu' terminology equates fathers and uncles, mothers and aunts, and siblings and cousins. However, a person addresses a sibling or cousin of the same sex *(suwod)* differently from a sibling or cousin of the opposite sex *(tabbay).*

Aging parents move in with a married daughter, usually the one with the least children. The eldest son inherits the greatest part of the property (including the heirlooms), but he is obliged to support younger siblings to the extent of providing bride-wealth for his brothers (but he also receives part of the bride-wealth due for his sisters).

Manuvu' keep cats and dogs as pets, and *limukon* doves for predicting the future.

¹¹CLOTHING

Manuvu's wore bark-cloth until the mid-19th century, when they adopted the costume of their Attaw trading partners. In addition, captured women and children from other groups brought the art of weaving. Traditional clothing consists of tight knee-length trousers and long-sleeved jackets for men, and tube skirts and blouses for women. Family members commonly borrow or exchange clothing and extra clothing is seen as communal property.

¹²FOOD

Manuvu's subsist on a basic diet of corn; *salog,* (an indigenous rice); vegetables, and cassavas. Seeds are derived from the farmer's own saved seeds from the previous season that have been dried and stored. Unhusked corn cobs are hung on clotheslines and corn cobs are hung above the cooking area (*abuhun*) after harvest until the following planting season. Threats to Manuvu' agricultural traditions include a rapidly changing environment, depletion of the soil, and the opening of the Manuvu' homelands to commercial markets.

¹³EDUCATION

Traditional Manuvu' education takes place in the home. From a young age Manuvu' children stay by their mother's side. Young girls are taught household chores and agricultural tasks reserved for females, while boys assisted their fathers in the fields. After puberty, girls are eligible for marriage. In the 1950s and 1960s government-operated public schools were established, but student enrollment remains low as students drop out of school at a young age.

¹⁴CULTURAL HERITAGE

Dance and music traditions (including gong-playing and the singing of the *Tuwaang* epic, a highlight of most social gatherings) resemble those of other Mindanao-Sulu peoples.

Traditionally tattooing was common. Men wore tattoos on the chest, upper arms, forearms, and fingers, while women had tattoos on the same parts of the body as well as on their calves, where the most elaborate tattoos were done. Tattoo designs mimicked the embroidered patterns on clothing, with the addition of figures of *binuaja* (crocodile), *ginibang* (iguana) and *binuyo* (betel leaf).

Traditionally men carry *bolos,* knives with long blades and a wooden handle that are used to clear vegetation in agricultural land or cutting trails in the forest.

¹⁵WORK

Before World War II, agriculture provided about 75% of food, while hunting, fishing, and gathering provided the remainder. Since then, as commercial logging (by non-Manuvu') depletes game and otherwise upsets the ecology, the proportion of food obtained through hunting, fishing, and gathering has fallen to 5%.

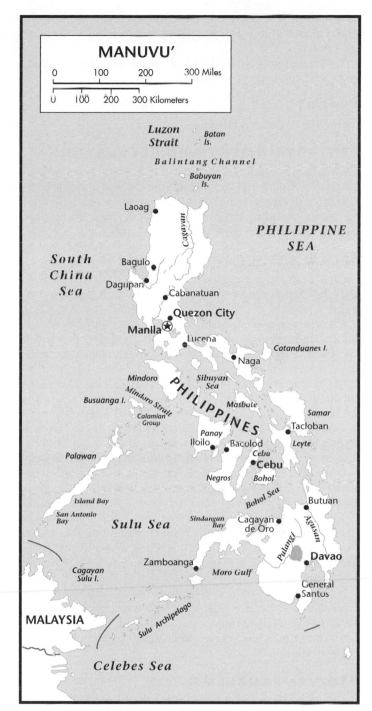

Families own two or more swidden fields, rotating their cultivation in two- to three-year cycles; tools consist of machetes, wooden spades, and digging and dibble sticks. The staples are maize, rice, and sweet potatoes, supplemented by squash, beans, sugarcane, bananas, and tubers. Some areas have begun to grow abaca and coffee as cash crops in recent decades. Families keep chickens for food and sacrifices. Wild boar having once been abundant, Manuvu' had no need to keep domestic pigs and learned hog-raising from Visayans only recently. Horses, water buffalo, and now cattle are obtained from coastal peoples as measures of wealth used in the paying of bride-wealth, debts, and fines. Game includes wild boar and deer (speared or trapped), and monkeys, small game, and birds (shot with arrows or blowdarts, or trapped). Fishing techniques include damming, poisoning, and piercing with spears and arrows.

Traditional society held blacksmiths, weavers, healers, midwives, and epic singers in high esteem.

[16] SPORTS

See the article entitled **Filipinos**.

[17] ENTERTAINMENT AND RECREATION

The Manuvu's practice a subsistence agricultural economy and the chores of daily life leave little time for recreation. A common form of entertainment is music played on traditional instruments, including the *dwagay* (violin-like instrument), *togo* (bamboo guitar), and the *kubing* (harp).

[18] FOLK ART, CRAFTS, HOBBIES

Though Manuvu' wear modern clothing and have access to mass produced goods, they continue to utilize traditional crafts.

Common ornaments include brass or silver rings, bracelets, anklets, and earrings. In addition, beads, mother of pearl, wild cat's teeth, and the seeds of the *saguya* tree are used in traditional ornaments.

Many Manuvu' crafts are utilized in agriculture. Large containers named *lukong* or *liwit* are made from the bark of the red lauan tree and can store five to six sacks of rice. A single tree can produce three to five pieces of *lukong/liwit*. The bark is sewn together with *uway*, a variety of calamas plant, and the bottom of the *lukong/liwit* is made of *uway* mesh. The *lukong/liwit* are placed in a traditional storage house (*payag sa humay*) constructed of wood or bamboo and covered with a grass roof. The *payag sa humay* is elevated several feet off the ground by four posts that have milk cans or flat, round wooden discs placed on them to prevent rats from climbing into the storage areas. The structures have only one door, no windows, and a removable ladder. The Manuvu' keep separate storage houses for rice and corn.

Another seed container is the *laban* or carrying basket. This is made of *uway* and is used to carry harvested crops or firewood. Other seed containers include the *tabungos*, which can carry two *taros* (45 lbs) of rice seeds, and the *langkap*; both are made of bamboo.

[19] SOCIAL PROBLEMS

The most pressing social problem for the Manuvu' is the civil war that has taken place on Mindanao since the late 1960s. The local Muslim population of Mindanao rebelled against the central Filipino government because of land distribution inequalities and official corruption. The mountainous homeland of the Manuvu' is ideal terrain for an insurgency, and both the rebels and government have attempted to recruit Manuvu' villagers. In 1993 the government used the military to force the Manuvu' to back down from opposition to a geothermal project on Mount Apo. In the late 1990s the government armed a village of Manuvu' who in 2000 engaged in a battle with insurgent forces from the Moro Islamic Liberation Front (MILF). The civil war has pitted the Manuvu' against their neighbors, and Manuvu' villages have negotiated *dyandi*, or peace pacts, with their neighbors.

[20] GENDER ISSUES

Manuvu' society is male-dominated and men and women are assigned distinct social roles.

When preparing for marriage, women have little choice in choosing their future husbands. While females may express resistance to an initial marital suggestion, it is the role of the male suitor or the parents to decide a match. Marriages can be arranged in any of the following ways: (1) either the man's or the woman's family makes the proposal (sometimes, a man will hint at his preferred bride); (2) parents arrange the betrothal of a child (or even a fetus); (3) the woman's family holds the man prisoner in their house until the marriage is consummated or the man's family "buys" him back or provides a replacement; (4) the man abducts the woman (sometimes with her consent); (5) the man provides his prospective in-laws with live-in bride service; (6) the man courts the woman (clandestinely, as she is not supposed to talk to men); or (7) a senior wife selects a junior wife for her husband.

New brides are directed by their fathers to not quarrel with their husbands, talk to any male strangers, and to be faithful to their partner until death. In marriage there is a division of labor according to gender. The activities of the wife are centered in the home: house cleaning, cooking, raising children, making clothes, and weaving baskets and mats. Men work in the fields, hunt, and fish. When the family leaves home to visit relatives the woman usually is loaded with a child or goods in her carrying basket, where as the man carries a weapon and is responsible for defending the family against attack. While both men and women may on occasion exchange assigned gender roles, hunting is exclusively assigned to the husband. Women do not even play a part in preparation of the carcass. Historically, wife-stealing took place between villages and tribes. *Datus* who had more than one wife were often the victims, and incidents of wife-stealing could ignite inter-communal warfare.

Women play a large role in the Manuvu' agricultural economy. They tend to rice plants, removing weeds and picking crops. An important task of Manuvu' female farmers is the selection of seeds for the following year's crop. Storing and preserving seed material for the next planting season is exclusively the role of women in the Manuvu' community.

[21] BIBLIOGRAPHY

LeBar, Frank M., ed. *Ethnic Groups of Insular Southeast Asia.* Vol. 2, *The Philippines and Formosa.* New Haven, CT: Human Relations Area Files Press, 1972.

Lopez, Regolio M. *Agricultural Practices of the Manobo in the Interior of Southwestern Cotabato (Mindanao).* Cebu City, Philippines: University of San Carlos, 1968.

Manuel, E. Arsenio. *Manuvu' Social Organization.* Diliman, Quezon City: University of the Philippines Press, 2002.

Parreno-de Guzman, Lucille Elna. "Caring for Seeds: Learning from the Manuvu Women in the Philippines." *Appropriate Technology.* Vol. 29. No. 3. (September 2002): 54-55.

Sevilla, Ester Orlida. *A Study of the Structure and Style of Two Manuvu Epic Songs in English.* Cebu City, Philippines: University of San Carlos, 1979.

—revised by D. Straub

MAORI

PRONUNCIATION: MOW-ree
LOCATION: New Zealand
POPULATION: 565,329 in 2006 census
LANGUAGE: Maori; English
RELIGION: Christianity; traditional Maori, based on ancestor worship
RELATED ARTICLES: Vol 3: New Zealanders

¹INTRODUCTION

The ancestors of the present-day Maori created an outpost of Polynesian culture on the North and South islands of New Zealand. They remained relatively isolated from external contact until 1769, when Captain James Cook initiated a permanent European presence in New Zealand. In less than a century, Maori culture changed dramatically as a result. The Maori have been striving to revive aspects of their traditional culture, reclaim artifacts of their cultural history from foreign museums, and regain their ancestral homelands. As of 2006, the Maori of New Zealand numbered over 565,000, or about 15% of New Zealand's total population. While the overall number of Maori has risen over the past decade, the percentage of the total population has remained the same. The term "Maori" covers a number of different tribal and sub-tribal groups that view themselves and each other as very distinct. The Maori word for each tribal unit is *iwi*, and there are well over one hundred Maori iwi. The largest Maori iwi is Ngapuhi, which had a total enrollment of 122,211 according to the 2006 census. Not all Maori know their iwi; a situation that parallels Americans of American Indian descent who do not know their tribal affiliations.

²LOCATION AND HOMELAND

The islands of New Zealand are the present-day homeland of the Maori. New Zealand consists of two islands, the North Island and the South Island. The topography of the North Island is hilly with areas of flat, rolling terrain. The South Island is larger and more mountainous than the North Island. The vast majority (86%) of present-day Maori live on the North Island. Prior to human habitation of the islands, there were extensive forests. These forests provided a resource for the ancestors of the Maori that ventured there from parts of present-day French Polynesia.

Maori oral history states that the original homeland of the traditional Maori was in the Society Islands of Polynesia, and that the Maori migrants left to escape warfare and the demands of excessive tribute. Archaeologists refer to two branches of Maori, the archaic and the traditional. The archaic Maori were likely the original inhabitants of New Zealand who relied on the moa, a large, flightless bird that they hunted into extinction. The artifacts that remain of this culture can be dated to around AD 1000 and are significantly different from those of the traditional Maori. The traditional Maori are believed to have migrated to the North Island around the 14th century. This is confirmed by archaeological dating techniques as well as the genealogical histories of the Maori.

In 1840, some 500 Maori chiefs signed the so-called Treaty of Waitangi with the British government. The treaty promised the Maoris that they would keep their lands and property and have equal treatment under the law as British subjects. However, the British later confiscated Maori lands and made the people move to reservations. As a result of war and disease, the Maori population fell to 42,000 by 1896. Since World War II, the government's policies have been more favorable to the Maoris. In recent years, the government of New Zealand has acknowledged its responsibility after a series of protests and court rulings. Since 1991, negotiations over specific claims have been underway. In October 1996, the government agreed to a settlement with the Maoris that included land and cash worth $117 million, with the Maoris regaining some traditional fishing rights.

³LANGUAGE

Maori belongs to the Tahitic branch of Eastern Polynesian; Eastern Polynesian is, in turn, a branch of the larger Austronesian language family. Maori and Tahitian are very closely related, and earlier European explorers to the region commented on the similarity of the two languages. In fact, these were the first two Polynesian languages to have printed books in the early 19th century.

The Maori of today speak English and Maori. Prior to European colonization of New Zealand, there were two distinct Maori dialects: North Island Maori and South Island Maori, which is now extinct. Preschools that offer instruction in Maori language have sprung up all over the country at a rapid rate

A Maori warrior with moko (facial tattoo) waits for the coffin of Maori Queen Te Arikinui Dame Te Atairangikaahu near the sacred Taupiri Mountain near Hamilton, New Zealand. Thousands gathered along the funeral route to bid farewell to the queen. (AP Images/ NZPA, Wayne Drought)

as a result of Maori activism. In 2006, nearly 25% of the Maori population indicated that they could hold a conversation in Maori.

⁴FOLKLORE

Traditional Maori folklore describes an original couple, Rangi (sky) and Papa (earth), who were locked in copulation until the god Tane was able to push them apart and provide for the creation of human life. The god Tane was responsible for the creation of the first woman and the first man. Maori folklore focuses on oppositions between pairs, such as earth and sky, life and death, and male and female.

⁵RELIGION

Like other New Zealanders, many Maori today are Christians (primarily Anglicans, Presbyterians, and Roman Catholics). Precontact Maori religion was based on the important concepts of *mana* and *tapu*. Mana is an impersonal force that can be both inherited and acquired by individuals in the course of their lives. Tapu refers to a sacredness that was ascribed by status at birth. There was a direct relation between the two: chiefs with the most mana were also the most tapu. The English word "taboo" derives from this general Polynesian word and concept. Ancestor worship was important in traditional religion.

⁶MAJOR HOLIDAYS

Christian Maori celebrate the major Christian holidays as do other New Zealanders. Holidays as Westerners view them did not exist in precontact Maori society. Rituals were performed according to the religious calendar and the harvest and collection of foodstuffs.

A controversial New Zealand national holiday for the Maori is Waitangi Day (6 February), which commemorates the 1840 signing of the treaty that was supposed to guarantee their rights and privileges. In 1994, Maori radicals disrupted the Waitangi Day national celebration, forcing the government to cancel the festivities.

⁷RITES OF PASSAGE

Modern Maori rites of passage are similar to those of other New Zealanders, but specific Maori traditions are still practiced at certain events. At weddings, for example, a relative of the groom traditionally challenges the father of the bride to a fight. The bride's father then approaches the challenger and is welcomed.

The Maori once practiced what anthropologists call "secondary burial." Secondary burial involves two interments of a corpse or its remains. When a person died, the body would be laid out on ceremonial mats for viewing by relatives and other members of the village. After a few days, the body was then wrapped in mats and placed in a cave, a tree, or buried in the ground. Different Maori groups had different practices. After one year had passed, the body was removed from the primary burial and the bones were cleaned and painted with red ochre. These remains were taken from village to village for a second period of mourning. Following that, the bones were interred in a sacred place.

8 INTERPERSONAL RELATIONS

Maoris today, like other New Zealanders, typically address each other informally and emphasize cordiality in relationships.

Feasting, called *hakari* in the Maori language, was an important aspect of precontact Maori culture. The Maori feasts brought together a number of different families and other social groups where a man of status would provide food and gifts for those who attended. In the end, he and his family would be left with very little in the way of material possessions or reserves of food, but instead would have gained enormous enhancement to his status.

Premarital sexual relationships were considered normal for Maori adolescents. Both males and females were expected to have a series of discreet relationships before they were married. When Maori females became sexually active, they were to publicly acknowledge this so that they could become tattooed. Tattooing marked their ritual and public passage into adulthood. It was also considered extremely attractive and erotic.

9 LIVING CONDITIONS

Today, 80% of the Maori live in the urban areas of New Zealand. However, until the 1920s, they lived almost primarily in rural areas. Maori housing today therefore typically reflects that of other urban New Zealanders [*see* **New Zealanders**].

In coastal areas, Maoris traditionally relied on travel by canoes of various types, including both single-hulled outriggerless canoes as well as large double-hulled canoes. *Waka taua* were large Maori war canoes that were powered by both sail and paddles. As with other New Zealanders, travel today is by modern road, rail, water, and air transport.

10 FAMILY LIFE

Since most Maoris live in urban industrialized areas, family life is similar to that of other urban New Zealanders. Intermarriage between Maoris and Pakehas (the Maori term for whites) is common. Most Maoris have Pakeha cousins or other Pakeha relatives. Maori households may include relatives besides the nuclear family, such as grandparents, uncles, and aunts.

The traditional social unit of Maori society was the *whanau*. The whanau included both the nuclear and the extended family, oftentimes including up to four generations within on large social unit. Within the whanau, the grandparents were primarily responsible for the cultural socialization of their grandchildren. A special relationship holds between grandparents and grandchildren that is called *mokopuna* in Maori. The concept of mokopuna is that when a grandparent looks at a grandchild, the grandparent sees his/her reflection. Mokopuna is a powerful concept that guides the care and upbringing of grandchildren by their grandparents.

There were four distinct levels of descent groups in traditional Maori culture. The highest ranking was called *waka*,

meaning "canoe," referring to a group of people who share descendants on both their mother's and father's sides who came on the same canoe in the historical migration to New Zealand recounted in Maori oral history. The lowest level was the *whanau*, which were households that represented as many as four generations of people related through the male line. Individuals chose their spouses from outside this group, but usually from within the village.

The system of naming members of the immediate and extended family in Maori culture differs from that found in American culture. In the Maori system, a person's brothers, as well as the cousins on both the mother's and father's side, would be called by the same term "brother." A person would call his or her sister, as well as his or her cousins, by the same term "sister." This lumping of relatives together within a generation continues across the generational divisions. Therefore, a Maori child would have as many mothers as his biological parents had sisters.

11 CLOTHING

Maoris typically wear modern Western-style clothing, but still wear their traditional clothing for special occasions. Traditional Maori clothing was some of the most elaborate in Polynesia. Elaborately decorated cloaks were an important item of dress for individuals of high status within Maori society.

12 FOOD

Maoris typically eat the same kinds of foods as other New Zealanders [*see* **New Zealanders**]. The traditional Polynesian foodstuffs of taro, yams, and breadfruit were not well adapted for cultivation on the temperate islands of New Zealand.

13 EDUCATION

Public education has now become the norm for most urban Maori, although a number of preschools based on Maori cultural education have been established throughout New Zealand. Education is state-supported and compulsory in New Zealand between the ages of 6 and 15. Students planning to attend one of the country's six universities continue their secondary education until the age of 17 or 18, when they have to take university qualifying exams.

14 CULTURAL HERITAGE

The *haka* dance of the Maori is one of the best-known cultural traditions of Polynesia. These dances are accompanied by song and body percussion created by clapping hands, stamping feet, and slapping thighs. There is a leader and a chorus that responds to his lead vocal line. The dance itself involves energetic postures, which represent warlike and aggressive poses.

Maori chanting follows very strict rules for performance and rhythmic structure and continuity. To break a chant in midstream would be to invite disaster or even death for a community. These chants often recounted genealogies or the exploits of ancestors.

15 WORK

Maoris today work at the same types of jobs and professions typical to any urbanized industrial economy, with about two-thirds engaged in services.

Traditional Maori culture developed a high degree of specialization in terms of the division of labor in society. Craftsmen in the form of tattoo artists, canoe builders, house builders, and carvers, were all classified as *tohunga* in Maori—a title that conveys the qualities of sacredness and translates best into English as "priest." These craftsmen paid homage to the gods of their various occupations and were initiated through a series of rituals into their craft. All craftsmen were descended from chiefly lines in traditional Maori society.

[16]SPORTS

New Zealand, like its neighbor Australia, has rugby and cricket as national sports. Maori boys and men participate in and follow rugby in New Zealand. New Zealand Maori is the name of a rugby league team that traditionally plays teams touring New Zealand. The prerequisite for being a member of this team is that the player has to be of at least 1/16th Maori descent. New Zealand Maori competes in international competitions and it has participated in the Rugby League World Cup. There were traditional competitions among men in Maori society that stressed aggressiveness and provided practice for real-life conflicts.

[17]ENTERTAINMENT AND RECREATION

The modern Maori have become not only consumers of video, television, and film, but also producers of their own stories in these media. Traditional storytelling and dance performance have been preserved by the Maori and serve as form of entertainment at the present.

[18]FOLK ART, CRAFTS, AND HOBBIES

The New Zealand Maori are accomplished artists in a number of media. Collectors and the general public are most familiar with Maori carving and sculpture. However, the Maori also have a tradition of figurative painting dating back to the late 19th century. Each Maori sub-tribe is an art-producing and art-owning unit. Therefore, while there are certain similarities in style in Maori art, there are also a number of differences between the styles of different sub-tribes.

Large meeting houses of the Maori were decorated with elaborately carved facades containing figures of their ancestors. The entire structure was conceived as representation of an ancestor.

[19]SOCIAL PROBLEMS

The vast majority of all contemporary Maori are urban dwellers. The social problems that accompany urban life in conditions of poverty continue to beset the Maori. In some urban areas, Maori unemployment rates exceed 50%. The critically acclaimed film *Once Were Warriors* (1994) provides a Maori perspective on the social problems of alcoholism, domestic violence, and underemployment/unemployment.

[20]GENDER ISSUES

Tattooing among the Maori was highly developed and extremely symbolic. Male facial tattooing, called *ta moko,* was done in stages in a male's life through adulthood. Maori facial tattoos were not only created by piercing and pigmenting the skin with a tattooing comb, but also by creating permanent grooves in the face with a chisel-like instrument. Females were also tattooed in Maori society and there has been an increasing revival of the art among younger women nowadays. Female facial tattooing was known as *ta ngutu.* Designs were placed on the chin and lips. *Ngutu* means "lips" in Maori and *ta* means "to strike."

A controversial gender topic in modern Maori society is that of role of homosexuality in precontact times. *Takatapui* is a Maori word that is defined in the earliest dictionary of the Maori language as "an intimate companion of the same sex" (Williams 1834). The word had fallen into disuse following colonization and the impact of Christian missionaries, but in recent times, takatapui has become part of the vocabulary of the Lesbian Gay Bisexual Transgender (LGBT) community in New Zealand. The controversy revolves around whether or not homosexuality was part of precontact Maori gender relations. The most current and comprehensive accounts clearly demonstrate the important roles of takatapui in precontact Maori society, and their incorporation into iki and whanau.

[21]BIBLIOGRAPHY

Bangs, Richard. *Quest for Kaitiakitanga: The Ancient Maori Secret from New Zealand that Could Save the Earth.* Birmingham, AL: Menasha Ridge Press, 2008.

Best, E. *The Maori.* Wellington, New Zealand: The Polynesian Society, 1924.

Bishop, Russell. *Maori Art and Culture.* London: British Museum Press, 1996.

Gell, A. *Wrapping in Images: Tattooing in Polynesia.* Oxford: Clarendon Press, 1993.

Hazlehurst, Kayleen M. *Political Expression and Ethnicity: Statecraft and Mobilisation in the Maori World.* Westport, Conn.: Praeger, 1993.

Tregear, Edward. *The Aryan Maori.* Papakura, N.Z.: R. McMillan, 1984.

Williams, William. *A Dictionary of the Maori Language.* Paihia: Mission Press,1834.

—by J. Williams

MARANAO

PRONUNCIATION: mah-ruh-NOW
ALTERNATE NAMES: Meranao or M'ranao
LOCATION: Philippines (island of Mindanao)
POPULATION: 1.1 million
LANGUAGE: Maranao
RELIGION: Islam
RELATED ARTICLES: Vol. 3: Filipinos

¹INTRODUCTION

The Muslim Maranao, the largest non-Christian ethnic group in the Philippines, have lived around Lake Lanao in western Mindanao since at least the 13th century, having separated from kindred coastal people at that time. Some Maranao maintained relations with these Ilanun, joining them in slave-raiding in the Philippine and Indonesian archipelagos. Legends, however, locate Maranao origins in Bembaran, a kingdom that sunk to the bottom of the sea because it rejected Islam. Sarip Kabongsoan of Johore (in Malaya) converted the neighboring Magindanao; his descendants went to the Lanao region and intermarried with descendants of refugees from Bembaran.

In contrast to the Magindanao and Tausugs, the Maranao never established a single state but rather divided into a great number of small "sultanates" in continual warfare with each other. They, however, successfully resisted incorporation into the Spanish colonial state, and only the Americans early in the 20th century managed to subdue them. The influx of Christian Filipino settlers, particularly from the nearby Visayas, has threatened to marginalize the Maranao in much of their ancestral land. The region has been one of the hotbeds of the Muslim (Bangsa Moro) separatist movement since the 1970s. A major episode of that struggle was the 1972 MNLF attack on the Maranao city of Marawi (Dansalan before 1956). Under the Marcos' martial law regime, many traditional activities virtually ceased due to curfews strictly enforced by a government army suspicious of all Maranao gatherings. The influence of the many Maranao educated in the Middle East in recent decades has constituted an even greater challenge to Maranao customs, which often do not conform to standard Islamic practice.

The separatist movement notwithstanding, prominent Maranao participate in Philippine national politics, and, under the Aquino administration, an Autonomous Region in Muslim Mindanao including Lanao del Sur province (but not now Christian-majority Lanao del Norte province) was established in 1989. Maranao culture (like Moro and non-Christian cultures more generally) have contributed key icons to the national identity of the predominantly Christian and Hispanized Philippines: the Maranao epic, the Darangen, was put on the UNESCO list of Masterpieces of the Oral and Intangible Heritage of Humanity in 2005, and the artisan village of Tugaya was nominated as a UNESCO World Heritage Site in 2006.

²LOCATION AND HOMELAND

Maranao (in their own pronunciation, *Meranao* or *M'ranao*) means "people of the lake," referring to Lake Lanao, which lies 670 m (2,200 ft) above sea level in western Mindanao. Numbering 776,000 in 1990 and as many as 1.1 million currently

(2008), the Maranao, the largest non-Christian ethnic group in the Philippines, inhabit the lands around the lake, dominating the province of Lanao del Sur (609,000 or 91% of the population in 2000) stretching to its south. However, Visayan immigrants now outnumber Maranao in Lanao del Norte province (169,000 or 35.8% of the population). About 61.8% of the Visayan immigrants are of people speaking closely related Visayan dialects, such as Cebuanos, Binisaya, and Boholanos. The Maranao in turn are moving into the highlands to the south of the lake, which are already inhabited by other peoples. 21.9% of households in the Autonomous Region in Muslim Mindanao (to which Lanao del Sur belongs, but not Lanao del Norte) identified Maranao as their first-language. Small Maranao communities can be found in towns throughout Mindanao and the Sulu Archipelago. In recent years, many Maranao have settled in Manila (as many as 35,000 by 1984).

³LANGUAGE

The Maranao language is an Austronesian language whose closest similarities are to other indigenous languages of Mindanao (though not to the Visayan-type language of their fellow Muslim Tausugs). In the past, a version of the Arabic script was used to preserve genealogies *(salsila)*, religious literature, and Islamic tales.

Most names derive from Arabic, but native Maranao words referring to desired traits or lucky objects (e.g., Macacuna, "robust," or Bolawan, "gold") are also chosen (now usually as an addition to an Islamic name). Some Maranao have even named their children after prominent Filipino national leaders (e.g., Marcos). Young people often take American nicknames, e.g., "Mike" for Ismail or Macacuna. Among themselves, Maranao do not use surnames, but in dealing with Philippine educational or bureaucratic systems, individuals use the name of a father, grandfather, brother, or prominent ancestor as a second name. In one community, a person may register under one relative's name as a surname; in another, he or she may register under another. This allows Maranao to vote in different jurisdictions, something they understand not as electoral fraud but as a right of descent.

⁴FOLKLORE

According to legend, Radia Indarapatra married the water nymph Potri Rainalaut and sired two children: one became the ancestor of the Maranao and the other the ancestor of the *tonong*, invisible beings that protect the Maranao from illness and their crops from pests. Traditional Maranao place offerings of food and betel nuts for the tonong in the *lamin*, a 1-m (3-ft-long) long box wrapped in yellow cloth and hung from a house beam. The tonong have names (e.g., Tomitay sa Boloto, Apo a Bekong) and inhabit bodies of water, mountains, and especially the *nonok* (a tree that wraps around other trees like a vine). Maranao who have been educated or influenced by Middle Eastern Islamic universities equate appeasing the tonong as honoring the offspring of the Devil.

Other spirits include: *saytan*, evil spirits; the *inikadowa*, a person's invisible double; the *malaikat*, an angel who guides a person in his or her work; *arowak*, the souls of the dead who visit their kin on Muslim holidays; *gagamoten*, a human poisoner; *langgam*, a ghoul who eats the insides of fresh corpses; and the *balbal*, one type of which at night splits into a lower

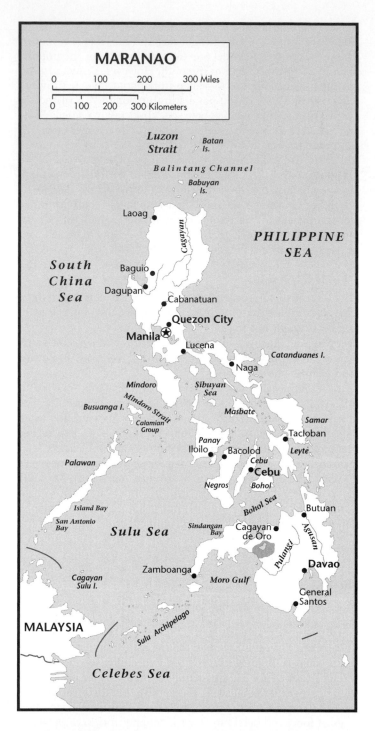

MARANAO

0   100   200   300 Miles

0   100   200   300 Kilometers

Luzon
Strait   *Batan*
              Is.

Balintang Channel

                    Babuyan
                    Is.

Laoag •   **PHILIPPINE**
                              SEA

South   Baguio •
China
Sea   Dagupan •
                • Cabanatuan

                Quezon City

           Manila ☆
                • Lucena
                                  Catanduanes I.
                      • Naga

           Mindoro   *Sibuyan*
                         Sea
Busuanga I.
        Mindoro Strait   *Masbate*
           Calamian
           Group   *Samar*
                     Panay   • Tacloban
                  Iloilo • Bacolod •   *Leyte*
                              Cebu
Palawan   • **Cebu**

                  Negros   *Bohol*

                        Bohol Sea
                              • Butuan
        Island Bay
San Antonio   *Sindangan*
Bay   *Bay* Cagayan
                             de Oro •   *Agusan*
           Sulu Sea   *Pulangi*
                                        Davao
        Cagayan   Zamboanga •
        Sulu I.   *Moro Gulf*
                                        General
                                        Santos
MALAYSIA
              Sulu Archipelago

    Celebes Sea

half that stays in the house and an upper half that flies off. Tales abound of people being led off by spirits, never to return.

⁵RELIGION

The Maranao are Muslim. In recent years, Maranao who have studied in Islamic universities in the Middle East have worked towards the elimination of traditional spirit beliefs and associated rituals. In addition to the religious merit, much social prestige comes from sponsoring the construction of religious buildings, such that every community now has a mosque and *madrasah* (Islamic school). Moreover, large numbers of Maranao make the pilgrimage to Mecca.

In addition to Muslim religious officials, such as the *imam* (prayer leader) and *kali* (judge), there are *pandarpa'an*, usually old women, through whose possessed bodies spirits speak and *pamamantik*, practitioners of magic and counter magic.

⁶MAJOR HOLIDAYS

On certain Islamic holidays, the souls of the dead visit their kin; the latter offer the souls food, which is later distributed to neighbors or given to the *tuan*, who recite prayers for the dead. At the end of the fasting month of Ramadan, people clean their family graves and at night light them with candles. They also light candles or lamps in their houses so that they might catch a glimpse of the Lailatol Kadr, an angel with a turban and a long white beard who has the power to grant wishes (some enter trances in order to see him). This is the "night of power" when God will answer any prayer.

⁷RITES OF PASSAGE

After birth, the umbilical cord is kept to ward off evil spirits. The placenta is buried near the house, as a guardian for the child, or cast into a body of water, where it can save the child from drowning. On the third or seventh day after birth, the child receives his or her name. After this, a boy can be circumcised, although he may be as old as 10 years of age when this takes place; clitoridectomy for girls persists as well.

Many marriages are still arranged by the parents; even if partners select each other, family approval is necessary. The man's side sends an intermediary to initiate the negotiations. If the woman's side's response is positive, the go-between, the man's parents, and the man visit the woman's family. The parents express the proposal in indirect language, and the go-between mentions the *betang* (bride-price) that the man's side is willing to pay. The woman's side defers the decision (perhaps for months) but claims a cash fee for opening the discussion. Subsequently, the man's parents gather the money or convene a meeting where other kin will contribute to the betang. On their part, the woman's relatives (who have a right to a portion of the betang) gather to decide the amount to be asked, considering also what advantages an alliance could provide their kingroup. They also investigate the man's genealogy; finding an ancestor who was a slave, a *balbal* or *gagamoten* (evil spirits), or a non-Maranao could cancel the wedding. The go-between carries on the bargaining on the betang and the setting of the wedding date.

During the engagement period, the man's relatives may give food to the woman's family, which the latter will share with fellow villagers and, if possible, with neighboring villages. The man may now eat with the woman in her house (though someone else will always be somewhere in the house); he may also sleep there (but not with her), using for a blanket a *malong* (a type of sarong), which his prospective in-laws give him. The future bride now must ask her fiancé for permission to go out of the house; he must accompany her and cover her expenses.

Some families hold the wedding ceremony in hotels or rented halls (the richest even use hotels in Manila and invite national figures); most build a stage by their house and decorate it with lots of flags. The groom and his kin may travel to the bride's house in a motorcade filmed on a video camera. The groom wears a malong and a shirt (possibly a *barong tagalog* [see **Filipinos**]) or a Western coat and tie (or, following a new fashion, he may adopt Arab or Pakistani clothing). The bride dresses traditionally or puts on a Western wedding gown. She is not present at the wedding ceremony itself, which does include the groom, the *imam* (prayer leader), and four witnesses, one for each grandparent's lineage. After this, the groom goes to the bride's room and, after paying a fee to the attendant girls, he touches her for the first time. During the ensuing feast, more cash is given out to guests who do not share in the *betang*.

Following Islamic regulations, a dead body cannot stay overnight in the house and is buried as soon as possible. Close kin wash and enshroud the body while other relatives arrive to give monetary aid; the immediate family serves food to the relatives. In the gravepit, the imam asks the deceased the questions that an angel will ask him or her later; this is an unorthodox custom, as is the planting of flowers, laying of stones, or laying of cement to mark the grave. The imam reads a prayer and pours water on the four corners and center of the now-sealed grave to "awaken" the deceased. Relatives may guard the grave so that balbal or *langgam* (corpse-eating ghouls) will not defile the body.

The dead soul lingers on earth for 100 days. Mourning rituals last for three (formerly seven) days; these include having *tuan* (the community's religious men) recite prayers for the dead and receiving guests in the evening, who entertain themselves with eating, playing parlor games, or sometimes gambling with cards. Tuan offer prayers on every Friday or every 10 days until the 100th day after the death, when a large feast is held where several tuan recite prayers.

⁸INTERPERSONAL RELATIONS

A Maranao's sense of *maratabat* requires that he avenge wrongs done to him, his kin, and his friends. In the past, this led to public combat in spots marked by a red flag, but now ambush is the common method. Maranao will risk their own lives in defense of a sworn friend (quasi-kindred): "Your blood will be on top of mine," i.e. I will die before I let someone lay a hand on you.

Public image is important: a person who spends little on personal comforts will lavish extravagant sums on a family rite-of-passage celebration or the community *madrasah* building fund. Maranao use euphemistic language or grant concessions in order to avoid embarrassing or humiliating others. Maranao tend to flatter people by addressing them with the highest title associated with their profession (e.g., one might call a schoolteacher "professor").

Each hamlet has two or more descent lines (*bangsa*), one of which claims superior status to the others and is led by a title-holder (often "Sultan"; there are as many as 43 "royal houses"). Hamlets are grouped into ever-larger associations, which culminate in one of the *pat a pangampong a ranao* ("the four encampments of the lake") into which the Maranao people are divided.

Although titles are inherited by descent lines, only the most qualified member can hold the title (by virtue of wealth, knowledge of customary law, and the ability to settle disputes without shaming any parties). Today, individuals win titles by surpassing others in contributing to mosque and madrasah building funds. A title-holder must also be prepared to hold a *kandori* where food is served and cash is distributed. The formal receipt of a title is an occasion of great ceremony preceded by *kalilang* (traditional music), *kambayoka* (singing contests),

kasipa (kickball), other games, and the slaughter of cattle or water buffalo for feasting.

Boys and girls are strictly segregated, even in school activities. In the evening, a boy visits a girl he likes at her house, but directly courts her kin rather than her. It is older relatives who entertain the boy; both sides display their skill in delivering short love poems in classical Maranao (*pununuruon* or *tobadtobad*), though today the former may simply tell stories. The boy, the girl, and often the girl's relatives may play music together. A boy can also send the girl a poetic love letter, which she shows her parents for their advice. It is also common for them to exchange notes secretly at school.

⁹LIVING CONDITIONS

Houses are made of wood, raised 0.3 m to 2 m (1–7 ft) from the ground and have steep roofs of galvanized iron. From 2 to 20 families reside in a house; each has its own sleeping area, though there are no partitions. Traditional structures included a separate room for unmarried women. A kitchen shed contains a large hearth.

A descent line has a *torogan,* a large house where the senior kin-group lives and gatherings are held. Having names such as Bantog (Honorable), Kompas (Guide), Lumba (Center), or even Malacañang (after the presidential palace in Manila), the torogan boasts intricate prow-like carvings on the external beams. However, most traditional torogan were destroyed in a 1955 earthquake.

Hamlets include 3 to 30 multifamily homes strung out along a road or river, along with a mosque and at least one torogan. Until the American conquest, each hamlet contained a fortress of earthen walls reinforced by thorny plants and trees.

Average family income in the Autonomous Region in Muslim Mindanao, of which Lanao del Sur province is a part, amounted to 89,000 pesos (us$1,745) in 2006, the lowest in the country, cf. the national average of ₱173,000, the National Capital Region's ₱311,000, Southern Tagalog's ₱198,000, and those of the neighboring Davao and Zamboanga regions, ₱135,000 and ₱125,000 respectively. In 2000, Lanao del Sur had the fifth lowest Human Development Index, 0.464 (combining measures of health, education, and income) in the country (above Ifugao and the provinces in the Sulu archipelago, cf. the Philippines' national HDI of 0.656); Lanao del Norte was ninth lowest (at 0.512).

According to the 2000 census, the proportion of houses in Lanao del Sur with a roof of galvanized iron/aluminum reached 81.1%, with a roof of grass or palm thatch 5.8%; 54.9% of houses had outer wooden walls, and another 11.9% outer walls of bamboo or thatch. In 2000, 11.7% of households in Lanao del Sur had access to a community faucet, 12.7% to a faucet of their own, and 4.8% to a shared deep well, while 53.3% obtained their water from springs, lakes, rivers, or rain. Almost half of households (47%) disposed of their garbage by burning it, 11.9% by composting it, and 10.5% by burying it; only 2.3% had it picked up by a collection truck. 42% of houses were lit with kerosene lamps, 49% with electricity, and 5.9% with firewood. 72.8% possessed a radio, 31% a television, 12.7% a refrigerator, 8.3% a VCR, 7.5% a telephone or cell phone, 4.9% a washing machine, and 5.1% a motorized vehicle.

[10]FAMILY LIFE

An individual's kin-group comprises paternal and maternal relatives up to and including third cousins, although the most important relationships do not go beyond the circle of first cousins. For kinship solidarity, marriage is preferred with second and third cousins (but taboo with first cousins). A person can also claim as many as 15 descent lines for the purpose of inheriting titles.

Until the bride-price is paid in full, the groom lives with the bride's family, only later establishing his own house. Within the multifamily dwellings, a single family eats together and has its own sleeping area. At least one married child remains in the house to take care of the parents.

Because fathers are the disciplinarians, children tend to be closer to their mothers. Close relatives may also correct or punish a child. Parents will not physically punish an older child in public. Children learn skills by assisting their parents in work.

Though permitted under Muslim law, taking more than one wife is not common because it would shame the first wife's family. Physical abuse by a husband or an insult from him in public are grounds for divorce. If a husband cannot tolerate his wife's actions, he is supposed to appeal to her relatives or to community leaders. Because families mediate conflicts, and custom stipulates a "cooling off" period before the finalization of divorce, which requires return of the bride-price if the wife has no sufficient grievance, divorce is rare.

[11]CLOTHING

In towns, many Maranao wear nontraditional clothing, not just Western clothing but also the Filipino *barong tagalog* [see **Filipinos**], Malay fashions, and most recently Arab and Pakistani garb. The *malong,* a sarong whose edges are often connected by a *langkit,* a second piece of cloth of contrasting design, is the main article of traditional clothing for both sexes. Ceremonial apparel for a *datu* (male title-holder) consists of an embroidered coat and long, tight-fitting pants; a tobao, a matching silk cloth; and a dagger tucked into a 12-cm wide (5-in-wide) waist sash. A *bai* (female title-holder) wears a long-sleeved blouse (often embroidered); a malong of locally woven silk; a necklace of gold coins; and a *kobong* veil (formerly, a crown and a special coiffure). Colors range from yellow for sultans to red or maroon for other titles. An attendant holds a large umbrella over the title-holder, while others carry a *kris* (sword) and a brass basin, symbols of authority and wealth, respectively.

[12]FOOD

With rice as the staple, Maranao food resembles that of other Filipinos, particularly Muslim groups [see **Filipinos**].

[13]EDUCATION

A *madrasah,* a school stressing the reading of the Quran, stands in every community, built with community funds, sometimes with additional money from Arab countries. Suspicious of English-language schools as institutions for Christianization, Maranao initially avoided them. Nowadays, however, parents send their children to such schools, often making great sacrifices to do so. Formal education used to be so rare that families celebrated graduations very lavishly. Considerations of family prestige exert high pressure on individuals to obtain degrees. Degree-holders are so numerous that many cannot obtain appropriate employment. Many Maranao have obtained degrees in Middle Eastern Islamic universities, which qualifies them to teach in madrasah.

According to the 2000 census, the literacy level in the Autonomous Region in Muslim Mindanao was 68.9%, very low by national standards. In Lanao del Sur, nearly one in three (32.8%) had completed elementary school, over one in five (21.5%) high school, and nearly one in eight (11.8%) college or university, though the percentage for elementary was somewhat lower, those for secondary and tertiary education were dramatically higher than in fellow ARMM province, Sulu). *See Tausug*

[14]CULTURAL HERITAGE

Musical instruments include the *kulintang* (a horizontal series of eight knobbed gongs played with two sticks), a *dabakan* (a wooden drum also played with two sticks), various hanging gongs (*agong, pamulsan,* and *babandir*), the *insi* (a bamboo flute), *kobing* (jew's-harp), and *kotyapi* (a two-stringed instrument with a soundbox in the shape of an abstract crocodile). In the *kalilang* ensemble, females play the kulintang with its subtle melodies while men strike the hanging gongs. Formerly, all girls and boys learned to play so they would be proficient by the time they were of marriageable age. Girls could display their expertise to boys; a boy would accompany a girl he was courting, considering it a shame if rivals outdid him in skill.

Among Maranao dances, the *singkil* is the most famous, mastering it having once been a requirement for aristocratic girls. Two pairs of bamboo poles are crossed; the dancer, maintaining a grave expression and waving a fan, steps in and out of the poles as they are rapidly clapped together. Another well-known dance is the *sagayan,* a male war dance.

Kambayoka are all-night contests in oratorical singing held as part of the celebrations of high-status people. The Maranao also have an epic, the *Darangen.*

[15]WORK

Mostly relying on rainfall for irrigation, wet-rice is grown in the lowlands. Other crops are maize and sweet potatoes on marginal lands; taro, squash, cassava, peanuts, and chilies in gardens; and betel nut, papayas, and bananas on trees. Livestock include water buffalo, goats, chickens, and ducks. As lake stocks are now depleted, most fish is obtained from trade with the coast.

Maranao peddlers, particularly of brassware, frequent town markets throughout Mindanao and have long been the commercial link between pagan hill peoples and maritime traders.

Acquiring an aristocratic title or bureaucratic job that frees one from manual labor is greatly esteemed.

[16]SPORTS

See the article entitled **Filipinos**.

[17]ENTERTAINMENT AND RECREATION

See the article entitled **Filipinos**.

[18]FOLK ART, CRAFTS, AND HOBBIES

Of all non-Christian people of the Philippines, the Maranao are the most famous for their crafts. Male artisans produce *okir,* intricate carving for household objects, canoes, and the projecting beams (*panolong*) of *torogan* (senior kin-group) houses. Emphasizing plant and floral motifs in delicate scroll-work, there are numerous named designs, including the *nia-ganaga* (a stylized dragon) and *pako rabong* (representing a growing fern). The *sari-manok* is a stylized bird situated, among other places, on the top of banner poles. Contemporary artists incorporate "Bugis" (i.e., Bornean or Malay) designs and Arab forms, such as the *borak* (a flying horse with the head of a beautiful woman); they also produce lions, eagles, and peacocks for the tourist market. High-status families will commission famous artists to decorate their *torogan*.

Women weave cloth with complex geometric patterns (which have poetical names), often using *andon*, a tie-dying technique (*ikat*). They also produce mats and baskets.

Metalwork is another art, encompassing gold- and silver-smithing as well as the production of swords, such as the *son-dang* (a short dagger) and *kampilan* (a long-bladed sword), both of which are longer and larger than their Malay-Indonesian counterparts. Much artistry is lavished on the handles, which may be in the shape of a hornbill beak or a swallow tail.

[19] SOCIAL PROBLEMS

See the article entitled **Filipinos**.

[20] GENDER ISSUES

In 2000, in Sulu the ratio between men and women was 94.27 men for every 100 women, though women were more numerous in the age group from birth to 35 years (which may be partly the result of male insurgent casualties). Literacy levels in the Autonomous Region in Muslim Mindanao, low by national standards, were somewhat higher for men (69.8%) than for women (67.7%). In Lanao del Sur, however, more of those completing all levels of education were women than men. In contrast to other parts of the country, such as Southern Tagalog, more overseas workers from the ARMM were female (56%) than male; the median age of those female overseas workers was 24 years (there are hiring quotas for Muslim domestic workers employed in Saudi Arabia and other Muslim Middle Eastern States).

[21] BIBLIOGRAPHY

Disoma, Esmail R. *The Meranao: A Study of Their Practices and Beliefs*. Marawi City: Mindanao State University, 1990.

Gordon, Raymond G., Jr. (ed.). *Ethnologue: Languages of the World*, 15th ed.. Dallas: Texas: SIL International, 2005. http://www.ethnologue.com (November 21, 2008).

LeBar, Frank M., ed. *Ethnic Groups of Insular Southeast Asia*. Vol. 2, *Philippines and Formosa*. New Haven, CT: Human Relations Area Files Press, 1972.

National Statistics Office: Republic of the Philippines. "Autonomous Region in Muslim Mindanao: Nine Out of Ten Persons Were Muslims." http://www.census.gov.ph/data/pressrelease/2003/pr0301tx.html (November 21, 2008).

_____. "Lanao del Norte: Population Growth Rate Decreased to 1.53 Percent." http://www.census.gov.ph/data/pressrelease/2002/pr02162tx.html (November 21, 2008).

_____. "Lanao del Sur: 94 Males for Every 100 Females." http://www.census.gov.ph/data/pressrelease/2002/pr02156tx.html (November 21, 2008).

—revised by A. J. Abalahin

MARĀTHAS

PRONUNCIATION: muh-RAHT-uhz
ALTERNATE NAMES: Mahrattas; Mahrattis
LOCATION: India (Maharashtra state)
POPULATION: c. 70 million (estimate) (50% are of the population of Maharashtra belong to the Marātha and Kunbi castes)
LANGUAGE: Marāthi
RELIGION: Hinduism
RELATED ARTICLES: Vol. 3: People of India

[1] INTRODUCTION

The Marāthas (also Mahrattas, or Mahrattis) are a people of partly non-Aryan stock inhabiting the Deccan Plateau of western India. Outside the area, the term Marātha loosely identifies the entire regional population who speak the Marāthi language. Within the region, however, it specifically refers to the dominant landowning and cultivating castes, the Marāthas and the Kunbis. The precise distinction between these two groups is unclear, though some believe they are descended from the same stock. All Kunbis are Marāthas, but not all Marāthas are Kunbis. Marāthas typically have *ksatriya* status, that is, they trace their origins to the chieftains and warriors of ancient India and see themselves as superior to the Kunbis. The Kunbis are mainly cultivators and predominantly *sūdras* (the lowest of the four major caste groups) by caste, though some also claim ksatriya descent. There is some hypergamy (i.e. intermarriage between the two groups), but this tends to be one-way. Thus a Kunbi female, provided her dowry were large enough, might be married into an impoverished, aristocratic Marātha family, but Marāthas would never give a daughter in marriage to a family of the Kunbi castes.

The Marāthas first rose to prominence in the 17th century. One writer characterizes them as a hardy, capable, and rough-hewn people who lived in a poor country and had achieved little of note prior to that time. This was all changed by the meteoric rise of Shivaji (1627–80), who united the Marātha chieftains against the Muslim rulers of India. By the time of his death, Shivaji had carved out a Marātha kingdom in the Konkan (the coastal and western areas of Maharashtra State) and laid the grounds for further Marātha expansion. During the 18th century a powerful Marātha Confederacy arose. Led by the Peshwas and including the houses of Bonsla, Sindhia, Holkar, and Gaekwar, the Marāthas extended their territories as far as the Punjab in the north and Orissa in the east. Marātha power was greatly weakened by the shattering defeat inflicted on them by the Afghans at the Third Battle of Panipat in 1761. Nonetheless, marauding bands of Marātha horsemen, feared by Muslim and Hindu alike, continued to raid as far afield as the Punjab, Bengal, and southern areas of the Indian peninsula. A series of defeats by the British in the early years of the 19th century led to the final collapse of the Marātha Empire.

The sense of Marātha identity generated during the 17th and 18th centuries survives in modern times. After India's independence, Marāthas were active in promoting the formation of states based on language. Popular sentiment led to the creation of Maharashtra State in 1960 to include the bulk of the Marāthi-speaking peoples within its borders. A major platform of the Shiv Sena, a modern regional political party, is the ouster of non-Marāthas from the state.

2 LOCATION AND HOMELAND

The population of Maharashtra in 2001 was 96.9 million people, making it the second-largest state in the Indian Union in terms of population (it is third largest in area). Of this total population, perhaps 50% belong to the Marātha and Kunbi castes. Only 11 countries in the world (including India) have populations greater than Maharashtra's.

The Marātha homeland, i.e., Maharashtra, falls into three broad geographic divisions. The Konkan is the coastal lowland running from just north of Bombay (Mumbai) to Goa. Inland from this are the Western Ghāts, the line of hills that parallels the entire west coast of India. Generally between 760 m and 915 m (2,500–3,000 ft) in elevation in Maharashtra, they reach a height of 1,646 m (5,400 ft) inland from Bombay. These hills are actually a steep escarpment facing west, making access to the interior difficult. Many isolated peaks in the Ghāts are crowned by hill-forts that were strongholds of the Marāthas in their struggle with the Muslims. To the east of the Ghāts lie the plateaus and uplands of the Deccan lava region, at elevations varying between 300 m and 550 m (1,800–1,000 ft). This region is drained by the eastward-flowing Godaveri River and tributaries of the Krishna. In the extreme north is the Tapti River, which flows west to the Arabian Sea.

Average monthly temperatures at Bombay range from 24°C to 30°C (75°F – 86°F), with annual precipitation totaling 207.8 cm (82 in). The west-facing Ghāts receive the full force of the summer monsoon, and some hill areas receive as much as 660 cm (260 in) of rainfall. East of the Ghāts, however, there is a rain-shadow effect, and rainfall over much of the plateau region is in the range of 50–100 cm (20–40 in).

3 LANGUAGE

Marāthi, the language spoken by Marāthas, is a member of the Indo-Aryan branch of the Indo-European language family. It is derived from Maharashtri, a form of Prakit (or language spoken by the common people, as opposed to the classical Sanskrit). According to the 2001 Census of India, 62,481,681 people in Mahasrashhtra spoke Marāthi and its dialects, which include Konkani, Varadhi, and Nagpuri. The standard form of Marāthi is spoken in the Pune area. Marāthi is written in the Devanagari script or a cursive form of Devanagari called Modi.

4 FOLKLORE

The greatest folk hero of the Marāthas is Shivaji, who is seen as the champion of the Hindu peoples against the oppression of the Muslims. Developing guerrilla warfare to a fine art, Shivaji challenged the might of the Mughal Empire and founded the last of the great Hindu empires in India. Many incidents in his life have entered local lore. A Muslim general, feigning friendship, arranged a meeting with Shivaji in order to kill him. In an incident still remembered by both Hindus and Muslims, Shivaji embraced the general and killed him with steel claws attached to his hands before the Muslim could stab him with a concealed dagger. On another occasion, a prisoner of the Mughal emperor Aurangzeb, Shivaji escaped by being concealed in a fruit basket. Shivaji's men are reputed to have captured the hill-fort of Singadh (southwest of Pune) from the Muslims by

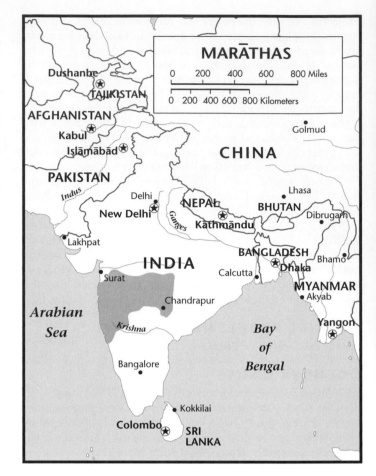

sending trained lizards up its perpendicular walls, carrying ropes for the attackers to climb.

5 RELIGION

The Marāthas and Kunbis are Hindu. Although most worship one or more gods as a "family deity," Shiva is of particular importance among the group. In villages, Shiva is worshiped in specific incarnations, e.g., as Khandoba, the guardian of the Deccan, or as Bhairav, the protector of the village. Khandoba has an important temple at Jejuri, not far from Pune. Shiva's consort Parvati is also revered by the Marāthas. She is worshiped in the form of Bhavani, Janni Devi, or one of the other local mother-goddesses found throughout the region. It is common for a goat or a cock to be sacrificed as an offering to these deities. Maruti is the monkey god, and no village in the Deccan is without a shrine to this kindly deity who provides protection from evil spirits. The Marāthas believe in witchcraft, the evil eye, and in ghosts and evil spirits, who can harm the living. Mashoba is the most widely feared of the evil spirits and when wronged can bring sickness and ill-fortune to the village. Some Marāthas worship Vishnu as well as Shiva. The temple of Vithoba at Pandharpur, for example, is an important Vishnu shrine and a major pilgrimage center. Though Brahmans officiate at most temples, some deities are served by non-Brahman priests. A Khandoba temple generally has a Marātha or Dhangar priest, while Lingayat or Gurav priests serve at shrines dedicated to Shankar (a form of Shiva).

⁶MAJOR HOLIDAYS

Although Marāthas observe all the major Hindu festivals, they also have their own regional celebrations. At Divali, for example, they sing hymns in praise of the Asura king Bali and worship cow-dung images of this demon-god. The birthday of Ganesha, the elephant-headed god of the Hindus, is a major event in Bombay. Specially made images of the god are worshiped for the three days of the festival (Ganesha Chaturthi) then carried to the seashore to be immersed in the ocean. Nag Panchami, when snakes are worshiped, is celebrated widely in Maharashtra. Bendur or Pola, a festival at which bulls are decorated, worshiped, and taken in procession through the villages, is popular in the interior of the state. The Marātha hero Shivaji's birthday (Shivaji Jayanti) has been declared a public holiday by the government of Maharashtra.

⁷RITES OF PASSAGE

Among the rituals of the Marāthas is the birth ceremony (jātakarma), held a few days after a child is born. Marāthas believe the fifth and sixth days after birth are particularly dangerous for the newborn child, who may be attacked by evil spirits during this time. Thus, "Mother's Fifth" and "Sixth" are extremely important and are accompanied by rituals to protect the infant. The period of ritual pollution after birth lasts for 10 days, after which a purification ceremony is performed. The first anniversary of the child's birth is celebrated by a feast, at which the hair-cutting ceremony (chaula karma) is often held. Marāthas who claim ksatriya (warrior) status will perform the sacred-thread ceremony for their sons between the ages of 10 and 12.

The death rites of the Marāthas closely follow those of the Brahmans. The corpse is bathed, wrapped in a white shroud, and placed on a bier. The funeral procession, sometimes led by musicians of the Mahar caste, makes its way to the burning ghāt (cremation ground), which is usually on the banks of a river or stream. In the days following the cremation, the ashes are gathered and taken to some holy place or river where they are thrown in the water. A purification ceremony is undergone by the relatives of the deceased on the eleventh day, and the funeral feast (srāddha) is held on the thirteenth day following the death.

⁸INTERPERSONAL RELATIONS

Marāthas use the "Namaste" greeting common among Hindus in India. This is accompanied by the gesture of joining of hands, palms together, in front of the body.

⁹LIVING CONDITIONS

There are regional variations in settlement patterns and house types between the coastal areas of Maharashtra and the upland plateaus. Plateau villages are tight clusters of houses, with no gardens or compounds. Smaller houses are simply a rectangular block of four walls forming a single room. Larger houses are made of several such blocks arranged so they make a hollow square, with a sun-court (chowk) in the middle. Rooms include living quarters, a kitchen, storerooms, and the devgarh, a room where images of the family gods are kept. Such village houses are in sharp contrast to the expensive luxury tower apartments that line the oceanfront along Bombay's Marine Drive.

¹⁰FAMILY LIFE

Although Marāthas claim to have gotras (clans), they are of little importance and appear to have been adopted from north India. The basic kin unit for Marāthas is the kul, literally "family," which is a lineage made up of extended families. Members of the kul worship a common totemic symbol called devak, a term that is also used as an alternative for kul. The devak symbol is a material object such as a bird, a tree, or an artifact. Examples of devak include the cobra, the elephant, and the blade of a sword. One cannot marry someone who worships the same devak. Other than kul exogamy, Marāthas have few of the marriage restrictions common among Hindus in northern India. They can marry within the village, cross-cousin marriage is allowed, and a man may have more than one wife. Marriages are arranged, and a bride price is paid to the girl's family. The actual marriage is elaborate, involving 24 separate ceremonies. The most important of these is the installation of the devak.

¹¹CLOTHING

Traditional clothing for Marātha men is the turban, a coat, a shoulder cloth, and a dhotī (Indian loincloth) or short trousers known as cholnās. The coat is distinctive, fitting tightly around the arms and chest. The sleeves are longer than the arms and form numerous small folds between the elbow and wrist. The coat is fastened by tying it in front, below the right shoulder. From the chest, the coat falls in loose folds to the knee. Formerly, a sword was a regular part of the Marātha dress. Women wear the bodice (cholī) and sārī. Peasant women, especially when working in the fields, often draw one end of the sārī through their legs and tuck it in at the back of the waist. Marātha women share the characteristic fondness of South Asian women for jewelry and ornaments.

¹²FOOD

The standard diet of the Marāthas consists of flat, unleavened bread (rotī), with pulses and vegetables. Among the poor, a typical meal consists of millet bread eaten with chopped chilies and lentils (dāl). Among the more-affluent, bread is made from wheat flour, while rice and a greater variety of vegetables are served at meals, along with condiments and ghī (clarified butter). Marāthas are nonvegetarian, eating fish, mutton, and chicken, although only the better-off eat meat on a regular basis. For the poor, meat is a festival food, to be eaten only on special occasions and religious holidays. There are no specific caste rules prohibiting the use of alcohol or narcotics.

¹³EDUCATION

According to the 2001 Census of India, literacy in the state of Maharashtra is 77.27%. As is to be expected in South Asia, significant differences in literacy rates exist between males and females (86.27% and 67.51% respectively) and between urban and rural populations. In Bombay, for example, literacy is over 86%, but only around 60% of women in rural areas are literate, although among some rural, female Kunbis, this figure drops below 40%. Bombay, with the University of Bombay, the Indian Institute of Technology (IIT), and the Tata Institute of Social Science, is one the country's major educational centers. Maharashtra State provides free, compulsory education for children between 6 and 14 years, with attendance at the primary level being above 90%. Maharashtra State has numerous universities and institutions of higher learning, though actual participation in this system is largely a matter of economics and the choice of the population.

¹⁴CULTURAL HERITAGE

Marāthi regional literature dates from around AD 1000. The devotional poetry and songs of Maharashtrian saints such as Namdev (1270–1350) and Ramdas (1608–81) are among its greatest achievements. The 18th century saw the rise of two other literary forms: the love lyric and the heroic ballad (powada), based on the exploits of Shivaji and other Marātha heroes. The 19th-century paintings of the Peshwa period were derived largely from the Rajasthani tradition. It should be remembered that these form part of a regional cultural tradition that the Marāthas did not develop themselves, but adopted from the traditions of others. The poet-saint Ramdev, for example, was of the Brahman caste. Marātha history in western India abounds with the military exploits of the great Marātha dynasties. But the overall Marātha record is more one of destruction than of construction.

¹⁵WORK

In the past, the chieftains, nobles, and landowners of Maharashtra were drawn from the ranks of the Marāthas. Some were soldiers, and the Marātha cavalry was renowned throughout the subcontinent during the 17th and 18th centuries. Many Marāthas continue this tradition of military service in the armed forces of modern India. The bulk of the Marāthas and Kunbis were cultivators and continue to be so today. Many of the village headmen (patels) in the central Deccan are of the Marātha caste. Maharashtra is one of the most heavily urbanized Indian states. Its cities include Bombay, one of the world's major urban centers (with a population of over 18 million people), Pune, and Nagpur in the eastern part of the state. This fact is reflected in the numbers of Marāthas who now live in cities and towns and follow urban occupations, e.g., commerce and government service, and professions such as teaching, medicine, and law.

¹⁶SPORTS

Marātha children play games that are common in Maharashtra and the rest of India. Young children enjoy role-playing, boys pretending to be horse-drivers, engine-drivers, etc., while girls play with dolls or at housekeeping. Organized games include various versions of tag, blind man's bluff, and hide-and-seek. Traditional Indian games such as Gullī dandā (Indian cricket) and Kabaddī (team wrestling) are popular. Cricket is perhaps the most important spectator sport, with other modern games such as field hockey, soccer, tennis, and badminton played in cities and towns. Popular indoor games include chess, cards, and carrom (a board game in which counters are used to knock one's opponent's counters into pockets).

¹⁷ENTERTAINMENT AND RECREATION

Many Marāthas depend on local festivals, fairs, and traditional folk entertainment for their recreation. The Nandivala, for example, is a traveling performer who entertains village audiences with sound effects, tricks, soothsaying, and trained-animal shows. The Bahrupi, literally "one with many disguises," is a professional entertainer known for humorous impersonations. Modern forms of entertainment such as radio, television, and

movies are readily available to those who can afford access to them. Bombay, India's equivalent of Hollywood, is one of the world's largest centers of movie-making and produces films in both Hindi and Marāthi. Bombay is also one of India's major intellectual and cultural centers, with museums, performances of modern and classical music, theater, and other cultural activities.

¹⁸FOLK ART, CRAFTS, AND HOBBIES

As landowners and cultivators, the Marātha and Kunbi castes arc not themselves involved in arts and crafts. Within Maharashtra State, however, traditional crafts include weaving and metalwork, as well as local specialties such as Kolhapuri leather sandals, and the Muslim himsa (weaving) and bidri (metal inlaid with silver) work of Aurangabad.

¹⁹SOCIAL PROBLEMS

The dominant landowning and cultivating caste in their region, the Marāthas and Kunbis are unified by a shared history and a common culture rooted in the Marāthi language. This sense of identity resulted in agitation for a linguistic state that led to the creation of Maharashtra as a Marāthi-speaking state. Though Marāthas essentially make up the bulk of the rural peasantry in the state, a Marātha elite has risen to positions of political power in Maharashtra. Marātha nationalism has led to anti-foreigner sentiments, with calls for non-Marāthas such as Gujaratis and Tamils to be expelled from the state. The recent renaming of Bombay as Mumbai, the Marāthi name for the city, is another expression of this sense of Marātha consciousness.

When Maharashtra State was created as what was primarily a linguistic state, there was an upwelling of pro-Maharashtrian, anti-foreigner sentiment fuelled largely by the Shiv Sena, a conservative, Hindu, regional political party with strong Marātha support, which was founded in 1966 by Bal Thackeray (a relative of the English writer William Makepeace Thackeray). Feeling against Gujaratis, of whom there were many in Bombay, and the Gujarati language were strong, and between 1956 and 1960, protests, sometimes accompanied by fatalities, occurred in favor or a Marāthi-speaking state. The Samyukta Maharashtra Samiti demanded unification of all Marāthi speaking regions in one state, and on 1 May 1960 the current Maharashtra state was formed from Marāthi-speaking areas of Bombay State, the Deccan states (the Deccan State Agency, an association of princely states, was an administrative unit of British India, which was incorporated into Bombay State at Independence in 1947) and Vidarbha (which was then part of Madhya Pradesh). There are various interpretations as to what the term "Maharashta" means. Some say it translates as Great (mahā) Country (rashtray), others that it probably derived from rathi meaning "a chariot driver," referring to drivers and builders of chariots who were called "Maharathis" or "fighting force," while still others say it means "Country of the Mahars," an untouchable caste found in the area.

The Shiv Sena gained in strength in Maharashtra in the last decades of the 20th century, and, although the state has traditionally been a stronghold of the Indian National Congress, even formed the State government from 1995–1999. With Bal Thackeray as one of its leaders, it continues to promote its policy of "Maharashtra for Maharashtrians." However, Maharashtra's government remains in the hands of the Indian National

Congress. Vilasrao Deshmukh serves as chief minister, even though the Bharatiya Janata Party (BJP), the Hindu nationalist party committed to Hindutva ("Hinduness"), won 54 out of 288 seats in the Maharashtra Vidhan Sabha (lower house) in the 2004 elections.

The Shiv Sena appears to be in a state of decline, even though it once proudly claimed to be the only genuine Hindutva party in India, and Bal Thackeray even asserted publicly that his boys struck first blow at Babri Masjid. The Shiv Sena came to power by trashing minorities and was responsible for the Bombay riots of 1992-93 that, like the Gujarat riots of 2002 in which numerous Muslims were killed, shook the conscience of the whole nation in the concept of India as a secular state. Bal Thackeray's hold on the Marāthi people, however, has been seriously weakened and his followers, in whom he took great pride, are deserting him. The Shiv Sena vote base is fast being eroded, and it may soon find itself on the margins of Maharashtra politics.

Despite their position as the dominant cultivator caste in Maharashtra, Kunbis are classified as Other Backward Castes (OBCs), whereas other groups such as the Marāthi Brahmins are not. Kunbis reap the benefits of this status and, being upwardly mobile, tend to dominate the other groups, like the Malis and Ahirs, which are accorded the same OBC status. In addition, Kunbis and Marāthas dominate politics in Maharashtra. As recently as June 2008 the Sambhaji Brigade, a militant pro-Marātha organization whose membership consists primarily of Marātha youth from the interior of the state and which is named after a son of the warrior Shivaji, has demanded Other Backward Classes status for Marāthas in Maharashtra. Taking a cue from the Gujjars in Rajasthan, the brigade has warned of a violent agitation if Marāthas are not granted OBC status soon.

20 GENDER ISSUES

The status of women in Maharashtra from the rise of the great Marātha hero Shivaji to the present was basically not different from that of women in other parts of India. Here, too, women were dependent on men and had to play a secondary and subordinate role. Yet, in certain respects, the situation in Maharashtra was different from that in other parts of India. Women belonging to aristocratic and ruling families were taught the art of horse-riding. They not merely used swords effectively on the battlefield but also led armies. Englishmen such as Captain Thomas Broughton admired the Marātha women for their bravery and courage. Broughton—in 1809—wrote "At no time is the difference in the treatment of women between the Marāthas and other natives of India more strikingly displayed. Such as can afford it here ride on horse without taking any pain to conceal their faces; they gallop about and make their way through the throng with as much boldness and perseverance as the men. The Marātha women have a bold look that is to be observed in no other women of Hindustan." Though women belonging to the aristocratic families had to observe *purdah* in the presence of strangers, the practice was relatively less rigorous in Maharashtra. The Rani of Jhansi, who, with her armies, opposed the British during the 1857 sepoy uprising, was a Marātha.

Being Hindus, Marātha and Kunbi women, especially in rural contexts, experience the social restraints typical of Hindu society. Thus, arranged marriages are common, child marriage (once the norm and now illegal) still occurs, and a dowry is often demanded by the groom's family among Marāthas who claim an upper caste status. However, among some low caste groups a *dej* (bride-price) is paid to the girl's father. Except for the Deshmukh families of the Sirole sub-caste, Kunbis allow the remarriage of widows. However, Marāthas do not allow widow remarriage or divorce.

The President of India in 2008, Pratibha Devisingh Patil, is a Maharashtrian. She is the first female President of the country.

21 BIBLIOGRAPHY

Dhekane, K. D. *Agrarian System under Marathas*. Bombay: Himalaya Pub. House, 1996.

Doshi, Saryu, ed. *Maharashtra*. Bombay: Marg Publications, 1985.

Enthoven, R. E. "Marathas." In vol. 3 of *The Tribes and Castes of Bombay*, edited by R. E. Enthoven. Bombay: Government Central Press, 1922.

Karve, Irawati. *Maharashtra—Land and Its People*. Maharashtra State Gazetteer. General Series. Bombay: Directorate of Government Printing, Stationery and Publications, Maharashtra State, 1968.

Kulakarni, A. Ra. *Maharashtra: Society and Culture*. New Delhi: Books & Books, 2000.

————. *Marathas and the Marathas' Country*. New Delhi: Books & Books, 1996.

Prakash, Om, ed. *Marathas and their Administration*. New Delhi: Anmol Publications, 2004.

Walker, Benjamin. "Maratha." In *Hindu World: An Encyclopedic Survey of Hinduism*. Vol. 2. London: George Allen and Unwin, 1968.

—by D. O. Lodrick

MARONITES

PRONUNCIATION: MA-ruh-nites
LOCATION: Lebanon
POPULATION: 1.5 million (2006 estimate)
LANGUAGE: Arabic; French; English
RELIGION: Maronite (Uniate Catholicism)
RELATED ARTICLES: Vol. 4: Lebanese

¹ INTRODUCTION

Maronites take their name either from the 5th century AD saint, John Maroun, or the 8th century AD monk who took his name and became the first Patriarch of Antioch. Although their origins are obscure, the Maronites believe that their heritage goes back to the time of Jesus. Their ancestors lived when Jesus did in the land then known as Palestine, heard him preach, and were among the first Christians. Whatever their origins, they were one of the Christian sects in the Middle East to remain intact after the Islamic revolution of the 7th century AD. (For the first 100 years of Islamic rule, Arabs more often than not considered Islam an "Arab" religion and did not expect non-Arabs to convert.) The Maronites were the only Christian sect to use Arabic for their church records right from the start.

To distinguish themselves from "Arabs," Maronite versions of their history claim that they fled Muslim persecution during the Islamic revolution. Records show, however, that at first the Maronites welcomed the Muslims as saviors from the hated Byzantine rulers of that time, and the Muslims in fact treated the Maronites fairly well. The Maronites ingratiated themselves with these new overlords and set up tax-farming arrangements that provided the Maronites with a decent living. It was not until the European Crusaders sacked Alexandria and the Maronites supported them that the Muslims questioned Maronite loyalty and punished them along with other Christians. The Maronites eventually fled to the hills of Mount Lebanon to escape persecution by the Ottoman Turks in the 15th century. They stubbornly survived there for the centuries to follow.

Maronite support of the Crusaders established ties to the West that became a defining factor for the Maronite community. They entered into partial communion with the Roman Catholic Church in the 12th century AD and came into full communion in 1763. During the Ottoman rule of the mid-19th century, Lebanon had been divided into two states, one Christian and one Druze. The Druze religion dates back to the 11th century and is separate from Christianity or Islam. Its adherents were often persecuted as heretics by Muslims. The French supported the Maronites in their war with the British-supported Druze. After the Druze massacred a large number of Maronites in 1860, an international commission decided to reunite the country under a non-Lebanese governor. The French later allied themselves again with the Maronites during the French mandate years (1920–1943), cementing the Maronite identification with the West, particularly France. This Western identity has led to a sense of separateness from other Arabs on the part of the Maronites and resentment toward them on the part of their Arab-identified neighbors. In the last ten years, however, Maronites have become more comfortable with a Lebanese identity as nationalism has increased among Lebanon's population.

The Maronites have campaigned for an independent homeland since the 7th century AD, but they are no longer attempting to convert Lebanon into a Maronite state today. Based on the confessional system of government (where political authority is divided up according to population percentages of religious faiths), the Lebanese presidency is designated as a Maronite post because Maronites were in the majority at the time of the 1932 census. A civil war began in Lebanon in April 1975 due to increasing instability of a system of government that allowed Christians majority rule despite the fact that Muslims had become the majority of the population. This was especially true after the influx of Palestinian refugees from Palestine and Jordan in 1948, 1967, and 1970. The unwillingness of the French and the Maronites to consider the concerns of the majority in a period of strong Arab nationalism led to increasing conflict, which was promoted in part by outside players. Initially, the Muslims had the upper hand in the fighting, but Syria, with the support of Israel, the United States, and most Arab states, entered Lebanon with a "peacekeeping" force to maintain the status quo. With Syria's support, the Maronites were able to preserve their position in Lebanon until a new government was formed at Taif (in Saudi Arabia), which, under Syria's tutelage, formally ended the civil war. Maronite Christians still retain the presidency position in Lebanon's governing structure. However, the sect's political power has diminished considerably since the 1990s as the Druze and Shia Muslims has grown more united.

² LOCATION AND HOMELAND

Most ethnic groups living in the Levant region have intermingled with other groups. The territory known as Lebanon today has a diverse society, due in part to numerous foreign armies passing through over the centuries. Some Maronites claim descent from the European Crusaders, such as the major northern families of Franjiehs and Douaihis. The Franjiehs say their name means "Franks," and the Douaihis link their name to the French city of Douai, the home of some of the knights of the Crusades. It appears from what records exist that the Maronite sect began in northern Syria in the valley of the Orontes River, near the present-day city of Hama, in the 6th century AD. The Maronites moved south to the coast of northern Lebanon in the 8th century, then fled into the hills of Mount Lebanon to escape persecution by the Ottoman Turks in the mid- to late-15th century. Holing up in small, isolated communities, the Maronites became clannish and fiercely self-protective. After surviving in the high mountains of northern Lebanon for many centuries, the Maronites then spread south throughout the mountain range during the 18th and 19th centuries. The Maronite Church acquired a great deal of land and became the largest, most organized, wealthiest institution in the Mount Lebanon area. By the mid-19th century, the Maronite Church owned one-fourth to one-third of all the land in Mount Lebanon. During the 20th century, some Maronites began to move out of the mountains to the cities and coastal plains, especially to Beirut, but they continued to be clannish and isolated from their neighbors in their new locations.

During the Lebanese civil war, more than 600,000 Maronites were driven out of their homes and off their lands. Of the 850,000 inhabitants of the Maronite enclave in Lebanon sometimes called "Marounistan," 100,000 fled abroad, and 150,000 fled to other parts of Lebanon. As Muslims gain more political

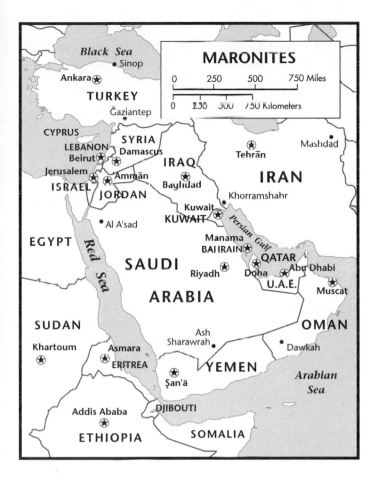

MARONITES

0   250   500   750 Miles

0   250   500   750 Kilometers

dominance in Lebanon, more Maronites are emigrating from their homeland to Europe and the United States.

³ LANGUAGE

Although Arabic is the official language of Lebanon, many Maronites also speak French. Economic and military ties have led most residents of Lebanon to learn French and English in addition to Arabic. Syriac is used for the church liturgy, but Maronites have used Arabic for church records since their beginnings.

⁴ FOLKLORE

The door of the Maronite church in Beit Meri is never locked because it is believed that the hand of any thief there would be miraculously paralyzed.

⁵ RELIGION

The Maronites are Uniate Catholics: they recognize the authority of the Roman Catholic Pope, but they have their own form of worship. Their priests can marry, and monks and nuns are housed in the same building. Even after becoming a Uniate church in AD 1180, the Maronites continued to use the Syriac language for their liturgy instead of Latin (as in the Roman church). Syriac is the Maronite liturgical language to this day. The Maronites did quietly drop their belief in monothelitism, branded heresy in AD 680 by the Roman church, after becoming a Uniate church in 1180. Monothelitism proposes that Christ has two natures that are so blended with each other that they produce one will. The orthodox view, called dyothelitism,

holds that Christ has two natures and two wills, one human and one divine, which are inseparable, yet unconfused: Christ is at one with God in his divine nature and at one with humanity in his human nature. The Qadisha (Holy) valley is the Maronite spiritual center.

⁶ MAJOR HOLIDAYS

The Maronites celebrate the usual Christian holidays, such as Christmas (December 25), Easter (moveable, in March or April), the Feast of the Ascension (40 days after Easter), and the Feast of the Assumption (August 15). On the Festival of the Cross (September 14), Maronites set fires on high places all over Mount Lebanon and light candles at home and in churches. A special Maronite holy day is St. Maroun's Day (February 9), the feast of the Maronite patron saint, St. John Maroun of the 5th century AD.

⁷ RITES OF PASSAGE

The Maronites mark major life events, such as birth, marriage, and death, within the traditions of Christianity.

⁸ INTERPERSONAL RELATIONS

Centuries of life in isolated mountain communities, hiding out from persecution by various attackers, has led to the development of clan loyalties and fierce feuding among the Maronites.

⁹ LIVING CONDITIONS

Maronite villages have a style of architecture common around the Mediterranean area. Homes are small and simple, yet elegant, often with a balcony overlooking the mountains or the Mediterranean Sea. Since the 18th and 19th centuries, the Maronites have been fairly affluent. During the Lebanese civil war, many Maronites fled from the cities (especially Beirut) back to their ancestral homes in Mount Lebanon. As a result, business boomed there, housing construction soared, and the area became quite prosperous.

¹⁰ FAMILY LIFE

Although modernization has led to an increased emphasis on the nuclear family, the Maronites, like other Arabs in Lebanon, still have a strong sense of extended family. Men spend quite a bit of time at home with the women and children. There is some intermarriage between Maronites and members of other religious groups. Divorce is forbidden by Maronite law.

¹¹ CLOTHING

Maronites wear Western-style clothing, as do the Druze, Shiites, Sunnis, Armenians, and Greek Orthodox in Lebanon. The more devout Maronites tend to wear conservative clothing. Apart from slight differences in headgear, even the religious leaders of all the communities in Lebanon tend to dress alike.

¹² FOOD

Maronites eat typical Middle Eastern and Mediterranean food, with French and European elements blended in. For example, breakfast might consist of either Lebanese flatbread or French croissants with cheese and coffee or tea. Lunches and dinners usually consist of meat (mutton is a favorite) with onion, spices, and rice. Mutton is often ground and served as meatballs or in stews, or mixed with rice and vegetables and rolled in grape leaves. The Middle Eastern tradition of *mezze* (small portions of a wide variety of foods served all at once for diners to pick and choose from) is popular with Maronites, as is *arak*, the anise-flavored alcohol produced in the region.

13 EDUCATION

By the 17th century, European missionaries had established Catholic schools in Lebanon. The Maronites had an initial advantage with the missionary schools established for them, but eventually the schools began accepting Muslims as well. In 1788, a monastery was converted to a secondary school that taught secular subjects, and American Protestant missionaries set up schools for both boys and girls in Lebanon in the 1820s and 1830s. However, the Uniate Catholic Maronites were more inclined toward the schools set up soon after by French Catholic missionaries. Most Maronites today still receive their primary and secondary schooling in French-language schools, then generally go to the University of St. Joseph in Beirut, founded by French Jesuits in 1875 to compete with the Syrian Protestant College (now called the American University of Beirut) established in 1866.

The Lebanese government requires students to have a functional knowledge of Arabic in order to graduate from secondary school but only recently has this been enforced. Many older Maronites speak only French.

14 CULTURAL HERITAGE

The poet Maya Angelou published an essay on the Maronites in Lebanon in 1984. At the time, civil war had been raging in Lebanon for nine years and would continue for six more years. Angelou described the Maronites as a people with "a split personality." "They are Arabs who often look to the West for inspiration and assistance," Angelou wrote. "A minority that insists it must rule in order to survive and nationalists in a land that is so fracture it can hardly be called a nation."

Angelou's words continue to describe the cultural heritage of the Maronites today. Lebanon contains people of many different religious and ethnic backgrounds. Maronite leaders have joined with leaders of other factions within Lebanon to try and unify the country. Yet, the Maronites also wonder where they fit in the Lebanon of the early twenty-first century. They are an Arab people, but they have strong cultural ties to the West, and many have ancestral ties to the West as well. In 1585 a religious school for Maronite men was established in Rome. A short time later, European Catholic missionaries settled in Lebanon and began schools there. To this day, Maronites continue to send their children to French-language private schools in Lebanon [see **Lebanese**]. As former president Camille Chamoun, a Maronite, told Angelou: "We are part of the Arab world, but we are also apart from the Arab world because so much of our identity comes from the West."

15 WORK

Many Maronites are wealthy, and Maronites have long held powerful positions in Lebanese government, business, and education. With the aid of the French, the Maronites developed Mount Lebanon's greatest money-making venture of the past—the silk industry. The mountainsides are dotted with old silk-reeling factories.

16 SPORTS

Maronites enjoy the same sports as other Lebanese. These activities include soccer, basketball, volleyball, horseback-riding, cross-country running, martial arts, skiing, rock-climbing, and caving. Maronites, like other Lebanese, also go swimming and fishing in the lakes, rivers, or visit beaches along the Mediterranean coast.

17 ENTERTAINMENT AND RECREATION

Maronites, like other residents of Lebanon, watch television avidly. Many stations emphasize all Christian programming, though others offer a mix. Maronites also watch American, European, and Lebanese films in theaters, and enjoy the dramatic theatre tradition of their home country.

18 FOLK ART, CRAFTS, AND HOBBIES

Traditional crafts among Lebanese Maronites include basketry, carpet-weaving, ceramics and pottery, copper and metalworking, embroidery, glass-blowing, and gold- and silver-smithing. Lebanon is also known for its finely crafted church bells. Wine-making can also be considered an art, dating back for thousands of years in Lebanon.

19 SOCIAL PROBLEMS

The Maronites suffered under Ottoman rule from the 16th century to the end of World War I. The arrival of European colonizers in the early 20th century worked to their advantage, especially because the Maronites shared the same Christian faith as the Europeans. The privileges that the Maronites acquired under European colonial rule are treated with disdain by other Lebanese who see their acquisition of wealth as a product of their favorable access to Lebanese politics. Although other communities (such as the Sunnis and Shiites) have also benefited from the traditional Lebanese system of government created by the French, there have been tensions as these groups seek more equitable representation in the Lebanese government. Within the Maronite community itself, centuries of clannish mountain life has led to perpetual feuding and in-fighting, continuing today among the different Maronite militias.

The long civil war damaged Lebanon's economic infrastructure. National output was cut in half, and the country has struggled to rebuild its economy through heavy borrowing from domestic banks and international sources. The economic difficulties have made the plight of the Maronite minority more precarious, especially since many Lebanese Muslims see the Maronites as hostile to their people. The end of the civil war and the end of Maronite political dominance has made many Maronites uncertain about their future place in Lebanon. As a result, many Maronites have begun to migrate out of Lebanon in recent years.

20 GENDER ISSUES

Maronite women experience the same kind of discrimination in public and private life that other Lebanese women face. In general, Lebanese laws and court systems do little to help women. Lebanese laws allow for each religion to have a separate court system to handle matters of marriage, divorce, and inheritance. Frequently, these religious customs, whether they are Christian or Muslim, fail to protect women from domestic violence.

²¹BIBLIOGRAPHY

Amnesty International. *Amnesty International Report 2008: State of the World's Human Rights*. http://thereport.amnesty.org/eng/Homepage (October 26, 2008).

Angelou, Maya. "Arabs who look to the West; with guns and crosses, Lebanon's Christians try to survive." *Time* 123 (5 March 1984): 29-30.

Background Note: Lebanon. United States Department of State. www.state.gov/r/pa/ei/bgn/35833.htm (October 25, 2008).

Dreher, Rod. "Out of Lebanon: The fate of Christians, the fate of a country." *National Review* 54.24 (Dec 23, 2002).

Foster, Leila Merrell. *Enchantment of the World: Lebanon*. Chicago: Children's Press, 1992.

Johnson, Marguerite. "Arabs Who Look to the West: With Guns and Crosses, Lebanon's Christians Try to Survive." In *Time* 123 (5 March 1984): 29.

Keen, Lynda. *Guide to Lebanon*. Old Saybrook, CT: Globe Pequot Press, 1995.

Lebanon. CultureGrams: World Edition. Ann Arbor, Mich.: ProQuest LLC, 2008.

Marston, Elsa. *Lebanon: New Light in an Ancient Land*. New York: Dillon Press, 1994.

Moss, Joyce, and George Wilson. *Peoples of the World: The Middle East and North Africa*, 1st ed. Detroit: Gale Research, 1992.

Phares, Walid. *Lebanese Christian Nationalism: The Rise and Fall of an Ethnic Resistance*. Boulder, CO: Lynne Rienner Publishers, 1995.

Randal, Jonathan. *The Tragedy of Lebanon: Christian Warlords, Israeli Adventurers and American Bunglers*. London: Hogarth Press, 1990.

—revised by H. Gupta-Carlson

MELANESIANS

PRONUNCIATION: mel-uh-NEE-zhuns
ALTERNATE NAMES: Papuans
LOCATION: [Papua] New Guinea, Vanuatu (the former New Hebrides), New Caledonia, the Solomon Islands, and some smaller neighboring islands
POPULATION: Unknown
LANGUAGE: English; Tok Pisin, Hiri Motu (Papua New Guinea); Bislama (Vanuatu); Solomon Islands Pidgin English (Solomon Islands); Bahasa Indonesia (Papua and West Papua provinces of Indonesia); other native languages
RELIGION: Christianity; some native religions

¹INTRODUCTION

Melanesia is not a socio-political unit, but instead a *culture area*. Culture area is a term used by anthropologists to refer to a geographical region where people share many of the same cultural traits, such as family structure, marriage rules, socio-political organization, or subsistence strategies. Melanesia itself is part of a larger culture area called Oceania which includes Melanesia, Polynesia, Micronesia, and Australia. The native inhabitants of Melanesia, called Melanesians, are characteristically dark-skinned with frizzy hair. They are sometimes referred to as "Papuans," from the Malay word "papua" meaning "frizzy haired."

²LOCATION AND HOMELAND

Melanesia includes the islands of New Guinea, Vanuatu (the former New Hebrides), New Caledonia, the Solomon Islands, and some smaller neighboring islands. The island of New Guinea is divided politically down the middle. The western half of the island is comprised of two provinces of Indonesia called Papua and West Papua, while the eastern half is the independent nation of Papua New Guinea. New Caledonia is a *departmente* of France, and Vanuatu became an independent nation in 1980. All of Melanesia lies within the tropics of Cancer and Capricorn and is south of the equator. Melanesians migrate locally to other nearby islands or to Australia. A small percentage does leave the region entirely and take up residence in the United States, Canada, or Europe.

³LANGUAGE

In many of the island nations that comprise Melanesia, there is more than one official, national language. For instance, Papua New Guinea has three official languages: English, Tok Pisin, an English-based pidgin language, and Hiri Motu, an Austronesian-based pidgin language. Tok Pisin has a history based in colonialism and forced plantation labor in the 1800s in the South Pacific. The language ultimately derives from a kind of nautical English that was spread throughout the Pacific by sailors. The structure of the language is somewhat like English and somewhat like the Austronesian languages that were spoken by the plantation laborers. A sample sentence in Tok Pisin looks like this: "Bai mi kaikai wanpela kaukau" (translated, "I will eat a yam.").

Within the region of Melanesia, the island of New Guinea alone has over 1,000 different languages. Some of these languages have as few as 50 speakers, while others, such as Enga, have a few hundred thousand. Many of these languages remain undocumented and undescribed. Melanesia is truly a linguistic frontier.

⁴FOLKLORE

Oral history is important to the peoples of Melanesia since none of these cultures ever developed a native writing system. In the Sepik River region of Papua New Guinea, the origin myth of many groups tells of a mythical crocodile that split in two, with his upper jaw becoming the heavens and his lower jaw becoming the earth. For many of these groups, there was also an original pair of humans that sprang from the mud and are responsible for populating the Earth. In this origin myth, however, the original pair are brothers.

⁵RELIGION

Christianity has spread throughout Melanesia. Missionaries are very active in this region, learning the native languages and translating the New Testament into those languages. Native religions are still practiced, although in modified form, by many groups. In many societies in the Sepik River region of Papua New Guinea, the original belief systems incorporated aspects of both headhunting and cannibalism. The two practices have been illegal in the region since the late 1920s. Most groups believe in a variety of spirits which inhabit the forests, mountains, and swamps. They also believe that the ghosts of their ancestors inhabit the same plane of reality that they do. In fact, in the highlands of Papua New Guinea, when Melanesians saw the first Europeans they believed them to be the ghosts of their dead ancestors returning to the community. Some groups jokingly refer to "white" tourists in the same way.

⁶MAJOR HOLIDAYS

Independence Day is a major holiday for the independent Melanesian nations of Papua New Guinea and Vanuatu. For those that belong to the Commonwealth, British holidays such as the Queen's birthday are celebrated in urban areas. Banks and schools are closed for those holidays, but in areas where there are no banks or schools, these holidays have little meaning.

⁷RITES OF PASSAGE

There are many important rites of passage in Melanesian societies. Puberty is an especially important rite in all Melanesian societies; however, these societies differ in regards to which sex undergoes initiation rites. In the Sepik River region, males used to undergo extreme and elaborate initiation rites. These involved extensive scarification as well as brutal treatment by older males. Scarification has all but disappeared in the Sepik region, except for the few males who can afford to have the process done. It is an expensive proposition to pay the fees of the scarification experts who perform the operations. In some societies, males were expected to commit a homicide and take their first head at puberty. This process was halted by colonial administrators in the 1920s, soon after the first European contacts in the region. Girls generally had less harsh puberty rites, often undergoing only a brief period of seclusion with the onset of menstruation. Funerals were also important rites of passage in Melanesian societies involving much feasting and display of emotion.

⁸INTERPERSONAL RELATIONS

There are extreme differences between urban Melanesians and rural Melanesians in terms of how they greet and take leave of each other. In parts of the highlands of Papua New Guinea, males would greet each other by rubbing each other's groin region. In most of these cultures, the Western handshake has replaced this traditional form of greeting. Since trade was such an important part of daily life in parts of Melanesia, special ceremonial greetings took place when one group went to trade with another. Special languages were used and the participants placed specific roles with each other.

Many groups require that marriages occur between persons who come from different villages. Special courtship rituals still take place between men and women in these instances. Among the Chimbu of Papua New Guinea, men woo women through their ability to sing. They would also decorate their bodies in elaborate ways to look beautiful for the women whom they are trying to court. Marriages, however, have to be negotiated between the families and usually involve the payment of a "bride price" to the bride's father by the prospective son-in-law.

⁹LIVING CONDITIONS

Melanesia is a tropical region and its inhabitants experience the hardships of life in an environment where rain, heat, and mosquitoes are ever-present. Malaria is endemic to the region and most local inhabitants of the low-lying areas are afflicted with this debilitating disease. Healing is a long process in the tropics and, as a result, infection is a serious problem. Most of Melanesia, though, is a relatively healthy region of the world.

Transportation varies from region to region within Melanesia. In areas where flooding is common, roads are of little value in the rainy season. During that time of year almost all transportation is by dugout canoe. Some people are wealthy enough to buy outboard motors for their canoes so that they do not have to paddle. In the cities of Melanesia, automobiles are common, especially taxis and minibuses which transport people as far as the roads will allow. In rural areas there are no posted speed limits, and travel by bus can be considered a dangerous activity. Drivers with a schedule to keep seem to have little regard for hazardous road conditions or the possibility of oncoming traffic. Small propeller aircraft are an important means of travel between the cities and the isolated mountain valleys. It is not uncommon to share a row on a plane with an individual in traditional dress.

¹⁰FAMILY LIFE

In many Melanesian societies, there is a great deal of antagonism between men and women. It is common in many villages to have men's and women's houses. In the Sepik River region, men's ceremonial houses are off-limits to all women and to uninitiated (non-adult) males. Men would traditionally spend most of their time in this large house where matters of ceremonial importance were often planned. Men would also often take their meals here. There were no real "family meals" in traditional societies along the Sepik. Food for the day is often placed in a woven basket that is suspended from the house rafters. People just eat when they get hungry.

Women are the primary caregivers of children and the primary food producers. Women play important roles in ceremonial and political life in many Melanesian societies. In some

Melanesian children float on a bamboo pontoon on the Coral Coast, Fiji. (AFP/Getty Images)

societies, a child's maternal uncle is the most important male figure.

Households vary in size from society to society. In some very small societies, everyone in the group lives in one house. Antagonism between the sexes is not as dramatic among these groups as it is among larger groups. In all societies, however, the domestic space is divided between males and females.

¹¹CLOTHING

Traditional clothing in Melanesia was scant by Western European standards. In the highland societies of New Guinea, men went naked except for their "penis sheath" made from the gourd of a vine. Nowadays, in only a few remote societies do men continue to dress in this manner; instead, they wear Western-style shorts or long trousers and shirts. In these societies, women wear skirts made from handmade fiber. An important aspect of adornment in these societies was body decoration, which involved elaborate painting and the use of various headgear, wigs, and other items. The most elaborate adornment took place when exchanges between groups were to occur. These were a time of feasting and boasting and beauty was an important aspect of the event. Some individuals still adorn themselves in this manner at these events, while others choose to refrain from the traditional activity.

In many parts of Melanesia the all-purpose *laplap* has become the standard unisex item of clothing. Laplap refers to a piece of cloth, usually store-bought, which can be wrapped around the waist or up under the armpits to cover the body, somewhat like a sarong. In the lower altitude areas, women still prefer to not wear any covering on their upper body; however, when tourists are in the village, they can adjust the laplap to cover their breasts.

¹²FOOD

Food varies in Melanesia but there are some similarities. In parts of the lowland areas of the region, the sago palm is an important foodstuff. The pith of the palm is processed into a starch which can be made into pancakes or dumplings. A sago pancake has the appearance of a freshly cooked soft tortilla and the consistency and texture of a rubber-soled shoe. They are, however, very filling and taste quite nice with peanut butter. In the higher elevations, yams are the staple diet, with pork being consumed on ceremonial occasions.

¹³EDUCATION

Many parts of Melanesia do not have access to formal, European-style education. Education focuses on traditional ways of life and the values of the society. Schools have reached some remote areas and are part of urban life for Melanesians. Education in schools revolves around literacy in the national language(s) and preparation for urban life, such as civil service careers. In Papua New Guinea, the educational system is based on the Australian model, where formal required education ends at grade 10. Grades 11 and 12 are not mandatory; they are only for those students who have a desire to pursue higher education at the university level. The University of Papua New Guinea offers a variety of degrees in a number of fields. Many of its faculty are indigenous Papuans who trained both in foreign and domestic institutions. Literacy in Tok Pisin is growing among the urban population in particular, while literacy in English is lower. Children who attend school have at least basic proficiency in written English.

¹⁴CULTURAL HERITAGE

There are a number of musical traditions within Melanesia. In the Solomon Islands, there is a tradition of panpipe orchestras that is well-known to ethnomusicologists (scholars who study the role of music in its cultural contexts). These panpipes look and sound very similar to those played by the Aymara and Quechua of the Andean region of South America. Drums are nearly universal in the musical traditions of Melanesia. Melanesian drums are usually hand-held, hourglass-shaped, and single-headed. The Tok Pisin word for this type of drum is *kundu*. In many highland societies of Papua New Guinea, large groups of men play drums together at large ceremonial gatherings called *sing sing*.

Dance is an important part of ritual life in Melanesian societies. Both men and women dance; however, in many societies there are separate men's and women's dances.

Written literature is a recent development in Melanesia. Many pieces of written literature are the transcriptions of folklore and oral history. Nationalism in island Melanesian nations has resulted in the production of modern literatures in the national languages of the countries, such as Tok Pisin and Bislama.

¹⁵WORK

Wage labor was introduced to Melanesia by European colonists. Prior to this, work was often cooperative and reciprocal, and for village-based projects it still remains so to this day. Individuals have certain responsibilities to their relatives and in-laws which typically include working for them on cooperative projects such as house building. In some societies, a son-in-law has to work in his father-in-law's gardens for a fixed period of time after his marriage. This practice is called "bride service" by anthropologists.

¹⁶SPORTS

Soccer, rugby, and cricket are important sports in Melanesia. Some societies have transformed these sports in unique ways or adapted them to meet local conditions. In a well known case in the Trobriand Islands off the coast of Papua New Guinea, cricket is played by local rules which do not allow for a winner. In many other remote villages of the various islands in the region, these sports are no more than names to the people.

¹⁷ENTERTAINMENT AND RECREATION

Electricity does not reach many Melanesian homes, so television is a luxury of the urban folk. There is one television sta-

tion in Papua New Guinea called *Em TV* in Tok Pisin, one of the national languages of the country. *Em* in Tok Pisin means "it, he, or she," so the station's name means something close to "It's TV." Australian, American, and locally produced shows are aired during a restricted viewing schedule. Cable and satellite service are available to the wealthy locals as well as the expatriates of the islands.

Traditional recreation involves storytelling and performances of music, dance, and song. No recreational event is complete without betel nut chewing, a favorite recreation of most Melanesians.

¹⁸FOLK ART, CRAFTS, AND HOBBIES

Art in most Melanesian societies is utilitarian: there is no saying "art for art's sake." In the Sepik River region, there is an extremely well developed tradition of artistic expression involving sculpture and painting. Every item is elaborately decorated with important animals and birds as well as geometric and abstract designs. Masks were an important aspect of ritual performances, but have now become important items of tourist art. Every year, several thousand tourists visit this area of New Guinea to purchase the art and artifacts of these people. It is not an industry that creates any wealthy Papuans, however.

¹⁹SOCIAL PROBLEMS

Like every other group of people, Melanesians are dealing with the modern world. Alcoholism is becoming a more serious problem in parts of Melanesia where males have access to money and find time on their hands. AIDS poses a serious health threat in Papua New Guinea, where condoms were not available until recently, and again, more predominately in the urban areas. The social phenomenon of "rascals" in parts of Papua New Guinea is a cause for concern for locals and visitors alike. Rascals are unemployed, disenfranchised youth who rob people as well as businesses, often assaulting their victims. Guns are rarely used in these robberies since they are difficult to come by and ammunition is illegal by Papua New Guinea law.

²⁰GENDER ISSUES

The relationships between males and females are highly varied within the Melanesian culture area. While initiation for males certainly dominates the cultural landscape of Melanesia, there are several societies in which female initiation is found. One complaint that has leveled in feminist anthropology is that the male-bias of most modern ethnography has obscured the roles of women in Melanesian societies.

Among the Abelam of the East Sepik Province of Papua New Guinea, there is both male and female initiation. For a female, adulthood is marked through a public ritual that celebrates the girl's first menses. For a period of a month or two after that, the young woman is called *naramtaakwa*, meaning "decorated woman." During this time, she wears particular decorations, follows a set of social restrictions, and avoids work. At the end of the *naramtaakwa* period, a young woman is called *taakwa* and is now eligible for marriage. For a male in Abelam society, on the other hand, adulthood is attained through a gradual social process that does not reach completion until a man is in his forties.

Segregation of the sexes is common throughout Melanesia and recent interpretations of the ethnographic data provide new insights into the reasons why this pattern is common. Previous explanations focused on the concept that women, and by extension children, were seen as polluting to men. This pollution stemmed from menstruation and fear of male contact with menstrual blood. Recent ethnographic studies in parts of Papua New Guinea have shown that men are believed to be equally polluting to women. Among the Abelam, for instance, virile men are seen as dangerous to certain female activities. The Abelam believe that sexual intercourse is detrimental to the growth of yams, which are their staple crop. During yam growing season, the young men and women are kept apart to insure their adherence to the prohibition on sexual intercourse. The reinterpretation of the ethnographic facts place a dual equality on the "dangerous" aspects of male and female in Abelam society.

Gender differences are also signaled through grammar in some of the languages spoken in Melanesia. The language of the Trobriand Islanders, Kilivila, has a complex system of gender. In Kilivila, every noun—even inanimate nouns—has a defined gender that is signaled by the use of a suffix that is attached to the noun.

In 2005, the Melanesian island nation of Vanuatu instituted a law that girls and women could be fined for wearing trousers or jeans in public. The law stemmed from concerns that traditional dress is being abandoned by ni-Vanuatu girls and women in favor of western styles. A further deterrent is that the family of the female violating the law will have to kill one pig, and pigs are items of wealth for ni-Vanuatu families.

[21] BIBLIOGRAPHY

Codrington, Robert Henry. *The Melanesians: Studies in Their Anthropology and Folklore.* New Haven: HRAF Press, 1957.

Harrison, Simon. *The Mask of War: Violence, Ritual, and the Self in Melanesia.* Manchester: Manchester University Press, 1993.

Holdsworth, David. *Festivals and Celebrations in Papua New Guinea.* Bathurst: Robert Brown & Associates, 1982.

Knauft, Bruce M. *South Coast New Guinea Cultures: History, Comparison, Dialectic.* New York: Cambridge University Press, 1993.

Ryan, P., ed. *The Encyclopedia of Papua New Guinea.* Melbourne: Melbourne University Press, 1972.

Sillitoe, Paul. *An Introduction to the Anthropology of Melanesia: Culture and Tradition.* Cambridge; New York: Cambridge University Press, 1998.

Spriggs, Matthew. *The Island Melanesians.* Oxford: Blackwell, 1997.

Strathern, Marilyn. *The Gender of the Gift: Problems with Women and Problems with Society in Melanesia.* Berkeley: University of California Press, 1988.

———. *Dealing with Inequality: Analysing Gender Relations in Melanesia and Beyond.* Cambridge: Cambridge University Press, 1987.

—by J. Williams

MELPA

PRONUNCIATION: MEL-pah
ALTERNATE NAMES: Medlpa; Hageners
LOCATION: Papua New Guinea
POPULATION: 130,000
LANGUAGE: Melpa; Tok Pisin
RELIGION: Christianity; native Melpa religion

[1] INTRODUCTION

The Melpa (also spelled Medlpa) are some of the first Papuans that tourists and visitors to the island of New Guinea see when they step off the plane in Mount Hagen. "Hageners," as the Melpa are often called, frequent the airport at Mount Hagen offering modern "stone axes," colorful string bags, and other artifacts for sale. Some of them also provide taxi and bus service to the local hotels and guesthouses. Historically, the Melpa were the first highlands group to be encountered by Europeans in 1933. Up until this time, the highlands of New Guinea had been unknown to the outside world, and, conversely, the highlanders had never before seen people who lived beyond their mountain valleys and plains. The first contact between these two groups was recorded on film and provides an invaluable and extremely interesting record of this monumental time of discovery for both groups.

[2] LOCATION AND HOMELAND

The Melpa live in the Western Highlands Province of the independent Pacific nation of Papua New Guinea. They are highlands-dwelling people with most of the area they inhabit ranging between 1,200 and 2,000 m (4,000–6,500 ft) above sea level. The Melpa occupy the areas north and south of the important town of Mount Hagen. There are about 130,000 Melpa, with the greatest area of population density just outside Mount Hagen in the Wahgi Valley and nearby Ogelbeng Plain. The climate in the area is relatively mild, especially by tropical standards. The temperature rarely exceeds 30°c (86°f) in the summer months and rarely falls below freezing in winter. Rainfall is heaviest between October and March, with a dry period from April until September. Mosquitoes are nonexistent here and malaria is, therefore, not a problem.

[3] LANGUAGE

The Melpa speak a Papuan language belonging to the East New Guinea Highlands stock. Melpa is closely related to the well-known Chimbu language spoken by the people of the same name located to the east of the Melpa region. Melpa has over 130,000 speakers and a portion of that population speaks Tok Pisin as a second language. Tok Pisin is one of the official languages of Papua New Guinea. Melpa is not under threat from Tok Pisin, as some other languages in the country are. It is still the case that most Melpa children grow up speaking Melpa as their first language.

[4] FOLKLORE

Myths relating the origins of the clans were and still are told within Melpa society. Sacred objects or living beings associated with these myths and clans are called mi. Extended or-

A Melpa tribe member has a head scarf adjusted at a SingSing festival. (Sylvain Grandadam/Getty Images)

atory and epic stories are performed to recount the deeds of clan heroes and ancestors. "Female Spirit"—called *Amb Kor* in Melpa—stories are important and widespread in Melpa oral literature.

5 RELIGION

Ghosts are the focal point of non-Christian religious practice among the Melpa. Pork sacrifices are made to placate the ghosts of dead family, lineage, and clan members on the occurrence of illness within the village or prior to the undertaking of any dangerous event. The Melpa have religious experts who are responsible for curing the sick and act as intermediaries between the human world and the spirit world. Women are not allowed to be curers but can be possessed by spirits and can also foretell the future. Christianity has existed in the Melpa region ever since the founding of Mount Hagen as an administrative, trade, and missionary center after the first Leahy expedition in 1933. A number of the Melpa are now practicing Christians and attend the local churches on a regular basis.

6 MAJOR HOLIDAYS

The Mount Hagen Show is an important local holiday for Hageners. At the show groups from all over the highlands re-

gion attend to perform traditional songs, music, and dance adorned in ceremonial attire. Body decoration reaches it pinnacle for this event. The Mount Hagen Show takes place every two years. National holidays such as Independence Day are recognized by the Melpa who live and work in Mount Hagen. More rural Melpa do not recognize these events since they do not directly affect their daily lives.

The most important and well known ceremonial event in traditional Melpa society was the *moka*. The *moka* was an exchange process in which an individual male gave an initiatory gift to another male, who in turn gave a gift back to that individual plus something more. Exchange partnerships developed in this way continued through the adult lives of men. Before the introduction of European goods into the highlands, the major items of exchange in the *moka* were pigs, both living and cooked, and pearl shell necklaces. In the post-colonial period, cash, machetes, and even four-wheel drive vehicles were exchanged in increasingly competitive *moka* ceremonies. The goal of the exchange was to gain status and prestige in the eyes of the larger society by giving more than one received. Men who are accomplished at achieving this goal are known as "big-men" in the community and viewed as leaders, and although the traditional *moka* has all but disappeared from Melpa society, "big-manship" is still important Within the *moka* system, true "big-men" were able to arrange large-scale, multiple *moka* exchanges involving many pairs of exchange partners. Anthropologists refer to this type of exchange as "redistribution." In redistributive exchange, the goal is not to accumulate goods or wealth for personal use, but instead to accumulate items to redistribute them within the community. Modern-day taxation is also classified as a type of redistribution.

7 RITES OF PASSAGE

In most societies in the world, a female's passage into adulthood is marked by the onset of menstruation. This event is usually recognized by the community through ceremony, seclusion, or a set of initiation/maturation rites. The Melpa people are different in that they did not socially recognize or celebrate a girl's first menstruation. Most other highland groups from Papua New Guinea have rites centered on a girl's first menstruation. The Melpa are like other groups in the area that do focus on the necessary segregation of males and females due to the fear of pollution of males by females, especially through menstrual blood.

In the past, the Melpa did have elaborate initiation rites for males, although through contact with the outside world these have been greatly modified and have all but disappeared.

8 INTERPERSONAL RELATIONS

In some parts of the highlands, hamlets are separated by valleys and mountain ridges. Especially in the more rural Melpa region, hamlets may be widely separated from each other. In these areas greetings are accomplished long distance via yodeling. Requests, directions, commands, and challenges are often yodeled back and forth by men across a ravine or a ridge, completely out of visual range of each other.

Inheritance is based on patrilineal principles: sons inherit from their fathers. The most important item for inheritance is land. A father's land is parceled out to his sons at the time of their marriage. His daughters may receive cultivation rights to a parcel of land after they are married.

⁹ LIVING CONDITIONS

There are two main types of traditional Melpa houses: men's and women's houses. Men's houses are round with conical roofs. This is where men and pre-teenage boys live once they have been separated from their mothers around the age of eight years old. Women and their unmarried daughters live in the rectangular-shaped women's house. There are pig stalls built inside the women's house to keep the pigs from wandering off at night or being stolen. A hamlet consists of at least a men's house and a women's house. Members of a clan resided in the same territory, which was near gardening areas and linked together by paths. Missionaries advocated the building of family homes among the Melpa where a husband, a wife, and their children would sleep together. Some Melpa have adopted this new form of residence while others have chosen not to. Roads often link hamlets together and further link these to the Highlands Highway, which bisects the Highlands Range.

¹⁰ FAMILY LIFE

Marriage involves the exchange of valuables by both families. The majority of the goods are given by the groom's family to the bride's family and constitute what anthropologists refer to as "bride wealth" or "bride price." Traditionally, the groom's family and kinfolk would provide a number of pigs and shells to the father of the bride in compensation for the loss of his daughter. Nowadays, cash payments are included in the calculation. The bride's family provides a number of breeding pigs that their daughter will have control over in her new family. The negotiation of a "bride price" is a significant part of the marriage transaction and can derail a potential marriage.

The Melpa trace their genealogies through the male line. Clans are created through common descent from a shared male ancestor. Individuals choose their spouses from clans outside their own. After marriage, the couple moves into the groom's father's hamlet. Later, they will build a new women's house for the bride near the groom's men's house. Divorce consists of repayment of part of the bride price, especially if the woman is seen to have been at fault.

¹¹ CLOTHING

The Melpa that live or work in Mount Hagen wear Western-style clothing. Men usually wear shorts, a T-shirt, shoes if they own them, and a knitted cap, and carry a string bag. Women wear A-line dresses often made of a floral print fabric. They also carry string bags, but much larger than those of the men. Women also wear shoes if they own them, but one is much more likely to see a man with shoes than a woman. Concepts of owning a wardrobe of clothing do not exist for the vast majority of Melpa. In fact, most people own only one change of clothing. It is still possible to see Melpa dressed in traditional attire, including the traditional wig made from human hair that adult Melpa men wear on important occasions. In some cases, Melpa from rural hamlets will take a plane to another highland community traditionally dressed and carrying implements of traditional life, such as stone axes and digging sticks. The airport at Mount Hagen is truly a meeting place of the jet age and the Stone Age.

¹² FOOD

Like other Highland cultures in Papua New Guinea, the Melpa traditional subsistence was based primarily on sweet potatoes and pork. Sweet potatoes are still an important staple, although Western-style foodstuffs have gained in importance due to their ready availability in trade stores and the central marketplace in Mt. Hagen. There is also a prestige associated with their consumption.

¹³ EDUCATION

Traditional education consisted of socializing young boys and girls to become competent members of adult Melpa society. Although this is still true today, public and parochial educational venues are also open to Hageners. In the highlands region, Western-style education has been integrated with traditional ways of life to create individuals who seem to exist in two very different worlds.

¹⁴ CULTURAL HERITAGE

Vocal music is especially important in Melpa society. Courtship songs are prevalent in many highland cultures in New Guinea. Men woo their mates by composing and performing songs that have double entendre lyrics. When men go to sing to women in other villages they paint and decorate themselves very elaborately.

Mt. Hagen hosts the annual Mt. Hagen Cultural Show, which has been in existence since 1961. The Mt. Hagen Cultural Show is a form of friendly competition in which performance groups from dozens and dozens of tribes from across the country perform traditional songs.

¹⁵ WORK

The traditional division of labor was between the sexes. Men are responsible for creating gardens and fencing them. The fences serve to keep out the pigs that graze and root in the area. Women tend the pigs, plant the staple crop of sweet potatoes and other foodstuffs such as greens and taro, and weed and harvest the garden plot. Beyond small-scale subsistence farming, coffee is the primary cash crop for Hageners.

The modern Melpa work in a variety of jobs in the town. Driving taxis and buses, porting baggage at the airport, and working in shops are only a few of the types of employment that the Hageners pursue.

Tourism is one of several areas of economic growth and development that the regional governments within the Melpa traditional homeland targeted after the 2000 national census.

¹⁶ SPORTS

As in other parts of Papua New Guinea, rugby is an important sport in the area around Mount Hagen. Mount Hagen is the venue for many rugby games involving Hageners and other Papuans from throughout the island.

¹⁷ ENTERTAINMENT AND RECREATION

Town-dwelling Melpa have access to electricity and many of them enjoy watching television. There are very few locally-produced television shows in the country and only one local television broadcast station, EMTV. Satellite television broadcasts a wide range of Australian, British, and American programs.

[18] FOLK ART, CRAFTS, AND HOBBIES

Body decoration is the major art form in the Hagen region. The body is painted with paints produced from local dyes mixed with pig fat. Traditional materials such as feathers and shells are used to decorate elaborate headdresses. Relics of the modern world have become part of the traditional headdresses, including the labels of various products and the tops of cans. The American product Liquid Paper has also become a favorite substitute for pigmented white paint; the intensity of whiteness is cited as the reason for the switch. In the past, *moka* exchanges were important times for elaborate decoration to take place.

[19] SOCIAL PROBLEMS

Revenge was the basis for many violent actions taken by the Melpa in the time before pacification. Revenge murders often pitted the male members of one clan against those of another. This mentality has not completely faded from Melpa culture. Hundreds of men dressed in full war regalia can occasionally be seen running along the Highlands Highway toward a neighboring village to exact revenge for a death or wrongdoing that took place in the past. Events like these alarm tourists and government officials and warnings are sometimes issued regarding travel in the region as a result.

Mortality rates are very high among the Melpa. The infant mortality rate is 57 deaths per 1,000; the child mortality rate is 15 deaths per 1,000; and the maternal mortality rate is 80 deaths per 1,000. The main causes of death among the Melpa are pneumonia, malaria, and typhoid. Life expectancy for the Melpa as derived from the 2000 national census are 53 years for women and 54 years for men.

[20] GENDER ISSUES

Like many of the groups in Papua New Guinea, Hageners exhibit sexual opposition and separation. Differences between males and females are often exaggerated to the point of ambivalence, antagonism, mistrust, and even fear. Nevertheless, Melpa girls have considerable autonomy in choosing a spouse. Although a girl's family might want her to marry into a particular family, they know that forcing their daughter will only result in unhappiness for everyone. Women control the production in Melpa society, including the cultivation of gardens and the all-important pig husbandry that is the center of the Melpa exchange universe. Men must rely on their wives as producers and as such, women wield considerable political power in Melpa society.

[21] BIBLIOGRAPHY

Robbins, Joel and Wardlow, Holly, eds. *The Making of Global and Local Modernities in Melanesia.* Burlington: Ashgate, 2005.

Sillitoe, Paul. *An Introduction to the Anthropology of Melanesia: Culture and Tradition.* Cambridge: Cambridge University Press, 1998.

Stewart, Pamela J. and Strathern, Andrew. *Gender, Song, and Sensibility: Folktales and Folksongs in the Highlands of New Guinea.* Westport, CT: Praeger Publishers, 2002.

Strathern, Andrew. *The Rope of Moka.* Cambridge: Cambridge University Press, 1971.

—by J. Williams

MIAO IN CHINA

PRONUNCIATION: mee-OW
ALTERNATE NAMES: Hmong; Hmu; Meo
LOCATION: China [also Vietnam, Laos, Kampuchea, Thailand, Myanmar and about 1 million migrants to the West]
POPULATION: 8.94 million
LANGUAGE: Miao
RELIGION: Shamanism; ancestor worship; Catholicism and Protestantism
RELATED ARTICLES: Vol. 3: China and Her National Minorities

[1] INTRODUCTION

The Miao have a very long history. They are mentioned in the most ancient Chinese sources, dating from about the 12th century BC. The events related are even more remote. According to these legends, the Miao lived along the Yellow River Valley and the Yangzi River Valley as early as 5,000 years ago. It was said that they were defeated in a fierce battle by the Yellow Emperor (Huang Di, the legendary ancestor of the Chinese people) and had no alternative but to migrate south of the Yangzi River. Nonetheless, they continued to fight against the rulers. Once they were defeated, they moved again. After tens of centuries, they entered the deep forests and mountainous regions of southwest China, especially Guizhou Province. It was from there that they dispersed, under military pressure during the 18th and 19th centuries, especially into the adjacent provinces of Guangxi, Hunan, Hubei, and Yunnan and even across the Chinese border into Vietnam, Laos, Kampuchea, Thailand, and Burma. From time immemorial, the Miao engaged in primitive farming, practicing slash-and-burn cultivation. Families lived in the same house no more than five years. As the soil of the nearby land became impoverished, families would then move away. This method of cultivation required repeated displacement. The Miao have been famed for their "perpetual motion." However, since the mid-20th century, the great majority of the Miao have settled down.

[2] LOCATION AND HOMELAND

The Miao are distributed in more than 700 cities and counties of 7 provinces of south China and numbered 8.94 million in 2000. The main characteristic of their inhabitation is "wide distribution and tiny colonies." Their largest area of concentration is the Wuling and Miaoling mountain range in Guangxi Autonomous Region, where nearly one-third of the Miao population of the Peoples' Republic of China lives. "Birds nest in trees, fish swim in rivers, Miao live in mountains," says an adage of the Miao. Generation after generation, the Miao have dwelled in mountainous areas with mild climate and abundant rainfall both in China and in countries on the southwest Chinese border. In the 1970s and '80s, more than 100,000 Miao migrated from Laos to the United States, Canada, Australia, France, and Guyana. The Miao expatriates amount to more than one million.

[3] LANGUAGE

The Miao language belongs to the Sino-Tibetan system, Miao-Yao family, Miao branch. It is typologically akin to the Thai language. There are 3 dialects, 7 subdialects, and 18 regional idioms. A written language was created by an English missionary about 100 years ago, but its use was limited to only a few counties. In the 1950s it was revised and another three written scripts were created in correspondence with the three dialects. Today, the Miao use the Chinese *pinyin* phonetic system based on the Western alphabet. Language is an important criterion to distinguish the many Miao groups. Each has its own self-given name, such as Kanao, Mo, Mao, Guoxiong, Daisou, Shuang, and Daji. The ancient Chinese books, identifying these groups by clothes and hairstyles, described them as Red Miao, White Miao, Black Miao, Flower Miao, Blue Miao, Long-skirt Miao, Short-skirt Miao, Red-head Miao, Tip-top Miao, etc.

⁴FOLKLORE

The creation of nature, the existence and development of every animal, plant and artifact, the origin of the Miao people, and the battles and migrations they experienced are all illustrated in Miao mythology. For example, the ancient "Maple Song" said that White Maple was an immortal tree that gave birth to Butterfly Mama. She married a water bubble and thereafter laid 12 eggs. The treetop changed into a big bird, which hatched the eggs during a period of 12 years. The eggs finally hatched, giving birth to a Thunder God, a dragon, a buffalo, a tiger, an elephant, a snake, a centipede, a boy called Jiangyang, and his sister. Thus, Butterfly Mama was the mother of God, animals, and human beings. Then the flood came, which destroyed everything. As it receded, Jiangyang and his sister, alone in the world, were confronted with the dilemma of human progeny and incest. To know Heaven's will, they rolled down from the mountain two millstones. Since the millstones laid one on top of the other when they came to rest, the brother and sister were bound to marry. Three years after the marriage, the woman gave birth to a fleshy lump. Her husband cut it into pieces and spread them apart. Every piece of the fleshy lump turned into a man or a woman. Human beings thus multiplied.

The Miao folklore and mythology contains a great wealth of stories. Shelang and Ayi are the hero and heroine of a love story. The woman Naliaowan invented pottery. Meishan is a female hunter. Wumoxi is the heroine of an insurrectionary army. There is an endless stream of tales and songs about heroes and heroines.

⁵RELIGION

The Miao believe that there is a supernatural power that exists in everything surrounding them and dominates or influences their destiny. They also believe that everything that moves or grows has its own spirit. They revere the sun, moon, lightning and thunder, fire, rivers, caverns, large trees, huge stones, and some animals, praying for their protection. According to the Miao, the spirit of the dead will become a ghost, which may come to haunt their families and livestock, make them sick, or even cause death. The shamans play the role of intermediary, allowing people to communicate with ghosts; they resort to magic arts, practice divination, treat various illnesses, eliminate personal misfortune, and bring about good luck. The earliest shaman was one of the Miao's ancestors, whose name (Xianggao) was frequently mentioned in the shamans' incantations. The Miao also worship their ancestors because they are deeply grateful for having been granted life; they also pray for protection and for the multiplicity and prosperity of their off-

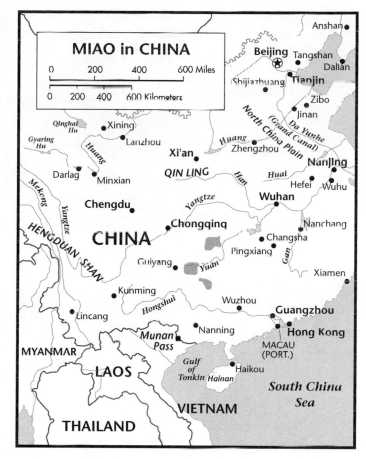

spring. Since the 19th century, a sizable number of Miao have converted to Catholicism and Protestantism.

⁶MAJOR HOLIDAYS

There are dozens of Miao festivals. Among the most important is the offering of sacrifice to ancestors, performed at fixed dates during the year. Other sacrifices are for the purpose of social intercourse and collective celebration after a busy farming and hunting season. Chiguzhang is a grand ceremony held every 13 years in certain Miao districts, accompanied by the sacrificial slaughter of buffalo in honor of the ancestors. The Miao use their own calendar as well as the Gregorian and lunar calendars. The main purpose of the Miao calendar now is to fix the Miao New Year, a very jubilant festival. The Spring Festival (lunar New Year; Western calendar, between January 21 and February 20) is now a major holiday common to all of China's nationalities. There are songs, dances, horse races, reed-pipe wind music, and dating.

⁷RITES OF PASSAGE

To the Miao, a huge stone is a symbol of a strong child. As the child grows to three years of age, the parents will bring offerings to a huge stone, burn joss sticks and kowtow, and pray for blessings and protection. This rite is repeated three times annually. If it does not work (for example, if the child is unhealthy), the parents will turn to a large tree or cavern.

There is an ancient custom that right after a boy is born, his father would bury a piece of iron equivalent to the body weight of the baby, forge it every year, and finally hammer it into a

Miao people in Yunnan, China. ((c) Panorama/The Image Works)

sword when the child reached the age of puberty. Miao girls learn embroidery early at five or six years of age. When they reach adolescence, they are good enough to brocade, cross-stitch, and tailor clothes and skirts. Thereafter, they begin sewing their embroidered bridal clothes.

Miao boys and girls are allowed to date from 13 or 14 years of age. In some districts, when a girl reaches 12, she is believed to have passed through childhood and thus is allowed to participate formally in any dating activities.

According to custom, the Miao bury the dead underground. The family announces the sad news to all the village people, who spare no effort in the funeral arrangements. A shaman is invited to sing the mournful songs, to lead the soul of the dead back to live with the family, to bless and protect the offspring and, last but not least, to tell the dead how to be reunited with their ancestors in the future.

⁸INTERPERSONAL RELATIONS

The Miao are a very hospitable people, always keeping their house open for guests, who are greeted with wine and song. The host comes outdoors to greet the guests and proposes a toast immediately. Then they sing, drink, and eat, enjoying themselves to the fullest. On the fifteenth of February or March (lunar calendar; Western calendar, between March 8 and April 6 or between April 7 and May 5) each year, the whole

village will receive young males from outside. This so-called Sisters' Feast Festival lasts about three days. The parents prepare meals, which their daughters will offer to the boys. Girls dress up, use makeup and wear a yellow flower in their hair. Blowing the reed-pipe wind instrument (*lüsheng*), peculiar to the Miao, boys come to the village and wait for the girls to come and meet them. The group dating of the Miao is called *youfang (yaomalang), tianyue, zuoyue, or caiyueliang* in different Miao districts, but the meaning of the words and the ritual patterns are similar. Singing in antiphonal style and dancing form the initial rite through which a boy and a girl might gradually pay tender regards to each other and fall in love. Group dating is held on many occasions, especially during festivals. During the Sisters' Feast Festival, each girl offers food to the boy of her desire, who sings for his meal. He may find in the rice a token of affection. If he is not the boy chosen by the girl, a little food will be carelessly offered.

⁹LIVING CONDITIONS

Engaged in agriculture, the Miao are self-sufficient for their livelihood. They live in houses of one or two stories, the rear built on the mountain slope and the front resting on stilts. The roof is made of straw. The grain is stored in the ceiling. The bottom of the house is for the livestock and poultry. There are three to five rooms. Sons and daughters are separated. The infants live with their parents. Their furniture includes a bed, cupboard, case, table, and stool, all made of wood. In addition, there are big bamboo baskets for food storage and pottery vessels for water and wine. The living conditions of the Miao residing in urban areas are not very different from their neighbors of other nationalities.

¹⁰FAMILY LIFE

The Miao family is monogamous and patrilineal, consisting of parents and their children. The property is inherited by the man, but the housewife has power in the family. There is enough freedom to allow young people to choose their spouses, and marriage is usually the result of dating and falling in love. Although an old custom favored arranged marriages or cousin marriage, the union took place only when the boy and the girl both agreed. There is a custom that the bride goes back to her own family immediately after the wedding ceremony and will return to live with her husband only during festivals or after the busy season. If she gets pregnant, she will then move to her husband's house. Otherwise, she should move three years after the wedding. A rite will be held for the change of dwelling. The Miao enjoy a healthy demographic growth, and, like the other national minorities in China, are not restrained by the one-child policy of the Chinese state.

The Miao are fond of pets, especially dogs, cats, and birds.

¹¹CLOTHING

There are a variety of costumes corresponding to the numerous Miao branches (in fact, the difference in costumes and hairstyles is the best symbol to distinguish one branch of Miao from another). As a result, there are hundreds of styles that have no parallel among the other nationalities in China. Brilliant embroideries and silver ornaments are a distinctive national feature. The accordion-pleated skirt is a cultural trait of Miao women.

¹²FOOD

The Miao's principal food is rice (glutinous rice during festivals), supplemented by yams, millet, corn, wheat, buckwheat, and sorghum, all cooked in a rice steamer. The Miao like hot pepper. In fact, every dish is spicy. They also like sour condiments. Proteins come from poultry, eggs, beef, veal, pork, frog, fish, snail, eel, snake, crab, and shrimp, but their diet is mainly vegetables. No food is taboo. They use chopsticks and bowls. Wine is made at home with rice. The kitchen is provided with a cooking range, burning firewood, or sometimes coal. Filling the bowl with rice is the duty of the housewife, her unmarried daughter, or a daughter-in-law who lives in the house. Men and guests should not do it. A married daughter still staying at her parents' home can fill the bowl, but not if she has already lived at her husband's house.

¹³EDUCATION

All children are able to receive formal education. Miao scholars, professors, and other intellectuals are not uncommon. Some parents, however, hold the traditional view against girls' education: "It would be better to send a girl to a piggery than to send her to study," "Girls eventually marry and leave," etc. Quite a number of girls drop out of school after puberty. That is why female intellectuals are so few and the rate of illiteracy and semi-illiteracy among Miao women is as high as 95%.

¹⁴CULTURAL HERITAGE

Song and dance are deeply rooted in Miao life. Without them, one is no longer a Miao. In addition to songs sung on specified occasions (love songs, funeral songs, wedding songs, sacrificial offering songs, etc.), a great variety of songs are sung impromptu to express in a touching manner an individual's true feelings. On the occasion of a wedding ceremony, aged persons are invited to sing in antiphonal style, continuing for days and nights. In antiphonal singing during group dating, the appropriate answer, unique metaphor, beautiful voice, and poetic wording of a singer will definitely attract attention from the opposite sex.

Just like their songs, dances also display the distinctive features of Miao culture. Dance is not only an expression of joy, but also of grief. The Miao dance not only for entertainment and recreation, but also for physical health and sentimental expression. Blowing the wind reed-pipe, accompanied by the graceful movement of the performer, is a unique combination of music and dance.

The Miao have a rich tradition of folk tales, represented mainly by ancient songs; an ancient song, Jia, sung in ancient Miao language, is considered a gem of ancient Miao culture.

¹⁵WORK

All the work of Miao is dedicated to ensuring a constant supply of food and daily necessities. They are self-sufficient agriculturists, with rice as their staple crop. In addition, they grow corn, yams, millet, sorghum, beans, wheat, buckwheat, fruits, vegetables, cotton, hemp, tobacco, indigo, castor, peanut, sunflower, rapeseed, and sesame. They grow an abundance of hot peppers. In the past, weeding was thought to be women's duty and plowing was left to men. Nowadays, women also work with the plough. Needless to say, many other farm chores are also done by women. Only harrowing and building raised paths through fields are men's duties. In addition, all the housework, including cooking, laundry, spinning and weaving, tailoring, and livestock and poultry raising, is left to the females, while the males sometimes join together for hunting in the off-season.

¹⁶SPORTS

The Miao like horse races, which are usually held on festivals. Teenagers love basketball, table tennis, and Chinese chess. The dragon boat regatta is a traditional competition of the Miao. The participants of a team usually come from the same village. The distance of the race is about 2 km. Other popular sports are kicking the shuttlecock and Chinese shadowboxing (wushu).

¹⁷ENTERTAINMENT AND RECREATION

Dancing and singing for nights and days only takes place during festivals and wedding or funeral ceremonies. In normal times, dining together, chatting, calling on relatives, and the visit of a married woman to her parents' home are the joys of life. Movies, television, videos, libraries, and cultural centers are popular in cities, counties, and small towns.

[18] FOLK ART, CRAFTS, AND HOBBIES

Embroidery, wax printing, brocade, and paper-cuts are four famous crafts of the Miao. Silver ornaments elaborately wrought by craftsmen display their great attainments and sophisticated artistic conceptions.

[19] SOCIAL PROBLEMS

Because of their mountainous environment, the Miao are still confronted with the problems of poverty and isolation. Migration of Miao youngsters from their villages to urban and coastal areas is a widespread and ambivalent phenomenon. The positive aspect is that the migrants may bring back new knowledge and experience, which is helpful to their native place; the negative aspect is that their migration runs counter to the immediate needs of talent and skills for local development. Today, the trend of migration to the outside world grows stronger and stronger.

[20] GENDER ISSUES

The Chinese constitution states that women have equal rights with men in all areas of life, and most legislation is gender neutral. However, there are continued reports of discrimination, sexual harassment, wage discrepancies, and other gender related problems. The gap in educational level between women and men is narrowing with women making up 47.1% of college students in 2005, but only 32.6% of doctoral students.

China has strict family planning laws. It is illegal for women to marry before 20 years of age (22 for men), and it is illegal for single women to give birth. The Family Planning Bureau can require women to take periodic pregnancy tests and enforce laws that often leave women with no real options other than abortion or sterilization. Though minority populations were previously exempt from family planning regulations, policy has changed in recent years to limit minority population growth. Today, urban minority couples may have two children while rural couples may have three or four.

Prostitution and the sex trade is a significant problem in China involving between 1.7 and 5 million women. It involved organized crime, businessmen, the police, and government workers, so prosecution against prostitution has limited success. In 2002, the nation removed homosexuality from its official list of mental illnesses, and though it is still a taboo topic, homosexuality is increasingly accepted, especially in large, international cities.

[21] BIBLIOGRAPHY

Bai Ziran, ed. *Mœurs et coutumes des Miao*. Beijing: Éditions en langues étrangères, 1988.

Cheung, Siu-woo. "Millenarism, Christian Movements, and Ethnic Change among the Miao of Southwest China." In *Cultural Encounters on China's Ethnic Frontiers,* edited by Stevan Harrell, 217–47. Seattle: University of Washington Press, 1994.

Chiao, Chien, Nicholas Tapp, and Kam-yin Ho, ed. "Special Issue on Ethnic Groups in China." *New Asia Bulletin*, no. 8, 1989.

Diamond, Norma. "Defining the Miao, Ming, Qing, and Contemporary Views." In *Cultural Encounters on China's Ethnic Frontiers,* edited by Stevan Harrell, 92–116. Seattle: University of Washington Press, 1994.

Dreyer, June Teufel. *China's Forty Millions*. Cambridge: Harvard University Press, 1976.

Eberhard, Wolfram. *China's Minorities: Yesterday and Today.* Belmont: Wadsworth Publishing Company, 1982.

Gustafsson, Bjorn A., Shi, Li, and Sicular, Terry, eds. *Inequality and Public Policy in China*. New York: Cambridge University Press, 2008.

Heberer, Thomas. *China and Its National Minorities: Autonomy or Assimilation?* Armonk, NY: M. E. Sharpe, 1989.

Lebar, Frank, et al. *Ethnic Groups of Mainland Southeast Asia.* New Haven: Human Relations Area Files Press, 1964.

Lemoine, Jacques. "Les Miao-Yao." In *Ethnologie régionale II* (Encyclopédie de la Pléiade). Paris: Gallimard, 1978.

Ma Yin, ed. *China's Minority Nationalities*. Beijing: Foreign Languages Press, 1989.

Miller, Lucien, ed. *South of the Clouds: Tales from Yunnan*. Seattle: University of Washington Press, 1994.

Ramsey, S. Robert. *The Languages of China*. Princeton: Princeton University Press, 1987.

Shin, Leo Kwok-yueh. *The Making of the Chinese State: Ethnicity and Expansion on the Ming Borderlands*. New York: Cambridge University Press, 2006.

Wiens, Harold J. *Han Chinese Expansion in South China*. New Haven: The Shoestring Press, 1967.

—by C. Le Blanc

MICRONESIANS

PRONUNCIATION: mye-cro-NEE-zhuns
LOCATION: Federated States of Micronesia (comprising Guam, Republic of Belau, Kiribati, Marshall Islands, Republic of Nauru, Chuuk State, the Northern Mariana Islands, and thousands of smaller islands)
POPULATION: Approximately 108,000
LANGUAGE: Chukese, Pohnpeian, Yapese, Kosrean, Ulithian, Woleaian, Nukuoro, Kapingamarangi, English (official language)
RELIGION: Catholicism; Protestant sects

¹INTRODUCTION

Most of the nearly 2,500 islands that comprise Micronesia were administered by the United States until 1986, when the Trust Territory of the Pacific Islands was dissolved into four constitutional governments. The Federated States of Micronesia, the Republic of Belau (Palau), the Republic of the Marshall Islands, and Commonwealth of the Northern Mariana Islands all still retain political and economic relationships with the United States, some to a greater degree than others. However, each of these constitutional political units relies economically on the United States almost completely.

The name "Micronesia" comes from the Greek, meaning "small islands." The culture area of Micronesia is a parallelogram-shaped region in the North Pacific Ocean. Its corners are formed by the Republic of Belau in the southwest; Kiribati, formerly the Gilbert Islands, in the southeast; Guam in the northwest; and the Marshall Islands in the northeast.

The capital of the Federated States of Micronesia was relocated in 1989 from Kolonia, Pohnapei to Palikir, only about six miles west of the former capital.

²LOCATION AND HOMELAND

Volcanic and coral islands make up Micronesia's islands. The largest of these is Guam, with 225 sq mi and about half of the total population of Micronesia. Only half of Guam's total population is indigenous; the other half are mostly American military personnel. Guam has been a territorial possession of the United States since 1898, when the island was acquired from Spain.

Almost all of the islands within the region of Micronesia are located north of the equator. As it happens, the richest and poorest islands of the region are the only ones located south of the equator. The Republic of Nauru is one of the smallest countries in the world with a total area of nine sq mi. It is also one of the least populous, with only around 13,500 people, and an island rich in phosphate rocks that provide almost all of the national income for the country. Nauruans have lived in a virtual welfare state with no taxes but an extremely high unemployment rate (nearly 90%).

³LANGUAGE

The languages of the Micronesian region belong to the large family of Austronesian languages that are spread throughout the Pacific Basin. Micronesian languages fall into two types, nuclear and nonnuclear languages. The nonnuclear languages show close affinities to other Austronesian languages outside of Micronesia such as Philippine languages and languages of Indonesia. The nuclear languages are all closely related to each other and create a chain of languages across the middle of Micronesia. Linguists look at these patterns of relationships to help determine the prehistoric settlement history of the area. From this pattern we can posit that there were at least two migrations into the region: one from the Indonesian archipelago into the western section of the region and a second from the eastern Melanesia. The migrations from eastern Melanesia were later than those from the Philippine and Indonesian regions.

The Pacific and Asian Linguistics Institute of the University of Hawaii administers a program that provides linguistic documentation of the languages of Micronesia in the form of dictionaries and language learning materials. The work of this institute has vastly increased knowledge of the languages of the region.

⁴FOLKLORE

Micronesian mythology reflects concern for the social and natural order of things. One Palauan myth recounts the story of a magical breadfruit tree that the child of sun provides for his mortal mother. In order to provide fish for her to eat, the son cuts a hole in the center of a breadfruit tree that grows outside his mother's house and next to the sea. Fish were thrown through the hole by the waves of the sea and the mother need only walk out of her doorway to collect fish. Her neighbors became jealous and cut down the breadfruit tree, which caused a catastrophic flood engulfing the whole island. Only the mother was saved by her son, who flew her through the sky on a raft.

⁵RELIGION

Christian missionaries in Micronesia have converted most of the indigenous population to either Catholicism or Protestant sects. Religion in traditional Micronesian cultures involved beliefs in ghosts, in ancestor worship, and in spirits that inhabit places and natural objects and that are associated with specific activities. Canoe builders, for instance, had patron spirits who would control the outcome of their work on canoe construction. Chants and offerings were directed to these patron spirits to help insure their successful participation in human projects.

⁶MAJOR HOLIDAYS

Major religious holidays in Micronesia now revolve around the Christian calendar. Many Micronesian states celebrate Christmas, Easter, Ash Wednesday, and All Saints Day. On the Republic of Nauru, Angam Day is held on October 26. Angam Day celebrates the threshold births of the 1,500th Nauruan at two points in the island's history. The first was in 1932. The population was recovering from two major epidemics that had reduced the population to an all-time low of just over 1,000 in 1920. The second cause for celebration came in 1949, when the 1,500 mark was reached again following a decline in 1941. American secular holidays are all observed in many parts of Micronesia and some islands even recognize American Thanksgiving. Precontact holidays would likely have been occasions of celebrations for auspicious events or the accomplishment of certain feats. A major event for the display of traditional culture is the South Pacific Arts Festival, which rotates

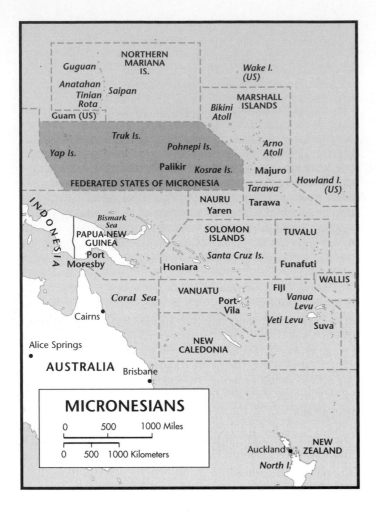

MICRONESIANS

0   500   1000 Miles

0   500   1000 Kilometers

between venues in the Pacific Ocean. At this festival performing groups from a number of Pacific Island nations come together to put on shows for the enjoyment of tourists, the local populations, and the participants themselves.

7 RITES OF PASSAGE

Christianity has altered many of the traditional celebrations associated with changes in social status that accompany events like birth, puberty, marriage, and death. Birth on the island of Belau was accompanied by a series of ritual exchanges prior to and following the birth of the first child of a wealthy couple. The attainment of puberty by males on the island of Yap is accompanied by a hair cutting ceremony that has been retained to the present day. In other parts of Micronesia, the passage through puberty was marked only by a change in attire. In Chuuk State (formerly Truk), following puberty both males and females were permitted to engage in sexual relationships. Trial marriages were also permitted. Christian ideology has altered these patterns of sexual relationships considerably, and they do not continue in the present time.

8 INTERPERSONAL RELATIONS

Long distance exchange was part of the life of some Micronesian groups. Definite rules of etiquette dictated the behavior of visitors to another island or atoll. However, little is known about precontact behavior in most Micronesian societies. Social class dictated marriage rules and likely influenced pat-

terns of day-to-day social intercourse. In most societies, there were three distinct social classes that individuals were born into; however, in some societies, individuals could "marry up," while the converse was not possible. Status still determines social etiquette in Micronesian societies. Greetings in many societies translate into English as "welcome." In the Chamorro language of the Northern Marianas, the greeting is *hafa adai*.

9 LIVING CONDITIONS

Micronesian communities are located near the coastline on both the "high" volcanic islands and the "low" atolls. Some islands have several types of houses that served different functions. In the era before European influence on Ponape, where there was a fairly large population and a highly stratified polity, there were guesthouses for visiting dignitaries.

Many Micronesian societies also have canoe sheds where canoes are stored. These structures function as men's clubhouses where men could congregate and would occasionally sleep. These structures are not like the Melanesian men's houses where women are prohibited. Western-style housing has become common in Micronesia, although some houses are still constructed out of traditional materials save the corrugated tin roof.

Electricity and running water are present in those Micronesian islands where the European and American presence is most heavily felt. Gasoline-powered generators are also owned by families to run electrical appliances.

Traditional transportation in Micronesia is by canoe and by foot. Automobiles and buses are now common on most islands in the region. Micronesian cultures are famous for their highly specialized and technologically sophisticated outrigger canoes.

10 FAMILY LIFE

Families in traditional Micronesian societies are based on a husband, a wife, and their unmarried children. In many societies such as those in precontact Belau, a woman would move away from her traditional land and into a house that her husband had built on land he had inherited from his mother.

In Belau, there are women's councils and women's clubs organized in an identical fashion to those of the men. The only difference is that women do not have elaborate ceremonial houses in which to conduct their business. Women's councils continue to play an important role in village decision-making in Belau.

11 CLOTHING

Traditional Micronesian cultures typically made use of some sort of clothing. Early Spanish accounts of the Marianas Islands describe the population there as going naked. Typical attire involved either a loin cloth for men or a type of fiber skirt for women. In the Marshall Islands women wore plaited skirts that resembled mats spanning the waist to the ankles.

A number of items of body adornment were also manufactured in Micronesian societies. Carved combs and flower arrangements often decorated the hairstyles of Micronesian men and women. Coconut oil was also spread on the skin to make it shiny and sweet smelling. A yellow dye made from the root of the turmeric plant was also applied to the skin in some Micronesian cultures. Turmeric, a relative of ginger, is an important ingredient in Indian curry, giving the food its distinctive color.

In parts of Micronesia, tattooing was an important part of body adornment. The most extensive tattooing occurred in the Caroline Islands, now the Federated States of Micronesia.

Colonization has changed clothing patterns among most Micronesian groups. Western-style clothing now predominates on almost every occasion. However, ceremonial occasions often warrant a return to traditional styles of dress.

12 FOOD

Traditional foodstuffs in Micronesia are fairly uniform across the region. There are some local differences due to patterns of rainfall and island topography. Taro root, breadfruit, coconuts, and yams were the most important in precontact times and continue to be staples in many households throughout the region. Since European contact with the region, corn, sweet potato, and manioc (cassava) have also become important staples. Fish is the most important source of protein in all parts of Micronesia. Since animal life was limited on most islands, hunting played a very small role in the subsistence of Micronesian peoples. Although rats and lizards were omnipresent, they were not utilized as a source of food by any groups.

Western foodstuffs have become important, especially to younger people. Prepared and packaged American foods such as breakfast cereals are part of many Micronesian daily meals.

13 EDUCATION

Western-style education has been introduced throughout Micronesia. The American presence in the region has produced a number of American schools where expatriates send their children. Graduation ceremonies often include addresses from high-ranking American military personnel present on the island. Opportunities for higher education must be sought in the United States or in other developed countries.

14 CULTURAL HERITAGE

Micronesian music is dominated by the human voice; there are very few musical instruments produced by Micronesian cultures. The shell trumpet and the nose flute are the most common instruments in the region. The Marshall Islands also made use of the hourglass-shaped drums that were common in most of Melanesia.

Gesture was important in traditional Micronesian vocal music. Dances were often only gestures performed while in a seated posture. In other instances, line dances were performed by a number of individuals in unison.

Musical traditions of other cultural regions of the world have gained importance in Micronesia. Polynesian-style music from Hawaii has become popular in parts of Micronesia. American music and dance has been introduced via television and the resident American population in the islands.

15 WORK

Traditional patterns of work entailed a division of labor along gender lines. In some islands, males engaged in fishing and harvesting the products of trees such as breadfruit, coconuts, and betel nut, while females were responsible for gardening and activities that took place in the household including plaiting mats and making clothing. In some other islands, women provided most of the fish. However, in all parts of Micronesia women were forbidden to fish from canoes.

Wage labor in a variety of industries is now the norm in Micronesia. Both women and men are in the wage-earning workforce in Micronesian society. Many states have set minimum wage standards that are at odds with the U.S. federal minimum wage standards. In the Northern Marianas Islands, the minimum hourly wage for 2007 was $3.55, which was less than the federal minimum wage of $5.85.

16 SPORTS

Traditional forms of competition in Nauru consisted of singing and dancing competitions and kite flying. The competing "teams" were organized along lines of genealogical descent. These activities have all but ceased in most parts of Micronesia. Sports introduced from other nations, such as the United States and Japan, have become important.

A traditional sport on the island of Nauru is catching Noddy birds. The Brown or Common Noddy bird (Anous stolidus) is a member of the tern family. Noddy birds feed on fish caught out and sea. At sunset, when the birds return to land after feeding at sea, Nauru men stand on the beach ready to throw their lassos on the returning birds. The Nauruan lasso is constructed of supple rope and weighted at one end. When a bird flies over, the lasso is thrown up to knock the bird from the sky. The fallen Noddy birds are then cooked and eaten.

17 ENTERTAINMENT AND RECREATION

Television and videos have become important forms of entertainment in many Micronesian societies. Most of the programming is foreign and often out of date, coming from the United States and, in some cases, Japan. Local programming for news and community information is limited. Television and videos have made an impact on traditional ways of life in Micronesia. Movie theaters in many islands run current American and other foreign releases; however, the runs of these movies are often very short, only a few days in many cases.

18 FOLK ART, CRAFTS, AND HOBBIES

Belau, in western Micronesia, is well known for the elaborately incised and painted facades of the chiefly collective houses, called bai. The degree of decoration and ornamentation was directly related to the degree of status and amount of wealth the group possessed. Each plank of the facades at either end of the house was painted with a separate narrative relating aspects of cultural history or mythology. Beginning in the late 1800s, planks were cut away from bai to give to foreigners. In the 1930s, the Palauans began to create replicated as well as new "storyboards" for sale to tourists.

Carved bowls of various shapes and sizes were utilitarian in function but decorative in design. These are now produced for the tourist industry in Micronesia. Finely plaited mats for sleeping and sitting were items of status among many Micronesian groups. These items are now also produced primarily for sale to tourists.

The construction of single outrigger canoes was the outstanding technological achievement of Micronesian cultures. Many were over 40 ft long and their hulls were made of hewn planks lashed together with coconut fiber rope. The production of canoes has greatly diminished in post-contact times in Micronesia.

[19] SOCIAL PROBLEMS

Economic self-sufficiency and cultural survival are two of the major problems facing Micronesian countries. Creating compromises between various factions both within islands and between islands is a challenge that will continue for many years to come. The immense differences that separated the various islands linked together through the weak infrastructure of the Trust Territory of the Pacific Islands have been diminished through the creation of independent socio-political units in the mid-1980s. Success of the islands will be a balancing act between modernization and the maintenance of traditional cultural patterns and institutions.

[20] GENDER ISSUES

The Micronesian culture area exhibits considerable variation in terms of gender. At the highest level of social organization, eastern Micronesia societies trace descent matrilineally and form clans based on these principles. In western Micronesia, societies are patrilineal both in descent and social organization. Under the social influences of Western societies, the strong principles of matrilineal social organization have been gradually eroding in eastern Micronesia.

Rank and status are important concepts that interact with the cultural construction of gender in Micronesian societies. On Yap, gender is conceptualized as part of the bipartite distinction between "pure" or "sacred" and "polluted" or "profane." Males and females and members of the nuclear family are placed into this scheme, which exhibits a degree of relativity. In general, males are *tabugul*, "pure" or "sacred," while females are *ta'ay*, "polluted" or "profane." Fathers are tabugul to their wives and children; women are ta'ay to their husbands and post adolescent sons, but tabugul to their other children. As in so many other societies in the Pacific, menstrual blood is the source of ta'ay in Yap society.

Village space in Yap is also gender specific. Every village has at least one men's house as well as at least one menstrual house. Menstrual houses are restricted to menstruating women who spend at least one week per month there. Upon a girl's first menstruation, she enters the menstrual house (*dapal*) for a period of time ranging from six to 18 months. The men's house is restricted to adult men and the post adolescent boys who reside there and are socialized into the roles of adult males.

[21] BIBLIOGRAPHY

Alkire, W. *An Introduction to the Peoples and Cultures of Micronesia.* 2nd ed. Menlo Park, CA: Cummings Publishing Company, 1977.

Barnett, H. *Being a Palauan.* New York: Holt, Rinehart and Winston, 1960.

Ferreira, Celio. *Palauan Cosmology: Dominance in a Traditional Micronesian Society.* Goteborg: Acta Universitatis Gothoburgensis, 1987.

Thomas, S. D. *The Last Navigator.* New York: Henry Holt, 1987.

—by J. Williams

MINAHASANS

PRONUNCIATION: mee-nah-HAH-suns
ALTERNATE NAMES: Menadonese
LOCATION: Indonesia (Sulawesi)
POPULATION: 650,000 to 1.25 million
LANGUAGE: Malay (Manado dialect and Bahasa Indonesia); various indigenous languages (Bantik, Ponosakan, Tombulu, Tonsawang, Tonsea, Tondano, Tontemboan).
RELIGION: Christianity
RELATED ARTICLES: Vol. 3: Indonesians

[1] INTRODUCTION

Although the Minahasans produced no pre-colonial kingdoms, as other Indonesian ethnic groups can boast, since the Dutch period they have enjoyed one of the highest standards of education and economic development in the whole country. The term *Minahasa* itself means "made one," referring to an early confederation of tribes formed to resist the neighboring Bolaang-Mongondow people. Deriving from these nine tribes are the sub-ethnic groups recognized among the Minahasa today: Tonsea, Tombulu, Tontemboan, Tondano, Tonsawang, Pasan Ratahan, Ponosakan, Babontehu, and Bantik. The people of the regency (*kabupaten*) are also commonly called Manadonese, after the principal city, Manado.

Such as it is known, early Minahasa history is one of constant warfare among clans and villages, marked by headhunting. The Muslim sultanate of Ternate to the east exercised some influence on the Minahasans, though the latter, unlike the Gorontalo farther west, resisted Islamization. In the mid-16th century, the Portuguese, with the first Christian missionary, a Catholic priest, among them, visited the region. From bases in the Philippines, the Spanish also made contacts among the Minahasans, leaving American food crops and horses (the local Malay lingua franca takes its word for the animal from the Castilian *caballo*).

In the 1650s, the Dutch East India Company drove the Spanish out of Minahasa in pursuit of the spice monopoly. They built Fort Amsterdam in 1673, around which would grow the city of Manado. However, it was only in 1808–09 that the Dutch penetrated very far beyond that strategic outpost; in those years, they subjugated the surrounding highlands. This opened up lands for the forced cultivation of coffee and began a cultural transformation, which would include rapid mass conversions to Christianity. While losing a great part of their indigenous culture, the Minahasans took advantage of the opportunities offered by the Dutch colonial government and European missionaries. By 1930, the region had the highest literacy rate in both Malay and Dutch in the whole country. In disproportionately high numbers, Minahasans staffed the bureaucracy throughout the colony. They also served in the colonial military, feeling more solidarity with the Christian Dutch than with their Muslim fellow "natives."

Indeed, the struggle for independence from Dutch rule in the aftermath of World War II received a far from unanimous welcome in the region. However, despite its reputation as the "twelfth province of Holland," Jong Minahasa ("Young Minahasa") was one of the early 20th century regional associations that merged into the Indonesian nationalist movement. Dur-

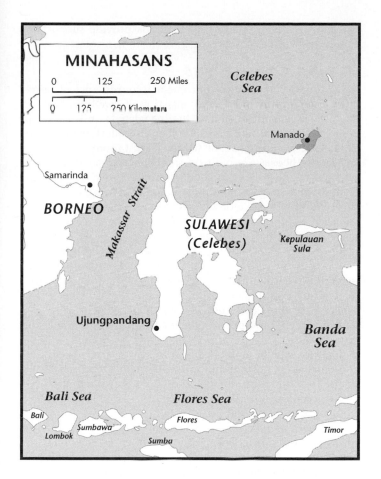

MINAHASANS

0   125   250 Miles

0   125   250 Kilometers

Celebes
Sea

Manado

Samarinda

BORNEO

Makassar Strait

SULAWESI
(Celebes)

Kepulauan
Sula

Ujungpandang

Banda
Sea

Bali Sea   Flores Sea

Bali

Sumbawa   Flores

Lombok   Timor

Sumba

ing the revolution, Sukarno and Hatta sent a Minahasan, Dr. Sam Ratulangie, to establish a republican administration for all of Sulawesi. Today, the Minahasa region is well integrated into the Indonesian nation, at a distance from the Java and Islam-dominated mainstream but without separatist ambitions. According to one official index, North Sulawesi, of which Minahasa is the most advanced part, ranks only after Jakarta and Yogyakarta in quality of life. Already an increasingly popular tourist destination, particularly for its spectacular venues for scuba-diving, Manado is slated to become one of the principle nodes in a "growth triangle" that will include Malaysian Sabah and Philippine Mindanao.

²LOCATION AND HOMELAND

The Minahasa region occupies the very tip of the Sulawesi's northern peninsula (corresponding to Minahasa regency within the province of North Sulawesi). The landscape is mountainous, dominated Mt. Klabat, which is 1,995-m (6,000-ft), and Mt. Soputan (which erupted in 1989). There is also a sizable upland lake, Tondano, along whose shores wet-rice cultivation flourishes. According to the 2000 census, Minahasans made up 33% of the population of Sulawesi Utara (North S.) province, equaling over 650,000; the province's total population had risen to 2.85 million in 2008. The population density of the Minahasa region, at 750 persons per sq km (1,940 persons per sq mi) is half of Java's but exceedingly high for the Outer Islands. Many Minahasans have settled in Jakarta and other parts of Indonesia, as well as in the Netherlands.

The region, especially the city of Manado, has long attracted outsiders. The common physical stereotype of the Minahasans is that they are strikingly attractive examples of racial blending, though this may not accurately apply to the generality. There is a small community of mixed European and indigenous descent, the Borgo. Intermarriage with Chinese has also been very frequent with noticeable results; anti-Chinese feeling seems to be much lower in Minahasa than in the rest of the country.

³LANGUAGE

Like most other Indonesian languages, those of North Sulawesi are Austronesian. However, they display closer affinities to the Austronesian languages of the Philippines to the north than to their neighbors farther south on Sulawesi. Despite the Minahasa region's small size, seven distinct languages are spoken, each associated with a particular district (Bantik, Ponosakan, Tombulu, Tonsawang, Tonsea, Tondano, and Tontemboan).

The regional lingua franca is a localized dialect of Malay called "Manado Malay" after the multiethnic provincial capital. Daily speech in the indigenous languages is freely mixed with Manado Malay and, increasingly, with Bahasa Indonesia. The lingua franca may drive the Minahasan languages into extinction over the course of the next few generations.

In a pattern atypical of Indonesia, Minahasans use family names, with married women placing their maiden names after their husband's surname.

⁴FOLKLORE

According to legend, the ancestress of the Minahasans, Lumimuut, was born from foam thrown up by the sea. Lumimuut was impregnated by the wind and bore a son, Toar. Hoping to find mates, the two set out in different directions. After years of wandering, they met again but failed to recognize each other. They married and had many children, among whom Lumimuut divided her realm, the Minahasa land. The sacred stone, Watu Pinawetengan, to which she summoned her offspring for this division, can still be seen, covered with carvings of unknown meaning.

⁵RELIGION

Some 90% of the population of Minahasa is Christian (the majority subscribe to several Protestant sects led by the [Dutch] Reformed Church; a small minority is Catholic). Catholicism was first introduced in the 16th century by a Portuguese priest, Father Diego Magalhaens. Protestantism arrived with the Dutch in the 17th century but massive conversion occurred only in the 19th century.

Belief persists in a wide range of supernatural beings that are believed to have memory, feeling, and energy: *opu* or *dotu,* ancestral spirits; *murku,* the spirits of the dead, which remain near human dwellings; and *panunggu, lulu, puntianak,* and *pok-pok,* various categories of demons or ghouls. Good people are believed to become benevolent spirits; evil people, suicides, and accident victims become malevolent ones. Propitiatory rituals attend important life events, times of danger or disease, and the full moon. These rituals are led by mediums *(tonaas* or *walian)* and require offerings of eggs, betel nuts, palm wine, cigarettes, and rice. Mediums heal with potions of water in which magical objects have been soaked; they locate these herbs, stones, or wood pieces in places indicated by ancestral spirits through visions. Divination is performed by examining an animal's gall bladder. Some shamans specialize as midwives, thief-detectors, and spell-casters; they are often consulted on political strategy.

⁶MAJOR HOLIDAYS

See the article entitled **Indonesians**.

⁷RITES OF PASSAGE

Whereas formerly parents arranged their children's marriages, nowadays young people choose their own spouses. Preliminary to the wedding, the man's family sends a representative to meet with an intermediary named by the woman's family. The delivery of the bride-price formalizes the engagement. On the Sunday before the wedding, representatives of both families announce the wedding and reception in church. On the day itself, the groom goes to the bride's house, knocks on the door of her room, and, usually very embarrassed, they kiss each other in front of onlooking family and friends. The groom escorts the bride to the church, where the wedding ceremony takes place, to be followed by a reception at the bride's house. After church the following Sunday, the groom brings his bride for a visit to his parents' house.

⁸INTERPERSONAL RELATIONS

Since the Minahasans never knew an indigenous kingdom, high status was traditionally not inherited but had to be won by demonstrating excellence to one's fellows (who in turn were always eager to challenge those who had managed to win prominence). In conditions of constant petty warfare, this meant personal prowess in battle and the ability to recruit fighters. Agricultural success was also a sign of divine blessing. A man seeking recognition would mount a great feast; completing a cycle of nine such feasts would qualify a man for a *waruga* stone burial chamber (carved with human figures, whose shape suggests a house with a gable roof). Waruga are no longer being built, but modern people still leave coconuts in front of them, said to be a substitute for human heads; replacing these are ostentatious modern mausolea, sometimes in the shape of boats or cars to reflect the source of the deceased's wealth.

According to Minahasan mythology, three status groups were distinguished: the *tonaas* or *walian,* religious specialists; *makatelupitu,* the leaders and warriors; and ordinary people. In addition to respecting *walian* and now Christian ministers, modern Minahasans recognize informal social status based on government office, wealth, inheritance, and education (a basic classification is between *tou siga,* "clever," i.e., educated, people and *tou lengei,* the "still stupid," i.e., uneducated).

A village *(kampung)* headed by a *hukum tua* is traditionally divided into subvillages headed by a *kepala jaga,* which break down further into groups of houses led by a *meweteng* who distributes work duties. Other village officials include a clerk, a land surveyor, an irrigation supervisor, a town-crier, and a police chief.

People belong to mutual aid associations *(mapalus)* that assist their members in holding funerals, weddings, and other major celebrations, as well as with agricultural tasks. Similarly, organizations for kin and people from the same locality play an important role, flourishing among Minahasans in Jakarta and elsewhere outside their homeland. In hotly contested village-head elections, these organizations provide support for candidates who must mount large feasts to win votes.

⁹LIVING CONDITIONS

According to 17th-century European accounts, ancient Minahasan villages were fortified, consisting of dwellings built on massive pillars and housing six to nine related families, each in a separate room with its own kitchen; the eldest, who was the head of the kin group, possessed the largest room.

Modern houses are built on smaller wooden or limestone piles (2.5 m or 8 ft high) and house a single family. An unwalled front room as long as the rest of the house is edged by a simply carved railing. A corridor with rooms on either side runs down the middle of the walled part of the house. The space under the house is walled in for storage or left open for a cart. Roofs are made of palm thatch or zinc; the latter, along with glass windows, expensive woods, and a cemented undercroft floor, is the mark of a richer family's house. Separate outbuildings are used for cooking, bathing, and toilet functions. Reminiscent of Europe, local houses are renowned for their hedged yards, well-tended gardens, and potted plants adorning window sills and porch railings.

As fields may be some distance from the family house, rural Minahasans make use of *sabuwa,* small, simple houses for shelter from the rain, storing produce before taking it to market, and cooking and sleeping when crops need to be guarded from animals for days at a stretch.

Villages *(wanua)* consist of houses arranged along a main road (or also down side roads in larger settlements); the church, market, headman's office, police, shops, and food stalls are concentrated on this axis. Ox- and horse-drawn carts are still common.

The Minahasans' home province, North Sulawesi, has a Human Development Index (combining measures of income, health, and education) of 74.2 (2005 score), far higher than Indonesia's national score of 69.6 and second only to that of the region of the national capital, Jakarta (76.1). North Sulawesi's GDP per capita is us$8,360, moderately high for Indonesia (cf. us$10,910 for North Sumatra, us$6,293 for Central Java, and us$2,919 for North Maluku). In 2000, the level of infant mortality, at 27.77 deaths per 1,000 live births, was the third lowest in country, after the national capital region of Jakarta and the highly urbanized Yogyakarta region.

¹⁰FAMILY LIFE

Kinship is bilateral, with equal emphasis on connection to maternal as well as paternal relatives. The family includes parents and their unmarried children; a daughter and her husband may live with the parents before setting up their own house. A couple, their children, and their children's families constitute the basic kinship unit, the *patuari* or *famili* (a Dutch term), which is exogamous (wider kin-groupings have lost their function in modern times). Divorce is common, governed by modern laws. Inheritance is divided equally among heirs, who may include surviving spouses and biological, adopted, and stepchildren; the eldest son oversees the rotation of non-divisible property.

¹¹CLOTHING

Heavily Europeanized, modern Minahasa is not known for distinctive costumes, because indigenous weaving died out in the 19th century.

¹²FOOD

Maize is the staple food for most Minahasans. While papaya fruit is fed to pigs, people eat the cooked leaves. Dishes are accompanied by *rica-rica*, a mixture of chili peppers, tomatoes, onions, garlic, and ginger. Regional specialties include pork *sate*, *tinoransak* (another pork dish), *kawaok* (fried forest rat), *kelulawar pangang* (bat stew), *RW* (*rintek wuuk*, "fine hair," a euphemism for spiced dog), and cat (*tusuk* or "*eveready*" as in the battery with the cat logo). Fish is common fare, the best-loved preparations being fried carp dipped in *dabu-dabu* sauce (chili, tomato, onion, and lime) and smoked tuna (*cakalang fufu*), fried or cooked in coconut milk. *Tinutuan*, famed throughout Indonesia as *bubur Manado*, is a rice gruel with greens and dried fish. *Milu* is a clear soup with young corn kernels and small shrimp, slightly sour from lime. A common snack is *panadu*, Iberian-style meat-and-vegetable turnovers. Desserts include *halwa kenari* (kenari nut with brown sugar), various confections (*bagea* and *wajik*), and fried ice cream.

¹³EDUCATION

Compared to other ethnic groups, Minahasans have long enjoyed superior access to modern schooling. The Dutch colonial government and Christian churches promoted education; by 1900, there was 1 school for every 1,000 people in Minahasa, while Java's ratio was 1 school for every 50,000 people. Because of this educational advantage, Minahasans have been disproportionately represented in the bureaucracy. Disdaining manual labor and commerce, Minahasans migrate to fill positions in areas with a shortage of civil servants.

In 2005, North Sulawesi's level of literacy stood at 98.87%, high by Indonesian national standards and even higher than in the region of the national capital, Jakarta (*see also* the article entitled **Indonesians** in this volume).

¹⁴CULTURAL HERITAGE

Throughout Indonesia, Minahasans are famous for their singing skills (which they readily display at parties), as well as for the *kolintang*, an orchestra of wooden xylophones; their music, widely available on cassette, is Western in style. A legacy from the Dutch colonial military of which Minahasa, along with Ambonese, formed an important component, marching band music on bamboo versions of brass and other wind instruments (trumpets, trombones, tubas, saxophones, and clarinets) accompanies festivals. Early Spanish influences survive in a tradition of Christmas mumming (masked dance) and *katrili*, a kind of square dancing. For competitions and the reception of important guests, a number of dances of a more indigenous character have been secularized and modernized. Group dancing (*maengket*) includes: the *maowey kamberu*, depicting the rice harvest; the *marambak*, depicting housebuilding; and *lalayaan*, a dance offering the sexes a chance to interact. Also performed in the Moluccas, the *cakalele* (also called *kubasaran* or *mahsasuh*) is a war dance consisting of red-clad men waving swords and shields and emitting fierce cries.

¹⁵WORK

Some 76% of the population earns a living from agriculture. Inland valleys with volcanic soils support wet-rice, but swidden (shifting-cultivation) field maize is the staple food, grown along with tubers and peanuts. Cabbage, Chinese cabbage, onions, tomatoes, water spinach, and chili are also grown for market. Important cash crops are coffee (declining in importance since the 19th century), coconut for copra and oil, and, since the 1970s, cloves. The domestic cigarette industry's demand for cloves has enriched many farming families; the short harvest time pulls in all available labor, closing schools and offices. Most land is owned by individuals (aside from a diminishing amount of land owned by kin-groups), and conflicts over inheritance frequently erupt. Sharecropping is common. Villagers may use communal lands after informing the village head.

Other occupations include livestock-raising and fishing (usually by families, from outrigger and non-outrigger canoes). Each village has a carpenter. *Tibo* brokers sell produce purchased from farmers, transporting it in carts.

¹⁶SPORTS

See the article entitled **Indonesians**.

¹⁷ENTERTAINMENT AND RECREATION

See the article entitled **Indonesians**.

¹⁸FOLK ART, CRAFTS, AND HOBBIES

Gardening is a major leisure activity; roses, hibiscus, bougainvillea, and citrus are grown.

¹⁹SOCIAL PROBLEMS

See the article entitled **Indonesians**.

²⁰GENDER ISSUES

Minahasan women enjoy among the highest levels of wellbeing and empowerment in Indonesia. North Sulawesi's Gender-Related Development Index (combining measures of women's health, education, and income relative to men's) is 62.1, higher than Indonesia's national GDI of 59.2. The province's Gender Empowerment Measure (reflecting women's participation and power in political and economic life relative to men's) is 55.1, also higher than the national GEM (54.6).

²¹BIBLIOGRAPHY

Badan Pusat Statistik: Statistik Indonesia. http://demografi. bps.go.id (November 9, 2008).

Dalton, Bill. *Indonesia Handbook*. Chico, CA: Moon Publications, 1991.

Jonge, Nico de, ed. *Indonesia in Focus: Ancient Traditions—Modern Times*. Meppel: Edu'Actief, 1988.

Koentjaraningrat, ed. *Manusia dan Kebudayaan di Indonesia* [Man and Culture in Indonesia]. Jakarta: Djambatan, 1975.

LeBar, Frank M., ed. *Ethnic Groups of Insular Southeast Asia*. Vol. 1, *Indonesia, Andaman Islands, and Madagascar*. New Haven, CT: Human Relations Area Files Press, 1972.

Melalatoa, M. Junus. "Minahasa, Suku Bangsa." In *Ensiklopedi Nasional Indonesia* (ENI), vol. 10. Jakarta: Cipta Adi Pustaka, 1990.

Profil Propinsi Republik Indonesia: Sulawesi Utara. Jakarta: Yayasan Bhakti Wawasan Nusantara, 1992. Volkman, Toby Alice and Ian Caldwell, ed. *Sulawesi: Island Crossroads of Indonesia*. Lincolnwood, IL: Passport Books, 1990.

—revised by A. J. Abalahin

MINANGKABAU

PRONUNCIATION: mee-NAHNG-kah-BOW (as in "bow down")
LOCATION: Indonesia (Sumatra and other areas)
POPULATION: 5.5 million
LANGUAGE: Minangkabau
RELIGION: Islam
RELATED ARTICLES: Vol. 3: Indonesians

¹INTRODUCTION

The Minangkabau (also called "Minang") are one of the few matrilineal cultures surviving into modern times (and the largest currently existing), a distinction even more striking as theirs is virtually the only such society within the Islamic world. Their very name ("victorious [*menang*]" "buffalo [*kabau*]") reflects their independent spirit. According to legend, for a bullfight held in lieu of battle, the Minangkabau pitted a tiny water buffalo calf against the giant beast representing the Javanese invaders. The Minangkabau secretly affixed blades to the calf's horns; the calf, taking the larger animal as its mother, knifed it to death while seeking an udder.

Wet-rice agriculture made its earliest debut on Sumatra in the Minangkabau home valleys, but it was the region's gold that first attracted foreigners. In the 14th century, the half-Javanese, half-Sumatran prince Adityavarman established the first kingdom near the coveted mines. This was probably the distant ancestor of the Pagurruyung monarchy (actually, three co-rulers of limited power) of later centuries.

Increased external trade, with Gujerat (India), Aceh, and Malacca, brought Islam to the Minangkabau by the 16th century. By the end of the 18th century, the new religion had spawned the Paderis, puritanical reformers bent on purging the Minangkabau lands of everything contrary to Islam as they understood it, including the matrilineal Pagurruyung aristocracy. Although, after more than three decades of war (1803–1837), the reformers largely succeeded, the upheaval invited the intervention of the Dutch. The Dutch East India Company had made its first appearance in the Minang region in 1663.

Under Dutch rule, the Minangkabau, to a greater extent than most other Indonesian peoples, pursued modern education. Minangkabau intellectuals were to play key roles in the nationalist movement; one of them, Muhammad Hatta, became Indonesia's first vice-president. Nonetheless, independence disappointed Minangkabau desirous of regional autonomy and an Islamic state. In 1958, Minangkabau and Toba Batak military leaders backed the establishment of the "Revolutionary Government of the Republic of Indonesia" (PRRI); Jakarta crushed the rebellion swiftly but left Minangkabau feeling no better than a conquered people. Stability and prosperity under Suharto's New Order reconciled the once-disaffected with the central government.

²LOCATION AND HOMELAND

Numbering 5.5 million (2000 census), the Minangkabau locate their original homeland in the fertile volcanic highlands of West Sumatra, specifically in three valleys, Tanah Datar, Agam, and Limapuluh Kota. From there they spread outward into neighboring mountainous areas, reaching into other Sumatran provinces and down into the swampy western coastal plain as far north as Meulaboh in Aceh and as far south as Bengkulu. In addition, Minangkabau can be found in cities throughout the archipelago, particularly Jakarta. Minangkabau constitute 88% of the population of their home province of West Sumatra (3.74 million out of 4.25 million) and are the sixth largest ethnic group in Indonesia; a 1.76 million-strong diaspora lives in other provinces (constituting 15% of the population in North Sumatra, 11% in Riau, and 5% in Jambi). Crossing the Straits of Malacca as early as the 15th century, they founded Negeri Sembilan in the 18th century, now one of Malaysia's states; 300,000 Minangkabau were estimated to be living in that country in 1981.

This wide distribution results from the *merantau* tradition: because women possess the rights to village lands, men wanting to acquire wealth for themselves have long migrated from the Minangkabau homeland to do so, either temporarily or permanently. Increased land scarcity beginning in the 19th century has led more and more Minangkabau to *merantau*.

³LANGUAGE

The Minangkabau speak a language very close to Malay, but it is readily distinguishable from Malay, e.g., cognates differ usually in the final syllable: Malay *pusaka, pasisir, perut* versus Minang *pusako, pasisie, paruik*. The important Malay particle *yang* ("that" or "which") is *nan* in Minang.

⁴FOLKLORE

Remote mountain or jungle spots may be *tampek-tampek nan sati*, places charged with supernatural power. Spirits feared by the Minangkabau include *puntianak*, women who from afar suck the blood out of an infant through the soft spot in its skull (the fontanel). *Palasik* are women who have an innate power (which, however, they cannot control) to render children sickly. People may enlist the services of *dukun*, practitioners of magic and herbal medicine, to combat malevolent spirits or to victimize others (as in *menggasing*, sending poison to another's bloodstream through the air). As a defense, many carry amulets, a particularly potent one being crystallized elephant sperm.

⁵RELIGION

The Minangkabau are among the peoples most-committed to orthodox Islam in the archipelago. Despite conflicts between that patriarchal religion and their own matrilineal traditions, Minangkabau consider both integral to their culture. Islamic reform movements over the last two centuries have eliminated virtually all traces of pre-Islamic beliefs, although there are Minangkabau who recognize various types of spirits as well as the power of magic.

⁶MAJOR HOLIDAYS

Minangkabau observe the major Islamic holidays [*see* **Indonesians**]. One festival, which because of its Shi'ite character has very few counterparts elsewhere in predominantly Sunni Indonesia, is the colorful and lively *tabuik* (*tabut*) of the West Sumatra coast, a celebration in commemoration of the death of the Prophet Muhammad's kinsmen Hassan and Hussein at the battle of Karbala (AD 680).

MINANGKABAU

0   125   250 Miles

0   125   250 Kilometers

Gulf
of
Thailand

MALAYSIA

Medan ●

Strait of Malacca

SINGAPORE

Nias

Pekanbaru ●

Padang ●

Kepulauan Mentawai

SUMATRA

Palembang ●

⁷RITES OF PASSAGE

Surrounding birth are several rites (of waning importance nowadays): one at the sixth month of the pregnancy; the playing of the *talempong* (metallophones) to greet the birth; the burial of the placenta; the infant's first touching earth (at 40 days of age); its first haircut; and, at three months of age, a formal visit to its father's family. Corresponding to circumcision for boys, a "doing up the hair" (*menata kondai*) ceremony is held for a girl who has experienced her first menstruation.

Because of matrilineal traditions, the wedding process among the Minangkabau does not conform to the pattern general to Indonesia. Not only men but also women may issue a proposal (via intermediaries, as usual elsewhere). Despite the requirements of Islamic law, a Minangkabau man does not pay a bride-price. On the other hand, the bride's family may pay the groom's an *uang jemputan* (handed over during the ceremony). Of greater importance is the exchange of symbolic goods, such as krisses (short daggers), between the two families.

Funerals follow general Islamic guidelines. Before the deceased is carried to the cemetery, the coffin is raised so the deceased's children may pass under it three times in order to prevent excessive grief (and dreams about the dead) from afflicting them.

See also the article entitled **Indonesians**.

⁸INTERPERSONAL RELATIONS

Villages (*nagari*) consist of clusters of houses belonging to different matrilineal lineages (local branches of far-flung *suku*). A lineage that descends from the original founders (*urang*

asa) of the village possesses rights to more land than other lineages, and its head has the exclusive privilege of bearing a title. Among the lineages that settled later, those (usually related to the *urang asa* line) that enjoyed some status in their native place were eventually able to buy land and gain equality, except for being barred from holding the above title, with the dominant lineage. Other lineages, on the other hand, suffer an inferior status in the village, obliged to serve the dominant lineages in various capacities, and, in the case of those lineages with known slave ancestry, their members may be shunned as marriage partners.

A council composed of the heads (*penghulu*, males) of all the lineages manages village affairs (though under the modern Indonesian state this amounts to little more than dispute arbitration). Traditionally, four groups share leadership responsibilities in the village: *niniek mamak* (heads of *paruik*, the extended matrilineal family); religious officials (*imam* and *khatib*); the *cerdik pandai* (individuals with education); and *bundo kanduang* (senior women). Wealth and education, both secular and religious, have become as or more important than hereditary titles in determining status. Indeed, only some of the Minangkabau traditionally recognized aristocratic principles (those following the Koto-Piliang norms, as well as those in Aceh-influenced Pariaman); others, those adhering to the Bodi-Caniago pattern, preferred egalitarian practices, such as having elected rather than hereditary *penghulu*.

Etiquette requires that one's language and behavior express deference to older people, a careful formality to relatives by marriage, and affectionate patience to those younger; people of the same age, even strangers, should show mutual respect. Parents prefer to correct a child out of the hearing of others, though sometimes they may judge it suitable for these others to hear. Women who are blood relations or on intimate terms may embrace each other after a long separation, but it is not proper for a man to greet even a related woman with an embrace. According to some, a man and a woman should never shake hands. Women should not squat as men do, nor sit unaccompanied on the roadside or elsewhere frequented by men.

Traditionally, young men and women (e.g., a boy and his uncle's daughter) could exchange glances only at large celebrations. One opportunity for interaction (in the Pesisir Selatan area) is afforded at weddings where young men enter a house playing tambourines while the young women, sitting above in the *pagu* (open attic), rain flowers down on them. A young woman lowers a flower and a cigarette on a string down to the young man of her desire; he replies by sending her a ring or other valuable wrapped in a cloth.

⁹LIVING CONDITIONS

Raised 2 m (6.5 ft) off the ground on numerous pillars, the traditional Minangkabau house, or *rumah gadang* ("big house"), is famous for the ridge beams of its roof sections that sweep up to a sharp point at both ends, evoking water buffalo horns. Stretching out north to south, the house is entered through a roofed staircase to the door on one of the long sides. A room for receiving guests runs the length of the house. Behind it along the back wall are the rooms (*bilik*) for the married sisters of the family (added when each weds); the house pillars, 3 m (10 ft) apart, determine where the partition walls of each bilik will be. At one end of some houses, the floor is raised to provide a sitting place (*anjueng*) for those of superior status. Where there

Minangkabau children play with kites in Belubus, Indonesia. Anthropologist Pegge Reeves Sanday has studied and lived among the Minangkabau people for 16 years. She calls the group the largest and most modern matrilineal society in the world. (AP Images/Peggy Reeves Sanday, File)

is no anjueng, the spot is occupied by a room for the youngest sister and her husband. The kitchen occupies a small building, usually at the back, accessible by a small bridge.

Nowadays, most people occupy single-family houses; traditional ones are called *tungkuih nasi* ("rice packet," referring to the hornless roofs).

The village (*nagari*) consists of the nagari proper (houses and wet-rice fields) and the *taratak* (forests, dry-crop fields, and sometimes the dwellings of non-owning caretakers). The nagari proper includes a mosque, a village council hall, a place for a weekly or twice-weekly market, and *surau*, halls for daily prayer that is also where the community's unmarried men sleep.

West Sumatra has a Human Development Index (combining measures of income, health, and education) of 71.2 (2005 score), higher than Indonesia's national score of 69.6 and the ninth highest in the country (out of 33 provinces). West Sumatra's GDP per capita is US$9,784, very high for Indonesia (cf. US$10,910 for North Sumatra, US$6,293 for Central Java, and US$2,919 for North Maluku). In 2000, the level of infant mortality, at 52.66 deaths per 1,000 live births, was moderate for Indonesia, worse than provinces on Java but better than most in eastern Indonesia.

10 FAMILY LIFE

A Minangkabau belongs to his or her mother's clan (*suku*) and traditionally lives in an extended family (*paruik,* meaning "[common] stomach or womb"), which consists of all individuals who trace their ancestry back to a common great-grandmother matrilineally.

The 96 named suku trace back to an original four: Bodo, Caniago, Koto, and Piliang. One must marry outside one's suku. Custom preferred a man to marry his maternal uncle's daughter, though he might also choose his paternal aunt's daughter or the sister of his sister's husband; today, the choice is not so restricted). Within the paruik, children's interaction with their mother's siblings is hardly less close than that with their parents.

Formerly, a husband visited his wife only at night, retaining residence in his mother's village; these days, he moves into her house after the wedding. If a man takes more than one wife (a practice condemned by younger people), he commutes between their houses, which may mean between one house in his native place and another where he has migrated. For children, it was the mother's eldest brother (*mamak*) who served as the male authority figure; the mamak, moreover, managed the affairs of the paruik in general. The mamak's relations with his sister's husband tends to be formal. Parents-in-law, on the other hand, are known to spoil their children-in-law. If a man migrates with his wife, his parents-in-law may join them, while his own parents will not. After divorce, the husband must move away, leaving the children with his wife.

As the nuclear family increasingly displaces the extended family as the norm, the role of the father and his kin grows proportionately. It has become common for a deceased man's wife and children to challenge his sister's children's traditional claim to his property. Custom traditionally distinguished between *harato pusako*, property (mainly land and heirlooms) retained by the *suku* or its branches in perpetuity, and *harato pacarian*, (usually moveable) property earned by a man that he could bequeath as he wished.

¹¹CLOTHING

As everyday wear, men wear shirts, trousers, and a *peci* cap [*see* **Indonesians**]. Older men still wear *serawa* (long pants with a drawstring) and a *teluk belanga* (tunic) or a "Chinese" shirt and sometimes a head cloth rather than a peci. Women wear a sarong and *baju kurung* (long-sleeved *kebaya*) and a *tingkulak* (head wrap covering the hair); urban women who wear modern clothing put on traditional clothing while in the village.

Ceremonial attire for men consists of: a tunic with short sleeves that widen towards the opening; trousers; a *songket* (gold- and silver-embroidered) cloth wrapped around the waist to hang just below the knee; a sash over the shoulder; a *saluak* headdress; and a *kris* (short dagger) tucked in the front. Women wear the baju kurung; a songket sarong with a matching sash over the shoulder; earrings; several necklaces, one on top of another; and bracelets on both arms. Most distinctive is the women's headwear: the cloth is folded (the precise manner is unique to each village) to look like horns (*tanduk or tilakuang*). Brides don elaborate headdresses of gold.

¹²FOOD

Rice is the core of the Minangkabau meal. The usual side dishes (*samba*) are (often salted) fish and boiled vegetables, such as cabbage, water spinach, cassava or papaya leaves, eggplant, amaranth, and banana blossom. Less often, Minangkabau eat dishes of meat (except pork) fried in coconut oil or stewed in coconut milk and heavily spiced with lots of chili and such seasonings as garlic, onions, ginger, galangal, pepper, salt, turmeric, and lemon grass. The most renowned Minangkabau dish is *rendang*, chunks of water buffalo meat stewed for hours in coconut milk and spices until the liquid reduces to a thick coating; the meat keeps for a very long time and sustains travelers on long journeys. Other dishes are *gulai kambing* (goat meat in a coconut milk sauce), *dendeng* (spicy dried beef), and *singgang ayam* (fried chicken). Drinks include *kopi daun*, a "tea" of dried coffee leaves.

"Padang" restaurants throughout Indonesia serve Minangkabau food. A waiter lays out several dishes at once on the customer's table; the customer is only charged for the portions that he or she has taken. Their great popularity among non-Minangkabau in Muslim-majority Indonesia is partly due to the assurance that the meat served there is *halal*, prepared in conformity with Islamic dietary regulations.

¹³EDUCATION

In 2005, West Sumatra's level of literacy stood at 95.98%, high by Indonesian national standards (*see also* the article entitled **Indonesians** in this volume).

¹⁴CULTURAL HERITAGE

Vocal music includes *dendang* (singing), *zikir* (Arab-style chanting), and *selawat* (invocations from the Qur'an). Instruments include bamboo flutes (*saluang and bansi),* the tambourine (*rebana),* the drum, the *kecapi* (a zither), and the violin.

Dances (all dynamic) include: the fan dance, portraying the interaction of young men and women; the umbrella dance, depicting a couple's love, often danced by a bride and groom; *rantak,* consisting of martial arts moves; and *sauik randai,* representing the happy mood upon finishing a day working in the fields or fishing. *Dabus* is *pencak silat* martial arts movements performed as an artistic expression.

At ceremonies such as weddings, people are quick to improvise poems (*pantun* and *syair*) and aphorisms. Traditional literature includes an epic, *Kaba Cindur Mata.* Although writing in Malay for publication by the Dutch colonial government's Balai Pustaka publishing house, early 20th century Minangkabau writers produced novels depicting conflicts between tradition and modernity within their native Minangkabau society; many of these became the first classics of modern Indonesian literature.

¹⁵WORK

Agriculture provides the majority with a livelihood. Rice from irrigated fields is the main subsistence crop, while dry-field vegetables (peanuts, potatoes, cabbage, tomatoes, and chili) are grown for the market. In outlying hilly areas, Minangkabau open the land with swidden (shifting-cultivation) methods, planting first dry rice, maize, cassava, pumpkins, or the like, then leaving the plots fallow for a couple of years, and finally planting perennials, such as rubber, cloves, cinnamon, pepper, coffee, and coconut, sugar palm, or fruit trees. With these perennials, farmers are able to participate in the cash economy.

Minangkabau raise chickens, ducks, cattle, water buffalo, and goats for meat. Fishing (in the sea, lakes, and artificial ponds) provides farmers with supplementary income.

Lacking sufficient land, or unsatisfied with the limited returns from farming, and, because of the merantau tradition (migration to acquire wealth), open to an itinerant lifestyle, many Minangkabau seek wealth through commerce. Minangkabau business owners, rather than Chinese as elsewhere in Indonesia, dominate the local economy, marketing agricultural products and the craft specialties of individual villages.

¹⁶SPORTS

The local form of martial arts is called *kumango*, a version of the pan-Malay-Indonesian *silat*. One common game played by 5–15 year olds is *galah*, in which one team (variable numbers) attempts to block the members of the other team from running a course from a starting point to the end of the playing field and back to the starting point. Males (very rarely females) of all ages enjoy *catur harimau* ("tiger chess"), a board game with stone playing pieces where one player's "tigers" attempt to eat up the other player's "goats" (the moving and placing of pieces requires skill and strategy).

[17] ENTERTAINMENT AND RECREATION

See the article entitled **Indonesians**.

[18] FOLK ART, CRAFTS, AND HOBBIES

Intricate carving, often painted, decorates the pillars and walls of the *rumah gadang* (the traditional Minangkabau house). Particular (usually plant) motifs correspond to different parts of the structure and symbolize virtues (e.g., the *tangguak lamah* design signifies humility and courtesy).

A few villages continue to produce the ceremonially important *songket*, cloth brocaded with gold and silver threads.

[19] SOCIAL PROBLEMS

See the article entitled **Indonesians**.

[20] GENDER ISSUES

West Sumatra's Gender-Related Development Index (combining measures of women's health, education, and income relative to men's) is 60.7, higher than Indonesia's national GDI of 59.2. The province's Gender Empowerment Measure (reflecting women's participation and power in political and economic life relative to men's) is 54.2, almost as high as the national GEM (54.6).

Contemporary Minangkabau notions of gender relations are influenced by distinct and often conflicting discourses: Minangkabau matrilineal values and customary law (*see Interpersonal Relations* and *Family Life*) and patriarchal pan-Islamic and Indonesian nation-building/modernizing ideologies. Mothers, for instance, continue to advise and guide their children even when they are adult, and, if they are senior women (bundo kanduang) within their lineage, they wield authority beyond their own immediate household (Islamic values, however, do not extend her power into children's adulthood and to households other than her own). As the ultimate controllers of property (most importantly of rice lands), women regularly speak up in kinship group and community decision-making gatherings, as they would not generally in other Indonesian cultures. At the same time, as in many other Indonesian cultures, aggressive verbal self-assertion is looked down upon as displaying powerlessness rather than power, with the result that male elders can have their way simply by saying as little as possible.

The genuinely central place of women and especially of mothers in Minangkabau culture is countered by the authority positions traditionally given to men (a man would have authority over his sister's property but not over his wife's) and by Islamic notions. For example, the idea that women unlike men attain adulthood before learning to master their passions, or that a person gets his or her essential character and status from his father's sperm, and, therefore, family's seek men of "good seed" for their daughters. Dutch colonial and later Indonesian national governments have favored the male lineage head (penghulu) over other types of community member traditionally participating in community decision-making processes, including the bundo kanduang through whom property was inherited. The Indonesian national government recognizes the father as the head of the household and channels forms of development aid, such as instruction in new agricultural techniques, to men rather than to women. It has applied the title "Bundo Kanduang" to "model mothers" judged according to an Islamic/Western patriarchal framework, shifting it away from its traditional Minangkabau meaning of a senior woman with great power and authority within her lineage. Women who are junior according to traditional matrilineal lineage hierarchies may raise their status by invoking their husbands' rank within non-traditional hierarchies, such as the Indonesian bureaucracy. Modernization, including increased emigration and the increased value of remittances from migrants, is increasing the importance of the nuclear family as the expense of the extended family and of the lineage and proportionally reducing the power of senior women.

[21] BIBLIOGRAPHY

Ayatrohaedi, et al. *Tatakrama di Beberapa Daerah di Indonesia* [Etiquette in Some Regions of Indonesia].Jakarta: Department of Education and Culture, 1989.

Azmi. *Adat Istiadat Daerah Sumatra Barat* [Customs of West Sumatra]. Jakarta: Project for the Study and Recording of Regional Cultures, 1977.

Badan Pusat Statistik: Statistik Indonesia. http://demografi. bps.go.id (November 9, 2008).

Blackwood, Evelyn. "Senior Mothers, Model Mothers, and Dutiful Wives: Managing Gender Contradictions in a Minangkabau Village." In *Bewitching Women, Pious Men: Gender and Politics in Southeast Asia*, edited by Aihwa Ong and Michael G. Peletz. Berkeley, CA: University of California Press, 1995.

Irwan. M. H. "Minangkabau, suku bangsa." In *Ensiklopedi Nasional Indonesia.* Vol. 10, Jakarta: Cipta Adi Pustaka, 1990.

Junus, Umar. "Kebudayaan Minangkabau" In *Manusia dan Kebudayaan di Indonesia* [Man and Culture in Indonesia], edited by Koentjariningrat. Jakarta: Djambatan, 1975.

Karman, Ummy. "Minangkabau, arsitektur." In *Ensiklopedi Nasional Indonesia*. Vol. 10, Jakarta: Cipta Adi Pustaka, 1990.

Krier, Jennifer. "Narrating Herself: Power and Gender in a Minangkabau Woman's Tale of Conflict." In *Bewitching Women, Pious Men: Gender and Politics in Southeast Asia*, edited by Aihwa Ong and Michael G. Peletz. Berkeley, CA: University of California Press, 1995.

LeBar, Frank M., ed. *Ethnic Groups of Insular Southeast Asia.* Vol. 1, *Indonesia, Andaman Islands, and Madagascar.* New Haven, CT: Human Relations Area Files Press, 1972.

Oey, Eric M. *Sumatra: Island of Adventure.* Longwood, IL: Passport Books, 1991.

Profil Propinsi Republik Indonesia. Vol. 23, *Sumatra Barat.* Jakarta: Yayasan Bhakti Wawasan Nusantara, 1992.

Yunus, Ahmad, ed. *Permainan Rakyat Daerah Sumatra Barat* [Folk Games of West Sumatra]. Jakarta: Department of Education and Culture, Regional Cultures Inventorization and Documentation Project, 1982.

—revised by A. J. Abalahin

MINAS

PRONUNCIATION: MEE-nuhs
ALTERNATE NAMES: Meos; Mewati
LOCATION: India (primarily Rajasthan state)
POPULATION: 5 million (estimate)
LANGUAGE: Various dialects of Rajasthani
RELIGION: Hinduism; some Islamic practices
RELATED ARTICLES: Vol. 3: People of India

¹INTRODUCTION

The Minas, also known as the Meos, or Mewati, are a tribe and caste inhabiting parts of western and northern India. Early views of the Minas held that they were among the oldest inhabitants of the region and represented pre-Dravidian elements in the population. More recently, however, it has been suggested that the Minas may have migrated to this region from inner Asia in the 7th century along with various Rajput groups. Some Minas even claim Rajput descent.

According to Mina tradition, the Minas ruled most of what is now eastern Rajasthan, an area they referred to as "*mindesh*" (country of the Minas). They subsequently were replaced by Rajput clans, the most recent being the Kachhwaha Rajputs who founded the state of Amber, later known as Jaipur. The last important Mina ruler, the Raja of Naen, was defeated by the Rajputs in the 16th century. However, the Minas continued to play a prominent role in the affairs of the region. Like the Bhils in Mewar (Udaipur) State, it was formerly the custom for a Mina to participate in the *tika* ceremony, placing a ceremonial mark with his own blood on the forehead of a new ruler of Amber State. Minas held important positions in Amber, guarded the person of the prince at night, and were given charge of the women's quarters.

In the 11th century, when Muslim invaders gained control of northwestern India, some Minas converted from Hinduism to Islam. This branch of the Mina tribe is called the Meos. Further conversions to Islam occurred among the Minas during the 13th and 17th centuries. Despite their conversion, however, Meos continued to follow many of their original Hindu practices, and their culture remains a blend of Hindu and Muslim traits.

Political events since the middle of the 20th century have seen the Meos take on a stronger Muslim identity. British India was partitioned in 1947 and Pakistan was created as a separate country for Muslims. At this time, many Meos migrated from territory that was assigned to the Republic of India to West Pakistan, the western "wing" of the new Islamic state. The Meos who remained in India, a Muslim minority in an overwhelmingly Hindu population, found themselves facing pressures to abandon Hindu traits and conform to traditional Islamic customs.

²LOCATION AND HOMELAND

The Minas, along with their allied groups, number some nearly 5 million people and rank among the largest tribes of South Asia. The current estimate of the Mina population is 4,482,000, of which 3,834,440 are found in Rajasthan. The main concentrations of Minas lie in eastern Rajasthan, in Alwar and Bharatpur Districts, spilling over into the Gurgaon District

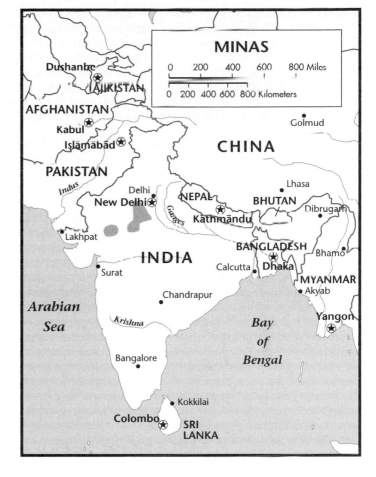

of Haryana State. This area is known as Mewat, reflecting the prominence of the Meos in the region. The name Mewati, i.e., a resident of Mewat, is sometimes used as a synonym for Mina and Meo. Considerable numbers of Minas are also found in Madhya Pradesh State.

The Minas of Rajasthan identify 12 *pals* in the state. Pals are historical territorial units settled by Minas who shared a common ancestry and, often, similar cultural and linguistic attributes. Beyond this geographic distinction, there are several divisions among the Minas based on factors such as occupation and status. In addition, all Mina groups are divided into numerous clans (*gotras*), which are exogamous social units.

The Mers, the hill peoples of central Rajasthan, are also considered to be a branch of the Minas. They trace their descent to Rajput chiefs who married Mina women and are known as Rawat Minas. Like the Rajputs, the Mers are divided into clans. Some Mer clans converted to Islam, while others remained Hindu, but in the past all Mers intermarried. It was only with the introduction of communal representation in British India, and the events leading to independence in 1947, that the two groups began to move apart. Significant numbers of Minas also live in southeastern areas of Rajasthan.

In Rajasthan, Minas are second in number only to the Bhils and are classed as a Scheduled Tribe. Mina populations have spread from their Rajasthani homeland to adjacent states, although there they are less numerous, may not be recognized as a tribal group, and are sometimes called by different names. In Uttar Pradesh, the state lying to the northwest of Rajasthan, for instance, Minas are known as "Pardeshi Rajputs." This literally means "Rajputs from a foreign land," and no doubt refers to the claims of Mina groups migrating from Rajasthan to Rajput descent. In Madhya Pradesh, Minas are known as Rawats and are regarded as a Scheduled Caste because they eat meat and consume alcohol. Minas are also found in small numbers in Haryana and Punjab States. The Meos who migrated to Pakistan after partition in 1947 settled in the eastern region of that country's Punjab Province.

The areas of Rajasthan inhabited by the Minas include the Aravalli Range and the semiarid plains lying to the southeast of these hills. The Aravallis are the most prominent relief feature of Rajasthan, a narrow belt of precipitous hills and ridges running northeast–southwest through the center of the state for a distance of over 600 km (approximately 375 mi). Ridges in the north, in Mewat, scarcely reach 400 m (approximately 1,300 ft). In the south, however, the mountains increase in width and elevation, rising to 1,722 m (5,650 ft) at Mount Abu. The Aravalli Range separates the arid lands of the Thar Desert in northwestern Rajasthan from the slightly more humid regions to the southeast, which are drained by the Banas and Chambal rivers. In the extreme southeast of Rajasthan, rainfall exceeds 80 cm (30 in), but over most of the area it averages around 65 cm (25 in). As is true of all semiarid climates, rainfall is highly variable and the region is prone to frequent droughts and famines. Mean maximum temperatures in May, the hottest month, exceed 40°C (104°F). Natural vegetation, where land has not been cleared for cultivation, is drought-resistant scrub forest.

Minas in Rajasthan are divided into the Mina Zamindar, the landowning Minas, and the Mina Chowkidar. Both groups claim *ksatriya* status, and the 2001 Census of India puts their number at between 2,800,000 and 3,000,000 (the estimate given above includes natural increase since 2001, Bhil Minas, Meos, and related groups). The Zamindar Minas occupy a higher ritual status in the Hindu caste system than the Chowkidar Minas. The Bhil Mina are said to be descendants of Bhils and Rajputs who fled Muslim domination elsewhere in northern India.

³LANGUAGE

The Mina homeland lies in the "Hindi belt" (the area where Hindi, an Indo-Aryan language descended from Sanskrit, is widely spoken) of northern India. However, linguistic patterns in India are such that people commonly speak the dialect of their immediate locality rather than the "proper" or official form of the regional language. Minas, depending on where they live in Rajasthan, speak various dialects of Rajasthani, which itself is a regional variant of Hindi. The major dialects spoken in the Mina areas are Mewati, Shekhawati, Harauti, Talhati, Dhundari, and Pachwari. Minas living in other states speak the dialect of their local region.

⁴FOLKLORE

The derivation of the name Mina is uncertain, but some suggest it means "fish." The Minas claim an association with *Matsya* or *Minavatar,* the first incarnation of Vishnu in which the Hindu god assumed the form of a fish. According to a legend related in several ancient texts, a *ksatriya* king named Manu was fishing in a river when he caught a small fish. The fish promised to protect Manu from coming misfortunes if he took it home rather than return it to the river. The king placed the fish in a small earthen vessel, but it started growing and eventually had to be moved to a pond, then to a lake, to the sea, and finally to the ocean. By now, King Manu realized that the fish was an incarnation of a god. The deity warned the king that a devastating flood was coming and that he should build a boat and embark on it with the seeds of all living things. Forewarned, Manu survived the flood. After the waters subsided, Manu performed a sacrifice to the gods. A woman was created from this sacrifice, and the entire human race is descended from the union of this woman and Manu.

The legend of the flood is found in many cultures, but the Mina tradition that they are descendants of King Manu achieves two goals specific to the Indian context. First, it gives a degree of legitimacy to the Mina claim of *ksatriya* status and, therefore, to an advantageous place in the caste structure of Indian society. Thus, where Mina groups have assumed a caste identity, they rank just below the Brahman caste and above the service castes and hill peoples. Second, identification with Vishnu through his Matsya incarnation confirms the Minas as Hindu, an important goal for tribal groups that may have their origins outside Hindu society. Even today, Minavatar remains a major deity for the Minas.

⁵RELIGION

The Minas are Hindus, and worship at the temples and shrines of Hindu deities is an important part of everyday life. Most Minas are Shaivites, meaning they are followers of the god Shiva. But, like all Hindus, they also worship other gods and goddesses of the Hindu pantheon. These gods and goddesses include Rama, Sita, Hanuman, and Bhairon. In addition, Minas revere local deities and construct shrines to these lesser gods on the outskirts of their villages. Daily prayers are offered to Balavji, who represents Hanuman and protects the inhabitants of the village. Shitala Mata (the goddess of smallpox), Pipla Mata, and other lesser village goddesses are also worshipped. The Minas pay special attention to the presiding deities of their clans.

Minas are highly superstitious people and place great meaning on omens. For example, the braying of an ass on the left, the hooting of an owl on the left, and the cry of a jackal on the right mean good fortune. Hearing the cry of the Saras crane, or meeting a cat, sheep, or hyena, is unlucky.

The Meos, the Muslim branch of the Minas, follow Muslim practices, such as male circumcision and burial of the dead. They celebrate Muslim festivals, such as Id and Muharram. But in many others aspects, the Meos in India continue to preserve elements of their Hindu past. Meos often worship at the shrines of Hindu gods and goddesses and keep Hindu household deities. Hindu epics, such as the *Mahabharata* and the *Ramayana,* are as well-liked as readings from the Quran. Popular given names for both males and females are often Hindu names, with the Muslim title "Khan" added. Sometimes the Hindu name "Singh" is added to a Muslim name, as in "Fateh Singh." Until recently, Meos' dress differed little from their Hindu neighbors. In addition, despite pressures for change, the Meos continue to follow traditional Hindu kinship patterns and marriage rituals. The Meo community is divided into at least 800 exogamous clans, and its clan structure resembles that of the Hindu Minas, Rajputs, Jats, and other Hindu castes.

Meos do not follow purdah, the custom of secluding women, which is the practice in Muslim society.

⁶MAJOR HOLIDAYS

As Hindus, the Minas observe many of the major festivals of the Hindu calendar. The spring festival of Holi is celebrated in typical fashion, with the burning of the demoness Holika and the throwing of colored water and powder. Dasahara is celebrated in October. The Divali festival, the Festival of Lights, occurs in the fall after the summer harvest has been collected. Hundreds of lamps are placed around the houses, which are often newly plastered and decorated with designs. Men indulge in gambling and drinking. Govardhan Puja, a festival dedicated to the welfare of cattle, is celebrated a day or so after Divali. At this time, cattle are bathed in the village pond and decorated with ornaments and colored paint. Women pray to the cattle for wealth and feed the animals special food. Cow dung, a symbol of wealth, is placed on the steps of each house and offerings are made to it.

In addition to these Hindu observances, Minas celebrate certain festivals that are specific to the Mina community. The Minas go to great lengths to appease their ancestors and set aside a special day for ancestor worship. On this day, special foods are cooked in each household, and the village priest is invited to the house to receive an offering. Another day is set aside to honor local village deities.

Two local festivals in Rajasthan—Tej, the Festival of Swings, and Gangaur, which honors the goddess Gauri—are popular events. Fairs held at various religious shrines in eastern Rajasthan are regularly attended by the Minas. The fair of Mata near Rewasa in Sikar district is a Mina fair marked by offerings of liquor and the sacrifice of buffaloes to the Goddess.

⁷RITES OF PASSAGE

As with other Hindus, the first shaving of a male child's head (handukadi) is a major ritual for the Minas. But perhaps the most important Mina ceremony is the funeral feast (nukta). As is the custom in Hindu India, the Minas cremate their dead. At the end of a period of mourning after a death, the bereaved family holds a feast for relatives and the entire community. In the Mina tradition, the nukta is obligatory, and the scale of the feast a mark of a family's economic status. Thus, in addition to its ritual function, the feast fulfills social and economic obligations. However, the heavy expenditure involved in holding this feast has resulted in many Mina families acquiring a lifelong burden of debt. This has become such a problem that some Mina tribal associations have attempted to ban the ceremony in their communities.

⁸INTERPERSONAL RELATIONS

The Minas follow the traditions of hospitality that are found throughout rural India. Guests are received cordially and served tea and other refreshments. During events such as marriages and death feasts, however, Minas maintain a social distance between themselves and other non-Mina communities.

⁹LIVING CONDITIONS

Mina villages are usually comprised of the members of one or more clans or gotras, along with service castes essential to an agricultural settlement. The village is generally unplanned, with a wide, unpaved main street cutting through its center. Houses of both Minas and other castes are constructed along this street. The village temples are often located in this central area. Minas who own land may build their houses on the edges of the village to be close to their property. In some areas, small hamlets (dhani) made up exclusively of the members of one family are scattered around the outskirts of the village. A council or Panchpatel, composed of the headmen (patels) of the various lineages (kutumbs) and settlement groups in the village, looks after community affairs.

The typical Mina house has mud walls and thatched roofs. A thick mud wall with only one entrance encloses a central courtyard around which are found rooms, one for each married male member of the household. These living rooms are used for storing family possessions and food grains and contain a niche for the family deity. On cold winter nights, the men sleep in these rooms, but otherwise they lie in the domain of the women of the household. Kitchen hearths are built under a thatch shed outside each living room. A large room containing a few wooden cots built outside the walls at the entrance to the main courtyard, acts as the men's living quarters. Behind the courtyard, and with a separate entrance, is the cattle shed where animals are kept and fodder and agricultural implements are stored. Fuel, in the form of cow dung cakes, is kept outside the walls of the house near the cattle shed.

Many Mina villages are located off the main communication routes, and transportation in these areas is difficult. A few private buses keep to somewhat unreliable schedules, but even then villagers may have to walk several kilometers to reach a drivable road. Transport is commonly undertaken by bullock cart, camel cart, and bicycle.

¹⁰FAMILY LIFE

The basic family unit among the Minas is the extended family. It may include several brothers, often of advanced age, along with their married and unmarried children. As many as three or four generations of a family may be in residence in a single household. Mina society is patrilocal and married daughters reside with the family of their husbands. Child marriage is the norm among the Minas, who believe that the ideal age for marriage is between 6 and 10 years old. A newly married girl remains with her family until she reaches puberty, when she moves to her husband's home. A typical Mina household may also contain divorced and widowed daughters.

Minas are endogamous and marry within the tribal group. Marriage partners have to be found outside one's own clan and thus often come from another village. Most marriages in Mina society are arranged by the parents of the prospective bride and groom. The girl's father negotiates a bride-price to be paid by the family of the husband. This used to consist of a cash sum or a specific number of cows, bullocks, or camels. More recently, however, marriage negotiations in India have expanded to include consumer goods such as watches, radios, and household appliances. In addition to the bride-price, Mina marriage is accompanied by the exchange of gold and silver ornaments between the two families.

Marriage rites as practiced by the Minas are similar to Hindu marriage rites. Brahman priests are used to fix an auspicious day and to officiate at the marriage rites. The groom travels to the village of the bride, accompanied by some elders of his family. The bridal party receives the hospitality of the bride's family for the one or two days it takes for the marriage rituals to be completed. At the appointed hour, a fire is lit and the bride and groom walk around it in the circumambulation rite. On the following day, the newlywed couple and their party return to the groom's home. Within a few days, the female relatives of the bride visit the groom's family and bring the girl back from her in-laws. The bride stays with her family until she reaches puberty, when she returns to live with her husband permanently.

Widow remarriage is accepted by the Minas. The preferred partner is a deceased husband's brother or paternal cousin. Another type of marriage accepted by Mina society is one in which a woman with a living husband can remarry another man, with the second husband paying compensation to the first husband. Both men and women are allowed to seek divorce on grounds ranging from adultery to the inability to have children.

11 CLOTHING

The dress of the Minas differs little from that of other Hindu groups in eastern Rajasthan. Men wear a *dhotī*, a single piece of white cloth about 5 m (16 ft) long and 1 m (3–4 ft) wide. About half the length is wrapped around the waist, and the remainder is drawn through the legs and tucked into the waist behind the body. A loose shirt or *kurta* and a turban complete the outfit. Women wear a skirt, a blouse that leaves the midriff bare, and a long wrap that can cover the head and be pulled across the face if necessary. Young children generally go naked, wearing a type of shirt during the colder winter months.

Meos traditionally wore similar dress until relatively recently, when they adopted Muslim style clothes. These are typically loose pants *(salwar),* a long tunic *(kamiz),* and a scarf *(dupatta)* for women, and a kurta and *tahband,* a long piece of cloth wrapped around the waist in the manner of a sarong, for men.

12 FOOD

Rajasthan lies in that part of India where cereals rather than rice are the main food crops grown, and this is reflected in the food of the Minas. The typical meal consists of unleavened bread *(rotī)* made from wheat, or millets called *jowar* and *bajra.* This is eaten with pulses such as lentils, which provide protein in the diet. Locally grown vegetables include onions, potatoes, spinach, and eggplant. The food is seasoned with chilies and other spices. Milk and curds and clarified butter *(ghī)* form part of the diet, although the cost of these products limits their use. Mustard oil is used for cooking. Tea is consumed at all times of the day.

Like all Hindus, especially those who aspire to higher caste status, the Minas are vegetarian and do not eat beef. The killing of a cow is considered by most Minas to be a heinous crime and subject to punishment. But some groups such as the Melia Minas or the Dhedia Minas are said to eat beef. The Padihar Minas received their name because of their supposed practice of eating buffalo meat *(pada* means buffalo calf). Mina groups that eat meat are regarded as socially inferior by other Minas, who will not intermarry with them.

13 EDUCATION

Despite the availability of state-supported schools, illiteracy and lack of education remain problems among many rural communities, including the Minas, in India. Distance, poor transportation facilities, inadequate resources in local primary and secondary schools, and a reluctance among many Minas to send their children to school result in low levels of education among the community. The literacy rate for Rajasthan in 2001 was 60.41%. However, this average masks a tremendous variation in literacy in the state. In the Virat Nagar block of Jaipur District (a rural area), for instance, literacy among girls is only 4.6% (2001). Among the Mina community, literacy is 52.2%, while for females, this figure drops to 31.8%, which is higher than the Bhils and most tribal communities in Rajasthan except for the Dhanka. Some Mina community associations have attempted to impose fines on Minas who do not send their children to school. The high costs of sending a child away for higher education is prohibitive for most Mina parents. But 62% of Mina children between the ages of 5 and 14 years attend school, although only around 5% ever graduate from high school.

14 CULTURAL HERITAGE

The Minas do not have a written literature but share in the regional traditions of Rajasthani folk culture. They participate in local fairs and festivals, and women sing appropriate folksongs at ceremonies, such as weddings. The Minas are fond of social gatherings and celebrate these events with song and dance. Many of the songs and dances of the Minas are considered to be obscene, and modern reformers have tried to ban these activities.

15 WORK

The Minas are primarily agriculturalists, depending on cultivation and animal husbandry for their livelihood. The Minas themselves make distinctions between the Zamindari Minas (agriculturalists) and Chowkidari Minas (watchmen), who in the past made their living as village night watchmen. The Chowkidari Minas have traditionally been associated with theft and robbery. Under the British, they were classified as criminals under the Criminal Tribes Act and required to report to the nearest police station every day. Some reportedly continue to follow a life of crime, but the old distinctions between the two communities are blurring. The Zamindari Minas see themselves as socially superior, and in the past the two groups did not intermarry. Such marriages do occur today.

Some Minas, especially those who have large landholdings, are fairly prosperous. They have accepted agricultural innovations and use modern equipment such as tillers, tractors, and irrigation pumps. Many Minas, however, have small, uneconomic holdings and lack modern equipment. Their agricultural efforts are greatly hampered by the frequent droughts of the region, and they often must supplement their income by working as laborers. It is common for all able-bodied men in a village to work at building roads once their seasonal agricultural activities are completed.

Small numbers of Minas are engaged in service and other occupations, but an overwhelming 75% are recorded as cultivators in 2001 census returns.

16 SPORTS

There are no sports, in the modern sense of the word, associated with traditional Mina society.

[17] ENTERTAINMENT AND RECREATION

Until recently, many Mina villages lacked electricity, and entertainment and recreation was derived primarily through traditional village festivities. With the development of rural areas and the advent of radio and even satellite television, such entertainment is available to those who can afford it. Urban areas provide access to popular Hindi movies, though again this is a luxury few villagers can afford.

[18] FOLK ART, CRAFTS, AND HOBBIES

Minas are known for their skill in areas such as basketry, ropemaking, embroidery on cloth and leather, and wall-painting. One Mina community living near Agra, in Uttar Pradesh State, makes its living from crafting the brightly colored, embroidered shoes and sandals worn by Rajasthanis. They are known as the Chamaria Minas, the Chamars being the traditional leatherworking castes of India.

[19] SOCIAL PROBLEMS

The Minas face many problems typical of tribal or conservative rural communities attempting to deal with the modern social and economic environment of India. Until the mid-20th century, the Minas lived under a feudal system that placed little emphasis on the social improvement of the people. Partly due to the indifference of their former rulers and partly due to their own resistance to change, the Minas continue to face problems of illiteracy and lack of education. Alcoholism is a problem among some Minas. Customs such as the paying of the bride-price and the death-feast have resulted in a considerable debt burden for many Minas.

Though they achieved little success, movements for social reform among the Minas date back to the 1920s, when Mina chiefs in Jaipur State founded the Mina Reformist Committee. Since then, many Mina associations aimed at social reform have been started. A summary of the social problems facing the Minas as perceived by the Minas themselves is provided by a list of offenses, to be punished by fines, set out by a Mina association in 1974. These included holding the death feast; distilling, selling, or drinking alcoholic beverages; taking work as a guard; failing to send children to school; and participating in group singing and dancing.

In 1950, when the president of India announced the list of peoples who were to be categorized as "Scheduled Tribes," the Minas were surprised to find they were not on it. However, following representations to the Government of India through the Mina Mahapanchayat and a visit to Mina country by a member of the Backward Caste Commission, the Minas were included on the list, giving them reserved government jobs and places in educational institutions. The Minas have generally made good use of the advantages accorded to them by Scheduled Tribe status and rank among the highest in the state among tribal groups in most socio-economic indicators.

Minas in Rajasthan object to the agitation by Gujars to be reclassified as a Scheduled Tribe (ST), as was promised by the Bharatiya Janata Party (BJP). Such agitation was taking place in 2008. Because of caste politics people vote en bloc as a community and they benefit as a bloc. This is what happened when Jats in Rajasthan were granted Other Backward Classes (OBC) status in 1999. Since they are powerful and generally well off, they cornered the benefits of reservations. The Gujars, who also have OBC status had to compete with the Jats, were later

promised ST status by the BJP. The community voted and BJP came to power in Rajasthan. The Gujars now want the promise fulfilled. Now, if Gujars get included as an ST then the other ST communities, including the Minas, suffer because someone else will come to share the ST reservation pie. Hence they protest to maintain their benefits. "Meenas in Rajasthan are the only Scheduled Tribe and we would not tolerate any inclusion into our community," the president of Rastriya Meena Mahasabha is supposed to have said. However, even though Minas have cornered most of the reservations for Scheduled Tribes in the state, groups such as the Bhils and Garasias are also classed as Scheduled Tribes in the state.

Rajasthan State has reservation quotas of 49% (16% for Scheduled Castes, 12% for STs, and 21% for OBCs). In June 2008 the state legislature was to meet to consider enacting a 14% job and education quota for the Economically Backward Category (EBC), which would make Rajasthan the first state in the country to have this quota. The Rajasthan government offered a 5% special reservation to the Gujar, Banjara, Gadia Lohar, and Raika communities, bringing an end to a nearly month-old stand-off over the Gujar community's demand for inclusion in the Scheduled Tribes category. If enacted, the additional 5% and 14% would bring the total of reservations in Rajasthan to 68%, one of the highest in the country.

The Gujar-Mina confrontation in Rajasthan, which has turned violent at times, has prompted a nationwide rethink of India's policy of reservations based solely on caste. Yet, this is not just a case of Gujars or Minas wanting to gain more reservation privileges. It is also the story of how politicians are attracted to quotas and reservations as vote banks. Once contemplated as a temporary measure to ensure equality for historically disenfranchised communities, reservations have become a permanent tool for vote-bank politics—and have, in the process, been excessively divisive.

[20] GENDER ISSUES

Women among the Mina have a lower status then their men. A woman has no right to inherit property, though she does have an important role in the socio-economic area. She has a strong influence in family decisions, although the final decision is always made by the head of the family, who is invariably male. Women involved themselves in matters like school enrolment (education is seen by most Minas as a means to better oneself), diarrhea management and campaigning for safe drinking water. Where there is no supply of safe drinking water in a village, it is the women who have to sometimes walk miles to get it, carrying the water in pots on their head—a common scene in Rajasthan. And women do important agricultural work in the fields.

The Minas have been strongly influenced by the Hindu groups amongst whom they live, which leaves them open to the usual abuses (occasionally the press reports the death of a Mina woman, though this is clearly more of a problem among caste Hindus). Thus Mina women observe *purdah* and marriages are arranged, though divorce is rare and usually has to be sanctioned by the local *panchayat*. A woman's family pays a dowry (which is quite high for a suitable match). A widow or widower may remarry, a junior levirate or junior sororate type of union being considered the most appropriate arrangement. Child marriage, though now technically illegal in India, is traditional among Mina groups, who think the ideal age of marriage for a girl is between 6 and 10 years of age.

Tuberculosis and death during delivery is common in the villages, which often lack adequate medical facilities. As income from agriculture is meager, many Mina women suffer the consequences of poverty and illiteracy. Yet they are open to modernization, seeing education and development as a way out of their situation.

[21] BIBLIOGRAPHY

Ali, Hasim Amir. *The Meos of Mewat: Old Neighbours of New Delhi.* New Delhi, Bombay, Calcutta: Oxford & IBH Publishing Co, 1970.

Gahlot, Sukhvir Singh, and Banshi Dhar. *Castes and Tribes of Rajasthan.* Jodhpur. Jain Brothers, 1989.

Gupta, Basant. *Environmental Perception and Tribal Modernization: A Study of Meena Landscape.* Jaipur: Ritu Publications, 2007.

Jain. P. C. *Planned Development Among Tribals: A Comparative Study of Bhils and Minas.* Jaipur and New Delhi: Rawat, 1999.

Sharma, S. L. *Social Stratification among the Tribes.* Delhi: Himanshu Publications, 2004.

Rizvi, S. H. M. *Mina: The Ruling Tribe of Rajasthan.* B. R. Publishing Corporation: Delhi, 1987.

Vetscher, Trande. "Bethrothal and Marriage among the Minas of South Rajasthan." *Man in India* 53 (1973): 387–413.

—by D. O. Lodrick.

MONGOLS IN CHINA

PRONUNCIATION: MAHN-gohls
ALTERNATE NAMES: Mengwushiwei
LOCATION: China (primarily Inner Mongolia Autonomous Region)
POPULATION: 5.81 million
LANGUAGE: Mongol
RELIGION: Lamaism
RELATED ARTICLES: Vol. 3: China and Her National Minorities

[1] INTRODUCTION

The expression "Mongol" originated from a tribe called Mengwushiwei in the Chinese book *Jiu Tang Shu* (The Ancient History of the Tang Dynasty), written in the 10th century. It seems the term was transliterated "Mongol" for the first time in the Yuan Dynasty (1271–1368). It gradually became the common name of many tribes. The east bank of the Erguna River (in central Inner Mongolia) was the cradle of the ancient Mongol people. Around the 7th century, they started to move toward the grassland in the west. In the 12th century, they dwelled in the upper reaches of Onon River, Kerulen River, and Tola River, east to the Kente Mountains. They made up a tribal group in which a large number of aristocrats gradually emerged from the nomads. Their leader, Temujin, was a powerful man whose strength came from the loyalty of his army and his own ability to command it. He conquered the other tribes and set up the Mongol empire. He took the title of Genghis Khan, Mongolian writings were created, and laws were codified. From 1211 to 1215, Genghis Khan expanded his territory to Central Asia and to the southern part of Russia. From 1227 to 1241, his successors swept west as far as Vienna. From 1253 to 1258, the Mongolian cavalry pushed deep into the Middle East. Before long, the occupied territory split into independent countries, including the Chinkai Empire, the Chagatai Empire, the Ogedei Empire, and the El Empire. In 1260, Kubilai (grandson of Genghis Khan) became the fifth supreme Khan and founder of the Mongol Yuan Dynasty (1271–1368), which had its capital in China (in present-day Beijing). He destroyed the Southern Song Dynasty in 1279 and established China as the center of his immense empire. After the fall of the Yuan Dynasty in 1368, the Mongols suffered from internal division and conflict for a very long time.

Lamaism, the Tibetan form of Buddhism, entered the Mongolian society in the 16th century. Thereafter, it had a strong impact on the Mongolian culture and socio-economic situation for centuries.

Under the influence of Soviet Russia, a revolutionary government was set up in 1921. Three years later, a large part of the traditional homeland of the Mongols became the People's Republic of Mongolia, established with the support of Soviet Russia, but it did not receive diplomatic recognition from many countries for decades. The other portion of the former Mongolian homeland remained within the Chinese border and was called Inner Mongolia. After 1949, it became the "Inner Mongolia Autonomous Region."

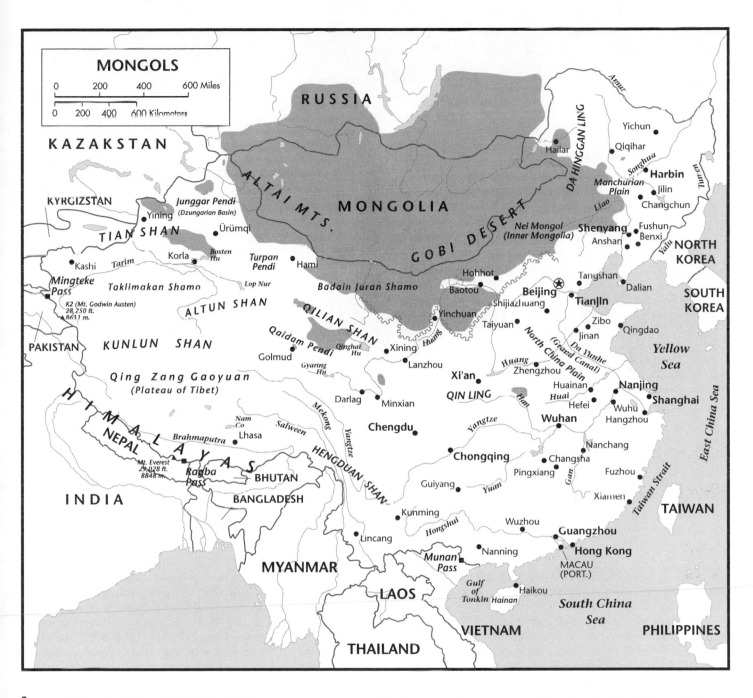

²LOCATION AND HOMELAND

The Mongols living in China numbered 5.81 million in 2000. They are mainly concentrated in Inner Mongolia Autonomous Region, but many also live in autonomous prefectures and counties in Xinjiang, Qinghai, Gansu, Heilongjiang, Jilin, and Liaoning. There are also Mongol communities scattered in Ningxia, Hebei, Sichuan, Yunnan, and Beijing. The territory of Inner Mongolia Autonomous Region covers some 460,000 sq mi, mostly hilly grassland and desert.

³LANGUAGE

The Mongol language belongs to the Altaic family, Mongolian group. There are three dialects. The writing system was created in the 13th century. Kubilai Khan ordered a Buddhist monk from Tibet to reform an ancient writing system, which

had been used to record oral literature but had ultimately been abandoned. The Mongolian writing system was revised several times by native Mongol linguists so as to conform to the spoken language. The Mongols in Xinjiang have used a variant of the Mongolian writing system since the 17th century.

⁴FOLKLORE

A large number of Mongolian myths are related to the origins of the Mongol people. One of their more important myths describes a tribe called Mongu fighting with other tribes for many years. Finally, the Mongu was defeated and all their people were killed, except two men and two women who escaped death by sheer luck. They went through many hardships and ultimately took refuge in a remote, thickly forested mountain, where only a narrow winding trail led to the outside world.

Mongolian herders emerge from a polling booth in a yert (a traditional nomadic tent) at Birjin, Mongolia. The polling station was set up to allow herders in the area to vote without the inconvenience of riding their horses long distances to the nearest city. (AP Images/Greg Baker)

This was a place with plenty of water and lush grass. They married. Many years later, the population grew to such a size that the land could not produce enough grain to nourish all the people. They had to move but, unfortunately, the narrow trail was obstructed. However, an iron mine was found by surprise. They cut down the trees, killed bulls and horses, and made a number of bellows. Then, they exploited the mine. This way, they not only opened an outlet to the outside world but also got plenty of iron. A vast expanse of grassland awaited them. They are the ancestors of the Mongols. To commemorate their heroic undertakings, the Mongols used to smelt iron at every year-end.

Some myths about the flood and sun-shooting are Mongolian versions of Chinese or Tibetan mythology.

⁵RELIGION

Originally, the Mongols believed in Shamanism. The shaman is a witch doctor, a dream reader, and an intermediary between the living and the spirit world; he is also skilled in divination and astrology. Up to the present, the remnants of Shamanism, such as sacrificial offerings to ancestors and reverence for the sun, moon, and nature, still exist.

Lamaism brought about a strong influence from Tibet, such as the integration of religion with politics. Built here and there,

Lamaist temples became independent manors possessing land, livestock, and manpower. The Mongols gradually turned to Lamaism. They sought the counsel and help of the *lama* for every aspect of their life: migration, marriage, childbirth, disease, and death. During the Qing Dynasty (1644–1911), the number of lama increased to almost one third of their population. Since the lama were not engaged in material production and not allowed to marry, the economic and demographic development of the society was greatly inhibited. Since 1949, Lamaist beliefs and practices have decreased drastically.

⁶MAJOR HOLIDAYS

The Spring Festival (lunar calendar; Western calendar, between January 21 and February 20) is an important holiday for the Mongols, as it is for the other nationalities of China. In preparation for this holiday, the Mongols tailor new clothes and store large quantities of mutton, wine, and dairy products. On the eve of the lunar New Year, all members of the family sit cross-legged in the center of the *yurt* and begin their dinner at midnight. They offer toasts to the senior persons, eat and drink extravagantly, and listen to storytelling all night long. Early the next morning, they dress up and call on relatives' and friends' homes. They kowtow to the senior persons. According to their custom, it is the duty of the son-in-law of the host to propose the toasts, which are never refused. Heated with wine, they dance while singing.

The Feast of Genghis Khan is April 23 (lunar calendar; Western calendar, between May 17 and June 16). On this occasion there are commemorative activities, exchange of commodities, theatrical performances, and sport games.

In June or July of each year, the Mongols celebrate a special ritual, called Aobao, which seems to go back to an ancient shamanistic practice. Aobao is a kind of altar or shrine made of a pile of stone, adobes, and straw, believed to be the dwelling of the gods in shamanism. During the ritual, tree branches are plucked into the Aobao, which is surrounded by lit joss sticks. Wine and horse milk are sprinkled over the mound, and mutton and cheese are placed on it as sacrificial offerings. While performing the ritual, the shaman dances and enters into a trance. Wrestling and horse racing follow the religious ceremony.

The "Nadam Rally" is a traditional holiday of the Mongols. Nadam means recreation and play. It is a happy festival of the herdsmen, held annually on a selected day in the summer or in the fall.

7 RITES OF PASSAGE

Depending on local custom, the Mongols practice cremation, burial in the ground, or funeral in the wilderness. In the west nomadic area, the last form of burial is the most common. The body of the dead is placed in an open horse-drawn cart and carried over rough terrain until the corpse drops down due to the bumps. Then the body is laid in the wild. It is believed that when it is eaten by wolves or vultures, the soul of the dead rises to heaven. If the body is still there after a week, it is regarded as unlucky: the soul was not accepted in heaven. A lama is then invited to recite the scriptures and pray for the dead. A donation is necessary. In case of the burial in the ground, the deceased is wrapped in white cloth and put in a plank cabinet or in a wicker basket, then buried.

8 INTERPERSONAL RELATIONS

There are no inns in the boundless grasslands, but one can always count on the Mongols for help. Their hospitality displays the lavishness that is characteristic of nomadic peoples. The master of a *yurt* will put up a stranger for the night. He offers milk tea, mutton, and wine. Surrounding the guest, the whole family will show its concern by making detailed inquiries. Upon leaving, the guest will be accompanied for quite a distance and then told the direction of his destination. If a herdsman calls at his friend's home, the host will offer his snuff-bottle to the guest, who will offer in turn his bottle for exchange. Each takes a sniff at the bottle of the opposite side and then gives the bottle back.

The Mongols in Yunnan have a special custom called "to meet the firewood-cutter." When it is about the time for someone to return home after cutting firewood for a whole day, one member of the family will go ahead to meet the tired person halfway, showing loving care for the family member engaged in hard labor.

9 LIVING CONDITIONS

The *yurt* is the traditional housing of the Mongols. It can be dismantled and transported on horseback, thus being suitable for nomadic life. The yurt is like a cylinder covered by an um-brella. The wall can be split into several pieces. Each is about 2.75 yards long and 1.5 inches high, made of long narrow pieces of wood arranged in networks. To set it up, one connects the separate pieces into a cylinder, which is covered by an umbrella-like roof also made of separate pieces. The wall exterior is covered with large pieces of felt, which are tied together by ropes. Only a round skylight and a doorframe toward the southwest are left open. The yurt may be as small as 4 yards in diameter, but the large ones may house hundreds of people. Stationary yurts are common in semi-nomadic districts and are mostly made of wood and adobes. In agricultural areas, the Mongols usually dwell in one-story houses like the Chinese, within the confines of a village. The Mongols living in towns and cities have, to a large extent, adopted the Chinese way of life.

The Mongols are adept at horse riding. Whenever they can ride instead of walking, they do so. Recently, however, bicycles, motorcycles, and cars have entered Mongol towns and villages, transforming the mode of transportation.

10 FAMILY LIFE

A Mongolian family generally consists of a man, his wife, and their young children. The sons, after wedding, move out of their parents' home. However, their yurts are relatively close to each other, so that they may move together with their parents in search of new pastures. In semi-nomadic districts, one finds large families, including parents, sons, and their spouses.

The Mongols are monogamous. The family is dominated by the man, but herdsmen usually consult their wives when matters arise. Furniture, clothes, and ornaments brought to the family by the wife during the wedding ceremony remain her own property.

A custom of "denying entrance on wedding" has been prevalent among the nomadic and semi-nomadic Mongols. The bridegroom, accompanied by relatives, rides to the bride's yurt. He finds the door slammed in his face. After repeated requests, the door is finally opened. He presents a *hada* (a ceremonial silk scarf) to his parents-in-law on entering and is given a banquet with a whole lamb. After the meal, the bride sits with her back to the others. The bridegroom kneels behind her and asks her pet name in childhood. He drinks at her house all night long. The following day, the bride leaves the yurt first. She rides a horse and circles the yurt three times, then speeds along to the bridegroom's house. The bridegroom and his relatives ride after her. The door is also slammed in her face and is only opened after repeated requests.

11 CLOTHING

Mongol dress varies with the environment and the seasons. In winter the Mongols living in pastoral areas usually wear a worn-out sheep fur coat with silk or cloth on the outside; in summer, they wear loose robes, usually in red, yellow, or dark navy, with long sleeves and a silk waistband. Knives with beautiful sheaths, snuff-bottles, and flint are worn as pendants at the waist. Long leather boots are often worn. All these items are related to the nomadic style of life. Mongolian peasants wear a cloth shirt, underwear and robes, or cotton-padded clothes and trousers. Felt boots are worn in winter. The old habit of wearing a waistband has been retained. Men like black or brown hats. Some of them wrap their heads with silk.

Women wrap red or blue cloth on their heads and wear a cone-shaped hat in winter.

¹²FOOD

The main traditional foods of the Mongols include beef, mutton, and milk products, supplemented by grain and vegetables. Roasted mutton and yogurt are popular. Breakfast usually consists of stir-fried millet with milk tea. Butter and salt are always added to the milk tea. Beef, mutton, and noodle soup are eaten for lunch and dinner. They drink the milk of horses, cows, and sheep, as well as brick tea and wine. Rice and flour are the staple foods of the peasants. Common dishes include dumplings, steamed stuffed buns, and meat pie.

¹³EDUCATION

According to data collected in 1978, there were 15 universities and colleges, more than 80 technical schools, about 5,000 middle (junior and senior) schools and 30,000 primary schools in Inner Mongolia. The cultural and educational level of the Mongols is higher than average among the national minorities of China.

¹⁴CULTURAL HERITAGE

There are quite a number of Mongolian folk songs, which may be divided into two different groups. One is prevalent in pastoral areas, slow in tempo and free in rhythm. The other is popular in semi-nomadic districts, with quicker tempo and regular rhythm. Haolibao is a style of singing performance, very popular in Mongolian areas. The melody is rather fixed, but the words are impromptu, usually inspired by a sudden event that touches the singer. Songs are usually sung by two singers in an antiphonal style but sometimes by a single performer. Matouqin ("horse-head stringed instrument") is a traditional instrument of the Mongols. The Chopstick dance and Winecup dance, soft and gentle, are frequently seen during festivities. The Horse dance and Saber dance, bold and generous, reflect well the nomadic styles.

Literature in the Mongolian script includes a heroic epic "Life of Jiangger" written in the 15th century and a "Historical Romance" written in the 19th century.

¹⁵WORK

Most of the Mongols are engaged in livestock husbandry, raising mainly sheep, cows, and horses. Mongolian horses, small and tough, serve the herdsman for transport, as a source of milk, and as subject of dance and songs. The Mongols develop a reverence for horses from childhood. It seems the expression "flying horse" is of Mongolian origin.

¹⁶SPORTS

In addition to horse racing and arrow-shooting, wrestling is one of the favorite pastimes of the Mongolian men. After a day of work, kids, young fellows, and male adults under 50 frequently gather before the yurt and wrestle under the sunset. For a match, they wear a black vest and sing as they wrestle.

¹⁷ENTERTAINMENT AND RECREATION

Movies and television have become popular and widespread over the last decades. Publications, broadcasts, drama, and films in the Mongolian language are flourishing. The Inner Mongolia Autonomous Region boasts a state-of-the-art film studio. Cultural centers and libraries disseminate the Mongolian language and cultural productions in cities, towns, and even in the pastoral areas.

¹⁸FOLK ART, CRAFTS, AND HOBBIES

Snuff-bottles are treasured among the Mongolians. They are made of gold, silver, copper, agate, jade, coral, or amber, with fine relief of horse, dragon, rare birds, and animals. Another artifact is the pipe bowl, made of five metals, with delicate figures and designs. Supplemented by a sandalwood pole and a red agate holder, it is considered very precious. A Mongolian saying states: "A pipe bowl is worth a sheep."

¹⁹SOCIAL PROBLEMS

One notices a strong trend among the Mongols to engage in trade. An urgent problem facing the Mongols at present is how to stabilize livestock husbandry and how to introduce scientific methods to breed the livestock. As breeding livestock is the mainstay of the Mongolian society, the modernization of their traditional mode of production is one of the keys to economic success.

²⁰GENDER ISSUES

The Chinese constitution states that women have equal rights with men in all areas of life, and most legislation is gender neutral. However, there are continued reports of discrimination, sexual harassment, wage discrepancies, and other gender related problems. The gap in educational level between women and men is narrowing with women making up 47.1% of college students in 2005, but only 32.6% of doctoral students. Mongols have achieved higher-than-average levels of education when compared to the national minorities of China.

China has strict family planning laws. It is illegal for women to marry before 20 years of age (22 for men), and it is illegal for single women to give birth. The Family Planning Bureau can require women to take periodic pregnancy tests and enforce laws that often leave women with no real options other than abortion or sterilization. Though minority populations were previously exempt from family planning regulations, policy has changed in recent years to limit minority population growth. Today, urban minority couples may have two children while rural couples may have three or four.

²¹BIBLIOGRAPHY

Borchigud, Wurlig. "The Impact of Ethnic Education on Modern Mongolian Ethnicity, 1949–1966." In *Cultural Encounters on China's Ethnic Frontiers*, edited by Stevan Harrell, 278–300. Seattle: University of Washington Press, 1994.

Chiao, Chien, Nicholas Tapp, and Kam-yin Ho, ed. "Special Issue on Ethnic Groups in China." *New Asia Bulletin*, no. 8, 1989.

Dreyer, June Teufel. *China's Forty Millions.* Cambridge: Harvard University Press, 1976.

Eberhard, Wolfram. *China's Minorities: Yesterday and Today.* Belmont: Wadsworth Publishing Company, 1982.

Gustafsson, Bjorn A., Shi, Li, and Sicular, Terry, eds. *Inequality and Public Policy in China.* New York: Cambridge University Press, 2008.

Heberer, Thomas. *China and Its National Minorities: Autonomy or Assimilation?* Armonk, NY: M. E. Sharpe, 1989.

Khan, Almaz. "Chinggis Khan: From Imperial Ancestor to Ethnic Hero." In *Cultural Encounters on China's Ethnic Frontiers,* edited by Stevan Harrell, 248–77. Seattle: University of Washington Press, 1994.

Lebar, Frank, et al. *Ethnic Groups of Mainland Southeast Asia.* New Haven: Human Relations Area Files Press, 1964.

Lemoine, Jacques. "Les Mongols." In *Ethnologie régionale II* (Encyclopédie de la Pléiade). Paris: Gallimard, 1978.

Ma Yin, ed. *China's Minority Nationalities.* Beijing: Foreign Languages Press, 1989.

Ramsey, S. Robert. *The Languages of China.* Princeton: Princeton University Press, 1987.

Schwarz, Henry G. *The Minorities of Northern China: A Survey.* Bellingham, WA: Western Washington University Press, 1989.

Shin, Leo Kwok yuch. *The Making of the Chinese State: Ethnicity and Expansion on the Ming Borderlands.* New York: Cambridge University Press, 2006.

—by C. Le Blanc

MONS

PRONUNCIATION: MOHNS
LOCATION: Myanmar (Burma)
POPULATION: Estimated 5 to 8 million in Myanmar
LANGUAGE: Mon; Burmese
RELIGION: Buddhism; some Animist and Hindu beliefs

[1] INTRODUCTION

Mons were among the original inhabitants of the lands now known as Thailand (formerly Siam) and Myanmar (called Burma until 1989), migrating south from the Mongolian steppes as far back as the 3rd century BC. The kings and queens of the ancient Mon civilization founded the cities of Thaton, Bassein, and Pegu in Burma. Their empires spread as far as northern Siam (Thailand) and Vietnam, and their trade routes stretched to India and Malaysia. Absorbing cross-currents of Asian culture, the Mons embraced the new Buddhist religion and then spread it to neighboring states. Conflict with those neighbors—Burmese (Burmans), Shans, and Siamese—was always a feature of Mon life. Sometimes expanding their territory, the Mons also endured periods of conquest. When the rulers of Upper Burma vanquished the Mons in the 11th century, Mon craftsmen and scholars were brought north to enhance the Burmese city of Pagan. Lower Burma retained its predominantly Mon character until the Burmese King U Aungzeya conquered it completely and began killing thousands of Mon Buddhist monks and other civilians. Many Mons fled to Thailand, and they became a minority group in central Burma.

The Mons had formed alliances with the French and later with the British against the Burmese, but found themselves increasingly marginalized. After World War II, when Burma gained independence from Britain, Mon dissatisfaction led to Mon nationalist insurgent groups taking up arms. Based in a narrow strip of southern coastline now called the Mon State, those groups fought a guerrilla war for decades, while trying to promote a revival of Mon culture. As human rights abuses of Mon civilians by the Myanmar military government became extremely widespread, the main Mon rebel group, the New Mon State Party entered into a ceasefire agreement in 1995. Many Mon dissident politicians and Buddhist monks have been imprisoned in Myanmar. Prominent Mons born in Thailand have actively supported their cause.

The related tribespeople of the Shan State, the Was and Palaungs have had turbulent histories as well. Buddhist tea growers, the Palaungs have had small insurgent groups, which are now in ceasefire agreements with the government. The Was, notorious for their headhunting in the past, were exploited as troops for the Burmese Communist Party insurgency after World War II. An opium-growing area from the British colonial days, the Wa homeland now produces the biggest share of Myanmar's opium poppies, the raw material for heroin. A large Wa nationalist group, the United Wa State Army (UWSA), involved in the narcotics trade, has a ceasefire agreement with the Myanmar government. The impoverished region controlled by the UWSA has been Southeast Asia's main source of opium refined into heroin as well as methamphetamine production, and casinos there are patronized by Chinese gamblers from across the border.

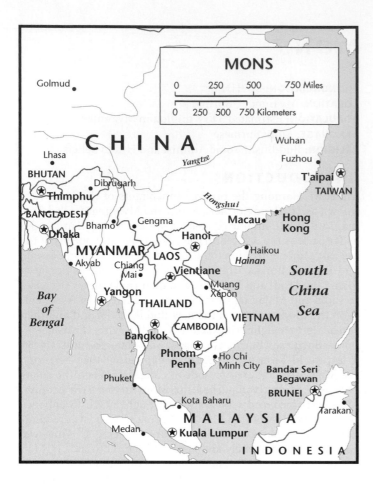

2 LOCATION AND HOMELAND

The Mons are an Austro-Asiatic people, closely related to the Khmers of Cambodia. Estimates of Mon population in Myanmar range from 5 to 8 million (no proper census has been done and many people of Mon ancestry only speak the Burmese language), and as many as 3 million Thais of Mon ancestry, as well as Mon populations in coastal Cambodia, Vietnam, and Malaysia. Thousands of Mons from Myanmar live as refugees or migrant workers in Thailand, Malaysia, and other countries. Other Mon-Khmer ethnic groups include the Palaungs (about 400,000) and the Wa mountain people who number perhaps 1 million, half in Myanmar's Shan State and half in China's Yunnan Province.

While the old Mon empires covered immense areas of Southeast Asia, today Myanmar's Mon State is the only official Mon homeland. Located in Myanmar's southern Tenasserim region, the Mon State has a string of mountains separating it from Thailand, and flat coastal plains with farmland, fruit orchards, and mangrove wetlands. Numerous small islands lie offshore in the Andaman Sea, which has huge reserves of natural gas. The main cities of the Mon State are Thaton, Moulmein, Amherst (Kyaikkami), and Ye, all on or near the sea. Since the 1990s, deforestation has affected the Mon State as rainforest and mangroves have been cleared for timber and agricultural development.

3 LANGUAGE

The Mon-Khmer language group is distantly related to some in India and the South Pacific. It is very different from the neigh-boring Sino-Tai and Tibeto-Burmese groups. As learning Mon is discouraged by the current educational system of Myanmar, many Mons are only Burmese-speakers. To greet each other in their own language, Mons say "*Mange rayaw,*" meaning "prosperity." They also ask, "*Mo'ng mip ha?*" ("how are you?"). "Thank you" in Mon is "*Tang kun.*"

The Mon alphabet, based on the Sanskrit-related Pali script, has 35 letters. Mons taught their script to the Burmese, who devised an alphabet later adapted by many of Myanmar's ethnic groups.

4 FOLKLORE

Mons believe in a supernatural world, inhabited by spirits of the trees and fields, household and village spirits, ghosts of ancestors, and demons such as the "*kalok daik,*" a spirit from the sea that devours children. A yearly "spirit dance" may be held to honor village spirits, with trance dancing by women possessed by the ghosts of their ancestors. Mon shamans, witches, and astrologers interpret messages from the spirit world and bad omens such as the cry of an owl. Buddhist monks may be called on to exorcise ghosts or other bad spiritual elements.

5 RELIGION

The Mons discovered Buddhism through contact with India. They practice a conservative form of Theravada Buddhism, emphasizing the study and interpretation of scriptures. Meditation, uncluttered ritual, and the merciful rule of law are important features. The monasteries are important centers of learning in Mon villages, and many young men and women become Buddhist monks or nuns for a short period or for life. During the September 2007 "Saffron Revolution" protests by Buddhist monks throughout Myanmar, Mon monks and their supporters marched in the towns and cities. In spite of their faith in a rigorous form of Buddhism, many Mons believe in old Animist or Hindu elements as well, such as possession by ghosts, and astrology.

The Shan State's Mon-Khmer relatives, the Palaungs, practice Buddhism along with the worship of *Nats* (guardian spirits), and the Was are largely animists with some Christians and Buddhists. In past times, the Was cut off the heads of victims who crossed their paths, leaving the skulls on posts leading to their villages. This was thought to protect the village and ensure a good rice crop. Their headhunting gave the Was a reputation as fearsome warriors that has lasted through their service in various insurgent groups and drug-trade militias.

6 MAJOR HOLIDAYS

Mons celebrate Buddhist holidays, including the full moons that begin and end Lent (a three-month period of Buddhist prayer and study that coincides with the monsoon season). At the Buddhist New Year in the Spring, Mons enjoy the Water Festival with music, dance, and playful water-throwing. There are also individual festivals held yearly for the temple structures called pagodas. These have all-night dance and theater performances, sports events, and special foods. Overseas Mons celebrate Buddhist holidays and Mon National Day, a commemoration of the founding of the last Mon kingdom.

7 RITES OF PASSAGE

Traditionally, after a baby is born, the Mon mother and baby have turmeric, a yellow spice, rubbed on their skin as a healing potion. The mother rests near a fire for three days afterwards. Babies have their ears pierced, and women wear earrings all their lives. Boys stop wearing them at around age 10, when most become novice Buddhist monks for one to three months. At age 20, most Mon men become monks again for a short period. Some choose after age 21 to take vows and remain monks for life. The monks are greatly respected in Mon society for their self-discipline and learning. Some girls and older women become Buddhist nuns. Both monks and nuns keep their heads shaved, wear simple robes, and eat only vegetarian food.

Mons believe that the soul can leave the body, even when someone is asleep. Sometimes, it is said the soul takes the form of a butterfly. The soul leaves for good when someone dies, which is considered a step on the way to rebirth through reincarnation. If they can afford it, Mons prefer large funerals for family members, with music and a feast for guests and the Buddhist monks who chant prayers. The body is usually cremated.

8 INTERPERSONAL RELATIONS

Mons use honorifics in front of their names, usually *Nai* for men and *Mi* for women. When they meet, they put their hands together in a "prayer" position and bow slightly. If greeting an older person or a monk, the hands are held up in front of the face and there is more of a bow.

Guests are served tea or at least water. People take their shoes off inside the house. Older people are to be treated with the respect that you would show your own parents or grandparents, and should not be touched on the head or spoken to impolitely.

Boys and girls meet at festivals, and sporting or school events, which they attend in groups. Rather than dating, a boy usually visits a girl at her parents' house. Once a relationship has begun, love-letters are often exchanged.

9 LIVING CONDITIONS

The Mons in rural areas have suffered from efforts by the Myanmar military government to control their region for resource exploitation. Logging companies from neighboring Thailand decimated forests in the Mon State, and a pipeline bringing natural gas from offshore to Thailand traversed the area. Human rights groups accused the Myanmar military of abusing local people while securing the pipeline route, and a lawsuit was filed in the United States on behalf of affected villagers against one of the petroleum companies involved, Unocal. During the 1990s, Mons were moved to new settlements near Myanmar army bases and were used for forced labor as military porters and road/railway builders. Many thousands fled this treatment to Thailand, only to be pushed back across the border. Others have gone to Malaysia and other counties, seeking safety and work. The displaced Mons in rural Myanmar are especially susceptible to tropical diseases such as malaria, typhoid, and dysentery. Even in the cities, there is a severe shortage of medical facilities, personnel, and medicines. Malnutrition has been increasing steadily. In 2007–2008, steep increases in prices of essential commodities including fuel and rice further narrowed the margins of survival for the Mons in Myanmar.

In the countryside, Mon houses are built of wood or bamboo. On short or tall stilts, they are one or two stories high, with a sloping thatched roof and a verandah along the front. In the cities, Mons live in wood, brick, or cement houses, with ornamental carvings and balconies. Families with money now prefer brick or cement houses, as seen by people on trading journeys to Malaysia or Singapore, even though the electricity supply is not reliable enough to keep them cool with fans or air conditioning. Often there is a shop on the first floor and family living quarters upstairs. Mon-related ethnic groups, the Palaungs live in multi-family wood and bamboo longhouses, and the Was live in houses of woven bamboo.

A railway line runs through Mon State as far south as Tavoy. A highway runs parallel to it. Much transport is by shared jeep or truck, small riverboats, or ocean-going vessels. In the countryside, ox-carts and small motorbikes are the main forms of transportation, and travel in the mountains is done on foot.

10 FAMILY LIFE

When a Mon couple wants to marry, they usually ask their parents' permission. A simple ceremony is held in which the couple joins hands. The couple may exchange vows. Buddhist monks often attend, but it is not a religious ritual. Friends give wedding gifts and refreshments are provided.

Mon families are large, especially in the village. Having six or seven children is average. Child mortality is now high because of malnutrition and infectious diseases. Divorce is allowed in Mon society, and any children usually live with the mother.

Mons keep cats in their houses as pets, as well as colorful songbirds in bamboo cages. Dogs are considered very low and dirty animals and so aren't considered good household pets. Stray dogs sometimes live in the monastery yards.

11 CLOTHING

The Mons, living in a tropical climate, wear light-weight cotton clothes. Men dress in shirts with trousers or sarongs called *nein*, often with a checked pattern. Mon women wear short jackets, blouses, or T-shirts with sarongs called *kloit*. For special occasions, they wear silk sarongs embroidered with gold or silver threads and a matching sash that crosses over one shoulder. The sarongs are made by simply sewing the fabric with one seam into a wide tube. Men knot theirs at the waist, and women wrap theirs tightly and then tuck them in at the waist. Mon girls decorate their hair with orchids and other flowers, and use a sunscreen or face powder made from a fragrant wood. Mon men used to have their legs and arms elaborately tattooed with Buddhist inscriptions and symbolic animals, but this practice is now uncommon.

The Mons' relatives in the mountains of the Shan State, the Palaungs and Was, have their own distinctive styles of dress. Palaung men wear loose trousers and jackets of homespun indigo with bright-colored sashes and turbans. The women wear short cotton jackets with striped sarongs. Rattan, bamboo, and silver hoops circle their waists, and they wear masses of beaded necklaces and large, circular silver earrings. More beads are wound around their turbans. Wa men, when not in olive drab military uniforms, wear dark homespun cotton clothing. The women wear sleeveless jackets, short wraparound sarongs, and bracelets and headbands made of silver.

[12]FOOD

Mons who can afford to enjoy curries of beef, pork, or chicken served with many dishes of rice, and seafood including crab, lobster, shellfish, prawns, and many varieties of river and ocean fish. *harrok*, a paste made of fermented fish, is a favorite accompaniment to any meal. Fish soup with noodles is a popular breakfast. Plain tea is served with meals, and tea or coffee with sweetened, condensed tinned milk is served between meals. Cookies, small cakes, and orange- or coffee-flavored hard candies can be bought in the shops. Fruits are the most popular snacks, especially mango, durian (a pungent large fruit with a hard spiky shell), pineapple, and watermelon. Mons make a cooling snack by mashing watermelon pulp in a bowl and mixing in sweetened condensed milk. Mon cuisine influenced Burmese cooking in the days of the royal courts and has in turn been influenced by the dishes of India, Thailand, and Malaysia. Mons consider their food spicier than that of the Burmese (Burmans).

[13]EDUCATION

In villages, Mons rely on the local monasteries to teach their children. There is a shortage of schools, teachers, and educational materials in the government schools, and instruction there is carried out in Burmese. The Mons value literacy and education highly, and resent what they consider to be the deliberate suppression of their language and culture by the predominantly Burmese (Burman) government of Myanmar. The idea that the Mons are an assimilated people who have become absorbed into the Burmese mainstream has been promoted by the government. Mon schools supported by the New Mon State Party following the 1995 ceasefire have been shut down by the Myanmar government. Nonetheless, many Mon people, especially in the Thai border area, still speak and read their ancient language, which is mostly taught at monastery schools. The Mon political underground promotes Mon literacy and the study of ancient history.

[14]CULTURAL HERITAGE

Mon classical music is played by ensembles of horns and percussion instruments. Two distinctively Mon musical instruments are a U-shaped frame with a series of metal gongs suspended along it, and the *mi-gyaung*, a long zither in the shape of a crocodile. "Mon songs" are one of the categories of Burmese classical music and are usually faster in tempo than other compositions. Mon dance, influenced by Indian classical dance, includes solo forms and the group "candle dance," performed by girls holding lit candles in each hand to reenact a courtly welcome to the Buddha.

Most of Mon literature is Buddhism-related. In centuries past, Mon monks wrote detailed interpretations of Buddhist theory and hid them away when rival ethnic kingdoms were in power. In the 20th century, Mons revived and published these old works. Religious texts in Mon are tolerated by the Myanmar government, but other Mon writing is discouraged. Underground writers, and those in exile, have written essays about Mon history. Exiled journalists formed the Independent Mon News Agency and Kaowao News Group to provide updates online. An exile group, the Human Rights Foundation of Monland, publishes a newsletter called "The Mon Forum."

Mon woodcarvers, metal sculptors (specializing in Buddha images), mural painters and architects deeply influenced Burmese, Shan, and Thai culture. Their work can be seen in the ruins of Myanmar's ancient capital, Pagan, and in art museums around the world. The famous Shwedagon Pagoda, a massive golden spire in Myanmar's largest city, Rangoon, was established by a Mon queen, Shin Saw Bu, in the 15th century.

[15]WORK

The Mons have traditionally been wetland rice farmers, although forced relocation and demands for crop quotas by the Myanmar military have greatly disrupted their agricultural production. Mons also raise coconut and betel palms and other fruit trees. On the coast, Mons have fished and gathered shellfish, but this occupation has been diminished by overfishing by foreign trawler fleets. Logging of the remaining forests by foreign timber firms has made it difficult for Mons to hunt or gather rattan and other forest products. Mon farmers have had their land confiscated for military-owned plantations and the cultivation of jatropha, an introduced bio-fuel crop, which takes away land that was used for food production.

The economy has also been depressed in the cities, where people try to make their living in shops or offices, or through sea trade with Malaysia and Singapore. Many people have to hold more than one job just to buy enough rice for their families. Numerous educated Mon professionals have emigrated to Thailand or elsewhere overseas.

The Palaung people are known for their tea growing and are also hill rice cultivators. The primary cash crop for the Was has long been opium poppies. They gain a minimal profit from raising heroin's raw material, the value of which increases the more it is refined and the further it is transported. A great many Wa men serve in the United Wa State Army (20,000 strong), while the women raise and harvest hillside rice and opium poppies.

[16]SPORTS

Young Mons enjoy practicing a style of kick-boxing similar to Thai boxing, but even less restrained. Soccer is extremely popular, as is *chinlone* (a game like "hacky-sack" played with a woven rattan ball).

[17]ENTERTAINMENT AND RECREATION

All-night theater shows, with comedy and musical performances, are a traditional form of entertainment. Cities, towns, and some villages have "video parlors" that show foreign movie DVDs, or homemade productions in the Mon language. Numerous Mon pop music groups make and distribute their own recordings. Songs by some Mon recording artists, like the pop band *Anat Ghae*, have been purchased and released with Burmese-language lyrics by Burmese (Burman) singers for national sales. With satellite television and the Internet severely restricted by the government, shortwave radios are still important sources of news and international music.

[18]FOLK ART, CRAFTS, AND HOBBIES

Mon woven cotton blankets from the town of Mudon are well-known in Myanmar. Mons in Myanmar and Thailand make pottery, often of a red-orange clay. The Mons are also skilled goldsmiths. The Palaungs craft lacquered baskets, textiles, and silver jewelry.

[19] SOCIAL PROBLEMS

Heroin addiction is quite widespread among young people in the Mon cities and in the Palaung and Wa regions where opium is refined into heroin. Along with the trafficking of young women to Thailand and China for prostitution, intravenous heroin use has contributed to an extremely high rate of HIV/AIDS infection. There is still not enough educational material available about the disease and not enough medicine to treat those who have contracted it.

The Mon people have long resented the downfall of their ancient civilization and the suppression of their culture at the hands of outsiders, but now, due to Myanmar military government efforts to push them aside and obtain their natural resources, many of the Mons of Myanmar have struggled for their daily survival.

[20] GENDER ISSUES

Mon society is tolerant of gay and transgender individuals. The status of women among the Mons is traditionally high, and the ancient Mon empires were from time to time ruled by queens. However, warfare and human rights abuse have left many Mon women victimized. Rape by the Myanmar military forces has been common, and Mon refugee girls and women have been forced into prostitution in Thailand.

[21] BIBLIOGRAPHY

Asia Watch. "A Modern Form of Slavery: Trafficking of Burmese Women and Girls into Brothels in Thailand." New York: Human Rights Watch, 1993.

———. "The Mon: Persecuted in Burma, Forced Back From Thailand." New York: Human Rights Watch, December 1994.

Human Rights Foundation of Monland. http://rehmonnya.org/ (29 May 2008).

Independent Mon News Agency. www.monnews-imna.com (29 May 2008).

Kaowao News Group. http://www.kaowao.org (29 May 2008).

Lang, Hazel J. Fear and Sanctuary: Burmese Refugees in Thailand. Ithaca NY: Southeast Asia Program Cornell University, 2002.

LeBar, Frank, ed. Ethnic Groups of Mainland Southeast Asia. New Haven, CT: Human Relations Area Files, 1964.

Mirante, Edith T. Burmese Looking Glass: A Human Rights Adventure. New York: Human Grove Press, 1993.

"Mon Music of Burma," CD, Nai Htaw Paing Ensemble (San Francisco: Fire Museum Records, 2006).

Mon Unity League. "The Mon People: A Noble Past, An Uncertain Future." Burma Debate III, no. 6 (Nov/Dec) 1996.

Smith, Martin. Ethnic Groups in Burma. London: Anti-Slavery International, 1995.

South, Ashley. Mon Nationalism and Civil War in Burma: The Golden Sheldrake. London: Curzon Press, 2002.

Takano, Hideyuki. The Shore Beyond Good and Evil: A Report from Inside Burma's Opium Kingdom. Reno NV: Kotan Books, 2002.

—by Edith Mirante

MORO

LOCATION: Philippines
POPULATION: 2 million
LANGUAGE: Marano, Maguindanao, Tausag, other Malayo-Polynesian languages
RELIGION: Islam

[1] INTRODUCTION

The Moro are the indigenous Muslim population of the Southern Philippines and are composed of more than a dozen ethno-linguistic groups of Islamic faith that occupy Mindanao Island, the Sulu archipelago, and Palawan Island. The Spanish were the first to refer to the Muslim Filipinos as Moros, derived from the name used to describe Spanish Muslims, Moors. The term Moro held a derogatory meaning until the 1970s, when Islamic insurgent groups embraced the appellation.

The history of the Moro is traced back to the arrival of Islam in Southeast Asia. Beginning in the 9th century, regional trade between the Philippine archipelago and Southeast Asia expanded rapidly. Muslim traders from Arabia and India situated in Southeast Asia were the first to introduce Islam into the southern Philippines. By the 1300s the conversion to Islam was in progress among the western most islands situated nearest to the sultanates of Melaka and Johor in modern Malaysia. The first Islamic sultanate in the modern day Philippines was established around 1450 on Jolo by an Arab named Syed Abu Bakr. According to Moro legend, Sharif Muhammad Kabungsuwan, a prince from the Sultanate of Johor, first introduced Islam to Mindanao Island in the early 1500s. By the early 16th century, Islam had spread across the Philippine archipelago, from Mindanao in the south to Luzon Island in the north. During this period the Moro were ruled by local leaders known as datus or sultans.

In the early 16th century, the Spanish began to colonize the Philippine archipelago. The new possession was named the Philippines after the Spanish King Phillip II. In 1565 Miguel López de Legazpi arrived in the Philippines, overthrew the Sultanate of Manila, and commenced the conversion of the northern Philippine islands to Catholicism. The Spanish zeal to extinguish Islam from the Philippines led to stiff resistance in the southern Islands, particularly on Mindanao and the Sulu archipelago. Military bases were established on the southern islands, and Catholic missionaries succeeded in converting some of the population, in particular in the northeastern sections of Mindanao, but the Spanish presence in the Moro homeland remained minimal, and the Catholic and Muslim communities remained divided.

In 1898 the United States defeated Spain in a brief war and took control of the Philippines. The United States adopted secular rule, and the new colonial government maintained the territorial unity of the Philippines. The 1899 Kiram–Bates Treaty granted the Sulu Sultanate political and cultural autonomy, while recognizing that the island chain remained part of the Philippines. Over the next several decades, the United States initiated development projects throughout Moro territory in order to integrate the region into the Philippines.

The Philippines gained self-rule in 1935 and control of the Moro homeland came under the control of the Catholic-domi-

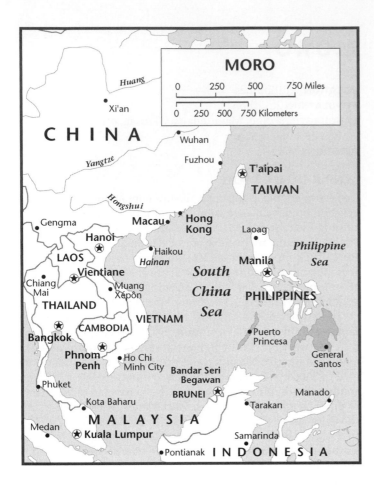

escalated on both sides and tens of thousands of Moros and Christians became internally displaced.

The most prominent anti-government organization was the Moro National Liberation Front (MNLF), which was comprised of Moro nationalists and Islamic revivalists. By 1972 the conflict on Mindanao had worsened to the point that the Filipino government declared martial law. The Libyan government lent its support to the MNLF and by the mid-1970s as much as a third of the Filipino military was deployed to Mindanao. In 1976 Marcos signed the Tripoli agreement, which granted autonomy to the Muslim-majority areas of Mindanao. The Marcos regime adopted a conciliatory stance towards the Moro. The Moro autonomous regions were determined by plebiscite. Regions in Palawan and Mindanao opted not to join either of the two autonomous regions.

The MNLF continued their resistance against the Marcos regime into the 1980s. This was in spite of the government development projects implemented in the late 1970s and early 1980s that were meant to alleviate the economic hardships suffered by the Moro. In 1987 a new constitution provided for a second round of autonomy plebiscites, but only four of thirteen regions opted to join the new Autonomous Region in Muslim Mindanao. In 1996, President Fidel Ramos signed a major peace accord with the MNLF, yet the issues of land rights and Christian settlers on traditionally Moro tribal territory remained unsettled.

In the early 2000s, the Islamist fundamentalist group Abu Sayyaf (al-Harakat al-Islamiyya) grabbed headlines with bombings, kidnappings, and killings of Filipinos and foreigners, and through daring battles with the Filipino armed forces. Situated in western Mindanao and the Sulu archipelago, Abu Sayyaf has fought to establish a Muslim homeland in the traditional Moro homeland. After the 11 September 2001 terrorist attacks in the United States, the U.S. military began assisting the Filipino military in their fight against Abu Sayyaf. In 2006 Abu Sayyaf's leader was killed in battle, and the government's counter insurgency campaign succeeded in expelling the group from a number of their strongholds. In spite of these setbacks, Abu Sayyaf remained capable of carrying out lethal raids and, in 2008, Filipino intelligence agencies revealed a plot by the group to assassinate President Gloria Arroyo.

²LOCATION AND HOMELAND

The Moro occupy the southern islands of the Philippines, including Mindanao Island, the Sulu archipelago, and Palawan Island, as well as numerous smaller islands. The Moro homeland is referred to as Bangsamoro, or nation of the Moro. The term Moro refers to Filipinos of Islamic faith and encompasses communities that are divided by long distances and speak distinct languages. While the Moro are the indigenous inhabitants of the Southern Philippines, the arrival of a large number of Christian migrants from the northern islands has reduced the Moro to a minority across much of their homeland.

The Moro ethno-linguistic group includes the Tausag, Badjao and Sama of the Sulu archipelago; the Magindanao, Maranao, Iranun, Kalagan, Kalibugan, and Sangil of Mindanao Island; the Yakan of Basilan Island, off the coast of Mindanao; the Palawani and Molbog of Palawan Island, and the Jama Mapun, situated in southern Palawan and the Sulu archipelago. Of these groups, the largest populations of Moros are the Maranao and Maguindanao, both over 700,000, and the Tausug, more

nated government in Manila. That year, the new Filipino government passed the Quirino-Recto Colonization Act, opening Mindanao to mass immigration of Catholic settlers. In 1903 the census recorded that 78,000 non-Muslim immigrants lived in Muslim majority regions. Official government support of migration ensured that by the end of the 20th century more than 9 million non-Muslims resided in what had been Moro-majority territory. In addition, the Filipino government abolished the sultanates and ended Moro political autonomy. The Muslim Moro population came under the direct administration of Catholic bureaucrats appointed by Manila, which only inflamed Moro resentment against Filipino rule.

By the 1960s, official corruption, economic underdevelopment, and increased Catholic migration led to deep resentment towards the Filipino government and the Catholic majority. Control of economic resources lay in the hands of non-Muslims and international conglomerates dominated the agricultural industry. The abolition of the traditional sultan-based rule and the social hierarchy that supported it had led to a power vacuum, which was filled by Moro insurgent groups who espoused a revival of Islamic beliefs. The relations between Muslims and Christians worsened considerably during the administration of Ferdinand Marcos, who ruled the Philippines from 1965–1986. Corruption reached extreme levels under Marcos, and Christian settlers aggressively pushed Muslim tribes off their land on Mindanao, which often resulted in violence. In the 1970s, in Cotabato province, Mindanao, the Filipino military armed Christian militias, which attacked Muslim villages. Violence

A Filipino boy stares at a former member of the Moro National Liberation Front (MILF) rebels, who are now integrated with the Philippine military while he patrolls in Basilan province. (© Reuters/Corbis)

than 300,000. In addition, there are Moro migrant communities located in major urban centers across the Philippines.

The islands occupied by the Moro are mountainous and traversed by tropical forests, rivers, and lakes. The regional climate is dry during the winter months and receives heavy rainfall in the summer, when monsoon rains inundate the Philippines. The region is often struck by typhoons, which can cause extensive damage. Hydropower stations along regional river systems provide the majority of electricity on Mindanao. The Moro homeland also has potential for geothermal energy and may contain substantial petroleum deposits.

³LANGUAGE

The Moro speak more than a dozen languages. With the exception of Chavacano, the Moro languages fall within the Malayo-Polynesian branch of the Austronesian language family. Marano, Maguindanao and Tausag are spoken by more than 1 million individuals each, though not all native speakers of these languages are Moro. There are several Spanish Creole languages, which are known commonly as Chavacano. In addition, English is widely spoken as a second language.

The Austronesian languages of the Moro share a high degree of intelligibility. The intelligibility between Marano and Maguindanao speakers is more than 50%. Common terms shared across several languages include *ina* (mother), *ama* (father), *isa* (one) and *dua* (two). Common Tausag phrases include *Hisiyu in ngan mu?* (What's your name?), *Maunu-unu nakaw?* (How are you?), and *Daing hain kaw?* (Where are you from?).

⁴FOLKLORE

Moro folklore has been preserved in oral epics that are composed of communal histories, genealogies, origin stories, and tales of ancient heroes, as well as stories of the Prophet Muhammad and other Islamic figures. Epics are often sung and epic singers undergo lengthy apprenticeships that often include memorization of the Quran and training in traditional music instruments.

Epics are known to only a small minority who have been trained by elders. Among the Sama of the Sulu archipelago and Yakan of Basilan Island, epic poems called *kata-kata* are only recited by important individuals who have the authority to conduct rituals. During communal festivals and holidays epics are recited for days on end. The *kata-kata* is sung by Sama narrators during a period over several nights that coincides with a full moon and serves as the main highlight of an important public gathering.

Moro epics often share striking similarities with non-Islamic epics. The epic *Tutolan ko Radia Mangandiri* (*Story of Radia Mangandiri*), first recorded by modern scholars in 1939, contains components of the Hindu epic *Ramayana*. In the epic, the hero Mangandiri searches for Tuwan Potre Malano Tihaia, who has been kidnapped by Maharadia Lawana. Lawana has himself transformed into a golden goat and Mangandiri is aided by his son Laksamana, who takes the form of a monkey. Other epics include the *Radya Indara Patra* and the *Diwata Ksalipan* of the Maguindanao, and the *Darangen* of the Maranao.

⁵RELIGION

The Moro are adherents of Islam and their religion is a defining characteristic of their ethnicity. The Islamic-Christian divide in the Philippines is both religious and cultural in nature. Once an individual or community has left Islam, they are no longer considered Moro.

In the 14th century, Islam was introduced to the Philippine archipelago by missionaries from Southeast Asia. Sufi missionary Makdum Karim is credited with Islamizing the population of Jolo in the Sulu archipelago. The Islamic concept of *din wa daula*, or unity of religion and state, was adopted by pre-colonial Moro leaders, who held positions of both political and religious significance.

The Moro are Sunni Muslims and Moro communities observe common Islamic norms. Friday is the holiest day of the week in Islam and Muslims must conduct prayers at specific hours of the day, from dawn until dusk. The Friday noon service *zubor* (prayers) open with a *adhan* (melody) sung by the imam. Prayers are often accompanied by singing and chanting. Common religious musical texts include poetic verses that recount the lessons of Prophet Muhammad. On Jolo Island the *luguh Maulad* is sung commemorating the birth of Muhammad. Islamic education prescribes the memorization of the Quran and Moro who are able to recite the entire Quran are held in high regard. Annual Quran-reading competitions choose Filipino representatives to international competitions, where Filipinos have won major prizes in recent decades.

The Moro, as is the case with Muslims across the world, practice a mixture of Shariah (sacred Islamic law) and *adalat* (customary pre-Islamic traditions). Filipino Muslims hold common beliefs with their animist and Christian neighbors that appear to contradict Islamic teachings. This includes the notion that the world is filled with sprits (*dewas* and *hantus*) that are to be feared and must be appeased through offerings. It is commonly believed among the Tausag that *mangilit* (a head ghost) haunts humans and that precautions must be taken to prevent *lagtaw* (evil beings) and *balbalan* (witches) from harming infants. On Mindanao, illness and mental disorders are attributed to evil spirits that can only be appeased through *kalilang* (honorific ceremonies). Among the Tausag, local imams (Islamic religious leader) participate in food offering ceremonies meant to excise sprits from the body. The Moro also often fail to observe basic Islamic customs, including *salat* (ritual daily prayers) and *zakat* (annual alms-tax).

6 MAJOR HOLIDAYS

Most Moro holidays are Islamic, and their date is determined by the lunar calendar, thus the days of celebration fall on different dates each year. Ramadan (*puwasa*) is a major Islamic holiday that celebrates the revelation of the Quran to Prophet Muhammad and takes place during the ninth month of the Islamic calendar. During this period Muslims refrain from eating or drinking from dawn to dusk. Pregnant women, children, the elderly, and the ill are exempt from fasting. Eid is the celebratory feast held at the end of Ramadan.

The Kabunsuan Festival is celebrated on December 15 in Cotabato City on Mindanao. The day celebrates the arrival of Sharif Muhammad Kabungsuwan in the early 16th century and the introduction of Islam to Mindanao Island. During the harvest season, celebrations are held throughout the agricultural areas of the Moro homeland. Music is played on percussion beams, bamboo clappers, and log drums and starts immediately after the planting of rice seedlings until the time they break from the ground.

7 RITES OF PASSAGE

While the Moro are composed of various ethno-linguistic groups with distinct cultures, the Moro as a whole share some traditions of rites of passage, including the initiation of children into a community, circumcision, and marriage.

Among the Moro there is no particular ritual for naming newborn children, but local Moro have ceremonial acknowledgement of an infant as a member of the community. The Tausug of Sulu practice *paggunting*, or the ceremonial haircut, is conducted on male children around the age of two. The ceremony takes place in the father's home, and a pillar of woven leaves or a pot of rice is placed in the center of the room. Imams are invited, and passages from the Quran are chanted. At the end of the ceremony, perfume is poured on the child's head, and a lock of hair is cut. The child's head is kept shaven for several years following the ritual.

Circumcision is performed on pre-pubescent children around the age of 12. The male circumcision includes the cutting of the foreskin and religious ceremonies. Among the Tausug, quasi-circumcision is practiced on females, whereby a knife is rubbed on the girl's genitalia but no incision is made. Circumcisions may be performed by imams or laypeople, though the practice of circumcision was introduced along with Islam.

Moro youth are often married at a young age, in the mid to late teens. Negotiations are initiated by the groom's father and a go-between is frequently employed to negotiate the dowry. The value of the dowry is determined by the social class of the bride's family, with upper class brides receiving the most money. The dowry is considered compensation to the bride's family for the time and effort spent raising her.

8 INTERPERSONAL RELATIONS

In traditional Moro society, interpersonal relations are determined by a hierarchy of relationships. These relationships help establish alliances and regulate conflicts when communities resort to communal warfare, which still occurs between Moro groups. Among the Tausug of Sulu, relations can vary from *bagay magtaymanghud* (blood brother) and *babay* (good friend) to *tao ha'ut* (neutral) to *tao hansipak* (opponent) and *bantah* (personal enemy). *Bagay magtaymanghud* swear a personal allegiance on the Quran that, in theory, cannot be broken without risk of supernatural sanctions. A *bagay magtaymanghud* relationship can be established either by two friends who decide to cement their friendship to prevent betrayal and increase solidarity or on the order of a legal official who finalizes an amiable conclusion between enemies. Blood brothers have strong obligations to support each other in fighting, assisting with debts, and providing food and shelter. Conversely, *bantah* are sworn enemies that hold personal grudges and seek vengeance for a past wrongdoing. Often, a bantah is a person held responsible for the killing of a kinsmen or a friend. In battle a man should seek out and kill a bantah. Through mediation, bantah can become blood brothers. In a lifetime, relations between individuals experience numerous changes.

Among Moro youth, courtship between men and women is played out in part through music. Young men play narrower rimmed-gongs called *gandingan* to communicate their love to young women. Common love songs include the *baqat* of the Tausug, which incorporates archaic language, and the *kapranon* of the Maranao, a highly sentimental ballad. The Jew's harp, a bamboo wind instrument called *kubing* by the Maguindanao and Maranao and *kulaing* by the Yakan, is a favorite instrument of courtship and recreation. Nearly every young Yakan has a kulaing tucked in their headband.

9 LIVING CONDITIONS

Seventy-five percent of the Moro live in rural areas and are primarily employed in agriculture, while a quarter of Moro live in urban areas. Poverty is widespread among the Moro, and even those who find employment subsist off of meager wages. In many Moro communities, multiple families, as many as five, may live in a single household. The majority of Moro are subsistence farmers and fishermen and Moro families can afford few amenities.

10 FAMILY LIFE

The diversity of culture among the Moro precludes drawing a stereotypical image of Moro family life. The division of labor within the family runs along gender lines. The task of raising the children is primarily the responsibility of the females in the family, while the males in the household work in the fields or fish. One important aspect of many Moro communities is that women often have an equal role in decision making within the household. On the island of Sisangat, near the town of Siasi in Sulu, the Sama women are recognized as the heads of the households. Women on the island marry in their early teens and, in the first years of marriage, the wives play a more obedient role and follow the model of the elders in the home. But, as women mature, they take on more responsibilities, including handling money and making purchases; men on the island must ask their wives for permission before making purchases.

Childrearing is primarily the responsibility of women, though men do assist in caring for the children. Among the Tausag, lullabies are sung by both mothers and older men in the family. Among the Maguindanao, special lullabies (*sangel*) are sung for either male or female children. The Sama *aembo-aembo* lullaby is sung by the mother while rocking the baby between the mother's raised feet. At the end of the song, the mother's legs are straightened, and the baby slides into the mother's lap.

Divorce is sanctioned among the Moro, and both women and men can initiate divorce proceedings. Among the Sama of Sisangat, the community will attempt to reconcile the couple seeking a divorce, but if reconciliation is not possible a local agama court will judge and settle the divorce proceedings. The *panglima* (religious functionaries) will divide the communal property and decide who is at fault for the divorce. The guilty party pays the *panglima* a fee. Divorces can be initiated because of adultery, stealing from one's spouse or their relatives, quarreling, domestic violence, the husband's gambling, and when a man does not surrender his earnings to his wife. The community does not ostracize divorcees; however, adulterers and those who steal from spouses or relatives are frowned upon.

11 CLOTHING

Until recent decades, the Moro maintain traditional styles of clothing, including sarongs, scarves, sashes, and headdresses made of traditional fabrics, weaves, and designs. Materials used in clothing included cotton, silk, grasses, and bark. Designs were composed of plaid, stripes, and cloud-like backgrounds of various colors and images. Each community had their own distinct styles of clothing, and across the entire Moro homeland there was a wide diversity in clothing. The making of clothes was the responsibility of the women in the household and pieces of elaborate weaving could take months to complete. Today, mass-produced clothing has displaced traditional homemade Moro textiles.

12 FOOD

The diet of the Moro homeland consists of rice, fish, and sago, a powdery starch made from the pith of the Sago palm tree. Food is not eaten with utensils, but by hand. Common crops produced on Mindanao are banana, coconuts, mango, coffee, durian fruit, seaweed, and pineapple. In coastal areas fish provide the bulk of the daily diet, and fisherman may spend many days on fishing expeditions in search of reef fish and deepwater fish.

13 EDUCATION

Moro education generally lags behind non-Muslim Filipinos. Only 66% of Moro are literate, compared to more than 80% of non-Muslims. Less than 40% of Moro graduate from elementary school and only 18% have achieve a high school degree. The number of Moro university degree holders is very small.

Traditionally, the Moro educated their children in Islamic religious schools (*madrasahs*). The Spanish colonial government actively discouraged Moro from sending their children to madrasahs and went so far as to close Islamic religious schools and destroy their materials. Children were encouraged to attend Catholic missionary schools, which contributed to the social and economic inequalities between Muslims and non-Muslims.

In the early 20th century, the U.S. government introduced modern schools into Moro territory. These schools were for the children of the Moro elite who cooperated with the U.S. administration and only a small minority of Moro received an education. In 1900, about 25 such schools with 2,000 pupils operated in Moro areas. In 1903, that number had increased to 52 schools and by 1918 over 8,000 Moro children received a public school education. One factor limiting enrollment in public schools was that the administrators were often Christian missionaries and, thus, parents were reluctant to enroll their children in schools. Girls were encouraged to attend school and in 1916 a girl's dormitory was established in Jolo.

In the post-colonial era, new madrasahs and Muslim private schools opened to serve the Moro. The Muslim private schools, which are operated by religious organizations and private foundations, offer six years of elementary course work, four years of secondary schooling, and a two-year collegiate degree that includes courses in reading, writing, math, history, Arabic, and Islamic studies. The Egyptian government has supported these schools by sending Egyptian religious scholars to work in the madrasahs and private schools. In addition, Cairo has awarded hundreds of scholarships to Moro students.

One of the earliest Muslim private schools is Kamilol Islam Maahad Ulom in Murawi City, capital of Lanao del Sur province on Mindanao. The school was opened in 1938 by the Kamilol Islam Society and in 1952 it began to offer both Islamic and western style education. The institute's Arabic department was upgraded to an independent institution, the Jamiatul Philippine al Islamiya. Other notable schools in the Mindanao Arabic Institute, a madrasah in Marawi City run by the Agama Islam Society. Many of the teaching materials used in the schools have been donated by Arab countries in the Middle East and North Africa.

The first university on Mindanao, Mindanao State University, opened in Marawi City in 1961. The institute offers dozens of graduate and undergraduate degree programs.

14 CULTURAL HERITAGE

The Moro communities in the Philippines share rich musical traditions. The principle musical instrument of the Moro is the *kulintang*, a set of graduated gongs laid in a row in a wooden frame. The number of gongs in a set can vary according to culture, with the Tausug using 11 or 13 and the Yakan on Basilan island utilizing as few as 5. The musical tone of each kulintang set differs. The lowest (*pangandungan*) and the highest (*pamantikan*) gongs are cast first and the tones of the other gongs are then adjusted accordingly. Young boys and girls practice on a *sarunay*, a miniature copy of the kulintang made of metal plates with rounded protrusions. The kulintang is important social property owned by individual families and ownership indicates high social status and cultivated taste. The value of a kulitang set is high and can serve as marriage dowries.

Other gong instruments include the *agung*, a large, deep-rimmed gong; the *gandingan*, gongs with narrower rims that are played in pairs, and the *babandil*, a gong with a narrower, turned-in rim. In addition, a drum called the *dabakan* often accompanies gongs. In Lanao del Sur province on Mindanao the Maranao people play deep-rimmed gongs called *pumalsan* and the *penanggisa-an*, and the Tausug people on the island Jolo play a pair of hanging gongs called *duwahan*.

15 WORK

More than 80% of the Moro population is employed in the forestry, agriculture, and fishing sectors or as laborers. Only a quarter of Moro live in urban settings, where it is more common to open small shops or trade goods. Few Moro work in mining, manufacturing, construction and finance, forms of employment dominated by non-Muslims. Unemployment among Moro is just below 60%, which is slightly above the national average. Non-employed Moro are mostly subsistence farmers who work a small plot of land and have a higher standard of living than their urban, unemployed counterparts. In coastal areas, especially in the Sulu archipelago, many residents are subsistence fisherman.

Unemployment on Mindanao has been exacerbated by an electricity crisis that struck the island in the early 1990s. The hydroelectric plants that supplied 90 % of the regions electricity had their production cut in half when water levels in a lake that fed one of the main plants reached dangerously low levels, which was caused by abnormally hot weather and deforestation in the watersheds that fed the lake. The result was that the region suffered frequent brownouts, causing factories in the region to run at lower capacity. The ongoing conflict between the local Moro and government forces on Mindanao and the Sulu archipelago has further hindered economic development and frightened off outside investment.

16 SPORTS

Basketball, a legacy of the U.S. occupation of the Philippines, has a strong following in the Philippines and several teams from the Mindanao Visayas Basketball Association are situated on Mindanao. The Filipino marital art *Eskrima*, also known as *Kali*, putatively has its origins in Moro culture and history. The sport has its origins in the tribal warfare that was widespread across the Philippines in the pre-modern period. The term *Eskrima* is derived from the Spanish word for fencing. *Eskrima* practitioners strike with their hands, feet, swords, and sticks and grapple or throw opponents.

17 ENTERTAINMENT AND RECREATION

The Moro have a mix of traditional and modern forms of entertainment and recreation. In larger cities, particularly on Mindanao, all forms of modern entertainment are available, including theaters, bars and professional sports. In rural areas and remote islands, traditional music remains a popular form of entertainment. Music is often performed at weddings and other social gatherings.

Music frequently accompanies agricultural work and it is believed that songs not only pass time but also encourages plant growth. Farmers often employ music to pass the time, including drums and wind instruments. The Yakan utilize a log drum (*tuntungan*), while the *oniya-niya* wind instrument of the Maranao is made of a coconut leaf and a stalk of rice,

which when blown on produces a sound thought to frighten away wild animals. Sama children sing the *puk lara* while sitting in a circle and playing a game of catch.

18 FOLK ART, CRAFTS, AND HOBBIES

Until the mid 20th century, Moro artistic creativity was expressed through in traditional weaponry, namely swords and daggers. Moro edged-weapons often were ornate, carved from fine woods, and included silver and gold overlay and inlay. Weapons made for wealthy elite had handles made of ivory, inlayed jewel, and were formed in the shape of birds or spirits.

The *kris* is a double-edged dagger that is more than a foot in length and has a blade with multiple curves that form a pattern of waves, which enhances the blade's ability to cut flesh. The *kris* was a common weapon among Moro warriors, who used the daggers to slash their enemy. *Kris* blades contain nickels, which form grainy patterns, and the finest blades are reportedly made from iron extracted from meteoroids. *Kris* swords were commonly thought to hold spiritual powers that could be good or evil in nature. Other common Moro weapons include the *kalis*, a sword similar in style to the *kris*, and the *kampilan*, a single edged sword several feet in length.

19 SOCIAL PROBLEMS

The primary social problems amongst the Moro remain lack of economic opportunities and violence tied to the Christian-Muslim conflict and anti-government insurgency. Since the traditional Sultanate system of government in Moro territories was abolished in the 1930s, the Filipino government has favored the consolidation of arable land into the hands of non-Muslims with close ties to the government. Wealth derived from large plantation style agricultural projects on Mindanao often is not reinvested in the local community and is funneled into the hands of non-Moro elite. The local Moro population remains impoverished and has little access to higher education.

20 GENDER ISSUES

In Moro society there is a clear division of gender roles. While 75% of all employed men work in agriculture, only 40% of employed women are engaged in agriculture; 45% of employed women are employed in retail business or social services, mostly in urban areas. Women are more likely than men to have no educational degree and are much less likely to have a higher educational degree.

The division between genders carries over into musical traditions. Among the Sama of Sulu, women play the *kulintangan* gongs, while men play the hanging gongs. Wooden castanets are used exclusively by female dancers. The *tariray* dance is performed by young women with subtle erotic movements of the hands and body, the *titik tabawan* is usually performed by older women. The Maranao *kulintangan* is composed of two principle instruments: the *kulintang*, played by a young woman, and the *dubakan*, reserved for men. The musical performance is likened to a dialogue or courtship between the performers.

21 BIBLIOGRAPHY

George, T. J. S. *Revolt in Mindanao: The Rise of Islam in Philippine Politics*. Kuala Lumpur: Oxford University Press, 1980.

Gowing, Peter G. and Robert D. McAmis eds. *The Muslim Filipinos*. Manila: Solidaridad Publishing House, 1974.

Rodil, B.R. *The Minoritization of the Indigenous Communities of Mindanao and the Sulu Archipelago*. Davao City, Philippines: Alternate Forum for Research in Mindanao, Inc., 1994.

Santos, Ramón P. "Islamic Communities of the Southern Philippines." in Terry E. Miller Sean Williams *The Garland Encyclopedia of World Music*. Vol. 4. New York: Routledge, 1998: 889-912.

Stark, Jan. "Muslims in the Philippines." *Journal of Muslim Minority Affairs*, vol. 23, no. 1, (April 2003): 195-209.

—-by David Straub

MOTU

PRONUNCIATION: MOH-too
LOCATION: Papua New Guinea
LANGUAGE: Motu (Hiri Motu); Tok Pisin; English
RELIGION: Christianity

¹INTRODUCTION

The Motu are an Austronesian-speaking group who live on the southern coast of the independent nation of Papua New Guinea. They occupy a stretch of coastline that was the first area of permanent European settlement on the island of New Guinea. The Motu are well represented in literature because of their elaborate annual trading expeditions in distant parts of the Gulf of Papua. The Motu men constructed large sailing craft called *lagatoi*. The lagatoi were multihulled rafts built out of large logs and lashed together. These rafts were propelled by crab claw-shaped sails made of coconut fiber. The crew needed to sail one of these vessels was around 30 men. Although the annual *hiri* expeditions are no longer undertaken by the Motu, there are annual ceremonies and events that commemorate the tradition.

²LOCATION AND HOMELAND

The Motu homeland is in the Central Province of Papua New Guinea. Papua New Guinea has been an independent nation since 1975 and occupies the eastern half of the island of New Guinea, the third largest island in the world. The capital of Papua New Guinea is Port Moresby, a city that divides the traditional Motu territory in half. Port Moresby is built on the land traditionally belonging to two peoples, the Motu and the Koitabu. The Motu were the subject of one of the earliest ethnologies of the region that was published in the latter half of the 19th century. The first European accounts of the Motu record the same 14 villages that are still occupied by the Motu today. The Motu coastline has two distinct seasons: a hot, dry period from April to November, and a wet, humid period from November to March. Some Motu have left their villages and moved to small settlements on the outskirts of Port Moresby, while others live in the city itself in modern homes with running water and electricity.

³LANGUAGE

The language of the Motu is related to the other Austronesian languages of New Guinea and the South Pacific region. Austronesian languages are in the minority in Papua New Guinea, and speakers of these languages are usually only found in coastal regions. The Papuan languages are the majority languages of this island nation and found mostly in non-coastal areas. The distribution of these two language families reflects the prehistoric migration of these two populations to the island. The ancestors of the present-day Austronesian speaking populations, such as the Motu, were later migrants to the island.

During their annual trading expeditions, the Motu used a special form of their language referred to now as "Hiri Motu." Recognizing the importance of this language in the south coastal region of the country, the government made Hiri Motu one of the three official languages of Papua New Guinea. Hiri

Motu is losing ground to Tok Pisin, another one of the official languages of the country.

⁴FOLKLORE

The existing body of folklore and mythology of the Motu is dwindling at a rapid rate due to urbanization and, in some cases, education. In many cases, children no longer have the opportunity to learn the traditional stories of the past. Many Motu stories recount conflict between the Motu and their neighbors. Stories of the successes of ancestors in raiding neighboring villages are still remembered by some older Motu. Traditional myths concerning the origins of the Motu, the development of fire, the history of the hiri trading expeditions, and others have been written down and published as small booklets. Many other groups in Papua New Guinea have done the same thing in an effort to preserve the traditions, although in an altered form.

⁵RELIGION

The vast majority of Motu are regular church-going Christians. Missionaries have been active in the area since the earliest history of Motu-European contact and the London Missionary Society dominated this activity. While some of the traditional beliefs and ceremonies are maintained in Motu society, the United Church—the descendant of the London Missionary Society—has transformed much of traditional Motu practice. For instance, the Motu once believed in witchcraft and sorcery, but they did not practice it; instead, they believed that neighboring groups had this power and the Motu would have to enlist the services of outsiders if they wanted to inflict illness or death on one of their own.

⁶MAJOR HOLIDAYS

The Motu celebrate Christian holidays. Most Motu also recognize and, in some cases, celebrate the secular national holidays since they participate in the nation's wage-earning work force. The Hiri Festival is also an important holiday. It gives the Motu a chance to celebrate their traditional heritage and enjoy the dress and entertainment of traditional Motu society.

⁷RITES OF PASSAGE

The Motu have experienced the effects of modernization more than many other groups in Papua New Guinea. As a result, many of the traditional aspects of their culture have been lost. The traditional stages of life that were part and parcel of Motu traditional society no longer exist. Only the payment of "bride price" still exists as part of a traditional rite of passage. The transitions from infant to adolescent, adult, and then onwards to death, are marked more in the European manner. Birthdays are celebrated in Motu homes in Port Moresby. Traditional mortuary practices are no longer observed, although a traditional mourning period of about four weeks is observed in regards to non-essential activities.

⁸INTERPERSONAL RELATIONS

Since many Motus live and work in the capital city, greetings and leave-takings are based on urban patterns of social interaction. The choice of language for the greetings is the most important aspect of the interaction. Motus will usually greet each other in Hiri Motu. They can choose other languages as well,

usually choosing either English or Tok Pisin. In each case, the choice of language directly reflects the nature of the social relationship between the parties involved.

The kinship terminology of the Motu is the "Hawaiian" type. A kinship terminology is the set of terms that a person uses to refer to or address a relative. In American English, one distinguishes between one's mother and one's aunts, but typically does not distinguish between maternal aunts and paternal aunts. In the Motu system, there is no distinctive word for "mother" and another for "aunt." Instead, both are referred to by the same term. The Motus do distinguish between relatives on the father's side from relatives on the mother's side.

⁹LIVING CONDITIONS

Traditionally, the Motu built their houses in lines connected to each other by walkways over the tidal shallows. The line of houses corresponded to a descent group—that is, a group of people related to each other by shared descent from a common ancestor. Some Motus have chosen to remain in the village area but have built houses on land. Motu village houses often have corrugated sheet metal walls and thatched roofs with plank floors. Some of the Motu who live in traditional villages do not have electricity and rely on kerosene lanterns for lighting and battery-operated radios to keep in touch with the larger society and the outside world. The urban Motus live in a range of styles of house. Wealthy, professional Motus have large houses with all of the amenities that most Americans are accustomed to having in their homes.

Before Europeans colonized the Motu region, transportation between Motu villages was by canoe and sometimes by foot. Now, all Motu villages are connected by road to Port Moresby. Many Motus still use canoes to visit other villages. The Motus are well known to anthropologists for their large ceremonial canoes used in the hiri trading expeditions.

¹⁰FAMILY LIFE

The nuclear family is the basic unit of social organization among the Motu. Households were linked together by a shared walkway and a shared cooking area.

Marriage among the Motu today has changed from when Europeans first encountered them. Today, the Motus are monogamous. In pre-colonial times, men of status and wealth often had several wives. Motu marriages were arranged in traditional times, and there were many restrictions on potential spouses. Child betrothal was quite common, and gift exchange occurred often until the final bride price was paid and the marriage was finalized. The modern Motus are free to choose their marriage partners; however, wealthy Motu families have inflated bride prices and it now often takes quite some time for a marriage transaction to become finalized. The Motu have garnered a reputation in Papua New Guinea for demanding the highest cash bride prices in the country, topping 60,000 kina.

¹¹CLOTHING

Traditional clothing for Motu women consists of a grass fiber skirt. They did not wear any footwear or any covering on their upper bodies, which were frequently tattooed. For ceremonies and other important occasions, both men and women would oil their skin. Feathers, flowers, and the leaves of croton plants were used to decorate women's hair and were also placed in armbands that they wore on their upper arms. Traditional dress is still used by the Motu for ceremonial events such as bride price payments, weddings, and canoe races. Urban Motus wear Western-style clothing all the time.

12 FOOD

The traditional foods of the Motu were fish, yams, and bananas. They also collected shellfish and crabs. The Motu traded with their neighbors and also on trading expeditions to farther villages for food. A vibrant tuna fishing industry exists in some Western Motu villages, based on an important myth regarding its origins. Nowadays, Western foodstuffs have become staples. Tinned fish and canned Indonesian curry dishes are popular foods. Rice and tea are also important foods that are purchased in local shops and grocery stores in Port Moresby. American food products such as boxed cereals, soft drinks, and hot dogs can be purchased in the Port Moresby stores. Although families often pool their foodstuffs and cook communally, the Motu nuclear families eat separately.

13 EDUCATION

Traditional education was structured along sex lines. Boys learned adult male activities from their male relatives and females learned adult female activities from their female relatives. Nowadays, public education is available to the Motu and almost all families take advantage of it. Some Motus go on to college at one of the national colleges or universities, such as the University of Papua New Guinea in Port Moresby.

14 CULTURAL HERITAGE

Traditional Motu dances were very impressive. Men and women wore elaborate face paint and feather headdresses. The dancers performed intricate group dances. Dancing was accompanied by drumming and sometimes singing. The Motu use hand-held, hourglass-shaped drums called *kundu* throughout Papua New Guinea. Dancing was discouraged by Christian missionaries, and, as a result, many of the traditional ceremonial dances are no longer performed and are lost to memory. Some dances are still performed on important occasions and for the tourists that regularly visit Motu villages.

15 WORK

The traditional division of labor in Motu society was along sex lines. Men built houses and canoes, constructed fishing nets, and did the fishing and participated in the trading expeditions. Women made the pottery that the men took to trade on the hiri voyages. Women also cooked, fetched water, and gathered terrestrial foodstuffs and marine resources. Both men and women tended the garden where the Motu grew limited crops. Today, both men and women seek wage labor outside the village, usually in nearby Port Moresby. Many of the Motus hold white-collar professional jobs. Traditional industries are all but lost and only few still remain for resuscitation at festivals and ceremonies.

16 SPORTS

Rugby is both a spectator and participant sport all over Papua New Guinea. The Motus are able to watch league (semi-professional) rugby since many of them either live or work in Port Moresby.

17 ENTERTAINMENT AND RECREATION

Canoe races are an important form of recreation for the Motu. The canoes are modeled on the traditional styles, but are constructed out of modern materials. For the Motu who live in the surrounding areas of Port Moresby, movie houses, clubs, and pubs are places for entertainment of various sorts. The national beauty pageant that crowns "Miss Papua New Guinea" for her competition in larger, regional pageants is an important event for all of those living in Port Moresby. The Motus are always well represented in this event.

18 FOLK ART, CRAFTS, AND HOBBIES

Art among the Motu was limited to the styles of pottery that were manufactured by women and the elaborate body tattoos of women. Although many Pacific societies have given up the practice of tattooing, some Motu girls and young women are still being tattooed. Patterns are geometric in nature with some Christian motifs having become part of the imagery.

19 SOCIAL PROBLEMS

Maintaining the distinctiveness of their culture in the shadow of urbanization and modernization represented by the capital city of Port Moresby is a challenge for the present-day Motu. Their language has lost some ground to the popularity of Tok Pisin among young people, especially those that migrate to the city and its suburbs. Larger problems that face the entire nation are alcohol and drug abuse, the spread of HIV, and enforcement of laws which forbid the importation, sale, or possession of ammunition and pornography of any kind. The law against pornography exists in an effort to maintain respect for the traditional dress of women. In fact, every participant in the Miss Papua New Guinea must dress in traditional attire as part of the competition. For most, this will mean that they will have to appear topless. The government and society are striving to maintain the appreciation of this form of dress for its cultural value, and to not allow for its objectification.

The Motu Koitabu are the group of people indigenous to areas in and around the coastal city of Port Moresby and the National Capital District. They are the traditional owners of the land upon which the city of Port Moresby is located, and number about 30,000. After Papua New Guinea (PNG) obtained its independence from Australia, on 16 September 1975, Port Moresby became the nation's capital. Large numbers of people from other provinces moved into the city, making it the business, commercial and administrative center of the nation. Increasingly all aspects of the lives of the Motu Koitabu—political, economic, social and cultural—have become marginalized. In 1999 the Inaugural Summit on Motu Koitabu was held in Baruni village. Recommendations for social, economic, and ecological change were unanimously agreed upon and adopted by the members of the summit, and those are now referred to as "The Baruni Declaration."

Garbage build-up and pollution are increasingly serious problems in Port Moresby and in the surrounding villages. These problems directly impact the Motu Koitabu.

20 GENDER ISSUES

As a coastal culture of Papua New Guinea, the Motu do not evidence the types of sexual antagonism and segregation that are common in the Highlands cultures of the nation (see the *Dani* and *Melpa*). The extensive tattooing of Motu women is particularly noteworthy. While men were only tattooed across their chests in recognition of exploits in headhunting raids, Motu women were tattooed from head to toe. The elaborate patterns of the tattoos are handed down from mothers to daughters. As early as the age of five, Motu girls would receive the first tattoos on the backs of their hands. From then on, and following a strict age pattern, further tattoos were added to a girl's body until she would be completely tattooed by the time the girl married after puberty. Nowadays, many Motu girls use felt markers to draw the elaborate designs on their bodies instead of undergoing the painful and permanent traditional inking.

Men and women had distinct roles in the important hiri trading expeditions. Women would make the pots that were in turn traded for sago as part of the trade. While the men were away on a hiri trading expedition, the unmarried females would remain secluded in their homes until the men returned. During that time, these girls would continue receiving elaborate tattoos and they would be instructed in the ways of being a proper Motu woman by their elderly female relatives. During their seclusion, the young women were not allowed to bathe, comb their hair, and were required to eat only vegetables using special chopstick-like utensils called *diniga* in Motu.

[21] BIBLIOGRAPHY

Dutton, Tom. *Police Motu: Iena Sivari*. Port Moresby: University of Papua New Guinea Press, 1985.

Groves, M. "Hiri." In *The Encyclopedia of Papua New Guinea*, ed. P. Ryan. Melbourne: Melbourne University Press, 1972.

Holdsworth, David. *Festivals and Celebrations in Papua New Guinea*. Bathurst: Robert Brown & Associates, 1982.

Lister-Turner, R. *A Dictionary of the Motu Language of Papua*. 2d ed. Sydney, A. H. Pettifer, 1941?

—by J. Williams

MOUNTAIN MON-KHMER GROUPS

PRONUNCIATION: mountain MOHN kuh-MER groups
ALTERNATE NAMES: Hill tribespeople
LOCATION: Cambodia; Laos; Thailand; Vietnam
POPULATION: 210,000 (estimate)
LANGUAGE: Mon-Khmer; Austronesian
RELIGION: Traditional spirit-based beliefs

[1] INTRODUCTION

As well as the ethnic Khmer, Chinese, Vietnamese, and other groups who live in Cambodia, there are the hill tribespeople who are not ethnic Khmer, as are the vast majority of Cambodians. Numbering less than 2% of the Cambodian population, they add a colorful and fascinating chapter to Cambodian life.

The tribespeople of Cambodia were originally called, by the Khmers, *phnong* or *samre*, meaning "savage." The Cambodian government began calling them Khmer Loeu ("Upper Khmer," or "Highland Khmer") in the 1960s, ostensibly to create unity among the highland tribal groups and the lowland Khmer. The French often referred to all the mountain people in Cambodia and Vietnam as *montagnards* ("men of the mountains"), and some Communist Cambodians called them the *Khmers Daeum* ("original Khmers") highlighting that they had been "untainted" by western civilization. While some hill groups speak languages related to Khmer, most come from a very different language and cultural background. Most have very different appearance, customs, survival strategies, and religion from lowland Cambodians.

Among the hill tribes of Cambodia are the Brao (or Lave, Love), who numbered about 18,000 in 1984. The Kui (Kuoy, Soai) number more than 100,000 in east-central Thailand, northeast Cambodia, and Laos. The Saoch numbered about 500 in 1981. These are located in southwest Cambodia and are closely related to the Pear and the Chong. The Pear numbered about 1,000 in 1981. Also known as the "Bahr" or "Pohr," they live in southwest Cambodia. The Krung and Kravet totaled about 12,000 in 1984. The Stieng of Cambodia number approximately 25,000, with about double that number in Vietnam. According to official Cambodian government figures for 2002, there were 211,851 hill tribespeople in the country.

The origins of the hill tribes are not clear. Some scholars think that the tribes who speak Mon-Khmer languages, such as the Kuy, Mnong, Stieng, Brao, and Pear, were originally part of the long-term migration of peoples from the northwest. The Austronesian-speaking groups of Rade and Jarai may have migrated first to coastal Vietnam and then west into the highlands of Cambodia. The Suoi may be the remnant of the population who lived in Cambodia before the Khmer. Some scholars think they could be the original Cambodians.

During the French Protectorate which started in 1863, the colonizing French recruited some tribesmen to serve as soldiers with the French army, mainly as trackers and to help locate Communist jungle hideouts. Some young men continued this tradition after independence in 1953 by joining the Royal Cambodian Army.

During the 1960s, the Cambodian government had the army take part in a broad-based civic action program among the hill tribes, which included teaching them the Khmer language and culture in an effort to eventually assimilate them into Cambodian society. Most of this involved making schooling compulsory for all children including those of the Khmer Loeu.

Many tribespeople resented these efforts, as they had resented lowland Khmer for many decades. In 1963 when he fled the Cambodian capital, Phnom Penh, to go into the jungles and organize a Communist resistance group, Saloth Sar, later better known as Pol Pot or "Brother Number One," found refuge in the tribal areas of the province of Ratanakiri. Three years later he had gained the trust and confidence of some of the hill tribespeople and established his office for the Central Committee of the Communist Party of Kampuchea in Ratanakiri. In the late 1960s and early 1970s, the Khmer Communists, or Khmer Rouge, were able to recruit a number of young tribesmen to their cause. The illiterate tribal youth, unfamiliar with any element of civilization, became the prototype of the Khmer Rouge army, first a target of ridicule and then an object of fear after the Khmer Rouge takeover of Cambodia in April 1975.

Although they had supported the Khmer Rouge, largely because of their marginalization during the Khmer Republic (1970–1975), many tribal groups suffered at the hands of Democratic Kampuchea, the government established by the Khmer Rouge. Like other Cambodians, tribespeople were forced to abandon their traditional religious rituals, customs, and activities which Communist rulers thought took tribal attention away from the revolution being conducted by Democratic Kampuchea.

In December 1978, the Vietnamese invaded Cambodia and by mid-January they controlled most of the country. The new Vietnamese-backed government of Cambodia then struggled through the 1980s to reestablish institutions and a society destroyed by the Khmer Rouge who mounted attacks at them from jungle strongholds.

The Khmer Rouge gradually regained control of much of northeastern Cambodia in the 1980s, and the Kuy in particular, helped protect Pol Pot's jungle base at Anlong Veng. In most areas, however, the tribespeople were allowed to live in their village societies, with the new pro-Vietnamese Communist government of Cambodia also eager to incorporate tribes into mainstream Cambodian life. An attempt is now being made to teach the Cambodian language and culture to the various tribespeople, although the government claims that tribal languages and customs will continue to be respected.

At the same time, both legal and illegal harvesting of timber in the forests of northeastern Cambodia have brought many tribespeople into Cambodian culture as they are deprived of the forest areas needed for agriculture. As their homeland rapidly shrinks, their way of life is changing also.

For centuries, tribal peoples have recognized the political superiority of the lowlanders surrounding them. Highlanders acknowledged the domination of the lowland people by rendering obeisance to the lowland political leaders in exchange for lowlanders' recognition of them being the descendants of the region's first residents. Between 1600 and 1860, this relationship was symbolized in a triennial exchange of gifts between lowlanders and highlanders, specifically the Cambodian king and Jarai sorcerers, called "Lords of Fire and Water."

More tangible relationships also existed between many highland tribes and lowland Cambodians. Highlanders traded products which they gathered from the forest to the lowlanders, such as wild animal skins, herbs, exotic flowers and feathers, beeswax, lac resin used for shellac, and tusks and horns used as medicine. In exchange, the hill groups received metal, pottery, salt, and bronze drums. Tribal peoples were also frequently used by the lowlanders as voluntary or involuntary laborers. Lowlanders raided the tribes themselves or pitted tribes against one another in a search for slaves.

In some areas and for much of the past, however, tribal peoples were able to live in isolation from lowlanders.

²LOCATION AND HOMELAND

In the late 1960s, the hill people were estimated to number between 70,000 and 100,000. Present-day estimates of their number are much higher, around 210,000. Population figures are difficult to determine because of the geographical roughness of the terrain and its isolation from lowland Cambodians.

The hill tribes live in remote highland areas in the plateaus and mountainous areas on the western, northern, and eastern periphery of Cambodia. Most highland people are located in the northeast provinces of Ratanakiri, Mondulkuri, Kratie, and Stung Trung. Indeed, most of the population of Ratankiri and Mondulkuri are still highland peoples.

The Khmer Loeu of Cambodia include 13 distinct minority groups. The major tribal groups are the Kuy, Mnong, Stieng, Brao, Pear, Jarai, and Rade. Each group resides not only in Cambodia but in a neighboring country, Laos, Vietnam, or Thailand. This is possible because of the isolation and ruggedness of the terrain, making political control of the plateaus and mountains difficult. Hill people down through the centuries have been able to avoid contact with lowlanders and to travel fairly freely across political boundaries.

Some 14,186 Kuy, according to the 1995 Census, live in north central Cambodia in the provinces of Kampong Thom, Preah Vihear, and Stung Trung and in neighboring Thailand. Maybe half that number live in Cambodia-proper.

The Brao tribes live in northeastern Cambodia and just across the border in Laos. The total Brao population is between 10,000 and 20,000, about evenly divided between Cambodia and Laos.

The Mnong live in eastern Cambodia along the border with Vietnam. They number between 20,000 and 25,000. The Stieng also number between 20,000 and 25,000 and live along the Cambodian-Vietnamese border.

The Pearic group is made of numerous smaller tribes totaling about 10,000 people. The Pear live in north central and Western Cambodia. The Chong live in the Cardamom Mountains in Battambang Province in northwest Cambodia and in neighboring Thailand. The Saoch live in southern Cambodia. The Samre live in northwestern Cambodia and the Suoi live in central Cambodia.

The Jarai people live in northeastern Cambodia and are related to even larger numbers of Jarai in central Vietnam. The 1995 Census identified 11,549 Jarai in Cambodia, while over 200,00 Jarai live in Vietnam. The Rade are closely related to the Jarai. Approximately 20,000 Rade live in Cambodia with more than 100,000 Rade living across the border in Vietnam.

The turmoil of the Vietnam War and rule by Democratic Kampuchean that followed has deeply affected the hill tribes of Cambodia. While some groups were recruited by the Khmer Rouge as soldiers, others fought to escape conscription and control by the Communists. Many tribal people escaped the war and horrors of Cambodia by slipping over the border into neighboring countries where they lived with fellow tribespeople with whom they shared culture, language, and often family ties. When conditions improved in Cambodia, they moved back across the border.

Some tribal people escaped to Thailand to live with fellow tribespeople or were placed in refugee camps and were then eventually resettled in the United States or other Western countries.

³LANGUAGE

The hill tribes of Cambodia belong to two very different language groups. The Mon-Khmer speakers include the Mnong and Stieng. The Brao language is also a Mon-Khmer, Austroasiatic language, and is closely related to Krung and Kravet languages also spoken in Cambodia. The Chong, who numbered approximately 5,500 in 1984, are related to the Pear and Saoch, all three of whom speak Mon-Khmer languages.

Austronesian language speakers include the Rade, Jarai, both closely related to Cham. Each is spoken by the several thousand members of both tribes in northeastern Cambodia.

Names vary greatly from group to group. A person may carry an individual name, a nickname, and may change names frequently according to life situations and events. In some groups, people are called by the name of their father, mother, child, or spouse. Sometimes the name of a relative is added to the individual's name.

⁴FOLKLORE

The heroes and myths of the hill tribes of Cambodia are religious and familial in nature. Heroes are actual or fictional ancestors whose deeds and characteristics are passed down from generation to generation. Many of these heroes are considered to have originated particular clans and are respected, even worshipped, by their descendants not only as great people but as the founders of their tribal or descent group.

The myths of particular groups relate largely to these founding ancestors. Other myths relate stories of the spirits, landscape, animals, and flora of a group's environment and explain their surroundings. The myths of the highland groups thus form part of their traditional religious beliefs.

⁵RELIGION

The Mountain Mon-Khmers continue the traditional beliefs and practices of their ancestors. They believe that magical spirits live in the natural world, thus inhabiting rocks, mountains, rivers, and trees.

Most religious leaders are also spirit healers who lead ceremonies to cure illness and other physical and mental misfortunes. They do so by communicating with the spirits who have caused the difficulty or have allowed it to happen.

Among Pearic tribal groups, each village has two important sorcerers whose main duty is to control the weather. By so doing, they protect the community from natural calamities and aid in the timely development of the crops.

Sorcerers among the Jarai and Rade of northeast Cambodia in the past held extensive religious and political power. These became known as "kings of fire and water," and their power

extended beyond an individual village and over numerous villagers. Stieng religious beliefs focus on spirits and are conducted at the family level.

⁶MAJOR HOLIDAYS

The holidays of the tribal groups of Cambodia are primarily religious celebrations. Festivals are held to propitiate the spirits and exorcise evil spirits. The beginning of the lunar New Year is always an important festival. Life-cycle events such as birth, puberty, marriage, and death are celebrated by families and villages. These are often major festivals involving multiple families and villages and considerable money and preparation.

⁷RITES OF PASSAGE

Among most hill groups, infants and small children are greatly desired and are treated with great indulgence. Seldom reprimanded or hit, they are carried constantly by parents, siblings, or extended family members.

The children of most hill groups are socialized primarily by the immediate family, with assistance from extended family members and fellow villagers. By the time girls are five or six years of age, they are assisting their mother in the home and with younger siblings, and boys are assisting with garden duties and caring for the family's livestock. By the age of eight or nine, both boys and girls are helping in the fields.

Many youth marry while they are still teenagers. Among most groups, girls generally marry after puberty, when they reach 13 or 14. Boys marry a little later, at 16 or 17. This is the case because by the time most hill tribespeople have reached their early teens, they are fully socialized into adult life. By 13 and 14 years of age, boys and girls are acting as adults. After marriage, then, they have the skills to support their new family.

The lives of adult hill people center on family, making a living, and dealing with the spirits or gods who rule the earth.

At death, ceremonies are held to help the soul of the deceased as it makes its move to the afterlife. These consist, for most people, of prayers and ritual offerings made at regular intervals. For people who die unnatural deaths, special ceremonies must be conducted to exorcise their spirit and prevent it from doing similar harm to living relatives. Some tribal groups bury their dead, others cremate them. Among the Saoch of the Pearic group, the corpse of a dead person is buried and not cremated like among the neighboring majority Khmers who are Buddhist.

⁸INTERPERSONAL RELATIONS

For tribal people, like most traditional people living in small villages, interpersonal relations are based on fairly strict rules of etiquette. Since most villagers have known one another since birth and will continue living with one another for years to come, people treat one another as extended family and try to avoid conflict in their everyday relations.

Greetings are important, for they assist villagers in acknowledging one another, keeping harmony, and preventing conflict. With strangers, most tribespeople are usually modest and reserved. With family and fellow villagers, they are more demonstrative. Always, however, there is an emphasis on getting along with one another. Men and women, even closely related, seldom display affection openly. Women must be respectful and cautious, especially with strangers.

Visiting among hill peoples is a major activity and predominant form of entertainment. Visiting between families within a village appears casual, but is less so than it appears. While neighbors go to one another's homes often and apparently without announcement, they are careful to go only at acceptable times. Visiting between villages is even more formal. While relatives may visit from one village to another fairly casually, visits by larger groups of people for ceremonies or festivals are arranged ahead of time as to place, time, and the obligations of both hosts and guests.

Young people do not date as do youth in the West, or indeed in Phnom Penh. Courtship may be brief and involve little contact between the future bride and groom in some groups, with parents or matchmakers doing most of the visiting and arranging. In other tribes, courtship may occur over years and involve relatively frequent contact between the couple. Usually, contact between young men and women is careful, supervised, and understood to be leading to marriage.

⁹LIVING CONDITIONS

Most hill groups live in regions remote from the lowland cities and towns and denser population areas of Cambodia. In Ratanakiri Province, for example, the only way into much of the province during the rainy season is by airplane and elephant: the airport transports travelers to a town, where travel is halted unless one can find elephants. In the elections from 1958 when Long Boret, then a novelist (and later prime minister), was campaigning for his seat in Sung Treng (the province which at that stage included Ratanakiri), he conducted much of his electioneering from an elephant. Motor vehicles are still virtually unusable for much of the year because the roads are too muddy or flooded. Even foot traffic is difficult.

The distance from the centers of Cambodian life and the difficulty in travel, especially at certain times of the year, have isolated many tribal groups also from governmental services, including health and education.

Health facilities remain much less available to hill tribes than to Cambodians of the central plains, and life expectancy is lower than among fellow countrymen. Most hill groups attribute illness and physical and mental misfortune to supernatural causes, especially spirits, and much health care is directed at preventing and curing spirit action. Most illness and accidents thus continue to be dealt with through local healers rather than medical clinics which operated well in towns in the 1960s, but were destroyed in the war and not rebuilt until the early 1990s.

In all tribes, most people have extensive knowledge of traditional medicinal plants and herbs which are grown in backyard gardens or gathered in the nearby forest. Among some groups, in addition, community specialists are available to treat serious illness.

The Khmer Loeu live in widely scattered villages near their fields. When they abandon their fields to seek new ones, they also abandon their village sites, sometimes returning a generation or two later when the nearby fields have regained their productivity.

Houses vary in size from huge dwellings in which many families live to small single-family structures. The multi-family longhouses generally are divided into sections, one per family, with each family also keeping its own hearth for cooking

its own food. Houses may be built close to the ground or high on stilts.

The Brao, for example, live in a communal house in large villages. The Mnong live in villages, each of which contains several longhouses. Each longhouse is divided into compartments and each compartment is occupied by a nuclear family consisting of father, mother, and their children.

The Jarai and Rade in northeast Cambodia on the Cambodian-Vietnamese border live in longhouses, between 20 and 60 to a village. Each longhouse is divided into family compartments.

Most hill people have few consumer items and live much as their ancestors did without the electricity, running water, and appliances available to many Cambodians who live in the central plains, especially those in urban areas and people who live in industrialized countries.

The degree of contact with the ethnic Khmer of the plains determines the kind of transportation: the more contact, the greater the reliance of hill people on motor vehicles, motor scooters, and bicycles. For many groups still living in isolated villages, transportation is primarily by foot.

¹⁰FAMILY LIFE

Hill tribespeople observe a strict division of labor. Women have the primary responsibility for domestic chores, child care, carrying water, and looking after the domestic animals. They also gather food and weave. In agricultural villages, they are also involved in some rice cultivation chores, such as transplantation, irrigating, weeding, harvesting, and husking. Men, on the other hand, do the hunting and the heavy agricultural tasks. They clear the ground, plow, and thresh. They also make and repair tools and build and repair houses.

Families tend to be large, for most hill people continue to rely on their children to assist with household and subsistence activities. As their contact with ethnic Khmer increases, along with the expense of educating their children and the availability of family planning and contraceptives, more tribal people are choosing to have smaller families.

Marriages tend to remain traditional. In many groups, for instance, the choice of a partner and wedding arrangements are made by parents, often before the youth reach puberty. The family of the groom gives large quantities of pork and alcohol and a few silver coins to the bride's family. Among the Mnong in eastern Cambodia, most marriages are monogamous.

Among the Jarai and Rade of northeast Cambodia, marriage is initiated by women, who also do the marriage negotiations. Residence is matrilocal, so the new couple goes to live with the parents of the wife.

Two of the Mnong subgroups also recognize matrilineal descent, with family recognition and property inheritance descending through females rather than males. Residence among the Mnong is predominantly matrilocal, with the young couple going to live with the wife's parents after marriage. The Jarai and Rade of northeast Cambodia also have matrilineal descent groups. These groups are exogamous, so they do not marry within the matrilineal group.

The Stieng, also straddling the Cambodian-Vietnamese border, differ from the Mnong in being patrilineal and patriarchal. Descent is recognized through males and property is inherited through the male line. After the bride-price has been paid to the family of the bride, the young couple then moves in with the husband's family. In contrast to both the groups above, the Brao have a bilateral kinship system.

The Pearic groups have totemic clans, which are kin groupings that trace their descent to a common ancestor generally believed to be a legendary figure with supernatural powers. Each clan is headed by a chief who receives his office through inheritance from his father. The Pearic tribes recognize patrilineal descent, so children belong to their father's clan and inherit through their father. Young married couples observe either matrilocal residence until the birth of the first child or patrilocal residence, as among the Saoch.

Villages among the hill groups of Cambodia traditionally have been the basic political unit of social life—thus autonomous and self-governing. Each Jarai and Rade village, for instance, is autonomous and is governed by its leading families. In some villages, the basic unit is even smaller than the village. Among the Stieng, for example, the family constitutes the basic social and political unit and there is no political organization at a higher level.

The Mnong along the Cambodian-Vietnamese border measure status by wealth, and wealth is measured by the number of buffalo a person sacrifices on funeral or other ceremonial occasions. The greater the number sacrificed, the greater that person's standing in his and neighboring communities. In the past, slavery existed among the Mnong; under certain conditions, a slave could gain his freedom.

Most tribespeople have little regard for pets although they keep domesticated animals, such as buffalo, pigs, and chicken, but these are kept to trade, eat, or sacrifice on special ritual occasions. Dogs are kept by some for protection both from other humans and from wild animals. Some families keep cats as a countermeasure to rats.

11 CLOTHING

Most Khmer Loeu continue to wear traditional clothing. Men wear a short loincloth and strings of beads, while women wear a variety of skirts.

The hill tribes of Cambodia weave their traditional colorful clothing on homemade looms. Each tribe has a different style of clothing and jewelry. Clothing is made of cloth which repeats thousands of tiny patterns, with decorations such as silver hoops added. Just one dress can take weeks to make. In addition to their colorful dress, some highland groups file their front teeth and also wear tattoos just as their ancestors did.

The decrease in isolation from ethnic Cambodians has resulted in the use of imported clothing, so that tribespeople increasingly wear a combination of traditional, Cambodian, and European clothing.

12 FOOD

The primary food of a group depends foremost on its major means of subsistence. Hill groups who are primarily rice cultivators have rice as their central food. Groups who raise root crops, such as cassava, taro, and yams, depend primarily on those crops as well as maize, eggplant, beans, sugar cane, bananas, and other fruits and vegetables.

Rice and vegetable crops are supplemented by greatly valued meat either from domestic animals, such as pigs and poultry, or game and birds from the neighboring forests. Additional valued foods include fish and eggs. Every group has a method for making beer or rice from the products close at home. Rice wine and cassava beer are common and are consumed primarily on ritual occasions.

Because modern appliances are few and packaged goods a rarity, much time and energy goes into the growing, preservation, and preparing of a family's daily meals. Women are primarily responsible for everyday food preparation, while men often bear the responsibility for making alcoholic beverages and cooking ritual foods.

The preparing of food is also important for ritual. Virtually every ceremony includes an offering of food and drink to the spirits and a communal feast by the participants. A sacrifice of a valued animal, such as a buffalo or pig, marks an important ceremony. Buffalo, in fact, are kept primarily for ritual sacrifices and become the central food at religious festivals.

Food taboos are common among all the tribal groups and vary considerably according to group, age, sex, and situation. Thus, pregnant women, women after childbirth, and hunters, to mention just a few, may be required to consume or refrain from consuming particular foods for specific periods of time.

13 EDUCATION

Formal schooling for the hill people started after independence in 1953 when King Norodom Sihanouk sought to make education compulsory and available to all the people in the country. These programs continued until 1970, but many school buildings were destroyed in the war and it was not until the 1990s—ironically when Sihanouk returned to rule the country—that new school buildings were erected. While schools and teachers from the lowlanders are increasingly available for highland children, most continue to be taught traditional skills in traditional ways by parents and relatives. The more contact a village has with Cambodians from the central plains, the more likely their exposure to schools and education in Cambodian subjects and language.

The hill groups were traditionally oral rather than literate societies, in which tradition and knowledge were passed on verbally rather than through writing. Recently, however, several of the hill languages have been put into romanized form: the Rade and Jarai are two of these. Several epic tales in the Rade language have been transcribed and published.

14 CULTURAL HERITAGE

Music among hill people is played primarily in the service of religion, but also on ritual occasions such as marriage and funerals, and for popular entertainment.

Musical instruments include drums, flutes, gongs, xylophones, and horns of various kinds, traditionally made from wood or horn. More recently, instruments have been made of modern metals and some plastic ones are also used.

The literature of the hill tribes has traditionally been oral, consisting of the myths, legends, stories, and entire body of group knowledge passed on from generation to generation. In the absence of writing and modern entertainment, youth learned the beliefs and events of their past from their elders, in turn passing them on to their children.

15 WORK

The hill people of Cambodia are either sedentary or nomadic. Sedentary groups, which are more populous, are primarily wet rice cultivators. Some are engaged in growing industrial crops.

Nomadic groups, on the other hand, are swidden farmers growing their own crops. The system used for agriculture is also called slash and-burn agriculture which is a better description of what happens. After finding a good garden area, the men cut the trees down or cut them severely enough so that they die. The large logs are often used to build houses. The rest of the fallen trees are then burned so that the bush cover is to ash. The ashes help enrich the soil in which sticky rice, root crops, and cash crops are then sown.

The hill men tend their crops and harvest them over the next two to four years using hand implements, for they have no plows or other modern tools. Over a few years, the soil loses its nutrients, and the group moves on to establish new garden areas, following the same slash-and-burn techniques. After a few decades, the original plot of soil has regained its nutrients and can again support crops.

Thus the hill people move through the forest over the years, stopping to build a village in which they live for several years, moving on when the soils are exhausted to reestablish a village some miles away near their new gardens. Some groups raise primarily rice, others primarily root crops. Groups who raise root crops, such as cassava, taro, and yams, also raise maize, eggplant, beans, sugar cane, bananas, and other fruit and vegetables.

The Brao on the Cambodia-Laos border, for instance, cultivate dry season rice, while the Mnong along the Cambodian-Vietnamese border practice dry season rice farming. The Mnong also cultivate a wide variety of vegetables, fruit, and other plants for use as food and in handicrafts. The Stieng, Pearic, Jarai, and Rade tribes are also swidden farmers, growing primarily rice. They also hunt, gather, fish, and grow secondary crops such as maize and root plants to supplement their diets.

In addition to horticulture, hill men also raise a few domestic animals, including pigs, poultry, and buffalo. Among the Lahu, for example, pigs are the most important domesticated animal, but chickens are everywhere. They also raise ducks and geese. The Mnong are noted for trading pigs and poultry for buffalo.

Men hunt game and birds in the surrounding forests, obtaining almost everything they need by their own hand. Muong men hunt with guns, crossbows, traps, snares, and nets. Men organize communal hunts on festival days. A successful hunt is seen as a good omen for the rice harvest. In addition, Muong men fish with scoop nets, lines, bows, and knives.

Women do most of the vegetable and herb gathering. Muong women collect edible tubers, leaves, mushrooms, bamboo shoots, vegetables, berries, and fruit. When food is scarce, they gather breadfruit and eat it as bread. They also collect wood for fuel, materials for building houses, medicinal plants, and other products such as feathers and skins for trade.

16 SPORTS

Tribal children spend much of their time assisting their parents in hunting, gathering, horticulture, and rice cultivation. Whatever ways of making a living are followed by their village and parents, those are their major activities. Boys learn from an early age to help their fathers, and their play centers on learning to do what their fathers do. Thus, boys practice with tiny bows, shooting small animals, trying to catch birds and fish, and in numerous ways imitating the activities of their

elders. Girls, also, learn from their elders, assisting their mothers and other village women in caring for smaller children, looking after the house, and preparing food.

Children spend many nighttime hours listening to the stories and legends of their people. As they sit around their homes in the evening, they may listen to a story from a grandmother, an ancient tale from an older man, or hear the hunters relate their hunting experiences.

From the late 1950s, with the introduction of compulsory education, children at schools started learning to play soccer and also volleyball. Both sports, especially soccer, have continued to be popular, with boys from hill tribes in schools often playing against lowland Khmers, all participating barefoot.

17 ENTERTAINMENT AND RECREATION

Music is a major form of entertainment. The Kmhmu, for example, have a number of instruments on which they play any number of songs. Their instruments include flutes, mouth organs and harps, and percussion instruments, most made from bamboo. The bronze drum is not only a musical instrument but a symbol of wealth and status used in important communal ceremonies. Kmhmu songs are unique in featuring elaborate poetic verses with reverse parallelism.

Movies, television, videos, and other popular entertainment of Westernized countries—even radios—remain rare in much of highland Cambodia. Tribespeople rely on singing, dancing, and instrumentation for much of their entertainment.

18 FOLK ART, CRAFTS, AND HOBBIES

Hill women weave clothing such as skirts and blouses for themselves, loincloths for their men, and blankets. Using cruder materials, men weave mats and baskets. Embroidery and appliqué work is also done. Hill tribespeople make a number of musical instruments which include gourd flutes, mouth harps, guitars, and banjos. Men make agricultural, hunting, and gathering tools. The Kuy of northern Cambodia have a reputation for being excellent blacksmiths, while the Brao are noted for their pottery-making skills.

19 SOCIAL PROBLEMS

The hill tribes continue to struggle for more autonomy from the lowland Cambodians. They continue to be viewed by many ethnic Khmer as inferior, with strange customs that are best abolished. Their isolation has been lessened by the migration of lowland peoples into the highlands, but continues for many in slowing the spread of medical and educational facilities. The major threat to the culture and lifestyle of the hill tribes is, however, the logging which has reduced the jungles considerably.

Many Khmer Loeu and observers fear that within a few years, their cultures will have disappeared along with their environment. Many are gradually being incorporated into lowland Cambodian life. They have adopted many Khmer customs, clothing, and practices. Many of the youth are now being taught the Khmer language and are working on Cambodian farms.

Many tribal groups now practice wet rice cultivation rather than horticulture and frequently intermarry with Khmer. Most Chong and Pear, for example, are now assimilated into Cambodian society. Once hunters and gatherers, the Saoch are also now mostly assimilated into Cambodian society. Most

Kuy living in Cambodia have been assimilated into Cambodian culture, as Kuy living in Thailand have been incorporated into Thai society. Most Kuy practice wet rice cultivation, have converted to Buddhism, and speak both the national language and their tribal language.

[20] GENDER ISSUES

Generally in Mountain Khmer communities, women remained in the villages and were involved in traditional home-making. In recent years some have been involved in craft-work for sale in local towns.

[21] BIBLIOGRAPHY

Baradat, R. "Les Samre ou Pear, population primitive de l'ouest du Cambodge," *Bulletin de l'École Française d'Extrême-Orient* (1941) 1–150.

Bourdier, F. "Health, Women and Environment in a Marginal Region of Northeastern Cambodia." *Abstract for the Cuban National Committee of the IGU: Environment, Society, and Development*, 1995.

———. "Rapport d'une mission de recherche sur le theme de l'environnement au Cambodge dans le cadre de l'AUPELF/UREF. Connaissances et pratiques de gestion traditionnelle de la nature dans une province marginalisee." Unpublished manuscript, 1995.

Bourotte, Bernard. "Essai d'histoire des populations montagnards du Sud-Indochinois jusqu'a 1945." *Bulletin de Societeâ des Etudes Indochinoises* 30 (1955) 1–133.

Chandler, David P. *The Tragedy of Cambodian History: Politics, War, and Revolution since 1945*. New Haven, CT: Yale University Press, 1991.

Corfield, Justin J. and Laura Summers. *Historical Dictionary of Cambodia*. Lanham, MD: Scarecrow Press, 2003.

Hickey, Gerald C. "Pear." In *Ethnic Groups of Mainland Southeast Asia.*, F. M. LeBar, G. C. Hickey, and J. K. Musgrave, eds. New Haven, CT.: Human Relations Area Files Press, 1964.

———. *Shattered Worlds: Adaptation and Survival among Vietnam's Highland Peoples during the Vietnam War*. Philadelphia: University of Pennsylvania Press, 1993.

Kiernan, Ben. *How Pol Pot Came to Power: A History of Communism in Kampuchea, 1930–1975*. London: Verso. 1985

LeBar, Frank M., Gerald D. Hickey, and John K. Musgrave. *Ethnic Groups of Mainland Southeast Asia*. New Haven, Conn.: Human Relations Area Files, 1964.

Martin, Marie Alexandrine. *Les Khmers Daeum: Khmeres de l'Origine*. Paris: École Française d'Extrême-Orient, 1998.

Matras-Troubetzkoy, Jacqueline. *Un village en foret: L'essartage chez les Brou du Cambodge*. Paris: SELAF, 1983.

—revised by J. Corfield.

MUNDAS

PRONUNCIATION: MOON-duhz
LOCATION: India (Bihar state)
POPULATION: 3 million (estimate)
LANGUAGE: Mundari
RELIGION: Traditional animism; Hinduism; Christianity
RELATED ARTICLES: Vol. 3: People of India

[1] INTRODUCTION

The Mundas are one of the aboriginal peoples found in the Chota Nagpur region of eastern India. The tribe has lent its name to the Munda branch of the Austro-Asiatic language family, and sometimes *Munda* is used to designate the many tribes of the region (e.g., Munda, Santal, Ho) that speak Munda languages and share common spiritual and cultural values. These tribes are also sometimes called *Kolarian*. The following discussion, however, focuses specifically on the one tribe among this group that is identified as Munda.

The name *Munda,* which means "headman of a village," was originally applied to the group by outsiders. The tribe's own name for itself is *Hor-on*. The Mundas are a people of considerable antiquity, some scholars identifying them with the Mundas mentioned in the epic *Mahāhbhārata*. The origin of the Munda people is a matter of much uncertainty. Their own traditions indicate that they migrated to their current location from areas to the northwest. Linguistic evidence, however, suggests ties to northeastern India and Southeast Asia. Wherever they originated, the Mundas settled in the forest-clad uplands of the Chota Nagpur Plateau, perhaps as early as the centuries preceding the Christian Era. Here, they have remained in relative isolation until modern times.

[2] LOCATION AND HOMELAND

In 2000, the state of Jharkhand (*Jhārkhand*) was created out of the southern districts of the state of Bihar, largely to satisfy the aspirations of the local tribal population. Thus, over half of the Munda population of the subcontinent were included within the boundaries of the new state, Mundas being numerically the third largest tribal group in Jharkhand, after the Santals and Oraons. The 2001 Census of India reported over one million Mundas (1,048,886) in the state, with an equal number living in the state of Assam, and a considerable population in Bangladesh. Small numbers of Mundas are also found in Orissa, West Bengal, Bihar, Andhra Pradesh, Tripura, Madhya Pradesh and the Andaman and Nicobar Islands. Allowing for natural increase, and the numbers of Mundas living in other northeastern states, the Munda population is estimated to be around 3 million today.

The Mundas occupy the southern areas of what used to be Bihar State, but is now Jharkhand. The name Jharkhand comes from the Sanskrit "Jharikhanda," which is the ancient name of the region's dense forest. The demand for a separate Jharkhand state can be traced back to the early 1900s, though according to some historians, there was already a distinct geopolitical, cultural entity called Jharkhand even before the period of Magadha Empire (c. 6th century BC). In ancient days the northern portion of Jharkhand state was a tributary to the Magadha (ancient Bihar) Empire and southern part was a tributary to the Kalinga (ancient Orissa) Empire. According to a legend, Raja Jai Singh Deo of Orissa was accepted as the ruler of Jharkhand by its people in the 13th century. The Singh Deo's of Orissa have been very instrumental in the early history of Jharkhand. The local tribal heads had developed into barbaric dictators who could govern the province neither fairly nor justly. Consequently, the people of this state approached the more powerful rulers of Jharkhand's neighboring states, who were perceived to have a more fair and just governance. The turning point in the history of the region came when rulers from Orissa moved in with their armies and created states governed with the people and for their benefit. With this act, the barbarism that had marked the region for centuries ended. The good tribal rulers, known as the Munda Rajas, continued to thrive and exist to this day. Later, during the Mughal period, the Jharkhand area was known as Kukara. After the year 1765, it came under the control of the British Empire and became formally a state, under its present name, "Jharkhand"—the Land of "Jungles" (forests) and "Jharis" (bushes), at the beginning of the 21st century.

Mundas played a significant role in the creation of Jharkhand State. The Jharkhand movement was spearheaded by the Jharkhand Mukti Morcha., which sought to create a tribally-dominated state from the southern area of Bihar state. During the 18th and 19th centuries, Santals, Chero, Hos, Oraons, and Kols staged tribal revolts against the British, who were trying to destroy the traditional Adivasi (the "original inhabitants," or tribal people in India) institutions of self-governance and self-regulation. One such system the British tried to destroy was the *Munda-Manki* system. A *Manki* is an association of 12 villages that historically controlled the villages' land and resources. But in 1895, the last tribal revolt against the British overlords, the Birsa Munda Revolt, led by Birsa Munda (1875–1900), broke out throughout Munda country. It was the longest and greatest tribal revolt in Jharkhand history. During the 20th century, the Jharkhand movement was considerably more moderate, with the Adivasi Mahasabha, an association of tribals founded in 1939, being renamed the Jharkhand Party at Independence. Despite being denied a state in 1947, the Jharkhand Party never lost sight of its goals, and the state of Jharkhand came into being over 50 years later. Arjun Munda, formerly of the Jharkhand Party, served two terms as chief minister of the state (2003–2005 and 2005–2006), though as a member of the Bharatiya Janata Party (BJP). As of 2008 he was leader of the opposition in the state legislature.

Munda territory lies on the Ranchi Plateau of Chota Nagpur, extending south from the Damodar River Valley to the extreme northern part of Orissa State. The land is a jumble of plateaus and hills between 300 m and 760 m (1,000–2,200 ft) above sea level, with individual peaks reaching as high as 1,505 m (3,445 ft). The region is crossed by the valleys of numerous rivers draining south towards the Bay of Bengal. The area is heavily forested, with vegetation ranging from scrub jungle to denser subtropical and tropical deciduous forest. Rainfall, received mostly during the three months of the summer monsoon, averages between 120 cm and 160 cm (47–62 in). Humidity is high in summer, with maximum temperatures varying between 35°C and 40°C (95°F–104°F).

³LANGUAGE

Mundari is the mother tongue of the Munda peoples. Mundari, along with the languages of neighboring tribes, such as the Santal and Ho, belongs to the Munda branch of the Austro-Asiatic language family. Mundari thus forms part of the group of isolated languages of eastern India that are linguistically related to languages spoken in mainland Southeast Asia rather than to the major language families of the Indian subcontinent. Historically, the Mundas had no system of writing. The Roman script and regional scripts are now used for this purpose. Many Mundas are bilingual and use Hindi, Sadri, or other local languages for intergroup communication.

⁴FOLKLORE

A Munda legend explains the creation of the Earth in the following way. In the beginning of time, the Earth was covered with water. Sing Bonga, the Sun God, brooded over the waters and created the first creatures: a tortoise, a crab, and a leech. Sing Bonga commanded these animals to bring him a bit of clay from the ocean depths. Both the tortoise and the crab tried and failed, but eventually the leech managed to bring up a piece of clay from the deep. Out of this clay, Sing Bonga fashioned the Earth. At his bidding, the Earth brought forth all kinds of trees and plants. Sing Bonga next filled the Earth with birds and beasts of all sorts and sizes. Then a memorable incident occurred. The bird *Hur* or swan laid an egg, and out of this, there emerged a boy and a girl, the first human beings. These were the ancestors of the *Hor-on Honko*, or "sons of men," as the Mundas still call themselves.

⁵RELIGION

Although their religion is basically animistic, the Mundas believe in a supreme being they call Sing Bonga. He is widely revered but only invoked at the time of major calamities, when a white fowl is sacrificed to him. Two lesser classes of deities *(bongas)* are the village gods and the household gods. The former influence every aspect of Munda life, from their daily activities to their agriculture. The village priest, the *pāhān*, is responsible for presiding over the worship of these gods at the sacred grove of the village. The blessings of the household gods—who are the spirits of deceased ancestors—are sought at every social and religious ceremony. The head of the family leads the worship of the household gods in the *āding*, the room set aside for this purpose in every Munda house. There are, in addition, several types of lesser godlings and spirits inhabiting the Munda universe. Some, such as deities who guard the family or protect the interests of married women, are benevolent. Others are evil and bring disease and misfortune to the Mundas. These have to be identified and appeased by the ghost-finders or shamans, who are often drawn from non-Munda groups. Animals are sacrificed to the gods, and the Mundas are reported to have offered human victims in the past. The Mundas are great believers in magic, witchcraft, and the power of the "evil eye."

Some Mundas have accepted Hinduism and Christianity, although they preserve many of their earlier religious practices. Census data regarding religion in India is unreliable, because specific data has not been collected since 1951. However, according to the 2001 Census, some 73% of Mundas are Hindu, 17% follow Christianity (this figure is much higher than the average for India [around 2.5%] and reflects the work of Christian missionaries among the Munda), and the remaining 10% are animists following the traditional religion.

⁶MAJOR HOLIDAYS

Two important Munda festivals are the Magh Porob and Sarhul. The first of these is dedicated to honoring the spirits of deceased ancestors. It is held on the full moon day of January, after the winter harvest has been gathered. Sarhul, also known as the "Flower Feast," is celebrated in the spring when the *sāl* trees (*Shorea robusta*) are in flower. All the gods of the Munda pantheon are worshiped in the village's sacred grove, where chickens are sacrificed by the priest. The villagers return home dancing and singing, carrying *sāl* blossoms in their hands. Garlands of *sāl* flowers are hung around the houses, and people wear *sāl* flowers in their hair.

Some festivals of the Mundas are clearly borrowed from the Hindus, though celebrated with rituals that are traditional in nature. The Phagu festival corresponds to the Holi festival of the Hindus, while Dasai is the Hindu Dasahara. Sohorai is another festival of Hindu origin, when a black fowl and rice-beer are offered to the deity presiding over cattle.

⁷RITES OF PASSAGE

When a woman is discovered to be pregnant, the Mundas sacrifice a chicken to Garasi Bonga. This is the deity who protects both women and children during pregnancy and birthing. A woman is considered unclean for eight days after childbirth, after which the relatives gather for rituals to purify the mother, the newborn child, and the house. On the following day, the baby is named (the *sākhi* ceremony), and a girdle of thread is tied around its waist. Within a year or two, the baby's ears are ritually pierced. All of these ceremonies are accompanied by feasting and drinking.

Young unmarried Mundas generally do not sleep in their family residences but, rather, in village dormitories. While these institutions are not exactly like the dormitories of the nearby Oraon tribe, boys and girls will gather separately at a house in the village designated for this purpose. There, during the evening they will pose riddles, listen to songs and fables, and acquire knowledge of the customs and beliefs of their community until it is time to retire to bed.

In the past, Mundas cremated their dead, but many now resort to burial. Traditionally, the corpse was burnt and the bones collected to be interred in the family grave. Every village has its burial ground or *sasān*, or if there is more than one clan in the settlement, one for each clan. Big stone slabs are placed on the ground, and the bones of a family's ancestors are placed underneath the family's stone slab. If a Munda dies away from his village, her or his relatives will convey the bones to his or her ancestral village, where they will buried in the family grave. No one who does not belong to the clan is allowed to use the burial ground.

⁸INTERPERSONAL RELATIONS

Among the virtues of the Mundas are hospitality, respect for elders and those with social authority, affection for family members, and general friendliness.

⁹LIVING CONDITIONS

Munda villages are made up of scattered homesteads built together on the higher elevations of land where there is enough available space. The Munda home consists of at least two huts. One is used for sleeping and, among the poorer families, houses the livestock as well. The other is the eating house and contains the kitchen, a pen for the chickens, and also the sacred room where the family gods reside. The homes of the better-off may comprise three or four huts, arranged around a square and having a compound at the back. The walls of the houses are generally windowless and built of mud, with a tiled or thatched roof. Household utensils and furnishings are simple. The Mundas eat off wooden or metal dishes, while earthenware jars and baskets are used for storage. Wooden stools and a sleeping mat or string bed complete the household belongings.

In addition to its homesteads, a village has its sacred grove (*sarnā*), the public meeting space in the center of the village (*ākhrā*), and the village burial ground. On the outskirts of the village are cultivable uplands, which are regarded as part of the village itself and are used mainly for growing garden vegetables. Lying further down the slopes are the terraced lands used for wet-rice cultivation.

¹⁰FAMILY LIFE

The Mundas are divided into totemic clans (*kili*) such as the Nag (Snake) Kili and Bagh (Tiger) Kili. The Mundas are endogamous, i.e., they marry within the tribe, but they practice clan exogamy, i.e., they have to marry outside the lineage. Traditionally, Mundas do not marry before the boy can build a plow and the girl can weave and spin, but instances of child marriage are known to occur. Marriages are usually negotiated and depend on the consent of the involved parties. The actual ceremonies are quite elaborate and appear to have absorbed many Hindu rituals. A bride-price is paid in both cash and goods. Although the newlyweds may take up residence in the husband's father's house, the nuclear family is preferred. Monogamy is the norm, and both divorce and widow remarriage are allowed.

¹¹CLOTHING

Munda dress is very simple. Men ordinarily wear nothing more than a cotton loincloth with colored borders known as *botoi*. A piece of cloth or a blanket may be wrapped around the upper body during cold weather. Young men place a belt of silk or plaited thread around the waist. The dress of Munda women is a long piece of cloth wrapped around the waist, with one end passed diagonally across the upper body to cover the breasts. Young women are fond of ornaments and wear earrings, bracelets, anklets, and toe rings. Ornaments are usually made of brass, with only the wealthier among the population wearing silver or gold. Young girls are tattooed on the face, arms, back, and feet. Men don colored turbans for festive occasions when dancing is performed. Hindu Mundas are often indistinguishable in dress from their Hindu neighbors, while Christian Mundas sometimes wear European-style clothes.

¹²FOOD

Boiled rice forms the staple food of the Mundas. The more well-to-do eat this with vegetables (e.g., onions, eggplant, radishes, beans, and roots such as the sweet potato) and pulses. Spices used include turmeric, garlic, and chilies. The poorer Mundas eat their rice with green leafy vegetables and may substitute millets for the rice. Chickens and goats are raised for food, but they are usually killed and eaten only at festivals and sacrifices. The eating of beef, pork, and buffalo meat is not unknown. At each meal, the Mundas drop a few grains of rice on the ground in the name of their deceased ancestors. The Mundas are fond of drinking rice-beer (ili), each family brewing its own supply. They also enjoy chewing tobacco and betel leaves.

13 EDUCATION

Mundari is essentially a spoken language, and few Mundas have learned to read and write the regional languages that they use for intergroup communication. Literacy in Jharkhand (54.1% in 2001) is below the average for India as a whole and that for Mundas is still lower, measuring 47.9% for males, and only 34.9% for females. However, these figures usually refer to literacy in a second language. While government schools are available to them, their isolation and the need for children to help in agricultural work means that the Mundas' exposure to formal education is limited. Though 50% of the 5 to 14 year old *Mundas* attend school, only about 17% ever graduate from school and only 3.6% ever continue on to higher education.

14 CULTURAL HERITAGE

Like most tribal groups, the Mundas have a rich oral folk tradition. This includes historical myths (e.g., the Asur Legend), folk tales, riddles, and proverbs. There are love songs, and songs and dances appropriate for specific religious festivals and social events. The Lahsua dances, performed at the time of the Karam festival, are of a kind known as "stooping" dances. The dancers form a circle, join hands, and stoop forward. Keeping this position, they advance towards the circle's center, then retire, all the time circling towards the left. The musical instruments that accompany the singing and dancing include drums, tambourines, various stringed instruments, and bamboo flutes. For weddings, the Mundas employ musicians of the Ghasi tribe.

15 WORK

Although in the past they practiced shifting cultivation, most Mundas are involved in permanent, wet-rice agriculture today. They supplement this with hunting and gathering in the jungle, although this is decreasing in importance. Both men and women work in the field, but some activities—e.g., plowing—are restricted to men. Many Mundas work as agricultural laborers or in the mines and factories of Bihar's industrial area. Those few Mundas who have the necessary education work in white-collar jobs, in government, and in the professions.

16 SPORTS

Munda children play a variety of games, some apparently traditional and others introduced by European missionaries. Pastimes include games of tag such as *Chhūr*. The players divide themselves into two teams. Parallel lines are drawn on the ground, and one team guards the lines. The players on the other team try to penetrate the guarded territory and reach an area designated as the "salt-house" (non-gharā) without being touched by the defenders. If they succeed in this, the opposing teams switch roles. Other games include marbles, spinning

tops, hide-and-seek, and blind man's bluff. *Phodi* is a type of indigenous hockey game.

The Mundas also have a type of dramatic game that combines amusement with instruction in which children assume roles and act out situations from real life. One such game is the Jackfruit Game (*Kantara-Inu*). The actors pretend to be a jackfruit tree, its fruits, its owner, the owner's dog, and a thief. The game is played out by the thief stealing the fruit, cutting down the tree, and various other episodes that conclude with a mock *pūjā* or worship ceremony.

17 ENTERTAINMENT AND RECREATION

Living in remote villages, most Mundas derive their entertainment from their religious festivals and social events, which are invariably accompanied by singing, dancing, feasting, and drinking.

18 FOLK ART, CRAFTS, AND HOBBIES

The Mundas are not known for their arts and crafts. While they weave cloth, spin cotton, and make baskets, they rely on Hindu artisan castes to provide many of their material needs.

19 SOCIAL PROBLEMS

Like many tribal peoples in South Asia, the Mundas are faced with conflicting social pressures. It is to their advantage to promote their "tribal" identity because of the benefits of being designated a Scheduled Tribe. On the other hand, those Mundas who overcome the disadvantages of their tribal status (e.g., illiteracy and lack of education) and succeed economically tend to lose touch with their tribal roots. Historically, Mundas have resented what they see as exploitation by outsiders, and such feelings continue today. Many, for example, see current development schemes such as the Bihar Plateau Development Project (BPDP), which now, of course, falls within the area of Jharkhand, as serving the interests of the World Bank and transnational corporations, rather than those of the local tribal peoples.

Ruled by Bharatiya Janata Party-led Arjun Munda government, Jharkhand witnessed serious violations of international humanitarian laws both by law enforcement personnel and Naxalites rebels during 2005. Naxalite or Naxalism is an informal name given to revolutionary communist groups that were born out of the Sino-Soviet split in the Indian communist movement. Ideologically, Naxalites belong to various trends of Maoism (the Communist Party of India-Maoist [CPI-M] is outlawed in many states in India) and recently have spread into less developed areas of rural central and eastern India, such as Chattisgarh and Jharkhand from their state of origin in West Bengal. Naxalites are considered terrorists by the government of India. The Maoist problem continues to plague the state of Jharkhand with the guerrillas reportedly being active in 16 of the state's 22 districts. More than 500 people have been killed in the state by the Naxalites in the early 2000s. At least 15 villagers were killed and six others injured during an attack by alleged Naxalites at Bhelbadari village under Deuri police station in Giridih district on the night of 11 September 2005.

In parts of rural Jharkhand, many Mundas do not have access to health care, while starvation continues to be a problem. The conditions of women and children are deplorable. Mundas believe in witchcraft and the evil eye, and women (and men) are killed and tortured for practicing witchcraft. Despite the existence of anti-child labor legislation, bonded child labor is still found in Jharkhand. Conditions of Munda child laborers, such as those doing mica mining in the districts of Koderma and Giridih, continue to be grim. Many children have reportedly died due to mine collapse, while diseases such as silicosis, asthma and bronchitis, tuberculosis, and malnutrition are common. Violence often accompanies the electoral process in Jharkhand, with violations of human rights being committed by both security forces and the Maoist guerrillas.

Mundas continue to be victims of development projects and land alienation. The Jharkhand government has signed over 42 Memorandum of Understandings (MoUs) with investors including Mittal Steel, Tata Steel, and Jindal Steel and Power Company Limited since Jharkhand became a state in 2000 (Jharkhand is blessed with abundant mineral wealth). These projects would require approximately 47,445 acres of land in the mineral-rich Kolhan Region, which could affect about 10,000 families and cause deforestation of 5,715 square kilometers of land. A study by the People's Union for Civil Liberties (PUCL), a human rights organization, shows that over 740,000 tribals, including Mundas, were displaced in Jharkhand by different projects between 1950 and 1990. Only 184,500 were rehabilitated and the remaining 562,600—-over two-thirds of the displaced—have been left to fend for themselves. According to the report, industries had displaced 260,000 tribals, including *Mundas,* while different animal sanctuaries had forced about 500,000 tribals to leave their homes.

Mundas are also victims of land alienation through the illegal transfer of land to non-tribals in violation of the Chotanagpur Tenancy Act. The most popular method is by marrying tribal girls, buying tribal land in their names and, after dumping the tribal wives, selling the land to non-tribals. The tribals are also victimized under various forest laws. They face forcible evictions, harassment and imprisonment by the police and the forest officials.

[20] GENDER ISSUES

As with most tribal groups in South Asia, *Munda* women tend to have equality with men. Attitudes towards sex among young girls is quite relaxed, and girls often sleep in mixed village dormitories rather than at home. Marriages, though usually arranged, require the consent of both parties involved, a bride price is paid, and divorce and re-marriage are permitted. Given the creation of Jharkhand State as what is essentially a tribal state, the *Mundas* form a significant element in the state population and are quite well represented (Scheduled Tribes make up 26.3% of Jharkhand's population and Mundas account for 14.8% of the ST population).

However, along with taboos and restrictions on women, such as exclusion from rituals and witch-hunts that often target widows, *Mundas* continued to be victims of sexual abuses in Jharkhand. *Munda* girls are easy targets of sexual violence, especially in the context of the current Maoist insurgency. Women cannot inherit land, because they can marry outside the clan. Many women are migrants, leaving their homes to seek work as unskilled labor (*reja*). Poverty, illiteracy, and inheritance laws contribute greatly to the marginalization of *Munda* women in Indian society.

[21] BIBLIOGRAPHY

Basu, Sunil Kumar. *The Mundas: A Profile.* Calcutta: Cultural Research Institute, 1987.

Lal, Manohar. *The Munda Elites: Recruitment, Network, Attitudes, Perception & Role in Social Transformation.* Delhi: Amar Prakashan, 1983.

Nandi, Arati. *Mundas in Transition: A Study in Cultural Geography.* Calcutta : Paritosh Nandi, 1993.

Pandey, Ajit Kumar. *Kinship and Tribal Polity: A Comparative Study of the Mundas and Oraons of Bihar.* Jaipur: Rawat Publications, 1989.

Roy, S. C. *The Mundas and their Country.* 1912. Reprint, Bombay: Asia Publishing House, 1970.

Yamada, Ryuji. *Cultural Formation of the Mundas: Hill Peoples Surrounding the Ganges Plain.* Tokyo: Tokyo University Press, 1970.

—by D. O. Lodrick

MUSLIMS IN SOUTH ASIA

PRONUNCIATION: MUHZ luhms
LOCATION: Pakistan; Bangladesh; India; Sri Lanka; Nepal; Bhutan; other countries of South Asia and worldwide
POPULATION: 1.65 billion worldwide (estimate); 456 million in South Asia
LANGUAGE: Arabic (language of Islamic ritual); Urdu (South Asia)
RELIGION: Islam

¹INTRODUCTION

For over one and a half billion people in the world today, there is only one God: *Allah*. Allah made his will known to humankind when he revealed the holy scriptures (the *Quran*) to the world through his messenger Muhammad. Muhammad, who is seen as the last in a line of prophets that included Abraham and Jesus, was born around AD 570 in Mecca in the Arabian peninsula. The Arabic word *Islam*, literally meaning "submission," describes the religion whose followers submit to the will of Allah. One who submits to the will of Allah, as revealed by the Prophet Muhammad, is called a *Muslim* (or *Moslem*).

Islam, one of the world's great religions, spread rapidly across Arabia and then through the vast expanse of deserts and steppe lands that cuts a path across the Old World from the Atlantic Ocean to the China Sea. It spread along the maritime trade routes and caravan routes that carried the commerce of the times. Islam was first introduced into South Asia in AD 711, when an Arab naval expedition sailed to the mouth of the Indus River (now in Pakistan) to suppress piracy against Arab shipping. The most significant Muslim incursions into South Asia, however, began at the start of the 11th century, when Afghan rulers sent military expeditions into the plains of India. In 1021 the Punjab was annexed by Mahmud of Ghazni to form the eastern province of his empire. Lahore, its capital, emerged as a major center of Islamic culture, and mass conversions to Islam among the common people began at this time. By the end of the 12th century the Afghans had captured Delhi, which remained a center of Muslim power in South Asia for over 650 years. During this period of Muslim domination, large numbers of Hindus and Buddhists converted to Islam. Under Akbar (r. 1556–1605), the greatest of the Mughals, Muslims brought virtually all of the Indian subcontinent under their control. The final remnant of imperial Muslim power in India disappeared in 1858 when the last Mughal Emperor of India was exiled from Delhi by the British. However, independent states ruled by Muslims survived in the region until the middle of the 20th century.

By 1947, Muslims in South Asia numbered an estimated 100 million people, roughly 24% of the peoples of the region. With the withdrawal of the British from their Indian Empire at this time, the political boundaries of South Asia were redrawn. The Islamic state of Pakistan (later to break up into Pakistan and Bangladesh) was created. Mass movements involving as many as 10 million people saw Muslim populations flee to Pakistan, while Hindus and Sikhs migrated to India. This was a period of communal violence and bloodshed that saw an estimated one million people murdered because of their religion.

Pakistan, an avowed Muslim state, and India, a secular democracy—even though its population is primarily Hindu—have fought several wars since Independence. Independence itself was accompanied by a conflict that saw the Pakistani and Indian armies fighting in Kashmir, a problem that has yet to be resolved. In fact, supposed Pakistani infiltration of Indian-held territory in Kashmir led to the 1965 Indo-Pakistani War, which involved air and naval units as well as ground forces in Kashmir and along the entire Indo-Pakistani border in western India. Despite heavy losses in both men and materials on both sides, the war was essentially inconclusive. Not so the next conflict in 1971, which saw Indian forces intercede in the civil war in East Pakistan, the surrender of the Pakistan military in the region, and the birth of Bangladesh as an independent nation. The summer of 1999 again saw fighting between India and Pakistan, this time over Kargil in Kashmir. Allegedly the brainchild of the Pakistani Army Commander-in-Chief, General Pervez Musharraf, the plan involved infiltration of Indian-held territory in Kashmir by Pakistani soldiers and Kashmiri militants (despite the Pakistan government and military denying any involvement). The resultant Kargil War saw Indian regulars pitted against the Pakistani Army, and it is thought that only the threat of Pakistan's newly-developed nuclear weapons prevented Indian forces from pressing home the advantage they ultimately gained on the ground in Kashmir. Later in 1999, Musharraf mounted a military coup against Pakistan's civilian government and took the reins of power, becoming president of Pakistan.

²LOCATION AND HOMELAND

Muslims in South Asia today number around 456 million people, with Pakistan, India, and Bangladesh representing the 2nd, 3rd, and 4th most populous Muslim states in the world. Of these, almost two-thirds live in the two Muslim states in the region. Pakistan, in the west of the subcontinent, has 154.5 million Muslims, while Bangladesh, in the east, has a population of 127.3 million Muslims.

Although only 13.4% of India's population is Muslim according to the 2001 Census, the total number of Muslims in India today is estimated at 154.5 million, third in the world after Indonesia and Pakistan. Muslims in India are concentrated in the areas adjacent to Pakistan and Bangladesh, on the plains of the Ganges Valley, and in the interior of the Deccan. The Moplahs, a Muslim community descended from Arab traders who settled the area in the 7th century AD, are found along the coast of Kerala and also in Lakshadweep, an island group in the Indian Ocean that is Indian territory.

Muslim minorities are found in the remaining countries of South Asia, but in total numbers these communities are quite small. In Sri Lanka, Muslims make up 7.5% of the population, or about 1.8 million people. These include both Sri Lankan Moors (descendants of Arab seafarers) and Malays from Southeast Asia. Nepal has roughly 900,000 Muslims (3.8% of the population), located mainly in the southern lowland belt. In Bhutan, Muslims number around 91,000 (5% of the population).

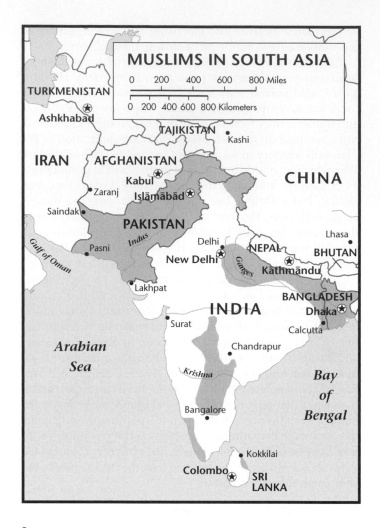

MUSLIMS IN SOUTH ASIA

³LANGUAGE

Arabic is the language used for ritual throughout the Islamic world. Outside the Arabic-speaking countries, ritual passages are memorized for the purposes of worship. This is the case in South Asia, where Muslims generally speak the language of their region, community, or cultural group. Thus Muslims in Pakistan speak Punjabi, Sindhi, Pashto, or one of the numerous other languages current in the country. In India, Muslims speak Urdu or regional languages such as Malayalam or Tamil. Most Bangladeshi Muslims are Bengali speakers.

If there is one language associated with Muslims in South Asia, that language is Urdu. Urdu, which means "language of the camp," is an Indo-Iranian language that evolved, during centuries of Muslim rule, from the Hindi vernacular spoken in the region of Delhi. It contains numerous Persian and Arabic words and is written in the Perso-Arabic script. In the 18th and 19th centuries it replaced Persian as the language of the upper classes and of administration in northern India. During the early decades of the 20th century, it came to be seen as a symbol of Muslim culture. Figures concerning the number of Urdu speakers in South Asia are unreliable. Estimates vary from 130 to 270 million speakers around the world, though perhaps an estimate of around 60 million individuals speaking Urdu as a first language across northern areas of the Indian subcontinent is reasonable. Urdu is not identified with any specific ethnic group or community, although in Pakistan it is associated with

muhajirs, Muslim immigrants from India. In Bangladesh also, Urdu is the language of immigrants from India. Urdu has been adopted as the national language of Pakistan. In India, Urdu is recognized as an official language. Urdu is associated with a tradition of literature and poetry in South Asia that extends back to the 14th century.

⁴FOLKLORE

A strictly monotheistic religion such as Islam does not allow much room for the development of myth and legend. However, commentators on the Quran trying to fill in the details of Muhammad's life inevitably wove strands of myth and legend into their works. Thus Muhammad, his relatives, and almost every person mentioned in the Quran are all associated with legends and miraculous deeds. On his death, for example, Muhammad is said to have ascended to heaven mounted on the winged horse Buraq and accompanied by the angel Gabriel.

In addition to beliefs that are common to the entire Muslim community, Islam, as it spread out of Arabia, developed regional mythological traditions. These often focused on the lives of the Sufi mystics, who played such an important role in converting the peoples of South Asia to Islam. The poetical works of the Sufis also blended classical Muslim motifs with popular legends in the folk traditions of Punjabi-, Sindhi-, and Bengali-speaking areas of South Asia.

⁵RELIGION

Islam originated with Muhammad. When Muhammad was about 40 years of age, an angel came to him in a vision and told him he was chosen to be the messenger of God. At frequent intervals until his death, he received further revelations that he believed came directly from God. These were gathered together and written down into a book called the Quran around AD 650. Because the Quran is literally the word of Allah, it is the unalterable source of authority for all matters relating to Islam.

Muhammad began his ministry around AD 610, and gathered around him a group of followers who accepted his teachings. However, the rich merchants of Mecca saw the new religion as a threat to the political and social stability of the city. They persecuted Muslims and eventually forced Muhammad to seek refuge elsewhere. In AD 622, Muhammad and his followers fled Mecca for Medina, an oasis city some 350 km (217 mi) to the north. This event is known as the *hijrah* ("emigration") and marks the beginning of the Islamic calendar. The year AD 622 in the Western calendar is AH 1 (Anno Hegirae, or the Year of the Hegira) in Muslim history.

The new religion combined contemporary Arab beliefs with elements of Judaism and Christianity. The veneration of stones and the keeping of many wives (polygyny) were Arab customs of the time. The monotheism (belief in one God) of Islam appears to have its origins in the Judeo-Christian religious tradition. The banning of usury (lending money for interest), of gambling, and of the use of human images in mosques also appears to be borrowed from Judaism or Christianity. Some Muslim practices, such as circumcision and avoidance of pork, were traditional among many peoples in the Middle East.

The basic beliefs of Muslims are set out in the "Five Pillars of Islam": 1) the profession of faith *(shahadah)*; 2) frequent prayer; 3) the obligatory religious tax *(zakat)*; 4) fasting during the month of Ramadan; and 5) pilgrimage to Mecca *(hajj)*.

All those who perform the tasks set out in the Five Pillars are members of the Muslim community, no matter what their nationality, caste, or color.

The profession of faith requires that one make a commitment to Islam. At least once in one's lifetime the following words have to be said with a full understanding of their meaning: "There is no God but God [Allah]; Muhammad is the prophet of God." Muslims are also expected to participate in congregational prayers five times a day. In towns all over South Asia, the *muezzin* in the mosques can be heard calling the faithful to prayer (nowadays the use of microphones and loudspeakers is common). After washing themselves, members of the congregation stand in rows behind the prayer leader *(imam),* facing Mecca. In South Asia, Muslims face towards the west. As the prayers are said, the congregation performs a series of movements involving standing, kneeling, and touching the head to the ground. The words "God is Great" accompany each change of posture. Friday is a day when special prayers are offered at mosques.

The religious tax *(zakat)* was originally intended to be collected by the state to be used for the poor. This has become largely a matter of voluntary contributions to charity, though Pakistan recently introduced a zakat tax on savings accounts.

The fourth pillar requires that Muslims fast between daybreak and sunset during the month of Ramadan. Eating, drinking, smoking, and even sexual activity are forbidden during daylight hours, although a light meal can be taken after sunset. It is also customary to make charitable offerings to the poor at this time. The end of Ramadan is celebrated by the festival of Id ul-Fitr.

The Hajj is the fifth pillar of Islam. It is the duty of every Muslim, if healthy and able to bear the expense, to make the journey to Mecca once in his or her lifetime. In Mecca, the pilgrim participates in various rituals, including walking around the Kabah, the shrine that contains the sacred Black Stone, and kissing the Black Stone itself. The pilgrimage ends with the sacrificial offerings of animals at Mina. Muslims who make the pilgrimage to Mecca are entitled to wear the coveted green turban as a sign that they have fulfilled this duty. For many Muslims in South Asia, completing the Hajj to Mecca is a lifelong ambition.

In its early years, Islam experienced divisions that saw the emergence of several sects and subsects. The most important split occurred at the end of the 7th century over the question of succession to the caliphate. *Sunnis* claimed that the caliph, the head of the Muslim community, should be elected. *Shias,* or *Shi'ites,* held that the caliph should be a descendent of the Prophet Muhammad. The majority of South Asian Muslims are Sunnis, though there are significant Shia minorities in the region. In Pakistan, some 25% of the population are Shias, belonging mostly to the Ismaili and Ashariya sects. The Ahmadiya sect originated in the Punjab in the late 19th century and today forms a minority group in Pakistan. The Shias are represented in India by the Khoja and Bohra communities of Gujarat. Sizable Shia communities are found in Indian cities such as Bombay, Hyderabad, and Lucknow.

Islamic mysticism, called *Sufism* in Western literature, played a significant role in the spread of Islam in South Asia. Wandering Sufi ascetics brought Islam to the common people and are held to be responsible for mass conversions in the region. Sufi saints and their poetry and music are particularly important in the cultural traditions of the Punjabis, Sindhis, and Bengalis. Sufi shrines are major centers of pilgrimage for Muslims in South Asia.

⁶MAJOR HOLIDAYS

The Muslim New Year begins with the sighting of the new moon in the month of Muharram. This month is associated with the period of mourning Shias observe for the martyrdom of Hussein, Muhammad's grandson, on the 10th day of Muharram in the year AD 61 (AD 680). Observances continue over 10 days, with the last day marked by processions with *ta'zias,* wooden towers decorated with tinsel, colored paper, and flowers that are meant to represent Hussein's mausoleum. The use of these towers is a particularly Indian tradition. Young men in the procession, stripped to the waist, will beat themselves with whips or even cut themselves with knives and razor blades in a ritual of mourning for Hussein.

Id ul-Fitr marks the end of Ramadan. It begins with the sighting of the new moon. People make the prescribed offering of alms to the poor then proceed to the 'idgah (a special place of worship for the Id festivals) or the mosque for prayers. At the end of prayers, members of the congregation embrace and salute each other by saying, "Id Mubarak" ("Blessed Feast"). The rest of the day is taken up with giving gifts to children, visiting relatives and friends, and entertaining guests. Id ul-Adha, known in South Asia as Bakr-Id, is celebrated in the last month of the Muslim year during the time of the Hajj. Muslims throughout the world sacrifice animals (goats, sheep, camels) at the time that pilgrims to Mecca are performing the sacrifice at Mina. The Feast of Sacrifice commemorates Abraham's willingness to sacrifice his only son, Ishmael, to God.

Whereas Muharram and the Ids are celebrated throughout the Muslim world, South Asian Muslims have festive days linked to the veneration of Sufi saints. These are celebrated at the shrine *(dargah)* where the saint is buried and may last several days. The annual *urs* (literally "wedding" because the Sufi believes at death his or her soul is united or wedded to Allah) festival commemorates the death anniversary of the saint. Worshipers file before the tomb in the mausoleum; they say prayers and offer money, incense, flowers, sweets, and sometimes a *chaddar,* a decorated cloth used as a covering for the tomb. The Quran is read in its entirety, and *qawwalis* are sung through the night. Free food is distributed to the poor. The most important *urs* in all South Asia is that of Khawaja Mu'in-ud-din Chishti, a 12th-century Sufi saint, held at Ajmer in India's Rajasthan State. As many as 300,000 people attend this annual festival.

⁷RITES OF PASSAGE

In their rites of passage, Muslims in South Asia follow the outlines prescribed by Islamic law (the *Shariah),* but they often combine these rites with local customs. At the birth of a baby, a *mullah* (Muslim priest) or a family elder repeats the Call to Prayer *(azan)* into the baby's right ear and a similar prayer into its left ear. On the seventh day after birth, or soon thereafter, the head-shaving ceremony is performed, often accompanied by the sacrifice of sheep or goats. At this time, the child is usually named as well. Some names are common throughout the Muslim world. Children may be named after the Prophet or his family (e.g., Muhammad, Ali, Hussein) or after the prophets (Ishmael, Ibrahim, Yusuf). Some common

Muslim names have the prefix "abd" (servant), as in Abdullah, the servant of Allah. There are, however, certain local South Asian traditions followed in naming children. The names of revered saints or shrines might be used, as in Sabir Bakhsh or Qalandar Bakhsh. Bakhsh means "bestower of gifts," and the first part of the name refers to a local saint. In southern parts of the country, last names such as Desai, Patel, or Majumdar that denote the occupation or office held by one's forefathers are common to both Muslims and Hindus. In Kashmir, last names such as Pandit that are specifically Hindu names may be used by Muslims.

Circumcision *(sunnat)* is a ritual that every male Muslim undergoes. The operation was normally performed by a barber, although today it is increasingly done in the hospital immediately after birth. Although the ceremonies associated with circumcision vary throughout the region, the rite is seen by many to be an initiation into the Muslim community.

Physical puberty is not marked by any special ceremonies. From this time, however, both boys and girls are expected to observe the customs set out in religious law. The education of both sexes in social and religious practices begins at an early age and is initiated by the *Bismillah* ceremony soon after a child is able to speak and understand things. Older children receive more formal religious instruction. In some Muslim communities, girls reaching puberty adopt *purdah* and are generally secluded from the company of males who are not close family members.

Burial rites follow the rules laid down in the Shariah, although local customs and traditions sometimes result in regional variations. Immediately after death, the body is ritually bathed and wrapped in a white shroud in preparation for burial. Mourners, led by a priest, say prayers over the corpse, which is then taken in procession to the graveyard. The body is buried with its face turned towards Mecca. Various ceremonies are performed for the deceased, lasting a minimum of 40 days and as long as a year after the time of death.

8 INTERPERSONAL RELATIONS

The most common greeting of Muslims in South Asia, and the world over, is "Salaam alaikum" ("Peace be with you"), often accompanied by a gesture in which the hand is touched first to the chest, then to the forehead. The correct reply to this is the sentence, "Wa alaikum as Salaam" ("And also unto you"). In the towns of northern India, especially in Lucknow, the secular phrase, "Adab arz" ("I pay my respects to you") is common. Less formally, men shake hands and friends embrace each other. "Sahib" and "Begum" are the Muslim equivalents of "Mr." and "Mrs."

9 LIVING CONDITIONS

Muslim lifestyles in South Asia vary according to factors such as occupation, social status, and regional cultural traditions. For example, the Bohras were a Hindu trading caste who converted to Islam. They remain a prosperous, mercantile community in the towns and cities of western India. The agricultural laborer or peasant farmer in rural Bangladesh, by contrast, has quite a different existence. Muslims living in cities in India tend to gather in distinct neighborhoods. In rural areas, although Muslims may be found in mixed-caste settlements, it is more common to find villages in which the entire population is Muslim.

Muslim devotees buy food in a market to break the first day of fasting for Ramadan in Dhaka, Bangladesh. Ramadan is the holy month of fasting for Muslims. (AP Images/Pavel Rahman)

10 FAMILY LIFE

Despite the doctrine of equality taught by Islam, Muslim society in South Asia shows the caste structure that is typical of other South Asian communities. Though it does not have the religious dimensions of the Hindu caste system, it does influence social and economic relations. The highest-ranked Muslim groups *(ashraf)* include the Sayyid, Shaikh, Mughal, and Pathan, who trace their ancestry to the Muslim invaders who conquered South Asia. Ranked next are Muslim Rajputs, followed by the occupational castes, and then the lowest group, the Muslim sweepers.

Caste groups marry within their own castes, although the specific details of kinship systems and marriage tend to follow regional patterns. For example, Muslim society in South Asia is patrilineal and patrilocal, yet the Moplah community of South India is matrilineal and matrilocal like their Hindu neighbors. Under Islamic law, marriage is a legal contract *(nikah)* and should be an austere and simple affair. Local customs, such as dancing, the use of music, telling bawdy jokes, and ceremonial visits paid by the bride and the groom to each other's houses, are often followed. Marriages are arranged and a dowry given to the bride by her parents. Islamic law allows up to four wives, although monogamy is usually the rule. Divorce is also permitted.

¹¹ CLOTHING

The *salwar*, loose baggy trousers, along with the *kurta*, a long tunic-like shirt, is the common form of dress for Muslim men in South Asia. In rural areas, the salwar may be replaced by a *tahmat*, a length of cotton wrapped around the lower body like a sarong. A variety of headgear is worn, from different styles of turbans to round cotton caps. On formal occasions, the kurta is replaced among the upper classes by an *achkan* or *serwani*, a long tunic-like coat that buttons up to the neck. Women commonly wear the salwar, *kamiz*, and *dupatta* (scarf), or the *sārī*. Orthodox women in *purdah* cover themselves from head to foot in the tent-like *burqa* when they go out in public.

There is, however, an infinite variety of dress styles in South Asia that identifies the individual as a Pathan, a Punjabi, a Bengali, or a Sri Lankan. Regional dress is more a facet of regional culture than of religion.

¹² FOOD

Muslim food in South Asia reflects broad dietary traditions that are determined by factors like geographical location, climate, and local agricultural conditions. Thus, for Muslims in the north and west, wheat and other grains are the staple. In the wetter regions of the subcontinent, rice forms the basis of every meal. Even within these wheat and rice belts, there are regional variations in cuisine. There are, however, some food customs that are prescribed by religion. Pork is considered unclean and is never eaten by Muslims. Muslims are nonvegetarians and will eat the flesh of goat, sheep, and other animals. However, Muslims will only consume *halal* meat, i.e., the flesh of animals slaughtered by having the throat cut and drained of blood. For many Muslims, the cost of meat is prohibitive, and it does not form a regular part of their diet. Beef is not eaten by Indian Muslims in deference to Hindu feelings concerning the sanctity of cattle. Beef and buffalo-meat are available in Pakistan and Bangladesh. Alcohol is forbidden to Muslims by their religion, though many are lax in keeping this taboo.

In the northern areas of the subcontinent one finds the "Mughal" style of cooking. This emerged from the royal kitchens of the Mughal Emperors of India and uses a blend of herbs and spices rather than the hot spices of regular Indian cuisine. Mughal food includes a selection of meats and poultry served in sauces or cooked in yogurt; tandoori dishes baked in a hot, clay oven; flat breads; and rice dishes.

Muslims use no utensils, consuming food with their hands. Only the right hand touches food because, like all other peoples in the region, the left hand is used for personal ablutions. Unlike other groups, Muslims often take food from communal platters rather than from individual plates.

¹³ EDUCATION

Muslims form part of a broader social community and share in the educational characteristics of the general populations of South Asia. For example, low literacy rates in Pakistan (49.7%) or Bangladesh (43.1%) result in part from the rural nature of the population and the role children play in the agricultural economy. By contrast, Muslims in Sri Lanka show the same high levels of literacy as the population at large (90.1%). There are certain features that can be attributed to religion. The Muslim tendency to keep girls at home after puberty, for example, results in an imbalance of the sexes in secondary and higher education. This is also seen in lower literacy rates for women than for men.

Muslim institutions of religious education known as *madrasas* are found in most countries in South Asia and provide an alternative to state-run educational systems. Madrasas in Pakistan have been accused of promoting radical Islam and are seen as recruiting grounds for extremist terrorists.

Education opportunities for Muslims vary considerably throughout South Asia. The reform of Muslim education, in particular bridging the gap between "religious" and "worldly" knowledge, has been one of the main focuses of the efforts of a range of South Asian Muslim reformists and revivalists over the past century. Major problems in the countries of South Asia have been the focus on the "religious" and the general neglect of schools. In Pakistan, for example, even though federal government assists in curriculum development, accreditation and some financing of research, public education lies in the bailiwick of the provincial governments. There are reports of public schools that receive no books, no supplies, and no subsidies from the government. Thousands more are "ghost schools" that exist only on paper, to line the pockets of phantom teachers and administrators. By contrast, in the Indian state of Kerala, educationalists estimate that almost all Muslim children are in school, at least up to the 10th standard, numbers that compare well to that of other communities. Even though numerous small madrasas exist throughout the region, South Asia can still boast of institutions of higher education such as Aligarh Muslim University in India, the University of Karachi and the Bangladesh University of Engineering and Technology (BUET).

¹⁴ CULTURAL HERITAGE

Islam has made significant contributions to South Asian civilization during the 1,000 years it has been present on the subcontinent. Muslims in India achieved their greatest accomplishments under the Mughal emperors, and Akbar ranks among the great figures of India's past. He united virtually the entire continent under his rule, effected administrative reforms to run his huge empire smoothly, raised many Hindus to positions of high office in his government, and was a great patron of the arts. However, the Mughal Empire is but one thread of Islam in the tapestry of India's history. Urdu poetic traditions, Mughal miniature painting, Indo-Islamic architecture culminating in the Taj Mahal, the impact of the Sufi saints on Hinduism, and the custom of *purdah* are to name but a few Muslim elements in Indian culture and life. The heritage of Islam in South Asia is to be seen in areas as diverse as language and literature, art and architecture, science and medicine, dress, food, and social customs.

There is also a less positive aspect to the Muslim presence in the Indian subcontinent. Islam contributed to the virtual destruction of Buddhism in the land of its birth. Also, the historical legacy of conflict between Muslims and Hindus continues to find expression in the territorial fragmentation and communal violence of South Asia today.

¹⁵ WORK

Religion plays little role in determining the occupation of South Asian Muslims, who engage in activities ranging from agriculture to nuclear science. The occupational structure in rural society shows the caste hierarchy so typical of South Asia. The upper-class groups are mainly involved in agriculture. Ranked beneath them are the "clean" occupational groups, including the service castes and artisans such as goldsmiths, weavers, and stoneworkers. On the lowest rung of the ladder are the "unclean" menial groups.

[16] SPORTS

No popular or spectator sports are specifically associated with Muslims in South Asia.

[17] ENTERTAINMENT AND RECREATION

Muslims throughout South Asia have access to the modern entertainment and recreational facilities of the general populations among which they live. Poetry readings and performances of *qawwalis* are popular among educated urban Muslims.

[18] FOLK ART, CRAFTS, AND HOBBIES

Folk arts and crafts in South Asia are activities associated with particular occupational castes in specific regions, rather than with religion. For instance, the marble workers around Agra are descendants of stonemasons who were brought to the area by Shah Jehan to build the Taj Mahal. Today, they continue to produce the semiprecious stone-inlay work that graces the Taj itself. The designs are Muslim, the workers are Muslim, but this could hardly be called a Muslim craft. The Patua of Bengal are a Muslim caste that paints pictures of Hindu gods and goddesses for the local population. All that can be said is that across South Asia there are Muslim artisans engaged in carpet-making, weaving, painting, stone-masonry, and the numerous other arts and crafts that form part of the rich folk tradition of the Indian subcontinent.

[19] SOCIAL PROBLEMS

Among the many challenges faced by Muslims in South Asia are those related to the general social and economic character of the region. The bulk of the population, both Muslim and non-Muslim, live off the land. They face the problems of subsistence cultivators in any developing country—low productivity, land fragmentation, poverty, and illiteracy. Rates of population growth are high, and low standards of living are compounded by high population densities and pressure on available resources. Bangladesh, in particular, ranks among the lowest of the developing countries in many demographic and socioeconomic categories.

South Asian Muslims also face problems unique to their own countries. In Pakistan, for instance, certain Muslim sects are subject to discrimination from others in the Muslim community. Conflict between Sindhis (native Pakistanis) and muhajirs (Muslim immigrants from India) has resulted in violence and a breakdown of law and order, especially in the southern city of Karachi. Kashmir continues to be a problem for both Pakistan and India. Pakistan is also undergoing a political upheaval, with the assassination in December 2007 of Benazir Bhutto, leader of the Pakistan People Party (PPP), and the ouster of the Musharraf government in the general election held early in 2008.

Indian Muslims are faced with social and economic discrimination. Increasing hostility from Hindu fundamental-ists and the rise of Hindu political parties threaten the secular nature of India and the position of the country's Muslim minorities, although the last President of the country, A.P.J. Abdul Kalam, belonged to the Muslim community. The rise of the Bharatiya Janata Party (BJP), which controls six state governments and is involved in a ruling coalition in another six, is a Hindu fundamentalist party that promotes "Hindutva" (Hinduness). It was involved in the destruction of the Babri Masjid mosque in Ayodhya (Uttar Pradesh State) by Hindus in 1992, and the subsequent violence and bloodshed that left hundreds of Muslims (and Hindus) dead across northern India. The BJP, with Narendra Modi as Chief Minister, formed the state government of Gujarat when hundreds of Muslims were killed after the burning of a train containing Hindu pilgrims at Godhra in 2002. Modi was accused of standing by and doing nothing while Hindus killed Muslims in revenge for the train burning. Communal and sectarian conflict remains one of the most widespread problems facing Muslims in South Asia today.

In Sri Lanka and Bangladesh, the problems facing Muslims are somewhat different. In Sri Lanka, Muslims are caught up in the civil war between the Sri Lankan government, which is primarily Buddhist, and the Tamil Tigers, Hindu rebels who want a homeland for Tamils on the island of Sri Lanka. In Bangladesh, where the majority of the population is Muslim, the situation they face is political instability. The leaders of both major political parties, Sheikh Hasina of the Awami League (AL) and Khaleda Zia of the Bangladeshi Nationalist Party (BNP), are under indictment on charges of corruption and the country is in the hands of a caretaker government that is supposed to oversee elections at the end of 2008.

[20] GENDER ISSUES

Muslim women in South Asia face the restraints of the Islamic religion. Thus, even though Islam espouses gender equality, women tend to be treated as second class citizens. Some groups favor *purdah* and many Muslim women wear the *burqa*, a robe that covers the woman's entire body with just netting through which she can see out. Honor killings are quite common in Pakistan—though men can be killed, the victims are usually female, because they have gone outside the community to pursue relationships. Divorce is easy for men to obtain, as Muslims in most South Asian countries live under Shariah law, while widow remarriage is permitted.

At least in Pakistan Muslims do not have to endure the communalism and casteism that is found in India. Despite India being a secular society, Muslims face discrimination of all kinds. With the rise of Hindutva, Muslims have faced hostility and animosity from Hindus. From Moradabad in 1980 to Gujarat in 2002, it is Muslim women who bear the brunt of Hindu anger, being sexually assaulted, raped, and burned to death. Moreover, since many Muslims in India were of the lower castes who converted from Hinduism to escape the inequities of the caste system, they are treated very much like lower caste Hindus. While many Muslim groups qualify for Scheduled Caste and Other Backward Class status, and thus are eligible for reservations, lack of education and political clout put them at a disadvantage. As usual, poverty, illiteracy and sociocultural customs place Muslim women at a considerable disadvantage in many societies in South Asia.

21 BIBLIOGRAPHY

Ahmad, Imtiaz. *Caste and Social Stratification among Muslims in India.* New Delhi: Manohar, 1978.

Akhtar, Shaheen. *The State of Muslims in India.* Islamabad: Institute of Regional Studies, 1996.

Engineer, Asghar Ali. *Muslims and India.* New Delhi: Gyan Publishing House, 2006.

Friedmann, Yohanan, ed. *Islam in Asia.* Vol. 1, South Asia. Boulder, CO: Westview Press, 1984.

Hasan, Mushirul. *Islam in the Subcontinent: Muslims in a Plural Society.* New Delhi: Manohar, 2002.

Ikram, S. M. *Muslim Civilization in India.* New York: Columbia University Press, 1964.

Jackson, Paul, ed. *The Muslims of India: Beliefs and Practices.* Delhi: Published for the Islamic Studies Association by Theological Publications in India, Bangalore, 1988.

Jain, M. S. *Muslim Political Identity.* Jaipur: Rawat, 2005.

—by D. O. Lodrick

NAGA

PRONUNCIATION: NAH-guh
ALTERNATE NAMES: Specific tribe names
LOCATION: India (Arunachal Pradesh, Assam, Manipur, and Nagaland states)
POPULATION: around 2 million (estimate)
LANGUAGE: Over 60 Naga dialects
RELIGION: Christianity; remnants of traditional religion
RELATED ARTICLES: Vol. 3: People of India

¹INTRODUCTION

Naga is a generic term used to designate a group of tribes inhabiting the hills and jungles of India's eastern borderlands. The name *Naga* may be derived from the Assamese word for naked (*naga*). Other possibilities are that it originates from *nāg* (mountain) and means hill people, or from *nok*, a local Naga word for "folk" or "people." The peoples of the area use the name of their specific tribe rather than "Naga," and their acceptance of this term is relatively recent.

The origins of the Naga tribes are veiled in obscurity. They are of Mongoloid stock and formed part of the successive waves of peoples who migrated into northeastern India over the centuries. Scholars suggest their original homeland may have been in central China, in the region between the Hwang He (Yellow) and Ch'ang (Yangtze) rivers. The Naga tribes have had prolonged contact with the Ahom peoples of the Assam Valley. Mention is made of them in Assamese chronicles dating from the 13th century AD onwards. British expansion into Assam in the 19th century led to conflict with the Naga and eventual annexation of the Naga region. At India's independence in 1947, the Naga tribes were unwilling to accept New Delhi's rule. On 14 August 1947, one day before India became a nation, the Naga National Council (NNC) declared the Naga people to be independent, and on August 15, when the Indian flag was hoisted at Kohima, headquarters of the then Naga Hills District, it was pulled down by the Nagas. Because of the Nagas' boycott of the first elections held in India, the Naga people were not represented in New Delhi in the first Parliament. During the 1950s, the Nagas set up the Naga Federal Government and took up arms against the Indian government. New Delhi could not allow any specific people on the Union's periphery to unilaterally declare themselves independent and, in 1955, sent in the Indian Army to restore order. Since then, Indian government troops have been fighting Naga rebels demanding an independent Naga state in the region. In 1957 the Indian government began diplomatic talks with representatives of Naga tribes, and the Naga Hills district of Assam and the Tuensang frontier were united in a single political entity that became a Union territory—directly administered by the central government with a large degree of autonomy. In July 1960 a further political accord was reached at the Naga People's Convention that Nagaland should become a constituent and self-governing state in the Indian union. Statehood was officially granted in 1963, and the first state-level democratic elections were held in 1964. This was not satisfactory to the tribes, however, and soon agitation and violence increased across the state—including attacks on Army personnel and government institutions—as well as instances of civil disobedience and non-payment of

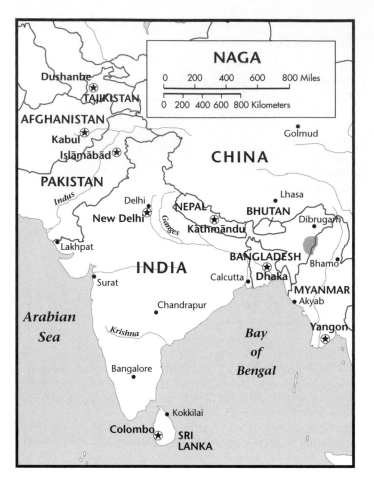

NAGA

0   200   400   600   800 Miles

0   200 400 600 800 Kilometers

taxes. An agreement, known as the Shillong Pact, was reached by the Indian government and the NNC in 1975. However, a section of hardcore militants in the NNC disapproved of the Shillong Pact and decided to go underground to start a more radical separatist movement. This led to the formation of the Nationalist Socialist Council of Nagaland or the NSCN in the late 1970s. The nucleus of the group that founded the NSCN included Isaac Chishi Swu, T Muivah, and Khaplang. The NSCN started an underground Naga government, complete with a council of ministers led by a prime minister. The NSCN received plenty of support in the form of arms, ammunition, cash and other resources from the People's Republic of China, Pakistan, and Bangladesh. However the NSCN suffered from a split in the late 1980s and broke into two factions, the NSCN (IM), led by Isaac Swu and Muiviah and the NSCN (Khaplang). The peace process in Nagaland has been complicated by violence and conflict between the rebel group factions. On 25 July 1997 Indian Prime Minister Inder Kumar Gujral announced after talks with the Isaac group of the Nationalist Socialist Council of Nagaland that the Indian government was declaring a cease-fire or cessation of operations with effect from 1 August 1997 for a period of three months. The cease-fire has been extended (it was in effect in 2008), while talks between the Indian government and Naga rebels continue. However, violence—mainly between Naga and Naga—also continues, with a third armed Naga faction, the National Socialist Council of Nagaland (Unification), or the NSCN(U), appearing in late 2007. There has been much violence in the Naga-inhabited ar-

eas of India, mainly involving conflict between different rebel factions. The violence between these factions led to more than 40 deaths in April–May 2008 alone.

²LOCATION AND HOMELAND

Naga tribes are present in four states of northeastern India (Arunachal Pradesh, Assam, Manipur, and Nagaland), as well as in neighboring areas of Burma (Myanmar). Their main concentrations, however, are in Nagaland where they make up over 90% of the state's population. The 2001 census reported a population of 1,990,036 people on the state of Nagaland, of whom 1,741,992 were Nagas, divided between 16 tribes. The more important of these are the Ao Naga, Sema Naga, Konyak Naga, Lhota Naga, and Angami Naga (the discussion presented in the following pages is based primarily on the Angami Naga). Most of the major ethnographic works on the Nagas have been undertaken by J. H. Hutton, J. P. Mills, and Christoph von Fürer-Haimendorf. Allowing for demographic increases and including Naga tribes outside Nagaland, the current Naga population in India is estimated to be just over 2 million people.

The Naga homeland lies in the rugged hills southeast of the Assam Valley that form the border between India and Burma. Its landforms consist of tightly packed parallel ridges and valleys, covered with dense tropical and subtropical forests, running in a general north–south direction. The elevations of the ridges increase from 600 m (2,000 ft) in the west to 2,100 m (7,000 ft) in the east. Mt. Saramati, located in eastern Nagaland on the India-Burma border, rises to an altitude of 3,826 m (12,553 ft). The region experiences a monsoon climate, with annual rainfall varying between 180 cm and 250 cm (70–100 in). Temperatures are influenced by altitude and in summer range from 20°C to 40°C (68°F–104°F). Winters are relatively mild. The thermometer rarely drops below 4°C (39°F), although frosts can occur at higher elevations.

³LANGUAGE

Virtually every Naga tribe speaks its own language, and some 60 spoken dialects have been identified. Dialects might even vary from village to village. All of the Naga tongues belong to the Tibeto-Burmese branch of the Sino-Tibetan language family. The language used for intertribal conversation is a form of broken Assamese or pidgin called Nagamese. (A pidgin language is a simplified form of speech used for communication by people who speak different languages.) This is widely spoken in the region of Kohima, the capital of Nagaland. Many Naga are also familiar with Hindi or English.

The Naga languages are essentially oral, with the literary tradition being limited to folk songs. However, Christian missionaries in the area developed alphabets and grammars for some of the Naga tongues during the late nineteenth century, with the objective of making the Bible available to the Nagas.

⁴FOLKLORE

The Angami Naga myth of origin centers on a village of the eastern Angami Naga called Kezakenoma. There was once an old couple, so the story goes, who lived in the village with their three sons. Every day they used to spread their paddy (rice) on a great flat stone to dry. Because the stone was inhabited by a spirit, their grain had doubled when they came to gather it up in the evening. The three sons used to take turns spreading their paddy on the stone, but one day they quarreled bitterly over whose turn it was. The parents, fearing bloodshed, broke eggs on the stone, covered it with wood, and set it on fire. The stone burst with a crack like thunder, releasing the spirit, which rose to heaven in a cloud of smoke, and the stone lost its magical properties. The three sons then left the village and became the ancestors of the Angami, Lhota, and Sema tribes of the Naga.

5 RELIGION

The Naga see their world as alive with supernatural forces that influence every aspect of their lives. They believe in a supreme creator named Kenopfu ("birth spirit"). She is always seen as benevolent, and when Angami Naga live good lives, their souls go to her dwelling place in the sky. There are also gods called *terhoma*, who vary from deities with specific functions to vague spirits of nature inhabiting jungles, streams, and stones. Among the more important of these are Rutzeh (the bringer of sudden death), Maweno (the goddess of prosperity), and Tekhu-rho (the god of tigers). Gods and spirits can be either good or evil and have to be worshiped, appeased, or even challenged by humans. The Naga spirit world is also inhabited by the souls of the dead.

There are many kinds of specialists who deal with the religious aspects of Naga life. One of the most important of these is the *Kemovo*, who must be a direct descendant of the village or clan founder. The Kemovo directs all public ceremonies and is a source of genealogical and historical knowledge for his village and clan. The *Zhevo*, on the other hand, is indispensable for performing certain personal rituals. The term *genna* refers to the complex of magico-religious ceremonies around which Naga life centers. Some gennas are communal, e.g., relating to the agricultural cycle or the prevention of illness, while others are individual and are associated with life-cycle events. Various prohibitions on individual behavior *(kenna)* and community activity *(penna)* form part of the genna observances. Ritual acts of offering associated with the genna are called *nanu*. The Naga sacrifice both chickens and pigs, but of particular note is their custom of sacrificing the *mithan*, a species of domesticated cattle *(Bos frontalis)*.

Although many elements of traditional religion survive among the Naga, most are Christian. Missionaries (American Baptists, in particular) who entered the Naga Hills in the 19th century set out to convert the naked, headhunting tribes they found living there. By 1947, about half of the Naga population had accepted Christianity. This number has been increasing in recent decades, and the 2001 census showed 90.01% of the Naga in Nagaland State as Christian.

6 MAJOR HOLIDAYS

Gennas (rites of worship) make up the festival cycle of the Naga. The Angami Naga observe 11 of these annually, with others celebrated at less frequent intervals. Gennas vary in duration but are invariably accompanied by *penna* (community restrictions) and *kenna* (personal restrictions). The Sekrengi genna, for example, is performed to protect the community from illness during the coming year. At this time, the village is in strict penna for five days. Work and travel to and from the village are prohibited. Men are kenna and have to eat separately and abstain from sexual relations. Five more days of *nanu* (ritual offerings) are observed, when work in the fields is totally banned. Gennas commonly involve animal sacrifice, the eating of special foods, such as dog-flesh, the wearing of ceremonial dress, and dancing and singing.

7 RITES OF PASSAGE

Every stage of a person's life is accompanied by individual *gennas* (rites). Immediately after birth, and before the cutting of the umbilical cord, a mother is fed on rice-beer, rice, and the flesh of a hen that has been touched by the newborn child. The husband, and sometimes the entire household, is under *kenna* (personal restrictions) for a period of time. Birth ceremonies end on the ninth day, when the father and mother take the baby to the fields. There, they pretend to work, take some food and drink, and then return to the village. Ears are pierced at a young age, although no formal ear-piercing ceremony is held. A name is given to the child after omens are read. The root *vi* ("good") is common in Angami Naga names, as in Vinile ("keeping good") or Viyale ("let your share be good").

At the age of about six years, a boy takes his place with the men in the community. He is expected to strangle a cock with all the other males of the village as part of the Sekrengi genna and stays with the men in ceremonies where the sexes are segregated. There is no ritual to mark puberty or the first wearing of men's clothes. The *Morung* or dormitory where young, unmarried men sleep is an important institution among tribes such as the Ao Naga and Memi Naga, though less so for the Angami Naga. Youth are allowed a considerable degree of sexual freedom before marriage.

When a death occurs, mourners gather, bringing cattle, rice, and rice-beer. The cattle are sacrificed and the meat distributed in a manner that would reflect the wishes of the deceased. The body is placed in a wooden coffin, along with the seeds of various crops, rice-beer, and the person's own drinking cup. A fire-stick (a piece of wood used for making fire), spears, an ax, and a live chicken are buried with the corpse. These are for the dead person to use in the next life. A bitter seed known as *gadzosi* is placed between the dead person's teeth. This is so the soul may pass by Metsimo, the spirit who guards the path to paradise. The Naga dig their graves either in front of the house or along a village path. Burial takes place at dusk. The following day, men come to the grave site in ceremonial dress to challenge the spirit who has carried off the dead person. They place the skulls of slaughtered cattle on the grave, as well as the dead person's shield and weapons (if a man), and personal belongings. Sometimes a life-sized wooden effigy wearing the ceremonial dress of the dead person is erected over the grave. A tomb of stone slabs is often built up over the grave site. Various feasts and animal sacrifices complete the funeral rituals.

8 INTERPERSONAL RELATIONS

Any Naga who can afford it performs a series of social *gennas* (rites) that confers on him or her high social status in the community. These "Feasts of Merit," each of which is more elaborate and costly than the preceding one, must be performed in a particular sequence. The rituals include ceremonial pounding of paddy rice (from which rice-beer is made) and sacrifices of pigs and *mithan* (cattle) whose flesh is consumed by the entire community. Those who perform the second-most important of these gennas *(Lisu)* are entitled to mount massive wooden horns *(kika)* on the roof of their house. The skulls of the sacrificed mithan may be hung on the house, and stylized mithan horns carved on its walls. Two wooden posts, the man's being Y-shaped, are erected in honor of the husband and wife who carried out the genna. The highest of the social gennas is *Chisu,* or "stone-pulling." The young men of the village or clan (sometimes hundreds in number) don their ceremonial dress, go out into the jungle, and pull a large stone back to the village. The stone is erected as a monolith to commemorate the genna. The event is, of course, accompanied by drinking, singing, and dancing.

⁹LIVING CONDITIONS

Naga settlements are located on hilltops. In the past, the villages were heavily fortified against attack by neighboring tribes. Wooden or stone walls and defensive ditches surrounded the village, with access limited to a heavily guarded gate or a few protected entrances. Even within the village, a clan neighborhood *(khel)* would be protected by a wall. Although the need for these is gone, their remains can be seen throughout the region. Near the entrance to the part of a village occupied by a particular clan is often found a large stone that is venerated by the clan and that formerly played a role in the headhunting *genna* (rite). Other features of the Naga village are its graves, as well as the stone pillars erected as memorials to individuals or to commemorate gennas. Angami Naga villages have lookout posts, once used to watch for approaching enemies, which rise over 9 m (30 ft) above the village itself.

In an Angami Naga village, houses are arranged in no particular order (although among some tribes they have an easterly orientation). A typical Angami Naga house has one story and measures 10–20 m (30–60 ft) in length and 6–12 m (20–40 ft) in width. The floor consists of leveled earth. The front half of the house is used for storage and contains a bench for pounding rice. A wooden partition sets this off from a room that contains the hearth and also low platforms used for sleeping. At the very back, there is another compartment extending the entire width of the hut that holds the beer vat, which is made of a hollowed log. Household utensils and furnishings include earthen pots for cooking, baskets for storage, jars for carrying water, wooden platters for eating, and rough wooden stools.

There are four "degrees" of houses that reflect the social position of its occupant. Typically, a house has a frame of wooden posts to which bamboo matting walls and a thatched roof are fixed. The eaves extend low to the ground, so that the structure has the look of an A-frame, but with a less-steeply angled roof. A person who has performed certain social gennas lives in a house of the second degree. He or she is entitled to place bargeboards (ornamental boards that hide the beams) along the front gable. One who has performed the *Lisu* genna may extend these boards to form "house horns" above the roof line that may stand 10 m (30 ft) above the ground. This is a house of the third degree. The rare house of the fourth degree has a roof made of wooden shingles in addition to the house horns. The houses of the wealthy are carved with stylized motifs including *mithan* (cattle) heads and "enemies teeth," a sign of the successful headhunter.

¹⁰FAMILY LIFE

The Angami Naga are divided into exogamous clans *(thino).* In modern times, however, the real exogamous unit seems to be a subdivision *(putsa* or "kindred") of the clan. Marriage may be informal, a man simply taking a woman into his house, where they remain *kenna* (under personal restrictions) for a day.

The ceremonial marriage, however, is a matter of status and is much more elaborate. Marriage negotiations are concluded between the families involved, omens are read, sacrifices are made, and a bride-price is paid. Although individual practices vary among the Naga tribes, there is usually a fair degree of freedom in the selection of a mate. The Angami Naga are monogamous, but divorce is allowed and common. The position of women in Naga society is generally low. Among some tribes, a woman is not allowed to inherit land. On the other hand, a woman is very much an equal partner in domestic affairs and also participates in the family's agricultural activities and trade.

¹¹CLOTHING

There is some variation in the dress of the Naga tribes. Some tribes go naked, like the Naked Rengma. Others, such as the Lhota, wear a type of loincloth called a *lengta.* Worn by males, this is a narrow girdle that is wrapped around the waist. One end is drawn down at the back, brought through the legs, and then tucked into waist at the front, where it hangs down like a flap. The lengta widens at the front to conceal the wearer's genitals.

The traditional dress of the Angami Naga man is a short black kilt that reaches to mid-thigh. Three or four lines of cowry shells are generally sewn on the kilt. In the past, three lines meant the wearer was a warrior; and four, that he had taken a head in battle. A long cotton cloth is wrapped around the body over the kilt. Among the Angami Naga, this is usually black, with broad, vertical red and yellow stripes running down the border. The color of the cloth and the stripes vary among the Naga tribes. Ornaments include a wide, multistrand necklace of beads, ivory armlets, and black cane rings worn just under the knees. The Angami Naga woman wears a type of sleeveless bodice, formed by wrapping a piece of cloth under one arm and fastening it on the opposite shoulder. Another piece of cloth wrapped around the waist and falling to the knees creates a skirt. Necklaces and bracelets are common, but usually there are no ornaments on legs or feet. The hair of unmarried girls is shaved or cropped short. Ao Naga girls are tattooed upon reaching puberty.

For ceremonial occasions, a woman simply adds to her everyday dress two scarlet tassels of dyed goats' hair hanging down from the ears and puts on as many bracelets as she can find. Ceremonial dress of men, however, is quite striking. A bearskin fringe surmounted by a wheel of hornbill feathers is worn on the head. A warrior might wear a headdress of *mithan* (cattle) horns, boar tusks, tiger claws, and hornbill feathers. Wooden rosettes are placed at the ears, and colored cane armlets and gauntlets, leggings, sashes, and other ornaments and decorations are added. Spears and shields complete the ceremonial dress, which clearly harks back to the warlike character of the Naga tribes in the past.

¹²FOOD

Rice is the main food of the Naga, with potato, maize (corn), wheat, and millets also supplementing their starch intake. Meat plays a much more important role in the Naga diet than it does among other rice-eating peoples of South Asia. Pork, chicken, and beef are commonly eaten. The entire community feasts on *mithan* (cattle) after sacrifices, and dog-flesh is regarded as a delicacy. The Angami Naga are essentially omnivorous and will eat almost anything that can be hunted and caught in the jungle, from elephant (now rare) to crows and snakes. Some foods are *genna* (i.e., forbidden) because it is believed that some of their qualities pass on to the person who eats them. Thus, the Angami Naga prohibit their women from eating male goat meat because they fear that they will acquire the animal's "lecherous" tendencies. Certain prohibitions also exist on the eating of tiger meat. Meat is usually cooked together with vegetables (e.g., tubers, beans, spinach, gourds, etc.) along with chilies. Food is served on large wooden platters from which people help themselves with their fingers. Rice-beer (*zū*) is drunk throughout the day. Some tribes chew tobacco, while others smoke it through a water pipe.

13 EDUCATION

Christianity is closely identified with modernity by the Naga, and followers of the Christian religion tend to be better educated than non-Christians. This, of course, reflects the importance Christian missionaries placed on education as a means of spreading their faith. Literacy among the Naga tribes varies, but it is on average higher than among other tribal groups in India, being reported as 65.8% in the 2001 Census of India. Literacy among the Konyak Naga was reported as low as 40.2% in the 2001 census, but it reaches as high as 85.9% among the Ao Naga. The value placed by the Naga on education is seen in the fact that some 80% of children below the age of 14 years were attending school in 2001.

14 CULTURAL HERITAGE

Much of Naga heritage focuses on the warlike past of the Naga tribes. The taking of a head was a sign of a warrior's courage and skill and entitled him to the appropriate insignia on his clothing and even on his grave. The elaborate ceremonial dress of the Naga, and some of their dances, also hark back to a time when the Naga tribes were in constant conflict. Singing and dancing are an important part of Naga life. The Angami Naga, for example, have love songs, songs to be performed at particular *gennas* (rites), songs to be sung in the fields, songs for pounding rice, etc. All the Naga tribes have oral traditions of myth, folk tales, and songs that embody the legendary history and beliefs of the Naga people.

15 WORK

The Naga practice shifting cultivation (*jhum*) and terraced agriculture by which they grow crops for trade as well as for their own consumption. They raise animals such as the *mithan* (a species of cattle, also known as the *gayal*), other types of cattle, and pigs for food. Their resources are often supplemented by hunting and gathering in the forest, though this is becoming less important. Dogs are kept for hunting as well as for food, although a Naga will never kill and eat his own hunting dogs. Spears, and now guns, are the weapons used for hunting. Killing fish by poison is common among the Naga tribes. With the spread of education, many Naga have taken to trade, government service, and other professions.

16 SPORTS

Naga engage in athletic contests very much like those found in the West. These include the high jump and the long jump. High-kicking is a game in which young men aim at a mark set on a tree, using either one leg or both legs. The mark is raised when it has been reached by the contestants. Some sports reflect the warlike past of the Naga. Wrestling is popular, as are spear-throwing competitions. The *Kedohoh* is a type of war dance, in which a young man, armed with shield and weapons, spins and utters shouts as if challenging enemy warriors. Young boys play fighting tops, the object being to set one's top spinning and knock over an opponent's top with it. Gambling with cowry shells is a popular pastime.

17 ENTERTAINMENT AND RECREATION

Access to modern forms of entertainment is restricted to those who can afford it. Otherwise, the Naga find their entertainment in their rituals and folk traditions. These include tribal legends, ceremonial dances, songs, community rituals, and the observance of religious and social ceremonies. Christians participate in the social activities of their churches.

18 FOLK ART, CRAFTS, AND HOBBIES

The Naga weave cotton cloth, each tribe having its identifying colors and striped patterns. Their artistic and aesthetic sense is seen in their elaborate ceremonial dress, ornaments, woodcarvings, ritual objects, such as forked (Y-shaped) memorial and sacrificial posts, the abstract designs of animal heads that decorate their houses, and tattoos. The more utilitarian Naga crafts include the making of iron spearheads and weapons, clay pots, bamboo mats, and cane basketwork.

19 SOCIAL PROBLEMS

The Naga are caught up in the problems of political instability and ethnic conflict that characterize much of India's northeastern region. The dream of independence is still strong in the minds of the Naga, and separatists in Nagaland continue to resist the presence of India with force. Recently, several insurgent groups have coordinated their activities under the banner of the National Socialist Council of Nagaland (NSCN). Indian security forces are carrying out operations against the guerrillas and have been accused of serious human rights violations by foreign observers. Matters are complicated by intertribal warfare. In Manipur State, for example, numerous incidents have occurred in which Naga have killed members of the Kiku tribe, and the Kiku have retaliated in kind. In addition, corruption and extortion are said to be commonplace in the government. The generally unsettled conditions have reportedly led to an increase of alcoholism and drug use among the Naga population.

The Naga Nationalist Union, a popular underground organization, put forward the following four reasons why Nagas should have a separate state:

a) the Mongoloid Nagas are physically different from the Aryan Indians

b) the Nagas are not Hindus and, therefore, do not practice Hinduism's prohibition on beef-eating

c) the Hindu caste system goes against the egalitarian tribal system of the Nagas

d) the Nagas should live in a democratic state that allows the free exchange of goods rather that a state that imposes taxes.

All these reasons are based on the differing nature of Naga tribal society compared to the Hindu-dominated Union of India. One of the greatest fears of the Nagas is that they will lose their tribal identity in the face of domination by New Delhi.

The violent conflict among Naga rebel groups that differ on the future of the Naga people and state continues to be a problem. A Naga civil society tired of the ongoing violence continues to denounce the violence and condemns the killings, factional clashes and loss of innocent lives and loss of properties, and appeals for dialogue, peace, reconciliation, unity and good sense continue to pour in from greatly troubled Naga mass-based organizations. As recently as the summer of 2008, the Naga Students' Federation (NSF), an organization of 21 student unions, demanded that the ongoing violence in the Naga family must cease. However, the National Socialist Council of Nagaland (IM) General Secretary Thuingaleng Muivah has said the group would keep up its agitation as no alternative solution was in sight: "Nagas will have to go on fighting for their rights. This is a hard reality. So, we will have to go on resisting."

It seems no end is in sight to the struggle in Nagaland, though it is unlikely that New Delhi can accede to demands for Naga independence.

20 GENDER ISSUES

Even though Naga society is patriarchal in nature, the rigid hierarchical structure of Hindu society, based on caste is non-existent in Naga society. The Nagas have a marked sense of "equality" based on community participation irrespective of sex, and they have hardly been influenced by the social stratification endemic in Hinduism and the Hindu caste system. By all considerations the Nagas still have a traditional society, although Christianity, education, urbanization have made considerable inroads into Naga society.

Women are regarded as playing a significant role in society. Traditional Naga culture and custom expect women to be obedient and humble, to perform the role of wife, mother, childbearer, food producer and household manager. The mother is the first to rise before the crack of dawn and start a day's work and has the prime responsibility for looking after the children, caring for the sick, cooking, storing food, feeding domestic animals, fetching water, and cleaning and washing. Women do not inherit ancestral property and, though they do have the vote, are not well represented on the political scene. There is, however, no emphasis on the bearing of male children—in fact, Naga families tend to prefer that their firstborn be daughters.

Naga women have played an important role in keeping the peace process on track in Nagaland. Women have helped stop violence between competing Naga factions and also between Nagas and the Indian security forces. Women's organizations such as the Naga Mothers' Association (NMA) and the Naga Women's Union have been actively involved in negotiating and mediating for peace and justice for the Nagas, and, today, the NMA and Naga Women's Union, Manipur (NWUM) are participating in the on-going cease-fire between the government of India and the Naga insurgents. The Indian government and the NSCN (I-M) would find it difficult to walk away from the peace table without provoking widespread public disaffection, largely as a result or pressure brought by organizations such as the NWA and NWUM. Such women's groups were integral to sustaining the current cease-fire, despite the strains following the arrest of Muivah in Bangkok, Thailand, in 2000, tension over the territorial extension of the cease-fire to all Naga areas, and endemic cease-fire violations. The continued support of women's organizations will be critical to the success of any political solution negotiated between the government of India and the Naga insurgents.

However, despite their advantages, Naga women have to overcome the effects of the ongoing civil war. In addition, like many women in South Asia, they have to struggle with poverty, illiteracy, sexual discrimination, lack of inheritance, poor nutrition, and difficulty of access to health care facilities.

21 BIBLIOGRAPHY

Aier, I. L. *Contemporary Naga Social Formations and Ethnic Identity.* New Delhi: Akansha Pub. House, 2006.

Elwin, Verrier. *Nagaland.* Shillong: P. Dutta, 1961.

Hutton, J. H. *The Angami Nagas.* 1921. Reprint, London: Oxford University Press, 1969.

Ramunny, Murkot. *The World of Nagas.* New Delhi: Northern Book Centre, 1988.

Vitso, Adino. *Customary Law and Women: the Chakhesang Nagas.* New Delhi: Regency Publications, 2003.

Zehol, Lucy, ed. *Women in Naga Society.* New Delhi: Regency, 1998.

—by D. O. Lodrick

NAXI

PRONUNCIATION: NAH-SEE
ALTERNATE NAMES: Muoshayi, Moxieman, Nari, Naheng,
    Malimasha, Yuanke, Bangxi, Muoxie, Moshu, and Wuman
LOCATION: China
POPULATION: 308,893
LANGUAGE: Naxi and Chinese
RELIGION: Dongba, Lamaism, Taoism, and Christianity
RELATED ARTICLES: Vol. 3: China and Her National Minorities

¹INTRODUCTION

As early as the 4th century AD, the ancestors of the Naxi lived around Yanyuan in south Sichuan. They were called Muoshayi in Chinese ancient books. Later on, they reached the Jinsha River and Yalong River and gradually migrated south to areas around Lijiang and Binchuan in northern Yunnan. There, they became prosperous and called the Moxieman. They established their own political administration, Moxiezhao, which was later integrated into the Nanzhao Kingdom in the first half of the 8th century. Areas around Lijiang, however, became an area of fierce rivalry between Nanzhao and Tubo (the ancient regime of the Tibetans). In the mid-13th century, the army led by Mongolian aristocrats passed the Lijiang area to attack the Dali Kingdom and were welcomed by the Mu clan, ancestors of the Naxi. Thereafter, hereditary headmen of the Mu clan were appointed by the Yuan (1271–1368), Ming (1368–1644), and Qing (1644–1911) dynasties. They represented a great force at the juncture of Yunnan, Sichuan, and Tibet, and played the role of a strong pillar of the Chinese central government to rule over this area. Owing to the close contact with various nationalities over many centuries, the economy and culture of the Naxi have been greatly influenced by those of the Chinese, the Tibetans, the Yi, and the Bai.

²LOCATION AND HOMELAND

Amounting to 308,893 in the 2000 census, the Naxi mainly inhabit Lijiang Naxi Autonomous County; they also form an important part of the ethnically composite population of Weixi, Zhongdian, and Ninglang counties in Yunnan Province and Mangkang County in Tibet. Jinsha, Lancang, and Yalong are three important rivers flowing through the areas inhabited by the Naxi and criss-crossing a varied topography of high mountain areas, plateaus, basins, and canyons, with an average height of 8,800 ft above sea level. Although the climate fluctuates considerably depending on altitude and season, rainfall is abundant and the land suitable for cultivation. The Jinsha River winds through a famous forested area. The Tiger-Leaping Gorge of Jinsha River is one of the deepest gorges in the world. The river cuts a deep course between the Yulong and Haba mountains, which reach an altitude of some 13,000 ft. Powerful torrents gush down a drop of more than 1,000 ft.

³LANGUAGE

The Naxi language belongs to the Sino-Tibetan family, Tibeto-Burman group, Yi branch. There are two dialects, eastern and western. Many people are bilingual (Naxi and Chinese). There were two traditional writing systems. The first was ideographic as well as pictographic (Dongba writing); the second was syllabic (Geba writing). These writing systems were not used by the Naxi people at large but were usually reserved for the priests of the Dongba religion (Bon shamanism originating from Tibet) to record poems, folklore stories, and rituals. An alphabetic writing based on romanization was created in 1957.

Naxi is a self-given name. "Na" means "big and black" and "Xi" means "men." Different branches of the Naxi call themselves Nari, Naheng, Malimasha, Yuanke, Bangxi, Muoxie, and Moshu. In China, the Naxi were traditionally known as Wuman (Black people). Naxi has been their unified name since 1954.

⁴FOLKLORE

Tradition has it that the first man of the world, Hengu, had five sons and six daughters. They married each other, incurring the wrath of the Supreme God, manifested by earthquakes and volcanic eruptions. All the brothers and sisters died except the youngest brother, Li'en, who hid in remote, thickly forested mountains. The Supreme God sought to kill him. In despair, he met a lesser god who gave him a goat, a dog, a rooster and 10 kinds of cereal crops. Following the god's instructions, Li'en killed an ox, made a bag with its skin, and put the animals and the crops inside the bag. Knowing about it, the Supreme God tried to destroy the bag and its content by fire, thunder, and turbulent streams. The leather bag floated in the air for seven months and finally dropped on a cliff. Li'en cut it open and let out the animals. He busied himself by planting crops and sometimes hunting, but lived in solitude. He sought help again from the lesser god, who told him: There were two celestial women living on the Twin-Star Cliff. One of them was very beautiful but not good, while the other was very good but not beautiful. The god repeatedly admonished him that the latter was the one he should marry. However, when he met the beautiful fairy maiden, he fell under her spell. After the marriage, the beautiful maiden had four children. The first time she gave birth to a pine and a chestnut; the second, to a snake and a frog; the third, to a bear and a pig; and the fourth, to a monkey and a chicken. Li'en was deeply disappointed. He asked for help again. After he implored for a long time, the lesser god finally promised to help him propose to the good fairy maiden. He succeeded in marrying her after innumerable hardships. She gave birth to triplets, but after six years, they still could not talk. Li'en and his wife offered sacrifices to the gods of heaven and earth. One day, the children began to speak, but in different languages. The eldest spoke Tibetan; the second spoke Moxie (Naxi); the youngest spoke Chinese. They became the ancestors of the Tibetan, Naxi, and Chinese peoples.

⁵RELIGION

Most Naxi believe in a religion called "Dongba"; others believe in Lamaism (the Tibetan version of Mahayana Buddhism) or Taoism. Since the 19th century a small number of them have converted to Christianity.

Dongba is a primitive polytheistic religion. Its name comes from its founder, Dongba Shiluo. He was a precocious child, endowed with many supernatural gifts. He killed an ogress and a number of malevolent ghosts, delivering the people from many evils. Another theory, however, says that Dongba is originally a branch of the original, pre-Buddhist Tibetan religion, called "Bon" (a form of Shamanism). The Naxi believe that the innumerable spirits that fill the world are ambivalent, hav-

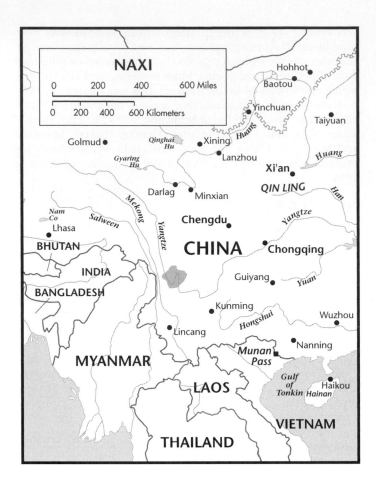

NAXI

should be put on the table. Thus, the whole family is reunited. They feed the dog rice and meat; based on the dog's appetite, they forecast the production and the price of rice and pigs. On the first of January, they offer sacrifice for boys and girls who have reached 13 years of age.

The twentieth of January (lunar calendar; Western calendar, between February 11 and March 9) is the Farm Tools Festival. It is a fair of farm tools, originating from a temple fair in the Ming Dynasty (1368–1644). Since the busy spring season is coming, an endless array of farm tools made of iron, wood, and bamboo, a wide variety of articles of daily use, as well as children's toys are exhibited on the square in front of the temple and on side streets.

The fifteenth of March (lunar calendar; Western calendar, between April 7 and May 5) is the Dragon King Festival, originally the date of a sacrificial offering to the Dragon King, now a fair of commodities among different nationalities.

From June 25–27 (lunar calendar; Western calendar, between June 22 and August 22) is the Torch Festival. Buffalo fighting, wrestling, and antiphonal singing are held in the daytime. In the evening, each household places a big torch on a nearby tree and many small ones in the courtyard. Children hold torches while dancing. Youngsters gather to dance while playing the reed-pipe wind instrument (*lüsheng*).

July 15 (lunar calendar; Western calendar, between August 9 and September 7) is the Mule and Horse Meeting. It is a colorful fair of large animals, among which the Lijiang and Yongning horses account for the greater part of the business (bidding). On this occasion, horse racing, antiphonal singing, and other recreational and sporting activities are also held.

⁷RITES OF PASSAGE

Among the Naxi around Lake Lugu, a rite of "adulthood" for boys and girls having reached 13 years of age is held on the morning on the first day of the lunar New Year. All families having a child of that age kindle a big fire in the firepool. The boy stands by a "male column" and the girl by a "female column." They stand with one foot on a grain bag and the other foot on the fat of a pig. Silver coins are put in their hands. This rite means that they will have endless fortune in the future. Helped by her mother, the girl puts on a new skirt; the boy, helped by his uncle (mother's brother), puts on new trousers; the *dongba* (shaman) recites the prayers. Finally, the boys and the girls kowtow to their mother, uncle, and other elder members of their family. After the rite, they are allowed to participate in some major productive labor and social intercourse.

The Naxi burial customs vary in different districts. Cremation is traditional. Around Lake Lugu, the funeral is organized by the *lama* as well as by dongba. As soon as someone dies, the family informs relatives and neighbors. The body is washed. Bits of silver, tea, and butter are put into the mouth of the dead. Butter is also applied to the nose and ears. Linen bands are used to tie the body up into a squatting posture; it is then put inside a linen or white cloth bag. A cave is dug beforehand in the rear of the central room. The bag containing the body is put down into the cave, with its face toward the gate. The cave is covered by a plank or an iron pan, which is further covered by a layer of earth. It is the exclusive duty of the son or nephew of the dead to cover the plank or pan with earth. This is called the "temporary stay of the corpse," the duration of which is decided by the lama, but it should not exceed 49 days. During these days, rela-

ing the power to bring disaster upon them and to grant them good fortune. They ascribe spirits to the sky, earth, sun, moon, mountain, water, fire, wind, rain, thunder, lightning, wood, snow, etc., and believe that the spirits never die. Therefore, they hold frequent offerings to various gods, even the Livestock God and Crop God. Images of gods appear on the instruments of the shaman (called *dongba*), including drums, bells, swords, chains, forks, bows, arrows, and conch. The religious activities involve almost every aspect of the Naxi's life, such as offering sacrifices to spirits and ancestors, marriage, birth, naming, burial, festival, divination, selection of dates for important events, exorcising ghosts, curing disease, praying for a good harvest, expiating the sins of the dead, etc.

⁶MAJOR HOLIDAYS

Besides seasonal sacrificial offerings, major holidays are the Spring Festival, the Farm Tools Festival in January, the Dragon King Festival in March, the Torch Festival in June, and the Mule and Horse Meeting in July (all according to lunar calendar).

The Spring Festival (lunar New Year; Western calendar, between January 21 and February 20) is a grand holiday. The New Year's Eve is a very important occasion. The traditional custom of cooking a pig's head and butchering chickens is still followed. These sacrificial rituals aim at honoring the Kitchen God and welcoming ancestors to return to celebrate the New Year together with the family. Various dishes and fruits are prepared for the dinner party. If a family member is away, a bowl and a pair of chopsticks symbolizing his/her presence

The youngsters are free to meet socially. During festivals and fairs, girls band together and prepare to meet boys. Holding catkins in their hands, the young men also get together in groups. According to custom, girls always bring some candies or cakes with them. The young men beg the girls they like for some refreshments. They make an appointment to meet in the evening by the riverside or by the bonfire. They express their passions through singing, but they are not allowed to sit side-by-side or face-to-face. A distance of 2–3 m (7–10 ft) is necessary for their conversation or antiphonal singing.

⁹LIVING CONDITIONS

There are two traditional types of housing. One is a wood-arris house. The walls are built by piling up logs and roofed with planks, which are pressed by stones. A firepool is at the center of the room. The beds are set up on frames. The second type is a tile-roofed house. The foundation is built by piling up hewn rocks. The lower portion of the wall is built with bricks or adobes, and the upper portion with planks. The roof is rather large, with eaves stretching outward to protect the wooden walls. There are many compounds of houses around a common courtyard, similar to the quadrangle of Beijing. There are also storied houses for large families.

Highways have been built in recent decades. Most of the Naxi townships and villages have bus stops. There are well-equipped hospitals in counties and cities. Pestilence and epidemic diseases have been eradicated since 1949.

¹⁰FAMILY LIFE

There are three types of families. One is the patrilineal family, usually an extended family consisting of three to four generations. The property is handed down from the father to his sons. The eldest son will be the patriarch when his father is old and infirm. When they break up the big family and live apart, an "old-age field" is provided for the parents and will be cultivated on their behalf by their sons. The position of women in a family is rather low. They have no right of inheritance. This type of family is now mostly replaced by small monogamous families, and the position of men and women in a family is more or less equal.

Naxi families living around Lake Lugu are matrilineal. For instance, a woman lives with her brothers and sisters, her mother with her mother's brothers and sisters, and so on for women of each generation. All the family members are generations of women with their sons and daughters. In the family, there are no husbands and wives, because they practice a unique form of friendship marriage called *azhu* ("friend"). An adult man goes to a woman's house at night and they sleep together. He returns to his mother's house at dawn to participate in productive labor there. The man and the woman call each other azhu. Their relationship is by no means stable. It may last as long as several years, or as short as one or two nights. Most of the men or women have six or seven azhu in their lives. The men usually begin to have an azhu at 17 or 18 and the women at 15 or 16. If the boy and girl are offspring of the same maternal ancestor of less than five generations, the azhu relationship is taboo; if more than five generations, there is no prohibition. Difference in age, seniority in the family or clan, and nationality are not limitations. To renounce the azhu relation is easy: either the woman closes her door to the man or the man ceases to call at her house. In some cases a simple message is sent to

Naxi ethnic minority people practice traditional dance in Suhe village near Lijiang, China. Lijiang is a popular tourist destination. (AP Images/Eugene Hoshiko)

tives and friends bring oblations and offer their condolences. When the days are over, the dongba priest is invited to read the scriptures to open a way for the soul of the dead. At the same time, the body is taken out of the cavern and put inside a cubic wooden coffin. When the coffin is sent to the crematorium, eight lama sit cross-legged while reciting the scriptures. Then, the body is again taken from the coffin and placed on firewood for cremation. They bury the ash in a secluded place. The Naxi in Lijiang District have exchanged the fire burial for a ground burial. There are four or five successive rituals during the funeral, which is organized mainly by the dongba.

⁸INTERPERSONAL RELATIONS

When entertaining guests, the host usually offers buttered tea, corn candy, millet candy, and stir-fried sunflower seeds. An alternative is bitter tea, potato, and stir-fried cornmeal. If the host gives a banquet, stewed chicken, fried eggs, pork, bean curd, and wine are served.

the opposite side stating that the azhu relation is terminated. The children born from the azhu relationship are members of the woman's family. The man has no concern for the children. A family usually consists of two to four generations, with an average of seven or eight people. In rare cases, the family members amount to as many as 20 to 30. The head of the family is usually an aged or a capable woman. She is also the organizer of the sacrificial offerings. The work is divided according to age and sex. The property is distributed according to a principle of egalitarianism.

The third type is the bilateral family, in which patrilineal and matrilineal families coexist. The children borne by the woman before and after marriage live in the same family, but only those who were born after her marriage are counted on the paternal side. All the family members have equal inheritance and proprietary rights. The bilateral family appears to be the combination of the matrilineal (linked to the azhu relationship) and of the patrilineal family structure of the Naxi.

In areas where the Naxi do not practice azhu, the wedding is an elaborate ceremony and the matrimonial customs show a marked influence of the Chinese traditional model.

11 CLOTHING

The men's dress is not very different from that of the Chinese. In winter, men wear a short garment of worn-out fur or a wool cloak. The middle-aged and the aged wear a long robe buttoned on the side, which was the traditional male dress of the Chinese and the Manchus during the Qing Dynasty (1644–1911). Men always put on a cap or a hat; if not, they wrap their head with a cloth. Women's clothes vary in different districts. In some areas, they wear a vest and a loose garment over their knees and a pair of trousers that is covered by a multipleated skirt. In other areas, they wear a short garment and a multipleated skirt with a broad waistband of cloth. Girls comb their hair into braids or wear a kerchief. Married women always wrap their head with a long cloth. The colors of their dress are mostly black, blue, and white.

12 FOOD

The staple foods of the Naxi include wheat, rice, and corn. In mountainous areas, highland barley, buckwheat, and potato are added as a supplement. They usually take rice only at dinner. Wooden tablewares are used. Meat is served in equal portions by the man of the house. Daughters are in charge of other dishes. The Naxi like sour and spicy food, drinking, and smoking. Ham cakes and sour fish are some of their main delicacies; these will be served to guests or offered as gifts.

13 EDUCATION

In Lijiang, 94% of school-age children attend local schools. In areas around Lake Lugu, primary schools have been set up in larger villages and middle schools in the counties. However, school attendance is not as high as that of the Lijiang District. There are a number of college students and scholars of Naxi nationality throughout China and some studying or teaching abroad.

14 CULTURAL HERITAGE

A major feature of Naxi culture is the combination of poems, songs, music, and dance, such as "Wenmaida," "Arere," and "Sanduo." There is also ancient orchestral music performed on indigenous or Chinese instruments including bamboo flutes, vertical flutes, reed-pipe (lüsheng), two- and three-stringed violins (huiqin and sanxian), plucked string instruments (pipa, zheng, and se) conches, and drums. "Dongba Classic Dance" (performed during rituals) and folk dance follow the general pattern of dancing while singing. A number of Naxi dances are imitations of animal movements: "White Lamb Dance," "White Deer Dance," Lark Dance," "Ox Dance," "Golden Peacock Dance," etc.

The Naxi have a rich literature including myths, folklore, stories, long poems, folk songs, fables, fairy tales, proverbs, riddles, and children's songs. Among them, "The Creation," preserved intact in Dongba scripture, is the most famous. It describes the story of Li'en, the earliest ancestor of the Naxi. Narrative poems, such as "The War of Black and White" and "Hunting Song," are also masterpieces of Naxi literature.

15 WORK

The main occupation of the Naxi is agriculture. Because of their long tradition of livestock husbandry, they are also experts in raising horses. Their horses are small and tough, good for climbing hills and mountains. Some people grow Chinese medicinal herbs. Ludian in Lijiang is the "home of medicinal herbs."

16 SPORTS

Swinging, horse racing, wrestling, and arrow shooting are traditional sports of the Naxi. In addition, there are two unique sports. One is the "Rotating Race" (damoqiu), for which the teenagers are most enthusiastic. A pole is erected on the ground. Its upper end is pared in a concave hemispherical pit. A transverse pole is pared at the middle point into a round ball-like shape to fit in the hemispherical pit of the vertical pole. Some vegetable oil is added for lubrication. Two players facing each other prostrate the upper part of their body on the transverse pole. They exert their strength on tiptoe in turn when touching the ground, thus making the ends of the transverse wave up and down as it rotates faster and faster. It requires much skill and is physically quite exhausting. The other sport peculiar to the Naxi is the "Dongba Jump." The athletes dress like warriors, imitating the martial practice of the ancient dongba, who were both priests and warriors.

17 ENTERTAINMENT AND RECREATION

Movies and television are quite popular in the Naxi districts. The public cultural events in their cities are not different from those of the Chinese. But, the Naxi still prefer their traditional forms of entertainment, singing, dancing, swinging, and damuoqiu.

18 FOLK ART, CRAFTS, AND HOBBIES

Carpets, brass and copper ware, embroidery, ornaments, silver plated wooden bowls, and tanned leather products are famous Naxi crafts. The ancient Naxi architecture (as is found in the governmental offices of local officials, temples, ancestral halls, arches, pavilions, stone tablets, and pagodas) are universally admired. The Naxi talent for sculpture and carving is vividly demonstrated in the wooden statue of the thousand-arm Buddha in Dajue Palace and in the openwork of the doors and windows of civilian houses. The thousand-arm Buddha in Fuguo Temple, the Sakyamuni in Longquan Temple, and group of warring animals in Beiyue Temple are masterpieces of clay sculpture.

[19] SOCIAL PROBLEMS

The Naxi have succeeded in maintaining their socio-economic sovereignty. They live in quite compact communities, cut off from the main lines of communication and transport in China. There is a marked rural/urban imbalance in their overall development. For instance, the Naxi around Lake Lugu still preserve their ancestral matrilineal type of marriage and family, while the Naxi living in and around Lijiang City have been integrated in the "Chinese way of life."

[20] GENDER ISSUES

The Chinese constitution states that women have equal rights with men in all areas of life, and most legislation is gender neutral. However, there are continued reports of discrimination, sexual harassment, wage discrepancies, and other gender related problems. The gap in educational level between women and men is narrowing with women making up 47.1% of college students in 2005, but only 32.6% of doctoral students.

China has strict family planning laws. It is illegal for women to marry before 20 years of age (22 for men), and it is illegal for single women to give birth. The Family Planning Bureau can require women to take periodic pregnancy tests and enforce laws that often leave women with no real options other than abortion or sterilization. Though minority populations were previously exempt from family planning regulations, policy has changed in recent years to limit minority population growth. Today, urban minority couples may have two children while rural couples may have three or four.

Prostitution and the sex trade is a significant problem in China involving between 1.7 and 5 million women. It involved organized crime, businessmen, the police, and government workers, so prosecution against prostitution has limited success. In 2002, the nation removed homosexuality from its official list of mental illnesses, and though it is still a taboo topic, homosexuality is increasingly accepted, especially in large, international cities.

[21] BIBLIOGRAPHY

Chiao, Chien, N. Tapp, and Kam-yin Ho, ed. "Special Issue on Ethnic Groups in China." New Asia Bulletin, no. 8, 1989.

Dreyer, June Teufel. China's Forty Millions. Cambridge: Harvard University Press, 1976.

Eberhard, Wolfram. China's Minorities: Yesterday and Today. Belmont: Wadsworth Publishing Company, 1982.

Gustafsson, Bjorn A., Shi, Li, and Sicular, Terry, eds. Inequality and Public Policy in China. New York: Cambridge University Press, 2008.

Heberer, Thomas. China and Its National Minorities: Autonomy or Assimilation? Armonk, NY: M. E. Sharpe, 1989.

Lebar, Frank, et al. Ethnic Groups of Mainland Southeast Asia. New Haven: Human Relations Area Files Press, 1964.

Lemoine, Jacques. "Les Nashi." In Ethnologie régionale II (Encyclopédie de la Pléiade). Paris: Gallimard, 1978.

Ma Yin, ed. China's Minority Nationalities. Beijing: Foreign Languages Press, 1989.

McKhann, Charles F. "The Naxi and the Nationalities Question." In Cultural Encounters on China's Ethnic Frontiers, edited by Stevan Harrell, 39–62. Seattle: University of Washington Press, 1994.

Miller, Lucien, ed. South of the Clouds: Tales from Yunnan Seattle. University of Washington Press, 1994.

Ramsey, S. Robert. The Languages of China. Princeton: Princeton University Press, 1987.

Shin, Leo Kwok-yueh. The Making of the Chinese State: Ethnicity and Expansion on the Ming Borderlands. New York: Cambridge University Press, 2006.

Wiens, Harold J. Han Chinese Expansion in South China. New Haven: The Shoestring Press, 1967.

—by C. Le Blanc

NEGRITO (PINATUBO AETA GROUP)

PRONUNCIATION: nuh-GREE-toh (pee-nah-TOO-boh EYE-tah)
LOCATION: Philippines (Luzon); Malay Peninsula
POPULATION: Over 7,600 (2000)
LANGUAGE: Dialect of Sambal
RELIGION: Traditional animism
RELATED ARTICLES: Vol. 3: Filipinos

¹INTRODUCTION

Before the advent of the Austronesians, small hunter-gathering bands of Australo-Melanesians inhabited islands in Southeast Asia and the Malay Peninsula. The modern Negritos (Spanish for "little blacks") represent a remnant and physical specialization of this stock. "Pure" Negritos differ from the dominant Southern Mongoloid populations of the region in being shorter of stature (less than 1.5 m or 5 ft tall), darker in complexion, and having kinky rather than straight hair. They can be found in the Sierra Madre (Dumagat), in the Ilocos Mountains, and in the greatest numbers in the Zambales Mountains, all on Luzon. Outside the Philippines, they are found on the Malay Peninsula (Semang) and, formerly, in the Andaman Islands in the Bay of Bengal. Possible mixed groups characterized by wavy hair can be found in Panay, Negros, Palawan (Batak), and Mindanao (Mamanua). Of all these, only the Andaman Islanders spoke in historical times a language unrelated to a neighboring Austronesian language (as in the Philippines) or an Austro-Asiatic one (on the Malay peninsula). In the Philippines, lowlanders generally refer to Negritos as "Aeta" or some variation thereof (the word seems to be a garbled form of the Malay word for "black," *hitam*). Upon the Spanish arrival, Negritos appeared to inhabit the edges of highlands throughout the archipelago (for instance, the Visayan island of Negros received its name because its mountains were particularly, but not uniquely, full of them); legends such as those of Panay [*see* **Hiligaynon**] honored Aeta as the original possessors of the land.

This article will focus on the Zambales Negritos in general and the Poon Pinatubo Aeta ("the people of the thigh of Mount Pinatubo") in particular; henceforth, all uses of the word "Aeta" will refer only to this group.

In their reliance on swidden (shifting-cultivation) agriculture, among other characteristics, the Pinatubo Aeta show more prolonged contact and intermarriage with lowlanders than do other Negrito groups. They may have originally lived in the lowlands themselves, as the plants they know are lower-altitude species (most Aeta know 450 types of plants, 75 types of birds, and most types of mammals, snakes, fish, and insects, including 20 kinds of ants). The Aeta have been in particularly intimate contact with the lowland Sambals, adopting the Sambal language, agricultural techniques, spirit beliefs, curing rites, and burial customs, but adapting them to their own culture.

Although older Spanish documents record Aeta working as woodcutters for Sambal and as companions of Sambal chiefs, the relation has overall not been a peaceful one. Sambals regularly made raids into Aeta territory in order to capture slaves (some to be sold as far away as Batangas until fairly recent times); the indemnity for murder could be paid with an Aeta slave. Moreover, as each Sambal man had to prove his worth by killing someone, Aeta often fell prey to their headhunting. To be sure, Aeta also abducted other Aeta in order to sell them to lowlanders, and parents even sold their children (after lowlanders had plied them with liquor).

Lowlanders often dispossessed Aeta of land, buying it with blankets, rice, or machetes. In the 18th and 19th centuries, Pampangans drove Aeta from the lands under Mt. Pinatubo in order to open fields for rice and sugarcane; a Don Angel Pantaleon acquired the forest that would later become Clark Air Force Base in this way.

Some Aeta did submit to Spanish administration, but the unsubjugated majority fled deeper into the mountains, particularly after raiding lowland villages that would in turn send revenge expeditions after them. The Spaniards attempted to mediate these conflicts, granting the title of *capitán* to cooperative Aeta leaders but on the whole failing to get the Aeta to settle in the lowlands.

In 1917, the American regime established a 4,720-hectare (11,660-acre) reservation for the Pinatubo Aeta; this, however, in practice remained accessible to lumber companies and sugarcane planters. World War II is a well-remembered time of chaos among the Aeta. Japanese ambushed Aeta, while the Aeta protected shot-down American pilots. In gratitude, General MacArthur himself granted Aeta the right to free movement through the base boundaries so they could scavenge; he also had food distributed to them from time to time. During the Vietnam War, Aeta taught American pilots how to survive in the jungle (e.g., camping in the forest, making fires, cooking without smoke, getting water from vines and trees, hiding from enemies, etc.).

The eruption of Mt. Pinatubo during the Aquino presidency disrupted Aeta life, perhaps irrevocably. A great number of Aeta perished under the falling ash and lava. Many of the survivors drifted to Manila, earning money by selling souvenirs, such as stones from Pinatubo. The conversion of the former U.S. military base at Subic Bay (between Zambales and Bataan provinces) into a resort area, as well as an export-processing zone, has opened up some new opportunities for Aeta, for instance, as guides for eco-tourists exploring the nature reserves on former base lands, or at least giving them the chance to sell souvenirs to tourists in front of hotels, shopping centers, and bus stations much closer to home than Manila.

²LOCATION AND HOMELAND

According to 1975 figures, 23,000 Negritos lived in the Philippines. Of these, 15,000 inhabited the Zambales mountains along the west coast of central Luzon, concentrated especially on the lower slopes of the 1,610-m-high (5,280-ft-high) volcano, Pinatubo. Except for the inaccessible places, the mountain was deforested and covered with cogon grass. Its recent eruption has catastrophically changed these Aeta's homeland. According to the 2000 census, 7647 inhabitants of Zambales province identified themselves as "Aeta."

In contrast to other Negrito groups whose numbers are declining due to disease, malnutrition, and assimilation, the Zambales Aeta population is actually growing rapidly. The surrounding lowlands have nonetheless come to be occupied by Sambal, Pampangan, Ilocano, and Tagalog settlers. In Zambales province in 2000, 27% of the population was Sambal, 27.5% Ilocano, 37.8% Tagalog; Cebuano immigrants were already half as numerous as Aeta.

³LANGUAGE

The Zambales Aeta speak a dialect of the Sambal, the language of the surrounding Christian lowlanders that is most closely related to Kapampangan.

⁴FOLKLORE

Other than the *anito* and *kamana* (good and bad spirits, respectively) Aeta recognize a variety of other supernatural entities and phenomena. When traveling beyond his or her local area, a person must pray to the *laman nin lota*, the spirit of the earth; otherwise, he or she might end up walking around the same place forever. A *balanding* is a spirit that, if it catches a person in the forest, immediately kills him or her. A *binagoonan*, another evil spirit, appears as a big man (described as resembling an American) who sits on the bough of a tree and has a body that glimmers like fire.

A benign spirit is the *patianak*, a dwarf resembling a child. The *balandang* is a powerful spirit, leader of the wild pigs and deer, who greatly influences the outcome of hunting. *Timbi* are thunder (*kilat*) attacks whose effects can be averted through medicines; kilat strikes when it is angered by people teasing earthworms or laughing at mating animals. Aeta carry talismans, such as stone tools left behind by ancient people.

⁵RELIGION

Aeta distinguish generally well-disposed spirits (*anito*) from inherently malicious ones (*kamana*). Anito dwell in forests, bamboo thickets, streams, rocks, huge tree trunks, etc., and only harm people when provoked. Kamana, on the other hand, have no fixed place and roam around, either victimizing the dead or actually being the dead themselves.

Those violating the property rights of spirits (e.g., by cutting down a tree belonging to one) suffer misfortune and illness; they must compensate the spirits with gifts (*langgad*) of tobacco, wine, and red cloth (procured from lowland traders). Burning certain plants creates smoke that drives off evil spirits (today kerosene lamps are favored for this).

Some Aeta believe that each person has a single soul (*kaelwa* or *kalola*) that can leave the body: if the soul leaves temporarily, it causes sickness; if it leaves permanently, it causes death. Others say that a person has multiple souls: if one leaves, sickness results; if all go, death occurs. The Aeta avoid the spirits of the dead, making offerings to them only at *patay* harvest festivals. The spirits of the dead ascend to Mt. Pinatubo and there lose their individual identity, merging into "all the dead" (*minaci*).

Manganito are male or female spirit mediums who can procure the rights from spirits to use land and can cure illnesses through *anituwan* rites. The better-known healers are greatly respected and feared by lowland Filipinos in neighboring areas. Actually, only groups that have adopted much lowland culture have such spirit mediums; in more isolated groups, a person with an ailment simply consults another who is more knowledgeable about medicinal plants.

In order to diagnose a patient's condition, the manganito blows on the sick person's body to send his or her guardian

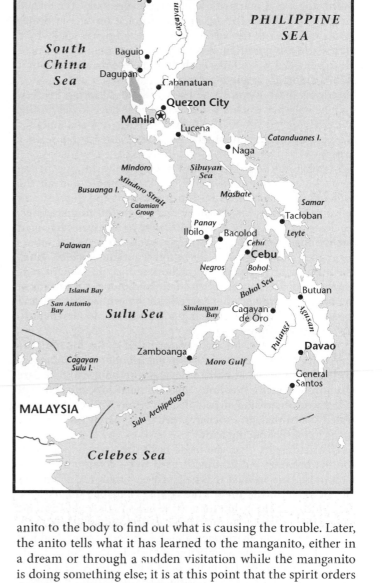

anito to the body to find out what is causing the trouble. Later, the anito tells what it has learned to the manganito, either in a dream or through a sudden visitation while the manganito is doing something else; it is at this point that the spirit orders that the anituwan séance be held.

During the séance, someone plays the *gitara nin lae* (handmade lowland guitar) in a quick rhythm (*magteteg*); this stirs another person to dance the *talipe* (jumping and making swift hand movements) until he or she tires out, and another dancer replaces him or her. Eventually, the manganito joins the dancing and soon dominates it. When the spirits possess the medium, the medium's body stops trembling, and he or she enters a trance and assumes a somewhat arrogant tone when questioned by those present as to what the spirit causing the disease wants. The séance also provides participants the opportunity to mention sources of group tension that might be causing the disease, which they normally would not be able to express.

⁶MAJOR HOLIDAYS

In December or January when food stocks are plentiful, large numbers of Aeta gather together in *iwi* or "fiestas of the spirits."

⁷RITES OF PASSAGE

The ideal pattern for marriage entails a gradual transition between single and married life in three stages: *hogo*, the formal marriage proposal; the *suson*, the negotiation of the bride-price; and *banhal*, the wedding feast. The hogo is made by a man's father or guardian. It is now more common for two people to get to know and like each other before marrying than it is for parents to arrange marriages. However, a man may on his travels meet a woman he likes without declaring his feelings; he will then ask his father to make the hogo to her family. In delivering the proposal, the father brings rice and a pig (or at least a chicken or can of sardines) to the woman's house after sunset.

Members of both kin-groups attend the suson, for all the man's kin contribute to the bride-price (*bandi*), and all the woman's kin partake in it. The negotiators use pebbles and twigs to represent the number and height of animals (pigs, chickens, and recently water buffaloes) to be given (delivered one by one as acquired). Formerly, bandi consisted of tobacco, maize, rattan, knives, cloth, forest products, *paltik* guns, and even cash. Today, bandi includes radios, portable phonographs, and rice, as well as machetes and money. The terms of the bandi agreement are generally set by oral agreement and remembered, but now Aeta might ask an Ilocano merchant to write them out in Ilocano.

After the suson, the man performs labor for his fiancée's family (bride-service, *manoyo* or *mangampo*) as a voluntary expression of his good will and to show his ability to take care of a family. During this time, the man must appear indifferent to the woman, avoid her, and behave properly. The wedding is sealed at a banhal, an expensive feast that is rarely held because of the burden of paying bandi.

Disagreements over the bride-price are a major source of conflict between kin-groups. It used to be common for Aeta men to capture women for their brides. Today, if the families do not agree to the union, the couple can elope (*mipowayo*); they hide in a remote hut for a while or go to the man's parents or relatives.

Formerly, Aeta abandoned a house where a person had just died. The corpse was wrapped and buried either horizontally or vertically beneath the house or at a distance. After a death, men would go on a headhunting raid (*mangayau*, perhaps a Sambal influence).

Today when a person dies, relatives, especially the women, gather around the deceased to wail. The family sends messengers to distant relatives and waits to bury the deceased until the relatives arrive or until the body begins to smell, whichever comes first. At least one night of mourning is observed for which the deceased is dressed in its best clothes or wrapped, with a glass of water and a plate placed next to the head. Close relatives sit around the body, while children and young people sit outside in a circle singing Tagalog or Ilocano love songs to drive away spirits (they pass around a firebrand, the one holding it having the turn to sing). Those Aeta under greater lowland influence observe nine days of mourning, ending with a final banquet (*pamisa*).

More-settled Aeta now use cemeteries, although the paths to them are overgrown because Aeta avoid them. Each mourner throws a clod of earth on the coffin before the grave is covered over, saying to the deceased, "*Agkayna mag-orong*," "Please don't come back." Some stamp their feet on the ground to drop their sorrow. The mourners may wash their face, hands, and feet in a river and step over a fire in front of the house to cleanse themselves of death.

⁸INTERPERSONAL RELATIONS

An encampment consists of 3 to 10 related families headed by the eldest male, who is assisted by other closely related males. Among more traditional groups, the encampment is an extended family that farms, hunts, and fishes together and sometimes cooks and eats together, using common utensils. Less traditional groups consist of families that function separately but remain in close association. The encampment is an exogamous unit, i.e., its members marry partners from outside the community, all of whose members contribute to and partake in bride-prices.

Aeta values stress harmony and downplay competition within the local community. Individuals in conflict with others tend to move away from the community before tensions become unmanageable. An informal council of older men resolves disputes through appeal and persuasion. The pressure of public opinion and the fear of supernatural punishment (e.g., for violating spirits' property rights without making a subsequent acknowledgment and offering compensatory gifts) also exert control on individual behavior. An offended party may publicly threaten the offender or his family; the threat pushes the community as a whole to put pressure on the parties to resolve their differences.

Aeta keep dogs for hunting and the occasional wild pig as a pet.

⁹LIVING CONDITIONS

Aeta live in scattered settlements or encampments of rarely more than three to four households (20–40 individuals). They move between a relatively fixed village and shifting swidden sites. The villages relocate every year or so after exhausting local resources or in case of epidemics or bad omens; they do relocate within a defined territory, however. The arrangement of dwellings follows no set pattern, although some anthropologists have noted that some villages take the form of a circle of huts around a central dancing place.

Houses are semipermanent structures of bamboo, banana stalks, and leaves. They are tent-shaped with one walled side where a low sleeping platform stands, with a hearth on the ground at the other end beneath a low sloping roof. Some more-settled Negritos have built houses of lowland style (*see* **Filipinos**). While traveling or hunting, Aeta use crude, floorless lean-tos for temporary shelter.

Zambales province is the poorest of the provinces of Central Luzon, which itself ranked third out of 17 regions in average annual family income). According to the 2000 census, 78.9%

of houses are lit with electricity, compared to 90.4% in Pampanga. 4.4% of households obtain water from springs, lakes, or rivers, compared to 0.5% in Pampanga. The proportions for those possessing their own household faucet were 20.8% and 27.2% respectively.

¹⁰FAMILY LIFE

Among the Pinatubo Aeta, the *mitata-anak* or nuclear family is less important than the grouping of related families living in the same encampment; this grouping is known by the name of its dominant male individual, e.g., "Hilay Pan Hokli" or "Mitata-Pan Hokli," which can be extended to include his children-in-law and grandchildren.

Parents traditionally contract marriage for the children while the latter are still young. Marriages are more often between people of different villages than those of the same village. First-cousin marriage is permissible after the performance of cleansing rituals. A man is permitted to take more than one wife, but this is rare. Divorce also seldom occurs because the relatives of the couple prevent it; if the woman is at fault, her family must return the bride-price (*bandi*).

¹¹CLOTHING

Traditional Aeta clothing was made of bark-cloth, but now people generally wear clothes bought from lowlanders, such as (for adult men) tee-shirts to accompany loincloths. Necklaces made of Job's tears (hard white seeds) are worn. Men used to wear tight boar's-hair arm and leg bands as a sign of bravery and as magical protection against injury. Formerly, Aeta beautified themselves with teeth-chipping, -pointing, and -blackening, as well as by cicatrization (making decorative scars, also a protection against disease).

¹²FOOD

About 85% of the Aeta diet comes from agricultural products: sweet potatoes, cassava, maize, dry-rice, taro, yams, and bananas. Following lowlanders, Aeta have developed a taste for rice, but, because dry-field varieties are not as productive, they still rely on root crops for the major part of their sustenance. Gathering supplies 7% of the diet: wild bananas and banana flowers, mushrooms, bamboo shoots, poisonous yams (*kalot*, requiring a long soak or several boils before they are safe to eat), fruits, nuts, berries, roots, honey, larvae, small frogs (*egik*), and insects (especially a certain kind of beetle). Hunting and fishing provide the remaining 8% of the diet: wild pigs, deer, birds, fish, and now pigs and chickens.

¹³EDUCATION

More-settled Aeta send their children to modern schools [*see* **Filipinos**].

¹⁴CULTURAL HERITAGE

Aeta dances include those imitating the actions of animals. They are also fond of telling stories (*istorya*) about their history or personal experiences, as well as those recounting folk legends.

¹⁵WORK

Aeta practice a highly inefficient form of swidden agriculture, intercropping root crops, maize, and rice (traditionally only root crops). They also gather a wide variety of wild plants.

Aeta traditionally hunt wild pigs and deer with dogs, fire, and bows and arrows. Crude homemade shotguns (*paltik*) were coming more and more into use (and nearly exterminating game animals in the process) until the government confiscated all firearms under martial law (declared in 1972). A wide variety of traps are used to catch smaller game and birds. Aeta now keep domestic pigs and chickens.

Fishing techniques include damming off streams, poisoning, trapping, and shooting with bows and arrows. Today, underwater fishing with spear guns has become popular; the swimmers use goggles made of wood and scavenged glass.

Traditional trade consisted of forest products, beeswax, and tobacco exchanged for lowlanders' salt, rice, metal, ceramics, and cloth. Scavenging from the dumpsites of American bases also provides Aeta with useful materials, such as scrap metal.

¹⁶SPORTS

See the article entitled **Filipinos**.

¹⁷ENTERTAINMENT AND RECREATION

More-settled Aeta may have access to modern entertainments; many now have radios and phonographs and enjoy Filipino pop music [*see* **Filipinos**].

¹⁸FOLK ART, CRAFTS, AND HOBBIES

Smithing is a major specialty, producing arrows, machetes, and even crude shotguns (*paltik*); arrowheads made in the Pinatubo area are traded all over the Zambales range. Aeta smiths follow taboos and rituals no longer observed by lowland Sambal smiths.

The skills to make bark-cloth are widely known but currently little used.

¹⁹SOCIAL PROBLEMS

See the article entitled **Filipinos**.

²⁰GENDER ISSUES

There is a strict sexual division of labor. Women occupy themselves with agriculture, gathering, and small-scale fishing, men with occasional hunting, and young men with underwater spear fishing. In planting a field, a line of men does make seed holes with dibble sticks, followed by a row of women inserting the seeds. Men spend most of their time away from home, trading, paying visits to relatives and friends, and participating in marriage negotiations. Although spirit mediums can be either men or women, the informal council that arbitrates disputes is composed only of older men, and the encampments to which Aeta families belong are identified by the name of the most dominant man.

According to the 2000 census, among the Aeta, men and women were about equal in number (50.9% vs. 49.1%). In the Zambales population as a whole, there were more females (50.9%) than males in elementary education, even though females were only 49.5% of the population over the age of 5 years—female predominance also characterizes all higher levels except high school.

²¹ BIBLIOGRAPHY

LeBar, Frank M., ed. *Ethnic Groups of Insular Southeast Asia*, Vol. 2, *The Philippines and Formosa*. New Haven, CT: Human Relations Area Files Press, 1972.

Scott, William Henry. *Barangay: Sixteenth-Century Philippine Culture and Society*. Quezon City, Manila: Ateneo de Manila University Press, 1994.

Shimizu, Hiromu. *Pinatubo Aytas: Continuity and Change*. Quezon City, Manila: Ateneo de Manila University Press, 1989.

—revised by A. Abalahin

NEPĀLĪS

PRONUNCIATION: nuh-PAW-leez
ALTERNATE NAMES: Nepalese
LOCATION: Nepal
POPULATION: 30 million (2008 estimate)
LANGUAGE: Nepālī (Gorkhali) is official language; over 36 other languages and dialects
RELIGION: Hindu majority (86.2%); Buddhist; Muslim; Christian; Jain

¹INTRODUCTION

The term "Nepālī" (also "Nepalese") describes the peoples of the mountain kingdom of Nepal. It includes a number of distinct ethnic and caste groups that have their own separate identities and customs, but who also share certain common cultural attributes and an historical association with Nepal. Of the modern nations of South Asia, Nepal is unique in that it is the only country of any size to have maintained its independence during the period of British colonial rule.

The Kathmandu Valley is the political and historical heartland of Nepal, and evidence points to cultures centered here as early as the 8th or 7th century BC. Indian inscriptions dated to the 4th century AD refer to a kingdom called "Nepala" in the Himalayan Mountains. Dynasties such as the Licchavis, Thakuris, and Mallas ruled the region at various times, but the birth of modern Nepal can to be traced to the rise of the Gurkhas in the 18th century. The ancestors of the Gurkha rulers are thought to have been Rajput princes fleeing from Muslim persecution in Rajasthan in western India. They established themselves in the mountains of what is now western Nepal in the mid-16th century. In 1768, Prithvi Narayan Shah, the ninth king in the Gurkha dynasty, conquered the Kathmandu Valley and moved his seat of power there.

By the beginning of the 19th century, the kingdom of Nepal extended along the Himalayas from Kashmir to Sikkim. However, disputes over its southern border led Nepal into conflict with the British in India. Defeat during the Anglo-Gurkha wars (1814–1816) saw Nepal's expansion halted and its borders fixed in their present locations. Sikkim, to the east, became a British protectorate. Much of the western part of the kingdom, and some territory in the productive lowlands in the south, were lost to British India. Following 1816, Nepal closed its borders to foreigners and did not reopen them until 1951.

In 1846, a young general named Jung Bahadur Rana seized power in Kathmandu. He appointed himself prime minister and made the office hereditary. For the next century, the kings remained nominal figureheads, but the Ranas were the real rulers in the country. Some instituted social changes, such as abolishing slavery and banning *satī* (suttee), which is the custom of wives burning themselves alive on their dead husband's funeral pyre. Most of the wealthy and autocratic Ranas, however, did little to improve the lot of the commoners and ruled very much as feudal overlords.

By the mid-20th century, the winds of political change sweeping across India were beginning to be felt in Nepal. The Indian National Congress, the nationalist political party that fought for India's independence from Britain, had its counterpart in the Nepālī National Congress. This organization

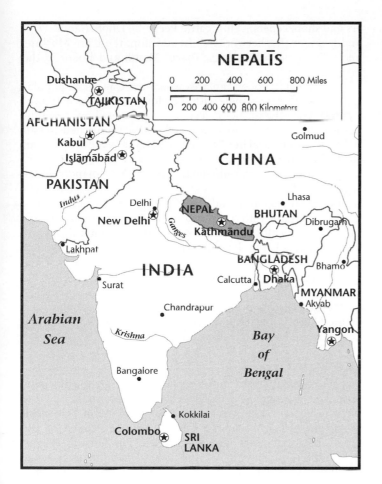

NEPĀLĪS

0   200   400   600   800 Miles

0   200 400 600 800 Kilometers

became the focus of opposition to the Ranas. The powerless king, a virtual captive in his palace, emerged as a symbol of the democratic hopes of his subjects. In 1950, the King of Nepal managed to escape to India. At this point, the Nepālī National Congress called for the overthrow of the Rana and proclaimed its own provisional government. After some inconclusive fighting, a compromise between the two rival parties was mediated by India. King Tribhuvan was restored to power and returned from exile in 1951, committed to establishing democracy in Nepal.

Although a representative form of government was instituted in 1959, within two years King Mahendra, Tribhuvan's successor, dismissed the parliament and banned political parties. He introduced a system of indirect government in which the prime minister and cabinet were chosen by the king. This system continued under King Birendra, who succeeded to the throne in 1972. Following two decades of periodic political unrest, a new constitution was proclaimed in 1990. This created a true parliamentary democracy, legalized political parties, and made provisions for a popularly elected legislature. The first general election under the new system was held in May 1991. King Birendra Bir Bikram Shah Dev continued to rule as a constitutional monarch, although his former powers had been severely curtailed.

On 1 June 2001 however, Crown Prince Dipendra was officially reported to have shot and killed his father, King Birendra; his mother, Queen Aishwarya; his brother; his sister; his father's younger brother, Prince Dhirendra; and several aunts,

before turning the gun on himself. Gyanendra, Birendra's brother, succeeded as King. However, on 1 February 2005 suspended the Parliament, appointed a government led by himself, and enforced martial law. The King argued that civilian politicians were unfit to handle the Maoist insurgency current in Nepal at the time. Telephone lines were cut, and several high profile political leaders were detained. Other opposition leaders fled to India and regrouped there. A broad coalition called the Seven Party Alliance (SPA) was formed in opposition to the royal takeover, encompassing the seven parliamentary parties who held about 90% of the seats in the old, dissolved parliament. A countrywide uprising began in April 2006, resulting in massive and spontaneous demonstrations and rallies held across Nepal against King Gyanendra's autocratic rule. Eventually, an agreement was made for the monarchy to be abolished, which it was on 25 May 2008, therefore ending 240 years of royal rule. Nepal became a Federal Democratic Republic with the prime minister becoming head of state.

The last decade of the monarchy was marked by the "Nepalese People's War," fought between Maoist insurgents and the Nepalese police and, later, the Royal Nepal Army. More than 12,800 people were killed during this conflict and an estimated 100,000 to 150,000 people were internally displaced during this time. The conflict disrupted the majority of rural development activities and led to the emergence of a deep and complex Left Front which, together with the Nepali Congress, was the backbone of the broadbased movement for democratic change in Nepal. In 1994 the Communist Party of Nepal (CPN) split, with the militant faction later renaming itself as the Communist Party of Nepal (Maoist). The war was started by the CPN (M) on 13 February 1996, with the aim of establishing the "People's Republic of Nepal." For 10 years the country was in the grip of civil war, with the Maoist insurgency initially commencing in the districts of Rolpa, Rukum, and Jajarkot in western Nepal and eventually spreading to 68 of the country's 75 districts. At first, the insurgency as seen as a police matter, but after Maoists attacked an army barracks in western Nepal in 2002 following failure of peace talks, the Army was called in to fight the insurgents. A considerable number of retired Gurkha soldiers of the British and the Indian Army inhabit many of the Maoist-affected areas and Nepalese security agencies suspected that these former soldiers along with retired soldiers and deserters from the Royal Nepalese Army (RNA) were involved in training the insurgents. Government estimates provided in early 2003 on the CPN-M strength indicated that there were approximately 15,500 combatants, 18,000 militia, 24,500 active cadres, 33,000 hard core followers, and 800,000 sympathizers, with Brahmans and Chhetris providing the political and military leadership. The war ended with a Comprehensive Peace Agreement signed on 21 November 2006.

As a result of the civil war, Nepal's greatest source of foreign exchange, its tourism industry, suffered considerably. A travel company, which published rankings of the popularity of tourist destinations based on sales, indicated that Nepal had gone from being the tenth most popular destination among adventure travelers, to 27th. The conflict also forced the young and able to seek work abroad in order to avoid the Human Rights Violations committed by the Government forces and the crimes committed by the Maoists.

²LOCATION AND HOMELAND

Nepal is a landlocked state on the northern mountain rim of South Asia. Its inhabitants number 29.5 million people (2008 estimate), living in an area of 145,391 sq km (56,139 sq mi), which is roughly the size of Iowa. Nepal extends 800 km (500 mi) in a generally east–west direction, but its north–south dimensions vary between only 125 and 225 km (approximately 80–140 mi). The country is surrounded on the east, south, and west by Indian territory, while China lies to the north.

Nepal is truly a mountain kingdom, with a quarter of its land over 3,000 m (9,843 ft) in altitude. The only lowland of note lies in the extreme south, where the country extends into the Ganges plains. A narrow belt, rarely exceeding 40 km (25 mi) in width and at one time a swampy, malaria-infested jungle, is known as the Terai. Over a third of Nepal's population and much of its agriculture and industry are found in this part of the country. The Terai is also the richest wildlife zone in Nepal and the home of several government wildlife reserves. The best-known of these is the Royal Chitawan National Park (now Chitawan National Park), designated a UNESCO World Heritage Site in 1984, which is a sanctuary for the endangered Bengal tiger and one-horned rhinoceros.

North of the Terai, the land rises to the Shiwalik Hills (750–1,500 m or 2,450–4,900 ft in elevation), before descending to a series of east–west running valleys known as *dūns*. From the dūns, the terrain rises steadily northwards through the Mahabharat Lekh, the Pahar (hill) zone, and the imposing main ranges of the Himalayas. The Nepal Himalayas contain eight peaks over 8,000 m (26,247 ft), including Mt. Everest, the world's highest mountain at 8,848 m (29,028 ft). Kanchenjunga, Dhaulagiri, and Annapurna are among the better-known peaks of this group.

The Kathmandu Valley lies north of the Mahabharat Lekh ranges at around 1,300 m (4,300 ft) above sea level. Formed by an old lake-bed, it is intensively cultivated and supports a dense population. It is the cultural and historical heart of Nepal, containing the modern capital of Kathmandu, as well as the medieval cities of Patan and Bhaktapur.

Nepal's climate and vegetation reflect the country's wide range of elevations. The Terai experiences conditions typical of the middle Ganges Valley. The mean temperature in June, the warmest month, exceeds 35°C (95°F), while winter temperatures drop to 10°C (50°F). Rainfall is received during the summer monsoon, with amounts varying from 200 cm (approximately 80 in) in the east to 100 cm (approximately 40 in) in the west. The natural vegetation consists of grasslands and *sāl (Shorea robusta)* forests. As one moves northwards into the mountains, temperatures decrease and rainfall increases. Vegetation changes to temperate pine and mixed forests. Above 4,000 m (13,100 ft), the climate is alpine, with short summers and long, severe winters. The higher elevations are under perpetual snow.

The ethnic composition of Nepal reflects its location between South Asia and Central Asia. The peoples of the Terai and southern Nepal are little different from their Indian neighbors. Caste remains the prime factor in social relations, and there is considerable freedom of movement and intermarriage across the border between Nepal and India. The mix of peoples in this area is typical of the Ganges plains. Brahmans, Rajputs, and Kayasths are the main land-owning castes. They are served by occupational castes such as the Nuniyar (trad-

ers and shopkeepers), Ahir (cattle-keepers), Dhobi (launderers) and Chamar (leatherworkers). In addition, there are Muslims and tribal populations (e.g., Tharu, Majhi, and Bodo) in the area.

Nepal's Pahar zone is an area where the Caucasoid populations of South Asia mingle with the Mongoloid physical type of Central Asia. The former category is represented by the Brahmans and Chhetris, upper castes who have dominated Nepālī political and cultural life. The powerful Ranas were drawn from the Chhetri (i.e., *ksatriya* or warrior) caste. The term "Newar" is used to describe the inhabitants of the Kathmandu Valley regardless of their ethnic origin. Peoples of Mongoloid descent in this Pahar region include the Gurung, Magar, Rai, Limbu, and other groups who traditionally have served as Gurkha soldiers. (Technically, there is no single ethnic group called Gurkha, the name being derived from soldiers of the Kingdom of Gorkha whose ruler conquered the Kathmandu Valley in the 18th century.) Other ethnic groups in the middle hills include the Tamang and the Thakalis.

The northern mountain belt is inhabited by peoples such as the Sherpas and Bhutia who are physically and culturally closely related to the Tibetans.

³LANGUAGE

Nepal's ethnic diversity is accompanied by linguistic diversity, with over 36 languages and dialects currently spoken by the Nepālī people. Groups in the northern mountain belt speak languages belonging to the Tibeto-Burmese branch of the Sino-Tibetan language family. These include Tamang, Magar, Rai, and Limbu. Sherpa and Thakal are Bhutia dialects virtually indistinguishable from Tibetan. Newari, a Tibeto-Burman language written in the Devanagari (Hindi) script, is spoken in the Kathmandu Valley. Nepālī, also known as Gorkhali, is spoken by 49% of the population (2001 census) and is the country's official language. It is the lingua-franca of Nepal and the Indian state of Sikkim, has official language status in West Bengal's Darjeeling district, and is also one of India's 23 official languages. An Indo-Aryan language related to Hindi, it, too, is written in the Devanagari script. Hindi, Bhojpuri, and Maithili, which are languages prevalent in adjacent areas of India, are widely spoken in the Terai. Also in the Terai are groups such as the Tharu and Danawar whose language shows elements of the Austro-Asiatic tongues widely associated with tribal groups in India.

⁴FOLKLORE

While each ethnic group has its own folk traditions, all Nepālīs share in the mythology of Hinduism and Buddhism. The Himalayas, for example, are regarded as the home of the gods. Here, in the "snow-abode" *(hima-ālaya),* is Gauri-Shankar, the peak where the god Shiva and his consort, Parvati, dwell. Annapurna, with her many peaks, is goddess of plenty. Ganesh Himal is named for Ganesh, the elephant-headed god of Hinduism. In Indian legend, every *rishi,* or yogi, who possesses divine power has a retreat in the mountain fastness of the Himalayas.

Another legend has it that, at the beginning of time, the Valley of Kathmandu was a beautiful turquoise lake. On this lake floated a lotus flower, from which shone a magnificent blue light. This was a manifestation of Swayambhu or Adi-Buddha, the first incarnation of Buddha. The lake was so beautiful, and

Nepalese farmers plant paddy in a field in Kathmandu, Nepal. More than 80% of people in the country make their livings by farming the steep terraced hills of the lower Himalayas. (AP Images/Binod Joshi)

the flame so sacred, that the devout came from far and wide to live along its shores, to meditate, and to worship. One such devotee was the sage Manjusri, who came from Central Asia to worship the flame. Wishing to approach the flame more closely, he sliced open the valley wall with his sword of wisdom. The waters of the lake drained away and the lotus settled on the valley floor. At this site, Manjusri built a shrine that was to become the sacred site of Swayambhunath.

⁵RELIGION

Nepal used to be the only Hindu kingdom in the world, before it was declared a "secular state" in 2006. However, although Hinduism is the dominant religion in the state, Nepālīs are highly tolerant of other religious beliefs. Freedom of religion is enshrined in law, which makes it illegal to proselytize (i.e., actively try to make converts) in the country. According to the 2001 Census of Nepal, the religious makeup of the population is: Hindu (80.6%), Buddhist (10.7%), Muslim (4.2%), Christian (0.5%), Jain (0.1%), and others, mainly adherents of local religions (3.9%).

Hinduism and Buddhism in Nepal have so influenced each other that it is sometimes difficult to distinguish between the two religions. Both Hindus and Buddhists, for example, worship at the Buddhist shrine of Swayambhunath. In addition, religion in Nepal has absorbed other elements that give it a

unique character. These include Tantric beliefs, aspects of the pre-Buddhist religion of Bon, and local animistic cults. Animal sacrifice accompanies almost every ritual and ceremonial event in Nepālī life. Nepālīs also worship *Kumārī,* the "living goddess," a young girl believed to be an incarnation of the Hindu goddess Parvati.

Swayambhunath and Bodhnath are major Buddhist shrines and centers of worship. The temple of Pashupatinath in Kathmandu, dedicated to the Hindu god Shiva, is viewed as one of the most sacred in all of South Asia. It is one of the few Hindu temples from which non-Hindus are barred.

⁶MAJOR HOLIDAYS

Nepal is a land of festivals. All the major Hindu and Buddhist celebrations are observed, as well as many that have their origins in ancient animistic cults. At the Seto Machhendranath festival held in Kathmandu in March, the image of the deity Seto Macchendra is placed in a towering chariot *(rath)* and pulled through the streets by hundreds of young boys. Gai Jatra is a festival when cows are decorated and led through the streets in procession. At Indra Jatra, the *Kumārī* (living goddess) is worshiped and carried through the streets in a special chariot. Many of the Buddhist festivals, such as the Mani Rimdu of the Sherpas, are accompanied by masked monks performing devil-dances.

One of the major celebrations of the Nepālī festival year is Dasain, which is the Nepālī name for Dasahara. It celebrates fertility and the victory of good over evil in the form of the goddess Durga's slaying of the buffalo-demon Mahisha. The festival lasts 10 days, with numerous rituals and offerings to the gods. The ninth day of the festival is marked by the sacrifice of animals (chickens, ducks, goats, and buffalo) by every household and by organizations such as the police force and military.

In March 2008 the Government of Nepal announced a new line up of public holidays, canceling former holidays such as the King's birthday and National Unity Day, and adding some such as Christmas, the Muslim "Ids," and the two Lhosars (Tamu and Sonam). The holiday situation is very much in a state of flux.

⁷RITES OF PASSAGE

Nepālīs practice the rituals and ceremonies of their respective communities, with Hindu and Buddhist customs predominating. High-caste Hindu boys, for example, undergo the sacred thread ceremony as an initiation into adulthood. Among Buddhists, on the other hand, this initiation consists of boys adopting the saffron clothes and lifestyle of the novice monk for a short period. Both Hindus and Buddhists cremate their dead, except for important *lāmās* (Buddhist spiritual leaders), who are buried. Some groups at higher elevations where wood is not available dispose of their dead by exposing the corpses to be consumed by vultures and wild animals.

⁸INTERPERSONAL RELATIONS

Nepālīs have a reputation of being an open and friendly people. The normal Nepālī form of greeting is the "Namaste," said while joining one's own hands together, palms touching, in front of the body. A common greeting on the mountain trails is "Khana Khaiyo," literally, "Have you eaten?" This is an indication of the difficulties in obtaining the most basic necessities in the country.

⁹LIVING CONDITIONS

Nepal is among the poorest and least developed countries in the world, a fact that is reflected in the nation's health and vital statistics. The average life expectancy at birth is just under 61 years. The leading causes of death are infectious and parasitic diseases and respiratory problems. Infant mortality rates are high, amounting to 62 deaths per 1,000 live births. Fertility rates are also high, with 3.9 average births per childbearing woman in the population. The natural increase of population is over 2% per year.

Nepālīs are a rural people, with over 90% living in villages. These are usually clusters of houses sited on a hilltop or hillside, surrounded by agricultural land, and located near a source of water. Terracing of hillsides is quite common. Typical houses in the Pahar zone are two-story, mud-brick structures with thatched or tin roofs. Stone and wood are the main construction materials in the mountain belt. Creature comforts vary, though standards of living are generally quite low. Per capita income stands at US $1,630 per year (2008 estimate), considerably less than India's $3,800 per year.

Nepal's mountainous terrain makes for difficult transportation and communications. Goods are often transported by pack animals or carried by porters over mountain trails. Highways total a mere 17,280 km (10,800 mi), of which only 9,829 km (6,142 mi) are paved. The rail system has only 59 km (37 mi) of track and is of little economic significance. Nepal Airlines, formerly Royal Nepal Airlines, the country's air carrier, operates a schedule of domestic and international flights. Of interest is Nepal Airline's daily mountain flight (weather permitting) from Kathmandu to view Mt. Everest. Regional Airlines include Gorkha Airlines and Yeti Airlines.

¹⁰FAMILY LIFE

Social organization and family life differ among the various ethnic groups of Nepal. However, all practice some form of clan exogamy, with descent most commonly traced though the male line. Hindus follow typical practices in terms of arranged marriages and the extended family structure. Monogamy is the norm, although some Tibetan-speaking peoples practice fraternal polyandry (i.e., two brothers may marry the same woman). Wife-capture is a practice among Tibetan-speaking groups. Customs concerning divorce and remarriage vary according to the community.

¹¹CLOTHING

Nepālī clothing reflects the variety of peoples and cultures in the country. Each community has its own particular style of dress, although certain broad patterns can be seen. Peoples of the Terai are virtually indistinguishable from their Indian neighbors. Groups in the northern mountain belt wear Tibetan-style clothes. The traditional Nepālī dress is typically worn in the middle hills region. For men, this comprises trousers that taper from the waist to tight-fitting legs. Over this is worn a blouse-type shirt that reaches to mid-thigh and is tied at the waist with a belt and a Western-style jacket. The Nepālī cap, with its peak offset from the center, giving it a slightly lopsided look, completes the outfit. Ex-soldiers wear the badges of their former regiments with much pride. Women wear blouses

and *sārīs,* and they adorn themselves with gold ornaments and jewelry.

¹²FOOD

Nepālī food is generally similar to Indian cuisine. Rice, the staple cereal, is boiled and eaten with lentils (*dāl*) and spiced vegetables. Beef, of course, is not available, but poultry, goat, and buffalo meat are consumed. Meat is consumed mainly on special occasions and at festival times. Rice, too, is often out of the reach of the average rural Nepālī family. It is replaced by a dough made by mixing flour with boiling water, which is eaten with one's fingers just like rice. A flat bread (*chapātī*), which is dry-roasted on a hot skillet, is a staple of the diet in the Terai. Milk products such as *ghī* (clarified butter) and curd form part of the diet, and hot, sweet tea made with milk and water is drunk everywhere. Sweets such as *jalebīs* and *laddūs* are popular.

In the mountains, a ground cereal known as *tsampa* takes the place of rice. It is sometimes eaten dry, or sometimes mixed with milk or water into a gruel. In the higher elevations, yak meat is consumed. Among the Sherpas, potatoes have replaced rice as the staple food starch. Tibetan foods include *momos,* a boiled or fried stuffed dumpling, and *thukba,* a thick soup. Tibetans drink their tea with butter and salt added.

¹³EDUCATION

Education levels in Nepal are low, with over a third of the adult population having no formal schooling. Although primary education is free, government schools are often inadequate and overcrowded. Many schools in remote areas are very basic and sometimes unsafe, and many communities have cultural inhibitions against sending children, especially girls, who often leave school by the age of 12, to school. Enrollment in secondary schools is less than 35%. Literacy among the adult population is low (53.7%) with that for the male population over 15 years being 65.1%, and the figure for females dropping to 34.5% (2001 Census of Nepal). Kathmandu is the site of the Tribhuvan University, until 1985 the only doctoral-granting institution in the country, but since then another five universities, such as Mahendra Sanskrit University and the National Academy of Medical Sciences, have been established.

¹⁴CULTURAL HERITAGE

Past cultures in the Kathmandu Valley have left behind a rich artistic heritage. The magnificent religious stone sculptures of the Licchavi period (4th to 9th century AD) are matched by the elaborate wooden carvings of the early medieval period. The distinctive multi-tiered, pagoda-style roofs so typical of East Asia have their origins with Newar architects of the late 13th century. Nepālī painting encompasses illuminated manuscripts of the 11th century to more recent Tibetan-style *thankas.* Traditions of music range from the sonorous chanting and huge horns, thigh-bone flutes, and conch shells of Tibetan sacred music to the songs and folk music of wandering professional troubadours. Dance forms include the classical *kumārī* of the Newars and the masked devil-dances performed at Tibetan Buddhist festivals to scare off devils and demons.

Buddhist monks march for peace in the Nepalese capital Kathmandu. (AP Images/Binod Joshi)

¹⁵WORK

Nepālīs are overwhelmingly agricultural, with 93% of the labor force engaged in this sector of the economy. Subsistence cultivation dominates, although pastoralism based on the yak, a hybrid bovine, is important in higher altitudes. One unique tradition in Nepal, however, is military service in the Gurkha regiments of the British and Indian armies. The fighting abilities of the Gurkhas were recognized during the Anglo-Gurkha war of 1814–1816, after which they were recruited into the army of the East India Company. The Gurkha regiments of the British Indian Army were divided between Britain and India in 1947. Famous for their curved knives or *khukhrīs,* the Gurkhas have fought with distinction in campaigns around the world.

Historically, trade between India and China was important for the Nepālī economy. Another group that has carved out an occupational niche for itself is the Sherpas, who are well known as guides and porters for mountain-climbing expeditions. It was a Sherpa, Norgay Tenzing, who accompanied Sir Edmund Hillary in 1953 to become the first climbers to scale Mt. Everest. Tourism, trekking, and mountain expeditions are major earners of foreign exchange in Nepal.

¹⁶SPORTS

Modern sports popular among Nepālīs include soccer, cricket, basketball, table tennis, and badminton. Despite the mountainous nature of the country, altitude and the rugged terrain make skiing impractical.

¹⁷ENTERTAINMENT AND RECREATION

Most Nepālīs are restricted to traditional forms of entertainment and recreation, such as festivals, folk dances, and folk music. Radio Nepal broadcasts news and music, and for those who can afford television sets, Nepal Television commenced service in 1985. The cinema is popular in the cities, with most movies being supplied by India. Occasionally, Western films are shown. There is an ancient tradition of theater in Kathmandu.

¹⁸FOLK ART, CRAFTS, AND HOBBIES

Many of the traditional arts of Nepal are practiced today, though often the goods are of lesser quality and are manufactured for the tourist market. These items include woodcarvings, folk objects such as *khukhrīs* (curved knives), prayer wheels, *thankas,* musical instruments, and dance masks. Some of the Tibetan-speaking peoples are known for their weaving and make colorful clothes, bags, and carpets.

[19] SOCIAL PROBLEMS

Many of Nepal's social problems are related to poverty, over-population, and the nature of the country's environment. Only 17% of the country's land area is arable land, and Nepal has to import food to feed its population. Much of the population is engaged in subsistence agriculture, but the numbers of farmers unable to meet their basic food requirements is growing rapidly. More than 40% of the population is undernourished. An expanding population, and the added pressure this places on agricultural resources, is likely to increase levels of poverty in the next few decades. Poor transportation and natural hazards, such as flooding, landslides, and drought, intensify the problems of agricultural production.

Low levels of industrialization, lack of mineral resources, a severe shortage of skilled labor, and heavy reliance on foreign aid imposes restrictions on future economic expansion. Even existing resources are being threatened. Reliance on wood for fuel and construction has led to extensive deforestation, which in turn has resulted in widespread soil erosion and severe flooding. The country's important tourism industry may suffer if environmental degradation along trekking routes and at tourist centers continues unchecked. The Kathmandu Valley, for example, is currently experiencing major problems with air and water pollution.

Among Nepal's assets are its magnificent scenery and its newfound tradition of democratic government. However, the country is still dealing with the aftermath of 10 years of civil war, with the resultant decline in the tourist dollar and the associated decline in agricultural production in rural areas. It remains to be seen how the new government will deal with the serious social, economic, and ecological problems facing the peoples of Nepal today.

[20] GENDER ISSUES

Gender problems in Nepal differ considerably according to community in Nepal. However, with over 80% of the population of the country professing Hinduism, the problems of women in Hindu society are common to most women in Nepal. Most societies in Nepal are patriarchal, and males dominate. Nepalese women do all the house work, feed the children, clean the house, take care of the livestock, wash dishes, and do laundry. Men don't do dishes and don't do laundry. Girls are usually limited in their access to education and are kept home to help in the house and in the fields. Child marriages are common, with some girls being married before they reach 10 years of age, dowry giving is the norm (incidents of dowry death are occasionally reported, especially from the *terai*), and widow remarriage is prohibited. Low caste women are subjected to sexual and domestic violence and trafficking of young Nepali girls as young as 11 years to the red light districts in Indian cities is common. Many such victims remain until they get sick or contract diseases like HIV; then, they are dumped out of the brothels with nowhere to go. Most commit suicide, though some return back to Nepal to get help from some social organizations, such as the Women Foundation of Nepal, which helps with education, child labor, prostitution, and abuse resulting from witch hunting. In some cases, largely because of poverty, young girls are sold as wives in Indian states, such as the Punjab, where the imbalance between sexes makes finding a suitable wife difficult.

Nonetheless, women have been prominently involved in the recent civil war in Nepal. Available reports indicate that one-fifth to one-third of the insurgents' cadre and combatants may be women. Reportedly, every village had a revolutionary women's organization. According to a Jane's Intelligence Review report of October 2001, there were usually at least two women in each unit of 35–40 men, and they were used to gather intelligence and act as couriers. Durgha Pokhrel, Chairman of the National Women's Commission, who visited more than 25 Maoist districts, stated on 3 July 2003 during a talk delivered at the Nepal Council of World Affairs that the percentage of women among insurgent cadres could be as high as 40. A women's group, the All Nepal Women's Association (Revolutionary), was alleged to be a front for the CPN (M).

In addition to the recently ended civil war, Nepalese women have to deal with poverty, illiteracy, lack of access to medical facilities, poor nutrition, poor education, discrimination, and casteism.

[21] BIBLIOGRAPHY

Annamanthodo, Priscilla, ed. *Red Light Traffic: The Trade in Nepali Girls*. Kathmandu: ABC/Nepal, 1992.

Bhattarai, Govind Raj, trans. *Selected Nepali Essays*. Kathmandu: Jiba Lamichhane, 2003.

Bista, Dor Bahadur. *People of Nepal*. 2nd ed. Kathmandu: Ratna Pustak Bhandar, 1972.

Karan, Pradyumna P. *Nepal: A Cultural and Physical Geography*. Lexington, KY: University of Kentucky Press, 1960.

Maslak, Mary Anne. *Daughters of the Tharu: Gender, Ethnicity, Religion, and the Education of Nepali Girls*. New York: Routledge Falmer, 2003.

Rose, Leo E., and John T. Scholz. *Nepal: Profile of a Himalayan Kingdom*. Boulder, CO: Westview Press, 1980.

—by D. O. Lodrick

NEW CALEDONIANS

PRONUNCIATION: n(y)oo kal-uh-DOHN-ee-uhns
ALTERNATE NAMES: Kanaks (indigenous Melanesians)
LOCATION: New Caledonia (island chain in South Pacific between Australia and Vanuatu)
POPULATION: 224,824 (July 2008 estimate)
LANGUAGE: 39 indigenous languages; French (official), Javanese, Tahitian, Vietnamese, Wallisian
RELIGION: Christianity (Roman Catholic, Protestant); Islam

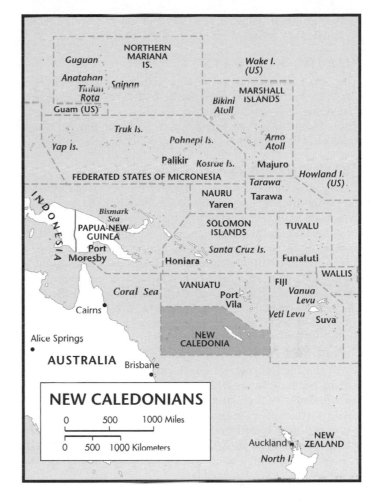

¹INTRODUCTION

The island chain of New Caledonia presents a cosmopolitan mix of cultures from many parts of the world. The original inhabitants are Melanesians, sometimes called "Kanaks." The term "kanaks" can have both positive and negative associations, depending on who is using it and in what manner. There have been French settlers in the islands since the 19th century, and their impact in terms of culture, language, and food can be clearly seen. Asians from Vietnam and Indonesia have also settled in New Caledonia and created their own immigrant communities. Lastly, Polynesian migrants from other parts of the French Pacific, especially Tahiti and the Wallis and Futuna islands, have relocated to New Caledonia in hopes of finding economic prosperity.

²LOCATION AND HOMELAND

New Caledonia is part of the Melanesian culture area of the South Pacific. New Caledonia is situated east of Australia and west of Vanuatu. New Caledonia is the third largest island in the South Pacific following New Guinea and New Zealand. There is a large chain of mountains that runs north and south and divides the island into two regions: a dry west coast area and a wet, tropical east coast area. The entire island is encircled by a barrier reef, creating the world's largest lagoon around the island. The main island of New Caledonia is referred to as "Grande Terre." There are several smaller islands and chains of islands that belong to the Territory of New Caledonia and Dependencies. New Caledonia has been an overseas territory of France since 1956. The French have had some sort of political control over the island group since the first French missionaries landed and settled at Balade in 1843. French settlers took land away from the indigenous Melanesians of New Caledonia and relocated them to reservations just as the Native Americans were. This history has left permanent scars for many New Caledonians and can be a source of friction between the two groups. The current population of New Caledonia is nearly 225,000.

³LANGUAGE

By the latest count, there are 39 living indigenous Austronesian languages spoken in New Caledonia. Some of these languages have been described by missionary linguists, are now written, and have been used to translate the New Testament. Many others have not been studied by outsiders. Other languages spoken in New Caledonia include French, Javanese, Tahitian, Vietnamese, the Malayo-Polynesian language Wallisian, and Tayo, a French-based Creole. Tayo has about 2,000 speakers who live primarily in the village of St. Louis. Over 50,000 New Caledonians speak French as their first language.

⁴FOLKLORE

Indigenous New Caledonian groups have large bodies of myth regarding their social histories and genealogies. Many groups have totemic myths that recount how the natural symbol of the group, an animal, plant, or mineral, came to stand for that group. These myths also describe the migrations of the splinter groups that have left the original group over time. Indigenous New Caledonians have an unusual metaphor for this relationship. While most Austronesian groups in the Pacific use the branches of the tree as a metaphor for genealogical relationships, the New Caledonians use mounds of earth to describe them. Each clan house is built on a mound that is named. The names of all the clan house mounds are recounted in story form to tell the migration history of the clan and to demonstrate the social ties that bind distant communities.

⁵RELIGION

Christianity is the majority religion in New Caledonia, with around 90% of the population claiming to be Christian. Of these, 60% are Roman Catholic and the other 30% are Protestant. Islam is the religion of approximately 4% of the New Caledonian population, and the vast majority of the Muslims are from Indonesia. The remaining 5% of the population follows traditional religious practices and has not been affected by missionary activity.

⁶MAJOR HOLIDAYS

The only national holiday in New Caledonia is Bastille Day, celebrated July 14. The various ethnic groups that live in New Caledonia all celebrate their own secular and religious holidays. Indigenous New Caledonians celebrate certain rituals that could be considered the equivalent of religious holidays.

⁷RITES OF PASSAGE

Passage through the various stages of life is marked by ceremony and the exchange of commodities among the indigenous New Caledonians following traditional cultural patterns. Other groups on the island recognize culturally significant events such as birth, marriage, and death in their own ways. The Javanese tradition of *slametan*, or feasting, has been brought to New Caledonia. This feast is performed on important days within the ritual calendar and marks the passage of time within certain events. For instance, slametan are given seven days after a birth and also seven months after a birth.

⁸INTERPERSONAL RELATIONS

Until the French colonial administration pacified hostilities among the indigenous New Caledonians, warfare and raiding were endemic to the island. The New Caledonians hesitated to take control of the land of a group they had beaten in battle because of fear of retribution by the ghosts and spirits of the group. The victors would encourage the village priest to placate the spirits, and only then might they consider taking up residence on the newly acquired land.

Kinship relations dictate the nature of interpersonal relations among the indigenous New Caledonians. The maternal uncle is extremely important for indigenous New Caledonians; he must be given gifts at the occurrence of births, deaths, and marriages.

⁹LIVING CONDITIONS

There are a wide range of living conditions among the New Caledonians. Those people that live in the capital city of Noumea may experience a very cosmopolitan lifestyle. The amenities of life are essentially the same as those of most middle class Americans. Socio-economic status determines what lifestyle a family will have in the city.

Indigenous groups in New Caledonia have villages arranged around a rectangular plaza that is flanked by beehive-shaped family houses. At the end of each line of family houses is the larger, beehive-shaped clan-house, or men's house. This house is off-limits to women, except during special events. As opposed to other groups in Melanesia, the indigenous New Caledonians do not store their clan artifacts and treasures in the clan house; instead, they build separate small houses to store them. These structures are fenced in to keep women and children from seeing the items of ritual significance that are stored inside. Behind the houses, running parallel with the plaza space, are street-like spaces. Beyond these spaces are small, rectangular-shaped work sheds where the activities of pottery making, wood carving, and mask-making take place. At the furthest point away from the plaza are the huts for menstruating women.

Most of the roads in New Caledonia are unpaved. Railroads do not exist on the island. Transportation for the indigenous New Caledonians that still follow traditional ways of life include travel by foot, by canoe, and, in some cases, by light truck or bus. Airfields have been built in many parts of the islands to facilitate economic development and increase mobility.

¹⁰FAMILY LIFE

Indigenous New Caledonians have separate living quarters for men as opposed to women and children. Men spend most of their time in the clan house. Each married woman has her own separate house where she lives with her unmarried children. Marriage partners are typically chosen from members of the mother's clan, and the preference is for a man to marry his mother's brother's daughter. In the most traditional New Caledonian villages, these arrangements are made by infant or child betrothal. This means that a baby girl will be betrothed to a man or boy much older than she. The marriage will not be formally transacted until after she has reached puberty; however, it does mean that the ages of the married couple will be wildly divergent and the wife will greatly outlive her husband.

¹¹CLOTHING

The cosmopolitan nature of New Caledonian society presents wide variety in terms of clothing and adornment. In Noumea, a range of styles of dress can be found, in many cases related to the ethnicity of the individual. Modern French fashion coexists alongside peasant attire adopted by some of the resident indigenous New Caledonians of the city. Traditional attire is worn only by a few indigenous groups on the island nowadays.

¹²FOOD

The traditional foods of the indigenous New Caledonians are taro root and yams. Taro is classified as a "wet" food and is associated with females, while yams are classified as a "dry" food and associated with males. Yams are the focus of much symbolic and ritual activity for traditional New Caledonians. Indigenous New Caledonians also keep domesticated chickens as a food source for special occasions. Fishing is important, while hunting is far less so.

Urban New Caledonians eat a wide variety of foods and have an extensive array of restaurants at their disposal. There are grocery stores as well as specialty shops that sell specific kinds of foodstuffs.

¹³EDUCATION

As a French possession, public education is conducted within a French framework. Noumea has many educational opportunities, especially for the French population. The indigenous New Caledonian population has less access to formal education. The literacy rate among both adult men and women in New Caledonia is approximately 96%. The remaining 4% is constituted by the indigenous New Caledonians that have not been integrated into the larger society.

¹⁴CULTURAL HERITAGE

Traditional forms of dance and music are still performed in indigenous New Caledonian villages. Popular music from France and French Polynesia can also be heard in New Caledonia. The various ethnic groups that have immigrated to the island also brought their music traditions with them. The culture of compact disk music guarantees a continual stream of new musical influences into Noumea.

15 WORK

Nickel mining and smelting is one of the major industries in New Caledonia. New Caledonia possesses about 35% of the world's total nickel deposits. Many mine workers, however, are not from New Caledonia, but are instead immigrant workers from other parts of the South Pacific, especially Wallis and Futuna Islands. The tourist industry also employs many workers in New Caledonia. The majority of workers in the service area of tourism are New Caledonians. Most of New Caledonia's tourists come from Japan to spend their honeymoons.

16 SPORTS

There is a wide range of sports available in New Caledonia, and, again, socio-economic status dictates the spectra within which any individual can participate. Golf, tennis, and soccer are all popular sports, especially among the French New Caledonians.

17 ENTERTAINMENT AND RECREATION

There are broadcast television stations as well as a handful local radio stations in New Caledonia. In Noumea and other areas that have electricity, television, video, and DVDs are popular forms of entertainment.

18 FOLK ART, CRAFTS, AND HOBBIES

New Caledonian indigenous groups are very well known for their distinctive style of masks. The nose of New Caledonian masks forms a hooked beak. This style of mask is very well represented in museums throughout the world.

Indigenous New Caledonians also make carvings and sculptures that decorate the village houses. Some of these items are now marketed for tourist consumption.

19 SOCIAL PROBLEMS

Land rights are an important issue for indigenous New Caledonians. A large portion of their traditional lands were confiscated by French settlers in the colonial period. Efforts to reclaim those lands are underway by groups that were displaced. Other groups that were able to maintain their traditional lands and ways of life are struggling to continue their cultural patterns into the next century.

20 GENDER ISSUES

New Caledonia belongs to the Melanesian culture area, which is characterized by sexual segregation and antagonism. The degrees to which sexual segregation and antagonism were part of precontact culture are not well understood by anthropologists. However, it is clear that in contemporary New Caledonian Kanak society, aggression towards women is a major social and medical problem. One issue of concern is the increasing risk of the transmission of HIV/AIDS and STDs to women through patterns of sexual aggression and assault by men. The emerging pattern is one of gender violence towards women perpetuated by spouses, relatives, and colleagues.

21 BIBLIOGRAPHY

Duituturaga, Emele. "New Caledonia: Fatal Intimacy: Gender Dynamics of STD and HIV/AIDS." *Pacific AIDS Alert Bulletin* 19: 14-15, 2000.

Leenhardt, Maurice. *Do kamo: Person and Myth in the Melanesian World.* Trans. B. M. Gulati. Chicago. University of Chicago Press, 1979.

—by J. Williams

NEW ZEALANDERS

PRONUNCIATION: new ZEE-lun-duhrs
ALTERNATE NAMES: Kiwi (nickname)
LOCATION: New Zealand
POPULATION: 4,115,771 (2007)
LANGUAGE: English; Maori
RELIGION: Christianity (Church of England, Presbyterian, Roman Catholic, Methodist, and Baptist); New Zealand Christian sects (Ratana and Ringatu); Buddhism; Hinduism; Judaism
RELATED ARTICLES: Vol. 4: Maori

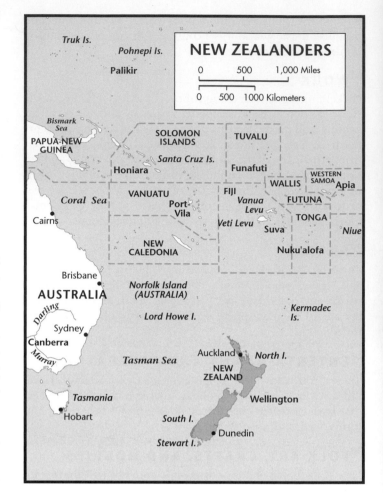

¹INTRODUCTION

New Zealand is an island nation in the southwestern Pacific Ocean, separated from Australia by the Tasman Sea. A small country, New Zealand is also a young one: it was a British colony until 1907 and did not achieve full independence from Great Britain until 1947, although it had been essentially self-governing since the middle of the previous century. New Zealand's history of human habitation is also relatively short. Its original inhabitants, the Maori, migrated from Polynesian islands in three separate waves between AD 950 and 1350. Calling their new homeland *Aotearoa* ("land of the long white cloud"), they settled in communities called *kaingas*, mostly located on North Island, passing on their culture and history orally to succeeding generations. The first European to discover New Zealand was Abel Tasman, a navigator for the Dutch East India Company, who sighted the west coast of South Island in 1642. In the 1790s, the islands began to attract whalers from Europe who established the first settlements on the coast, and in 1814 the first missionary station was set up in the Bay of Islands.

Europeans and Australians began arriving in New Zealand in large numbers in the 1830s. In 1840, the Maori chieftains entered into a compact, the Treaty of Waitangi, under which they granted sovereignty over their land to Britain's Queen Victoria while retaining territorial rights, and New Zealand became a British colony. More settlers arrived after gold was discovered in 1861. After the Maori Wars (1860–70), resulting largely from disputes over land rights and sovereignty, New Zealand rapidly increased in wealth and population. With the introduction of refrigerated shipping in 1882, New Zealand became one of the world's great exporters of dairy, produce, and meat. In 1907, New Zealand was made a Dominion of Great Britain. Its troops served in World Wars I and II at the side of the British, fighting in Europe in both wars and in the Pacific in World War II. In 1947, the New Zealand government formally claimed complete independence while remaining a member of the British Commonwealth. Troops from New Zealand fought with United Nations forces in the Korea conflict and with U.S. forces in South Vietnam.

Since 1984 New Zealand has actively pursued an anti-nuclear policy, refusing to admit a U.S. warship to one of its ports because of the possibility that there were nuclear arms on board. In 1986 the U.S. responded by suspending its military obligations to New Zealand under the 1951 ANZUS (Australia, New Zealand, and the United States) agreement. The U.S. also banned high-level contacts with the New Zealand government, a ban that was rescinded in 1990. In December 1989, a Cabinet-level committee was established to formulate a government policy toward extensive Maori land claims (the country's entire coastline, 70% of its land, and half of its fishing rights).

²LOCATION AND HOMELAND

Situated in the southwest Pacific Ocean, New Zealand consists of two main islands—North Island and South Island—and several dozen minor ones. With a total area of 268,680 sq km (103,738 sq mi), it is about the size of Colorado. Most of New Zealand's large cities, including Auckland and the capital city of Wellington, are located on North Island, which is home to three-fourths of the country's population. North Island is also known for its volcanic activity, including two active volcanoes as well as bubbling mud pools, hot springs, and geysers. South Island is the larger of the two islands and the location of the scenic Southern Alps, which run almost the entire length of the island from north to south and include New Zealand's highest peak, Mount Cook, which is 12,349 ft (3,766 m) high.

The most recent estimate (July 2008) of New Zealand's population is 4,173,460. The largest urban areas are Auckland (1,158,891 in 2001 census); Wellington, the capital (423,765 in 2001 census); and Christchurch (316,227 in 2001 census). Approximately 70% of the population is of European (mostly British) descent. The Maori, who were New Zealand's first inhabitants, are presently the country's most significant minority group, representing close to 8% of the population. In the 2006 census there were 565,329 Maoris or part-Maoris (those reporting a Maori ancestry of 50% or more), about 90% of whom live on North Island. The non-Maori Polynesian population in 2006 was 265,874. People of Chinese, Indian, and Southeast Asian ancestry account for the remainder of New Zealand's population (between 1 and 2%).

³LANGUAGE

English is the universal language of New Zealand, although Maori, which belongs to the Polynesian language family, is still spoken by the Maoris and taught in Maori schools. Maori became an official language of the country in 1987 through the Maori Language Act. New Zealand English resembles British English in a number of ways. In addition, New Zealanders have many unique words and expressions of their own. Both males and females are addressed informally as "mate," and the word "she" is used for "it" in a very general sense, as in "she'll be right," which means "everything will be all right."

COMMON ENGLISH WORDS AND PHRASES

bach (or crib)	cottage or vacation house
fizzy	soda pop
mob	herd of sheep or cattle
rousterer	professional sheep shearer
panel beater	auto body shop
hogget	year-old lamb
gumboots	rubber rain boots
hotel	a public bar
mozzies	mosquitoes
peckish	slightly hungry
prang	car or bicycle accident
sandshoes	sneakers

MAORI WORDS AND PHRASES

aotearoa	land of the long white cloud (Maori name for New Zealand)
aroha	love and understanding for others
Maoritanga	the Maori tradition and way of life
marae	a Maori meeting house or the area surrounding it
pakeha	a white, or non-Maori, New Zealander

⁴FOLKLORE

Guy Fawkes Day, an institution with English roots, was celebrated by burning an effigy of Guy Fawkes, who in 1605 was discovered lurking in the cellar of the Parliament building with barrels of gunpowder, waiting to blow up Parliament as it opened in the morning. In parts of New Zealand, children would recite Guy Fawkes rhymes in a type of competition and adults would throw pennies to the children who recited the loudest or the best. Sometimes, certain adults would heat pennies on a shovel held over a fire before throwing them. The anxious children would pick up the hot pennies, regardless of the burns they would receive. Some children carried painful reminders of Guy Fawkes Day for weeks.

The Maori have a rich folklore tradition that is reflected in their native art, song, and dance. Some of their legends involving journeys contain highly detailed and accurate descriptions of New Zealand's terrain and of the surrounding waters.

⁵RELIGION

The majority of New Zealanders are Christians. In the 2006 census, over 2 million New Zealanders reported Christianity as their religion. The next largest group includes those who reported no religion, with a total of approximately 1.3 million. In the same census, most of the population belonged to one of three main churches: the Church of England, 17%; the Presbyterian Church, 11.0%; and the Roman Catholic Church, 14%. There are many other Protestant groups, and two Christian sects that are native to New Zealand (Ratana and Ringatu). The largest growth in religions reported in the 2006 census was for Hinduism and Buddhism. The number of Buddhists in New Zealand increased by 255% between the 1991 and the 2006 census.

⁶MAJOR HOLIDAYS

Nationwide legal holidays in New Zealand include Christmas and Boxing Day (December 25 and 26), Easter, New Year's Day, Labor Day (the fourth Monday in October), and the official birthday of Britain's Queen Elizabeth, celebrated on the first Monday in June. A holiday unique to New Zealand is Anzac Day (April 25), on which New Zealanders and Australians who died in both world wars are honored at dawn services throughout the country. Another date with national significance is Waitangi Day (February 6), commemorating the signing of the Treaty of Waitangi between the Maori and Great Britain in 1840.

⁷RITES OF PASSAGE

Rituals marking major life events such as birth, marriage, and death are generally observed within the Christian religious tradition, as well as within Buddhism, Hinduism, and the other faiths represented in New Zealand.

⁸INTERPERSONAL RELATIONS

New Zealanders like to refer to themselves as "kiwis," a name derived from the kiwi, a rare flightless bird unique to their country. (The distinctive kiwi fruit, with its green center and fuzzy brown skin, was originally known as the Chinese gooseberry and renamed to reflect its connection with New Zealand. However, the popularity of the name "kiwi" comes from the bird, not the fruit.) People from New Zealand also refer to themselves as "En Zedders," a name based on the abbreviation "NZ" ("Z" is pronounced "zed" in New Zealand, as it is in Britain). The Maori word "pakeha" is used for New Zealanders of European descent.

A common greeting among New Zealanders is "good day," pronounced so that it sounds like "geday." New Zealanders often address each other informally as "mate," a term that reflects the British ancestry that many of the country's inhabitants share. The Maoris have a traditional greeting, called *hongi*, in which they touch faces so that their noses are pressed together. It is believed that their spirits mingle through this gesture.

⁹LIVING CONDITIONS

Most people in New Zealand live in single houses with large yards and flower or vegetable gardens that New Zealanders enjoy tending during their leisure time. The average home has three bedrooms, a living room, dining room, kitchen, laundry, bathroom, and garage. Most are built of wood and have sheet-iron or tiled roofs. Besides the garden, a common sight outside a New Zealand house is a clothes-drying rack covered with laundry spinning in the wind. Most families own their own homes. However, high-rise apartment buildings can be found in the major cities. More than half of the total housing stock has been constructed since 1957.

New Zealand's life expectancies showed continued increase since the 1991 census. In the 2002 national data, the life expectancy of non-Maori females was 81 years while that of non-Maori males was 76 years. For Maoris, the average life expectancies were about 8.5 years less than those of non-Maoris in 2002. The principal causes of death are heart disease, cancer, and stroke. Alcoholism and related health problems are significant public health concerns in New Zealand. In a national study whose results became available in 2004, alcohol consumption has decreased for adult New Zealanders. Older New Zealanders (over the age of 55) consume alcohol at the highest rates of all groups that were surveyed. Most doctors practice under the National Health Service, established by the Social Security Act of 1938, but private practice is also permitted. New Zealand's health care system has been undergoing a restructuring since the mid-1980s, when area health boards were established to combine primary and hospital care facilities for each region under a single administrative unit.

New Zealand's mountainous terrain has made the development of rail and road communications a challenge, especially on South Island. The automobile is New Zealand's primary mode of transportation. There is one car for every two people, and teenagers can get their driver's licenses at the age of 15. While there is little traffic on roads in most parts of the country, the major cities have begun to experience the traffic congestion common to metropolitan areas in other countries. People travel between North and South Islands on ferries that can transport both them and their cars. A government-operated railroad system links New Zealand's major cities. Auckland and Wellington are the nation's two main ports, and there are international airports at Auckland, Christchurch, and Wellington.

10 FAMILY LIFE

Most families in New Zealand have two or three children and enjoy a high standard of living, often owning a home with three or four bedrooms and an attached garage. Maori families are larger than those of the *pakeha*, or white, population, and Maori households may include relatives besides the nuclear family, such as grandparents, uncles, and aunts.

11 CLOTHING

New Zealanders wear modern Western-style clothing. They prefer to dress casually, and men in white-collar jobs sometimes even wear shorts and knee socks to work with their white shirts and ties. Maoris generally dress like other New Zealanders, but still wear their traditional costumes for special occasions. The most distinctive feature of these costumes is the striped, fringed skirt woven from flax that is worn by both men and women (women wear them over brightly colored dresses consisting of snugly fitted bodices with shoulder straps and either knee-length or longer skirts). Over their dresses the women may also wear long white capes decorated with black fringes.

12 FOOD

New Zealanders eat three main meals a day—a hearty breakfast of eggs, sausage, and bacon; lunch, often consisting of a meat pie, hamburger, or sandwich; and a full meal at dinnertime, generally featuring some type of meat dish, often lamb. In addition, it is common to have a mid-morning snack called morning tea between ten and eleven o'clock and a bedtime snack called supper. British-style afternoon tea is still popular, complete with scones, cakes, and other pastries, especially as an occasion for entertaining guests. The most popular traditional dinner entrée is roast lamb with mint sauce, typically served with roasted potatoes, roast *kumara* (New Zealand's sweet potato), and roast pumpkin. A distinctive New Zealand dish that is considered a real delicacy is the dark-green soup made from the *toheroa*, a rare clam found on the country's beaches. For dessert, New Zealanders enjoy tarts and various other pastries topped with fruit, including the distinctive kiwi fruit. Ice cream also comes topped with chunks of fruit. A special favorite is *pavlova*, made of meringue covered with fruit and whipped cream.

The most famous Maori culinary tradition is the *hangi*, a meal prepared in the traditional manner that used to characterize most Maori cooking. The term *hangi* also refers to the cooking method itself: a covered pit filled with red-hot, fire-heated stones on which meat and vegetables are left to steam for several hours.

13 EDUCATION

New Zealanders are a well-educated people, with an adult literacy rate of 99%. Education is free and compulsory for children between the ages of 6 and 15, although most children attend school from the age of 5, many at state-subsidized preschools. Most state schools are coeducational, but some private schools are not. For children in isolated areas, there is a public correspondence school, which enables them to send in their homework assignments by mail. In some regions there are special state primary and secondary schools for Maori children, but most Maori children attend public schools.

Although young people may leave school at 15 to work, most stay in school through the eleventh grade (called the fifth form), earning a school certificate. Students planning to attend college continue their secondary education until the age of 17 or 18, when they take university qualifying exams. New Zealand has six universities: the University of Auckland, University of Waikato (at Hamilton), Massey University (at Palmerston North), Victoria University of Wellington, University of Canterbury (at Christchurch), and University of Otago (at Dunedin).

14 CULTURAL HERITAGE

New Zealand enjoys the rich cultural heritage provided by both its Maori and European traditions. In recent years Maori weaving and wood carving have enjoyed a revival, and many galleries and museums display Maori art. The Maori also preserve their traditional songs and dances. Since World War II, a lively art scene has grown up in New Zealand, with leading artists including Frances Hodgkins, Colin McCahon, and Sir Toss Woollaston. The New Zealander with the greatest literary reputation worldwide is probably the 20th-century short story writer Katherine Mansfield. Other well-known authors include Frank Sargeson, Janet Frame, and Sylvia Ashton-Warner.

A farmer and his dog look over a valley in Waikato County, North Island, New Zealand. (© Evan Collis/Corbis)

Native New Zealander Kiri Te Kanawa is an internationally acclaimed opera singer. New Zealand's motion picture industry, assisted and promoted by the New Zealand Film Commission, has produced a number of internationally acclaimed movies. Notable New Zealand films include *The Piano, Once Were Warriors, Whale Rider, Lord of the Rings,* and *Heavenly Creatures.*

15 WORK

In 2003, New Zealand had a total labor force of 1,985,100 people. Due to slow economic growth in the early 1990s, unemployment climbed into the double digits in the early 1990s. The 21st century saw boosts in the New Zealand economy and employment and the 2003 labor statistics show that unemployment hovered around 5% in the first three years of the century. Since 1977 employers have been required to pay men and women the same minimum wage.

16 SPORTS

New Zealanders enjoy many kinds of sports. Rugby, a game similar to football in the United States, is the national game. The national team, called the All Blacks (a name that refers to their uniform of black shirt and shorts), plays teams from Australia, France, Britain, and other countries, and is well-known throughout the world. Cricket is also very popular, as are a variety of water sports including sailing, surfing, kayaking, canoeing, and rafting. Bruce Kendall, a New Zealander, won an Olympic gold medal in yacht racing in 1988, and in 1995, New Zealand won the coveted America's Cup yachting trophy. In the winter, skiing is a favorite pastime in New Zealand, where the ski season runs from June to late October.

17 ENTERTAINMENT AND RECREATION

Almost every household in New Zealand has a television set, and New Zealanders enjoy watching both local programming and popular shows from Britain and the United States. Camping is a universal summertime activity among New Zealanders, who take advantage of their vacation time to enjoy their country's beautiful scenery, including its national parks. Beach houses (called "bachs" or "cribs") are also popular vacation spots. Most family trips are taken during summer vacations from school, which run from late December to early February.

[18] FOLK ART, CRAFTS, AND HOBBIES

The Maoris are known for their weaving and their intricate wood carving, a skill that is transmitted from one generation to the next. Other New Zealand crafts include stained glass, glassblowing, and pottery.

[19] SOCIAL PROBLEMS

Free market reform policies instituted by New Zealand's government since the mid-1980s, while lowering inflation and increasing economic growth, have resulted in high unemployment and led to cutbacks in educational spending and social services. New Zealand, a country proud of its traditionally egalitarian ways, has seen a growing division between rich and poor, accompanied by rising tensions between the Maori and pakeha (white) populations and an increase in violent crime.

[20] GENDER ISSUES

New Zealand is generally considered a progressive, tolerant community in regards to sexual and gender expression. Several members of the New Zealand Parliament and Ministers of Cabinet belong to the Lesbian Gay Bisexual Transgender (LGBT) community. In the 1999 election, Kiwi Georgina Beyer became the world's first transsexual member of parliament. She retired from parliamentary politics in 2007. In 2004 the Civil Union Act was passed that provides the right for same sex couples a legal equivalent of marriage. The Act took effect in 2005.

In 1893, New Zealand became the first country in the world to grant women the right to vote in parliamentary elections.

[21] BIBLIOGRAPHY

Bangs, Richard. *Quest for Kaitiakitanga: The Ancient Maori Secret from New Zealand that Could Save the Earth*. Birmingham, AL: Menasha Ridge Press, 2008.

Dobbin, Murray. "New Zealand Nightmare." *Canadian Dimension*. April-May 1995: 21.

Fox, Mary Virginia. *New Zealand*. Chicago: Children's Press, 1991.

Gall, Timothy, and Susan Gall, ed. *Worldmark Encyclopedia of the Nations*. Detroit: Gale Research, 1995.

Hanke, Steve. "A Revolution that Paid Off." *Forbes*. 20 May 1996, 121.

Hanna, Nick. *Fodor's Exploring New Zealand*. 4th ed. New York: Fodors Travel, 2008.

Hawke, G. R. *The Making of New Zealand*. Cambridge: Cambridge University Press, 1985.

Johnston, Carol Morton. *The Farthest Corner: New Zealand, A Twice Discovered Land*. Honolulu: University of Hawaii Press, 1988.

Keyworth, Valerie. *New Zealand: Land of the Long White Cloud*. Minneapolis: Dillon Press, 1990.

King, Jane. *New Zealand Handbook*. Chico, CA: Moon Publications, 1990.

Lealand, Geoffrey. *A Foreign Egg in Our Nest?: American Popular Culture in New Zealand*. Wellington: Victoria University Press, 1988.

MacDonald, Margaret Read, ed. *The Folklore of World Holidays*. Detroit: Gale Research Inc., 1992.

McLauchlan, Gordon, ed. *The Illustrated Encyclopedia of New Zealand*. Auckland: D. Bateman, 1992.

The Oxford Illustrated History of New Zealand. New York: Oxford University Press, 1990.

—by J. Williams

NEWARS

LOCATION: Nepal (Kathmandu Valley)
POPULATION: 1,245,232 (Census of Nepal 2001)
LANGUAGE: Newari; Nepālī
RELIGION: Mixture of Mahāyāna Buddhism, Hinduism, and older animistic beliefs

¹INTRODUCTION

The Newar are the indigenous population found in the Kathmandu Valley in Nepal. The name *Newar* has no ethnic implications, but refers to the mixed peoples of both Mongoloid and Mediterranean stock who have settled the region over a period of more than 2,000 years. Over the centuries, the Newar have evolved a distinctive culture that has come to be seen by many as typically Nepālī.

The beginnings of Newar civilization may date back as far as the 8th or 7th century BC, when the Kathmandu Valley was conquered by the Kirati tribe. Since then, many peoples have settled the area, each making its own contributions to Newar history and culture. In the years following AD 300, for example, the Licchavis brought the Hindu caste system to the peoples of the Kathmandu Valley. Some of the Malla kings (from the 13th to the 18th centuries) were great patrons of art and literature. The Gurkhas gained control of the Kathmandu Valley in 1768. Using the valley as a base of power, in the next few decades they succeeded in establishing the outlines of the modern state of Nepal. The term *Newar* is derived from *Nepal,* and the Kathmandu Valley, the heart of Newar territory, remains the political and cultural focus of the kingdom to this day.

²LOCATION AND HOMELAND

Newars make up roughly 5.5% of Nepal's population, or some 1,245,232 people (Census of Nepal 2001). Allowing for natural increase, the current population is estimated at just over 1.4 million. More than two-thirds of this number are concentrated in the Kathmandu Valley. The remaining Newar are found spread through the eastern and western hill (Pahar) zones and the belt of lowlands in southern Nepal known as the Terai.

The Kathmandu Valley is one of the largest of a series of Himalayan valleys that lie between the foothills and the high ranges of the Great Himalaya. Formed by an ancient lake-bed, the valley is an amphitheater roughly 24 km (15 mi) across and about 1,300 m (4,300 ft) above sea level. The climate is very pleasant, with average temperatures ranging from 10°C (50°F) in January to 26°C (78°F) in July. Most of the 140 cm (55 in) of annual rainfall falls during the summer monsoon period from June to September. South of the Kathmandu Valley, the Mahabharat Lekh mountains bar the route to the Terai and the Ganges Plains. To the north, visible from many places on the valley floor, tower the snow-clad peaks of the Himalayas.

³LANGUAGE

Newari, the mother tongue of the Newar, is a Tibeto-Burman language. Several dialects of Newari are spoken in the Kathmandu Valley, with the standard form being that of Kathmandu. There are numerous loan-words in Newari, the result of a long history of contact with Sanskrit, Nepālī, and other Indo-Aryan languages. Today, Newari is written in Devanagari, a script used to write Sanskrit, although several alphabets derived from ancient Indian systems of writing have been used in the past. Many Newars also speak Nepālī, which is used for official purposes and for inter-group communication. Although other groups in South Asia who speak Tibeto-Burman languages have given up their mother tongues, the Newar appear to be committed to preserving Newari as their language.

Newari is one of the few languages of Nepal to possess a distinct literature. Early works in Newari were translations from Sanskrit, but by the 14th century AD, Newari histories started appearing. There is a tradition of Newari literature dating to that time, a tradition that is being maintained by modern writers such as Dhushwan Salami.

⁴FOLKLORE

Newars share Nepālī myths and traditions such as those relating to the origins of the Kathmandu Valley and the founding of the sacred shrine of Swayambhunath. There is, however, an unusual story in the Newar Buddhist literature that bears a resemblance to the biblical account of the creation of mankind. According to this legend, the earth was originally uninhabited by humans, but half-male/half-female creatures from the Abode of Brahma used to visit the earth. One day, Adi Buddha (the primordial Buddha of Mahayana Buddhism, the sect of Buddhism that reveres Buddha as divine) created in these beings a longing to eat some of the earth, which tasted to them like almonds. Once they had eaten earth, they lost their power to fly back to their home. Doomed to remain on earth, they ate fruits for sustenance. This aroused in them strong sexual urges that resulted in the earth being peopled with humans.

⁵RELIGION

Newar religion is a mix of Mahāyāna Buddhism (the sect of Buddhism that reveres Buddha as divine), Hinduism, and older animistic beliefs. Buddhists are essentially monotheistic (believe in one god), but Newar Buddhists also recognize the Hindu gods Shiva, Vishnu, and other Brahmanical deities. (Brahma is the Supreme Soul revered in Hinduism.) Newars visit and worship at both Hindu and Buddhist temples. Images of Hindu goddesses, for instance, are found at the sacred Buddhist *stupa* (shrine) at Swayambhunath. Newar Buddhists have castes, or a hierarchy of social classes, just as Hindus do, with the *Gubhaju* being the equivalent of the Brahman priestly class. Likewise, Hindu Newars share Buddhist practices such as the worship of the living goddess, *Kumārī.* Of great significance in everyday life are numerous lesser godlings and their female counterparts, the latter known by terms such as *devi* or *mai* (mother). These are often served by priests from the lower castes, and their worship involves blood sacrifice and offerings of liquor. Surviving animistic beliefs may be seen in the Newars' veneration of frogs, snakes, and other animals. The Newars believe in the existence of witches skilled in the black arts and in demons, ghosts, and evil spirits that haunt cremation grounds and crossroads. Priests and magicians are called upon to deal with this spirit world.

⁶MAJOR HOLIDAYS

The main festivals of the Kathmandu Valley are inter-caste celebrations held at particular locations. These include many *jatras* (e.g., *Indra Jatra, Macchendra Jatra,* and numerous festivals for *Bhairava*), when images of the deities are carried through the streets in procession. Rituals often include the sacrifice of buffalo or goats, and the festivals are always accompanied by the lavish consumption of rice, meat, liquor, and home-made beer. *Gai Jatra,* when cows are decorated and led through the streets in a parade, is a festival of particular importance to Hindu Newars, as the cow holds a sacred place in Hinduism. A second category of observances includes the worship of clan gods as well as festivals of the Hindu calendar, such as *Holi* (the worship of Krishna) in the spring and *Divali* (a festival of lights that, in some areas, marks the beginning of the new year) in the fall. As with other Nepālīs, *Dasain (Dasahara,* a Hindu festival*)* is an important occasion marked by animal sacrifices. Newar practices differ slightly from other communities, however, and their offerings are made to the goddess Talleju.

⁷RITES OF PASSAGE

The birth of a child is a joyous occasion among the Newar, with a son being particularly welcome. A midwife from the barber caste *(Nau)* attends the birth, cuts the umbilical cord, and completes certain important rituals. Two names are given to the Newar child, one by the astrologer *(Joshi)* based on a horoscope, and the other by the family. Around the age of seven months, a first-feeding ceremony (known as *Maca Jankwa*) is held in the presence of family and priests. Childhood is a carefree time for Newari children, but they are soon initiated into adult life. Before they reach puberty, young girls are "married" to the god Narayan in the *Ihi* ritual. Dressed as a bride, a girl undergoes the symbolic rituals of a typical marriage. As a result, she will never (in theory) be a widow, and divorce in a real marriage thus becomes a mere formality. The puberty ceremony for Newar girls is called *Barha*. The initiation ceremony for boys is called *Kayta Puja,* and among the higher Hindu castes, it is often accompanied by the putting on of the sacred thread, a rite viewed as a symbolic rebirth. Buddhists require a boy to put on saffron-colored clothes and lead the life of an novice monk for a period of four days. After this, he resumes his normal life as a full-fledged adult of his community.

An unusual feature of the Newar life-cycle rituals is a series of ceremonies *(Bura Jankwa)* marking the attainment of old age. The first of these ceremonies is observed when a man reaches 77 years, 7 months, and 7 days (an age few reached in the past). In the last of these rituals, held at 99 years of age, a man enters his house through a window on the top floor (he is placed on a wooden shrine that is hoisted up by ropes). This is symbolic of going to heaven.

Death ceremonies generally follow Hindu or Buddhist rites, although there are some differences in specific practices. Unlike other Hindus, Newars offer *pindas* (cakes made from barley) to the soul of the deceased before cremation. Musicians from the *Nau* (barber) and *Jyapu* (farmer) castes accompany the procession to the cremation ground, which is usually on the banks of a river. Following ceremonies presided over by priests, the chief mourner—usually the eldest son—walks three times around the pyre before setting it alight. Death-pollution rituals are performed for a period of 10 to 12 days, and the mourning period ends with a feast and a purification ceremony *(ghasu)*.

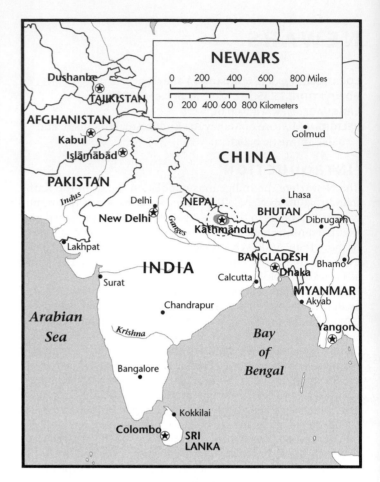

⁸INTERPERSONAL RELATIONS

When Newars meet, they use the typical Nepālī word of greeting, *"Namaste,"* accompanied by the joining of hands, palms together, in front of the body.

⁹LIVING CONDITIONS

In the Kathmandu Valley, Newars are engaged in agriculture, trade, and many traditional service occupations. The *Jyapu* is the farming caste, while *Shresthas* and *Udas* are merchants. Other artisan and service castes include barbers *(Nau),* potters *(Kumha),* blacksmiths *(Kau),* and sweepers *(Chami).* Almost all Newar settlements in the Kathmandu Valley are built on plateaus above the general level of the valley floor. Houses are built of brick and may be several stories high. Their roofs are of slate or tile, and angled wooden beams support the overhang of their eaves. Houses line the streets and alleys of towns and villages with no gaps between them, their brick walls pierced by many windows, doors, and perhaps a veranda overhanging the street. Houses are often built around squares *(chowks)* that may have temples built in the middle. Elaborately carved windows and wooden doors adorn the houses of the Newar aristocracy. Patan and Bhaktapur are medieval cities with many fine examples of traditional Newari architecture.

¹⁰FAMILY LIFE

Newars marry within their own caste, but lack the clan structure and strict rules of clan exogamy (marrying outside one's group) associated with other Hindu groups. Descent is patrilineal (traced on the father's side), and the *phuki* (a term meaning "brother" but usually applied to cousins and their families) defines what is essentially an exogamous lineage. A man may not marry a woman who is related to him through blood for seven generations on both his father's and his mother's side. Thus the cross cousin (i.e., father's sister's daughter, or mother's brother's daughter) marriages found among the Gurungs, Bhutias, and other Nepāli groups are not permitted. Marriages are typically arranged, although urban youth are increasingly choosing their own mates. Marriage ceremonies are elaborate and may last for the better part of a week. The groom sends the bride's mother a gallon of milk as a symbolic act of repayment for her having suckled his future wife. Following the wedding, the young couple moves in with the husband's family. The extended family is typical of Newar society. Just above the level of the family is an important Newar socio-ritual organization known as the *guthi*. *Guthis* are associations often—although not always—based on common descent and organized for religious, social, and public-service purposes.

¹¹CLOTHING

The traditional dress of Newar men is the same as that of all Nepālis. It consists of tight-fitting trousers (*suruwa*) that flare out to a very loose fit around the upper thighs and seat. Over these is worn a blouse-type shirt (*laa*) tied with string on one side of the chest and falling to mid-thigh, with a cloth belt tied around the waist. Newar women wear the *parsi*, a garment like a *sārī* except that it is wrapped around the waist rather than having one end over the shoulder. With the parsi is worn the *misa-laa*, a long-sleeved blouse that fastens at the side of the chest; the *jani*, a wide sash tied around the waist; and the *ga* or scarf. The Indian *sārī* and blouse are also popular with Newar women. Young men typically wear Western-style shirts and pants.

¹²FOOD

The Newar follow the Nepāli habit of eating two main meals a day. A light breakfast of tea and snacks may be taken, but the first heavy meal of the day is consumed in the late morning. This typically consists of boiled rice, lentil curry, and one or two dishes such as potatoes and green-leafed vegetables. This meal is accompanied by pickled chilies, radishes, or other condiments. The second main meal of the day is eaten after sunset and is similar to the morning meal but may include some meat dishes. Buffalo, goat, and chicken are eaten, although pork is avoided, as is yak, which is considered as on a par with the cow. The *momocha*, a steamed, meat-filled pie much like the Tibetan *momo*, is popular among the upper castes. Sweet dishes are also popular and tea is drunk at any time of the day. Liquor, mostly brewed at home from rice, is indispensable in Newar social as well as ritual life.

¹³EDUCATION

Education levels in Nepal are low, with more than one-third of the adult population having no formal schooling. Literacy among the general population over 15 years old is only 45.2% (2001), but for women it is only 27.6%.

The education system in Nepal is characterized by large disparities in primary and secondary school attendance. School attendance rates are higher among boys, residents of urban areas, and children from wealthier households. Among the Newar, some 88% of households have children in primary school, while 52.3% have children in secondary schools—both values considerably higher than those for Nepal as a whole. This no doubt reflects the fact that the bulk of the Newar live in the Kathmandu Valley, where access to educational institutions is easier than in the rest of the country.

The 10 years of the Maoist insurgency have played havoc with the education system in Nepal. "The situation with regard to education has become so bad that it will take several decades to restore what we had achieved before the conflict started," said Dipendra Roka, a schoolteacher in Salle village in Rukum district, about 300 km northwest of the capital, Kathmandu. Like many rural hill districts, Rukum has experienced very low school attendance since the conflict started, due to abductions by rebels who have often forced students and teachers to march to the remotest parts of the district to attend their cultural and "revolutionary orientation" programs. Most schools in the district are also running out of books, other teaching materials and even decently-built classrooms, as the government has failed to use the education budget to maintain infrastructure and supplies, local teachers say.

¹⁴CULTURAL HERITAGE

Buddhist *stupas* (shrines) dating to the 3rd century BC are all that is left of the early cultures of the Kathmandu Valley, but numerous magnificent stone sculptures survive from the subsequent Licchavi period. Malla rule ushered in another era of artistic achievement. Under the Mallas (13th to 18th centuries), Newar artisans carried woodcarving, metal work, and stone sculpture to new heights. This work can be seen in temples, palaces, and courtyards throughout the Kathmandu Valley. In the late 13th century, a Newar architect introduced the Valley's distinctive multi-tiered, pagoda-style roof into Tibet, and from there it spread to East Asia. Tibetan influences on Newar art can be seen in the Golden Gate of Bhaktapur, a mid-18th century gilded copper gate considered the single most important work of art in the valley. Newari painting is religious in nature and encompasses the illuminated manuscripts of the 11th century to more recent Tibetan-style *thankas* (painted scrolls). *Kumārī* is the classical dance form of the Newars, and folk songs and dances play an important role in Newar life.

¹⁵WORK

Newars have traditionally been involved in agriculture, commerce, and crafts, and these remain their main occupations today. With the modernization of Nepal, however, many have found their way into government, administrative, professional, and clerical occupations. An expanding tourism industry has also created opportunities for employment.

¹⁶SPORTS

Sports and games of the Newars tend to be of the indoor variety, many of them involving gambling. The upper classes enjoy chess and other board games. Cards are popular with both adults and young people. Young boys fly kites, play marbles, spin tops, and also play a game called *khopi*, which involves betting on a coin tossed into a scoop. Girls enjoy playing with dolls. Outdoor sports such as soccer are played in Kathmandu and other major cities.

A young Newar girl and an older relative at the girl's Ihi ceremony in a Buddhist temple in Kathmandu. The Ihi is a mock-marriage with the god Vishnu and every Newar girl goes through the ceremony sometime between the age of five and ten. (© Anders Ryman/Corbis)

¹⁷ ENTERTAINMENT AND RECREATION

Living where they do, Newars have access to the modern amenities offered by the city of Kathmandu and nearby towns. Government-controlled radio and television programming is available to those who can afford receivers. Theaters in the cities show movies, mostly Indian. Many Newar cannot afford modern entertainment, however, and turn to religious festivals and folk traditions of song, music, and dance for their recreation.

¹⁸ FOLK ART, CRAFTS, AND HOBBIES

Many of the traditional handicrafts of the Newar focus on religious objects. Artisan castes are known for their skill in casting images in bronze, brass, copper, and other metals. Carving in stone and wood is also commonplace. Among the numerous items available are statues of deities, prayer wheels, *thankas* (painted scrolls), Nepālī *khukhrīs* (curved knives), and paper maché dance masks. More utilitarian crafts include weaving, pottery, and basketry.

¹⁹ SOCIAL PROBLEMS

Many of the Newars' social problems are typical of populations in other developing countries. It has been less than 50 years since Nepal, which was closed to the outside of the world since 1816, abandoned its policy of isolation. Despite efforts by

the government, Newars are faced with problems of poverty, overcrowding, poor sanitation and inadequate health facilities. Political instability and problems with the structure of Nepal's economy (low levels of industrialization, a lack of mineral resources, a severe shortage of skilled labor, and heavy reliance on foreign aid) hinder solutions to many of these problems. Environmental problems are increasing, with the Kathmandu Valley facing severe air and water pollution.

In Nepal, there are certain groups of people who for historical, social, or cultural reasons have become, or remained poor, and the government of Nepal has classed these people as "*janajatis*" (similar to *adivasis* or "indigenous peoples" in India). Janajatis are defined as persons who have their own language and traditional culture and who are not included under the conventional Hindu hierarchical caste structure and are accorded reserved seats in terms of political representation, educational institutions, and jobs. There are umbrella janajati organizations such as Federation of Indigenous Nationalities (NEFIN), which are lobbying for more rights for janajatis to break the dominance of high caste Hindus (i.e. the Brahmans and the chhetris) in the country.

One problem facing the Newars, who are classed by the government as janajatis, is whether or not to take advantage of the benefit offered by this status. "Newars with their proud cultural history and economic status were never janajatis and will never claim that status," wrote Pradip Shrestha, a Newar, in the weekly *Nepal Jagaran*. Accepting Shrestha's views would mean giving up the "special arrangements for education, health and employment" that the Nepali Constitution promises for "economically and socially" disadvantaged janajatis.

[20] GENDER ISSUES

Newar women's roles are both like and unlike those of women in patrilineal households in other cultures in South Asia. They have greater freedom than their Brahman and Chhetri counterparts in Nepal, but nonetheless occupy the same subservient status in society. Newar women's restrictions at menstruation—a time of impurity for higher caste Hindus—are considerably less. Menstruating Newar women can comb their own hair, and may continue to sleep in their usual place, although they sometimes go to another household woman's sleeping area to sleep. They can cook all foods except rice to be used for ceremonial purposes and can attend ceremonial family feasts, although they are not supposed to carry water or touch god images, sacred utensils, or priests.

Women are able to move outside the house with greater ease than Brahman and Chhetri women and also are able to start up their own businesses. Newar women cannot inherit property, but retain personal control over their dowry, often investing it in businesses such as money-lending or renting out livestock. There are women's organizations, such as the Kathmandu Federation of Business and Professional Women, which serve as forums to articulate the interests and problems of women in Nepal, particularly those related to working women.

Nonetheless, Newar women still fulfill the roles of running the household and bearing children, preferably sons to continue the lineage, which are so typical of women in South Asian societies.

[21] BIBLIOGRAPHY

Bista, Dor Bahadur. *People of Nepal*. 2nd ed. Kathmandu, Nepal: Ratna Pustak Bhandar, 1972.

Chattopadhyay, K. P. *An Essay on the History of Newar Culture*. Kathmandu: Educational Enterprise, 1980.

Lall, Kesar. *The Newar Merchants in Lhasa*. Kathmandu: Ratna Pustak Bhandar, 2001.

Nepālī, Gopal Singh. *The Newars: An Ethno-Sociological Study of a Himalayan Community*. Bombay: United Asia Publications, 1965.

Rose, Leo E. and John T. Scholz. *Nepal: Profile of a Himalayan Kingdom*. Boulder, CO: Westview Press, 1980.

Toffin, Gerard. *From Kin to Caste: The Role of Guthis in Newar Society and Culture*. Lalitpur: Social Science Baha, 2005.

Vergati, Anne. *Gods, Men, and Territory: Society and Culture in Kathmandu Valley*. New Delhi: Manohar, 2002.

—by D. O. Lodrick

NGAJU DAYAK

PRONUNCIATION: NGA-joo DAH-yahk
LOCATION: Indonesia (Kalimantan/Borneo)
POPULATION: About 800,000 (2003)
LANGUAGE: Ngaju
RELIGION: Traditional animism; Christianity (Protestant, Catholic); Islam
RELATED ARTICLES: Vol. 3: Indonesians

[1] INTRODUCTION

Originally meaning "inland" or "upriver," *Dayak* is a catch-all term to distinguish traditionally animist peoples of the interior of Borneo from the Islamized and Malayified coastal population. Despite centuries of cultural exchange through trade and the mixing of populations through migrations across the island, Dayak groups maintain distinct traditions and identities from one another, often more linked with peoples across the seas than those across the mountains. Individuals tend to identify with ancestral valleys; thus, for example, a Ngaju Dayak of Central Kalimantan calls her or himself an *oloh* ("person [of]") *Kahayan*, an *oloh Katingan*, or an *oloh Serayun*, depending on his or her locality of origin. Even a rough classification of Dayak peoples yields several groupings: the nomadic Punan of the deep interior forests; the Murut-Kadazan of Sabah and adjacent territory in Indonesia, whose languages have their closest relatives in the Philippines; the Lun Dayeh and Lun Bawang, who are linked to Sarawak's Kelabit; the Kayan and Kenyah of eastern Kalimantan; the Land Dayaks and Sea Dayaks (Iban) of western Kalimantan, who speak Malay dialects but do not share in Islamized Malay culture; and the large Barito-river groups of central Kalimantan, including the Ma'anyan, Ngaju, Ot Danum, Benuaq, and Tunjung.

This article will focus on the Ngaju of Central Kalimantan, the largest Dayak group in terms of population and the most influential politically and culturally. The name "Ngaju" signifies upriver (as opposed to *ngawa*, downriver). The Ngaju distinguish themselves from the Ot Danum, related but more conservative peoples living even further upriver (*Ot* itself means "upriver" and *Danum* means "water" or "river").

Austronesian peoples from the Philippines, farmers and seafarers, had arrived in Borneo by 3000 BC. Beginning in the 6th century AD, iron metallurgy provided Dayaks with the tools with which they could clear tracts in the dense interior forests for the cultivation of rice and taro, which was more nutritious than their former staple of sago palm starch. Since the early centuries AD, Dayak peoples have supplemented their subsistence agriculture by procuring forest products. These include gold, diamonds, gutta-percha, *illipe* nuts (source of a valued oil), aloeswood (an aromatic), resins, and camphor and bezoar stones (the hardened gall bladders of certain monkeys) and other ingredients for Chinese herbal medicines. Dayak traditionally traded them to coast-based brokers in exchange for such goods as Javanese gongs and Chinese porcelain and silk. The greatest brokers of all were the sultans (such as the ruler of Banjarmasin [*see* **Banjarese**]) who controlled the river mouths and thus all traffic between the Borneo interior and the outside world. Despite Banjarese claims to suzerainty over the upriver peoples in central Kalimantan, these latter, living in small semipermanent settlements scattered over a vast area, remained de facto independent.

Beginning in the 1830s, the Dutch colonial government promoted Protestant missionary efforts among the Dayaks; this slowed the progress of Islamization, reinforced among interior peoples a sense of a distinct identity, and created a Christianized Ngaju elite. Included within the Banjarmasin-centered province of South Kalimantan under the newly independent Indonesian republic, animist as well as Christianized Ngaju feared they would end up at the mercy of a Muslim Banjarese majority. After fighting a small-scale guerrilla war against the central government, the Ngaju were able in 1957 to achieve their goal of a province of their own (Central Kalimantan) and toleration of their traditional religion. Their ultimate success can be attributed in great part to the esteem in which the national military held the Ngaju leader Tjilik Riwut, an ex-parachutist and hero of the revolution.

Despite these political successes, the Ngaju still face being outnumbered within their own province. The New Order regime (1966-1998) greatly increased transmigration into Central Kalimantan (as into other parts of Kalimantan) of Javanese, Balinese, Madurese, and others (from 13,000 between 1971 and 1980 to 180,000 in 1981-1990 and a similar number in the following decade). The government's aggressive development program promoted a highly destructive logging industry that reduced forest land from 84% of the total area of Central Kalimantan in 1970 to 56% in 1999, dramatically diminishing the territory available to Ngaju swidden farming.

In 1996-1997, as Suharto seemed to be preparing to retire and a succession struggle appeared eminent, violence erupted in neighboring West Kalimantan where Dayaks targeted one group of transmigrants, the Madurese. Sparked by an incident between Malays and Madurese, fighting resumed between Dayaks and Madurese in 1999 after the fall of Suharto in the wake of the Asian/global emerging markets financial crisis of 1997-1998; the conflict killed 186 people and displaced at least 26,000 Madurese. Dayak-Madurese conflict broke out in Central Kalimantan in 2001, spreading from Sampit, a town that had become majority-Madurese, to the provincial capital of Palangkaraya, 220 km away. From February to May, almost 500 hundred Madurese were killed, and almost the whole Madurese community of over 100,000 fled the province. Dayaks in West and Central Kalimantan were not only exacting revenge on Madurese for perceived grievances but also scapegoating them for all that Dayaks had suffered under the New Order (other groups, Malays [including recently Islamized Dayaks], Bugis, and even Chinese reportedly joined in the anti-Madurese attacks). Central Kalimantan has remained quiet since, but the conflict between the interests of the indigenous peoples of Borneo and the goals of the national government persists.

2LOCATION AND HOMELAND

The terrain of Central Kalimantan province consists of several river valleys running north–south from the Schwaner and Muller Mountains to the Java Sea. Swamps extend from the coast deep into the interior, where they give way to dense jungle.

From a homeland along the Kahayan River, the Ngaju have spread as far west as the valley of the Seruyan. They have settled down to the mouth of the Kapuas, but, as one approaches the sea, they become more and more mixed with non-Day-

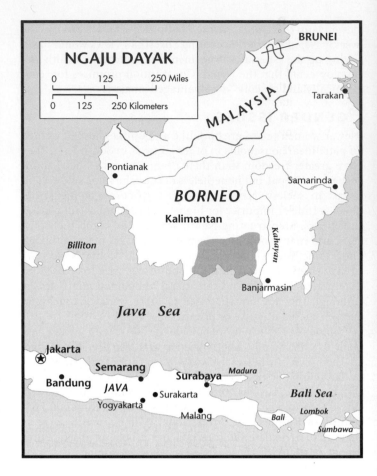

ak. The upper courses of the rivers are largely the preserve of the related Ot Danum Dayak. According to the 2000 census, Ngaju constituted 18% of the population of Central Kalimantan, 334,000 out of 1.86 million; they were outnumbered by Banjarese (24%) and equaled by Javanese (18%) transmigrants. A 2003 estimate places the number of Ngaju speakers as high as 800,000.

3LANGUAGE

The Ngaju language is one of a group of closely related Austronesian languages (the Barito family) spoken from the Schwaner Mountains and the upper Mahakam valley to the southeast corner of Borneo (minus Banjarese-speaking territory). The Kahayan dialect (called Bara-dia after its words for "have" and "not") has become a lingua franca throughout much of Kalimantan. Other major Barito-group languages are Ot Danum, Lawangan, and Ma'anyan. Incidentally, a dialect of Ma'anyan appears to be an ancestor to the languages of Madagascar; apparently, around the 5th century, Barito Dayaks were living closer to the coast and participated in long-distance seafaring under Malay leadership.

For the last five generations, Ngaju have had a system of given and family names (the Ot Danum adopted this only very recently). A man's full name will consist of his given name, the name of his father, and the name of a patrilineal ancestor. Upon marriage, a woman will keep her given name but replace the rest with the full name of her husband, e.g., a woman named Luise H. Tuwe marries Alex Banda Mambay and becomes Luise A. B. Mambay.

4FOLKLORE

See the article entitled **Indonesians**.

5RELIGION

According to the 1980 census, 17.71% of the population of Central Kalimantan (and a much larger percentage of the specifically Ngaju portion thereof) adhered to traditional animism, predominating in the more upriver villages. Some 14.27% of the provincial population was Protestant and 1.94% was Catholic. Because the schools were initially established by missionaries, the Ngaju elite is largely Christian. The rest of the provincial population is Muslim. In the past, conversion to Islam meant exchanging a Dayak identity for a Banjarese or Malay one. In recent times, however, many Dayaks (such as the Bakumpai, a Ngaju subgroup) have adopted Islam but remained Dayak in language and culture.

The traditional Ngaju religion recognizes *ganan*, spirits who dwell in house posts, in big rocks or trees, in the dense forest, and in bodies of water. These spirits divide into *sangiang* or *nayu-nayu* (benevolent spirits), *taloh* or *kambin* (malevolent spirits), and *liau* (ancestors). Gods include supreme deities of the upperworld (male) and the underworld (female). Various rituals are performed, from small offerings to the ancestors, to ceremonies marking major transitions in the individual's life, to community rites to ensure abundant harvests or cure epidemics. *Balian* (priestesses) and *basir* (transvestite priests) speak an esoteric language while being possessed by spirits. The abode of the dead is visualized much like that of the living, as a settlement consisting of houses strewn along a riverbank (though in former time the most privileged dead, those whose heirs were able to offer human sacrifices, would enjoy a hill-top estate).

The Indonesian state's requirement that all citizens adhere to a monotheistic religion has threatened the practice of the Ngaju's traditional animism. In response, Ngaju have formalized their religion under the name of Kaharingan (taken by Tjilik Riwut from the name of an "elixir of life" spring, *Danum Kaharingan Belum*) and to have the religion classified as an "offshoot" of Balinese Hinduism [*see* **Balinese**]. Kaharingan claims 330,000 adherents, including many Dayak who are not Ngaju. There is a 16-member council (almost all Ngaju) to coordinate theology and rituals; however, this does not include balian or basir. Through a 300-page study book (published in 1981), Hindu-Balinese–style meeting halls, and sermons, prayers, and hymns, the council aims to instill concepts of individual salvation and a supreme being. For instance, it promotes the already widely accepted identification of the important god Tempon Telon with Jesus Christ. Nowadays, no *tiwah* celebration takes place without being registered with the council, which directs the police to issue the required permit.

6MAJOR HOLIDAYS

See the article entitled **Indonesians**.

7RITES OF PASSAGE

Men wed at the age of 20, women at 18. Formerly, parents chose a child's partner, but now school-educated young people choose their own spouses. Bringing a sum of cash, the man's parents deliver the proposal for him to the woman's parents.

The woman's parents call their kin together to discuss the proposal. They try to discover whether the man is of good character and has no blood of slaves. If the woman's kin decide to refuse the proposal, they return the money. If they accept it, they arrange the betrothal ceremony and feast, bearing the whole cost thereof.

The two sides negotiate a bride-price (*palaku*), the wedding expenses to be paid by the man's family, and the date of the wedding. The woman's side may set a very high palaku as an assertion of its own status; too high a palaku may cause the man's side to withdraw the proposal. The man's side must first present *bahalai* (cloth for a woman's sarong), cloth for a *kebaya* (blouse), *perfume*, gold rings, etc., to the woman's side. The palaku is often returned to the husband later if he has shown himself to be a good man who loves his wife. In addition, the man presents *saput*, a gift consisting of an heirloom gong or porcelain, to the wife's siblings as a sign of gratitude for their having taken care of his future wife. Moreover, a *panangkalau*, a similar gift, is given to any older sister of the wife who is not yet married; this is to ward off any disaster that would follow upon a younger sister daring to marry before an elder sister. The wedding contract (*surat pisek*) is sealed with the taking of medicinal herbs. From one month to three years may elapse between the betrothal and the wedding itself, depending upon the financial resources of the man's side.

Funerals unfold in two stages. The primary burial rite sends the soul of the departed to the lower part of heaven; the secondary ceremony (*tiwah*) enables the soul to pass into the highest heaven, Lewu Tatau, where it meets the supreme god Ranying and will never again suffer disasters, difficulties, or fatigue. First, the corpse is laid in a wooden coffin in the shape of a boat or a trough for pounding rice. This first burial includes masked performers dancing to ward off evil spirits, and priests chanting to the accompaniment of drumming.

A tiwah costs the equivalent of $6,000–$12,000; it requires the sacrifice of many water buffalo and pigs, and the feeding of numerous visitors who come in from villages scattered over a wide area. The expense is such that groups of families can mount tiwah only every seven years or so; those dying within that interval are given a common tiwah that takes from one to three weeks. *Balian* sing legends and genealogies from memory for hours and hours and perform dances. To take advantage of the gathered crowds, individuals set up stalls to sell prepared food and other goods, as well as venues for gambling nearby.

The bones of a deceased person are exhumed from the *raung* (sometimes, the corpses need to be cremated first) and deposited in *sandung*. These are houses, 2 m (6.5 ft) high, intricately carved with representations of the hornbill, symbolic of the upperworld, and of the lower world's *naga* serpent (the Ma'anyan inter the bones of whole families in the larger *pambak* mausolea); modern sandung are often of concrete. Sacrificial animals are slaughtered while tied to a *sepunduq*, a post carved with images of demons with fangs, huge protruding tongues, and long noses. Another piece of funerary art is the *sengkaran*, a 6-m (20-ft) pole representing the "tree of life" (a symbol of the cosmos); at the top is a hornbill flying over a forest of spears stuck into the back of a naga that lies on a Chinese heirloom jar. Also important are "ships-of-the-dead," small, model sailing ships with a crew of benevolent spirits made of gutta-percha (a kind of latex); these are now produced throughout Kalimantan for tourists.

[8] INTERPERSONAL RELATIONS

Traditional Ngaju society was divided into three classes: the *utus gantong* or *utus tatau*, the *utus rendah,* and slaves. Living in the upriver part of the village, the utus gantong were people of influence and wealth, status inherent in their possession of gongs and porcelain; the *demang* (chieftains) came from this group. Living downriver, the utus rendah were free persons but lacked such prestige goods. *Balian* or *basir* (religious specialists) could come from this group; specializing in, among other duties, chanting at funerals, they did not labor in the fields, and offenses against them were doubly punished. The slaves were either *jipen* (accepting bondage to pay off a debt) or *rewar* (captured in war and sometimes designated as human sacrifices); slavery was abolished in 1892, but the stigma of slave ancestry remains.

Prominent individuals took noble titles of Banjarese (Javano-Malay) origin. Under the current Indonesian government scheme, the *demang* (named for life because of their personal qualities) stand between the village heads (*kepala desa*) and district heads *(camat).* The kepala desa is elected for life, has an assistant *(sekretaris),* and a subordinate in charge of agriculture and land holdings (*kepala padang*). A council of elders advises him, but everyone has the right to give an opinion on matters of common interest (individuals who have experience of the outside world are listened to the most eagerly). Many villages, particularly those farthest upriver, are in effect autonomous from higher administration. Unwritten customary law emphasizes fines and rites to propitiate offended spirits; the village council with the village head presiding decides punishments.

The Dayak have had a reputation (often exaggerated by Westerners) for relatively free sexual relations. It is clear that a women's pleasure was given priority, as when men wore the penis pin (*palang,* in historical times known among the Ngaju only in the Katingan valley). Young men and women can interact freely, for instance joke and dance, when older people are watching. A man can speak with another's wife as long as a third party is present. If a man is found alone in a deserted place with a woman other than his wife or sister, he must pay a fine (*singér*).

[9] LIVING CONDITIONS

Villages are on or near rivers (generally the only way to get between settlements) and include a central community house and a place to dock boats.

Most people spend as much as half the year away from the main settlement in smaller ones near their respective swidden (shifting-cultivation) fields, returning only for major ritual celebrations. Houses are built either directly along the river shore or along a road parallel to the river. Long-houses (*betang*) are only found now among the Ot Danum (those of other Dayak peoples may house the equivalent of an entire village in as many as 50 single-family rooms [*bilik]*). Among the Ngaju, longhouses were only built by the rare individuals who were able to amass the capital necessary to build them, and they represented so huge an investment that they were not abandoned even when the owners needed to farm increasingly distant swidden fields. Contemporary Ngaju live in large extended family dwellings (*umah hai*) housing one to five nuclear families (a couple, unmarried children, and their married daughters and their families). Raised on 2.5-m (8-ft) pillars, houses have walls of wooden shingles or pieces of bark. Wealthier families build houses in a "Dutch" style, complete with chairs, coffee tables, china cabinets, and the like (traditional houses have no furniture).

The Ngaju home province, Central Kalimantan has a Human Development Index (combining measures of income, health, and education) of 73.5 (2005 score), far higher than Indonesia's national score of 69.6 and the fifth highest in the country (after Jakarta, North Sulawesi, Riau, and Yogyakarta). Central Kalimantan's GDP per capita is us$10,976, among the highest in the country (cf. us$10,910 for North Sumatra, us$6,293 for Central Java and us$2,919 for North Maluku). In 2000, the level of infant mortality, at 47.68 deaths per 1,000 live births, was the third lowest in country (after the national capital region of Jakarta and the highly urbanized Yogyakarta region).

[10] FAMILY LIFE

The basic kin group consists of a nuclear family expanded to include the families of married daughters; kinship is reckoned on both the mother's and father's sides. According to custom, the ideal marriage is between the grandchildren of two brothers; also preferred are matches between the children of two sisters and between the children of a brother and a sister. Taboo, however, are matches between the children of brothers and especially between generations, as between an uncle and a niece. In the latter case, the infringing couple is required to eat from a pig manger with the entire village as witnesses, otherwise, the couple *and* the village will suffer calamities as supernatural punishment.

As taking a second wife is too expensive, polygamy rarely occurs. The divorce rate is high (one Ma'anyan village counted as many as one in four marriages ending in divorce). Infidelity by the husband or the wife is the usual reason; barrenness is not sufficient cause because childless couples adopt. In the case of divorce, younger children stay with the mother, while older children can become the responsibility of other kin of either side, depending on the circumstances.

[11] CLOTHING

In earlier times, Ngaju made cloth from bark or wove it from cotton. Nowadays, they wear manufactured clothes imported via the coastal ports.

Traditional ceremonial clothing for men includes a head cloth decorated with hornbill feathers; a sleeveless shirt; short pants; two pieces of cloth to cover the front and back of the body down to the knees; a *penyang,* or belt made of leopard claws; bead necklaces; a *mandau* sword; and a richly carved wooden shield. Women's attire is essentially the same, except that gold thread and beads are worked into the front and back cloths, the *penyang* is of copper plates, and numerous bracelets are worn.

Though much less so today than in the past, Ngaju (as other Dayaks) have intricate tattoos and stretch their earlobes down to the shoulders with numerous earrings.

[12] FOOD

The staple foods are rice, cassava, and various tubers. Cassava leaves are commonly cooked as a side dish, as are river fish (game is eaten only rarely; this includes wild pigs, monkeys, snakes, and wild fowl). Regional specialties include: *sayur rimbang,* a large eggplant cooked with river fish; *sayur ambut,* a pungent dish combining fish and tender shoots of rattan; and *wadi* and *paksem*, fermented mixtures of meat (fish, wild pig, deer, or deermouse) and rice. Durian is a popular sweet, preserved as *tempoyak* or made into *dodol* taffy.

Anding, an alcoholic drink made from glutinous rice, is used in rituals and is an indispensable part of all celebrations. Tea and coffee are drinks for everyday consumption. One makes *barum gula* by fermenting 4 kg (8.8 lbs) of boiled glutinous rice in a jar with cloves, cinnamon, and peppers and adding sugar after a week. Both men and women are fond of chewing betel nut.

13 EDUCATION

In 2005, North Sulawesi's level of literacy stood at 98.87%, high by Indonesian national standards and even higher than in the region of the national capital, Jakarta (*See also* the article entitled **Indonesians** in this volume).

14 CULTURAL HERITAGE

All ceremonies feature the playing of an *ije karepang*, an ensemble of five Javanese gongs; to this are added the *tarai* (a flat gong), the *tangkanong* (a xylophone), and *gandang* (drums).

Each of the many traditional dances serves a particular function. The *deder ketingan* offers young people an opportunity to mix at traditional feasts. The *enggang terbang* ("flying hornbill") honors the ancestors. The *kunjan halu*, originally a post-harvest dance of thanksgiving to the gods, serves now as a *tiwah* funeral feast entertainment. The *kinyah kambe* is a trance or possession dance. The *balian bawo* heals sickness. The *giring-giring* greets guests. The *munambang pangkalima* celebrates victory in battle.

15 WORK

Most Ngaju support themselves by practicing swidden shifting-cultivation agriculture, growing dry rice and other plants, such as cassava, *ubi rambat* (a kind of tuber with a creeping vine), taro, eggplant, pineapple, banana, sugarcane, chili, gourds, and sometimes tobacco. This requires cooperation between families; men generally do the work in the fields, but women do also, if their family has lost its adult men through death or for some other reason. Among Dayak groups, the Ngaju have pioneered the growing of cash crops on permanent fields, primarily rattan and rubber but also cloves, oil palms, coffee, pepper, and cacao. Pigs and chickens are kept for ritual consumption. Catching river fish provides the main source of protein, more important than hunting wild pigs with spears and dogs and shooting down fowl with blowguns; hunters also use snares, as well as traps employing wooden or bamboo spikes.

Ngaju also sell forest products to brokers from the coast, including valuable woods, such as ironwood *(ulin)*, damar resin, *kulit gemur* (used for cosmetics and insect repellant), and *illipe* nuts.

16 SPORTS

Cockfighting and *kinyah* (a form of *silat* [see **Malaysian Malays**] martial art) are popular sports.

17 ENTERTAINMENT AND RECREATION

See the article entitled **Indonesians**.

18 FOLK ART, CRAFTS, AND HOBBIES

Traditional arts include mat- and basket-weaving, textile-weaving, canoe-making (especially among the Ma'anyan), pottery, and tattooing. Particularly noteworthy is the production of *mandau* swords and *sumpitan*, blowguns unique because they consist of a shaft of ironwood through which a hole has been drilled. Non-Dayak blowguns consist of split wood or bamboo tied back together. Woodcarving is also highly developed. Dayak artwork features repeated geometrical forms, such as spirals (an influence from the Dong Son culture of ancient northern Vietnam) and densely packed yet harmonious combinations of stylized motifs, especially fantastical animals, reflecting inspiration from Chinese art of the late Zhou dynasty.

19 SOCIAL PROBLEMS

See the article entitled **Indonesians**.

20 GENDER ISSUES

Central Kalimantan's Gender-Related Development Index (combining measures of women's health, education, and income relative to men's) is 60.9, higher than Indonesia's national GDI of 59.2. The province's Gender Empowerment Measure (reflecting women's participation and power in political and economic life relative to men's), however, is 51.8, significantly lower than the national GEM (54.6).

21 BIBLIOGRAPHY

Bertrand, Jacques. *Nationalism and Ethnic Conflict in Indonesia*. Cambridge, UK: Cambridge University Press, 2004.

Danandjaja, J. "Kebudayaan Penduduk Kalimantan Tengah" [The Culture of the Inhabitants of Central Kalimantan]. In *Manusia dan Kebudayaan di Indonesia* [Man and Culture in Indonesia], edited by Koentjaraningrat. Jakarta: Djambatan, 1975.

Darity, and Djongga L. Batu. "Kalimantan Barat, propinsi." In *Ensiklopedi Nasional Indonesia*, Vol. 8. Jakarta: Cipta Adi Pustaka, 1990.

Data Statistik Indonesia. http://demografi.bps.go.id/ (November 8, 2008).

LeBar, Frank M., ed. *Ethnic Groups of Insular Southeast Asia*. Vol. 1, *Indonesia, Andaman Islands, and Madagascar*. New Haven, CT: Human Relations Area Files Press, 1972.

Loveband, Anne and Ken Young. "Migration, Provocateurs and Communal Conflict: The Cases of Ambon and West Kalimantan." In Charles A. Coppel, ed., *Violent Conflicts in Indonesia: Analysis, Representation, Resolution*. London: Routledge, 2006.

Muller, Kal. *Borneo: Journey into the Tropical Rainforest*. Lincolnwood, IL: Passport Books, 1990.

Profil Propinsi Republik Indonesia, Vol. 11, *Kalimantan Tengah*. Jakarta: Yayasan Bhakti Wawasan Nusantara, 1992.

Sevin, Olivier. *Les Dayak du Centre Kalimantan: Etude Géographique de Pays Ngaju de la Serayun a la Kahayan*. Paris: Orstom, 1983.

Waterson, Roxana. *The Living House: An Anthropology of Architecture in South-East Asia*. Singapore: Oxford University Press, 1990.

—revised by A. J. Abalahin

NIASANS

PRONUNCIATION: nee-AHS-uns (Nias: "NEE-ahs")
LOCATION: Indonesia (island of Nias, off the northwest coast of Sumatra)
POPULATION: over 700,000
LANGUAGE: Nias
RELIGION: Christianity (Protestant, Catholic); Islam; Pelebegu (indigenous religion)
RELATED ARTICLES: Vol. 3: Indonesians

¹INTRODUCTION

While most Indonesian ethnic groups identify themselves with a named place or, at the very least, with a general direction such as "upstream," the indigenous inhabitants of the island of Nias call themselves *ono niha*, "children of the humans." Lumping all other Indonesians as *dava*, the language itself reflects the isolation in which Niasan culture has developed over the millennia. The Niasans' Austronesian ancestors arrived as early as 3000 BC. This inward orientation also manifests itself in the fact that, despite the myth of a common origin in central Nias, each Nias village has virtually been a world unto itself, cultivating traditions distinct from even its nearest neighbors.

From genealogies and myths going back 30 to 40 generations, scholars calculate that Nias' aristocratic, megalith-raising culture dates back to the 8th century AD. It may well have been fueled by the export of slaves from the very beginning. The first reference to Nias (from an Arab travelogue) dates to AD 851–13th-century Arab sources describe its slave trade as already ancient. When the island first drew the attention of the Dutch East India Company (VOC), the Muslim Acehnese satisfied a Niasan chief's insatiable appetite for gold in exchange for Niasan slaves, whose paganism made them a valuable commodity in a by then largely Islamized archipelago (Islamic law forbade Muslims to enslave Muslims). The VOC gained entry to the island by concluding pacts with coastal chiefs needing protection from slavers; the slave trade was depopulating the north of the island and militarizing society (slavery would persist long after Dutch abolition in 1860).

Although the Dutch established their first garrison at the port of Gunung Sitoli in 1840 and enjoyed nominal control of the entire island by 1857, it was not until 1906 that, with the costly Acehnese war over [*see* **Acehnese**], they achieved a complete subjugation. Of even greater long-term significance was the arrival in 1865 of the Rhenish Missionary Society (German Lutherans). Conversions were few until the crumbling of traditional society in the face of colonialism threw the indigenous ideology into question; South and Central Nias submitted to the new religion only after the devastation of epidemics and brutal colonial repression.

In the mid-1910s, apocalyptic Christian revival movements convulsed Nias, throwing up native prophets to challenge the authority of the German missionaries. Nativist schisms continued after the end of colonialism, and Roman Catholic missionaries came to break the Protestant monopoly. Although the Indonesian state has provided some basic infrastructure and services and the dava (non-Niasan) population has grown, Nias remains isolated and underdeveloped. The level of infant mortality is high, and the incidence of malaria and cholera is very grave despite the operation of government health clinics.

The earthquake and tsunami of 26 December 2004 and the earthquake of 28 March 2005 (the world's second most powerful since 1965) devastated much of Nias, leaving hundreds dead and thousands more homeless as nearly every dwelling on the island sustained some degree of damage; the coastline in many places receded as much as 50 meters, and much of the island's infrastructure of harbors, bridges, and roads was destroyed as well as over 700 schools and 1,000 places of worship. Just as in nearby Aceh, many international organizations are assisting in the reconstruction.

²LOCATION AND HOMELAND

The island of Nias is 130 km (81 m) long by 45 km (28 mi) wide, slightly smaller than Bali (which is about the size of Delaware). Across a 125-km-wide (78-mi-wide) strait, one can see Sumatra's volcanic peaks. The terrain is rugged, and, with a growing population of 712,000 (2005, up from 200,000 in 1959, an increase of more than 3.5 times), deforestation is becoming a problem. About 200 years ago, Niasans also settled on the Batu Islands to the south.

For Niasans, the important reference points are not the cardinal directions but *raya*, "upstream," and *yu*, "downstream," added even in mentioning the house next door. "Left" and "right" are not specified; one simply says *mi sa* or *tan sa*, "to the side" or sometimes *raya* and "*yu*." The *ulu*, the river source, is considered the origin of all things sacred, while the sea is seen as the abode of monsters and evil spirits.

³LANGUAGE

The Nias language is Austronesian and is probably most closely related to Mentawai and Batak, but centuries or millennia of isolated development have given it a coincidentally "Polynesian" phonetic appearance, as in its having only open (vowel-final) syllables. Three dialect-groups (North, Central, and South) are distinguished, of which the Laraga dialect of the North was chosen to translate the Bible, and subsequently became the standard form for all secular publications.

Although most ordinary adult villagers do not have a mastery of Bahasa Indonesia beyond the ability to sing a few patriotic songs, all children, as recipients of an elementary education and listeners of the radio, are fluent in it.

After the birth of a child, his or her parents are no longer known by their personal names but as *Ama* [child's name, e.g., Rosa] or *Ina* [child's name] ("Father of …," "Mother of …").

⁴FOLKLORE

According to the current version of the Niasan creation myth, the god Lovalangi created the world and placed on it Tora'a, the tree of life. Tora'a grew two fruits, cared for by a golden spider. From the fruits hatched out a god and a goddess; their divine descendants populated heaven, living under the kingship of one of their number, Sirao Uwu Zihönö.

Sirao took three wives and sired three sons by each. When he wanted to retire, his nine sons began to quarrel over the succession. So he had them compete for the throne in a contest of dancing on nine spears. The youngest, Luo Mewona, won. In order to avoid further conflict, Sirao sent Luo Mewona's eight older brothers down to earth.

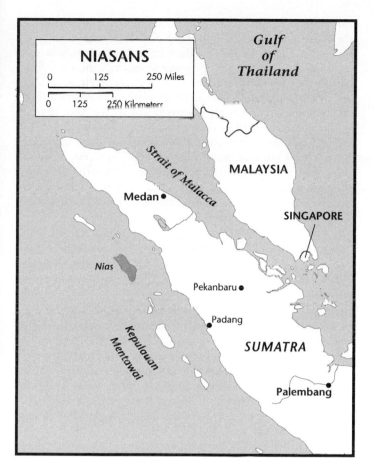

NIASANS

0   125   250 Miles

0   125   250 Kilometers

Gulf of Thailand

MALAYSIA

SINGAPORE

Strait of Malacca

Medan •

Nias

Pekanbaru •

Padang •

Kepulauan Mentawai

SUMATRA

Palembang •

Of the eight, only four reached the earth (i.e., the island of Nias) safely; they became the ancestors of the Niasan clans. Of the other four, one, being too heavy, pierced the earth, becoming a giant serpent, the "supporter of the earth and the cause of earthquakes." Another fell into the water and became the spirit of the rivers, to be worshipped by fishers. Yet another was carried away by the wind and became the spirit of the forest, to be worshipped by hunters. The last hit earth at a stony area in the north of the island, becoming the ancestor of experts in invulnerability magic.

⁵RELIGION

Six out of seven inhabitants of Nias are Protestant; the remainder is about evenly divided between Muslim (mostly immigrants from elsewhere in Indonesia) and Catholic. The folk Christianity that has developed emphasizes a relationship between God and humanity that focuses on prohibitions, which are largely compatible with the traditional value system. Nonetheless, the colonial abolition of slavery, headhunting, and ancestor worship forever changed the context of those values.

A few thousand Niasans register themselves as adherents of Pelebegu, used first by non-Niasans, evidently from the Karo Batak *perbegu*, or Molohe adu, the Niasan expression, both meaning "worshipping the ancestral spirits." Before iconoclastic campaigns early in the century, the people took reverent care of the wooden statues of the *adu* ancestral spirits, filling shrines and the public rooms of their houses with them and making daily offerings to them. The mythology continues to be handed down in the *hoho* songs sung at feasts, even by

Christians. Originally, the highest god and creator of the world was Sihai. However, Protestant missionaries chose to translate the name of the Christian God with the name of another god, Lovalangi, whom the Niasans worshipped most as the deity responsible for their welfare. Thus, Niasans came to attribute the role of highest god and creator to Lovalangi.

According to traditional belief, a person has two bodies: a physical one *(boto)* and a spiritual one, consisting of "breath" *(noso)* and "shadow" *(lumölumö)*. At death, the boto becomes dust, the noso goes to Lovalangi, and the *lumölumö* becomes a *bekhu,* a ghost. The indigenous conception of the other world described it as opposite to this world in every detail (night here is day there; sentences here run backwards there) except that the rich and powerful of this world enjoyed the same high status in the other world—provided their kin mounted expensive funerary ceremonies (otherwise, bekhu remained in the vicinity of the grave). The Christian-influenced scenario that has become current is that a soul reaches heaven (Teteholi Ana'a) only after crossing a bridge blocked by a guardian god and his cat. A person who has sins on his conscience *and* who has not been given the proper ceremonies is pushed off the bridge into hell, which is below.

Priests *(ere),* who are considered to be representatives of Silewe Narazata, one of the high gods, can be either men or women. A person destined to become an *ere* first disappears for a time, i.e., is carried off by spirits. After returning, he or she learns from an experienced *ere* how to perform ritual chants, sacrifice cocks, make spirit images, and cure disease. Also important are *kataruna,* women and girls specializing in trance, who provide oracles and also heal diseases.

⁶MAJOR HOLIDAYS

In the *boro n'adu* ceremony, traditionally held every 7 or 14 years, priests destroy totemic symbols at the spot where the Niasan ancestors descended from the upperworld, e.g., a giant tiger representing a ruler was carried on a high platform and cast into the Gomo River. Missionaries outlawed the ceremony in 1913, but it has recently been revived as part of Indonesian Independence Day festivities.

⁷RITES OF PASSAGE

Boys undergo *fumoto* (circumcision); Christianized Niasans vehemently opposed the German missionaries' attempts to ban the practice, long predating Islamic influence.

In addition to considering social status, a man tries to confirm that the woman of his choice for marriage is indeed his "predestined match" *(tambali)* by looking for omens. In the past, he would resort to divination to discover whether the ancestors had joined the couple.

The wedding process involves the following stages. The man's kin issues the proposal, presenting the women's kin with betrothal wealth of three *pao* (30 g or 1 oz) of gold; the latter gives them in turn a basketry container *(bola)* containing the lower jaw, heart, and liver of a pig. The man's kin must return the bola to them full of boiled pork. Once resources for the wedding expenses have been accumulated, a *fangötö bongi* ceremony is held at which the two sides decide the wedding date and the amount of the bride-price. In some areas, this can still be quite substantial, for example 100 large pigs. Men who cannot afford the bride-price must work for the bride's family for a specified time. At the *fangowalu,* the wedding ceremony itself, huge numbers of pigs are slaughtered to serve guests and display wealth. The groom brings the bride back to his house on a litter. In the *famuli nucha* ceremony, the couple, after two weeks, pays a call on the bride's parents, bringing boiled pork and returning the bridal jewelry that had been borrowed earlier. The bride's parents in turn present them with a specially bred sow, seed rice, and a *balewa* (a large machete), the basics with which to start a household.

When a man knows his death is imminent, he gives his blessing to and prays over his sons; this *famalakhisi* ceremony ensures that the sons, who serve the father pork, will not have lives full of obstacles. Customs for handling the corpse differ from region to region. In some areas, bodies are exposed on a platform in the graveyard until the bones are picked clean, at which time a secondary burial can be held. In others, the body is put into a coffin. The bodies of slaves were simply thrown into the forest.

The *fanörö satua*, or secondary burial, is necessary for the soul's passage to heaven (Teteholi Ana'a). Including the slaughter of pigs (and formerly the sacrifice of slaves), these ceremonies are the opportunity for the display of wealth.

⁸INTERPERSONAL RELATIONS

At the end of the 18th century, Nias had more than 50 constantly warring *öri*, independent confederations of villages (*banua*). Leading each confederation was a *tuhenöri*, and heading each village was a *salawa*, drawn from the founding and dominant clan of the community.

Niasan society was composed of a number of the following social strata: aristocrats, priests (*ere*), commoners, and slaves. Among aristocrats, called siulu, literally "those of the river source," further distinction was made between rulers (*balö ziulu*) and the rest. Likewise, the commoners (*ono mbanua*, "children of the village") divided into *siila*, commoner leaders and various specialists, and *satö*, the ordinary people. Slaves (*sawuyu*) included three categories: *binu*, those captured in war or through abduction; *sondrara-hare*, those selling themselves to pay off a debt; and *hölitö*, those delivered from a death sentence by another in exchange for servitude. Slaves might end their life as a sacrifice, accompanying their master to the grave.

The aristocrats met together to determine the tasks to be done every Wednesday by the whole community. Moreover, commoners were bound by obligations of debt to the aristocrats (for the most part incurred at feasts).

Although generally an individual could not cross class lines, e.g., a commoner could not become an aristocrat, within the two classes one could raise one's status by mounting "feasts of merit" (still given only in Central Nias). Anyone but the poorest can hold a small-scale feast (slaughtering up to 30 pigs) in order to pay off debts acquired in attending other people's feasts and to gain honor. The much more ambitious ovasa feast earns the *ovasa*-holder the position of village elder (*satua mbanua*), with the right to join the salawa in governing the village. The host's wife-givers confer on him a title, such as "Lamp of Flame" or "Heard and Obeyed"; the host may erect a stone monument in front of his house. In order to mount an ovasa, a man must call on the assistance of relatives and his wife-takers, persuading them to contribute to the feast (actually, to pay off previous debts to the host) through oratorical skill. The ovasa itself includes competing poetical speeches; various entertainments;

carrying of the ovasa-holder and wife in a procession through the village on a litter; slaughtering pigs; and distributing prestige-payments to the host's wife-givers. As aristocrats serve as channels for fertility-giving power from on high, their feasts benefit the whole community.

Contact between the young of opposite sexes is very difficult and, if dared, requires an intermediary. In the past, sex outside of marriage was punished with death (a couple could be bound and cast into a river). Illicit sex is assumed to damage the woman's kin and her own prospects for marriage. Thus, if the couple is not separated by taboo restrictions, the simplest solution is for the man to marry the woman. Otherwise, the man pays fines to her patrilineal kin (and, should she have one, to her husband's patrilineal kin).

⁹LIVING CONDITIONS

The village (*banua*, also meaning "sky") contains members of several clans (*mado*) and is usually built on a height for defense (for this reason too, villages in south Nias encompass as many as 3,000 people). Each village has a paved rectangular plaza (*evali* or, more poetically, *olayama*, "ceremonial dancing ground") that can be extended into a central avenue. On one end of the evali stands the *omo sebua* ("great house") of the chief lineage. On either side of the evali leading away from it are the ordinary houses (*omo niha*). The opposite end is left open (graveyards are often located there). By the omo sebua stands the village gate, which leads down a flight of stone steps to the valley below.

Niasans distinguish between *omo* (proper houses in the village), *ose* (the temporary huts of exiles from other villages), and *halama* (substantial huts near the fields). "Great houses" and ordinary houses differ only in size. The omo sebua are on a monumental scale, supported on massive, almost 1-m-thick (3-ft-thick), vertical and diagonal (bracing) pillars of ironwood, grounded in large foundation stones as proof against earthquake. With its great projecting eaves, the roof reaches much higher than the rest of the house, going as far up as 30 m (98 ft), while the room height would only be 4 m (13 ft). In north Nias, houses are smaller and have an oval plan.

Traditional houses (*omo hada*) possessed in front a large, light, and airy public room (*tavolo*) with a long bench built into the inner front wall for elders to sit on. Tavolo are otherwise empty, though formerly they were crowded with wooden ancestral figures. In the back is the private area for the dark, musty bedrooms or apartments for different related families (also separate sleeping areas for boys and unmarried men), and the kitchen with a big wood-framed hearth and utensils and other tools hanging from the walls.

In front of some houses stand various stone monuments. *Behu* are megaliths raised to commemorate feasts of merit. *Daro-daro* or *harefa* are stone slab seats. *Osa-osa* are thrones of honor with monster faces carved into their backs. Simulating the walls of enemy villages, stone pylons are raised for *zawözawö* jumping. Dancing women slap their feet on *ni'ogazi*, mushroom-shaped stones that produce a musical tone.

Central Nias villages used to have an *osali nazu*, a house for idols (as well as sacred weights and skulls taken for rituals) erected on a paved embankment. The chief's house served as the community meeting hall and place for rituals (often with space for 200 dancers); elsewhere on the island these functions took place in a separate structure called an *osali* (north) or *bale* (south). Churches also go by the name *osali*.

Modern extensions to traditional villages include houses on the general Indonesian model (*omo ndrava* or *omo pasisir*).

The two regencies into which the island of Nias is divided, Nias and South Nias, have Human Development Indices (combining measures of income, health, and education) of 66.1 and 63.9 respectively (2005 score), considerably lower than the national HDI of 69.6 and dramatically lower than the HDI for North Sumatra as a whole (72, in the top third in the country). Nias regency's GDP per capita is us$3,514, and South Nias regency's us$3,702, very low for Indonesia when compared with us$10,910 for North Sumatra as a whole, us$6,293 for Central Java, and us$3,427 for East Nusa Tenggara. In 2000, the rate of infant mortality for the whole island stood at 55.66 deaths per 1,000 live births, which was moderate for Indonesia, worse than provinces on Java but better than most in eastern Indonesia and comparable to provinces on Sumatra with higher GDP's per capita.

10 FAMILY LIFE

Niasans belong to *mado* (*gana* in the south), large patrilineal clans that often trace their heritage to a common ancestor 30 to 40 generations back. A household consists of a *sangambatö sebua* (*sangambatö*, "nuclear family"; *sebua*, "great"), which consists of a married couple, their unmarried children, and their married sons and their families all living together.

The ideal marriage is between a man and his mother's brother's daughter. Taboo is marriage between a man and a woman of the same clan related back to 10 generations, as well as between a man and a woman whose mother, grandmother, or great-grandmother, is of his own clan. Marriage creates a relation (expressed in flows of gifts) between a man as a "wife-taker" and the woman's brother, father, and her father's father-in-law and brother-in-law, her maternal grandfather's father-in-law and brother-in-law, and so on, as the "wife-givers." In pre-Christian times, a man might take more than one wife, usually due to the obligation to marry his deceased father's wives (other than his own mother). It was also common, but not mandatory, for a man to wed his brother's widow. If a man has no sons, he adopts one of his brother's sons. Sons, especially the eldest, and not daughters receive inheritance.

11 CLOTHING

Contemporary Niasans follow the mode of dress of other Indonesians, from the Western-style short-sleeve shirts and long pants of the men, to the sarong and *kebaya* combination for women. Colonial authorities forbade the "indecent" traditional clothing (which consisted of a loincloth of beaten bark; Niasans had no indigenous weaving). Today's war-dancer attire consists of a loincloth of brightly colored woven cloth hanging down to the calf at both front and back, an open jacket, and a head cloth. Ceremonial wear for women includes long-sleeved or sleeveless long dresses in solid colors with appliqué trimmings. Women's jewelry (genuine gold or copper imitation) comes in large pieces in simple designs (crowns, broad headbands, pectorals, bracelets, and petal-shaped earrings).

12 FOOD

Currently the staple food is rice, but formerly it was yams (*ubi rambat* in Bahasa Indonesia); on the Batu Islands it is sago.

Supplementary starch comes from yams, maize, and taro. The yam is boiled or roasted and eaten with sliced or grated coconut. Niasans make little use of coconut milk except to stew cassava leaves, a common side dish. Most other preparations, including pork for feasts, involve only boiling the raw food with salt. Snacks made from fruit are becoming common under *dava* influence.

13 EDUCATION

In 2005, the level of literacy stood at 87.77% for Nias regency and 62.19 for South Nias regency. The latter was among the lowest in Indonesia by Indonesian national standards, but the former was comparable to the more developed provinces of Bali and Central Java (*See also* the article entitled **Indonesians** in this volume).

14 CULTURAL HERITAGE

Funerals and feasts of merit feature *hoho*, narrative poems (hero tales or genealogies) sung by a leader and three two-man choruses in four-tone melodies. A simpler form, the *maena* from north Nias, has become a popular replacement for the hoho, consisting of a humorous verse in praise of the feast-giver sung by a leader and answered by a chorus. Various traditional dances are performed by both sexes, the most famous of which is the war dance which accompanies high-stone jumping.

15 WORK

Except for the few who have completed enough education to qualify for government jobs, Niasans support themselves through dry-field, swidden agriculture, growing yams, rice, maize, and taro. Wet-rice is cultivated only in swamps. Every house raises pigs, so as to be able to contribute to the feasts of merit, the funerals, and the bride-wealth needed by kin and wife-givers. In the past, dried pork served as a standard of value, rather like money. Other livestock includes chickens, ducks, water buffalo, goats, and horses. Hunting and fishing are of only secondary significance. Nias' main exports are copra, rubber, and pigs (slaves used to be one of their main exports as well).

16 SPORTS

Zawözaw consists of jumping over a 2.1-m-high (7-ft-high) stone structure (these are located in the village's central plaza). Formerly, zawözawö was a test of skill for young men, and being able to make it over the stone was a prerequisite to entering the marriageable age. Now, it is performed for government ceremonies or tourist entertainment.

17 ENTERTAINMENT AND RECREATION

See the article entitled **Indonesians**.

18 FOLK ART, CRAFTS, AND HOBBIES

Valued specializations include gold-smithing, copper-working, and woodcarving (house wall panels and statues). Basketry is also a common skill.

19 SOCIAL PROBLEMS

See the article entitled **Indonesians**.

[20] GENDER ISSUES

In 2002, the Gender-Related Development Index (combining measures of women's health, education, and income relative to men's) for the whole island of Nias was 61.5, significantly above Indonesia's national GDI of 59.2 though the same as that of North Sumatra as a whole. The island's Gender Empowerment Measure (reflecting women's participation and power in political and economic life relative to men's) was 59.3, dramatically higher than the national GEM of 54.6 and the provincial GEM of 48.4.

While men, particularly older ones, spend much of their time debating points of customary law or just chatting (when not performing occasional or seasonal tasks such as hunting or clearing swidden [shifting-cultivation] fields), women are occupied all day either working in the fields or preparing food. In gatherings, women sit either on the floor or serve betel to the men seated on benches; however assertive they might be in private with their husbands, in public women keep silent.

[21] BIBLIOGRAPHY

Beatty, Andrew. *Society and Exchange in Nias.* Oxford: Clarendon, 1992.

Beawiharta. "Nias, arsitektur." In *Ensiklopedi Nasional Indonesia,* Vol. 11. Jakarta: Cipta Adi Pustaka, 1990.

Data Statistik Indonesia. http://demografi.bps.go.id/ (November 9, 2008).

Koentjaraningrat, J. Danandjaja. "Penduduk Kepulauan Sebelah Barat Sumatera" [Inhabitants of Islands to the West of Sumatra]. In *Manusia dan Kebudayaan di Indonesia* [Man and Culture in Indonesia], edited by Koentjaraningrat. Jakarta: Djambatan, 1975.

LeBar, Frank M., ed. *Ethnic Groups of Insular Southeast Asia.* Vol. 1: *Indonesia, Andaman Islands, and Madagascar.* New Haven, CT: Human Relations Area Files Press, 1972.

Miharza, ed. *Adat Istiadat Daerah Sumatra Utara,* Vol. 2. Jakarta: Project for the Inventorization and Recording of Regional Cultures, 1977.

Oey, Eric M. *Sumatra: Island of Adventure.* Longwood, IL: Passport Books, 1991.

Profil Propinsi Republik Indonesia. Vol. 25, *Sumatera Utara.* Jakarta: Yayasan Bhakti Wawasan Nusantara, 1992.

—revised by A. J. Abalahin

NICOBARESE

PRONUNCIATION: nik-uh-bahr-EEZ
ALTERNATE NAMES: Holchu (self-reference)
LOCATION: India (Nicobar Islands)
POPULATION: 28,785 (2001 Census)
LANGUAGE: Nicobarese; Hindi
RELIGION: Animism; Christianity mixed with indigenous beliefs; Islam; Hinduism
RELATED ARTICLES: Vol. 3: People of India

[1] INTRODUCTION

The term Nicobarese describes the dominant tribal peoples of the Nicobar Islands, an island group located in the Bay of Bengal. Although the inhabitants of each island have their own specific name, the Nicobarese refer to themselves as "Holchu," meaning "friend." The people are of Mongoloid stock from mainland Southeast Asia, possibly originating in Burma (Myanmar). The date of their arrival is uncertain. The islands are mentioned in 11th century inscriptions from South India as Nakkavaram, the "Land of the Naked," suggesting that people were present by that time. The Nicobarese were probably not the first inhabitants of the islands. When they arrived, they came into conflict with peoples of Malay descent who were already there and forced them into the interior. The Shompen, another tribal group in the Nicobars, are believed to be the descendants of these earlier inhabitants. Though relatively isolated, the Nicobarese were exposed to contact with various European maritime powers as they expanded into Asia after 1500. Great Britain laid claim to the islands in 1869 and governed them (except for the 1942–45 Japanese occupation) until they passed to India in 1947. Today, the islands are administered by India as part of the Union Territory of the Andaman and Nicobar Islands.

[2] LOCATION AND HOMELAND

The 2001 Census of India recorded a population of 28,784 Nicobarese in the Andaman and Nicobar Islands. Because of population pressure, 163 families were resettled from the Nicobars to Little Andaman Island in 1973 by the government.

The Nicobar Islands are a chain of 19 islands in the Bay of Bengal that runs southeast from the Andaman Islands towards Indonesia. Their total area is 1,841 sq km (710 sq mi), though only 12 of the islands are inhabited. The largest of these is Great Nicobar (863 sq km or 333 sq mi), which lies only 145 km (95 mi) from the Indonesian island of Sumatra. Other populated islands include Car Nicobar, Little Nicobar, and Nancowry. Some of the islands have flat, coral-covered surfaces, but others are hilly. Great Nicobar, for instance, rises to 642 m (2,105 ft) and is the only island in the entire group that has permanently flowing streams. The Nicobar Islands lie between 6°N and 10°N latitude and experience a near-equatorial climate. Monthly temperatures vary from 33°C (91°F) to 18°C (64°F). Rainfall totals between 230 cm and 340 cm (90–135 in) a year, with maximum amounts coinciding with the two monsoon seasons. Dense tropical evergreen forest covers Great Nicobar Island.

³LANGUAGE

The populations of different islands in the Nicobars speak different languages, which are all considered to be dialects of the Nicobarese language. These are usually classified into four (sometimes six) separate groups. The North Nicobar group, for example, includes the Car, Chowra, Teressa, and Bompaka languages. Nicobarese is a member of the Austro-Asiatic language family. Some linguists place Nicobarese in the Mon-Khmer branch of the family, while others consider the various languages spoken in the Nicobar Islands to form a separate branch of the Austro-Asiatic family. Most Nicobarese understand the Car dialect. A variant of the Roman script is currently used for writing. Hindi is used for intergroup communication.

⁴FOLKLORE

The Nicobarese have many legends concerning their first arrival in the Nicobar Islands. One story relates that when the land was totally uninhabited, a boy came down from the sky and entered the earth. After a few days, the shoot of a lemon tree emerged from the ground. This soon grew into a huge tree, with flowers and fruits. Peoples of the northern islands, e.g., Kondul, Teressa, and Nancowry, originated from the lemon seeds of the northern branches of the tree. The people of Great Nicobar came forth from the seeds of the tree's southern branches. After many years, differences in opinion about how they should live split this southern group in two. Some of them (believed to be the Shompen) retreated to the dense forest of the interior, while the others are the coastal Nicobarese of Great Nicobar.

⁵RELIGION

Traditional religion in the Nicobar Islands is animistic in nature. The Nicobarese of Great Nicobar, for example, believe in the existence of the soul, ghosts, and spirits. The soul (*iyum*) has no form and is immortal. A person turns to a ghost (*huihe*) when the soul leaves the body after death, and there are ghosts in and all around the island. Spirits (*shaitan*) are thought to be the cause of storms, natural disasters, and disease. Shamans are called upon to identify the spirits responsible for a bad storm or an illness and to pacify them with rites that include the sacrifice of a chicken or a pig. The island of Chowra is known particularly for the skill of its shamans. All young Nicobarese males are expected to pay a ritual visit to Chowra for their initiation into manhood.

Few Nicobarese follow their ancient religion today. The 1981 census records that 94.23% of the Nicobarese identified themselves as Christian. The spread of Christianity in the islands was in large part due to the work of the Nicobarese Christian John Richardson in the early decades of the 20th century. He was responsible for the idea of educating the Nicobarese in their own language, produced the first Nicobarese primer, and translated the New Testament into Nicobarese. Richardson emerged as a respected leader of the Nicobarese, particularly during the Japanese occupation, and eventually attained the rank of bishop. However, Christianity in the Nicobar Islands embraces many elements of the pre-Christian beliefs of the people. For example, all Nicobarese keep *kareus* in their huts. These are human figures made from clay, old clothes, straw, and wood that serve to scare away ghosts.

There are small numbers of Muslims and Hindus among the Nicobarese.

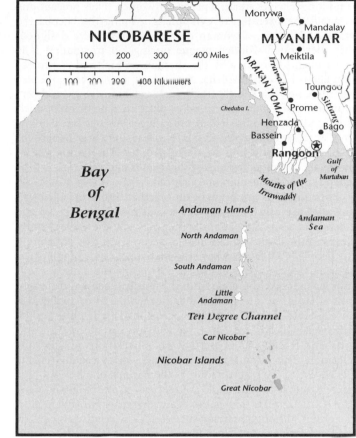

⁶MAJOR HOLIDAYS

Religious festivals such as Christmas and Easter are celebrated by the Christian Nicobarese, while Muslims observe Id ul-Fitr and Id ul-Adha. On the other hand, traditional festivals are mostly seasonal events, held for the community's benefit and to protect it from evil spirits and from outsiders. In January of every year, for instance, a ceremony is performed by the shaman in the gardens to increase their yields. This is accompanied by a communal feast, along with singing and dancing. Specific rituals are kept to mark events such as the first sailing of a canoe. *Hānu-cheroi* is the worship of the canoe before it sets out on its maiden voyage. The shaman enters the house of the canoe's owner, where he sets out a green coconut and covers it with a betel leaf. He then sacrifices a chicken and marks the coconut and betel leaf with the chicken's blood, at the same time chanting spells. A boy is sent to stand in one end of the canoe. He grasps a stick in the middle with both hands, so that it is horizontal and aligned at a right angle to the hull. Starting at one end, he walks the length of the canoe moving the stick up and down so it touches the two side walls of the boat. He chants incantations while doing this. The coconut and betel leaf are then placed in the canoe. The ritual ends with the slaughter of a pig and a feast for the relatives. The shaman receives a leg of the pig for his part in the ritual.

⁷RITES OF PASSAGE

Many of the magical beliefs of the Nicobarese come into play during critical times in the Nicobarese life-cycle. Although the traditional idea that pregnancy is caused by a *shaitan* (spirit) is no longer widespread, a pregnant women takes precautions to avoid the attention of evil spirits. Among the Nicobarese of Great Nicobar, a woman carries an artistically designed, thin, perforated wooden plaque during her pregnancy. It is given magical potency by the shaman and is used as protection against harmful spirits. A pregnant woman cannot enter a garden, nor can she eat foods such as lemons, eggs, and certain kinds of fish. Delivery takes place in a birth-hut, which is located on the outskirts of the village. Various birth pollution rituals are observed in Car Nicobar, but these are absent among the central and southern peoples. The naming ceremony, accompanied by a feast for friends and relatives, is held when the baby is around one year old.

Boys and girls are brought up together. From the age of 12 onwards they are taught about sexual matters by the village elders and also learn about it indirectly, as the entire family sleeps in the same room. Puberty is known as *cho-cho* among the people of Great Nicobar. The first appearance of menstruation is a cause for grief, because it means the daughter will soon be married and gone from the family. Relatives from distant villages are informed and gather within 25 or 30 days for an elaborate feast to mark the occasion. This is quite unlike marriage, which is not associated with any ceremony. Boys and girls mix freely, and premarital sexual relations are not uncommon. This often leads to marriage, which usually reflects the choice of the girl. As soon as the parents of a boy and girl agree to a match, the couple are accepted as husband and wife. The Nicobarese are endogamous and can marry anyone within the group, although marriage between close relatives is considered incestuous and is forbidden.

At the time of death, the corpse is bathed and dressed in pieces of cloth provided by family members. The body is then placed in a wooden box, along with items such as a basket and a spear that are provided for the future use of the deceased. (It is believed that after death, everyone goes to another world where they hunt, fish, and garden, living very much like they did in this one.) The coffin is taken to the funeral ground, where it is buried. Death rites are performed by the shaman. The mourning period usually lasts for 30 days, and its end is marked by a feast for family and friends. The funerals of Christian and Muslim Nicobarese follow the normal patterns of their respective religions.

[8] INTERPERSONAL RELATIONS

The Nicobarese of Great Nicobar welcome strangers to their village with coconuts. The village captain greets the visitor by extending the right arm and shaking hands (possibly learned from visiting naval officers in the past!). When kin meet, they raise their right hands above their heads and shout "Ho!" meaning "Hello." Both host and guest partake of food and drink, usually toddy (fermented palm sap). When leaving, Nicobarese again raise their right hands above their heads and say "Kāyengose!" which means "Goodbye."

[9] LIVING CONDITIONS.

The Nicobarese villages on Great Nicobar Island are strung out along the island's western shoreline. Although tracks link the villages, the only practical means of transport between these settlements is the canoe. Each village has a headman called a captain, selected by the village elders. In the past, the captains of the villages selected one of their number to be the chief captain, although this has now become a hereditary post. A council, made up of the village captains, is responsible for maintaining law and order in the community.

A village on Great Nicobar is usually a shapeless cluster of huts and also may contain a church, a school, a store, a burial ground, and perhaps a sports field. Traditional huts are round in shape, with the walls and dome-shaped roof built of thatch. They are constructed on poles at a height of about 120 cm to 150 cm (4–5 ft) above the ground and are reached by a short ladder, which is drawn up at night. Each hut consists of only one all-purpose room, with an area set aside for hearth and kitchen. Furnishings are simple and, except for the kitchen utensils, are most likely made by the hut's inhabitants. They may consist of a few stools, a table, and some storage cabinets. Most families sleep on the floor on sleeping mats. There are no arrangements for sanitation; people use the beach or nearby gardens for their daily bodily functions.

[10] FAMILY LIFE

Both nuclear and extended families are found among the Nicobarese. Rules of residence after marriage are not closely followed, and both patrilocal (residence with the husband's family) and matrilocal (residence with the wife's family) patterns are found. Women are considered a valuable economic asset, and the birth of a daughter is as welcome as that of a son. Besides her household duties, a woman spends much of her time tending the garden and the coconut plantation. In Nicobarese society, women enjoy almost equal status with men in the social, religious, economic, and political spheres of life.

[11] CLOTHING

Traditional dress for the Nicobarese is a brief loincloth for men and a girdle of leaves for women. This has changed, however, and nowadays the usual dress of the male is a pair of shorts called *paijam*, sometimes worn with a vest. Women wear a blouse (*kānjut*) and a long skirt known as a *lungi*. Weaving is not known to the Nicobarese, so they have to purchase clothes or buy cloth and sew the clothes themselves. People commonly go barefoot but may put on sandals when leaving the village. In the past, women wore ornaments made from local products such as wood and bamboo, though cheap costume jewelry is now popular. Both men and women are fond of tattoos and have pictorial designs indicating their name inscribed on their forearms.

[12] FOOD

The staple foods of the Nicobarese are the coconut (*koā*) and pandanus (*lārop*). The kernel of the coconut is cut into pieces or grated and eaten with a paste made from the nuts of the pandanus, the Nicobar Island's breadfruit tree (*Pandanus lerum*). Previously unknown to the Nicobarese, rice and wheat (in the form of *rotī* or unleavened breads made from wheat flour) form part of the modern diet. Naturally, for an island people, fish, turtles, and octopus are important foods for the Nicobarese. These are usually eaten with curried vegetables and lentils (*dāl*). Vegetables include yams, eggplant, okra, and various types of gourds. Chicken and pork are also consumed, often after the animal has been offered as a sacrifice. The water of the green coconut is drunk, and so is tea (sometimes with honey), but milk is totally absent from the diet. Toddy, an alcoholic drink made from fermented coconut water and palm sap,

A Nicobarese tribal woman joins others in prayer at a tsunami refugee camp in Port Blair, India. A devastating tsunami hit India's Andaman and Nicobar Islands in December 2004. (AP Images/Aijaz Rahi)

is popular with both men and women. Toddy is also drunk as a part of ceremonial rituals. Both men and women chew betel nut and tobacco.

¹³EDUCATION

Many of the older Nicobarese are nonliterate. Today, however, education is free and available to the Nicobarese through government-run schools. Education is seen by many as a means of obtaining employment in government service or in local businesses. The 2001 census showed the literacy rate for the Scheduled Tribes in the Andaman and Nicobar Islands to be 46% and that for women to be 40%. The last data available for the Nicobarese are in the 1981 census and showed literacy to be 31.46% (38.84% for males and 23.54% for females), though no doubt these values have increased over the last three decades.

¹⁴CULTURAL HERITAGE

The Nicobarese have a tradition of oral literature, embodying the legendary history, customs, and beliefs of the people. They also have a complex system of magical beliefs and practices that influence many aspects of their lives and daily behavior. Music and dance are elements of traditional culture and a necessary part of festive and ceremonial occasions. On Great Nicobar, young and old dance together, irrespective of sex, but on some other islands men and women dance separately. Dancers lock arms with their neighbors and move in a circle with rhythmic steps, lifting the right and left legs alternately. The beat of the dance is kept on the *tallag,* a big metal gong that is struck with a padded stick.

¹⁵WORK

The traditional economy of the Nicobarese is horticulture, based on the growing of coconuts, pandanus, areca palms, bananas, mangoes, and other tropical fruits. In the past, the collection of wild roots and tubers supplemented the food supply. Fishing and hunting wild game are important activities. Dogs are kept for the hunt. The Nicobarese rear pigs, and any important occasion is marked by the slaughter of a pig and a feast of pork (except among the Muslims). The inhabitants of Chowra Island specialize in the making of earthen pots and large seagoing canoes. As more Nicobarese acquire the necessary education, they move into jobs as teachers, clerks, and similar occupations.

¹⁶SPORTS

Canoe-racing, pig-fighting, and wrestling are popular pastimes among the Nicobarese. They have also taken to modern sports, such as soccer, volleyball, and track-and-field with enthusiasm.

17 ENTERTAINMENT AND RECREATION

The Nicobarese find their entertainment primarily in the music, song, and dance that accompanies their festivals. Some listen to Hindi film songs on their transistor radios, but most Nicobarese do not understand the language well enough to do other than enjoy the music.

18 FOLK ART, CRAFTS, AND HOBBIES

There are no specialist carpenters in traditional Nicobarese society, and everyone develops skills in woodworking. Men build huts and make spears, harpoons, digging implements, furniture, and other wooden objects (the metal heads are purchased from traders). They are efficient canoe-builders, constructing dugout outrigger canoes that are capable of crossing the stretches of ocean that separate the islands from each other. The outer hulls of the canoes are decorated with carved geometrical designs. A sense of aesthetics is seen in the miniature canoes they carve for pleasure and in the wooden effigies made for various ritual purposes.

19 SOCIAL PROBLEMS

Largely because of their isolation, the Nicobarese have managed to preserve much of their traditional way of life. They have maintained a sense of cultural and linguistic identity, as well as their social and political institutions. They have not yet experienced the dramatic changes brought about by rapid contact with outsiders that other tribal peoples in South Asia have undergone. Change, however, is inevitable and is occurring. The advent of Christianity has brought new religious beliefs and practices. The traditional barter economy has been replaced by a cash economy. Contact with the outside world has brought with it schools and better health facilities, but it has also brought concerns such as alcohol addiction and fear of theft. Only time will tell how well the Nicobarese will adapt to the modern world they are now entering.

In December 2006, as a result of the *adivasis* of India's long struggle for rights, the Indian Parliament passed the Scheduled Tribes and Other Traditional Forest Dwellers (Recognition of Forest Rights) Act of 2005, seeking to recognize and vest the forest rights and occupation of the land in forest-dwelling Scheduled Tribes and other traditional forest-dwellers. Yet some see the act as a potential disaster for the Nicobarese rather than as one protecting India's forests. The Nicobarese already enjoy total and unfettered rights over the tribal reserves of Nicobar Islands, accorded them by the Andaman and Nicobar Islands Protection of Aboriginal Tribes (ANPTR) Act, passed in 1956. The new federal act could pose a potential danger to their enjoying these rights. At a later day, some could argue why can't the Nicobarese be content with 2.5 hectares of land in the forest, as the New Delhi bill allows, like all the other tribes of India? Why should so few Nicobarese have such a large chunk of land available to them? It is even possible that since the central act is being passed to protect tribal rights, the ANPTR could even be declared null and void or rescinded. Even now the Defense establishment is eyeing the Nicobars for possible firing ranges.

Nicobarese tribals are growing increasingly uneasy with people settling on their islands, outnumbering them and putting pressure on scarce land and water resources. They have now formally demanded that thousands of illegal settlers from the mainland leave the islands. Traditionally represented by tribal councils that work along with the government, the Nicobarese have formed an alliance known as the Federation of Tribal Councils of Nicobar. The remote Andaman and Nicobar islands have for long been targeted by poachers and pirates and are geographically much closer to several Southeast Asian nations than to the Indian mainland. Illegal settlements are threatening to overwhelm indigenous people on islands that are supposed to be strictly protected tribal areas. In 2005 the Indian government repatriated 129 Myanmarese fishermen who were involved in poaching, illegal fishing and illegal immigration in the Andaman and Nicobar Islands to Burma.

On the morning of 26 December 2004 the Andaman Islands were struck by a devastating tsunami originating as a result of the earthquake of Indonesia. At least 850 people died on Car Nicobar Island and another 3,000 Nicobarese were missing (some put this figure as high as 7,000). Many villages were literally wiped off the map, and the core of the Nicobarese economy was virtually destroyed. Many Nicobarese fled inland to escape the tsunami and still remain there in relief camps. The Nicobarese used to fish, diving from dugout canoes with harpoons and masks, or casting lines in deeper water for bigger fish. Thousands of coconut trees, the lifeblood of the Nicobarese economy, were uprooted by the tsunami, and it will take 10 years for the plantations to grow back. The very cultural traditions—e.g. their economic activities, their villages, and the communal huts where family life was focused—of the Nicobarese are under threat.

20 GENDER ISSUES

Nicobarese women experience the freedom of most tribal women in South Asia and enjoy a status almost equal to that of men.

Although there is no institution such as the dormitory of other tribes, young people mix freely and pre-nuptial affairs are quite common. These often end in marriage. There is no such thing as an arranged marriage, the latter being the outcome of courtship initiated by either sex, although the families of the parties involved make the necessary arrangements, and child marriage is not practiced. There is no payment of either bride price or dowry. Widow re-marriage is permitted, and divorce, sometimes accompanied by payment of compensation determined by the village headman, is not uncommon. Grounds for divorce include adultery, incurable disease, chronic ill-health, a proneness to crime, misconduct, and insanity. Since the payment of a dowry or bride-price is not involved in a marriage, no repayment is necessary.

Women are considered a valuable economic asset, because of their assistance in economic activities. In addition to running the household, they spend much of their time tending gardens and working in the coconut plantations. There is no preference for male children in Nicobarese society, and, though few women enter politics, they have essentially equal status with men. They also have the right to participate actively in religious ceremonies, although there are restrictions during pregnancy and at the time of menstruation.

Property can be considered as communal, familial or personal. Every Nicobarese has the right to fish, hunt in the forest or draw water from a well, as these are considered communal property. Huts, canoes, gardens, weapons, and livestock are familial property and are to be used by the family. Women maintain the right to personal property such as ornaments, even after marriage, and after marriage they have the right to a share in the products of their parent's garden. A woman has the right to inherit property as long as she remains with the family and the marital tie is intact.

21 BIBLIOGRAPHY

Gautam, R. K. and A.N. Sharma. "The Nicobarese of the Har-minder Bay, Little Andaman, India." *South Asian Anthropologist* Vol. 4, No. 1, 2004: 1–11.

Justin, A. *The Nicobarese*. Calcutta: Seagull Books on behalf of the Anthropological Survey of India, 1967.

Malhotra, Om P. *Tribal Education in Andaman and Nicobar Islands*. New Delhi: S. Chand, 1986.

Mann, Rann Singh. *Andaman and Nicobar Tribes Restudied: Encounters and Concerns*. New Delhi: Mittal, 2005.

Mathur, Kaushal K. *Nicobar Islands*. New Delhi: National Book Trust, 1967.

Nandan, Anshu Prokash. *The Nicobarese of Great Nicobar: An Ethnography*. Delhi: Gyan Publishing House, 1993.

—by D. O. Lodrick

NI-VANUATU

PRONUNCIATION: nee-vahn-(y)uh-WAH-too
LOCATION: Vanuatu
POPULATION: 218,000 (estimated 2007)
LANGUAGE: English, French, and Bislama

1 INTRODUCTION

The Ni-Vanuatu are the Melanesian inhabitants of the island chain known today as the Republic of Vanuatu. From the time of its European discovery until the time of its independence in 1980, the Y-shaped chain of islands was known as the New Hebrides. Vanuatu is probably best known to Americans as the setting for the James Michener novel that was made into the musical "South Pacific." The American reality-television show "Survivor: Vanuatu" was filmed on the island in 2004. The American view of this island and the South Pacific in general does not do justice to the reality of the cultural diversity of this island group.

2 LOCATION AND HOMELAND

Vanuatu is located squarely in the heart of the Melanesian culture area. Vanuatu's nearest neighbors are New Caledonia, Fiji, and the Solomon Islands. A total of 83 islands make up the Republic of Vanuatu. Twelve of the islands are considered the main islands of the group. The islands are both of volcanic and coral formation, providing for a wide range of topography within the country. Some islands are very mountainous and are covered in lush vegetation. The climate ranges from oceanic tropical to subtropical depending on island type and geographical location. November through April is the hot, rainy season for the Ni-Vanuatu. This is also the period of the most hurricane activity that passes through the islands. The three largest islands are Espirtu Santo, Malakula, and Efate. The capital city of Vanuatu, Port Vila, is located on Efate and has a population of approximately 33,700. The only other town in the chain is Luganville, which is located on Espirtu Santo. Luganville has a population of only around 10,700. The total population of the Republic of Vanuatu was estimated to be 218,000 in 2007.

3 LANGUAGE

With over 100 distinct languages spoken in the Republic of Vanuatu, it ranks as one of the nations of the world with the greatest amount of linguistic diversity per square mile. Many of these languages have never been described by anthropologists, linguists, or missionaries. There are three official languages in the Republic of Vanuatu: English, French, and Bislama. The first two owe to the island's colonial history: it was jointly administered by Great Britain and France. Bislama is a contact language that is derived from a form of South Pacific English that spread with European economic activities in the region during the 19th century. The name Bislama comes from the English rendering of the French phrase "beche de mer" that refers to the edible sea slug that was economically important during that time.

[4] FOLKLORE

For many traditional communities in Vanuatu, the yam is a secondary source of food after the taro root, but of primary importance in terms of cultural ideology and symbolism. The cycle of yam cultivation in many communities dictates the sequence of ritual activities. Appropriately enough, there are important myths regarding yams. Among the speakers of the Sa language on South Pentecost Island, there is a myth recounting the origin of yams that goes essentially as follows:

> In the beginning, there was no food. There was an old man who stayed alone in his hut, lying down and never going out. One day, he was cutting his fingernails and toenails and he threw the pieces out the door. The nails sprouted a plant that grew out of the ground. He tasted the plant and it tasted good. He called to his children and told them to clear a spot in the forest but he would not tell them why they were doing the work. When the spot was cleared, he instructed his children to kill him, cut him up, and bury the pieces in the spot they had cleared. He had given them his buttocks as a charm and it caused the yams that grew from his body parts to be enormous.

Other tribal groups in Vanuatu have similar myths regarding important parts of the natural and supernatural world.

[5] RELIGION

The predominant religion of the Ni-Vanuatu is Christianity. However, a large number of Ni-Vanuatu still practice traditional, indigenous religion and there are certain cargo cults on the islands. The most well-known of those is the John Frum movement that started in the 1930s. The John Frum movement exists in opposition to the Christian church and its followers often see it as a way to better their material lives. The message of the John Frum movement has been to maintain the traditional ways of life that the Christian church tried to abolish, such as *kava* drinking, traditional dancing, and other behaviors that were viewed as "pagan" by church authorities.

[6] MAJOR HOLIDAYS

The largest national holiday in Vanuatu is Independence Day, celebrated on July 30. There are usually many local as well as national competitions that co-occur with Independence Day celebrations. In the community of Sulpher Bay, on the island of Tanna, John Frum Day is celebrated in February.

[7] RITES OF PASSAGE

In the tribal societies of Vanuatu, passage from one stage of life to another is often marked with rituals, symbolic behaviors, and overt physical alterations. Male initiation is widespread in the Melanesian culture area to which Vanuatu belongs. Not all tribal Ni-Vanuatu practice male initiation now or in the past. In groups where male initiation is practiced, it usually involves the cutting of the foreskin of the penis. The young man then wears a plaited fiber cover over the penis called a "penis-wrapper." Males who would refuse to undergo the operation may not be considered adult men.

In the northern islands of the chain, tribal Ni-Vanuatu have a cultural pattern of ranked status grades that primarily men pass through during adulthood. The named stages are entered through the purchase of various symbols associated with the grade and a large sacrifice of animals. Traditionally, pigs are the currency by which an individual accedes through the ranks. They are all the animals that are ritually slaughtered at the culmination of the event. In some cases, women may also pass through the stages of rank.

[8] INTERPERSONAL RELATIONS

The interpersonal relations of traditional Ni-Vanuatu are governed by the nature of the genealogical relationship between the participants. In some communities, there is a strict avoidance between brothers and sisters. They are not permitted to talk or even occupy the same space after passing puberty. Interactions between brothers and sisters in these communities must be accomplished by a young girl who acts as an intermediary.

[9] LIVING CONDITIONS

Over 85% of the population of the Republic of Vanuatu is rural. Most rural villages are now located in the coastal plain regions of the islands. Prior to European involvement in the islands, villages were located in the upland regions to provide for some defense against enemy raids that were endemic. Housing styles vary considerably from region to region. The urban Ni-Vanuatu occupy a range of dwellings comparable to those found in North America. Houses constructed of the remains of other buildings are found on the fringes of the city, while modern homes, apartments, and condominiums are found in the city itself. The rural housing ranges from traditional construction out of locally produced materials to mixed construction that utilizes traditional elements like woven bamboo walls and earthen floors as well as galvanized sheet metal for roofs.

Health treatment is limited for the Ni-Vanuatu. There are only two hospitals in the islands, one in Port Vila and the other in Luganville. These are most accessible to the urban Ni-Vanuatu. The rural Ni-Vanuatu do not have easy access to medical facilities or health care. There are several development agencies that work with the national government in an effort to improve health care delivery systems for the rural population.

The city of Port Vila has many of the amenities that Americans are accustomed to. There are several fine restaurants encompassing a fairly wide range of cuisine including Continental French, Vietnamese, and Chinese. Clubs, movie theaters, and other places for night time entertainment are available.

[10] FAMILY LIFE

For the rural Ni-Vanuatu who still reside in traditional villages, the choice of a marriage partner is determined by considerations of kinship and descent. Some societies divide the entire population into two groups, loosely related by descent, and the marriage partner must come from the opposite group. The marriage itself is usually accompanied by the exchange of certain products including woven mats and pigs. Among the Tannese of the TAFEA district of Vanuatu, sister-exchange marriage is practiced. Sister-exchange marriage requires that a male may not marry unless he has a sister to exchange in return for his prospective bride.

In the northern part of Vanuatu (Espiritu Santo, Sakao, Ambae and others), descent is reckoned along matrilineal lines. In the central and southern islands (Pentecost, Ambrym, Efate, Erromongo, Tanna, and others), descent is reckoned patrilineally.

¹¹ CLOTHING

There is a wide range of clothing found among the Ni-Vanuatu. The urban Ni-Vanuatu dress in a style that would be familiar to most Americans. Traditional villages often combine styles of Western dress with more indigenous forms of dress and adornment. Women often wear fiber skirts and go topless, while men might wear a traditional pubic covering or a pair of shorts and a T-shirt.

¹² FOOD

Food choices and food preparation varies between the rural and urban Ni-Vanuatu. The urban dwellers have a wide selection of food options. Shops sell imported food products while the large marketplace that operates in Port Vila brings in traditional food crops from the rural areas. Restaurants are also available to the urban population. The choice of food depends upon the income of the family. For the rural Ni-Vanuatu, the food choices are much more limited. Traditional food crops such as taro root and yams are prepared in traditional manners without the use of electricity or gas.

¹³ EDUCATION

Education has been provided by the mission schools that were run by the various Christian sects on the islands. Literacy is low for the overall population since many still do not have access to any form of public, institutionalized education.

¹⁴ CULTURAL HERITAGE

Dancing is an important part of the traditional culture of the Ni-Vanuatu. In many villages, a person's identity is tied to the family dancing ground called *nasara*. Musical instruments of the traditional cultures of Vanuatu include the slit gong, made from a hollowed-out tree trunk and carved on the ends. The slit gong is used to represent the voices of the spirits and also for long distance communication between the village and people who have gone off into the forest.

¹⁵ WORK

Ni-Vanuatu engage in a variety of types of work. In Port Vila there are bureaucratic jobs associated with the government and also with the work of foreign development agencies. Traditional forms of work were and, in some cases, still are, divided among tasks for males and tasks for females. Although females are often the main food producers, the work of men is typically more highly valued.

¹⁶ SPORTS

Tennis and golf are sports that the urban Ni-Vanuatu have some access to in Port Vila. Tennis matches on the international circuit are occasionally scheduled for Vanuatu.

¹⁷ ENTERTAINMENT AND RECREATION

For the majority of Ni-Vanuatu, entertainment and recreation follow traditional cultural patterns. Broadcast television was not available in the Republic of Vanuatu until 1992. Electricity has limited availability for the vast majority of Ni-Vanuatu, so they are not able to watch videos, television, or see movies. These pursuits are reserved for the urban Ni-Vanuatu and the numerous expatriates from other nations that reside in Port Vila.

An important form of traditional entertainment for adult Ni-Vanuatu men is the drinking of the intoxicating beverage called "kava." Kava is prepared from the roots of the domesticated kava plant (*piper methysticum*). This plant is related to the vine that produces peppercorns. The freshly dug root balls of mature plants are cleaned and then pulverized or ground, and the pieces are soaked in water and then strained through coconut fiber to produce the semi-liquid drink. On the island of Tanna, the roots are chewed and then spit out in wads to be placed in water to create the drink. Typically, adult men drink kava nightly. Kava is the favored intoxicating beverage for most Ni-Vanuatu, in part because it does not induce aggressive behavior. In fact, kava drinking is a quiet occasion and is usually completed within a couple of hours.

The popularity of kava drinking has lead to the development of local commercial kava bars in the villages, towns, and cities. The "nakamals," as they are called, are a local gathering place for men and women to drink kava. As opposed to the traditional kava drinking patterns, the nakamals permit women to drink, as long as the woman does not come from the same village as the owner of the bar. Large quantities of kava are produced nightly for the customers. Meat grinders are often used to process the large quantities more rapidly than the traditional methods of production. A half coconut shell of kava costs around 50 cents and on average, men only drink two or three rounds an evening.

¹⁸ FOLK ART, CRAFTS, AND HOBBIES

Tapa cloth was also a traditional product of many groups in Vanuatu. The process has now become part of the repertoire of folk arts that is produced for sale to tourists and collectors.

¹⁹ SOCIAL PROBLEMS

The maintenance of traditional culture in light of the influences of the outside world is one of the overriding problems facing the Ni-Vanuatu. Broadcast television has also introduced a new set of cultural images to the island nation. The economy is also a cause of concern for the Ni-Vanuatu. As opposed to other South Pacific nations, Vanuatu's tourism industry continues to show significant growth. In the late 1990s, the island nation received only about 35,000 visitors per year. The 2007 figures show that over 150,000 tourists visited Vanuatu in that year alone. Increased airline service, the development of boutique hotels, and a growing backpacker tourism focus has fueled the tremendous growth in tourism that Vanuatu has experienced.

²⁰ GENDER ISSUES

The role of women varies among the Ni-Vanuatu. Tribal groups divide into two main camps. In some areas male domination is manifested by a series of cultural institutions like male initiation, yam cults, and the wearing of penis wrappers. In other areas, especially parts of Espirtu Santo and Efate, women have greater control over their resources and genealogical descent is traced through the female line.

The Tannese, one of the southern ethnolinguistic groups of Vanuatu, recognize two genders: male and female. The opposition of male and female governs the Tannese understanding of most of the natural world. For instance, the two staple food crops, yam and taro, are classified as male and female respectively. The characteristics of maleness that apply to all items in this classification are hardness, dryness, heat, and the state of being closed. Femaleness is characterized by softness, wetness, cold, and the state of being open, which is equated with menstruation.

Like most other Melanesian groups, the Tannese believe that boys must be transformed into men through complex rituals that remove the female essence that was instilled in them through reproduction and birth and replace it with a new male essence. Circumcision is central to transforming boys into men and replacing the female essence with a new male essence.

There are two public activities that distinguish men from women; those are public speaking and kava drinking at the kava-drinking grounds. Only men are allowed to speak at the regular dispute settlement meetings and only men are allowed to be present at the public kava-drinking grounds.

[21] BIBLIOGRAPHY

Allen, Michael, ed. *Vanuatu: Politics, Economics and Ritual in Island Melanesia*. New York: Academic Press, 1981.

Kirch, Patrick V., and Jean-Louis Rallu, eds. *The Growth and Collapse of Pacific Island Societies: Archaeological and Demographic Perspectives*. Honolulu: University of Hawaii Press, 2007.

Küchler, Susanne, and Graeme Were. *The Art of Clothing: A Pacific Experience*. Portland, OR: Cavendish, 2005.

Vanuatu & New Caledonia. Footscray, Victoria; Oakland, CA: Lonely Planet, 2006.

—by J. Williams

OMANIS

PRONUNCIATION: oh-MAHN-eez
LOCATION: Oman
POPULATION: 3 million
LANGUAGE: Arabic; English
RELIGION: Islam: Majority Ibadi sect as well as Sunni and Shia

[1] INTRODUCTION

Archaeological evidence shows human activity in the present-day land of Oman as far back as 12,000 BC, with fairly advanced civilization showing up at about 5000 BC. From 3000 BC until AD 1500, the Omanis were a prosperous, seafaring, export-oriented people, with most of their wealth coming from the export of frankincense (a tree resin native to the area that was highly valued for medicine, perfume, and religious incense). In the 4th century BC, Oman came under the domination of Cyrus the Great, founder of the Persian Empire. Arab tribal groups from Yemen migrated to Oman and seized control of the country from the Persians. During the 6th to 7th centuries AD, Islam was brought to Oman by the Arabs. During the 1500s, the Portuguese invaded and built forts in the coastal towns to control the Arabian (or Persian) Gulf trade route.

The Portuguese occupied the area for about 100 years, until the Omanis, led by Imam Nasir ibn Murshid, drove them out. In 1646, the Omanis established friendly relations with the British and signed the first of a series of trade agreements. The strong British influence lasted for the next three centuries. The Dutch East India Company made its presence known in Oman from about 1660 to 1760, and the French became a force to reckon with in the mid-1700s. But except for a brief time during the Omani Civil War in the early 1700s, when Persia took control, Oman has not been under foreign rule since the Portuguese were driven out in the 1600s.

The Omani Civil War broke out after the death of Imam Sultan ibn Saif II in 1718. Two successors vied for the imamate, and then more complications arose. The Persians then took advantage of the situation and invaded. Ahmad ibn Said became an Omani hero when he drove out the Persians, and in 1747 he was elected imam. Small conflicts continued, but the civil war was over.

During the early to mid-19th century, Oman was ruled by Sayyid Said bin Sultan. Oman became an important commercial center for the Gulf area, and relations with other countries were developed. Oman established diplomatic relations with the United States in 1840.

In the 1860s, the invention of the steamship and the opening of the Suez Canal eliminated the demand for Omani sailing ships and the need to stop at Omani ports. Oman entered a time of economic hardship that lasted until oil production began in 1970. Till 1970, Oman had also been kept completely isolated by a succession of rigidly fundamentalist imams and sultans. Finally, on 23 July 1970, Sultan Said bin Tamir was forced into exile by his son, Qaboos, who then became sultan. Sultan Qaboos began the production of oil and used the profits to make much-needed improvements. He loosened the restrictions on contact with foreigners while trying to maintain traditional Islamic values. Sultan Qaboos has brought electricity and running water, free modern education and health care, and great improvements in housing and roadways to Omanis throughout the country, as well as modern technology, such as telephone and television services and satellite communications.

The first national census took place in December 1993, and its results were published in January 1995. The population of Oman was determined to be 2,018,074. Seventy-three percent are Omanis, and 27% are non-Omanis. The capital is Muscat, located on the northeast coast. Most of Oman's foreigners live in Muscat, where they make up 46% of the capital's inhabitants. The majority of Omanis are Arabs, but substantial minorities are of Persian and Indian descent.

² LOCATION AND HOMELAND

Oman is located on the southeast corner of the Arabian Peninsula. It is bordered on the west by Saudi Arabia, on the southwest by Yemen, on the east by the Arabian Sea, and on the northeast by the Gulf of Oman, and it is cut off from its northernmost tip by the United Arab Emirates. The northern tip of Oman lies on the east coast of the narrow Strait of Hormuz, the passageway between the Gulf of Oman (and the Arabian Sea) and the Arabian (or Persian) Gulf. The total area of Oman is about 310,000 sq km (about 120,000 sq mi), approximately the same size as the British Isles, or just slightly smaller than the U.S. state of Kansas. Oman has about 1,600 km (about 1,000 mi) of coastline. The landscape of Oman varies from a fertile coastal plain, known as the Batinah, to the mountains of the Al-Hajar range, to the deserts of the Empty Quarter (which covers a vast stretch of the Arabian Peninsula). The small northern tip of Oman on the Strait of Hormuz and the southern province of Dhofar both receive monsoon rains during the months of June through September. Rain also falls in the mountains. The rest of the country receives little or no rain, making water a very valuable commodity. An ancient water-management system dating back 2,500 years still operates, carrying water from the mountains down into the dry plains below. Oman is known for its extreme heat and humidity, with summer temperatures rising as high as 43°C (110°F) in the shade and humidity reaching a drenching 96%.

³ LANGUAGE

Omanis speak Arabic, with a few pockets of other languages including Kumzar (an Iranian dialect), and the Modern South Arabian languages, which are related to the Old South Arabian languages. English is taught as a second language to all students beginning in primary school. Other languages that are in usage include Swahili and Balochi (Pakistani dialect).

Arabic is spoken by up to 422 million people worldwide, both as native and non-native speakers. Arabic has many distinct dialects, so that people living as few as 500 km (about 310 mi) apart may not be able to entirely understand one another. The written form of Arabic is called Classical Arabic, or, for today's literature and press, Modern Standard Arabic. It is the same for all literate Arabs, regardless of how different their spoken dialects are. Arabic is written from right to left in a unique alphabet that makes no distinction between capital and lower-case letters. It is not necessary for the letters to be written in a straight line, as English letters must be. Punctuation rules are also quite different from those of English.

"Hello" in Arabic is *marhaba* or *ahlan,* to which one replies, *marhabtayn* or *ahlayn.* Other common greetings are *As-salam*

OMANIS

0   250   500   750 Miles

0   250   500   750 Kilometers

'aluykum, "Peace be with you," with the reply of *Wa 'alaykum as-salam,* "and to you peace." *Ma'assalama means* "Goodbye." "Thank you" is *Shukran,* and "You're welcome" is *'Afwan;* "yes" is *na'am* and "no" is *la'a.* The numbers one to ten in Arabic are *wahad, ithnayn, thalatha, arba'a, khamsa, sitta, saba'a, thamanya, tisa'a,* and *'ashara.*

Arab names consist of a first name, a father's name, and a paternal grandfather's name. Women do not take their husband's name when they marry but rather keep their father's family name as a sign of respect for their family of origin. First names usually indicate an Arab's religious affiliation: Muslims use names with Islamic religious significance, such as Muhammad and Ahmed for men, and Fatima and Khadija for women.

⁴ FOLKLORE

Folktales include the legends of Sinbad the Sailor. There is also a legend that King Solomon of Israel flew to Oman on a magic carpet with his jinn (a spirit who can take on human or other animal form) and built 10,000 channels for the ancient water-carrying system in 10 days.

⁵ RELIGION

The original inhabitants of Oman were pantheists, worshiping various goddesses and gods. Many later converted to Christianity. When the Islamic revolution swept through in the 7th century AD, Omanis were among the first to adopt the new religion. All Omanis are Muslims, most belonging to the Ibadi sect, one of the oldest and most traditional branches of Islam. Ibadis believe in maintaining the original purity of Islam as conceived by the Prophet Muhammad. Outside Oman, Ibadi Muslims are found only in North and East Africa.

Islam is the youngest of the world's Abrahamic religions, having begun in the early 7th century AD when the prophet Muhammad received his revelations from Allah (God). Within just a few years of Muhammad's death in AD 632, Islam had spread through the entire Middle East, gaining converts at a dynamic rate.

Born into the Koreish tribe of Mecca (c. AD 570), in what is now Saudi Arabia, Muhammad was later driven from the city because of his vigorous denunciation of the pagan idols worshiped there (idols that attracted a profitable pilgrim trade). The year of Muhammad's flight from Mecca, AD 622 (July 16), called the *Hijra,* is counted as the year one in the Muslim calendar. Muhammad fled to the city now known as Medina, another of the holy sites of modern-day Saudi Arabia. Eventually Muhammad returned to Mecca as a triumphant religious and political leader, destroyed the idols (saving the Black Stone, an ancient meteorite housed in the *Ka`aba,* or Cube, building, which has become a focal point of Muslim worship), and established Mecca as the spiritual center of Islam.

The Islamic religion has five so-called "pillars": 1) Muslims must pray five times a day; 2) Muslims must give alms, or *zakat,* to the poor; 3) Muslims must fast during the month of Ramadan; 4) Muslims must make the pilgrimage, or hajj, to Mecca; and 5) each Muslim must recite the *shahada: "ashhadu an la illah ila Allah wa ashhadu an Muhammadu rasul Allah,"* which means, "I witness that there is no god but Allah and that Muhammad is the prophet of Allah." Arabs say all their prayers facing in the direction of Mecca. Both men and women are expected, and greatly desire, to make the pilgrimage at least once in their lifetime. Ramadan, the ninth month of the Muslim year, during which Muhammad received his first revelations, is observed by complete fasting from dawn until dusk each day of the entire month.

Islam is a simple, straightforward faith with clear rules for correct living; it is a total way of life, inseparable from the rest of one's daily concerns. Therefore, religion and politics and faith and culture are one and the same for Muslims. There is no such thing as the "separation of church and state." In theory, there should be no distinction between private religious values and public cultural norms in an Islamic country; in actuality, history, geography, and daily life have influenced the cultures of Islamic countries, resulting in standards of social behavior and interaction that are not always in agreement with religious codes of conduct.

6 MAJOR HOLIDAYS

The one secular holiday in Oman is National Day on November 18. Otherwise, all the holidays are Muslim ones. Muslim holidays follow the lunar calendar, moving back by eleven days each Western year, so their dates are not fixed on the standard Gregorian calendar. The main Muslim holidays are *Eid Al-Fitr,* a three-day festival at the end of Ramadan; *Eid Al-Adha,* a three-day feast of sacrifice at the end of the month of pilgrimage to Mecca, during which families who can afford it slaughter a lamb and share the meat with poorer Muslims; the First of *Muharram,* or the Muslim New Year; *al-Mawlid An-Nabawi,* the prophet Muhammad's birthday; and *Eid Al-Isra' wa Al-Mi`raj,* a feast celebrating Muhammad's nocturnal visit to heaven. Friday is the Islamic day of rest, so most businesses

and services are closed on Fridays. All government offices, private businesses, and schools are closed also during Eid Al-Fitr and Eid Al-Adha.

7 RITES OF PASSAGE

Omani boys are circumcised at either 15 days or 6 years of age. In the past, circumcision was performed at the age of 15 years in a ceremony involving both women and men. After the boy's foreskin was cut off, the boy had to dance around the circle of people to show his threshold for pain. Today, this practice is far less prevalent and circumcisions are often done under medical supervision in a hospital or by a midwife, or *daya.*

Births are an occasion for celebration, particularly if the child is a boy. Weddings are perhaps the most elaborately celebrated occasions, with great feasts and dancing. Ornate decorations for the bride are prepared well in advance. Death is also a complicated ritual that is governed by Islamic code and often adhered to very closely. A dance known as *dan* is the highest expression of grief in Omani culture and is a common genre in Dhofar region. A female dancer moves very slowly to the seven-unit rhythm to express her grief. The performance involves crying and lamentation.

8 INTERPERSONAL RELATIONS

Arab hospitality reigns in Oman. When talking, Arabs touch each other much more often, and stand much closer together, than Westerners do. People of the same sex will often hold hands while talking or walking. In earlier days, members of the opposite sex, even married couples, never touched in public; this is changing today. Arabs tend to be very expressive and talkative, often employing many hand gestures in their communication. It is not unacceptable to interrupt one another in a conversation.

9 LIVING CONDITIONS

Before Sultan Qaboos took over in 1970, conditions in Oman were extremely primitive. There was no electricity or running water; houses were built of either mud brick or woven and knotted palm fronds; there were only 10 km (6 mi) of paved roads, and the only means of transportation were camels and donkeys; and there were no newspapers and no television or radio stations. Since the coup in 1970, Sultan Qaboos has introduced electricity and running water to most of the country; built many new buildings of cement block (and started a booming business in cement-block production in many towns and villages); constructed about 35,400 km (about 22,000 mi) of paved roads, including multilane divided highways; and modernized communications, health care, and education, all of which are provided free of charge. In 1970 there was only one trained Omani doctor, and he practiced outside the country. In 1993, almost seven years after the opening of a faculty of medicine in the Sultan Qaboos University, 48 Omani doctors completed their training in Oman; 28 of these were women. Beginning in 1997, Oman had 80 new Omani doctors per year.

The number of Omanis practicing medicine is not sufficient to meet the needs of the population, so Omanis still depend on the services of health workers from outside the country. Today, the total number of physicians working in Oman is 3,478. A major immunization initiative introduced in the 1980s has reduced the prevalence of many diseases and has ended diphtheria, poliomyelitis, and neonatal tetanus. Trachoma and malaria

An Omari camel rider stands confidently on his animal during a show race in a village in Oman. The race is one of the most exciting and interesting traditional races in Oman. It stresses the beauty and breed of camels. (AP Images/Hamid al Qasmi)

remain public health problems although the number of cases has been reduced dramatically. Also, major developments in the field of genetics have made it easier to prevent congenital disorders. There has also been a campaign against marriage of close relatives, a prevalent practice that has often increases the likelihood of genetic disorders in newborns. The estimated life expectancy for Omani nationals in 2006 was 72.4 years for men and 74.1 years for women.

The first earth satellite station in Oman opened in 1975. Today, most Omani homes have access to satellite stations and can choose from hundreds of regional and global stations, both news and entertainment. Some 80% of homes are owned by their occupants. Since Omanis now own cars and trucks, the distance from the capital city of Muscat in the northeast to the city of Salalah at the other end of the country can now be crossed in one day. The same trip used to take two weeks by camel caravan.

¹⁰ FAMILY LIFE

Omanis are a tribal people, and family is the center of their life. Marriages are traditionally arranged by parents, with first cousins being the preferred match. The groom pays the bride a dowry, or *mahr,* which becomes her property no matter what happens. The mahr consists of two stages. The first stage is the *muqaddam,* which is a dowry given preceding the wedding to allow the bride to buy things for herself and her new home. The second stage, the *muta'akhir,* is a form of insurance for the woman in the event of divorce; the groom pledges in a contract that he will pay the bride an agreed-upon amount if he should divorce her. Polygamy is legal though it is rarely practiced. A man may have up to four wives, if he guarantees that all will be equally loved and cared for. Divorce is a fairly simple procedure, but it does not happen very often. In a divorce, the father is given custody of all children over the age of five, and the mother takes the younger ones with her back to her parents' house, where she will live until she remarries. Girls can be betrothed as young as 11 or 12 years of age.

A traditional Omani woman's role is domestic, while the man's is public. Men take care of all business and public transactions, even doing much of the food shopping. Women take care of the home, doing all the cooking, cleaning, and childcare. Women and children do most of the sheep, goat, and poultry herding. On farms, women do most of the work in the fields. Weaving and embroidery are also women's tasks. Although Oman is one of the most traditional Islamic countries, women are actually much less restricted in Oman than in other Arab nations. Today, there is a mixture of lifestyles in Oman, some of which starkly contrast with this traditional domestic labor arrangement. Increasingly, as the sultanate has experienced an economic spurt in the last decade, many Omani families rely on live-in domestic workers from south Asia and east Africa to assist with upkeep, care-giving and other domestic chores.

¹¹CLOTHING

Omani men wear the traditional *dishdasha,* an ankle-length robe, usually white. Sometimes they wear a *bisht,* a kind of cloak that is usually black with gold trim, over their dishdasha. On their heads they wear a skullcap or a turban. Many Omani men carry a camel stick, which is the length of bamboo with a curved handle, like a cane. Almost all Omani men wear a curved dagger called a *khanjar* through their belt. Khanjars have ornate silver handles and are an expression of traditional folk art. Most Omanis wear leather sandals on their feet.

Women in Oman wear very colorful dresses over loose-fitting pants that are gathered tightly at the ankles. They wear scarves on their heads, and much jewelry everywhere. In public, most Omani women wear a black ankle-length robe called an *'abaya,* and many wear a traditional Islamic veil over their heads. Some opt to wear the *niqab* that covers the entire face, with holes for the eyes.

¹²FOOD

Staple foods in Oman consist of rice, dates, fruit, fish, and meat. Most meat is cooked in a *tanour,* a hole in the ground where a fire is built, then allowed to burn down to ashes, after which meat wrapped in leaves is placed on the ashes and the hole is covered with earth. After 24 hours, the cooked meat is dug up, unwrapped, and served. Omanis eat their meals on the floor or ground, the dishes spread on a cloth. Food and drink are always taken with the right hand. Families eat together, except on special occasions when men and women eat separately. The main meal of the day is at noon; breakfast and supper are light meals. A favorite dessert is *halawa* (halvah), a sweet, flaky dessert usually made of crushed sesame seeds and honey. Coffee is drunk strong and black, sometimes flavored with cardamom. Bedu (or bedouin) nomads eat the locusts that swarm over farmers' crops.

¹³EDUCATION

Before Sultan Qaboos took over in 1970, there were only three schools in Oman, with a total of 900 students, all boys. Today, there are over 1,100 schools, with a total enrollment of 800,000 students, half of whom are girls. Until recently, girls and boys went to separate schools despite having the same educational curriculum. Education is free to all Omanis from the preschool through postgraduate levels. Children's education goes through three stages: primary, preparatory, and secondary. Primary school begins at six years of age and continues until the child passes a sixth-grade examination. Of all children between the ages of 6 and 11, 86% attend elementary school. Those who pass the examination go on to preparatory school, which is completed after three years with another examination. Passing students then attend secondary school, where the focus of study is determined by the grade they have achieved

in their preparatory-school exam. Some students attend college or technical training institutes after secondary school. The Sultan Qaboos University was inaugurated in 1980 and opened for classes in September 1986. Sixty-five percent of its more than 10,000 students are female who are enrolled in five colleges: Engineering, Medicine, Agriculture, Education, Art and Islamic Studies and Science. The literacy rate in 1995 was determined to be about 59% for those over 15 years of age. Hundreds of adult-education and literacy centers have been established to help eradicate illiteracy. A testament to the success of these programs, the current literacy rate is approximately 82%.

¹⁴CULTURAL HERITAGE

The Ministry of National Heritage and Culture was established in 1976. By 2000, it had restored more than 100 historic buildings, which included forts, castles, citadels, and ancient houses. Some of these restored buildings have become tourist attractions, such as the castle at Jabrin, built in the 17th century. The Ministry has also built numerous historical museums, libraries, and cultural centers, and organized excavations of ancient remains. Excavations have uncovered pottery jars, beads, and arrowheads dating back to the 3rd millennium BC.

Music is not encouraged by the Ibadi sect of Islam. Yet, some folk music has developed in Oman, and the Oman Center for Traditional Music was founded in August 1983 to collect and document Omani folk music. It serves as a repository of video tapes, audio recordings, and pictures and slides of songs and dances handed down through generations. Folk music is played on traditional instruments, such as drums, a trumpet made out of horn, a straight pipe, and the *rebaba,* a stringed instrument. Sea chanteys have been sung throughout the seafaring Omanis' history. The traditional men's sword dance has its origin in a series of military exercises. In 1985, Sultan Qaboos established the Royal Oman Symphony Orchestra and a music-training school. The school, located in Bayt al-Barakah, is a boarding school attended by both sexes. Since the advent of satellite television, much of the music scene in Oman has been influenced by popular trends from other countries in the region and English-language music.

Until recently, visual arts in Oman were mostly confined to utilitarian objects, such as kitchen utensils, rugs, ceramic pots, and clothing. However, recent artistic exhibitions have focused on contemporary Omani painters and sculptors whose works now grace many public areas in the capital Muscat.

¹⁵WORK

In the fertile areas of Oman, such as the Batinah (coastal plain) and the inland valleys beneath the mountains, most people are farmers.

About 10% of Omanis are fishers in the Gulf of Oman and the Arabian Sea. Boatbuilding is an ancient craft passed down from generation to generation. Traditionally, boats were built from palm fronds, although larger ones were built from wood. These traditional boats are still used, although recently many fishers have purchased aluminum boats. Sails and oars were the means of propulsion until the past two or three decades; most boats now have motors.

Omani nomads are sheep, goat, and camel herders. Oman is the camel-breeding capital of the world.

Although most of Oman's revenue currently comes from oil, that industry employs only a few thousand Omanis. Out of a total of 730,000 laborers in the work force, only about 260,000 (36%) are Omanis; the rest are expatriates. The government has set the objective of "Omanization" of the labor force, hoping to replace foreign workers with Omani nationals.

16 SPORTS

Since 1970, Sultan Qaboos has increased the scope of sporting activities in the country. Sports complexes and sports clubs have been built throughout Oman. The traditional sport of camel racing is very popular, as is horse racing. Hockey was introduced into Oman from India in the 19th century and is very popular. Many Omanis enjoy marksmanship, and some have won regional or international shooting competitions. Omani national teams have also competed in the Olympic games.

17 ENTERTAINMENT AND RECREATION

Omanis enjoy plays and concerts performed by the national Youth Theater, established in 1980. Boys have joined Boy Scout groups since 1948; girls have been able to be Girl Scouts since 1970. The National Organization for Scouts and Guides, established in 1975, aims to develop in youth a sense of service, self-reliance, responsibility, and public spirit. There are 10 Scout camps in the country.

18 FOLK ART, CRAFTS, AND HOBBIES

All art in Oman is utilitarian and can therefore be seen as folk art. Silver-, gold-, and copper smithing are perhaps the most highly developed arts, although weaving, embroidery, and woodcarving also are highly intricate and require great skill. Pottery is also a well-developed utilitarian art.

19 SOCIAL PROBLEMS

Ecologically, Oman is very environmentally responsible in some ways but not in others. Although it is a very clean country, with stiff fines for littering (or even for having a dirty car), there is a great deal of coastal pollution from oil tankers dumping or leaking oil offshore, from the mining of sand to build new roads, which then encroach on wilderness territory, and from the dumping of wastes. The government is attempting to address these problems with various measures, but the problems still exist.

The once nearly extinct white oryx, an antelope, has been successfully reintroduced into the wild in Oman, but several species of sea turtles continue to be endangered by the Omani taste for turtle soup. Groundwater reserves that have existed since prehistoric times, when the climate was much wetter, are being rapidly depleted, and the dry climate of today will not provide enough rain to replenish them. The digging of wells is regulated, but not strictly enough.

Politically, the traditional sultanate structure, in which family members are given all the positions of authority and decision-making, is quickly becoming obsolete and detrimental to Oman's welfare. Many commoners are now much better educated and trained in the skills needed for government posts than members of the ruling family. Since the production of oil began in 1970, the ruling family has kept Oman's citizens quiet by giving them great benefits and subsidies. In return for this lavish treatment, citizens have not questioned the way the government is run. But those days are quickly disappearing. Oman has very limited oil reserves that are anticipated to run out soon, and the wealth will not flow so freely after that. Omanis are becoming dependent on government handouts that will have to be severely cut back once the oil runs out. Sultan Qaboos Is trying to develop non-oil industries, but he has had limited success so far.

Modernization has been new to Oman, but it seems Omanis have developed a culture that is a unique amalgam of both traditional and modern social norms.

20 GENDER ISSUES

While the *niqab* (full facial covering worn by women) has been increasingly popular throughout the region, in an interesting turn in the expression of religion, Sultan Qaboos has banned the niqab by all women in public office. Furthermore, he has decreed that all women are allowed to vote and run for Majlis Al-Shura (Consultative Council) seats. In the first election of the council in 2003, two women won seats. Furthermore, Qaboos also appointed a cabinet comprised of three women ministers whose portfolios are Higher Education, Social Development, and Tourism. Also, the Omani ambassador to the United States, Hunaina bint Sultan al-Mughairyah, has become the most prominent woman in a diplomatic mission. Various projects to empower Omani woman have proven successful. The Omani Women's Association (OWA) is a very active organization that collaborates with government initiative and local grassroots groups. Notable Omani women include artist Mariyam Mohamed and writer Rafiah Altalei.

21 BIBLIOGRAPHY

Allen, Carl. *Oman Under Qaboos: From Coup to Constitution, 1970-1996*. Routledge, 2002.

Bequette, France. "Environment-friendly Oman." *UNESCO Courier* (April 1995): 39.

Berger, Gilda. *Kuwait and the Rim of Arabia*. New York and London: Franklin Watts, 1978.

Dutton, Roderic. *An Arab Family*. Minneapolis: Lerner Publications Co., 1985.

"The Gulf's Uneasy Rulers." *World Press Review* 42, no 8 (August 1995): 6–7.

Hawley, Sir Donald. *Oman and its Renaissance*. London: Stacey International, 1990.

Hunt, Carla. "Land of Sinbad Proves Irresistible to Some U.S. Tour Firms." *Travel Weekly* 54, no 103 (28 December 1995): 28.

Iskandar, Adel. *The Oasis of Frankincense, Gold and Peace*, Ambassadors Online Magazine, Volume 3, Issue 2, July 2000.

Moss, Joyce, and George Wilson. *Peoples of the World: The Middle East and North Africa*. Detroit: Gale Research, 1992.

Zahlan, Rosemarie Said. *The Making of the Modern Gulf States: Kuwait, Bahrain, Qatar, the United Arab Emirates and Oman*. London: Unwin Hymen, 1989.

—revised by Adel Iskandar

ORANG ASLI

PRONUNCIATION: oh-RAHNG ahss-LEE
LOCATION: Malaysia
POPULATION: 132,873 (in 2000)
LANGUAGE: Orang Asli; Malay; Thai; other dialects
RELIGION: Animism; Islam; Christianity
RELATED ARTICLES: Vol. 3: China and Her National Minorities; Iban; Kelabit; Vol. 4: Malaysian Malays

¹INTRODUCTION

As a collective, the term *Orang Asli* can be transliterated as "original peoples," or "first peoples." The word *orang* means "people" and the term *asli* comes from the Arabic word "*asali*," meaning "original," "well-born," or "aristocratic." The Orang Asli of Malay Peninsula (or West Malaysia) are divided into a great number of different tribal groups, some of which have very little contact with each other. The various Orang Asli tribes, which include 19 subethnic groups, have traditionally been grouped for administrative purposes under three main categories: the Negritos, the Senoi, and the Aboriginal-Malays (refer to Table 1). Each group is unique in that it has a language and a mode of living quite different from the others. Each group includes a number of related tribes who speak similar languages and who follow a similar way of life, although some of the tribes are rather mixed. Differences between the Negritos, the Senoi, and the Aboriginal-Malay groups are also shown by their physical appearances.

In spite of differences in languages and physical appearances, all Orang Asli tribes share one thing in common, which is that they are the descendants of the earliest known inhabitants who occupied the Malay Peninsula. In other words, the Orang Asli lived in West Malaysia long before the arrival of the other races, that is, the Malays, the Chinese, and the Indians. Some authorities claim that the Negritos came to the Malay Peninsula about 25,000 years ago. There are different opinions as to the origin of the Senoi. Some suggest that they are related to present-day Cambodian and Vietnamese mountain tribes, while others propose that they are related to indigenous groups from southern India and Sri Lanka. They are believed to have arrived in Malaysia in a second wave of migration about 6,000 or 8,000 years ago. The third group, the Aboriginal -Malays, is often called "Jakun." They are thought to have migrated about 4,000 years ago, constituting the third wave of Orang Asli migration to Malaya. Their ancestors are believed to have migrated from the Indonesian islands to the south of the peninsula and, prior to that, are believed to have come from a location in Yunan, in present-day China.

Because of their small population, the Orang Asli are insignificant players in present-day political spheres. One parliamentary seat is reserved solely to look into the affairs of the Orang Asli. Nonetheless, there is a need to have more representatives in both the parliament and state assemblies. This could be done through elections for seats where Orang Asli represent a sizable section in the constituency, or through appointment.

²LOCATION AND HOMELAND

Numbering 132,873 people in 2000, the Orang Asli constitute an extremely small segment of the population of Malaysia,

making up only 0.5% of the total population (21.9 million in 2000). The Senoi are by far the largest subgroup, constituting 53.4% of the Orang Asli population. The Aboriginal-Malays, with a population of 40,117 people, form about 43.3% of the total, while the remaining 3.3% consists of the Negritos, who form the smallest segment of the population. The Semai-Senoi represent the largest subethnic group among the Orang Asli, numbering 34,248 people or 29.4% of the total Orang Asli population in 1999.

The Orang Asli are found in all 11 states of Peninsular Malaysia. Many of the Negrito groups, and most of the Semai-Senoi, live in the northern parts of the Malay Peninsula, while the Aboriginal-Malays are concentrated in the center and southern part of the Peninsula. The Orang Asli subgroups and their locations are:

SUBGROUP	LOCATION
Negrito	Northeast Kedah
Kensiu	Kedah-Perak Border
Kintak	Northeast Perak and West Kelantan
Jahai	North Central Perak
Lanoh	Southeast Kelantan
Mendriq	Northeast Pahang and South Kelantan
Batek	
Senoi	
Semai	Northwest Pahang and South Perak
Temiar	North Perak and South Kelantan
Jah Hut	Central Pahang
Chewong	Central Pahang
Mah Meri	Coastal Selangor
Semoq Beri	South Central Pahang
Aboriginal Malay	
Temuan	Selangor and Negri Sembilan
Semelai	Central Pahang and East Negri Sembilan
Jakun	South Pahang and North Johor
Orang Kanaq	East Johor
Orang Kuala	West and South Coasts of Johor
Orang Seletar	West and South Coasts of Johor

Traditionally, most of the Orang Asli were forest dwellers. However, official statistics by the Department of Orang Asli suggest that today not all groups live in the deep jungle. Out of 840 Orang Asli settlements in 1997, 387 were in forested areas, while 440 were in forest fringe areas, and the rest (13 settlements) in urban areas. In a sense urbanization seems to be encroaching faster and closer onto Orang Asli settlements.

³LANGUAGE

None of the Orang Asli groups have a written language. Therefore, they do not have a written history. Their histories are passed down through generations by word of mouth.

It is very common for Orang Asli to speak more than one language. A great number still speak their own language and practice tradition, while at the same time also speak Malay, Thai, or other Orang Asli languages. Some of the northern Orang Asli groups, for instance, the Semai-Senoi and Negrito groups, speak languages now termed Aslian (Mon-Khmer speakers). Members of the Aboriginal-Malay tribes speak dialects that belong to the Austronesian family of languages (as

An Orang Asli child carries her brother in the rural village of Lembah Belum, Perak, Malaysia. (AP Images/The Eng Koon)

does the Malay dialect), with the exceptions of the Semelai and Temoq dialects. Some Aboriginal-Malays speak nothing other than standard Malay.

⁴FOLKLORE

The Orang Asli, like many other indigenous people in Malaysia, have a rich folklore tradition. This tradition includes legends, fables, tales, and myths. One of their popular myths is the story of creation from the Jah Hut ethnic group. According to this myth, people originally inhabited an unnamed primeval land. Soon, however, the land became overcrowded, compelling some to leave. Some left in a ship with many decks. Some took with them a pair of every animal species and enough food for the journey. They left without really knowing where they were heading. After a while, turbulent waters caused the ship to break on a coral reef. In the confusion, those who happened to be at the top of the ship managed to cling to a few planks and to their blowpipes. Those inside the ship held onto tools, iron, and cloth and drifted away to other islands and other places. Thus, people were spread through the islands and mainland and moved from one island to another and from place to place.

⁵RELIGION

Unlike other major religions of the world, the Orang Asli religion does not possess any written sacred script. Traditionally, the Orang Asli are animists and believe that there are spirits that dwell in inanimate objects, such as trees and rocks, and also in various natural phenomena, such as thunder and lightning. Beliefs in shamanism are still very strong among some of the tribes. Shamans are ritual specialists who have the gift of going into a trance. A shaman plays an important role in the life of Orang Asli as an intermediary between humans and the world of spirits, to combat evil spirits, cure illnesses, and also to strengthen the morale of the group.

Aside from shamanism, dreams occupy an important place in the spiritual life of the Orang Asli. Dreams are believed to foretell the future and are also used to control social behavior. Everyone in the tribe is encouraged to share their dreams, which are then interpreted by an expert in the community. Children are encouraged to mention their dreams to their fathers. As an agent of social control, a dream bestows obligations on its dreamer to warn his or her friends of any forthcoming danger. For instance, if a person dreams that one of his or her friends is attacked by a wild animal, the dreamer is responsible for warning his or her friend of the danger.

Today, some Orang Asli have embraced other major religions, particularly Islam and Christianity. Aboriginal-Malays have been Muslim for over 100 years.

⁶MAJOR HOLIDAYS

See the article entitled **Malaysian Malays**.

⁷RITES OF PASSAGE

Socialization among the Orang Asli is an informal, natural, and gradual process. It is a major concern of the parents. The father is responsible for training the male children, while the mother concerns herself primarily with her daughters. A son is normally under the care of his mother until the age of five or so. At this age, a son begins to look upon his father both as an example and as a teacher. The father teaches the son how to hunt and use the blowpipe, and the son gradually begins to follow the father on hunting expeditions. The mother, on the other hand, is responsible for bringing up her daughters. As her daughters become older, she teaches them how to prepare food and look after the family's dwelling. Also, at this period, they begin to accompany the older women on their food-gathering forays.

In all the tribes, men and women marry at an early age. A man will normally marry at the age of 18 or so, while his bride may be a few years younger. Even though most marriages are informal arrangements and are not marked by any special ceremony, marriage as an institution is still highly regarded by the Orang Asli.

⁸INTERPERSONAL RELATIONS

Sharing whatever one can afford with others in the community is highly valued among the Orang Asli. If one has only a little surplus over one's own immediate needs, one shares it with one's nuclear family. If the surplus is larger, it is shared with people in one's house or neighboring houses. If the surplus is very large, it is shared with all of the people in one's settlement.

Besides sharing, all the tribes stress values like cheerfulness, a lighthearted attitude to life, and a willingness to cooperate with others, especially with one's friends and kinfolk. These are very important attitudes for surviving in the Orang Asli's difficult and at times rather grim environment.

The Orang Asli are peace-loving and friendly people. Thus, they set a high value on nonviolence and avoidance of disputes. They are also very shy, and their first response to threat is flight rather than hostility. Respect for older people is also highly regarded, and children are taught from a very young age to respect their elders.

⁹LIVING CONDITIONS

It is important to note that the majority of the Orang Asli are not jungle-dwellers or nomads although many live in forest or forest-fringe areas. The only exception is the Negritos, who lead a nomadic or seminomadic existence. These people normally live in remote areas of the jungle. Therefore, they are considered materially poorer and less developed than the others. Some of these tribes live together or in bands. Others have settled and live in villages, much like the Malays.

Most of their dwellings, called "wind screens," are made from jungle materials, such as bamboo, wood, leaves, sticks, and rattan. A very simple dwelling usually consists of a small and rather narrow sleeping platform. However, others, such as the Temiar, live in longhouses. Every longhouse has a number of divisions or compartments, each with a separate hearth or fireplace.

The Orang Asli have a great deal of variation in their ways of life. However, as a community, the Orang Asli are not always well-off from a material and a nutritional point of view. There is a degree of malnutrition, as their diet is insufficient in protein. They normally supplement their starchy diet by hunting and fishing. Animals and fish provide the much-needed protein, but normally the amount is insufficient. This is aggravated by the need to share the food among the population.

Certain settlements lack basic amenities, such as piped water and electricity, and have to depend on water from the streams and kerosene for light. Nonetheless, at present, many own transistor radio sets.

¹⁰FAMILY LIFE

The social structure of the various tribes is essentially similar. The most basic kinship unit is the nuclear family; a husband, wife, and their own children. This is considered to be the most important unit of the social structure. Besides being a social structure, the nuclear family is an economic unit and a basic working group. The father is always the leader of the family and will be replaced by his wife only if he dies.

A division of labor between men and women exists within the households. The father and sons are responsible for providing meat for the family and thus go out hunting together, while the mother, accompanied by her daughters, provides the jungle fruits and vegetables. The mother usually cooks the food for the whole family.

The concept of dating in the Western sense does not exist among the Orang Asli. When a young man is in love with a girl and wants to marry her, he will approach her father, but he will only do this after he has already reached a clear understanding with the girl.

¹¹CLOTHING

Traditionally, children up to the age of five or so generally went naked, but nowadays all Orang Asli wear clothes of some kind. The traditional skirt of the Negrito women is a short, fringed skirt, which is commonly made from pounded tree bark. Sometimes belts, headbands, and bracelets are also worn. While the women wear skirts, the men's traditional clothing consists essentially of a loincloth, called *chawat* in Malay, which again is made from pounded tree bark. In addition, the men frequently wear rattan belts, which are used for the carrying of knives and other small items such as tobacco pouches. Traditional clothing of this kind has become increasingly rare.

Orang Asli's contacts with other communities, especially with the Malays, facilitated the introduction of a Malay-type of cloth that is made from cotton and is of a Western dress code. For instance, the women today usually wear sarongs made from cotton, and men will normally wear a pair of trousers or shorts, putting on a shirt when he goes into the jungle.

¹²FOOD

Some groups of Orang Asli are able to survive in the jungle for years, without resorting to the cultivation of any crops. They rely on varieties of tubers, rattan roots, different kinds of jungle fruits, and many other jungle shrubs and vegetables as their staple diet. For example, for the Negritos, wild tubers are the basis of their diet, cooked in a variety of ways.

Some other tribes, such as the Temiar, cultivate two staple crops: hill rice and tapioca. Other vegetation, such as millet, bananas, maize (corn), and other vegetables, are also grown. Some tribes also domesticate animals, mostly chickens, for domestic consumption.

¹³EDUCATION

The government encourages formal education among the Orang Asli, as it does for other Malaysians. The Aboriginal Peoples Act of 1967 and 1974 stipulates that no Orang Asli child should be precluded from attending any school only by reason of being an Orang Asli. As a result, the overall enrollment of Orang Asli in school has increased. Nonetheless, there is still low rate of literacy and proportionally small number have attained tertiary education. For instance, by 1997, only 138 Orang Asli obtained tertiary education with government assistance, while 99 persons were still pursuing their education. Low educational attainment is mainly because of high dropout rate among Orang Asli children at the primary level. For the period 1971–1995, an average of 62.1% of Orang Asli students dropped out annually.

¹⁴CULTURAL HERITAGE

The Orang Asli, like many other indigenous peoples across the world, depend partly on the forest for their living. All sorts of jungle products are put to good use as raw materials. Various jungle products, such as bamboo and wood, are used to build houses and to make household utensils and vessels, ornaments, and different kinds of musical instruments (such as flutes made from bamboo, and wooden and bamboo xylophones). Bamboo is used to build houses and for the construction of tools, weapons, baskets, waterpipes, rafts, traps, and hunting implements.

¹⁵WORK

The Orang Asli have varied occupations and ways of life. For example, those who live close to the coastal areas are mainly fishermen and women This includes the Orang Laut, Orang Seletar, and Mah Meri. Others, such as some members of the Temuan, Jakun, and Semai, are involved in permanent agriculture and manage their own rubber, oil palm, or cocoa farms. There are also others who are engaged in traditional economic activities like shifting cultivation, cassava swiddening, and hunting and gathering. These are subgroups who still live close to or within forested areas, such as the Temiar, Chewong, Jah Hut, Semoq Beri, and all the Negrito groups. There are others who also engaged in some trading with the Malays, with jungle produce (such as petai, durian, rattan, and resins) being exchanged for salt, knives, and metal axe-heads. These groups live very close to, or within, the forest area.

As a result of urbanization and migration trends a fair number also live in urban areas and are engaged in both waged employment and salaried jobs. These include the fields of agriculture, animal husbandry, forestry, fishing, and hunting. There are others being employed in production and production-related activities, such as in electronic, textile, and rubber-products factories. Some are employed by the government, and some engage in seasonal work in Malay villages or work as laborers in the tea estates in places like the Cameron Highlands.

¹⁶SPORTS

Hunting animals (by men) and gathering wild fruits and vegetables from the jungle are considered sports among the Orang Asli, as is true among many indigenous people in the tropics. Swimming in the rivers is a sport mainly enjoyed by the children. Other games, such as soccer, volleyball, and *sepak takraw*, are becoming popular among the Orang Asli.

¹⁷ENTERTAINMENT AND RECREATION

Most Orang Asli, particularly those who still live close to or within forest areas, do not have televisions, compact discs, or tape players, though some do possess transistor radio sets. Traditional dances serve as a form of entertainment. These dances are always held after nightfall and are accompanied by public singing or chanting. Hunting, besides providing a reliable source of animal protein, generates much excitement for the hunters, who are invariably male, and is thus treated as a form of recreation as much as a task.

¹⁸FOLK ART, CRAFTS, AND HOBBIES

Orang Asli material culture consists of various types of household utensils woven by women and tools and weapons made by men. Women weave baskets from various pandanus leaves. This requires skill, knowledge, and experience. Some of the baskets are carried in the manner of a rucksack. Larger baskets are used to carry various household goods and clothes, while small baskets are used as tobacco pouches and for carrying other personal articles.

The blowpipe is an important weapon among the Orang Asli. The construction of a blowpipe is a very skilled job, and it sometimes takes longer to make a blowpipe than it does to build a house. Another work of art that is considered unique, particularly among the Negritos, is the beautifully incised and decorated comb, which is primarily used by women. These combs, with anywhere from 12 to over 20 teeth, are cut from a piece of split bamboo. The possession of these combs is a source of great satisfaction and pride to their owners.

Wooden statues and carvings, and beautiful wooden masks that are worn during dances and other ceremonies, are also highly valued by the Orang Asli.

¹⁹SOCIAL PROBLEMS

Because of their geographical isolation, and also because of their relatively small population, the Orang Asli are economically and politically disadvantaged when compared to the rest of their Malaysian fellow citizens. The official statistics classify 35.2% of Orang Asli as extremely poor, and they lag behind in basic infrastructure and in political representation. However, today, the greatest threat to the Orang Asli culture, identity, and livelihood is their dispossession from their traditional homelands. Their lands are often used for development schemes, plantations, mining concessions, highways, dams, and various other forms of development. Land dispossession is a persistent issue facing the Orang Asli, and insecurity of land ownership is the most threatening social problem the Orang Asli have ever encountered.

²⁰GENDER ISSUES

Females comprise almost 49% of the Orang Asli population in Peninsula Malaysia. Traditionally there was a sexual division in roles and functions whereby women held important responsibilities as *shamans* and influential leaders in society. However, the spread of sexual differentiation and social inequality through contacts and internalization of external cultures have affected gender relations and the present position of women in Orang Asli society. This is made evident through the exclusion of women in most political functions and official meetings. Since all Orang Asli village heads (*batins*) are men, only the men attend official meetings with government representatives. In other words, Orang Asli women's involvement in the social and political domains is increasingly restricted and limited.

²¹BIBLIOGRAPHY

Carey, Iskandar. *Orang Asli: The Aboriginal Tribe of Peninsular Malaysia.* Oxford University Press, 1976.

Nicholas, Colin. *The Orang Asli and the Contest for Resources. Indigenous Politics, Development and Identity in Peninsular Malaysia.* Copenhagen: International Work Group for Indigenous Affairs, 2000.

Nicholas, Colin. *Pathway to Dependence: Commodity Relations and the Dissolution of Semai Society.* Monash Papers on Southeast Asia No. 33. Centre for Southeast Asian Studies, Monash University, 1994.

Nicholas, Colin, Chopil, Tijah Yok, and Sabak, Tiah. *Orang Asli Women and the Forest. The Impact of Resource Depletion on Gender Relations among the Semai.* Subang Jaya, Malaysia: Center for Orang Asli Concerns, 2003.

Nicholas, Colin, and Raajen Singh. *Indigenous Peoples of Asia: Many Peoples, One Struggles.* Bangkok: Asia Indigenous Peoples Pact, 1996.

—by P. Bala

ORAONS

PRONUNCIATION: oh-RAH-ohns
ALTERNATE NAMES: Uraons; Kurukh, Dhangar
LOCATION: India (primarily Bihar, Orissa, aand Madhya Pradesh states)
POPULATION: Nearly 3.5 million (estimate)
LANGUAGE: Kurukh; Hindi; other languages of regions in which they live
RELIGION: Mixture of magic, animism, and elements of Hinduism; Christianity

¹INTRODUCTION

The Oraons (Uraons) are one of the five largest tribes in South Asia. They live in the forested uplands of east-central India, occupying the Chota Nagpur region of Jharkhand and adjoining states. Scholars have speculated that they migrated there in the distant past from the Konkan coast of South India. In the centuries preceding the Christian era, the Oraons were established around Rohtas, to the northwest of their present home. According to their own traditions, the Oraons were forced out of their lands by invading peoples and migrated to Chota Nagpur, where they settled among the Munda tribes of the area. Historians indicate this may have occurred around 100 BC.

The origins of the name "Oraon" are unclear. Some Oraons say that the name is derived from *Ur* (chest), because they believe they were born of the blood from the chest of a holy man. Many see the name as a disparaging one given by caste-conscious Hindus who considered the tribe to be unclean. The Oraons themselves use the name "Kurukh," possibly after a mythical Oraon king called Karakh.

Oraons are, as a rule, short of stature and dark-complexioned, broad-nosed, and thick-lipped. They are considered to be of Proto-Australoid stock, descended from a race that influenced the peoples and cultures of a wide area of South Asia, Southeast Asia, and the islands of Polynesia. In South Asia, the Proto-Australoids form an old, pre-Dravidian element in the population. The physical traits associated with this group are found among tribal peoples and also, to varying degrees, among the lower castes of the Hindu populations of peninsular India.

²LOCATION AND HOMELAND

Population estimates of the Oraon are clearly unreliable. The Joshua Project estimates that Kurukh speakers in India number around 4,390,000 people while Oraons in Nepal, Bangladesh, and Bhutan would bring this total to close to 4.5 million. However, by totaling the Oraon populations in the states where they were found for the 2001 Census of India, and allowing for a natural increase in the region of 1.7% per year, this figure is estimated to be closer to 3.5 million people. Part of the confusion may be that in some states the Oraons are called Dhangar, Kisan, or Kuda. So, the total population of Oraons numbers between 3.5 and 4.5 million people. The creation of the new Indian states of Jharkhand and Chhattisgarh in 2000 resulted in the inclusion of over one million Oraon in each state, thus giving them greater political representation. In addition to Jharkhand and Chhattisgarh, Oraons are also found in neighboring areas of Orissa and in Madhya Pradesh State. In Mad-

hya Pradesh, they are also known as Dhanka and Dhangad. Numbers of Oraons have migrated from their homeland to areas of West Bengal, with many settling in Jalpaiguri District in the north. A few Oraon live in Tripura State and Assam in northeastern India, where their ancestors were taken in the early 20th century to work as laborers on tea plantations.

Chota Nagpur, the homeland of the Oraons, is the name given to the northeastern section of the great peninsular mass of India known as the Deccan (literally the "South"). In Jharkhand, the Deccan pushes north and east towards the Himalayas, constricting the alluvial plains of the Ganges River to their narrowest extent. The Ganges flows from west to east across Bihar, but once the river leaves the state it turns southeast towards its delta in the Bay of Bengal.

The Chota Nagpur region lies south of the Ganges plains, extending eastwards from the River Son, a tributary of the Ganges, to the lowlands of West Bengal. The terrain assumes the aspect of open plateaus and steep-sided, mesa-like hills between 300 m and 760 m (approximately 1,000–2,200 ft), surmounted by peaks reaching as high as 1,505 m (3,445 ft). Though much of the area has been cleared for cultivation, extensive areas of forest remain. These vary from scrub jungles to denser subtropical and tropical deciduous forests. Rainfall averages between 120 cm and 160 cm (47–62 in) and is received mostly during the three months of the summer monsoon. Humidity is high during the summer, with maximum temperatures varying between 35°C and 40°C (95°F–104°F).

³LANGUAGE

The Oraons' language is Kurukh, which is a member of the northern subgroup of the Dravidian language family. However, many Oraons are bilingual or even multilingual. They use Hindi, the widely spoken language of northern India, or Shadri, a local dialect, to communicate with non-Oraon groups. Oraons living in other parts of northern India commonly speak the language of the region in which they live. Thus Bengali, Oriya (the language of Orissa), and Assamese, in addition to lesser dialects, are all reported as second languages spoken by Oraons.

As with many tribal groups, the Oraons originally had no written form of language. (The Oraons themselves believe that at one time they did possess a script but that it was lost during one of the many crises in their history). The Oraons now write in Devanagari, which is the script used by Sanskrit, Hindi, and some related Aryan languages.

⁴FOLKLORE

Oraon folk tradition tells of how the tribe was driven out of the ancient kingdom of Rohtas (called Ruidas in Kurukh). For many years, so the story goes, the Kurus had attempted to dislodge the Oraons from Ruidas but had never been able to defeat them in open combat. So the Kurus sent a milkmaid into the fort to gain intelligence. When she returned, the spy informed the Kurus that if they attacked while the Oraons were celebrating the Xaddi (Sarhul) festival, the men would be drunk on rice-beer. The plan worked and when the Kurus attacked, all the Oraon men were intoxicated and asleep. But the women, led by Princess Singi Dai, dressed up as men and repeatedly fought off the invaders. It was not until the Kurus discovered that they were fighting women that they succeeded in capturing the fort.

Many Oraons were killed, but one man sobered up and managed to escape. He fled, pursued by Kuru warriors, until he reached Chota Nagpur. The region was already inhabited by the Munda tribe. On reaching a village, the fugitive begged for help from some Mundas who were about to sit down and eat a cow they had just slaughtered. The Mundas told the Oraon that if he threw away the "sacred thread" he was wearing and joined them in their meal, they would protect him from the Kurus. The Oraon remained in Chota Nagpur, and it is his descendants who live in the land to this day.

The ending of this tale is of interest in the Indian social context. High-caste Hindus wear the sacred thread and do not eat meat. By discarding the sacred thread and eating the Mundas' food, the Oraon was essentially abandoning his caste status. Also, commensal relations (the willingness to eat with people of a particular caste or group) are a symbol of social status in India. People will not take food with others whom they see as socially inferior. By dining with the Mundas, the Oraon was, in effect, accepting them as his equals. This is how the Oraons explain their low standing in the social hierarchy of the Chota Nagpur region. It is also worth noting that the Oraons and Mundas have coexisted for centuries and share many cultural traits.

⁵RELIGION

Oraons follow a Hindu form of worship, although their deities are non-Sanskritic, that is to say, they are not found in the sacred Sanskrit texts of Hinduism. Many of their gods, e.g., Chandi, Chauthia, Dadgo Burhia, Gaon Deoti, and Jair Budhi, are local in character and are not found anywhere else in India. Oraon religion can best be described as a mixture of magic, traditional animistic beliefs and practices, and elements of Hinduism.

The Oraons recognize the existence of a supreme being, symbolized by the sun and known as Dharmes. Dharmes is the master of all that exists in the universe and controls the fate of all beings, both physical and spiritual. Beneath Dharmes, there is an array of lesser deities, nature spirits, the souls of dead ancestors, evil ghosts, and impersonal forces of good and evil. Elements of totemism (belief in an ancestral relationship with plants, animals, and other objects) and shamanism (belief that the spiritual world can be manipulated through a shaman) complete the belief system of the Oraons.

The world of lesser deities and spirits is divided into several categories. First, there are the ancestor spirits, souls of departed relatives who protect the living during illness and guard them from mischievous spirits. Ancestor spirits are honored every year at the *Harbora* ("Bone-drowning") ceremony. At this time, the bones of every Oraon who died during the previous year are laid to rest. Second, there are the tutelary deities *(deotas)* and spirits *(bhuts)* of the village. These include the benign Chala Pachcho, a popular goddess who protects the village and is sometimes known as Gaon Deoti. Pat or Pat Raja is the master of all the village spirits. In this role, he protects the village from disease and other misfortune. In addition, there are six or seven other categories of spirits ranging from Chandi, a goddess of hunting and war, to various household spirits.

Stray spirits that haunt the village have to be driven off by exorcism. This is undertaken not by the village priest *(pahan)* but by diviners who identify the malevolent spirits, and shamans who exorcise them. "Black" magic is known, but its practitioners are feared and detested. They are punished or driven from the village when they are discovered. Oraons also believe in the "evil eye" *(najar)* and the "evil mouth" *(baibhak)*, both of which can bring misfortune to their victims.

Many deities and spirits, including the ancestor spirits, are honored or propitiated by the sacrifice of animals. A white fowl or goat is the appropriate offering to Dharmes, the supreme deity. Buffalo, sheep, and pigs are also used as sacrificial victims. The actual sacrifice is carried out by the village priest and his assistants. These offices can be hereditary or elective. The priests are usually Oraons, but in some villages they may be from another tribe, such as the Mundas or Baigas.

One unusual feature of traditional Oraon religion is human sacrifice, a custom also found among the neighboring Gond and Munda tribes. S. C. Roy (1928) writes that the sacrifice was performed by the Oraons to appease a powerful village spirit, who would otherwise bring terrible epidemics and destruction to the villagers. Others suggest the offering was made to a vindictive goddess who controlled the fertility of the soil. In some instances, parts of the victim's body were buried in the fields and the blood mixed with seed to ensure a good harvest. Human sacrifice was widely reported among the tribes of the region during the 19th century. Though it is now rare and is considered to be murder by the government, human sacrifice may occasionally take place. Killings are occasionally reported to the police that have all the telltale signs of ritual sacrifice.

Oraon religion has clearly been influenced by Hinduism. The purely Hindu name Bhagwan is sometimes used to refer to Dharmes, perhaps because he shares many attributes of the Hindu supreme deity. Mahadeo (literally, "Great God"), which is a name Hindus use for Shiva, has become an Oraon village deity. The village goddess Devi Mai ("Goddess Mother") is the Hindu mother-goddess who has been absorbed into the Oraon pantheon, complete with her Hindu name. Although the Oraons build no temples for their own gods, they erect a thatch structure over Devi Mai's shrine as they have seen done by their Hindu neighbors. In the Oraon myth of origin, the wife of the supreme deity is sometimes called Parvati (consort of the Hindu god Shiva) or Sita (consort of Rama, an incarnation of Vishnu). In addition, many Hindu religious festivals have been introduced into the Oraon festival calendar.

There are a number of Hinduized cults, known as *bhagats*, found within traditional Oraon society. The earliest of these date back to perhaps the 18th century AD. Their members have abandoned rituals, such as sacrifice to the spirits or village deities, and have taken up vegetarianism, abstinence from alcohol, and other Hindu customs. Some use the services of Brahmans for social and ceremonial purposes. They usually will not marry with non-Hindu Oraons. The Kabirpanthi sect (followers of the 15th-century Hindu reformer Kabir) and the Tana Bhagat are two of the more important of these Hindu groups among the Oraons. Census returns show that nearly 60% of Oraons are now Hindu.

Christianity, too, has its followers among the Oraons. Christian missionary activity was discouraged by the East India Company, which administered British possessions in India until 1858. Missionary groups were admitted in the early 19th century, but they met with little success in established Hindu or Muslim society. It was among the tribal peoples of the subcontinent that their work flourished. The first converts among the Oraons were made in 1850. Census returns in Jharkhand

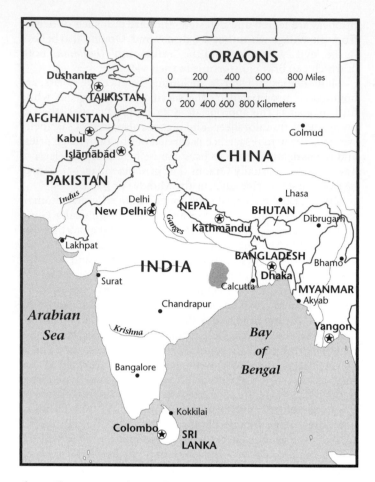

ORAONS

| 0 | 200 | 400 | 600 | 800 Miles |

| 0 | 200 | 400 | 600 | 800 Kilometers |

No one is concerned about the ownership, nor can one complain about his pet being killed or carried away. Armed women hunters move from village to village in search of prey.

The former importance of hunting in Oraon life is seen in the Oraon hunting festivals. These are religious ceremonies, dedicated to Chandi, the goddess of the hunt, that are accompanied by hunting expeditions and are held several times a year. They are performed to secure an abundant harvest through the magical influence of a successful hunt.

Other festivals observed by the Oraons have been adopted from the Hindus, although Oraon elements have been added to them. The celebration that marks the end of the old year and the beginning of the new, called Phagu by the Oraons, is really a Hindu festival. But it has been combined with the important ceremonial spring hunt. The Sohorai festival is a cattle festival that has been adopted from the Ahirs, a local Hindu pastoral caste. Similarly, the Karam and Jitia festivals are agricultural festivals borrowed by the Oraons from their Hindu neighbors.

7 RITES OF PASSAGE

Oraon society believes that gods and spirits influence every aspect of an individual's life. It is necessary, therefore, to maintain good relationships with them, especially at the time of major life events, such as birth, marriage, and death. This may be ensured by performing the appropriate rites and ceremonies.

A pregnant woman must restrict her activities to avoid the attention of evil spirits or the evil eye. During a first pregnancy, a sacrifice is performed to sever a woman's ties with the ancestor spirits and village deities of her father. The birth itself is followed by the sacrifice of a chicken. The days following the birth are a period of impurity when special care has to be taken to guard the mother and child from evil spirits. After four or five days, the mother and her newborn child, and the entire house, are ritually purified. The name-giving ceremony is held anywhere from a few weeks to a year after birth. Until this takes place, the baby is called after the day of the week on which it was born, or after a festival if born on a festival day. On the day of the name-giving ceremony, the child's head is shaved except for a small tuft of hair. The name is chosen by divination. A man recites the names of the child's ancestors while another man drops three grains of rice into a leaf-cup of water. When the rice grains touch in a certain manner, the child receives the name of the ancestor being spoken at the time.

When young people reach puberty and before they are married, they leave their family homes to sleep in the village dormitory (dhumkuria). The period of residence in this institution involves instruction by elders in folklore, traditions, tribal beliefs and practices, sexual matters, and communal activities. The initiation ceremony when a youth enters the boys' dormitory includes scarring on the arm. The dormitory itself may contain certain emblems and objects of ritual significance. One of the wooden posts supporting the roof of the dormitory may have a cleft, representing the female sexual organ, carved in it. Another ritual emblem found in the Oraon dormitories is the bull-roarer. This is a slat of wood or bamboo up to 23 cm by 7.5 cm (9 in by 3 in) in size, with a hole at one end so a string can be tied to it. When swung around the head, the bull-roarer produces a humming or roaring sound. Although the Oraon no longer remember the ritual or magical uses of the bull-roarer, it is possible it was used to scare away spirits.

show Christians make up about a quarter of the Oraon population, while the figure for the total Oraon population amounts to 23.66% Christian and 62.32% Hindu, with 13.93% following the ethnic (i.e. original) religion. Conversions of Oraons to Christianity have continued, even though states such as Andhra Pradesh, Chhattisgarh, and Madhya Pradesh have laws on the books against proselytizing.

6 MAJOR HOLIDAYS

The most important festival of the Oraons is the Sarhul festival, the Feast of the Sal Blossoms (the *sal* is a tree widely used in India for its timber). It is held in the spring when the sal trees are flowering and is, in reality, a spring agricultural festival celebrating a renewal of vegetation growth. Among the rituals associated with the Sarhul are the invocation of the ancestor spirits and a ceremonial procession to the village's sacred grove, where animals are sacrificed to Gaon Deoti and other gods and spirits. After feasting on the flesh of the sacrificed animals, the entire village gathers to sing and dance through the night. Rice-beer is drunk and loose sexual behavior, which is believed to stimulate the fertility of the earth, is permitted.

A unique tribal festival celebrated by Oraon women once every twelve years is the *Mukka Sendra* (also known as *Janni Shikar*). Supposedly celebrated in memory of the role of women in the defense of Rohtasgarh against the Afghans, women of the tribe dress up as males, wear turbans, and equip themselves with arrows, sticks, spears, axes, or any convenient tool that may prove handy during a daylong hunt when they are entitled to kill any animal, anywhere, and carry it back home.

Girls have their own dormitories and follow their own initiation rites.

The Oraons cremate their dead, except for young children and pregnant women who are buried. If a death has occurred before the onset of the monsoon rains, cremation takes place immediately. However, if the death takes place during the monsoon months, the corpse is buried in a temporary grave. The body is then dug up after the harvest and cremated in the usual manner. After the cremation, the remnants of bone left in the ashes of the funeral pyre are gathered by women relatives and placed in an earthenware jar. The jars are kept until the Harbora ceremony is held. At this time, they are taken in procession by female relatives of the deceased to a specially designated spot near water. The bones are then "drowned" by being thrown into the river, stream, or pond. After the men and women take ritual purifying baths, they return to the village where the young men and women assemble for a dance-meeting. A few days later, the village priest goes about the village pacifying the ancestor spirits and purifying the village itself. This ritual is accompanied by the sacrifice of a pig or white chicken. Important or elderly Oraons may have memorial stones erected in their honor.

[8]INTERPERSONAL RELATIONS

On meeting relatives and friends, Oraon men raise the right hand slowly to the forehead, saying *Gor-lagi Aba* (father), *Gor-lagi Dai* (sister), or whatever the appropriate relationship is. Like many groups in India, the Oraons have an elaborate terminology for kin relations. "Gor-lagi" can be roughly translated to "Greetings." Women perform Gor-lagi by cupping both hands and raising them towards the forehead, accompanied by the appropriate greeting.

[9]LIVING CONDITIONS

Oraon tribal society is divided into a number of territories (*parha*) containing anywhere from 7 to 20 villages. The territory more or less coincides with clan groupings, although members of several clans may reside in a territory. Each village, however, has its dominant clan. One of the village headmen is chosen to act as chief (*parha raja*) of the confederacy. He and all the other village headmen form a council to deal with inter-village matters. Each village has its own leader and village council to handle its own affairs. The village may also contain members of other castes (e.g., herders, potters, and metalworkers) who provide the Oraons with services essential to the agricultural economy.

A typical Oraon house has mud walls and a tiled roof. Its orientation is east–west, and a veranda runs around the house on the east, south, and west. There are no windows and only one door. Generally, there are two rooms, one used for storage and the other for sleeping. The family sleeps on mats, which are laid out at night and picked up in the morning. One corner of the house is used as a kitchen. Poultry may roost in the house at night, although separate structures are erected close by for pigs, sheep, goats, and cattle. There is no running water, and villagers draw water from streams and ditches for drinking and for bathing.

[10]FAMILY LIFE

The Oraons practice village and clan exogamy. The family is a patrilineal extended family, but nuclear families are found as well. A typical family contains five to seven members. In the past, young Oraons would select their own marriage partners, but it is more common for marriages to be arranged. This is, in part, a result of exposure to Hindu practices. The best age for marriage is considered to be between 16 and 20 years for males and 13 and 16 years for girls, which violates national laws against child marriage.

Once a suitable match is found, elaborate marriage negotiations are undertaken between the two families. Omens are watched, and the marriage is often called off if they are seen to be bad. A token bride-price, often a small amount of cash and some clothes, is paid. Among the many ceremonies associated with marriage, the central ritual is the anointing with vermilion (a red pigment). The bride and groom stand on a yoke (the crosspiece used to harness cattle to ploughs) and a curry-stone (a stone used to grind condiments). The groom applies vermilion to the bride's forehead and to the parting of her hair. The bride, in turn, applies vermilion to the groom's forehead. Marriage is considered a lifelong undertaking by Oraons, and divorce is rare.

As a tribal group, the Oraons do not possess the caste structure so typical of Hindu society. There is, however, a division into two occupational groups: the Kisans (cultivators) and Kudas (unskilled laborers). These groups tend to marry among themselves.

[11]CLOTHING

Traditional dress for Oraon men is a loincloth—a long piece of cotton fabric with red borders at each end, which is wrapped around the waist. A hair band of brass or silver is worn around the head. Rings are placed in the ears, necklaces (often made of silver coins) are strung around the neck, and a silver bangle is worn on the forearm of the right hand. A shawl is sometimes wrapped around the shoulders.

For the all-important dance festivals, men wear turbans. A feather or a strip of brass or silver is inserted into the turban. A peacock feather or a yak's tail is tucked into the waistband, and bells are tied around the waist or ankles.

Traditional Oraon dress is being replaced by local Hindu items, such as the *dhoti,* and Western-style shirts and pants.

Women's dress consists of a white cotton *sari,* with five red lines decorating one end. They wear earrings, necklaces, bangles on the arms and ankles, and toe rings. These ornaments are commonly made of brass, copper, silver, or gold. Tattoo marks are worn on the forehead and temples. Oraon women have no special dress for festivals.

[12]FOOD

The Oraons are nonvegetarian and eat the flesh of pigs, goats, chickens, and buffalo. Much of this meat is consumed at feasts following the sacrifice of animals at religious ceremonies. The staple cereal is rice, supplemented by wheat and maize. Vegetables, pulses, and spices are cultivated. Mustard oil is used for cooking. Both men and women consume alcohol. Rice-beer is brewed at home and drunk at many festivals. Men chew tobacco, while women smoke the *hukka* or bubble-pipe.

[13]EDUCATION

Literacy levels among the Oraon are higher than those of other Scheduled Tribes. This is particularly true among Oraons who are Christians, whose better education give them access to better jobs. The Anglican, Lutheran, and Roman Catholic missionary movements in the region have placed great emphasis on the social welfare of their converts. In addition to spreading Christianity, they have opened hospitals and dispensaries and run high-quality schools throughout the tribal area. Ranchi, the largest city of Chota Nagpur, is an important regional educational center. Formal education is also spreading rapidly among non-Christian groups. Literacy rates amongst the Oraon in Orissa exceed 54.2% (2001), although they are less than half this among females. This figure hides considerable regional differences between the north and the south of the state and between genders. Literacy figures from Oraon villages in Bangladesh show a female literacy rate at just over 20%.

One problem faced by the Oraon is that literacy is often in a language other than the Kurukh mother tongue. Many Oraon professionals who have good positions are concerned that the Oraons are losing their mother tongue and have asked parents to teach their children Kurukh, even though it does little to prepare them for competitive employment in the "real world."

14 CULTURAL HERITAGE

Like most tribal groups in South Asia, the Oraons have no written literature. Singing and dancing play an important role in their ritual life and accompany almost every social and religious occasion. Musical instruments, such as the pipe or drum, are thought to possess special powers. When they are first acquired, they are "married" by anointing them with vermilion.

Of special interest is the *jatra,* or dance-meeting, of the Oraon. Every Oraon village has its dancing ground *(akhra)* where the dance-meetings are held. They often occur as part of the rituals associated with village festivals, such as Harbora, and thus have socioreligious significance. Sometimes, several villages will participate in a jatra. Each village has its jatra flags, which are taken to the jatra gathering place. Carved images of animals such as the tiger, horse, or tortoise are carried to the dance ground on the shoulders of young men. Both flags and animals are totems before which sacrifices are made and libations of beer and milk are offered.

Oraons believe in witchcraft and sorcery and the power of the evil eye. Even though Jharkhand laws forbids the accusing of people as witches, women who are accused of being witches are often subjected to violence, torture, and even death by the local populace.

15 WORK

In the past the Oraons were hunters and gatherers, living off game and edible plants found in the forests. However, hunting and fishing have become mostly ceremonial, and the forests play a minor role in the economic life of the people. Most Oraons (around 67%) are farmers and cultivate their own land, or they work as sharecroppers or agricultural laborers. A few have found their way into government service, or work in the manufacturing and service industries.

16 SPORTS

There are no organized or spectator sports in traditional Oraon society.

17 ENTERTAINMENT AND RECREATION

Entertainment and recreation among the Oraons is traditionally associated with the socioreligious festivals of Oraon tribal life. For urban Oraons who are Christians, the typical varieties of church-related social and educational activities are available.

18 FOLK ART, CRAFTS, AND HOBBIES

The Oraons are not particularly well known for any folk arts. Some groups had a tradition of spinning thread from cotton, while modern craft activities include mat-weaving, rope-making, and carpentry.

19 SOCIAL PROBLEMS

The Oraons have been designated as a Scheduled Tribe, and the problems they face reflect, to a greater or lesser extent, those of tribal peoples throughout India. They occupy less productive lands, are often heavily in debt, and suffer from high levels of poverty. Many lose their land altogether and have to turn to manual labor. Tribal families that move to urban areas to seek work face disruptions and the loss of their traditional village support systems. Discrimination and exploitation are common.

One segment of the Oraon population that has improved its social conditions, however, is the Christian community. Christian Oraons tend to have higher levels of education, possess a greater degree of literacy, have access to better medical facilities, and be more open to modern ideas of health and public hygiene.

Considerable friction exists between the Christian and non-Christian Oraons, largely reflecting the better education and socioeconomic position of the Christians. As recently as 2004, the press reported that Hindus in a village in Ranchi District in Jharkhand State beat and drove out some Christian families, while reportedly police did nothing regarding complaints filed on their behalf. In Jharkhand and Andhra Pradesh, some politicians do not want Christians to receive the benefits of being classed as a "Scheduled Tribe." Similarly members of the Hindu nationalist Bharatiya Janata Party (BJP) believe that Christian converts should not be included in the tribal category and are not entitled to the benefits that belong to that group.

Development in Oraon lands is another cause for social dissent. States like Jharkhand are rich in mineral resources, but development of these resources usually involves disruption of Oraons from their lands and, in addition, projects are designed to generate profits for large companies or to serve the needs of state governments. However, organizations, such as the Jharkhand-Chhattisgarh Tribal Development Programme, focus on tribal people in Jharkhand and Chhattisgarh, targeting marginal households, women, landless people, hill cultivators and tribal people. Their goal is to empower tribal people to participate in their own development through local self-government. Specific activities promote increased production and productivity of land and water resources, alternative sources of income and sustainable management of natural resources.

Perhaps one of the major problems faced by the Oraons and other tribal peoples in Chota Nagpur is political rather than social—a lack of political unity. Oraons have participated in the various tribal movements that have emerged in the region since the beginning of the 20th century. They have supported political parties such as the Jharkhand Party and the

Jharkhand Mukti Morcha, which claim to represent the local tribes. There remains, however, a lack of political leadership among the Oraons (ascribed by some to the egalitarian nature of Oraon society). The local political parties, which have their roots in attempts to end tribal exploitation, have become radicalized. Even the creation of states such as Chhattisgarh and Jharkhand has not helped matters much. Some have argued it is too late to rescue the tribal communities of Jharkhand and their culture, ethnography, lifestyles, and livelihood from slow extinction The area of Jharkhand, specifically, and eastern India as a whole is of increasing significance for the Maoists (Naxalite) rebels due to its rich forest and mineral resources, and is an area that is seeing increasing Naxalite violence.

[20] GENDER ISSUES

As is common among the tribal peoples of South Asia, Oraon women generally are treated with a degree of equality that is rare in Hindu society. Except where they have been Hinduized, they usually have a say in their marriage, lack the preference for male offspring so typical of Hindu society, and do not have a dowry system, a small bride price being paid by the groom's family. Widow re-marriage is allowed and so is divorce, though the latter is rare. (Cases of adultery are uncommon, and the offenders are usually beaten and fined according to their means.) Traditionally, women in Chhattisgarh enjoy a higher status than seen in other states. This is largely due to their tribal culture and greater financial independence through participation in the labor market. Men and women share housework, including cooking, house cleaning, and childcare. However, women disadvantaged by heavy workloads and lack of time, have literacy rates far below those of men and are often excluded from community organizations.

Arranged marriages are the norm among the Oraon, though generally marriage requires the consent of the involved people. However, it is customary among the Oraons for only the family of the male to initiate negotiations, and often women's parents force their daughter into a marriage fearful there will no other opportunity to marry her off. Age is significant because most Oraons look for a young bride. If a woman is not married by a certain age, the parents are blamed for failing in their duty of arranging a suitable match for their daughter. One consequence of this is the number of unmarried Oran women found in the Chota Nagpur area.

Women are seen as economic assets. In addition to running the household, they help the men in agricultural tasks, though among the Oraon there is a tradition that if a women ploughs a field, dire consequences will follow. Oraon women sometimes work as agricultural laborers and are commonly found in the tea plantations of Assam, West Bengal and Tripura.

Oraon society is patriarchal in nature, and it is customary that women are not allowed to inherit land or property. However, this situation is changing. The UN ratified the Vienna Convention on Elimination of all forms of Discrimination Against Women (CEDAW) in 1979 and the Government of India ratified and acceded to CEDAW in 1993. The convention reiterates that discrimination against women violates the right to equality and acts as an obstacle to the participation of women on equal terms with men in political, social, economic, and cultural life. Discrimination has been defined as any distinction, exclusion, or restriction made on the basis of sex that impairs or nullifies the exercise by women (irrespective of their marital status) of the same rights as men. India's Protection of Human Rights Act, 1993, defines human rights as "the right to life, liberty, equality and dignity of the individual guaranteed by the Constitution [of India] or embodied in the International Covenants and enforceable by courts in India." The principles embodied in CEDAW and the concomitant right to development thus become enforceable as part of Indian law. The Government of India is obligated to take appropriate measures including legislation and modification of the law to abolish gender-based discrimination in existing laws, customs and practices, but the actual enforcing of such protections is a different matter. For instance, state laws throughout the country prohibit the sale of land in tribal areas to non-tribals, but land alienation (i.e. sale to non-tribals) remains a problem.

Illiteracy and poverty, with their resulting limitations on access to education, good employment, and health care facilities are major problems facing Oraon women in their drive for upward mobility.

[21] BIBLIOGRAPHY

Ayub, Mallick. *Development Programmes and Tribal Scenario: A Study of Santal, Kora, and Oraon*. Kolkata: Firma KLM, 2004.

Campion, Edmund. *My Oraon Culture*. Ranchi, Catholic Press, 1980.

Dhan, Rekha O. *These Are My Tribesmen—The Oraons*. Ranchi, Bihar Tribal Research Institute, Government of Bihar, 1967.

Ghosh, Abhik. *The World of the Oraon: Their Symbols in Time and Space*. New Delhi: Manohar, 2006.

Lakra, Christopher. *The New Home of Tribals*. Faridabad: Om Publications, 1999.

Oraon, Karma. *The Spectrum of Tribal Religion in Bihar: A Study of Continuity and Change among the Oraon of Chotanagpur*. Varanasi, Kishor Vidya Niketan, 1988.

Roy, S. C. *The Oraons of Chota Nagpur: Their History, Economic Life, and Social Organisation*. Ranchi: S.C. Roy, 1915.

———. *Oraon Religion and Customs*. Ranchi, Industry Press, 1928.

—by D. O. Lodrick

ORIYA

PRONUNCIATION: aw-REE-(y)uh
LOCATION: India (Orissa state)
POPULATION: 31 million
LANGUAGE: Oriya
RELIGION: Hinduism
RELATED ARTICLES: Vol. 3: Hindus; People of India

¹INTRODUCTION

The Oriya are the dominant ethnic group in India's eastern state of Orissa. They speak the Oriya language and share historical and cultural traditions that date to the 6th century BC, if not earlier. The Oriya are identified with the Odra (or Udra), a people mentioned in ancient Sanskrit texts and the *Mahabharata* epic. The lands to the north of the Mahanadi River, which flows into the Bay of Bengal, were known as Odradesha, or the "country of the Odra."

The hilly nature of Orissa allowed the existence of numerous small kingdoms in the region. From the 4th century BC on, however, important regional states, such as Kalinga, extended their control over much of the area. During the 4th and 5th centuries AD, a foreign people (possibly Greeks) rose to power in the region, to be followed by a series of local dynasties. The end of the 11th century saw the rise of the Eastern Gangas, whose rule ushered in a golden era in Orissa's history. This dynasty was able to resist the spread of Muslim power into eastern India. The region remained a stronghold of Hinduism until it was conquered by the Muslim rulers of Bengal in 1568. Orissa subsequently became part of the Mughal Empire, but with the decline of Mughal power, its western areas fell to the Marathas. The British acquired the coastal regions in 1757 and the Maratha-held lands in 1803. Under the British, the region consisted of both directly administered territory and independent princely states that accepted British political rule. Orissa assumed its present form in 1947 when India gained its independence from Britain.

²LOCATION AND HOMELAND

The Oriya make up some 75% of Orissa's population, the remaining people belonging to the numerous tribes that live in the state. The 2001 census reported Orissa's population as 36.7 million. Based on projected growth rates and including the small numbers of Oriya who live in adjacent areas of neighboring states, the current number of Oriya is estimated at 31 million people.

The traditional home of the Oriya and the historical core of Orissa State is the alluvial delta of the Mahanadi River and the adjacent coastal lowlands that run along the shores of the Bay of Bengal. Inland from the coastal plains lie the Garjat Hills and the Eastern Ghats, the hills that form the edge of India's Deccan Plateau. Elevations in these hills vary from around 900 m (3,000 ft) in the north to almost 1,525 m (5,000 ft) in the south. To the west of this line of hills are the interior plateaus of western Orissa. The hills and plateaus of Orissa are among the most heavily forested regions left in India. The Mahanadi River flows in a southeasterly direction across the middle of the state. The open basin of the middle Mahanadi Valley forms the only area of extensive lowland in the interior. Climate is monsoonal, with rainfall averaging around 150 cm (60 in) over the region. The rainy season (July–October) is followed by cool winters, with mean temperatures around 20°C (68°F). In mid-February, the thermometer begins to climb as the hot, humid summer weather approaches. In June, average temperatures approach 30°C (85°F).

The location of Orissa on the Bay of Bengal makes it vulnerable to the deadly cyclones that periodically sweep up from the south from May to November. In October 1999, for instance, what came to be known as the Orissa Cyclone hit Orissa with winds peaking at 250 kmh (155mph), causing the deaths of over 10,000 people and affecting another 12 million. Thousands of cattle were killed and over a million animals were lost. Damage in the path of the cyclone amounted to about $2.5 million, and 7 million people were left homeless. Relief agencies immediately sent assistance, and operations extended well into 2000. Unfortunately, many people died of starvation and diseases after the storm because rescue workers could not reach everyone in time.

³LANGUAGE

Oriya is an Indo-Aryan language closely related to Bengali, Assamese, and other languages of eastern India. It shows less Muslim or British influence than do other Indo-Aryan languages because the region where it is spoken was one of the last to be conquered by these foreign powers. The language is one of the 23 languages spoken in India that are recognized as official languages and appears in the list of these languages printed on Indian rupee notes. Although written Oriya does not vary, the spoken form differs over the region. Standard Oriya is spoken in the Cuttack and Puri districts of Orissa.

There is a long literary tradition in Oriya, which is written in its own script. It dates back to the 14th century AD, and the early works consist of accounts of the Natha-cult, which replaced the Siddha-cult around this time. The literary tradition in Oriya is almost continuous from this time, consisting largely of songs and poetry, most of which is religious in nature. A major change in Oriya literature occurred towards the end of the 19th century, coinciding with the advent of the British administration and Western education. During the early 20th century, freedom fighters, such as Gopabandhu Das, came to the fore. In the immediate post-Independence era, writers, such as Chandrasekhar Rath, Shantanu Acharya, Mohapatra Nilamani Sahoo, and Gopinath Mohanty, became known for their fiction and short stories. In the 1970s, a reaction to the earlier fiction writers saw the emergence of literary figures, such as Jagadish Mohanty, but the latter part of the 20th century saw the appearance of feminist writers (e. g. Sarojini Sahoo) and new authors of Oriya fiction and drama.

⁴FOLKLORE

Puri, a town located on the coast at the southern end of the Mahanadi Delta, is the site of a shrine dedicated to Krishna in his form of Jagannath (*jagan-natha,* "lord of the universe"). According to Puranic legend, the god Krishna was mistaken for a deer in the forest and killed by a hunter. His body was left to rot under a tree. It was found by a pious person, who cremated it and placed the ashes in a box. The local king was directed by Vishnu to make an image from these sacred relics. The king approached the divine artisan Vishvakarman, who agreed to do the work, provided he was left undisturbed until its completion. The king became impatient after 15 days of waiting and went to see how the work was progressing. The divine artisan became enraged and left the image incomplete, a mere stump without arms or legs. The god Brahma gave the image its eyes and a soul and acted as chief priest at its consecration. The king sacrificed 100 horses in honor of the occasion. The image at the temple in Puri, the most important Jagannath shrine in the country, perpetuates this tradition by representing the deity as a crudely carved block of wood.

⁵RELIGION

The Oriya are overwhelmingly Hindu. They have the caste structure typical of Hindu society, with Brahmans performing their traditional role in ritual and religion. They accept the authority of the Vedas and the other sacred Sanskrit texts of Hinduism. The Oriya worship Shiva, the Mother Goddess, the Sun God, and many other Hindu deities. The most important sect, however, is the Vaishnava sect that reveres Krishna in his form as Jagannath.

In addition to the classical forms of Hinduism practiced by the Oriya, there is a level of popular belief embracing local deities and spirits that influence everyday life and activities. These spirits have to be appeased or otherwise dealt with through the services of shamans (kulisi), who identify and mediate with disease-causing spirits. Magicians (guni) are skilled in witchcraft and sorcery.

⁶MAJOR HOLIDAYS

As Hindus, the Oriya observe the usual pan-Indian festivals celebrated by their co-religionists across the country, as well as some that are regional in character. However, there is one festival celebrated in Orissa that is of national importance and attracts pilgrims from all over the country. This is the Chariot Procession (Ratha Yatra) of Jagannath held at Puri in Orissa every year in June or July. The images of Jagannath and two lesser deities are taken from the Jagannath temple to a country house some 3 km (2 mi) away. The images are placed in cars or chariots and pulled by pilgrims. Jagannath's car is roughly 14 m (45 ft) high, with wheels over 2 m (7 ft) in diameter. The other images travel in smaller chariots. The English word "juggernaut" comes from "Jagannath" and refers to the god's massive chariot that crushes all before it.

⁷RITES OF PASSAGE

Certain superstitions are observed by pregnant women in rural areas. For example, they are not allowed to go out in the dark in case they become frightened and have a miscarriage. Most babies are born at home. Village women give birth squatting, with a piece of cloth tied tightly around the abdomen, and gripping a wooden pole during the labor pains. Male babies are greeted with special joy. The entire family is ritually unclean until the seventh day, when rites of purification are observed. The name-giving ceremony is held on the twenty-first day. Villagers are invited to a feast, where the family Brahman performs the necessary pujas. Children are the center of family life. They are spoiled and fussed over, until such time as they begin to share in the family household tasks. Girls are usually segregated for a period of seven days at the time of their first menstruation. In some communities, they rub turmeric paste on their bodies and bathe, before resuming their domestic and social activities.

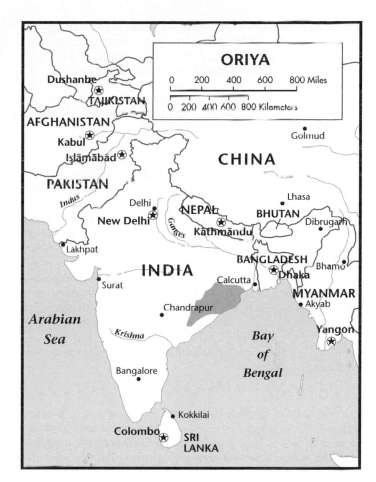

The dead are cremated, although children and unmarried persons are usually buried. The corpse is anointed with turmeric, washed, and wrapped in a shroud. It is carried to the cremation ground by relatives and placed on the funeral pyre with the head toward the north. Some groups place women facing up and men facing down. Funeral rituals follow Hindu customs, with ceremonies being performed on the seventh, ninth, and eleventh days after death. A Brahman priest is engaged to perform these rites. Near blood-relatives shave their heads and don new clothes, and on the eleventh day a feast is held for caste members and Brahmans.

⁸INTERPERSONAL RELATIONS

As is common in India, when people meet a stranger, the first question they always ask is, "What caste do you belong to?" This is the usual practice, and no one feels embarrassed or offended at the question. Caste plays an important role in interpersonal relations, particularly in rural areas, and determines the nature of social contacts between people.

⁹LIVING CONDITIONS

The Oriya are a rural people, with only 14.97% living in areas classified as urban (2001 Census of India). Villages are typically linear in form, with houses built along either side of a single street. There is often a tributary hamlet near the village, where members of the Untouchable or service castes live. The Oriya house is rectangular in shape and has mud walls and a gabled roof thatched with straw. Affluent families may have a double roof (providing insulation and some protection against fire), a small guest house, and a fence enclosing the compound. Rooms serve as cattle shed, grain store, bedroom, and kitchen. In traditional houses, the northeast corner of the kitchen is reserved for family worship. Furnishings include wooden beds, tables, and chairs. Living rooms may be decorated with pictures of gods and goddesses, important political leaders, and even film stars.

10 FAMILY LIFE

The Oriya follow the normal North Indian traditions of marrying within one's caste or subcaste and outside one's clan. The preference is to marry outside the village or immediate area. An Oriya proverb states: "Marital relatives from distant places are beautiful, as distant hills are enchanting." Marriages are arranged, and although child marriage was common in the past, the age of marriage is increasing. The marriage ceremony and rituals follow the Hindu form. The daughter-in-law takes up residence with her husband's family, where she assumes various responsibilities in the household. Her status, of course, is considerably enhanced when she gives birth to a son. Divorce is uncommon, although legal under Indian law. In urban areas, there is a trend away from the extended family toward the nuclear family structure.

11 CLOTHING

The usual dress for men is the *dhoti* (loincloth) and *chaddar,* a shawl that is draped over the shoulder. Sometimes a *kurta,* or shirt, is worn as an upper garment. Younger men, especially in the towns, favor Western-style clothes. Women wear the *sari* and *choli* (bodice). Orissa is known for its tie-dyed saris, and these are gaining in popularity across the country. Despite Orissa being known for its silver filigree ornaments, these are not popular among village women but tend to be favored, rather, by urban middle-class women. Village women display the usual array of ornaments and jewelry. Women of lower castes sometimes sport tattoos as decoration.

12 FOOD

Rice is eaten by Oriya at every meal. At breakfast, cold rice, puffed rice *(mudhi),* or various types of rice cake *(pitha)* are taken with molasses or salt, and the meal is completed with tea. Thin rice pancakes are a specialty of Orissa and are frequently served to guests. A typical meal in an Oriya household consists of rice, *dāl* (lentils), and vegetable curry using eggplant, spinach, and seasonal vegetables, such as cauliflower, cabbages, or peas. For those who can afford it and who are not vegetarian, fish or goat meat may be served. Food is cooked in mustard oil, except for offerings to the gods, which are prepared in clarified butter *(ghi).* A particular favorite in villages is a rice dish called *pakhala bata.* Rice is boiled in bulk, and whatever is not consumed is stored in cold water. The rice ferments a little and is later served cold with fresh green chilies. This dish is popular in summer, when it is eaten with curds and green mangoes. Bananas, coconuts, and limes are the main fruits of the region. People are fond of sweets, cookies, and drinks, such as sherbets. Alcohol is avoided by caste Hindus, although the Untouchables drink toddy made from fermented dates. Hashish is made into a drink *(bhang)* and taken socially and at festivals.

Food has an important role in Oriya ritual. At the feast for Shiva, for example, villagers prepare a huge, steamed rice cake

made in the shape of a *lingam* (Shiva's phallic symbol) and stuffed with cheese, molasses, and coconut. It is colored red with vermilion dye and is worshiped before being eaten. Similarly, there are over 50 types of rice cake prepared and offered to the deity at the Jagannath Temple at Puri.

13 EDUCATION

Education is seen by middle- and upper-class Oriya as a means to economic advancement. Education levels in Orissa State, however, are among the lowest in India. Literacy rates in 2001 were 63.08% for those seven years of age and older (about the average for India as a whole), but this figure masks considerable differences between rural-urban populations and also gender differences. Male literacy in Orissa is 75.96% where as only 50.51% of females are literate. As against State literacy rate averages, districts like Koraput had only 35.72% literate, Malkangiri 30.53%, and Nawarangpur 33.93%.

Education is free and supposedly compulsory up to age 14, but attendance at schools is very much a matter of family choice. Girls rarely proceed beyond primary school, especially among the tribal populations. As is to be expected, test results from private schools far exceed those of government schools, and nongovernmental organizations (NGOs) are getting involved in educational projects. For instance, Mahila Vikas, an organization with experience in tribal development and one that has successfully executed other social welfare projects in the Gajapati district of Orissa aimed at ameliorating the economic and social status of women, is undertaking a project titled "Promotion of Girl Child Education of Primitive Tribals." The Gajapati District is one of the most backward areas of Orissa and is occupied by Saura tribals. Because of limited school capacity and the inability of parents to send their girl children to government schools located some distance away, an estimated 2,000 girl children in the area are school dropouts. Mahila Vikas has established a learning center for these children and transitions them into a government school. There is a great degree of community support for the project and a strong desire to remedy the situation.

There are numerous government-run colleges and five universities in Orissa. One of these, the Shri Jagannath Sanskrit University at Puri, is devoted to Sanskrit learning and culture.

14 CULTURAL HERITAGE

Chronicles of the Jagannath Temple at Puri, written in Oriya, date from the 12th century AD. The most productive period in Oriya literature began in the 14th century. Important contributions to Oriya literature were made by medieval *bhakti* (devotional) poets. Modern writing in Oriya, however, suffers from comparison with Bengali achievements. Orissa is famous for its traditions of dance, music, and architecture. The classical dance of Orissa, known as *Odissi,* originated as a temple dance performed for the gods. The *Chhau* dance, performed by masked male dancers in honor of Shiva, is another feature of Oriya culture. Cuttack is a major center for dance and music. Painting of icons (*patta* paintings), palm leaf painting, and woodcarving are important artistic traditions in Orissa. Orissan temples, ornamented with carvings and sculptures, are built in a distinct style regarded by some as the climax of North Indian temple architecture. Several important temples are found at Bhubaneshwar, though the Sun Temple at Konarak is considered to be the masterpiece of medieval Orissan temple architecture.

¹⁵WORK

Most Oriya are involved in rice cultivation. Orissa State accounts for around 10% of India's total rice output. Agriculture in the region is still fairly traditional, depending on animal power for traction and requiring considerable inputs of labor. Cash crops include oilseeds, pulses, sugarcane, jute, and coconuts. Fishing is important in coastal areas. Many families are engaged in producing traditional handicrafts. Industrial development in the state has occurred only in the decades following independence (following 1947).

¹⁶SPORTS

Children amuse themselves with typical games, e.g., ball, tag, hide-and-seek, spinning tops, and kite flying. Traditional games for adults include cards, dice, and other games of chance. Body-building and wrestling are common sports for men and *kabaddi* (team wrestling) is very popular. Modern sports, such as cricket, soccer, and field hockey, are played in schools.

¹⁷ENTERTAINMENT AND RECREATION

Although modern forms of entertainment are found in towns, the Oriya are mostly rural and draw on the rich traditions of folk entertainment associated with Oriya culture. These include folk dances and songs, puppet plays, shadow plays (where the shadows of the characters are projected onto a screen using puppets), and folk opera (*jatra*), as well as the activities associated with fairs and religious festivals.

¹⁸FOLK ART, CRAFTS, AND HOBBIES

Orissa is well known for its handicrafts, particularly its little carved wooden replicas of Jagannath and the other gods at the temple in Puri. Painted masks and wooden animal toys for children are also very popular. Local sculptors make soapstone copies of temple sculptures for pilgrims and tourists. Textiles include appliqué work, embroidery, tie-dyed fabrics, and various types of hand-loom cloth. The artisans of Cuttack are skilled in filigree work and the making of gold and silver filigree jewelry. Brassware and items made from bell metal (an alloy of copper and tin) are also produced by local artisans.

¹⁹SOCIAL PROBLEMS

Some social problems that plague Orissa stem from the "super cyclone" that affected the region in 1999. Some of the survivors, especially from the Jagatpur District that was hard hit by the storm, suffered from post-traumatic distress syndrome, experiencing symptoms like restlessness and sleep disorders. The number of suicides and attempted suicides following the cyclone was quite high and, in a survey taken in the region after the storm, a staggering 11% of the respondents expressed a death wish.

Access to land is another problem in Orissa. While land reform legislation has reduced the share of agricultural land held under large holdings (more than 6 hectares) in Orissa since the 1950s, the proportion of households operating no land, whose livelihoods are based principally on agricultural labor, increased substantially following the widespread eviction of tenants from former landlord estates. Around a quarter of all households in Orissa still have no land. In spite of land reforms, formidable obstacles continue to prevent the rural poor from improving their access to land.

Orissa is one of a few states in India that has attempted legally to abolish tenancy (land-leasing), except in the case of persons of disability (the definition of which includes widows, divorcees, and other unmarried women). Land rights may pass to any cultivator who can demonstrate continuous occupation over a period of at least 12 years. However, tenancy remains widespread, and restrictions have led to concealed forms of tenancy (e.g. with oral contracts) that give tenants little or no protection in law. A ceiling on individual land holdings also applies and currently stands at 10 "standard acres" (depending on land quality). In addition to these provisions, which fall under land reforms legislation, three major acts govern land administration and respectively provide the basis for land survey and settlement, land consolidation/prevention of land fragmentation, and prevention of encroachment on government land.

Development also causes problems for rural people in Orissa. For instance, the giant Pohang Iron and Steel Company (POSCO) of South Korea's steel plant and port in Jagatsinghpur district of Orissa will displace 471 families in 11 hamlets. For the last several years, local communities have been fighting to retain the land they have been cultivating for generations but which, after Independence, has been deemed government forest land. It is doubtful that the recent Forest Rights Act will give them the ability to assert their rights over this land. The local people assert that their vibrant and self-sufficient local economy based on betel leaf, cashew, and paddy cultivation, pisciculture and fishing will be destroyed, rendering them homeless and jobless if the steel plant and port come up. The government and the company in question have been doggedly pursuing efforts to "clear the land of people," with the argument that the plant, port, and mines together will generate 45,000 jobs and unprecedented revenue for the state. The pressure on local communities is based on the contention that much of the occupation and cultivation in the area is illegal because it is on government land under the jurisdiction of the forest department.

The Scheduled Tribes and Other Traditional Forest Dwellers (Recognition of Forest Rights) Act of 2006 is a key piece of forest legislation passed in India on 18 December 2006. It has also been called the "Forest Rights Act," the "Tribal Rights Act," the "Tribal Bill," and the "Tribal Land Act." The law concerns the rights of forest dwelling communities to land and other resources denied to them over decades as a result of the continuance of colonial forest laws in India and affects the 25% of Orissa's population that are tribal, though some critics argue that the law does more to harm tribals than to defend their traditional rights.

Land alienation among the tribals of the state, i.e. the sale of tribal land to non-tribal peoples, continues to be a problem, despite the existence of legislation designed to prevent this.

Orissa is one of the poorest states of India, and many of the problems faced by its people reflect this. Illiteracy and poverty in rural areas are commonplace. Much of the region lacks a safe drinking-water supply, adequate schools, roads, and electricity. The use of child labor is common, and of concern to foreign organizations funding development projects in the region. Alcoholism in rural areas is such a problem that there is a groundswell, especially among low-caste women, for the imposition of prohibition. Modern social conditions, however, can be expected to improve as Orissa modernizes in the future. Today's social problems detract nothing from the important contributions the Oriya have made to Indian culture in the past.

20 GENDER ISSUES

As a predominantly Hindu, rural people, the Oriya experience many of the problems associated with Hindu society. Purdah, child marriage, dowry payment and casteism were traditionally the lot of rural Oriya women and little has changed since the past. Sons are still preferred as offspring and feticide is not uncommon, as seen in the disparity of local sex ratios. Low-caste women are subject to sexual violence and rape, and the sale of poor girl children, either into prostitution or as wives in richer parts of India, is not uncommon.

Oriya women may appear, as in other parts of South Asia, to enjoy certain land rights in law, but legal protections rarely translate into effective control over land in practice, owing to embedded, gender-biased social norms and customs. It has been suggested that women's access to and effective control over land may be enhanced through joint land titling. This measure is rather limited in scope, since ideally what need to be promoted are women's independent land rights. But while the principle of joint titling is readily accepted at the level of the government of India, it has yet to be realized in practice in Orissa.

The life of urban, middle- and upper-class Oriya is, naturally, quite different. However, Oriya women find poverty, illiteracy, lack of rights to inheritance, lack of access to education, poor health services and lack of economic resources as barriers to improving their status in society.

21 BIBLIOGRAPHY

Beruhia, Nrusinha Charan, ed. *Orissa State Gazetteer.* Vol. 1. Bhubaneshwar, India: Gazetteers Unit, Government of Orissa, 1990.

Das, Binod Sankar. *Life and Culture in Orissa.* Calcutta: Minerva Associates, 1984.

Jena, A. C. *Devolution of Functions and Finances on Panchayats in Orissa.* Hyderabad: National Institute of Rural Development, 2003.

Jena, B. B. *Orissa: People, Culture and Polity.* New Delhi: Kalyani Publishers, 1980.

Mohanti, Prafulla. *My Village, My Life: Portrait of an Indian Village.* New York: Praeger, 1973.

Mohanty, Jatindra Mohan. *History of Oriya Literature.* Bhubaneswar: Vidya, 2006.

Pandey, Balaji. *Trafficking in Women in Orissa: An Exploratory Study.* Bhubaneswar: Institute for Socio-Economic Development, 2003.

Pati, Rabindra Nath. *Tribal and Indigenous People of India: Problems and Prospects.* New Delhi: A.P.H. Pub. Corp., 2002.

—by D. O. Lodrick

PAKISTANIS

PRONUNCIATION: pak-is-TAN-eez
LOCATION: Pakistan
POPULATION: 169.3 million (mid-2007 est.)
LANGUAGE: Urdu (official national language); English; Punjabi (60%); Sindhi (13%); Pushto (8%); Baluchi (2%); more than 20 total
RELIGION: Islam (majority); Hinduism; Christianity; Buddhism; Baha'i; Parsi (Zoroastrian)
RELATED ARTICLES: Vol. 3: Brahui; Vol. 4: Pathans; Sindhis

1 INTRODUCTION

Pakistanis are citizens of the Islamic Republic of Pakistan *(Islam-i Jamhuriya-e Pakistan).* This political identity is relatively recent, because the state of Pakistan only came into existence in 1947. Prior to that time, the region formed part of the British Indian Empire. It has a complex history that extends back nearly 5,000 years to one of the world's first urban civilizations that grew up along the Indus River. Pakistan is settled by peoples of varied ethnic and cultural backgrounds who today find a common sense of unity in their commitment to the Islamic faith. In the Urdu language, the name "Pakistan" translates as "Land of the Pure."

Modern Pakistanis are heirs to a cultural tradition going back to the Harappan (or Indus Valley) civilization, which emerged on the plains of Indus River around 3000 BC. From about 1700 BC onwards, however, nomadic invaders from Central Asia settled on the plains of the Punjab, displacing the Harappans. These peoples introduced the Aryan languages into northern India and eventually developed Hindu civilization. Subsequent history is one of wave after wave of invaders sweeping through the passes of the northwest into the plains of the Punjab. This region saw a succession of peoples come and go, including the Persians, Greeks, Parthians, Kushans, and the White Huns. The Mauryas, Hindu (and later Buddhist) kings whose capital lay far to the east near the city of Patna in India, extended their empire (321–181 BC) to include virtually all of what is now Pakistan. By the end of the 9th century AD, most of the northern region was ruled by the Hindu Shahis.

Islam first reached Pakistan by sea from the south in AD 711, but the more significant introductions occurred in the north. At the beginning of the 11th century, Turkish rulers from Afghanistan (the Ghaznavids and later the Ghurids) mounted military campaigns over the mountain passes into the Indian subcontinent. In 1193 Afghan forces captured Delhi. For over 650 years from this time, a regional or imperial Muslim power based in Delhi ruled much of the area that makes up modern Pakistan. The Mughal emperor Akbar even made Lahore his capital for a short while towards the end of the 16th century.

The early 19th century saw the rise of a powerful Sikh state in the Punjab under Ranjit Singh. Sikhism is a religion combining elements of Islam and Hinduism that originated in the Punjab in the 15th century. However, conflict with the British resulted in wars that eventually led to the annexation of the Punjab by the British in 1849. The British had already conquered Sind in the south. Over the next 100 years, the British government in India gained control over virtually all the lands and peoples that were to make up Pakistan.

The modern state of Pakistan was created in 1947 when the British colonial possessions on the Indian subcontinent were divided between Pakistan and India. Muhammad Ali Jinnah, the founder and leader of the Muslim League, became Governor-General of Pakistan, and to all intents and purposes, the new country's political ruler. But Jinnah, who came to be known as *Quaid-e-Azam* ("Great Leader") and *Baba-e-Quam* ("Father of the Nation"), died in September 1948. Liaquat Ali Khan, also a leader of the Muslim League, became Pakistan's first prime minister in 1947, but he was assassinated, allegedly by an Afghan, in 1952. The first constitution of Pakistan was adopted in 1956 but was suspended in 1958 by General Ayub Khan, marking the first of several takeovers of the government by the military. Zulfikar Ali Bhutto, founder and leader of the Pakistan People's Party, became the president of Pakistan from 1971 to 1973 and was elected prime minister from 1973 to 1977. However, he was ousted by the military in 1977 and was later executed (1979), despite international protests, by General Zia-ul Huq. Muhammad Zia-ul-Haq, who suspended Pakistan's constitution and declared martial law in 1977, became the president and military ruler of Pakistan from July 1977 to his death in August 1988 in a mysterious plane crash. Benazir Bhutto, Zulfikar Ali Bhutto's daughter and leader of his Pakistan People's Party, was elected prime minister in 1988 and again in 1993, but on both occasions was removed from office for alleged corruption. The only other civilian leader of this time was Nawaz Sharif of the Muslim League, who served two non-consecutive terms as prime minister (1990–1993 and 1997–1999). In 2000, Sharif, also, was convicted of corruption and banned from participating in politics for life.

In 1999, General Pervez Musharraf, chief of staff of the Pakistani army, seized power as president of Pakistan and remains in that office, though his power was much curtailed following elections held in Pakistan in 2007. In an attempt to retain power, on 3 November 2007 Musharraf, who was supported both financially and materially by the United States and the West in the War on Terror, fired the chief justice of the Pakistan Supreme Court, the popular Iftikar Chaudhury—who was about to declare the 2007 reelection of Musharraf as president unconstitutional—suspended the constitution, and declared a state of emergency. Chaudhury was reinstated and Musharraf—who survived several assassination attempts—stepped down as army chief on 28 November 2007 (appointing General Ashfaq Pervez Kayani as a replacement), hoping his political party would win the general elections to be held in 2008.

Both Benazir Bhutto and Nawaz Sharif, who had fled Pakistan to exile in Saudi Arabia, returned to Pakistan to contest the elections to be held early in 2008, but Benazir Bhutto was assassinated—Al Qaeda claimed responsibility—on 27 December 2007, causing the elections to be postponed from January to February. In the 8 February 2008 general elections, the PPP (now led by the late Bhutto's husband, Asif Ali Zardari) gained the majority of the popular vote and along with the Muslim League-N [ML (N)], Nawaz Sharif's faction of the Muslim League, formed a coalition civilian government with Yousaf Raza Gilani as prime minister. In June 2008 a Pakistani High Court disqualified Sharif and his younger brother Shahbaz from contesting by-elections, but allowed the latter to continue to hold his office as chief minister of Punjab Province.

In April 2008, much against the wishes of the United States, the Pakistani government signed an agreement with the pro-

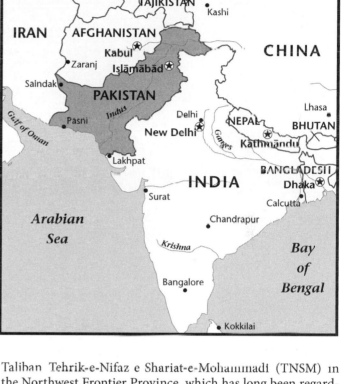

Taliban Tehrik-e-Nifaz e Shariat-e-Mohammadi (TNSM) in the Northwest Frontier Province, which has long been regarded as a Taliban safe haven and allows the imposition of Shariah law in Swat and Malakand districts. Similar agreements for South Waziristan and other areas of the border region were being negotiated as of mid-2008.

The Muslim League-N faction of the ruling coalition said in May 2008 that it would quit the government in a dispute over when and how to reinstate judges fired by Pervez Musharraf. The leader of the PPP, Zardari, expressed a willingness to work with Musharraf as president, though with considerably reduced powers, while Sharif wanted Musharraf's ouster. The announcement by former Prime Minister Nawaz Sharif raised the prospect of the splintering of the alliance that defeated the U.S.-backed Musharraf and his pro-Musharraf political party, the PML (Q) party (Pakistan Muslim League [Quaid]), though Sharif said his party would continue to support the government for the time being. If the PML (N) party were to quit the government, the only way the coalition could survive is with the support of opposition parties, such as the Muttahida Qaumi Movement (MQM) and PML(Q). As of July 2008 it remained to be seen how this political crisis in Pakistan would play out.

²LOCATION AND HOMELAND

Pakistan lies in the northwest of the Indian subcontinent. It has an area of 796,095 sq km (307,304 sq mi), excluding the territory of Jammu and Kashmir that it occupies. In size, Pakistan is slightly larger than Texas, or roughly half the area of

Pakistani women sit outside a relief camp as they wait for clothes and food. Pakistan was devastated by a major earthquake in late 2005. (AP Images/Anjum Naveed)

Alaska. Its southern border is formed by a 1,046-km (650-mi) stretch of coastline along the Arabian Sea. From there, the country extends northwards for 1,600 km (1,000 mi) to the mountains that lie along its northern border with China. To the west, Pakistan shares borders with Iran and Afghanistan. India lies to the east, and in the northeast is the disputed territory of Kashmir.

The political outlines of Pakistan are the result of two historical forces. The western boundaries coincide with those fixed between 1875 and 1900 as the British stabilized the western frontier of their Indian Empire. The eastern boundary, however, reflects events that occurred in the mid-20th century. Muslims in the Indian subcontinent were concerned that they would be a minority in a Hindu-dominated state when the region became independent, and they demanded their own country. Efforts at compromise failed. When the British left India, Muslim majority areas in the northwest and the northeast of the subcontinent were separated to form Pakistan.

This created several problems. Pakistan comprised two "Wings" separated by 1,600 km (1,000 mi) of Indian territory. East Pakistan, even though it had a Muslim majority, was culturally different from the western Wing. Eventually, civil war erupted and East Pakistan broke away (with Indian help) as the independent nation of Bangladesh in 1971. In the west, the new boundary between India and Pakistan divided the historical and cultural region of the Punjab in two. Partition in 1947 was accompanied by the mass migration of Sikhs and Hindus into

India, and Muslims into Pakistan, with an estimated 1 million lives lost in the process. Muslims from India who crossed into Pakistan at this time are known, along with their descendants, as *muhajirs*. They form a distinct element in Pakistan's population, and tensions between muhajirs and other ethnic groups have contributed to recent social instability in the country.

The Kashmir problem also has its origins at this time. Even at the height of the British Empire, there were several hundred princely states in the Indian subcontinent that were governed by their own rulers under overall British control. These states were required to "accede" to either Pakistan or India when the countries became independent. Naturally, Muslim states that were located in territory assigned to Pakistan merged with Pakistan, and Hindu states joined India. One of the largest and most important of the princely states was Jammu and Kashmir, located in the strategic northern mountains and having a common border with China. Kashmir had a Muslim majority population but a Hindu ruler, who was reluctant to accede to either Pakistan or India. After Muslim tribes from Pakistan entered Kashmir in October 1947, the Hindu Maharaja of Kashmir appealed to India for help. The Indian government sent military aid, which was in turn countered by Pakistan. A cease-fire was negotiated by the United Nations in 1949, but Kashmir remains divided with Pakistani and Indian troops facing each other across the cease-fire line.

Despite the unifying influence of the Islamic religion, the 169.3 million (2007 estimate) people of Pakistan encompass a range of distinct ethnic groups, each with its own language, customs, and cultural traditions. Baluchis are found in the southwest, and Sindhis in the south. The Punjabis of the northern plains of the Indus are the most numerous, and politically influential, group in the country. In the northwest, the old North West Frontier of British days, Pathans (also called Pushtuns or Pakhtuns) dominate. The largest among the numerous Pathan tribes are the Afridis, Waziris, and Yusufzais. Further north, in the mountains that stretch to the Chinese border, are a bewildering array of tribal groups that include the Khowar, Kohistani, and Shina. Tribal areas are administered federally rather than by provincial governments. Areas of Kashmir occupied by Pakistan include Baltis and Kashmiris. The ethnic mix of Pakistan is further modified by the muhajirs, who represent perhaps 10% of Pakistan's population. During the recent Soviet occupation of Afghanistan, there were an estimated 3 million Afghani refugees (mainly Pathans) in northwestern areas of Pakistan.

Pakistan falls into three broad geographical regions: the Indus plains, the northern mountains, and the hills and plateaus that extend from the Khyber Pass to Baluchistan. The Indus plains, and especially the northern region of the Punjab, form the heart of the country. Despite an arid climate (Karachi receives 20.4 cm or 8 inches of rain a year) and maximum temperatures that may hover above 40°c (104°F) for months at a time, the plains support the bulk of Pakistan's population. Agriculture, of course, is heavily dependent on irrigation and the waters of the Indus River system. The northern mountain zone has some of the most rugged and difficult terrain found anywhere in the world. Nearly all the region lies above 2,400 m (approximately 7,800 ft) and the Karakoram Mountains contain some of the highest peaks in the world. More than 50 peaks are above 6,500 m (21,000 ft) in elevation, and even the passes into China lie above 4,900 m (16,000 ft). The area is a difficult one to cross, especially in the winter months, and is sparsely populated with tribespeople who display a fierce sense of independence from the government in Islamabad. The northwestern hills and western plateaus, too, are barren, rugged regions sparsely populated by tribal groups.

³LANGUAGE

The linguistic patterns of Pakistan reflect the ethnic diversity of the Pakistanis, with over 20 languages spoken in the country. The majority of the languages belong to the Aryan branch of the Indo-European language family. Punjabi (including Siraiki, a Punjabi variant) is spoken by almost two-thirds (58%) of the population. Other languages include Sindhi (13%); Pushto, the language of the Pathans (8%); and Baluchi (4%). Kashmiri is the language of the disputed areas of the former Jammu and Kashmir State. In terms of numbers of speakers, the languages in the tribal areas in the north (e.g., Kafiri, Kohistani, Khowar, Wakhi, and Shina) are relatively minor, although they do have political significance. Balti, spoken in the extreme northeast, belongs to the Sino-Tibetan rather than the Indo-European language family. The origins of the Burushaski language that is spoken in the Hunza region is as yet unknown. Brahui, spoken by some 2.5 million people in Baluchistan Province, is of interest. Unlike most languages of Pakistan, it belongs to the Dravidian language family. It is linguistically related to the languages of southern India. Brahui may be the last survivor of

the languages spoken in the region before the Aryan invasions following 1700 BC.

With this diversity, and especially given the role of language in cultural identity, it is perhaps fortunate that Urdu has been adopted as Pakistan's national language. Urdu, written in the Perso-Arabic script, evolved during the 16th and 17th centuries from the mix of languages spoken by Muslim soldiers (Persian, Turk, Arab, and Afghan) and the local speech. It is thus not identified with any particular ethnic group and avoids the issue of the cultural supremacy of a specific segment of the population. On the other hand, this national language is the native tongue of only the muhajirs and is spoken by only about 10% of the population. It has been adopted by the intelligentsia and the educated, urban elite, but in terms of numbers of speakers, it can by no means be viewed as "national." Urdu and English—the latter a legacy of the colonial era—are official languages in which government and business affairs are conducted.

⁴FOLKLORE

Given that the "Pakistani" was created by a political decision only half a century ago, it is not surprising that the peoples of Pakistan tend to identify with their communities before their nation. One is a Punjabi, Baluchi, Sindhi, or Pathan before one is a Pakistani, and individuals follow the folk traditions and folk heroes of their own community. However, Muhammad Ali Jinnah (1875–1948) has achieved the status of a national hero among many Pakistanis. It was Jinnah, Pakistan's first leader, who demanded a separate Muslim state in India and was ultimately responsible for the existence of Pakistan

⁵RELIGION

Pakistan is an Islamic state, and Pakistanis are overwhelmingly Muslim in religion. There are, however, small religious minorities in the country. These include Hindus, Christians, Buddhists, and Baha'is of Iranian descent. There is a small Parsi (Zoroastrian) community, concentrated in Karachi. Minority religions account for only 3.3% of the population.

Within the Muslim community, there are also minority groups. For instance, some 25% of the population are Shia (or Shiite) Muslims, who are often at odds with the Sunni majority. The Shia community is splintered into numerous sects. The Ismailis, a Shia sect that recognizes the Aga Khan as its leader, have a strong presence in the northern mountain region. The Ahmadiyas are a modern Islamic sect whose beliefs are so unorthodox that many Muslims view them as non-Muslim. Numbering over 2 million people, they face considerable discrimination and anti-Ahmadiya sentiment from other Pakistanis.

⁶MAJOR HOLIDAYS

The two great religious festivals celebrated by the Pakistanis are Id-ul-Fitr, celebrating the end of Ramadan, and Bakr-Id, the feast of sacrifice. Ramadan, the month of fasting, is observed by all Muslims, and Muharram is a major day of remembrance among the Shias. The Urs festivals, commemorating the death-anniversary of Sufi saints, are important festivals celebrated at the saints' shrines. The calendar dates of Muslim religious holidays change because of differences between the Islamic and Western calendars.

In addition to religious holidays, Pakistanis observe certain national holidays. These include Independence Day (August 14), Pakistan Day (March 23), Defense of Pakistan Day (September 6), and the birth- and death-anniversaries of M. A. Jinnah, the Quaid-e-Azam (December 25 and September 11, respectively).

⁷RITES OF PASSAGE

As Muslims, Pakistanis follow the rites of passage associated with the Islamic faith. The newborn child is sanctified by prayer and undergoes the head-shaving and naming ceremonies. All males undergo the ritual of circumcision (sunnat). Among some Muslims, a ceremony known as Bismillah marks the beginning of a child's education in religious matters.

Ceremonies associated with death and burial combine practices laid down in the Shariah, the body of Islamic law, with local customs and traditions. The shrouded body is then ritually bathed and wrapped in a white shroud in preparation for burial. The body is brought out of the house, and the face of the deceased is shown to relatives and neighbors. Mourners, led by a priest, say prayers over the corpse, which is then taken in procession to the graveyard. There are certain customs observed by the family during the days and weeks following burial.

⁸INTERPERSONAL RELATIONS

Traditional Pakistanis use the formal greeting of Muslims the world over, "Salaam alaikum" ("Peace be with you"). The correct reply to this is the sentence, "Wa alaikum as Salaam" ("And also unto you"). Less formally, men shake hands and friends embrace each other. Pathans embrace twice, once from the left side and once from the right. Men are addressed as "Sahib" (Mr.), though when used with a name, the word "Sahib" comes last (as in "Johnson Sahib"). The equivalent form of address for a woman is "Begum." Khan, although a name, is also a title of respect.

⁹LIVING CONDITIONS

Despite improvements in the nation's health standards since independence, many Pakistanis continue to face major health hazards. Leading causes of death include malaria, childhood diseases (measles, diphtheria, whooping cough), typhoid, gastrointestinal problems, and respiratory infections. Inadequate sewage disposal, lack of safe drinking water, and malnutrition contribute to health problems. Infant mortality rates are high, with 66.9 deaths per 1,000 live births. Fertility rates are also high, with 3.6 average births per childbearing woman. The natural increase of population is 2.3% per year, the highest rate in South Asia.

Many Pakistanis live in cities. Karachi has a population approaching 16 million inhabitants, and Lahore exceeds 10 million people. The modern city of Islamabad was built specifically to be the nation's capital. Yet, Pakistanis are essentially rural, living in villages scattered from the high mountain valleys in the north to the desert areas in the southeast. Rural house types, construction materials, furnishings, and creature comforts vary according to region. Standards of living in Pakistan vary considerably. The prosperous urban elites live in large, air-conditioned houses with the latest modern conveniences, whereas the rural poor live very much in the manner of underprivileged classes the world over. Per capita income stands at $2,600 per year (2005 estimate).

Pakistan has 259,758 km (c. 160,000 mi) of road, of which some 65% is paved. State-run bus services and private minibuses are available to the traveling public. Pakistan inherited a substantial railroad network from colonial days, and the train still remains the most common means of long-distance travel for Pakistanis today. Pakistan also has a state-run airline that operates scheduled domestic and international flights.

Of special note is the Karakoram Highway. Completed in 1978, this paved road connects Islamabad with Kashgar, in China. For much of its 1,200-km (800-mile) length, it follows the ancient Silk Route along which trade passed between India and China. It crosses some of the highest and most rugged mountain terrain in the world.

¹⁰FAMILY LIFE

Despite the principles of equality embedded in Islam and its specific rejection of caste in South Asia, social relations among Pakistanis are very much influenced by caste. This is less true of urban Pakistanis and the tribal groups of the north and west, but it is quite evident in the main agricultural regions. The system, based on the jati (or zat) and the biradari (patrilineage), does not have the religious dimensions of the true Hindu caste system. But it does define the occupational roles of specific groups in the village economy. It is also important in terms of selecting a marriage partner.

Pakistanis follow the general customs of Islam in marriage (nikah), but details vary according to community and region. Parents take great care in arranging marriages for their children. Pakistani society is patrilocal, with the daughter-in-law entering the household of her husband. In the early years of marriage a woman has very little status, but this soon changes with the arrival of children, especially sons. The role of women in traditional Pakistani society is clearly defined. It is to bear sons, to manage the affairs of the household, and to see to the needs of the male members of the family. However, behind the scenes, women do have considerable say in family matters.

Purdah is the Islamic custom of keeping women in seclusion. When practiced to its fullest extent, it prohibits all social contact between women above the age of puberty and men outside the immediate family. Women in purdah who go out of the house wear the burqa, the long garment that covers them from head to toe.

¹¹CLOTHING

The standard dress of men all over Pakistan is the salwar, loose baggy trousers, and kurta, a long tunic-like shirt. This is worn with a variety of headgear, from turbans to caps. On formal occasions, the kurta is replaced by an achkan or serwani, a long tunic-like coat that buttons up to the neck. Women commonly wear the salwar, kamiz, and dupatta (scarf), or the sari. Orthodox women cover themselves from head to foot in the tent-like burqa.

There is, however, a bewildering variety of local dress that identifies a person as coming from a particular region or ethnic group in Pakistan. For example, the Pathan man wears a velvet jacket, trimmed with gold braid, over a homespun salwar-kurta. His cap, the kulah, is made of finely woven straw and gold thread. Over the cap is wrapped a turban or pagri, and the distinctive way in which the turban is tied will identify his tribe. It is not unusual for this outfit to be completed with an assortment of weapons. Men from Hunza and the northern mountains favor the *pakol*, the flat, round woolen cap worn by the Afghan freedom-fighters so often shown on American television during the Soviet-Afghan war. Sindhi men wear a round, embroidered cap with a section cut out in the front, while fabrics sewn with tiny mirrors are popular with Sindhi women. The kurta of Baluchistan has a unique underarm gusset that gives it extra fullness, while the front, cuffs, and pocket are elaborately embroidered. The Jinnah cap, headgear favored by M.A. Jinnah, is popular among politicians, bureaucrats, and other urban groups in Pakistan.

¹²FOOD

It is difficult to identify food that is specifically Pakistani because the region shares in broader subcontinental dietary traditions. Perhaps the only broad distinction between Pakistani and Indian food is that the former tends to be less spicy. Pakistani dishes are often made with yogurt, which reduces the effect of the hot spices commonly used in cooking.

Wheat is the staple food for most of the population. It is eaten in the form of flat, unleavened bread called *chapatis* or *roti*, along with spiced pulses (*dāl*), and seasonal vegetables. Sweetened tea, buttermilk, or *lassi*, a drink made from yogurt, rounds out the meal. Those who can afford it eat meat or poultry, although in rural areas this is usually a festival food. Goat meat is a favorite. No Pakistani, of course, will eat pork, which is regarded as unclean by Muslims.

Within Pakistan, there are also numerous regional specialties and dietary preferences. Thus, Sindhis are known for their seafood dishes, Punjabis for their bread and dals, and the northern areas for their fruits. The long life-expectancy of people in the Hunza Valley is ascribed to the importance of apricots in their diet. A favorite of Pathans is *nan-kebab*, a thick bread baked in an oven, eaten with cubes of meat, fish, or poultry. All Pakistanis enjoy sweets, and a wide variety of milk-based sweets are consumed. The giving of sweets to celebrate happy events is very common.

No mention of Pakistani cooking would be complete without mention of "Mughal" dishes. This style of cooking was developed in the Muslim courts of India. It uses a blend of herbs and spices rather than chilis and offers a selection of meats and poultry served in sauces; tandoori dishes baked in a hot, clay oven; breads such as *nan*, and various rice dishes.

¹³EDUCATION

Despite the expansion of educational facilities since independence, just over one half of all Pakistanis over 15 years of age are literate (49.9% in 2005). This breaks down to 63% for males and 36% for females. The variation in literacy between urban and rural populations is also quite considerable. Attendance at school remains low in rural areas because many children must work in the fields, and the dropout rate is high. Over two-thirds of the adult population have no formal schooling. Only 2.34% of the population between 16 and 23 years of age are enrolled at university campuses (2004). The corresponding figure for the United States is around 75%, although this figure includes two-year colleges, part-time students, and on-line enrollments. The Pakistani figure is quite low, despite a 1999 higher education initiative that provided for scholarships for Ph.D. students studying both at home and abroad.

¹⁴CULTURAL HERITAGE

Pakistanis' can trace their cultural heritage back 5,000 years to the Harappan civilization. This urban society, with its planned cities, irrigation systems, script, system of weights and measures, complex social and religious organization, and advanced material culture, rivals the civilizations of ancient Egypt and Mesopotamia. Most scholars believe the Harappans were Dravidian peoples, and that Harappan elements survive mainly in the Dravidian cultures of South India. However, similarities in toys, musical instruments, and pottery suggest that, at least in folk culture, some elements of Harappan traditions may be seen in modern Pakistan.

Buddhism, too, has left its mark on Pakistan. The ancient kingdom of Gandhara, in northern Pakistan, was a major center of Buddhist learning and artistic endeavor from the 1st to the 5th century AD. Exposed to influences from the West, Buddhists developed a tradition of Gandhara art that combined motifs from Persia, Greece, and Rome with Buddhist forms. Early Gandharan sculptures of Buddha had Greek faces and pleated robes patterned after the Roman-style toga.

It is Islam, however, that dominates the cultural landscape of Pakistan. The Indo-Islamic style of architecture, the numerous shrines of the *pirs* (Sufi saints), and mosques such as the Badshahi Mosque in Lahore are visual evidence of the presence of Islam in the land. Literature is perhaps the most important of the art forms. The poetry and music of the Sufis are known in every household in the land. The singing of *qawwalis*, devotional songs, is extremely popular, and some qawwali singers enjoy the fame reserved for pop stars in the West. There is a rich tradition of poetry in Urdu and other regional languages.

¹⁵WORK

Pakistan is primarily an agricultural nation, with 68% of its peoples living in rural areas. Government efforts at economic development saw a rapid expansion in the industrial sector and a rise in output in the decades following independence. However, several factors have acted to slow economic expansion. Pakistan's population has experienced relatively high growth rates, placing a heavy burden on food resources and slowing economic expansion. It has, however, meant a surplus of labor. This has given rise to such unique ventures as the world's largest ship-breaking operation on the beaches of the Arabian Sea coast that is done virtually entirely by hand. The traditional hostility with India has resulted in several military confrontations, with wars being fought in 1947, 1965, and 1971 and 1999. One consequence of this is seen in Pakistan's expenditure on its armed forces which, as a percentage of its GNP, is more than twice the world average.

Growing numbers of Pakistanis work in the labor-short, oil-exporting countries of the Middle East, earning much higher incomes than is possible in Pakistan. This forms an important source of outside currency for the country.

¹⁶SPORTS

Sports enjoyed by children in rural areas include hide-and-seek, marbles, kite-flying, *gulli-danda* (a stick game played by boys), and *kabaddi*, a wrestling game. For men, cock-fighting, partridge-fighting, and pigeon-flying (and betting on the outcome) are favorite pastimes. Polo, of a much less restrained form than that found in the West, is popular in northern areas such as Gilgit.

Pakistanis also play modern sports. The entire country is addicted to the game of cricket, a relic of British colonial days. In recent years, the Pakistani national (Test) cricket team has regularly defeated the England team, as well as those of other cricketing nations. The Pakistani national field hockey team is also one of the best in the world, a frequent winner of the Olympic Gold Medal in the sport. Games such as soccer, tennis, badminton, and table tennis are also played. Pakistanis have regularly won the world championship in squash, a court game similar to racquetball.

[17] ENTERTAINMENT AND RECREATION

Radio and television are available in Pakistan, although these forms of communication are controlled by the government. Television broadcasts during limited hours, and the programming is often uninspiring. The standard fare includes popular quiz programs, dramas highlighting the country's social problems, soap operas, and reruns of old sitcoms from the West. Urdu- and English-language films are popular and attract large audiences. Many well-to-do households have VCRs, and video rentals are readily available in the bazaars.

Movie houses abound in Pakistani cities and towns, showing Punjabi and Urdu films. The films, starring well-known actors and actresses, tend to be melodramas, with much action, singing, dancing, and predictable plots. Film music is popular and can be heard on the radio, in buses, and in the bazaars at all hours of the day.

[18] FOLK ART, CRAFTS, AND HOBBIES

Every region in Pakistan specializes in local arts and crafts too numerous to discuss in detail here. These include rugs and carpets, embroidered and appliquéd bedspreads and table linen, colorful fabrics and mirror work, leather goods, copper and brassware, onyx ornaments, woodwork and inlaid furniture, lacquerware, and gold and silver jewelry.

[19] SOCIAL PROBLEMS

Pakistanis face many of the social and economic problems typical of developing nations. Poverty, illiteracy, unemployment, inflation, and a widening gap between rich and poor are but a few of the country's ills. These problems have been intensified by wars with India, high expenditures on the military, the continuing conflict in Kashmir, and the current War on Terror. The frequency with which the Pakistani Army has displaced democratically elected governments has added to political instability in the country. There has been some sentiment for the creation of an independent Pashto-speaking state ("Pakhtunistan") on Pakistan's northwest frontier. In recent years, the presence of 3 million Afghan refugees has placed an added burden on the country. Punjabis are viewed as wielding too much power and influence, and discord between muhajirs and Sindhis has led to communal unrest in the south, especially in Karachi. In addition, the government's policy of Islamization, combined with the outspoken fundamentalism of many religious leaders, has resulted in conflict between segments of the Muslim community.

Under Musharraf, Pakistan supported President George W. Bush's War on Terror following 11 September 2001. In return, the United States supported President Musharraf and channeled some $10 billion in civilian and military aid to help fight Muslim radicals. However, a problem facing Musharraf was that many Pakistanis, especially those along the border with Afghanistan, tended to support the Muslim radicals and the Taliban because they are Muslim and culturally and perhaps even ethnically related to them. The result has been a virtual civil war pitting the Pakistani government and its security forces against the Pakistani population. In addition, there are those in the United States who claim that Musharraf did not do all he could to aid the United States and who argue that U.S. aid to Pakistan be stopped. It is not unlikely that U.S. support for Musharraf, who as of July 2008 was under pressure from the civilian government to resign as president, led indirectly to the defeat of his political party in the 2008 elections held in Pakistan.

Sectarian conflict is common in Pakistan. Karachi, for instance, has a history of religious and ethnic violence between the minority Shia and majority Sunni communities. The press periodically reports bomb blasts at mosques belonging to one sect or the other.

The most difficult task facing Pakistanis today seems to be creating a sense of "nation" among the diverse communities and ethnic groups that make up the country's population, a task that is complicated by political events in Afghanistan, Iraq, and Pakistan itself. On 6 July 2008, a suicide bomber killed at least 11 policemen near the Red Mosque in Islamabad in apparent retaliation for the government's security forces' attack on the mosque in 2007, which was aimed at driving out hard-line Muslim clerics and their supporters.

[20] GENDER ISSUES

Pakistani women, because they live in a country that is officially Muslim, suffer from the restrictions of a Muslim society. Some writers argue that the South Asian subcontinent is the most gender insensitive region in the world. Thus, women in Pakistan are not only subject to the norms of Muslim society (*purdah*, the wearing of the *burqa*, arranged marriages and child marriage [called "*vani*" in Pakistan]), they are also discriminated against financially and by being the victims of inhuman customs and laws such as *karo-kari* ("honor killings") and the 1979 Hudud Ordinance (which designated punishment such as stoning for adultery) [this Ordinance has since been amended by the National Assembly of Pakistan in 2006 and replaced by the Women's Protection Bill, which eliminates some of the apparent inequities of the Hudud Ordinance]. Needless to say, the Women's Protection Bill was applauded by women's organizations but strongly opposed by traditional Islamists.

Women are often treated like slaves subject to drudgery, performing chores such as looking after the children, cleaning the house, cooking, washing and many other forms of domestic labor. They are there just to obey their fathers, brothers and husbands. They do not have the right to decide about themselves because women are considered as foolish creatures according to the dominant social and cultural norms. Likewise, marriage is also a sort of trade between different families both in the rural and urban areas.

Women are also subject to domestic violence (one report states that 82% of women in the Punjab are subject to some kind of domestic violence), rape, and trafficking. The legal code discriminates against women and girls (according to law, a female witness in the courts is only worth half a male witness) and creates major obstacles in seeking redress for acts of violence. Proof of rape generally requires the confession of the accused or the testimony of four adult Muslim men who witnessed the assault. If a woman cannot prove her rape allegation she runs a very high risk of being charged with fornication or adultery, the criminal penalty for which is either a long prison sentence and public whipping, or, though rare, death by stoning.

In general, with obvious exceptions such as Benazir Bhutto who rose to become Pakistan's prime minister before her assassination, women—especially poor women—in Pakistani society are treated (according to Western standards) like second-class citizens.

[21] BIBLIOGRAPHY

Aziz, Khursheed Kamal. *The Making of Pakistan: A Study in Nationalism*. Lahore: Sang-e-Meel Publications, 2002.

Blood, Peter R., ed. *Pakistan, a Country Study*. 6th ed. Washington, D.C.: Federal Research Division, Library of Congress, 1995.

Burki, Shahid Javed. *Pakistan: The Continuing Search for Nationhood*. Boulder, CO.: Westview Press, 1991.

Eglar, Zekiye. *A Punjabi Village in Pakistan*. New York: Columbia University Press, 1960

National Institute of Folk Heritage. *Folk Heritage of Pakistan*. Islamabad: National Institute of Folk Heritage, 1977

Quddus, Syed Abdul. *The Cultural Patterns of Pakistan*. Lahore: Ferozsons, 1989.

—by D. O. Lodrick

PALESTINIANS

PRONUNCIATION: pal-uh-STIN-ee-uhns
LOCATION: Israel and the Occupied Territories (West Bank and Gaza Strip); Jordan; Lebanon; Syria; worldwide
POPULATION: 4.5 million
LANGUAGE: Arabic
RELIGION: Islam; Christianity; Druze

[1] INTRODUCTION

Palestine is the historical name for the region between the Mediterranean Sea and the Jordan River. The land was first inhabited as long ago as 9000 BC on the West Bank of the Jordan. The Hebrews (ancestors of today's Jews) settled in Palestine in 1900 BC and had formed the kingdom of Israel, ruled by King David, by 1000 BC. Palestine was then taken over by a succession of foreign powers, including the Assyrians (722 BC), Babylonians (597–587 BC), Greeks (332–140 BC), and finally Romans (63 BC–7th century AD). Greeks ruled Palestine from 332–140 BC. In 140 BC, Simon Maccabaeus, following an earlier revolt led by Judas Maccabaeus against the Greeks, asserted Jewish theocratic rule over Palestine. From 140 to 63 BC, a Jewish kingdom was in power. The Romans drove the Jews out of Palestine after two revolts, one in AD 70 and the second in AD 135. The Arabs took control of the area during the Islamic expansion of the 7th century AD, and it is from these Arabs that modern-day Palestinians are descended. The Arabic word for Palestine is "Falastine," which reflects the ancestry of the Palestinians, who are believed to be descendants of the "Philistines," who were of Mycenaean origin. In 1516, the Turks invaded, and Palestine became part of the Ottoman Empire for the next 400 years, until the Empire was defeated in World War I (1914–19). During the war period, both the Arabs and the Jews were made promises by the British concerning the future fate of Palestine. In 1915, in the MacMahon-Hussein correspondence, the British pledged support for postwar Arab independence over a region understood by the Arabs to include Palestine. In 1917, in the Balfour Declaration, the British pledged support for a national home for the Jewish people in Palestine. These promises ultimately supported the national aspirations of both people to the same land, a situation that resulted in the political impasse that still exists today in Palestine. Palestine was handed over to the British in 1920. The British, as the mandatory power, then controlled the land of Palestine until 1948. Britain relinquished the mandate and withdrew from Palestine on 14 May 1948, following prolonged and sporadic fighting between the Jews and the Arabs and attacks by both groups against the British.

In 1947, the United Nations divided Palestine into two states, one Jewish, and one Arab. When the independent state of Israel was declared on 15 May 1948, the Arab forces of Egypt, Iraq, Lebanon, Saudi Arabia, Syria, and Transjordan advanced into Palestine. After the ensuing war, the West Bank came under Jordanian rule, the Gaza Strip came under Egyptian rule, and the remainder of Palestine came under Israeli rule. Many Palestinian Arabs fled during this time, but others stayed and continued to live in now-Israeli territory. In 1964, the Palestine Liberation Organization (PLO) was formed in Jerusalem un-

PALESTINIANS

0　　20　　40 Miles

0　　20　　40 Kilometers

LEBANON

Damascus

SYRIA

Qiryat Shemona

Al Qunayṭirah

Golan Heights

'Akko

Hefa

Teverya

Sea of Galilee

Nazerat

MEDITERRANEAN SEA

Qishon

Jordan

Janin

Netanya

West Bank

Nābulus

Herzliyya

Petah Tiqwa

Tel Aviv-Yafo

Rām Allāh

'Ammān

Ramla

Rehovot

Soreq

Jericho

Ashdod

Jerusalem

JORDAN

Bayt Lahm

Ashqelon

Dead Sea

Gaza

Al Khalil (Hebron)

ISRAEL

Khān Yūnis

Gaza Strip

Be'ér Sheva'

Al Karak

EGYPT

Dimona

der the leadership of Ahmad Shukairy. Yasser Arafat became the head of the PLO in 1969.

In the June 1967 war, Israel captured the West Bank (which had been under Jordanian rule since 1948) and the Gaza Strip (which had been under Egyptian rule since 1948). In 1967, Israel annexed East Jerusalem. The West Bank and Gaza Strip have since been called the Occupied Territories. Most of the residents there are Palestinian Arabs. The Israeli government and the PLO signed the Declaration of Principles (DOP) in September 1993, resolving that Israeli troops would leave the West Bank and Gaza Strip areas. In 1994, limited Palestinian self-rule was established in Jericho and the Gaza Strip. Fighting continues over the question of a fully independent Palestinian homeland.

The term *Palestinian* used to refer to anyone who lived in the land of Palestine, Arab and Jew included. With the establishment of the modern state of Israel, however, the term *Palestinian* has narrowed to mean only those Arabs (both Christian and Muslim) and their descendants who lived in Palestine during the time of the British mandate (1920–48). For those Muslim and Christian inhabitants of the land who were incorporated into the Israeli state, many continue to identify themselves as Palestinians while holding Israeli citizenship but are often referred to as the "Israeli Arabs" or "1948 Arabs." Because of the initial exodus of Palestinians following the establishment of the state in 1948 through forced evacuation by Israelis and escape, and through subsequent exiling from their

homeland, up to 6 million refugees and their descendents have a legitimate claim for right of return under international law. With more Palestinians outside of historic Palestine than inside it, a large component of the contemporary political identity is a product of various resistance campaigns, migrant estrangement, and attempts at reinstatement.

The Palestinian territories (now comprising the West Bank and Gaza Strip) have been the site of several democratic elections, including that of January 2006, when the Islamic political militia group Hamas won a majority of the parliamentary seats. Since that time, frequent attacks by Israel on Hamas strongholds and infighting between Palestinian factions has been prevalent. Today, there are two Palestinian parties, the Palestinian Authority (Fatah) and Hamas, each in charge of a territory, the former in the West Bank and the latter in the Gaza Strip. Recent Israeli attempts to oust the Hamas government and gain control in the Gaza Strip have escalated to a full siege of the territory, preventing supplies from entering. Various Human Rights groups and intergovernmental agencies have declared it a humanitarian disaster. In January 2008, effectively the "largest open-air prison," became impossible to seal as tens of thousands of Palestinians, starved for food, medicine, fuel, and supplies breached a border crossing with Egypt and the border town of Rafah.

²LOCATION AND HOMELAND

There are more than 11 million Palestinians in the world, about half of them in Israel and the Occupied Territories—the West Bank and Gaza Strip. The rest are scattered across the globe, although most live in neighboring Arab countries, such as Jordan, Lebanon, and Syria. The United Nations lists 7 million Palestinian refugees. During the war years of 1947–49, 700,000–800,000 Palestinians were driven from their homes. When Israel occupied the West Bank and Gaza Strip in 1967, another 300,000 Palestinians became refugees (and 150,000 who were already refugees were forced to move again).

Refugees live in camps or slums. Refugee camps set up by the UN Relief Workers Agency (UNRWA) originally consisted of simple shacks and unpaved alleys. Today, they are built of concrete, galvanized steel, and aluminum. Most camps are very overcrowded and become more so as time passes, more refugees pour in, and more children are born to the families already there. Some refugee camps in the Gaza Strip have more than 80,000 people living in them.

Many Palestinians continue to live as small subsistence farmers in rural villages. Others have managed to find good jobs and live quite well in the lands to which they have moved. There are also many urban centers in Palestine. The village of Ramallah serves as a commercial center for surrounding villages and is now the main hub of Palestinian economic, cultural, and political life. It houses banking establishments, construction companies, private schools, technical colleges, shops, restaurants, and so on. Ramallah has undergone a construction boom since the DOP was signed, reflecting the hope and conviction that peace would bring stability and prosperity to the West Bank. East Jerusalem is the center of political and intellectual leadership in the West Bank, housing human rights organizations, think-tanks, and the famous "Orient House," owned by the family of political leader Faisal Husseini, where many meetings of political leaders take place. Over the years, some Israelis protested asking that Orient House should be shut down because Palestinian leaders should not convene in East Jerusalem, which is not under Palestinian control. In 2001, Israel forces entered Orient House and confiscated most of its contents, effectively shutting down operations from the house.

Because Jerusalem holds symbolic political and religious importance for both Muslim and Christian Palestinians, discussions of its future fate are often heated. Both Jews and Palestinians insist on controlling East Jerusalem and instituting a capital for each of their states in the Holy City. The Israeli government has pledged to maintain sovereignty over it. Starting in 2002 and 2003, the Israeli government began erecting an extensive concrete and reinforced wall to separate the West Bank from Israel, under the claim of ensuring the security of Israelis from Palestinian attacks. The wall, which covers an extensive area of land, severs Palestinian land and cuts some areas off from water supplies and vital transport routes. In some instances, this wall that the Palestinians refer to as the "Apartheid Wall" wraps around cities, such as Qalqilya, and effectively prevents their growth. The wall has become a prominent symbol of Palestinian dispossession and Israeli security, a geographic landmark, and a source of much controversy. The wall itself has become a famous canvas for Palestinian, Israeli, and international artists and activists to express their discontent with the partition.

³ LANGUAGE

Palestinians speak Arabic. "Hello" in Arabic is *marhaba* or *ahlan*, to which one replies, *marhabtayn* or *ahlayn*. Other common greetings are *As-salam alaykum* ("Peace be with you") with the reply of *wa 'alaykum as salam* ("and to you peace"). *Ma'assalama* means "goodbye," with the literal translation being "go with peace." "Thank you" is *Shukran*, and "You're welcome" is *'Afwan*. "Yes" is *na'am*, and "no" is *la'a*. The numbers one to ten in Arabic are: *wahad, ithnayn, thalatha, arba'a, khamsa, sita, sab'a, thamanya, tis'a,* and *'ashara.*

Common names for boys are: Ahmad, Shukri, Isma'il, and Ibrahim. Muhammad is a very common Muslim name. Hanna is a very common Christian name. 'Isa (Jesus) is used by both Muslims and Christians. Common names for girls are: Samia, Sawsan, Maysoon, Muna, and Fatima. On rare occasions, girls are given politically significant names, such as Al-Quds (Jerusalem).

⁴ FOLKLORE

Palestinians are very religious people, regardless of their faith or denomination. For this reason, much of the local folklore grows out of religious superstitious interpretations. Many believe in *jinns*, evil spirits who can take on the shapes of natural forms and cause trouble, and take extra measures to safeguard their homes from these. They also use amulets, household decorations and various rituals to deter jinns and people who are perceived as "evil" or envious.

A famous fictional character is Juha. School children read about Juha's exploits in fables that teach some sort of lesson. For example, in one story, Juha buries a treasure in the ground and tries to remember its whereabouts by remembering the clouds that hover over it. Naturally, he loses his treasure because clouds move about and disappear.

A famous true story in which Palestinians take pride is the capturing of Jerusalem by Arab Muslims in the 7th century. In AD 636, a few years after the Prophet Muhammad's death (AD 632), Muslim armies led by Khalid Ibn al-Walid defeated the Byzantine army at the Battle of Uhud in Jordan. Shortly thereafter, Jerusalem was captured in AD 638.

Many Muslim stories cherished by Palestinians are similar to those in the Judeo-Christian tradition. For example, the stories of Noah and the Ark and Adam and Eve are important to Muslim and Christian Palestinians. Noah is known as the Prophet Nuh, Adam's name remains the same, and Eve is known as Hawwa.

Today, Palestinian folklore is tied to feelings of estrangement, exile, and longing for home. Many of the stories from contemporary Palestinian literature and poetry deal directly with losing a homeland, feeling dispossessed, and glorifying resistance to the status quo. Traditional music and dance, Palestinian *dabke,* are a common way of expressing heritage and are enacted in weddings, festivals, and celebrations in Israel, the Occupied Territories, and the diaspora. The rituals continue in every location in the world where a Palestinian presence is prominent.

⁵ RELIGION

Most Palestinians (75%) are Muslim, the majority belonging to the Sunni sect. Islam is the youngest of the world's Abrahamic religions, having begun in the early 7th century AD when the prophet Muhammad received his revelations from Allah, the one true God (according to Islam). Within just a few years of Muhammad's death in AD 632, Islam had spread through the entire Middle East, gaining converts at a dynamic rate.

Born into the Koreish tribe of Mecca (c. AD 570) in the Hijaz (modern-day Saudi Arabia), Muhammad was later driven from the city because of his outspoken denunciation of the pagan idols worshipped there (idols who attracted a lucrative pilgrim trade). The year of Muhammad's flight from Mecca to Medina (AD 622), called the Hijra (or Hegira), is the first year of the Muslim calendar. Eventually Muhammad returned to Mecca as a triumphant religious and political leader, destroyed the idols (saving the Black Stone, an ancient meteorite housed in the *Kaaba,* or Cube, building, which has become a focal point of Muslim worship), and established Mecca as the spiritual center of Islam. All prayers are said facing Mecca, and each Muslim is expected, and greatly desires, to make a pilgrimage there (called a *Haj* or *Hadj*) at least once in his or her lifetime.

Islam is a simple, straightforward faith with clear rules for correct living. It is a total way of life, inseparable from the rest of one's daily concerns. Therefore, religion, politics, faith, and culture are one and the same for Muslims. There is no such thing as the "separation of church and state," or any distinction between private religious values and public cultural norms.

About 17% of Palestinians are Christians whose ancestors have lived in that land since the time Jesus Christ was born, ministered, and died there. There are sites in Palestine, especially in Jerusalem and Bethlehem, which are visited by Christian pilgrims from around the world. The Church of the Holy Sepulchre, the room of the Last Supper, the Via Dolorosa, and the town of Nazareth are all important Christian attractions. Although some of these are located in East Jerusalem, which has been annexed by Israel, supervision of the individual sites is maintained by Palestinians, and Christian Palestinians hold Jerusalem's holy places to be central to their Palestinian national aspirations. Palestine's Christian population is comprised of many different denominations, from various Eastern Orthodox to Catholic and Protestant.

Palestine is also important to Muslims from around the world. It is believed that the Prophet Muhammad ascended to heaven from Jerusalem on a night's journey known as *al-Isra' wa al-Mi`raj*. On this site, Muslims built the Dome of the Rock and al-Aqsa Mosques, which also gives Muslims cause to demand Muslim control over East Jerusalem. This site is believed to be the third holiest shrine to Muslims after Mecca and Medina in Saudi Arabia.

Some 8% of Palestinians are Druze [*see* **Druze**].

6 MAJOR HOLIDAYS

Islam uses a lunar calendar, so Muslim holidays occur on a different date of the Gregorian calendar each year. The major Muslim holidays are `Eid al-Fitr, the end of Ramadan (a three-day festival); `Eid al-Adha, a feast at the end of the *Hadj* (the pilgrimage month to Mecca); the First of *Muharram*, the Muslim New Year; and the prophet Muhammad's birthday.

`Eid al-Fitr and `Eid al-Adha are celebrated by visiting close friends and relatives throughout the day. At least one family member, usually the mother, remains home to greet guests, and the rest of the family travels from home to home delivering holiday greetings. Children are usually showered with money from most of the adults they encounter. At every home, pastries called *Ka`k al-Id* are served. These are made of a flour called smeed, similar to semolina flour, mixed with lots of butter. The dough is shaped into small round forms and stuffed with a mixture of walnuts, cinnamon, and sugar, or with dates. They are baked and then sprinkled with powdered sugar. During the three-day `Eid celebration, everyone eats lots of ka`k.

The Christian holiday of Easter is also moveable, being calculated on a lunar basis. It always occurs sometime during March or early April. Other Christian holidays are: the Day of the Ascension; the Feast of the Assumption (August 15); and Christmas and Boxing Day (December 25–26). New Year's Day (January 1) is a secular holiday.

In 1977, an International Day of Solidarity with the Palestinian People was declared as a political observance (November 29). Some politically significant events are observed each year by a general strike and demonstrations. Two examples are November 2, in protest over the 1917 Balfour Declaration, and May 15, in protest over the declaration of the state of Israel.

7 RITES OF PASSAGE

Males of both Christian and Muslim background are circumcised, and the family holds a great feast to celebrate the occasion. Marriages are another important rite of passage. A simple wedding is followed by a huge feast and celebration attended by family and friends, who bring gifts. Childbirth is considered an important function of marriage, in part because the Islamic religion favors having children, but also because Palestinians feel that reproduction is an important nationalist duty.

Education is highly valued, and families compare the grades of their children. The highest achievers are noted in newspapers. It is a great honor to be the highest achiever on both banks of the Jordan River (i.e., in both the West Bank [Palestine] and the East Bank [Jordan]).

After completing high school, many go on to college, and many get married. A Palestinian wedding ceremony consists of a simple exchange of vows, which is taken in the presence of a Muslim clergyman and witnesses representing the two families. This ceremony is called the *Katb al-Kitab* or *Imlak*. Following the ceremony, there is a huge celebration and feast attended by families and friends. In some cases, candy is distributed at the reception; in other cases, a dinner is served, which most often features the meal called *mansaf*. This consists of layers of thin bread called *shraj*, topped with a layer of rice, and then drenched in a sauce made with yogurt and lamb stock. This is served in a large round pan and is covered with enough lamb chunks to feed all the guests.

When a Palestinian dies, there is a three-day mourning period for the family of the deceased. During this time, family and friends pay their condolences and recite passages from the Quran. The closest neighbors serve meals to the bereaved family and their guests for the three-day period. The next observance of the death is at the 40-day point, and once again the Quran is recited and meals are served to guests. *Mansaf* is often served as part of the meal.

8 INTERPERSONAL RELATIONS

When two Palestinians greet one another, they usually shake hands. It is also common for two women to kiss one another on the cheeks in greeting.

Neighbors have very cordial relations and look out for one another's interests. Palestinians in the West Bank generally live with their parents in the home of their birth until they are married or move abroad in search of work or education. Once an adult settles down and gets married, it is common for the couple to live out their lives in one house or apartment. Thus, because they do not move from home to home, neighbors get to know one another and establish life-long relationships. They celebrate happy occasions together and share in losses, such as deaths, together. Palestinians are known for their hospitality. One cannot visit a Palestinian home without being offered refreshment, at the minimum a soft drink or a cup of coffee or tea with a pastry.

Despite the hospitality and neighborly relations, it is considered impolite to impose on a neighbor by overextending one's visit. Invitations to dinner are often heartily declined so as to avoid imposing on the host, to which the host responds with an equally hearty insistence on the invitation.

Because Palestinian society is very conservative by Western standards, dating as it is understood in the West is not tolerated. If a man and woman are interested in one another, it is customary for the man to first declare his intentions to the woman's family. Dating to socialize or get to know one another is not allowed; the intent must be marriage. If a woman and her family approve of the prospective husband, there is a formal engagement, followed by a getting-to-know-one-another period. The marriage takes place at a time convenient to both parties. Increasingly, it is becoming common for two people to "fall in love" before approaching the woman's family, but the social norm is to "protect" the woman by having the man "screened" by her family before the courting period.

9 LIVING CONDITIONS

Palestinians live in a variety of conditions, from refugee camps to comfortable, middle-class (or even wealthy) homes in modern towns and cities. Traditional villages have one-story houses made of white stone, with a kitchen, a room for bathing, a *li-*

wan (sitting room) for receiving guests, and a few small rooms for sleeping.

Floors are covered with pieces of carpet, linoleum, or tile. Some of the wealthier homes now have wall-to-wall carpet. The houses have interior wooden doors, and exterior doors and window frames are usually made of a strong metal. Houses are often surrounded by small gardens separated from the street by a high wall (called a *sur*) with a gate. Wealthier families often have two stories, an upstairs for living and entertaining, and a downstairs area (called a *makhzan*) for storage and utilities. Such homes have indoor plumbing and electricity, whereas other families get their water from local wells and cook on small charcoal stoves. Most urban Palestinians have radios, cassette players, and stoves and ovens for cooking. Most also have refrigerators and televisions sets. Videocassette recorders are frequently brought into the country by Palestinians traveling abroad. To this day, few Palestinian homes in the West Bank and Gaza have computers and regular, reliable internet access. Most Palestinians of different ages rely on cell phones as an indispensible means of communication.

Refugee camps set up by the UN Relief Workers Agency (UNRWA) provide small, cement-block homes with corrugated metal roofs and doors. Some have no running water or electricity. Families cook on a metal grate laid over a tin container filled with charcoal, sleep on thin mats on the floor (which are then rolled up and out of the way during the day), and bathe and wash their clothes in metal drums filled with water from a hose at community faucets.

In most instances, whether in the cities or refugee camps, Palestinian nuclear and extended families live within close quarters and sometimes even under the same roof. It is generally discouraged for a son or daughter to move out of the family house prior to marriage.

¹⁰FAMILY LIFE

The family is the central organizing unit of Palestinian society. Traditional village life used to be regulated by the *hamula*—a male-dominated extended family system, or clan-based operation. The hamula is disappearing as ancestral clan-controlled lands are taken away or lost, but families are still very important, and extended family members often live near or with each other.

Arranged marriages continue to be the norm in some places, with first cousins or members of the same village being the preferred match. Marriage by individual choice is becoming common in other areas, however, especially as more males and females meet in universities, which are all co-educational. Child-marriage and polygamy still occur, although not in great numbers. Palestinians have one of the highest birth-rates in the world, and approximately 45% of the population is under the age of 14. Children are taught to use good manners and to respect their elders. In fact, the elderly continue to live with the family of their sons or daughters. There are very few nursing homes, and it is rare and a dishonor to send one's elderly parent to a nursing home. Women are expected to fulfill the traditional role of homemaker, doing all the cooking, cleaning, laundry, and so on, as well as taking care of the men's and children's needs. Women are beginning to break out of these roles, however; 44% of the students at the five West Bank universities are women. Particularly under Israeli occupation, as more and more men were arrested by the military government

for political activities hostile to the state of Israel, women were forced to fill in for men who were detained in prison. Women thus assumed jobs and became heads of households. Having attained prominent social and professional roles, many women now insist on equality of the sexes.

Women are to be highly respected in a family. Brothers must show respect for their sisters and are obligated to look out for the welfare of their sisters even into adulthood. On holidays, brothers are expected to give their sisters gifts, although sisters do not have to reciprocate.

¹¹CLOTHING

Palestinians of the older generation still wear traditional clothing. Men wear a long loose robe called a *jallabiyeh* and the common Arab headscarf, or *kaffiyeh*, held in place with a twisted band called an *ogaal*. Women wear a long black peasant dress, known as a *thob*, with an embroidered bodice, and a shawl over the head and shoulders. Women from different towns can be distinguished by the embroidery and style of the thob. The designs are cross-stitched, sometimes by the woman herself, and sometimes by a professional seamstress. The latter can charge hundreds of dollars for each bodice she embroiders, because each one takes days of sewing by hand to prepare. Thobs are made either of linen or velvet. A particularly fancy velvet dress, known as the *malaka*, is traditionally worn by brides. It is often made of burgundy and green velvet and has silver or gold embroidery.

Most younger Palestinians wear Western-style clothing, with traditional headscarves that cover the hair for young women. Religiosity increased during the years of the Intifada (beginning 1987), and this has been reflected in an increase in religious attire, known as *shari'a* clothing or *jilbab*, for young women. This is basically a long jacket-like dress that covers the entire body, with a scarf worn on the head to cover the hair.

¹²FOOD

Palestinians eat typical Middle Eastern food, such as *falafel* (deep-fried chickpea balls or patties), *hummus* (ground chickpeas with garlic, lemon juice, and *tahini*, a sesame paste), lamb, chicken, rice, nuts, and eggplant. A favorite Palestinian candy is *halvah*, a sweet nougat made of sesame seeds and honey. For meals, some rural Palestinians sit on mats or cushions around a cloth laid on the floor and scoop up their food with pieces of pita bread, called *khubz*. They drink lots of strong black Turkish coffee. A recipe for khubz follows.

Khubz (Pita Bread)

2 teaspoons dry yeast
1 tablespoon salt
2½ cups warm water
5 to 6 cups whole wheat flour
or 3 cups whole wheat and 2 to 3 cups white flour
or 5 to 6 cups white flour

Dissolve yeast in half a cup of warm water. Cover and let sit until yeast ferments, about 10 minutes. Stir 3 cups of flour, salt, dissolved yeast, and remaining 2 cups of water in a large bread bowl or mixing bowl. Add remaining 2 to 3 cups of flour in small portions, kneading well with the hands after each addition. Keep adding flour until the dough holds together well and stops sticking to your hands.

Knead very well on a lightly floured surface for 8 to 10 minutes. The dough should be smooth and elastic. Return the dough to the mixing bowl and cover with plastic wrap. Wrap the entire bowl, including the bottom, in a blanket or heavy towel, and allow dough to rise until doubled in size, about 2 to 3 hours.

On a lightly floured surface, cut the dough into 8 balls. Cover the balls and let rest for 30 minutes. Preheat the oven to 400°F. While the oven is heating, use a rolling pin to flatten each ball of dough into a circle about ¼ inch thick and 8 to 9 inches in diameter.

Beginning with the first loaf you rolled, set each loaf directly on the oven rack. You can bake two loaves at a time, one on each rack. When the loaves begin to brown, turn them so that they brown evenly on both sides (about 3 minutes per side). (If you find it difficult to drop the dough directly onto the oven shelf, use a pizza pan or a pizza stone to lay the loaf on.)

As each loaf comes out of the oven, wrap it in a clean cloth or towel to keep it soft until the baking process is complete. After the loaves have cooled, store in plastic bags.

Other Palestinian favorites are zucchini and grape leaves, both stuffed with a rice and meat mixture. Because olive trees are plentiful in the hilly terrain, Palestinians also enjoy olive oil, and preserved olives, harvested in the summer, are eaten year round. Almonds, plums, apples, cherries, and lemons are enjoyed in many households fresh off the trees in family gardens. Pork is prohibited in the Muslim religion, as is alcohol. Many Palestinians are Christian, however, so alcoholic beverages are served in some restaurants and sold in some stores, generally in urban centers, such as Ramallah and Jerusalem.

The most traditional Palestinian meals are *maqluba, musakhan,* and *mansaf. Musakhan* is a common main dish that originated in the Jenin and Tulkarm area in the northern West Bank. It consists of roasted chicken over bread, topped with pieces of fried sweet onions and pine nuts. *Maqluba* is a rice and baked eggplant casserole mixed with cooked cauliflower, carrots, and chicken or lamb. Dating back to the 13th century, *maqluba* is eaten throughout the Levant, it has a particular significance among Palestinians. *Mansaf* is a traditional meal in the central West Bank and Negev region in the southern West Bank, having its roots from the Bedouin population of ancient Palestine.

¹³ EDUCATION

Palestinian children attend schools similar to those in the West. Children begin school in kindergarten and attend elementary, preparatory, and high school. There are many types of school systems, due in large part to the history of foreign rule and influence over Palestine. For refugee children, the United Nations Relief and Works Agency (UNRWA) runs schools in which children receive a free education and some assistance with educational materials. The majority of Palestinian children attend free public schools. There are also many private schools for those who can afford them. Private schools tend to be predominantly religious. Islamic schools were established by local Muslims, but Christian schools were established by foreigners with the assistance of local Palestinians. The latter include Friends' schools (run by Quakers from the United

States), and the Frere and Rosary schools (run by French Catholics). All girls, whether in UNRWA, public, or private schools, wear uniforms. Boys dress as they wish within limits reflecting the social norms. Palestinians have the highest percentage of university graduates in the Arab world. The five Palestinian universities on the West Bank have a combined enrollment of about 5,000 students. These universities are hotbeds of social and political activism and have been closed down from time to time by the Israelis to try to put a stop to the students' revolutionary ideas and actions. Today, the most prominent Palestinian university is Beirzeit University outside of Ramallah. Recent high-caliber campuses have developed throughout the West Bank, including the Arab-American University in Jenin.

The average literacy rate for Palestinians is one of the highest in the region and the Arab world. The overall literacy rate is reported at 93%.

¹⁴ CULTURAL HERITAGE

Traditional Palestinian dancing is segregated by sex. Men dance in a semicircle with their arms around each other or holding hands as they perform the *dabka*. In the dabka, which is performed at all wedding receptions, dancers circle the dance floor following the lead and instructions of a designated leader. Women also perform the dabka at social events, and in professional performances men and women do the dabka together. Dancing is often done to the rhythm of a drum called a *derbakah*. Other musical instruments are the lute and the *shebabah*, a reed instrument. Afif Bulos is a popular contemporary Palestinian musician.

Contemporary Palestinian writers include literary critical and intellectual Edward Said, who is Palestinian-American. The famous Palestinian poet and short story writer Ghassan Kanafani. His poetry and stories, like much Palestinian literature, features themes of protest against the Israeli occupation and reminiscences of times predating the occupation. Poet Mahmoud Darwish wrote the protest poem "Investigation" and many other poems that have become iconic in Palestinian life. Rashid Khalidi, a historian, political commentator and professor is a renowned voice on the Palestinian-Israeli situation. Numerous radio and television personalities, many of whom work for Arabic satellite stations Al-Jazeera and Al-Arabiya, as well as Western news agencies. Sabri Jiryis, a radio personality, is the author of *The Arabs in Israel*, a book about events in 1956 in the Palestinian town of Kafr Qasim. The famous cartoonist, Naji Al-Ali, is famous for his character *Handala,* a small impoverished Palestinian boy, who is omnipresent in his work and acts as the witness to Palestinian suffering. Painter Jammana al-Husseni is also internationally known.

¹⁵ WORK

It is difficult for Palestinians in the Occupied Territories to find work. Unemployment is a serious problem among the many refugees. When they do find jobs, they are often paid low wages.

Many Palestinians from Gaza and some from the West Bank cross over into Israel for employment. In Israel, they hold low-wage jobs as restaurant waiters, street cleaners, construction workers, and dishwashers. Since the signing of the DOP, the borders between Israel and the Palestinians have often been closed, causing extreme hardship for the Palestinians who once relied on Israel for jobs.

Palestinian school children walk back to their home in Rafah, southern Gaza Strip. Because of the shortage of school classrooms and teachers, some Palestinian children have to study in two shifts. (AP Images/Laurent Rebours)

Although many Palestinians hold college degrees, jobs compatible with those degrees are difficult to find. This leads to much of the frustration that is ultimately expressed in riots and demonstrations against the Israeli occupation. Under Prime Minister Yitzhak Rabin, who died in 1995, discussions were underway to develop an industrial complex along the borders to solve the unemployment problem. Under the consecutive governments of Benjamin Netanyahu, Ehud Barak, Ariel Sharon, Ehud Olmert, and now Tzipi Livni, the situation has gotten progressively worse for Palestinians seeking work. The construction of the wall throughout the West Bank has made it more difficult for Palestinians to seek and attend work in once-adjacent areas.

In Jordan, Palestinians who were once escapees from the West Bank dominate the private sector, holding 60 to 65% of the jobs in banking, 60 to 75% in retailing, and 75 to 80% in the import-export business.

16 SPORTS

Although Palestinians in the Occupied Territories have little time or space for organized sports activities, soccer is popular. It is played in schools and during free time in the many fields of the West Bank. There has been little attention given to organized, professional sporting events. An Israeli professional soccer team comprised of both Jews and Palestinians won the Israeli league championship and received much coverage. Fledgling Palestinian athletics and the struggle to succeed under dire circumstances have become topics of several documentary films.

17 ENTERTAINMENT AND RECREATION

Informal street-side games of soccer are a popular form of recreation among Palestinians. They also enjoy listening to poetry and music and playing the very popular Middle Eastern version of backgammon. Men smoke the *narghila*, or water-pipe (like a hookah) at corner cafés and coffeehouses. Only men go to coffeehouses, where they socialize, make business deals, and play cards and backgammon.

Children play hopscotch, jump rope, and marbles on the sidewalks. Families take evening walks, especially during the month of Ramadan after breaking the fast at sundown. There are outdoor parks, called *muntazahs,* where families order ice cream or a meal and eat outdoors.

Palestinians watch television programs broadcast from Egypt, Israel, Jordan, and sometimes Syria. One of the favorite television characters is Ghawar al-Tosheh, a Syrian comedic character who often criticizes government policies in his storylines. Popular music videos are frequently viewed by Palestinian youth along with Arab and international soccer matches. Today, satellite television is immensely popular throughout the

Palestinian territories and is watched for news, entertainment and religious programming. Several Palestinian television and radio stations now broadcast and have gained increasing popularity. On Fridays, the noon prayer is broadcast on television for Muslims.

[18] FOLK ART, CRAFTS, AND HOBBIES

Some Palestinians are skilled in the art of calligraphy, and they sketch Quranic verses and expressions in beautiful designs. Calligraphy shows are held at universities and associations, and artwork is sold for profit. Other artists draw pictures of political protest, predominantly against the occupation. One popular pastime is to memorize and recite verses of the Quran. Children begin this process at an early age, and it continues through adulthood. Women can often be seen sitting on their front porches knitting for their families, cross-stitching or embroidering the bodices for their traditional dresses, or cross-stitching items for craft shows, such as wall decors or Quranic verses. In Jerusalem, Ramallah, or Bethlehem, tourists can purchase crafts made of olive wood or ivory, two of the most common materials used by craftsmen. Jewelry boxes, crosses, scenes of the Last Supper, camels, mosques, and other items are handcrafted from olive wood and ivory.

[19] SOCIAL PROBLEMS

The main social problem for Palestinians is the war with Israel over rights to the Palestinian homeland. Palestinians are a people without a country, living at best as displaced persons and at worst as refugees in crowded camps. The war with Israel has been going on for decades, and younger generations of Palestinians have never known a time when their people were at peace. They grow up with a consciousness shaped by conflict and violence. Although the PLO and the Israeli government signed the Declaration of Principles on September 1993, and limited Palestinian self-rule began to be established in Jericho and the Gaza Strip on 18 May 1994, the agreement is opposed by extremists on both sides, and the peace that existed is very shaky. The Palestinian fight for an independent homeland, the tempo of which increased with the *intifada* (or "uprising") begun in December 1987, continues. The number of casualties has been enormous, and the problems—physical, social, psychological, and spiritual—caused by the perpetual unrest are too numerous to count. The major grievance of Palestinians is that their political and civil rights are not being upheld by the occupation. They assert that the right to self-determination, which has been affirmed by the United Nations, gives them the right to decide their own system of government and to establish statehood. A 1995 poster distributed by a Palestinian human rights organization refers to the Universal Declaration of Human Rights with the caption stating: "The Palestinians are also part of this universe."

The 1994 agreement, which gave Palestinians self-rule, soon crumbled as the Israeli counterparts refused to abide by the accord and discontinue building settlements in the West Bank and Gaza. Increasing frustration and anxiety came to a head when the Israeli candidate for prime minister, Ariel Sharon, visited the Old City of Jerusalem's Temple Mount, which is adjacent to the Dome of the Rock (Mosque) in September 2000. Palestinians revolted and protested his visit, clashes ensued, with casualties sustained by both sides. The violence escalated and spread beyond the holy sites and to other areas in the Palestinian territories. Sharon was elected as prime minister in 2001 with the agenda of controlling the Palestinians. The period that followed saw ruthless attacks, arbitrary Palestinian home demolitions, an expansion of Israeli settlements in the West Bank, an increase in targeted killing of Palestinian politicians, and the construction of the wall separating Israeli and Palestinian villages and restricting Palestinian movement. Whilst the first Intifada was called on by Palestinian leader, Yasser Arafat, it is commonly understood that the second Intifada, known as Al-Aqsa Intifada was spontaneous.

[20] GENDER ISSUES

With very large numbers of Palestinian men detained in Israeli prisons, the predicament of Palestinian women is rather complicated. They are often thought of as the symbol of Palestinian resistance and perseverance, as even the nation, Falastin, is often depicted as a woman. The burden of living under occupation is often magnified for Palestinian women, who find themselves as caregivers and breadwinners. The frequency at which they must face the death or lengthy detainment of males in the family and uncertain futures have forced many women to take on enormous responsibilities as spouses, mothers, and the sole source of income.

However, the plight of Palestinian women has not gone unnoticed. Many solidarity groups between women of Israeli and Palestinian background have sprung up in the early 2000s and have become increasingly influential, including some that resist Israeli occupation of the West Bank and Gaza, house demolitions, and violations of Palestinian rights.

Palestinian women are now becoming increasingly prominent on both the political and cultural stages. Academic, diplomat, and consummate politician, Hanan Ashrawi, has been a prominent figure of the Palestinian struggle for representation. Also, feminist, activist, and humanitarian, Samiha Khalil (known commonly as Umm Khalil), is among the notable Palestinian women of the late 20th century. A growing number of popular Palestinian women figures, including musicians, artists, and authors such as Ghada Karmi, have been influential in placing their people in the spotlight.

[21] BIBLIOGRAPHY

Ganeri, Anita. *Why We Left: I Remember Palestine*. Austin, TX: Raintree Steck-Vaughn, 1995.

Khalidi, Rashid. *The Iron Cage: The Story of the Palestinian Struggle for Statehood,* New York: Beacon Press, 2007.

———. *Palestinian Identity*. New York: Columbia University Press, 1998.

Khalidi, Walid. *Before Their Diaspora: A Photographic History Of The Palestinians 1876-1948*. Washington, D.C. : Institute for Palestine Studies, 2004

Melrod, George, ed. *Insight Guides: Israel*. Boston: Houghton Mifflin, 1994.

Sabbagh, Suha. *Palestinian Women of Gaza and the West Bank*. Bloomington: Indiana University Press, 1998.

Said, Edward W. and Mohr, Jean. *After the Last Sky: Palestinian Lives*. New York: Columbia University Press, 1998

Stannard, Dorothy, ed. *Insight Guides: Jordan*. Boston: Houghton Mifflin, 1994.

—reviewed by A. Iskandar

PAMIRI

PRONUNCIATION: pa-MIR-ee
ALTERNATE NAMES: Mountain Tajiks
LOCATION: Tajikistan
POPULATION: 150,000
LANGUAGES: East Iranian language variations; Tajik; Russian
RELIGION: Islam (Ismailism and Sunni Muslim)

¹ INTRODUCTION

The Pamiri peoples, also called the Pamirian or Mountain Tajiks (*Pamirtsy* in Russian) comprise seven ethnic groups of Tajikistan in formerly Soviet Central Asia. They go by the names of Shugnis, Rushanis, Wakhanis, Bartangis, Yazgulemis, Khufis, and Ishkashimis. Although their histories tie in to the history of the Tajiks of Afghanistan and Tajikistan, there are some unique features.

Local tradition has it that the Pamiris are descendants of Alexander the Great from his 4th century BC invasions into the remote and inaccessible Pamir mountain valleys. Pamiris have strikingly European features for people living in so remote an area of Central Asia. Reference to Shugnis and Rushanis of these high valleys shows up in Chinese chronicles by the 2nd century AD. What is also known from the archaeological and historical sources in Classical Greek and Old Persian is that ethnic groups such as the Saka and Dari, who lived in the Pamirs approximately 3,000 years ago, helped give rise to today's Pamiris. Anthropologists refer to such processes as ethnogenesis, or the birth and growth of ethnic groups.

The Pamiris have never really had their own country or lived independently of surrounding powers, although tiny independent kingdoms existed for a short period after Tibetan rule during the 8th and 9th centuries. Pamiri history is marked by conflicts over territory and scarce natural resources. Neighboring Kyrgyz have been a persistent rival. While Afghani and Uzbek rulers vied for control over the Mountainous Badakhshan region where the Pamiris lived throughout the 18th and 19th centuries, so too were these lands coveted by the Russians and the British, whose imperialistic challenges to one another were relaxed by 1905. By 1904 Russia had annexed the Pamiri lands from the Emir of Bukhara.

After three years of incessant struggle, the Pamiri lands were brought under Soviet rule and in 1925 designated the Special Pamir Province. Just a few months later, the area was redesignated the Mountainous Badakhshan Autonomous Province that was later joined to the Tajik Soviet Socialist Republic, created in 1929. From 1992 to 1997, independent Tajikistan was wracked by civil war, and the Pamiris played a major role in fighting against Kuliabi Tajiks of the Kurgan-Tiube region. Pamiris and Garmis are allies in a very complicated and violent conflict that left hundreds of thousands of people homeless, injured, and dead. The dispute concerned political power, the control of economic resources, and organized crime. In the end, the Pamiris gained little from the conflict, but from the late 1990s onward they have benefited from international aid, so while poor and struggling their cultures and identities remain fairly stable.

² LOCATION AND HOMELAND

Small numbers of Pamiris live in Afghanistan, China, and Pakistan, but the vast majority live in their autonomous enclave within Tajikistan. Overall, Pamiris number about 150,000, most of whom live in the high mountain valley of the Western Pamirs, in the southwestern part of the Badakhshan province. These mountains, known as the "Roof of the World" in Persian (*Bam-i Dunya*) are the second highest in the world after the Himalayas. Several peaks there top 7,000 m (20,000 ft). The area's climate is dry and continental: winters are long and cold, and summers short and cool. Snowfalls may block roadways as early as mid-September.

Pamiris live in close geographical proximity to one another. On the south side of their territory runs the Pyandzh River, separating them from Afghanistan. On the west the Afghanistani province of Badakhshan borders, and to the north and east is greater Tajikistan and Kyrgyzstan. Only two major roadways link the Pamiri territory to major centers, connecting Dushanbe and Osh with Mountainous Badakhshan. Few places in the entire former USSR are as remote as this.

Although these harsh lands yield little agricultural production, there is cultivation of cereals, potatoes, tobacco, and melons and squashes in the lowest valleys. Water resources are good and hydroelectric power plentiful. There are few natural resources aside from small deposits of gold, asbestos, and rich pastures for animal husbandry. Sheep, goats, cattle, and yak are the main herds.

³ LANGUAGE

The Pamiris speak East Iranian languages closely related to the modern Persian of Iran, Tajik, and Pashto/Dari (spoken by the majority of Afghanis). These languages are known as the Galcha group. Close relations and geographical nearness aside, most of these languages are mutually incomprehensible. Tajik and the Shugni-Rushan dialect serve as variants of a common language among the people. Yazgulemi, Wakhi, and Ishkashimi are very distinct dialects. Although attempts have been made to create alphabets for theses languages, they remain non-literary. Children learn in Tajik and Russian. Across international borders, Pamiris communicate in Persian and Dari. All of the people are multi-lingual. These modern languages display a clear connection to some of the great Iranic languages of the distant past, including Sogdian, Bactrian, and Saka, which had flourishing literary traditions.

Some examples of Tajik phrases include: *"Turo chi lozim ast?"* ("What is it that you need?"), and *"Shumo chi mekhured?"* ("What would you like to eat?").

⁴ FOLKLORE

Pamiri folklore takes the form of tales, legends, proverbs, and sayings. Heroism relating to bravery in battle and in combating nature's harsh elements commonly appears in the tales and stories. However, most concrete information about Pamiri folklore generally appears under Tajik folk culture.

⁵ RELIGION

National consciousness is strongly based on the Islam of the Pamiris. They are members of the Ismaili sect, which was accepted in the 11th century and spread through the great mystic poet Nasir-i Khoshrow. Ismailism is a secretive sect charac-

deal of feasting. People generally wear very colorful clothes on this day, or new clothes if they have them. The foods served contain the first vegetables or greens, as *Novruz* is a harbinger of the land coming back to life after a long period of dormancy. The celebratory atmosphere of Novruz usually continues for two or three days after the initial celebrations.

"First Furrow" marks the beginning of the planting season. People address the saint of farming, known as *Bobo-m-Dekh-tona* ("Grandpa Farmer"). A public feast is held, and people commemorate the origins of irrigation. Another public holiday marks the time in early summer when women take flocks out to be pastured.

⁷RITES OF PASSAGE

Rites of passage include parties for the circumcision of little boys, and women celebrate a girl's first menstrual period. Other rites include marriages and those marking death. Unfortunately, none of these rites are well documented in the scant literature available about the Pamiris. Specific rites of passage for the Pamiris appear to be similar to those of the Tajiks and the peoples of Afghanistan.

⁸INTERPERSONAL RELATIONS

"Assalomu alaikum!" is the standard way of saying hello. After that, people proceed to ask one another about their families and their work. Surprise or pleasure in eating may be expressed by lolling one's head from side to side. If told of something unexpected or strange, people are likely to let out a high-pitched "Uhhhhhhhh!". Use of the hands to emphasize and be descriptive is also common. One favorite gesture that all Central Asians use is moving a cupped hand back and forth across the mouth. This signifies going for something to eat.

Spending time with extended family and friends who live nearby is very common as is visiting relatives who have moved away from Badakhshan. Young people do not date, as this would be considered immoral behavior. However, young people may meet clandestinely while out working in the fields or doing chores on behalf of their families. Intimacy between the young is reserved for marriage.

⁹LIVING CONDITIONS

As in so many other parts of the former USSR, declining health standards prevail. The overall decline in the economy coupled with the Tajik civil war made it much harder for people to find good foodstuffs, medicines, or medical treatment, although this has taken a gradual turn for the better since about 2000. Basic health care is now provided by relief agencies such as the International Red Cross/ Red Crescent, the Aga Khan Foundation, and the France-based *Medecins Sans Frontiers* (Doctors Without Borders). Under Soviet rule, all public health care was free of charge. Diseases and illnesses of the past, such as leprosy, trachoma, syphilis, and typhus were eradicated after World War II. Opium smoking was also common and created very debilitating conditions. Indications are that some Pamiris have become addicted to opium once again.

Consumer goods have greatly improved Pamiri life, especially with regard to food, since variety has been introduced to the traditional diet. All sorts of housewares and clothing also became available through the Soviet state stores, but this development has since been reversed.

terized by the divine worship of Ali, who was the son-in-law of the prophet Muhammad. Ali is believed to be Muhammad's divinely inspired successor. Although closely related to Shi'ism, Ismailism broke with mainstream Shi'ism in the 8th century AD. Pamiris do not believe in the need for mosques or clergymen, but there are rather informal houses of prayer and de facto, wandering holy men. These people maintain contact with the principal Ismaili center in the world, located in India, whose spiritual leader is the Aga Khan. Most Bartangis and Yazgulemis practice Sunni Islam (through their contact with the Bukharan Emirate), which predominates throughout the world.

Many traditional Pamiri beliefs and rituals relate to agriculture and the herds. All sorts of prohibitions and practices determine when planting and watering may be done and what will lead to the best conditions for agricultural success. Rituals connected with the threshing of grain ensure that people will be full and satisfied with the bread baked from the grain. A scarecrow symbolizing an ancient deity helps purify the area near the piles of wheat while people pour sweets atop the pile and burn sacred grasses around its perimeter. Once the flour is finally made and the first loaf baked, everyone from a given family partakes until they say *"bas"* ("enough"). The bread from the first piles of newly threshed grain is known as *basik*.

⁶MAJOR HOLIDAYS

Pamiris celebrate *Novruz*, which falls on the vernal equinox (around March 21) and marks the beginning of the Persian new year. *Novruz* is celebrated with music, dances, and a great

Most Pamiri villages exist at the triangle of a river delta. Main houses are not arranged on streets, but rather stand amid the agricultural fields and orchards. Doors to houses and other farm buildings open inward toward an interior courtyard. From outside the settlement complex, only bare walls are visible. Ordinarily, the inner courtyards contain small gardens and apricot and mulberry trees.

Most homes are made of unworked stone with wooden roofs. Stone workers use clay to cement pieces together. Walls are made either from stone or from the clay from loess soils, which men mold into bricks for the wall construction. The roofs are put together with boards and beams. From outside, the roof appears as a layered vault, and from within it forms a stepped ceiling. The central beam in the house, the most important roof support, is known as the *shashtan*. It is carved and decorated, and plays a role in people's spiritual lives. Upon entering an empty house, one pays respects to the *shashtan*.

One room of a house contains alcoves in which these people eat, sleep, and receive guests when the weather turns cold. Today Pamiri homes always have well-equipped guest rooms with rugs, quilts, furniture, and often a television or radio. Wall niches often serve as a place for drawers, dishes, or knick-knacks.

The standard of living for all Tajiks has decreased markedly since the advent of the civil war, and conditions for the Pamiris would certainly have been even worse over the past few years had it not been for international relief.

10 FAMILY LIFE

Pamiri women traditionally enjoy fewer restrictions than is true of Tajik women. They participate in public gatherings on a par with men and work both outside and inside the home. They never wore veils, nor were they ever relegated to a particular part of their houses. Still, their work in the household is arduous. Among their specialties are pottery (made without potter's wheels) and all aspects of milking and milk product preparation.

In a typical Pamiri living arrangement, several patrilineal extended families would live together and cooperate economically. Often all married sons and their families would live in their father's house. Pamiris traditionally married a first or second cross or parallel cousin of either the father's or mother's lineage. The mother's brother is considered more closely related than the father's, and plays a major role in arranging marriages and helping his nephews and nieces if they encounter hardships. One Yazgulemi saying states: "Wherever you find an uncle on your mother's side, you don't need one from your father's."

Marriages today are increasingly based on Quranic law. Members of the patrilineal group provide all sorts of gifts to ensure an easy start for the newlyweds. Most young women do not marry before the age of 18. Weddings are always accompanied by huge parties.

Pets are not kept, and even shepherds have no dogs to help them protect their flocks from wolves.

11 CLOTHING

Pamiri clothes today are Western in style for the most part. Headwear is important to both men and women. Men are distinguished by Central Asian skullcaps (*toki*), around which are often wrapped thin wool turbans, or by Russian-style fur or woolen hats, depending upon the season. Women wear either light or heavy woolen kerchiefs and shawls. Summertime kerchiefs are either all white or full of sparkling gold thread. Historically, most clothing was made from rough-hewn cotton or hemp, but some elite Pamiris wore white silk.

In warm weather, farming men typically wore a *kurta iaktagi* (a loose open-necked white shirt) and *tambun* (baggy trousers). In slightly cooler weather, a light woolen robe (*gilim*) was added. Younger men often wore an Afghani-style vest known as a *voskat*, around which a belt (*miend*) was affixed. Boots of wool and leather were handcrafted, as were wooden galoshes for wet and snowy weather. Both men and women wore these.

Women's garments were also quite simple, consisting of woolen, shirt-like dresses with tunic-like outer robes. Women's pants, *sharovari*, were narrower than men's. Although they also wore shawls as head wraps, they apparently never had heavy winter outer garments. Women adorned themselves with jewelry made from animal antlers, along with bronze bracelets and earrings. They braided their hair and kept their braids in different positions and at different lengths depending on their age and the number of children they had.

12 FOOD

Until the mid-20th century, bread was literally the staff of life in the Pamiri diet, and people ground whatever grain or legume was available for bread, including peas, millet, and wheat. Pamiris also ate noodle dishes with occasional pieces of mutton, beef, or yak meat added. Milk products were common in the form of sour cream and butter from cows and yaks. In the lower valleys, some squashes and melons have been cultivated. Salt and tea were relatively unknown until the recent past. During the Soviet period, potatoes and cabbage were added to the Pamiri crop repertoire, and these nutritious foods greatly enhanced local diets. The Soviet administration also introduced canned and fresh goods that were regularly delivered to state stores.

For feasts and holidays, the main culinary specialty is boiled meat, which people tend to eat in large quantities because they dine on it so rarely. Meat and other dishes are ordinarily consumed with one's fingers, but soups or porridges made from peas or mung beans are eaten with spoons or pieces of bread. In the late summer and early fall, fruits such as apricots and plums, along with walnuts and almonds, are available. A typical breakfast includes bread, butter, and tea with perhaps occasional honey, because some small apiaries are kept.

Today, Tajik foods are a regular part of the Pamiri diet. Following is a recipe for a typical Tajik dish, "Beef and Peas":

Cut beef into large pieces and place in a pot. Add water and bring to a boil. Then add chopped onion and pre-soaked peas. Let all of these boil till cooked. Ten minutes before turning off the flame add salt and spices. Serve the peas piled atop the meat, and add green onions and red pepper. Serve a bullion separately.

13 EDUCATION

Most children finish high school, but very few go on to university or technical schools unless they leave Mountainous Badakhshan. Those who do attend university must move to Dushanbe, the Tajik capital. Although parents encourage both boys and girls to finish their required education, they do not necessarily encourage university training as it has little bearing on Badakhshani existence. Recently, the Aga Khan Foundation, an international Ismaili relief organization, laid plans to build the "University of the Mountains" in Central Asia, and they plan to build the first affiliate in Khorog, which is the regional capital of Badakhshan province (Gorno-Badakhshan) in Tajikistan; this university would be a huge boost for higher education among the Pamiri peoples. Nearly everyone is able to read and write Tajik, but a far smaller percentage know Russian well. What Russian they do know is from contact with television and radio.

¹⁴CULTURAL HERITAGE

Singing accounts for the bulk of Pamiri musical culture. Several types of poetical songs are popular among the Pamiris, including the *lalaik* and *duduvik*. Recently renowned Bakakhshani instrumental and vocal ensembles have toured the world, especially the United States. The *zhurni* is a common kind of comic love song among the Shugnis. Pantomime dances accompanied by music, and *bobopirak* satirical dances take place from time to time. The most common instrument is the guitar-like *rubob*. Literature does not exist per se, but storytelling is a common pastime.

¹⁵WORK

Pamiri work is dominated by collectivized agricultural chores, and there are few tasks that are solely the domain of either men or women. One notable exception is that only women shear sheep, whereas only men shear goats. Women also tend to all of the milking, whereas men act as the shepherds, even though women initially take the animals out to pasture.

During the warmer months, Pamiris practice vertical transhumance—that is, they move their flocks up and down the mountains in accordance with weather conditions and the availability of grasses for their animals. Choice of crops depends very much on the elevation of a particular valley. The lower the elevation, the greater the variety of crops. The few non-agricultural jobs that do exist relate to town life and transportation. Some men and women work in clerical and administrative professions and some as gold miners, power-plant workers, and as long-distance truckers.

The elaborate systems for much of the terraced agriculture that is practiced in the Pamirs require constant maintenance. The canals must be cleared of rocks and debris, especially after the winter thaw. Farmers must work fast after the snow has melted on their fields, and people help one another out to clear the fields of rocks as they dig up and turn the soil over twice.

¹⁶SPORTS

Soccer was introduced to the Pamiris relatively recently, along with other sports, such as basketball and volleyball. Traditionally, women play a ball game with a roll of tightly wound wool. Slingshots, tag, bow and arrow competitions, and polo are all favorites. Polo is played by two teams with up to 40 people in total, and players use long makeshift sticks and a wooden ball.

¹⁷ENTERTAINMENT AND RECREATION

A relatively small number of these isolated people own televisions, but those who do are exposed to world culture via Russian television stations. Movie theaters exist in all of the major settlements, including Khorog and Ishkashim, and these also serve to broaden people's perspective on the world "below them." Much of popular culture today is dominated by grade-B karate movies and violent American cinema.

¹⁸FOLK ART, CRAFTS, AND HOBBIES

Pamiris historically produced textiles made of wool and imported cotton. Vertical looms were employed for crafting the *palas*—a local rug. Smiths and metalworkers made decorative jewelry. Millstones were another craft item made by the Pamiris for their water-driven grain mills.

Wakhanis, Yazgulemis, and Rushanis are well-respected for their wooden containers and pots, particularly for large serving plates. Women potters make fine pottery from a unique gray clay that they strengthen by tempering with goat hair. Men create textile threads by spinning and weaving yak and goat hair, and women make heavy socks from camel and sheep hair.

¹⁹SOCIAL PROBLEMS

The Tajik civil war destroyed thousands of lives and ruined any chance for national economic growth until the early 2000s. Social problems are substantial, and the human rights situation has deteriorated greatly because Pamiris are suspected of being criminals in organized gangs. The Tajik and Russian military forces engaged in the fighting have dealt with many Pamiri communities rather severely. These communities are very loyal to one another, so they are very reluctant to report on the whereabouts or doings of any of their members. Civil rights became a casualty of war, and their full restoration requires a prolonged period of peace and development; fortunately, the signs that this is happening gradually are encouraging.

Along with organized criminal activities and links to criminal groups in Russia, social problems involving drugs and alcoholism have occurred, but this is no indictment of Pamiri society as a whole. The vast majority of the Pamiri population is poor and in desperate need of international food relief, medicines, jobs, and reconstruction. This area was always one of the most impoverished in the USSR, and the outlook for the near future shows that improvements will be incremental but significant. It will be possible that the survival of these remote peoples and languages has some chance, but most depends on the decisions that young people make, either staying in Badakhshan or moving to other parts of Central Asia and Russia.

Tajikistan has experienced a labor migration that includes 10-12% of its overall population, and the Pamiris must be included in these ranks. While people have enjoyed international aid, cultural preservation projects, and development work, they still are impoverished, and this is why many young men and women have taken to traveling to Russia in the main, to try to make better lives for themselves. Many Tajik citizens are now settling permanently in Russia, too.

²⁰GENDER ISSUES

Pamiri people show few gendered differences from many other Central Asian peoples, although men and women tend to keep less of a separation from one another in social affairs, than say, Uzbeks, Tajiks, and Turkmen. Owing to the nature of Pamiri dwellings, men and women actually share the same living and sleeping spaces. Their sex segregation in this sense is rather exceptional compared to most other Central Asian peoples.

Culturally, men and women have a division of labor around the home, with women being responsible for most domestic chores, as well as many of those dealing with agricultural work.

Pamiri girls are encouraged to get basic grammar schooling, but usually not much beyond this. Of course, it tends to be similar for boys.

As mentioned above, many Pamiris have joined the ranks of other Tajik labor migrants, but little accurate data seems to be available on just how many Pamiris work abroad, and what the overall effects have been on Pamiri linguistic, social, and economic life. This is an area that needs to be watched.

21 BIBLIOGRAPHY

"Endangered Pamiris." *Neweurasia.net*, http://tajikistan.neweurasia.net/2007/10/18/endangered-pamiris/ (May 2008).

Friedrich, Paul, and Norma Diamond, ed. *Encyclopedia of World Cultures*. Vol. VI, Russia and Eurasia/China. Boston: G. K. Hall, 1994.

Olson, James S., ed. *An Ethnohistorical Dictionary of the Russian and Soviet Empires*. Westport, CT: Greenwood Press, 1994.

Tolstov, S. P., ed. *Narody Srednei Azii i Kazakhstana I* (The Peoples of Central Asia and Kazakhstan, Vol. I). Moscow: Izdatel'stvo Akademii Nauk, 1962.

—by R. Zanca

PARSIS

PRONUNCIATION: PAHR-seez
ALTERNATE NAMES: Parsees; Farsis
LOCATION: India (mainly Bombay); Pakistan
POPULATION: 69,601
LANGUAGE: Gujarati; English
RELIGION: Zoroastrianism
RELATED ARTICLES: Vol. 3: People of India

1 INTRODUCTION

Parsi (Parsee) is the name by which Zoroastrians in South Asia are known. Zoroastrians are followers of an ancient Persian religion founded in the 7th century BC by Zarathusthra (Zoroaster). The word "Parsi" means "a man from Pars," or Persia, and refers to the fact that the Parsis emigrated to the Indian subcontinent from Persia (Iran), where Zoroastrianism was the established religion. The Parsi community in India is also known as "Farsi," Fars being another name for the area from which they originated.

In the 7th century AD, the homeland of the Parsis was overrun by Arabs, who compelled the defeated Persians to accept the Islamic religion or face extinction. Tradition has it that a small band of Zoroastrians, faithful to their religion, fled into the mountains of Khorasan for safety. After a century or more, still facing persecution, they eventually made their way south to the island of Hormuz in the Persian Gulf. From there, they pressed on eastwards to India. After stopping for two decades at Diu, a port on the Kathiawar Peninsula, they continued to the coast of Gujarat in western India. Parsi tradition gives the date of their arrival as AD 936 (this is subject to debate, some claiming AD 716 as the year the Parsis arrived in India).

The Parsis petitioned the local Hindu ruler for permission to stay, and this was granted subject to certain conditions. These included the Parsis adopting the customs and language (Gujarati) of the country, renouncing the carrying of arms, conforming to Hindu marriage practices, and respecting Hindu sentiments concerning the slaughter of cows. The Parsis agreed to these terms and founded a settlement near the coast where they had landed, about 160 km (100 mi) north of Bombay. They named their new home Sanjan, after their hometown in Persia. The story of the Parsis' migration to India is found in the *Kisseh-e-Sanjan*, a narrative poem dated to around AD 1600.

2 LOCATION AND HOMELAND

Parsis in South Asia are a small community, numbering 69,601 people according to the 2001 Census of India. The original settlers at Sanjan were farmers, and though they soon migrated to nearby Navsari and Surat, they remained essentially in rural occupations. With the arrival of the Europeans, however, the Parsis began to assume the role of intermediary agents and brokers, laying the groundwork for their later rise to prominence in the business world. Today, the community is almost exclusively urban, concentrated mainly in the city of Bombay. Lesser numbers are found in the cities of Gujarat State, while some 5,000 Parsis live in Pakistan (mostly in Karachi). Tata and Godrej, two of India's biggest business families, are Parsis.

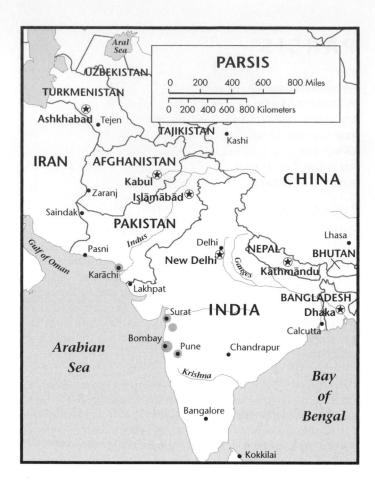

³LANGUAGE

The original Zoroastrians who settled in India spoke Farsi (Persian)—from which the name Parsi is derived. But most Parsis speak Gujarati, the language of their adopted homeland, although most are bilingual and also speak fluent English. Many Bombayites switch between languages, often employing a mish-mash of Hindi/Urdu, Marathi, Gujarati and English called "Bambaiya," but Gujarati and English remain the dominant languages used by the Parsis. In Pakistan, Gujarati has been replaced by Urdu as the language in which Parsis carry out their daily business. Religious ceremonies are performed in Avestan, the language of the Zoroastrian scriptures. Some secondary literature is written in Pahlavi or Middle Persian, the official state language of the Persians during the 4th century AD.

⁴FOLKLORE

The religion of the Parsis has its roots in the beliefs of the Indo-European peoples. As a result, many similarities are found in the mythologies of Zoroastrianism and the Vedic religion of northern India. Both traditions, for example, make a distinction between the "heavenly" gods (*daevas* or *devas*) and those that possess special occult powers (*ahuras* or *asuras*). In India, the devas later entered the pantheon of Hindu gods while the asuras were reduced to the rank of demons. In Iran, however, it was the ahuras (literally "Lords") who were revered as gods and the daevas who were viewed as evil. One particular ahura, Mazda or the "Lord of Wisdom," was eventually elevated to the position of the supreme deity in Zoroastrianism.

The similarities between the ancient Iranians and Indians extend also to their heroes and legends. For instance, the Yama Raja of the *Vedas* becomes Yima Khshaeta (Jamshed) of the *Avesta*, the Zoroastrian sacred texts. In the Iranian tradition, Yima was a king of the golden age and happy ruler of the Iranian tribes. Many of the myths and legends of the Zoroastrians are to be found in the *Shahnamah* of the poet Firdausi.

⁵RELIGION

In many aspects, the ancient religion of Iran resembled that of the early Vedas of northern India. This in itself is not surprising, since the peoples who inhabited the two regions were closely related. They were probably descended from a common ancestral race, they both spoke Aryan tongues, and their sacred books showed many parallels in religious beliefs and practices. These included polytheism, worship of the same gods (the Iranian god Mithra, for instance, is the Indian Mitra), the cult of fire, and the *hoama* sacrifice (*soma* in India). The subsequent development of religion in each area, however, was different. The Vedic religion ultimately evolved into Hinduism, the complex religious, social, and economic system that numbers close to 800 million people among its followers. In Iran, religious beliefs and practices were reformed by Zoroaster. Zoroastrianism rose to become the state religion of three great Persian Empires, but today there are less than 200,000 members of the religion spread throughout the world.

Zoroaster was born in northeastern Persia. His dates are given as 628–551 BC, although some scholars argue he may have lived as many as eight centuries earlier. He is known to us from the *Gathas*, 17 hymns composed by Zoroaster and faithfully handed down through the generations by his followers. These were not works of instruction but rather inspired poetic utterances, many addressed directly to God, attempting to express a personal understanding of the divine. The Gathas and a few other ancient texts in the same language are collectively known as the Avesta, the Zoroastrian scriptures.

The Gathas themselves reveal that Zoroaster was trained as a priest, well versed in the rituals, doctrines, and religious practices of the time. Tradition holds that he spent years in a quest for truth. During his wanderings he witnessed much of the violent conflict typical of northeastern Persia in that era, with fierce nomadic bands from the steppes pillaging and slaughtering peaceful farming communities. As a result of this, he developed a deep longing for justice, for the moral law of the ahuras (gods) to bring peace to weak and strong alike. Eventually, at the age of 30, he was at a gathering to celebrate a spring festival. He had a vision on the banks of a river, a shining Being who led him into the presence of the god Ahura Mazda and five other radiant figures. It was from these seven Beings (the heptad) that Zoroaster received his revelation, namely that he was chosen to serve Ahura Mazda. He wholeheartedly obeyed this call and set out on the path that was to give the world a new religion.

Though rooted in the ancient Persian religion, Zoroaster's teachings were fundamentally new. He proclaimed, for example, that Ahura Mazda (one of many ahuras worshipped by the Persians) was the one uncreated God, who was the Creator of all things good, even other divinities. Coexisting with Ahura Mazda (later known as Ohrmazd) was another primal Being, Angra Mainyu (Ahriman), the source of all evil. The world is thus a battleground between Good and Evil. Ahura Mazda evoked six lesser divinities to aid him in this struggle, and together they form the heptad of Zoroaster's revelation. Each of the heptad is responsible for one of the seven creations, including humans. Although humans are the chief creation, they are linked to all other creations, and even to the gods, through their ultimate purpose—the defeat of Evil.

Zoroaster's teachings concerning death also represented a departure from the old religion. According to Zoroaster, at the time of death the individual soul is judged on its ethical achievements. Mithra and a tribunal of gods wait at the Chinvat Bridge that separates this world from the next. Depending on the balance of good and evil deeds performed in life, the soul enters Paradise, Purgatory, or Hell. There it awaits the coming of a Savior who will undertake the resurrection of the dead and a Last Judgment. At this time, all the metal in the mountains will be melted into a glowing river through which all humankind must pass. The good will survive and live forever, but the evil will perish. The demons and their legions of darkness will already have been defeated in a last great battle with the forces of Good. The molten river will flow into Hell and destroy Angra Mainyu, thus removing the last vestige of Evil in the universe.

Zoroaster was the first to teach that the individual would be judged on the basis of his or her deeds, that there is a Heaven and Hell, that a future Savior will resurrect the dead for a final Judgment Day, and that the pure at heart will have life everlasting. These doctrines, monotheism, and the dualism (i.e., the coexistence of Good and Evil) found in Zoroastrianism are now fundamental to the beliefs of many peoples in the world. They spread from Persia to influence Judaism and were inherited from Judaism by Christianity and Islam.

If Zoroaster's teachings were new, many of the devotional forms and practices of his faith were adapted from the old religion. The Zoroastrian reverence for fire, for instance, seems to have its origins in a much older cult of fire prevalent among the Indo-European ancestors of the Persians. It was also, apparently, the custom among these groups for men to wear a cord on their initiation into the religious community. Even today, the upper castes of India wear the "sacred thread" as a sign of their status. Zoroaster appears to have modified this practice: all Zoroastrians, both men and women, wear a sacred cord wrapped around the waist three times as a symbol of their faith. Similarly, whereas the local custom was to pray three times a day, Zoroaster required his followers to pray five times a day. The method of prayer seems to have changed little over the centuries. Believers prepare themselves by ritually washing their hands, face, and feet; they untie the cord from their waist and stand, holding it in both hands, staring into the sacred fire. They pray to Ahura Mazda, they denounce Angra Mainyu while at the same time contemptuously flicking the ends of the cord, and then retie the cord around the waist. Regular prayer is an integral part of humanity's fight against Evil in the world. Zoroaster also made it binding that his followers celebrate the seven feasts of obligation that are the major events of the community's religious calendar.

In its early years, it seems Zoroastrianism had no temples or places of worship. By the 4th century BC, however, the fire temple had emerged as a center of Zoroastrian ritual. All Zoroastrians maintained a sacred hearth fire at home, but now the fire temple became a symbol of the community. The oldest fire temple in South Asia was established at Sanjan, the first Parsi settlement in India. Soon after their arrival, the inhabitants sent back to Persia for ashes from their original fire temple and the necessary ritual objects to consecrate a new one. This remained the sole Parsi fire temple in South Asia for around 800 years. It contained the most sacred (Atash Behram) of three categories of fires in Parsi temples. Today, there are some 35 fire temples (called agiyari) around Bombay, but only 4 have the Atash Behram. Parsi temples are tended by hereditary clergy, divided into high priests (dasturs) and those of lesser rank (mobeds). Non-Parsis are not allowed to enter the fire temples.

⁶MAJOR HOLIDAYS

The principal Parsi festivals are the six seasonal festivals known as Gahambars. Tradition ascribes their origin to Zoroaster, but they appear to be earlier agricultural celebrations he redefined as part of the new faith. They occur irregularly through the year and are: Midspring; Midsummer; Feast of Bringing in the Corn; Feast of the Homecoming, i.e., of the herds from pasture; Midwinter; and a feast honoring Ahura Mazda celebrated the night before the spring equinox.

Each festival lasts for five days and is an occasion for congregational worship dedicated to Ahura Mazda. Religious services are held early in the day and are followed by assemblies devoted to feasting, fellowship, and general goodwill. Rich and poor gather together, quarrels are resolved, and friendships are renewed and strengthened. This is a time for strengthening the ties that bind the Parsi community.

The six Gahambar festivals celebrate one of the creations of the gods (the heavens, water, the earth, plants, animals, and humans), but the seventh creation, fire, stands apart. As the life-force of all creation, fire is honored at the most joyous of the Zoroastrian festivals, Noruz. Literally "New Day," Noruz falls on the spring equinox and marks the beginning of the Zoroastrian New Year. At noon on this day, Rapithwina, the spirit of noon who retreated into the earth during the dark days of winter, emerges to usher warmth and light into the world.

Together, the Gahambars and Noruz make up the seven high feasts of obligation whose observance was enjoined on his followers by Zoroaster. Mehragan, the festival dedicated to Mithra, is also an important occasion. Among the Parsis, jashans are celebrations of important events (both happy and tragic) observed by prayers and a sacramental meal.

⁷RITES OF PASSAGE

The birth of a child is a joyous event in a Parsi household. No particular rites are observed during pregnancy, but at birth a lamp is lit in the room where mother and baby are confined, to ward off demons. The newborn child is given a first drink of consecrated haoma juice (nowadays pomegranate juice), a symbol of immortality. When named, a Parsi child is given three names. The first is the personal name; the second, the father's name, and the third, the family name. Male names end in "ji" (from the Avestan "to live") and female names end in "Bai."

At the age of about 6, a Parsi child begins to prepare for the important Naojot ceremony. This is of special significance because it marks initiation into the religious community. In Iran it is performed around 15 years of age, but Parsis hold the ceremony when the boy or girl is around 7. Like all Parsi rituals, the ceremony is performed in the presence of the sacred fire, upon which sandalwood and incense are burned. At this

A Parsi woman and her child at a fire temple on Parsi New Year in Ahmadabad, India. Parsis are descendents of Persian Zoroastrians who migrated to the Indian subcontinent over 1,000 years ago. (AP Images/Ajit Solanki)

time, the child receives the sacred symbols of Zoroastrianism, the *sedrah* and the *kasti,* which must be worn at all times. The sedrah is a shirt made of white muslin that represents the garment made of light worn by Ahura Mazda. Sewn into the neckline is a small pocket, a reminder to the wearer that he or she should be continually filling it with good thoughts and deeds. The kasti is the sacred cord, a hollow tube made of natural wool that is wrapped around the waist over the shirt. It has 72 threads and ends in several tassels, the numbers of each having specific religious significance. The kasti is untied and retied as part of the daily prayer ritual, before meals, and after performing bodily functions.

Parsi death rituals are quite unlike those of any other group in South Asia. After death, a dog is brought to view the corpse. It is preferable that the dog be "four-eyed," i.e., having spots over each eye. In ancient times, it was believed that the glance of a dog would scare away any demons or evil spirits that might be hovering near the body, and the extra "eyes" increase the effectiveness of its look. Later tradition has it that the presence of a dog will ease the passing of the soul to heaven. By contrast, Hindus and Muslims in South Asia regard the dog as unclean. The rite is repeated five times a day, and after the first time, fire

is brought into the room and kept burning until three days after the corpse is removed.

The dead are placed in Towers of Silence *(dakhma).* These are usually built on a hill, and the interior consists of three concentric circles, one each for men, women, and children. Corpses are exposed naked in the Towers where they are rapidly consumed by vultures. Within an hour or so, the flesh has been stripped from the body, leaving only the bones. After several days, the bones are swept into a central well filled with sand and charcoal. It is believed that the charcoal protects the earth from the pollution of death. Various ceremonies are performed during the next three days. The morning of the fourth day is of particular significance because this is the time of the soul's final departure to the other world.

8 INTERPERSONAL RELATIONS

The Parsi code of conduct may be summarized by the phrase, "Good thought, good words, good deeds." Living proof of this is seen in the strong tradition of philanthropy found in the community. This includes not only the support and endowment of schools, hospital and charitable institutions, but also a concern for the welfare of the less fortunate members of the Parsi community.

⁹LIVING CONDITIONS

Parsis have a reputation for prosperity, and indeed they count some of the wealthiest Indians among their numbers. They are a highly-educated, urbanized, Westernized group, who enjoy the high standards of living and consumerism that go along with their social and economic status. They live almost exclusively in Parsi housing estates. There are, however, many Parsis who are not so successful and are supported by charitable contributions from their community. In Bombay, for instance, there are numerous tenements and apartments operated by Parsi-established trusts for low-income and indigent Parsis.

¹⁰FAMILY LIFE

Parsis are an endogamous group, and in such a small community it is not surprising that marriages with close relatives (e.g., cross-cousin and parallel-cousin marriages) are permitted. Some marriage rites, such as the tying together of the bride's and groom's hands and the recitation of Sanskrit prayers, are clearly borrowings from Hinduism. The ceremony concludes with a visit to the fire temple to pay homage to the sacred fire. Divorce is permitted.

Today, Parsi households are generally based on the nuclear family, although in the past the extended family was the norm. The problem of a low birthrate and declining population means that many elderly Parsis live alone. However, wealthy Parsis have endowed several secular charities and given their community free housing, education, health care, and religious infrastructure worth more than $500 million as of 2008.

¹¹CLOTHING

During much of their residence in South Asia, Parsis wore the dress of their Gujarati neighbors, though with small differences that distinguished them from Hindus. For instance, women who wore the *sārī* also covered their hair with a small cloth underneath the *sārī*. Today, the Parsi community is one of the most Westernized in all of South Asia, and Western dress is the norm. Priests wear white robes, white turbans, and a mask while performing rituals, and men generally wear white for religious purposes.

¹²FOOD

There are few food restrictions in Parsi culture, though some Hindu customs, such as the prohibition on beef, have been adopted voluntarily. Parsi food blends Persian, Gujarati, and Western influences to create a distinctive cuisine. From Persia comes the tradition of combining meat with dried fruits and a fondness for eggs. Two typical Parsi dishes are *Bharuchi akuri* and *dhansakh*. The former is a dish in which eggs are baked on a layer of herbs, with added ingredients, such as potatoes, tomatoes, almonds, raisins, cream, and butter. Dhansakh is a kind of stew made with at least three kinds of lentils, meat, and vegetables.

The Parsi wedding banquet is a veritable feast. It starts with drinks (men like whiskey, while women tend to stay with wine and soft drinks) and continues with course after course of delicious Parsi-style food. A fish dish, usually made from pomfret, is always served at weddings—fish is considered a symbol of good fortune. Potato sticks and sweets are particular favorites.

¹³EDUCATION

Parsis are highly educated, with literacy rates reaching 90% in the community. Literacy among females marginally exceeds that among males, a situation unique among the peoples of South Asia. Both girls and boys are encouraged to pursue higher education in preparation for their careers. Parsis recognized the value of Western education at an early date, and many have earned degrees and advanced degrees in professions such as medicine, law, and engineering. Parsis also supported their own schools, until sectarian education was abolished by the Indian government in the 1950s.

¹⁴CULTURAL HERITAGE

There are no artistic or cultural traditions associated specifically with the Parsi community. Individual Parsis have made contributions to Gujarati literature and theater and have also written in the English language. In keeping with their Westernized outlook, many have become involved in modern art and classical music. The world renowned conductor, Zubin Mehta, for example, was born in 1936 into a Parsi family in Bombay. He is the son of Mehli and Tehmina Mehta, Mehli being a violinist and founding conductor of the Bombay Symphony Orchestra. Following a stellar career as an international conductor, Mehta was named "Honorary Conductor" by several of the world's major symphony orchestras, including the Vienna Philharmonic, Munich Philharmonic, and Los Angeles Philharmonic Orchestras.

Rohinton Mistry, who as of 2008 lived in Canada and is considered one of the foremost authors of Indian heritage writing in English, was born into the Parsi community in Bombay. Several of Mistry's novels, which tend to deal with the Parsi community in India, have been short-listed for the prestigious Man Booker Prize.

¹⁵WORK

Unlike Hindus, Parsis are under no religious constraints in terms of their economic activities. This, combined with their openness to Western education, permitted them to enter the modern professions that emerged during the 19th century. Parsis achieved great success in business, engineering, trade, finance, and similar occupations. The Tata family built perhaps the most important private industrial empire in India during the late 19th and 20th centuries. Tata Iron and Steel has formed the backbone of Indian heavy industry for nearly a century, while almost every gaily-decorated, overloaded truck that plies India's roads today carries the Tata name. The Wadias and the Petits were other important industrial families. Dadabhoy Naoroji (1825–1917) was a leading Indian politician of his day. Sir Jamsetji Jejheebhoy, a noted 19th-century philanthropist, made his fortune in the China trade. Other Parsis who have achieved a degree of fame include Dr. Homi Sethna, the nuclear physicist; Field Marshal Sam Manekshaw, chief of staff of the Indian Army from 1969 to 1972; and the internationally renowned classical musician and conductor, Zubin Mehta.

¹⁶SPORTS

There are no sports linked specifically to the Parsi community, although Parsis readily took to all forms of sports introduced to South Asia by the British. For a community of its size, the Parsis produced a large number of outstanding Indian Test (international) cricketers, including Polly Umrigar and Nari Contractor. In recent years, Parsis in Karachi have made a name for themselves in international yachting competitions.

¹⁷ENTERTAINMENT AND RECREATION

As a highly Westernized, urbanized group, Parsis have full access to the modern entertainment and recreational facilities of Bombay and the other cities where they reside.

¹⁸FOLK ART, CRAFTS, AND HOBBIES

There are no particular folk arts or crafts associated with the Parsi community in South Asia.

¹⁹SOCIAL PROBLEMS

The Parsis, a small band of Zoroastrians fleeing Muslim persecution, brought their religion to South Asia over a millennium ago. For over 1,000 years, they have managed to preserve their identity, resisting the all-embracing reach of Hinduism and the coming of Islam to South Asia. Yet today, the Parsis are facing a very real threat to their existence—declining numbers. It is estimated that only 99 Parsis were born in the year ending August 2007, and the Zoroastrian population in India is expected to fall to 25,000 by 2020.

"'We must become more broad-minded," said a reformist priest in Bombay, "we must welcome children of mixed parents and maybe even some new converts into our community." With the faith losing thousands of would-be members, some priests have started performing the *navjote*, an initiation ceremony for children born of Zoroastrian mothers and non-Zoroastrian fathers. Conservatives reacted fiercely. A coterie of powerful priests called for the excommunication of all Zoroastrians married to non-Zoroastrians. Although the priests backed off their stand after its legality and practicality were questioned, the episode emphasized the chasm within the community and some conservatives still cut their ties with family members who marry outside the faith. "Purity is more important than numbers," said a Zoroastrian scholar in Bombay. "Our religion is interwoven with our ethnicity [and] can only be passed on through a Zoroastrian father."

Thus, declining numbers are caused by several factors. At some stage in their stay in India (possibly at the very beginning), Parsis stopped actively seeking converts to their religion. In a sense, this brought the Parsis closer to Hindu traditions, and in some ways Parsis function very much like a caste in Indian society. Parsi women, however, have an equality with men rarely seen in South Asian society, but this is a double-edged sword. Their involvement in higher education and careers leads to later marriage and lower fertility rates. Furthermore, if a Parsi woman marries outside the religion she and her offspring are excluded from the Parsi community. Since the mid-20th century, the Parsi population in South Asia has been decreasing at about 1% per year. With declining economic opportunities, especially after the departure of the British from South Asia, there has been emigration to the United States, Canada, and Britain, further reducing numbers.

There are also other problems facing the Parsi community in South Asia. The sons of priests no longer follow in the footsteps of their fathers, seeking better-paying jobs elsewhere. The advent of electricity means that the sacred fire no longer burns in the hearths of many Parsi households. With the "golden age" of Parsi prosperity in the past, increasing poverty is found in the Parsi community. Young Parsis are asking, "Who is the Parsi?" as well as questioning the traditions of the past. Finally, above all, there is the matter of declining numbers. Should current trends continue, the Parsi community in South Asia may eventually disappear entirely.

The situation is best summarized in the words of one writer discussing the Parsis who have emigrated to the West: "Parsis have found themselves increasingly called upon to articulate their religious faith and practice intellectually in order to explain it to others. A sense of the need for the maintenance of tradition through adaptive change, including the admission of non-Zoroastrian spouses to membership and certainly a sophisticated presentation of Zoroastrian faith and practice, is one of the recent contributions of the overseas Parsis. With them may lie the chapters of Parsi history still to be written." (Oxtoby 1987: 201).

²⁰GENDER ISSUES

Many Parsi women claim that, despite the activities of reformist priests, the one change that could stem the decline in population will never come. When men marry outside the community, their children are considered to be Parsi. But the children of women who enter mixed marriages cannot be considered Parsi. Other than this, Parsi women are highly educated, have a high literacy rate, and are generally treated as equal to men (as far as this is possible in South Asia). Many have emigrated to the West, where they have been highly successful in their chosen careers.

²¹BIBLIOGRAPHY

Boyce, Mary. *Zoroastrians: Their Religious Beliefs and Practices*. London and New York: Routledge & Kegan Paul, 2001.

Luhrmann, Tanya M. *The Good Parsi: The Fate of a Colonial Elite in a Postcolonial Society*. Cambridge, MA.: Harvard University Press: 1996.

Modi, Jivanji Jamshedji. *The Religious Ceremonies and Customs of the Parsees*. Bombay: Jehangir B. Karani's Sons, 1937.

Oxtoby, Willard G. "Parsis." In *Encyclopedia of Religion*, editor-in-chief Mircea Eliade, Vol. 11, pp. 199–201. New York: Macmillan, 1987.

Palsetia, Jesse S. *The Parsis of India: Preservation of Identity in Bombay City*. Leiden: E. J. Brill, 2001.

Schermerhorn, R. A. "Parsis: Asian Puritans in Transition." In *Ethnic Plurality in India*. Tucson, AZ: University of Arizona Press, 1978.

Taraporevala, Sooni. *Zoroastrians of India. Parsis: A Photographic Journey*. New York: Overlook Press, 2004.

—by D. O. Lodrick

PASHTUN

PRONUNCIATION: PASH-toon
ALTERNATE NAMES: Pushtun, Pakhtun, Pashtoon, Pathan, Afghan
LOCATION: Southeastern Afghanistan; northwestern Pakistan
LANGUAGE: Pashtu
Population: approximately 35 million
RELIGION: Islam (Sunni Muslim)

¹INTRODUCTION

Pashtun (also spelled Pushtun, Pakhtun, Pashtoon) are Pakhtu- or Pashto-speaking people inhabiting southeastern Afghanistan and the northwestern province of Pakistan. Outsiders often referred to them as Pathan or Afghan. Pashtun (Afghan) constitute one of the largest ethnic groups in Afghanistan and the term *Afghan* until recently referred exclusively to the Pashtun peoples before it came to denote all citizens of Afghanistan.

Pashtun are traditionally pastoral nomads with a strong tribal organization. Each tribe, consisting of kinsmen who trace descent in male bloodlines from a common tribal ancestor, is divided into clans, subclans, and patriarchal families. Tribal genealogies establish rights of succession and inheritance, the right to use tribal lands, and the right to speak in tribal council. Disputes over property, women, and personal injury often result in blood feuds between families and whole clans; these may be inherited unless settled by the intervention of clan chiefs or by tribal council.

²LOCATION AND HOMELAND

Pashtun have lived for centuries in the corridors between Khurasan and the Indian subcontinent, at the crossroads of several historically great civilizations. Their mountain homes have been overcome by conquering armies repeatedly, and have been subjected to the rule of great empires including the empire of Alexander the Great and the Persian Empire. However, the Pashtun's story has never been put in perspective. There is no true written history of the Pashtun in their own land. Pashtun traditions assert that they are descended from Afghana, grandson of King Saul of Israel, although most scholars believe it more likely that they arose from an intermingling of ancient Aryans from the north or west with subsequent invaders.

The Pashtun are divided into about 60 tribes of varying size and importance, each of which occupies a particular territory. In Afghanistan, where Pashtun are the predominant ethnic group, the main tribes are the Durrani or Abdali south of Kabul and the Ghilzay east of Kabul.

In Pakistan, the Pashtun predominate north of Quetta between the Sulaiman Ranges and the Indus River. The areas of Pakistan in which Pashtuns are prevalent include the Northwest Frontier Province and the Federally Administered Tribal Areas, or FATA. In the hill areas, the main tribes are, from south to north: the Kakar, Sherani, and Ustarana south of the Gumal River; the Mahsud, Darwsh Khel, Waziri, and Batani, between the Gomal River and Thal; the Turi, Bangash, Orakzay, Afridi, and Shinwari from Thal to the Khyber Pass; and the Mahmand, Uthman Khel, Tarklani, and Yousufzay north and northeast of the Khyber. The settled areas include lowland tribes subject to direct administration by the provincial government. The main tribes there are, from south to north: the Banuchi and Khattak from the Kurram River to Nowshera; and the Khalil and Mandan in the vale of Peshawar.

³LANGUAGE

Pashtu is language of Pashtun. It belongs to the North-Eastern group within the Iranian branch of Indo-European. It is the language of the major ethnic group of east and south Afghanistan adjacent to Pakistan. Pashtun make up 40 to 60% of the population of Afghanistan, but reliable census figures are not available. Pashtu is one of the two official languages of Afghanistan. It is the language of 12 million Pashtun in Pakistan also, the majority of whom live in the North West Frontier Province and the rest in Baluchistan Province.

Two cities in the Pashtu area are important centers of Pashtu language: Kandahar in Afghanistan and Peshawar in Pakistan. In literary works, the trend is to avoid the dialectal differences and use the form of Pashtu used in the urban centers.

Pashtu has always been written in the Perso-Arabic script, with the addition of consonant phonemes of Pashtu. The name of the language, *Pashtu,* denotes the strong code of customs, morals, and manners of the Pashtun, which is also called *Pashtunwali.* There is a saying: "A Pashtun is not he who speaks Pashtu, but he who has Pashtu." Hospitality (*Milmastia*) is important to Pashtun, as is a reliance on the tribal council (*jirga*) for the resolution of disputes and local decision making. Other Pashtu codes include: courageousness (*Tureh,* which is also the word for sword in Pashtu); the spirit of taking revenge *(Badal);* protection of honor (*Ghuyrul);* and *nanawati,* a method of terminating hostility, hatred, and enmity (i.e., when a person, family, or tribe goes to the hostile people through elderly people, they will accept their apology and the feeling of hatred and enmity are dissolved). Important elements of Pashtunwali code are personal authority and freedom. Political leadership is based on personalities rather than structures and ideologies.

It is perhaps the power and leadership of individuals that divides the Pashtun not only into tribes but also into numerous sub-tribes, each isolated within its own boundaries. Interference in each other's affairs has caused conflicts among the different sub-tribes throughout history. Yet any external interference—Russian, British, American, etc.—has resulted in immediate unity of Pashtun tribes.

⁴FOLKLORE

Many traditional stories, thoughts, and beliefs exist among the Pashtun. The numerous clans and families that comprise the Pashtun population have specific characteristics. Famous stories, such as "Adamkhan and Durkhani," are common, and many Persian stories are also used by the Pashtun. Pashtun have characteristic folksongs, marriages, and funerals. Certain quatrains, known as *matal,* are very popular. Chorus singing also exists among the Pashtun.

⁵RELIGION

Pashtun tribes are Sunni Muslims, except for a few tribes or parts of tribes on the eastern border near Waziristan. In this region, the Turi tribe is Shia Muslim, as is the Muammad Khel branch of Orakzai. Islam was introduced to the Pashtun in the 8th century, but the rule of Islam within Pashtun traditional culture is different from other Islamic groups, as it is tempered

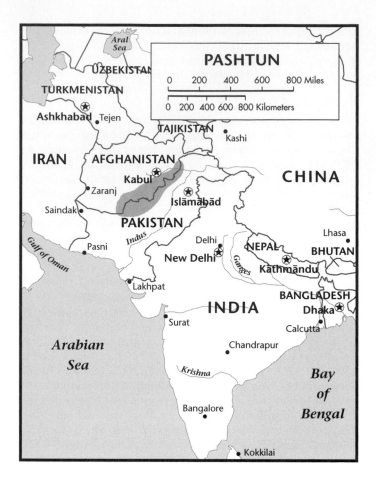

by the influence of the *Pashtunwali* code of conduct. Pashtun believe they are more Pashtun than Muslim. Sufism, particularly of the *Naqshbandi* order, maintains an influence among some Pashtun groups.

⁶MAJOR HOLIDAYS

As all Pashtun are Muslims, they celebrate the two major festivals of the Islamic lunar calendar year. The first of these is *Eid al-Fitr,* which is celebrated for three days after the month of Ramadan (the fasting month)—i.e., the first three days of Shawwal, the 10th month of Islamic calendar. They also celebrate *Eid al-Aa,* which is on the 10th of Dhu-l-ijja (the 12th month of the Islamic calendar). In addition, they observe the 10th of Muarram, which is the first month of the Islamic calendar, in commemoration of the martyrdom of the grandson of the prophet. Pashtuns also celebrate the traditional Persian new year, *Novruz,* a holiday that continues to be observed throughout most of the Persian/Turkic world every March.

⁷RITES OF PASSAGE

Each child of a Muslim family is a Muslim by birth; therefore, all Pashtun are Muslims by birth. After a baby's birth, Pashtun whisper the call for prayer in the baby's ear. The male circumcision ceremony used to be held when a boy was seven years old, but now it is held at the age of about one week and is merged with the birth celebration.

Male and female children are taught the prayers at an early age by parents or grandparents. In addition to the profession of faith and the rituals of prayers, preschool children are taught

about the other obligations of Islam: charity, fasting, and pilgrimage. Prayers and fasting officially start with sexual maturity, but in practice they begin much earlier.

⁸INTERPERSONAL RELATIONS

Both tribal society and Islam prescribe the conduct of man to his human environment in so much detail that there is little room for individual variation. Pashtun society is largely communal and attaches tremendous importance to the unwritten tribal code, which defines the way tribesmen should behave lest they endanger the cohesion and therefore the very life of the tribe. So completely is this code transmitted to each child born into the tribe that it becomes an ineradicable structural part of his personality, and to depart from it is almost unthinkable. *Pashtunwali* (the customs and ethics of the Pashtun), *Tureh* (courageousness), *Nanawati* (method of terminating hostility, hatred, and enmity), *Badal* (the spirit of taking revenge), *Milmastiya* (hospitality), *Jirgeh* (council of elderly men to decide disputes), liberty, and freedom are some of the characteristics of their interpersonal relationships.

⁹LIVING CONDITIONS

Pashtun belong to different clans and families with varying relationships to each other and differing social statuses. Pashtun migrated to different places during the 18th century due to their increasing population and lack of food, water, and grazing land for their animals. Many Pashtun of Afghanistan are not big landowners but make a living in agricultural fields despite having low incomes. Many groups of Pashtun along the border between Afghanistan and Pakistan live nomadic lifestyles.

Many Pashtuns suffer from a low standard of living, particularly due to the many years of conflict suffered by Afghanistan, beginning with the Soviet invasion in 1979. Many Pashtuns became refugees during these years of conflict and left for neighboring countries, particularly Pakistan where they were accepted by their co-ethnics. Since the removal of the Taliban from power in 2001, many of these Pashtun refugees are encouraged to return to Afghanistan but often find themselves in a worse living situation as the homes they left were destroyed or occupied.

¹⁰FAMILY LIFE

The Pashtun family is an extended family. The household normally consists of the patriarch and his wife, his unmarried children, and his married sons and their wives and children. It is a patrilineal system in that descent is through the paternal side, and family loyalty is to the paternal line. A married woman must transfer complete allegiance to her husband's family. Married sons live in their father's household rather than establishing homes of their own. The eldest male possesses complete authority over the extended family. The preference for marriages is within the extended family or with other close relatives.

Economically, the Pashtun family is a single unit. Wealthy family members contribute to the support of those who are poorer, and the family maintains an appearance of well-being. Old people depend on their children for care and support, and the whole family shares the expense of a child away at school.

Obedience and respect for elders are the main points of an Pashtun child's upbringing. Almost everything an individual does is a matter of concern to the family, for in Pashtun society the family is judged by the behavior of its individual members.

An Pashtun woman helps a girl tie a baby to her back in front of their tent in the outskirts of Kabul, Afghanistan. The Pashtun are nomadic herders. (AP Images/Tomas Munita)

¹¹ CLOTHING

Traditional Pashtun dress is a somber-colored, loose-fitting shirt worn to the knees *(qmis)* and full trousers tied at the waist with a string *(shalwar)*. Over the shirt there is usually a vest, and for footwear there are thick leather shoes *(chaplay)*. Most Pashtun farmers and almost all adult males in tribal areas wear turbans *(pagray)*, long lengths of cotton cloth wound around the head and fastened so that one end dangles. They also usually wear a wide, long piece of cloth called a *chadar* on their shoulders.

Country women wear baggy black or colored trousers, a long shirt belted with a sash, and a length of cotton over the head. City women wear the same type of trousers and long shirt *(qmis)* and cotton over the head. They also usually wear a veil, a loose garment that covers a woman from the head to below the knees *(burqa)*. Women wear colored clothes printed with flowers and other designs. For footwear, they use sandals, shoes, or embroidered slippers.

¹² FOOD

Religious prohibitions prevent Pashtun from eating pork and drinking alcoholic beverages. Staples in their diet include bread, rice, vegetables, milk products, meat, eggs, fruits, and tea. A favorite dish is *pulaw,* a rice and meat dish flavored with coriander, cinnamon, and cardamom.

¹³ EDUCATION

Traditionally, education took place in religious institutes and mosque schools *(madrassa* or *maktab)*. In addition to these institutions, free secular education was available in most villages, at least prior to 2001. In Afghanistan, the entire educational system was disrupted due to Russian invasion in 1978, and since the pullout in 1989 to 1992, due to the civil war. During the period of Taliban control (1996–2001), education was again restricted to religious institutions, and girls were not allowed to attend school. Since the Taliban were removed from power, many schools have been rebuilt, and many girls have returned to school. However, schools that allow girls are often targeted by the Taliban insurgency. These problems tend to affect Pashtuns greatly, as they make up the majority of the population in those areas most threatened by the insurgency.

In the North West Frontier Province of Pakistan and Baluchistan there are boys and girls schools in almost in every village and government colleges for boys and girls in every town. (These are affiliated with various universities.)

In 2007, half of Afghan children were thought to attend school. Of those who attended, 35% were girls. Eleven million Afghans were thought to be illiterate.

Higher education and universities were available in Afghanistan but were greatly disrupted due to the many years of conflict and by the strict laws of the Taliban. Since 2001 some universities have again begun to operate, such as Kabul State University.

¹⁴CULTURAL HERITAGE

Pashtun social groups are well-organized. In increasing size, they are: Qabila, Taifa, and Khail. The males are the dominant members of a household. For example, if a husband dies, the widow is required to marry someone within her husband's family, even if the only person available happens to be only one year old. In this case, it appears that culture is given more weight than religion. Pashtun leaders convene to discuss and to solve major problems in the community. The *jirga* is the community assembly that is used to solve disputes and problems. The *shura* is an Islamic council that is also relied upon by Pashtun in Afghanistan for organization. Respect for the elderly is very important to the Pashtun.

¹⁵WORK

Pashtun work at a variety of occupations in agriculture, business, and trade. Women and children also play a role in agricultural work. Generally, the Pashtun of Afghanistan do not have very high living standards. The working conditions of Pashtun in Afghanistan and Pakistan differ, being generally better in Pakistan.

Naiza bazi, a game involving riding horses and throwing spears, is a sport enjoyed among the Pashtun. Some Pashtun also have rock-throwing competitions. *Atan* is a famous group folkdance of the Pashtun. Pashtun have also adopted some of the sports of Northern Persian speaking Afghan nationals such as *buzkashi,* a form of polo played with a sheep or goat carcass.

¹⁷ENTERTAINMENT AND RECREATION

Social get-togethers are the major form of entertainment. The *Eids,* religious holidays occurring twice a year, are also times of celebration and entertainment. Certain card games are played amongst Pashtun as well. Kite flying and pigeon flying were popular among Afghans of many backgrounds including Pashtun. Banned under the Taliban, since 2001 these recreation forms have been revived. One novelistic account of two Afghan boys and their love of kite-flying is Khaled Hosseini's *The Kite Runner* (2003) and the film of the same name (2007).

¹⁸FOLK ART, CRAFTS, AND HOBBIES

Pashtun clothes differ from province to province, but they are often highly decorated. The people of Kandahar sew characteristic designs on their clothes and wear small hats made of thread or silk. In Paktia, people generally wear large hats with turbans. Vests are very common among Pashtun, but styles differ from location to location. For example, the people of Nangahar wear vests with bright designs.

¹⁹SOCIAL PROBLEMS

Because the Pashtun do not all live within one country, they have differing social conditions, although they generally live in societies with tight religious restrictions. Differences among Pashtun clans and families have led to much violence and killing both in Afghanistan and Pakistan.

Narcotics, particularly opium, production has become a serious problem in Afghanistan due to the chaos and poverty caused by the years of conflict. Afghanistan was the largest producer of opium in the world in 2005, 2006, and 2007. Much of the production takes place in the predominately Southern Pashtun areas. Use of narcotics has remained minimal among Pashtuns due to religious beliefs.

²⁰GENDER ISSUES

Women have traditionally had few rights under the strict code of Pashtunwali. *Purdah,* or separation of men and women, is traditionally practiced. At times throughout history, such as during the years of Communist rule, women were encouraged to take part in society more openly. However, during the years that the Taliban controlled Afghanistan, women were restricted from participating in almost every form of public life, forced to adhere to a strict dress code that included the wearing of the *burqa,* and were restricted to their homes unless accompanied by a male family member. Since the Taliban were removed from power, such restrictions have been lessened, and some Pashtun women have regained their careers and even hold public office. However, many continue to follow these restrictions due to social pressure or because of their own choice.

²¹BIBLIOGRAPHY

Afghanistan Ministry of Education. 1386 School Survey Summary Report. Afghanistan Ministry of Education. http://www.moe.gov.af/index.htm (June 2008).

Hosseini, Khaled. *The Kite Runner.* NY: Riverhead, 2003.

Jawack, Nassim. *Afghanistan: A Nation of Minorities.* N.p.: Minority Rights Group, 1992.

Layiq, Sulaiman. *A Short Account of the Pashtun Tribes.* Kabul, Afghanistan: DRA Academy of Sciences Social Sciences Center, 1986.

Leonard, Thomas, ed. *Encyclopedia of the Developing World.* New York: Routledge, 2005.

Thompson, W. Kenneth. *Encyclopedia of the Modern Middle East and North Africa.* New York: Macmillan Reference, 2004.

Wilbur, N. Donald. *Afghanistan.* New Haven, CT: Human Relations Area Files, 1956.

Wirsing, G. Robert. *The Baluchis and Pathans.* N.p.: Report Minority Rights Group, No. 48, 1981.

—revised by M. Kerr

PENAN

PRONUNCIATION: peh-NAHN
LOCATION: Malaysia (Sarawak state)
POPULATION: 14,000 (2004)
LANGUAGE: Penan
RELIGION: Animism; Christianity
RELATED ARTICLES: Vol. 3: Iban; Kelabit; Vol. 4: Malaysian Malays

¹INTRODUCTION

The Penan are among the last of the nomadic hunter-gatherers living in the world's tropical rain forests today, and have been described as the true aborigines of the island of Borneo. They are believed to have originated from the upper Kayan River, Today the Penan are a subgroup of the Orang Ulu in the state of Sarawak. They can be categorized into two groups: Western Penan (those who settle along the Rajang River) and Eastern Penan (those living along the Baram River).

²LOCATION AND HOMELAND

There are about 14,000 Penan. The Western Penan, which consists of Penan Silat (Baram District), Penan Geng, Penan Apau, and Penan Bunut, are centered in the Belaga District and the Silat River basin in the Kapit and Bintulu divisions. The Eastern Penan, also known as Penan Selungo after the Selungo River, live mostly in the Baram River basin in Miri and Limbang divisions.

About a quarter of the population is settled, half is semi-settled, living part of the time in small, scattered villages, and the rest are nomadic (about 2,000 people). The settled Penan, like many other indigenous communities in Sarawak, lives in either longhouses or single houses in village settlements. Whereas the nomadic Penan, who live in bands, are still practicing a lifestyle by which they rely heavily on the forest to provide most of what they need to live. Each band usually consists of 2 to 10 families, or 20–40 people, who move around together within their own territory. Unless they are invited by a neighboring group to eat a meal of fruit together, other groups are not supposed to encroach on the territory of a nomadic group.

The Penan, like some other tribes in Sarawak, have a Mongoloid cast to their features, but their skin coloring is noticeably lighter than that of most of the locals. This is because of their dislike of the sun and preference for jungle shade. Unlike their neighbors, the settled Dayaks, the Penan have been less influenced by the outside world.

³LANGUAGE

The Penan speak their own language, called Penan, with dialectical variations. Even though they do not have a written language, the Penan have a very interesting method of relaying messages. Various items, such as shoots, leaves, stones, sticks, and feathers, are used to leave messages along the paths in the jungle. They are used to show directions, to give instructions to wait or to follow, and to indicate danger, hunger, disease, death, or food. The Penan usually poke sticks in the ground to which they attach leaves or feathers to show direction, time, and number of families passing through.

In the 1970s, missionaries tried for the first time to put the Penan language into writing. One of their accomplishments was to write and compile a Penan Bible.

⁴FOLKLORE

The Penan, like every other tribe on Borneo, have many myths, epics, and legends. *Oia Abeng* is their most popular epic poem. Unfortunately, all but small fragments of the epics have been forgotten. This is both because the lyrics are orally transmitted, and because the younger generations are losing interest in oral traditions.

One of the Penan's popular folk tales is that of the god of thunder, Bale Gau, who has the power to turn people into stone. The Penan believe that when the spirit of an animal, dead or alive, is angered, the spirit may call upon Bale Gau to inflict its curse on people. Most ancient rock formations are believed to have once been people who were punished by the god of thunder for mocking an animal spirit dressed with human clothes.

⁵RELIGION

Many Penan have chosen to embrace Christianity, with the support of Borneo Evangelical Mission, while the rest remain animist, believing in a supreme god called Bungan, and that nature itself has a soul. They also believe that forests are filled with powerful spirits, and that these spirits must not be disturbed. They get angry and inflict disease on people if they are deliberately disturbed. Therefore, the Penan leave these spirits in peace, appease them with sacrifices, or threaten them using magic words.

The Penan also believe strongly in taboos and omens. Dreams, animals, such as deer and snakes, and bird sounds and flights are omens indicating the correct course of action. For example, a Penan will turn back if he or she hears a king-fisher's call at the start of a journey. He or she will continue the journey only if the call of the crested rainbird is heard. They believe if they disobey the taboos and omens, they will experience hardships, illness, or death.

6 MAJOR HOLIDAYS

See the articles entitled **Kelabit, Iban,** and **Malaysian Malays.**

7 RITES OF PASSAGE

Childbirth is usually done at home with the help of a midwife or an experienced elder. All children grow up without birthday parties, graduations, or other ceremonies that mark the passage of time.

Since the Penan believe that knowledge is acquired through experience, their children receive training from their elders at a young age. The importance of sharing and showing respect for elders is also instilled at a young age. Since selfishness is considered a serious crime by the Penan, their children are taught to share everything with other people. Even a tiny fruit is sliced in enough pieces so that everyone can have a bite.

Penan children learn how to survive in the jungle at a young age. They learn the names and uses of myriad plants and animals in the forest. They learn how to navigate through the jungle without compasses or maps, how to start a fire, build a shelter, and make tools. By watching and helping his father and grandfathers, a boy learns how to make blowpipes and darts. He learns to hunt with his friends in the forest. A girl learns to weave by watching and helping her mother and grandmothers. She learns to gather fruits, nuts, and fish with her friends.

A person usually gets married at the age of 16, when she or he has mastered the skills and knowledge needed to support a family. A marriage does not involve a ceremony. With the consent of their parents, a young woman and man may simply decide to live together as husband and wife.

When a person dies, the body is wrapped in woven mats, which will later be buried near the camp or under the hearth of the dead person's hut. In order to soften their grief, the Penan will leave the place and build new shelters in another part of the forest. They believe in an afterlife. Their heaven is a rain forest above the sky where human souls hunt and harvest sago palm without illness, hardship, or pain.

8 INTERPERSONAL RELATIONS

The Penans are gentle, shy, and timid people, in contrast to their primitive and savage image in the eyes of others. They are the only tribe that never practiced headhunting in Sarawak. They avoid conflict, and resort to negotiation if there is a misunderstanding.

A Penan turns away his or her gaze when greeting someone, and avoids eye-to-eye contact with a stranger. Their normal way of greeting is to shake hands, and the hands are never tightly squeezed. It is taboo to mention someone's real name in his or her presence. Therefore, expressions such as "brother" *(pade)*, "father" *(mam)*, "respected man" *(lakei dja-au)*, and "respected woman" are used.

It is impolite to walk directly towards another person. The Penan bend slightly and make a bow when they pass by someone or a group of people. Usually a bow is also made before a meal. It is taboo to step over food served for a meal, as this pollutes the meal, as well as the host and the person herself or himself.

Sharing is a central value and survival tactic for the Penan, so, all wild game and collected forest products are shared equally within the community. When food is short, a hunter will march for hours to bring food for the group. This will ensure the survival of the children, the old, the sick and less fortunate, and the community as a whole.

9 LIVING CONDITIONS

The nomadic Penan live in the forest, while the settled Penan live in longhouses and are agriculturalists. While the nomadic are hunters and gatherers of forest products, like fruits, mushroom, game, and wild sago, the settled Penan are farmers. The settled Penan grow hill rice and rear chicken and pigs for domestic use. There are some groups that are now cultivating cash crops, such as rubber, pepper, palm oil, and cocoa. These groups settle in villages and do have access to the market and modern infrastructure. Meanwhile, the nomads do not have permanent houses but live, rather, in simple shelters or huts *(selap)* that are built to last only for three to four weeks. By that time, they will need to move on. These huts are constructed with wooden sticks as supports, palm leaves for roofing, and split bamboo pieces or small sticks for flooring. Strips of rattan are used to hold these materials together. The huts in the settlement can be built very close together or very far from each other.

A nomadic "village" usually consists of about 30 persons, though the number may vary from 5 or 6 to as many as 160 persons. These temporary settlements are built on the tops of hills to avoid the risk of being hit by a falling tree. Thus, water has to be carried some distance in bamboo containers. These settlements will be moved when the supply of sago palm, their staple diet, is exhausted, or when game or jungle produce becomes scarce and difficult to find in the area.

The nomadic Penan household goods and personal possessions are very few and most are carried in backpacks made from rattan. They include a spear, a bamboo container of wooden darts, a small gourd containing the dart heads, one or two machetes encased in wooden sheaths, a couple of cooking pots, several rattan baskets, and a couple of woven rattan mats.

10 FAMILY LIFE

Penan women never hunt. Most foraging is done by men, while the women's primary sphere is the encampment. A woman is responsible for raising children, preparing food, gathering wood and water, and weaving baskets and mats from rattan and bamboo strips. A Penan woman exercises her influence through relating with her husband, who will in turn relate her wishes to others. However, she is allowed to indicate her desires to the community when necessary.

The family size of nomadic Penan is smaller in comparison to those of both the settled Penan and other tribes in Sarawak. The rate of infant mortality is high, due to the rigors of their existence. There are, on average, three children per family among nomadic Penans, while settled Penan families may average five

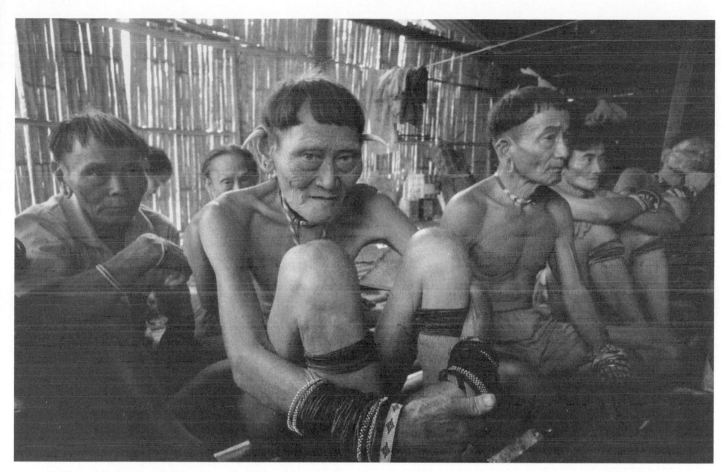

Members of the Penan tribe sit in the village of Long Block in the Baram district of Sarawak on Borneo Island. The Penan are fighting to preserve their culture, waging a war against the government and loggers. (AP Images/Richard Vogel)

children. A family consists of a mother, a father, and at least one child. Sometimes a family is joined by the grandparents.

Traditionally, polygyny and polyandry were practiced, whereby a man could have two wives and a woman could have two husbands. However, monogamy is the norm today. A marriage may happen without any celebration or ceremonial event. Two people are considered married as soon as they establish their own household.

Each Penan family owns about a dozen dogs. Dogs are important in the life of the Penan. They are neither kept as pets nor eaten. They are, rather, used in the hunting and tracking of wild game. Some other animals are kept as pets. There are times when a hunter will return with a live baby animal, such as a bear, a monkey, or a bat. These animals are kept as pets by the children. A Penan will never kill and eat an animal that has been fed, even when the animal is mature, ready for slaughter, and the Penan are hungry. It is unthinkable for a Penan to keep and raise an animal for the purpose of living off its meat or its milk.

¹¹CLOTHING

There is no known Penan group that ever went about totally naked, although the primary, and sometimes only, article of clothing for most Penan groups is the loincloth or *chawat*. Even though loincloths traditionally were made of bark-cloth, today they are made of cotton. These materials are obtained

through trade with other tribes such as the Kayans, Kenyahs, Kelabit, and the coastal Malay and Chinese traders. These days, few Penan go barefoot. In fact, only Penan elders still maintain traditional dress of *chawat*, bands on their legs and wrists, and large holes in their earlobes. Many others are wearing Western-style clothes of T-shirts, shirts, pants, and shorts.

¹²FOOD

The semi-settled Penan depend partially on rice and tapioca from their plantations for food, while the nomadic Penan depend entirely on the forest for their survival. Their staple food is wild sago palm, which is supplemented with wild game and wild fruits gathered from the jungle. With their blowpipes and hunting dogs they roam the forest in search of wild sago while hunting animals, fishing, and gathering wild fruits for their daily existence. The wild game hunted by the Penan includes mousedeer, wild boar (Borneoan bearded pig), five different kinds of monkey, barking deer, birds, and occasionally bear and python. The wild boar is the most valuable catch, as it is a source of both protein and fat. Other food includes the pith of the sago palm, fish, and shrimp from the river.

Sago flour is usually cooked with water. The starchy flour is poured into the water and is cooked until it congeals into the consistency of paste. It is then eaten with wooden "forks" out of a common pan. Sago can also be baked or fried in lard, and it is also used to thicken soup. The Penan eat sago with wild game, like Americans eat potatoes with meat.

¹³ EDUCATION

Traditionally, the Penan did not go to school. However, through the government's persuasions, more and more Penan are attending government schools. In 1987, about 250 Penan attended primary schools, while about 50 others attended other schools farther away. At the beginning of the 21st century, it was estimated that less than 12 Penan youth attain a tertiary education. These are mostly the children of the settled Penan. While the children of the settled Penan are attending government schools, the children of the nomadic Penan get their lessons from their parents, grandparents, uncles, and aunts. The elders are perceived as full of knowledge and wisdom that need to be imparted to the younger generations. The Penan also believe that knowledge is taught by experience; therefore, from a young age a child is taught the skills to survive in the forest.

¹⁴ CULTURAL HERITAGE

Even though they have a very simple lifestyle, the Penan are a musical people. All their musical instruments are made of wood and bamboo. There are five different kinds of musical instruments that are widely played: the mouth organ (kellore/kelure), jaw-harp (oreng), flute (kringon), four-stringed instrument (pagang), and lute (sape). The kelure is made from a dried gourd with six bamboo pipes, three long and three short, each with finger holes at the base. It produces a sound similar to a flute. The oreng is made of wood, about 18 cm (7 in) long and 2.5 cm (1 in) wide. The wood is well carved and weighted with resin. Slots are cut in the wood to make a long tongue for vibration. More slots are cut in the tongue to enhance the sound. While the oreng is made of wood, the pagang is made from a piece of bamboo about 60 cm (24 in) long and 10 cm (4 in) wide and is only played by women. Group and solo dances are danced to the rhythmic strumming or sound of these various instruments.

Part of Penan cultural heritage is their wide knowledge of nearly everything they need in the forest. They use about 30 different kinds of plant drugs to dress wounds and treat headaches, stomachaches, poisoning, rashes, and other ailments. Although some have a slower effect compared to chemically derived drugs, there are others that have an immediate effect on certain ailments. For example tongue and mouth rashes in small children disappear within a few minutes after chewing a leaf stem of benua-tokong. Different kinds of vines and barks are crushed and used as soap. More than 20 kinds of fruit leaves, bark, and skin are used for dyeing rattan. The Penan also know more than 30 different kinds of rattan, which are used for weaving and handicrafts.

¹⁵ WORK

The nomadic Penan earn their living primarily by hunting and gathering. They are considered to be the real masters of the forest, being expert hunters and trackers. Hunting is done with dogs and with simple weapons such as spears, blowpipes, and poison arrows. It can be done in small groups, pairs, or alone, depending on the kind of animal they are seeking. Large animals such as deer and wild boars require a group of hunters and their dogs.

Besides hunting, the Penan gather a wide variety of nuts, fruits, mushrooms, and leaves. These provide them with additional foods. They eat more than 100 different kinds of fruits, and 30 different species of fish. Fishing is usually done by the women. There are several ways this is carried out. Fruit-eating fish are lured into the fishing nets by throwing stones that make the same size splash as falling fruit. Another way is to dump poison made from crushed plants into a slowly moving stream. This will cause the fish to die and float to the surface of the water, where they can be picked up.

Weaving mats and baskets is also work done mostly by the women. They spend a large amount of their time slicing rattan into strips of various sizes, dyeing the strips, and then weaving them by hand into intricate geometric patterns.

¹⁶ SPORTS

Hunting and gathering are not only tasks that need to be done daily, but the Penan also treat them as sport or as forms of entertainment and recreation. While the older people spend most of their time away from the camp, the children play games within the settlement areas. They climb trees, splash in the streams, and slide down muddy slopes.

¹⁷ ENTERTAINMENT AND RECREATION

Deep in the jungle where a supply of electricity is impossible to obtain, movies, and television as forms of entertainment do not exist. Therefore, the nomadic Penan's forms of recreation and entertainment are very different from those of settled tribes in Sarawak. Hunting and gathering food are their major forms of recreation in the daylight. In the night when all their tasks for the day are complete, musical instruments are played, accompanied by dances and songs. They have good reason to be merry when their surroundings are safe and they are in good health. Every wild boar caught during this time provides a reason for a party at night.

¹⁸ FOLK ART, CRAFTS, AND HOBBIES

The Penan are some of the best craftspeople in Borneo. They produce superb handicrafts, and some of Borneo's finest rattan mats and baskets are woven by the Penan women. While their women weave fine rattan mats and baskets, their men are excellent blacksmiths and make the best blowpipes, which are much coveted by members of other tribes in Sarawak. Besides baskets and mats, the Penan women weave intricate and beautifully patterned artifacts such as backpacks, arm and leg bracelets, and ornate mats, which are adorned with lively black and white designs.

These handicrafts are traded, along with jungle products such as camphor and gaharu (a scented wood), for salt, metal, clothing, and cooking utensils. Like most of the tribes in Borneo, the Penan adopted the custom of having elongated and perforated earlobes with earrings.

¹⁹ SOCIAL PROBLEMS

Like many other indigenous people worldwide, the Penan's traditional lifestyle is threatened by so-called modernization. Modern government policies promoting settled agriculture and systematic logging may gradually force these forest-dwellers to abandon their way of life. The nomadic Penan have been affected by large-scale selective logging since late 1970s. They have find it more and more difficult to survive in the forests because of the relentless encroachment of logging companies and the creation of palm oil and acacia wood plantations. They have to cope with a new or modern lifestyle that is making its way along newly built roads into the most remote areas. Their once self-sufficient lifestyle is slowly being replaced by a dependent one.

20 GENDER ISSUES

The Penan are well known for being highly egalitarian with little gender division. Nevertheless, there is a clear division of labor in certain areas. Among the nomadic Penan, women never hunt and most foraging is done by men. The women's primary sphere is the encampment while the men are free to roam the forest to hunt game and to collect forest products. At home, a Penan woman is expected to raise the children, prepare food, gather wood and water, and weave baskets and mats from rattan and bamboo strips. However, a Penan woman can exercise her influence through relating them to her husband, who will in turn relate her wishes to others. Furthermore, she is allowed to indicate her desires to the community when necessary.

21 BIBLIOGRAPHY

Langub, Jayl. "Penan community and traditions." In Hood Salleh (ed.) *The Encyclopedia of Malaysia, Peoples and Traditions*. Kuala Lumpur: Editions Didier Millet, 2006. (pg. 100 -101)

Lau, Dennis. *Penans: The Vanishing Nomads of Borneo*. Inter-State Publishing Company Sdn. Bhd., 1987.

Manser, Bruno. *Voices from the Rainforest: Testimonies of a Threatened People*. Bruno Manser Foundation and INSAN, 1996.

Munan, Heidi. *Culture Shock: Borneo*. Times Books International, 1988.

Siy, Alexandra. *The Penan: People of the Borneo Jungle*. New York: Dillon Press, 1993.

—by P. Bala

POLYNESIANS

PRONUNCIATION: PAHL-uh-nee-zhuns
LOCATION: Polynesia, a vast string of islands in the Pacific Ocean, including Hawaii, New Zealand, Easter Island, Tonga, Tuvalu, and French Polynesia
POPULATION: Unknown
LANGUAGE: Native languages of the islands; Maori; Tahitian; Hawaiian; Samoan; French; English
RELIGION: Christianity with elements of native religion

1 INTRODUCTION

The Polynesians are the original inhabitants of a vast string of islands in the Pacific Ocean that spans from New Zealand in the south to Hawaii in the north. The western boundary is Easter Island, and the Fiji Islands are generally considered to lie just beyond the western boundary of the region. Polynesia means "many islands" in Greek and the cultures of the region share many traits with each other. This does not mean there is no diversity within Polynesia; however, the differences are often subtle and not readily perceived by outsiders.

Independence for Polynesian peoples under colonial rule began with Western Samoa in 1962. Many other island nations have followed suit, the main pocket of colonial possessions being the territories of French Polynesia, which includes Tahiti and the Marquesas. The Kingdom of Tonga is unique in Polynesia since it is a constitutional monarchy and was never a colonial possession. Tonga was a British protectorate during the first half of this century. In 2006 the Tongan king of 41 years died and was succeeded by his eldest son Siaosi Tuou V.

2 LOCATION AND HOMELAND

In the Pacific region, there is an important distinction made between "high" islands and "low" islands. Tahiti is a typical high island in Polynesia, being relatively large with steep slopes, luxuriant vegetation, and abundant waterfalls and rushing streams. Coastal plains are absent or extremely limited on high islands. Low islands are of a few different types. Atolls are the most common low islands in Polynesia. These are typically "desert islands" that are low-lying, narrow, and sandy with few, if any, surface streams. Low islands have less biodiversity than do high islands.

At the time of the first known European contact with the Polynesian world in the 1500s, there were probably around half a million people scattered throughout the region. European powers vied for ownership of most of the inhabited islands of Polynesia. The indigenous populations suffered at the hands of the Europeans, with the loss of their traditional lands and resources, as well as discrimination against their cultures and languages. On the North Island of New Zealand, increasing European encroachment into interior lands inhabited by the Maori led to a decade of armed conflict referred to as the "Maori Wars" of the "Land Wars." The result of the conflict was the decimation of those Maori who sided against the Europeans and the absorption of their traditional lands into the larger pool available to European settlers.

Polynesians migrate within the region, especially to New Zealand, where there is a large population of Cook Islanders resident in Auckland. In fact, there are more Cook Islanders resident there than in the Cook Islands themselves. Polynesians also immigrate to California, parts of Europe, and Australia. Samoans migrate to Hawaii and California. Residents of French Polynesia immigrate to France.

³LANGUAGE

The Polynesian languages are part of the larger Austronesian language family that encompasses most of the languages of the Pacific Basin. Polynesian forms a sub-group of this extensive language family; all of these languages are more closely related to each other than they are to other languages spoken in the Pacific. Linguists believe that Proto-Polynesian, the ancestral language of all the current Polynesian languages, was spoken in the area of Fiji-Tonga-Samoa around 300 to 400 years ago. At that time, the original speakers began to migrate to different islands and, as a result, the proto-language began to diverge and change. This movement is responsible for the current language situation in the Polynesian area.

Many Polynesian languages face an uncertain future. Attempts have been made to revitalize the Hawaiian language through educational initiatives at the university and the elementary school levels. Tahitian has been used as a lingua franca (common language) throughout the Tuamotuan Islands, the Marquesas, the Gambiers, and the Austral Islands since before European contact and is threatening the viability of the native languages of those islands. In New Zealand, all speakers of Maori—the indigenous Polynesian language of the island chain—are bilingual in English. There has been considerable progress in the revitalization of the Maori language, and a bilingual Maori-English television station was launched in New Zealand in 2004. Maori Television has undertaken a block of completely Maori broadcasting for three hours each evening.

⁴FOLKLORE

Polynesian societies have an exceptionally rich body of folklore and mythology. There are myths relating the origins of human beings as well as the origins of cultural practices and institutions. There is a considerable body of mythology regarding the origins of tattooing in Polynesian cultures. Some origin myths describe the process of migration via ocean-going canoes from one island to another. Cultural heroes are important figures in the folklore of Polynesian societies.

⁵RELIGION

Polynesian religion changed dramatically with the coming of European missionaries to the region in the early part of the 19th century. From what we do know of precontact practices, there was considerable variation in religious ideas and practices throughout Polynesia. In Hawaii, for instance, priests performed sacrificial rites at monumental temple complexes to provide legitimacy for the authority of the chief. Chiefs were genealogically related to gods and, as a result, were believed to possess sacred power called *mana*. The Hawaiian system recognized four major gods and one major goddess. Ku, the god of war, fishing, and other male activities, ruled the ritual calendar of ancient Hawaiians for eight months out of the year. Ku was the patron god of the well-known Hawaiian king Kamehameha.

The concept of *tapu*, English "taboo," was important in all Polynesian societies, generally meaning forbidden or prohibited due to sacredness. There were things that were tapu such as certain body parts of particular individuals—the head of the first-born, for example. There were also rules that served to protect through the prohibition of certain actions. In the Marquesas Islands, a woman's menstrual cloth was not tapu; however, it was tapu to touch it.

Today, most Polynesians are followers of Christianity, both Catholicism and Protestantism. Some traditional beliefs and mythologies have been incorporated into Christian ideology.

⁶MAJOR HOLIDAYS

Holidays in most contemporary Polynesian societies are events related to the state or the church. In the French possessions like the Marquesas, Bastille Day (July 14) is an important holiday. Many islanders now celebrate a number of Catholic holidays due to influence of missionaries in the colonial era.

⁷RITES OF PASSAGE

From the novels of authors such as Herman Melville, we know a considerable amount about the ways of life in Polynesian societies at the advent of European influence and colonization. For example, we know that the Marquesas Islanders had a birth feast on the day a child was born. On that occasion, the maternal uncles and the paternal aunts of the newborn would cut their hair and an ornament maker would fashion hair ornaments for the child to wear later in life. The newborn was brought presents by family and friends and a type of shrine was built by the infant's father.

Passage into puberty was often accompanied by tattooing rituals in many Polynesian societies. In some societies, such as Samoa, only men were tattooed. In others, both men and women were tattooed, but one group less elaborately than the other. The practice of tattooing in Polynesia is very complicated. It carried with it a number of cultural meanings. There have been recent revivals of the art of tattooing in societies such as the Maori of New Zealand.

Another puberty ritual performed in some Polynesian societies was fattening. Male and female youths were secluded, kept inactive and out of direct sunlight, and fed excessive amounts of food for a period of time to make them more sexually desirable. In the Society Islands these young people were called *pahio,* which derives from the word for "lazy." These puberty rituals are no longer performed.

Death was accompanied by ritualized wailing on the part of women and the performance of formalized chanting on the part of men in the Marquesas. Women would also perform a specific dance called *heva* in which they would shed all of their clothes and move in an extremely exaggerated manner. Finally, the female relatives of the deceased would do physical harm to themselves by cutting their hands and faces with sharks' teeth and other sharp implements. Christian missionaries saw these behaviors as "pagan" and quickly found ways to put a stop to them.

⁸INTERPERSONAL RELATIONS

Greetings in Polynesian societies vary from island to island. Status determines the nature and extent of the social interaction of individuals in these societies. In rural Tahiti, for example, the standard greeting is, "Where are you going?" There are two expected responses: either "Inland," if the person is headed away from the coast, or "Seaward," if the person is headed towards the coastline. The interaction can continue with a fairly standard second level of interchange that includes the question, "What's new at the inland/seaward end?" This is usually an opener for a conversation.

Premarital relations between the sexes are typically very relaxed in most Polynesian societies. However, once a permanent relationship is established, unconstrained sexual relations are not permitted. The choice of a marriage partner is less fixed than in many cultures of the world. In the times before Christian influence, the preference in some Polynesian societies such as the Marquesas Islands was for cross-cousin marriage. In other words, a woman would marry one of her mother's brother's sons or her father's sister's sons: in English kinship terms, a cousin. Missionaries forbade this type of marriage pattern and the present patterns allow for freedom of choice in marriage partners, not unlike that found in American society.

⁹LIVING CONDITIONS

Traditional Polynesian societies did not possess large villages. Instead, families clustered together in neighborhoods that focused on a set of shared structures that were at the center of social, ceremonial, and religious life. Like many Melanesian cultures, many Polynesians had separate sleeping quarters for bachelors. However, Polynesian bachelor houses were not off-limits to females as they were in most parts of Melanesia. In some parts of Polynesia, households were built on elevated stone platforms. Religious shrines, whether communally- or family-owned, were important parts of the household structure.

Households of the nobility had carved items of furniture including headrests and stools. Sleeping mattresses were also available for members of noble households. In many parts of Polynesia, illumination by torches or coconut oil lamps was common inside houses at night. Polynesia seemed like a virtual paradise to Europeans who ventured there.

Nowadays, Polynesian houses and communities are the products of indigenous design and Western materials. Houses constructed of modern materials are frequently found in Polynesian communities. In rural communities, Polynesian houses may be made in the traditional manners of precontact times, yet utilizing some Western building products.

Transportation was by foot and canoe in precontact times. There were many different types of canoes in Polynesia, and Polynesians are especially well-known for their navigational skills. Polynesians spread throughout the Pacific Basin via ocean-going canoes. War canoes were elaborately decorated and treated with special care when not in use. The war canoes of chiefs were stored in special structures on land in times of peace. Although outrigger canoes are associated with Polynesian seafaring, they probably did not originate in that region, but in Micronesia.

Polynesians enjoy typical modes of transportation, such as driving cars, riding buses, bicycling, boating, and walking.

¹⁰FAMILY LIFE

In societies like Tahiti where there were discrete social classes, marriage was prohibited among individuals from different classes. Children born of sexual relations between members of different classes were killed at birth in traditional Tahitian society. Again, these practices were discontinued as a result of missionary activity in Tahiti.

A Polynesian man with his baby son on Tuvalu, South Pacific. (Tim Graham/Getty Images)

In many Polynesian societies, polygamy was practiced. The Marquesas Islanders were unique in the region because in traditional society, a woman could have more than one husband at a time, a practice called "polyandry" by anthropologists and fairly rare in the cultures of the world. It was very uncommon to find a man who had more than one wife in the Marquesas. Monogamy, having only one spouse at a time, is now the universal practice in Polynesia.

The role and status of women in relation to men varies between island societies in Polynesia. In a place like the Marquesas, women have always enjoyed a status nearly equivalent with men. One evidence of this equality is in the extent of tattooing that was permitted for both sexes in the precontact society. Men and women were tattooed almost equally as much. In many other Polynesian societies, this was not the case, as women held positions of lower status than men.

¹¹CLOTHING

Typical Polynesian attire in precontact times was similar for men and women. A section of bark cloth that was worn as a loincloth by men or a waistcloth by women was the standard piece of clothing. The bark used to make the cloth came from various types of trees including the mulberry, banyan, and breadfruit trees. In some cases certain classes of women would protect themselves from exposure to the sun by wrapping themselves in a sheet of bark cloth. On ceremonial occasions, men of high status would also wrap up in sheets of decorated bark cloth. Decorated bark cloth known as *tapa* was the main item of traditional clothing in Tahiti, although it is no longer manufactured there. There were a number of ornaments that were worn for ceremonial events. Elaborate feather headdresses were signs of nobility. Ear ornaments were worn by both men and women in Polynesia. Traditional patterns of dress have disappeared except for performances or special ceremonial or cultural events. Fashion in Polynesia spans the range that it does in any Westernized developing country.

12 FOOD

Most traditional Polynesian societies rely on fishing and horticulture. We know from early European accounts of the region that the Marquesas Islands were unique, for they relied on the production of breadfruit. Breadfruit was preserved and fermented in deep pits. Each family had its own pit for making the fermented breadfruit called *ma*.

Taro root is another important foodstuff in Polynesia. Early Hawaiians relied on taro as a staple starch in their diet. In Hawaiian mythology, the taro plant originated from the corpse of the first-born of Wakea, a high god in Hawaiian cosmology who had died from premature birth.

In some parts of Polynesia, Hawaii, Tahiti, and the Marquesas in particular, men and women ate separately. In general, this pattern is no longer followed except in the most traditional communities and in certain ceremonial contexts. In rural Tahitian society, young women are not allowed to eat food that has been prepared for adult men. The idea is that male interaction with the spiritual world could have some residual effects that would pass via the food to the young, vulnerable women.

13 EDUCATION

Western-style education has become the standard in Polynesia. Many Polynesians attend colleges and universities both inside and outside the region.

14 CULTURAL HERITAGE

Polynesia has a rich tradition of vocal and instrumental music. Some genres of musical expression have been lost and some new ones have been created as a result of missionary activity in the region. Christian hymns have had considerable influence in the style of vocal music in Polynesia. The Tahitian vocal music known as *himene* (from the English word "hymn") blends European counterpoint with Tahitian drone-style singing.

One of the most well-known Polynesian musical instruments is the Hawaiian *ukulele*. It is the Hawaiian version of the Portuguese mandolin that came to the islands with Portuguese immigrants in the 1870s.

The primary use of Hawaiian flutes and drums was to accompany the dance known as the *hula*. There is a complex structure to the musical accompaniment to the graceful and erotic dance that most Westerns think of when they think of "hula dancing." Hawaiian hula were usually named after the instruments that accompanied them: *hula ili ili* was accompanied by a pair of smooth lava pebbles that are clicked together like a pair of castanets called *ili ili*.

15 WORK

Throughout the Polynesian world there is a traditional division of labor along the lines of gender. Men are responsible for fishing, construction, and protection of the family units, while women are responsible for collecting and processing horticultural products and the manufacturing of basketry items and bark cloth. Both sexes participate in gardening activities. Throughout Polynesia, modern contexts of employment are to be found in the cities and towns. As in American society, the type of employment a person has depends on the level of education and training they have received.

Tourism is not a major source of economic support for most modern nations within the Polynesian culture area. Samoa, for example, receives less than 14% of its GDP (gross domestic product) from tourism and tourism accounts for just under 10% of all employment in Samoa. French Polynesia and Hawaii are the two most active participants in global tourism in Polynesia, although their tourism profiles differ considerably. Bora Bora, in particular, has become an exclusive tourism destination where rates for hotel rooms range from $1,000 to $15,000 per night.

16 SPORTS

Arm wrestling was a traditional Polynesian form of male entertainment as a competition of strength. Other forms of competition between males were common throughout the region as ways to prepare for battle. These forms have either disappeared or been modified, since indigenous warfare is no longer practiced in Polynesia. Surfing was also popular in many parts of Polynesia, although it was only in Hawaii that surfers stood on their surfboards. The world-wide sport of surfing originated through European observation of this traditional Polynesian past-time.

17 ENTERTAINMENT AND RECREATION

Most parts of Polynesia have running water and electricity. Television has made its way into most Polynesian communities. In some parts of the region, Polynesian peoples are taking control of the images of themselves presented in the popular media, producing popular films as well as documentaries.

18 FOLK ART, CRAFTS, AND HOBBIES

Decoration of objects of utilitarian nature is common in most Polynesian societies. Wood carving has been particularly well developed among the Maori of New Zealand. In most Polynesian societies, the designs and patterns that appeared on bark cloth or wood carvings also appeared on the human body in the form of tattoos. In some societies, tattooing was the primary art form. Many traditional art forms, including tattooing, are being revived in many Polynesian societies.

19 SOCIAL PROBLEMS

The right to self-determination is important for many Polynesian peoples. Increased nuclear testing in French Polynesia has been a central concern for the region and the world. In September 1995, France sparked widespread protests by resuming nuclear testing on the Mururoa atoll, which is part of the Tuamotu Archipelago, after a three-year moratorium. Nuclear testing was suspended in January 1996. As a result of widespread international pressure and extensive social protests, French Polynesia's autonomy has been greatly expanded.

Many Polynesian groups like the Maori continue to deal with the social problems of alcoholism and domestic violence. The 1994 film *Once Were Warriors* is a moving, insightful portrayal of modern, urban life for the Maori.

20 GENDER ISSUES

There is some debate in the scholarly literature about gender roles in traditional (precontact) Polynesian societies and their manifestations in post-contact environments of urbanization and a wage economy. Most scholars agree that in traditional Polynesian societies, the concept of *tapu* governed the interactions of males and females. *Tapu* dictated that men and women should eat their meals segregated from each other to prevent any form of pollution. The tapu system did not, on the other hand, stipulate that women were subservient to men. There were several mechanisms by which women attained high status in traditional Polynesian societies.

Traditional Tahitian society has recognized a transgendered role for men who dressed and assumed the social roles of women since precontact times. *Mahu* as the role is called in the Tahitian language also observe the taboos and restrictions of women; however in modern Tahitian society, *mahu* no longer dress like women although they do engage in occupations that are considered as female, such as household care. The category of *mahu* is considered to be natural in Tahitian sexual ideology, although an individual does not have to remain *mahu* throughout the course of his entire life. *Mahu* are not socially stigmatized in Tahitian society and neither are their heterosexual male partners.

21 BIBLIOGRAPHY

Gell, A. *Wrapping in Images: Tattooing in Polynesia*. New York: Oxford University Press, 1993.

Goldman, I. *Ancient Polynesian Society*. Chicago: University of Chicago Press, 1970.

Hooper, Anthony and Judith Huntsman. *Transformations of Polynesian Culture*. Auckland, New Zealand: The Polynesian Society, 1985.

Melville, Herman *Typee*. New York: Wiley and Putnam, 1876.

Thomas, N. "Complementarity and History: Misrecognizing Gender in the Pacific." *Oceania*, 57(4):261-270, 1987.

—by J. Williams

PUNJABIS

PRONUNCIATION: puhn-JAHB-eez
LOCATION: Pakistan (Punjab province); India (Punjab state)
LANGUAGE: Punjabi
RELIGION: Hinduism; Islam; Buddhism; Sikhism; Christianity

1 INTRODUCTION

Punjabis derive their name from a geographical, historical, and cultural region located in the northwest of the Indian subcontinent. "Punjab" comes from the Persian words *panj* (five) and *ab* (river) and means "Land of the Five Rivers." It was the name used for the lands to the east of the Indus River drained by its five tributaries (the Jhelum, Chenab, Ravi, Beas, and Sutlej). Culturally, the Punjab extends beyond this area to include parts of the North West Frontier Province of Pakistan, the foothills of the Himalayas, and the northern fringes of the Thar (Great Indian) Desert in Rājasthān.

The Punjab is an ancient center of culture in the Indian subcontinent. It lay within the bounds of the Harappan civilization, the sophisticated urban culture that flourished in the Indus Valley during the 3rd millennium BC. Harappa, one of the two great cities of this civilization, was located on the Ravi River in what is now Pakistan's Punjab Province. The Punjab has also been one of the great thoroughfares of South Asian history. Aryan-speaking nomadic tribes descended from the mountain passes in the northwest to settle on the plains of the Punjab around 1700 BC. Subsequently, Persians, Greeks, Huns, Turks and Afghans were among the many peoples who entered the Indian subcontinent through the northwestern passes and left their mark on the region. Punjabis, who are of Aryan or Indo-European stock, are the modern descendants of the many peoples that passed through the region.

At times in the past, the Punjab and its population have enjoyed a distinct political identity as well as a cultural one. During the 16th and 17th centuries AD, the region was administered as a province of the Moghul Empire. As recently as the 19th century, much of the area was united under the Sikh state of Ranjit Singh. Britain administered the Punjab as a province of its Indian Empire. However, the redrawing of political boundaries in 1947 saw the Punjab divided between India and Pakistan. Punjabis, despite their common cultural heritage, are now either Indians or Pakistanis by nationality.

2 LOCATION AND HOMELAND

Punjabis number about 120 million people, of whom around 90 million live in the Pakistan Punjab and just over 30 million in the Indian state of Punjab. Migrant Punjabis form important communities in Indian cities, such as Delhi, as well as overseas in Southeast and East Asia, Australia, Africa, Europe, and North America. Punjab Province in Pakistan includes virtually all of the Punjab (i.e., West Punjab) that was assigned to Pakistan in 1947. The Indian Punjab (East Punjab) State extended from the international border with Pakistan to Delhi. In 1966, however, agitation for a Punjabi-speaking state saw the creation of the present Punjab State. This is less than half the size of the former East Punjab and only 14% of the area of the undivided Punjab. The location of India's Punjab State

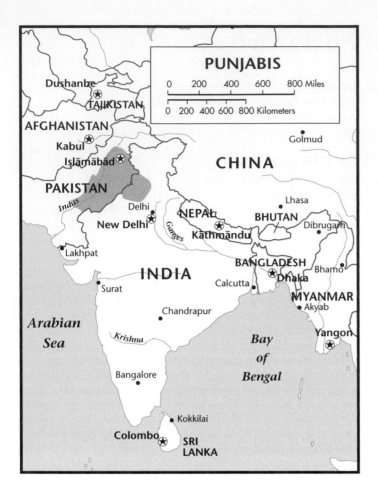

PUNJABIS

0   200   400   600   800 Miles

0   200   400 600 800 Kilometers

mums drop close to freezing and hard frosts are common. Rainfall varies from 125 cm (approximately 49 in) in the hills in the northeast to no more than 20 cm (8 in) in the arid southwest. Precipitation has a monsoonal pattern, falling mainly in the summer months. However, weather systems from the northwest bring valuable amounts of rain in the winter.

³LANGUAGE

Punjabi is the name of the language, as well as of the inhabitants, of the Punjab region. Punjabi belongs to the Aryan branch of the Indo-European language family. In Pakistan, Punjabi is written using the Perso-Arabic script introduced to the region during the Muslim conquests. Punjabis in India use the Lahnda script, which is related to Devanagari, or the Gurmukhi script in which the Sikh sacred books are written. Punjabi is spoken by two-thirds of the population of Pakistan. In India, Punjabi is the mother tongue of just under 3% of the population. Punjabi was raised to the status of one of India's official languages in 1966.

There are six major dialects of Punjabi localized on the *doabs*, the areas lying between the rivers, which tend to be cultural and historical as well as geographical regions. Majhii, one of the more important dialects, is spoken in the region of the cities of Lahore and Amritsar. The other important Punjabi dialects are Malwa, Doabi, Powadhi, Dogri, and Bhattiani. To the west, Punjabi gives way to Lahnda, which is also known as Western Punjabi. Urdu, rather than Punjabi, is favored by city dwellers in Pakistan. Seraiki, sometimes called Multani, is a Punjabi dialect (some say it is a separate language) spoken by some 30 million people in Pakistan in the southern Punjab and northern Sindh. Like Punjabi, it is written in the Perso-Arabic script, the Gurmuki script, or the Devanagari script.

⁴FOLKLORE

Punjabis have a rich mythology and folklore that includes folk tales, songs, ballads, epics, and romances. Much of the folk tradition is an oral one, passed on through the generations by traditional peasant singers, mystics, and wandering gypsies. Many folk tales are sung to the accompaniment of music. There are songs for birth and marriage, love songs, songs of war, and songs glorifying legendary heroes of the past. The *Mahiya* is a romantic song of the Punjab. *Sehra Bandi* is a marriage song, and *Mehndi* songs are sung when henna (a red dye) is being applied to the bride and groom in preparation for marriage. *Heera Ranjha* and *Mirza Sahiban* are folk romances known in every household in the Punjab. Wandering Sufi holy men, such as Bullhe Shah, are well known in the Punjab for their poetry and music. They contributed a verse form that became distinctive of Punjabi literature. The mixture of Hindu, Sikh, and Muslim themes in Punjabi folklore mirrors the presence of these different religious traditions in the region.

⁵RELIGION

The religious composition of the Punjabis reflects the Punjab's long and varied history. Early Hinduism took shape in the Punjab, Buddhism flourished in the region, and Muslims wielded political power in the area for nearly six centuries. Sikhism had its origins in the Punjab, which saw the existence of Sikh states that survived until the middle of the 20th century.

Sikhism was a syncretic religion combining the monotheism of Islam with many of the social features of Hinduism. Al-

along the border with Pakistan and only some 40 km (25 mi) from the city of Lahore, gives it great strategic significance.

The Punjab is an agricultural region and Punjabis, whether in India or Pakistan, share the agrarian social structure based on caste that is found throughout South Asia. The Jats, mainly landowners *(zamindars)* and cultivators, are the largest caste in the Punjab. Other agricultural castes include Rājputs, Arains, Awans, and Gujars. Among the lower-ranked service and artisan castes are the Lohars, Tarkhans, and Chamars.

The homeland of the Punjabis lies on the plains of the upper Indus Valley, covering an area of roughly 270,000 sq km (104,200 sq mi). It stretches from the Salt Ranges in the north to the fringes of the Thar Desert in the southeast. The western margins lie along the base of Pakistan's Sulaiman Range. The Shiwaliks, the outer foothills of the Himalayas, define the Punjab's eastern boundary. The region is a vast alluvial plain, drained by the Indus River and its tributaries. In the northeast, the plain lies at around 300 m (just under 1,000 ft) above sea level, but it declines to under 75 m (250 ft) in elevation along the Indus River in the south. The hills bordering the plain exceed 1,200 m (approximately 4,000 ft) in the Shiwaliks and 1,500 m (approximately 5,000 ft) in the Salt Range.

The Punjab experiences a subtropical climate, with hot summers and cool winters. The mean temperature for June is 34°C (93°F), with daily maximums often rising much higher. The mean maximum temperature for Lahore in June is 46°C (115°F). Dust storms are a common feature of the hot weather. The mean January temperature is 13°C (55°F), although mini-

though its founder, Guru Nanak Dev (1469–1539), preached for a classless society and the equality of women, Sikhs have to all intents and purposes adopted the Hindu caste system and treat women in a similar manner. Born into a Hindu caste in a village in the Punjab (now in Pakistan), Nanak founded a religion that today has most of its adherents in the Punjab. The British annexed the Punjab in the 19th century and introduced Christianity to the region. Thus, Hinduism, Islam, Buddhism, Sikhism, and Christianity are all represented among the Punjabi population.

Religious distributions in the Punjab were the result of historical processes at work over many centuries. These patterns were, however, dramatically altered by the mass migrations that accompanied the creation of India and Pakistan in 1947. Hindus and Sikhs fled Pakistan for India, while Muslims traveled in the other direction seeking refuge in Pakistan. Communal strife at this time between Hindus, Sikhs, and Muslims left as many as 1 million people dead. Today, Punjab Province in Pakistan is 97% Muslim and 2% Christian, with small numbers of Hindus and other groups in the population. Sikhs account for 63.9% of the people in India's Punjab State, while 34.7% are Hindu and roughly 1% each are Muslim and Christian. Small numbers of Buddhists, Jains, and other groups are also present.

⁶ MAJOR HOLIDAYS

Festivals in the Punjab are communal events shared by the entire community, no matter what their religion. Many are seasonal or agricultural festivals. Thus, Basant, when the mustard fields are yellow, marks the end of the cold weather. Punjabis celebrate by wearing yellow clothes, organizing kite-flying, and feasting. Holi is the great spring festival of India and a time for much gaiety, throwing of colored water and colored powder, and visiting friends and relatives. Vaisakh (Baisakh), in April, marks the beginning of the Hindu New Year and also is of special importance for Sikhs, as it commemorates the founding of the Sikh Khalsa. Tij marks the beginning of the rainy season and is a time when girls set up swings, wear new clothes, and sing special songs to mark the occasion. Dasahara, Diwali, and other festivals of the Hindu calendar are celebrated with much enthusiasm. The Sikhs have their "gurpurbs," holidays associated with the lives of the Gurus, while Muslims commemorate the festivals of Muharram, Id-ul-Fitr, and Bakr-Id.

⁷ RITES OF PASSAGE

Punjabi rites of passage follow the customs of the community to which a person belongs. Thus, among Muslims, the *mullah,* or priest, will visit a house within three days of the birth of a male child to recite holy words, including the Call to Prayer, in the baby's ear. The traditional period of impurity after childbirth ends with a fast. The child is named in consultation with the mullah. Males undergo circumcision *(sunnat)* any time before 12 years of age. Sikh birth rituals are simpler, with the child being taken to the temple for offerings, prayers, and the naming ceremony. The *Adi Granth,* the sacred book of the Sikhs, is opened at random and the parents choose a name that begins with the first letter of the first word on the left-hand page. An important ceremony for the Sikhs, however, is the baptism or initiation into the Sikh religion. This usually takes place in the late teenage years. For Hindus, it is important that a child be born at an auspicious time. A Brahman priest is con-

sulted and, if the time of birth is deemed unfavorable, special ceremonies are held to counter any harmful consequences that might result from this. In the past, a mother remained in isolation for a period of 40 days, though this custom is beginning to disappear. The ritual shaving of the head of the child is usually performed during the first five years of the child's life.

At death, Muslims wrap the corpse in white cloth before taking it to the mosque. White is the color of mourning throughout South Asia. At the mosque, the mullah reads the holy words over the body, which is then buried in the graveyard. Sometimes a stone slab is placed on the grave and each of the mourners places a handful of earth on the grave. This symbolizes the breaking of the link with the deceased. The mullah prays for the dead for three days. Hindus and Sikhs cremate their dead. On the fourth day after cremation, Hindus collect the ashes and charred remains of bones from the funeral pyre and immerse them in the sacred Ganges River, at Haridwar if possible. Sikhs usually immerse the ashes at Kiratpur Sahib, on the River Sutlej.

⁸ INTERPERSONAL RELATIONS

Forms of greetings and address vary according to circumstances and social context. In rural areas, a man is usually referred to as Bhaiji or Bhai Sahib (Brother) and a woman as Bibiji (Mistress) or Bhainji (Sister). Sikhs are addressed as Sardar (Mr.) or Sardarni (Mrs.). When they meet, Sikhs join the palms of their own hands together and say the phrase, "Sat Sri Akal" ("God is Truth"). Hindus accompany the same gesture with the word "Namaste" ("Greetings"). The common Muslim greeting is "Salaam" ("Peace" or "Greetings"), or "Salaam Alaikum" ("Peace be with you").

⁹ LIVING CONDITIONS

Punjabi villages are compact nucleated settlements, with houses clustered around a mosque, temple, or gurdwara. Typically, the houses on the outside edge of the village are constructed so as to present the appearance of a walled settlement with few points of access. The main entrance to a village is through an arched gateway called a *darwaza* (door or gate), which is also a meeting place for the village. Houses are built close together, often sharing common walls, with rooms built around a central courtyard where animals are tethered and agricultural implements are stored. Most villages are made up of the various communities that are essential to a functioning agricultural economy—landowners, cultivators, artisans, and service castes.

The prosperity brought to the Punjab by the agricultural advances of the Green Revolution in the late 1960s and 1970s is clearly seen in local housing and creature comforts. In the Indian Punjab, houses are now built of brick, village streets are often paved, and every village has electricity. Households commonly have comfortable furniture, ceiling fans for the hot summers, and conveniences like telephones, radios, televisions, and even refrigerators. Many farmers have tractors. Scooters and motorcycles are common, and the more affluent families have cars and jeeps. Although the Pakistani Punjab has not achieved quite the same levels of prosperity, it too is a fertile agricultural region, and Punjabis enjoy some of the highest standards of living in Pakistan. However, being of a considerably larger size, there are areas lacking the transportation infrastructure and amenities that characterize the rest of the province.

¹⁰ FAMILY LIFE

Caste, or *jati*, is the most important social grouping among Punjabis, defining social relations, marriage pools, and often occupation. Castes exist even among Muslims and Sikhs, whose religions specifically deny the legitimacy of the caste system. Castes are divided into numerous *gots* or clans, which are exogamous social units. One cannot marry into the gots of any of one's four grandparents. Among Muslims, castes are known as *qaums* or *zats*, but at the village level it is the *biradari*, or patrilineage, that is the more significant social unit. All males who can trace their lineage to a common ancestor belong to the same biradari, and all members of the biradari are regarded as kin. Members of a biradari often put up a united front in village affairs and disputes, for they share a sense of collective honor and identity.

The family is the primary unit of Punjabi society. The joint family dominates, with sons and their wives and children, along with any unmarried offspring, living in the household of the parents. The men have the responsibility of overseeing the agricultural or business activities of the family. Women, under the direction of the mother-in-law or senior wife, see to the running of the household, food preparation, and the care and raising of children. Among peasant cultivators, women as well as men participate in agricultural activities. Both men and women from laboring castes work for hire, as agricultural workers or at other manual labor.

Marriage and the bearing of children are expected of women in Punjabi society. Marriages are arranged by the parents of the boy and girl, though each community follows its own marriage rituals and customs. Among Muslims, for instance, the best match is considered to be a marriage between first cousins. The months of Ramadan and Muharram are avoided as marriage dates, the former being a month of fasting and the latter being a period of ritual mourning. The Muslim marriage ceremony is termed the *Nikah* ceremony. The girl is given a dowry, which explicitly remains her property. Hindu Punjabis seek marriage partners according to the limitations of caste endogamy and clan exogamy. Dowry is an important factor in negotiating a Hindu marriage. Hindu rituals include the traditional journey of the *barāt* (marriage party) to the bride's house, the garlanding of the bride and groom, and the ritual walking around the sacred fire. Sikhs, on the other hand, do not give or take dowries and solemnize their marriages before the Granth, their sacred book. In all communities, however, residence is patrilocal—the new bride moves into the home of her husband's family.

Different Punjabi communities have different customs regarding divorce and remarriage. Although Islam has provisions for a man to divorce his wife, in rural society divorce is intensely disapproved of and there are strong social pressures against it. Nor do Muslims approve of widow remarriage. Sikhs do not permit divorce, but do allow widow remarriage. Widow remarriage is not common among Hindus, although Jats permit the union between a widow and the younger brother of her husband. Divorce is not customary among Hindus, although there are ways in which marriages can be informally brought to an end.

¹¹ CLOTHING

The standard dress in the rural Punjab is the *kurta, tahmat,* or *pyjama,* and turban. The kurta is a long shirt or tunic that hangs down to the thighs. The tahmat is a long piece of cloth that is wrapped around the waist and legs like a kilt. The pyjama, from which the English word "pajamas" is derived, is a pair of loose-fitting trousers. Turbans are worn in different styles in different localities and by different communities. Among cultivators, the turban is a relatively short piece of cloth, perhaps 1 m (3 ft) in length, wrapped loosely around the head. The formal Punjabi turban worn by men of social standing is much longer, with one end starched and sticking up like a fan. The Sikhs favor the peaked turban found around Patiala. Leather shoes, which are locally made, complete the outfit. During the winter a sweater, woolen jacket, or blanket is added. Men wear rings and sometimes earrings.

Women wear the *salwar* (baggy pants drawn in at the ankles) and *kamiz* (tunic), along with the *dupatta* (scarf). Sometimes a *ghaghra*, a long skirt dating back to Mughal times, replaces the salwar. Ornaments decorate the hair, rings or jewels are worn in the nose, and earrings, necklaces, and bangles are popular.

In urban areas, traditional dress is giving way to modern styles. Jackets, suits, and ties may be worn, with women wearing saris, dresses, skirts, and even jeans.

¹² FOOD

The basic diet of Punjabis consists of cereals (wheat, maize, or millets), vegetables, pulses, and milk products. Goat meat is eaten, but this tends to be consumed on special occasions, such as weddings or other celebrations. A typical meal consists of flat bread *(roti)* made from wheat, a cup of lentils or other pulses *(dal),* and hot tea or buttermilk. In winter, the bread is made of maize, and vegetables, such as mustard greens *(sag),* may be added. Dal and sag are prepared in a similar way. Sliced or chopped garlic and onion are fried in butter, along with chilies, cloves, black pepper, and ginger. The vegetables or pulses are added and the food cooked, sometimes for several hours, until it is tender. No utensils are used because the food is eaten with the fingers. Only the right hand is used, with a piece of roti torn off to scoop up dal or the vegetable and place it in the mouth. Tea, which is drunk in generous quantities at all times of the day, is made with half water and half milk and sweetened with three or four teaspoons of sugar. Fish, chicken, and eggs are rarely eaten.

¹³ EDUCATION

Punjabis have made great strides in education in recent years, although there is still room for improvement, especially in Pakistan. Assisted by organizations, such as the World Bank, Punjab Province has some 58% (2005 estimate) of the population under 10 years of age attending school, but less than 25% completed high school and only some 3% of this population attended university. The literacy rate in the population over 10 years of age in the Pakistan Punjab was 57% (2005 estimate). However, this varied from 60% among urban males to only 25% among females in rural areas. This is significant as some two-thirds of Punjab's population live in rural areas. 2001 figures for the Indian State of Punjab are 69.7% overall—75.2% for urban males and 57.7% for rural females.

Punjabi women perform Giddha, a traditional Punjab dance for women and girls, during the second heritage festival in Amritsar, India. (© Munish Sharma/Reuters/Corbis)

Both Punjabs have a tradition of education, with many institutions of higher learning. The University of the Punjab and the University of Engineering and Technology are located in Lahore in Pakistan. Among the institutions of higher learning in the Indian Punjab are Punjab University in Chandigarh, Punjabi University in Patialia, and Guru Nanak University in Amritsar.

14 CULTURAL HERITAGE

Though Punjabis never developed any classical traditions of dance, they are known for several forms of folk dance. These are usually performed at religious fairs and festivals or at harvest time. The most famous is the Bhangra, which is identified with the Vaisakh festival. Today, it may be performed at marriages, on the occasion of the birth of a son, or at similar events. Young men of the village, dressed in brightly colored clothes, gather in a circle around a drummer who beats out the rhythm of the dance. Moving around the drummer, slowly at first, then faster as the tempo of the drum quickens, they dance and sing with great abandon. The Giddha is a dance for women and girls. Jhumar, Sammi, Luddi, and the sword dance are all popular folk dances of the Punjab.

In addition to the music associated with folk culture (songs, epics, and dances), Punjabis share in the traditions of Sikh sacred music and Sufi mysticism. The religious compositions of the Sikh Gurus combine aspects of classical Indian music with popular Punjabi folk tunes. Among the mystics and holy men who wandered India spreading the Islamic faith were poets who composed in the language of the region and set their works to music. Their contributions, along with the devotional songs of the Hindus and Sikhs, became part of the Punjabi regional musical tradition. More formal Muslim music forms, such as the *qawwali* and *ghazal,* continue to be popular in the region today.

Folk epics and romances, the Sikh sacred literature, and the poetic compositions of the Sufis are all part of a literary tradition that continues today. Modern Punjabi literature has its beginning in the mid-19th century, with writers like Charan Singh and Vir Singh. Noted modern writers include Amrita Pritam, Khushwant Singh, Harcharan Singh, and I. C. Nanda.

15 WORK

Most Punjabis are agriculturalists. With its development as a center of modern commercial agriculture, the Punjab (both Indian and Pakistani) is one of the most important agricultural regions of South Asia. However, the Punjab also has a proud martial tradition that extends back several centuries and continues in modern times. Between the two world wars, Sikhs made up 20% of the British Indian Army, though they accounted for only 2% of the Indian population. This tradition of military service continues today, with Sikhs making up an unusually high proportion of the Indian armed forces. In Pakistan, too, Punjabis—especially Jats and Rājputs—have a distinguished tradition of military service.

16 SPORTS

Games that are popular with children include hide-and-seek, kite-flying, and Indian cricket (*gulli-danda*), a stick-game played by boys. *Kabaddi,* a team wrestling game, is played by boys and men. Wrestling, partridge- and cock-fighting, pigeon-flying, and gambling are favorite pastimes of Punjabi men.

Modern sports, such as soccer, cricket, and field hockey, are widely played and watched in the Punjab. Punjab State in India has a government department to organize and promote sports and athletics, and the National Institute of Sports is located at Patiala. Punjabis are well represented in Indian national sports teams. In Pakistan, too, Punjabis have a strong presence on the country's national sports and athletics teams.

17 ENTERTAINMENT AND RECREATION

In the past, Punjabis derived much of their entertainment and recreation from their traditional sports and games, from religious fairs and festivals, and from their rich tradition of folklore and folk culture. They had their songs, romantic epics, folk dances, and castes of traveling entertainers such as the Mirasi. This has changed in recent times with the advent of radio, television, and movies. Film music is popular and the Indian Punjab even has a small film industry producing feature films in Punjabi.

¹⁸FOLK ART, CRAFTS, AND HOBBIES

Contemporary folk arts in the Punjab represent traditions that may extend back several thousand years. Village potters make clay toys that differ little from figurines recovered from Harappan archeological sites. Peasant women follow a tradition of painting intricate designs on the mud walls of their houses for festival days. The Punjab is noted for its elaborate embroidery work. Local crafts include woodwork, metalwork, and basketry.

¹⁹SOCIAL PROBLEMS

Despite the Punjab's overall prosperity, problems exist, ranging from alcoholism in rural areas to unemployment in the cities. Illiteracy is still high in villages, especially among women. Punjabis who have migrated from rural areas to cities in search of work form an urban underclass that are cut off from the ties and support system of their families and village communities. The cities are full of high school and university graduates who lack the technical training for success in the modern economy. If they are fortunate enough to obtain employment, it tends to be in low-level clerical jobs. The Indian Punjab has also been faced with civil unrest and disruptions caused by the confrontation between Sikh extremists and the central government over the last several decades. The 1970s and 1980s saw the emergence of the Khalistan movement in the Indian Punjab to create "The Land of the Pure" as an independent Sikh state in all Punjabi-speaking areas, which include Indian Punjab, Haryana, Himachal Pradesh, and some other Punjabi speaking parts of states like Gujarat and Rājasthān. The 1980s saw militants undertake an insurgency against the government of India. However, under the Constitution of India, secessionism is forbidden, and the Indian government sent in security forces to counter the insurgency. The Indian Army's Operation Blue Star, involving an attack on the Sikh's holy shrine at Amritsar, where some militants had taken refuge, led ultimately to Prime Minister Indira Gandhi's assassination by her Sikh bodyguards in 1984 and the subsequent indiscriminate killings of Sikhs by Hindus throughout India. Various rebel groups in favor of Khalistan fought an insurgency against the government of India in the early 1990s, an insurgency that was suppressed by Indian security forces. Human rights groups have reported numerous atrocities, especially against Sikh women, carried out by the Indian security forces at this time.

Punjabis in Pakistan are subject to the chronic political instability that affects the state. Punjabis, who are the most populous group in the state, are viewed by other peoples as dominating the state of Pakistan, and Nawaz Sharif, Benazir Bhutto's chief protagonist until her assassination in December 2007, has had his power base in the Punjab. The radicalism associated with militant Islam and Pakistan's (apparently reluctant) involvement in the West's War on Terror is a cause of social problems, as is sectarian conflict and both internal and external disputes over water resources. The dispute with Sindh Province over the use of the waters of the Indus River and its tributaries extends back to the middle of the 19th century, but Pakistan's Water and Power Development Authority's (WAPDA) proposed plan known as Vision-2025 will essentially give Punjab Province control of the Indus' waters, extremely important in a country irrigated agriculture is the dominant economic activity.

When the Punjab was partitioned between India and Pakistan in 1947, a bone of contention remained which country had the right to use the waters of the Indus River and its tributaries. This issue was finally resolved by the Indus Waters Treaty, signed between the two countries in 1960. The Treaty provided that the waters of the contested rivers, the Ravi, Beas, and Sutlej would be for the exclusive use of India. However, India would have to make a one-time financial payment to Pakistan as compensation for the loss of water from the rivers in India. The countries also agreed to exchange data and co-operate in matters related to the treaty, creating the Permanent Indus Commission, with a commissioner appointed by each country.

In 1958 the government of India started construction on what came to be called the Indira Gandhi Canal, which carried water from the Harike Barrage, a few kilometers below the confluence of the Sutlej and Beas rivers in Punjab state into desert areas of Rājasthān. While the Canal has certainly succeeded in dramatically changing the face of agriculture in Rājasthān, some see this as stealing water from the water-short Punjab, and this was a contributing factor to the Punjab's resistance to the central government.

²⁰ GENDER ISSUES

The situation facing women in the Punjab tends to vary according to which (i.e. Pakistani or Indian) Punjab they inhabit, although in both locales they are accorded inferior status. In the Indian Punjab, for instance, where Hinduism is well-entrenched, women face all the problems of Hindu society—arranged marriages, child marriages (these still occur even though they are illegal according to both national and state law), payment of dowries, and abuse and even deaths arising from dowry disputes. In 2001 Punjab had a child sex ratio (for 0–6 years) of 874 girls for 1,000 boys, showing the impact of sex selective abortion despite the passage of the Pre-Conception and Pre-Natal Diagnostic Technique (Prohibition of Sex Selection) (PCPNDT) Act by the government of India in 2003. This is a trend for Hindu India, with the 2001 Census showing a sex ratio of 933 women for 1,000 males. One social consequence of this is the sale of young girls from poor countries, such as Nepal, or states, such as West Bengal or Assam, to wealthy peasants as wives due to the lack of girls of marriageable age in the Punjab. This same situation applies to the Sikhs, who tend to mirror Hindu attitudes towards women, despite the protestations of freedom and equality their religion supposedly grants women. The situation regarding female feticide among Sikhs became so bad that five Head Priests of the "Akal Takht," the highest seat of Sikh religious authority in the Golden Temple at Amritsar, issued a *Hukumnama* (edict) in April 2001 preaching excommunication of those involved in this practice.

Women face a serious law and order situation in the Indian Punjab, with numerous cases of murder, rape, and attempted rape recorded. Kidnapping and suicides are common, with many cases of dowry deaths reported and still more going unreported. With revenge as their sole motive, a growing number of women in Punjab are landing themselves on the wrong side of law. Police officials say that a rise in the number of cases of well-to-do women getting entangled in murders, attempts to murder, and even in assisting rapes reveals a new trend in the state.

Detriments, such as lack of inheritance and economic discrimination stemming from the patriarchal social systems, exist on both sides of the border, but women in West Punjab suffer from the general place of women in Muslim society. Under Muslim law, a man can have up to four wives, and divorce is relatively easy for him to obtain. High-class women are required to maintain *purdah,* and village women commonly wear the *burqa.* Women (and men, too) are subject to "honor killings" and, despite passage of the Women's Protection bill of 2006, live under Muslim law and are sentenced to the legal penalties set out in the 1979 Hudud Ordinance. It is not uncommon for women to be subjected to physical abuse by their husbands and other male members of the family.

Societal norms, poverty, illiteracy, the dominance of a patriarchal society, and the constraints of Hindu or Muslim religious practices influence all but the most affluent women in the Punjab.

21 BIBLIOGRAPHY

Ahmad, Sagir. *Class and Power in a Punjabi Village.* New York: Monthly Review Press, 1977.

Aryan, K. C. *The Cultural Heritage of Punjab: 3000 BC to 1947 AD.* New Delhi: Rekha Prakashan, 1983.

Bajwa, Ranjeet Singh. *Semiotics of Birth Ceremonies in Punjab.* New Delhi: Bahri Publications, 1991.

Banerjee, Himadri, ed. *The Khalsa and the Punjab: Studies in Sikh History, to the Nineteenth Century.* New Delhi: Tulika, 2002.

Eglar, Zekiye. *A Punjabi Village in Pakistan.* New York: Columbia University Press, 1960.

Fox, Richard Gabriel. *Lions of the Punjab: Culture in the Making.* Berkeley: University of California Press, 1985.

Gill, M. S., ed. *Punjab Society: Perspectives and Challenges.* New Delhi: Concept, 2003.

Mann, Vijepal Singh. *Troubled Waters of Punjab.* New Delhi: Allied Publishers, 2003.

Nadeem, Farooq. *Chaos: Research Articles on History and Socio Economic Situation of Pakistani Punjab.* Lahore: World Institute of Literature and Culture, 2005.

Nadiem, Ihsan H. *Punjab: Land, History, People.* Lahore: al-Faisal Nashran, 2005.

Sekhon, Iqbal S. *The Punjabis: The People, Their History, Culture and Enterprise.* 3 vols. New Delhi: Cosmo, 2000.

Singh, Mohinder. *History and Culture of Punjab.* New Delhi: Atlantic Publishers and Distributors, 1988.

—by D. O. Lodrick

QATARIS

PRONUNCIATION: KAHT-uh-reez
LOCATION: Qatar
POPULATION: 907,000 (2007)
LANGUAGE: Arabic; English
RELIGION: Islam (Sunni Muslim)

1 INTRODUCTION

Qataris live on a small peninsula that juts into the Persian Gulf, in the Middle East. Qatar is one of the "oil states," a country that moved quickly from poverty to riches with the discovery of oil reserves. There is archaeological evidence that the land now known as Qatar was inhabited by humans as long ago as 5000 BC. Pearling in the oyster beds just off shore began back in 300 BC, and continued to be Qataris' main source of income until the early 20th century. The Islamic revolution arrived in Qatar in AD 630, and all Qataris converted to Islam. For most of its history, Qatar was a sparsely populated land whose people followed three different lifestyles: some Qataris were fishers in the Gulf; others made their living through pearling; and the rest were Bedu (or Bedouin) nomads (*see* **Bedu**). The modern state of Qatar can perhaps be said to have begun when the Arab tribe of Utub settled there around 1766. The years following their arrival were marked by constant shifts in power between two ruling families: the al Khalifa family, who are now the ruling family of Bahrain; and the al Jalahima family. Other forces who were involved in these centuries of conflict include the Sultan of Oman, Wahhabi Muslims from Saudi Arabia, the Persians, and the Ottoman Turks. When Britain made its treaties with other Gulf states (which then became known as the Trucial States), Bahrain and Qatar were left out because Britain did not want to get involved in the conflicts between them. Qatar, therefore, became a stronghold for the pirates that terrorized the Gulf at that time.

After a series of naval battles between Bahrain and Qatar (initiated by Bahrain) in 1867–68, Britain decided it was in their best interests to try to negotiate a settlement between them. In this settlement, the al Thani family were established as the rulers of Qatar, which they continue to be to this day.

The Ottoman Turks occupied Qatar in 1871 and stayed until August 1915. As soon as they left, Qatar began to negotiate a protective treaty with Britain, and officially became one of the Trucial States in November 1916. When Japan developed the cultured pearl in the late 1920s, Qatar's economy sank. Cultured pearls were a much easier way to obtain pearls than diving for them in the wild oyster beds, so demand for Qatar's wild pearls fell drastically. The Qatari people lived in great poverty for the next two decades, until oil was discovered. World War II (1939–45) delayed production of the oil for a few years, until 1947. Since that time, Qataris have become some of the wealthiest people in the world. Qatar became fully independent on 3 September 1971.

Toward the end of the 20th century, Qatar began establishing itself as a reforming, democratizing force among the countries of the Gulf Cooperation Council (Bahrain, Kuwait, Oman, Qatar, Saudi Arabia and the UAE). The country allows no political parties, but does sponsor regional conferences on civil liberties and does allow elections to regional coun-

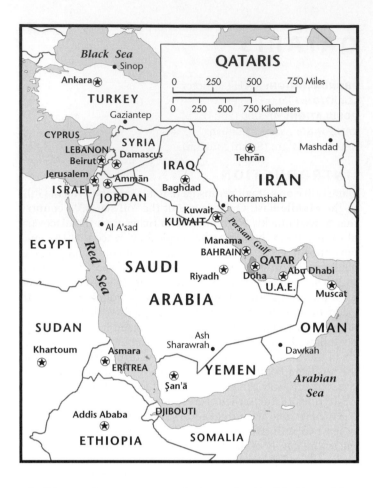

QATARIS

0   250   500   750 Miles

0   250   500   750 Kilometers

cils. These reforms were mostly driven by Sheikh Hamad bin Khalifa al Thani, who overthrew his father in a bloodless coup in 1995. He introduced municipal elections in 1999 and a new constitution enacted in 2005 created a national assembly, one third of whose members are appointed by the emir.

²LOCATION AND HOMELAND

Qatar is a small peninsula that juts due north into the Arabian (or Persian) Gulf. The peninsula is about 160 km (100 mi) long, and 88 km (55 mi) across at its widest point. The total area is 11,437 sq km (4,427 sq mi), which is about the size of the US states of Connecticut and Rhode Island combined. The north, east, and west sides of the peninsula are bordered by the Gulf waters. To the south lie Saudi Arabia and the United Arab Emirates. Qatar and Bahrain have long disputed ownership of the Hawar Islands, which lie between the two states.

The climate in Qatar is generally hot and dry. In the winter months it gets somewhat cooler, but much more humid. Temperatures can go as high as 43°C (110°F) in the summer (between May and October). In the winter, the humidity can reach 100%. A hot desert wind, or *shamal*, blows almost constantly all year long, bringing with it frequent sand- and duststorms. There is very little rainfall, only 7.5 cm (3 in) per year on average, all of which falls during the winter months. Qatar's terrain is flat, with some sand dunes in the southeast. There are also extensive salt flats in the south, indicating that the land there was once under the sea, making Qatar an island in the remote past.

Little plant or animal life exists in Qatar, beyond hardy forms of desert life, such as thorn bushes, cacti, and scrub grass; insects, spiders, and some butterflies; and lizards, snakes, and scorpions. Mammals in the desert include fox, rabbits, hedgehogs, gerbils and other rodents, and bats. The Gulf waters support a greater amount and variety of life. Sea turtles, sea cows, dolphins, and an occasional whale can be found there, as well as a myriad of fish. Shrimp are harvested in large numbers as well. Flamingoes flock along the shores, along with other sea and shore birds. The Arabian, or white, oryx is almost extinct in the wild but is being bred in captivity in Qatar and elsewhere. The same is true for the gazelle.

The human population of Qatar is about 907,000. Of those, at least three-fourths are foreign workers. There are only about 173,000 native-born Qataris. Most people in Qatar live in the cities; 80% of the total population lives in the capital city of Doha. Doha is on the east coast of the Qatar peninsula, as are most of the larger towns and cities.

³LANGUAGE

The official language of Qatar is Arabic, the native language of native-born Qataris. Many Qataris are also fluent in English, which is used as the common language for business transactions, etc.

Arabic, spoken by 100 million people worldwide, has many dialects which are very distinctive, so that people living as little as 500 km (300 mi) apart may not be able to understand one another. The written form of Arabic is called Classical Arabic, or, for today's literature and press, Modern Standard Arabic. It is the same for all literate Arabs, regardless of how different their spoken forms are. Arabic is written from right to left in a unique alphabet which has no distinction between upper and lower cases. It is not necessary for the letters to be written on a straight line, as English letters must be. Punctuation conventions are also quite different from English.

Arabic speakers tend to use emotional appeal, exaggeration, repetition, and words instead of action (for example, making threats with no intention to follow through on them). They are more interested in the poetry of the language than in communicating "cold, hard facts." "Hello" in Arabic is *Marhaba* or *Ahlan,* to which one replies, *Marhabtayn* or *Ahlayn.* Other common greetings are *As-salam alaykum,* "Peace be with you," with the reply of *Walaykum as-salam,* "And to you peace." *Ma'assalama* means "Goodbye." "Thank you" is *Shukran,* and "You're welcome" is *Afwhan.* "Yes" is *na'am* and "no" is *la'a.* The numbers 1 to 10 in Arabic are *wahad, itnin, talata, arba'a, khamsa, sitta, saba'a, tamania, tisa'a,* and *ashara.*

Arabs have very long names, consisting of their given name, their father's name, their paternal grandfather's name, and finally their family name. Women do not take their husband's name when they marry, but rather keep their mother's family name as a show of respect for their family of origin. Given names usually indicate an Arab's religious affiliation: Muslims use names with Islamic religious significance, such as Muhammad and Fatima, whereas Christians often use Western names.

⁴FOLKLORE

Many Muslims believe in *jinns,* spirits who can change shape and be either visible or invisible. Muslims sometimes wear amulets around their necks to protect them from jinns. Stories of jinns are often told at night, like ghost stories around a campfire.

⁵RELIGION

At least 95% of the total population of Qatar is Muslim, and native-born Qataris are mostly of the Sunni branch of Islam and adhere to a modified, slightly less conservative branch of Wahhabism, the fundamentalist and puritanical branch of Islam that is prevalent in Saudi Arabia.

⁶MAJOR HOLIDAYS

As an Islamic state, Qatar's official holidays are Islamic ones. Muslim holidays follow the lunar calendar, moving back by 11 days each year, so their dates are not fixed on the standard Gregorian calendar. The main Muslim holidays are *Ramadan*, the month of fasting from dawn until dusk each day; *Ayd Al-Fitr*, a three-day festival at the end of Ramadan; *Ayd Al-Adha*, a three-day feast of sacrifice at the end of the month of pilgrimage to Mecca (known as the *Hajj*; the First of Muharram, or the Muslim New Year; *Mawoulid An-Nabawi*, the Prophet Muhammad's birthday; and *Ayd Al-ism wa Al Miraj*, a feast celebrating the nocturnal visit of Muhammad to Jerusalem. Friday is the Islamic day of rest, so most businesses and services are closed on Fridays. All government offices, private businesses, and schools are also closed during Ayd Al-Fitr and Ayd Al-Adha.

⁷RITES OF PASSAGE

Qataris mark major life transitions such as birth, puberty, marriage, and death with Islamic ceremonies and feasting.

⁸INTERPERSONAL RELATIONS

Arab hospitality reigns in Qatar. An Arab will never ask personal questions, as that is considered rude. It is expected that a person will say what he or she wishes, without being asked. A direct refusal is also considered rude, so one must learn to read the indirect signals that are given. Food and drink are always taken with the right hand because the left hand is used for "unclean" purposes, such as wiping oneself after using the toilet. When talking, Arabs touch each other much more often, and stand much closer together, than Westerners do. People of the same sex will often hold hands while talking, even if they are virtual strangers. (Members of the opposite sex, even married couples, never touch in public.) Arabs talk a lot, talk loudly, repeat themselves often, and interrupt each other constantly. Conversations are highly emotional and full of gestures.

⁹LIVING CONDITIONS

Qatar has engaged in a rapid modernization program since the 1970s, when income from the oil industry rose dramatically. All villages and towns can now be reached by paved roads which are well-maintained. The constantly growing population in the cities leads to a continual campaign of expansion and road construction, so travel there is sometimes delayed. There is little public transportation available in Qatar, so nearly everyone drives a car. Housing, utilities, and communication services are all modern. Health care is up-to-date and free to all Qataris. Health clinics, both public and private, are located throughout the peninsula so that medical care is readily available to all. The general health of Qataris is good, although there are some problems with rat and insect control—and their accompanying diseases—in the larger cities.

The two largest cities, the capital city of Doha and the west-coast city of Umm Said, have a water-main system that provides running water to all residents. In other places, water is delivered by tankers and stored in water tanks in gardens or on roofs, or is pumped into homes from deep-water wells. All foreign workers are provided with free housing. Even the formerly nomadic Bedu (or Bedouin) now live in air-conditioned villas built by the government. The government also provides social welfare programs for the sick, elderly, and disabled.

Qatar's population increased rapidly in the 1990s and early in the first decades of the 21st century. This has caused some housing shortages but the country is rapidly building new housing and is even allowing some foreign ownership in newly developed properties.

¹⁰FAMILY LIFE

The family is the central unit of Qatari society. Qataris are only recently removed from a tribal way of life, so tribal values and customs still prevail.

¹¹CLOTHING

Qataris wear traditional Arab clothing. For men, this is an ankle-length robe called a *thobe* or *dishdasha,* with a *ghutrah* (a large piece of cloth) on the head which is held in place by an *uqal* (a woven piece of rope). Women tend to wear very colorful long-sleeved, ankle-length dresses, with a black silk cloak called an *abaya* covering them completely in public. Some older Qatari women still wear a face mask, called a *batula,* but this custom is dying out.

¹²FOOD

Rice is a staple food for Qataris. It is usually fried (or sautéed) first, then boiled. Saffron is often added during the frying stage to make the rice yellow. Bread is served at almost every meal, especially pita bread (known in Qatar as *khubus arabi*). *Hummus,* a spread made from ground chickpeas, is also eaten at most meals. *Hamour,* a type of fish caught in the Gulf, is frequently served baked, or cooked with rice. Mutton (sheep) is the favorite meat—pork is forbidden by Islam (as is alcohol). Shellfish, particularly shrimp which are caught in great numbers off Qatar's shores, is a popular dish. Tea and coffee are the beverages of choice. Tea is never drunk with milk added, and coffee is always made from Turkish beans and is often flavored with saffron, rosewater, or cardamom. Coffee and tea are usually sweetened with sugar.

¹³EDUCATION

Education is highly valued by Qataris. Attendance at primary and secondary schools is 98%, and the literacy rate is more than 65% and rising. In the public school system, which was established in 1956, education is compulsory from age 6 to age 16 and it is free all the way through university-level. The government even provides full scholarships (including travel costs) for university students who wish to study abroad. Over 40,000 students, both boys and girls, are enrolled in primary and secondary schools, and another 400 or so study in vocational training institutes and religious schools. Adult education was introduced in 1957, and 40 adult education centers

Qataris play traditional percussion instruments in central Doha. (AFP/Getty Images)

now provide literacy courses to about 5,000 adult students. Qatar University was founded in 1973 and offers state-of-the-art degree programs in many subjects. Computer courses are required for all university students, as is physical education.

Qatar has been developing an international hub of higher education since early in the 21st century. By 2008 the country hosted branch campuses of such US universities as Cornell, Virginia Commonwealth University, and Texas A&M.

14 CULTURAL HERITAGE

Arab music is much like the Arab language—rich, repetitive, and exaggerated. The *oud* is a popular instrument; it is an ancient stringed instrument that is the ancestor of the European lute. Another traditional instrument is the *rebaba*, a one-stringed instrument. A traditional Arab dance is the *ardha,* or men's sword dance. Men carrying swords stand shoulder to shoulder and dance, and from among them a poet sings verses while drummers beat out a rhythm.

Islam forbids the depiction of the human form, so Qatari art focuses on geometric and abstract shapes. Calligraphy is a sacred art, with the Quran being the primary subject matter. Muslim art finds its greatest expression in mosques. The Islamic reverence for poetry and the poetic richness of the Arabic language inform much of Qatar's cultural heritage.

15 WORK

The most profitable industry in Qatar is the oil industry, and natural gas production. The government runs both. Other industries include cement, power plants, desalinization plants (making drinking water out of sea water by removing the salt), petrochemicals, steel, and fertilizer. The government is trying to encourage private industry by offering grants, low-interest loans, and exemption from customs duties to private entrepreneurs. There is almost no agriculture in Qatar, although irrigation systems are being developed to increase the amount of arable land. Fishing continues to be a way of life for many Qataris, one that they have followed for millennia.

16 SPORTS

Qataris love outdoor sports, both on land and on water. Football ("soccer" in the US) has become the most popular sport, although auto-racing is also a favorite. Basketball, handball, and volleyball are modern sports that are beginning to catch on in Qatar. Ten-pin bowling and golf are also enjoyed by some Qataris. The traditional sports of horse- and camel-racing and falconry are still pursued passionately in Qatar.

17 ENTERTAINMENT AND RECREATION

Qataris enjoy playing chess, bridge, and darts. Tea shops and coffee houses are popular spots for socializing. Most are inside malls due to the intense heat of the Persian Gulf. Going to the movies is a very popular pastime as is simply driving around. Most modern Qataris have free time and considerable amounts of disposable income (the country has the fifth highest per capita income in the world, higher than the US) and the streets and mall and cinema parking lots are overflowing with the best luxury automobiles in the world.

¹⁸FOLK ART, CRAFTS, AND HOBBIES

The national government generously subsidizes folk arts such as rug making and basket-weaving. Goldsmithing is an ancient art among Qataris that continues to be practiced today. Folk music is also performed in Qatar. The National Theater produces both Arabic and English language productions at a modern performance space in Doha.

¹⁹SOCIAL PROBLEMS

The rapid modernization of Qatar in the last few decades has created a huge generation gap between the pre-oil boom elders and the post-oil boom young people. Older people who grew up in Qatar before oil wealth made modernization possible do not understand or like many of the changes that modernization has brought about. They often lament the loss of the "good old days." Young people, on the other hand, have grown up in the more-industrialized era of high technology and are comfortable with it, seeing only the benefits and none of the losses. The two generations often find it very difficult to communicate with each other.

Qatar is a politically and religiously moderate country, but there was at least one incident of a terrorist bombing in Doha in 2005. A British citizen was killed outside of a theater in Doha. The bombing occurred on the second anniversary of the US invasion of neighboring Iraq. The US maintains an enormous military presence in Qatar. The US Central Command is headquartered there and this has caused some unease among some Qataris due to the great unpopularity of the US occupation of Iraq.

²⁰ GENDER ISSUES

The rights of women in Qatar are limited by Islamic teachings and Arab tradition. The wife of the emir, Sheikha Mozah bint Nasser al Missned, has been a strong advocate for women's rights in the country. Qatar is one of a very few Arab countries with a personal status law, passed in 2007, which codifies personal and family law in such areas as divorce, inheritance, and child custody. Women in Qatar have the right to divorce their husbands and the 2007 personal status law also ended the ancient tradition of "temporary marriage." Women are represented in the government to a greater degree than in other Gulf countries but their participation is low by Western standards.

²¹ BIBLIOGRAPHY

Albyn, Carole Zisa, and Lois Sinaiko Webb. *The Multicultural Cookbook for Students*. Phoenix: Oryx Press, 1993.

Background Notes: Qatar. Washington, D.C.: US Department of State, Bureau of Public Affairs, Office of Public Communication, April 1992.

Cordesman, Anthony. *Bahrain, Oman, Qatar, and the UAE: Challenges of Security*. Boulder, CO. Westview Press, 1997

McCoy, Lisa. *Qatar: Modern Middle East Nations and Their Strategic Place in the World*. Broomall, PA: Mason Crest Publishers, 2002.

Orr, Tamra. *Qatar*. New York: Marshall Cavendish Benchmark, 2008.

Post Report: Qatar. Washington, D.C.: US Department of State, 1991.

Qatar. London: Stacey International, 2000.

Rickman, Maureen. *Qatar*. New York: Chelsea House, 1987.

Vine, Peter, and Paula Casey. *The Heritage of Qatar*. London: IMMEL Publishing, 1992.

—revised by J. Henry

RĀJASTHĀNIS

ALTERNATE NAMES: "Marwaris"
LOCATION: the northwest Indian state of Rājasthān
POPULATION: 56,473,122 (Census of India, 2001, for Rājasthān state)
LANGUAGE: Rājasthānī and various languages and dialects spoken in Rājasthān
RELIGION: Hindu

¹ INTRODUCTION

Rājasthān, the sixth most populous state in India, is inhabited by numerous groups, but it is the Rajputs (*Rājpūts*) and Rajput culture that give the region its distinct identity. The state was called *Rājputāna* ("Land of the Rajputs [Sons of Kings]") in colonial British days, while its present name Rājasthān ("Land of Kings") reflects the fact that the former states in the region (most are currently districts in the state) were ruled by Rajas (*Rājas* [kings]) who, once they accepted British paramountcy in the 19th century, were allowed to rule their territories from that time with no British interference in their domestic affairs. In the past, the region was also called Rajwara (*Rājwāra*) and Raethana (*Rāethāna*) ["Land of Kings"], reflecting its association with the Rajput rulers. The independent states of Rājasthān virtually remained feudal kingdoms until they were incorporated into the Republic of India in 1947. In the post-Independence era, Rājasthān is known for the success of its Panchayati Raj—a system of local government based on *panchayats*, or local caste, village or tribal councils.

In addition to the Rajputs, who are relatively small in number and make up under 6% of the state's population, other groups in Rājasthān include Charans and Bhats, castes that provided hereditary services to the Rajputs, tribals (Bhils, Minas, Meos), the nomadic Lohars and Rabari, and Brahmans, Banias, Jats, Chamars and Muslims.

² LOCATION AND HOMELAND

Rājasthān, territorially the largest state in India, covers some 342,239 sq km (about the area of Germany) in the north west of India. The state is bounded by Gujarat to the south, Madhya Pradesh to the south east, and Uttar Pradesh, Hayana and Punjab to the northeast. The western border of Rājasthān is the international frontier with Pakistan, which given the history of India and Pakistan, makes the state, especially Rājasthān's western areas, important from a military perspective.

Rājasthān is an arid region, with the Aravalli range of mountains running for over 600 km northeast-southwest though the middle of the state. Rising from "the Ridge" at Delhi, the mountains rarely exceed 1,000 m in the north. For much of their length, the Aravallis assume the form of a narrow belt of low, though often precipitous, parallel ridges rather than a continuous mountain system, though they reach a maximum elevation of 1,722 m at Mount Abu in the south. The Aravallis have the distinction of containing the oldest rocks in the world that present any elevation as a mountain system and separate the Thar Desert to the west from the more well-watered, agricultural plateaus of southeastern Rājasthān. The barren plains of the Thar (also known as the "Marusthali" or "Region of Death") extend north and west from the Aravallis

to the Indus and Sutlej Rivers in Pakistan. This region gets less than 10 inches of rainfall a year, with mean maximum temperatures in summer averaging around 45°C (113° F). To the south and east of the Aravallis, an area drained by the Banas and Chambal Rivers receives close to 25 inches of precipitation a year and, with its relatively fertile soils, provides one of the more environmentally productive regions of the state.

The Rajputs are believed to be descended from numerous warlike clans such as the Scythians, Huns and Gujjars who entered India from the northwest from Central Asia in the years preceding the 6th century AD. Once they established military supremacy over the local inhabitants, they set out to establish themselves as *kshatriyas*, as belonging to the ruling, warrior caste. They accomplished this in Rājasthān by having genealogies developed for them by Charans, a caste whose traditional occupation is as bards and genealogists to the Rajputs. No doubt such genealogies were mythological, but they legitimized the position of the Rajputs in Hindu society, providing them with an ancestry that was linked to the Rajputs in the ancient Vedas. Thus Rajput clans such as the Sisodiyas and Rathors in Rājasthān claim to be descended from the sun (the Suryavansha lineage), the Bhati from the moon (the Chandravansha lineage), and the Chauhans and Pratihara find their origins in the "agnikula" or firepot of a sage on Mount Abu, in southern Rājasthān (the Agnivansha linage). By the 7th century AD, kingdoms ruled by Rajputs extended from the Arabian sea to the head of the Bay of Bengal. However, the successful invasions of Muslims from the northwest in the centuries following the 12th century AD changed all this. Though resisted by the Rajputs, successfully at first, the Muslims established themselves at Delhi.

The Rajput kingdoms along the Ganges Valley were destroyed, with Rajput kingdoms surviving in the foothills of the Himalaya. The Rajputs of what is now Rājasthān retreated into the barren wilderness of the Thar desert to wage a guerrilla war against the Muslims, who were never able to inflict a decisive defeat on them. Reverses, such as the sacks of Ranthambore and Chittorgarh, accompanied by Rajput *jauhar*, when the men rode out in saffron robes (a symbol of Hinduism) to meet their death at the hands of the besieging Muslim forces and the women burned themselves in a massive funeral pyre, served only to add to the romantic myth of the Rajput. It was from this time that the image of the fearless, Rajput warrior, defender of Hinduism and cows against the marauding Muslims dates. It is also from this time that the political outlines of modern Rājasthān was formed. The Muslims skirted the region and went on to conquer Gujarat to the south, but independent Rajput states such as Jaipur, Jodhpur (Marwar) and Udaipur (Mewar) retained their independence. It was only through a combination of force and marriages that the Mughal Emperor Akbar was able to bring the states of Rājasthān to heel and make them his allies.

The major former independent states of Rājasthān, ruled by separate Rajput clans include Jaipur (founded by the Kachhwaha clan of Rajputs), Jodhpur or Mawar (ruled by the Rathors) Jaiselmer (ruled by the Bhatis) and Udaipur (the Sisodiyas) remained essentially independent feudal kingdoms until India gained its Independence from British rule in 1947. Udaipur is considered the most senior of the former states, because the Sisodiyas never came to an accommodation with the Muslims ruling in Delhi. In fact, though it can be argued there is no such thing as "Rājasthāni" culture and that the Rājasthān government is trying to promote a sense of being Rājasthāni (most people in the area identify with a particular caste or community rather than the state), some scholars feel that the Rajput imprint on the region is distinctive enough to talk about a "Rājasthāni" culture.

³LANGUAGE

Numerous dialects are spoken in Rājasthān, most of which form part of western Hindi. Along the borders of the state, the dialects show the influence of neighboring tongues such as Sindhi, Punjabi, and Gujarati. In the "core" of Rājasthān, however, spoken dialects tend to correlate with the boundaries of the former Rajput states. Thus Harauti is the dialect spoken in the areas of the former Rājpūt states of Kota, Bundi, and Jhalawar, Jaipuri is the dialect of the state of Jaipur. Mewari is spoken in what used to be Udaipur (Mewar), and Marwari is spoken in what used to be Jodhpur and much of the western part of the state. In 1908 George Grierson was the first scholar who gave the designation "Rājasthāni" to the languages of the region. Today, Rājasthāni as spoken is essentially the Marwari form of speech. Although the Union (i.e. central) government does not recognize Rājasthāni as one of India's official languages, the Sahitya Akademi, India's National Academy of Letters, and the University Grants Commission do recognize it as a distinct language. It is also taught as such in the Universities of Jodhpur and Udaipur. Since 1947, several movements have been going on in Rājasthān for its recognition as an official language of India, but today Rājasthāni is still considered a "dialect" of Hindi.

A tradition of literature exists in Rājasthān dating back to the 6th century AD. A major element in this tradition is the poetry written by the Charans, hereditary bards and genealogists to the Rajputs, extolling the virtues, accomplishments, victories and sometimes the glorious deaths of Rajput heroes. This bardic poetry reaches it greatest heights in medieval times, when it was strongly influenced by the religious *Bhakti* (Devotional) movements. Mirabai, a 16th century authoress of numerous poems and songs of the Bhakti movement extolling the virtues of the god Krishna, was born in Rājasthān, as was Dadu Dayal, a 16th century saint who founded the Dadu Panth, a sect that still has numerous followers in Rājasthān.

The writings of many of the poets of the Independence period are full of patriotic and nationalistic fervor, while since Independence, traditional romantic, lyrical works co-exist with those that attempt to raise the reader's consciousness of the plight of the common man.

⁴FOLKLORE

While each ethnic group in Rājasthān, (e.g., the Chamars, Bhils, Banias, Bishnoi, Meos, and Minas) has its own folk traditions, once can argue that the region's folk culture is essentially that of the Rajputs. Thus, the view of the brave, martial Rajput as the defender of the faith (Hinduism) and of the common man against the depredations of the Muslims lies at the heart of Rājasthāni folklore.

There is the village tradition, for instance, of the Bhopa, who travels from village to village with his *phad*, a cloth backdrop 30 feet in length painted with episodes from the life of Pabuji, a local folk deity. The Bhopa (priest singer) and his wife tell the tale of Pabuji in front of the phad, which itself is a form

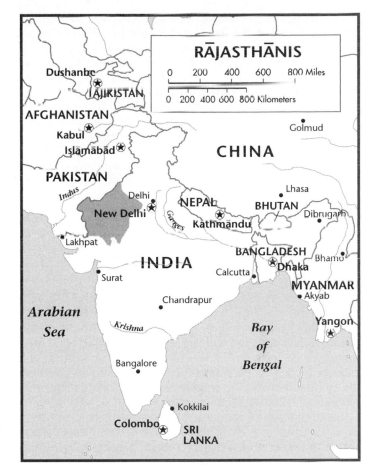

of folk art, in a performance that might take a week to complete. Pabuji, himself a Rajput, offered to protect the herds of the Charan woman Deval (again, an example of the ties between the Charans and the Rajputs). Deval asks him to retrieve her stolen herd, and Pabuji leaves his marriage ceremony to do so, but is killed in the process of rescuing the herd. Again, this is a story about honor and responsibility, whatever the consequences. All the villagers are familiar with the Pabuji story, but the Bhopa and the phad form a distinctly Rājasthāni element in local culture. Dev Narayanja is another folk deity, though in this case the hero is an incarnation of the god Vishnu. He is revered by local villagers in Rājasthān, and his tale, also, is told by traveling Bhopas before a phad depicting his exploits. Tejaji (a Jat whose story is similar to Pabuji's in that he put his life and family at risk but kept his pride and values like loyalty, freedom, truth, and social reform etc. intact) and Gogaji (a snake god, originally a Chauhan Rajput, revered by Hindu and Muslim alike) are folk heroes with whose tales every villager in Rājasthān is familiar.

⁵RELIGION

Although a sizeable Muslim minority (8.5%) exists in Rājasthān, 88.7% of Rājasthānis are Hindus. This figure, however, glosses over the wide range of religious beliefs among Hindus in Rājasthān. The non-sectarian Dadu-Panth has a strong presence in the state, following the teaching of the 16th century Rājasthāni saint Dadu Dayal, who preached the equality of all men, strict vegetarianism, total abstinence from intoxicating liquor, and lifelong celibacy. Although followers of Shiva are found in the state, most Rājasthānis follow Vishnu and, in particular, Vishnu in his incarnation as Krishna. A major shrine of the Vallabhacharya sect of Krishna exists at Nathdwara, on the banks of the Banas River, north of Udaipur (Mewar). Tradition has it that, while the image of Krishna was being moved from its home in Brindaban (Uttar Pradesh) to Dwarka in Gujarat, the cart carrying the icon broke down at Nathdwara, and the Rana (ruler) of Mewar gave his permission for the Sri Nathji temple to be built at the site—hence the presence of the temple, which is a major pilgrimage center for Vaishnavas in India. Nathdwara's devotional music and art forms, such as *pīchhavāī*, temple hangings painted with scenes from the life of Krishna, contribute to the uniqueness of Rājasthāni culture.

The Dargah (tomb) of Kwaja Mu'in ud-Din Chishti, an important Sufi saint, in Ajmer is the most important pilgrimage center for Muslims in India outside of Mecca and the annual Urs attracts over 300,000 pilgrims to this city in central Rājasthān, including some from Pakistan and the Middle East. Hindus as well as Muslims visit the shrine. In addition to Muslims, small numbers of Christians, Sikhs, and Buddhists contribute to the religious diversity of Rājasthān. Jains, though numerically few (only 1.2% of the population) and concentrated along the borders of Gujarat, have left their mark on the cultural landscape in magnificent temples such as those at Ranakpur, Palitana, and Mount Abu.

In addition, one finds numerous shrines to folk heroes such as Tejaji and Gogaji scattered across the state. There is one shrine to Gogaji near Ajmer, in central Rājasthān, where the head of the snake is in the shrine, and the rest of the snake's body extends several feet beyond the retaining wall in the rear of the shrine.

⁶MAJOR HOLIDAYS

Rājasthānis celebrate all major holidays of the religious calendar in India. Holi and Diwali are, perhaps, the most important. Holi, a spring festival, is marked by the throwing of colored water and the burning of bonfires. At Diwali, which is the major autumn festival of the Hindus, lights (traditionally butter lamps in small earthenware pots, though in modern times these have been replaced by electric lights) are used to decorate houses, houses are whitewashed or painted, and friends play cards and gamble together. For the Bania castes, Diwali marks the beginning of the New Year—financial books are closed and debts are paid. In villages, Govardhan Puja, a festival related to the Hindu deity Krishna, is celebrated on the day following Diwali. Villagers clean and resurface their hearths with cow dung, and make crude figures (of Krishna), also out of cow dung (in the more important temples of the Krishna sect, such figures of Krishna are much more elaborate). These images are destroyed by driving cattle across them. Different legends are attached to the dung figures in different parts of Rājasthān. According to local tradition in the Udaipur District of Rājasthān, for example, the dung figure represents a local farmer named Govardhan who was sleeping outside his hut. The god Krishna, bent on amorous adventures, attempted to enter the house and disturbed the cattle, which stampeded and trampled the farmer to death.

For the Rajputs in Rājasthān, Dassehra is an important festival. It is the custom at this time for Rajputs to sacrifice male

buffalo by beheading them, the meat being distributed to the local people.

Gangaur is an extremely important festival of Rājasthān. It commences on the day following Holi and continues for 18 days. The festival is celebrated by womenfolk with great enthusiasm and devotion for Gauri, the consort of Shiva. While married women worship Gauri, the embodiment of perfection and conjugal love, for the success of their married life, unmarried women worship the Goddess for being blessed with good husbands. Gangaur Festival also celebrates the monsoon, the harvest and marital fidelity. Numerous rituals, such as the collection of ashes from the Holi fire and burying of wheat and barley seeds in it, the making of clay images of Gauri, to the accompaniment of traditional folk songs sung in praise of the goddess, and processions of women, accompany the festival. Gangaur aptly reflects the rich cultural heritage of Rājasthān and is celebrated with great pomp and show in Bikaner, Jodhpur, and Jaisalmer.

Teej is the festival of swings. It marks the advent of the monsoon and is celebrated in the month of Shravan (July/August). Swings are hung from trees for the enjoyment of girls and brightly-attired women hold processions, sing, and generally engage in much merriment. This festival is dedicated to the Goddess Parvati, commemorating her union with Shiva, and she is worshipped by seekers of conjugal bliss and happiness.

Numerous fairs are held throughout Rājasthān, some coinciding with religious events. Thus the Baneshwar Fair, which is a favorite among Bhil tribals, is a celebration of Shiva. Other events, such as the Nagaur Fair, are primarily a chance to trade in cattle. But perhaps the best known fair in Rājasthān is that held in the fall at Pushkar, near Ajmer in the central part of the state. Pushkar, is an important pilgrimage site, containing the only active temple in all of India dedicated to the Hindu god Brahma. It is also an important event for locals to trade camels and cattle and to experience bazaars, music, and various sports. Pushkar has become an attraction for foreign tourists.

Muslims celebrate Muslim holidays such as Ramadan and Id, Sikhs celebrate the birthday of Guru Nanak, Buddhists observe Buddhist holidays, Jains celebrate the birth of Mahavira, and Christians keep Christian festivals such as Christmas and Easter. All of these holidays are observed as public holidays by government offices.

⁷RITES OF PASSAGE

Rājasthānis tend to follow the norms of their particular communities in rites of passage. Thus these will be different for Rajputs, Brahmans, Jats, and the numerous other ethnic groups represented in the state. Male babies among Muslims are circumcised, for example, while Sikhs are baptized into their religion, and Brahmans officiate at Hindu rituals. Sikhs and Hindus cremate their dead, while Muslims resort to burial. But, the majority of Rājasthānis being Hindu, rites of passage follow those of Hinduism in general outline (see *Hindus*).

There are, however, differences between communities. The Bishnois, for example, are a Hindu sect found around Jodhpur. They abstain from tobacco, drugs, and spirits, and are noted for their regard for animal life, which is such that not only will they not themselves kill any living creature, but they do their utmost to prevent others from doing so. Among the Bishnois, who are very particular about ceremonial purity, a child, whether boy or girl, is baptized 30 days after the birth by the

A Rājasthāni woman, dressed in traditional attire, smiles for the camera during the annual cattle fair in Pushkar, Rājasthān, India. Pushkar is a popular Hindu pilgrimage spot and tourist attraction for its cattle fair and camel races. (AP Images/Rajesh Kumar Singh)

priest (*sādh*), this ceremony also having the effect of purifying the house that has been made impure by the birth (*sutak*). At the same time, the barber clips off the child's hair. Bishnois do not wear a scalp-lock (*choti*) like other Hindus and when an adult is baptized this is cut off and the head shaved, for the Bishnois shave the whole head and do not leave the scalp-lock like the other Hindus. But they allow the beard to grow, only shaving the chin upon the father's death.

Bishnois marry among themselves only and by a ceremony of their own. Unlike most Hindus, they do not revere Brahmans, but have priests of their own, chosen from among the laity. These priests are celibates. The Bishnoi do not burn their dead, but bury them below the cattle-stall or in a place frequented by cattle, such as a cattle-pen. Bishnois go on pilgrimage to the place where Jhamba-ji, their founder, is buried, in the south of Bikaner, where there is a tomb built over his remains and a temple (*mandīr*) with regular attendants (*pugāris*). A festival takes place here every six months, when the pilgrims go to the sand hill on which Jhamba-ji lived and there light sacrificial fires and make offerings of burnt barley, til, *ghī* (clarified butter), and sugar, at the same time saying the prayers set for the occasion. They also make presents to the attendants of the temple and distribute grain for the peacocks and pigeons that live there in numbers. Another place of pilgrimage is a tomb called Chhambola in the Jodhpur area, where a festival is held once a year. There the pilgrims bathe in the tank and sing and play musical instruments and scatter grain to peacocks and pigeons.

8 INTERPERSONAL RELATIONS

Being Hindus, most Rājasthānis use the standard "Namastee", or "Namaskar" to greet each other, the words said while touching one's palms together. However, occasionally, local terms and phrases, such as "Khamaghani," which stands for hello, or "Ram Ram" are used to greet one another. People of the Muslim faith use the traditional greeting of "Salaam Akcikum" ("Peace be with you"), often accompanied with an obeisance, performed by bowing low and placing the right palm on the forehead.

9 LIVING CONDITIONS

Living conditions in Rājasthān reflect the community traditions of Rājasthānis. Thus Rajputs who were rulers and local landowners (*jagirdars* and *istimradars*) live in forts and palaces that may date back to the 14th century or earlier. Village Rajputs who are agriculturalists follow local traditions. In central Rājasthān, a typical farmhouse consists of a square walled structure, with a gateway that can be closed at night, with living quarters and quarters for cattle within the complex. Regular houses in villages have compounds encircled by hedges of impassable thorns (often from the *khejri* [*Prosopis cinereria*] tree, a local type of acacia) in which to keep livestock at night. Villages are nucleated, with fields of varying quality of soils, scattered around the village lands.

The city of Jodhpur is sometime referred to as the *Blue City*, due to the indigo tinge of the whitewashed houses around the Mehrangarh Fort. The blue houses were originally for Brahmins but non-Brahmins soon joined in, as the color was said to deflect the heat and keep mosquitoes away.

Where Bhils have not adapted *pukka* (i.e. stone) structures for their houses from their neighbors, they build their house from thatch and bamboo. Perhaps reflecting their origins as shifting cultivators, Bhil settlements tend to be dispersed, with houses built near the land they are farming. Similarly, the round mud huts with thatched roofs of Jaisalmer District in the extreme west of the state differ significantly from the modern, stone house being built in Jaipur, the state capital, an urban area of nearly 5 million people.

10 FAMILY LIFE

This varies according to community. People usually take meals four times a day—a light breakfast, the main meal about 11 AM or noon consisting of bread (*roti*) made from various types of grain, vegetables and curry, roti and vegetables in the late afternoon, with dinner after sunset usually including roti, chilies, *dāl* (lentils) and *chhach* (buttermilk). Agriculturalists are often so poor they have only two main meals a day.

Rājasthānis follow the customs of their own communities when it comes to marriage. Thus, among caste Hindus, one marries into one's own caste, marriages are arranged, and the giving of dowries is common. Widows may or may not be allowed to marry, but divorce is rare. Marriage rules among tribal groups are different.

Except for the very rich, *purdah* is not kept.

11 CLOTHING

Reflecting the colorful Rājasthāni culture, Rājasthāni clothes have a lot of mirror-work and embroidery, and Rājasthāni dresses are usually designed in bright colors like blue, yellow, and orange. This forms a striking contrast with the dun landscape and green vegetation of the region.

Turbans, called variously *pagari, pencha, sela* or *safa* (the safa is 39 feet in length and 4 feet wide), are a must for men and one can usually identify caste and community, and sometimes even location down to the village level, by the dress an individual wears. The age-old dress worn in Rājasthān is the turban (white or colored red or orange or multi-colored [bright or spotted turbans signify a birth or marriage in the family]), coat (*angarkha*) and loincloth (*dhoti*), the last two usually being white in color. Men will wear sandals (*chuppals*) or a leather shoe (*jutti*), with the toes curled up, that may be bought at a fair or made locally. Traditional dress for females comprises an ankle length skirt (*gaghra*) and a short top, also known as a *lehenga* or a *chaniya choli*, tied in the back with string. In the hot summer, it is common for village women to go bare breasted, omitting the choli. A piece of cloth (*odhani*) is used to cover the head, both for protection from heat and maintenance of modesty, peasant women usually covering their faces when in the presence of strangers or males who are not in the immediate family. Tribals tend to wear only a dhoti and a pagari with the rest of the body being kept bare. Banias wear a distinctive type of pagari, as do Rajputs from different states. Thus, the Jaipuri-style turban is tied with a long tail hanging down the back, while the Mewar-style turban is closer to the bania turban in appearance. The Jodhpuri safa is quite distinctive. In formal dress, Rajputs wear their own style of turban (usually colored), an ornate, sometimes embroidered *sherwani* (tunic) and *churidar* (tight pants). A sword completes the outfit. Jats usually wear white turbans.

Both women and men are fond of ornaments and wear gold and silver. Women commonly wear bangles and anklets (these used to be made of silver or ivory, but nowadays tend to be plastic).

The usual dress for Muslims is the pyjama, which is sometimes worn by non-Muslims as well. A coat known as an *achkan*, along with a distinctive cap (*topi*) is donned for special occasions. Muslim women may wear the *burqa*, a long robe that covers them from head to toe.

In urban areas, Rājasthānis who work in offices or for the government commonly wear Western style clothing.

12 FOOD

As is to be expected in an area with numerous ethnic and caste groups, cuisine in Rājasthān varies widely, with some areas of Rājasthān known for certain foods. Thus, Jodhpur is known for its *katchori*, a spicy snack consisting of fried gram flour, usually filled with Urad dal. Banias, Jains and some Jats in Rājasthān will not eat meat, and so their diet is strictly vegetarian, consisting mainly of *roti* (unleavened breads made from cereals such as wheat and *bajra* [pearl millet] or *jowar* [sorghum]), lentils, local vegetables such as onions, potatoes, eggplant, carrots and cabbage, and milk and other dairy products). Rajputs and some other castes will eat meat—goat, chicken, and pork, but caste Hindus will never eat beef. Rajputs commonly eat game birds, such as duck, partridge, and goose and other animals they bring down in the hunt. Muslims, of course, will eat goat but never pork.

But the typical Rājasthāni cuisine found in the countryside is *dāl, bāti*, and *churma*, all of which is made from locally-grown crops. Dal, of course, is made from lentils; bati is a ball of dough, usually *jowar*, roasted in the fire, and churma is coarsely ground wheat crushed and cooked with *ghee* and sugar. Typically, a villager eats twice a day, the man taking vegetables and roti out into the field with him for his midday meal.

13 EDUCATION

Rājasthān's improvement in respect of literacy has been spectacular during the last decade. In the 1991 Census, literacy in Rājasthān was recorded at a mere 38.5%, but this improved to over 61% in 2001. Among men, literacy (76.5%) actually exceeds the all-India average, though women still lag behind the rest of the country.

Rājasthān is rapidly emerging as one of the most favored destinations for education in the country. Growth in the industrial sector of Rājasthān in recent years has encouraged the government as well as private institutions to pay close attention to the educational infrastructure. Under its Rājasthān Education Initiative (REI), for example, the government of Rājasthān seeks to engage global and local partners from private foundations and nongovernmental organizations (NGOs) in innovative multi-stakeholder partnerships to support education in the state. The main educational objectives identified for Rājasthān under the REI are as follows:

100% enrollment in primary education by 2010, 100% enrollment in secondary education by 2020

Increase numbers finishing primary school to 100% by 2010 and for secondary to considerable higher levels

Increase access and retention of girls in primary education near 100% levels and in secondary to levels that will enable them to lead productive lives with employment opportunities

Increase the quality of learning, especially in areas of Math, Science, and English

Expanding curricula to provide ICT skills to secondary school students and to enable formation of human capital for the economy

Many institutes of management, engineering, medicine and, law allow students to pursue higher studies in the state. The University of Rājasthān in Jaipur, for instance, is a premier educational institution in India and attracts students from all over the country. Jodhpur, Kota, Udaipur, and Ajmer also play pivotal educational roles in the state. Ajmer, for example, is the location of Mayo College, one of the major "public" (in the British sense) schools in India. Originally founded by the British to turn the sons of local Rajput rulers into "proper British gentlemen," it nonetheless continues to provide students with an excellent secondary education.

Many private primary and secondary institutions across the state are "English medium" schools, i.e. they teach their students in English. Knowledge of English is seen as a *sine quae non* for good jobs in government and industry.

14 CULTURAL HERITAGE

Despite the low numbers of Rajputs in the state, elements of Rajput culture, such as *jauhar* and *sati*, have come to be associated with Rājasthān. As one exits the Mehrangarh fort in Jodhpur, for example, one can see the handprints (in stone) of past satis who chose immolation, throwing themselves on the funeral pyres of the Maharajas of Jodhpur. The handprints still bear red ochre and silver paper, evidence that local women come to worship the satis. Although sati was apparently a custom primarily associated with Rajputs rulers, in 1987 Roop Kanwar, a Rajputs villager from Sikar district in northwestern Rājasthān, gained international notoriety by committing sati. Local people came to the cremation site in Deorala village to worship Kanwar as a *sati mata* ("sati mother") and the government had to ban crowds from the sati site. One result was the passing of the Rājasthān Sati Prevention Ordinance in 1987 that makes the glorification of sati a crime, though the enforcement of this ordinance obviously raises many issues. Women from Rājasthān marched in opposition to the ordinance and local Rajputs plan to build a temple at the site of the sati.

Another aspect of Rajput culture that is identified with Rājasthāni culture is Rajput miniature painting. It was a matter of status that the courts of the erstwhile Rajputs states be centers of patronage of the arts, and one area for which they are famous is painting. Combining traditions of the Moghul court, though often depicting Hindu themes or typical Rajput activities, and sometimes employing Persian and Muslim painters as well as local Rājasthānis. Each Rajput court developed its own school of painting, and the cognoscenti can tell at a glance where a particular painting originated. Thus, paintings that are characterized by a dark border are usually from the state of Kota (Kota and Bundi paintings are known collectively as Haudati paintings). More typical is the red borders of the Jaipur and Mewar schools. Though many of the paintings are miniatures, following the Moghul style, in palaces such as the City Palace of Mewar there are paintings that are of mural size.

A feature of Rājasthāni culture is the architecture of the region. The Rajputs developed a unique style of architecture, which incorporated Muslim elements such as arches and domes and came to be known as the Indo-Islamic style, blending features of indigenous architecture with elements of Muslim architecture. Although each of the former Rajput state (i.e. Jaipur, Jodhpur, Mewar, Jaisalmer, and Bikaner) has its own unique style of architecture, the imprint of Indo-Islamic architecture is plain to see throughout Rājasthān. The Rajputs tended to build palaces and forts, while Muslims built tombs and mosques.

Although Rajput palaces, Indo-Islamic architecture, the Rajput ethos, the traditions of *jauhar* and *sati*, Rajput paintings, and relations between Rajputs and Muslims and tribals in the area is a major part of Rājasthāni culture, this is not to say that Rājasthāni culture is the same as Rajput culture—there are other distinctly Rājasthāni elements in the region's cultural tradition. For instance, there is the traditional performance of puppetry in the villages—narrating an event from history, myths, folklore, or legend, complete with music and speech usually performed by Bhats, another community in Rājasthān. The performances are the repository of traditional wisdom, knowledge, and social mores and within them are contained the oral history of the region. In addition, there is the existence of caste groups in addition to the Charans and Bhats that fulfill specific roles in Rājasthāni culture. The Manghaniyars (Muslim musicians in western Rājasthān), the Bishnoi (around Jodhpur), the Minas (in the region north of Jaipur) all add to the "Rājasthāni" mystique, as do the wall murals of the Shekhawati region, the banias (many of them Jains), and the Muslims. *Mehndi*, the tradition of painting hands and feet and *Mandana* (a folk tradition of decoration and painting), festivals such as Gangaur, popular dramas (*khyals*), the folk music of the region, folk heroes such as Pabuji and Dev Narayanji, dress, the ethnic mix of the region—all contribute to what might be called a distinctive Rājasthāni culture.

15 WORK

Rājasthān is primarily agricultural and rural, with 77% of the population living in rural areas, and agriculture—much of which is subsistence in nature—accounting for 22.5% of the gross domestic product (GDP). Cattle, sheep and goat rearing are important activities, while camel herding is found in the more arid areas of the west. The construction of the Indira Gandhi Canal in the west—bringing water from the Sutlej and Beas Rivers in Punjab State to arid regions of western Rājasthān, and terminating near Jaiselmer—has given agriculture in the state a boost. Otherwise, agriculture in Rājasthān is dependent on the monsoon, there being no natural bodies of water in the state. The state also grows cotton and the textile industry has grown up in several places in Rājasthān.

Rājasthān is also well-endowed with mineral resources, resulting in a large number of small-scale industrial units springing up all over the state. Large deposits of zinc and copper exist and these are being exploited for the development of industries dependent on these metals. It also has large deposits of gypsum and lignite and mica is produced in substantial quantities. The marble industry is significant in places like Kishangarh and Makrera, marble from the latter's mines being used in the construction of the Taj Mahal in Agra. Among the other private sector industries are cement, ball bearings, sugar, caustic soda, and other chemicals.

Rājasthān, in particular Jaipur, forms part of the "Golden Triangle," the commonly traveled tourist trail that includes Delhi, Agra, and Jaipur. As a result, along with the luxurious Palace on Wheels that takes tourists out into the western desert, tourism is a major employer in Rājasthān. With Jaipur being the state capital, the service industries form a significant element in the Rājasthāni economy, accounting for 40% of the state's GDP.

[16] SPORTS

There are no sports uniquely Rājasthāni. However, Rajputs tend to hunt on their former lands, even though hunting has been banned in India by the government in Delhi. In the past, Rajputs shot tiger and panther, as well as various types of deer and game birds, keeping careful records of each kill in notebooks. Pig-sticking, i.e. killing wild boar from horseback with a lance—a dangerous pastime, tended to develop the military skills so loved by Rajputs. Polo is also a sport played by those who can afford it. (The term "jodhpur," i.e. a type of riding breeches, is taken from the city and state of Jodhpur.) Jaipur, which is a polo center and has several polo clubs, has the 61 Cavalry Regiment—the only horsed cavalry unit in the Indian Army—with its polo team stationed there.

Kabadi is a traditional Indian sport played throughout Rājasthān, while popular modern sports include soccer, (field) hockey and cricket.

[17] ENTERTAINMENT AND RECREATION

Urban Rājasthānis go to the cinema to see "Bollywood" movies. In villages, where movies are not available, entertainment is provided by traveling entertainers, such as Bhopas and puppeteers. Local fairs and festivals, and religious celebrations are important events in the countryside, and provide recreation and entertainment. Nowadays, almost all villages have television sets, and even satellite dishes to access international TV programming. Almost everyone, even in villages, has a cell phone if they can afford it.

[18] FOLK ART, CRAFTS, AND HOBBIES

Rājasthān is known for its handicrafts, with every region having its specialty. Thus, Bikaner is known for its woolen fabrics, carpets, and leather vessels made from camel hide. Japiur is an international center for the jewelry trade, with diamond cutting being its *forte*, but is also known for its hand block printed cotton fabrics, gold enamel work, paintings, and blue pottery ware. Areas in the western desert are known for fabrics and mirror work, while weaving, enamel work, lacquer work , embroidery and carving are also Rājasthāni traditions. The paint-

ing of *phad* is done in Devgarh, but the making of puppets, originally associated with the Bhats of Nagaur in Marwar, is now found throughout the state. *Thewa*, gold filigree work on colored glass is associated with Patarbgarh. Mandana is the folk craft of decorating houses. Red sand and chalk powder are used to make designs on floors and walls. This art is quite popular in the rural areas of Rājasthān. Different types of square, rectangular and floral designs are made, appropriate to the particular season or festival. Another popular form of folk art prevalent among women is *mehndi*. The use of mehndi (henna) designs on the palms and feet is symbolic of welfare, artistic taste, and religious attitude. There is hardly a function or festival in Rājasthān when women do not apply mehndi.

[19] SOCIAL PROBLEMS

Social problems in Rājasthān have their roots in poverty and the large proportion of tribal peoples in the state. Despite efforts at improvement and development by the government, and advances in education, tribal peoples such as the Bhils and Minas are still economically and socially disadvantaged. The arid environment makes agriculturalists dependent on monsoonal rains, and several bad monsoons can lead to famine and farmers going heavily into debt to moneylenders, who often charge exorbitant rates of interest. Land fragmentation, a result of inheritance systems common in the state, is also a problem in rural area. Access to safe drinking water, overgrazing, relations between caste and non-caste Hindus, and the place of women in society remain issues in Rājasthān.

[20] GENDER ISSUES

Women in Rājasthān tend to suffer the same discrimination as other Hindu women, a discrimination that has its roots in the religious and cultural practices of India. There are several clear indicators of the fact that Indian women continue to be discriminated against in Hindu society: for instance, the sex ratio is skewed against them. In Jaipur, according to the Census of India, 2001, the sex ratio was 909:1000. A recent study blames this decline in the number of females on sex determination by ultrasound machines, Hindu society placing a premium on male babies. The implication is that female fetuses are aborted. Maternal mortality is high, female literacy is low, female children tend to have a high mortality (even if female infanticide is not practiced any more, this is often the result of neglect of the health of girl children) and crimes against women are on the rise.

It is a paradox of modern Rājasthān that women wield power and hold positions at the topmost levels (in 2008 the Chief Minister of Rājasthān was a woman, Vasundhara Raje Scindia of the BJP) yet large sections of Rājasthāni women are among the most underprivileged. While attempts have been made to address issues such as sati, child marriage, widow remarriage and dowries, the status of women in contemporary Rājasthān is reflected in the state of their health, education, employment, and life in society.

[21] BIBLIOGRAPHY

Chandana, Saha. *Gender Equity and Equality: Study of Girl Child in Rājasthān*. Jaipur: Rawat Publications, 2003.
Held, Suzanne and Amina Okada. *Rājasthān: A Land of Splendor and Bravery*. Bombay: India Book Distributors, 2000.

Martinelli, Antonio. *Princely Rājasthān: Rajput Palaces and Mansions.* New York: Vendome Press, 2004.

Rudolph, Lloyd I. and Susanne Hoeber Rudolph. *The Political Modernization of an Indian Feudal Order: An Analysis of Rajput Adaptation in Rājasthān.* Chicago: University of Chicago Committee on Southern Asian Studies, 1968.

Schomer, Karine et al., eds. *The Idea of Rājasthān: Explorations in Regional Identity.* Columbia, MO: South Asia Publications, 1994.

Tod, Col. James. *Annals and Antiquities of Rājasthān, or The Central and Western Rajput States of India.* 3 Vols. London: Oxford University Press, 1920.

—by D. O. Lodrick

RĀJPUTS

PRONUNCIATION: RAHJ-puts
ALTERNATE NAMES: Ksatriya caste
LOCATION: India (Rājasthān state and elsewhere)
POPULATION: 138 million (estimate)
LANGUAGE: Language or dialect of their region
RELIGION: Hinduism (majority)

[1] INTRODUCTION

"Rājput" identifies numerous castes in northern and western India that claim *ksatriya* or "warrior" status in the Hindu social hierarchy. They trace their descent to the ksatriyas of ancient times and thus legitimize their standing as superior to all social groups except the Brahmans in modern society. The term "Rājput" is derived from *rājapūtra*, literally meaning "son of kings." Rājputs are famed for their fighting abilities and until India gained its independence, Rājput kings ruled numerous states in the Indian subcontinent. The British grouped many of the largest and most powerful of these states in western India into the Rājputana Province. Rājputana, i.e., "the land of the Rājputs," survives virtually intact as the modern Indian state of Rājasthān.

The origins of the Rājputs, who appear suddenly on the Indian scene during early medieval times (approximately 5th–7th centuries AD), are obscure. It is generally accepted, however, that they are mainly of foreign stock. They are descendants of the numerous tribes from Central Asia (e.g., the Parthians, Kushans, Shakas, and Huns) that entered India at this time, conquered local peoples, and settled down as part of the ruling political elite. The integration of these groups into Hindu society was accomplished by marriage with high-caste women or by conversion to acquire the benefits of a ksatriya status sanctified by the Brahmans. By the 9th century, Rājputs controlled an empire that extended from Sind to the lower Ganges Valley, and from the Himalayan foothills to the Narmada River. Following the disintegration of this empire in the mid-10th century, various Rājput clans rose to prominence in the region. The Chauhan Rājputs, for example, ruled the lands around Delhi, while the Chandellas controlled the central Indian region of Bundelkhand.

Rājputs in northern India were the first to face the Muslim invasions of the late 12th century. However, the rival Rājput clans were never able to present a united front against the Muslim threat. In 1192, the Rājputs under Prithviraj Chauhan were defeated by Muhammad Ghuri at the second battle of Tarain, near Delhi. This firmly established Muslim power in India and marked the end of Rājput dominance in the region. As the Muslims moved down the Ganges Valley, they conquered the Rājput kingdoms in their path. Muslim penetration south and west to Gujarat isolated the Rājput states in the west. It was here, in the arid regions of the Thar Desert, that Rājput kingdoms survived to challenge the might of the Mughals. For four centuries, states such as Mewar (Udaipur) and Marwar (Jodhpur) were able to preserve their independence from the Muslims. Akbar, the Mughal emperor, succeeded in enlisting many prominent Rājput rulers (e.g. Man Singh of Amber and Jaswant Singh of Marwar) to his cause, using diplomacy rath-

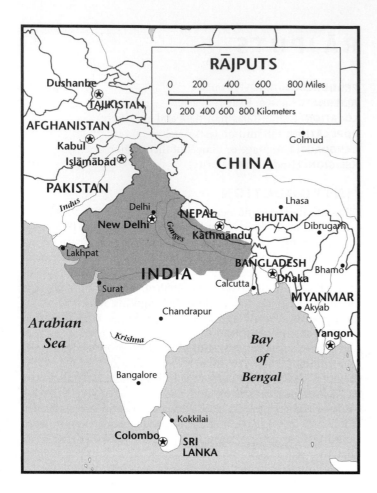

comprise more than 10% of the population include the Ganges Valley in eastern Uttar Pradesh and western Bihar and western Madhya Pradesh. Surprisingly, in Rājasthān, with its strong historical and emotional ties to the Rājputs, the caste ranks only fifth in numbers, with less than 6% of the population. Other states with sizeable Rājput communities include Uttaranachal, Gujarat, Haryana, Himachal Pradesh, Maharashtra and Delhi.

³LANGUAGE

Rājputs speak the language or dialect of their region. Thus, Rājputs on the Ganges plains use the local dialect of Hindi current in their locality. The language spoken in the foothills of the western Himalayas is Pahari. In Rājasthān, Rājputs speak one of the dialects of Rājasthāni, which is itself a variant of Hindi. Many of the former Rājput states in this area are historical and cultural regions as well as political regions and have evolved their own distinctive regional dialects. Jaipuri, for example, is the dialect used in the former Rājput state of Jaipur. Marwari, the dialect spoken in Marwar State, has come to be regarded as the standard form of Rājasthāni.

⁴FOLKLORE

As descendants of the many invaders who conquered local peoples and set themselves up as the ruling class, the Rājputs of northern and western India have no common ancestry. However, various myths have evolved to give legitimacy to their status as rulers and their claims to ksatriya status. One relates that a ksatriya chieftain learned that his father had been killed by a Brahman. Enraged, he embarked on a series of campaigns to eliminate Brahmans from the face of the land. With the depletion of Brahman males, however, Brahman females had to accept ksatriya men as husbands. This gave rise to the various ruling dynasties of Rājputs. (It is interesting to note that the orthodox Hindu would find a union between ksatriya and Brahman totally unacceptable). Another legend tells that the gods created a new order of pure ksatriya clans in the fire-pit of the sage Vasishtha on Mt. Abu in Rājasthān. Their purpose was to help the Brahmans in their struggle against the Buddhists and *mlechchhas* (foreigners). These *agnikula* ("fire-race") Rājputs were the forerunners of clans such as the Chauhan, Solanki, and Ponwar Rājputs. Other Rājput clans trace their ancestry to the Sun or the Moon.

Rājput culture is replete with heroes who accomplished great deeds of honor, bravery, and self-sacrifice. Some of these have entered local folk traditions and have even come to be worshipped in many rural areas. In Rājasthān, for example, Pabuji, Gogaji, and Ramdeoji are Rājput figures who are revered as gods by the local population.

⁵RELIGION

Although there are Muslims and Sikhs among the Rājputs, most are Hindu. In fact, Rājputs came to be seen as the champions of Hinduism against the challenges of Buddhism and Islam. In matters of ceremonial purity and caste, Rājputs were as rigid as the most orthodox of Hindus. Writers note that Eastern Rājputs, i.e., those found on the Ganges plains in Uttar Pradesh and Bihar, are more strongly subject to Brahmanical influences than the Western Rājputs of Rājasthān.

Today, in their religious practices, Rājputs differ little from other high-caste Hindus. They use Brahmans for ceremonial

er than force. Mewar, however, claims the distinction of never having submitted to Muslim rule.

With Mughal power in decline during the 18th century, many of the Rājput states in western India came under the control of the Marathas. In the early 19th century, however, following the British defeat of the Marathas, they accepted British dominance. By recognizing Britain as the sovereign power in India, the rulers of these states were able to retain their independence and preserve their feudal way of life until India gained its independence in 1947. Rājput states existed elsewhere in India, for example, Jammu and Kashmir and the Pahari (Hill) states in the foothills of the Himalayas. It is the Rājput states of Rājasthān, however, with their history of resistance to Muslim rule, that have come to be seen as the upholders of Rājput tradition and culture.

²LOCATION AND HOMELAND

Estimates of the Rājput population vary considerably, especially since the last census that gathered data on caste was the Census of India in 1931. Using the average rate of natural increase for India during the last decade, an estimated 138 million people in India belong to the Rājput or ksatriya castes (the low figure given for Rājputs in India is about 65 million). They are distributed throughout northern India, although their greatest concentrations lie in the foothills of the western Himalayas. Here, in a belt extending from the border of Nepal through the former Hill States to southern Kashmir, Rājputs make up as much as 40% or more of the population. Areas where Rājputs

and ritual purposes, though they see themselves as inferior only in spiritual matters. They may follow any of the many Hindu sects and they worship all the major Hindu deities. The majority of Rājputs, however, are Shaivites, or devotees of the god Shiva (S´iva). These Rājputs are nonvegetarian, smoke opium and tobacco, and are fond of alcohol. In addition, they worship other deities such as Surya (the Sun God) and Durga in her aspect of the Mother-Goddess. It is customary in Rājasthān, for example, when Rājputs open a bottle of liquor, to pour the first few drops on the ground as an offering to the Mother, saying "Jai Mataji" ("Long live the Mother-Goddess"). In addition, nearly every Rājput clan has its own patron deity, to whom it pays special respect and to whom it turns for protection.

In every household, Rājput men and women worship their *kuldevi* (goddess of the *kul* or lineage). This deity, who is always female, is seen as the protector of the household and is also something of a fertility goddess—women of the household worship the kuldevi to help them conceive sons, who continue and expand the kul. All Rājput women in the household know kuldevi stories and foundation myths of the kuldevi, which is seen has having the character of the ideal *patrivrata* (husband-protector). Formerly, the kuldevi would protect Rājput men in battle, though with the demise of the Rājput states, the domestic functions of the kuldevi have become of increasing significance.

⁶MAJOR HOLIDAYS

Rājputs celebrate all the major Hindu holy days, keeping to the festival calendar of their region. Thus Shivratri ("Shiva's Night"), the holy spring festival, and Divali (the Festival of Lights), are all observed with great enthusiasm. Of particular importance to Rājputs is Dasahara, the festival dedicated to Durga. It is customary for Rājputs to sacrifice a buffalo to the goddess, in commemoration of her victory over the evil buffalo-demon Mahisha. The animal is killed by being beheaded with one stroke of a sword. Although Rājputs are nonvegetarians, they do not eat buffalo and the meat is usually distributed to servants or the lower castes in the area.

⁷RITES OF PASSAGE

The major stages in the life of a Rājput are celebrated by 12 ceremonies called *karams*. These commence before birth and continue through to the final rituals after death. The more important of these include the ceremonies relating to birth, the sacred thread, marriage, and death.

On the birth of a male child, the family Brahman is summoned to record the details for the infant's horoscope and determine if the moment of birth is auspicious. The family barber is sent to inform relatives and friends of the event and there is much feasting and celebration in the family. The Brahman fixes a propitious day for the naming of the infant. The head-shaving ritual is carried out when the child is around two years of age. Among many Rājputs, the birth of a daughter is regarded as a misfortune and is observed with a minimum of ceremony. Female infanticide was a common practice of Rājput society in the past.

As with all higher-caste Hindus, one of the most important rites of passage for the Rājput male is the investiture with the *janeū* or sacred thread. This marks his formal admission to the rank of the twice-born, that is, to high-caste status. Worn over the left shoulder and under the right arm, the sacred thread is a constant reminder of the Rājput's aristocratic origins and of his duties as a member of the warrior caste. The actual ceremony is rather elaborate and is performed by the family's Brahman priest.

When possible, certain rituals are prescribed for a Rājput when death is approaching. The sick person is laid on a bed of sacred *kusa* grass on a spot that has been circled by cow dung. A sprig of the *tulsī* plant, a piece of gold, or a few drops of Ganges water are placed in his or her mouth. This is to delay the messengers of Yama, the God of Death, until the proper rites have been carried out. A cow is brought to the side of the dying person so that he or she can grasp its tail and be carried safely across the mythical River Vaitarani to the other world. A Brahman recites the appropriate mantras from the sacred literature. After death, the corpse is washed and prepared for cremation. In the case of an important landowner or *thākur*, the entire population of the region may join the funeral procession to the cremation grounds. The body is seated or laid on the funeral pyre, facing north. Though Brahmans perform the necessary funeral rites, the pyre is lit by the eldest son. He is also responsible for cracking open the skull after the corpse is burnt to allow the soul to depart from the body. After the cremation, the mourners undergo the required purificatory bath.

A death is followed by a period of mourning. On the third day after cremation, bones and ashes are collected from the funeral pyre and taken to be placed in the Ganges or some other sacred river. The *srāddha* ceremonies usually commence on the eleventh day after death. These include offerings to the ancestral spirits, the feasting of relatives and friends, and the feeding of Brahmans. The soul of the deceased is held to depart this world on the thirteenth day. No marriages can take place in the months following a death in the family.

⁸INTERPERSONAL RELATIONS

Rājputs follow the customary greeting practices of their religious communities and region.

⁹LIVING CONDITIONS

Rājputs traditionally formed the landowning classes of northern and western India and as such they maintained a lifestyle and standard of living in keeping with their station. In the past, the Rājput rulers of princely states such as Kashmir, Jaipur, and Jodhpur were known for the splendor of their courts. Like the other princes in India, Rājput *Mahārājās* often lived luxuriously in ornate palaces, surrounded by retainers, with servants at their beck and call. Even Rājputs of lesser rank had an enviable lifestyle. One can hardly travel through Rājasthān, for example, without being in sight of the fort (*garh*) of a local *thākur*. Following India's independence in 1947, however, the princes lost their titles and privileges. Government reforms reduced the amount of land an individual could own, limiting the resources available to the Rājput landowning class.

Not all Rājputs live in palaces and forts, surrounded by weapons and armor and the trappings of the Rājputs' former glory. In the village in Uttar Pradesh studied by Leigh and Minturn (1966), for example, the custom of sons inheriting equal shares of land has reduced landholdings to the point that most Rājputs have to farm the land themselves rather than support tenants or sharecroppers. With their self-image as former warriors and rulers, they regard this as somewhat demeaning.

They have stories to justify this situation, sometimes blaming it on a conscious effort of Muslim conquerors to scatter and subdue their Rājput opponents.

In the Rājput neighborhood of the village, the men's quarters are the most conspicuous buildings. These consist of a courtyard containing a platform about 1¼ m to 2 m (4–6-ft) high, reached by a series of steps and often shaded by trees. The men of the family and their friends gather together on the platform, chatting and perhaps smoking the *hukkā*. At the far end of the platform is a roofed porch, behind which is a large central room used by the men for sleeping during the winter months, and smaller side rooms for storage. Because of the custom of *purdah,* the keeping of women in seclusion, the women's quarters are separate. They are enclosed by walls, with all the rooms facing the inner courtyard and lacking outside windows. A hearth—a mud, U-shaped fireplace about 30 cm (1 ft) square and about 15 cm (6 in) high—is built against one of the courtyard walls for cooking. Stairs provide access to the roof. The interconnecting roofs of the houses provide Rājput women with a means of visiting each other out of the sight of males. Buildings are built of brick or of mud, depending on the economic circumstances of the individual family.

¹⁰FAMILY LIFE

A distinctive feature of Rājput society is its division into a hierarchy of ranked clans and lineages. Over 103 clans have been identified in all. Among the more important Rājput clans are the Chauhans, whose former capital was Ajmer; the Gehlots of Mewar; the Rathors of Marwar; and the Kachhwaha of Jaipur. These groups are found mainly in Rājasthān. The Bundelas and Chandellas are distributed in Madhya Pradesh and on the Ganges plains. The Gaharwar and the Surajbansi Rājputs are concentrated on the Ganges plains in Uttar Pradesh.

Rājputs follow clan exogamy, i.e., they marry outside the clan. They also practice hypergamy. This means that they marry their daughters into clans of higher rank than their own, while accepting daughters-in-law from clans of lower rank. Although the specific ranking of individual clans might vary from region to region, rank increases as one goes westwards. The Rājput clans of Rājasthān have the highest standing. There is thus a distinct geographical component in the movement of brides in Rājput society. This also raises difficulties in finding suitable husbands for girls in the highest-ranking Rājput clans.

Rājputs traditionally have their own marriage rituals. As is typical in South Asia, Rājput marriages are arranged by the parents, often with the assistance of a professional matchmaker. Once a suitable spouse is identified, certain preliminaries have to be settled. The Bhats or family genealogists verify the pedigree of both parties, while astrologers determine that the horoscopes of the potential bride and groom are favorable. Should everything be in order, a dowry is negotiated and the betrothal (*tilak*) is announced. Marriages among Rājputs are occasions for great pomp and ceremony. The most reckless extravagance is not only permitted but is almost required as a point of honor. Many go deep into debt and spend the rest of their life paying off the moneylenders (the cost of marriage was a contributing factor to the Rājputs' former practice of female infanticide).

The actual marriage ceremony is held on a day determined by the Brahmans to be auspicious and follows the normal Hin-

A folk artist dances during a procession for World Tourism Day. Rājasthān's independent kingdoms created a rich architectural and cultural heritage, seen today in its numerous forts, palaces, and havelis. (STR/AFP/Getty Images)

du rites. The groom, accompanied by male friends and relatives, sets out in the *barāt* (procession) for the bride's house, where he is received by the family of the bride (*Sehla* and *Dhukav* ceremonies). Mounted on a horse, he is dressed in colorful robes, with turban and sword. Among the higher Rājput clans, the groom may be mounted on the back of a gaily decorated elephant. Preliminary ceremonies are carried out, accompanied by the giving of gifts and distribution of money to the crowd of onlookers that usually assembles. At the appointed time, the marriage is solemnized with the *agni pūjā* (fire-worship ceremony). The clothes of the bride and groom are tied together and the couple walks around the sacred fire three times while Brahmans chant the appropriate prayers from the Vedas. Several more days are spent in feasting and celebrating, before the groom and bride return home. In the past, when child marriage was customary, the bride would return to her family after a few days and remain there until an age when she could enter normal relations with her husband.

In the past, certain Rājput groups permitted more than one wife and the keeping of concubines in the *zenānā* (women's quarters). *Purdah* is customary, limiting the outside activities of Rājput women among all but the lowest classes. Among Rājputs, as with most classes of Hindus, women occupy a status inferior to men. Unless she belongs to a wealthy family that employs servants, a Rājput woman's household chores differ little from those of other Hindu women. Bearing sons is of particular importance to the Rājput woman.

Marriage alliances between the upper classes traditionally were important ritual symbolic forms through which the power and authority of *rajas* (kings and rulers) were established or extended. Women, marriage and power were integrally linked. Thus, during the 16th century, the Mughal Emperor Akbar was able to bring the Rājput state of Amber to heel by marrying the eldest daughter of the Rājput ruler, Raja Bharmal. From this time on, the Rājputs of Amber State were drawn into the Mughal power structure and some, such as Raja Man Singh I of Amber, became trusted generals in the Moghul Army. On 26 August 1605, Man Singh became a *mansabdar* of 7,000, i.e., a commander of 7,000 cavalry in the Mughal forces, which was the maximum command for anyone other than a son of the Mughal ruler. He fought many important campaigns for Akbar and led the Mughal army in the well-known battle of Haldighati fought in 1576 between the Mughal Empire and the Rājput ruler of Mewar (Udaipur), Maharana Pratap Singh. The Mughal Emperor Jahangir married a Rājput princess of Marwar, thus cementing relations between the Mughals and the State of Marwar (Jodhpur). Several of the Marwar rulers were trusted generals of the Mughals and Abhay Singh of Marwar served as the Mughal governor of Gujarat during the 18th century.

Widow remarriage is not customary in Rājput society. Certain Rājput clans that do allow widows to marry a younger brother of the deceased husband are regarded by other Rājputs as degraded and impure. One custom that was formerly widespread among the Rājputs was *sati*, the self-immolation of a widow on her husband's funeral pyre. When a Maharaja died, all his wives and concubines were expected to commit sati. Near the gateways to forts in Jodhpur and other cities in Rājasthān, one will find the handprints of Rājput women who followed their husbands and masters to their deaths in the cremation fire. These, along with the stone sati memorials that are found all over Rājasthān, are revered as shrines by the local population. The British suppressed the practice of sati during the 19th century and it is illegal in India today. But the rite is still deeply embedded in the Rājput psyche, even though the ritual was, in the past, limited to the women of Rājput rulers. In 1987 one Roop Kanwar, a Rājput villager from Sikar district in northwestern Rājasthān, gained international notoriety by committing sati. Local people came to the cremation site in Deorala village to worship Kanwar as a *sati mata* ("sati" mother) and the government had to ban crowds from the sati site. One result was the passing of the Rājasthān Sati Prevention Ordinance of 1987 which makes the glorification of sati a crime, though the enforcement of this ordinance obviously raises many issues. Women from Rājasthān marched in opposition to the ordinance and local Rājputs plan to build a temple at the site of the sati a young girl in a village in Rājasthān committed, and within days over 100,000 people had gathered at the site to pay homage to her act. Some authors see sati as a means of removing a family's burden of maintain a widow, since widow remarriage is not permitted by most Rājput groups, and suggest that most satis in the past were forced rather than voluntary. In the case of Roop Kanwar, 45 people were charged with her murder, though they were later acquitted.

Closely related to sati was the Rājput rite of *jauhar*. It was the custom when Rājputs were facing defeat for the women to burn themselves on funeral pyres to avoid captivity or worse. In 1303 when the fort of Chittor in Rājasthān was about to fall to the Muslims, the Rājput Rani and all the women in the fort burned themselves to death before the men rode out for their final battle.

¹¹CLOTHING

The principal item of dress for the Rājput male is the *dhotī*, a length of white cotton cloth wrapped around the waist, pulled between the legs, and tucked in at the back. The upper body is covered by a cotton tunic, or a short jacket that fastens on the right side that Rājasthānis call an *angarhkā*. A turban or *sāfā* is worn on the head, tied by each clan according to its own fashion. The turbans may be white, red, or of other bright hues, providing a splash of color against the browns and tans of the Rājasthān desert. Yellow is a favorite color of the Rājputs. In ancient times, when a Rājput donned saffron robes before entering battle, it meant he was prepared to fight to the death. For ceremonial occasions, Rājputs may wear tight *chūrīdar pyjāmas* covered by a long, embroidered coat similar to the Mughal *sherwani (serwānī)*. A ceremonial turban and a curved Rājput sword completes the outfit.

In addition to the *sārī*, everyday dress for Rājput women includes loose baggy pants worn with a tunic, or a blouse and long skirt, both accompanied by a headcloth. Rājput women are fond of jewelry, wearing bangles, perhaps a stud in the nose, and a variety of rings on fingers, ears, and toes. Formal dress is invariably a *sārī*, often bright red, with gold thread running through the material. The best gold and silver jewelry is worn on such occasions.

Rājput men, especially in urban areas, have taken to wearing Western clothing. However, one item of Rājput clothing has made its way to the West—the tight riding breeches of Jodhpur State's Rathor Cavalry Corps, introduced by the British as "jodhpurs."

¹²FOOD

Rājputs' dietary patterns are determined partly by agricultural ecology and partly by cultural preferences. With their broad distribution in the drier parts of India, the Rājputs' staple diet consists of various unleavened breads *(rotī)*, pulses, and vegetables. Rice *(chāwal)*, which is usually grown rather than purchased in the bazaar, and milk products are also important. Some Rājputs are vegetarian by choice, but many eat meat. Beef, of course, is taboo. Rājputs are fond of hunting and will eat venison and game birds such as goose, duck, partridge, and grouse. Alcohol, both store-bought and country liquor such as *kesar kastūri*, is consumed in great quantities.

¹³EDUCATION

Formal education was of little significance among the ruling and landowning Rājput clans of India. Boys were brought up in the traditions of Rājput culture, trained in the martial arts and in a code of conduct based on valor and honor. The sons of Rājputs became huntsmen and polo-players, horsemen, and swordsmen rather than scholars.

An educational institution of particular note is Mayo College, the "Eton" of India, in Ajmer in Rājasthān. This was founded by the British in the early 1870s as a school for the sons of the ruling (mostly Rājput) princes and *thākūrs* of Rājputana. Its purpose was to impart the "proper" British values to the future ruling elites in the region. Though many Rājputs still attend the school today, it has become an exclusive private school for the children of the Indian upper classes.

¹⁴ CULTURAL HERITAGE

The Rājput heritage in India is one of the most colorful of any group in India. Fostering the fighting traditions of their ancestors, Rājputs have developed a mystique of the brave warrior—champion of the Hindu *dharma* (faith) fighting the Muslim invader in the desert sands of Rājasthān. This romanticized view of the past is perpetuated to a considerable degree by Colonel James Tod in his classic 19th-century study of the Rājputs.

However accurate this picture, Rājputs have left their distinctive imprint on India, particularly on the peoples, culture, and landscape of Rājasthān. In fact, Rājasthānī culture is to a considerable degree Rājput culture. For instance, certain castes exist in Rājasthān to serve the specific needs of Rājputs. Bhats are genealogists who keep family records and can trace a Rājput pedigree all the way back to a clan's mythical ancestors. Charans are bards and poets who for centuries, under Rājput patronage, have recorded the deeds and accomplishments of Rājput rulers. Rājput courts were centers of culture where literature, music, dance, painting, and sculpture flourished with the support of the Rājput elite. A specific style of Rājput painting, often focusing on religious themes, portraiture, or miniatures, emerged at Rājput courts in the Himalayas (the Pahari school) and in the western desert (the Rājasthānī school). Bardic literature such as *Prithvirāj Rāso* recounted the deeds of Rājput heroes of the past. But not all Rājasthānī writing was about Rājputs. Mira Bai, a noted poet born in the 15th century and known for her contributions to the Hindu *bhakti* (devotional) literature, was herself a Rājput princess.

The Rājputs were great builders and took pride in their engineering achievements. They built irrigation canals, dams, and reservoirs throughout their lands. The temples at Khajuraho, best known for their erotic carvings, were built by the Chandellas in the 10th and 11th centuries. The Solankis patronized the Jains and constructed many temples in Gujarat and western Rājasthān. Later Rājput palaces and forts represent a pleasing blend of Hindu and Muslim architectural styles. Among the more notable of these are the forts at Chittor, Gwalior, and Jodhpur, and the Palace of the Winds in Jaipur. Maharaja Jai Singh II of Jaipur constructed astronomical observatories in Jaipur and Delhi in the early 18th century.

¹⁵ WORK

Rājputs are hereditary landowners and soldiers and continue to follow these traditional occupations. Many have been reduced to farming their lands themselves, but, where possible, they hire laborers to perform the agricultural work. Agriculture remains the primary occupation of the group today. Opportunities for soldiering are much reduced in modern India, although Rājputs still serve in the Rājput Rifles and other regiments of the Indian Army. Many serve in the other branches of armed forces or pursue careers in the police or other government service.

¹⁶ SPORTS

Rājputs participate in modern sports and athletics in India today. However, they are particularly fond of shooting and in the past hunted tiger and panther, as well as deer and game birds. Pig-sticking, the dangerous sport of hunting wild boar on horseback with a lance, was also a popular pastime. Riding skills were sharpened by playing polo.

¹⁷ ENTERTAINMENT AND RECREATION

Historically Rājputs have taken great pleasure in the elaborate rituals and ceremonies associated with their religion and their community. Weddings and other festive occasions are observed with much enthusiasm and are often celebrated with feasting, drinking, and sometimes with the presence of *nautch* (dancing) girls.

¹⁸ FOLK ARTS, CRAFTS, AND HOBBIES

Rājputs themselves are not identified with any specific folk arts or crafts. However, Rājputs are the central figures in many folk traditions. The exploits of Amar Singh Rathor, a Rājput, are a favorite theme of string-puppet shows in Rājasthān. In the same region, professional storytellers called *bhopās* travel around the countryside relating ballads to entertain the villagers. One such ballad tells of Pabuji, a 13th-century Rathor chieftain. A Charan woman lends Pabuji her mare to ride to his wedding, on condition that Pabuji will protect her herd of cows from thieves from the desert. Soon after the wedding ceremony has begun, Pabuji learns that the thieves are making off with the cows. He leaves his wedding to keep his word and recovers all the herd except a single calf. He risks another battle for the calf and is killed by the enemy. When word is brought to his bride, she prepares to commit *sati,* leaving her handprint on the gate of Pabuji's residence.

This story is sung in front of a cloth backdrop, up to 9 m (approximately 30 ft) in length and 2 m (over 6 ft) wide, on which scenes from Pabuji's life are depicted. The painting of the backdrop is itself a Rājasthānī folk art. Though the ballad of Pabuji is sung by non-Rājputs for a primarily non-Rājput audience, it embodies Rājput ideals. Pabuji is depicted as the brave warrior, the defender of sacred cows, who puts duty and honor before all else at the risk of his very life. His bride shows the virtues of the dutiful wife in preparing to commit sati.

¹⁹ SOCIAL PROBLEMS

As hereditary landowners of high caste, Rājputs do not face the social discrimination and problems of poverty that confront many of lower status in Indian society. While some may have fallen on hard times, as a result of factors such as land-fragmentation or excessive spending, Rājputs as a community are relatively prosperous. Alcoholism is a problem among some groups. One of the biggest challenges faced by Rājputs in recent years, however, is adjustment to the democratic environment of post-independent India. After over a millennia of rule as feudal overlords, Rājputs have faced threats to their position of power and prestige in the community. Their economic resources have been threatened by government attempts to redistribute wealth. They have faced challenges from castes seeking economic and political independence from Rājput control. Rājputs are beginning to enter politics, from the local *panchāyat* (village council) to the national arena. However,

800 years after Rājput unity might have stemmed the Muslim tide in India, Rājputs still lack the unity that would give them a powerful voice in modern Indian politics.

The historical role of Rājputs as defenders of the Hindu faith against the Muslims and their overt anti Muslim views have tended to result in the Rājputs supporting *Hindutva* ("Hinduness") and the political parties such as the Bharatiya Janata Party (BJP) that espouse Hindu nationalism. Thus in Rājasthān, the BJP formed the state government from 1990–1998 under Bhairon Singh Shekhawat, himself a Rājput. As of 2008 the government in Rājasthān (since 2003) was formed by the BJP, led by Vasundhara Raje Scindia.

20 GENDER ISSUES

As Hindus, Rājput women (Rājputnis) have to deal with the inequities of the Hindu social system. Moreover, as members of the *ksatriya varna*, the second of the major class groupings of Hindu society, they are expected to maintain the restrictions of "purity" expected of people of their social standing. Thus, there is a tradition that in AD 1303 , after she had thwarted the designs of Sultan Ala-ud-Din Khilji, Padmini, the queen of Chittor and the wife of king Rawal Ratan Singh, and the women in Chittor committed *jauhar* rather than be raped and dishonored by the Muslim besieger's army. In this, they were truly following their roles as *pativrata*, by selflessly serving their husbands and their families.

The concept of pativrata is central to the role Rājput women see themselves as performing in society. Literally meaning "one who has taken a vow (*vrat*) to [protect] her husband (*pati*)" and sometimes used loosely to refer to any wife, pativrata (or being a good husband-protector) is behind much of the behavior of Rājput women, even the committing of sati, and many of their religious rituals.

In the past, Rājput women faced child marriage, sati, polygamy, purdah, and female infanticide. Though many of these are illegal in modern India, today they still face the issues of dowry death, purdah, and female feticide. Again, socio-economic status plays a significant role in the extent to which Rājput women have to deal with such issues. Most Rājputs, as former landowners, do not have to face the problems of poverty and illiteracy that other communities face. The daughters of good Rājput families are sent to good schools and tend to marry into Westernized families. It is the poor village Rājput women who, mindful of their social status, have to face the worst aspects of life in rural India.

21 BIBLIOGRAPHY

Bahadur, K. P., ed. *Caste, Tribes & Culture of Rājputs*. Delhi: Ess Ess Publications, 1978.

Harlan, Lindsey. *Religion and Rājput Women: The Ethic of Protection in Contemporary Narratives*. Berkeley, Los Angeles and Oxford: University of California Press, 1992.

Joshi, Varsha. *Polygamy and Purdah: Women and Society among Rājputs*. Jaipur: Rawat Publications, 1995.

Khan, Rana Muhammad Sarwar. *The Rājputs: History, Clans, Culture, and Nobility*. Lahore: Rana Muhammad Sarwar Khan, 2005.

Minturn, Leigh, and John T. Hitchcock. *The Rājputs of Khalapur, India*. New York: John Wiley & Sons, 1966.

Saxena, R. K. *Rājput Nobility: A Study of 18th Century Rājputana*. Jaipur: Publication Scheme, 1996.

Schomer, Karine, Joan L. Erdman, Deryck O. Lodrick, and Lloyd I. Rudolph, eds. *The Idea of Rājasthān: Explorations in Regional Identity*. 2 vols. Columbia, MO: Manohar and American Institute of Indian Studies, 1994.

Tod, James. *The Annals and Antiquities of Rajast'han, or the Central and Western Rajpoot States of India*. 2 vols. New Delhi: K. M. N. Publishers, 1971 (reprint of 1829-32 ed.).

—by D. O. Lodrick

RAKHINES

PRONUNCIATION: rah-KINES
LOCATION: Western Myanmar (Burma)
POPULATION: Estimated 3.5 million
LANGUAGE: Rakhine dialect of Burmese
RELIGION: Buddhism

1 INTRODUCTION

Living in Western Myanmar (which was known as Burma until 1989), the Rakhines are descended from the Pyu people of ancient Burma and peoples of India. Their coastal land gave rise to the powerful empire of Arakan around the 4th century. They built the fortified capitol of Mrauk-U, which had streams and canals for streets and artificial lakes. A great variety of goods, including precious stones and metals, incense, indigo, and forest products, were bought and sold there. Seafarers and traders from much of Asia frequented Mrauk-U, while Portuguese pirates raided the coast. The kings of Arakan repelled many invaders until a ruthless Burmese ruler, King Bodawpaya, took advantage of internal disorder in Arakan and conquered it in 1784. Bodawpaya took the Rakhine king captive and had many of his subjects massacred. The Rakhines' most cherished treasure, a 12.5 foot bronze Buddha statue called the Mahamuni, was carried off to the Burmese city of Mandalay, where it remains today. The Rakhine capitol, Mrauk-U became an abandoned ruin, eventually replaced by a new city, Akyab, founded by British colonizers.

Resentment of British colonization was strong among the Rakhines, and an articulate Buddhist monk from Akyab named U Ottama organized a pro-independence movement in the first three decades of the 20th century. During the 1930s and 1940s, ethnic tensions grew between the Buddhist Rakhines and the Rohingya Muslims of Arakan. World War II brought fierce fighting to the area and increased inter-ethnic conflict.

Violence continued when Burma became independent following the war. Rakhine and Rohingya insurgent groups were formed to fight the central government. The Rakhine rebels mostly aligned themselves with Burma's Communist underground and hoped for an independent, or at least autonomous, Arakan State. Their ranks increased with the military takeover of Burma in 1962, then waned in later years, dividing into many factions. Some Rakhine rebel groups signed ceasefire agreements with the government in the 1990s. Those that are still active are small in numbers and have few weapons. A Rakhine rebel group, the Arakan Army, attempted to buy arms in 1998 on an island belonging to India, but its leader was killed and 34 of its members have remained in India's prisons ever since.

Numerous Rakhine political dissidents are now in prison in Myanmar or in exile for espousing the cause of democracy for Myanmar and their home state. During the September 2007 "Saffron Revolution," thousands of Buddhist monks and other people participated in mass nonviolent street marches in Akyab and other Rakhine communities. Rakhine students were arrested in 2008 for opposing the regime's constitutional referendum, which was designed to legitimize the role of the military in government.

2 LOCATION AND HOMELAND

The Rakhine population of Myanmar has been estimated at around 3.5 million, but there are no reliable recent census figures. A few thousand more Rakhines live in border villages and cities in Bangladesh and in India. There are many Rakhines in Myanmar's largest city, Rangoon, as well. Because their language and religion are very similar to those of Myanmar's ethnic majority, the Burmese (Burmans), Rakhines have sometimes been considered just a Burmese sub-group. Therefore many Rakhines fear complete assimilation into the ethnic majority. Their pride in the rich history of their people leads them to resent such a cultural absorption. They feel that the Burmese (Burmans) took Arakan by force, and have continually mistreated the Rakhines, so that becoming indistinguishable from the conquering nation would be the ultimate defeat.

Arakan is a long, narrow state, following Myanmar's Western coastline on the Indian Ocean's Bay of Bengal. It shares a northern border with Bangladesh, and Tripura State of northeast India is not far away. The mountain range called the Arakan Yoma runs through the state and separates it from the rest of Myanmar. The coastline is rugged, and rivers including the Kaladan and Lemro flow down from the mountains. Many islands, large and small, lie offshore. Most Rakhines live in villages, on the mainland, or on the islands. Akyab, also known as Sittwe, is the main city, and there is a beach resort town called Sandoway. Some tourists visit the beaches and the ancient ruined city of Mrauk-U.

In 2003 immense natural gas reserves were discovered in deep water off the coast of Arakan, and India competed with China for drilling and export rights, which would be granted by Myanmar's military government. The Shwe Gas Movement, a group formed by Rakhine exiles, voiced concerns that the revenue from gas sales would benefit Myanmar's regime instead of the people, and that transport of the gas might involve pipelines across Arakan to India, Bangladesh, or China. Port facilities in Arakan were upgraded by China and India to facilitate natural gas extraction and shipment.

3 LANGUAGE

The Rakhines speak a language that is considered a dialect of Burmese. The Rakhine alphabet has 33 letters, which are the same as the Burmese alphabet. There are some significant differences, mainly in pronunciation, such as the fact that Rakhines pronounce the letter "r," while Burmese do not (they use "y" in its place, calling the Buddhists of Arakan "Yakhines").

The Rakhine greeting is *Nay Kaung pha laa* ("How are you?"), and "thank you" is *Chyee zu thon ree.*

4 FOLKLORE

The pre-Buddhist culture of the Rakhines survives in a widespread belief in *Nats,* which are spirits of the sky and earth. Locations such as villages, fields, and bodies of water can have resident guardian Nats who may behave beneficially or harmfully. Ancient temples of Arakan are said to still be a place where rites of *yattara,* magic to ward off misfortune, are performed by spirit-mediums called *Nat kadaws.*

5 RELIGION

The Rakhines are an overwhelmingly Buddhist people. Buddhism seems to have appeared in Arakan around the 6th century bc. The Rakhines were Animists prior to conversion to Buddhism and were also influenced by India's Hindu Brahmanism. Buddhist missionaries from Ceylon (Sri Lanka) are thought to have brought the faith that now pervades Rakhine culture.

The ancient kings of Arakan built huge temple complexes and fortified them against invaders. Rakhines have continued to build Buddhist monasteries and pagodas and to maintain many of the old ones. Each Rakhine community has a Buddhist monastery that shelters a population of monks, including those putting on the robes for a short period of time. Rakhine Buddhism is very close to that of the Burmese, including study of Buddhist scriptures, respect for life, the importance of feeling compassion, and the inevitability of a cycle of reincarnations.

6 MAJOR HOLIDAYS

Rakhines celebrate festive occasions at least once each month, using the lunar calendar. Gatherings are held at temples, with food booths and theatrical entertainments. Some festival features are: boat races on the river (April and September), watering banyan trees (May), a tug-of-war between men's and women's teams (February), a contest of weaving robes for monks (October), parades of elephants and horses (January), and honoring the elders (October).

A festival of lights occurs in October, with people's houses lit by candles or (for those who can afford it) strings of electric lights.

The Rakhine New Year, Thorn Garan, is the highlight of the festival calendar. At the height of the hot season, usually in April, this Buddhist New Year is celebrated for a week with singing, dancing, and feasting. Buddha statues in monasteries are bathed in scented water on the first day. Later, boys and girls meet to splash each other with water. A girl may dress up in her best outfit, only to end up soaked with water thrown by a boy who has been admiring her. Rakhines who live overseas like to gather as a community for the major traditional holidays such as the New Year water festival.

7 RITES OF PASSAGE

The Rakhines have several taboos for pregnant women: they should not attend weddings or funerals, or even send gifts or donations to them. A pregnant woman is advised not to sit in the doorway, plant trees, or bathe after dark. After giving birth, the mother stays by a fire for seven days in the room where she gave birth. Then a naming ceremony is held. A female elder carries the baby out of the house and shows it the earth, the sun, and the moon. Baby girls then have their ears pierced.

Between age seven and the early teens, all Rakhine boys become monks for at least a few days. An elaborate feast is held, and the boys are dressed like ancient princes and paraded to the monastery. Then their heads are shaved and they put on the unadorned red robes of Buddhist monks.

When Rakhines die, they are cremated or buried. Accident victims or those who died from violence are traditionally buried in separate cemeteries, away from the village. The most elaborate funerals are those of senior monks, whose bodies are kept, embalmed, at their monastery, until an auspicious (according to astrology) day when they are cremated.

8 INTERPERSONAL RELATIONS

Rakhines shake hands when they meet. Guests are welcomed into a house with tea or a cold beverage. People always remove their shoes when entering a home or a Buddhist temple.

Young people meet at festivals, religious occasions, and at school. Friends introduce boys and girls to each other, or a boy who is interested in a girl may visit her at her parent's house. Traditionally, he'll stay outside and try to talk to her; she may ignore him or she may show that she likes him by deciding to converse with him. Few people have telephones, so love notes, passed along by friends, are a typical way for a couple to communicate. Rakhines have a special vocabulary called *zaam*, which is used only for romance.

9 LIVING CONDITIONS

The Rakhines suffer from a lack of health care, due to a shortage of trained doctors and nurses and a lack of medical facilities. In Arakan's hot, rainy climate, malaria (spread by mosquitoes) and other tropical diseases are common. Malnutrition is serious in the countryside and even in the cities, where workers struggle to earn enough to buy rice, the staple food. As a worldwide food crisis took hold in 2008 and the price of rice soared in Asia, Rakhines found it harder and harder to feed their families. The May 2008 Cyclone Nargis disaster in Myanmar affected Arakan indirectly with drastic increases in the price of rice, other foods and fuel.

Traditional Rakhine houses are built above the ground on stilts. They are usually made of bamboo, many varieties of which grow in Arakan, or of wood. The houses generally have a shaded verandah in the front and sleeping quarters in the back. Those who can afford it use mosquito nets to keep away the carriers of malaria. Meals may be prepared and eaten in the cool area under the elevated house.

Living standards for the Rakhines tend to be low. Farmers are harassed by the Burmese government forces to turn over major quotas of their rice crop. Whole villages are forced to relocate, sometimes to predominantly Muslim areas that the military wants to surround with Buddhist "settlers." The inland and coastal forests of Arakan are under some threat from logging enterprises, and new shrimp farms set up by the government along the coast cause pollution and the destruction of mangrove forests.

Travel within Arakan is mainly by riverboat. Arakan has no railway, and few road links exist to the rest of Myanmar. To travel to regions outside of Arakan, Rakhines usually go by boat. There are some airplane flights in and out of Akyab and Sandoway, but plane tickets are too expensive for most Rakhines. There are few roads in the state, although the Burmese government has used Rakhines and Rohingyas as forced laborers to build more.

10 FAMILY LIFE

Families with five or more children are the norm among the Rakhines, who tend to marry in their late teens or early twenties. Parents often arrange marriages, but unarranged "love matches" are very common as well. The groom's family gives a dowry, and the couple's horoscopes must be found compatible. Before the wedding, Buddhist monks recite prayers at the homes of the bride and the groom. A well-off married couple with children is asked to perform the actual wedding ceremony by tying the hands of the bride and groom with a thread.

Then the newlyweds bow to their parents. Gifts of money are put in a silver bowl by parents, relatives, and other guests. A feast follows, with the married couple eating food in pairs: two prawns, two eggs, and so on. The couple afterwards lives at the bride's parents' house for a while. If a couple has problems, they may be counseled by village elders. Divorce is permissible, but rare.

Rakhine families sometimes have cats and caged songbirds as pets, and dogs are kept outside to guard the house.

11 CLOTHING

Rakhines wear an ankle-length sarong called a *cheik thamein*. For men it is knotted at the waist, and women wrap it tightly and tuck it in at the side. The fabric is heavy cotton or silk, woven in a thick, brocade-like pattern. Men wear shirts or T-shirts, and women wear traditional or modern blouses or T-shirts. Women's clothing is often vividly colored, especially at festival times, and they decorate their hair with orchids and other flowers. For formal occasions, a long jacket of thin material is worn. Girls wear lipstick, nail polish, and *thanaka,* a sunscreen and face powder made from a fragrant wood. People often carry umbrellas as shelter from the sun as well as from the monsoon rain. They wear flip-flop sandals made of velvet and straw, or plastic or rubber.

12 FOOD

Rakhine cuisine is closely related to that of the Burmese and has strong Indian influences. The Rakhines eat two or three rice-based meals a day. Soups, vegetable dishes including string beans, squash, and baby eggplant, and curries accompany the rice. Popular curries include chicken, beef, fish, and prawns, but these ingredients are becoming increasingly hard for most people to afford. Unlike the Muslim Rohingya people of Arakan, the Rakhines eat pork in the form of curry, pork chops, meatballs, or sausage. Rakhines use chilies, garlic, ginger, and fish-paste for flavoring. They eat rice dishes by scooping up mouthfuls with the fingertips of the right hand. For a snack or dessert there are tropical fruits such as mangos and sweet cakes made of flour or sticky rice, served with tea. Rakhines who are strict Buddhists avoid alcohol, but others drink toddy palm wine or beer.

13 EDUCATION

The Rakhines have traditionally been a learned people, valuing intellectual and artistic achievement. Ethnic discrimination and the general decline in educational standards have made it hard for Rakhines to pursue higher learning elsewhere in Myanmar, and schools in Arakan have often been shut down as a measure by the Burmese government to curtail student unrest. During Myanmar's pro-democracy uprising of 1988, Rakhine and Rohingya students took over government of most of Arakan's towns and cities for several months, until their movement was brutally suppressed by the military.

Elementary to high school education is in bad condition as well. Teachers and teaching materials are in short supply. Buddhist monasteries provide some education, mainly for boys. Some Rakhine student refugees from the 1988 uprising founded and staffed schools for refugee children and poor villagers in India and Bangladesh. Others, including young Buddhist monks, continued their studies at universities and colleges in India, and have documented the human rights situation and history of Arakan.

14 CULTURAL HERITAGE

The ancient palaces and temples of the Rakhine kings at Mrauk-U and elsewhere were built with elaborate stonework, much of which remains. Stone terraces and bell-shaped pagodas overlook the landscape, along with remains of old fortification walls. These had been surrounded by dwellings made of bamboo or more costly materials, such as fragrant sandalwood. Large Buddha images and carved-stone reliefs abound in these archeological sites, and frescoes depicting Buddhist stories and daily life in past centuries can still be seen.

Rakhine dance, poetry (the lyrical *E-gyin* style), and music are derived from performances at the ancient royal courts. The Rakhines have a variety of songs composed for specific occasions, from courtship to weddings to lullabies. Rakhine orchestral music is similar to Burmese classical music and emphasizes percussion instruments including xylophones, drums, and cymbals. A particularly Rakhine instrument is the *hne*, a shawm (metal horn) with a double reed. Such orchestras play for dramas, comedies, marionette theater, and classical dance. Rakhine dance, influenced by India, includes large ensemble pieces such as the "spider" dance with as many as 40 dancers, and the *Don Yin* dance with as many as 100. There is also a dramatic Rakhine dragon dance.

15 WORK

Most Rakhines make their living as farmers, fishermen, or as shopkeepers and traders in towns. Women often travel by riverboat to bring goods to and from central Myanmar for sale. A highly educated Rakhine elite, including doctors, teachers, and other professionals, lives largely outside of Arakan. Those who have attempted political action within Arakan have been in considerable danger. U Tha Tun, a noted Rakhine historian, died in 1991 in prison in Akyab, where he had been sent while a pro-democracy political candidate. A Rakhine dissident helped to found "Green November," Myanmar's first environmental action group. Rakhine exiles operate the Narinjara News online information service, and several overseas Rakhines have blogs about political, cultural, entertainment, and personal topics.

16 SPORTS

The Rakhines enjoy playing and watching soccer, volleyball, and *chinlone*, a fast kickball game played with a woven rattan ball. Young men sometimes stage a contest to see which team can climb highest up a pole or tree by standing on each other's shoulders. A traditional form of wrestling, *kyun* ("quick like a tiger") can be seen at festivals. Karate, judo, and other martial arts are popular with young people in the towns and cities.

17 ENTERTAINMENT AND RECREATION

Rakhine young people enjoy listening to pop songs from Western countries or Myanmar and singing them with guitar accompaniment. Towns and cities have movie theaters or "video parlors" where foreign or local video discs are played. Students are avid readers, sharing books, which are in short supply, and many play chess. Satellite television has limited availability, so shortwave radios are an important source of information on local and foreign news and cultural developments. Internet access is often censored and few people own home computers, but the urban centers have cyber-cafes where computer games are popular.

[18] FOLK ART, CRAFTS, AND HOBBIES

The Rakhines are known throughout Myanmar for their woven, brocade-textured fabrics. Basketry and pottery are other Rakhine crafts.

[19] SOCIAL PROBLEMS

Forced relocation and forced labor at the hands of the Burmese government military have disrupted traditional Rakhine society in the countryside, while suppression of dissent and economic decline have created a climate of fear and frustration in the towns and cities. In addition to these ongoing problems, ethnic friction between Rakhines and Rohingyas continues. While the groups worked together for the democracy cause in 1988 and afterwards, the Burmese military has played one off against the other, through actions such as moving Rakhines onto confiscated Rohingya land. Animosities from the period around World War II, and farther back into ancient history, have been allowed to resurface. Many, if not all Rakhines will insist that the Rohingyas are an alien people with no real right to live in Arakan. In this matter alone, they agree with the Burmese central government. The Rakhines have their own insecurity, which hinges on the fear of assimilation by the much larger Burmese ethnic group, to which they are so closely related. Many real and perceived wounds will have to be healed before the Rakhines can live in peace and security with all their neighbors.

[20] GENDER ISSUES

In the Buddhism practiced by Rakhines, women are considered an inferior incarnation to men, and Rakhine families are dominated by the father, who makes important decisions. Rakhine women are, however, very active in the life of their communities. Rakhine women are active in business as entrepreneurs and market vendors. They own and run shops and travel great distances to trade in rice and consumer goods, often while their husbands stay at home. Rakhine women are also involved in health care, education, and underground pro-democracy political activities. In exile, Rakhine women participate in political life, more often in leadership roles than women from other ethnic groups of Myanmar. A Rakhine women's rights activist, Mra Raza Linn, won the 2007 Yayori Award for human rights. Although Rakhine society is somewhat conservative, gay and transgender individuals are treated with tolerance. Sometimes transgender people perform as *Nat kadaw* spirit-mediums.

[21] BIBLIOGRAPHY

All Arakan. www.allarakan.com (May 21, 2008).

Collis, Maurice. *The Land of the Great Image.* New York: Alfred A. Knopf, 1943.

Gutman, Pamela. *Burma's Lost Kingdoms: Splendours of Arakan.* Bangkok: Orchid Press, 2001.

Klein, Wilhelm. *Burma.* Hong Kong: Apa Productions, 1982.

Maung, Shwe Lu. *Burma: Nationalism and Ideology.* Dhaka, Bangladesh: University Press, 1989.

Mirante, Edith. *Down the Rat Hole: Adventures Underground on Burma's Frontiers.* Bangkok: Orchid Press, 2005.

Narinjara News. www.narinjara.com (21 May 2008).

Rakhapura.com. www.rakapura.com (21 May 2008).

Smith, Martin. *Ethnic Groups of Burma.* London: Anti-Slavery International, 1994.

—by Edith Mirante

ROHINGYAS

PRONUNCIATION: roh-HIN-juhz
LOCATION: Western Myanmar (Burma) (
POPULATION: Estimated 1.5 million in Myanmar
LANGUAGE: Rohingya
RELIGION: Islam (Sunni Muslim)

¹ INTRODUCTION

The Rohingya people of western Myanmar (the country called Burma until 1989) are closely related to the Bengali people of neighboring Bangladesh and India. Like those in Bangladesh, the Rohingyas are Muslims. In addition to their Bengali heritage, the Rohingyas are thought to have descended in part from Persian, Moorish, and Arab seafarers. A coastal people on the trade route between Arabia and China, the Rohingyas converted to Islam around the 12th century. Their knowledge of science and the arts influenced the Buddhist Rakhine kings of Arakan in past centuries, when Bengal and Arakan were allies. The Muslims and their Buddhist Rakhine compatriots generally coexisted peacefully.

During British colonial days, northern Arakan was at first part of India's Bengal province, but then the British decided that Arakan was to be part of Burma. When World War II reached Burma, the Rohingyas helped the British to fight their way back into Burma through Arakan and to repel the Japanese invaders. Anti-Muslim rioting broke out in Arakan in 1942, causing tens of thousands of Rohingyas to flee across the border to Bangladesh (then called East Pakistan). At Burma's independence in 1948, the Rohingyas hoped for their own Muslim state, but they were combined with predominantly Rakhine areas in Arakan State. Tensions between Rakhines and Rohingyas, unresolved from World War II, continued, and government discrimination against the Rohingyas, in terms of travel restrictions within Burma and citizenship laws, commenced.

With the 1962 military takeover of the central Burmese government, conditions worsened for Arakan's Muslims. They were viewed as a threat to the predominantly Burmese (Burman) power structure and a holdover from colonial times when the British brought many workers from India to Burma. In 1978, Operation *Nagamin* ("Dragon King") took place. It was a systematic campaign of human rights violations by the government military against the Rohingyas, who were declared "illegal immigrants." Over 200,000 fled across the border to Bangladesh. Thousands starved to death in deliberately under-supplied refugee camps until the survivors were forced to return to Burma.

After the suppression of the 1988 pro-democracy uprising throughout Burma, Muslims were again targeted for mistreatment. A government military build-up in northern Arakan in 1991 was accompanied by murder, land confiscation, rape, torture, destruction of mosques, and large-scale forced labor. Again, this led to a huge flight to Bangladesh. Over 250,000 Rohingya refugees sought sanctuary in border camps this time. Eventually, most were convinced or coerced to return to Arakan, although forced labor and other forms of abuse have continued there. The estimated 27,000 Rohingya refugees who remain in the official camps in Bangladesh endure miserable conditions, and there is a constant influx of new arrivals who struggle to survive outside of the camps.

Exiled Rohingyas promote the preservation of cultural identity and support democracy for Myanmar, and a small group of insurgents still fights for political autonomy. Rohingyas have also become "boat people" in recent years, fleeing Arakan by sea for Thailand or Malaysia. In 2008 Thailand's Prime Minister Samak Sundaravej proposed confining all Rohingya migrants on an island detention camp. Rohingyas in Malaysia (a predominantly Muslim country) have been a useful part of the workforce making up for that country's labor shortage, but are subject to abuse, detention and forced repatriation, as they are considered illegal immigrants.

A "third country" program has had some success in sending Rohingya refugees from the Bangladesh camps to other countries, particularly Canada. The United Nations High Commissioner for Refugees (UNHCR), the agency overseeing the camps in Bangladesh, announced in May 2008 that an agreement with the governments of Bangladesh and Myanmar to repatriate the remaining occupants of official camps back to Myanmar would be revived. With other regions of Myanmar devastated by Cyclone Nargis that month, and the whole country facing a rice shortage, there was some question about the practicality of such a mass repatriation.

² LOCATION AND HOMELAND

There may be as many as 1.5 million Rohingyas in Myanmar, but no reliable census figures exist for them or other ethnic minorities. Hundreds of thousands more Rohingyas live in exile. At least 127,000 live in Bangladesh, inside and outside of established refugee camps. An estimated 200,000 reside in Pakistan, another 200,000 in Saudi Arabia, and thousands more in the Persian Gulf states and Jordan. Tens of thousands of Rohingyas live as illegal immigrants in Malaysia. Besides the Rohingyas, Myanmar has other Muslim populations of Chinese, Indian, and Burman lineage.

The Rohingya homeland is at the northern tip of Arakan State, bordering Bangladesh's Chittagong and northeast India's Tripura. The main towns are Buthidaung and Maungdaw, a river port. Most Rohingyas live in villages surrounding them. Others live in and around the cities of Akyab and Rathedaung, to the south in Arakan and on islands in the Bay of Bengal. In recent years, the Myanmar government has brought in families of Buddhist settlers, often poor people from other parts of Myanmar, to farm land confiscated from Rohingyas or abandoned by those who left as refugees.

The Kaladan, Mayu, and Seindaung Rivers run through flat farmland surrounded by mountains and the Bay of Bengal coastline. The Naaf River forms Arakan's border with Bangladesh. Forests of bamboo and mangrove exist, but they have greatly decreased due to logging and the government's shrimp farming projects.

³ LANGUAGE

The Rohingyas' language is closely related to the Bengali dialect spoken in Bangladesh's southern Chittagong Province and has some Persian and Arabic influences. The written language is close to that of Bengali.

The usual Rohingya greeting is to ask "How are you?": *Ken ahsaw?* with the reply, *Balah aasee,* ("I am fine"). "Thank you" in the Rohingya language is *Shu kuria.*

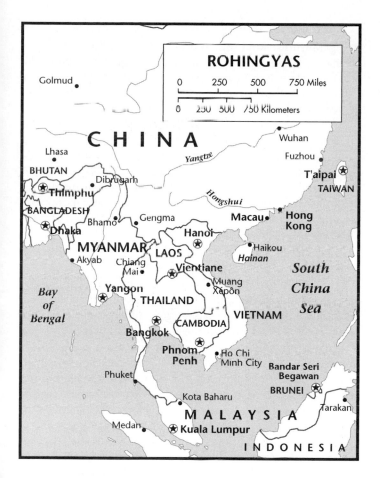

ROHINGYAS

0   250   500   750 Miles

0   250   500   750 Kilometers

is nearly impossible for most Rohingyas due to the cost and government travel restrictions.

6 MAJOR HOLIDAYS

Rohingyas observe the Ramadan fast of Islam (according to the lunar calendar) during the first half of the year, when they consume no food or drink during daylight hours for one month. At the end of Ramadan, the celebration called *Eid Al Fitr* takes place. People who can afford to do so buy new clothes and provide food for visitors who drop in. Children go from house to house with bags to collect small gifts of money. Seventy days after Ramadan, *Eid Adha* is celebrated. Animals, usually goats, are bought by those who can afford them. The goats are sacrificed and a third of the meat is given away to the poor. The rest is shared with family, friends, and neighbors.

7 RITES OF PASSAGE

Rohingya mothers usually give birth at home, assisted by a midwife. Traditionally, the new mother would stay by a warm fire for several days after the birth. For about 40 days she stays at home and sleeps apart from her husband. Within a week or two of the birth, the baby's head is shaved. Children who are sick with fever sometimes have their head shaved because the parents believe the illness will make their hair fall out and shaving will help it to grow back properly.

Boys and girls from ages 4 to 12 attend mosque schools called *madrasahs* to learn to read the Quran in Arabic. From their early teen years, they work alongside their parents, in the home if girls, or farming and fishing if boys. Because of increasing economic hardship, child labor has become common as well, and children have been used for forced labor on military projects such as road or barracks building.

When Rohingyas die, they are, according to Islamic tradition, buried. The funeral is simple, and those who can afford to mark the grave with a stone bearing the deceased's name. After seven days, recitations of the Quran are held to honor the dead, and families who can afford to sacrifice an animal and give part of the meat to feed the poor.

4 FOLKLORE

Because of their adherence to Islam, the Rohingya people tend to reject the serious belief in ghosts and nature-spirits prevalent elsewhere in Myanmar. People do enjoy the "Arabian Nights" fairytales, though, translated into Bengali. Local customs include considering it impolite to point your feet at people or objects and not leaning your forehead on your hands, as this is considered a sign of severe depression.

5 RELIGION

From the 8th to 14th centuries, Islam took hold in northern Arakan. The Rohingya people are a traditionalist Sunni Muslim society, believing that Allah is the only God and adhering to the code of morality set down by his prophet Muhammad. While not obviously "fundamentalist" or "militant," for most Rohingyas, life revolves around the practice of their faith. Daily prayers and study of the Quran are of great importance, although many religious schools have been closed down by Myanmar's military government. Each community would normally have a mosque, but many have been destroyed in recent years by the government. Communities donate money and materials to build and maintain the mosques, which are built of wood, or in larger communities, whitewashed cement, but it is very difficult to get the necessary government permission to make repairs. Each functioning mosque has an Imam, in charge of worship, and a Muezzin, who calls the faithful to prayer. They are paid support by the community. The government has banned amplified calls by the Muezzins. The traditional Muslim pilgrimage, the Haj, to Mecca in Saudi Arabia,

8 INTERPERSONAL RELATIONS

Rohingyas greet each other by shaking hands, and family members hug each other. People remove their shoes when entering a Rohingya house. The host will bring tea or other refreshments to a guest, without asking, as an inquiry such as "Would you like some tea?" would receive a polite refusal.

Shoes are always taken off, and a person's head is kept covered when visiting a mosque. Men and women occupy separate sections of the mosque, with a curtain between them.

9 LIVING CONDITIONS

Throughout Arakan, living conditions are hard; this is particularly so for Rohingyas, who, viewed as less than full citizens, tend to lack access to education, medical care, and other social services. Some outside help from the United Nations and a few foreign voluntary agencies has been allowed as part of the agreement to resettle Rohingya refugees from Bangladesh back in Arakan. Malaria, dysentery, and other tropical diseases are widespread among the Rohingyas, as is malnutrition.

In normal times, most Rohingyas live in thatch-roofed one- or two-story houses built of wood and raised up on stilts. They use chairs and tables in their dining areas and sleep on platform beds, with mosquito nets if they can afford them. The displaced people built bamboo huts with plastic sheets for roofing material to keep out the monsoon rainfall.

Many Rohingyas have lost the land left to them by their families because of outright confiscation by the military, forced resettlement of Rakhine villagers onto Rohingya land, or the inability to prove ownership because papers got lost during the escape to Bangladesh. A council of elders called the *Samaj* traditionally made important decisions in Rohingya villages, but such authority has now been taken over by Burmese military officers from bases established in the area.

Transportation for Rohingyas is mainly on foot or on small riverboats. Bicycles are a luxury owned by some. Arakan has no railway, and the few roads are in poor condition. Travel for Rohingyas within northern Arakan is difficult because of military checkpoints, and their access to the rest of Myanmar remains restricted.

¹⁰ FAMILY LIFE

Under normal conditions, Rohingyas tend to marry and start a family in their late teens or early twenties. Marriage is usually arranged by the parents, so dating is rare and is usually kept secret. If a couple falls in love without parental consent, they might elope. Some couples never meet at all before their wedding. The relatives negotiate for jewelry, usually gold if they can afford it, to be given to the bride by both sides of the family, as the newlyweds' "bank account." On the morning of the wedding day, the bride's relatives attend a lunch and bring gifts for her, and then the groom's relatives attend a dinner in the evening. In Arakan, the Rohingyas are subject to marriage restrictions, as a bride and groom must apply for marriage permission from several government agencies. That permission is often denied, and there are many cases of arrest for illegal marriage between consenting adult Rohingya men and women in Arakan.

Divorce is rare and is considered shameful for women. The children are often raised by the husband's mother in cases of divorce. Widows are looked after by their own family and their husband's family.

Five children is an average size for a Rohingya family. Infant and child mortality rates, due to diseases and malnutrition, are high. Ideally, a Rohingya household is self-sustaining, with its own rice paddy, vegetable garden, and domestic animals such as chickens and goats. Cats and songbirds are popular house pets, and dogs are kept outside to guard the house.

¹¹ CLOTHING

Rohingyas wear ankle-length cotton sarongs. The men's sarong is called a *longi* and is knotted in front, and the women's is called a *thain* and wraps tightly around the waist. Cotton shirts and blouses are worn with the sarongs. Women have pierced ears and wear bangle bracelets of gold, glass or plastic. Some married women wear a gold ring called a *Nag-pool* ("nose-flower") in one nostril. In former times, Rohingya women always wore full veils when outdoors. Now, women and older girls generally wear a large scarf that covers most of their hair and wraps around the shoulders. The scarves are often quite colorful, except for those of older women, who wear white. Men over age 40 or so grow beards.

¹² FOOD

Being Muslims, Rohingyas do not eat pork. They also have their own taboos against eating hawks, eagles, and (from the sea) rays. Many Rohingyas are fishermen, and a variety of river fish are available. Chicken and goat are favorite curries, always served with rice. Common vegetables include potatoes, tomatoes, okra, and eggplant, with chili peppers for flavoring. Rice is served twice a day by those who can afford it, for lunch and dinner. In the morning, tea or coffee is served with flat bread called *roti* or other types of bread and biscuits. *Biryani*, an Indian spiced rice dish with goat or chicken, is a favorite dish for weddings and other celebrations. Rohingyas eat cakes, cookies, and rice puddings, often made with coconut. Fried garbanzo beans are sold as a snack.

¹³ EDUCATION

Aside from the religious schools where boys and girls learn the Quran and some higher-level religious training for men, education in Arakan consists of government schools, where instruction is conducted in the Burmese language. Very few Rohingyas are able to continue their education past primary school, and only 5%, nearly all male, go on to study after high school. The cost of education, the difficulty of going away to school due to travel restrictions, and discrimination against Rohingyas contribute to the current shortage of highly educated people.

¹⁴ CULTURAL HERITAGE

As early as the 7th century, small mosques known as *Badr Moqam* were built along the Arakan coast as shrines to a Muslim saint. Important mosques were built in Arakan during the 14th, 15th, and 16th centuries. The largest mosque in Akyab, the Musa Dewan, and the Jam-e-Mosque of Akyab, which has many domes and spires, were constructed in the 17th century.

Rohingya literature blossomed in the ancient courts of Arakan, when Muslim poets including Daulat Qazi, Magan Siddiqi, Mardan, and Shah Aloal wrote in Bengali, Persian, or Arabic. The 17th century poet Shah Aloal, who led an adventurous life as a warrior, scholar, and scientist, is considered one of the great poets of Bengali literature. He translated and adapted romances and epics from Hindi and Persian, and composed his own lyrical and mystical poems as well. "Poetry," he wrote, "is full of fragrance. It brings the faraway near, and takes the near to the distant." His romantic poems are noteworthy for being realistic depictions of human emotions rather than the spiritual allegories prevalent at the time. Shah Aloal wrote, "After sifting all matters, I find that love can be compared to nothing. Full of sharp pain is love, yet blessed is he who has been fortunate to experience it."

Little is being written in the Rohingya language at present, although exiled Rohingya dissidents in Bangladesh have been researching the history of their ethnic group. Likewise, Rohingya art, architecture, and music await historical research and contemporary revival. Rohingya exiles have devised a way to write their language in the Roman alphabet for computer use, and have established the Bangladesh-based Kaladan Press Network, which reports news of Arakan online.

[15] WORK

The Rohingyas are mostly rice farmers and fishermen. Some own cattle for plowing or for meat and milk. Rohingya entrepreneurs run small shops and river transport services. Boatbuilding is a skilled trade in northern Arakan, producing small wooden vessels to be rowed with oars, for the most part, and some sailboats. The few Rohingyas who have achieved higher education work as doctors, lawyers, and business persons, mainly overseas. Rohingya women are far less likely to work outside the home than those of other ethnic groups of Myanmar.

[16] SPORTS

Soccer and volleyball are the most popular sports for Rohingya young people to play or watch. Arakan's climate is often very hot, so children particularly like to go swimming in the rivers.

[17] ENTERTAINMENT AND RECREATION

In Arakan's towns and cities there are movie theaters and small "video parlors" where Burmese, Indian, and other films are shown on disc. In the villages, people like to go for an evening stroll after dinner and gather on a soccer field or other open space to listen to music, usually Indian pop songs, on portable compact disc players. Old folk songs are sung while working in the rice fields or vegetable gardens. Many communities have tea shops where men gather in the morning or afternoon to talk.

[18] FOLK ART, CRAFTS, AND HOBBIES

Rohingyas make baskets from cane and bamboo and weave straw mats for their houses. Rohingya women knit, or embroider their clothing. Some of the mosques in Arakan have ornamental tile-work.

[19] SOCIAL PROBLEMS

The Rohingyas have had to endure a concerted campaign of human rights abuse by Myanmar's military government, denial of full citizenship rights, and even routine discrimination by other ethnic minority groups that are otherwise democratic in nature. Mosques and other Islamic religious sites have been burned or desecrated by the government forces and access to Islamic texts and pilgrimage severely restricted. The traditional rural society has been thrown into chaos by demands for forced labor, crop and property confiscation, and the flight to temporary sanctuary in Bangladesh. Rice goes unplanted and children go unfed. The Rohingyas' present poverty and the pattern of risky escape to other countries have made the survival of the Rohingyas in Myanmar very precarious. Even if this ongoing crisis is resolved, relations with the Rakhines, with whom the Rohingyas share geography and history, must be greatly repaired for Arakan to return to any level of peace and prosperity. Government programs settling Buddhist families in Rohingya areas have increased friction between the religious/ethnic groups, rather than understanding or acceptance.

[20] GENDER ISSUES

Rohingya women tend to live more homebound lives than most women in Myanmar. Men work in the fields and sell goods in the market, while women take care of children, the home, vegetable gardens, and domestic animals. After age 12 or so, girls mostly stay at home except when they are attending school. Few Rohingya women in Myanmar have gone on to higher education, but some have become teachers and nurses. In recent years, according to documents by human rights groups such as Amnesty International, Rohingya women and girls have been targeted for rape by Burmese government troops. Such use of rape as a military tactic appears to be intended to humiliate the ethnic minority group and instill fear of the uniformed authorities. This danger adds to the tendency of Rohingyas to keep girls at home and even to keep them out of school.

Homosexuality is generally disapproved of in the conservative Islam that is intrinsic to Rohingya society. However, gay and transgendered individuals are often treated with tolerance and acceptance in Rohingya households.

[21] BIBLIOGRAPHY

Amnesty International. "Human Rights Violations Against Muslims in the Rakhine (Arakan) State." New York: Amnesty International, 1992.

———. "Myanmar—The Rohingya Minority: Fundamental Rights Denied." New York: Amnesty International, 2004. http://www.amnesty.org/en/library/info/ASA16/005/2004 (26 May 2008).

Asia Watch. "The Rohingya Muslims: Ending a Cycle of Exodus?" New York: Human Rights Watch, 1996.

Human Rights Watch. "Rohingya Refugees from Burma Mistreated in Bangladesh." New York: Human Rights Watch, 27 March 2007. http://hrw.org/english/docs/2007/03/27/bangla15571.htm (26 May 2008).

Kaladan Press Network. http://www.kaladanpress.org/ (26 May 2008).

Lewa, Chris. "We Are Like a Soccer Ball, Kicked by Burma, Kicked by Bangladesh." Bangkok, Thailand: Asian Forum for Human Rights and Development (Forum-Asia), 2003. http://burmalibrary.org/docs/KICKED-June2003.htm (26 May 2008).

Lintner, Bertil. "Distant Exile." *Far Eastern Economic Review.* 28 January 1993.

Mirante, Edith. *Down the Rat Hole: Adventures Underground on Burma's Frontiers.* Bangkok: Orchid Press, 2005.

Refugees International. "The Rohingya: Discrimination in Burma and Denial of Rights in Bangladesh." Washington D.C.: Refugees International, 2006 http://www.refugeesinternational.org/content/article/detail/9137?PHPSESSID=468353286602b680cd5c10502f47fe0b (26 May 2008).

Smith, Martin. *Ethnic Groups in Burma.* London: Anti-Slavery International, 1994.

U.S. Committee for Refugees. *The Return of the Rohingya Refugees to Burma.* Washington, D.C.: U.S. Committee for Refugees, 1995.

U.S. Department of State. "International Religious Freedom Report 2007." Washington D.C.: Bureau of Democracy, Human Rights, and Labor, U.S. Department of State, 2007 http://www.state.gov/g/drl/rls/irf/2007/90131.htm (26 May 2008).

Yunus, Mohammed. *A History of Arakan.* Chittagong, Bangladesh: Magenta Colour, 1994.

—by Edith Mirante

SA'DAN TORAJA

PRONUNCIATION: Toh-RAH-jah
ALTERNATE NAMES: Toraja
LOCATION: Indonesia (Sulawesi)
POPULATION: 650,000
LANGUAGE: Sa'dan Toraja (Bahasa Tae')
RELIGION: Christianity (64% Protestant, 12% Catholic); Aluk To Dolo ("the Way of the Ancestors")
RELATED ARTICLES: Vol. 3: Indonesians

¹ INTRODUCTION

Since converting to Islam in the 17th century, the lowland peoples of South Sulawesi have applied the term "Toraja" to all highlanders who retained their ancestral animism. Dutch colonial anthropology began to distinguish numerous distinct ethnic groups in the mountains at the heart of Sulawesi, roughly grouping them into "Eastern," "Western," and "Southern" Toraja. Of these groups, only the "Southern Toraja," associated with the valley of the Sa'dan River and the most well known internationally, have taken the originally pejorative term as their own (in this article, "Toraja" will only refer to the Sa'dan Toraja).

While substantial kingdoms developed in lowland South Sulawesi as early as the 14th century or before, the Toraja knew no political units larger than village confederations (tondok) until the beginning of the 20th century. The Toraja remember only one fleeting episode of unity: a common front put up against Arung Palakka, the Bugis ally of the Dutch East India Company in the destruction of Makassar, whose hegemonic ambitions reached even into the highlands. The tondok was an association that could comprise as little as a cluster of two to three houses or encompass as much as a network of families stretching across the highlands; a tondok wove ties of marriage and ritual between often remote settlements while excluding nearby ones. In the highlands, possession of land and the slaves to work it were the key to social prominence, making an individual a to kapua, a "big man." The meat from animal sacrifices was (and remains) the medium that affirmed status and represented relations of obligation.

In the late 19th century, population growth made land ever scarcer, leaving the land-poor and land-less vulnerable to enslavement for nonpayment of debts. The slave trade flourished as labor was needed both in the lowlands and for growing coffee, the new and very lucrative export crop, in the highlands; one estimate counts as many as 12,000 Toraja sold into captivity. Slave raiding and warfare over land rights and trade routes became so intense that villages placed themselves on hilltops encircled by fortifications and connected themselves to neighboring settlements with underground tunnels.

As part of their general pacification of South Sulawesi, the Dutch sent armies into the Toraja highlands, by 1908 overcoming resistance led by the to kapua, Pong Tiku, master of the coffee traffic to Bone via Luwu (his only rival was the master of the alternate Sidenreng–to–Pare-Pare route to the west). The colonial peace ended the slave trade and introduced schools, clinics, and imported cotton cloth. In a pattern repeated all over the archipelago, the to kapua collaborated with the Dutch as officials in the newly imposed bureaucracy.

The years since World War II have transformed Toraja society. The lowland Kahar Muzakkar rebellion of 1950–1965 [see **Bugis**] washed up into the highlands. Under the fear of forced Islamization, thousands of Toraja sought the legal protection of conversion to Christianity (a trend accelerated under the New Order's "anti-communist" suspicion of paganism). In recent decades, voluntary emigration, including of educated professionals, has replaced the old efflux of slaves and has brought new wealth back into the Toraja homeland. Beginning in the 1980s, the Indonesian government heavily promoted the Toraja region as a destination for international tourism (even putting traditional Toraja noble houses, tongkonan, on the 5,000 rupiah note, about as common as sight to Indonesians as Lincoln on the $5 bill is to Americans, signaling that Torajan culture, like Balinese culture, had come to be viewed as emblematic of the national identity). Attracted to the dramatic landscape and to "exotic" rituals, mass tourism has also created new opportunities as well as problems for the Toraja.

Since the end of the Suharto regime in 1998, political instability in Indonesia, including internationally publicized inter-ethnic/sectarian violence in neighboring Central Sulawesi has caused a sharp decline in tourism to the Toraja homeland, challenging a local society that had become dependent upon it. Torajans have stood against the spread of ethnic violence to their region as when, soon after anti-Chinese rioting had burned down a thousand homes and businesses in Ujungpandang (Makassar), the capital of South Sulawesi in September 1997, Torajans linked arms to block Muslim agitators from outside the Toraja region from attacking Chinese shops in the major tourist town of Rantepao. At the same time, Muslim transmigrants, as elsewhere in Indonesia, started to consider returning to their homelands, fearing persecution by Toraja and Chinese for what other Muslims had attempted to do. In 2001, Toraja identity received international validation when the Ke'te' Kesu', the village showcasing the finest examples of tongkonan, was nominated to join the UNESCO list of World Heritage sites, alongside the monumental architecture of Java's Borobudur and Prambanan, also non-Muslim icons of identity for the world's largest Muslim-majority nation.

² LOCATION AND HOMELAND

The Sa'dan Toraja's mountain homeland lies in the extreme north of Sulawesi's southwestern peninsula. The highlands begin at 330 m (1,080 ft) above sea level, with the major towns of Rantepao and Makale at above 700 m (2,300 ft) and the highest peak (Mt. Sesean, abode of Suloara, the legendary first priest of the Toraja) at 2,000 m (6,560 ft). Paddy fields cover what patches of flat land there are, usually along the many small rivers, and rise in terraces up the thickly forested mountainsides.

The Sa'dan Toraja number over 650,000, of whom most still live in their homeland in South Sulawesi's Tana Toraja residency (2005 population: 437,000). As many as 200,000 Toraja have migrated, most settling in the provincial capital Makassar and in the national capital Jakarta. These migrants maintain close ties with their ancestral places. Their money has permitted commoner families to hold ritual celebrations that only aristocrats were permitted to perform in previous times. Indeed, the new wealth has increased the frequency and elaborateness of ritual activity to an unprecedented level.

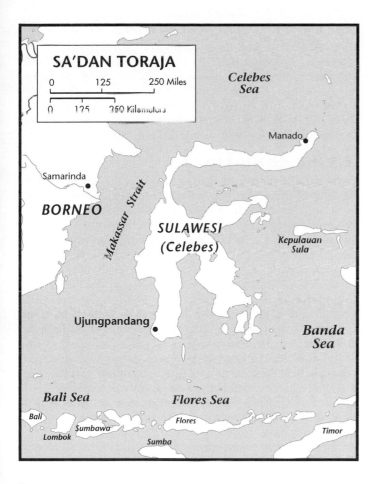

SA'DAN TORAJA
0   125   250 Miles
0   125   250 Kilometers

Celebes Sea

Manado

Samarinda

BORNEO

Makassar Strait

SULAWESI
(Celebes)

Kepulauan Sula

Ujungpandang

Banda Sea

Bali Sea

Flores Sea

Bali

Sumbawa

Flores

Lombok

Sumba

Timor

³LANGUAGE

Linguists have reconstructed the Austronesian language, Proto-South-Sulawesi, which is ancestral to Sa'dan Toraja, Bugis, Mandar, and Makassarese. Particularly close to the Sa'dan Toraja language is the speech of people in the neighboring Luwu and Duri regions; the latter are generally regarded as Bugis because of their adherence to Islam. The Sa'dan Toraja language is called Bahasa Tae', "tae'" being the word for "no." The traditional greeting is "Manasumorekka?" ("Have you cooked rice yet?"), to which the standard reply is "Manasumo!" ("The rice is cooked already!).

⁴FOLKLORE

One of a number of origin myths tells that the Toraja ancestors arrived in eight canoes (lembang) from an island in the southwest. According to the Bugis tradition, the Toraja descend from one of the lesser cousins of the supreme god Batara Guru, whose own descendants are the Bugis royalty. For their part, the Toraja claim that the Toraja Laki Padada was the ancestor of 100 noble lines, including the lowland kingdoms of Luwu, Bone, and Gowa; despite their adherence to Islam, surviving Luwu royalty sent pigs to the renovation of Laki Padada's house in 1983.

One tale offers the origin of one of the differences between the Toraja and their Muslim neighbors. The Toraja hero Karaeng Dua' was born of a pig mother. Karaeng Dua' traveled down to Luwu and there married a female chief (datu) of Luwu. A mischievous fellow highlander informed the chief that her mother-in-law was a pig. Infuriated, the chief scooped up all the sunlight into her house, leaving Luwu dark for three days, during which the people indulged in unlimited feasting on pig. After the three days, the chief released the light and all the remaining pigs were let loose in the forest, now taboo for Luwu people to eat.

⁵RELIGION

Since Indonesian independence, Christianity has grown rapidly among the Toraja, claiming 64% as Protestants and 12% as Catholics. The remaining population practices Aluk To Dolo, "the Way of the Ancestors." Before the 20th century, the Toraja had no separate word for religion, aluk meaning the totality of the correct ways of behaving and working, including those that outsiders would consider secular. The Indonesian state tolerates Aluk To Dolo by classifying it as a variant of Hinduism, one of the recognized five religions under Pancasila.

The Toraja distinguish between "smoke-rising rituals" (rambu solo), directed to the gods for the benefit of agriculture, and "smoke-descending rituals" (rambu tuka'), dedicated to the welfare of the dead. As Dutch missionaries condemned the former but tolerated the latter, funerals have increased in relative importance in modern times. Leading aluk rituals are a range of religious specialists: to minaa (priests, conversant in a special ceremonial language); to burake (priestesses and "hermaphrodite," i.e., transvestite, priests); funerary experts; healers; and heads of the rice cult.

Traditional cosmology divided the cosmos into three worlds. The upperworld, associated with the direction North, is ruled by the grandson of the supreme god Gauntikembong, Puang Matua, the creator and the giver of aluk. The middleworld (where humankind lives) is under the jurisdiction of Pong Banggairante. The underworld, associated with the direction South, is governed by Pong Tulakpadang, who has a fearful but not otherwise important wife, Indo Ongon-Ongon.

While the East is connected to the gods in general, the West is the direction of the spirits of the dead who are specifically believed to reside on Puya, an earthly island far to the southwest. Another god, Pong Lalondong, cuts the thread of life that determines each individual's fate. He guards the peril-fraught path running through the gravestone to Puya. The dead in Puya are sustained by burial offerings.

"Smoke-rising rituals" include offerings to the gods in paddy fields, at the roadside, and in front of houses. To thank or appease the gods, major animal sacrifices are held every 10 or 12 years on special ceremonial fields, highlighted by the exploding of bamboo stalks in bonfires. Mabugi rites are performed to request rain or deliverance from epidemics; going into trance, participants stab themselves with daggers without harm. Other rites such as the bua' kasalle ensure the welfare of humans, animals, and crops.

⁶MAJOR HOLIDAYS

See the article entitled **Indonesians**.

⁷RITES OF PASSAGE

After a child is born, the father buries the placenta (the child's "twin") in a woven reed bag on the east side of the house; because many placentas are buried by it, a house should never be moved.

Weddings are not as elaborate as funerals, only requiring the slaughtering of pigs and chickens for the feast, not the sacrifice of water buffalo.

If a person dies at sea or in a distant land, the family must still perform funeral rites, using a length of bamboo as a surrogate. The burials of low-status people are very simple; children dying before teething are buried in a tree to ensure the strength of the next child. High-status people, however, receive elaborate two-part funeral rites. The first part (Dipalamabi'i) takes place immediately upon death. Treated as merely "sick," the body is given food, spoken to, and put in a sitting position facing east–west. The mourning family fasts, wears black, makes an effigy of the dead (out of wood or bamboo, according to wealth), and sacrifices water buffalo and pigs. After time elapses, the body is considered officially dead and is reoriented north–south. The body is wrapped in cloth, traditionally of pineapple fiber, and banners are hung outside the *tongkonan* (ancestral ceremonial) house.

The second part (Diripa'i) takes place only after the deceased's kin have amassed funds for the ceremony and arranged for the arrival of even the most distant relatives. As this requires months and sometimes years, nowadays formalin is used to delay the decomposition of the corpse, which remains in the tongkonan. The funeral proper begins with the sounding of a gong and the beating of a drum that officially announces the death. The surviving spouse fasts for several days. Through the night, a circle of men chants *ma'badong*, dirges that commemorate events in the deceased's life, express grief, recount happenings during the funeral celebrations, tell how the deceased will be fashioned in gold like the first human, and describe what the journey to Puya and the life there will be like. At the same time, women chant separately (ma'londe).

Extending over several days or weeks, the major celebration takes place in a *rante*, a large field marked with large commemorative stones. A sizable procession brings the body, now in its coffin, to the rante, and, jostling it about a bit, installs it on a high tower, the *lakkean*. Singing, dancing, water-buffalo combats, and cockfights follow (the last were officially banned in 1981 but continue, nonetheless, amid furious gambling). Representing social ties and the payment of debts, water buffalo and pigs are brought and sacrificed (the former slaughtered with a single machete blow to the jugular vein); a *to mentaa* distributes cuts of meat to the guests according to their status and the indebtedness of the deceased's kin to them.

Images of the deceased are made; the simplest ones are temporary and made of bamboo and cloth. In some localities, high-status deceased are represented by statues (tau-tau) made from the wood of the jackfruit tree, the men dressed in a European shirt and a batik sarong, the women in a *kebaya* blouse and sarong; these *tau-tau* are displayed in cliff-side galleries. However, theft for the international market has forced many Toraja to store their family tau-tau under lock and key, leaving only crude concrete stand-ins in the galleries for tourist eyes.

In the final stage, the body is rewrapped amid further pig sacrifices and martial dancing; it is then put into an ornate casket and placed under the family rice barn. From there, a procession carries it to the gravesite, which may be a cave crypt at the bottom or on the side of a cliff, or a boat-shaped coffin suspended from an overhang. The spirits of the dead are believed to become the constellations that indicate phases of the agricultural cycle.

⁸INTERPERSONAL RELATIONS

The traditional social order distinguished three classes: the "big men," *to kapua* (semi-monarchical *puang* in the south, and free farmers, *makak*, elsewhere); the *tobuda*, the unexceptional majority; and the *kaunan*, landless slaves. The nobles possessed the privileges of leadership and the most elaborate types of house decoration and funerary celebration, though now wealthy commoners can enjoy them, too.

⁹LIVING CONDITIONS

Early in the 20th century, the Dutch forced the Toraja to abandon their fortified, hilltop villages and settle in the plains. Toraja villages divide into "high" and "low" halves, each a unit for ceremonial purposes. The poor live in bamboo huts, but the wealthy have elaborate houses raised 2.5 m (8 ft) off the ground on wooden pillars. These dwellings are oriented east–west and consist of several parts: on the north side, a raised floor where guests sleep; on the east, a low floor for the kitchen; on the west, a low floor for the dining area; and on the south, a raised floor higher than the northside floor for the sleeping area of the owner of the house. Animals are kept in the space under the floor. The entry ladder, once on the long side, is now at the short side. In front of the house, facing south, stands a rice barn, raised off the ground on round pillars that rats cannot climb; its decoration consists of carved scenes of death rites and of daily life, such as pounding rice, going to market, and hunting. The platform on which the barn stands provides shade for napping.

The *tongkonan,* an ancestral house (distinct from the *banua,* an ordinary house), symbolizing the living and dead members of a lineage, is the place to discuss important family matters (including upkeep of the tongkonan itself) and hold ceremonies. Representing water buffalo horns (but resembling a boat), the front and back ends of the roof project far beyond the house itself, often needing poles for support. The house front is ornately decorated, the center post (*tulak somba*) being hung with buffalo horns. The most prestigious tongkonan sport a *kabongo* (a carved buffalo head with real horns) and above it a *katik* bird, representing death and fertility. Carvings on the outside walls are painted in black, white, yellow, and red and consist of geometrical patterns, basket motifs, buffalo horns, animals, and the rooster-and-sun, all signs of prosperity; trailing plants symbolize many descendants. Building (particularly the raising of the tulak somba, the first step) and renewal of a tongkonan are occasions for sacrificial rituals and require the contributions of all families tracing descent from it.

As traditional houses tend to be cramped and dark, modern people prefer to live in concrete Western-Indonesian bungalows or Bugis wooden houses, though they may add a tongkonan-style saddle-roof.

Tana Toraja regency has a Human Development Index (combining measures of income, health, and education) of 69 (2005 score), higher than that of South Sulawesi province as a whole of 68.1, thus more closely approaching Indonesia's national HDI of 69.6. This is the case despite the fact that, in terms of GDP per capita, Tana Toraja (at US$2,335) is among the poorest regencies in South Sulawesi (the provincial figure is US$6,913, itself relatively low for Indonesia, cf. US$9,784 for West Sumatra and US$8,360 for North Sulawesi, but US$6,293 for Central Java and US$6,151 for West Nusa Tenggara). In 2000, the rate of infant mortality, on the other hand, stood at

34.73 deaths per 1,000 live births, little over half the rate for South Sulawesi as a whole (65.62) and among the lowest in the country.

¹⁰FAMILY LIFE

Kinship is traced back to the tongkonan as the "origin house." As kinship is bilateral, an individual may belong to several tongkonan, though his or her strongest ties will be with parents, grandparents, and in-laws. An individual activates lineage connections when rebuilding a house, staging major rituals, or deciding inheritance (the portion of the inheritance matches the number of water buffalo an heir contributed to the funeral). Tongkonan membership includes right of burial at the ancestral gravesite.

A newlywed couple lives with the wife's family. Early ethnographies reported that divorce was easy and premarital sex common (if a child was born out of wedlock, the father would be obliged to marry the mother). After a divorce, the man must leave the house, though he may claim the rice barn.

¹¹CLOTHING

Toraja everyday dress follows the Indonesian pattern of alternating sarongs with Western-style clothes, such as trousers. For ceremonial occasions, women wear long, single-color (dark red, green, etc.), short-sleeved dresses with beadwork belts, headbands, necklaces, and other jewelry.

¹²FOOD

Toraja food tends to be simpler than that of their lowland neighbors. Rice is the preferred staple, although because of its expense, the poor must supplement their diet with maize and tubers. Meat (water buffalo, pig, chicken, and, more rarely now, dog) is largely reserved for feasts. Some Toraja specialties are *papiong* (rice, meat, vegetables, and coconut milk stewed in a bamboo section), *songkolo* (a mixture of glutinous rice, chili, and coconut milk), and *baje* (fried coconut with brown sugar). Carried in bamboo tubes, *balok* is a popular palm wine whose taste ranges from sweet to sour; a bark extract gives it a red color.

¹³EDUCATION

Because of the considerable missionary presence in recent years, many Toraja have had greater access to modern education than (particularly rural) lowlanders in Sulawesi, a fact of which the Toraja are proud. In 2005, the level of literacy in Tana Toraja stood at 79.2%, significantly lower than the South Sulawesi provincial average of 84.6% (itself low by Indonesian national standards), but higher than several other South Sulawesi regencies with higher GDPs per capita (*See also* the article entitled **Indonesians**.)

¹⁴CULTURAL HERITAGE

Traditional instruments include the flute, water-buffalo horn, drum, gong, *geso-geso* (a two-stringed vertical fiddle), and the *karombi* (Jew's harp). For such occasions as funeral vigils, singing is mournful and monotonous, the chorus forming a circle linked by their little fingers or by arms around shoulders. One singer leads, and the chorus repeats the verses verbatim. By contrast, church singing in Western harmonies is spontaneous and lively. At funeral and other ritual feasts, boys and girls socialize by taking turns singing to each other (*kalinda'da', sengo, londe*), including riddles in the verses. Contemporary Toraja songs derive from storytellers' refrains and are accompanied by guitar or the Mandar/Bugis zither (*katapi*).

Noteworthy among traditional dances is the *Magellu*, a ceremonial dance in which several young girls in beaded costumes sway and flutter their fingers; and the *Magundu*, in which men attempt to dance wearing a black velvet headdress heavy with silver coins and buffalo horns, usually giving up after a few minutes.

¹⁵WORK

In their homeland, the great majority of Toraja farm for a living. Wet-rice paddies have progressively replaced the traditional swidden (shifting-cultivation) farming; maize, tubers, and vegetables are grown. Coffee, especially the fine local arabica, has been an important export crop since the mid-19th century, now joined by pepper and cloves. Pigs and water buffalo are largely kept for ritual sacrifice, rather than for daily consumption.

Education has allowed many Toraja to become bureaucrats, soldiers, business owners, and scientists, mostly employed outside the homeland. Migrants, known for their energy and ambition, also include mechanics, and shoe- and furniture-makers, for which occupations the Toraja enjoy a high reputation in eastern Indonesia's cities. Less esteemed are the many Toraja domestic servants in Makassar city, whom the Bugis and Makassarese point to as evidence for the "natural servility" of the Toraja (the Toraja region was once the lowlanders' main source of slaves). Tourism has provided new opportunities for employment as guides, hotel and restaurant staff, and makers and sellers of crafts.

¹⁶SPORTS

Although officially banned in 1981 for their association with gambling, cockfighting (for major ceremonies) and kick-fighting (for the harvest festival, in particular) are still enthusiastically pursued, betting and all.

¹⁷ENTERTAINMENT AND RECREATION

See the article entitled **Indonesians**.

¹⁸FOLK ART, CRAFTS, AND HOBBIES

Bamboo carving (flutes, tube containers, belts, necklaces, hats, and baskets) is a major craft, producing the most common souvenirs. Others are *ikat* (tie-dye) weaving and blacksmithing (local smiths make machetes from scrap metal such as automobile springs). Carved wooden panels integrating Christian iconography into traditional Toraja scenes and adapting traditional Toraja design motifs (such as the *pa' barre allo* sunburst motifs) to Christian uses have become popular in recent years as Indonesia's secular identity faces challenge from assertions of Islamic identity; Toraja Muslim artists (10% of the Toraja are Muslim) have responded by integrating Islamic symbols, such as the crescent and star into their carvings.

¹⁹SOCIAL PROBLEMS

See the article entitled **Indonesians**.

[20] GENDER ISSUES

Tana Toraja's Gender-Related Development Index (combining measures of women's health, education, and income relative to men's) is 60.9, substantially higher than South Sulawesi's provincial GDI of 56.9 and slightly surpassing Indonesia's national GDI of 59.2. The regency's Gender Empowerment Measure (reflecting women's participation and power in political and economic life relative to men's) is 50.8, also higher than the province's (45.6), but lower than the national GEM of 54.6.

[21] BIBLIOGRAPHY

Adams, Kathleen M. *Art as Politics: Re-Crafting Identities, Tourism, and Power in Tana Toraja, Indonesia*. Honolulu: University of Hawai'i Press, 2006.

Data Statistik Indonesia. http://demografi.bps.go.id/ (November 9, 2008).

Karman, Ummy. "Toraja, Arsitektur." In *Ensiklopedi Nasional Indonesia (EIN)*, Vol. 17. Jakarta: Cipta Adi Pustaka, 1991.

LeBar, Frank M., ed. *Ethnic Groups of Insular Southeast Asia*. Vol. 1, *Indonesia, Andaman Islands, and Madagascar*. New Haven, CT: Human Relations Area Files Press, 1972.

Pakan, Priyanti. "Toraja, Suku Bangsa." In *Ensiklopedi Nasional Indonesia (EIN)*, Vol. 17. Jakarta: Cipta Adi Pustaka, 1991.

Reid, Helen, and Anthony Reid. *South Sulawesi*. Berkeley: Periplus, 1988.

Volkman, Toby Alice. *Feasts of Honor: Ritual and Change in the Toraja Highlands*. Urbana, IL: University of Illinois Press, 1985.

Volkman, Toby Alice, and Ian Caldwell. *Sulawesi: Island Crossroads of Indonesia*. Lincolnwood, IL: Passport Books, 1990.

—revised by A. J. Abalahin

SAMOANS

PRONUNCIATION: suh-MOH-uhns
LOCATION: Polynesian archipelago comprising Samoa (former Western Samoa) and American Samoa; west coast of the United States (including Hawaii)
LANGUAGE: Samoan; English
RELIGION: Christianity (Methodist, Seventh Day Adventist, Catholic, Mormon)

[1] INTRODUCTION

Samoans are the residents of a chain of islands within the Polynesian culture area of the South Pacific. The Samoan archipelago is politically divided into the independent nation of Samoa and the unincorporated United States territory of American Samoa. In 1962, Samoa became the first Pacific Island nation to gain independence. The population of Samoa in 2007 was estimated at around 186,000 people, while that of American Samoa was only around 66,900 in the last (2006) census. There has been an extensive migration (an estimated 65,000) of Samoans from American Samoa to the west coast of the United States; another 20,000 have left American Samoa and now reside in Hawaii. However, since 2002 there has been no official record keeping of either migrations or returns. This chapter will focus on the Samoan way of life, or, as it is called by Samoans themselves, *fa'a Samoa*.

[2] LOCATION AND HOMELAND

Samoa is located about 2,300 mi southwest of Hawaii in the Pacific Ocean. Samoa is made up of two main islands, Upolo and Savai'i, and a few smaller surrounding islands. Samoa was a possession of the Germans, the British, and a trustee of New Zealand before gaining its independence and setting a political model for many other South Pacific societies. Samoa is located in the heart of Polynesia and, as such, has many cultural and historical ties with neighboring Tonga, the Cook Islands, and Tahiti.

The two main Samoan islands are of volcanic origin and, as a result, are mountainous with rocky soil and lush vegetation due to the tropical climate and ample rainfall. The average humidity in the Samoan archipelago is 80%. Of the two main islands of Samoa, Savai'i is more rural and has a much smaller population than Upolo. The only city in Samoa, Apia, is located on Upolo.

[3] LANGUAGE

The official language of Samoa is Samoan. Samoan belongs to the Polynesian group of the Austronesian language family and is closely related to the other languages of Polynesia including Tahitian, Tonga, Maori, and Rarotongan. Although English is spoken by educated Samoans in the city of Apia, it is rarely spoken by rural Samoans.

[4] FOLKLORE

Samoans have a creation myth very similar to that of the Christian faith. The creator god in Samoan cosmology is Tagaloa. Many of the traditional myths have been forgotten due to the massive conversion to Christianity in the islands. An important figure in Samoan history is the Scottish author Robert Louis Stevenson, who spent the final years of his life there and is buried there.

5 RELIGION

Christianity is the dominant, if not the only, religion practiced in Samoa. Ninety-eight percent of Samoans are professed Christians. Samoans are extremely proud of their devotion to the Christian faith and their adherence to its practices. Several Christian denominations including the Methodists, Seventh Day Adventists, Catholics, and Mormons coexist within Samoan villages.

6 MAJOR HOLIDAYS

Samoans celebrate holidays in the Christian calendar as well as some secular holidays. Samoan Mother's Day is celebrated on May 15 and is a public holiday. There are elaborate song and dance performances by the Women's Committees throughout the country in recognition of the contribution of mothers to Samoan society. Samoan National Independence celebrations are multi-day events.

7 RITES OF PASSAGE

Child rearing in Samoan society is hierarchically organized. Children, from the time they are toddlers, are expected to obey their elders without questioning or hesitation. There is no tolerance for misbehavior or disobedience. Older siblings are expected to take care of their smaller brothers and sisters. Adulthood in traditional Samoan society is marked by the tattoo.

In traditional Samoan belief systems, death was marked by the separation of the body and soul. The soul was believed to live on as an "ancestor spirit" called *aitu*. The placation of the aitu was an important part of religious life in precontact Samoa.

8 INTERPERSONAL RELATIONS

Status governs every interaction in Samoan society. Greetings are determined by the relative status of the individuals involved. A very informal greeting in Samoa is *talofa*. More formal greetings at a household dictate that neither party speaks until the visitor is seated. Then the host will begin a formal greeting and introduction with, "Susu maia lau susuga," which translates roughly as "Welcome, sir."

Individuals who have left their villages to take up residence in Apia will return to their villages for important ceremonial occasions.

Unmarried females are almost always chaperoned in Samoan society. Premarital sexual relationships are very difficult to arrange. "Sleep crawling," *moetotolo* in Samoan, exists as one solution to this problem for young Samoans. Typically a young man with an interest in a young woman will wait until her household and her chaperones are asleep and then crawl on all fours into her house and hope to have a sexual encounter with her. In some cases, the young woman will send the suitor away. In other cases, the woman will become pregnant and marriage may ensue.

9 LIVING CONDITIONS

Large amounts of foreign aid have come to Samoa since its independence. This aid has modernized even the most remote parts of rural Savai'i, where there are many European-style houses with wooden frames, corrugated iron roofs, and louvered glass windows. Some homes even have pickup trucks. There are, however, still traditional Samoan-style houses to be found in Samoa. Traditional Samoan houses are rectangular and built on black, volcanic boulder foundations. Traditional roofs are high-peaked and covered with thatch. There are no walls on traditional Samoan dwellings, but shutters or blinds of plaited coconut leaves can be lowered to keep out the blowing rain.

The Samoan standard of living is hard to describe. On the one hand, food is plentiful and the atmosphere is relaxed. On the other hand, people are always striving to find ways to make money. The economy of the country is very limited, with most money coming from foreign aid and private aid sent by relatives who work overseas. This third source of money accounts for the majority of the income of the average Samoan. Cash crop exportation is practiced widely, but it only accounts for a very small portion of a family's income.

Samoa has a chiefly socio-political system called the *matai* system. Matai is the Samoan word for "chief." Every Samoan extended family has a matai. In Samoa, there are two types of chiefs: high chiefs and talking chiefs. Talking chiefs are skilled in special forms of the Samoan language and are responsible for making public speeches. Talking chiefs are of lower rank than high chiefs. Within Samoan villages, the various matai from extended families meet regularly to discuss problems and issues and also to determine resolutions.

10 FAMILY LIFE

Traditional marriage in Samoan society consists of an exchange of goods between the two families with the bride and groom cohabiting afterwards. In the early period after the final exchange, the couple is likely to live with the bride's family, although later the couple will move near the groom's father's household. Marriage within the village is discouraged, and anyone from either the mother's or father's descent group is a prohibited partner. Prior to their conversion to Christianity, high-ranking Samoan men practiced polygyny (having many wives at once). Church weddings are important in Samoan society today, but they are expensive and not every family can afford to provide one for their children.

Households in traditional Samoan society were centered on the extended family. The nuclear family has now become the most common domestic unit. Nuclear families can be very large by American standards. Many women have as many as a dozen children. Couples want to have as many children as possible, and improved health care and nutrition have contributed to lower infant mortality rates.

The Samoan kinship terminology is of the Hawaiian type. This means that there is a single term for the mother, mother's sisters, and father's sisters, and a single term for the father, father's brothers, and mother's brothers. This pattern persists through each generation, so that female cousins (in the American sense) are called "sisters" and male cousins are called "brothers."

A Samoan man wearing the lavalava. Traditional Samoan tattoos can be seen on his legs and back. (© Neil Farrin/JAI/Corbis)

¹¹CLOTHING

Traditional Samoan attire has been adapted to modern life in Samoa. The wraparound skirt called *lavalava* is worn by men and children. Even important village leaders that work in the city may choose to wear a formal lavalava, a sport shirt, and a wide leather belt around their waist. Women wear dresses or matching long blouses and skirts called *puletasi*. Civil servants, both male and female, often wear uniforms of dark colors. Tattooing is an important aspect of body adornment in Samoa. Samoa is one of the areas of Polynesia that has seen a resurgence of the tradition of tattooing. Young men more than young women have returned to the custom of tattooing.

¹²FOOD

Traditional Samoan foods included taro root, yams, bananas, coconuts, breadfruit, fish, turtles, and chicken. Even though pigs are raised, pork is reserved for ceremonial occasions. Samoan meals are invariably accompanied by a salted coconut cream condiment called *pe'epe'e,* which is poured over boiled taro root and heated before serving. For many rural Samoans, this is the staple foodstuff and is served at the two daily meals. Coconut meat is not eaten in Samoa. For a Samoan, eating coconut meat indicates poverty and a lack of food. The favorite Samoan beverage is *koko Samoa* which is made from fermented cocoa beans, water, and brown Fijian sugar. It is an essential component of the village meal in Samoa. Imported American foods can also be purchased in Apia and in small village shops in the rural areas.

¹³EDUCATION

The literacy rate in Samoa is approximately 90%. Education is seen as essential by parents for the success of their children. Even in the most rural villages, parents will send at least some of their children off to school. Those that do not go to school will stay at home and help with the household chores and gardening.

¹⁴CULTURAL HERITAGE

In Samoa, as opposed to American Samoa, traditional Samoan songs are the favorites of young and old alike. In American Samoa, American popular music sung in English is the favorite form of music among young people. Polynesian dancing is still practiced in Samoa. Oratory is considered a verbal art among all Samoans. Political deliberations required well crafted oratory from senior male village leaders.

¹⁵ WORK

There are a number of occupations that Samoans engage in today. The urban center of Apia provides many of the modern careers that Americans are familiar with such as bureaucrats, teachers, nurses, clerks, entrepreneurs, and secretaries, to name a few. Men hold approximately 60% of the wage-earning jobs.

¹⁶ SPORTS

Cricket is an important game for Samoans and every village has a cricket pitch laid through the middle of the village green. Samoan-style cricket is a modification of the British form, in which the cricket bat now resembles a traditional war club and the teams number around 30–40 per side. Rugby is also a very big spectator and participant sport in Samoa. Boxing, wrestling, and American football are also important sports in both parts of Samoa. There are a number of professional football players in the United States who are of Samoan descent.

¹⁷ ENTERTAINMENT AND RECREATION

For Samoans that live in or near Apia, most of the amenities and pleasures of modern, urban living can be found. Long-boat races called *fautasi* are enjoyed at important festivals and public celebrations. Dominos are a favorite pastime of Samoan men in rural and urban areas alike.

¹⁸ FOLK ART, CRAFTS, AND HOBBIES

The traditional art of barkcloth (*siapo*) manufacturing has been all but lost in Samoan culture today. The artists who specialized in house construction, canoe building, and tattooing were organized into guilds in traditional society. These individuals worked for families of high status who could afford to pay them.

¹⁹ SOCIAL PROBLEMS

Migration out of the area is a major problem for both Samoa and American Samoa. Over 60% of the American Samoan population has immigrated to the mainland and Hawaii. Samoans have immigrated to American Samoa and now, as a group, form the majority portion of the population. Limited economic opportunities are a problem for Samoans. The chance of finding economic prosperity in the United States drives Samoans to leave their home islands.

²⁰ GENDER ISSUES

Samoans conceive of gender as being a social role that an individual plays. In the Samoan conception of gender, there are five gender roles: boy, girl, man, woman, and male transvestite (*fa'afafine* in Samoan). The distinction between a girl and a woman in Christian Samoa centers on sexual activity. *Teine* (girls) are not sexually active while *fafine* (women) are sexually active. Although male transvestites are called teine, there is an assumption especially in urban areas of Samoa that fa'afafine are sexually active. There is no comparable female transvestite role for women in Samoan society.

Samoan gender is not seen as a temperament. Instead, Samoan gender is seen as a social role to be played by individuals. As a result, differences between the sexes are less significant than in societies where gender is a temperament. All adults are expected to be respectful, dignified, and strong. Adulthood is informally marked by the starting of a family and formally marked through the awarding of a title. In Samoa, status is determined by an individual's titles.

Brother-sister relations are the most important cross-sex relationships in Samoan society. It is important to remember that in Samoan kinship, all cousins are brothers and sisters. The Samoan word for the brother-sister relation is *feagaiga*. There was no word for the relationship of marriage in pre-Christian Samoa.

²¹ BIBLIOGRAPHY

Lockwood, Victoria S., Thomas G. Harding, and Ben J. Wallace, ed. *Contemporary Pacific Societies: Studies in Development and Change.* Englewood Cliffs: Prentice Hall, 1993.

Mageo, Jeannette Marie. "Samoans." In *Encyclopedia of Sex and Gender: Men and Women in the World's Cultures*, Volume 2. Edited by Carol R. Ember and Melvin Ember. New York: Springer, 2003.

O'Meara, Tim. *Samoan Planters: Tradition and Economic Development in Polynesia.* Chicago: Holt, Rinehart & Winston, 1990.

—by J. Williams

SANTALS

PRONUNCIATION: suhn-TAHLS
ALTERNATE NAMES: Santhal; Hor ko; Hor hopon ko; Manjhi
LOCATION: India; Bangladesh; Nepal
POPULATION: Over 6 million (estimate)
LANGUAGE: Santali
RELIGION: Native Santal religion with influences of Hinduism

¹INTRODUCTION

The Santals form the third largest tribal group in India. Their ancestral homeland is believed to lie in Southeast Asia, where they are associated with the old Champa Kingdom of northern Cambodia. The Santals are thought to have migrated to the Indian subcontinent long before the Aryans entered the Indian subcontinent around 1500 BC. They most likely reached their homeland, the Chota Nagpur Plateau of east-central India, through Assam and Bengal.

According to Santal traditions, following the famine of AD 1770, large numbers of Santals migrated from the Chota Nagpur Plateau and the plains south of the Damodar River and established a colony (Damin-i-koh) in what was later to become the Santal Parganas District, now in eastern Jharkhand. In June 1855, Santals in Damin-i-koh began protesting their mistreatment by landlords, moneylenders, and traders. Failing to get any redress from government officials (the settlement was located in territory administered by the East India Company), the protest turned into a full-scale rebellion. The uprising was quelled by British troops at the cost of hundreds (some say thousands) of Santal lives. Although unsuccessful, the rebellion eventually led to administrative reforms that saw the creation of Santal Parganas District. This has always remained at the center of Santal tradition and activities.

The Santals accept the designation "Santal," which is a term used by outsiders, but they call themselves *Hor ko* ("Man") or *Hor hopon ko* ("sons of Man"). They are also known as Manjhi. In Jharkhand, Orissa, and West Bengal, the Santals are classed as a Scheduled Tribe, but not in Assam.

²LOCATION AND HOMELAND

With a population of over 6 million the Santals are surpassed in number only by the Gonds and the Bhils among the tribes of India. The Santal heartland lies on the Chota Nagpur Plateau in Jharkhand, with large Santal populations also found in neighboring areas of West Bengal. This area of concentration extends southwards into the Mayurbhanj District of northeastern Orissa. Migrant communities are found working in the tea plantations of Assam and Tripura. Some 65,000 live in northeastern Bangladesh and a few thousand are found in the *terai* (low-lying swampy plains along the Himalayan foothills) of Nepal.

In 2000, as a result of popular pressure to create a state which reflected the aspirations of tribals in the region, the new state of Jharkhand was formed by the Government of India out of 18 districts of southern Bihar and became the 28th state of the Indian Union. Although the modern movement to create a state of Jharkhand dates to the 1900s, according to some historians, there was already a distinct geo-political, cultural entity called Jharkhand even before the period of the Magadha Empire (c. 6th century BC). In ancient times the northern portion of Jharkhand state was a tributary to the Magadhan (ancient Bihar) Empire and southern part was a tributary of the Kalingan (ancient Orissa) Empire. Subsequently, much of the area came under the Munda Rajas. During the Mughal period, the Jharkhand area was known as Kukara. After 1765 the region came under the control of the British and became formally known under its present title, "Jharkhand"—the Land of "Jungles" (forests) and "Jharis" (bushes).

The Santals occupy the easternmost segment of the Chota Nagpur Plateau, where the uplands jut out into the Gangetic plain. There is a great bend in the Ganges River as it skirts the edge of the uplands before swinging southeastwards towards the Bay of Bengal. Chota Nagpur lies on ancient, hard, crystalline rocks that have eroded into hills and undulating plateaus. In the Santal areas, these lie at elevations between 400 and 600 m (approximately 1,300–2,000 ft), with isolated peaks rising to 850 m (approximately 2,800 ft). In the northeast, along the Ganges River, the Rajmahal Hills rise steeply from the alluvial plains. At one time the whole area was extensively forested, though much of the forest cover has been cleared for cultivation. To the south, the land falls away towards the basin of the Damodar River Valley and the low-lying plains of West Bengal. The climate experienced is typical for this part of India—hot summers (maximum temperatures in May average over 35°C or 95°F), with three or four months of heavy rain associated with the summer monsoon (June–September) and cooler and drier winters.

³LANGUAGE

The language of the Santals is Santali, which belongs to the North Mundari group of the Austro-Asiatic language family. The Santals had no written form of the language until Christian missionaries introduced the Roman script during the late 19th century. As a consequence, many Santali works are written in the Roman script. Many Santals are bilingual, speaking the predominant regional language as well as their mother tongue and using the regional script for writing purposes. Thus the Bengali script is used in West Bengal, the Oriya script in Orissa, and the Devanagari script in Bihar. Recently, in an attempt to generate a sense of tribal identity, some Santals have begun advocating the exclusive use of a script called *Olchiki* for writing. The Olchiki script, also known as Olcemet ("language of writing") or simply as the Santali alphabet, was created in 1925 by Pandit Raghunath Murmu for the Santali language. Ol Chiki, which is written from left to right, has 30 letters, the forms of which are intended to evoke natural shapes. The Latin alphabet is better at representing some Santali stops, but vowels are still problematic. Unlike most Indic scripts, which are derived from Brahmi, like the Latin alphabet, Ol Chiki is a true alphabet, with vowels given equal representation with consonants. Additionally, because it was designed specifically for the Santali language, one letter could be assigned to each Santali phoneme (i.e. the smallest structural unit that distinguishes meaning).

⁴FOLKLORE

One of the legendary figures of the Santals is Kamruguru, who figures in many of their folk songs and myths. The details of his exploits differ from region to region, but all Santals believe Kamruguru was a great medicine man and sorcerer in ancient

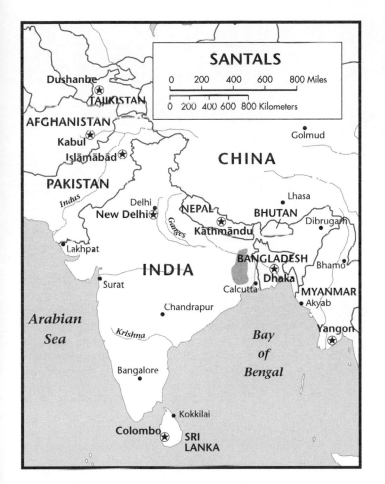

SANTALS

0   200   400   600   800 Miles

0 200 400 600 800 Kilometers

⁵RELIGION

The Santal universe is inhabited by supernatural beings and powers, both good and evil, which influence every aspect of Santal life. The Santal religion revolves around maintaining the correct relationship with this supernatural world through the appropriate rituals and magical practices.

Preeminent in the Santal pantheon is Thakur Jiu (also called Sin Bonga or Dharam), the Creator and Preserver of the universe. The Thakur (this is not a Santal word and is probably adopted from the Hindus) is a benevolent deity who receives no specific worship but is remembered at all religious festivals and important social occasions. He is invoked particularly at the time of famines and drought, when white fowl are sacrificed to him.

In addition to Thakur Jiu, the Santal recognize a host of spirits or *bongas*, estimated to be between 150 and 180 in number. The bongas are to be revered, feared, called upon to intercede for the welfare of the Santal, and propitiated with blood-sacrifice and other offerings. They must be worshiped at regular intervals, but also at religious festivals, at times of major life events, and during important economic undertakings. Bongas fall into several categories: village spirits, hill spirits, ancestor spirits, the deity of agriculture, mischievous spirits such as Baghut Bonga (the tiger spirit), household deities, and the secret deity of the family or subclan. Maran Buru, for example, is the most powerful of the Santal Bongas. He is identified with both good and evil spirits and is worshiped with the sacrifice of a white fowl or a white goat and offerings of rice-beer. He taught the first Santal couple how to engage in sex and how to brew rice-beer. Maran Baru (literally "Bonga of the Great Mountain") is propitiated at all festivals. He resides in the village's sacred grove of sal trees (*Shorea robusta*), along with other important bongas. The Santals have no temples but perform many of their religious ceremonies in this sacred grove, the *Jahirstan*.

Like the Oraon and Munda tribes, with whom they have much in common, the Santals have a number of individuals who perform specific roles in their religious and ritual life. The village priest (*naeke*), along with his assistant (*kudam naeke*), is responsible for rituals at festivals and religious ceremonies. He consecrates offerings to be made to the spirits and performs sacrifices. The medicine man or shaman (*ojha*), however, drives away malevolent spirits; he also diagnoses and cures diseases, either by magical incantations, exorcism, or administering medicines. An ojha, not the village priest, is selected to preside at the annual Dansae festival. The witch-finder (*Janguru*) divines which evil bonga or witch is responsible for diseases that no one else can cure. The annual hunt festival is led by the *dihru* or hunt-priest.

As with other tribal peoples who have been exposed to Hindu culture, the Santals have been influenced by Hinduism. They have adopted Hindu deities such as Shiva, Rama, Kali, and Durga in their pantheon of spirits and worship them along with their own deities. Festivals such as Pata, Chata, and Jatra are festivals borrowed from the Hindus, but they are celebrated in the Santal manner with sacrifice, drinking rice-beer, singing, and dancing. Santals may also participate in Hindu festivals such as Durga Puja. In the past, Hindu reformist movements such as the Kharwar movement gained some following among the Santals.

Santal society. A popular legend is told about Kamruguru's death. At the end of his life, according to this story, Kamruguru became seriously ill. Confined to his bed, he called his two disciples and ordered them to bring some herbs from the jungle of a distant hill. Only these herbs could effect a cure. While crossing a river on the way to the hill, they met an old woman who informed them that Kamruguru was already dead. They abandoned their search and returned, only to find their master alive. Kamruguru sent them out again to fetch some special fish from the river to make a medicine. At the river they met the old woman catching fish and she told them to go back as their master was no longer alive. This time, the disciples returned to find Kamruguru dead. Some Santals say that Kamruguru was killed by a witch and that the songs and dances of the Dansae festival are symbols of lamentation for his death.

One ritual of the Dansae festival requires that young men participate in the dancing and singing dressed as women. They place peacock feathers in their headgear and carry peacock feathers in their hands (in Santal belief, peacock feathers give protection from evil spirits and black magic). According to a Santal legend, a great Santal warrior named Hodor-Durga met a white-complexioned woman in battle. After a prolonged struggle, the woman killed Hodor-Durga. As was the custom of the time, the victor took the name of the vanquished warrior and became known to all as the Goddess Durga. Her warriors plundered every Santal village, killing all the men. To save their lives, the men disguised themselves as women and fled into the hills and jungles. The Dansae dancers dress as women in emulation of their ancestors.

Bangladeshi aboriginals from the Santal tribe perform a traditional dance to mark the 150 anniversary of rebellion in Dhaka. Two Santal brothers started a movement for social justice in 1855. Although the movement was suppressed, it brought about a shift in colonial policy. (Farjana K. godhuly/AFP/Getty Images)

Christian missionary efforts among the Santals began during the 19th century and just under 3% of Santals are now Christian.

⁶MAJOR HOLIDAYS

The most important of the Santals' festivals is the Sohrae festival, a harvest festival held in December or January after the winter rice crop is harvested. The festival usually lasts five days. On the first day, after fowl are sacrificed, the village cattle are driven over a hen's egg. The animal that treads on it is caught, washed, and its horns are decorated. The owner of the cow, it is believed, will have good luck. On the second day, each family in the village performs a *puja* (worship ceremony) in its cow shed, sacrificing chickens and a pig to Maran Buru, the household gods, and the ancestor spirits. The third day, a wooden pole with straw tied to the top is erected in the village. A bull is washed, its horns are anointed with oil and vermilion, and the animal is tied to the post. The bachelors and young boys of the village then proceed to bait the bull, drumming, dancing, and screaming to get it excited and make it buck. The remaining days of the festival are given over to feasting, dancing, and singing. Traditionally this a period of sexual license, although taboos against adultery and liaisons between members of the same clan are strictly followed.

Other important festivals celebrated through the year are Baha (the Flower Blossom Festival), Magh Sim, Erok Sim, Hariar Sim, Iri-Gundhi Nawai, and Janthar. These are all festivals connected to agriculture. Festivals such as Jom Sim and Mak Mor are dedicated to specific deities. Karam is celebrated to ensure increased wealth and progeny and to drive out evil spirits. The Dansae festival is held in the fall and corresponds to the Hindu Durga Puja. The annual hunting festival, Disom Sendra, is an important event for the Santals.

⁷RITES OF PASSAGE

A pregnant woman is subject to certain taboos to avoid harm from malevolent spirits or witches. Birth is attended only by female relatives and a midwife. After a birth, both the house and village are considered polluted. On the fifth day after birth (or third day if the baby is female), ceremonies are performed to remove this pollution and also to name the child. A male child takes the name of his father's father; a second son, that of the mother's father; a third son, that of a brother of the father's father; and so on. Girls take the names of their female relatives in the same sequence.

Santals have to undergo the Chacho Chetiar ceremony before they can take their place in society. No Santal can be married or cremated, participate in ceremonies, or claim any social rights without this. There is no prescribed age at which this occurs and Santals often perform the ceremony for several children at the same time. All the village officials and villagers attend the festivities, which are accompanied by singing, dancing, and drinking, and the retelling of the mythical history of the Santal people. The naming ceremony and the Chacho Chetiar are two of the rare Santal rituals that are not accompanied by animal sacrifice.

Around 8 to 10 years of age, boys are initiated into the tribe by having the five Santal tribal marks branded on their forearms by a maternal uncle. Girls are tattooed on their faces, foreheads, chests, and arms after they start menstruating, at which time they are considered to be sexually mature.

The Santals believe that the souls of the dead eventually become bongas, provided the correct rituals have been performed. The dead are cremated, but young children and pregnant women are buried. Bones are taken from the funeral pyre and kept in the house, where they are ritually fed with milk, rice-beer, and sacred water by female mourners. Periodically, the Santals take the bones of their dead relatives to a stream or river (many go to the Damodar River) and deposit them in the water. This ritual is completed by the sacrifice of a male goat. After returning from the river, the relatives of the deceased hold a feast for the entire village.

8 INTERPERSONAL RELATIONS

Santal children are taught proper manners at a very early age. When a son greets his father, he bows low, touches his left hand to his right elbow, raises his right fist as high as his forehead, and pauses slightly. The father responds by touching his right arm with his left hand, moving the right fist downwards and opening his hand. A daughter salutes her mother by bowing before her and touching the ground. Her mother returns the greeting by extending her hands, palms turned up, flexing them a few times, and raising them over her head.

These are the standard forms of greeting used not only between parents and children but by the community at large.

9 LIVING CONDITIONS

Santal villages usually consist of up to 30 or more houses built on either side of a single, wide, unpaved street, planted at intervals with shade trees. Villages are generally neat and clean, kept so by the villagers and also by scavenging dogs and pigs. The house of the village headman (*Manjhi*) is built close to the center of the village near the Majhisthan. This is a raised platform, covered with a thatched roof supported by poles, on which the business of the village is carried out. Every village also has its sacred grove of sal trees located within the village boundaries.

A typical Santal house is rectangular in form, roughly 5 m by 4 m (16 by 12 ft) in dimension, divided into two rooms. The floor is packed earth, while the walls are made of earth and cow dung, some 45 cm (18 in) thick, plastered over branches placed vertically between the wooden posts supporting the roof. The roof is gabled, made of a split-bamboo frame covered with paddy straw or grass, fixed on rafters. The sleeping

room is also used to store rice and other possessions and the chickens are penned in there at night. Although most activities, including cooking, take place outside the house or on the veranda under the eaves, there is a hearth for cooking indoors during the cold season. Every Santal house has a special area, banned to outsiders, that is sacred to the ancestors. A separate shed is constructed to house cattle and pigs. Santals keep dogs, primarily for hunting, and also cats to catch rats.

10 FAMILY LIFE

The Santal are divided into 12 patrilineal totemic clans, which are further subdivided into subclans. Violation of rules of tribal endogamy and clan exogamy are severely punished, with the offenders being expelled from Santal society. Clan names are commonly used as surnames.

Households can contain nuclear or extended families, although the latter is more usual. Though women are theoretically subordinate to their husbands, in practice they are almost equal partners in the economic affairs of the family. Matters of trade and the sale of agricultural products are entirely in their hands. Wives are acquired through negotiation (the preferred method), elopement, or capture. Girls are married between 16 and 18 years or age, while boys are anywhere from 16 to 22 years old. The consent of both parties to the marriage is sought. Marriage (*bapla*) is one of the most important of the Santal life-cycle rituals and it is celebrated with much dancing, singing, and drinking. Traditional Santal practices involved payment of a bride-price, but among the more affluent, urban communities today the dowry is becoming popular. Residence patterns are patrilocal and the bride moves into the household of her husband's family. Divorce is permitted with the sanction of the village council. Women have no rights of inheritance, with sons sharing equally in the property of the father.

11 CLOTHING

The traditional dress of the Santal male is the *lengta* or "little apron." This is a piece of white cloth, over 1 m in length and 25 cm wide (4 ft by 10 in). A string is tied around the waist, one end of the cloth is tucked into the string at the back, and the rest is drawn through the legs and tucked into the string at the front. Sometimes a larger piece of cloth covering the body from the waist to the knees is worn. Santal men generally wear no headgear and the upper body is bare, except in winter. Males wear no ornaments except small silver earrings.

Santal women wear two pieces of clothing. One is wrapped around the waist and lower body; the other, about 1 m by ¾ m (3 ft by 2½ ft) is worn over the torso so as to cover the breasts. This cloth, usually white in color, was formerly spun and woven by the Santals, but nowadays it is purchased in local markets. Women wear silver earrings, bead necklaces around the neck, and silver rings and ornaments in the nose. Heavy brass bracelets are worn on the arms and also brass or sometimes silver anklets on the legs. Every Santal girl wears flowers in her hair.

Dress styles are changing and Santals, especially those who live and work in towns, have adopted regional dress, such as the *sārī* for women or Western-style clothes for men.

12 FOOD

Rice is the staple food of the Santals. It is typically eaten boiled, with spiced vegetables such as sweet potato, eggplant, pumpkin, beans, radishes, and onions. Dishes are also prepared from edible roots, leaves, and mushrooms collected in the forest. The Santals cultivate a variety of pulses, which they boil in water and mix with spices and salt. This dish is called *dāl.* Fruits eaten by the Santal include jackfruit, guava, plantain, blackberry, tamarind, and papaya.

The Santals are fond of meat and eat beef, pork, and the flesh of wild animals, fish, and birds. The cost of meat is prohibitive, however, and the Santals usually subsist on a vegetarian diet. At festival times, the meat of sacrificed animals is eagerly consumed.

Milk is not an important element in the Santals' diet, although it is used for preparing curds and butter, from which *ghi* is made. The liquid left after the butter has been churned is drunk and considered to be very nourishing.

Rice-beer is brewed and drunk in large quantities. The Santals also distill liquor from the fruit of the Mahua tree (*Bassia latifolia),* although this is now banned by the government.

¹³EDUCATION

Levels of educational achievement among the Santals is generally low, except among the Santal Christian community. Despite the availability of government educational programs, Santals show literacy rates below the average for the Scheduled Tribes. In Jharkhand, for example, the 2001 Census returns show overall literacy among Santals standing at only 40.5%, with female literacy being less than half that of men. A recent study in a rural area of West Bengal showed literacy among local Santal women to be around 10%.

A major conflict in Santal education relates to the use of the Santali script. The Christian Santals are in favor of the Roman script whereas the non-Christian prefer the locally developed Ol Chiki script. However, Santali has already been recognised as one of India's 23 official languages by the central government and the state governments of Jharkhand, Bihar, West Bengal, and Orissa have already initiated action plans for imparting education in their mother tongue for the Santal students in primary schools. The University Grants Commission in Delhi has started teaching and conferring Post-Graduate degrees in Santali language and literature, while universities in Jharkhand and Bihar are offering post-graduate courses in Santali language and literature. In government schools in Bihar, Santali students are provided primary and secondary education in Santali, although there is a problem with obtaining the appropriate texts.

Despite these advances in Santali education, a flourishing modern literature in Santali, and the fact that many Santals see education as a way out of poverty and low socio-economic status, illiteracy is high among the Santals—especially women—and education is not high on the Santal priority list. Only some 37.6% of 5- to 15-year-old Santals attend school and only 13.2% of the population graduates from high school.

Even though Santali is known primarily for its oral traditions and despite the issue of which script is to be used, there is a modern tradition of Santali literature—especially poetry—with writers such as Nirmala Putul composing their works in Santali.

⁴CULTURAL HERITAGE

Santals have a rich tradition of oral literature. Myths tell of the creation of the world, of the first Santal man and woman (Pil-chu Haram and Pilchu Burhi), of the wanderings of the tribe, and of Santal heroes. Folk tales, riddles, and village stories add to lore of the Santals. Much of this material has been gathered and published over the last century. A tradition of modern Santali literature has also developed, with poems, novels, short stories, and plays being written by authors such as Ragunath Murmu, Balkishore Basuki, and Narayan Soren. Newspapers, literary magazines, and even school texts are now published in Santali.

Traditional songs are an integral part of Santal life and represent the very essence of Santal culture. There are songs for every occasion—songs to be sung at specific rituals, to accompany dancing, and for the worship of bongas. There are love songs, obscene songs for the licentious spring festival, songs for the ceremonial hunt, and songs expounding on Santal social customs. Dancing, too, is an important part of Santal life and there are specific dances that accompany the songs. Men and women dance separately, except when love songs are being performed.

In the past, Santals preserved knowledge of their traditions through institutions along the lines of "guru" schools. Every clan had its school headed by a *guru* (teacher), usually an elder who had intimate knowledge of the myths, lore, and customs of the people. It would be he who would pass on traditions of music, dance, and song from generation to generation. Similarly, the Santals have an extraordinary knowledge of folk medicine and herbal healing. The Raranic, or herb-doctor, learns his trade as an apprentice to an older man, jealously guards his secrets, and in turn passes his knowledge on to the next generation. Even today, Santals often seek the services of both the herb-doctor and modern medical doctors to treat illnesses.

¹⁵WORK

Santals were once hunters and gatherers, subsequently adopting the slash-and-burn cultivation still practiced by the Paharias (hill tribes) in the hills of Chota Nagpur. Today, the Santals are primarily settled cultivators, growing paddy rice and cereals, and keeping cattle, goats, pigs, and poultry. They fish where they have the opportunity and supplement their diet by hunting. Many Santals have left the land to work as agricultural laborers. Some work in the mines and factories of the Damodar Valley industrial region, while others have migrated further afield to find employment on tea plantations or as gardeners or domestic servants. Seasonal labor is important, even for those who cultivate their own land. More educated individuals work in government offices, schools, hospitals, and other service-sector industries, and a small elite have entered the professions as lawyers, doctors, engineers, and politicians.

¹⁶SPORTS

Boys play with bows and arrows, just as their fathers hunt with these weapons. Hide-and-seek is a popular pastime. Another game involves two small, semicircular pieces of wood and a stick about 1 m (3 ft) in length. A hole is dug in the ground and one of the semicircular pieces is placed standing on its straight edge by the hole. The other piece is stood on edge about 1.5 m (4–5 ft) away from the first piece. A batter takes the stick and tries to strike the second piece so that it knocks the first into the hole. The loser is penalized by having to run a short distance on one leg.

[17] ENTERTAINMENT AND RECREATION

The boundary between entertainment, recreation, and traditional life in Santal society is never very clear. The dancing, singing, music, and feasting associated with religious festivals and social occasions provide entertainment as well as strengthening village and family ties. Even the ceremonial hunt combines ritual meaning with a favorite pastime of the Santals.

Access to modern forms of entertainment, however, depends largely on individual circumstance. The more prosperous Santals living in urban areas, with the means and inclination to do so, can share in the radio-television-movie culture of the modern urban scene. Many Santals, however, living in relative isolation and faced with poverty and a lack of education, do not have access to such modern entertainment.

[18] FOLK ART, CRAFTS, AND HOBBIES

The Santals have a rich tradition of folk arts and crafts, including designs painted on walls, woodcarving, and the making of jewelry. Design motifs include figures of animals, birds, and trees, and scenes of humans hunting and dancing. Among the woodcarvings are representations of deer, peacocks, small sparrow-like birds, fishes, and frogs.

[19] SOCIAL PROBLEMS

A major problem faced by the Santals over the last few decades is land fragmentation. Smaller land holdings and the resulting poverty have led to the displacement of cultivators and increasing numbers of landless laborers. Many workers have migrated to towns to seek work, losing the immediate support provided by their traditional social environs. Emerging educated elites living in urban areas have lost contact with their roots in rural areas, depriving their communities of potential leadership. Alcoholism and belief in witchcraft remain a problem in traditional Santal society.

The Santals see themselves as neglected and exploited by non-Santals (*dikus* or outsiders). This was the driving force behind the 1855 Santal rebellion and it remained the driving force of Santal involvement in modern demands for a separate tribal state called Jharkhand. However, the creation of Jharkhand State was not a panacea for all tribal ills. Although Santals make up about 10% of Jharkhand's population (the total tribal population of Jharkhand is about 28%), Santals by no means have proportional political representation in the 81-seat legislature. Furthermore, in its short history, Jharkhand has seen it all: Naxalism, bribery cases and murder, not to mention five chief ministers in seven years as of 2008.

Jharkhand and central India is an area which has recently seen a surge in Naxalite activity—Naxalism is the communist-inspired insurgency in India that takes its name from Naxalbari, a small village in West Bengal that saw a violent Maoist uprising in 1967. Naxalites are said to be active in 15 of the original 18 districts of Jharkhand, with their activities ranging from attacks on villagers and Indian police and security forces and assassination of politicians to encouraging opium production to fund their operations. Some Santals, resenting their exploitation by "outsiders," naturally felt that the Naxalites sympathized with their condition on their side and joined them in insurgency, which is most pronounced in the "Red Corridor" of eastern India that includes Jharkhand and Chhattisgarh States. The vast gap between poor and rich and the underdevelopment of the tribal areas has fueled the insur-

gency and has revived and encouraged the ethnicity, indigeneity, and sub-nationalism so typical of the region.

Development itself has created problems for the Santals. Jharkhand is rich in mineral resources and to access this mineral wealth requires operations that inevitably result in the displacement of tribals from their ancestral lands. Thus Santals complain that at no point of time in the planning for the Pachwara Coalmines Project in Santal Parganas, which affected some 130 villages, did consultation in any form take place, either with the villagers or with the Gram Sahbas. Between 1950 and 1990 it is estimated that some 740,000 tribals were displaced by development projects in the area of what is now Jharkhand State. Even though compensation was offered, fewer than 200,000 of the displaced persons have been resettled.

Loss of tribal land to non-tribal peoples is a major problem facing Santals in Jharkhand and continues with the government turn a blind eye to it. Thus, the Punjab State Electricity Board (PSEB) was able to acquire the land for its Pachwara mining project in the Scheduled Tribal area, even though there are certain provisions in the Santal Parganas Tenancy Act of 1949 (SPT Act, 1949) prohibiting the transfer of tribal land through sale or mortgage or lease or any other agreement. Santals found out the hard way that their traditional rights over land meant little to the new government. Adivasi populations and also other poor peasants have routinely lost land for decades throughout India. This has been well documented. The Santals in Jharkhand are no exception.

In the years following the creation of Jharkhand, the state experienced unrest over what was termed the "domicile" controversy. At issue was who could be called a resident of Jharkhand and thus be eligible for "reserved" government jobs. Local residents, objecting to a Jharkhand High Court verdict that said that the state could conduct a country-wide search for qualified teachers, instituted a *bandh* (strike) that led to police firings and violence and even deaths. The chief minister at the time, Babulal Marandi, decided that 1932 would be the cutoff date and certificates of domicile would be issued to anyone who could provide documentation—e.g. land records—of residency at that time. Of course, many Santals, who had been in the area much longer, had no such documentation. Even the Scheduled Tribes and Other Traditional Forest Dwellers (Recognition of Forest Rights) Act of 2006, passed by the government of India in 2008 does little to protect the rights of Santals to their lands. Land alienation (i.e. the sale of tribal lands to non-tribal peoples) is a major issue in Jharkhand.

Santal religion, however, is a potent force in strengthening the social solidarity of the people. The Santal concept of righteousness is bound up with its social or tribal consciousness. They have an excellent and well-ordered village organization with a hierarchy of village officers and courts for dispensing their unwritten law.

The search for a new identity, both political and cultural, is a distinguishing feature of Santal society today.

[20] GENDER ISSUES

Despite living in a patrilineal society, the Santal woman is not subject to the negative elements usually associated with Hindu caste society. However, she does not have political or religious rights and cannot be a member of the village *panchayat*. In most cases, she runs the household as well as works with the men in fields, farms, and forests. She goes to the market and strikes bargains for the surplus produce of the family.

In the matter of inheritance Santals follow their own customs and do not follow the practices of the (usually Hindu) societies amongst which they live. A Santal woman does not have a share in her father's property but she can hold moveable property like money, goods, and cattle, and usually gets a cow when her father's property is divided between the sons. A widow may remarry, but it is thought the right thing for her to do is marry her late husband's younger brother (junior levirate). Divorce is allowed, although if a woman demands a divorce without just cause, the father returns the bride-price to the aggrieved husband and often pays a fine that is determined by the local *panchayat*.

Despite these disadvantages, Santal society is highly democratic and the Santal woman's social status is relatively high, though she still suffers from poverty, illiteracy, and lack of access to education or health care.

[21] BIBLIOGRAPHY

Archer, William G. *The Hill of Flutes: Life, Love and Poetry in Tribal India*. London: Allen & Unwin, 1974.

Biswas, P. C. *Santals of the Santal Parganas*. Delhi: Bharatiya Adimjati Sevak Sangh, 1956.

Bodding. P. O. *Traditions and Institutions of the Santals*. New Delhi: Gyan Publishing House, 2001.

Kaviraj, N. *Santal Village Community and the Santal Rebellion of 1855*. Calcutta: Subarnarekha, 2001.

Mahapatra, Sitakant. *Modernization and Ritual: Identity and Change in Santal Society*. Calcutta: Oxford University Press, 1986.

Ray, U. K., A. K. Das, and S. K. Basu. *To Be With Santals*. Calcutta: Cultural Research Institute, Scheduled Castes and Tribes Welfare Department, Government of West Bengal, 1982.

Sharma, B. K. *Habitat, Economy & Society of Tribal Core: A Case Study of Damin-I-Koh*. New Delhi: Inter-India Publications, 1992.

—by D. O. Lodrick

SASAK

Pronunciation: SAH-sahk
LOCATION: Indonesia (island of Lombok)
POPULATION: 2.6 million (2000)
LANGUAGE: Sasak
RELIGION: Native variations of Islam
RELATED ARTICLES: Vol. 3: Indonesians; Balinese

[1] INTRODUCTION

Until the recent boom in tourism, the Sasak people of Lombok have remained among Indonesia's least-known ethnic groups, even in comparison with some of their more "exotic" eastern neighbors in the Lesser Sundas, not to mention the Balinese. Nonetheless, Sasak culture is fascinating on its own terms, having developed along several cultural "fault lines," sharing much with the Sumbawans and Bimanese to the east but receiving strong influences from the Balinese, Javanese, Malays, and Makassarese as well.

The Sasak call their island *Bumi Gora,* or "Dry Farmland." *Selaparang* is another name, that of their earliest recorded kingdom, which lay on the eastern coast. In the early 17th century, the Balinese kingdom of Karangasem on the one hand, and the Makassarese kingdom of Gowa in alliance with the sultanate of Bima on Sumbawa on the other, established competing footholds on Lombok. The Balinese eventually prevailed, driving the Makassarese out in 1678 and completing the subjugation of the island by 1750. While the Sasak in the western half of the island lived harmoniously with the Balinese, sharing much of the same ritual life despite adhering to different religions, the Sasak aristocracy in the east resented this domination and led three peasant revolts under the banner of orthodox Islam against their "infidel" Balinese lords in the 19th century. The last of these rebellions invited the intervention of the heretofore distant Dutch colonial state. This ended in 1894 with the mass suicide of the Balinese Mataram court after heroic resistance. Although the Dutch built new dams for irrigation, the increased rice production could not sustain a rapidly growing peasant population in the face of an increased burden of taxes owed to the colonial government, in addition to obligations to traditional aristocrats. The average daily consumption of rice fell by 25% over the years 1900–1930, from 400 g to 300 g (14–10.5 oz).

Lombok still suffers from one of the highest illiteracy and infant mortality rates in the country, although conditions have improved with the rapid national economic development beginning in the New Order regime (1966–1998), temporarily interrupted in the wake of the 1997–1998 Asian/global emerging markets financial crisis, and the local growth of international tourism, a spillover from Bali, which has experienced temporary downturns due to instability in Indonesia as a whole and due to local outbreaks of communal violence. During the period 1990–2004, West Nusa Tenggara suffered 198 incidents of communal violence, almost all of them on Lombok with the exception of the riots that destroyed much of Kota Bima on Sumbawa in 1998. This is a high level if one considers that West Java, with over nine times the population of West Nusa Tenggara, only had 4.4 times the number of incidents and 2.3 times the number of resulting deaths (256 vs. 109). However, the scale of the communal violence on Lombok was miniscule compared to the conflicts in the Moluccas and Kalmantan and consisted mostly of vigilante groups exercising "popular justice" and intra-village brawling. A new type of communal violence has emerged since 2006. Members of the Sunni Muslim majority on Lombok (as in West Java) have launched mass demonstrations and attacks against members of the Ahmadi sect, including burning of mosques and houses. Ahmadis do not accept that Muhammad was the last prophet and recognize Mirza Ghulam Ahmad, who founded the sect in Punjab in India in 1889, as the Mujaddid, the "reformer" prophesied to come during the end times. Many Ahmadis continue to live in a refugee camp on Mataram.

²LOCATION AND HOMELAND

Lombok is about 80 km (50 mi) north to south and 70 km (44 mi) east to west, for a total of 5,600 sq km (1,815 sq mi). Gunung Rinjani, Indonesia's highest volcano and second-highest peak, dominates the north of the island. To its south is a rich agricultural plain, broadest along the western coast, which rolls up into hilly country in the south, which in turn breaks off abruptly in cliffs that fall down to the Indian Ocean. The rainy season runs from October to March.

The Sasak number around 2.6 million, forming 80% of Lombok's population (the rest being mostly Balinese in the extreme west) and 68% of the population of West Nusa Tenggara province as a whole. Overpopulation and rural poverty have included Lombok among the sources of transmigrants: Sasak transmigrants can be found on Sulawesi, and Sumbawa received its first Sasak transmigrants in 1930. In 2006, a total of 32,835 people from Lombok were registered with the Indonesian government as working in foreign countries (*see below* the section entitled "*Work*").

³LANGUAGE

Sasaks speak Western Malayo-Polynesian, an Austronesian language most closely related to the neighboring Balinese and Sumbawan languages. There are three caste-related language levels. Sanskrit vocabulary is prominent in the high level. Arabic words are more frequent in the speech of orthodox Muslim villagers.

The language has traditionally been written in the *jejawan* script derived from Java, which is virtually identical to Balinese letters. It is also written in Arabic script and increasingly in Latin script. Traditional writing was done on lontar palm leaves, though it is now also written on factory paper, and includes literature, records, chronicles, grants, wills, and village regulations.

⁴FOLKLORE

Seen most strongly among Wetu Telu Muslims, belief in a wide array of supernatural beings continues. These beings include village founders; past rulers; ancestral spirits; spiritual doubles (*jim*); and personified spirits of forest, mountain, and water (*samar, bakeq*). In addition, witches (*selaq*) are believed to exist; *balian* can communicate with spirits and heal. Wetu Lima Muslims are also known to fear *jim* and *bakeq*. Illness can result from spirit possession, black magic, and breaching taboos. Mystical power is held to reside in heirlooms, such as old weapons.

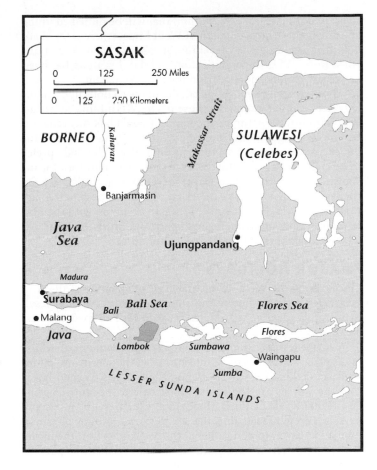

⁵RELIGION

Most Sasak adhere to Islam, introduced from Java (according to legend), by a Javanese holy man, either Sunan Giri or Pangeran Sangopati, in the late 15th century. It is claimed that Islam as initially introduced was already syncretic, as suggested by the fact that Pangeran Sangopati is also known in Bali as Pedanda (Priest) Bau Rau. There is a cleavage between syncretists who combine Islamic and pre-Islamic beliefs and practices, and purists who conform more strictly to Islamic orthodoxy. The former are referred to as *Wetu Telu* ("Three Time") Muslims and the latter as *Wetu Lima* ("Five Time") Muslims.

Because of persecution during the upheavals of 1965–66, exact figures for the Wetu Telu population are elusive; they may number as much as 30% of Lombok's inhabitants and are concentrated in the mountainous northern part of the island. The Wetu Telu religion stresses the veneration of ancestor and local spirits through village feasts. Wetu Telu observe only three days of Ramadan fasting, recognize three cardinal duties (to God, to the community elders, and to one's parents), and do not go on the *Hajj* pilgrimage, although they do bury their dead with the head towards Mecca. Many believe Gunung Rinjani to be the abode of ancestors and the supreme being and fast there for the three nights of the full moon. Religious specialists include village priests who perform rituals and fast at the beginning of Ramadan on behalf of the entire community, as well as *pemangku*, male or female spirit mediums and guardians of holy sites.

Wetu Lima Muslims, the majority, follow Islamic orthodoxy, such as the five daily prayers from which the label derives. Avoiding sinful acts *(haram)* that will be punished in the afterlife is the central concern of Weut Lima, whereas for Wetu Telu it is avoiding the breaching of taboos that will be punished in this life. The organization Nahdatul Wahtan has been active since independence in combating Wetu Telu.

Approximately 8000 Sasak adhere to indigenous non-Islamic beliefs, similar overall to those of the Wetu Lima Muslims; this community (going by the name "Boda") has succeeded in having its religious traditions officially recognized by the Indonesian government as a form of Buddhism. The Boda prefer to be classified as Buddhists rather than as Hindus (as, for instance, the animist Ngaju Dayak have done) in order to keep themselves separate from the Hindu Balinese, despite the fact that their own religion has very little in common with the Mahayana Buddhism of their only fellow Buddhists on Lombok, who are members of the Chinese community.

⁶MAJOR HOLIDAYS

Once during the Wetu Telu ritual cycle of eight years, the Alip Festival is held to honor the supreme being. Among Sasak Muslims in general, Maulid, the birth of Muhammad, is a major celebration.

A major festival unique to Lombok is the *Bau Nyale*, which takes place at the February appearance of the sperm and ovum segments of a sea worm *(nyale)* on the beaches. Legend has it that the worms are the transformed hair of a beautiful princess, Putri Nyale or Putri Mandalika, who, beset by too many suitors, threw herself into the sea. Separate groups of young men and young women gather at the beach to collect the nyale, which are eaten raw with grated coconut, grilled, or partially fermented in bamboo tubes. This is a rare occasion for the young of both sexes to meet in groups unsupervised by their elders: flirtation takes the form of poetic songs and subtle word play (if a girl accepts a present from a boy on this occasion, she is obliged to marry him).

⁷RITES OF PASSAGE

After birth, Wetu Telu fathers bury the placenta (thought to be the spiritual twin and guardian of the child) in a special place. A priest gives the child a name while scattering ash. The first haircut, 105 days after the birth, as well as tooth filing and, for girls, the first ear-piercing, are occasions for specific rituals and celebrations.

For his circumcision, a boy is first dressed in an elaborate costume and paraded on a wooden horse or lion with palm frond tails. No anesthetic is used for the actual operation, and the boy makes obeisance to an unsheathed *kris* (short dagger). As all life-passage rituals are held after the harvest, the party following often recycles glasses, chairs, and decorations from a previous wedding reception. The circumcision party is accompanied by bloody ritual fights.

For the wedding ceremony, which tends to be more complicated for aristocrats and Wetu Telu, the couple is carried on sedan chairs. The bride-price rises with the caste of the girl. The traditional inventory consists of strings of old Chinese coins; ceremonial gilt-tipped lances; rice bowls containing Chinese coins, covered by a large square of cloth with a small knife on it; and coconut milk and brown sugar.

Marriage by elopement is cheaper. The boy secretly takes the girl away to another village where he reports to the headman, receives 44 lashes as punishment, and is required to wear a black string on his wrist as a public sign. The village head informs the girl's family through their village's headman. The boy sends a delegation to the bride's family to set the bride-price, which will be distributed among members of the bride's family.

The coordinated pounding of rice mortars announces a death and solicits contributions of rice and labor for the funeral from fellow villagers. In addition to the conventional Muslim funerary rites [see **Indonesians**], Wetu Telu place offering trays of food and other goods on the grave. Hand carved pieces of wood for a man and decorative combs for a woman are also placed on the grave (after 1,000 days these are replaced with stones and a sprinkling of holy water). Wetu Telu hold a special feast at the graveside. At 3, 7, 10, 40, and 100 days after the death, ceremonies are held, which include Quran readings. Kinsfolk report to the ancestors before all important rituals. The bones are exhumed after 10 years and reburied elsewhere; the initial grave will be reused.

⁸INTERPERSONAL RELATIONS

Traditional society recognized three castes: aristocrats (two grades: *raden* and *lalu*); commoners *(bapa* or *buling);* and, in pre-colonial times, serfs and slaves *(jajar karang).* One properly married within one's caste (and especially not below it). Aristocrats may well be poor. Wetu Telu villagers all own land and possess roughly equal amounts of other goods.

Village authorities include the village head *(pemekel* or *pemusungan)*, neighborhood heads *(keliang* or *jero)*, the irrigation official, the chief religious official *(penghulu),* the clerk, the village guard, messengers, and others knowledgeable in *adat* (custom). Traditional punishments include ostracism and lectures by village elders. Villagers join together to perform collective tasks.

Houses are owned individually, while the land under them is village property.

Titles change upon marriage or the birth of the first child, e.g., a lower-level male aristocrat is addressed as "Lalu" before the birth of the first child, and "Mami" thereafter. Older or higher-status people are addressed as "Side" or "Epe" and are spoken to in respectful language, e.g., for "Please eat," "Silaq medaran" or "Silaq ngelor" is used instead of "Ke mangan." Younger siblings, or cousins whose parents are younger than one's own, are addressed as "Ante" or "Diq."

When greeting an older person, the younger person takes the older one's right hand with both of his or her hands; one kisses the hand of parents, uncles, and aunts. Disrespectful speech to parents and other elders will earn a child misfortune or disaster.

If a young man wants to meet a girl, he must visit the girl at her house under the eye of her parents. He sits at the *berugaq* meeting hall or on the house porch, talking around the subject, often joining the girl in whatever work she happens to be doing. They may chat using a special love language, or the boy may announce his feelings through an adult woman acting as intermediary. Tradition stipulates heavy fines on a man and his family if the man touches a woman in the sight of others. Aside from the *Bau Nyale,* harvest time was traditionally an opportunity for village boys and girls to meet; they approached in same-sex groups from opposite ends of the paddy field, singing to each other and flirting.

⁹LIVING CONDITIONS

The three regencies comprising Lombok, the home island of the Sasak, have an average Human Development Index, combining measures of income, health, and education, of 58.4 (2005 score), dramatically lower than that of West Nusa Tenggara province as a whole (62.4) and of Indonesia as a whole (69.6); though the HDI of Mataram, the capital of West Nusa Tenggara that is on Lombok, is only slightly under the national score. Lombok's GDP per capita is us$3,347.33, very low for Indonesia (cf. us$9,784 for West Sumatra, us$8,360 for North Sulawesi, us$6,293 for Central Java, and us$6,151 for West Nusa Tenggara as a whole). In 2000, the rate of infant mortality stood at 96.2 deaths per 1,000 live births on Lombok (minus Mataram), the highest in the country.

Traditional houses enclose a raised platform of clay, dung, and straw with walls of bamboo or palm leaf ribs and a thatch roof. There is an open veranda and two rooms, a lower one for cooking and receiving guests and a higher for sleeping and storage. *Lumbung*, rice barns with a horseshoe profile, have largely disappeared.

Villages are laid out in a rough grid with a *berugaq* (meeting hall), family houses, rice barns, a mosque or a few prayer houses, a cemetery, and sometimes a playing field. Larger villages are marked off into neighborhoods (*gubug*); aristocrats sometimes live in a separate compound.

Cidomo, hand-drawn or horse-drawn carts that carry goods and passengers, are a common sight on Lombok's roads.

¹⁰FAMILY LIFE

Kinship is bilateral, although the paternal line is emphasized, particularly as concerns the inheritance of noble rank or other offices. Most privileges and obligations derive from the *wirang kadang*, comprised of the paternal grandfather, father, paternal uncles, and paternal cousins. The basic household unit is the nuclear family, sometimes including a widowed parent, a divorced child, and adopted children. Aristocratic brothers and their families often remain in the same compound after their parents' death.

The preferred marriage is between cousins, but marriage is taboo between uncles and nieces or aunts and nephews. Newlyweds live with either the bride's or the groom's family or establish their own separate house, though aristocratic couples stay with the man's side as a rule. Three divorces per lifetime is average. For Wetu Lima, children stay with the father after divorce; for Wetu Telu, they stay with either parent. One means of divorce is for the wife to leave her husband's house and return to her parents as a sign of dissatisfaction with a husband who is an adulterer or a deficient provider. She may refuse to talk to the husband when he comes looking for her, thus frustrating him and making his family lose face, such that a divorce becomes inevitable.

¹¹CLOTHING

For everyday wear, Sasak men traditionally wear a batik sarong in blackish colors, whose longer front-hanging edge is held up while walking. To this is added a breast cloth of white or gold thread and an open short-sleeved shirt. Above a sarong and a sash for the waist, women wear a black *baju lambung*, a shirt with wide sleeves that is cut short in the back. Old people and big smokers carry around containers for cigarettes and tobacco, while many women carry holders for betel-nut chew.

Ceremonial clothing for men adds a *sapu'*, a head wrap of batik cloth, which is white down the middle. Women wear a batik sarong, a long-sleeved *kebaya* shirt, and a belt of gold thread. A *kris* sword tucked into the belt often completes the ensemble.

¹²FOOD

Rice is the central item of the Sasak diet, supplemented by boiled cassava and sweet potatoes. The main meals are lunch between 12:00 and 2:00 PM and dinner from 7:00 to 8:00 PM. For those who can afford to have it, breakfast consists of rice, maize, or boiled bananas with coffee. A warming food for the rainy season is fried maize with coffee. Fruits are not yet a regular part of the peasants' diet, being sold in town instead.

For celebrating Muslim festivals, *reket rasul*, yellowed glutinous rice with chicken, is prepared, as are *jaja tuja'*, steamed glutinous rice cakes with grated coconut. *Berem*, a kind of rice wine, is still consumed by Wetu Telu villagers.

¹³EDUCATION

In 2005, the level of literacy stood at 74.65% on Lombok (average of the three regencies, not including the city of Mataram), which is very low for Indonesia, significantly below that for West Nusa Tenggara as a whole (78.79%), and dramatically below that for other densely populated provinces with large numbers of poor such as East Java and Bali (*See also* the article entitled **Indonesians**.)

¹⁴CULTURAL HERITAGE

Indigenous performing arts are encouraged in "traditional" villages and by tourism-promoting government policy but are discouraged in "modern," orthodox Muslim villages. The Sasak *gamelan* (metallophone) orchestras resemble their Balinese counterparts from the scales down to players' costumes. Processional gamelans similar to the Balinese *beleganjur* accompany many dances. The *gamelan gong Sasak* combines the modern Balinese *gong kebyar* with a native *oncer* ensemble. Another orchestra is the *gamelan grantang* of bamboo xylophones. An Islamic taboo on bronze instruments (which represent the voices of ancestors in pre-Islamic belief) has yielded both iron ensembles as well as an ensemble of *rebana* (Middle Eastern flat drums) that can play the gamelan repertoire.

Various types of sung poetry are performed: *cepuk*, the recitation and singing of the Panji legend to *suling* flute, *rebab* fiddle, and a chorus imitating the sounds of the gamelan; *tembang Sasak* and Malay *hikayat* (verse), the latter simultaneously translated into Sasak; readings of the *Barzanji* (lives of Muhammad and Islamic saints) in a call-and-response format; and popular Sasak poetry accompanied by a *cilokaq* (or *kecimol*) ensemble of a piercing *preret* oboe, plucked lutes, and rebana. Finally, the Jew's harp, played in duets, is a popular instrument.

Sasak dance includes the *tari oncer*, where two drummers play interlocking rhythms and strike dramatic poses; the *batek baris*, which imitates a Dutch military parade coupled with female *telek* dancers who play the roles of kings, ministers, and soldiers; the *barong tengkok*, where men inside a mythical lion play kettle gongs; the *pepakon*, a trance dance meant to cure the ill; and the *gandrung*, where a single female dancer invites men from the audience to dance with her.

Theater forms include the *kemidi rudat,* which depicts tales from the "1,001 Nights," resurgent despite strong orthodox Muslim disapproval; the *teater kayak* masked dramas (*Cupak Grantang, kayak sando,* and other forms); and *Wayang Sasak,* the shadow puppet play introduced from the western Javanese city of Cirebon in the 17th century.

[15] WORK

Wet-rice is the primary crop, now grown in rotation with soybeans. Tobacco is an important export as are betel nuts, cinnamon, chilies, coffee, medicinal plants, and more recently pepper, vanilla, cloves, pumice, pearls, carrageenan algae, and sea cucumber. Most fish is obtained by trade as the Sasak are not seafarers. Fruit, honey, edible leaves, and bamboo shoots are gathered from the wild. Chickens, ducks, and goats are raised; water buffalo are reserved for feasts. Wetu Lima villages have formal marketplaces, and itinerant peddlers are Wetu Lima Muslims because the Wetu Telu Muslims look down on trade. The recent growth of international tourism on Lombok has provided altogether novel opportunities for work.

In 2006, a total of 32,835 people from Lombok were registered with the Indonesian government as working in foreign countries. The largest number was found in Malaysia, where the overwhelming majority were men (26,142 compared to 690 women). Very few men, however, were working in the Middle East: 5,610 women (domestic servants) in Saudi Arabia (only 84 men), 108 in Kuwait, and 55 in Jordan (no men in the latter two countries). The gender ratio was more even in South Korea: the 108 Lombok workers there (all from Mataram city) numbered 64 men and 44 women.

[16] SPORTS

One traditional children's game still commonly played is *bawi ketik* ("kicking pig"). This game imitates a wild sow protecting her piglets from hunters. It is played in the daytime after chores are done. On all fours in the middle of a circle, the designated "pig" bends over a number of stones representing the "piglets," one for each of the "hunters." From five to eleven "hunters" attempt to grab their respective stones from under the "pig" who, remaining on all fours, can only ward them off with kicks to their calves. A "hunter" who gets kicked in the calf becomes the "pig." This continues until all "piglets" have been captured whereupon the "hunters" hide their "piglets" while the "pig" closes his or her eyes. The "pig" must then search for the "piglets," the owner of the first one that he or she finds becoming the next "pig." Thus, it continues until the children become bored or tired.

The Sasak are particularly fond of competitive sports, such as soccer and volleyball. *Lanca* is a type of boxing originating in Sumbawa in which two men use their knees to strike one another. The *peresehan* is a ritual fight that accompanies wedding celebrations and the rain ceremony. It commences with two men, finely attired in turbans and sashes, feigning combat with rattan sticks and buffalo skin shields to the accompaniment of a *gamelan.* The two then invite members of the crowd to fight, taking care to match them well. It is permissible to refuse, but winning brings great honor. The matches can get very bloody.

[17] ENTERTAINMENT AND RECREATION

See the article entitled **Indonesians**.

[18] FOLK ART, CRAFTS, AND HOBBIES

The Sasak are famous for their *ikat* (tie-dyed) textiles, basketry, and pottery. Women weave cloth and sleeping mats. Men make baskets, traps, hide containers, tools, painted house posts and doors, as well as the wooden horses used as ceremonial mounts.

[19] SOCIAL PROBLEMS

See the article entitled **Indonesians**.

[20] GENDER ISSUES

The Gender-Related Development Index (combining measures of women's health, education, and income relative to men's) for Lombok (average of the three regencies, not including Mataram city) is 44.7, dramatically below Indonesia's national GDI of 59.2 (Mataram's HDI is slightly higher, 60.2). The Sasak regencies' average Gender Empowerment Measure (reflecting women's participation and power in political and economic life relative to men's) is 37.33, also far lower than the national GEM of 54.6 (Mataram's GEM is only slightly lower at 52.3).

In some villages, women cannot inherit land; in others, they inherit it only at the ratio of one to three with men. Inheritance may include land, houses, and heirlooms, such as cloth, jewelry, and *kris* or daggers. Jewelry is the common property of the women of a family (*see also* "Family Life").

[21] BIBLIOGRAPHY

Badan Pusat Statistik: Statistik Indonesia. http://demografi.bps.go.id (November 9, 2008).

Cederroth, Sven. "From Ancestor Worship to Monotheism: Politics of Religion in Lombok." *Temenos* 32 (1996). 7–36.

Government of West Nusa Tenggara—Lombok and Sumbawa. http://ntb.go.id/ntb.go.id/demografi.php (November 14, 2008).

LeBar, Frank M., ed., *Ethnic Groups of Insular Southeast Asia. Vol. 1, Indonesia, Andaman Islands, and Madagascar.* New Haven, CT: Human Relations Area Files Press, 1972.

Muller, Kal. *East of Bali: From Lombok to Timor.* Lincolnwood, IL: Passport Books, 1991.

Project for the Inventorization and Documentation of Regional Culture. *Permainan Rakyat Daerah Nusa Tenggara Barat* [Folk Games of West Nusa Tenggara]. Jakarta: Department of Education and Culture, 1984.

Project for the Study and Documentation of Regional Culture. *Adat Istiadat Daerah Nusa Tenggara Barat* [Customs of West Nusa Tenggara]. Jakarta: Department of Education and Culture, 1978.

Situs Resmi Pemerintahan Propinsi Nusa Tenggara Barat—Lombok dan Sumbawa [Official Site of the

Varshney, Ashutosh, Rizal Panggabean, and Mohammad Zulfan Tadjoeddin. "Patterns of Collective Violence in Indonesia (1990-2004)." Jakarta: United Nations Support Facility for Indonesian Recovery, 2004. http://www.conflictrecovery.org/bin/Patterns_of_collective_violence_July04.pdf.

Wheeler, Tony, and James Lyon. *Bali and Lombok: A Travel Survival Kit.* Hawthorn, Australia: Lonely Planet Publications, 1992.

—revised by A. J. Abalahin

SAUDIS

PRONUNCIATION: SOWD-eez
LOCATION: Saudi Arabia
POPULATION: 28,161,417 (July 2008 estimate; includes 5,576,076 non-nationals)
LANGUAGE: Arabic
RELIGION: Islam

¹ INTRODUCTION

Modern-day Saudis are descended from ancient nomadic tribal peoples of the desert who were fiercely independent. One tribal family, the Al-Saud, finally rose to dominance. By the early 1800s, they ruled much of the Arabian Peninsula from their base in the city of Diriyah. When the Ottoman Empire captured Diriyah in 1818, the reign of the Al-Saud family was ended, but only for a few years. By 1824, they had regained control of central Arabia and ruled again, this time from the city of Riyadh, Saudi Arabia's modern-day capital. In 1891, the Al-Saud family was forced into exile in the Empty Quarter (Rub Al-Khali) by the Al-Rashid family with the support of the Ottoman Turks. The Al-Saud family then moved to Kuwait. In 1901, Abdul Aziz Bin Abdul Rahman al-Saud left Kuwait, at the age of 21, to recapture the Arabian Peninsula. Retaking Riyadh in 1902, Abdul 'Aziz-Saud used it as his headquarters from which to unite the different regions of the peninsula into one nation.

The Kingdom of Saudi Arabia was officially declared on 23 September 1932, with Arabic as its official language and the Islamic holy book, the Quran (or Koran), as its constitution. When King 'Abdul 'Aziz died in 1953, his son Saud Bin 'Abdul 'Aziz took the throne, followed by Faisal Bin 'Abdul 'Aziz in 1964, Khalid Bin 'Abdul 'Aziz in 1975, and Fahd Bin 'Abdul 'Aziz in 1982. A major trade route that has been used extensively since 3000 bc lies across the western part of Saudi Arabia, generating significant wealth for Arabians in that part of the country. The discovery of oil in the 1930s led to rapid economic growth and development for the entire nation. Saudi Arabia is a founding and principal member and largest supplier of the Organization of Petroleum Exporting Countries (OPEC), established in 1960. With months of strong sunlight each year, Saudi Arabia is also developing the technology of solar energy. The land receives 105 trillion kilowatt hours of sunlight per day, the energy equivalent of 10 billion barrels of crude oil.

King Fahd ruled from 1982 until 2005, when he was replaced by his son, Abdullah bin Abd al-Aziz. Fahd devoted much of his energy in the 1980s and mid-1990s to establishing himself as well as his kingdom as a leading player in the Arab and Islamic world. His initiatives included the Middle East plan in 1982 and the 1989 Taif Agreement, which ended a long-running civil war in Lebanon. He also founded the World Muslim League and declared himself the custodian of Islam's most holy places, specifically the cities of Mecca (or Makkah), which is where Islam was founded around ad 610, and Medina, which the Prophet Muhammad established as the first Islamic capital. Mecca continues to be the spiritual center of Islam, and Saudi Arabia plays host each year to millions of Muslims who make a pilgrimage to Mecca.

Saudi Arabia's leaders remain powerful politically in the Arab world, but the nation faces threats from militants and the leaders of other Middle Eastern nations. These threats were heightened first during the 1980-88 Iran-Iraq war and intensified during the U.S. invasion of Iraq during the 1991 Persian Gulf War. The nation depends on the United States for military protection, and the United States has used bases in Riyadh as staging grounds for military personnel since the 11 September 2001, terrorist attacks. King Abdullah has initiated democratic reforms, and the first nationwide municipal elections took place in 2005. Nevertheless, Saudi Arabia remains tightly controlled by the ruling family.

² LOCATION AND HOMELAND

The Kingdom of Saudi Arabia makes up almost four-fifths of the Arabian Peninsula. The Saudi government estimates the size of the country to be 2,217,949 sq km (856,350 sq mi). Other estimates vary from 2,149,690 to 2,240,000 sq km (829,995 to 864,864 sq mi). It appears about one-third the size of the United States, yet the population is less than that of New York State. Most of the land is barren and harsh, unable to support large numbers of people; less than 1% of the land is suitable for cultivation. The national average for rainfall is four inches per year, with as much as 20 inches per year falling in the mountains of the southwest, and as little as none for 10 years or more in the Empty Quarter (Rub al-Khali), the largest contiguous sand desert in the world. Most rain falls in the winter, between October and April. There are only a few permanent streams and natural lakes in Saudi Arabia. In the desert, summer temperatures can reach as high as 44–50°c (111–122°F), with winter temperatures in the northern and central regions dropping to below freezing. Along the coast, humidity can approach 100%. In the midwinter and early summer, the *shamal*—a north wind carrying sand and dust—blows fiercely. The *kaus*—a southeast wind—blows less frequently.

Saudi Arabia is surrounded on three sides by water: the Persian Gulf and Gulf of Oman to the east, the Arabian Sea and Gulf of Aden to the south, and the Red Sea to the west. Lying at the junction of three continents—Europe, Asia, and Africa—Saudi Arabia has a wide variety of plants and animals, despite its vast areas of desert. The earliest human settlements in Saudi Arabia discovered so far date back to 5000 bc, on the Persian Gulf coast. Modern-day Saudi Arabia is bordered on the north by Jordan, Iraq, and Kuwait, on the south by Yemen and Oman, on the east by the United Arab Emirates, Qatar, and Bahrain, and on the west by the Red Sea.

³ LANGUAGE

The official language of Saudi Arabia, spoken by virtually all Saudis, is Arabic. Arabic, spoken by 100 million people worldwide, has many distinctive dialects, so that people living as little as 500 km (310 mi) apart may not be able to understand one another. Written Arabic, on the other hand, is classical Arabic and is the same for Arabic writers the world over. It is written and read from right to left.

"Hello" in Arabic is *marhaba* or *ahlan*, to which one replies, *marhabtayn* or *ahlayn*. Other common greetings are *As-salam alaykum* ("Peace be with you") with the reply of *Walaykum as-salam* ("and to you peace"). *Ma'assalama* means "goodbye." "Thank you" is *Shukran*, and "You're welcome" is *Afwan*. "Yes" is *na'am*, and "no" is *la'a*. The numbers one to ten in Arabic

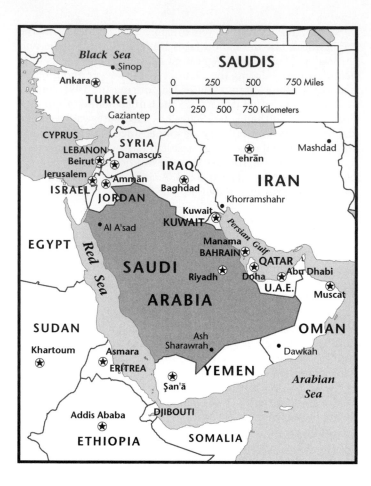

are: *wahad, ithnayn, thalatha, arba'a, khamsa, sita, sab'a, thamanya, tis'a,* and *'ashara.*

Saudis generally speak English in business dealings. About 5.6 million foreign workers also reside in Saudi Arabia and generally speak Arabic as well as their native languages.

⁴ FOLKLORE

The Arabs of Saudi Arabia, being Muslim, have much folklore in common with the rest of the Islamic world. Of particular significance to the Saudis, however, is that much of the common folklore glorifies the city of Mecca, the holiest place in Islam. The myths and legends concerning pre-Islamic Mecca were recorded during the early years of Islam. One such story tells the tale of the creation of Mecca and, following this, the creation of Adam and Eve. According to the tale, in creating the earth, Allah (God) first shaped the area around Mecca, laying the rest of the earth around Mecca to make this sacred city the center of the world. He then made the angels from light and the *jinn* from fire. The angels remained in heaven, circling Allah's Sacred House, and the jinn were sent to the earth. When Allah decided to create Adam as His vicegerent over the earth, the angels objected, making Allah angry. To gain His favor, the angels built on earth an imitation of Allah's Sacred House in heaven. This replica was the *Ka'ba* in Mecca, to which all Muslims should go for pilgrimage. Allah then created Adam from dry clay, molded him from black loam, and breathed His spirit into him, giving him life. When Allah ordered the angels to prostrate themselves to Adam, all but one angel, Iblis (Satan), did so. Iblis was then banished from paradise because

of his defiance. Allah created Hawwa (Eve) for Adam and allowed the couple to enjoy all the fruits of paradise except the fruit of one tree, which was forbidden. The resentful Iblis made his way back to paradise and tempted Adam and Hawwa to eat the fruit that Allah had warned them against. Both Adam and Hawwa ate from the fruit, and in return for disobeying Allah He ordered them to descend to the earth, where they and their descendants must remain until the Day of Judgment. Adam and his people worshiped Allah at the Ka'ba, and when the Ka'ba began to fall apart, Adam built a permanent House of Allah in the same spot. Centuries after the prophet Nuh's (Noah) flood, the prophet Ibrahim rebuilt the House of Allah.

There are many such legends illustrating the importance of the Saudi city of Mecca to the Islamic world. The Arab world also has thousands of proverbs and fables, many originating in ancient Arabia. Some are attributed to an ancient wise man known as Lukman, "the Aesop of the Arabs." According to Lukman: "He who does good has good done unto him"; "Walk quietly, lower your voice, for the voice of the jackass is the loudest and most ugly of voices"; and "A woman once owned a hen that laid a silver egg every morning. The woman thought, 'If I give her more food, she will surely lay more eggs.' She doubled the amount of food, but the hen, unable to take it, died of overfeeding."

⁵ RELIGION

Saudi Arabia is an Islamic state and no other religious practices are allowed by law. About 90% of Saudis are Sunni Muslims, and the remainder is Shia Muslim. Non-Muslim religious services were tolerated in Saudi Arabia for a long time. Although they were discouraged, they were not prohibited outright until after the 1991 Persian Gulf War. Christian prayer services used to be held in the country, including in the palace of King 'Abdul 'Aziz in the 1920s. From the 1960s until the 1980s, Christian services were held in private homes and foreign housing compounds. Since 1991, however, Christian services have been broken up by police, perhaps in response to the protests against the overwhelming Western presence in the country during and after the Gulf War.

The Al-Saud family supported the Islamic preacher Muhammad Ibn Abdul Wahhab in the 18th century, who advocated for the return of Islamic practices to their original "pure" state. The Wahhabi form of Islam is still followed in Saudi Arabia. The Wahhabis have been called the "Muslim Calvinists," for their literal interpretations of the Quran and *hadith* (sayings of the Prophet Muhammad). The Wahhabis decreed that the commands of the Quran must be enforced. For example, men are required to pray in a ritual manner, music and dancing are at times forbidden, and the type of clothing women wear is specified. This differs from Islam in other countries in that choices are not left up to the individual Muslim, but must follow the rules as they are interpreted by Wahhabis. In other countries (e.g., Egypt, Jordan, Iraq, etc.), the nature and extent of religious observance is more an individual matter.

Islam is the youngest of the world's Abrahamic religions, having begun in the early 7th century AD when the prophet Muhammad received his revelations from Allah, the one true God (according to Islam). Within just a few years of Muhammad's death in AD 632, Islam had spread through the entire Middle East, gaining converts at a dynamic rate.

Born into the Koreish tribe of Mecca (c. AD 570) in what is now Saudi Arabia, Muhammad was later driven from the city because of his outspoken denunciation of the pagan idols worshiped there (idols who attracted a lucrative pilgrim trade). The year of Muhammad's flight from Mecca, AD 622, called the Hijra, or *Hegira*, is counted as Year One in the Muslim calendar. Muhammad fled to the city now known as Medina, another of the holy sites of modern-day Saudi Arabia. Eventually Muhammad returned to Mecca as a triumphant religious and political leader, destroyed the idols (saving the Black Stone, an ancient meteorite housed in the *Ka'ba*, or Cube, building, which has become a focal point of Muslim worship), and established Mecca as the spiritual center of Islam. All prayers are said facing Mecca, and each Muslim is expected, and greatly desires, to make a pilgrimage there (called a *Haj* or *Hadj*) at least once in his or her lifetime. A central religious holiday is *Ramadan*, the ninth month of the Muslim year, during which Muhammad received his first revelations—celebrated by complete fasting from dawn until dusk each day of the entire month.

Islam is a simple, straightforward faith with clear rules for correct living. It is a total way of life, inseparable from the rest of one's daily concerns. Therefore, religion, politics, faith, and culture, are one and the same for Muslims. There is no such thing as the separation of church and state or any distinction between private religious values and public cultural norms in Saudi Arabia.

6 MAJOR HOLIDAYS

The one official secular holiday in Saudi Arabia is National Day (September 23), commemorating the founding of the modern Kingdom of Saudi Arabia in 1932. The rest of the official holidays are Muslim. Muslim holidays follow the lunar calendar, moving back by 11 days each year, so their dates are not fixed on the standard Gregorian calendar. The main Muslim holidays are: *'Id al-Fitr*, a three-day festival at the end of *Ramadan*; *'Id al-Adha*, a three-day feast of sacrifice at the end of the month of pilgrimage to Mecca (known as the *Haj*)—families who can afford it slaughter a lamb and share the meat with poorer Muslims; the First of *Muharram*, or the Muslim New Year; *Mawlid An-Nabawi*, the prophet Muhammad's birthday; and *'Id al-Isra' wa al-Mi'raj*, a feast celebrating the nocturnal visit of Muhammad to heaven from Jerusalem. Friday is the Islamic day of rest, so most businesses and services are closed on Fridays. All government offices, private businesses, and schools are also closed during 'Id al-Fitr and 'Id al-Adha.

7 RITES OF PASSAGE

Saudis traditionally have had their marriages arranged and often marry within their extended families. Although the practice of arranged marriage is changing among some Saudis in urban areas, dating remains unacceptable. A Saudi marriage contract must be signed by witnesses. The contract specifies an amount of money known as *mahr* (dowry) that the bridegroom pays to the bride. It might also specify a second amount of money known as *muta'akhir* (a postponed dowry), to be paid to the wife in case of divorce. In some cases, the requirement of an advanced dowry (which can range between 25,000 to over 40,000 riyals) makes it difficult for many young men to afford marriage. Some couples, however, stipulate only a token amount of mahr to fulfill the legal requirements. In case of di-

vorce, the woman not only receives the postponed dowry, but also her father and brothers are responsible for her well-being.

A Saudi woman does not take her husband's last name. She keeps her own family name because she is legally considered to belong to her own family for life. Chastity is regarded as the most important thing that a woman can bring to a marriage. Despite the fact that Saudi society is patriarchal, many Saudis interpret the retention of a woman's maiden name as an indication of her independence from her husband's control.

Upon the death of a parent or spouse, Islamic inheritance laws go into effect. A brother receives twice the share of his sister. Males are considered to be responsible for their families and thus need the larger inheritance, but a woman's inheritance, as with any personal property she owns, is hers to keep and do with as she wishes.

8 INTERPERSONAL RELATIONS

Arab hospitality reigns in Saudi Arabia. An Arab will never ask personal questions, as that is considered rude. A person is expected to say what he or she wishes without being asked. A direct refusal is also considered rude, so one must learn to read indirect signals. Food and drink are always taken with the right hand because the left hand is used for "unclean" purposes, such as wiping oneself after using the toilet.

The most widely used greeting in Saudi Arabia is *as-salamu 'alaykum* ("peace be with you"), to which one responds *wa 'alaykum as-salam* ("and peace be with you"). Men either shake hands or kiss on the cheeks during a salutation. Women do the same. However, a man and woman who are unrelated do neither.

Chastity and sexual modesty are highly valued, and many of the social restrictions on women in Saudi Arabia are said to be for the purpose of protecting a woman's honor and virtue. For example, the practice of preventing women from driving cars is not considered a restriction but is rather a means of protecting women from the indignity of driving.

Saudi values emphasize generosity and hospitality and helping those in need. Saudi society is tribal in nature, with a tribe consisting of groups of relatives traced through males. Members of the tribe take an interest in one another's well-being, and the more wealthy come to the aid of the indigent if the need arises. Each tribe has a leader known as a *shaykh*, who serves as a mediator in conflicts between tribal members. The *shaykhs* and their tribes give allegiance to the royal family—Al Saud—as a matter of loyalty.

It is very important to Saudis that they be hospitable to their guests. Respectability is maintained by extending generosity during a dinner party. Throughout dinner and dessert, (indeed, until the guests leave), the host or hostess acts as a server, continuously refilling plates and urging the guests to eat more. Serving the guests is known as *al-mubashara*. Even if the host or hostess has a domestic staff, it is his/her place to perform this service for guests.

9 LIVING CONDITIONS

Since the discovery of oil in the 1930s, money has been available for modernization and technological development, resulting in dramatic improvements in the Saudi standard of living. An extensive network of roadways makes almost every corner of Saudi Arabia accessible, and most families own at least one car. Camels are still used for transport in some desert areas.

Saudi men leaving a mosque after midday prayers in Riyadh, Saudi Arabia. (AP Images/Hasan Jamali)

Bus services link cities and towns and provide public transport within cities. Saudi Arabia has the only rail system on the Arabian Peninsula. The national airline, Saudia, was established in 1945 and is now the largest in the Middle East, with domestic and international flights to many destinations. In addition, two other Saudi airlines, Sama and Nas, operate in the country.

The Hajj Terminal at the King 'Abdul 'Aziz International Airport in Jeddah was built exclusively to handle Muslim pilgrims making their way to Mecca. (More than 2 million Muslims make the pilgrimage annually.) Saudi Arabia has many modern ports, the five largest being at Jeddah, Dammam, Yanbu, Jizan, and Jubail. The communications network is quite modern, with one of the world's best telephone systems. Telex, pager, and cellular phone services are also available. In 1985, Saudi Arabia launched the first- and second-ever Arab communications satellites. A well-developed postal system relies on post office boxes, rather than door-to-door delivery.

Modern health care and education are available free of charge to all Saudi citizens and pilgrims. Social services provide for workers and families in case of disability, retirement, or death. There are also provisions for social security pensions; elderly, orphans, or widows without incomes; home health care; rehabilitation of juvenile delinquents; nursing homes for the elderly; and orphanages for children. Low-income housing is available for public employees and students. The government also offers no-interest, long-term loans for the construction of homes. All adult Saudis, if not independently wealthy, are entitled to a plot of land and a loan to build a home.

Saudi homes traditionally were built for extended families, and this practice continues in rural areas. However, in cities, more married couples are living separately from their families. Houses are quite large and usually have separate quarters for men and women. Saudi architecture tends to use traditional Islamic designs. Adobe is common in Riyadh, the Nadj region, and the eastern province. Stone and red brick are generally used in the western districts. In Jeddah, corals from the Red Sea make for colorful buildings and homes.

There are at least 10 privately owned newspapers published in Saudi Arabia, 7 in Arabic and 3 in English. *Ar-Riyadh* and *al-Jazirah* have the highest circulation. Editors exercise self-censorship over their newspapers, in keeping with an unwritten press censorship code that restricts articles expressing opposition to the government. Foreign newspapers are heavily censored before entering the country, both to restrict politically sensitive material and to remove morally offensive items. There are millions of televisions and radios in the kingdom, hundreds of television stations, and dozens of radio stations. Internet access has been available in the country since 1999 and, as of 2006, approximately 26% of Saudi households had Internet access.

10 FAMILY LIFE

The family is central to Saudis. Extended families often live together in the same house. Marriages are usually arranged by families. A man is allowed up to four wives by Islamic law, if he can treat and love them all equally, but men rarely marry more than one woman at a time. Divorce is easy for men and possible for women and, since 1993, it has become commonplace. Women may write their own provisions into the marriage contract, and they may own and dispose of property freely.

Socially, women are very restricted. They must not mingle with men who are not close family members, at any time, in any way. They must wear a black veil over their heads, faces, and clothing whenever they are in public. Traditionally, women do not drive cars, and they are forbidden to travel alone. A woman may not attend a university lecture given by a man, but she may watch it on closed-circuit television; in this way, women may now earn advanced degrees at universities formerly closed to them.

11 CLOTHING

Saudis generally wear traditional clothing. Men wear a *thob*, a simple ankle-length robe of wool or cotton, usually in white or earth tones. On their heads they wear a *ghutra*, a large, diagonally folded cotton square worn over a *kufiyyah* (skull-cap) and held in place with an *i'gal*, a double-coiled cord circlet. Sometimes men wear a flowing floor-length outer cloak called a *bisht* over their thob; the bisht is made of wool or camel hair in black, beige, brown, or cream colors.

Women's traditional dress varies by region, but it always covers the body from head to toe. It is often embellished with coins, sequins, metallic thread, or brightly colored fabric appliqués. Some women wear a *shayla*, a black gauzy scarf wrapped around the head and held in place by a variety of hats, head circlets, or jewelry. In public, women sometimes wear a black outer cloak called an *'abaya* over their dress. In the southwest district known as the *Asir*, women wear brightly colored, long-waisted dresses and no veils.

12 FOOD

Traditionally, dates were the staple food of the Saudis. Dates form an integral part of many Saudi (and other Middle Eastern) sweets. To celebrate 'Id (or 'Eid) al-Fitr at the end of Ramadan, Saudis cook a sweet dish called *dubyaza*, which consists of cooked dates, dried apricots, dried figs, sultanas, and almonds. For 'Id al-Adha, commemorating the end of the Haj, Saudis make a pastry known as *ma'mul*. *Smeed,* a semolina-like flour, is mixed thoroughly in butter to make a granular pastry. This is then shaped into small balls and filled with either dates or almonds. The *ma'mul* is baked until golden in color and, after cooling, dusted with powdered sugar.

Although dates are still a supplement to the Saudi diet, with the modernization of agriculture and expanded trading opportunities, a wider variety of food is now available. A typical Saudi dish is lamb (or chicken) on a bed of seasoned rice. Pork is forbidden by Islamic law, as is alcohol. The possession of harmful drugs can actually carry the death penalty in Saudi Arabia. Tea and coffee are served at all gatherings, large or small. Buttermilk, camel's milk, and *laban*—a yogurt drink—are favorite beverages. Dessert generally consists of one or more types of seasonal fruit. A unique Saudi food is *arikah*, a bread from the southwest region (the *Asir*) that is broken off and formed into a spoon shape to be dipped into a dish of honey. Locusts, although terribly destructive when swarming, are considered a delicacy in the Saudi diet.

Meals that commemorate religious events, such as the birth of the prophet Muhammad, are served on a white tablecloth on the floor. Forks and knives are not used at these meals; either the right hand or a spoon is used on religious occasions. Everyday meals are served at tables and forks and knives are commonplace.

13 EDUCATION

Education is highly valued by the Saudis. It is a central aspect of family and community life, and parents are very involved in their children's education. Public education—from preschool through university— is free to all citizens. Government scholarships are also available for study abroad; most students go to the United States. Primary schooling begins at age six and continues for six years. Intermediate schooling begins at age 12 and lasts for three years. High school lasts from age 15 to 18 and is geared toward either the arts and sciences or vocational training.

Despite the importance placed on education, recent reports show that Saudi enrollment in schools lags that of other Arab nations. In 2004, for instance, the UN Development Program Human Development Report found that only 59% of Saudi children were enrolled in primary schools and only 52% in secondary schools. Nevertheless, the report also found that Saudi children had a literacy rate of 95.9%, which indicates that some children might be schooled at home or at private institutions.

Islamic studies are at the core of Saudi public education, but modern studies are also pursued. Formal primary education began in the 1930s, and the first university (now known as King Saud University) was founded in 1957 in Riyadh. A growth in the population of young Saudis and a need to equip Saudi youth with marketable skills prompted the government to increase the number of universities in Saudi Arabia from seven in the late 1970s to twelve as of 2008. Saudi Arabia also has 113 technical and vocational colleges and more than 18,000 schools. Boys and girls are educated separately; the first school for girls was built in 1960 under Crown Prince Faisal. About 58% of the 603,757 Saudis attending colleges or universities in 2005 were female.

Most Saudi Arabian schools are run by the government, which provides free tuition, books, and health services. There are a few private elementary schools. Government schools are also available for children and adults who are blind, deaf, or physically or mentally challenged. The Saudi Arabian government wants to eradicate illiteracy and has adult literacy programs in place across the country. As of 2003, literacy rates among men had reached 84.7%, compared with 73% in 1990. Among women, the literacy rate in 2003 had reached 70.8% compared with 48% in 1990.

14 CULTURAL HERITAGE

The national dance of Saudi Arabia is the *ardha*, or men's sword dance. Men carrying swords stand shoulder to shoulder, and a poet among them sings verses while drummers beat out a rhythm. The dance consists of a ceremonial procession and symbolizes the unity of the kingdom. *Al-mizmar* is the name of both a folk dance involving skillful stick movements and a musical instrument resembling an oboe. Other traditional instruments are the *oud*, or lute, and the *rebaba*, a one-stringed instrument.

Islam forbids the depiction of the human form, so Saudi Arabian art focuses on geometric and abstract shapes. Calligraphy is a sacred art, with the Quran (Koran) being the primary subject matter. The Islamic reverence for poetry and the poetic richness of the Arabic language inform much of Saudi Arabia's cultural heritage.

15 WORK

The Saudi work week runs from Saturday through Wednesday, with Thursday and Friday as the weekend. Working hours are usually 8:00 am to 7:00 or 8:00 pm, with a long break in the afternoon. Government offices are open from 7:30 am to 2:30 pm, and banks are open from 8:00 to 11:30 am or 8:30 am to noon, and again from 4:00 to 6:00 pm or 5:00 to 7:00 pm.

As part of the economic development plan, new industrial cities have been built near sources of raw materials and easy access to domestic and international markets. Eight such cities have been built so far, with the two major ones at Jubail on the Arabian Gulf, and at Yanbu on the Red Sea. Jubail is the largest industrial city, accommodating 30,000 workers at 15 large factories and other industrial facilities. It also has a desalination plant, a vocational training institute, and a college. All industrial cities are constructed with an emphasis on environmental and wildlife conservation.

The government offers many incentives to private businesses, including no-interest loans (with a 25-year repayment plan) to start up new businesses. Many jobs are not open to women because women are not allowed to mingle with men who are not close family members, even in the workplace, according to Wahhabi Islamic tradition. However, this is slowly changing, and women are beginning to enter all ranks of employment, from skilled labor to professional positions.

16 SPORTS

Soccer is the national sport of Saudi Arabia. Volleyball, basketball, and tennis are also popular modern sports. The traditional sports of horse- and camel-racing are still enjoyed as well. The annual King's Camel Race that began in 1974 draws 2,000 competitors and 20,000–30,000 spectators each year. Many other horse and camel races are also held throughout the country. Hunting with guns has been banned for the sake of wildlife conservation, but traditional hunting, with dogs or falcons, is still avidly pursued. The Saluki hound used for hunting is probably one of the world's oldest breeds of domesticated dogs.

Sports training programs are available to all Saudis in a wide range of activities. The government promotes sports through physical education in the public schools and the establishment of huge Sports Cities in large urban centers, smaller neighborhood Sports Centers, and Sports Clubs in rural areas. Fifteen Sports Cities already exist, and more are being built. Each contains a multipurpose stadium that seats between 10,000 and 60,000 people, a 5,000-seat indoor stadium, Olympic-size swimming pools, indoor and outdoor courts and playgrounds, cafeterias, conference facilities, and sports-medicine clinics. Exceptional athletes go to sports camps for serious training, and the best of the camp trainees enter international competitions such as the Olympic Games.

17 ENTERTAINMENT AND RECREATION

Entertainment is largely a private matter—there are no public cinemas, for example. Camping is very popular, and there is an extensive network of local and national parks and campgrounds across Saudi Arabia. Water sports are enjoyed in the Arabian Gulf and Red Sea. Many Saudis watch movies on video in their homes.

Saudi Arabia has more than 5 million radio receivers and 4.5 million television sets. There are more than 112 television stations and dozens of radio stations. The Saudi Arabian Broadcasting Service transmits programs to other countries in Arabic, Farsi, French, Indonesian, Somali, Swahili, and Urdu. Many of the domestic broadcast stations transmit English-language programs; the rest are Arabic-language. The strict Saudi moral standard restricts what can be broadcast, and programs are screened for scenes that contradict the codes of sexual chastity and religious observance.

18 FOLK ART, CRAFTS, AND HOBBIES

Saudi Arabia is famous for gold and silver handicrafts, particularly jewelry fashioned as both a decorative art and as a status symbol. Jewelry is treasured both for its beauty and for the monetary value it bears. Because jewelry can be traded in or sold for currency, it is regarded as insurance against hard times. One of the finest examples of gold and silver handicrafts is on the *kiswah*, a black cloth embroidered in gold and silver with verses from the Quran. The kiswah measures approximately 28,500 sq ft and covers the four sides of the *Ka`bah* (cube building). The kiswah is replaced every year and made in Mecca.

Pottery making is another Saudi craft. Using a pottery wheel, craftsmen fabricate beautiful storage and water urns. Urns are made with narrow necks to prevent the evaporation of water. Brass and copper crafts are also abundant. In the city of Riyadh, craftsmen can be seen making brass coffeepots over open flames. Since ancient times, Saudis have crafted goods from leather, including handbags, saddlebags, sandals, and shoes. Wood carving is another prized art. Geometric designs and religious inscriptions are carved with sharp knives to create both artwork and fixtures such as wooden plates and engraved panels for doors. Straw is also used in artwork, with straw hats, mats, containers, and cooking lids available at the *souk*, or market.

19 SOCIAL PROBLEMS

Crime rates have risen in Saudi Arabia with the presence of foreign workers and ongoing hostilities in the Middle East following the 11 September 2001 terrorist attacks on the United States. Amnesty International reported in its 2008 human rights report that the Saudi government arrested hundreds of people suspected of terrorism in 2007 as well as activists pressing for political reforms. At least 158 people were executed in

2007 and many others received punishments of flogging or amputation.

In the past, Saudi Arabia's severe penalties helped prevent severe crimes from occurring. Repeated theft is punishable by amputation of the right hand, and drunkenness and gambling are punishable by flogging with a cane. Many sentences are delivered in secrecy and information about individuals detained in Saudi prisons often goes unreported to the public. Saudi Arabia has been criticized by Amnesty International for its human rights record concerning prison conditions, and asked permission to visit the country in 2007 to discuss human rights. The government has initiated some reforms in its justice system and has indicated a willingness to discuss its human rights records. However, the government had not agreed to a date for an Amnesty International visit as of late 2007.

20 GENDER ISSUES

Women in Saudi Arabia suffer extreme legal discrimination. Women cannot study, work, travel, marry, testify in court, file a legal complaint, or even undergo medical treatment without the consent of a male guardian, such as a husband, father, grandfather, brother, or son. Saudis justify these restrictions on the basis of Islamic principles. However, women are beginning to protest the discrimination and human rights organizations, such as Human Rights Watch and Amnesty International, are bringing the plight of Saudi women to international attention.

The lack of legal rights has caused many Saudi women to suffer violence and abusive treatment from husbands, and has led to a rise in beatings, rapes, and non-payment of wages to foreign female workers in the kingdom. The government has signed international charters supporting women's rights, but has not significantly modified its laws. Although more than half of all college graduates in Saudi Arabia are women, few women enter the workforce or have the opportunity to use their education outside of the home.

Women's rights groups have formed in Saudi Arabia. One such organization petitioned King Abdullah in September 2007 for the right to drive vehicles and to compete in international sporting events. The government has indicated a willingness to allow women more rights, but has not put policies to end discrimination into place.

21 BIBLIOGRAPHY

Al-Hariri-Rifai, Wahbi, and Mokhless al-Hariri-Rifai. *The Heritage of the Kingdom of Saudi Arabia*. Washington, DC: GDG Publications, 1990.

Al-Saleh, Khairat. *Fabled Cities, Princes and Jinns from Arab Myths and Legends*. New York: Peter Bedrick Books, 1985.

Amnesty International Report 2008: State of the World's Human Rights. http://thereport.amnesty.org/eng/Homepage (retrieved August 3, 2008).

CIA World Book: Saudi Arabia, https://www.cia.gov/library/publications/the-world-factbook/geos/ir.html#People, 2008 (retrieved July 31, 2008)

Economist Intelligence Unit: Country Profile: Saudi Arabia. Economist Intelligence Unit Inc., 2007

Fattah, Hassan M. "Saudi Arabia Debates Women's Rights to Drive," *New York Times* 28 September 2007, www.nytimes.com (retrieved 1 August 2008).

Foster, Leila Merrell. *Enchantment of the World: Saudi Arabia*. Chicago: Childrens Press, 1993.

Kingdom of Saudi Arabia. Culture Grams: World Edition. Ann Arbor, Mich.: ProQuest LLC, 2008.

Metz, Helen Capin. *Saudi Arabia: A Country Study*. Washington, DC: Library of Congress, Federal Research Division, 1993.

"Our Women Must Be Protected," *The Economist* 24 April 2008. www.economist.com (retrieved 31 July 2008).

Saudi Arabia, pamphlet series. Washington, DC: The Royal Embassy of Saudi Arabia, Information Office, 1994.

Saudi British Bank Business Profile Series: Saudi Arabia, 5th ed. Hong Kong: Hong Kong and Shanghai Banking Corporation, Ltd., 1991.

Zubaida, Sami, and Richard Tapper, eds. *Culinary Cultures of the Middle East*. London and New York: I.B. Tauris Publishers, 1994.

—revised by Himanee Gupta-Carlson.

SHANS

PRONUNCIATION: SHAHNS
LOCATION: Myanmar (Burma); India; China; Laos; Thailand; northern Viet Nam
POPULATION: 5 to 7 million
LANGUAGE: Shan; Chinese; Burmese
RELIGION: Buddhism, with elements of Animism

¹ INTRODUCTION

A people known as the Tai have inhabited a vast area of Asia, including Thailand, Laos, and northeastern Myanmar (formerly called Burma.) The name for the Tai ethnic group of Myanmar is "Shan." The Shans migrated into Myanmar from China, to the north, many centuries ago, and settled in the valleys. They established kingdoms and expanded their territory, often in conflict with other ethnic groups such as the Burmese (Burmans). From the 15th century on, the Shan Plateau was their main homeland. The people were governed by hereditary princes called Sao-Phas in as many as 40 different principalities.

When the British Empire annexed Burma in the late 19th century, the Shan princes negotiated protectorate agreements which allowed them to continue to rule their domains, while acknowledging British supremacy. With time, the Sao-Phas became more educated and more willing to work together, and in the 1920s they formed the Federated Shan States. After World War II, the British granted independence to Burma, and Shan leaders participated in the Panglong Agreement with Burmese independence hero, General Aung San, ensuring a great deal of autonomy for the Shan aristocrats. The independent constitution of Burma created a Shan State and granted it the right to secede after 10 years.

Many Shans, including pro-democracy Sao-Phas, became disillusioned with being part of the Union of Burma. They felt that their culture was being suppressed by the majority Burmese and there were conflicts with central government troops. A military government took over Burma in 1962, and Burma's president—a Shan——Sao Shwe Thaike, was put in prison, where he died. Burma's military rulers renamed the country "Myanmar" in 1989.

Armed rebel groups promoting Shan nationalism sprung up throughout the Shan state. The Shan rebellion was characterized by many factional splits and by "warlords" who took advantage of the State's lucrative opium trade to form their own narcotic-trafficking armies. In the 1990s, some armed Shan groups surrendered to Myanmar's central government or reached ceasefire agreements. Khun Sa, the notorious warlord of one of the surrendered armies, died of natural causes in Myanmar in 2007. The Shan State Army led by Colonel Yod Serk has continued to fight a hit and run guerrilla war against the Myanmar government's army. Yod Serk has often spoken out against the narcotics trade.

² LOCATION AND HOMELAND

Although there are no sure census figures in Myanmar, the Shan population there has been estimated at more than 5 million, perhaps as many as 7 million. There are Shan-related ethnic people in India's Assam, China's Yunnan Province (the Dai people), Laos, Thailand, and northern Vietnam as well. Myanmar's Shan State has a border with Yunnan in the north, Laos to the east, and Thailand to the south. The region is often called "The Golden Triangle" and is associated with trade in opium, the raw material for heroin. In addition to the Shans, numerous other ethnic groups live in Myanmar's Shan State, mainly in the hills: Palaungs, Pa-Os, Was, Lahus, Akhas, and other tribal people, and the Kokang Chinese.

The Salween River flows from China down through the Shan State, and the Mekong River forms the border with Laos. Major cities include Taunggyi, Keng Tung, and Lashio. In the southeast of the state is Inle Lake, where the Intha people live in stilt houses above the water and grow vegetables on floating gardens. The Shan State has been green and fertile, but deforestation in recent decades, as Myanmar's military government sold off teak wood to neighboring countries, has badly degraded the terrain. Major population displacement took place in the Shan State during the late 1990s, as the Myanmar government's forces destroyed villages, confiscated or burned crops, and moved masses of civilians around for forced labor projects. These events and related rural poverty caused tens of thousands of Shans to flee to Thailand, where they sought work and safety in a land whose language and people were related to their own.

³ LANGUAGE

The Shans speak a language classified as Sino-Tai. It is distantly related to Cantonese and other Chinese dialects, and closely related to Lao and Thai. There are considerable regional differences in the Shan spoken in various areas. Throughout northeast Burma, Shan is used as a common language for trade among various ethnic groups. Many Shans speak some of the Yunnanese dialect of Chinese and some Burmese, as well as Shan. The traditional Shan alphabet has 18 consonants and 12 vowels; more letters have been added in a modernized version. The letters have a circular shape, like those of the Burmese language.

To say "Thank you very much," Shans say *Yin lii nam nam.* The usual greeting in a Shan village is *Kin khao yao ha?* meaning, "Have you eaten?" The reply is probably yes, so the follow up question asks what you had for lunch or dinner. A popular expression is *Am pen tsang*—meaning "No problem," because the Shans value a relaxed lifestyle. Sometimes you'll hear *am pen tsang* even during a crisis, as Shans try to stay calm to deal with any situation.

⁴ FOLKLORE

Shans often believe in ghosts and demons who haunt forests, graveyards, and other lonely places. Shamans or Buddhist monks can be called on to exorcise such ill-intentioned spirits. The forest can be inhabited by animals which are actually ferocious human ghosts, such as *were-tigers.*

⁵ RELIGION

Shans, like most Tai peoples, are Buddhists. They practice a religion based on compassion for all beings and the search for enlightenment within a reincarnation cycle of birth and death. Buddhist monks, revered for their learning and self-discipline, are important to Shan communities. Some Shan monks are particularly well-known throughout Myanmar for their teachings, and Shan monks participated in the "Saffron Revolution" against Myanmar's government in 2007. The power that stems from keeping precepts (abstaining from violent acts, intoxication, and other negative forms of conduct) can prevent evil and bring good fortune. Shan Buddhism also incorporates many Animist elements, such as belief in a fertility goddess known as "the Rice Mother," and local spirits known as "the Lord of the Village."

6 MAJOR HOLIDAYS

The Shans observe Buddhist holidays and more animist-related ones such as an annual "repairing the village" ceremony called *mae waan*, meant to drive away dangerous beings. On holy days, everyone is expected to keep the five main Buddhist precepts: no killing, no stealing, no improper sexual conduct, no lying, and no use of intoxicants.

Because generosity, especially to the Buddhist monasteries, is an important virtue for Shans, gifts for the monks are a feature of many special occasions. Often a "money tree" will be paraded through the village, its branches decorated with banknotes and small household items for the monks to use. Dancers and musicians accompany the tree on its way to the monastery.

Shans sometimes hold a "Rocket Festival" in hopes of bringing on the rainy season to provide water for the rice and other crops. Large homemade fireworks are launched into the sky. Buddhist Lent occurs during the monsoon season, for three months. The monks stay at their monasteries, concentrating on their prayers and studies. Marriages and other festivities do not take place during Lent.

7 RITES OF PASSAGE

It was the old Shan custom for a mother to spend a month indoors, near a fire, after giving birth. When that month was over, the baby would be given a special bath in water that had coins and pieces of gold dropped into it.

Young boys usually become novice monks for one to three months. A colorful ceremony called *Poy Sang Long* is held as Buddhist Lent begins. The boys are costumed as little Shan princes. They are carried through the village on relatives' shoulders, or on ponies (sometimes even on elephants). Golden umbrellas shade them from the sun. At the monastery, the boys' heads are shaved, and they put on plain orange robes and begin learning the Buddhist scriptures.

In their mid-teens, many Shan boys get their first tattoos, usually from a *sayah* who uses a brass-tipped stick to inject magical ingredients in symbolic patterns. The chest, back, arms, legs, and tongue are common places for tattoos. The ink and designs can give the wearer various powers against illness, evil-doers, or weapons, or for cleverness. The tattooed person should keep Buddhist precepts of self-restraint to ensure the power. Men may continue to be tattooed, sometimes making their entire arms and legs blue-black from the ink. Shan women also get tattooed, but usually to a lesser extent than men. Other ethnic groups often seek out the Shan *sayahs* as the most powerful tattooists.

Death is considered the path to another existence, perhaps a better one. The dead are usually buried in a wooden coffin. Cremation ceremonies are held for monks and those who can afford to pay for the elaborate ritual. Musicians accompany the body to cremation site or burial grounds.

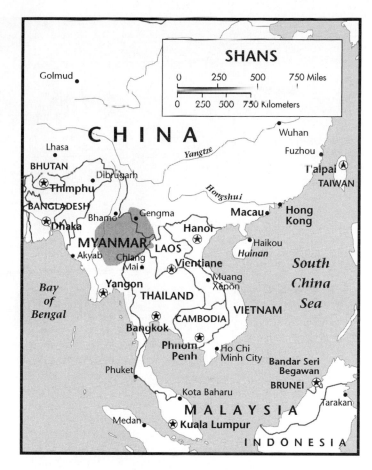

8 INTERPERSONAL RELATIONS

When visiting a Shan home, you remove your shoes to go inside. Traditionally this even applies to small shops. You also take your shoes off at Shan Buddhist temples and monasteries, and it is the usual practice to make an offering of money, flowers, or food for the resident monks. Shans treat the monks with respect, especially older monks or those known for their strict self-discipline.

Visitors to homes, or even offices or shops, are served tea. Shans are usually introduced using an honorific with their name, most often "Sai" for men and "Nang" for women, and it is polite to address them that way.

9 LIVING CONDITIONS

Currently there are many severe health problems among the Shans. There are few doctors or medical facilities, especially in rural areas. Malaria is prevalent, and children often die from it. Villagers suffer from tuberculosis and other respiratory diseases, and goiter (caused by iodine deficiency). Medicine is too expensive for most people, and traditional "spirit doctors" cannot keep up with the present health crisis. HIV/AIDS has spread through Myanmar's Shan State because of widespread injection of narcotics (heroin refined from the locally grown opium and locally manufactured methamphetamine) and because of the trade in young girls and boys to neighboring Thailand and China for prostitution. Generally ignorant about the disease, these young people forced into the "sex industry" have a very high rate of infection.

Shan women participate in a ceremony to celebrate the 61st Union Day in Yangon. (Khin Maung Win/AFP/Getty Images)

Military rule in Myanmar has caused a decline in living standards for the Shans. Many have fled their original towns and villages because of forced labor, or have had their homes burned down by government troops seeking to secure the area. To get away from the conflict, they often settle in the hill country where it is hard to grow any crop other than opium, or find their way to a neighboring country, usually Thailand. There are no refugee camps for Shans in Thailand; instead the Shan migrants try to find any kind of work and attempt to fade in among the Thai population.

In peaceful times, the marketplace is a center of Shan life. The markets are held quite early in the morning, and men, women, and children go there to buy food for the day, drink tea, and exchange information. Most of the vendors are women. Another center is the Buddhist monastery, where many occasions are celebrated. Often the monastery is located on a hilltop overlooking a village or town. Larger settlements have several, with tall whitewashed pagodas.

Shan houses are traditionally raised up on stilts, with the area underneath used for storage or a cool, shady place to sit. The roofs are thatched with leaf material. Inside, the Shans sit on the floor, eat at low tables, and at night sleep on mats. Cleanliness is very important to Shans, so yards and village streets are swept often. In villages, Shans bathe in nearby streams or with buckets of rainwater.

The Shans like to travel a lot, visiting friends and relatives or trading goods from town to town, but few have their own cars or motorbikes. Ox-carts are used for carrying farm products, and mules or ponies still carry loads and riders up in the hills. There are some flights into the Shan State and railway connections to Taunggyi and Lashio. A more common way to cover long distances is to share a ride on a truck, which may be carrying goods from China or Thailand.

10 FAMILY LIFE

The Shans have monogamous marriages, although in the old times of the aristocracy the *Sao-Phas* often had more than one wife. A "bride-price" paid to the bride's parents was traditional. Horoscopes are still important for determining if a couple is really meant for each other, and if so, when the wedding should take place. Shan weddings are not Buddhist ceremonies, although monks may attend. Usually, village elders or other respected persons will tie blessing strings around the couple's wrists. A feast is then held for families, neighbors, and friends. Married couples live on their own with their children, but may be joined by aging relatives or others needing help. Divorce is permissible in Shan society, especially in cases of domestic violence.

Shan families in Thailand have an average of two children, with parents hoping for one boy and one girl. In Myanmar, where birth control is rare, six children or more is a typical Shan family size. Shan families keep dogs, cats, and birds as pets. The dogs are used to guard houses and for hunting. Shan Buddhist monasteries often have many cats living there.

11 CLOTHING

Shan men traditionally wear baggy trousers, usually of indigo-dyed homespun. Called *koon*, the trousers have a huge waistband which is gathered and knotted in front. Women wear sarongs, called *phasin*, which are striped cotton or fancy embroidered silk sewn in a tube and wrapped tightly at the waist. There are traditional jackets and blouses to go with these, but younger people often wear them with T-shirts and denim jackets for a comfortable mix of old and new. Blue jeans and other western clothing are gradually replacing wrapped trousers and sarongs in the wardrobes of younger Shans, with traditional outfits saved for festivals and other special occasions.

Large conical bamboo or straw hats called *kup* provide shade for Shan men and women working in the fields or walking in hot sunlight. Older Shan men and women often wear large turbans wrapped from long lengths of cotton or bright terrycloth towels.

12 FOOD

Shans are fond of sticky rice, called *khao niw*. Eating with the right hand, they make a little ball of sticky rice and use it to soak up accompanying curry. *Khao niw* is also featured in the special treats the Shans make for seasonal festivals. In the cold season they cook *khao lam*, sweetened sticky rice, in bamboo tubes. A hot season specialty is *khao yak ku*, brown sugar-sweetened sticky rice with peanuts and grated coconut on top. As well as their fondness for sweets, Shans are known for their taste for sour foods, such as a spicy pickled cabbage similar to Korean *kim chee*.

Numerous varieties of fruit are grown in the Shan State, including temperate climate fruits like apples and strawberries not found elsewhere in Myanmar. Mango (*mak muang*) is a favorite fruit, both ripe and unripe, and is combined with meat such as pork for a Shan curry. Disks of fermented soybeans, called *thoo nao khep,* flavor many dishes. Corn and potatoes, originally from North America, are grown by Shan farmers.

Khao soi, Shan noodles with chicken-coconut curry, has become popular throughout Myanmar and Thailand. You can make a "fast-food" version of *khao soi:* prepare chicken-flavored ramen noodles according to the directions on the package. Mix in three tablespoons of canned unsweetened coconut milk, a half teaspoon of turmeric, a half teaspoon of paprika, a dash of hot chili sauce, and some diced cooked chicken. On top of the noodles put sliced green onion, chopped fresh cilantro, and some crunchy "chow mein" noodles; squeeze some lime juice before eating.

13 EDUCATION

Being able to read and write in their native language has been a political cause for many Shans, who feel that the Burmese-dominated central government of Myanmar has deliberately suppressed Shan culture as a way to control Shan rebellion. Very little material is being published in Shan, as even Shan children's books and health pamphlets are considered suspect by the government. In many villages there are *sayahs*, men or women who can read old Shan texts on subjects such as astrology and herbal medicine, and use them to make predictions, cast spells, or treat illness. The sayah's power comes from book-learning as well as from the self-discipline needed to keep many Buddhist precepts.

Educational standards in the Shan State are low, with schools and teachers in short supply at every level. In many villages, the monastery is a source of education, at least for young boys. Children who do attend schools run by the Myanmar government are likely to learn in Burmese rather than Shan.

14 CULTURAL HERITAGE

Shan literature has largely consisted of texts relating to Buddhist scripture, books of astrological and herbal lore, and histories of the aristocracy. "The Padaeng Chronicle" and "The Jengtung State Chronicle" are examples of such histories from the Keng Tung area which have been translated into English. In recent years, women of Myanmar's Shan aristocracy, including Sao Hearn Hkam and Sao Sanda have told their life stories in books published in other countries. Chinese-American author Amy Tan's 2006 best-selling novel, *Saving Fish from Drowning* was set around Inle Lake in Myanmar's Shan State.

Typical Shan dances include one in which two young men in a costume portray a lion or yak-like creature, and another in which children dance dressed as mythical birds. Solo dance is a part of ceremonies involving ghosts and other special occasions. A popular social dance is the *ram wong*, from Indochina. Couples move around in a large circle, using simple steps and graceful hand motions. Dance music can be played by musicians walking or dancing in a procession, and it features long drums, gongs, cymbals, and bamboo flutes. There is also the ensemble music of the old Sao Pha courts, which was influenced by Burmese classical music and is played by seated musicians. A framed series of gongs which can be hit all at once with a bamboo mallet is a particularly Shan instrument for such music.

Shan singers and musicians have had much influence on contemporary music in Myanmar. Their songs sometimes include political commentary disguised as love lyrics. Rock singer Sai Htee Saing died in 2008; his band The Wild Ones was popular throughout Burma and promoted Shan culture and a Shan point of view in urban settings. Popular Shan female singers include Nang Khamnong, who sings up-tempo pop ballads, and Nang Sara who belts out hard rock tunes.

15 WORK

The Shans have traditionally been an agricultural society, producing bountiful crops of rice and vegetables including soybeans, garlic, and corn. Villagers exchange labor to plant and harvest each others' rice fields. Government quotas, confiscation, and forced relocation of farmers have brought on a severe decline in agricultural productivity, however, and increases in cultivation of opium poppies for the heroin refineries.

In addition to farming, the Shans have been noteworthy traders. Men and women travel from village to village, peddling cloth, medicines, forest products, tools, and a great variety of other goods. Much of the trading stock is brought into Myanmar illegally from neighboring countries. Commodities including gemstones (rubies, sapphires, and jade), gold, cattle, and heroin, are smuggled out of the Shan State. Shans who cross the border to Thailand often find work on construction sites or as domestic servants. Some work in northern Thailand's orchards, where there are health concerns about their exposure to agricultural chemicals.

16 SPORTS

Soccer and volleyball are popular sports in the Shan State, as is *takraw*, in which a lightweight woven rattan ball is kept in play with the feet. Many Shans learn Lai Tai, their indigenous martial arts form, or a traditional Shan martial art in which swords are held with both hands. A more sedate game is *maknim*, in which the large seeds of the mucuna vine are set up in rows. Players take turns trying to knock them down by shooting another seed like a marble, kicking it off the top of the foot or rolling it off their clothing.

17 ENTERTAINMENT AND RECREATION

The Shans, like other people of Myanmar, enjoy marathon theater and dance performances that often last long into the night. Sometimes a traveling movie show comes to a Shan village, projecting a film (usually from Thailand) on an outdoor screen for everyone to watch. In recent years, the larger villages and towns have mini-movie theaters, small shops with a DVD player set up to show foreign movies or locally produced videos. Radio is very popular in the Shan State, especially short-wave broadcasts such as the BBC or Voice of America programs in Shan or Burmese. Satellite television is available in some towns and cities, although the Myanmar government sometimes cracks down on owners of satellite dishes. Towns and cities in Myanmar's Shan State have computer shops where games can be played, but Internet access is extremely restricted.

18 FOLK ART, CRAFTS, AND HOBBIES

In some areas, Shan women weave colorful silk fabrics. Embroidered cotton shoulder bags (useful, as Shan clothes usually don't have pockets) are made by Shans and used all over Myanmar. Silverware, including decorated knives and swords, and basketry are other Shan crafts.

19 SOCIAL PROBLEMS

While the Shans have a strong sense of themselves as a "free people" and the inheritors of a vibrant culture, they are also endangered by the breakdown of their society under military rule. In the late 1990s, tens of thousands of Shan villagers were driven out of their homes by Myanmar government troops, and the flow of refugees to Thailand from the Shan State has been steadily increasing for decades. Constantly under the threat of forced labor and caught in the crossfire of government troops, insurgent groups, and opium armies, normal life has been nearly impossible for Shan farmers. In Myanmar's towns and cities, Shan intellectuals and politicians have been imprisoned, killed, or exiled. The young people are in particular danger from the HIV/AIDS epidemic spread through the sex trade and narcotics injection. Drug abuse is particularly rife in ruby-mining areas of the Shan State.

20 GENDER ISSUES

In traditional Shan society, women had equal rights, although Buddhism viewed their status as somewhat inferior. Shan women took significant roles in commerce and family decision-making. Some Shan women, such as Sao Hearn Hkam, a member of parliament, were active in politics in Myanmar before the military government took over, and in rebel groups afterwards. Shan culture is usually tolerant of transgender, gay, and lesbian individuals.

During the time of military rule in Myanmar, the political status and security of Shan women has decreased and human rights organizations have documented a pattern of rape targeting Shan women and girls by the Myanmar government's army. In 2002 a group formed in exile, Shan Women's Action Network, released a report, "License to Rape," which brought international attention to the situation. One of the report's authors, a young Shan woman named Charm Tong, met with US President George Bush in Washington DC in 2005 to discuss human rights issues. Charm Tong received the Reebok Human Rights Award in 2005 and a Vital Voices Global Leadership Award in 2008.

21 BIBLIOGRAPHY

Elliott, Patricia. *The White Umbrella*. Bangkok: Post Books, 1999.

Lintner, Bertil. *Burma in Revolt: Opium and Insurgency Since 1948*. Boulder, CO: Westview Press, 1994.

Marshall, Andrew. *The Trouser People: A Story of Burma in the Shadow of Empire*. Washington DC: Counterpoint, 2002.

Mirante, Edith T. *Burmese Looking Glass: A Human Rights Adventure*. New York: Grove Press, 1993.

Sanda, Sao. *The Moon Princess: Memories of the Shan States*. London: River Books Press, 2008.

Sargent, Inge. *Twilight Over Burma: My Life as a Shan Princess*. Honolulu: University of Hawaii Press, 1995.

Shan Herald Agency for News. www.shanland.org (20 April 2008)

Shan Human Rights Foundation and Shan Women's Action Network. *License to Rape: The Burmese Military Regime's Use of Sexual Violence in the Ongoing War in Shan State*. Chiangmai, Thailand: Shan Human Rights Foundation and Shan Women's Action Network, 2002.

Sita, Sao Ying. "The Tradition of Democracy in Shan State." *Cultural Survival Quarterly*. 13, no. 4 (1989).

Smith, Martin. *Ethnic Groups in Burma*. London: Anti-Slavery International, 1994.

Tannenbaum, Nicola. *Who Can Compete Against the World: Power-Protection and Buddhism in Shan Worldview*. Ann Arbor, Mich.: Asian Studies Institute, 1995.

Yawnghwe, Chao Tzang. *The Shan of Burma: Memoirs of an Exile*. Singapore: Institute of Southeast Asian Studies, 1987.

—by E. Mirante

SHERPAS

PRONUNCIATION: SHER-puhs
LOCATION: Nepal
POPULATION: 55,000
LANGUAGE: Sherpa (or Sherpali); Nepali
RELIGION: Nyingmapa sect of Buddhism

¹INTRODUCTION

The Sherpas are a tribe of Tibetan origin who occupy the high valleys around the base of Mt. Everest in northeastern Nepal. In the Tibetan language, *Shar Pa* means "people who live in the east," and over time this descriptive term has come to identify the Sherpa community.

According to Sherpa tradition, the tribe migrated to Nepal from the Kham region of eastern Tibet. Over a thousand years ago, the Sherpas say, a great chieftain named Thakpa Tho was instructed through visions and divine oracles to lead his people on a journey from their homeland. The tribe traveled west to Tingri. After a brief stay there, Thakpa Tho and his people turned south, crossed the Himalayas through the Nangpa La ("La" means "Pass" in Tibetan), and settled in the fertile valleys around Namche Bazaar.

Historians present a slightly different view. They suggest that the Sherpas were nomadic herders who were driven out of their original homeland in eastern Tibet by warlike peoples sometime between the 12th and 15th centuries AD. They migrated to the area around Tingri, but conflict with the local inhabitants caused them to move on in search of fresh pastures. They crossed the Himalayas and settled peacefully in their present homeland in northeastern Nepal.

²LOCATION AND HOMELAND

The current Sherpa population is estimated to be around 55,000 people. They are found mostly in the Khumbu and Solu-Khumbu regions that lie to the south of the Everest massif. Sherpa populations also occupy lands to the east of this area in Kulung. In addition, Sherpas inhabit the valleys of the Dudh Kosi and Rolwaling Rivers west of Solu-Khumbu, and they are also found in the Lantang-Helambu region north of Kathmandu. Kathmandu itself has a sizable Sherpa population, while small numbers of Sherpas can be found throughout Nepal, even in the Terai. Sherpa communities are also present in the Indian state of Sikkim and the hill towns of Darjiling and Kalimpong. Small numbers of Sherpas are also found in Bhutan. However, Khumbu and Solu-Khumbu can be viewed as the traditional homeland of the Sherpa people.

The Sherpas are of Mongoloid stock. They are quite small in stature, relatively fair in complexion, with the distinctive facial features associated with peoples of Tibetan origin.

The Sherpas are a mountain people, living on the flanks of the hill masses that jut south into Nepal from the crestline of the high Himalayas. Rivers, such as the Dudh Kosi and Bhote Kosi, have carved deep gorges into the mountains, leaving a complex terrain of steep ridges and narrow valleys. Sherpa villages cling to the sides of sheer mountain slopes or sit on top of steep escarpments. Wherever Sherpas are found, their settlements lie at the highest elevations of any human habitation. In Khumbu, their villages are found between 3,000 and 4,300 m

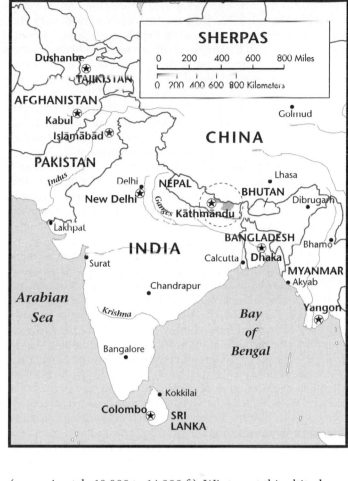

(approximately 10,000 to 14,000 ft). Winters at this altitude are severe, with snow covering the ground between November and February. No work can be done in the open. Most able-bodied Sherpas descend to lower elevations for the winter, leaving only the elderly in the villages. February sees the onset of spring, with warming temperatures and clear skies. People return to their villages for the New Year festival in late February and the next three months are spent preparing fields and sowing crops. Summer temperatures vary according to altitude. At Nauje village (elevation 3,440 m or 11,287 ft) in Khumbu, the July mean temperature is 12°C (53.6°F). May to August is the rainy season, with most of Nauje's annual precipitation of 104.8 cm (approximately 41 in) falling during this period. August to November heralds another period of fair weather, when the harvest is gathered in. Vegetation at lower elevations is dominated by mixed broadleaf and pine forests and rhododendrons, degraded in many places to scrub. This gives way to alpine tundra at higher altitudes.

As residents of Nepal, the Sherpas have been influenced by the communist uprising in the country, as well as by the dramatic political events that have occurred there recently. Though formerly the only Hindu Kingdom in the world, the country is now a secular state, becoming the Federal Democratic Republic of Nepal on 25 May 2008. This was largely the result of the "Nepalese People's War" fought between Maoist insurgents and first the Nepalese police and later the Royal Nepal Army. Almost 13,000 people were killed during this conflict and up to an estimated 150,000 people internally displaced during this time. The war was started by the Communist Party of Nepal (Maoist) (CPN [M]) on 13 February 1996, with the aim of establishing the "People's Republic of Nepal." For 10 years, Nepal was in the grip of civil war, with the Maoist insurgency initially commencing in the districts of Rolpa, Rukum, and Jajarkot in western Nepal and eventually spreading to 68 of the country's 75 districts. At first, the insurgency was seen as a police matter, but after Maoists attacked an army barracks in western Nepal in 2002 following the failure of peace talks, the Army was called in to fight the insurgents. The war ended with a Comprehensive Peace Agreement signed on 21 November 2006. The Sherpas make a lot of money from tourism and were generally unsympathetic to the rebel cause because the insurgency caused tourism to decline, but they were occasionally forced to provide young recruits to the rebels. Khumbu, at the base of Mount Everest, was generally considered as safe, though the lower Solu-Khumbu saw frequent rebel activity.

On 1 June 2001, Crown Prince Dipendra shot and killed his father, his mother, his brother and sister, one of his uncles, and several aunts, before turning the gun on himself. Gyanendra, Birendra's brother, succeeded as king. On 1 February 2005, Gyanendra suspended the parliament, appointed a government led by himself, and enforced martial law. The king argued that civilian politicians were unfit to handle the Maoist insurgency in Nepal. A broad coalition called the Seven Party Alliance (SPA) was formed in opposition to the royal takeover. This coalition included seven parliamentary parties that had held about 90% of the seats in the dissolved parliament. A countrywide uprising began in April 2006, resulting in massive and spontaneous demonstrations and rallies held across Nepal against King Gyanendra's autocratic rule. Eventually, an agreement was made for the monarchy to be abolished, which it was on 25 May 2008, ending 240 years of royal rule.

³LANGUAGE

The language of the Sherpas, called Sherpa or Sherpali, is a dialect of Tibetan, although it has borrowed heavily from neighboring languages. It belongs to the Tibeto-Burman branch of the Sino-Tibetan language family. Though Sherpali is primarily a spoken language, the Sherpas use the Tibetan script for writing. Sherpas use Nepali in their dealings with other peoples.

⁴FOLKLORE

A unique element in Sherpa folklore is the Yeti, better known in the West as the "Abominable Snowman." According to one tale, Yetis were far more numerous in the past and would attack and terrorize local villagers. The elders of the village decided on a plan to eliminate the Yetis. The next day, the villagers gathered in a high alpine pasture and everyone brought a large kettle of *chāng* (maize beer). They also brought weapons, such as sticks and knives and swords. Pretending to get drunk, they began to "fight" each other. Towards evening, the villagers returned to their settlement, leaving behind the weapons and large amounts of beer. The Yetis had been hidden in the mountains watching the day's events. As soon as the villagers left, they came down to the pasture, drank the rest of the beer, and started fighting among themselves. Soon, most of the Yetis were dead. A few of the less intoxicated escaped and swore revenge. However, there were so few left that the survivors retreated to caves high in the mountains where no one would find them. Occasionally, they reappear to attack humans.

⁵RELIGION

The Sherpas belong to the Nyingmapa sect of Buddhism. The oldest Buddhist sect in Tibet, it claims to adhere to the original teachings of Padmasambhava, the Indian monk who founded Tibetan Buddhism in the 8th century AD. It emphasizes mysticism and incorporates shamanistic practices and local deities borrowed from the pre-Buddhist Bon religion. Thus, in addition to Buddha and the great Buddhist divinities, the Sherpa pantheon embraces numerous gods and demons who are believed to inhabit every mountain, cave, and forest. These have to be worshiped or appeased through ancient practices that have been woven into the fabric of Buddhist ritual life. Indeed, it is almost impossible to distinguish between Bon practices and Buddhism.

Many of the great Himalayan mountains are worshiped as gods. The Sherpas call Mt. Everest *Chomolungma* and worship it as the "Mother of the World." Mt. Makalu is worshiped as the deity Shankar (Shiva). The Sherpas believe Mt. Khumbila is a white-faced deity who rides on his magical horse and protects the Sherpa people. Each clan recognizes mountain gods identified with certain peaks that are their protective deities.

The day-to-day religious affairs of the Sherpas are dealt with by Buddhist *lāmās* and other religious practitioners living in the villages. It is the village lāmā, who can be married and is often a householder, who presides over life-cycle ceremonies, undertakes purificatory rites, and occasionally conducts exorcisms. In addition, shamans *(lhawa)* and soothsayers *(mindung)* deal with the supernatural and the spirit world. They identify witches *(pem)*, act as the mouthpiece of gods and spirits, and diagnose illnesses.

An important aspect of Sherpa religion is the monastery or *gompa*. There are some two dozen of these institutions scattered through the Solu-Khumbu region. They are communities of *lāmās,* or monks, (sometimes of nuns) who take vows of celibacy and lead a life in isolation searching for truth and religious enlightenment. Their presence brings merit to the community at large, and they are supported to some degree by offerings from the general population. Their contact with the outside world is limited to the annual festivals to which the public is invited and the reading of sacred texts at funerals. One of the most famous and respected gompas is at Tengboche, north of Namche Bazaar. It is known for its *avatari*, a reincarnation of an important lama from a past life, as well as its library of religious texts and collection of objects, such as *thankas* (religious paintings).

⁶MAJOR HOLIDAYS

The major festivals of the Sherpas are Losar, Dumje, and Mani Rimdu. Losar, which falls towards the end of February, marks the beginning of the New Year in the Tibetan calendar. It is celebrated with much feasting and drinking, dancing, and singing. Sherpas who leave their villages to travel to lower elevations during the winter months hurry back to their homes in time for Losar.

Dumje is a festival celebrated for the prosperity, good health, and general welfare of the Sherpa community. It falls in the month of July, when the agricultural work is complete, the trading expeditions to Tibet have returned, and the Sherpas are preparing to take their herds into the high pastures. Over a seven-day period, Sherpas visit their local gompas to offer prayers to deities, such as Guru Rimpoche, Phawa Chere-

A Sherpa mother and daughter in the village of Ghat, Nepal. Thousands of climbers planned assaults on the summit of Mount Everest in 2003 to celebrate the 50-year anniversary of the conquest of Everest by Sir Edmund Hillary and Tenzing Norgay. (Paula Bronstein/Getty Images)

si, and Tsampa. Lāmās perform their devil-dances and villagers gather in the evenings to enjoy the occasion. There is much eating and drinking, and members of the younger generation participate in singing and dancing.

Equally important are the colorful Mani Rimdu celebrations, which are attended by enthusiastic onlookers from throughout the Sherpa country. These are held four times a year, twice in Khumbu (at the Tami and Tengboche monasteries) and twice in Solu-Khumbu (at the Chiwong and Thaksindhu monasteries). Monks don colorful costumes and elaborate masks to impersonate gods and demons and perform the religious dances intended to strike fear into the hearts of evil spirits.

Feasting and drinking accompany all Sherpa festivals and celebrations except for Nyungne. This is a penance for sins committed during the previous year. For three days, laypeople abstain from drinking and dancing and may even undergo a complete fast. They visit the gompa to recite sacred texts with the lāmās, or repeat the mantra *Om Mani Padme Hum*. The principal mantra of the Buddhists, it is also found inscribed on prayer wheels. It has many interpretations, one of which is "Om, the Jewel of the Doctrine is in the Lotus of the World." Monks and nuns keep to the restrictions of Nyungne for a full two weeks.

⁷RITES OF PASSAGE

Although a birth is not an occasion for formal observances among the Sherpa, the name-giving ceremony of the child is an important event. The local lāmā is informed of the birth and the time that it occurred. On the basis of this information, the lāmā determines the child's name and when the naming ceremony should take place. Children are often named after the day of the week on which they were born. Thus, a baby born on Friday would be called "Pasang." The lāmā, relatives, and neighbors are invited to celebrate the name-giving at a feast.

Children are usually brought up by their mothers, as the men are often away from home for much of the year. Young girls are introduced to household chores at an early age, while boys tend to have greater freedom for leisure and play. Boys undergo an initiation ceremony between 7 and 9 years of age, which is presided over by the lāmā and accompanied by feasting and drinking.

At the time of death, the body is washed and covered with a white shroud. The lāmā is sent for to commence the funerary rites. These include cutting off a lock of hair from the corpse so that the life breath (*prān*) of the departed may leave the body and reading from the sacred texts. Rituals include the making of *tormas*, conical dough figures that are placed on an altar set up behind the corpse. Both Buddhist and Hindu astrological books are consulted by the lāmā to determine in which direction the body should be taken and the manner of its disposal. The lāmā determines if the deceased is to be buried, cremated, or given a water-burial. The lāmā also decides when the time is auspicious for the removal of the corpse, which may not occur for several days. At the appointed time, the body is seated on a bier in the lotus position and taken for cremation or burial. The funeral procession is accompanied by flags and novice lāmās blowing conch shells and playing drums and cymbals. After death, the family performs rites for the benefit of the departed and undertakes a ritual purification of the home. Sherpas believe that the soul remains near the house for 49 days, and on the last of these days a grand feast is held to complete the last of the funeral rites (gyowa).

8 INTERPERSONAL RELATIONS

The Sherpas are a social and hospitable people. The cardinal rule of hospitality is that a visitor, even a casual one, must not leave the house with an "empty mouth." Guests are entertained with Tibetan tea or beer. Visitors of high standing will be served a snack, or even a complete meal. Unlike some communities in South Asia, guests in Sherpa homes have complete access to both the kitchen and the area set aside for worship.

9 LIVING CONDITIONS

Sherpa settlements range from villages with a few houses to towns, such as Khumjung or Namche Bazaar, with more than a hundred houses. In the higher elevations, a house is usually built in the middle of its owner's fields. Where more flat land is available, however, houses are clustered together in a group at the center of the village's agricultural land. Larger villages may have a community temple, a community mill, and religious monuments called stūpas and chorten. There are few proper roads, and villages are connected by tracks and trails. Goods are transported by pack animals or on the backs of the people.

Sherpa houses have two stories and are built of stone. The roofs are flat and usually made of wood, weighted down by heavy stones. The lower level is used to house livestock, fodder, food, and firewood, while the upper story holds the living quarters. The floor of this room is wooden, covered with carpets and rugs. The hearth is placed at the side of the room. It contains a simple woodstove used for cooking that also provides heat. Drawers and shelves line the walls and are used to store utensils, bedding, and personal effects. There is no furniture; platforms and benches are used for sitting and sleeping. One corner of the room holds a latrine and refuse-dump that opens into the stables below. A small area of the house is set aside for an altar. Here, one finds icons of the Buddha and various bodhisattvas and pictures of the Dalai Lāmā, the spiritual leader of Tibetan Buddhists. Incense and butter lamps are kept burning before the shrine.

10 FAMILY LIFE

Sherpa society is divided into a number of exogamous clans called ru. A person is required to marry outside his or her clan, but beyond this the clan is of little significance in Sherpa social organization. Although there is no ranking of individual clans, they fall into two endogamous groups, the khadeu and khamendeu. The former are of higher status and anyone marrying into the lower group loses this standing.

Sherpas choose their own marriage partners. The marriage process is a lengthy one that may stretch over several years. Following a betrothal, the boy has the right to sleep with his fiancée in her parents' house. This arrangement may continue for several years, during which the relationship may be broken off. Once the respective families feel that the marriage will be successful, a ceremony is carried out that formally confirms the marriage negotiations. Several months or even years may pass again before the wedding date is fixed. For the wedding ceremony (zendi), the boy's family dress in their best clothes and go in procession to the girl's house. There, they are entertained with food and drink and are expected to dance and sing in return. They visit houses of relatives, where the procedure is repeated. The feasting lasts for a day and a night, before the party returns home with the bride. The actual marriage is solemnized by putting a mark of butter on the forehead of the bride and groom. The bride is given a dowry by family and friends that usually consists of rugs, woolen carpets, yak-wool mats, and even cattle.

Sherpa families are small by South Asian standards. The nuclear family is the norm in Sherpa society, with households consisting of parents and their unmarried children. A newly married son is supposed to receive a house on completion of the marriage. Interestingly, a man does not return home until he has a child; he lives with his in-laws until such time as his wife gives birth. Most marriages are monogamous, although fraternal polyandry is permitted and is even considered to be prestigious. According to this practice, two brothers marry the same woman. Divorce is quite frequent among the Sherpas.

11 CLOTHING

Sherpa dress is similar to that worn by Tibetans. Both men and women wear a long inner shirt over a pant-like garment, both made out of wool. Over this, they wear a thick, coarse, wrap-around robe (bakhu) that reaches to below the knees and fastens at the side. A sash is belted around the waist. Both males and females wear high, woolen boots with hide soles. The uppers are colored maroon, red, and green (or blue), and the boots are tied on with colored garters. An unusual feature of women's dress are the multicolored striped aprons worn to cover the front and back of the bodies below the waist. Both married and unmarried women wear the rear apron, while the front apron is worn only by married women. Various ornaments and a distinctive cap called a shyamahu complete the dress of the Sherpa woman.

Traditional Sherpa dress is rapidly disappearing among Sherpa men. With the reduction in the availability of wool and woolen garments from Tibet, it is increasingly difficult to replace worn-out woolen clothing. Many younger men who have worked for mountaineering expeditions have acquired high-altitude clothing of Western manufacture. Older men, however, often have to make do with cotton clothing that is ill-suited to the cold climate of Sherpa country.

12 FOOD

The Sherpa diet is dominated by starchy foods, supplemented by vegetables, spices, and occasionally meat. In addition, Tibetan tea (tea served with salt and butter) is taken at all meals and throughout the day. A typical breakfast consists of Tibetan tea and several bowls of gruel made by adding tsampa, a roasted flour, to water, tea, or milk. Lunch is eaten in the late morning and may include boiled potatoes that are dipped in ground spices before being eaten. Sometimes a stiff dough made from a mixture of grains (sen) is eaten with a thin sauce made from spices and vegetables, or meat if it is available. A typical dinner is a stew (shakpa) consisting of balls of dough, potatoes, and vegetables cooked in spices, butter or animal fat, and water, and thickened with flour. Dairy products, especially butter and curds, are important in the Sherpa diet.

Sherpas eat meat, although they will not kill animals themselves in keeping with Buddhist beliefs. Meat and rice are special foods, eaten on special occasions. Often these foods are available only to the more affluent Sherpas.

A favorite beverage of the Sherpas is chāng, a beer made from maize, millet, or other grains. This is consumed not only at meals, but also at most social and festive occasions. It has considerable symbolic and ritual significance in Sherpa society. An anthropologist studying food among the Sherpa collected over 50 different names for chāng, depending on the context in which it is used. For instance, lāmās drink chachang when they put on a costume, but the beer they drink when they take it off is called silchang.

¹³EDUCATION

Although primary schools are slowly being introduced into Sherpa areas, few Sherpas have any formal schooling. As might be expected, literacy rates are low, as are parental expectations for their children. According to the census of 2001, the adult literacy rate (aged 15 years and above) of Sherpas is 37.4% (for women, this figure is in the low 20 percentiles) and attainment of the School Leaving Certificate (SLC) and above (16 years and above) is only 5%, which is very low in comparison with other ethnic and caste groups of Nepal (e.g. Kayastha [50.2%], Newar [24.7%], and Thakali [16.1%]).

The first modern schools were only introduced in the Sherpa areas in the 1960s, with the help of Sir Edmund Hillary, the New Zealander who, in the company of Sherpa Tenzing Norgay, became the first man to climb Mount Everest in 1953, and who devoted much of the remainder of his life to the welfare of the Sherpas. Prior to that, education was only available in the monasteries and was essentially Buddhist in nature.

The government school system in the Sherpa area is rather backward and consists mostly of primary schools. In recent decades, small schools have been established in a number of villages, but they are in a miserable condition: leaking or partly missing roofs; missing doors and windows or windows without panes; clay soil floors; missing or insufficient tables, chairs and benches; no drinking water and sanitary facilities; no electricity; no blackboards; insufficient teaching materials; curricula totally strange to Sherpa culture; insufficiently educated and badly paid teachers who usually don't speak the mother tongue of the children; no accommodations for teachers; and poor school participation, especially of girls. The poor and often irregular school attendance can be explained by many reasons—lack of understanding by parents who themselves did not have the chance to go to school; feelings against the teachers in general and especially toward those coming from far away villages and belonging to other population groups; the need for the children to work at home and in the fields; poor conditions of the school building and the resulting inefficiency of the classes; and missing perspectives after finishing school (hardly any chance to join secondary schools; no chances in

the administration or other government services dominated by Hindus). As it is typical for rural Nepal, Sherpa girls, too, are rarely sent to school. This is partly caused by the generally low social status of Nepali women that has been legally sanctioned by laws based on Hindu values, making women second-class citizens and depriving them of economic, property, and inheritance rights.

There are, however, organizations and nongovernmental organizations (NGOs) whose objectives are to promote education among the Sherpas. For instance, the Sherpa Association of Nepal (SAN) lobbies the Nepali government for reserved seats in government jobs for Sherpa candidates, scholarship for education of Sherpa students, and compulsory education up to the age of 14 years for Sherpa children. Some NGOs, such as The Sir Edmund Hillary Foundation of Canada and The Himalayan Trust, offer scholarships specifically for Sherpa students.

¹⁴CULTURAL HERITAGE

The Tibetan tradition of religious dance-dramas, known as 'cham, can be seen in the Mani Rimdu festivals of the Sherpas. Elaborately choreographed, with monks dressed up in costumes and masks, the Mani Rimdu dances enact the triumph of Buddhism over the demons of the Bon religion. The temple orchestras that accompany these dramas are unique in the makeup of their instruments, which include drums, cymbals, handbells, conch shells, 10-foot telescopic horns, large oboes, and flutes made from human thighbones. The distinctive chant used by monks in their religious observances is also in the tradition of Tibetan sacred music.

¹⁵WORK

Traditional Sherpa economic activities were centered on agriculture and trade with Tibet. Now, largely as a result of Trans-Himalayan trade having dried up as a result of the Chinese government's policies, agriculture is the mainstay of the Sherpa population. At lower elevations, such as in Solu-Khumbu, where conditions allow cultivation, Sherpas raise maize, barley, buckwheat, and vegetables. Potatoes were introduced to the Sherpas only 80 years ago but have now become the mainstay of their diet. In Khumbu, with its higher altitudes, farming gives way to pastoralism. Khumbu Sherpas raise cattle and the yak (Poëphagus grunniens), a bovine-like animal that does well at higher elevations. Hybrids of domestic cattle and the yak are known as dzo (male) and dzum (female) and play an important role in the economy. Yaks provide wool and milk by-products such as butter, which are sold or bartered for grain. Dzo are used as pack animals and are easily trained to the plough.

Despite the formidable physical barrier posed by the Himalayas, trade between Nepal and Tibet is of considerable historical importance in the region. Sherpas, because of their location and ability to handle high altitudes, have traditionally played a major role in the trade that moves through Nangpa La and other passes across the mountains. Salt, sheep's wool, meat, and yak are still brought from Tibet into Nepal, in exchange for food grains, rice, butter, and manufactured goods. Namche Bazaar, located at an elevation of 3,480 m (11,418 ft), is the main trading center on the route to Tibet.

Sherpas were first used as high-altitude porters in 1907, but it was Tenzing Norgay, Sir Edmund Hillary's companion on the first ascent of Everest in 1953, who was to bring the Sherpas to the attention of the world. Their role as porters and guides on mountain-climbing and trekking expeditions has brought the Sherpas a new source of income and, for some Sherpas, a comfortable living. There are Sherpas who have emerged as world-class mountaineers in their own right.

[16] SPORTS

Sherpas enjoy playing cards and gambling with dice. Wrestling and horseplay is popular among the young of both sexes.

[17] ENTERTAINMENT AND RECREATION

Sherpa entertainment and recreation is largely limited to their traditional pastimes of singing, dancing, and drinking beer.

[18] FOLK ART, CRAFTS, AND HOBBIES

Sherpas rely on the artisan castes to provide the material necessities of life. Some Sherpas have developed skills in religious painting and in liturgical (religious) chanting. The Sherpas have a tradition of indigenous folk songs and dancing.

[19] SOCIAL PROBLEMS

There are social problems that originate within Sherpa society itself. There is a high incidence of alcoholism, for instance, and the related medical problems that go with it. Similarly, although the situation is beginning to change, the lack of education among the Sherpas reflects to a large extent their isolation and the low level of development in Nepal as a whole. Perhaps the single greatest threat to traditional Sherpa society has been the coming of the tourist. Tourism in Sherpa country has been a double-edged sword. Its economic benefits helped compensate for the loss of the Tibetan trade in the 1950s; it helped spur development in the Khumbu region; and it provided many Sherpas with wealth far beyond their highest expectations. But this has occurred at a cost that goes far beyond the serious environmental degradation associated with tourism. Inflation, increasing dependence on a tourist-based economy, problems with drug-running, and the flight of wealthy Sherpas to Kathmandu are but symptomatic of broader changes in Sherpa society. How well the Sherpas adjust to these changes will determine the nature of the Sherpa identity they leave for future generations.

[20] GENDER ISSUES

Despite a generally low social status reflecting the influence of Hindu society, Sherpa women have become central to preserving centuries-old customs and traditions of Sherpa culture. In traditional Sherpa society, women assume the role of head of household for up to 10 months of the year while their husbands are away working as porters for foreigners. In addition to rearing the children, women are often left to farm and tend the livestock.

Social position is influenced by Hindu values. Thus, inheritance, ownership of property, and access (or the lack thereof) to education mirrors the situation of women in Hinduism. In recent years, women have tended to break the male monopoly on climbing. Thus, in 2000, Lhakpa Sherpa, from the village of Sankhuwasabha, scaled Everest in a historic all-woman Sherpa expedition and has since successfully climbed Everest several times. However, only a few Sherpas—men or women—benefit from working with as porters or guides with foreign tourists (a top Sherpa guide can earn up to $10,000 per expedition).

Generally, however, Sherpa women suffer from the poverty, illiteracy, poor education, overwork, and low socio-economic standing that is the lot of most women in South Asia.

[21] BIBLIOGRAPHY

Brower, Barbara. *Sherpa of Khumbu: People, Livestock, and Landscape*. Delhi: Oxford University Press, 1991.

Fisher, James B. *Sherpas: Reflections on Change in Himalayan Nepal*. Berkeley: University of California Press, 1990.

Fürer-Haimendorf, Christoph von. *The Sherpas of Nepal: Buddhist Highlanders*. Berkeley and Los Angeles: University of California Press, 1964.

Luger, Kurt. *Kids of Khumbu: Sherpa Youth on the Modernity Trail*. Kathmandu: Mandala Book Point, 2000.

Ortner, Sherry B. *Making Gender: The Politics and Erotics of Culture*. Boston, MA: Beacon Press, 1996.

———. *Sherpas Through Their Rituals*. Cambridge: Cambridge University Press, 1978.

Sherpa, Donna M. *Living in the Middle: Sherpas of the Mid-Range Himalayas*. Prospect Heights, IL: Waveland Press, 1994.

—by D. O. Lodrick

SIKHS

PRONUNCIATION: SEEKS
LOCATION: India (Punjab state)
POPULATION: 19,215,730 (Census of India, 2001)
LANGUAGE: Punjabi
RELIGION: Sikhism
RELATED ARTICLES: Vol. 3: People of India

¹INTRODUCTION

Sikhs are members of a religion that has its origins on the plains of the Punjab in the northwest of the Indian subcontinent. Founded by Nanak (AD 1469–1538) at the very end of the 15th century AD, Sikhism was a branch of the Hindu *bhakti* (devotional) movement that combined aspects of Hindu religious thinking with elements of Islam, in particular Sūfī mysticism. The word *Sikh* comes from the Sanskrit word for "disciple" (*sisya*), the Sikhs being disciples of Nanak and the nine other Sikh *gurus* (teachers) who followed him.

Although in its early years Sikhism was nonviolent in nature, the history of the Sikhs after Gobind Singh (1666–1708), the tenth and last guru, is one of continual strife and bloodshed. The 18th century saw the Sikhs in continual conflict with the Mughals in northern India, with bloody uprisings in the Punjab met with equal ferocity by Muslim imperial forces. Sikhs faced invasions by the Persian ruler Nadir Shah in 1738–39 and the Afghans between 1747 and 1769. In the power vacuum following these conflicts, Ranjit Singh (1780–1839) created a powerful Sikh state in the Punjab that extended from the Sutlej River to Kashmir. This marks the apex of Sikh power and prestige in northern India.

Following Ranjit Singh's death, the Sikh kingdom rapidly disintegrated, and the Punjab was annexed by the British in 1849. After almost a hundred years of relative stability, the Punjab again erupted into violence when British India was partitioned in 1947. Some 2.5 million Sikhs fled western areas of the Punjab that were to become part of Pakistan and settled in India. The communal strife that accompanied the creation of the independent states of India and Pakistan pitted Hindu and Sikh against Muslim, and an estimated 1 million people were killed attempting to cross the borders of the newly formed countries.

²LOCATION AND HOMELAND

Some 19.2 million people, or 1.9% of India's population, are Sikh. Sikhs (there are estimated to be c. 23 million world-wide) are concentrated mostly in and around the Indian state of the Punjab, in the northwest of the country. The general location of this homeland reflects the historical association of the Sikhs with the Punjab, but the political outlines of the Indian state of Punjab have come about relatively recently. The Punjab, literally meaning "Land of the Five Rivers," refers to the fertile plains in the northwest of the Indian subcontinent drained by the five great tributaries of the Indus River—the Jhelum, Chenab, Ravi, Beas, and Sutlej. This region was divided between India and Pakistan in 1947, with Sikhs migrating to the Indian Punjab, or "East Punjab" from Pakistani territory. Agitation over the next two decades by the Sikhs, who regarded themselves as culturally quite distinct from their Hindu neighbors, caused

the Punjab State of India to be divided in two in 1966 by the central government. The northwestern area was separated to create a smaller Punjab State in which Sikhs formed a majority, and the rest became Haryana State. Sizeable communities of Sikhs, i.e. greater than 200,000 people, are found in the Indian states of Haryana, Rajasthān, Uttar Pradesh, Delhi, Maharashtra, Uttaranchal, and Jammu and Kashmir.

The land occupied by the Sikhs today is but a remnant of their former homeland (the present Punjab State in India retains only 14% the size of the original, undivided Punjab territory). It is located on the Indo-Gangetic divide, an area of flat alluvial plains that separate the drainage systems of the Indus and Ganges rivers. Western areas are drained by upper courses of the Beas and Sutlej rivers, but most of the "Land of the Five Rivers" now lies in Pakistan. The region has fertile soils, and agriculture, based on canal and well irrigation, is extremely productive. Punjab is a major producer of wheat and other grains and is considered the "bread-basket" of India. Sikh farmers are regarded as among the best in India.

Sikhs are found in all the major cities of India, although their largest concentration is in Delhi. Sikhs have also migrated to East Africa, the United Kingdom, North America, and commercial centers of Asia, such as Singapore and Hong Kong.

³LANGUAGE

The language of the Sikh religion, as well as of Sikh culture, is Punjabi. A member of the Aryan branch of the Indo-European language family, Punjabi is written in the Gurmukhi script. This was developed during the 16th century by Angad, the second Sikh guru, for the purpose of recording the scriptures of the Sikhs.

⁴FOLKLORE

Sikhism, as a recent, monotheistic religion with a relatively complete recorded history, lacks the elaborate mythology and legend that characterize some other South Asian religions. However, a body of *sakhis* (stories) has grown up recounting the supposed miracles performed by the gurus. The "Hundred Stories" (*Sau Sakhi*) is a collection of prophecies ascribed to Guru Gobind Singh. The Sikh heroes are the gurus who died for their beliefs, and Sikh temples (*gurdwaras*) often have paintings or murals of the two gurus who were martyred by the Muslims. Sikhs, who are Sikh by religion, are also Punjabi in culture, and they share in the folklore and traditions of the Punjab region.

⁵RELIGION

All Sikhs are united by the common bond of religion, in particular their reverence for the Ten Gurus and the teachings that are set out in the sacred scriptures.

Nanak, the founder of Sikhism and its first guru, was born into a Hindu caste in a village in the Punjab. At the age of 30, he underwent a revelation that led him to commence his ministry among the peoples of the region. In his teachings, he embraced the concept of one God, the lack of any need for priests or ceremonial rituals, a classless society, and the equality of women. He worshiped at both Hindu and Muslim holy places and is even said to have gone on pilgrimage to Mecca and Medina.

At Guru Nanak's death, he was succeeded by Angad (1538–1552), who was followed by Amardas (1469–1574). Amardas appointed his own son-in-law, Ramdas (1534–1581), to succeed him and from this time, all the remaining gurus came from the same family. The fifth guru, Arjun Mal (1563-1606), son of Ramdas, began the compilation of the *Adi Granth,* the sacred book of the Sikhs, in 1604. This was a collection of verse containing the writings of the earlier Sikh Gurus, as well as that of Hindu and Muslim saints from northern India. This eventually led to Arjun Mal's death. He was ordered by the Mughal emperor Jehangir to remove all passages of the Granth that contradicted orthodox Muslim belief. Arjun Mal refused and was tortured to death in 1606.

The martyrdom of the fifth guru saw the beginning of the Sikh tradition of militarism. Hargobind (1595–1645), Arjun Mal's son, organized the Sikhs into a military brotherhood and often came into conflict with the ruling powers in northwestern India. Although the next two gurus, Har Rai (1630–1661) and Har Krishnan (1656–1664) are of minor importance, the ninth guru, Tegh Bahadur (1622–1675), was imprisoned and executed by the emperor Aurangzeb.

Gobind Singh, Tegh Bahadur's son, succeeded his father at a young age, becoming the tenth and one of the most important of the Sikh gurus. He announced that there were to be no more gurus after him because the Sikhs had an eternal guru in their scripture (the Adi Granth, also called the *Guru Granth Sahib*). But, as important, he was also responsible for converting the formerly pacifist Sikh religion into a powerful military and political movement. In 1699, he formed the *Khalsa* (the "Pure"), a fighting fraternity of Sikhs who all took the surname "Singh" ("Lion"). He required the Khalsa to wear their hair long and keep their beards unshaven and also to carry a sword on their person. The Khalsa were forbidden to smoke or drink alcohol. These, and other rules established by Gobind Singh, form part of the Sikh religion today.

Sikhism is a monotheistic religion. There is only one God, who is the Creator of the universe and all things in it. Humans alone in the universe have the ability to enter into a voluntary relationship of love with God. However, attachment to the physical world (*maya*) leads to rebirth (*samsara*) as a result of past actions (*karma*). The only way to achieve liberation (*mukti*) is to become God-conscious and God-filled (*gurmukh*). This can be achieved by following the path set out by the Gurus and the scriptures.

Worship, either at home or in the temple, is central to the Sikh community. At the gurdwara, Sikhs bow before the Granth with great reverence. The holy book is placed on a special altar, it is offered flowers, and a temple attendant fans it day and night. On special occasions it is carried in procession, accompanied by the singing of sacred songs. Gurdwaras are more than just places of worship, for they have meeting rooms, and kitchens (*langar*) for providing free food. Surmounting the building is a flag-staff flying a triangular yellow flag bearing the symbol of Sikhism, a quoit with a dagger in the center and two swords crossing beneath. Gurdwaras are found wherever there are Sikh communities, even outside of India. However, the Golden Temple at Amritsar in the Punjab is the most sacred site in the Sikh religion. It was the storming of the Golden Temple by the Indian Army in 1984 in an attempt to dislodge Sikhs opposing the central government that led to the assassination of India's then prime minister, Indira Gandhi.

⁶MAJOR HOLIDAYS

In the 16th century, Guru Amardas initiated the custom of assembling the Sikhs at the time of three important Hindu festivals (Vaisakhi, Divali, and Holi). His purpose was to wean them away from Hinduism, and today these occasions continue to be celebrated as Sikh festivals (*melas*). Vaisakhi, which falls in the middle of April, marks the beginning of the New Year in the Punjab. It is of particular significance in Amritsar, the traditional gathering place of the Sikhs, where it remains an important religious, political, and social occasion. Divali, the Festival of Lights for the Hindus, has much the same meaning for the Sikhs. Gurdwaras are decorated with oil lamps or electric lights, fireworks displays may be held, and small children receive presents. Holi, the spring festival of the Hindus, was originally a time for the Sikhs to gather and undertake military exercises. Today, the principal location of the Sikh Holi is Anandpur, where a fair is held, pilgrims gather, and the flags of all the local gurdwaras are taken out in procession.

The Sikhs also observe a number of *gurpurbs*, holidays related to events in the lives of the gurus. Many of these are local affairs, but three are celebrated worldwide: the birthdays of Guru Nanak (November) and Guru Gobind Singh (December) and the martyrdom of the fifth guru, Arjun Mal (May–June). At these times, the Granth is taken out in procession in the streets of the village or city, bands and speakers are arranged for entertainment, and free food is distributed. A complete reading of the Granth, which takes about 48 hours, is often held at this time.

⁷RITES OF PASSAGE

The birth of a boy or a girl is equally welcome among the Sikhs. After a baby is born, the entire family visits the gurdwara with traditional offerings of money, sweets, and a *rumala*, a piece of brocade or silk for the Granth. After readings from the Granth, the book will be opened at random, and the first word on the left-hand page is read aloud to the parents. The parents will then choose a name beginning with the first letter of the word. The *granthi*, the scripture reader, then announces the chosen name to the congregation, adding Singh ("Lion") after a boy's name and Kaur ("Princess") after a girl's.

In a strict sense, Sikhs are not born Sikhs but are baptized into the religion. (Converts to Sikhism in the West are known as *gora* Sikhs, or "white" Sikhs). Initiation rites are the same for Sikhs and non-Sikhs. Initiates should be over 14 years of age and in possession of the five "Ks" of Sikhism. These are the five symbols Guru Gobind Singh instructed his Khalsa to wear: uncut hair (*kesa*), a comb in the hair (*kanga*), a steel bracelet (*kara*), a sword (*kirpan*), and shorts (*kachha*). The ceremony includes readings from the Granth, an explanation of the principles of the Sikh faith, and the ritual preparation of *amrit* (nectar or sugar water), which is given to the initiates. A newcomer to Sikhism is given a Sikh name in the same manner as a child.

Sikhs cremate their dead, although burial is permissible. Ashes are usually placed in the nearest river. Death rituals are a family affair with the body being washed by members of the family, who ensure it is wearing the five symbols of the Sikh faith. Prayers may be offered in the gurdwara and, when the mourners return home, it is customary for a complete reading of the Granth to occur. The final act is the sharing of a meal by family and mourners, symbolizing the continuity of life and normal social activities in the face of death. Sikhs do not build funeral monuments.

8 INTERPERSONAL RELATIONS

The proper form of address for Sikhs is Sardar (Mr.) or Sardarni (Mrs.). If one does not know a man's name, he is addressed as Sardarji, or Sardar Sahib. Among the peasantry and the working class, a man is usually referred to as Bhaiji, or Bhai Sahib (Brother) and a woman as Bibiji (Mistress), or Bhainji (Sister). The title Giani is used for a scholar or a theologian.

Two forms of greetings are traditional among the Sikhs. In the more common one, a Sikh joins the palms of his or her hands and says "Sat Sri Akal" ("God is Truth"). The second form is practiced by men, especially when addressing large gatherings. The palms are joined and the man says "Wah Guru Ji Ka Khalsa" ("The Sikhs are the Chosen of God"). The response to this is "Wah Guru Ji Ki Fateh" ("God be Victorious").

9 LIVING CONDITIONS

Most Sikhs in the Punjab live in comfortable homes, built around a central courtyard. All villages in the Punjab are electrified, and most households have radios and televisions. Refrigerators and other conveniences of modern living are available to those who can afford them. Road and rail transportation facilities in the region are excellent.

10 FAMILY LIFE

Guru Nanak rejected the caste system of the Hindus. Features of the Sikh religion, such as the common surnames, the common kitchen, and the absence of priests, were intended to remove the distinctions of caste. Yet, Sikh converts were drawn from local Hindu castes, such as the Jats, and caste (*jat* or *zāt*) has not been completely eliminated from the Sikh community. Sikhs will eat together and worship together, but marriages are still usually arranged among the same subgroup or caste, such as Jat, Arora, or Ramgarhia.

Among Sikhs, marriage is not so much an arrangement as it is a joint decision based on considerations like the desires of the couple, caste, social status, and economic considerations. The Sikh family structure is based on the extended family, so the compatibility of the bride with her potential in-laws is a concern. Above all, however, a Sikh should marry a Sikh. The bride and groom may meet each other before the wedding but never alone; Sikhs disapprove of dating. An engagement may occur, but this is not necessary. Child marriage has always been shunned by the Sikhs. The legal age for marriage in India is 18 for women and 21 for men, and Sikhs generally adhere to this practice. Sikhism does not condone the taking or giving of a dowry.

The marriage ceremony is usually held before sunrise. It takes place in the bride's village and can occur anywhere, as long as the Granth is present. The ceremony is accompanied by the chanting of hymns that give advice on marriage, and readings from the Granth. The bride and groom give their consent to the union by bowing towards the Granth. The bride's father ties the end of his daughter's scarf to one worn by the groom, and the couple, led by the groom, circles the Granth four times. At the last circling, flower petals may be thrown. Following the marriage ceremony and further celebrations at the bride's home, the marriage party leaves for the groom's home where

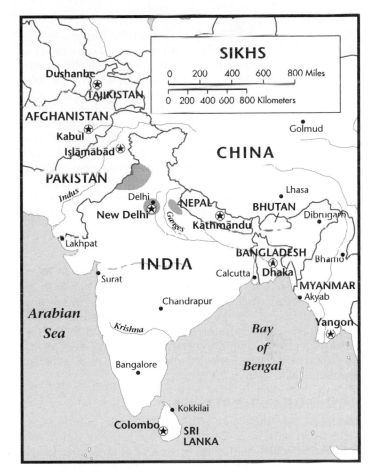

the bride begins her new life. Sikhism does not recognize divorce and has no restrictions against widow remarriage.

11 CLOTHING

Traditional dress for the Sikh is tight-legged trousers, covered by a long shirt (*kurtā*) worn hanging down outside the trousers. This is accompanied by a turban, most commonly the peaked "Patiala" style, the most distinctive item of a male Sikh's clothes. The turban, which is a symbol of religious and social identity, may be of any color. White is often worn at a time of mourning, pink at weddings, and yellow at the spring Basant festival when the mustard crop is flowering. The hair is uncut, tied into a topknot under the turban, and the beard is worn full. Traditional Sikh dress is completed by the remainder of the five "Ks," the comb, the bracelet, the sword, and the shorts. (The wearing of traditional Sikh dress has sometimes raised legal issues in the West, for instance, in countries and states that have motorcycle helmet laws or laws against carrying concealed weapons.)

Sikh women wear the trousers and tunic (*salwar-kamiz*) that is usually associated with Muslims but that is really the regional dress of the Punjab. Along with this, they wear a scarf (*dupattā*) over their shoulders or around their heads.

Western-style dress (pants, shirts, and suits) has become common among men, although the turban is still worn with it. Women have taken to wearing the Indian *sārī*, although only the elites in large cities have adopted modern women's styles of clothing.

[12] FOOD

The staple diet of the Sikhs is typical of the Punjab—wheat, buffalo milk, and milk products. A typical meal consists of flat bread (*rotī*) made from wheat or maize, a cup of lentils or other pulses (*dāl*), and hot tea or buttermilk. In winter, vegetables made from mustard or other greens and served with butter may be added. Though Sikhs are nonvegetarian and are particularly fond of goat meat, the cost of meat means it is only eaten on special occasions. Sikhs are forbidden to eat *halal* meat, that is, meat from an animal whose throat is ritually cut (Muslims can only eat halal meat). Sikhs share the Hindu view on eating beef, and many devout Sikhs will not eat meat, fish, or eggs.

Most Sikhs observe the prescribed taboo on tobacco, but not on liquor. Opium and hashish (*bhang*) are also widely used in rural areas.

[13] EDUCATION

Education, both traditional and modern, has come to be an important aspect of Sikhism. One of the aims of the Singh Sabha, an organization founded in the late 1800s, was to promote education. The Singh Sabha opened hundreds of schools and a college in Amritsar where Sikh religion and Khalsa traditions were included in the curriculum. The Sikh Educational Conferences, meeting annually since 1908, are responsible for promoting education in the community.

[14] CULTURAL HERITAGE

The Sikhs have their own traditions of music, painting, and architecture. The sacred music of the Sikhs is called *Kirtan,* which means singing the praises of God in melody and rhythm. The gurus based their compositions on classical Indian music, combined with elements of popular Punjabi folk tunes. Importance is placed on vocal music, although hymns are accompanied by the drum, the harmonium, and other musical instruments. Although there is no distinct Sikh school of painting, Sikh artists have been part of the Pahari, Kangra, and other traditions of painting that have flourished in northwestern India. A Sikh tradition of portrait painting flourished for a short while under the patronage of Maharaja Ranjit Singh. Sikh architecture, as seen in the gurdwaras, represents a combination of Mughal and Hindu styles, developed in a uniquely Sikh manner.

Beyond their own traditions of sacred literature, Sikhs have also made important contributions to modern Punjabi literature. Sikh writers include Vir Singh, Nanak Singh, and, more recently, the poets Purana Singh, Amrita Pritam, and Prabjhot Kaur. Khushwant Singh, a noted author and journalist, has devoted much of his life to the study of Sikh culture.

[15] WORK

The majority of Sikhs are peasant farmers living in hamlets and villages scattered across the Punjab plains. It was the Sikhs and other peasant farmers in the Punjab who were largely responsible for the success of the Green Revolution in India during the 1960s, when India went from "famine to plenty, from humiliation to dignity." The Green Revolution tripled food production, and the Punjab became known as the "breadbasket of India," with Sikh farmers adapting their farming methods to more mechanized techniques, using high-yielding hybrid seeds, the application of fertilizer, and irrigation. One consequence of this was an in increase in the material wealth of the Sikhs—the

Punjab had the highest per capita income of any state in India during the 1960s. However, many Sikhs are now leaving the land. India's 2001 Census found that only 39% of the working population of Punjab State was employed in agro-business.

There is a strong martial tradition among the Sikhs dating to the formation of the Khalsa by Guru Gobind Singh in 1699. The fighting qualities of the Sikhs were acknowledged by the British after the Anglo-Sikh wars of the 19th century when the British incorporated the Khalsa regiments into their fighting forces. The Sikh regiments remained loyal to the British during the 1857 sepoy uprising and saw distinguished service during the two world wars of the 20th century. At this time, Sikhs made up 20% of the British Indian Army, though they accounted for only 2% of the Indian population. The tradition of military service continues today in the police and armed forces, in which Sikhs have reached the highest officer ranks. Today, Sikhs make up an element in India's armed forces, which is out of all proportion to their population in the country.

Sikhs have also achieved high office in politics and government service. Swaran Singh was appointed to Prime Minister Jawarharlal Nehru's cabinet after Independence and served in various ministerial capacities in several Indian governments. Manmohan Singh, the prime minister in 2008, was finance minister in the Union (central) government from 1991 to 1996, and Giani Zail Singh was president of India from 1982–87.

Manmohan Singh was born in the Punjab in 1932. He is considered one of the most influential figures in India's recent history, mainly because of the economic liberalization he had initiated in 1991 when he was finance minister under Prime Minister Narasimha Rao. Manmohan Singh, as of 2008, headed a rather weak government formed by the United Progressive Alliance (UPA), a coalition of 12 political parties led by the Indian Congress, but which only retained power with the support of the Left Front (which was not a part of the coalition), a group of Indian Communist parties. This caused problems for the prime minister. Since the 1980s, India has been under a nuclear trade embargo by the United States, primarily because it is not a signatory to the Nuclear Non-Proliferation Treaty. The United States has tended to favor General Pervez Musharraf and Pakistan as a result of their assistance in the War on Terror. In early 2006, however, President George W. Bush of the United States visited India and negotiated a treaty, highly favorable to India, which would allow for U.S. nuclear trade with India and cooperation in the areas of domestic nuclear development. Ratification of this treaty by the Indian Parliament, was blocked by the Left Front, which threatened to withdraw its support from the government if the UPA were to bring the treaty to a vote. But Manmohan Singh persuaded the Samajwadi Party (SP), a former adversary based in the eastern state of Uttar Pradesh, to back it over the nuclear deal. So as of 2008, the treaty might be salvaged after all.

[16] SPORTS

There are no sports associated specifically with the Sikh religion. However, Sikhs, who as a group are of impressive physical stature and among the more imposing of the peoples of India, have excelled in the sports arena. Bishen Singh Bedi, the Test (international) cricketer, and Balbir Singh, the Indian field hockey player, are just two of the many Sikhs who have achieved national and international honors in Indian sports.

¹⁷ENTERTAINMENT AND RECREATION

There are no forms of entertainment and recreation associated specifically with Sikhs, although they enjoy Punjabi games, folk songs, and dances. In keeping with the Sikh martial tradition, sword-play is a popular pastime among men. Sikhs are also fond of telling jokes about themselves.

¹⁸FOLK ART, CRAFTS, AND HOBBIES

Among the arts and crafts for which Sikhs are known is hand embroidery work on cloth known as *Phulkari*. The Rumala offered to the gurdwara on the occasion of a birth is a piece of brocade or silk embroidered with religious symbols and lettering that is used to decorate the Guru Grant Sahib. In Amritsar there is a tradition of ivory-carving, with images of Hindu deities, Sikh portraits, and replicas of the Golden Temple being offered to the pilgrim visiting the city.

¹⁹SOCIAL PROBLEMS

A major problem that the Sikh community faced in the recent past was that of Sikh separatism. Despite the creation in 1966 of a Punjabi-speaking state with a Sikh majority, a section of the Sikh community continued to demand a greater degree of autonomy. The Akali Dal, a religious movement originally founded in 1920 to gain control of the community's gurdwaras but that has since developed into a political party, set out its demands in the Anandpur Sahib Resolution in 1973. Implicit in this resolution was the idea that the Sikhs were a nation separate from the Hindus, and this eventually led to extremist demands for an independent Sikh state of "Khalistan."

For over 20 years, the Punjab was the scene of a struggle between Sikh militants and the central Indian government, with moderates from both sides caught in the deadly crossfire. In the 1970s and 80s, a movement, which was probably not supported by most Punjabis, began in the Punjab to secede from the Indian Union and create a separate, sovereign Sikh state of "Khalistan." Allegedly supported by the Pakistani Inter-Services Intelligence agency, the movement reached its peak during mid 1980s under Jarnail Singh Bhindranwale. It then slowly ebbed, primarily due to the loss of popular support. The movement also hindered economic investment, became increasingly militant, and threw Punjab into a state of anarchy with increased levels of terrorism. The movement resulted in counter-terrorism operations conducted by the Indian Army and the Punjab Police which caused the deaths of thousands of innocent Sikhs according to Human Rights Watch. Politicians and leaders were assassinated, the lives of common people were disrupted by terrorism, and hundreds—if not thousands of Sikhs were murdered. In Operation Blue Star, the Indian Army was sent to attack the Golden Temple in Amritsar to dislodge the followers of Bindranwale, the extremist Sikh religious leader who opposed the government in Delhi. This violation of the most sacred of Sikh holy places led directly to the assassination of Prime Minister Indira Gandhi by two of her Sikh security guards. In reprisal for her death, hundreds of Sikhs were killed by Hindus in Delhi and other northern cities. After the bombing of Air India Flight 182, an alleged attack by Sikh separatists that claimed the lives of 329 Canadian civilians over the Irish Sea in 1985, support for Khalistan lessened considerably.

However, the anti-Sikh riots across Northern India in 1984 had repercussions in Punjab State. Thousands of innocent Hindus and Sikhs were killed by extremists of both religions,

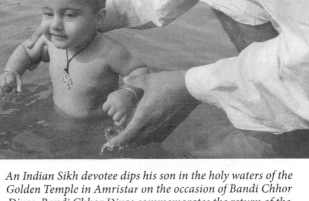

An Indian Sikh devotee dips his son in the holy waters of the Golden Temple in Amristar on the occasion of Bandi Chhor Divas. Bandi Chhor Divas commemorates the return of the sixth guru to the holy city of Amristar after his release from detention. (Narinder Nanu/AFP/Getty Images)

trains were attacked, and people were shot after being pulled from buses. In 1987, 32 Hindus were pulled out of a bus and shot, near Lalru in Punjab by Sikh militants. According to Human Rights Watch, "In the beginning of the 1980s, Sikh separatists in Punjab committed serious human rights abuses, including the massacre of civilians, attacks upon non-Sikhs in the state, and indiscriminate bomb attacks in crowded places." Indira Gandhi's son, Rajiv Gandhi, who succeeded his mother as India's prime minister, tried unsuccessfully to bring peace to the Punjab. In 1985 an Accord was signed between Rajiv Gandhi and Sant Harchand Singh Longowal, president of the Akali Dal, yielding to many of the Sikhs' demands (e.g. transfer of Chandigarh to Punjab as its state's capital), but Longowal was assassinated in 1985. Few of the Accord's terms were implemented by New Delhi. Between 1987 and 1991, Punjab was placed under the president's rule and was governed from the center. Elections were eventually held in 1992 but the voter turnout at 24% was very poor. A new Congress (I) government was formed, and it gave the police chief of the state K. P. S. Gill a free hand to quell the insurgency. Gill was ruthless against the insurgents, and his methods severely weakened the insurgency movement. However, Gill's reign is also regarded as one of the bloodiest in the history of the country: thousands of innocents were killed in fake encounters and countless disappeared from their homes. The Punjab police were also accused of crimes, such as rape and torture of women and children, according to several reports by Amnesty International and Human Rights Watch. Life in the Punjab is slowly returning to normal. Sikhs and Hindus have lived side by side for almost 500 years, and many deplore the violent events of the last several decades. But a lasting solution to the Punjab problem seems to depend on at least two fundamental issues: Sikh recognition that no Indian government could ever grant independence to such a strategically important region, and New Delhi's willingness to resolve legitimate grievances of the Sikhs. The third and, perhaps, unknown factor in this equation remains the Sikh religion itself.

[20] GENDER ISSUES

Although the Sikh gurus preached gender equality, in actual fact in Sikh society women are treated very much as they are by Hindus and Sikh women face many of the same issues as are found in Hindu society. Thus, Sikh families have a preference for male children and boys tend to be treated much better than girls. Female infanticide and sex selective abortions are a problem and the Census of India 2001 shows that the Sikh community has the lowest ratio of females to males of any religious community in India. The ratio of men and women in Punjab is so out of balance that young, light-skinned girls from poor areas such as Nepal are being brought to the Punjab where they are sold as wives to wealthy peasant farmers.

Women cannot participate in *Panj Piaray* and other Sikh rituals and the way they are treated by men certainly belies their theoretical "equality." Only in 2005 did the religious promotion and affairs committee of the Shiromani Gurudwara Prabandhak Committee (SGPC)—the governing body for Sikh shrines—decide that Sikh women would be allowed to perform *kirtan* (singing hymns) and *palki sewa* (carrying the Sikh holy book Guru Granth Sahib in a palanquin) on religious occasions, a decision that caused an outcry in the Sikh community.

It is not uncommon for Sikh women to be subjected to physical and sexual abuse by their husbands, while rape, torture, and killings—committed by both militants and Indian security forces—was a problem during the recent "troubles" in the Punjab.

[21] BIBLIOGRAPHY

Banerjee, Himadri, ed. *The Khalsa and the Punjab*. New Delhi: Tulika Books, 2002.

Cole, W. Owen, and Piara Singh Sambhi. *The Sikhs: Their Religious Beliefs and Practices*. 2nd rev. ed. Brighton: Sussex Academic Press, 1995.

Grewal, J. S. *The Akalis: A Short History*. Chandigarh: Punjab Studies Publications, 1996.

McLeod, W. H. *The Sikhs: History, Religion, Society*. New York: Columbia University Press, 1989.

Singh, Khushwant. *The History of the Sikhs*. 2 vols. London: Oxford University Press, 1991.

———. *The Sikhs Today: Their Religion, History, Culture, Customs and Way of Life*. Bombay: Orient. Longmans, 1959.

Singh, Patwant. *The Sikhs*. New Delhi: Rupa, 2002.

—by D. O. Lodrick

SINDHIS

PRONUNCIATION: SIN-deez
LOCATION: Pakistan (Sind province)
POPULATION: 35 million (estimate)
LANGUAGE: Sindhi
RELIGION: Islam (majority Sunnī Muslim)

[1] INTRODUCTION

Sindhis are inhabitants of Sind (or Sindh), the region of arid plains and deserts located along the lower course of the Indus River as it flows on its journey from the Himalayas to the Arabian Sea. Both the terms Sindhi and Sind are derived from "Sindhu," the ancient name of the Indus. Modern Sindhis are descendants of the many peoples who have settled in the area from earliest times.

The Indus is central to the history of the Sindhis. It was along this river that the Harappan (or Indus Valley) civilization developed during the 3rd millennium BC. Usually identified with Dravidian peoples, this sophisticated urban culture matched the achievements of Mesopotamia and ancient Egypt. The Harappans left an archeological record of contemporary life in Sind, but we know less of the centuries following their decline. From around 1700 BC onward, successive waves of Aryan invaders entered the Indian subcontinent from the northwest. The earliest of these nomadic tribes settled in the Punjab, where the outlines of Hindu Vedic religion and society emerged. This was quite different from urban Harappan culture. It was nonurban, based on the herding of cattle; its religion was dominated by male deities and sacrificial ritual; and its society was organized into a hierarchy of classes (castes), with the Aryans at the top and local non-Aryan peoples at the lowest levels. As the Aryans pressed steadily southward along the Indus Valley, their culture replaced that of the Harappans. The Harappan towns and cities disappeared, with Aryan (Hindu) civilization emerging as the dominant culture of Sind. Subsequently, groups such as the Persians, Greeks, Scythians, and White Huns who entered the region were absorbed into the existing structure of the Aryan-dominated society. During the 3rd and 2nd centuries BC, Sind formed part of the Mauryan Empire. At this time, Buddhism was the main religion in the region, though it was subsequently reabsorbed by Hinduism.

Arabs reached the mouth of the Indus by sea in AD 711 and within a few years gained control of Sind. From this time on, the region was dominated by Muslims and the culture of Islam. Around AD 900, the Arab governors of Sind—at first subject to the Caliph in Baghdad—established their own dynastic rule. Of mixed Arab and local blood, Sumra and Samma chieftains governed for several centuries, eventually being replaced by invaders from Afghanistan between 1518 and 1522. By the end of the 16th century, Sind was annexed by the Mughals. It remained part of the Mughal Empire until the mid-18th century. Sind was conquered by the British in 1843. (The British General, Sir Charles Napier, in charge of the operation, garnered a degree of notoriety when, after his successful campaign, he sent his superiors the one word dispatch "Peccavi," which is Latin for "I have sinned.")

Sind formed part of the Bombay Presidency of British India until 1937, when it was made a separate province. Following

Pakistan's independence, Sind was integrated into West Pakistan in 1955. In 1970 Sind was reestablished as a province of Pakistan.

²LOCATION AND HOMELAND

Sind lies in southern Pakistan. It shares a common boundary with the Republic of India on the east. The Pakistani province of Baluchistan lies to the west and north, while the Punjab is located to the northeast. Sind covers an area of 140,913 sq km (54,407 sq mi), which is slightly larger than New York State. Geographically, Sind falls into three distinct regions. In the west lies the Kirthar Range, a steep wall of mountains rising from 1,220 m (4,000 ft) in the south to nearly 2,400 m (approximately 8,000 ft) in the north. This forms a sharp line of separation between the rugged hills of Baluchistan and the fertile Indus plains. The Indus River flows in a southwesterly direction through the heart of Sind. It is here that agriculture and population, as well as Sind's major cities, are concentrated. To the east of the Indus plains, Sind extends into the Thar or Great Indian Desert.

The climate of Sind is subject to extremes. The mean maximum June temperature in Jacobabad in northern Sind is 45.5°C (114°F). Jacobabad has also recorded the highest temperature in the subcontinent, at 53°C (127°F). Temperatures drop to 2°C (36°F) in winter and fall below freezing at higher elevations. Annual rainfall averages less than 20 cm (approximately 8 in) and in some areas falls below 10 cm (4 in). This extreme aridity is reflected in the natural vegetation, which consists mainly of thorn scrub, acacias, and tamarisk.

Population statistics for Sind are notoriously inaccurate. In 1998 Pakistani government sources placed the population of Sind Province at 30,439,893, which, given natural increase since the beginning of the 2000s, led to 35 million as an estimate of the population of Sind by 2008. With several millions of Sindhis living in India and elsewhere (Hong Kong, Singapore, the United States, etc.), the world-wide population of Sindhis is estimated to be over 40 million. Although unified by religion and language, this population reflects the diversity of Sind's past in its ethnic composition. Many Sindhis are descended from Rājput and Jat groups of western India and are known as Samma Sindhis (descendants of Yadavs) and Sumra Sindhis (descendants of Parwar Rājputs). The Bhutto tribe, which gave Pakistan two prime ministers (Zulfikar Ali Bhutto and more recently his daughter, Benazir), are Sumras. Other Rājput and Jat groups are more recent converts to Islam. Some Sindhis, such as the Sayyids and Pathans, trace their ancestry back to Muslim invaders of the past. The Mallahs are fishing peoples settled along the river and in the delta region. The Talpurs, former rulers of Sind, are Baluchs from Baluchistan. However, they now speak Sindhi as a mother tongue and have been assimilated into Sindhi society.

Most Sindhis are Muslim, but before the creation of India and Pakistan some 20% of the Sindhi population was Hindu. In 1947, when the successor states to British India gained their independence, there was a mass exodus of Hindu Sindhis to India. Sindhi communities in India are concentrated in Delhi and the states of Gujarat, Rājasthān, Maharashtra, and Madhya Pradesh. At the same time, many Muslims in India fled their homeland and settled in Sind. Known as *muhājirs,* these immigrants and their descendants are culturally quite distinct from the Sindhis.

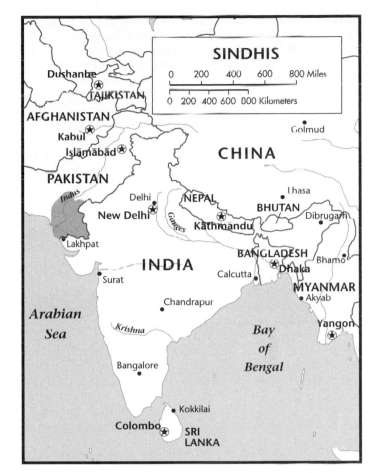

³LANGUAGE

The peoples of Sind speak the language known as Sindhi. It is an Indo-Aryan tongue but has a large number of Persian and Arabic words, reflecting centuries of Muslim influence in the region. Vicholi is the standard dialect of Sindhi, while Siraiki, Thareli, and Lari are other local forms of the language. Kachchi, a dialect of Sindhi, is spoken in neighboring areas of India (the Rann of Kutch, and the Kathiawar Peninsula). The Sindhi script is similar to that used for Urdu, yet different enough not to be read easily by a person who has learned Urdu. The script is Perso-Arabic in origin, even though Sindhi is an Indo-Aryan language. Hindus use a form of the Devanagari script for writing Sindhi. Some 2.5 million Sindhi-speakers lived in India as of 2008.

Perhaps the language closest to the original Prakit and Sanskrit of all the tongues of north India, Sindhi has a literary tradition that extends back to the 11th century. The earliest Sindhi works were poetry showing both Islamic and Hindu influences, though later epics emerged as important. Perhaps the best known Sindhi poet, Shah Abdul Letif (1690–1773) emerged during the early 18th century, while modern Sindhi literature consists of works of both poetry (dominated by the giant figure of Shaikh Ayaz [1923–1997]) and prose.

⁴FOLKLORE

Sind has a rich and varied folklore. One folk tale addresses the relations between Hindus and Muslims in the region. In the 10th century AD, so the story goes, a Muslim ruler in Sind began forcibly converting Hindus to Islam. The Hindus panicked and prayed to Darya Shah (Varuna, god of the Indus) to protect them. The answer to their prayers was Uderolal who, riding a horse and with a sword in his hand, struck terror into the hearts of the Muslims. He told people that there was only one god—Allah or Ishwar—and that both Muslims and Hindus should worship that one god. The Muslim ruler was suitably chastened and stopped his forcible conversions to Islam. Uderolal is identified with Zindapir (Sindhu Pīr), who disappeared into the river Sindhu along with his horse and sword. This water deity is worshiped by both Muslims and Hindus, who depend on the waters of the Indus for their livelihood.

5 RELIGION

Over 93% of the population of Sind is Muslim, mostly belonging to the orthodox *Sunnī* sect. As such, their religious practices and social customs follow the dictates of Islam as set out in the *Quran* (Koran) and summarized in the Five Pillars of Islam. Their modes of worship, religious festivals, rites of passage, family law and customs, and food taboos reveal the importance of Islam in Sindhi culture.

The worship of Muslim saints (*pirs*) is one aspect of Sindhi religion that deviates from orthodox Islam. Historically, the region has been extremely receptive to the Sūfī movement, and one of the most revered saints of Sind today is Lal Shabhaz Qalander, a 13th-century Sūfī. Saint worship and its attendant rituals reflect Hindu influences in Sind, and indeed in the past—especially at the level of folk religion—there was a great deal of mixing of Muslim and Hindu religious practices. It is not unusual for Muslims and Hindus to venerate the same saint. The patron saint of the Indus River, for example, is revered by Muslims as Khwajah Khidr, or Sheikh Tahir, and by Hindus, as Darya Shah, or Uderolal.

6 MAJOR HOLIDAYS

As orthodox Sunnis, Sindhis celebrate all the major Muslim festivals (e.g., Muharram, Ramadan, Id ul-Fitr, Id ul-Adha). However, festivals of particular importance in Sind are the death-anniversaries (*Urs*) of three local saints. Lal Shahbaz Qalandar, who is said to have died in AD 1345, is buried in the village of Sehwan, near Lake Manochar in central Sind. People from all over the country attend his Urs, which is an occasion for the gathering of musicians, *qawwālī*-singers, and dancers. The *melā* held to observe this Urs is, in effect, a festival of Sindhi culture, folk music, and dance. The Urs of Shah Abdul Latif, a mystic poet born in AD 1689, and Sachal Sarmast, an 18th-century poet, are also major festivals celebrated by Sindhis.

7 RITES OF PASSAGE

Three ceremonies are associated with birth in Sindhi life: naming, head-shaving, and circumcision. Naming takes place soon after birth, immediately after the father or an elderly male relation has whispered the Call to Prayer into the baby's ear. The head-shaving ceremony is held in the first few weeks after birth. Goats are sacrificed (one for a girl and two for a boy), and the meat is cooked and given to relatives. The goats' bones are buried with the infant's hair. Circumcision (*sunnat*) usually takes place in early boyhood. The boy is garlanded and taken around the town in procession before the circumcision

is performed by a barber at the family home. When the boy has recovered, a celebration is held for family and friends.

When a death is about to occur, relatives gather to participate in the death rituals. Passages from the Koran are read, the Muslim creed is repeated, and prayers are offered for the dying person. After death, the body is washed, the big toes are tied together, and the corpse is wrapped in a shroud in preparation for burial. The body is carried to the cemetery on a bier by close relatives. At the graveside the mourners, led by a *maulvī* (religious teacher), pray for the departed soul. The body is placed in the grave on its side with the face towards Mecca. Prayers for the dead, followed by a feast, are held on the third and tenth days after the death. The mourning ritual is completed with a feast for all relatives on the 40th day after the death.

8 INTERPERSONAL RELATIONS

Sindhis follow forms of greeting ("Salaam," "Salaam alaikum") used by Muslims throughout the Islamic world. Many, however, still use the Hindu "Namaste," echoing the former presence of a large Hindu population in the region. No visitors are allowed to enter a Sindhi home without the consent of the head of the family. A special room or building called an *otak*, which is often outside the walls of the house compound, is the center of Sindhi men's social life. Inside the otak, friends join together to pass the time chatting, discussing politics, drinking refreshments, playing cards, and in modern times listening to the radio or watching television.

9 LIVING CONDITIONS

Architecture in Sind has a pronounced Arab flavor. Villages consist of clusters of houses, surrounded by compounds, and walled for privacy. Wooden gates often shut off the compound from the outside world. Houses themselves are generally built of unbaked mud bricks, roofed with straw or bamboo. Poor people have a single room for eating and sleeping, and their houses are sparsely furnished. The houses of the landowners are more elaborate and may be built of brick and have tiled roofs. They have several rooms, with a cookhouse and a latrine in the compound (the poor go into the fields to perform their bodily functions). The otak of the wealthy are furnished with carpets, overhead fans that are swung by servants, tables, and chairs.

10 FAMILY LIFE

Sindhi society is predominantly Muslim. However, it shows the influence of its Hindu past in its organization into *zāts*. These are hereditary, occupational groupings (e.g., cultivators, blacksmiths, weavers, barbers) that function very much like Hindu castes. Zāts are further subdivided into *birādarīs,* groups of individuals within the *zāt* who can trace their lineage on the male side to a common ancestor. The biradari is an important social unit within the village.

The family is the basic unit in Sindhi society. It is organized along the lines of the patriarchal joint family. The male head of the family is the dominant authority, responsible for the family's affairs. His wife or wives, as Sindhis may have more than one, run the household. The wives of sons reside in the household, while daughters live with their husband's family after marriage. Marriages among Sindhis are arranged, with partners sought from within one's zāt or biradari. The ideal marriage is between first cousins (i.e., a male marries his fa-

Women of the Sindhi community carry earthen pots during a religious procession to mark the end of a festival in Ahmadabad, India. (AP Images/Ajit Solanki)

ther's brother's daughter). If a suitable bride is not available, a male can marry outside his clan, even into a zāt that is socially inferior to his. However, no father would allow his daughter to "marry down" into a zāt of lower social standing. Betrothal of infants was common in the past, although this is no longer practiced. The marriage ceremony (nikāh) is preceded by several days of festivities. The groom and his party travel to the bride's house in an elaborately decorated transport (car, donkey, or camel). The actual ceremony involves each partner being asked three times if he or she will have the other in marriage. The marriage settlements are agreed to and witnessed, and the ceremony is completed by readings from the Koran by a maulvī. (Hindus in Sind perform their marriage ceremonies according to the Vedic rites.) Divorce is permitted by Muslim law.

The custom of *purdah* is strictly observed by landowners and other groups who claim high social standing. Sindhi women are secluded behind the clay walls of the house and compound. If they leave the house, they go veiled or covered from head to toe in a cloak so that they are not exposed to the sight of men. In some rural areas, women are followed by a small boy ringing a hand bell and calling "Pass!" Men hearing the signal turn toward a wall until the party has hurried past. By contrast, purdah is ignored by many in urban areas.

¹¹ CLOTHING

The original dress of the Sindhi male is the *dhotī*, a type of coat (*jāmā*), and a turban. A round, embroidered cap, cut away in the front, is commonly worn by Sindhi men. As with many societies in South Asia, different communities within Sind have developed their own distinctive style of dress. Thus, Amils have adopted flowing pyjamas, high-topped caps, and leather slippers with their toes curled up. They follow the custom of tying a *kamarband* (i.e., cummerbund) around the waist. Muslim influence can be seen in the *salwar* (loose baggy trousers) and *serwānī* (a long, tunic-like coat). Hindu communities have their own styles of dress. Traders and businessmen, for example, favor the Marwari-style turban of Rājasthān.

Traditional dress for older Sindhi women consists of a white cotton tunic and a thick white or red skirt that reaches the ground. The head is covered with a thin muslin scarf that is larger than the modern *dupattā*. Slippers complete the ensemble. Sometimes, a white sheet (*chāddar*) is worn covering the entire body, with only a small peep hole (*ākhirī*) left open so that the wearer can see. Younger women wear the *salwār-kurtā*, or the *sūthan*, a pyjama-type outfit, along with slippers and the scarf. Mirrorwork on the kurtā is typical of Sind. Ornaments include ivory bracelets and bangles, silver anklets, and gold earrings and nose rings.

Sindhis, especially in urban areas, have abandoned traditional dress in favor of modern styles. Men wear Western-style jackets and pants, or the popular safari suit. The *sārī*, or salwār-kurta, is the dress of choice for women. Young women, especially in the cosmopolitan city of Karachi, are very style-conscious and adopt the latest fashions.

¹²FOOD

Sindhi food is typical of Pakistani Muslim cuisine, with distinctive Sindhi regional touches. Thus, wheat made into flat unleavened bread called *chapātīs,* or *rotī,* is the staple food for most of the population. It is eaten with spiced pulses *(dāl),* vegetable dishes *(sabzī),* and yogurt *(dahī).* Few poorer Sindhis can afford meat, except on special occasions. Lamb, goat, and chicken are eaten, though no Muslim Sindhi will eat pork. Fish is eaten by Sindhi communities who live along the Indus River or near the coast (Karachi is famous for its seafood). Sweetened tea, buttermilk, or lassi, a drink made from yogurt, rounds out the meal. Sindhis also prepare Mughal-style dishes such as *tandoorī* lamb or chicken, *biryānī* (lamb or chicken cooked with rice), and rice pilaf.

¹³EDUCATION

Though Sindhi literacy (56%) is higher than the Pakistani average (50% for Pakistanis over 15 years of age), Sindhis still face problems in education typical of the country as a whole. In rural areas, children must work in the fields, the school drop-out rate is high, and there is a Muslim antipathy to education for females. Literacy among males in rural areas is 39% but among women it is only 13%. However, urban males have the highest literacy in the country, with that in Karachi being over 90%, and reaching 100% amongst communities, such as the Parsis. Among the elite, education—even of daughters—is seen as a matter of prestige and a means of political power. For example, Pakistan's former prime minister, Benazir Bhutto, was educated at Harvard and Oxford. Sind University, located in Hyderabad, and Karachi University are the major academic centers in the province.

¹⁴CULTURAL HERITAGE

Important sites, such as Mohenjo-Daro, Amri, and Kot Diji, have left a record of the achievements of the ancient Harappan civilization in the areas of city-planning and building, economic production, social organization, and religion. It is generally held that there is little direct continuity of cultural tradition between the Harappans and modern-day society. However, some writers trace elements of modern Sindhi folk culture to Harappan times. They argue, for example, that the bullock carts used by farmers along the Indus today, or the pipes played by Sindhi shepherds, differ little from those used by the Harappans, as revealed by the archeological record.

Sindhis have a rich tradition of folk literature and mystical Sūfī poetry dating to the 14th century AD or even earlier. The legend of Dodo Chanesar, for example, an early Sindhi folk tale, is thought to date to the time of the Sumras. The most famous Sindhi poet, however, is Shah Abdul Latif, whose work, *Shāh Jo Risālo,* is known and recited throughout Sind. Sachal Sarmast (AD 1739–1829) is another eminent Sūfī in the Sindhi literary tradition. In addition to poetry, Sindhi folk culture embraces music, using instruments, such as the *sahnāī* (a wind instrument), dances, songs, and riddles.

¹⁵WORK

Traditionally, Sind lacked the pan-Indian four-tiered caste system (*Brahman, Kshatriya, Vaishya* and *Sudra*). Brahmans, who elsewhere in the Indian subcontinent enjoyed high ritual status, were numerically insignificant. They were neither learned nor affluent, functioning only as priests to the Hindu trading castes. There was no question of royal patronage as the region was under Muslim rule. Since no Sindhi Hindus formed part of the nobility or army, Kshatriyas were notably absent from the region, as were Sudras, the castes who were tillers of the soil (these were mainly Muslims) or the service castes. The main Hindu communities in Sind were, thus, of the trading caste—e.g. the Lohanas, Bhatias, Khatris, Chhaprus and Sahtas—and social hierarchies among these groups were primarily based on wealth. This social structure was unique to Sind, and regional identity became more pronounced than caste identity.

Around 70% of Sindhis, the majority of these being Muslims, derive their living from cultivation. Given the meager rainfall totals in the region, agriculture is dependent almost entirely on irrigation. The principal source of water is the Indus River, on which there are three major irrigation dams (called "barrages") in Sind. They are the Ghuddu and Sukkur Barrages in the north, and the Kotri Barrage in the south near Hyderabad. The major crops grown include wheat, millet, maize, rice, cotton, and oilseeds. Fruits, such as mangoes, dates, and bananas, are also cultivated. Away from the Indus Valley, herding sheep, goats, and camels has become the dominant economic activity. Fishing is important along the Indus River and the Arabian Sea coast, where prawns, shrimp, pomfret, shad, and catfish are caught.

Although Sind is essentially a rural province, the provincial capital, Karachi, is Pakistan's largest city, with a population of over 13 million inhabitants. Karachi is Pakistan's leading commercial and industrial center, giving Sind an important role in the country's economy. Industrial plants include cotton mills, sugar refineries, cement factories, steel mills, and automobile manufacturers.

¹⁶SPORTS

Sindhi children play local variations of games, such as hopscotch, marbles, and tag. Wrestling is a popular spectator sport in villages, while men indulge in traditional pastimes, such as cock-fighting, pigeon-racing, and camel-racing. Sindhis also play modern games, such as cricket, field hockey, tennis, and squash.

¹⁷ENTERTAINMENT AND RECREATION

Sindhis enjoy watching television or videos, seeing movies, playing cards, and socializing at cocktail parties. Such pastimes are, of course, more common among the Westernized Sindhis living in urban areas. Life is more restricted in the traditional village context.

¹⁸FOLK ARTS, CRAFTS, AND HOBBIES

Sind is particularly noted for its textiles, embroidery, pottery, and lacquered woodwork. Mirrorwork, the sewing of tiny pieces of mirror onto cloth, is typically Sindhi and decorates the brightly colored clothes of many Sindhi women. Blue-glazed tiles from Sind decorate mosques and shrines all over the country.

¹⁹SOCIAL PROBLEMS

Sindhis face many of the problems suffered by all rural, agricultural populations in developing countries. Population pressure, poverty, lack of education, and rural indebtedness contribute to low standards of living for the mass of the people. Migration of the rural poor to the cities has created huge squatter populations in Karachi and other towns, as well as an inadequate agricultural labor force in rural areas.

The most serious problems, however, relate to ethnic conflict in Sind and the volatility of Pakistan's politics. Sind's political fortunes have been closely linked to those of the Bhutto family. Sindhis have long resented the concentration of political power in the hands of Punjabis, along with perceived threats to Sindhi cultural identity. Attempts to replace the Sindhi language in schools with Urdu, and the national government's policy of Islamization, have both been strongly resisted. Conflict between Sindhis and Urdu-speaking muhājirs, who comprise an estimated 25% of Sind's population (and 70% of Karachi's population), has led to violence and many deaths. Murders, kidnappings, drug gangs, sectarian violence, and ethnic conflict are commonplace in Karachi, where even Pakistan's security forces have been unable to restore law and order.

Access to adequate supplies of water, both for drinking and irrigation, remains a major problem in Sind. The area is essentially desert, with precipitation averaging less than 8 inches a year, and the major source of water is the Indus River. However, the Punjabis seem to control most of the Indus water, and lack of water has provoked hundreds of angry demonstrations in Sind, with farmers and politicians alike charging that "water robbery" has been committed by Punjab Province. Even the Water and Power Development Authority (WAPDA), created by Pakistan after the 1960 Indus Basin Waters Treaty was signed with India, appears to be violating the 1945 Sind-Punjab agreement on water sharing, with total disregard for the lower riparian rights of Sindh. Virtually all of the crops grown in Sind (rice, cotton and cereals) depend on irrigation, and when water is not available, they are lost.

In addition to these economic losses, the reduced flows that characterize the River Indus as a result of water withdrawals in its Upper Basin, has resulted in severe water pollution. The river receives raw sewage from about 40 cities and hundreds of small towns and villages, untreated industrial wastewater from hundreds of industrial facilities, and irrigation returns from the millions of acres of agricultural lands spread along the riverbanks. Although it is attempting to reduce use because of health hazards, Pakistan still uses around 25,000 tons of chemical nutrients and pesticides in a year. With population growth and reduced water flows, Indus pollution is worsening. Levels of oxygen depleting organic contaminants from sewage, toxic compounds from industrial discharges, and pesticides and chemical nutrients from irrigation returns are increasing. Water borne diseases are on the rise. Many fish and other aquatic species have declined in number and diversity. If the situation is not reversed further water degradation will continue to occur, and its impact on aquatic life, public health, and other uses of water will be very significant.

The lakes and wetlands of Sind are being degraded at an alarming rate. The lakes in Sind are an important source of drinking water, recreation, fish, edible vegetables that grow in them, and employment for many people. With the lower Indus basin receiving reduced flows, the lakes and wetlands of the Sind are losing their inflow and slowly becoming polluted, and smaller ones are even drying out. Manochar, for instance, the largest lake in Sind is a source of drinking water and irrigation, but has become a dumping ground for discharge from salinity outfalls originating in Punjab and Baluchistan. Millions of people have been affected and thousands of Manochar fishermen have migrated to other areas of Pakistan. Furthermore, salt water intrusion into the plains of lower Sind is directly related to the decrease of flow in the Indus River. Salt-water intrusion has been witnessed inland up to 100 kilometers (over 60 mi) north of the sea.

In 2008, a breach appeared in the Rohri Canal at Tehsil, New Saeedabad, District Matiari, Sind Province, resulting in heavy losses to local peasants, including damage to standing crops, houses, roads, bridges, water courses, and embankments. The breaches inundated many villages nearby and caused extensive damage to houses in the vicinity. The floods affected 90% of the population of 50 villages involving over 19,000 persons. Over 300 houses were destroyed completely, and over 2,000 hectares (c. 5,000 acres) of cultivated land were inundated. The crops lost included both commercial and food staples, including rice. This was the third time in ten years that breaches occurred in this area, and the ministry of irrigation, which is responsible for checking the stability of the canal embankments on a regular basis, was tardy in providing assistance to the affected people. June 2007 saw torrential rains and flooding in Sind Province as it was hit by cyclone "Yemyin." The latter left vast areas of the region flooded with several hundreds dead and missing and substantial collateral damage to houses, livestock, and crops. Such natural disasters are not unique. In January 2001, when Gujarat—to the east—was hit by a devastating earthquake, Sind also experienced some deaths and significant damage to buildings.

On the political scene, Sindhis are outnumbered by Punjabis, who are seen as dominating the politics of Pakistan. However, Benazir Bhutto, a former Prime Minister of Pakistan, was a Sindhi and her Pakistan People's Party (PPP) was widely expected to win the 2008 elections outright. However, Bhutto was assassinated on 27 December 2007 and her husband, Asif Ali Zardari, replaced her as leader of the PPP. The elections in Pakistan were postponed for a month as a result of the assassination and the PPP emerged as the leader of an anti-Musharraf coalition. The PPP won a majority of seats in the National Assembly, though not enough to form the government by itself. However, the PPP, in association with Nawaz Sharif's Muslim League (N), formed the Pakistani government, with Yousaf Raza Gilani (Gilani was born in Karachi and thus is a Sindhi), a loyalist of slain leader Benazir Bhutto, as the nation's new prime minister.

²⁰GENDER ISSUES

Sindhī women live in either Hindu or Muslim societies, both of which are patrilineal in nature. As a consequence, they are generally prohibited by law from inheriting property and see their role in society as wife and home-maker, subservient to the wishes of their children, husbands, and in-laws. Marriages are typically arranged, according to local customs, and—even though it is illegal in India (Pakistan has no legal proscriptions against the practice)—dowry is usually given. Bride burnings are commonly reported in both India and Pakistan, and the press occasionally reports "honor" killings in Sind. In 1998 the adult sex ratio (i.e. among people over 6 years of age) in Sind was 891:1000, indicating the importance of males in Sindhi society. The low number of females is explained largely by sex selective abortion and neglect of young girl children.

Even though Sindhī women have emigrated to other parts of the world where they may be involved in business, Sindhī attitudes towards the role of women in society are mirrored in a marked lack of ambition.

Poverty, illiteracy, lack of education, and cultural attitudes are the greatest problems faced by women in Sind.

²¹BIBLIOGRAPHY

Bharadwaj, Prakash. *Sindhīs through the Ages*. Vols. 1 & 2. Kowloon, Hong Kong: World-Wide Publishing Co., 1988.

Jotwani, Motilal. *The Sindhis Through the Centuries*. New Delhi: Aditya Books, 2006.

Khan, Mubarak Ali. *Essays on the History of Sindh*. Lahore : Fiction House, 2005.

Khan, Zahid Ansar. *History and Culture of Sind*. Karachi: Royal Book Company, 1980.

Lambrick, H. T. *Sind: A General Introduction*. Hyderabad: Sind Adabi Board, 1964.

Thapan, Anita Raina. *Sindhi Diaspora*. Manila: Ateneo de Manila University Press, 2002.

—by D. O. Lodrick

SINHALESE

PRONUNCIATION: sin-huh-LEEZ
LOCATION: Sri Lanka
POPULATION: 14.5 million (2008 estimate)
LANGUAGE: Sinhala, Tamil
RELIGION: Buddhist (Theravada); small numbers of Christians and Muslims

¹INTRODUCTION

The Sinhalese are the majority ethnic group of Sri Lanka, an island situated off the southern tip of the Indian peninsula. Sinhalese are descendants of peoples believed to have come from northern India and settled the island around the 5th century BC. The name *Sinhalese* reflects the popular myth that the people are descended from the union of a mythical Indian princess and a lion (*sinha* means "lion" and *le* means "blood").

The ruler of Sri Lanka converted to Buddhism during the 3rd century BC, and since that time the Sinhalese have been predominantly Buddhist in religion and culture. Ancient Buddhist texts provide accounts of the early history of the Sinhalese people. By the 1st century BC, a thriving Sinhalese Buddhist civilization existed in the northern area of Sri Lanka. For reasons as yet uncertain, this civilization collapsed in the 13th century. Like many other peoples in South Asia, the Sinhalese later came under the influence of European powers. The Portuguese landed on Ceylon (the English name for Sri Lanka) in 1505 and soon gained control of much of the island. The Dutch replaced the Portuguese in the mid-17th century, but were driven out by the British in 1798. The island and its inhabitants formed part of Britain's Indian Empire until 1948, when Ceylon was granted its independence. The country adopted the name *Sri Lanka* in 1972.

²LOCATION AND HOMELAND

According to the 2001 Census, the Sri Lankan population was 16,864,544 people. The Sinhalese make up roughly 80% of Sri Lanka's population, so, allowing for natural increase at the average national rate of 0.078% per year, the current population of Sinhalese in Sri Lanka is estimated at around 14.5 million people. When overseas Sinhalese are added to this total, the world-wide population of Sinhalese is estimated at just over 15 million. Sinhalese are distributed over most of the island except the extreme northern districts near Jaffna and eastern coastal areas where the Hindu Tamil minority is concentrated.

Sri Lanka, an island 65,610 sq km (25,332 sq mi) in area, is separated from the Indian mainland by a strait only 35 km (22 mi) wide. The island is dominated by the Central Highlands averaging more than 1,500 m (5,000 ft) in altitude and reaching a maximum altitude of 2,524 m (8,281 ft) at Pidurutala Peak. The southwestern flanks of these mountains and the adjacent lowlands are known as the island's "wet zone." These areas receive as much as 500 cm (196 in) of rain a year from the southwest monsoon. The northern and eastern lowlands lie in the rain shadow of the mountains and form Sri Lanka's dry zone. In this area, rainfall averages less than 200 cm (79 in) and drops below 100 cm (39 in) in places. The island has an equatorial climate with little variation in temperature throughout the year. Mean monthly temperatures at Colombo range from 22°C (71.6°F) in the winter months to 26°C (78.8°F) in May.

Politically, the Sinhalese, who form the majority of the population and the government in Sri Lanka, have been engaged in what amounts to a civil war with the Tamils in the north of the island since the end of the 1970s. The Tamil United Liberation Front (TULF), an association of Tamil political groups that advocated a separate state for Tamils in the north of the island, was formed in 1972. Although TULF tended to be relatively conservative and consisted of Tamils who felt that Tamil objectives could be achieved without violence, TULF was frequently blamed by nationalist Sinhalese politicians for acts of violence committed by militant groups, such as the Liberation Tigers of Tamil Eelam (LTTE), during the 1970s and 1980s.

Violence in Sri Lanka became so bad that in 1983 the government declared a state of emergency. In 1987 Sri Lanka signed an agreement with India to provide security forces (the Indian Peacekeeping Force [IPKF]) to control the Tamils, but this was withdrawn in 1990. In 1994 Chandrika Kumaratanga won the presidential election, but a resurgence of violence led to a government offensive to secure the Jaffna peninsula, the Tamil stronghold in northern Sri Lanka. Despite the success of this operation, the LTTE reemerged in 2000 and, even though a cease-fire agreement was signed in 2002, the LTTE continues to bring pressure on the government, with random acts of violence and terrorism occurring. Bomb blasts on buses and trains are common, and in July 2008 several Sri Lankan police were killed in Colombo by a suicide bomber.

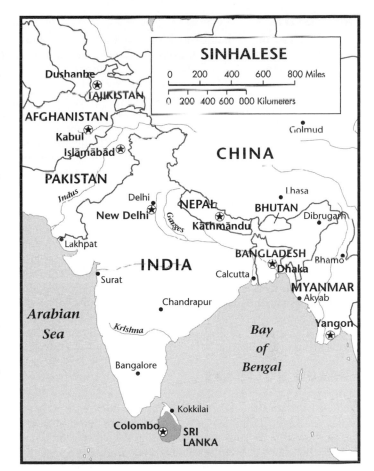

³LANGUAGE

The Sinhalese speak Sinhala, an Indo-Aryan language brought to Sri Lanka by the north Indian peoples who settled the island in the 5th century. Being geographically isolated from other Indo-Aryan tongues, Sinhala developed in its own way. It has been influenced by Pali, the sacred language of southern Buddhism, and, to a lesser extent, by Sanskrit. It also has borrowed words from Dravidian languages, mostly Tamil. Sinhalese is written in its own script (*abugida*) which, like other South Indian writing systems, is derived from the ancient Southern Brahmi script. Sinhala and Tamil are official languages in Sri Lanka, though English is also used.

Sinhala literature dates back well over 2000 years and is heir to the great Aryan literary tradition as embodied in the hymns of the *Rig Veda*, the collection of Sanskrit verses composed by the ancient Indo Aryans around 1500 BC. There is literary evidence to show that the *Mahavansa*, the great chronicle of Sinhalese royalty composed in Pali in the 5th century AD, has drawn heavily from the ancient commentaries in the Sinhalese languages known as the *Sihalatthakatha*. It is evident that many of the early Sinhala prose works, the earliest of which dates to the 9th century, were intended as accessories for Pali works. However, the golden age of Sinhala literature is widely considered to be the 13th century, with many stories and tales from this time dealing with the life of the Buddha. Sinhalese scholarship has traditionally been the domain of the clerical establishment, which accounts for the scarcity of good secular works in the language. It is not until the beginning of the late 19th century that we notice a surge in secular Sinhala literature—the novel appears during this period—with the works of writers, such as Albert Silva, Adara Hasuna, and W. A. Silva. Twentieth century Sinhala literature was based primarily on the Western model, with novelists like Martin Wickramasinghe (1891–1976) and his protégé G. B. Senanayake making names for themselves, but the situation changed in 1956, when Sinhala was adopted as the language in which education was carried out. Works of the late 20th century in Sinhala tended to return to Sinhalese religious roots though many assumed a political flavor in light of the Sinhalese-Tamil conflict in Sri Lanka.

⁴FOLKLORE

The Sinhalese have many legends about heroes and kings. When Prince Vijaya first came to the island of Lanka from northern India, so the tale goes, his men were imprisoned by the demon Kuveni. Kuveni was the queen of a Yaksha clan, the Yakshas being a class of often evil mythological creatures, who possessed magical powers. When Vijaya went to search for his men, he found Kuveni and threatened to kill her. Kuveni, who had assumed the guise of a beautiful maiden, pleaded for her life. She promised to release the men, give Vijaya a kingdom, and become his wife. Using her magical powers, Kuveni helped Vijaya destroy the Yakshas. Vijaya ruled as king in Lanka, the couple lived together for many years, and Kuveni gave birth to a son and a daughter. However, when a marriage was arranged for Vijaya with an Indian princess from the mainland, Vijaya banished Kuveni from his life. As she was leaving, Kuveni cursed the king for his act, and, as a result, he and his successor remained childless. It took a magical dance to remove the effects of the curse.

[5] RELIGION

Most Sinhalese follow Buddhism, accepting the religion's fundamental concepts of *dharma, samsara, karma,* and *ahimsa.* Dharma refers to the Law (the teachings of Buddha); samsara, the life cycle of birth-death-rebirth; karma relates to the effects of good or bad deeds on a person's rebirths and ahimsa is the doctrine of nonviolence toward living things. They believe that these Four Noble Truths point the way to achieving *nirvana* (the Buddhist equivalent of salvation). However, the Sinhalese follow the southern or *Theravada* (also called *Hinayana*) form of Buddhism. This form remains true to the original teachings of Buddha, holding that there is no God, that Buddha was an ordinary mortal who should be revered but not worshiped, and that everyone is responsible for working out his or her own salvation. Buddhism is reflected in every aspect of daily Sinhalese life. Buddhist monks (*bhikkus*) play an important role in the Sinhalese community and often wield considerable political power. Monks serve the religious needs of the people, but Sinhalese also worship at the temples (*devale*) of Hindu gods. The Sinhalese also believe in demons, ghosts, and evil spirits and have a number of folk practitioners to deal with such beings. Small numbers of Sinhalese are Christians (mostly Roman Catholic) or Muslims.

[6] MAJOR HOLIDAYS

Major festivals for the Sinhalese include the Sinhalese New Year in April and the *Vesak* festival in May, which commemorates the birth, enlightenment, and death of Buddha. During the *Esala Perahera,* a two-week festival held in the city of Kandy, the Tooth Relic of the Buddha is paraded through the streets on the back of an elephant. Thousands gather to see the relic and its accompanying procession of decorated elephants, temple officials, schoolchildren, dancers, and acrobats. A fire walking festival held at Katagarama attracts pilgrims from all over the island, as do other sacred centers of Buddhism.

[7] RITES OF PASSAGE

Sinhalese rites of passage involve a mix of Buddhist customs and folk traditions. In rural areas, difficulties in pregnancy are often ascribed to evil spirits or black magic, and a magician (*kattadiya*) may be called in to deal with the situation with charms and mantras. The birth of a child is eagerly anticipated, and male babies are preferred. The newborn is given a few drops of human milk with a touch of gold to endow it with strength and beauty, and offerings are made both at the temple and to Buddhist monks. There are few formal ceremonies, although the occasion when a child is taught to read letters (at about three years) is an important one. No special rites mark a boy's reaching puberty, but the first menstruation of a girl is observed with appropriate ceremony.

Death rituals are fairly simple. The Sinhalese do not believe in the existence of a soul, but rather that a human is an aggregate of five elements. At the time of death, these elements are dispersed and the most important one, consciousness, becomes reborn in a new existence according to the laws of karma. If possible, *bhikkus* (Buddhist monks) are called to the bedside of a dying man to chant from the Buddhist scriptures. After death, the deceased's face is covered with a handkerchief and the big toes tied together. Oil lamps are lit, flowers are spread on the bed, and religious books are read during the night. Bodies are prepared for disposal, then either cremated or buried.

Bhikkus preside at the funeral ceremony, and a white cloth is offered to the leading bhikku, who delivers a brief sermon. All those who attend the funeral take a bath to rid themselves of the pollution of death, and relatives gather for a simple meal. Close relatives wear white clothes, a sign of mourning in South Asia.

[8] INTERPERSONAL RELATIONS

"*Ayubowan*" ("Greeting") is the word used by the Sinhalese when meeting or parting. This is usually accompanied by holding one's hands clasped in front of the body, with a slight stoop of the body and head. The European style of shaking hands, however, is replacing traditional forms of greeting, and women often kiss friends and relatives on both cheeks. The Sinhalese are well known for their hospitality in entertaining guests. Typically, Sinhalese do not say "thank you," but something along the lines of "May you receive merit."

[9] LIVING CONDITIONS

Although many Sinhalese live in cities and towns, and their living conditions differ little from other urban populations in South Asia, the Sinhalese are by and large a rural people. They live in villages, hamlets, and isolated farmsteads scattered across the island. A typical agricultural village is made up of a cluster of houses situated on slightly elevated land and surrounded by paddy fields. Nearby, especially in the dry zone, may be one of the many "tanks" constructed over the centuries to store water for irrigation. The village itself will typically have a well, a temple, and perhaps a school and dispensary. Traditional building materials of mud and thatch are being replaced by cement and tiles. Each house stands in a garden in the midst of coconut, mango, papaya, and other trees. In front of the house is a veranda, where men sit during the day and sleep at night. A single door provides access to the house, where women and children sleep. There are typically two rooms and a kitchen, although sometimes the hearth is a lean-to attached to the back of the house. Most villagers sleep on mats, and only the more affluent have beds and simple wooden tables and chairs. Some households have their own well. Many houses have pit-latrines dug in the garden.

[10] FAMILY LIFE

Sinhalese have castes based historically on occupation, but the system is much less rigid than its Hindu counterpart. There are no Brahmans (priests), caste rankings are less significant, and in urban society caste observance is rapidly disappearing. Caste is, however, important in marriage. About half the Sinhalese population belongs to the agricultural *Govigama* caste. Other castes include washermen (*Hinna*), metalworkers (*Navandanna*), and drummers (*Berawa*). The *Rodiya* (formerly itinerant beggars) are considered by Sinhalese to be among the lowest castes.

Sinhalese marry within their caste, but also are subject to further limitations. Each caste is subdivided into microcastes (*pavula*), and women must marry men of equal or higher status within the caste. Marriages are usually arranged, with cross-cousin (i.e., father's sister's daughter, or mother's brother's daughter) marriages preferred. Preliminaries include the casting of horoscopes and negotiation of the dowry (if any is to be paid), but the actual ceremony is relatively simple. In some instances, there may be no formal ceremony. The bride usu-

A Sri Lankan Buddhist monk applies oil on an elephant during a religious observance to mark the traditional Sinhalese New Year in April.
(AP Images/Eranga Jayawardena)

ally moves in with the husband's family, although couples with the resources to do so prefer to set up their own household. A woman assumes the responsibility of running the household and perhaps contributing to the family income. Her prime role, however, is to bear and raise children, preferably sons. In general, women are treated with a considerable respect in Sinhalese society.

¹¹ CLOTHING

The traditional dress of the Sinhalese is the *sarama*, a type of sarong. Men may wear a shirt or, when they go bare-chested, throw a scarf around their shoulders. Women wear a tight-fitting, short-sleeved jacket with the sarama. Urban Sinhalese have adopted Western-style clothes. Women wear skirts and blouses, although they prefer the Indian *sārī* for formal and ceremonial occasions.

¹² FOOD

Rice, eaten with helpings of curry, is the staple food of the Sinhalese. A family usually has three meals a day, although "morning tea" may be nothing more than that—tea, perhaps taken with rice cakes, fruit, or leftovers from the previous evening's meal. Lunch consists of rice served with vegetable and meat curries and sauces, such as *sambol*, a spicy mix of grated coconut and chili, pickles, and chutneys. The evening meal is rice eaten with as many curry dishes as a family can afford. Although orthodox Buddhists are strict vegetarians, many Sinhalese eat meat, poultry, fish, and eggs. Many Sinhalese dishes are cooked in coconut milk. A meal is usually followed by fresh fruits or the sweets so popular among South Asians. Tea and coconut milk are common drinks. *Pan*, or betel nut (seed of the betel palm) eaten with lime, is taken after meals and often throughout the day.

¹³ EDUCATION

The Sinhalese literacy rate is around 92% (2001 Census), among the highest of any community in South Asia. Education is compulsory up to the age of 14, and it is the parents' responsibility to ensure a child's attendance. Schooling is free from kindergarten to the university level, although there is a shortage of places for qualified university entrants. Unusual for the region is the number of girls who remain in school to complete their educations. Because of the variety of ethnic groups in Sri Lanka, many schools teach only in either Sinhalese or in Tamil, though the elite schools also use English.

The University of Colombo is the island's most reputed university, while the Open University of Sri Lanka allows students to complete their degrees online. Sri Lankan universities include, among others, the South Eastern University of Sri Lanka, the University of Kelaniya, and the University of Moratuwa.

14 CULTURAL HERITAGE

The heritage of the Sinhalese is essentially that of Buddhist civilization in Sri Lanka. This includes early literary works (the *Dipavamsa* [AD 350] and the *Mahavamsa* [AD 550]) chronicling the history of Buddhism in the island, architecture, temple and cave frescoes, and massive sculptures such as the 14 meter long (46 foot long) reclining Buddha at Polonnaruwa. The Sinhalese evolved their own form of classical dance, usually performed by men, with rapid footwork and acrobatic movements. The "devil-dancing" of the southern coastal lowlands evolved from folk rituals to exorcise demons. *Kolam* is a form of dance-drama involving masked dancers retelling stories from myth and legend.

15 WORK

About 80% of the Sinhalese people are rural and engaged primarily in subsistence agriculture. Sri Lanka's commercial plantations (producing tea, coconut products, rubber, cinnamon, cardamoms, and pepper) provide some employment for the population. Industries in Sri Lanka are poorly developed and show only slow growth. However, the recently established clothing industry in a free trade zone near Colombo now accounts for nearly half the value of Sri Lanka's exports. Urban Sinhalese are engaged in government work, the professions, business, trade, and the service industries. Nonetheless, unemployment is a severe problem in Sri Lanka.

16 SPORTS

Sinhalese children play games typical of other young people in South Asia—tag, hide-and-seek, dolls, marbles, and so on. Indoor activities include board games and various string games, such as cat's cradle. Gambling is popular among adults, although many traditional sports, such as cock fighting, have been banned. Buffalo fights and elephant fights are still staged as part of Sinhalese New Year celebrations. Sports, such as cricket, soccer, field hockey, and track-and-field, were introduced by the British and are played in schools and colleges. Cricket is by far the most popular spectator sport.

17 ENTERTAINMENT AND RECREATION

Sinhalese have radio and television programming and can also see English and Sinhala movies. In rural areas, however, there is often little surplus income to spend on such activities, so villagers relax in more traditional ways. They spend time gossiping with their neighbors and visiting local fairs. They go on pilgrimages and watch religious processions, folk dances, folk theater, and puppet shows.

18 FOLK ART, CRAFTS, AND HOBBIES

Sinhalese crafts include wood and ivory carving, stone working, and metal work in brass, gold, and silver. Pottery and basketry are traditional cottage industries. Sri Lanka has been known for centuries for its gemstones, and jewelry making and the cutting of sapphires, rubies, and semi-precious stones continue to this day.

19 SOCIAL PROBLEMS

Sri Lanka suffered its worst natural disaster in centuries when it was hit by the December 2004 tsunami that originated in South East Asia. The Sinhalese areas in the south suffered severely from loss of life and livelihood, although the brunt of the tsunami was borne by the east and north-east coasts, populated mainly by Muslims and Tamils. Although sufficient relief funds were available, government mechanisms for distributing these funds to those in need were woefully inadequate, and the government received extensive criticism for its relief efforts.

Although in terms of certain social characteristics (e.g. health and education), the Sinhalese are atypical of South Asia, they nevertheless face problems endemic in the region. Sri Lanka is essentially an agricultural country, but self-sufficiency in food is a problem, and landlessness in rural areas is increasing. Unemployment and underemployment are serious problems, and slow industrial growth limits economic expansion and job creation. None of this is helped by the continuing ethnic conflict between Sinhalese and Tamil on the island. Tamil separatists in northern areas around Jaffna are engaged in an armed insurgency against the Sinhalese-dominated government. This has resulted in random terrorism, the assassination of a prime minister, considerable loss of life, and charges of human rights violations. Not only does this insurgency pose an economic burden, but millions of valuable tourist dollars have been lost. Until this conflict is resolved, it is unlikely that social and economic problems can be fully addressed.

20 GENDER ISSUES

Sinhalese are Buddhists by religion, and theoretically women in Buddhism have equal status with men. But Sinhalese women live in a patriarchal society that tends to subordinate women to men. There is, moreover, a caste system among the Sinhalese and while this division of society into strata differs somewhat from the classic *Varnas* of North India, it is similar in nature to the Jāti system found in South India. The fourfold caste model in Sri Lanka's pre-British period was: *Raja, Bamunu, Velenda* and *Govi*. Thus marriages among the Sinhalese are arranged and caste plays a significant role in the selection of potential partners. While inheritance laws are quite different from the rest of Asia—property is divided equally among all children, including daughters—it may be controlled by the family as an instrument of marital alliance; among wealthy families, dowry may be paid in lieu of inheritance. There is a strong preference for male children, who may receive better care, and the infant mortality rate for girls is higher than for males (21.2 deaths/1,000 live births for females and 17.63 deaths/1,000 live births for males [2007 est.]). There is a slight dominance of males in the sex ratio for the Sinhalese.

One problem Sinhalese women have to face is the civil war in Sri Lanka. The Tamil terrorists started a campaign of ethnic cleansing and genocide by killing Sinhalese in Jaffna and supposedly cut off the breasts of Sinhalese women. Reported human rights violations against Sinhalese women include both rape and murder. The conflict has also seen a change in women's role in traditional society, with women becoming heads of households with the loss of their spouses, through the conflict, divorce (which is relatively easy to come by), or desertion. The conflict has also seen a rise in alcoholism among men.

Nonetheless, the primary role of women in Sinhalese society is reproductive and to run the household. Despite high levels of education, Sinhalese women live in a male-dominated society and males make all the important socio-economic decisions The plight of women is even worse in rural areas where poverty and obtaining enough food are major problems.

[21] BIBLIOGRAPHY

Baker, Victoria. J. *A Sinhalese Village in Sri Lanka: Coping with Uncertainty*. Fort Worth, TX: Harcourt Brace College Publishers, 1998.

de Silva, Deema. *Life Cycle Rituals among the Sinhalese*. Dehiwala: Sridevi, 2002.

Gunasekera, Susan W. *The Sinhalese Have Met the Modernists*. Pannipitiya: Stamford Lake Publications, 2004.

Johnson, B. L. C., and M. Le M. Scrivenor. *Sri Lanka: Land, People, and Economy*. London: Heinemann, 1981.

Rajasuriar, G. K. *The History of the Tamils and the Sinhalese of Sri Lanka*. Australia: s.n., 1998.

Wijisekera, Nandadeva. *The Sinhalese*. Colombo, Sri Lanka: Gunasena, 1990.

Yalman, Nur. *Under the Bo Tree: Studies in Caste, Kinship, and Marriage in the Interior of Ceylon*. Berkeley: University of California Press, 1967.

—by D. O. Lodrick

SOUTH KOREANS

PRONUNCIATION: sowth kaw-REE-uns
LOCATION: Republic of Korea (South Korea)
POPULATION: 49 million
LANGUAGE: Korean
RELIGION: Mahayana Buddhism; Christianity (Protestantism and Roman Catholicism); Ch'ondogyo (combination of Christianity with native pre-Christian beliefs)

[1] INTRODUCTION

The Republic of Korea, generally called South Korea, lies south of an artificially demarcated line that divides the Korean peninsula in two, separating South Korea from the communist Democratic People's Republic of Korea to the north. Centrally located between China, Japan, and Russia, the Korean peninsula has been subject to foreign invasions throughout recorded history. Historically it was known as "the Land of the Morning Calm" *(Choson)*, and some of the Korean Peninsula was ruled by the Chinese for several centuries until the end of the Bronze Age (c. 200 AD), a period when China established a lasting influence on Korean culture, especially through its language and the Confucian belief system. Over the following centuries, the three Korean kingdoms that emerged after the long period of Chinese rule—Paekche, Silla, and Koguryo—were alternately unified and divided.

In 1876 the Kanghwa Treaty opened Korea to Japan and to the West. Japanese pirates had attacked the country since Medieval times, and Japan occupied it from 1910 to 1945. After World War II, the 38th parallel became the line of demarcation between the Soviet and United States occupation zones and, with some important changes, between the two Koreas that emerged after their governments were unable to reach a reunification agreement. In the Korean War (1950–1953), South Korea, with the aid of United States and United Nations multinational forces, repulsed an attack by the north and fought to maintain its independence from communist rule.

After a long period of successive military regimes, South Korea has undergone a series of political and economic reforms in recent years. However, North Korea—now one of the world's few remaining Communist countries—remains a secretive, authoritarian and relatively closed society. The border between the two nations is still guarded around the clock by armed troops, and reunification—the subject of continuing bilateral talks over the past 50 years—remains a distant dream, and technically there is still a state of war between the North and the South.

[2] LOCATION AND HOMELAND

South Korea is located in the southern half of the Korean peninsula in East Asia. Occupying 45% of the peninsula, which it shares with the Democratic People's Republic of Korea (North Korea), South Korea has an area of 38,023 sq km (98,484 sq mi). Hills and mountains cover about 80% of the country's terrain, separating its eastern and western regions. The east has a rugged coastline where the mountains meet the sea. The country's cultivated land, much of it planted with rice, is found in the south and west, where rivers flow westward to the Yellow Sea.

South Korea is one of the most densely populated countries both in Asia and in the world, with a population density of 438 persons per sq km (or 1,134 per sq mi). The nation's population estimate for July 2007 listed the population as 49,044,790, more than twice that of North Korea. In 2007, 9.8 million people—nearly a quarter of the total population—lived in Seoul, the capital and South Korea's largest city. Other major cities (with their 2007 populations) are Pusan (3.5 million people), Inchon (2.45 million), and Taegu (2.3 million). The Korean people are one of the world's most ethnically homogeneous nationalities, consisting almost exclusively of the Han, a people believed to be descended from the Mongols of Central Asia. There are no numerically significant ethnic minorities in South Korea.

³LANGUAGE

Korean is generally thought to belong to the Altaic language family, along with Turkish, Mongolian, Japanese, and other languages. China's far-reaching influence on Korean culture, especially in the form of Confucianism, is reflected in the large number of Chinese words found in the Korean language. Until the 15th century, Korean was written using Chinese characters. Then, in 1446, a mostly phonetic Korean alphabet, called Han'gul, was developed and it has been used ever since.

SOME COMMON KOREAN WORDS AND EXPRESSIONS ARE:

How are you?	*anahasiyo?*
Hello	*yoboseyo*
Goodbye	*aniyong ikeseyo*
Yes	*ye*
No	*anio*
Thank you	*kamsa kamnida*

NUMBERS:

one	*il*
two	*ee*
three	*sam*
four	*sa*
five	*o*
six	*yuk*
seven	*chill*
eight	*pal*
nine	*ku*
ten	*sip*
100	*paek*
1000	*chon*

⁴FOLKLORE

Korean folklore celebrates human longevity and the survival of the Korean people. A number of folktales involve either animals or heavenly beings who either become human or long to do so, and many have similar plots to those of early northern China. Others celebrate the figure of the wise hermit living a simple, secluded existence on a mountain top. Koreans have traditionally used special drawings called *pujok* as talismans in and around their houses to bring them luck and ward off evil. These talismans are usually printed in red, a color believed to have special beneficial properties and often seen in shamanistic rituals.

⁵RELIGION

There is a great deal of diversity in South Korean religious life. Koreans have traditionally combined elements from different belief systems, such as Taoism, Confucianism, and Buddhism. Today, about 25 million people are thought to be Christian, and most of these are members of the approximately 160 different Protestant denominations, with about 4.3 million being Roman Catholics. Some 24.5 million of the population are Mahayana Buddhist, approximately 1.5 million are Confucian, and there are also about 500,000 who follow Shamanist pre-Christian beliefs, or belong to newer religions that combine Christianity with native pre-Christian beliefs. The most widespread is Ch'ondogyo ("the Heavenly Way"), founded in 1860.

⁶MAJOR HOLIDAYS

Holidays in South Korea are celebrated either by the date on the modern solar calendar, or, in some cases, according to the lunar calendar that Koreans used for thousands of years in the past to reckon time. The New Year is one of South Korea's most important holidays, with bells usually ringing out at midnight. For the lunar New Year *(Sol),* which is either in late January or early February, there are three days set aside for family celebrations that include honoring parents and grandparents, shooting off firecrackers to frighten away evil spirits, and eating holiday foods.

The birthday of the Buddha (the eighth day of the fourth lunar month, usually early in May) is an important holiday for Korean Buddhists, who hang lanterns in the courtyards of Buddhist temples throughout the country. These lanterns are then carried through the streets in nighttime processions. *Tano,* held during the fifth month of the lunar calendar (around the beginning of June) is a major holiday in rural areas, where it is the traditional time to pray for a good harvest. It is celebrated with a variety of vigorous games and competitions, including wrestling matches for men and swinging contests for women (the holiday is also called Swing Day).

Other national holidays include Independence Movement Day (March 1), Arbor Day (April 5), Children's Day (May 5), Memorial Day (June 6), Constitution Day (July 17), Liberation Day (August 15), National Foundation Day (October 3), and Christmas (December 25). Mention should also be made of important festivals such as that of Snow, in January, and Cherry Blossoms in April.

⁷RITES OF PASSAGE

The harvest festival of *Chusok* in early September, often called the Korean Thanksgiving, is a legal holiday, although it, too, is based on the lunar calendar. Time-honored *Chusok* customs include exchanging gifts and staying up all night to watch the full moon. Another important holiday is *Hansik,* a special day for honoring ancestors, which is observed early in April (the 105th day of the lunar year). People carry food and wine to the graves of deceased relatives and picnic at the gravesite, during which time they ensure that it is well-tended.

Traditionally, Korean marriages were arranged, especially among the elite. Today, however, the popularity of arranged marriages, particularly in urban areas, has declined considerably, although many Koreans still follow the practice in a modified form: parents and other relatives locate prospective marriage partners, but the young people have the final say in approving their choices. Among the urban upper classes, the services of highly paid semiprofessional matchmakers are also becoming increasingly popular.

Ancestor worship plays a prominent role in Korean folk belief, which regards death as a rite of passage to a new state rather than a termination. Christian, Buddhist, and Confucian concepts also affect Korean attitudes toward death.

⁸INTERPERSONAL RELATIONS

Respect for parents and for elders in general is a central value for Koreans, and much of this and related tradition comes from Confucian values. There are detailed and elaborate rules governing one's speech and actions in the presence of older persons (although these rules are less rigidly observed than in the past). Even when not in the presence of their elders, Koreans are generally very courteous and emotionally reserved. Proper etiquette forbids strong displays of happiness, distress, or anger. When at home, Koreans have traditionally sat on the floor, although today chairs are becoming increasingly common. The most formal and polite posture when seated on the floor is to kneel with one's back kept straight and one's weight on the balls of both feet.

⁹LIVING CONDITIONS

The traditional Korean house was made of wood or clay with a thatched roof (later replaced by tile or slate). Today, most South Koreans in urban areas live in high-rise, multi-story dwellings, and most homes are built of concrete. Houses are generally built low, with small rooms. In order to keep out the cold, there are few doors and windows. The Koreans have a unique traditional heating system called *ondal* that is still found even in many of the most modern homes. Heat is carried through pipes installed beneath the floors, a system geared toward the traditional Korean custom of sitting and sleeping on mats or cushions placed on the floor.

Health care in Korea has improved substantially since the 1950s. Average life expectancy has risen from 53 to 77.4 years (2008). However, the infant mortality rate is still relatively high, and many doctors tend to emigrate after completing their training. Traditional causes of death, such as tuberculosis and pneumonia, have been replaced by conditions more typical of industrialized societies, such as cancer, heart disease, and stroke.

South Korea's transportation system has been continually modernized and expanded. Roads and highways, especially in the area of Seoul, underwent major improvements in the 1980s in anticipation of the 1988 summer Olympics. The country has an excellent rail network, and Seoul has a modern subway system which is gradually replacing buses as the major means of transport in the city and its environs. There are bus lines between all major cities, and bicycles are also a popular means of transport. Korean Airlines flies between the country's major cities and foreign destinations including Hong Kong, Japan, Taiwan, and the United States.

¹⁰FAMILY LIFE

The typical South Korean household consists of a nuclear family with two children. Although young children are nurtured and indulged, respect for one's parents—and one's elders, generally—is a central value in Korean life, and fathers in particular exercise a great degree of authority over their sons. Although divorce was not tolerated in the past, today it has be-

come quite common and no longer carries the stigma it once did.

¹¹CLOTHING

The majority of South Koreans wear modern Western-style clothing most of the time. During the country's very cold winters, warm clothing is a must, and most Koreans begin wearing long underwear early in the fall. Traditional garb (called *hanbok*) is still worn on a daily basis by some rural dwellers, and by all Koreans on special occasions such as weddings and holidays. For women, this type of clothing includes a long, full skirt called a *chima* and a short jacket (*chogori*) with a wide bow at the side (the entire outfit is also called *chimachogori*). The men's outfit is white and includes pants (*baji*) and a long coat or jacket (*turumagi*) worn over a sleeveless vest and adorned in front by a wide bow like that on the women's costume. In past times, the most distinctive item of male clothing was the *kat*, a high black horsehair hat with a wide brim and a chin strap. Today seen only occasionally on elderly men, it was once standard headgear for married men, who wore their hair in a braided topknot underneath it.

¹²FOOD

The Korean national dish is *kimchi*, a spicy, fermented pickled vegetable mixture whose primary ingredient is cabbage. A dietary staple, it is prepared in large quantities in the fall by families throughout Korea and left to ferment for several weeks in large earthenware jars buried in the ground. A typical Korean meal includes soup, rice served with grains or beans, and kimchi served as a side dish. (A recipe for kimchi follows.) Other common dishes include *bulgogi* (strips of marinated beef), *kalbi* (marinated beef short ribs), and *sinsollo* (a meal of meat, fish, vegetables, eggs, nuts, and bean curd cooked together in broth). Koreans eat with chopsticks and a spoon, often at small, collapsible tables that can be moved to any room of the house.

Kimchi

*Note: Kimchi needs to be prepared at least two days ahead of time so it can ferment and develop its full flavor

1 cup coarsely chopped cabbage
1 cup finely sliced carrots
1 cup cauliflower florets, separated
2 tablespoons salt
2 green onions, finely sliced
3 cloves garlic, finely chopped, or 1 teaspoon garlic granules
¼ tablespoon crushed red pepper
1 teaspoon finely grated fresh ginger or ½ teaspoon ground ginger

Place cabbage, carrots, and cauliflower in colander and sprinkle with salt. Toss vegetables and set in sink for about one hour. Rinse with cold running water, drain well, and place in a medium-sized bowl. Add onions, garlic, red pepper, and ginger and mix thoroughly. Cover and refrigerate for at least two days, stirring frequently. Yields about four cups.

13 EDUCATION

The Koreans' Confucian heritage has provided them with a great reverence for education, and literacy rates are some of the highest in the world: 97% for women and 99.3% for men. Education is free and compulsory in the primary grades between the ages of 6 and 12, and the great majority of students go on to six more years of middle school and high school. Discipline is strict, and children attend school five-and-a-half days per week. South Korea has over 200 institutions of higher education, including both two- and four-year colleges and universities. Ewha University is one of the world's largest women's universities. The leading public university in South Korea is Seoul National University.

14 CULTURAL HERITAGE

Chinese art, Confucianism, and Buddhism have all had a major influence on the arts in Korea. Some 80,000 art objects are collected in the National Museum and outstanding examples of Korean architecture can be seen in historic palaces and Buddhist temples and pagodas. The National Classic Music Institute trains its graduates in traditional Korean music and Korean folk painting (*min'hwa*) is still practiced. Western art forms have been very influential in South Korea. The Korean National Symphony Orchestra and the Seoul Symphony Orchestra perform in Seoul and Pusan. Western-style drama, dance, and motion pictures have also become very popular among South Koreans.

15 WORK

In 2005 some 6% of South Korea's labor force was employed in agriculture, forestry, and fishing and 27% in manufacturing, with the service sector employing 67% of the people. Unem-ployment was 3.7%. South Korea has been subject to continued labor unrest in recent years as living costs have outpaced wages, especially for manual laborers. Workers have struck for higher wages, shorter working hours, and improved safety conditions on the job. Working hours in South Korea are among the longest in the world, averaging nearly 55 per week.

16 SPORTS

Koreans enjoy a variety of internationally popular sports, including baseball, volleyball, soccer, basketball, tennis, skating, golf, skiing, boxing, and swimming. Baseball is especially popular, and South Korea has a professional baseball league, whose games are broadcast on television, as are competitions at the college and high school levels. The best-known traditional Korean sport is the martial art of *taekwondo,* taught by Koreans to people throughout the world as a popular form of self-defense. The 1988 summer Olympic Games were held in Seoul, and South Korea was the co-host of the 2002 F.I.F.A. Football World Cup.

17 ENTERTAINMENT AND RECREATION

Both traditional Korean forms of recreation and modern Western pastimes are enjoyed in South Korea. Age-old games and ceremonial dances are still performed at festivals and other special occasions. These include mask dances (*Kanggangsuwollae),* the *Chajon Nori* ("juggernaut") game, in which participants ride in wooden vehicles, and mass tug-of-war games involving as many as a hundred people.

Among more modern forms of entertainment, television is enjoyed throughout the country. Soap operas and detective programs are among the most popular types of programming. Outside the home, South Koreans enjoy gathering in the country's numerous coffeehouses (called *tabang* or *tashil*) and bars. Koreans enjoy Western classical music, and their country has produced many fine performers. They are especially fond of singing and it is common for Koreans to sing for each other at dinners and other social occasions. In addition to instrumental music, ballet and opera are also popular and South Korea's motion picture industry releases dozens of new movies every year.

18 FOLK ART, CRAFTS, AND HOBBIES

Fine Korean furniture, including wood and brass chests and lacquered items with mother-of-pearl inlay, is valued by collectors worldwide. Korean craftspeople are also known for their celadon ceramics, a term that refers to a type of greenish glaze that originated in China.

19 SOCIAL PROBLEMS

Most South Korean families face the common economic concerns of low wages, long working hours, and high rates of inflation. Few can afford to own their own homes. Korea's land has been eroded by poor farming practices and by deforestation during the country's occupation by Japan in the first half of the 20th century. In recent years, regional tension between Cholla and Kyongsang provinces has been a cause for concern.

In the 1980s, growing numbers of Koreans began to use the illegal substance crystalline methamphetamine, known as *hiroppon* in Korea and "speed" in the United States. By the end of the decade there were thought to be as many as 300,000 using

A South Korean family visits Changdeokgung Palace in Seoul, South Korea. (© Atlantide Phototravel/Corbis)

the drug, including many ordinary working people attempting to cope with high-pressure jobs and long work hours. Asian gangs were also engaged in shipping hiroppon manufactured in South Korea to other countries, including Taiwan, Japan, and the United States.

²⁰ GENDER ISSUES

The role of women in South Korean society has changed dramatically although much of South Korea is still very conservative. Women are not expected to smoke in public or in many areas drink alcohol in public. Many more women are in the work force than ever before—women make up some 34% of the total workforce—with women being found in all sectors, including the armed forces. There are some businesses run by women, although this remains rare, and there are some prominent women members of the National Assembly.

²¹ BIBLIOGRAPHY

Gall, Timothy, and Susan Gall. *Worldmark Encyclopedia of the Nations.* Detroit: Gale Research, 1995.

Hoare, James. *Korea: An Introduction.* New York: Kegan Paul International, 1988.

Kim, Choong Soon Kim. "Korean." *Encyclopedia of World Cultures.* Boston: G. K. Hall, 1992.

Korean Overseas Information Service. *A Handbook of Korea.* Seoul: Korean Overseas Information Service, 1993.

McNair, Sylvia. *Korea.* Chicago: Children's Press, 1994.

Nahm, Andrew; and Aidan Foster-Carter. "The Republic of Korea." *The Far East and Australasia.* London: Europa Publications, 2007.

Oliver, Robert Tarbell. *A History of the Korean People in Modern Times: 1800 to the Present.* Newark: University of Delaware Press, 1993.

Robinson, Martin; Andrew Bender; and Rob Whyte. *Korea.* Hawthorn, Australia: Lonely Planet, 2004.

Savada, Andrea Matles, and William Shaw, ed. *South Korea: A Country Study.* Washington, D.C.: U.S. Government Printing Office, 1992.

Steenson, Gary P. *Coping with Korea.* Oxford: Basil Blackwell, 1987.

—revised by J. Corfield

SRI LANKANS

PRONUNCIATION: sree-LAHNG-kuhns
LOCATION: Sri Lanka
POPULATION: 20.1 million (2007 estimate)
LANGUAGE: Sinhala; Tamil
RELIGION: *Theravāda* Buddhism (70%); Hinduism (15%); Islam (7.5%); Christianity (7.5%) (2001 Census)
RELATED ARTICLES: Vol. 4: Veddas

¹INTRODUCTION

Sri Lankans are inhabitants of the large island, formerly known as Ceylon, which appears to hang off the southern tip of the Indian peninsula like a teardrop. The modern name Sri Lanka is taken from the Indian epic *Ramayana,* in which the island is called Lanka. The prefix *"Sri"* is a common term of respect in South Asia. The island was named Taprobane by the ancient Greek mariners. Arab seafarers called it Serendib, from which has evolved our word "serendipity," meaning the ability to find good fortune without really looking for it. The English name Ceylon is derived from a Sanskrit word that means "Island of the Sinhalese."

Sri Lanka lies at the crossroads of the Indian Ocean. Its early history is one of repeated migrations of peoples from the Indian mainland. The first inhabitants of the island most probably included aboriginal peoples of Proto-Australoid stock who crossed the narrow straits from the southern tip of India. Peoples of Indo-European descent from northern India settled on the island around the 5th century BC, later evolving into the Sinhalese. Tamils from southeast India began to arrive in the early centuries AD and these migrations continued until about AD 1200. At times, kingdoms in South India were powerful enough to extend their control over parts of Sri Lanka.

At the beginning of the 16th century, Sri Lanka entered a new period in its history. This brought contact with the expanding maritime powers of Europe, and later domination by them. A Portuguese fleet landed on Sri Lanka in 1505, and in just over 100 years the Portuguese controlled most of the island. The Dutch replaced the Portuguese and, in turn, gave way to the British. From 1796 to 1948, Sri Lanka, called Ceylon by the British, remained a colony of Britain, forming part the British Indian Empire.

Ceylon achieved its independence from Britain without the communal violence that swept through the rest of the Indian subcontinent at the time. However, tensions between the Sinhalese and Tamil populations were later to lead to a full-fledged civil war. The island nation of Ceylon was officially renamed the Republic of Sri Lanka in 1972.

²LOCATION AND HOMELAND

Sri Lanka is an island in the Indian Ocean lying off the southern tip of India. It is separated from the mainland by the narrow Palk Strait. A string of shoals and islands known as Adam's Bridge crosses the strait, and here Sri Lankan territory is separated from India by only 35 km (22 mi). Sri Lanka is 65,610 sq km (25,332 sq mi) in area, roughly half the size of New York State.

Sri Lanka's topography is dominated by the central highlands, located in the south-central part of the island. Elevation in the highlands averages more than 1,500 m (approximately 5,000 ft) and reaches 2,524 m (8,281 ft) at Pidurutala Peak, the highest point on the island. The mountains play an important role in the human geography of the country through their effect on rainfall. The southwestern flanks of the mountains and the adjacent lowlands are known as the island's Wet Zone. These areas face the full force of the southwestern monsoon and receive as much 500 cm (196 in) of rain a year. The northern and eastern lowlands, the Dry Zone, in contrast receives less than 200 cm (79 in) with totals in some areas dropping below 100 cm (40 in). The island lies close to the equator, between 6°N and 10°N latitude, and so experiences an equatorial climate. There is little seasonal temperature variation, with daytime temperatures on the lowlands reaching between 29°C and 33°C (85°–92°F). Vegetation ranges from equatorial rain forest in the wetter upland to grasslands in the drier north.

The country's population is 20.1 million people (2007 estimate). Sinhalese form the bulk of this population, with 81.89% of the total (2001 Census). Within the Sinhalese community, a distinction is made between "up-country" and "low-country" branches. The former are Sinhalese in the interior mountains around Kandy who clung to their independence while the low-country population came under the influence of the Portuguese and the Dutch. Tamils, who make up 9.43% (2001 Census) of the island's people, are concentrated in the north and the eastern coastal lowlands. In Jaffna, on the northernmost tip of the island, they comprise over 90% of the population. Tamils, too, make a distinction in their own community. Sri Lankan Tamils trace their ancestry on the island back to the early centuries of the Christian Era, while Indian Tamils arrived during the 19th and 20th centuries to work on the tea plantations.

There are other minority communities present on the island. The Sri Lankan Moors are descended from Arab seafarers who arrived on the island in the 9th and 10th centuries. Moors, who have strong fishing and trading interests, form 8%(2001 Census) of the population. They are found along the coast, particularly in the southeast of the island. The Burghers, descendants of Dutch colonists from the 17th and 18th centuries, are a small but distinctive ethnic group. The term is also used to refer to Eurasians, i.e., any Sri Lankans of European descent. There is a small group of Malays in Sri Lanka. The Veddas, a primitive tribal people, are remnants of the oldest settlers of the island. They are Proto-Australoids, with racial affinities to groups such as the Bushmen of Africa and Aborigines of Australia. A primitive hunting and gathering people, they are rapidly being assimilated into Sinhalese society. In addition, there are bands of gypsies wandering the island, making their living from snake-charming, monkey-training, and tattooing.

Following Independence from Britain in 1948, Ceylon was ruled by Stephen Senanayake and his United National Party (UNP), which dominated the country's parliament in the immediate post-independence era. Ceylon, as a former British colony, inherited the British political system with power vested in the prime minister. It was fully expected that the new government would be threatened from the Left, but the island's Marxist parties were too divided to mount an effective challenge. A deteriorating economic situation combined with a rising Sinhalese nationalism, which was identified with Sri Lankan nationalism—a view that was rejected by minorities such as the Tamils—saw Solomon Bandaranaike sweep to power at the head of the Sri Lankan Freedom Party (SLFP) in 1956. Bandaranaike's government was unabashedly Sinhalese and Buddhist, but he was assassinated in 1959 and replaced by his wife, Sirimavo. Sirimavo Bandaranaike made a determined bid to secularize education, thus alienating the Roman Catholics, while her policies towards language alienated the Tamils. The Bandaranaikes created a new balance of political forces in Sri Lanka which saw the dominance of the Sinhalese and a decline in the status of minorities.

Despite a move to the left, Bandaranaike's United Front, a coalition of the old SFLP and several communist parties in Sri Lanka held power from 1970 to 1977. A combination of factors, such as unemployment, rising prices, and food scarcities, brought down the Bandaranaike government and in the general elections of 1977 the UNP under Junius Jayawardene won handily. In 1978 a new constitution was adopted, establishing a presidential form of government with Jayawardene as president. The constitution also improved the lot of minorities such as the Tamils. Nonetheless, the Tamil United Liberation Front (TULF), formed in 1972 from various Tamil political groups, became the main opposition and began advocating a separate state for Tamils on the island, a position to which the government was strongly opposed. The years 1983–1988 saw a period of ethnic violence and the emergence of the Liberation Tigers of Tamil Eelam (LTTE) as the main Tamil separatist group. The period was marked by numerous incidents of violence, with government security forces engaging the LTTE, and many civilians killed in the conflict. However, in 1987 Rajiv Gandhi visited Sri Lanka and agreed to provide military assistance in the form of the Indian Peacekeeping Force (IPKF). At first it seemed as if the Indian-Sri Lankan accord would be a success, with Tamil groups surrendering their weapons, but the Tamils continued their opposition, and the IPKF was withdrawn in 1990.

In 1988 presidential elections saw Ranasinghe Premadasa of the UNP returned to power and he repealed the state of emergency that had existed since 1983. Violence continued through the 1989 general elections and into the early 1990s, with the LTTE being banned in India, following Rajiv Gandhi's assassination in 1991 (Gandhi was supposedly killed by a LTTE suicide-bomber). Chandrika Kumaratunga of the People's Alliance (a political grouping consisting of the SLFP and various leftist parties), daughter of the Bandaranaikes, became prime minister in 1994 and immediately made overtures to the LTTE concerning unconditional peace talks. Kumaratunga won election to the presidency in late 1994 and resumed peace talks with the LTTE, which resulted in a formal truce between the government and the LTTE in 1995. However, following several rounds of deadlocked talks, the Sri Lankan government launched military offensives against the Tamils, while at the same time developing proposals for devolution, which would give Tamils in Jaffna a degree of autonomy. While successful at first, the Sri Lankan Army was frustrated by a resurgence of the LTTE in 1999–2000. In the meantime, violence continued, with an attempt on the life of President Kumaratunga herself. However, at the end of 2000 the LTTE declared a unilateral cease-fire as a prelude to talks with the government, and in 2002 Norway and several other Scandinavian countries agreed to monitor the implementation of the peace.

December 2001 saw the victory of a UNP-led coalition in general elections, with Ranil Wickremasinghe as prime min-

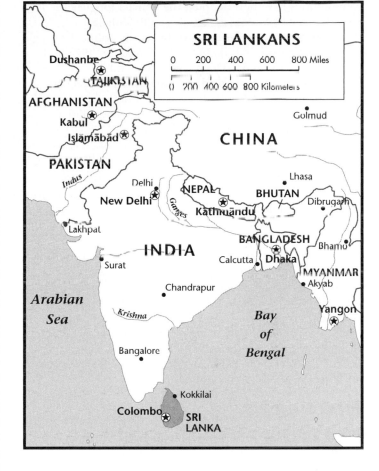

ister. One of the political consequences of this change in government was a strengthening of the peace process, which saw Norway's involvement. However, in 2004 the UNP coalition was defeated, and Mahinda Rajapakse became head of a rather unstable minority government. In 2005 Rajapakse secured a narrow victory in the presidential elections.

Despite a continued commitment to the peace process by the government and the Tamil separatists, acts of violence (probably carried out by the LTTE) still occur in Sri Lanka. In July 2008 a suicide bomber killed several people (both police and civilians) in Colombo. Even though the Sri Lankan government presented its proposals for devolution in 2007, by 2008 it was unlikely that peace would come to Sri Lanka in the near future.

³LANGUAGE

The linguistic patterns of Sri Lankans broadly mirror the ethnic composition of the island. Thus, Sinhalese speak Sinhala, an Aryan language of the Indo-European language family. This was introduced to the island by the peoples from northern India who settled in Sri Lanka around the 5th century BC. Tamils speak the Tamil language, a Dravidian language that is spoken in Tamil Nadu State on the Indian mainland. Arabic is the language of prayer and religious instruction for Sri Lankan Muslims, though the Moors use Tamil for everyday purposes and the Malays still speak their mother tongue. Although English was used in the past by the Burghers and Eurasians, these communities have now adopted the Sinhala tongue. The language spoken by Veddas is very similar to Sinhala.

Language has emerged as a symbol of the political struggle between Sinhalese and Tamils in Sri Lanka. In 1972 Sinhala was made the sole official language of Sri Lanka. This enraged the Tamils, who were denied the use of their own tongue for official purposes, and provided fuel for Tamils who wanted a separate Tamil state on the island. Today, both Sinhala and Tamil are official languages of Sri Lanka.

⁴FOLKLORE

The ethnic communities of Sri Lanka have their own traditions of myth and legend. The Sinhalese, for example, believe they are descended from a lion (*sinha* means "lion" and *le* is "blood") whose grandson, Prince Vijaya, came to the island from North India. The *Mahavamsa,* an important Buddhist work, relates how Vijaya conquered the demoness Kuveni and made her his queen, presenting the history of the island up to AD 350. Much of the Sinhalese folk tradition has its roots in Buddhism. Sri Lankan Tamils, however, take pride in being descended from South Indians who invaded the island nearly 2,000 years ago. As Hindus, their mythology embraces epics such as the *Ramayana*, which tells how the god Rama, assisted by the monkey-king Hanuman, destroyed the evil Ravana in his kingdom of Lanka (Sri Lanka).

⁵RELIGION

The ruler of Sri Lanka was converted to Buddhism during the time of the Indian Emperor Ashoka (3rd century BC), and since then the peoples of the island have been predominantly Buddhist in religion. Most, though not all Sinhalese are Buddhists, who make up 70% of the population. Buddhism in Sri Lanka is of the southern type, Theravāda Buddhism, which virtually requires becoming a monk to achieve salvation. The Buddhist Sangha, or order of monks, is an important element in Sri Lankan society.

Hindus make up 15% of Sri Lanka's population, and Muslims another 7.5%, or just over 1.5 million people. The effects of colonialism are seen in the 7.5% of Sri Lankans who are Christian (mostly Roman Catholic).

⁶MAJOR HOLIDAYS

Sri Lankans officially celebrate many Buddhist, Hindu, Muslim, and Christian holidays. In addition, most businesses are closed on full moon days, which are considered holidays.

One of the most colorful of the many Sri Lankan festivals is the two-week Esala Perahera that is held in Kandy, the ancient hill capital of the island. It is the occasion on which the Tooth Relic of the Buddha is taken out in procession (*perahera*). Thousands gather to see the sacred tooth (nowadays a replica), carried on the back of an elaborately decorated elephant, pass through the streets. The colorful procession consists of dozens of elephants, temple officials, school children, dancers, and acrobats. The festival held at Katagarama, an ancient place of pilgrimage, is attended by Buddhists, Muslims, and Christians, as well as Hindus. The regular festival calendars of all the religions present in Sri Lanka are observed by their respective communities.

⁷RITES OF PASSAGE

Although modernization has had its effect, many Sri Lankans still follow traditional customs in their life-cycle rituals. In rural areas, for example, when a Tamil girl experiences her first menstruation, she is kept isolated in a specially built hut for at least 16 days before she undergoes a ritual purification. For Muslims, the circumcision of male children is an important ritual. Christians solemnize baptisms and weddings in church. Hindus and Buddhists cremate their dead, while Muslims and Christians practice burial.

⁸INTERPERSONAL RELATIONS

Sinhalese are well known for their hospitality to friends, relatives, and even strangers. Guests are invited into the house and offered food and refreshment. This tradition of hospitality originates in Buddhist ideals of charity and compassion. Among the Sinhalese, the same general greeting, "Ayubowan" ("Greetings") is used both when meeting and parting from a person. "Vanakkam" is the Tamil greeting.

⁹LIVING CONDITIONS

Demographic and health statistics set Sri Lankans apart from the other peoples of South Asia because they are not typical of a developing country. Life expectancy for a man, for example, is close to 75 years, compared to 63 in Bangladesh. The annual rate of population increase is 0.78%, quite low when viewed against Pakistan's 2%. The infant mortality rate among Sri Lankans is only 11 deaths per 1,000 live births, whereas among Indians it reaches 58. Per capita income, however, is only US$4,100 (2007 estimate), which is below the average for Asia.

Sri Lankans living in major cities such as Colombo, Kandy, and Trincomalee have access to all the amenities of modern urban living. However, most people (78%) live in villages in the countryside. The typical Sinhalese village is built near a "tank," a reservoir that collects rainwater for irrigation. Houses are mud-walled, thatched, one-room huts, with no windows and a single door. A veranda runs along the front of the hut. Each hut stands on its own plot with a fence marking its boundaries, surrounded by a garden of fruit trees.

Town and country are linked by a network of paved roads and are served by a state-run bus system as well as by private mini-buses. A rail network, though not as extensive as in the past, serves many areas of the island.

¹⁰FAMILY LIFE

The Sinhalese, like their Tamil counterparts, have a caste system which determines ritual status, marriage partners, and even occupation. Marriages are generally arranged, and marriage rituals follow the customs of the community to which one belongs. The woman's role in the family is typical of South Asian societies—managing the household, preparing food for her husband, and above all, bearing children. Average household size is 4.3 persons.

¹¹CLOTHING

Standard dress among the rural Sinhalese is the sarong (*sarama),* which probably has its origins in Southeast Asia. Men wear this with a shirt, and today women use a jacket, though in the past they are reputed to have gone topless. Urban Sinhalese have adopted Western-style clothes. Women wear skirts and

A young Sri Lankan girl writes on a blackboard in Polonnaruwa, Sri Lanka. (© Keren Su/Corbis)

blouses, though they prefer the sari for formal and ceremonial occasions. Muslims wear the shirt and sarong, although the men can usually be distinguished by the caps they wear. In public, Muslim women cover the head and face with their sari in deference to the Muslim custom of purdah, the keeping of women in seclusion. Among Tamils, men wear the *verti*, a long length of cotton wrapped around the waist and falling to the ankles, with a collarless shirt. Tamil women wear the traditional Indian sari, though in a slightly different manner to the Sinhalese.

The "national" dress of Sri Lankans is basically a white verti and a long-sleeved shirt with a Nehru-style collar. It was popularized by politicians in the late 1950s but is hardly worn by anyone else.

¹²FOOD

The standard fare of Sri Lankans is rice, which is eaten at every meal. The rice is served on a plate, along with helpings of curry. A curry is a dish made with meat, poultry, fish, eggs, or vegetables, prepared in an assortment of spices. Sri Lankans cook their curries in coconut milk. The rice and curry is accompanied by an assortment of spicy sauces (sambol), pickles, and chutneys. The meal is usually followed by fresh fruits or, on special occasions, by the sweets so popular among South Asians. Hot tea and coconut milk are popular beverages. *Pan,*

or betel nut, is consumed after meals or, indeed, at any time of the day.

There are regional and also ethnic variations in diet among Sri Lankans. Muslim food, for example, is usually much sweeter than Sinhalese or Tamil dishes. Pork is never eaten because of Muslim religious beliefs. Food is also eaten differently, especially on ritual or ceremonial occasions. Men eat separately from women, sitting in groups and sharing food from a single plate. Among orthodox Buddhists, meat is never eaten because of the belief in the concept of nonviolence (ahimsa). It is common for housewives to offer a sampling of the food prepared for the noon meal (nothing containing meat, of course) to the statue of Buddha. Tamils, who regard the cow as sacred, will not eat beef. Rice cooked with coconut milk is an important festival food and is frequently an offering to the gods. At the time of Thai Pongal, a festival honoring the Hindu sun deity, Tamils prepare and ceremoniously consume a specially prepared dish of spiced and sweetened rice.

¹³EDUCATION

Sri Lankans are unique among South Asians in terms of literacy and educational levels. The overall literacy rate among the population over 10 years of age was 97.3% in 2003. This is the highest of any developing country, and of particular note is the high proportion of girls who remain in school. This figure drops only among Muslims, who tend to keep girls at home after puberty. Education is free, from kindergarten through the university level.

Ironically, the high level of education among Sri Lankans is the cause of some dissatisfaction. Many educated people cannot find suitable employment; they are often unwilling to accept lesser jobs and, therefore, add to the ranks of the unemployed on the island.

¹⁴CULTURAL HERITAGE

The cultural heritage of Sri Lanka is closely linked to the traditions of Theravāda Buddhism. An important event in the early history of Buddhism on the island was the arrival of a cutting taken from the sacred Bo tree under which the Buddha found enlightenment. The Emperor Ashoka sent it to the Island, and it was planted in the ancient capital of Anuradhapura. The tree still survives and, as the original Bo tree in Bodh Gaya no longer exists, it is the only living link with the Buddha. The tree is viewed with great reverence by Buddhists from around the world. The *Dipavamsa* (AD 350) and the *Mahavamsa* (AD 550) are two important works, written by Buddhist monks, chronicling the early history of Buddhism in Sri Lanka.

The artistic heritage of Sri Lanka is also strongly Buddhist in nature. The famous "cloud maidens" of Sigiriya, painted on a ledge high on the walls of a rock fortress, are Buddhist paintings that have survived from the end of the 5th century AD. Numerous Buddhist monasteries, temples, and sculptures are found all over the island. The Gal Vihara at Polonnaruwa, with its statue of the reclining Buddha (14 m or 46 ft long), represents one of the highest achievements of Sri Lankan art.

Sinhalese dance differs from Indian classical dance forms in its reliance on body movements, rapid footwork, and acrobatics to tell its story. It is usually performed by males. "Low-country" dancing, performed in the southern coastal lowlands is sometimes called "devil-dancing" because it evolved from folk rituals to exorcise demons. The "up-country" dancing found in the central highlands around Kandy is performed by women as well as men. *Kolam* is a form of dance-drama involving masked dancers retelling stories from myth and legend.

¹⁵WORK

On gaining independence, Sri Lanka inherited a well-developed plantation agriculture which remains a mainstay of the country's exports. Tea, coconut products, rubber, cinnamon, cardamom, and pepper are the major crops. For centuries, Sri Lanka has been known for gemstones and today still exports sapphires, rubies, semiprecious stones, and pearls. A relatively recent development has been the establishment of a Free Trade Zone near Colombo, the country's capital. Ready-made clothing produced there now accounts for nearly half the value of Sri Lanka's total exports.

¹⁶SPORTS

Sri Lankans are very fond of sports. Cricket is by far the most popular game, with many clubs participating in league play during the season, which lasts from September to April. Club matches draw large and enthusiastic crowds of spectators. On the international cricketing scene, Sri Lanka is emerging as a major power. In 1996 Sri Lanka achieved an important international honor by winning the World Cup of Cricket, beating countries such as the United Kingdom, Australia, and Pakistan.

Other popular sports include rugby, tennis, and soccer.

¹⁷ENTERTAINMENT AND RECREATION

Sri Lankans have access to radio and television, although television programming is scheduled only in the evening hours. Programs are broadcast in Sinhala, Tamil, and English. Sri Lanka has a small film industry producing movies in Sinhala.

¹⁸FOLK ART, CRAFTS, AND HOBBIES

Artisans in Sri Lanka carry on a tradition of fine craftwork that extends back many centuries. Woodcarving; lacquer work; ivory-carving; metalwork in brass, gold, and silver; jewelry; pottery; and basketry are all represented in the arts and crafts of the island.

¹⁹SOCIAL PROBLEMS

Sri Lankans have faced many of the problems typical of newly independent countries, for instance, the need to develop self-sufficiency in food, conversion of a colonial economy, inflation, and high unemployment. Heavy military expenditures, deficit financing, and high petroleum prices on the global markets increased inflationary pressures. Inflation was running at 19.8% in May 2008, the highest level in five years.

A number of Tamil refugees have fled the island to India and the West in order to escape the violence associated with the civil war.

The December 2004 Asian tsunami was an economic disaster for Sri Lanka. Not only were an estimated 40,000 lives lost, fisheries and tourism along the coasts were disrupted, and many people lost their livelihoods. The tsunami, along with political developments, interrupted promising economic policy initiatives and the progress of economic reconstruction.

In some areas, such as health and education, Sri Lanka is a model for the Third World. But the most divisive problem in the country is the conflict between the Sinhalese and Tamils. After independence, Tamil resentment at Sinhalese nationalism eventually led to armed insurgency on the part of Tamils in the northern areas around the Jaffna peninsula. Organizations such as the Liberation Tigers of Tamil Eelam (Eelam is the Tamil name for Sri Lanka), which has received support from Tamils in India, have been fighting for an independent Tamil state in the northern part of the island. India even sent a peacekeeping force to the region for a short time in the late 1980s. The problem remains unresolved today, with continuing armed conflict between the Sri Lankan Army and Tamil separatists.

²⁰GENDER ISSUES

The majority of women in Sri Lanka are Sinhalese, and as Buddhists they have theoretical equality with men. But like their Tamil counterparts, they live in patriarchies and thus tend to occupy subordinate roles in Sri Lankan society. Tamils are Hindus and share many characteristic of Hindu societies—arranged marriages, casteism, dowries, and the occasional dowry death. Many of these features are mirrored in Sinhalese society. Some Tamil teenagers marry when they are below the legal age in Sri Lanka (18 years) to avoid recruitment by the LTTE.

Sri Lankan women overall enjoy more equitable inheritance rights than women in many other parts of South Asia. The constitution provides for equal inheritance rights for men and women, but Islamic law discriminates against women in the area of property and grants them smaller inheritance shares than male heirs. A daughter, for example, inherits half as much as a son. In Kandyan law, males are also given precedence over females in inheritance of agricultural land.

Violence against women continues to be a problem and to a large extent is due to the long-running conflict between the Sri Lankan government and the LTTE. For the duration of the conflict—almost two and a half decades—women have experienced rape, detainment, harassment at checkpoints, and other violations of their personal security. Domestic violence, including marital rape, is another area of concern where legal protection, although strengthened through amendments to the Penal Code, is insufficient and incidents of domestic violence rarely reported.

²¹ BIBLIOGRAPHY

De Silva, K. M., ed. *Sri Lanka: A Survey*. London: C. Hurst, 1977

Ghosh, P. S. *Ethnicity Versus Nationalism: The Devolution Discourse in Sri Lanka*. New Delhi: Sage Publications, 2003.

Johnson, B. L. C., and M. Le M. Scrivenor. *Sri Lanka: Land, People, and Economy*. London: Heinemann, 1981.

Ludowyk, E. F. C. *The Story of Ceylon*. Rev. ed. London: Faber, 1985.

Tambiah, H. W. *The Laws and Customs of the Tamils of Jaffna*. Colombo: Women's Education and Research Center, 2001.

Uyangoda, J., Perera, M. ed. *Sri Lanka's Peace Process—2002: Critical Perspectives*. Colombo: Social Scientists' Association, 2003

—by D. O. Lodrick

SUMBANESE

PRONUNCIATION: SOOM-buh-neez
LOCATION: Indonesia (island of Sumba, Lesser Sunda chain)
POPULATION: 611,000 (island, 2005)
LANGUAGE: Wewewa (or Waidjewa) in the west, and Kambera in the east
RELIGION: Protestantism; Catholicism; traditional belief system
RELATED ARTICLES: Vol. 3: Indonesians

¹INTRODUCTION

The export of sandalwood and horses has linked Sumba to international markets since the earliest times; the 14th-century Javanese poem, the "Nagarakrtagama," lists Sumba as a Majapahit "vassal," though in actuality this meant little more than a commercial relationship. In the 17th century, the sultanate of Bima (on Sumbawa) extended a loose hegemony over the island's chiefdoms; at the same time, Makassarese influence also reached the island. Local rulers amassed great wealth, particularly in gold, through the sale of slaves to Muslim dealers from off-island. Reaching its peak in the 18th century but continuing well into the next, the slave trade virtually depopulated the center of the island.

In 1756, the Dutch concluded a contract with a coalition of Sumbanese chiefs. However, it was only around 1900 that the Dutch began to intervene in local politics, controlling the island through the chiefs already in power, renaming them "rajas." In 1886, a Catholic mission was established but soon abandoned. In 1906, the Dutch commenced the formal pacification of the island, installing an administrator six years later. The situation remained unsettled for some time, the garrison troops being replaced by police forces only in 1933. The Dutch ruled (and taxed) the island through its traditional elite, whose power colonialism actually increased; the elite also perpetuated their dominance by accessing the modern education newly introduced by Christian missionary organizations, education that gave their children the credentials to be appointed as officials. In 1962, the Indonesian republic replaced the old administrative divisions based on traditional "kingdoms" with a system of districts under district heads (*camat*).

Although the island remained the least developed part of one of Indonesia's least developed provinces, Suharto's New Order regime (1966–1978) did invest in schools, roads, electrification, and healthcare. Since subsistence agriculture has remained the primary means of livelihood (tourism grew but only minimally because of the limited infrastructure), infusions from the central government, particularly in the form of bureaucratic salaries, represent a relatively large portion of the local GDP. Thus, securing a government job not only for the salary itself but also for the opportunities for corruption, is the main way available for a person to lift himself and his extended family out of the poverty endured by the general population. Competition for government positions has been fierce between ethnic groups ("tribes," clans) on Sumba.

In the uncertain conditions after Suharto was forced to give up power and amidst national economic collapse and a regional drought, this competition erupted into one case of mass violence: in November 1998 in Waikabubak, the capital of West

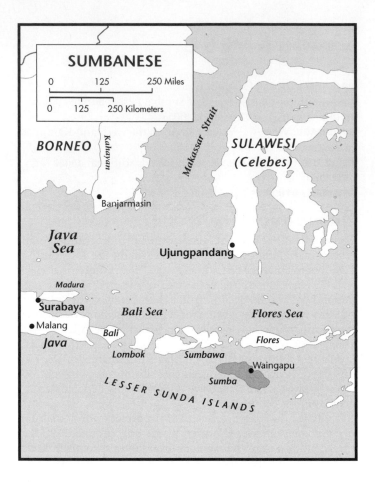

SUMBANESE

0   125   250 Miles

0   125   250 Kilometers

BORNEO

Kahayan

Banjarmasin

Makassar Strait

SULAWESI (Celebes)

Java Sea

Ujungpandang

Madura

Surabaya

Malang

Bali Sea

Flores Sea

Bali

Java

Lombok

Sumbawa

Flores

Waingapu

Sumba

LESSER SUNDA ISLANDS

Sumba regency, a protest against corruption in the civil service exams directed against the regency's current *bupati* (head administrator), a member of the Wewewa tribe, evolved into a battle between the Loli and Wewewa tribes, in which over a hundred people were killed. The bupati's chief opponent had long been the head of the regency parliament, a Loli. The town, once a magnet for tourists because of the traditional hilltop villages around which it had grown, was devastated. Traditional reconciliation ceremonies, appeals to Christian brotherhood, and police reinforcements from the East Nusa Tenggara provincial capital of Kupang in West Timor attempted to keep the peace thereafter.

²LOCATION AND HOMELAND

The island of Sumba (area: 11,153 sq km or 4,306 sq mi) belongs to the Lesser Sunda chain, lying south of Flores and Sumbawa across a narrow strait and east from Timor across the Savu Sea. Like Timor, the island lacks volcanoes. Much of the interior, especially towards the west, consists of irregular hills; the eastern part, in particular, is very hot and dry. The population (611,000 in 2005, up from 415,000 persons in 1988 and 250,000 persons in 1960) is concentrated in an interior plateau whose extensive grasslands can support grazing and small-scale agriculture. In the 19th century, the Dutch sponsored the settlement of Christians from the neighboring island of Savu; Muslim Endenese from Flores had already settled at points along the coast, originally engaged in the export of Sumbanese slaves.

³LANGUAGE

The Sumbanese speak several closely related Austronesian languages: Wewewa (or Wejewa), Anakulangu, Kodi, Lamboya, Laura, Mamboru, and Wanukaka in the west, and Kambera (divided into numerous dialects of its own) in the east. Outside the island, the Sumbanese languages find their closest affinities with Manggarai (Flores), Bimanese (Sumbawa), and Savunese.

⁴FOLKLORE

Traditional beliefs and mythology are still prevalent among the Sumbanese, even though Christianity has come to be the dominant religion. Sumbanese mythology includes many spirit figures, from the Creator to the ancestors (*see Religion*).

⁵RELIGION

In recent decades, Protestantism has come to claim 51% of the population in East Sumba and 34% in West Sumba, while the Catholic population now includes 20% of the total in West Sumba. Adherents of the traditional belief system, however, still number a relatively high 39% in East Sumba and a similar percentage in West Sumba.

Marapu is the generic term for the spirits and the spirit world. The highest deities include a Creator figure, a Mother Moon, and a Great Mother/Great Father. In addition, innumerable "Lords and Protectors" (of fields, houses, wells, etc.) are recognized. Some ancestral spirits are deified. Clan priests (*ratu*) communicate with the marapu through blood sacrifices, food offerings, and invocations at altars (racks, posts, or stones in houses, fields, and the bush). For instance, before hunting, one sacrifices a rooster to Marapu Ponda, the god of hunting. Religious celebrations accompanying hunting, house-building, weddings, and funerals provide an occasion for gift-exchange among linked kin-groups. Lengthy all-night recitals transmit stories (*li ndai*) about the creation of world, the descent of humans to a mythical mountaintop, the dispersal of ancestral clans, and the wanderings of clan founders.

Sumbanese social life is still in great part regulated by the Marapu religion and its rituals, and so even Sumbanese Christians living outside the clan "mother villages" where traditional practices are maintained continue to respect the authority of the ratu.

⁶MAJOR HOLIDAYS

The New Year's festival (*Wula Padu*) is celebrated at the beginning of the agricultural year (the start of the rainy season); a "first fruits" celebration is held at harvest time. Every four to eight years, village renewal festivals take place; ancestral spirits are invited to join.

The culmination of the annual fertility rites is the *Pasola*, timed for the first appearance of multicolored *nyale* seaworms (a delicacy) on shore (after the second or third full moon of the solar year). The worms are said to be the transformed body of Nyale, the beautiful daughter of the Moon King; taking pity on the sufferings of humanity, she threw herself into the sea as a sacrifice. The Pasola includes the ritual plowing of a sacred paddy field. Young men and women gather at the beach to watch boxing matches meant to draw blood to appease the spirits. Priests observe how abundant the worms are in order to determine prospects for the harvest. The highlight of the festival is a battle between two teams of 150 mounted warriors

A Rato (priest) of the Sumbanese culture is seen dressed for the Pasola ceremony in Sumba, Indonesia. The Pasola is a ceremony that is part of a fertility ritual. This culture remains one of Indonesia's last native groups to practice their traditional animist beliefs. (Getty Images)

each. Although the warriors use blunted spears, the fighting can get bloody. In the past, death was common and regarded as punishment meted out by the *marapu* for infractions of custom. The wounded could expiate their transgressions through sacrifices of chicken and pigs. The spilled blood purifies the participants' villages for the coming year and ensures the health of the crops.

⁷RITES OF PASSAGE

A child receives his or her name when one day old. Prayers to the *marapu* for an infant's safety and longevity accompany his or her first haircutting; an uncle brings a pig for the following feast, receiving a horse from the father in return. Boys undergo circumcision, while girls undergo tattooing and tooth filing.

Elders arrange marriages; for aristocrats, complicated negotiations are required. A representative of the boy's side, the *wunang*, delivers the proposal in euphemistic language, referring to the prospective bride as a "bundle of rice." Marriage by elopement is also common. Before taking the girl to his house, the young man leaves a gold chain under her pillow and a horse in the yard to inform her parents of the abduction. Upon arriving home, he beats a gong and distributes gifts to his relatives as a sign of the union. If amenable, the girl's side sends a wunang to negotiate, sending a cloth symbolizing their hav-

ing raised the girl; the boy's side replies by sending them water and wild figs. Now, the families can set the bride-price and the wedding date. Weddings entail the exchange of goods between the families: the groom's side gives "masculine" goods (gold, spears, slaves, horses), and the bride's side gives "feminine" goods (textiles, beads, pigs, ivory).

For the funerals of nobles, large numbers of water buffalo are slaughtered, and textiles and other valuable goods are destroyed as a display of status. Government regulations limit animal sacrifice to five animals so that no one bankrupts themselves. The rites extend over several years in order to accumulate wealth for a secondary burial. Aristocratic tombs consist of huge stone sarcophagi under enormous slabs; in West Sumba, 40 men labored two years to carve a 30-ton grave slab. The largest tomb on the island was built in 1971 at Gulabakul; 2,000 men were needed to drag the 70-ton slab.

⁸INTERPERSONAL RELATIONS

In East Sumba, an individual's identity traditionally derives from the independent domain (*tana*) to which he or she belongs (of which there are 50). Each tana has a fortified hilltop ceremonial center, the *paraing*. Within a tana, four clans share the title of *kabihu mangu tana* ("those who possess the land") and have the right to lead agricultural rituals. The *Tamu*

Umbu, the ruler of the tana, is determined theoretically by primogeniture, but oratorical skills and other leadership qualities may favor a younger son or other relative. The ruler's dwelling houses the treasure coming down from the *marapu* and serves as the temple for the whole tana. The ruler is empowered to deal with other tana and with foreign traders, on whom he levies duties on horse and cattle exports.

Society was traditionally divided into two broad endogamous classes: the *tau kabihu* ("humans") who possess land rights based on kin-group membership and clanless *tau ata* (slaves). The latter included *ata ndai* (servants) and *ata bidi* (war captives and violators of custom) and ranged from well-off household servants and artisans to field-hands and, formerly, the objects of human sacrifice. The elite (*maramba*) were descended most directly from the marapu, a status inheritable through paternal and maternal lines. This class had greater access to land, being able to afford to maintain wet-rice fields, as well as sumptuary privileges; lower-ranking tau kabihu were clients of maramba. An elite family traditionally gained prestige through sponsoring religious festivals at which it could display wealth in the form of water buffalo, horses, textiles, and jewelry, sometimes involving the potlatch-like destruction of these goods while extolling praise of the clan. Many former rulers have taken positions within the local administration under the Indonesian republic.

⁹LIVING CONDITIONS

In 2005, the two regencies of Sumba had an average Human Development Index (combining measures of income, health, and education) of 59.7, significantly less than that of East Nusa Tenggara province as a whole (63.6) but dramatically below that of Indonesia as a whole (69.6). East Sumba's HDI was much lower than West Sumba's in 1999, and now the former's GDP per capita is much higher than the latter's, us$3,507 vs. us$2,236, the third lowest in East Nusa Tenggara, whose provincial GDP per capita in turn is the second lowest in Indonesia (cf. us$9,784 for West Sumatra, us$8,360 for North Sulawesi, and us$6,293 for Central Java; and us$3,427 for East Nusa Tenggara as a whole). In 2000, the rate of infant mortality stood at 56.65 deaths per 1,000 live births for West Sumba, only slightly lower than the rate for the province as a whole (56.65), comparable to much more developed provinces, such as South Sulawesi and West Java. East Sumba, on the other hand, had an IMR of 65.62, comparable to Central Kalimantan and Banten, also more developed provinces.

Half of the year, people live away from the main village in scattered settlements near their swidden (shifting-cultivation) fields, although today more Sumbanese are living in riverside villages, while maintaining their clan ties and ritual obligations to the ancestral village. This fortified hilltop home village (the *paraing*) serves also as a ceremonial center. Clan houses face a central square containing the stone slab graves of prominent ancestors and a dead tree upon which skulls were formerly hung (the slabs are also used for tasks such as drying rice). Tombs, taking the shape of the canoes that brought the ancestors to Sumba, are also built on hillsides.

The clan house (*uma kabihu*) is a large rectangular structure supported on piles. Supported by four massive center posts, its thatched roof rises gently from all sides then rises sharply to a center ridge; a statue of a chicken (a fertility symbol) stands on the roof. High up under the roof is the place for storing the *marapu* heirlooms. A veranda runs along the front side. There are separate entrances for the sexes, as well as a gender-divided interior.

The uma kabihu housed members of a patrilineal clan segment and served as a clan temple; the right front corner post is where offerings are laid and the officiating priest stands near it at ceremonies.

Ordinary houses (*uma kamudungu*) are of wood and have nonpeaked roofs of plaited grass or bamboo (today often of corrugated iron).

¹⁰FAMILY LIFE

The *kabihu* is a patrilineal clan whose segments are scattered in different locales. Each clan has a senior branch, the "great house," most directly descended from the *umbu,* the founder who first obtained the right to settle the land of a given area (often in a mythical age).

A peculiarity of the kin terminology is that one's father's sister's daughter and one's mother's brother's daughter are distinguished from other cousins. At least one son in a family should be wedded to his mother's brother's daughter, although the uncle could be fictive kin. Each kabihu is exogamous, but marriage exchange is between kabihu within the same village with one clan wife-giving (*jera,* higher in status) and the other wife-taking (*laija*). Marriage links over generations impose numerous ritual and economic obligations. If a man dies before the bride-price is paid, his brother fulfills the obligation by marrying his brother's widow.

East Sumba regency has a Human Development Index (combining measures of income, health, and education) of 59.6 (2005 score), lower than that of East Nusa Tenggara province as a whole (63.6) but far below that of Indonesia as a whole (69.6). East Sumba's GDP per capita is US $3,507, above that of East Nusa Tenggara as a whole, us$3,427, the second lowest in Indonesia the second lowest in East Nusa Tenggara (cf. us$9,784 for West Sumatra, us$8,360 for North Sulawesi, and us$6,293 for Central Java). In 2000, the rate of infant mortality in East Sumba stood at 77.8 deaths per 1,000 live births, the highest in the province (provincial rate was 56.65). The corresponding figures for West Sumba regency (2005 HDI, 59.8) differed somewhat, with GDP per capital substantially lower yet the infant mortality also lower.

¹¹CLOTHING

Female attire consists of the *lau,* a tube skirt that includes some bands of warp *ikat,* a type of tie-dyeing (ceremonial skirts include other types of decoration, e.g., beadwork). In the villages, younger women are now wearing blouses. Men wear a *hinggi* consisting of two rectangular pieces of cloth sewn together; one piece is wrapped around the hips, the other draped over the shoulders as a mantle. One type is the *hinggi kombu,* a cloth of blue and rust ikat. Deeper shades are produced by tedious multiple dyeings. The dyes are derived from indigo and *kombu* tree bark; the cloth is treated with plant oils.

¹²FOOD

See the article entitled **Indonesians.**

¹³EDUCATION

In 2005, the level of literacy stood at 72.93% for West Sumba and 81.14 for East Sumba, both lower than that for the East Nusa Tenggara as a whole (84.95) and quite low for Indonesia (West Sumba's was only a little higher than Papua's, and East Sumba's was between West Nusa Tenggara's (78.79) and South Sulawesi's (84.6) (*See also* the article entitled **Indonesians**.)

¹⁴CULTURAL HERITAGE

Among the better-known performing arts are the *Kataga*, a war dance of West Sumba; and the *Lii Marapu*, tales of the creation of the first humans and the ancestors of the Sumbanese told during the *Wula Padu* (New Year) celebration by clan leaders.

¹⁵WORK

Sumbanese engage in small-scale farming supplemented by stock-raising and the exchange of goods. Rice is the staple food and is also ritually important, grown in aristocrat-owned irrigated fields in the valleys. Maize is cultivated in swidden fields. People keep year-round gardens and fruit trees. Large herds of wild horses roam the island; Sumbanese capture them for mounts or to trade off-island. Since the 1920s, Bengal cattle have been raised for export. Water buffalo provide meat for ritual feasts and serve as a measure of wealth. Sumbanese traded horses, buffalo, and *ikat* textiles for gongs, coins, gold jewelry, ivory, beads, and porcelain from Makassarese, Bimanese, and Endenese merchants. The intra-island exchange system, operating along ties of kinship and marital alliance, circulated regional craft products, rice, and imported goods.

¹⁶SPORTS

See the article entitled **Indonesians**.

¹⁷ENTERTAINMENT AND RECREATION

See the article entitled **Indonesians**.

¹⁸FOLK ART, CRAFTS, HOBBIES

Sumba is famous for its *ikat* (tie-dyed) textiles, exported off-island since the 19th century. Using home back-strap looms, women weave patterns from memory (learned from their mothers). Among the great variety of motifs are horses and buffaloes in profile, birds, lizards, open-mouthed dogs, climbing monkeys, rampant cats, Chinese-derived dragons, lions of Dutch origin, Indian patola patterns, standing human figures with arms akimbo or praying, and skull trees. Traditional colors were blue-and-white fabrics for commoners; nobles' cloths added reds. Ikat shrouds protect the body waiting for burial and ensure a safe journey and well-being in the afterlife.

Tombstones are often ornately carved, often with human figures.

¹⁹SOCIAL PROBLEMS

See the article entitled **Indonesians**.

²⁰ GENDER ISSUES

The Gender-Related Development Index (combining measures of women's health, education, and income relative to men's) for West Sumba (2002 score) is 51.6, far below both that of Indonesia as a whole national (59.2) and that of East Nusa Tenggara as a whole (56.3). The two regencies' Gender Empowerment Measures (reflecting women's participation and power in political and economic life relative to men's) were, respectively, 42.2 and 48.5, also far lower than the national GEM of 54.6 but close to the provincial GEM of 46.2).

Sumbanese culture, like those of eastern Indonesia generally, is characterized by allied clans exchanging brides and valuables. A Sumbanese woman's life is shaped by the experience of being moved from her father's house to her husband's house (as opposed to the case in many western Indonesian cultures where it is very often the husband who moves in with the bride's family or even remains virtually a temporary sojourner in his wife's family house). Men have access to the ancestral spirits of the patrilineal clan; women, as outsiders who have married in, do not have such access. On the other hand, women's ritual activity (including what is termed "witchcraft") focuses on "wild" spirits resident in forests, streams, coral reefs, and the depths of the sea and promotes the welfare of individuals and individual families rather than not that of the larger corporate groups defined by worship of common patrilineal ancestors.

²¹ BIBLIOGRAPHY

Badan Pusat Statistik: Data Statistik Indonesia. http://demografi.bps.go.id (November 9, 2008).

Gordon, Raymond G., ed. *Ethnologue: Languages of the World*, 15th edition. Dallas, TX: SIL International, 2005. http://www.ethnologue.com/ (November 16, 2008).

Hoskins, Janet. "Doubling Deities, Descent, and Personhood: An Explanation of Kodi Gender Categories." In *Power and Difference: Gender in Island Southeast Asia*, edited by Jane Monnig Atkinson and Shelley Errington. Stanford, CA: Stanford University Press, 1990.

Kuipers, Joel C. "Talking About Troubles: Gender Differences in Weyéwa Ritual Speech Use." In *Power and Difference: Gender in Island Southeast Asia*, edited by Jane Monnig Atkinson and Shelley Errington. Stanford, CA: Stanford University Press, 1990.

LeBar, Frank M., ed. *Ethnic Groups of Insular Southeast Asia*. Vol. 1, *Indonesia, Andaman Islands, and Madagascar*. New Haven, CT: Human Relations Area Files Press, 1972.

Muller, Kal. *East of Bali: From Lombok to Timor*. Berkeley: Periplus, 1991.

Project for the Study and Recording of Regional Cultures. *Adat Istiadat Daerah Nusa Tenggara Timur* [Customs of East Nusa Tenggara]. Jakarta: Department of Education and Culture, 1978.

Vel, Jacqueline A. C. "Tribal Battle in a Remote Island: Crisis and Violence in Sumba (Eastern Indonesia)." *Indonesia* 72 (October 2001).

—revised by A. J. Abalahin

SUMBAWANS

PRONUNCIATION: soom-BAH-wuhns
LOCATION: Indonesia (Sumbawa)
POPULATION: About 320,000 (2000)
LANGUAGE: Sumbawan
RELIGION: Islam
RELATED ARTICLES: Vol. 3: Indonesians

¹INTRODUCTION

The name "Sumbawa" originally referred only to the western part of the island of Sumbawa, to the home of the *Tau Semawa*, the Sumbawan ethnic group. The eastern part belongs to the distinct Bimanese people; relations between the regions were distant. As late as 1920, there was no intermarriage between the Sumbawan and Bimanese sultanates. The island received some early Hindu-Javanese influence; four places on the island appear in the 14th-century Javanese poem *Nagarakrtagama*. In the 16th century, the Balinese kingdom of Gelgel extended its hegemony to the Semawa, while Bima entered the Makassarese sphere of influence; both peoples adopted Islam.

On 12 June 1674, the sultanate of Sumbawa made an agreement with the VOC, which included ceding territory to the Dutch company, thus enabling it to monopolize the island's most renowned export, sappanwood (an ingredient in dyes). In 1820, an adventurer from Banjarmasin (South Kalimantan) seized the sultanate's regalia; his descendants ruled as sultans of Sumbawa until Indonesian independence. Dutch direct rule only began in 1905. The island had suffered from frequent famine before the 1980s, when the Indonesian government succeeded in doubling rice production.

²LOCATION AND HOMELAND

The island of Sumbawa (area: 15,448 sq km or 5,965 sq mi) lies between Lombok and Flores in the Lesser Sunda chain. The Gulf of Saleh virtually splits the island in half but for a narrow isthmus. Originating in the region of Sanggar, the Sumbawan ethnic group inhabits the land west of the gulf; their old sultanate was centered near the volcano Tambora before its catastrophic eruption in 1815 caused major population losses and displacements. Much of the island is covered by grasslands dotted with occasional clumps of trees and shrubs, partly the product of slash-and-burn agriculture. Wet and dry seasons contrast sharply.

According to the 2000 census, Sumbawans comprised 8% of the population of West Nusa Tenggara province or over 320,000; the two regencies of Sumbawa and West Sumbawa had a population of nearly 500,000 in 2006. Population is concentrated on the northern plains where wet-rice agriculture is possible; population density (2006 figures), at 59 persons per sq km (95 persons per sq mi, more than double 1990s estimates), remains low. By contrast, eastern Lombok counts 656 persons per sq km or 1,056 persons per sq mi. Although the coastline is highly indented, Sumbawan culture is not sea-oriented (most villages lie at least 5 km or 3 mi from the coast). A Southern Mongoloid people with minimal Papuan admixture, the Sumbawans are lighter in complexion than the more mixed Bimanese. Sumbawan communities can be found in eastern Lombok.

³LANGUAGE

A Western Austronesian language, Sumbawan is most closely related to Sasak and Balinese, while Bimanese links with the Central Austronesian tongues of Savunese and Manggarai. For example, "people" in Sumbawan is *tau*, but in Bimanese it is *dou*. In the past, Sumbawans used an Arabic-derived script (now little used) to set down charters and documents pertaining to the administration of land and livestock ownership. In addressing social superiors, one employs deferential language, such as substituting *kaku* for *aku* ("I"), and using aristocratic titles, such as *ruma, rato, dari,* and *ada.*

⁴FOLKLORE

See the article entitled **Indonesians**.

⁵RELIGION

The Sumbawans are reputed to be more orthodox in their practice of Islam than the highly devout Bugis-Makassarese and even more than the Bimanese who are widely seen as "fanatical." No Christian missionaries have ever been allowed to gain a foothold on the island. Southern Sumbawa, however, has only been Islamized for 100 years.

The sultan of Sumbawa retains his religious role despite having lost political power with the Dutch takeover at the beginning of the 20th century. Other religious officials include the *lebe,* the head of the mosque who is also responsible for leading agricultural rites; the *penghulu,* his assistant; the *ketip,* who delivers sermons at the mosque and otherwise directs worship; and the *marbat,* who is in charge of the mosque building and administration.

Remnants of pre-Islamic beliefs include *berempuk,* ritual boxing to spill blood to appease the spirit, and consulting a *sanro,* a healer who dispenses invulnerability treatments. The villages of Tepal and Ropang firmly maintain traditional customs, such as having heirlooms displayed to protect a bride and groom from witchcraft.

⁶MAJOR HOLIDAYS

See the article entitled **Indonesians**.

⁷RITES OF PASSAGE

Some parents still arrange *samulung,* marriages between their underage children, although this violates Islamic law. More usual is for a young man to propose marriage to a girl by sending a *penati,* an eloquent woman, to deliver his request in highly figurative language to the girl's representatives. The *pebeli* or bride-wealth is gauged to the bride's status and can be very high. *Adat* (customary) ceremonies precede the Islamic rites. On the eve of the wedding, there is all-night singing and *rebana* (Arab tambourine) playing.

⁸INTERPERSONAL RELATIONS

Traditional Sumbawan society consisted of the following classes: the *datu* or *dea,* aristocrats (divided further into upper and lower categories); the *tau juran(an),* the descendants of immigrants from Gowa (Makassarese), once influential at court; *tau kamutar,* subjects of the sultan; *sanak,* free commoners; and *ulin,* slaves. Like aristocrats, free commoners could own land but were obliged (though not compelled) to do labor for the kingdom as compensation. Among slaves, there were sharp distinctions between native Sumbawan debt-slaves *(tau mari-si)* and outsiders. Commoners were divided into "task groups" (often corresponding to kin-groups because of the tendency to endogamy), e.g., military or religious specialists, craftspeople, etc.

A village is defined by the presence of a mosque and is divided into wards, each with its own headman. These wards are often ethnically distinct, as in the case of the *kampung* Bugis in the capital of Sumbawa Besar. Under the sultanate, villages united into groupings headed by a *kepala gabungan*. A *wakil kepala* ("headman's deputy") governed each village with the help of a *mandur* (an enforcer) and a *malar* (an official in charge of distributing land titles and, formerly, a leader of agricultural rites).

9 LIVING CONDITIONS

The two regencies that comprise the homeland of the Sumbawan people, Sumbawa and West Sumbawa on the island of Sumbawa, have an average Human Development Index (combining measures of income, health, and education) of 63.7 (2005 score), considerably lower than the Indonesian national HDI of 69.6 though a little higher than that for West Nisa Tenggara as a whole). Sumbawa regency has a GDP per capita of US$5,248, very low for Indonesia (cf. US$9,784 for West Sumatra, US$8,360 for North Sulawesi, but US$6,293 for Central Java and US$6,151 for West Nusa Tenggara as a whole). In 2000, the rate of infant mortality stood at 87.55 deaths per 1,000 live births, among the highest in the country, though slightly less than the rate for West Nusa Tenggara as a whole, 88.55.

Houses on the coast resemble Bugis-Makassarese houses, consisting of four to six rooms with easily movable partitions; a room can be added for a newly married daughter and her husband. In the interior, houses are similar though smaller, resembling those in the eastern parts of the island.

A village is surrounded by its hamlets. Until harvest-time, the population lives in settlements near their swidden (shifting-cultivation) fields.

10 FAMILY LIFE

The Sumbawan lives within concentric circles of kin: his or her nuclear family; relatives up to and including first cousins on both paternal and maternal sides; relatives up to and including second cousins on both sides; and relatives up to and including third cousins on both sides. In the isolated mountain villages of 60–100 families, many people are third cousins, but villages do not correspond exactly to an individual's bilateral kinship group.

The desire to keep wet-rice lands in the family makes marriage between kin (first to third cousins) the preferred pattern. In 1967, only 19% of marriages were between non-kin in villages around Sumbawa Besar. A newlywed couple resides with the bride's parents at first while the husband performs bride-service. Divorce is common because many partners were brought together by their parents while still children.

11 CLOTHING

See the article entitled **Indonesians**.

12 FOOD

See the article entitled **Indonesians**.

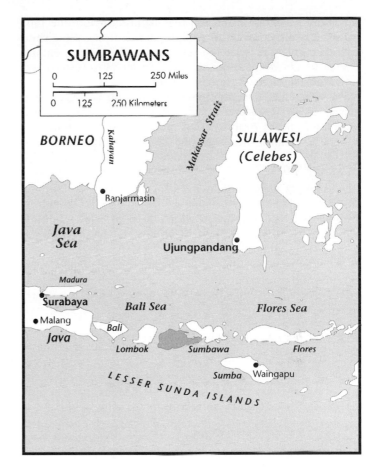

13 EDUCATION

In 2005, the level of literacy stood at 86.59% for Sumbawa regency and 88.4% for West Sumbawa regency, substantially higher than for most other parts of West Nusa Tenggara and is comparable to that for more economically developed if far more densely populated provinces such as East Java and Bali (*See also* the article entitled **Indonesians**.)

14 CULTURAL HERITAGE

See the article entitled **Indonesians**.

15 WORK

Since the Dutch takeover in 1905, there has been a significant expansion of wet-rice cultivation. Dry-rice (swidden farming) has become increasingly confined to the highlands where fields are worked for five years then left fallow for eight to ten years. Surrounding the villages are gardens with perennial crops, such as fruits and vegetables. The island exports onions, beans, and some tobacco and coffee.

Sumbawans raise small, sturdy horses (their export goes back at least to the 14th century). Some individuals own hundreds of cattle, and the island is one of the major areas in the archipelago for the raising of water buffalo. Sumbawans do not hunt the numerous wild boar (because of Islam) but often take deer. They leave fishing to Buginese, Bajau, and Selayar immigrants but do raise fish in fish ponds (alternately used for salt-making in the dry season). Arabs monopolize the horse and cattle trades, as well as money lending, while the Chinese buy up produce for resale and sell merchandise. Before the 1905 opening of a steamship line, Bugis-Makassarese sailing ships carried Sumbawa's trade (horses, water buffalo, hides, onions, beans) to its two main destinations, Surabaya in eastern Java and Makassar in southwestern Sulawesi.

In 2006, 10,280 people from Sumbawa and West Sumbawa regencies were registered with the Indonesian government as working in Saudi Arabia; almost all were women working as domestic servants (there were only 56 men among them).

[16] SPORTS

The racing of water buffalo yoked to a sled or plow through flooded fields has now become a spectator sport, though its original practical aim was to churn the mud before planting. A *sanro* helps prepare the buffalo with special oils and incantations on the night before the race.

Another sport is boxing after the harvest. The fights follow no rules and consist of wild flailing moderated by self-appointed referees. As no judges preside over the contests, each fighter assumes his own victory.

[17] ENTERTAINMENT AND RECREATION

See the article entitled **Indonesians**.

[18] FOLK ART, CRAFTS, HOBBIES

See the article entitled **Indonesians**.

[19] SOCIAL PROBLEMS

See the article entitled **Indonesians**.

[20] GENDER ISSUES

The Gender-Related Development Index (combining measures of women's health, education, and income relative to men's) for the ethnic Sumbawan region (average of the Sumbawa and West Sumbawa regencies) is 57.4, somewhat below Indonesia's national GDI of 59.2. Mataram's HDI, the average of the two residencies' Gender Empowerment Measures (reflecting women's participation and power in political and economic life relative to men's), however, is 45.4, far lower than the national GEM of 54.6 and slightly lower than the GEM for West Nusa Tenggara as a whole.

[21] BIBLIOGRAPHY

Badan Pusat Statistik: Statistik Indonesia. http://demografi. bps.go.id (November 9, 2008).

Government of West Nusa Tenggara—Lombok and Sumbawa. http://ntb.go.id/ntb.go.id/demografi.php (November 9, 2008).

LeBar, Frank M., ed. *Ethnic Groups of Insular Southeast Asia.* Vol. 1, *Indonesia, Andaman Islands, and Madagascar.* New Haven, CT: Human Relations Area Files Press, 1972.

Muller, Kal. *East of Bali: From Lombok to Timor.* Berkeley: Periplus, 1991.

Project for the Inventorization and Documentation of Regional Cultures. *Permainan Rakyat Nusa Tenggara Barat* [Folk Games of West Nusa Tenggara]. Jakarta: Department of Education and Culture, 1984.

Project for the Study and Recording of Regional Cultures. *Adat Istiadat Daerah Nusa Tenggara Barat* [Customs of West Nusa Tenggara]. Jakarta: Department of Education and Culture, 1978.

Situs Resmi Pemerintahan Propinsi Nusa Tenggara Barat—Lombok dan Sumbawa [Official Site of the

—revised by A. J. Abalahin

SUNDANESE

LOCATION: Island of Java in Indonesia
POPULATION: 35 million
LANGUAGE: Sundanese, Indonesian
RELIGION: Orthodox Muslim; Catholic, Protestant

¹INTRODUCTION

As the second largest ethnic group in Indonesia, the Sundanese have a complex history that has given rise to rich traditions of literature, music, dance, and other arts. This history can be traced with certainty back to the 5th century, when the Tarumanagara dynasty established its power and built up trade links extending as far as China. A succession of Sundanese kingdoms, with centers in various parts of western Java, was followed by 350 years of colonization by the Dutch, during which time Sundanese lands became an important source of exports of spices, coffee, quinine, rubber, and tea.

Dissatisfaction with colonization led the Sundanese to join with other peoples under Dutch rule to struggle for the formation of an independent, united Indonesian nation. They achieved independence on 17 August 1945, following a brief but painful period of occupation by the Japanese during World War II. Not all Sundanese were in favor of this unification, however, and some worked with the Dutch or Islamic rebel groups to try to establish an autonomous land for the Sundanese. These efforts were suppressed by Indonesia's first president, Sukarno, and by the late 1950s "Sunda-land" had been fully integrated into Indonesia as one of its richest provinces, called West Java.

Since that time the Sundanese have watched as urbanization and industrialization, punctuated by periods of civil unrest, have completely transformed their lives. Many of these changes took place during the authoritarian rule of President Suharto, who ruled the country from 1967–1998. He aimed to keep up this pace of change for West Java by building new industries, expanding communications services, and reducing the birth rate. Many Sundanese were skeptical of these plans, as a small minority of wealthy individuals gained enormous wealth while the majority remained poor.

In May of 1998, students rose in protest against the government. On May 12 soldiers in Jakarta opened fire on student protestors, killing more than a dozen individuals. This act elicited public outrage against the government and for days the capital was engulfed in rioting that left hundreds dead. The Sundanese homeland in Western Java suffered some of the most severe violence and President Suharto was forced to resign from power. A multiparty parliamentary democracy replaced the dictator and in the last decade Indonesia has seen expansive political reforms. The policies of the new government have permitted greater expression of rights for minority groups, including reform of the Sundanese language.

²LOCATION AND HOMELAND

The Sundanese number more than 35 million people, the vast majority of whom live on the island of Java. Java is the administrative and economic center of the immense Indonesian archipelago, it absorbs a large amount of traffic from other islands and other nations, so the Sundanese have grown quite accustomed to living and working alongside other peoples. This is especially so in the larger cities like Bandung and Cirebon, and in the area surrounding Indonesia's capital city, Jakarta.

Administratively, Java is divided into three provinces, with the central and eastern provinces inhabited predominantly by the larger Javanese ethnic group, and the Sundanese constituting a majority in West Java. West Java itself spreads over an area of 43,177 sq km (16,670 sq mi) and has a high population density, including a large rural population.

Ecologically, West Java enjoys a tropical climate and averages 125 days of rain per year, making it an extremely fertile place for agriculture. While the northern coast is flat and the southern coast is hilly, the central area is mountainous and is marked by spectacular volcanoes. The northwestern coast of Java island was devastated by the 1883 volcanic eruption on Krakatoa Island, which lies in the Sunda Strait between Java and Sumatra islands. The volcano released a large quantity of debris into the air and tens of thousands of people were killed in the ensuing tsunamis that devastated coastal areas.

The ecological diversity of the region makes it a good place to grow a variety of crops, such as rice, tea, coffee, coconuts, rubber, cloves, and vegetables. Western Java is an important center of biodiversity. Ujung Kulon National Park, located on the western most tip of Java Island, is home to more than 50 Javan rhinoceros, one of the most critically endangered mammals on the planet, as well as a stunning array of flora and fauna.

³LANGUAGE

Like other Indonesians, most Sundanese are bilingual, speaking both their mother tongue, Sundanese, and the Indonesian national language, Bahasa. Frequently, Sundanese is the language of choice among family members and friends, while in the public sphere, Bahasa Indonesian is used. Both languages are part of the Austronesian language family.

Sundanese is an extremely diverse language, with different regional dialects taking on words, intonations, and styles of their own. One thing that these dialects share is a division into different language levels. Each language level refers to a different social status. Thus, words used to address parents and elders will be different than those used when speaking to younger siblings and children. There is also a difference in verb usage. For example, Sundanese speakers use several words for the verb "to eat" depending on who is doing the eating. In everyday life, only two levels are used, or sometimes three, but some older people make use of four.

Latin script is primarily used in written Sundanese, but in 2003 the West Java government officially supported the use of the modern Sundanese script in daily activities. Adapted from historic scripts used by the Sundanese from the 14th to 18th centuries, the new script is associated with a revitalization of traditional Sundanese culture.

⁴FOLKLORE

Myths and heroic stories are an important part of Sundanese culture. Such stories are told through films, puppet shows, oral poetry, novels, and even comic books. Some of these stories are regional in character, explaining the history of a local kingdom, or the mythical origin of a lake or of a strangely shaped mountain. Others, like the Ramayana, are Hindu in origin but have been adapted over many centuries to suit the local culture.

If there is one myth that the Sundanese think of as distinctly their own, it is the legend of Nyi Loro Kidul, the Queen of the South Seas. This legend has been around for centuries and is told in a number of old Javanese chronicles. As the story goes, there was a princess in the Pajajaran kingdom in the 14th century whose thirst for power was so great that her father placed a curse on her. This curse gave her more power than he himself had, but it allowed her to wield it only over the South Seas. The princess was then reincarnated as the exquisitely beautiful Nyi Loro Kidul, who is said to live off West Java's south coast. More powerful than all the spirits, Nyi Loro Kidul is said to have received nighttime visits from Javanese kings and Muslim saints in her palace beneath the waves. Men who swim or fish off the south coast are warned not to wear green, for those who do are often spirited away by Nyi Loro Kidul and never return.

5 RELIGION

The overwhelming majority of Sundanese are Sunni Muslim, although some are Catholic or Protestant. Many Muslims pray five times a day, perform the pilgrimage to Mecca at some point in their life, and fast during the month of Ramadan. In towns and cities, there is a mosque in every neighborhood, and each day the calls to prayer are broadcast over public loudspeakers. It is estimated that Islam was first introduced to Java Island in the early 14th century. While embracing Islam, Javanese Muslims retained many of their pre-Islamic beliefs and practices. There are still many non-Islamic elements in Sundanese ceremonies and rituals, particularly in those surrounding the growing of rice. Such elements probably have their origins in the Hindu influence that preceded the spread of Islam, or in pre-Hindu Sundanese culture.

A minority of Sundanese are followers of the Sunda Wiwitan and Ahmadiyah faiths. Considered to be a religion that predates the arrival of Islam and Hinduism, Sunda Wiwitan incorporates traditional animistic beliefs with the belief that there is a God, or gusti, known by many names, including Sanghyang Kersa (the All-Powerful), Batara Tunggal (the One), Batara Jagat (Ruler of the Universe), and Batara Seda Niskala (The Unseen). Followers of Sunda Wiwitan worship the sun and believe that spirits reside in stones and trees. Most of the 3,000 practitioners of Sunda Wiwitan reside amongst the Badui tribe in West Java. Sunda Wiwitan is not recognized by the Indonesian government as an official religion, and followers of the faith have had difficulties obtaining identity cards and marriage registrations.

Ahmadiyah is an Islamic sect considered heretical by many Sunni Muslims. The Ahmadiyah faith originated in India in the late 19th century when the founder of the faith, Mirza Ghulam Ahmad, declared himself the promised Messiah of Islam. The Indonesian government has refused recognition of Ahmadiyah as an official religion, and followers of the religion have become victims of violence in recent years. In 2007, in the village of Manis Lor in West Java where Ahmadiyah have lived for generations, a number of mosques and homes were burned by extremist Sunni Muslims. In 2008, Indonesian president Susilo Bambang Yudhoyono signed a decree banning Ahmadiyah followers from practicing their religion or face arrest.

6 MAJOR HOLIDAYS

The Sundanese follow the calendar of Indonesian national holidays. In addition to holidays for each of the official religions, this calendar includes New Year's Day (January 1), celebrated the evening before with parties, street performances, and fireworks. Kartini Day (April 1) marks the 1879 birthday of one of Indonesia's most famous feminists and nationalists. Pancasila Day (October 1) is a holiday that celebrates the five founding principles of the Indonesian nation. Armed Forces Day (October 5) celebrates the anniversary of the founding of the Indonesian Armed Forces with military parades.

7 RITES OF PASSAGE

When a Sundanese child is born, a *paraji* (midwife with shamanic powers) is usually present to entertain and provide advice to the woman giving birth. The paraji also prays and says mantras so that the mother and the newborn get through the ordeal safely. Once the baby is born, its umbilical cord is cut with a special instrument called a *hanis,* the placenta is buried beneath a window at the rear of the house, and a ritual party is held in which family and neighbors gather to wish the child well and to thank God for its safe birth.

At the age of 7 or 8 years, boys undergo a circumcision ritual to usher them into adulthood. Before the circumcision takes place, the boy is bathed and dressed in a *sarung.* Two men then lift his legs, and a specialist performs the circumcision. The entire ceremony takes place at the boy's home and is frequently accompanied by a party. It is an event boys often look forward to, as it provides them with new found respect and responsibility.

Marriage is the most elaborate of Sundanese rites of passage. Formally, it involves nine stages. First, the parents of the groom visit the bride's parents to inquire whether the girl is eligible to marry. When it is clear that she is, the parents ask each other questions to determine whether it is a good match. When both sides are in agreement about the match, the groom comes with family and friends, bringing gifts and money, and then a representative of his family proposes to the bride's family. If the bride's family agrees, the couple is engaged and is subject to a whole set of restrictions on their interactions. A few days before the wedding, the groom is "given" to the bride, along with clothing, jewelry, and money. One day before the wedding, the parents of the couple formally provide them with advice about how to have a good marriage. On the day of the wedding, the groom is picked up at his home by representatives of the bride's family and taken to her house where he presents her with an agreed-upon amount of gold. Invitees of the bride's family come to see the couple, share food, and leave gifts. The parents of the couple ceremonially feed them the last bites they will receive from their parents' hands, as they are now independent and responsible for finding their own food. One week after the wedding, a gathering is held at the groom's house for his family and friends to meet the bride.

When death occurs among the Sundanese, friends and family immediately gather at the house of the deceased, bringing gifts of money and rice for the bereaving family. The women work in the kitchen, getting ritual offerings ready, while the men make a coffin and prepare a plot at the cemetery. Flowers are soaked in water, and this mixture is used for washing the body of the deceased. A religious leader *(kiai)* then reads a prayer over the body before it is carried in a procession to the cemetery. The death is later remembered, and the sins of the deceased lessened, by holding ritual gatherings on the third, seventh, fortieth, one-hundredth, and one-thousandth days after the person has passed away.

8 INTERPERSONAL RELATIONS

The important thing about Sundanese interpersonal relations is to show people the respect they deserve by following an unwritten code of behavior. Formal greetings, for example, are made by bowing the head and upper body, holding the hands together in front of the chest with fingers outstretched, and touching the tips of the fingers to the tips of the other person's fingers. In business settings, handshaking is quite acceptable. It is done with the right hand, and as one disengages one ought to touch one's heart briefly with that same hand.

When visiting someone, a person must ask permission to enter. The host will then invite the visitor to sit and offer something to drink and eat. It is considered polite to refuse such offers, although one will usually be given a drink anyway; however, the visitor should not drink it until specifically invited by the host to do so. A visitor should always announce his or her intention to leave, to which the host will inevitably reply that the visitor is leaving too soon, and has not even eaten yet (even if the visitor has been there for hours and the host had hoped to be doing something else).

The unwritten rule of dating is that a man must treat the woman he asks on a date with respect. This means he must pick her up at home, converse with her family, pay for any food and entertainment, and escort her home. The woman's family is involved from the beginning and will intervene if they feel a man is not appropriate or is taking too many liberties.

9 LIVING CONDITIONS

Living conditions in West Java are extremely diverse, with a small minority living in extreme wealth and many Sundanese residing in squatter settlements with no running water or electricity. Most people live somewhere between these two extremes, but the disparity in wealth among Sundanese is great.

Beginning in the 1980s, Indonesia has permitted a greater number of Sundanese to purchase cars, televisions, jewelry, and fashionable clothing. In urban areas, motorcycles and cars have become common, though a majority of the population continues to take public transportation for daily activities. Unemployment remains a widespread problem, and Sundanese are often forced to migrate in search of a job.

10 FAMILY LIFE

Kinship among the Sundanese is bilateral, meaning that descent lines are traced through both the mother and the father. There are special terms for seven generations of ancestors and descendants. For example, *gantung siwur* means the father's father of one's great-great-great-grandparent. In principle, all the descendants of a seventh-generation ancestor are members of one's extended family. While this extended family is the largest kinship group, the smallest is a nuclear family of parents and their children. Members of a nuclear family usually live in their own house, although it is not uncommon for relatives of either the husband or the wife to stay with them for a time.

Marriages are sometimes arranged by parents in the nine-step ritual, although this is becoming increasingly rare. More common is for the parents of a woman to prevent her from seeing someone they do not approve of, in the hope that she will find someone more to their liking. The preferred marriage partner should come from the same neighborhood and be a descendant of a common ancestor. Such a marriage is called *perkawinan gulangkep*. Urbanization has made such matches increasingly rare, as couples often meet at school or in the workplace rather than at family or neighborhood gatherings.

Sundanese society draws a clear line between male and female gender roles. Generally, this line places women in charge of the home and men in charge of earning cash. In rural areas, where life is sustained by subsistence agriculture, women are thus quite powerful. But, in cities where there is no space for gardens and all food must be bought, women find themselves economically dependent on their husbands. To combat this dependence and to increase their standard of living, many women have taken on careers or part-time jobs to help earn cash to support their families. It is now quite common for women to enter the workforce before they marry to help support their parents. If they marry, most stop working, but some do not. Even if they do not formally have a job, most women are engaged in informal income-generating work at home, such as catering or selling clothing.

11 CLOTHING

Traditional Sundanese clothing for women consists of a *kebaya* and a *sarung*. The kebaya is a long-sleeved, fitted lace blouse that is worn over a brassiere or another blouse. The sarung is a length of cloth, often batik, which is wrapped around the waist and hangs down to the ankles. Men also wear a sarung, but instead of a kebaya, they wear a long-sleeved batik shirt or a fitted, embroidered jacket.

Increasingly, such traditional clothing is worn only on formal occasions, such as weddings. Everyday dress follows either Western or Islamic styles.

12 FOOD

The Sundanese like to say, "If you haven't eaten rice, then you haven't eaten." While there are hundreds of different ways in which rice is prepared, it is simple boiled rice that serves as the centerpiece of all meals. Side dishes of vegetables, fish, or meat are added to provide meals with variety. These side dishes are spiced with any combination of garlic, *galingale* (a plant of the ginger family), turmeric, coriander, ginger, and lemongrass. Usually the food itself is not too spicy, but is served with a very hot sauce made by grinding chili peppers and garlic together using a mortar and pestle.

The contents of the side dishes depend on what region a Sundanese lives in. On the coast, saltwater fish are common, whereas in the mountains, fish tends to be either pond-raised carp or goldfish. The Sundanese, being Muslims, do not eat pork, but do eat the meat of goats, sheep, water buffalo, and cows. Preferred fowl include chickens, ducks, geese, and pigeons. A dish for which the Sundanese are known is *lalapan*, which consists only of raw vegetables (papaya leaves, cucumber, basil, eggplant, bitter melon, etc.).

Traditionally, Sundanese sit on the floor and eat using the fingers of their right hand. Guests and men are served first, with others following in shifts. Breakfast is generally eaten before the sun comes up, lunch before noon, and dinner about 5:00 PM.

[13]EDUCATION

The Sundanese follow Indonesia's national education system, in which nine years of compulsory primary and middle school may be followed by three years of high school, four years of college, and then studies toward graduate degrees. In the 1980s inadequate education was a wide spread problem. The percentage of the population that had, in 1985, finished primary school was 31%, while 15% had finished middle or high school. Data from 1987–88 indicates that the highest dropout rates occurred after primary school and after high school. In all, 42.8% of graduates from primary school went on to middle school, 75.6% of graduates from middle school went on to high school, and 20% of high school graduates enrolled in college. In 2003, the government of Indonesia mandated that all pupils complete nine years of education. In the post-Suharto era, a greater number of non-governmental organizations have been active in promoting and supporting education in poor regions of the country.

In general, education is very highly valued among the Sundanese, and parents will sacrifice a great deal to pay for their children's education. This is reflected in the better literacy rates in West Java compared with other areas of Indonesia. For example, in 1987, only 16.3% of people over 10 years of age were still illiterate in West Java, compared with over 20% in other provinces. The higher literacy rate may also be a reflection of the better facilities available in West Java, which has been a center of education since colonial times.

[14]CULTURAL HERITAGE

The Sundanese have an extremely rich cultural heritage with highly elaborate forms of music, dance, literature, and other arts. Musically, there is a whole range of styles, ranging from traditional orchestral music to Sundanese pop. One of the more traditional varieties is called *degung,* performed by a simplified *gamelan* orchestra blending soft-sounding percussion instruments with the melancholy sounds of a flute. Another type of orchestra is made up of an instrument called *angklung* (consisting of suspended bamboo tubes in different lengths that sound when shaken). The angklung is an ancient Sundanese instrument that once accompanied storytelling and marching but is now used to perform anything from a traditional tune to a melody by Beethoven. Indeed, the Sundanese are not conservative when it comes to the arts but are willing to try anything new that comes along. Many of Indonesia's most famous pop stars are Sundanese, and local music is sometimes set to the beat of House music.

Sundanese dance generally consists of movements that are smaller and fewer in number than in Western dance. Movements of the hands, fingers, eyes, head, and feet are very controlled and precise. Much of Sundanese dance is influenced by the martial arts, and some is accompanied by *gamelan* music. Some dances tell stories, like the Mask Dance, which tells of a king's hatred after his love was rejected. Other dances are more social, like *jaipong,* which combines elements of a number of different dances into an erotic whole.

Sundanese literature has traditionally been closely tied to oral storytelling culture. One of the oldest forms of literature still in existence is the *pantun cerita,* a kind of traditional poetry in which each verse consists of two couplets, the first of which suggests the second by sound, or by some other similarity. Such poetry tells of Sundanese heroes from ancient times,

often focusing on the age of Sundanese kingdoms. Such stories have been passed down for centuries. More modern forms of literature, such as the novel, have also emerged among the Sundanese. Unlike in the West, however, these novels have always been popular in character, as there is no "high" literary tradition. They are thus just as likely to be read by townspeople as by urban intellectuals.

[15]WORK

Unemployment is not as great a problem as underemployment in West Java. Most people have some way of generating income, either in the formal or the informal sector, but have a hard time making ends meet. This is particularly true for a new generation of college-educated youth who are having a hard time finding work. When a job does open up, it is often for very low pay at one of the new factories that produces sneakers, televisions, clothing, or furniture. Such positions are usually filled by young women and uneducated men, and often by migrants from Central Java who are more willing to work long hours without vacations than are the family-oriented Sundanese.

[16]SPORTS

The most popular sports in West Java are soccer, volleyball, badminton, and a martial art called *pencat silat.* Most neighborhoods have a small field in which kids play volleyball and soccer. Badminton is usually played in neighborhood front yards or in courts at a community center. Although all these sports draw spectators, soccer pulls in large crowds of local supporters. In larger cities like Bandung, riots are not unheard of when the local team meets with a team from another province.

Pencat silat is a martial art that blurs the line between dance and self-defense. It is usually taught to groups of children at Islamic boarding schools (*pesantren*) by a guru. Pencat silat emphasizes both the spiritual and the physical dimensions of the art and is sometimes tied to mystical practices that are said to give practitioners magical powers.

[17]ENTERTAINMENT AND RECREATION

The central form of entertainment in West Java is called *sore,* or "evening." People go out to movies, take strolls, eat in open-air cafes, and watch public performances. It is a chance "to see and be seen," so people put on their best clothes, women put on makeup, and motor vehicles become objects of envy and pride.

Going to the cinema can mean different things. Cinemas in West Java show a mixture of Indonesian and foreign movies, with the former being slightly more popular. While in city centers cinemas are air-conditioned and have plush seats, marginal areas of the country sometimes have open-air cinemas, which are like drive-ins without the cars. For those who prefer public performances, there is music and theater. One performance that always draws a crowd is *sinten,* in which magicians exhibit their powers. One can see, for example, people turned into birds, eggs cooked on someone's head, and people who are invulnerable to the stab of a sword. Another is *wayang golek,* a type of puppet show in which stories from the Ramayana and Mahabarata are performed, accompanied by singing and gamelan music.

At home, there is always television. Broadcasts include a peculiar blend of Indian movies, Latin American soap operas, American dramas, and Indonesian shows of all varieties. Television is sometimes considered a background entertainment like radio, with people going about their business while watching. It provides entertainment while people do their chores, and the soap operas make a great subject for discussion.

[18] FOLK ART, CRAFTS, AND HOBBIES

Like the neighboring Javanese, the Sundanese are known for the art of batik. Batik is a technique used to create patterns on textiles in which bee's wax is used to facilitate resist-dying. Originally, batik was made by painting the wax on by hand, using a special implement for that purpose, and then bathing the whole cloth in a dye. Using such a technique it could take up to six months to complete one *sarung*. Beginning in the mid-19th century, however, an industrial technique of stamping the cloth with wax was developed. This allowed for mass production and today, batik can be found in American and European stores.

[19] SOCIAL PROBLEMS

West Java has the usual problems associated with a society in which there exists a large gap between the rich and the poor. As in other urban environments, there is a certain amount of crime, a large number of industrial strikes, and occasional riots in which masses of people wreck and burn symbols of wealth and state power. During the Suharto years, the Indonesian government was known internationally for its high levels of corruption and its infringements on human and civil rights. The repressive and corrupt aspects of government made it almost impossible to improve social justice. In the last decade, political reforms have permitted unprecedented political and social freedoms for all Indonesians. Though corruption and poverty remain a problem, an independent judiciary has taken root and minority groups have been permitted to petition the government for reforms.

One persistent problem in West Java is alcohol and drug abuse. While alcoholism is not a serious problem, drug use in all segments of the population appears to be on the rise. Individuals of all religious, ethnic, and socioeconomic groups have been affected by substance abuse.

[20] GENDER ISSUES

Sundanese women in urban areas enjoy a great deal of social freedom, and West Java's modern cities ensure educational and career opportunities for middle class women. The situation in rural areas is quite different, where poverty is rampant, which fuels a sex trade crisis that entraps thousands of Sundanese women each year. High unemployment in West Java provides few job opportunities for young women. A cultural acceptance of prostitution has resulted in many families encouraging their daughters to enter the sex trade. Prostitution is endemic in Indonesian cities, and Sundanese women are found in brothels across the Indonesian archipelago. Local governments have attempted to crack down on the sex trade by refusing to issue identification documents to young women. Non-governmental organizations assist young women escape the sex trade.

In Indonesian society, homosexuals and transvestites neither enjoy legal protections nor are subjected to extreme forms of bigotry. In West Java, as in much of Indonesia, gay men and transvestites do not hide their sexual preferences, yet also have not achieved general social acceptance.

[21] BIBLIOGRAPHY

Moriyama, Mikihiro. *Sundanese Print Culture and Modernity in Nineteenth-century West Java*. Singapore: NUS Press, 2005.

Mustafa, R. H. Hasan. *Adat Istiadat Sunda*. Bandung: Alumni, 1991.

Republic of Indonesia. *Jawa Barat Dalam Angka*. Jakarta: Kantor Statistik, 1989.

Tamney, Joseph B. "Functional Religiosity and Modernization in Indonesia." *Sociological Analysis*, vol. 41, no. 1, (Spring, 1980): 55-65.

Weintraub, Andrew N. "Contesting Culture: Sundanese Wayang Golek Purwa Competitions in New Order Indonesia." *Asian Theatre Journal*, vol. 18, no. 1(Spring, 2001): 87 -104.

Williams, Sean. "Constructing Gender in Sundanese Music." *Yearbook for Traditional Music*, vol. 30 (1998): 74-84.

—revised by David Straub

SYRIAN CHRISTIANS IN INDIA

PRONUNCIATION: SIHR-ee-uhn Christians
ALTERNATE NAMES: Malabar Christians
LOCATION: India (Kerala state)
POPULATION: 3,083,884 (2001 Census)
LANGUAGE: Malayalam
RELIGION: Christianity (Syrian Orthodox, Catholic, and Protestant)
RELATED ARTICLES: Vol. 4: Syrians

¹INTRODUCTION

The term "Syrian Christians" is sometimes used to refer to the total Christian population of Kerala, which lies on the southwestern coast of the Indian peninsula. The presence of Christianity in most parts of India largely reflects the work of missionaries during the Western colonial period, particularly after the early 1800s. In a more restricted sense, however, Syrian Christians trace their origins to the 1st century AD, when St. Thomas the Apostle is believed to have landed in Kerala. As a result of this, they are also known as Christians of St. Thomas. The community derives its designation as Syrian Christians from its early association with the East Syrian Church of Christianity, and its traditional use of the Syriac language in church services. Syrian Christians are also called Malabar Christians, Malabar being the name for the coastal region of this part of India.

According to local tradition, St. Thomas landed on the coast of Kerala in AD 52 near Cranganur, some 30 km (20 mi) north of Cochin. He began to preach the gospel and is said to have established seven churches in the region. St. Thomas found a receptive audience among the local Hindu and Jewish populations, many of his converts coming from the high-caste Nambudiri Brahmans, the dominant landowning caste of Kerala. Many Christians in the region claim descent from these early converts among the local peoples. One group, however, traces its ancestry to Thomas of Cana (Knai Thoma), a merchant who led a party of Syrian Christians to Kerala in the middle of the 4th century AD. Some authorities, however, question the historical accuracy of these accounts. They suggest that Christianity was introduced to Kerala by Nestorian missionaries (a sect named after an heretical 5th-century bishop) during the 6th century. Further migrations from Syria during the 9th century invigorated and revitalized the Christian Church in Kerala. The Christian community in Kerala maintained its ties with the Christian homeland by continuing to get its bishops from Antioch, an ancient center of the Eastern Orthodox Church.

The arrival of the Portuguese in India in 1498 introduced the old conflicts of Christendom to the Indian subcontinent. As the Portuguese presence in India grew, so did the power of the Church of Rome. Condemning both the Syrian rites and many practices of the Syrian Christians, the Portuguese set out to "Latinize" the Church in Kerala. By the early 17th century, the Roman Catholic Church was dominant in the region. In 1653, however, some Syrian Christians reasserted their traditional beliefs, swearing before an open-air cross (an event known as the "Coonen Cross Oath") that they would never ac-

cept the supremacy of the pope and Western Christianity. One consequence of this and later splits within the community is that the Syrian Christians of Kerala are now divided between the Syrian Orthodox, Catholic, and Protestant Churches.

²LOCATION AND HOMELAND

Christians in Kerala are currently estimated to number over 6 million people. Around half this number are Christians who belong to non-Syrian Christian churches, for instance, the Protestant Church of South India (CSI). Syrian Christians (3,083,884 in the Census of India 2001) thus represent about 10% of the state's population (31,841,374 according to the 2001 Census), while Christians in Kerala make up nearly 30% of the total Christian population of India. It is by far the largest concentration of Christians found in the Indian subcontinent.

Kerala is a narrow, elongated state located in the extreme southwest of India. It extends for some 576 km (360 mi) along the shores of the Arabian Sea. The state's southern boundary lies a mere 55 km (35 mi) from Cape Comorin, the southern tip of the Indian peninsula. The state falls into three distinct geographical zones. In the west lie the fertile, alluvial lowlands of the Malabar coast. This is an important, densely populated, agricultural area, with lagoons, backwaters, and canals forming a network of waterways that are the region's main transportation routes. As one moves inland from the coastal plain, the land rises to low hills and plateaus at elevations between 60 m and 180 m (200–600 ft). Further to the east are the rainswept and forested slopes of the Western Ghats, the range of hills that parallels the entire west coast of the peninsula. The Ghats in Kerala average around 900 m (3,000 ft) in elevation, but peaks in the Cardamom Hills exceed 2,500 m (8,200 ft). The hills catch the full force of the summer monsoon blowing in from the sea, so that extremely high rainfall totals are received in the uplands. Annual rainfall amounts on the coast vary from about 300 cm (120 in) in the north to 100 cm (40 in) in the south. Because of its location between 8°N and 13°N latitude, Kerala experiences an equatorial climate. It is humid and hot all year, with maximum temperatures rarely exceeding 32°C (92°F) and minimums rarely falling below 21°C (70°F).

Kerala has given its name to the Kerala model or the Kerala phenomenon, which refers to a set of economic practices that have resulted in the state attaining a high level of standards in human development (no doubt influenced by the strong Christian presence), while compromising on its industrial development. Thus, Kerala has high literacy, a low birth rate, and demographic indices, such as life expectancy and infant mortality, that would place it among the developed nations, but it ranks behind many states in India in terms of industrial and economic development and in per capita income. Kerala also has the distinction of being one of the few states in the world that has regularly voted communist governments into and out of power. The state government in 2008, led by Chief Minister V.S. Achuthanandan, was formed by the Communist Party of India (Marxist).

³LANGUAGE

Malayalam is the language spoken by the Syrian Christians of Kerala. It is a Dravidian tongue, closely related to Tamil. Malayalam was, in effect, a dialect of Tamil until the 14th century, when it began to assume its own discrete identity. Both the written and spoken forms of the language use many words borrowed from Sanskrit. It differs from Tamil in aspects such as the absence of personal endings on verbs. Malayalam is thus the most recent of the four major Dravidian languages of South India (Kannada and Telegu are the remaining two) in terms of its development. Malayalam is the official language of Kerala and is spoken by 96% of the state's population. It is written in its own script, which is derived from the Tamil writing system. English is widely spoken as a second language. In fact, the winner of the 1997 Booker Prize (now the Man Booker Prize) for Fiction was Arundhati Roy, whose mother is a Syrian Christian and who was brought up in the Syrian Christian tradition.

[4] FOLKLORE

As a devout Christian community, the Syrian Christians lack the elaborate mythology and legendary heroes of their Hindu neighbors. Much of their lore centers on the important figures of their past. St. Thomas the Apostle, of course, occupies the major place in the traditions of the group. There are numerous stories of the miracles he performed through which many high-caste Hindus were converted to Christianity. It is said that St. Thomas was martyred in AD 72 near Madras, now called Chennai, in Tamil Nadu State. He was passing a temple dedicated to the Hindu goddess Kali, when the temple priests forced him to go inside. As he approached, a strong light shone from the temple, and it was destroyed by fire. The infuriated priests fell on St. Thomas and one of them thrust a spear into his heart. The Apostle died three days later. The Gothic San Thomé Cathedral stands on the site of his tomb on St. Thomas Mount.

[5] RELIGION

Whatever its origins, the Syrian Christian community was well established in Kerala by the 6th century AD. It is thus the oldest among the various Indian Christian groups found in the subcontinent. It also differs from the other Christian communities in the social categories from which its converts were drawn. The Portuguese, for instance, encouraged intermarriage with the local population. The early Christian communities of Goa and other Portuguese colonies were thus of mixed descent and derived primarily from Portuguese males marrying Indian women. Converts to Christianity during the 19th century, on the other hand, came largely from the lower and Untouchable castes or tribal peoples. The former were seeking to escape the Hindu caste system, while the latter were marginal to mainstream Hindu society. Many Syrian Christians, however, came from the landowning upper castes, and the community came to rank as equal to the Nairs, who claim warrior (ksatriya) status. Their social position was further enhanced through service to local rulers. Though Christian in religion and beliefs, Syrian Christians have managed to preserve many aspects of their Indian culture.

[6] MAJOR HOLIDAYS

Syrian Christians celebrate all the Christian holy days, with Christmas and Easter being especially important. Christmas is preceded by fasting for 25 days, although nowadays only the older generation follows this custom. During this period, no meat, fish, or eggs are eaten. Smoking, chewing betel nut, and drinking alcohol are totally forbidden. On Christmas Day itself, church services begin long before dawn. As part of the service on this day, the congregation goes in procession to

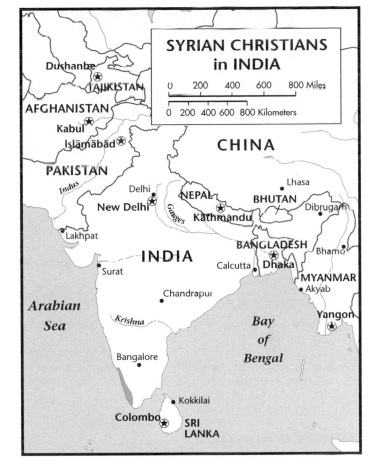

the churchyard, where a hole has been dug in the shape of the cross. Worshipers throw incense on a fire lit in this pit, a rite said to commemorate the offering of gifts to the child Jesus by the Three Wise Men.

Easter is another important festival. The Lenten fast is observed for 50 days prior to Easter. Easter Week itself is marked by church services the entire week. Good Friday is called Dukka Valliacha, which translates as "Friday of Sorrow" in Malayalam. Easter Sunday is a day of joyous celebration, when families gather to break the Lenten fast.

[7] RITES OF PASSAGE

Immediately after a child is born, a priest or male relative will whisper "Moron Yesu Masiha" (Jesus Christ is Lord) in the baby's ear. The child is given a few drops of honey in which some gold is mixed to ensure prosperity. The birth of a son is an occasion for great joy and is announced by the kurava (a shrill sound made with fingers moved up and down in the mouth). Care is taken to record the exact time of birth so that a horoscope may be cast. Baptism may take place soon after birth or be delayed for some months. Children are usually given Biblical names, though these have often been Indianized. Thus, Matthew becomes Mathai or Mathu, and Elizabeth becomes Eliamma.

A child's education begins at the age of three or four, when a ceremony initiating him or her to the world of learning is performed. From this time on, the child usually attends the local school. The ceremony was traditionally performed by a teacher who might be either Christian or Hindu. In modern times, however, a Christian priest is often called upon complete this ritual. Children are brought up to respect teachers and value education They also attend church regularly with their parents, a practice that continues into their adult life.

In the Syrian Christian Church, there is no such ritual as the "last rites." Prayers are said for the dying person, and a priest is usually at the bedside. When a death occurs, women weep and wail and beat their breasts. The kitchen fires are extinguished, and no cooking is done in the house until after the funeral. The body is washed, dressed, and anointed with oil. When the funeral procession is ready, the body is placed in a coffin and carried to the cemetery on the shoulders of friends and mourners. The women of the household usually do not accompany the procession. A simple meal known as *Pashni Kanji* is served to the relatives and mourners on their return from the churchyard. A *Qurbana* (Holy Communion) and a feast are held on the fortieth day after the death to complete the period of mourning.

8 INTERPERSONAL RELATIONS

Though Christian by religion, Syrian Christians are Indian in culture and use the traditional "namaskar" greeting. Despite the growing numbers of nuclear households, extended families keep in close touch with each other. They regularly get together to celebrate birthdays and religious holidays. There are no restrictions on consuming alcohol (except during fasts), and drinks are commonly served to guests or at social gatherings.

9 LIVING CONDITIONS

As a highly educated and literate community, Syrian Christians enjoy standards of health, housing, and material comfort that are among the highest in India. Houses are built facing east, in a compound abounding with mango, plantain, coconut, and other fruit trees. Traditional houses were built of heavy timber, such as teak, with the walls ornately carved and decorated. The roof resembled an inverted boat, to shed the heavy monsoon rains of the area. The people of Kerala have high standards of hygiene and houses have toilets, in contrast to much of India where villagers use the fields for their personal needs. All houses have a roofed entrance gate known as a *padipura*, a simpler version of the more elaborate gates leading to temples and churches. Settlements are dispersed, rather than forming nucleated villages.

10 FAMILY LIFE

Women are held in high esteem, reflecting perhaps the traditional matriarchal nature of society in Kerala. Education and opportunity mean that some women enter the professions and can lead relatively independent lives. However, many women continue in their traditional roles of wife, homemaker, and mother. Strict endogamy is maintained, with Syrian Christians marrying within their own community. Monogamy is the rule, and divorce is rare, in keeping with Christian traditions. The nuclear family consisting of husband, wife, and children is replacing the multigenerational extended family.

Arranged marriages are typical, although more and more young people are selecting their own spouses. There is no cross-cousin marriage. Girls were formerly married before puberty, although child marriage is now illegal in India. A dowry was paid to the bride's father, with a percentage going to the

church as a tithe. A betrothal feast is usually held on the day the banns, the formal proclamation of an intended marriage, are read by the priest in church. The actual marriage is solemnized in church according to the rites of the Syrian Christian Church. Some parts of the ceremony, however, such as when the groom ties a knot in a thread placed around the bride's neck, reflect local Hindu rituals. This is one instance of the many Indian customs that have been absorbed into Syrian Christian life.

11 CLOTHING

Syrian Christians dress in the same manner as do other people in Kerala. Men wear the *dhoti,* the long, white cotton cloth that is wrapped around the waist, then pulled between the legs and fastened at the back. Alternatively, they may wear a *mundu,* which falls to the ankles rather than being passed through the legs. In the past, the chest was left bare, but now shirts are common. A folded cloth known as a *kavani* is draped around the neck.

Women's clothing is generally white. It typically consists of three items: a mundu wrapped around the waist and reaching the ankles, a V-necked jacket or blouse, and a kavani with a narrow gold border draped on the left shoulder. This is used to cover the head when in church. One end of the mundu is folded and tucked into the back of the waist, to fall in the shape of a fan. Women wear earrings, necklaces, and bangles, but usually do not put rings in the nose.

Western dress is common in urban areas, especially among the younger generation. Young women favor the *sari* over traditional dress styles.

12 FOOD

Rice and fish are the staple diet of Syrian Christians in Kerala. Fish abounds in the rivers, lakes, and coastal waters of the region and is cooked in a variety of ways. It is made into fish curry or a fish *moillee* (stew), served in a *masala* (spicy) sauce, rubbed with spices and fried, and stuffed, to name but a few. What are seen as "Christian-style" fish dishes are cooked in tamarind and coconut sauce. A peculiarity of Kerala is that all food is cooked in coconut oil. Meals are eaten with an assortment of sauces and pickles. *Kalan,* for example, is a sauce made from yams, yogurt, and coconut. Rice flour is made into *vellappam* (known as *appam* elsewhere in South India), a mixture of rice and coconut similar to the "hoppers" of Sri Lanka. Tapioca and fish, boiled together with turmeric and chilies, provides a nourishing meal for the poorer classes in the region. Coconuts, plantains, jackfruit, mangoes, and other tropical fruits form an important part of the local diet. Wafer-thin banana chips are a specialty in many areas of Kerala.

13 EDUCATION

Syrian Christians have a strong commitment to education, and the community has virtually 100% literacy. Christian schools have the reputation of being among the best in the state, and parents encourage children—girls as well as boys—to pursue further education or professional qualifications. This is in keeping with, and no doubt contributes to, the educational characteristics of the general population of Kerala. Kerala has the most highly literate and educated population of any state in India It has eight universities, including the Universities of Kerala and Calicut (Kozikhode), numerous arts and sciences colleges, professional colleges, engineering colleges, and training institutes such as the Indian Institute of Management (Kozikhode).

14 CULTURAL HERITAGE

Religious dances and songs are part of the Syrian Christians' cultural heritage. However, they are rarely performed, and few still know them today. Songs told of the life of Christ, St. Thomas the Apostle, and other figures from the community's past. Folk dances presented dramas on Christian themes, or harked back to the days when Christians served in the armies of the local *maharajas* (princely chiefs).

15 WORK

Agriculture is the primary occupation of Syrian Christians. Many Christians own land, while labor is provided by low-caste Hindus. Christians dominate the plantation industry, growing cardamom, tea, coffee, and rubber. They are also successful entrepreneurs, owning factories that process agricultural goods (e.g., coconut fiber or coir, rubber, and cashews) and small businesses. Syrian Christians are well represented in government service, teaching, and professional fields, such as science and medicine. Many women enter nursing. Unlike other parts of South Asia where they have less access to education, women compete on relatively equal terms with men. The Gulf States provide high-paying job opportunities for many people from the region, and they regularly remit funds back to their families in Kerala.

16 SPORTS

In terms of sports, Syrian Christians are no different from their neighbors. They participate in modern games, such as soccer and cricket, and in traditional activities of the region. Many Christian families, for example, own "snake" boats that take part in regattas held to celebrate events like the Onam festival.

17 ENTERTAINMENT AND RECREATION

Syrian Christians enjoy all the amenities available to the people of Kerala—radio, television (color TV for the more-affluent), newspapers, and movies in Malayalam. Much of their social life revolves around church-related activities and events.

18 FOLK ART, CRAFTS, AND HOBBIES

No folk arts or crafts are identified specifically with the Syrian Christians of Kerala today. In the past, however, they were noted for their skill as woodcarvers, brass- and metalworkers, and jewelry designers and manufacturers.

19 SOCIAL PROBLEMS

Unlike many Christian communities in India, Syrian Christians are literate, educated, and relatively affluent. They rank high in the caste structure of Kerala and have a powerful voice in the affairs of the state. They do not suffer from the poverty, discrimination, and political underrepresentation that characterize many other minorities in South Asia.

One problem facing the community is that of fragmentation. There exist, for example, four denominations in the Syrian Church: the Romo-Syrians (Catholics), the Jacobites (Eastern Orthodox), the Reformed Syrians (Mar Thoma), and the Anglican (Protestant) denominations. The Syrian Christians are divided between these churches and often do not marry outside even their own branch of the Syrian Christian Church. Syrian Christians are also divided into two major sections, those that come from the north (Vadukkumbagars) and those from the south, Thekkumbagavars, also known as the Knayana Christians. Several theories exist as to the origins of these sects. One holds that Knai Thoma (Thomas of Cana) had two wives, one a Persian and one a Hindu from Kerala. On his death, he left his possessions north of Craganur to the children of his Hindu wife and his possessions in the south to the offspring of his Persian wife, hence the existence of the two sects of Syrian Christians. Another theory suggests the division came about as a result of two distinct migrations, with the Vaddakumbagars in the north reflecting the work of Knai Thoma on his original arrival in Kerala, and the Thekkumbhagavars in the south being the followers of two Nestorian Persians, who led a second immigration to Quilon in AD 822.

Whatever the origins of Syrian Christians in Kerala, they definitely do not interact with neo-Christians, recent converts from the low castes (some Christian churches in Kerala have separate pews for low-caste and high-caste members of the congregation). Conflicts between churches have sometimes ended up in the courts. Nonetheless, the Syrian Christian community has existed in Kerala for nearly 2,000 years, and no doubt will continue to do so for centuries to come.

Caste remains a problem among the Syrian Christians of Kerala. Early writings place them at the level of the matrilineal Nairs but below the patrilineal Namboodiris. Following efforts by the Christian Missionary Society in the 1880s to enhance the rights of "New Christian" low-caste converts, and their demands to equal status with Syrian Christians, the "delicate bonds" tying Syrian Christians to high-caste Hindus were broken. The effect of Hindu fundamentalist organizations and other upper-caste Hindus in regarding Syrian Christians as a polluting caste and banning their entry into Hindu temple grounds combined with Syrian Christian attempts to affirm assumed *savarna* (i.e. caste Hindu) status—which some were denying—to create a situation in which riots and mob attacks on Syrian Christians occurred. This led to a "chasm" opening between Syrian Christians and their high-caste neighbors. Anthropologists have noted that the caste hierarchy among Christians in Kerala is much more polarized than the Hindu practices in the surrounding areas, due to a lack of jatis. Also, the caste status is kept even if the sect allegiance is switched (i.e. from Syrian Catholic to Syrian Orthodox).

One way in which Syrian Christians differ from the society in which they live is that, unlike the matriarchies that dominate in South India, they are patriarchal. Thus, as in the North, cross cousin marriage is not permitted, although Kerala is one of the few regions in India in which females outnumber males. However, by the end of the 20th century, the fertility rate among Christians had dropped below that of Hindus and Muslims, largely because of the increasing age of marriage and the pursuit of education.

20 GENDER ISSUES

Syrian Christian women have high social status, reflecting perhaps the traditional matriarchal nature of society in Kerala. Education and opportunity mean that some women enter the professions and can lead relatively independent lives. However, many women continue in their traditional roles of wife, homemaker, and mother. Strict endogamy is maintained, with Syrian Christians marrying within their own community. Monogamy is the rule and divorce, though possible, is rare, in keeping with Christian traditions.

Christian society in Kerala mirrors many aspects of Hindu society. At one time, for instance, it was common for women to be married by the age of 15 years. Marriages are still arranged, though often this is done at the request of the individuals involved, and the custom of demanding (and giving) a dowry is well entrenched among the Syrian Christians. Traditionally, a woman received one quarter of the property sons received if a father died intestate, but, given some Supreme Court decisions regarding a woman's right to inherit equal shares, this is rapidly changing.

Syrian Christian women from Kerala, such as Nayantara, are suddenly hot items in the Tamil film industry. As Syrian Christian families are progressive and educated, they are not averse to the idea of the cinema as a career option for young girls.

Syrian Christian women tend to dominate the nursing profession in India. This is explained, in part, perhaps, by the fact that, unlike high caste Hindu women, Syrian Christian women do not have to deal with concepts of ritual purity and pollution relating to bodily secretions.

In general, Syrian Christian women in Kerala exist in a cultural milieu and have the socio-economic independence to allow them to follow their lives without the restrictions that circumscribe other women in South Asia.

21 BIBLIOGRAPHY

Balakrishnan, V. *History of the Syrian Christians of Kerala: A Critical Study*. Thrissur: Kerala Publications, 1999.

Pothan, S. G. *The Syrian Christians of Kerala*. Bombay: Asia Publishing House, 1963.

Thodathil, James. *Antiquity and Identity of the Knanaya Community*. Chingavanam: Knanaya Clergy Association, 2001.

Thomas, Anthony Korah. *The Christians of Kerala*. Kottayam, India: A. K. Thomas, 1993.

Visvanathan, Susan. *The Christians of Kerala: History, Belief, and Ritual of the Yakoba*. Madras: Oxford University Press, 1993.

Zachariah, K. C. *The Syrian Christians of Kerala: Demographic and Socio-economic Transition in the Twentieth Century*. New Delhi: Orient Longman, 2006.

—by D. O. Lodrick

SYRIANS

PRONUNCIATION: SIHR-ee-uhns
LOCATION: Syria
POPULATION: 19,747,586 (2008 estimate/includes approximately 1.5 million refugees from Iraq and 500,000 long-term refugees from the Palestinian Territories)
LANGUAGE: Arabic (official); French; English
RELIGION: Islam (Sunni, Alawi branch of Shia, Druze); Christianity; Judaism; Baha'i
RELATED ARTICLES: Vol. 4: Syrian Christians in India

1 INTRODUCTION

Syrians live in the Syrian Arab Republic, more commonly known as Syria, a land that has been inhabited for more than 7,000 years. The earliest human artifacts found in Syria date from the Middle Paleolithic age. Syria gets its name from the Assyrians, who controlled the area in the 14th through 10th centuries BC and again in the 8th century BC, until the Babylonians, under Nebuchadnezzar, conquered them in the 7th century BC. The city of Damascus has been continually inhabited longer than any other city on Earth, from as early as 3000 BC. The fertile land of Syria—lying at the crossroads of great trade routes between the East and West and the site of many holy places for Judaism, Christianity, and Islam—is a very desirable piece of property. It has been invaded, conquered, and occupied by many different peoples over its long history, including the Egyptians, Babylonians, Persians, Greeks, Romans, Arabs, European Crusaders, Mongols from Central Asia, Turks, French, and British.

The modern Syrian Arab Republic came about in 1946 when the French gave up the control they had been granted over an area known as Bilad al-Sham (the land of Syria) by the League of Nations in April 1920 at the end of World War I (1914–19). When the French gave up control, the area was divided into two countries, Lebanon and Syria. Damascus was named the capital of present-day Syria. In 1970, Hafez al Assad (*al assad* means "the lion" in Arabic), the then-minister of defense, took over the country in a bloodless coup and established himself as president. Hafez held control of Syria until his death in 2000. Although he was called president, Hafez was actually more like a dictator, wielding all significant authority in the republic and quashing any opposition. That tradition continued under the helm of Syria's leader, Hafez's son, Bashar al Assad. Bashar was elected unopposed to a second seven-year term, in 2007 in an election that international observers regarded as a sham poll. The dictatorial power held by the al Assad family led the Economist Intelligence Unit in 2008 to rank Syria 157th out of 167 nations in democracy. Syrians have few elections, civil liberties or opportunities to participate in the political system.

Syria's relationships with other Arab states are strained. Tension between Syria and its neighbors grew in September 2007 when Israel attacked an alleged nuclear facility in Syria. A peace agreement that was negotiated in May 2008 was hoped to help ease tension between Syria and its neighboring nations.

² LOCATION AND HOMELAND

The Syrian Arab Republic is a small country located on the eastern edge of the Mediterranean Sea, bordered by Turkey to the north, Iraq to the east, Jordan to the south, and Israel and Lebanon to the southwest. With a total area of 185,180 sq km (71,500 sq mi), Syria is just slightly larger than the state of North Dakota. Two-thirds of Syria is desert; the other third is part of the Fertile Crescent (or Levant) along the Mediterranean coast. Most of the population—about 80%—lives in that fertile region, within 80 miles of the sea coast. One Mediterranean island, Arwad, belongs to Syria. The country has a Mediterranean climate with four distinct seasons, milder along the coast than in the inland areas. Temperatures along the coast range from 10–21°C (50–70°F) in January, and 21–32°C (70–90°F) in July. The inland desert areas are much colder in the winter and hotter in the summer. Syria has several large rivers, the Euphrates being the most important. The largest river in western Asia, the Euphrates starts in Turkey and flows 3,360 km (2,100 mi) through Syria and into Iraq to join the Tigris River at Basra. Most large wild animals are now absent from Syria because of overhunting, habitat destruction, desertification, and the use of DDT and other pesticides. Lion-hunting used to be known as "the sport of kings" in the upper Euphrates area, but lions disappeared from the Syrian desert about a century ago.

The Syrian people are one of the most ethnically mixed of all Arab peoples, blending characteristics from their many conquerors and invaders. Most Syrians are a genetic mix of Phoenician, Babylonian, Assyrian, French, and Turkish. Syrians generally have olive skin, dark brown eyes, and black hair, but a wide variety of other physical characteristics exists as well: blond hair and pale skin; black hair and dark brown skin; blue eyes and brown hair; and even red hair and freckled, pinkish skin. The total population of Syria is nearly 19 million. About 90% are Arab, and the rest are Kurdish, Turkish, Armenian, and Circassian. Some Palestinian refugees also have made their home in Syria, and nearly 1.5 million Iraqi refugees have fled into Syria since the start of the Gulf War in March 2003. Half of the people live in cities, 4 million in Damascus alone. About one-third (36.2%) of the population is under age 14. In addition, several thousand Syrians have been internally displaced as a result of Israel's occupation of the Golan region.

³ LANGUAGE

Ancient Syrians spoke Syriac (a Semitic language) and Greek. Later Syrians spoke Aramaic, the language Jesus spoke. (Modern-day people in the small hill village of Maalula still speak Aramaic, and it is used in church liturgies there.) The earliest phonetic alphabet in the world, Ugarit, was discovered in Syria in ruins dating from the 14th century BC. Arabic is now the official language of the Syrian Arab Republic and the language spoken by nearly all Syrians. French is the second most common language, but it is beginning to be rivaled by English. Both French and English are taught in Syrian schools. Other languages spoken in Syria include Kurdish, Armenian, Aramaic, and Circassian.

Arabic, spoken by 100 million people worldwide, has many dialects that are so distinctive that people living as little as 300 miles apart may not be able to understand one another. Written Arabic, on the other hand, is classical Arabic and is the same for all Arabic writers the world over. It is written and

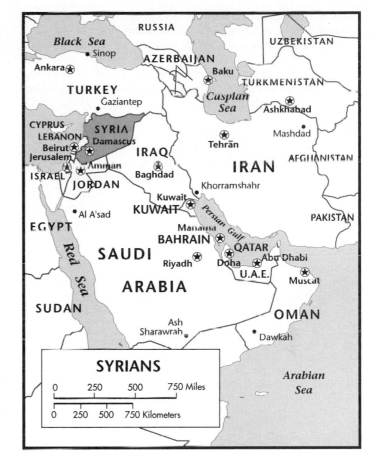

read from right to left. Oddly, Syrians do not use standard Arabic numerals but instead use numerals that came to them from India.

"Hello" in Arabic is *marhaba* or *ahlan*, to which one replies, *marhabtayn* or *ahlayn*. Other common greetings are *As-salam 'alaykum* ("Peace be with you"), with the reply of *Wa'laykum as-salam* ("and to you peace"). *Ma'assalama* means "goodbye." "Thank you" is *Shukran*, and "You're welcome" is *'Afwan*. "Yes" is *na'am*, and "no" is *la'a*. The numbers one to ten in Arabic are: *wahad, ithnayn, thalatha, arba'a, khamsa, sita, sab'a, thamanya, tis'a,* and *'ashara.*

At least half of Syria's men and boys are named Muhammad (they often use their middle names to distinguish themselves from each other). This name is common because of its association with the Prophet Muhammad. The next most popular male names are: Ahmad, Khalil, Khaled, Yassir, 'Imad, and Samer. Women's and girl's names commonly are Amal, Basima, Huda, Iman, Fatima (nicknamed Fatoum), Majd, and Sana.

⁴ FOLKLORE

Syrians are great believers in fate and frequently resign themselves to it. They also love proverbs, many of which reflect their strong attachment to family and intense involvement in social relationships. For example, "One who has no good for his/her family has no good for any other," and "Where there are no people, there is Hell."

One of Syria's heroes is Queen Zenobia of the ancient city of Palmyra who took control in AD 267 when her husband and her son were both assassinated. She managed to achieve full independence from Rome, then went on to attack Roman territories, taking over lower Egypt and all of Asia Minor before she was stopped by the Roman emperor Aurelius in AD 273. Aurelius took Zenobia back to Rome in chains the following year, where she lived as a respected former warrior and head of state until her death.

⁵ RELIGION

The majority religion in Syria is Islam: 91% of the population is Muslim. About 74% of Syrians follow the Sunni faith; however, many Syrians also follow Shia, Alawi, and Druze traditions of Islam. The Alawi branch of Islam is in the Shia tradition and is the branch to which Syria's leader belongs. The remaining 9% of Syrians are mostly Christians of the Greek Orthodox, Armenian Orthodox, Syrian Orthodox, Syrian Catholic, and Maronite sects. Small numbers of Jews, Baha'is and others also reside in Syria. The constitution guarantees freedom of religion, and it is illegal to try to convert others to your faith.

Syria was one of the first lands conquered by the Islamic expansionists in the 7th century AD. Damascus was taken by the Muslims in AD 635 and became the first capital of the Islamic empire in AD 661. Muhammad had earlier made Medina, Saudi Arabia, the first Islamic capital. Damascus, named the capital of the Umayyad Caliphate in AD 661, is also an important city for Christians. St. Paul was on the road from Palestine to Damascus when he was converted to Christianity by a miraculous blinding light, and he lived in Damascus for almost 20 years.

⁶ MAJOR HOLIDAYS

Muslim holidays, Christmas and Easter (both the Western and Orthodox dates), and the Christian New Year (January 1) are official holidays in Syria. There are also several political holidays, celebrated with fireworks, parades, military air shows, and/or Baath Party (the ruling party) speeches. Political holidays include: Union Day (February 22), Revolution Day/Women's Day (March 8), Arab League Day (March 22), Evacuation Day (commemorating the day French troops left in 1946 to give Syria full independence, April 17), Martyr's Day (May 6), Security Force Day (May 29), Army Day August 1), Marine's Day (August 29), Veteran's Day (October 6), Flight Day (October 16), Correction Movement Day (November 16), Day of Mourning (November 29), and Peasant's Day (December 14).

Friday is the Islamic day of rest, so most businesses and services are closed on Fridays. Muslim holidays follow the lunar calendar, moving back by 11 days each year, so their dates are not fixed on the standard Gregorian calendar. The main Muslim holidays are: *'Id Al-Fitr*, a three-day festival at the end of *Ramadan*; *'Id Al-Adha*, a three-day feast of sacrifice at the end of the month of pilgrimage to Mecca (known as the *Haj*)—families who can afford it slaughter a lamb and share the meat with poorer Muslims; the First of *Muharram*, or the Muslim New Year; *Mawlid An-Nabawi*, the prophet Muhammad's birthday; and *'Id Al-Isra wa Al-Mi'raj*, a feast celebrating the nocturnal visit of Muhammad to heaven from Jerusalem.

⁷ RITES OF PASSAGE

Marriage is the main goal in nearly every Syrian's life, so weddings are a major social event and rite of passage. The actual marriage, or exchange of vows, often takes place a few days or weeks before the wedding reception in the presence of a religious leader, the imam. A marriage contract is signed before witnesses, and a *mahr* (dowry) is paid by the groom's family to the bride's family. Christian marriages also require that a *mahr* be paid to the bride. The wedding reception is a festive event for which the groom's family provides dinner and sweets.

Children live at home until marriage and sons might bring their wives to live with their families. While some Syrians date before marriage, most are careful to choose a potential future mate whom their families would approve of. Marriages between Muslims and non-Muslims in Syria are rare.

Upon the death of one parent, an adult child, usually a son, is required to take care of the surviving parent until death. After a death, there are three days of mourning during which friends, relatives, and neighbors visit the family of the deceased. Close women relatives of the deceased wear black for many months, and then they can start wearing half black and half white. For traditional families, it can be up to a year before the women can wear colors again; more modern families wait only six months.

⁸ INTERPERSONAL RELATIONS

Syrians are generally very loud, aggressive people who may be very polite in their greetings but then cut in line, bump into people without apologizing, drive offensively, honk their car horns constantly, and blast music and talk loudly late into the night (right under someone's bedroom window). They love to laugh, joke, eat, talk, and dance, and will get a party going at any excuse. Haggling is a way of life; punctuality is of little concern. Both men and women are very affectionate with others of the same sex, often touching and holding hands, or even kissing on the mouth in public; this is not considered sexual behavior. Syrians are very interested in personal relationships, and they like to be part of a group. It is not a nation of fierce individuals; in fact, most Syrians hate to stand out in a crowd. Men enjoy a game of insults, where the object is to come up with an insult that is both clever and eloquently expressed.

Most Syrians are proud of their country's cultural heritage. Political opinions vary, however. Many Syrians would prefer to live under a more democratic regime, while others approve of the president's strong leadership.

Syrians stand close together, talk loudly, and use extravagant hand gestures. Holding the hand out with the palm facing up and the fingers together like a tent over the palm, then pumping the hand and forearm up and down, means "Wait a minute." Moving both open hands up quickly above the shoulders, palms facing the other person, means "That's my point!" or "That's my excuse!" Brushing the open palms together quickly as if to brush off dirt means "I'm finished with it (or you)." Patting the hand over the heart when meeting someone expresses affection for that person. A quick upward movement of the head with raised eyebrows, often with closed eyelids and a click of the tongue, means "No." A downward nod of the head to one side means "Yes." Shaking the head from side to side, often with a puzzled look on the face, means "I don't understand" or "I didn't hear you."

⁹ LIVING CONDITIONS

Nearly one-fourth of Syria's economy is agricultural. As a result, the country does not have a highly skilled labor force, which has made industrial development difficult to achieve.

A Syrian man buys nuts at a shop in Salihiya market in Damascus. (Louai Beshara/AFP/Getty Images)

Unemployment was about 9% in 2007, compared with higher rates of 35% in the 1970s and 1980s.

Although traditional Syrian homes were built around large courtyards, most Syrians today live in apartments. It is not unusual for a family of five people to share a unit that is 650 square feet or less. Those who are wealthy enough build villas or large vacation homes in the mountains or on the sea coast. There are no financing options for Syrians who wish to buy their own homes. All such transactions are paid for fully at the time of purchase in cash. Cities were once divided into ethnic and religious residential sections, but today they are divided more along lines of wealth and class: the wealthier people of all backgrounds move into the more modern sections of the city.

Syria's road system expanded in the late 1990s and early twenty-first century, and the nation has built two major ports and two international airports. Public transportation, however, is inefficient. Plumbing and telephone systems are unreliable. Trains are slow and crowded, and taxis and buses vary greatly in quality.

Health care is free for Syrian citizens but is somewhat limited. There are only 1.2 hospital beds per 1,000 people in Syria. The infant mortality rate is high at 26.78 deaths for every 1,000 births, and life expectancy is fairly low (69.5 years for men, 70 for women). Villages are poorer than cities and have even fewer modern conveniences available. Very few village residents own cars. Villagers live in small one- to three-room houses with a small courtyard, the older ones made of adobe bricks and plaster. The focal point of a village house is the front door, which is often huge and painted with multicolored geometric patterns. The interiors of all but the most modern Western-style Syrian homes are ornate and highly decorated. A favorite Syrian decoration is a massive crystal chandelier that hangs so that it can be seen from outside.

10 FAMILY LIFE

The family is the center of life in Syria. Children live with their parents until they marry and sometimes after. There are no nursing homes in Syria; the elderly are cared for at home by their families. There is some child abuse, and children are sometimes punished harshly, but children and parents also show a great deal of affection for each other. Getting married and having children is the top priority for almost all Syrians. Arranged marriages are still common, with first cousins being the preferred match. Polygamy is legal, although it is uncommon in the cities. Divorce is rare; when a divorce is granted, the father almost always gets custody of the children.

Women do practically all of the cooking in Syria; few Syrian men know how to cook. Most kitchens have no modern appliances, such as dishwashers, food processors, or microwave ovens, so food preparation and clean-up take much time and energy. Groceries are usually bought fresh every day because of limited refrigeration and the vast quantities of food required to feed a large family. There is a separate shop for each type of food and four different kinds of bakeries: one that sells only flat bread (a Syrian staple), one that sells baguettes and rolls, one specializing in European pastries, and one that sells Syrian sweets. Consequently, it can take most of the day just to purchase and prepare food and then clean up afterwards. Women are constitutionally guaranteed equal rights, but in actuality, traditional expectations and duties usually keep them from enjoying those rights.

11 CLOTHING

Syrians wear a mix of traditional Arab and Western-style clothing. However, casual Western clothes, such as jeans, T-shirts, and running shoes are rarely seen. Syrians, both men and women, almost always cover their legs to at least below the knee, and their arms to below the elbow. Women almost never wear their skirts or hair short, and men never have long hair or earrings. Neither men nor women wear shorts. Middle- and upper-class women, especially younger ones, tend to wear bright colors, lots of jewelry and make-up, high-heeled shoes, and "big" hair (teased and sprayed into bouffant styles). Young men have very short, closely-cropped hair and also dress stylishly.

The first royalty ever to wear purple robes were in Syria, the dye coming from a type of mollusk that is unique to the Mediterranean shore in that area.

12 FOOD

Syrians eat typical Middle Eastern food, such as *hummus* (a ground chickpea paste with lemon juice, tahina [sesame seed paste] and garlic), *falafel* (fried, spiced, ground chickpeas), and *shish kebab* (lamb chunks on skewers) or *shish tawouq* (chicken chunks on skewers). Unique to Syria is a dish called *farooj*, which is roasted chicken with chilies and onions. Ice cream is called *booza*, and fruity soft drinks are known as *gazooza*. All other soft drinks are called "cola." Syrians drink their coffee *(qahwa)* strong and sweet; tea *(shay)* is also drunk frequently. In general, Syrians love their food either very sweet or very sour. Most Syrian food uses some combination of the same basic ingredients: lamb, chicken, chickpeas and other dried beans, eggplant, rice, burghul (cracked wheat), olives, yogurt, Syrian cheese (white, salty cheese made of sheep's or goat's milk), garlic, and olive oil. Burghul (wheat that is parboiled, dried, and cracked) is a staple in the Syrian diet. It is cooked a variety of ways and is used as a cheap substitute for rice. When boiled, burghul can be combined with vegetables or meats or stews. Another use for burghul is in the making of *kibbeh*. To prepare kibbeh, burghul that has been presoaked in warm water is strained thoroughly and then combined with ground meat to form a paste. The paste is formed into small ovals the size and shape of an egg. A hole is poked down the center of the oval and is stuffed with a mixture of chopped onions, spices, ground meat, and pine nuts. The hole is then sealed by pinching the burghul paste over the top. Each unit of kibbeh is then fried in vegetable oil until brown and crispy. Kibbeh is served at social gatherings of all types.

Damascene gardens are known for their grape vines, and use of the grape leaf in Syria, as in all of the Middle East, is common. Leaves from the vine are picked, washed, and dipped briefly in boiling water. Each leaf is laid out on a flat surface. A mixture of rice, margarine, spices, and ground meat is prepared. A small portion of this is laid in a straight line across the bottom of the leaf, and the leaf is then rolled up over the rice mixture. The stuffed grape leaves are set in a pot, covered with water, salt, and tomato sauce, and cooked on the stovetop until tender, about ½ hour.

Meals last a long time in Syria, two to three hours or more. Most food is eaten by hand or is scooped up with flatbread. French fries are one of the few potato dishes eaten. They are served with every meal at restaurants and are eaten with a fork. Potatoes are also sometimes sliced and cooked in a pan with meatballs and onions. Syrians eat all parts of an animal, including the brains, sexual organs, and intestines. Small eggplants stuffed with spiced meat then pickled, or artichokes stuffed with meat but not pickled, are a Syrian specialty.

13 EDUCATION

Schooling is mandatory for six years, and higher education is paid for by the government at the four Syrian universities. These universities, however, have huge classes and outdated teaching methods, so those who can afford to study abroad. School children wear green, military-style uniforms and attend school six days a week. In high school, students must study either English or French for two years. The literacy rate in Syria is 83% for men, and 76% for women

14 CULTURAL HERITAGE

Syria's literary heritage includes mostly theologians, philosophers, and scientists, such as Jacob of Edessa (late 7th century AD), who is best known for his *Syriac Grammar*, and the philosopher Bar Hebraeus (mid 13th century AD), who wrote on logic, physics, mathematics, and astronomy. Only recently has there been any significant development of Syrian fiction writing. The Arab tradition of poetry remains strong in Syria. Ali Ahmad Said (1930–), pen-named Adunis, is an influential Syrian poet who was exiled to Beirut in 1956 and now makes his home in Paris. He uses poetry to inspire revolutionary change to create a new society, and he was considered for the Nobel Prize in Literature in 2006 and 2007. One of the most popular modern women writers in Syria is Ghada al-Samman, who was born in a Syrian village in 1942, studied in Damascus and London, and then moved to Beirut.

Arab music is much like the Arab language—rich, repetitive, and exaggerated. The 'oud is a popular instrument; it is an ancient stringed instrument that is the ancestor of the European lute. The Islamic prohibition against depicting the human form has greatly shaped Muslim visual art, which finds its greatest expression in mosques.

During the Middle Ages, sword-makers in Damascus became famous throughout the Middle East, Central Asia, and southern Europe for their extremely high-quality swords made from a secret alloy called Damascene steel. The hilts were elaborately decorated by a process known as "Damascening" in which the hilts were incised with intricate patterns and then inlaid with bronze, gold, and silver. In the 14th century, however, one of Damascus' conquerors captured all the sword-makers and put them in his own service, and the art of Damascene steel died out. The process of inlaying lives on, though, in Syrian woodworking.

15 WORK

Syrians worked mostly for the government or in agriculture until the mid-1990s when government efforts to privatize the economy opened up more opportunities. However, private companies have been slow to invest in Syria. Lafarge, a French company, is building a cement factory with the Syrian MAS Group, and oil and related industries are developing in the Deir al-Zour region. Most Syrians, however, continue to work in the government in large, inefficiently operated companies.

16 SPORTS

Syrians enjoy soccer as a spectator sport and also play the game in friendly street-side competitions. One can regularly spot boys playing soccer in open fields, school playgrounds, and streets—anywhere there is enough space for a game. Martial arts are very popular, with classes offered in many districts. Syrians also enjoying swimming (in both outdoor and indoor pools), tennis, track meets, and ping-pong tournaments. Body-building and weight-lifting clubs are frequented by the higher social classes. There are soccer and basketball teams, and camel-racing is a popular spectator sport.

17 ENTERTAINMENT AND RECREATION

Eating and socializing in coffee houses are the main forms of entertainment. Social activities involve whole families, only men, only women, or women and children. Some public activities are considered socially unacceptable for women. Men sit for hours in all-male tea houses drinking tea or Turkish coffee, smoking the water-pipe, talking, and sometimes playing a favorite board game—a Turkish form of backgammon. Young men often hang out on the streets, or if they have cars, they cruise the streets. Women generally spend their leisure time talking with other women or family members, exchanging recipes, doing crafts, or dancing together. On Fridays, the Islamic day of rest, Syrians with cars often drive to mountain resorts where they eat, talk, and stroll along the streets. When strolling through the streets at night, Syrians wear their finest clothes.

Cinemas show either tear-jerker Egyptian films or super-violent American or Asian action films. These are only attended by rowdy young men. Wealthy Syrians own VCRs and like to rent videos. All Syrians enjoy music concerts, from jazz to classical, and they love parties even more. Women will not belly-dance in public (they will sometimes dance in front of each other at home), but men at a party will show off their best moves in a hilarious belly-dance routine, laughing uproariously at each other's attempts to shake their bottoms and bounce their breasts. At celebrations such as weddings, both men and women, either separately or together, perform the *dabka* dance. The *dabka* is a line dance performed to the music of a band or a hand-held drum called a *tabla*. A leader guides the dancers by shouting out moves that they must make as he or she dances ahead of them.

18 FOLK ART, CRAFTS, AND HOBBIES

Syrian crafts include jewelry-making, characterized by extravagant gold- and silver-work (gold is considered higher class); mosaic, inlaid woodworking; glass-blowing; and weaving and embroidering textiles, such as clothing, tablecloths, pillow covers, and carpets. A special brocaded fabric called damask is named for the city of Damascus where it originated. Damask used to be made of silk with silver and gold threads woven through it by hand into a raised pattern that appears on both sides, making it perhaps the first reversible fabric. Modern damask is made from a variety of cloths but is still woven by hand. Syria is known for an alum charm that is supposed to ward off evil. The charm is colored blue and has a triangular shape. It is adorned with strands of beads and a symbolic blue hand that protects its owner. Taxis and buses have the charms hanging from their rear-view mirrors.

There is a well-attended international folk festival of music and dance every September in an ancient Roman amphitheater in Busra.

19 SOCIAL PROBLEMS

A struggling economy and the war in Iraq have made life difficult for many Syrians. Syria's population has doubled in 25 years and has been further swelled since 2003 by increasing numbers of Iraqi refugees, who now number around 1.5 million, almost 8% of the population. Syria's infrastructure has been expanding rapidly but remains poor by regional standards. The transport and energy sectors are antiquated and bureaucratic. The telecommunications and Internet sector is expanding rapidly, from a low base, following the easing of government restrictions. Many of the brightest students (particularly medical and engineering students) go abroad to study and never return. Syrian society is a fragmented one, made up of separate groups defined by language, region, religion, and ethnicity. There is little social cohesiveness or national loyalty. Violent acts of racism are rare, but there is pervasive stratification along skin-color lines, with the lightest-skinned people at the top and the darker-skinned at the bottom.

The chief of military operations for Hizbullah, an Iranian-backed Lebanese Shia group, was killed in Damascus on 12 February 2008. This action called attention to Syria's lack of internal security. The assassination followed an air raid by Israel five months earlier on an alleged nuclear facility in Syria.

President Haffez al Assad's dictatorship was brutal and oppressive to those who did not support him. Although his son, Bashar al Assad, has promised reforms, democratic participation is virtually non-existent in Syria. Opposing voices are silenced by imprisonment or death (or exile for the lucky ones), so few dare speak openly against the government. Nevertheless, some activists are beginning to fight for political reform. Several dozen opponents of Bashar were arrested in late 2007 and early 2008 for promoting the Damascus Declaration, a 2005 document that sought reforms.

20 GENDER ISSUES

When a Syrian man tells a woman that she cannot do something because women are not capable of it, she is said to retort, "What about our Queen Zenobia?" The reference is to Syria's legendary female warrior and national hero. Most Syrian women, however, do not have the power of Zenobia, and are confined to more traditional domestic roles. Women have few rights within marriages and often are at risk of violence from their husbands or other males.

The United Nations has begun to call attention to the poor status of Syrian women and, in June 2007, called on the government to reform its laws regarding marital rape, citizenship rights, and honor crimes. The UN also has called for the establishment of shelters and services for victims of violence. Little effort has been made by the government to improve the conditions for women, and there are some indications that conditions may be worsening. In January 2007, Syria's minister of social affairs and labor declared the Syrian Women's Association illegal and dissolved another women's rights group known as the Social Initiative Organization a month later. The government also has refused to license non-governmental organizations that support women's rights and services for victims of domestic violence.

²¹ BIBLIOGRAPHY

Amnesty International Report 2008: State of the World's Human Rights. http://thereport.amnesty.org/eng/Homepage (retrieved 3 August, 2008).

Economist Intelligence Unit: Country Profile: Iran. Economist Intelligence Unit Inc., 2007.

South, Coleman. *Cultures of the World: Syria.* New York: Marshall Cavendish, 1995.

Syrian Arab Republic. Culture Grams: World Edition. Ann Arbor, Mich.: ProQuest LLC, 2008.

Willard, Jed, ed. *Let's Go: The Budget Guide to Israel and Egypt 1996, including Jordan, Syria, and the West Bank.* New York: St. Martin's Press, 1996.

—revised by Himanee Gupta-Carlson.

TAGBANUA

PRONUNCIATION: tahg-BAH-nwah
LOCATION: Philippines
POPULATION: around 20,000
LANGUAGE: Tagbanua; Tagalog/Pilipino
RELIGION: Indigenous animist religion; some Catholicism and Protestantism
RELATED ARTICLES: Vol. 3: Filipinos

¹INTRODUCTION

The name Tagbanua derives from *tiga banua,* meaning "people of the village." There is evidence of early influence from Hinduized Brunei. In more recent times, Muslim traders and aristocrats, chiefly Tausug from Sulu, dominated Palawan. Although Magellan's expedition made a landfall on Palawan, and its chronicler Pigafetta recorded an impression of the natives, intense Spanish contact did not begin until the 1872 founding of the town of Puerta Princesa at the northern edge of Tagbanua territory. American contact with the Tagbanua only commenced with the 1904 founding of the Iwahig penal colony. Catholic and Protestant missionaries have had only limited success in converting the Tagbanua, even in comparison with the neighboring Palawan ethnic group. Like most peoples in the southern Philippines, the influx of immigrants from the overpopulated Tagalog and Visayan regions has had a profound impact on Tagbanua life, though the relationship in their case is not one of armed conflict.

²LOCATION AND HOMELAND

The Tagbanua inhabit both the eastern and western coasts of the central portion of Palawan Island, which lies between Mindoro and Borneo. The greater concentration of population is in the more extensive lowlands to the east of the island's mountain range that rises 760 m to 900 m (2,500–3,000 ft). The few mountain villages date from only the 18th century. Tagbanua also live on the Calamian Islands off the island's northern tip. The ethnic group numbered 14,000 in the 1980s (an 1985 estimate counted 2,000 speakers of the Central Tagbanua dialect). In 1990, speakers of the Agutaynen dialect of Tagbanwa (Agutaya island and nearby points in northern Palawan) numbered almost 10,400 and of the Calamian dialect almost 8,000. According to the 2000 census, 2.15% (over 16,000) of the population of Palawan identified themselves as Tagbanua.

The Tagbanua have much contact today with other ethnic groups, such as the Palawano and the Batak (not the same as the Sumatran people), both of which are animists like the Tagbanua themselves, as well as the Muslim Jama Mapun and Christian Tagalog and Visayan immigrants.

³LANGUAGE

The Tagbanua speak a language of the Central Philippine sub-branch of the Western Malayo-Polynesian branch of the Austronesian family. Significant differences exist between the dialects spoken on Palawan and that of the Calamian Islands. The Tagbanua on Palawan are one of the three groups (the others are in Mindoro) who use the pre-Hispanic alphabet (ultimately of Indic origin) once used by the Tagalogs and other Filipinos. They scratch the letters with a knife on pieces of bamboo. Many Tagbanua also speak the languages of neighboring peoples as well as the national language, Tagalog/Pilipino.

There is a strong taboo against mentioning the names of grandparents, especially deceased ones. Nor does one ever call parents by their names; this applies also to non-kin of the parents' generation, whom one addresses as "Amey" or "Manung" (uncle), or "Iney" or "Manang" (aunt). One even avoids using the names of adults of the same generation, calling them "Ungkuy" (friend) instead. One calls young boys "Duduy" and young girls "Nini."

⁴FOLKLORE

Diseases are caused by the *salakep*, small, dark, kinky-haired beings who once lived among the Tagbanua in the mythical past. Men who marry into a village fear magical poisoning (*ratyun*) by village natives. Against this and other harmful forces, men carry *mutya,* or amulets.

⁵RELIGION

Named deities dwell in a multilayered sky-world. The highest is Mangindusa, the "punisher of crime" (namely, incest). Upon clearing a forest for planting, offerings (*pagdasag*) are made to the *tawu tung talun* ("people of the forest"), spirits who will protect crops from pests and animals. Moreover, the rice plant itself has a soul (*kalag*), which is respected by the use of a special knife called the *kayed*. In the Calamian Islands, the *tekbeken,* a giant octopus, appears when someone is under a spell or breaks the incest taboo.

The *tiladmanin,* ancestral spirits, cause illness. The *pagsalaknan* ritual is performed for small children, entailing the sacrifice of a pig and six young chickens (*pitung kulu,* "seven heads") in an appeal for ancestral protection. Ceremonies for the ancestors are held from the level of the family to those of the entire Tagbanua people (by the Masikampu). Offerings include rice, chickens, and betel nuts placed on platforms or rafts decorated with leaf streamers affixed to upright poles. Ritual drink fests attract the spirits with rice wine; this is also an occasion for dancing, blood pacts, and courtship.

There has been some conversion to Catholicism and Protestantism in the Calamian Islands.

⁶MAJOR HOLIDAYS

The Tagbanua participate in the fiestas of non-Tagbanua communities.

⁷RITES OF PASSAGE

A pregnant woman observes numerous behavioral and dietary taboos lest the fetus become ill; certain plants are kept in the house as protection against witches and evil spirits (*mangaluk*). The midwife (a relative) puts the placenta in a bamboo tube and puts it on a tree or buries it under the house. The new mother continues to observe food taboos and on the third day after the birth bathes in water prepared by the midwife with boiled leaves. The new baby receives five secondary souls at another ceremony. The Tagbanua do not celebrate birthdays, but a father may swear to hold a *panaad* feast on the seventh birthday if he has lost many children already.

The Tagbanua are monogamous and marry early—as arranged by parents or other relatives, or today more often by picking their own partners. Parents must use a *talunga,* an in-

TAGBANUA

termediary, to negotiate a marriage. The man's side initiates the first meeting with the woman's side; at this time, they settle the bride-price (*begay*). The begay is delivered before the wedding and consists of two steps: the giving of money and fabric, symbolic of the anchor and back of a boat, and the payment of wealth ideally not less than the groom's father paid for his mother (knives, pigs, rice, cash, and recently coffee, sugar, gin, bread, and biscuits, and a sarong for the bride's mother and trousers for her father). Both sides share the cost of the uglun, a dancing party that lasts a whole day and night.

The sides exchange visits, beginning with the groom's kin to the bride's house; each time the visitors bring double the num-

Indigenous Tagbanua tribal elders perform a ritual to drive away evil aboard the Greenpeace flagship Rainbow Warrior in Puerto Princessa, Palawan, Philippines. (AFP/Getty Images)

ber of rice sacks they received before as hosts, until the bride's side decides to call it quits. The wedding can then follow. Each family holds an all-night dancing party to which relatives contribute. The groom's family asks for permission to enter the bride's house, which they get after they pay a ritual fee. They are greeted with a war dance (*saad*). Only at midnight does the groom himself enter. On the floor, he sits with his back to the bride. Everyone sits in silence waiting for an animal to make a sound; the longer the silence, the better the omen. After this, the bride holds a coin between her fingers, an old man puts the groom's hand on the bride's hand, and asks the groom if he will treat his wife as his own body. After the groom answers yes, the old man asks the bride the same question, to which she says yes. Then, he pours gin over their hands onto a plate. The couple drink from the plate, and the bride takes the coin for safekeeping.

A cheaper and faster alternative to the above process is *sudir*: the couple act intimate in front of the parents, who are thus pressured (for fear of scandal) to speed up the wedding process. Older people regard the children of such marriages as under a stigma.

In the Calamian Islands, upon death, the body is kept in the house on a mat. The family stops work, summons distant relatives, and keeps a vigil by the body. A large carrying pole is secured to the coffin. During the *pagtaliman* ceremony, an older man asks the deceased questions as to the cause of death. The old man tries to lift the carrying pole: if it feels light, the deceased's answer is yes; if heavy, it is no. This aims to allay feelings of guilt relatives and friends may have toward the deceased. Music accompanies the carrying of the coffin to the burial site. Three days after the burial, people gather in the yard of the deceased's home for a simple meal of rice and fish, then enter the house to listen to the singing of the *Dumarakul* epic, taking numerous breaks for coffee and gin.

Among the Tagbanua on Palawan, the surviving spouse is secluded for seven days; on the last day, a ceremony is held to sever the soul's connection to the world of the living. The soul then goes to *basad*, the underworld. If an epidemic caused the death, the soul travels in a spirit canoe to a special afterworld. Formerly, a second burial transferred the body to large earthen jars.

8 INTERPERSONAL RELATIONS

Tagbanua society is composed of autonomous villages recognizing an ethnic leader, the *Masikampu. Ginu'u*, community leaders, possess titles bestowed centuries ago by the Tausug rulers of Sulu and handed down father to son. The ginu'u base their power on a thorough knowledge of customary law and on the possession of supernaturally powerful heirlooms, such as old Chinese jars. Retaining their ritual and judicial authority, they have conceded political power to Philippine government officials. Villages are integrated into the national system of local administration via elected *barangay* captains and councils. *Surugudin* councils headed by ginu'u determine fines under a complex system of customary law and kinship obligations.

The traditional social order distinguishes between "high bloods" (the ginu'u, *bawalyan* [shamans], and their kin) and "low bloods" (everyone else). In the past, there was also a small number of debt-slaves (*uripen*). Personal qualities could qualify an individual born of a high-blood father and a low-blood mother for community leadership.

A boy may not visit a girl in the home or speak to her in public but must try to meet her secretly or give her small presents. Because of the grave consequences of incest, men and women avoid each other, feeling *inglaw* (discomfort) with each other, even with parents or children of the opposite sex. Brothers and sisters must observe formality with each other.

9 LIVING CONDITIONS

Consisting of a single room, houses are raised on 1.5 m to 2-m (5- to 6-ft) piles (0.5-m or 1.5-ft in the Calamian Islands). The floor, walls, and gabled roof are made of bamboo, rattan, and palm fronds. Cooking is usually done outside or under the house; if inside, it is done in a tin bucket filled with earth. The smoke drives away mosquitoes. Larger houses may have chairs on the veranda and benches in the yard. Household articles include baskets, a mortar, and wooden trunks or cardboard boxes for clothes. Today, Tagbanua use town-bought aluminum cookware, chinaware, plastic water containers, and tin cans for storing rice. Valued heirlooms consist of ritually important Chinese jars, brass betel nut boxes and trays, gongs, knives, and spears. Flowers are planted around the house. Houses used to be burned upon the death of an occupant.

More nomadic groups that live off the sea build houses of light materials and carry the roofs with them when they move, using them as a windscreen or sleeping place on the beach.

A village contains from 45 to 500 persons, usually around 150. It is divided into smaller units comprising the families of sisters. Water is taken from wells and springs.

Visits from government medical personnel are very rare. *Bawalyan* (shamans) and midwives provide most health care.

Average family income in the MIMAROPA region (Mindoro, Masbate, Romblon, and Palawan islands) amounted to 109,000 pesos (US$2,137) in 2006, the second lowest in the country (above the Autonomous Region in Muslim Mindanao), cf. the national average of P173,000, the National Capital Region's P311,000, and those of the neighboring regions, Southern Tagalog, P198,000, and the Western Visayas, P130,000.

In Palawan province, the proportion of houses with a roof of galvanized iron/aluminum increased from 11.63% in 1990 to 24.68% in 2000, with outer walls of concrete, brick, or stone from 4.31% in 1990 to 7.23%; this meant that the great majority of houses were still constructed of wood or of grass or palm thatch.

10 FAMILY LIFE

Kinship is reckoned on both the mother's and father's sides; the incest taboo extends to third cousins on both sides. People tend to identify with a prominent patrilineal or matrilineal ancestor. Nuclear families have one to two children, in contrast to the national average of four children per family. A household consists of a couple and unmarried children (sometimes also other relatives). A newlywed couple will live with the bride's family at first; exceptions to this rule for economic reasons cause friction between in-laws. The nuclear family remains under the influence of other kin in close residence.

Terminology distinguishes between older and younger siblings and among uncles and aunts with reference to birth order. In the Calamian Islands, mothers and aunts are addressed as "Nanay," fathers and uncles as "Tatay," siblings and cousins as "Putul," siblings-in-law and cousins-in-law as "Ipag," and grandparents and grandchildren as "Apu." When the mother is out, grandparents, older siblings, or other relatives take care of the children; fathers also watch the children after work. Children do not join adult conversation and are taught to respect authority and age. Childless couples do not adopt but rather "borrow" relatives' children for a day, returning them at night. Formal respect must be shown in-laws at all times, even in the midst of a drinking party.

Divorce may be demanded at the slightest incompatibility. Village elders try to mediate. If the husband is at fault, he pays a fine equal to the bride-price. If the wife is at fault, she pays back the bride-price.

The Tagbanua keep dogs for hunting and for guarding the house, as well as cats for catching mice.

11 CLOTHING

Traditional men's wear consists of fabric loincloths. In living memory, men wore *takwil*, loincloths of bark cloth. In town, men wear polo shirts and jeans or trousers, like other Filipinos. Women wear colorful sarongs (*gimay* or *patadyong*). It is not rare to see older and married women without a blouse on in the village, but schoolgirls always wear one. Female hair is kept long and in a chignon. In the village, earrings and chains of pearls are occasionally worn.

12 FOOD

Rice, a divine gift, is the most prized food and is the source of *tabad* (the "perfect drink," a ritually important alcohol). Tagbanua now buy rice in town. In the Calamian Islands, however, the *kurut*, a wild yam, is the staple food. It is poisonous, so hours must be spent processing it to get rid of the poison. In dried form, kurut can last for two years. Dried fish is the usual accompaniment to the main starch.

13 EDUCATION

To punish disobedience or disrespect, parents scold, pinch, beat, or lock up their children or put a curse (*gaba*) on them, threatening that the ancestors will cause the child illness or misfortune.

Children learn by observing and participating in the daily activities of adults. Illiteracy is high because school expenses (often requiring travel to a distant town) prevent most Tagbanua from sending their children to school, although Tagbanua value education. The first elementary school in the Calamian Islands dates to 1939. If parents can send their children, the children participate in school activities and celebrations, while the parents join in the P.T.A. Honors ceremonies are major events for such families.

According to the 2000 census, of persons over the age of five years in Palawan province, 47.5% had completed elementary school and 24.6% high school, but only 2.14% college or university (cf. 4.3% in Aklan province and 7.8% in Iloilo province, both on Panay in the neighboring Western Visayas region).

14 CULTURAL HERITAGE

Pasigem (riddles) and *ugtulen* (folk tales) serve not only as entertainment but also teach children social norms and history (explaining conflicts with other ethnic groups and the relationship with the Muslim peoples). The epic of *Dumarakul* (the hero's name) is sung after burial; all know the general story but few fully understand the archaic language of this long work. Traditional songs (*daluwasa, sablay, bagreng*) are gradually dying out. Today, people mix in lines in the languages of neighboring peoples and even prefer to sing entire songs in these languages. Also in decline are the playing of the Jew's harp, drum (*tambul*), and bamboo flute (*tipanu*), while great interest is shown in the guitar. Dancing to gong music is an important part of celebrations.

15 WORK

The Tagbanua practice slash-and-burn agriculture, growing dry rice, maize, millet, sweet potato, cassava, and taro. They build huts (*tangkungan*) near their fields so they can watch them. For this same purpose, tiptay, platforms light enough for children (who do the watching) to carry around, are set up in the fields. Yard gardens grow vegetables.

Fishing is the other important occupation. Methods include pole and line, poisoning with plant extracts, damming and drying up streams, and attracting fish with torches at night. Various types of harpoons and spears are being displaced by fishing guns. In addition to *barutu* (small outrigger canoes), motorboats are now used by the wealthiest Tagbanua.

Spear-wielding men hunt wild boars with the help of dogs. Fowl are also caught. It is customary to share game with relatives and neighbors. Water buffalo, perhaps only introduced in the 20th century, are kept for transport, as are cattle. Cattle and pigs are kept for ritual feasts. Certain types of chickens are raised solely for cockfighting or for their feathers, which can be made into fish bait.

The Tagbanua trade "Manila copal" (a mountain tree gum), split rattan, local rice, forest honey (as well as edible young bees and ritually important wax), and (in the Calamian Islands) edible bird nests taken at considerable risk from caves. For these, they obtain Moro goods (gongs, betel boxes, and stoneware) from Chinese or Christian shopkeepers.

Specialists include *bawalyan* (shamans), midwives, and drum- and flute-players. Some young men and women work as servants in non-Tagbanua houses, returning home to get married. Non-Tagbanua hire Tagbanua men to do carpentry or construction work.

16 SPORTS

Children play with toys they make themselves, such as boats and bamboo knives. They catch birds or butterflies. Girls weave small mats and play *sungka* with stones or shells; boys spin *ebeg*, wooden tops, as well as catch fish in shallow water with toy bows and arrows. Older children combine play with helping their parents.

17 ENTERTAINMENT AND RECREATION

Radios are now common, the most popular broadcasts being amateur singing contests and soap operas. Tagbanua watch films in town, mostly action and love stories in Tagalog/Pilipino, the national language, but also Westerns, kung fu movies, and the occasional pornographic film.

18 FOLK ART, CRAFTS, AND HOBBIES

The Tagbanua weave their own clothing from yarn bought in town.

19 SOCIAL PROBLEMS

See the article entitled **Filipinos**.

20 GENDER ISSUES

According to the 2000 census, Palawan province had a sex ratio of 107.07 men for every 100 women. Among those completing primary and secondary education, there were somewhat more men (53.6%) than women with an even greater gap than between percentages of men and women in the population as a whole. In tertiary education, the reverse was the case: women were more numerous than men (e.g. 59.7% of academic degree holders were women).

21 BIBLIOGRAPHY

LeBar, Frank M., ed. *Ethnic Groups of Insular Southeast Asia.* Vol. 2, *The Philippines and Formosa.* New Haven, CT: Human Relations Area Files Press, 1972.

National Statistics Office: Government of the Philippines. "Palawan: Population Rose to Three Quarter of a Million." http://www.census.gov.ph/data/pressrelease/2002/pr0290tx.html (November 21, 2008).

Talaroc, Edvilla R. *Tagbanua: Ein philippinisches Fischerfolk.* Münster: Lit, 1994.

—revised by A. J. Abalahin

TAHITIANS

PRONUNCIATION: tuh-HEE-shuns
LOCATION: Tahiti, in the Society Islands chain
POPULATION: 262,000 (2007)
LANGUAGE: Native languages of the islands; Maori; Tahitian; French; English
RELIGION: Christianity with elements of native religion

1 INTRODUCTION

The Tahitians are a Polynesian group inhabiting the island of Tahiti, the largest of a chain of islands called the Society Islands. The Society Islands are part of a larger sociopolitical unit called French Polynesia, an overseas territory of France. French Polynesians, including Tahitians, are citizens of France with certain voting rights and privileges.

Polynesians are thought to have first settled in the Society Islands in the 3rd century BC. The first contact by Europeans was made in the 16th century AD. In the late 1760s, both English and French seamen landed on and claimed control of Tahiti: the British Captain Wallis in 1767 and the French Bougainville in 1768. The first Protestant missionaries arrived in 1797 and began teaching the local populace to read and write and converting them to Christianity. In the 19th century Tahiti became an important distribution center for American and European whalers. In 1843 the ruling monarch of Tahiti's Pomare dynasty, Queen Pomare IV, signed a treaty making the island a French protectorate. In 1880 the last Pomare ruler abdicated and Tahiti became a French protectorate. It became a territory in 1957 and achieved internal self-rule in 1977. With the completion of Faaa International Airport in 1959, tourism became an important factor in the island's economy. French nuclear testing in the area began in the 1960s but ended in 1996. However, concerns about damage to local people's health resulting from the testing continued to reverberate in the 21st century. In 2006 it was revealed that French governments covered up for 40 years the fact that Tahiti was subjected to repeated fallout from atmospheric nuclear tests between 1966 and 1974.

2 LOCATION AND HOMELAND

The Society Islands are divided into two geographical and administrative clusters of islands: the windward group and the leeward group. Tahiti is part of the windward group. Tahiti is a "high" island in the typology of Pacific islands, having a volcanic origin. The landscape of Tahiti is punctuated with high peaks and a number of waterfalls. The climate is mild and tropical with an average temperature of about 25°C (77°F). The temperature rarely drops below 18°C (65°F). The rainy season lasts from November to April and the city of Papeete has an average yearly rainfall of 178 cm (70 in).

Tahiti had a total resident population of about 262,000 people as of 2007. The capital and largest city is Papeete, with a population of approximately 80,000 people. Persons of Polynesian descent made up the largest ethnic group in French Polynesia, accounting for 78% of the total population. The Chinese, who were originally brought to the islands in the 19th century to work in the cotton industry, accounted for 12% of the popu-

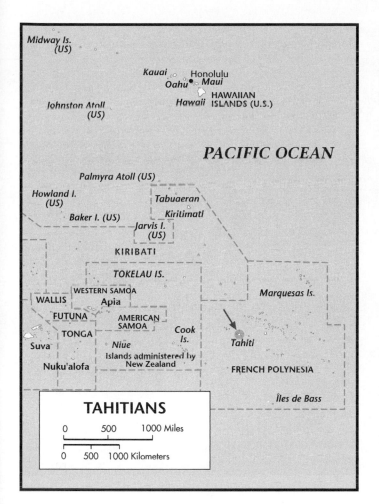

TAHITIANS

0   500   1000 Miles

0   500   1000 Kilometers

lation and Europeans (primarily French) accounted for about 10%.

³LANGUAGE

French and Tahitian are the official language of Tahiti. French is spoken widely and is the primary language used in official documents and in schools. Both social and economic status are affected by one's proficiency in French. However, most Tahitians speak a Tahitian dialect of French rather than Continental French. The Tahitian language, or Maohi, which is the official regional language of the Society Islands, is still used by a majority of the population and is the primary language spoken at home by older Tahitians. However, many young Tahitians have begun to use French exclusively. Tahitian is part of the larger family of Polynesian languages, which in turn belongs to the very large Austronesian language family. The Tahitian alphabet has 13 letters and all syllables in Tahitian end in a vowel. Forms of Pacific English are also spoken by Tahitians. Although there are a number of speakers of Chinese languages in the Society Islands, most Tahitians do not speak Chinese. Two popular Tahitian expressions are *"Aita e peapea"* ("no problem") and *"fiu"* ("fed up," or "bored").

⁴FOLKLORE

The history and lore of Tahiti's native people was passed down from one generation to the next in an oral tradition that included creation myths and stories of gods, heroes, and ances-

tors (many Tahitians can still list their ancient lineage). Epic poetry recounting the Polynesian past was recited in rhythmic chants and some legends were expressed in ritual dances accompanied by the beat of drums. A belief in ghosts *(tupapau)* still survives and some people leave lights on all night in their homes to protect themselves against these spirits.

⁵RELIGION

The conversion of the Tahitians to Protestantism occurred early in the history of European-Tahitian contact. In 1797 the London Missionary Society sent a group of evangelical Protestant missionaries to the island of Tahiti. By 1830 the vast majority of Tahiti and the whole of the Society Islands were Protestant. Even after the French takeover in the 1840s Protestantism remained the religion of the Tahitians. As of 2007 Protestants accounted for about 55% of the population and Roman Catholics for 30%. The largest single Protestant denomination was the Maohi Protestant Church (formerly known as the Evangelical Church of French Polynesia), which was established as an autonomous church in 1963. Services at the Maohi Protestant Church are presented in Tahitian. About 6% of the population was Mormon (members of the Church of Jesus Christ of Latter-day Saints) and 2% was Seventh-day Adventists. Some of the Chinese on Tahiti practice Buddhism.

The elements of the Christian faith, the church, and the pastor are central features of Tahitian village life. The church building and accompanying schoolhouse are reference points in every village. The village pastor shares in the political decision-making with the village chief. The Tahitian pastor is usually a native of the village where he or she holds a parish. The pastor presides over all of the religious activities of the village, conducts the Sunday school, teaches the Bible, conducts weddings and funerals, and provides communion. Some Tahitian church congregations are very well known for their hymn singing, which mixes European vocal style with traditional Tahitian style. Catholic services are conducted in French, while Protestant services are usually held in Tahitian.

⁶MAJOR HOLIDAYS

Tahiti's national holidays include New Year's Day (January 1), Good Friday, Easter Monday, Labor Day (May 1), Victory Day (May 8), Ascension Day, Whitmonday (Pentecost Monday), Bastille Day (July 14), Assumption of the Virgin Mary (August 15), All Saints' Day (November 1), Armistice Day (November 11), and Christmas. The biggest event of the year is Heiva I Tahiti, a celebration of Tahitian culture and the heroic Polynesian warriors of the past. Festivities last for about two weeks, beginning at the end of June, and include dancing, parades, dancing and singing competitions, sporting events, and feasting. On Bastille Day (July 14) there is a military parade in the capital. March 5 is celebrated by the Protestant communities throughout the island as Gospel Day, the day on which the first members of the London Missionary Society landed in Tahiti in 1797. The celebration includes religious services, discussions and religious and social issues, and banquets followed by singing and dancing. The Chinese New Year is also considered an important holiday in Tahiti.

A Tahitian woman in headdress in Tahiti, French Polynesia. (© Jean du Boisberranger/Hemis/Corbis)

⁷RITES OF PASSAGE

In the past, major life events were celebrated at religious gathering places called *marae*. Today rites of passage are generally observed within the Christian religious tradition.

⁸INTERPERSONAL RELATIONS

Tahitians, like other French Polynesians, are known for their *joie de vivre* (literally, "joy in life"), relaxed attitude, and unpretentious, courteous behavior. A favorite saying is, "If you act like old friends when you first meet, you will soon feel that you are." Visitors to Tahiti might receive a lei made from the Tiare Tahiti flower upon their arrival.

Tahitians typically greet each other by shaking hands, and women often exchange kisses on the cheek. The handshake is considered so important that if a person's hands are dirty, it is common to offer a wrist, elbow, or even a shoulder. Unless there are a large number of people present in a room (over 30), it is considered impolite not to shake hands with all of them. It is considered impolite to keep one's shoes on when entering another person's home. When guests are invited for a meal, the hosts are not necessarily expected to eat and may just sit and watch the guests eat. French greetings, such as *"Bonjour"* ("Good day"), are common in formal situations. A traditionally used Tahitian expression of welcome is *"La ora!"*

⁹Living conditions

Health conditions on Tahiti are generally good. Life expectancy for all of French Polynesia was about 76 years in 2008 with 74 years for men and 79 years for women. The rate of infant mortality was 7.7 deaths per 1,000 births (compared with a U.S. rate of 6.3 per 1,000). Medical care is paid for by the government.

Most Tahitians live in modern European-style homes with electricity and indoor plumbing. Housing styles range from the ultra-modern homes, townhouses, and condominiums of the wealthy in Papeete to the cement-walled, tin-roofed houses of the middle class. Wood-walled houses with thatch roofs can still be found among some of the poorest communities on the island.

Automobiles are commonly used for private transportation in Tahiti, and motorbikes are also popular. A widely used type of public transportation is called *le truck*.

¹⁰FAMILY LIFE

The traditional extended family has increasingly given way to the nuclear family in Tahiti, although it is not unusual for newly married couples to live with one set of in-laws for a period of time. Grandparents often play a prominent role in childrearing, and turning children over to adoptive parents (*faamu*) is also not unusual.

¹¹CLOTHING

Tahitians wear Western-style clothing as well as more traditional clothing consisting of simple cloths wrapped around the waist. Women ordinarily wear dresses rather than shorts. Thongs or sandals are commonly worn by both sexes without socks or hose. Traditional Tahitian dance costumes include grass or cotton skirts, necklaces, and headdresses made from local plants and grasses.

¹²FOOD

Staples of the Tahitian diet include pork, chicken, fish, and shellfish; root crops including yams and taro; coconut milk; breadfruit; rice; a type of spinach (fafa) and other locally grown vegetables; and fruits including papayas, pineapples, mangoes, and bananas. Bananas and papayas are pureed to create a popular dessert called poe'. Cooking in the traditional earth oven (himaa) remains popular in Tahiti. The food—which may include pork, chicken, fish, taro, or yams—is wrapped in leaves, placed over heated stones, covered with earth, and steamed for several hours. Also popular is poisson cru, a salad made with raw fish marinated in lime juice.

Village fare is basic. Breakfast typically consists of pancakes made from flour, coconut milk and sugar, coffee, and reef snails. Leftover pancakes accompany the other meals. Lunch is usually eaten around 1:00 or 2:00 in the afternoon and the meal centers on fish, usually fried, with taro root and cooked plantains. Supper is eaten around 7:00 PM. Leftovers from lunch and breakfast, as well as rice and canned vegetables, may form part of the evening meal. Coffee is an important part of supper.

In Papeete, lunch is the big meal of the day. Men and women arrive home from work about 11:30 AM to prepare the meal. After lunch, people typically sleep for an hour and then return to work by 1:00 or 2:00 PM. Supper in the city also consists mainly of leftovers or Chinese takeout food that is brought home by household members returning from the day's work. The Chinese are a major ethnic minority in Tahiti and as a result Chinese food is popular throughout the Society Islands.

¹³EDUCATION

Tahiti has a 98% literacy rate. Primary, secondary, and vocational schools were established on Tahiti by the French and conform to French educational standards. Schooling is free and compulsory between the ages of 6 and 14. There are also private schools, run by churches and subsidized by the government, that teach the same curriculum as the public schools. Adult education is also popular and offered at no charge. Tahitian students often attend college in France or other countries.

¹⁴CULTURAL HERITAGE

Performing arts competitions held in Tahiti every July during the Heiva I Tahiti festivities help preserve the traditional performing arts of song and dance in the Society Islands. The Society Islands also send performing troupes to compete in South Pacific arts festivals. Traditional Tahitian dances were once considered so lascivious by 19th-century Protestant missionaries that they were banned in the 1820s. In modern culture Tahitian dancing is extremely popular, with numerous dance competitions featuring troupes of between 20 and 50 dancers held during Heiva I Tahiti. In the aparima, the hands of the dancer express the story through movements and positioning.

The dance is generally performed in a standing posture and resembles the Hawaiian hula. It is accompanied by drums, guitar, and ukulele. Also popular is the sexually provocative tamure, in which young men and women dance around each other. The o'tea, performed by dancers lined up in two columns and accompanied by drums, consists of gestures based on specific themes, such as spear throwing. The pata'uta'u involves beating the ground with open palms.

The Tahitian word himene is used to denote all types of song. The word is borrowed from the English word hymn and shows the extent of the influence the early Christian missionaries had on the traditional culture of Tahiti. Himene tarava are songs performed by groups of approximately 100 male and female singers. In former times, the songs would recount the deeds of kings and gods, but now they tell popular tales from the Bible, sung in Tahitian. Guitars and ukuleles are important musical instruments for Tahitian males, as are a variety of drums including the toere, a slit drum made of tamanu wood and hit with a stick; the ofe, a split-bamboo drum; and the pahu, made from a hollowed section of coconut tree and covered with shark skin. Another traditional instrument is the bamboo nose-flute, or vivo.

The word tattoo originated in Tahiti. According to legend, Tohu, the god of tattoo, was responsible for painting the colors and patterns of all of the fish in the ocean. In Polynesian culture, tattoos are considered to be a sign of beauty.

¹⁵WORK

Since the establishment in the 1960s of France's Centre Experimental du Pacifique, which administered France's nuclear testing program, and the growth of tourism that began during the same period, the bulk of employment on Tahiti has shifted from subsistence agriculture to public and private services, each of which employs about 40% of the labor force. The Chinese are primarily employed in retail trade.

¹⁶SPORTS

Soccer is the most popular sport among Tahitians. Other favorites include basketball, volleyball, boxing, and cycling. Water sports are popular and include swimming, fishing, diving, canoeing, and windsurfing. Canoe races are the most popular sporting event of the Heiva I Tahiti festivities in July.

¹⁷ENTERTAINMENT AND RECREATION

The leisure-time pursuits of Tahitians include movies, music, dancing, and television. Radio Tahiti broadcasts programs in the Tahitian language.

¹⁸FOLK ART, CRAFTS, AND HOBBIES

Many traditional handicrafts, such as weaving, quilting, and carving, are learned and passed on from one generation to the next by "mamas," who are considered the guardians of such sacred traditions. In the past, the Tahitians used cloth made from the inner bark of mulberry, breadfruit, and banyan trees for clothing and other items. After being stripped from the tree and separated from the outer layer of bark, the inner layer was beaten with a mallet, dried in the sun, dyed, and hand-painted with floral or geometric patterns. A traditional craft still practiced is the making of two-layer patchwork quilts called tifaifai, often decorated with colorful floral patterns. Other crafts include needlework, seashell jewelry, and straw hats, mats, and baskets. *Pareu*—lengths of cotton cloth wrapped and tied to form sarong-like garments—are screened, blocked, and printed by hand with colorful patterns. Natural skin products, called *monoi* oils, are made from the oils extracted for the Tiare flower and tree fruits.

¹⁹SOCIAL PROBLEMS

The topic of independence has been part of many political debates since the 1970s. The island has a semi-autonomous government with an elected president and a great deal of control concerning internal affairs. However, the people are still dependent on France for services such as education and security and France offers economic stability as well. In 2004 the status of Tahiti was changed from an overseas territory to an "overseas country." While those groups promoting full independence are rather prominent, some reports indicate that only about 20% of the general population is in favor of independence.

²⁰ GENDER ISSUES

In traditional villages, men and women shared somewhat equally in the necessary tasks for daily life, particularly in finding and preparing food for the family. Both men and women assisted in maintaining the family gardens and fruit trees. Men were most often in charge of hunting and deep-water fishing while women were in charge of building and maintaining the outdoor ovens made of volcanic rock. Women worked by weaving baskets, mats, and other household items out of coconut leaves and creating jewelry out of shells. Handicrafts for men included carved tiki statues, drums, and other household items. In modern culture, both men and women have opportunities to work outside of the home, particularly in tourist-related services. Many men and women continue the tradition of making handicrafts, with products offered for sale to tourists.

²¹ BIBLIOGRAPHY

Cobb, Nicholas. *Tahiti & French Polynesia*. Maspeth, NY: Langenscheidt Publishers, 2002.

Ferdon, Edwin N. "Tahiti." *Encyclopedia of World Cultures*. Boston: G. K. Hall, 1992.

Grove, Arthur, ed. *The Lure of Tahiti: An Armchair Companion*. Honolulu: Mutual Publications, 1986.

Kuwahara, Makiko. *Tatoo: An Anthropology*. New York: Berg, 2005.

Levy, Robert. *Tahitians: Mind and Experience in the Society Islands*. Chicago: University of Chicago Press, 1973.

Polynesian Cultural Center. http://www.polynesia.com. (22 April 2008).

Sears, James. *Tahiti, Romance and Reality*. Wellington, New Zealand: Millwood Press, 1982.

—revised by K. Ellicott

TAIWAN INDIGENOUS PEOPLES

ALTERNATE NAMES: Formosan Aborigines, Taiwan Austronesians
LOCATION: Taiwan
POPULATION: 460,000 (2008)
LANGUAGE: 13 Austronesian languages
RELIGION: Christianity, Traditional Religions

¹INTRODUCTION

This article examines the place of the Indigenous peoples of Taiwan in contemporary society and political processes. For an ethnographic description of the traditional culture of one of these groups, please refer to the entry on Tao.

The 460,000 Indigenous Peoples of Taiwan (Taiwan Yuanzhuminzu) are several Austronesian Peoples who inhabited all of Taiwan before Chinese settlement began in the 1620s. Approximately 7000 years ago, horticulturalists making corded pottery and using polished stone tools began to cross the Taiwan straits from coastal areas of the Asian continent south of the Yangtze River. Their "proto-Austronesian" languages evolved in Taiwan along with cultural adaptations. Some 5000 years ago these cultures and languages began to spread through insular Southeast Asia, and the Pacific, becoming the large Austronesian linguistic and cultural family which extends from the Maori of New Zealand to Madagascar off the coast of Africa. Linguistic, archaeological, and genetic evidence now confirm that Taiwan is the original homeland of Austronesian languages and cultures. Some of the contemporary groups in Taiwan (Kavalan, Tao) appear to have been later migrants back to Taiwan from the Pacific or the Philippines.

What is beyond debate is that there were Austronesian peoples in Taiwan for centuries before they entered written history, and that they are very different from the Chinese, who now constitute 98% of Taiwan's population. These two traits make them "aboriginal" or "indigenous," and give them a collective identity beyond their varied languages, cultures, and forms of social organization. Although these differences are significant, it is their common historical experience and legal status in Taiwan today which allows us to discuss them together.

Through three centuries of Chinese immigration, the Austronesian peoples inhabiting the plains and hills of western Taiwan were gradually assimilated and intermarried with Chinese immigrants, so that today people whose ancestors were "Pingpu" (Plains Aborigine) are a major part of the "Taiwanese" population. The "savages" (*hoan-a*) who inhabited the mountains and east coast were feared as headhunters, and survived as distinct tribes who are today's Indigenous Peoples of Taiwan. Until 1875 Chinese sought to cordon off this area, but valuable camphor forests and the threat of Japanese designs led the Chinese to expand into the mountains, starting decades of "camphor wars" in which thousands of Aborigines and Chinese were killed.

In 1895 Japan took Taiwan from China. After 1908 they sent over 100 military campaigns into the mountains, ending with the conquest of the Truku in 1914. The Japanese excluded the

Chinese from Indigenous areas. Villages in the high mountains were moved out to facilitate control, modernization, and for shaping them into Imperial subjects. Indigenous people were used as forced labor in lumbering. In 1930 a large Tayal uprising at Wushe in central Taiwan was crushed with the use of poison gas.

After taking Taiwan in 1945 the Republic of China pursued a policy of economic improvement and cultural assimilation of the Indigenous People. Thus, while Indigenous People are poor and marginalized, their economic and educational situation is better than most indigenous peoples in the world.

²LOCATION AND HOMELAND

Traditional Indigenous territories are the rugged mountains and valleys which take up all of central and eastern Taiwan. Taiwan is a small island, 13,000 sq km (5,019 sq mi) (the size of Vancouver Island), and so even a "remote" village is never far from the densely populated western plain. Over one-third of Indigenous Peoples now live and work permanently in cities such as Taipei, Kaohsiung, and Taichung. But many retain homes in their villages, to which they return regularly.

The 460,000 Indigenous People make up only 2% of Taiwan's 23 million people. They are classified into 13 self-identified and officially recognized tribes, each with its own language and distinctive culture. They can be geographically and culturally grouped into six areas:

North: Tayal, 79,000; Truku, 22,000; Saisiat, 5,400

Central: Bunun, 47,000; Tsou, 6,200; Thao, 500

South: Rukai, 11,000; Paiwan, 82,000

East Coast: Pinuyumayan 10,500; Amis, 167,000,

Lanyu Island: Tao, 3,400

Plains Aboriginal: Kavalan 1000, Sakizaya 5000

(another 40,000 do not identify themselves with any one group, in part because of intertribal marriage)

Basic social structure roughly follows this geographic division.

The northern groups were simple band societies, based on hunting and semi-permanent hamlets. The central groups lived in larger villages organized into large extended households and clans that united people among many villages. The southern groups were unequal, chiefly societies divided into commoners and aristocrats who produced local hereditary chiefs. The Amis and Pinuyumayan were plains agriculturalists and fishermen, who lived in large settled villages organized into age group systems under village elders. Because of their unique features and location on a small island in the Pacific, the Tao are discussed in a separate entry. Two Plains indigenous groups, which were assimilated into Taiwanese culture in the late 19th century, and considered to have "disappeared," have now been revived, and achieved state recognition in 2003 (Kavalan) and 2007 (Sakizaya).

³LANGUAGE

There were at least 23 Indigenous languages in Taiwan in earlier times. Some 11 remain as living languages. The rest have died out or are limited to few speakers. These languages were highly diverse, but there are many cognate (shared) words such as *mata* (eye), *ina* (mother), *ama/tama* (father), *babui/vavui* (pig), *tulu/toro* (two), *pat* (four), *lima/rima* (five), etc., which are often found in languages of other Austronesian peoples.

As with all languages there are many borrowings, especially from Japanese. Names also reflect much diversity, such as Li'Bai (Amis F), Kui (Paiwan M), Walis Yugan (Tayal M) Yibu (Bunun F) Aroladen Pale (Rukai M). "Aroladen" means "river keeper," which shows that this family originally was responsible for collecting tribute for the chief from people fishing. Yohani (Bunun M) reflects Christian influence (John), while Sa'folo (Amis M) is from Japanese "Saburo" (third son).

⁴FOLKLORE

One myth shared among most Taiwan Indigenous cultures is about two suns. There are many versions, but the basic myth is that in early times there were two suns, so that there was no night and the world was very hot, and people were never able to rest. Life was hard. An archer travels to a high mountain and shoots one of the suns as it rises. The sun is wounded and becomes our moon. People now have day to work and night to sleep.

⁵RELIGION

The traditional religions included belief in various spirits. The northern group worshipped mainly ancestral spirits, the central and southern groups added many natural spirits, which involved many taboos. The eastern groups also believed in universal creator spirits, and the Pinuyumayan, influenced by Chinese folk religion, developed a hierarchy based on individual gods and spirit houses.

All groups had taboos and omens centered on hunting. A Bunun omen was that if you passed gas or sneezed while preparing to hunt, you should not go. Certain kinds of birds flying in front of you or singing were also good or bad omens for hunting among many tribes. All groups had women spirit mediums (shamans) and healers. In addition, there were ritual groups, usually based on extended kinship, for special ceremonies, including planting and harvesting of crops. The annual Amis harvest festivals (see below) are the best example of this. One of the most unusual rituals is the Saisiat "Dwarf Sacrifice" held every two years to honor the spirits of a race of small people whom Saisiat legend says their ancestors wiped out. It is suggested this is evidence that in prehistoric times there were Negrito peoples in Taiwan, as there still are today in the Philippines.

The Japanese forbade Christianity or Buddhism among Indigenous People, but in the early 1930s a Truku woman named Chi-oang became a Christian, and the new faith spread in secrecy. In 1945 Taiwan became part of the Republic of China, and with involvement of Taiwanese Christians and foreign missionaries, some 70% of the Indigenous People soon became Christian, mainly Presbyterian and Catholic. Christianity is now a significant marker of Indigenous identity in Taiwan, distinguishing them from the Chinese population, which is 90% folk religion, or Buddhist. Their churches, led by native clergy, and among the Presbyterians organized under self-governing tribal presbyteries, have played a key role in preserving Indigenous identity and promoting Indigenous rights. Clergy are often local political leaders.

⁶MAJOR HOLIDAYS

Today Indigenous People share the same public holidays as the Taiwanese, but Christmas and the Harvest Festival are uniquely important for them. Christmas is a major celebration in Indigenous villages. Almost everyone who is able will return from the city, some remaining to harvest and plant until the Lunar New Year in February. Christmas is marked with special services in churches, parties, and often a village sports day.

The Amis Harvest Festivals, marking the summer millet and rice harvest, are annual festivals, for which everyone must return to the village for several days. People who do not return may be fined by the village elders. The many rituals are capped by nightly majestic circle dancing accompanied by chanting. For younger men the dancing is compulsory and lasts all afternoon and all night. It marks a graduation into a higher age group status. Older men supervise this training and whip the legs of youths who are not putting enough effort into it. The festival is also a time for much feasting, drinking traditional millet wine, and for young people to begin courting. Boys dance wearing a small embroidered "lovers bag." If a girl is interested in a boy she will put some betel nuts into his bag during the dancing.

Other groups have their own harvest festivals, but none are as highly developed as the Amis ones, which are now big tourist attractions in Taiwan and have become the iconic symbol of aboriginality.

⁷RITES OF PASSAGE

In the past the birth of twins was considered very unlucky, and among the Bunun, twins were killed immediately at birth. This custom is no longer practiced, and births are generally occasions for many gifts.

Today Christian rituals mark the life passages of most Indigenous People in Taiwan. The disciplines of industrial work and school have replaced many traditional patterns. Older children take care of younger siblings, and young girls often carry infant brothers or sisters bound to their backs while parents work. Children are expected to take on responsibility from an early age. With many people in the village being kin, daily life is shared with cousins, and children may live with aunts and uncles as much as with parents.

In the past, relations between the sexes were closely controlled by many taboos, and premarital sex relations were completely forbidden. Ironically, the conversion to Christianity broke down these traditional taboos and many Indigenous youth follow Western-style patterns of dating and sex relations. Because the Taiwanese generally, and most Indigenous cultures, are strongly male-dominant, this often works to the disadvantage of Indigenous girls, who are seen as objects of male enjoyment and were even sold into prostitution.

Coming of age was marked in many ways. Tayal and Bunun would remove the front teeth of children, and the Tayal and Taroko tattooed the faces of both sexes. At a later age, taking a head was a sign of entry into adulthood for men in most tribes; this represented courage and skill in hunting. For women, it was ability to weave using a backstrap loom that marked adulthood. Both of these achievements were marked in the Tayal by additional facial tattoos which signaled readiness for marriage. Pinuyumayan had young men's houses where boys would live for their teens, receiving training and serving as the soldiers of the village. Coming of age was marked by a demanding series of tests of endurance. These customs have been revived in recent years, though the young men's house is now transformed into a summer camp. In 2008 a Tayal couple had their faces tattooed in the traditional way, so reviving this ethnic marker.

The typical day of a rural Indigenous high school student living in a village might involve getting up before 6:00 AM to do chores and study and to put lunch into a metal tin which will be heated at noon. They put on their student uniform, and then take the bus from their village to the high school in the nearby town. High schools in Taiwan are often separate for boys and girls. Students care for the school grounds and clean their classrooms before the morning assembly for flag raising at 8:00 AM. Classes usually last until 4:30. Arriving home after 5:30, they may have a bowl of noodles, and then go to the village basketball court to play basketball for a couple of hours. This is a time when boys and girls can socialize. There is much homework to do every night, and tests are frequent. Students may study until late at night or go to bed early and get up to study at 3:00 AM.

Compulsory military service is the universal rite of passage into adulthood for men in Taiwan. This occasion is more highly honored in Indigenous cultures than among the Chinese, and is usually marked by a special banquet for the male kin of the departing youth. For young women there is a quiet entry into the labor force, going to work in the city. Marriage usually takes place after a man's return from military service.

Traditional marriage customs differ from tribe to tribe, but all marriages are outside the kin group and monogamous. The Amis are a matrilineal culture, and the man marries into his wife's family and moves to her village. Betel nuts are an important part of the wedding gifts from the groom's family to the bride's family. Among the Rukai, the wedding includes a ceremony in which the groom pushes the bride on a rope swing, the directions of which were omens of a bad or good marriage. Learning how to position herself on the rope so as to move in the right direction was an important skill that a bride needed to learn. In the Bunun the new couple would usually live and work as part of a large household of an extended patrilineal lineage. Even today many young Bunun working away from home will give their earnings to the father, who then allots them an allowance.

In old age grandparents live with their children and are important caregivers for the grandchildren. As they become older, their children and grandchildren will sometimes carry them on their backs, thus completing the circle of life. Death is still a natural fact of life and often occurs at home, so that most Indigenous children have a much more mature understanding of death than Americans.

Traditional burials were under the floor of the house, except for the Paiwan and Amis, who buried the dead outside but near the house. If a person died unnaturally in the house (rather than by natural causes), then the house would be abandoned, as it would become haunted by the ghost of the victim.

Today most Indigenous People follow Christian funeral customs, but often with the adhesion of traditional rituals integrated into or added onto the Christian ceremony. Non-Christians may follow Taiwanese funeral rituals with similar adhesions. Burial is now in a cemetery. Most Indigenous People now follow the Taiwanese custom of wearing a small patch of mourning cloth on their clothes after a parent's death. A memorial is usually held one year after the death.

[8] INTERPERSONAL RELATIONS

Indigenous People are much more easygoing and openly friendly than their more formal Taiwanese neighbors. Even in the cities, they tend to associate most of the time with other Indigenous People, and will identify each other on the street by greeting a stranger who looks like a member of their tribe in their mother tongue. Generally Indigenous People make much use of body language, touching, and horseplay among friends. They are usually direct in speech, in contrast to the reserved Taiwanese, and visitors are often asked about things which Americans would never ask a stranger.

Dropping in unannounced for a visit is an important part of daily Indigenous social life. When visitors arrive, most homes immediately host them with beer, rice wine, and food. One problem with this is that many people become heavy drinkers, as the socializing may go on for hours. Unscrupulous merchants have often taken advantage of the openness and hospitality of the Indigenous People, tricking them into signing bad deals or even selling their land once enough bottles have been emptied.

[9] LIVING CONDITIONS

Traditional housing varied greatly, from the bamboo or wooden huts of the Tayal to the large stone houses of the Bunun extended family, to the Amis bamboo longhouse, to the substantial single family slate homes of the Paiwan. Today, urban Indigenous People tend to live in small concrete apartments in industrial areas, but may have used their savings and labor to build a nice home on their own land in their native village. Most Indigenous homes are a mix of Chinese and Japanese styles, the inhabitants often sleeping on tatami platforms. But in Indigenous villages there is a great variety of housing, with very poor and drafty wooden housing with rough cement floors beside new, two-story modern tile homes. However, these are often linked to high debt or the sale of land or of daughters into prostitution.

Motorcycles usually serve as the family car, and most Indigenous children can ride motorcycles by the time they are 12. This, and winding mountain roads, means that the rate of death and injury due to accidents is very high among Indigenous people, a rate made higher by industrial and mining accidents. Because of heavy social drinking there is a high rate of alcohol-related health problems. In some villages tuberculosis is still active. Gout is a common problem.

Thus, while in many ways the Indigenous People of Taiwan have a high standard of living for Asia, the quality of their lives is still poor compared to Taiwan generally. In 2006 average Indigenous household income in Taiwan was reported to be 47% of non-indigenous income (approximately US$17,000 to $36,000). This is a significant improvement over previous decades.

[10] FAMILY LIFE

Marriage in all Taiwan Indigenous groups is monogamous (one man and one woman) and exogamous (outside of the extended kin group). Marriage, past and present, is generally not arranged. All mountain-dwelling groups are patrilineal (kinship traced through the father), while the Pinuyumayan and Amis on the east coast are matrilineal (kinship traced through the mother), Tayal families are small and do not go beyond local lineages (kinship traced to a few generations), while Bunun families are organized into large patrilineal kinship groups extending across many generations and villages. Bunun nuclear families tend to be very large—seven children being quite common. Paiwan and Rukai families are clearly divided into the aristocrats, who traditionally married only other aristocrats, and commoners. In the Rukai the oldest son inherits the title of the father, while in the Paiwan the oldest child, male or female, inherits the position of chief.

Despite this, and the continuing strong matrilineal tradition of the Amis, the position and role of women in Indigenous society is still the homemaker, and, in many ways, under male domination. Indigenous women are generally more active in local political and church leadership than Taiwanese women, but in the home inequality. For example, often when guests come for dinner the husband and older sons will eat with them, while the wife and children wait until they are finished, and then eat the leftovers. Otherwise leftovers usually go to the dog. Tayal and Bunun households almost universally keep dogs used in hunting. Because monkeys are often caught in traps, many homes have pet monkeys.

[11] CLOTHING

Today Indigenous People wear the same clothes as everyone else in Taiwan. Because Taiwan is warm much of the year, traditional Indigenous clothes were quite simple, and 19th-century travelers reported that people often worked almost naked in their fields. Women in all groups wove ramie or hemp cloth on backstrap looms, the Tayal and Truku being famed for the quality of their weaving, which is still done today, but using commercial yarn. Bunun hunters wore leather caps and leather leggings. Amis men wore short kilts and vests, while Amis women are famous for their colorful red skirts and bodices with bells and fine needlework. The most exquisite clothes are black full-length dresses worn by Paiwan women, richly embroidered with beads in traditional patterns and small bells. Indigenous People are proud of their traditional clothes and almost everyone has a handmade set for special occasions.

[12] FOOD

For all tribes the principal traditional food staples were millet, taro, sweet potatoes, and rice. Meat was hunted, mainly wild pig and deer. The Amis especially eat a lot of fish. These are supplemented by wild greens, ginger, and wild fruits. Traditional utensils were wooden or bone spoons for soup. Meals were generally taken collectively from a large central pot. Many traditional Indigenous foods are still part of the daily diet. One of the most prized is Paiwan *avai,* meat in a soft cake of millet steamed in pandanus leaves. Tayal *tmmyen* is a delicacy of pickled raw meat.

A century of Japanese and Chinese rule have made their foods part of the daily diet of Indigenous People. Sashimi is a favorite food. Chicken and pork have replaced wild game, but when some is hunted it is an occasion for great celebration and everyone gets a share. In many homes a large Chinese dinner, often with wild greens and sweet potatoes, is the main meal. Breakfast is often a sweet potato and rice gruel eaten with leftovers from dinner. Rice and leftovers are packed in metal lunch tins for a noon meal, but people often eat at a noodle stand. In the last decade or so white bread and instant coffee have become very popular, and many now have coffee and toast for breakfast. Indigenous People tend to eat more meat and saltier food. This has led to widespread gout, high blood pressure, and heart problems as people eat heavy meat meals every day rather than only when game was available as in the past.

13 EDUCATION

Before missionaries created scripts after 1946, there was no Indigenous writing system. Today, however, Indigenous People in Taiwan actually have a slightly higher literacy level than the Taiwanese, mainly because of the high rate of Christian converts who learn to read the Bible and hymns in their own romanized writing, and often read Japanese as well. Most Indigenous People are multilingual, speaking their own language, Mandarin Chinese, Taiwanese, and often Japanese. School is taught in Mandarin, but Indigenous language classes are now a required course in Indigenous elementary schools. This is a great change from only the 1980s, when students were forbidden to speak their own language in school. However the hours dedicated to teaching mother tongue and the quality of teaching is less than ideal. There is now indigenous language television programming through the Public Television System. There is an Indigenous Peoples College located at National Tunghua University in Hualien.

After junior high school there is a high drop-out rate among Indigenous students, who end up in factories and construction jobs. Those that continue must take highly competitive entrance exams, and Indigenous children do not usually have the advantage of well educated parents or expensive urban tutoring schools to gain an advantage in these exams. Many Indigenous young people go to commercial or industrial schools, and far fewer into academic high schools. Many Indigenous young women go to nursing school. Those who graduate from high school also must face university entrance exams. While the government does allow them a 20% handicap on these exams, and free tuition in public universities, the proportion of Indigenous People with university education in Taiwan is much lower than Taiwanese with university education. In 2005, 28% of Indigenous People had some postsecondary education, up from 20% in 2000.

For these reasons, many Indigenous parents do not encourage their children to take the risky and costly route of postsecondary education, but to learn a technical skill and find a job. In school many Indigenous youth excel in athletics. A few lucky ones get athletic scholarships to universities and become physical education teachers.

14 CULTURAL HERITAGE

Group dancing and singing connected with Indigenous festivals are one of the great cultural contributions of the Indigenous People of Taiwan to the world. The circle dances and melodic songs are major cultural attractions in Taiwan and have been performed around the world. Amis and Paiwan dancing, Bunun eight-part harmonic singing, and Paiwan nose-flutes are some of the best known traditions. Many Indigenous singers have become top artists in Taiwan, often drawing from their traditional songs. The inclusion (without permission or compensation) of an Amis song in the music for the 1996 Atlanta Olympics became national news in Taiwan, and heightened awareness of the rich Indigenous musical tradition (and issues of intellectual property). In 2001 a Pinuyumayan pop singer, Amei, sang the national anthem at the inauguration of President Chen. Indigenous song and dance have become a

standard part of Taiwan's international self-representation and all public cultural events. There is a growing body of published Indigenous literature.

15 WORK

Indigenous people are at the bottom of Taiwan's socioeconomic ladder. About 40% of Indigenous households are considered farmers, though they may work off the farm as well in forestry and construction. But with the exception of highland temperate fruit farmers, the income of Indigenous farmers is much lower than the Taiwan average. Over half of all Indigenous People work in urban areas. Most of them are factory labor, construction workers, or miners. In construction whole families often move from site to site, living in temporary sheds. The large importation of foreign labor during the 1990s led to increased unemployment among aboriginal people (though the rate remained low by even American standards). Legal measures now guarantee preferred hiring of Indigenous People in many areas.

16 SPORTS

Sports are a major obsession in Indigenous society. Basketball is the universal sport, played daily in every village. Every social institution—schools, governments, churches, etc.—have endless rounds of basketball competitions for men and women, as well as frequent village sports days or county competitions. After basketball, baseball is most popular. This is especially so among the Amis and Pinyumayan, who live on the east coast plain. A number of Amis players are stars in professional Japanese baseball teams. The first Little League world champions from Taiwan were from a poor Bunun village where they made gloves from newspapers and practiced batting rocks. Indigenous youth have also excelled in track and field and produced two of Taiwan's few Olympic medalists.

17 ENTERTAINMENT AND RECREATION

Sports are the most popular recreation, but television and especially Japanese wrestling videos are very popular. In the late 1980s, video games invaded Indigenous villages, and by the late 1990s satellite dishes receiving stations from Japan and China, and computers with Internet access were found in every village. Trapping, fishing with javelins and nets, and hunting with homemade muskets are now recreational activities, but ones which are an important affirmation of continuing Indigenous cultural identity in modern Taiwan.

18 FOLK ART, CRAFTS, AND HOBBIES

In the decorative arts, the stone and wood carving of the Paiwan, created to decorate the homes and utensils of the aristocratic families, are the best known example of Taiwan Indigenous art and are purchased for high prices from Taiwanese and Japanese collectors. The dominant motifs in these carvings are ancestor figures, faces, and curled hundred-pacer snakes—symbols of aristocratic power. Weaving by Tayal and Taroko women is another highly prized art, but few women learn the use of the difficult and tiring backstrap loom today. However, weaving traditional textiles using modern looms is widely taught in some indigenous areas, becoming an income source for many women. Amis and Paiwan women's clothes have been developed by a few Indigenous women into elegant contemporary fashions. Many contemporary items made using traditional Indigenous crafts are widely marketed in Taiwan.

[19] SOCIAL PROBLEMS

Loss of their land, destruction of their cultural systems, and dislocation arising from rapid, enforced social change at the hands of an invader culture—the Chinese—are the basic experiences of the Indigenous People of Taiwan. The symptoms of high suicide rates, alcoholism, family breakdown, and low self-esteem are widespread.

Politically, they were militarily conquered and kept in subservience to the successive regimes ruling Taiwan. There are no treaties, and traditional leaders were rendered powerless. The government classifies some Indigenous land as "Mountain Reserve Land," presumably held in trust for Indigenous People, but much has been lost to the Forestry Department and illegal speculation. There are 30 Indigenous townships in which the mayor must be Aboriginal, but they have no autonomous fiscal or legislative power. Indigenous seats are reserved at every level of government, with Indigenous People as a separate electorate, so that they do have a voice in lawmaking.

In the 1980s the end of martial law (1987) and rapid democratization in Taiwan made a renewal of Indigenous culture possible. Indigenous leaders began actively advocating the rights of their own people. The 1987–89 "Return our Land" movement marked the beginning of Taiwan's Indigenous rights movement and identified the issues which continue to be the focus of Indigenous politics today: language, education, constitutional rights, and self-government. In 1996 a cabinet level "Indigenous Peoples Council" was established with a representative from each tribal group and a Chair who is a cabinet minister. Though it does not have administrative control over Indigenous affairs, it relates to all government departments which do, and develops policies implemented through them. It also provides generous funding to education, culture, research, international indigenous exchange, and infrastructure in Aboriginal Townships. The Council website www.apc.gov.tw is a rich source of information.

In 1999 Democratic Progressive Party (DPP) presidential candidate Chen Shui-bian signed a "New Partnership" agreement with Indigenous representatives during the election, promising to promote aboriginal self-government, recognize natural Indigenous rights, define Indigenous collective land rights etc. He was elected, and since 2001 a number of laws towards these goals were passed, including the Indigenous Education Law, Indigenous Job Protection law, and Indigenous Peoples Basic Law (2007), which mandates Indigenous self government and control of land and resources. An Indigenous self government law was proposed in 2003 but opposition control of the legislature stalled its passage. Many of the principles established in these laws await actual implementation, with political struggles between the DPP administration and mostly Kuomintang (KMT) local governments being a major problem. With the election of a KMT president in 2008 it remains to be seen whether things will change. Nonetheless, even for the KMT, Indigenous policy has changed from assimilation to multiculturalism, and the affirmation of Indigenous culture and identity is an important part of Taiwan's future.

[20] GENDER ISSUES

The appointment in 2008 of the first woman to be Chair of the Indigenous Peoples Council by KMT President Ma represents an important recognition of the role of Indigenous women as leaders and the continuing issues of gender equality in Indigenous cultures. As noted above, Indigenous cultures are male dominant, and even in the matrilineal Amis, decisions are made by male relatives. The status of women was helped by conversion to Christianity (women becoming leaders in churches and by extension in their communities) and state policies emphasizing formal gender equality and education for all. This is also reflected in the election of women to political office at all levels from town council to national legislature. Nonetheless, politics in Taiwan is a boys club, with much drinking and clubbing in which women are demeaned and marginalized. The sale of daughters into prostitution was a longstanding problem in indigenous villages until a major public campaign and enforcement of child protection laws in the late 1980s made it a national shame. On the other hand the incorporation of Indigenous People into the labor market and cash economy has made many women the financial managers in their households and so tended to equalize marriage partnerships. Especially with the development of local tourism in Taiwan, based on bed-and-breakfasts in indigenous villages, production and sale of aboriginal crafts, and Indigenous song and dance performance, while not without problems, have all highlighted and strengthened the role of women in traditional culture as well as contemporary society.

[21] BIBLIOGRAPHY

Barnes, R. H., Andrew Gray, and Benedict Kingsbury (eds.) *Indigenous Peoples of Asia*. Ann Arbor: Association for Asian Studies, 1995.

Bellwood, Peter. "The Austronesian Dispersal and the Origin of Languages." In *Scientific American*, July 1991, pages 88-93.

Chen Chi-lu. *Material Culture of the Formosan Aborigines*. Taipei: The Taiwan Museum, 1968

Government Information Office. *The Republic of China Yearbook*. Taipei: Government Information Office, 2007.

Harrison, Henrietta (ed.) *Natives of Formosa: British Reports of the Taiwan Indigenous People 1650-1950*. Taipei: Shung Ye Museum of Formosan Aborigines, 2001.

Mabuchi, Toichi. *The Ryukyus-Taiwan-Insular Southeast Asia. Asian Folklore and Social Life Monographs*. Vol. 59. Taipei: Orient Culture Service, 1974.

Rubinstein, Murray A. (ed.) *Taiwan: A New History*. Armonk NY: M.E. Sharpe, 1999.

Yeh Chuen-rong (ed.) *History, Culture and Ethnicity: Selected papers from the International Conference on the Formosan Indigenous Peoples*. Taipei: Shung Ye Museum of Formosan Aborigines, 2006.

—by M. Stainton

TAJIKS

PRONUNCIATION: tah-JEEKS
LOCATION: Tajikistan
POPULATION: More than 7 million
LANGUAGES: Tajiki; Russian; Uzbeki
RELIGIONS: Islam (Sunni and Shia); Orthodox Christianity; Judaism; Nonreligious

¹INTRODUCTION

The Tajiks are an Indo-European people who, after the breakup of the Indo-Iranian tribal confederation, occupied the upper reaches of the Amu River (territory of present-day Uzbekistan). In the 9th century AD, through the efforts of the Samanids (an Iranian family promoted by the Abbasid caliphs against Turkish invaders), they came to prominence and formed the Tajik nation. After the fall of the Samanids (999 AD), they became clients of the Turks and the Mongols.

During the latter part of the 19th century, the Tajiks were divided. Most of the population occupied what would become the republic of Tajikistan in the former Soviet Union and the rest became an integral part of Afghanistan. The Tajiks' desire to maintain their ethnic unity has made them vulnerable to manipulation by their neighbors, especially Russia and Uzbekistan. On 5 December 1929, Tajikistan became an independent republic in the USSR.

After gaining independence from the Soviet Union in 1991, clashes among clans and between Muslims and communists resulted in five years of civil war (1992–97) as a result of which thousands lost their lives, and more than 100,000 fled to Afghanistan. More than 35,000 homes were destroyed, either in battle or as a result of ethnic-cleansing actions. At present, the insecurity of the war has all but disappeared. The political situation, however, remains tense.

In November 1994, Tajikistan held its first presidential election. Imomali Rahmon (formerly Rahmonov), a former communist and the Head of Tajikistan's Supreme Soviet since 1992, was elected president. Elections of the Tajik Parliament (Majlisi Oli) have been held regularly and charges of ballot fraud and other irregularities have been leveled against the government (1999, 2000, 2005).

²LOCATION AND HOMELAND

Tajikistan covers 55,250 sq mi (143,100 sq km), an area slightly smaller than Illinois. Geographically, Tajikistan can be divided into two regions, north and south. The Zarafshan Mountains with their lush valleys and flat plains form the northern *kulturbund,* where Tajik and Uzbek cultures have become fused. The Hissar, Gharategin, and Badakhshan mountains form the southern *kulturbund.* Here, Tajiks live as members of major clan organizations. During the 1924 administrative divisions of Central Asia, the centers of the old Tajik culture (i.e., Samarqand and Bukhara) were given to Uzbekistan. Restoration of these cities to Tajikistan remains a goal.

Khorog, the capital of Gorno-Badakhshan and the up-and-coming cultural center of the south, is active in the development of Tajik culture, Badakhshani style. Aided by the Agha Khan, it has the potential to become a trendsetter for the region. The diverse peoples of Badakhshan——Ishkashims,

Roshans, Shughnans, Wakhis, and others—add color and zest to the linguistic and cultural developments of the region.

The major geographic feature in the south is the Panj River, which separates southern Tajikistan from northern Afghanistan. The river collects the waters of the Badakhshan and Gharategin highlands, irrigates a network of cotton plantations in Kulab and Qurqanteppe, and feeds the Aral Sea. At present, increasing use of the water upstream is creating chronic water shortages in Tajikistan.

Since the 1980s, the population of Tajikistan has grown from 3.8 million to more than 7 million. In addition, considerable numbers of Tajiks live in Uzbekistan, Kyrgyzstan, Afghanistan, and China. With a birth rate of 4.1 (per woman) and a death rate of 8.4 (per 1,000 people), the population of Tajikistan is expected to rise dramatically. This will no doubt put a great deal of strain on the Tajik economy, especially when prices are geared to world markets and salaries to Tajik scales.

³LANGUAGE

Tajiki is an Indo-European language, a close kin of Farsi and Pashto. The subtle semantic and structural differences often form the substance of interesting conversations; in fact, an ability to compare languages and explain oddities determines a person's grasp of the culture.

In 1989 Tajiki became the sole official language of the country, displacing Russian and Uzbeki. The act boosted Tajik morale, but failed otherwise. Viewing the future job market in Tajikistan, Russians, Ukrainians, and other Soviet contributors to Tajik prosperity left the country. Since 1995, Russian, which had retained its status as the language of international communication, has regained its previous status. Uzbeki, too, is allowed to flourish in regions predominantly inhabited by Uzbeks.

The current Tajik alphabet (in use since the 1940s) is a modified version of the Russian Cyrillic alphabet. Since the adoption of Tajiki as the national language, instruction in the Arabic-based Persian alphabet has been encouraged in schools. Materials for teaching the "language of the ancestors" are provided by the Islamic Republic of Iran. It is unlikely that the Tajiks will distance themselves from either the Russian language or the Cyrillic alphabet in the foreseeable future. The economic and security needs of the state require that Russian language and culture remain as a positive force in Tajik society. There is, however, an increasing use of the Latin alphabet for using email and Internet systems.

⁴FOLKLORE

Tajikistan, Iran, and Afghanistan enjoy a unique cultural heritage. Over the centuries, however, each has modified or developed new aspects of this culture. The major contribution to this shared heritage is the magnificent *Shahname* (Book of Kings) of Firdowsi—an account of the prehistory of the region, including the cosmic battle between Good and Evil, development of the "divine right of kings," and the dynastic reign of pre-Islamic Iranian monarchs. The exploits of Rustam, for instance, inspired a number of films produced by the Tajik Film Studios during the 1960s and 1970s.

Lesser myths, mostly based on Turkish prototypes, include the story of Nur, a young man who, to attain his beloved, tamed the mighty Vakhsh River by building a dam on it, and the story of a sacred sheep that was lowered from heaven to help the Tajiks survive.

5 RELIGION

In ancient times, present-day Tajikistan was a part of the empire of the Achaemenian Persians. The religion of that empire was Zoroastrianism. After the Arab conquest in the 8th century, Islam was introduced and remained unchallenged until the rise of atheism in the early years of the 20th century. Today atheists, Muslims, Jews, and Christians live together. The majority of the Muslims are Sunni (80%) of the Hanafi sect. The Shia (5%), primarily Isma'ili, live in Gorno-Badakhshan. There are also some Nonreligious groups (10%), and others (5%).

The Tajiks' religious beliefs dictate their choice of clothing. The more orthodox Muslims wear the *hijab*. Less orthodox Muslims wear modest, traditional Tajik attire. Those who work in offices wear typical Western clothing.

Sufism grew in strength during the Soviet era and, by creating a conduit between the Muslims of Afghanistan and Tajikistan, promoted Islamic teachings at the expense of the Society of the Godless. In 1992, the two ideologies clashed but the Communists, due to their access to the media and a competent propaganda machine, won.

6 MAJOR HOLIDAYS

Tajiks observe three different types of holidays: Iranian holidays that date back to the Zoroastrian times; Muslim holidays that, to a large degree, are the same as those elsewhere in the Muslim world; and Soviet holidays. The most important Iranian holiday is the *Navruz* (New Year). It begins on March 21 and continues for several days. This holiday, celebrated by Iranians, Afghans, and most Turkic peoples of the region, dates back to Iranian mythic times. It celebrates the victory of the forces of Good (warmth) over those of Evil (cold), marks the beginning of the annual sowing season, and commemorates the memory of departed ancestors.

The major Islamic holidays are *Maulud al-Nabi* (the birth of the Prophet Muhammad), *Id al-Adha* (celebrating the ancient account of Abraham offering his son for sacrifice), and *Id al-Fitr* (celebration of the end of the Ramadhan fast). These celebrations, observed in secret during the Soviet era, are now held in the open. Their dates are not fixed due to the rotating nature of the lunar calendar.

Holidays with origins in the Soviet era include the New Year's Day (January 1), International Women's Day (March 8), Labor Day (May 1), and Victory Day (May 9). This latter commemorates both the end of World War II and the victory over the 1991-attempted coup. Tajik Independence Day is celebrated on September 9.

7 RITES OF PASSAGE

There are both traditional and Soviet rites of passage. Boys are circumcised at the age of five. After marriage, Tajik women traditionally pluck their eyebrows and wear special ornate hats and distinctive clothing. Many connect the eyebrows together (*qosh*). Married Soviets, both men and women, wear their wedding rings on the third finger of the right hand. A ring on the middle finger indicates separation, or the death of a spouse.

8 INTERPERSONAL RELATIONS

The Tajiks recognize three privileged groups: children, the elderly, and guests. Children, like adults, participate in most gatherings and, within limits, contribute to the life of the party. The elderly, often referred to as *muysapid* (white hair) or *aksakal* (white beard), are highly esteemed, consulted in important affairs, and obeyed. Guests fall into various categories depending on the nature of the relationship.

Family visits and visits by colleagues and acquaintances require the preparation of a *dasturkhon*, a tablecloth spread over the floor or on a low table. Bread, nuts, fruits, various types of *halvo*, preserves, and homemade sweetmeats are placed on the *dasturkhan*. The guest of honor is seated at the head of the *dasturkhon*, farthest from the door. Tea is served by the host who serves himself first. The host offers the *piyola* to the guest with the left hand while placing the right hand on the heart. The guest drinks two or three less-than-half-full *piyolas* (cups). A *piyola* turned upside-down is the sign that a guest does not want it refilled. The offer of a full *piyola* indicates that the guest should drink and leave. Meetings outside the house occur in the *choikhona* (teahouse), where guests gossip, learn the news of the day, and listen to music.

When Tajiks meet, they shake hands and place their left hand on the heart or, if they are family or close friends, hug. Very close friends kiss each other on both cheeks. Holding hands among boys and young men is normal, a casual sign of friendship. The Tajiks have many unique and interesting customs. For instance, certain items such as money, keys, needles, and scissors are not passed from hand to hand. Rather, they

Two Tajik men talk in a square on the outskirts of Dushanbe, Tajikistan. (AP Images/Sergei Grits)

are placed on a table for the other person to pick up. It is believed that standing in the doorway will make a person go into debt, and spilling salt in the house will cause a person to get into a fight. A person who whistles in the house is likely to lose something valuable, and a person who twirls a key chain on his or her finger becomes a vagabond. If someone sneezes during a departure, the party should wait a while before leaving, and if one returns home for a forgotten item, one should look in a mirror before leaving the house again.

⁹LIVING CONDITIONS

Living conditions in Tajikistan, especially in Dushanbe, are challenging. The difficulty stems from shortages of water, gas, and electricity for everyday use. This, a nuisance for the visitor, is a nightmare for the Tajiks who lack purchasing power to buy commodities at exorbitant prices. The difficulty is compounded when the steady rise in prices is not compensated with a raise in salaries.

Housing in Dushanbe, the largest urban area, consists of many high-rise Soviet-era apartment complexes. In these complexes, which are usually surrounded by large courtyards and common spaces, elevators rarely work and water pressure is weak on the higher floors and the buildings in disrepair. Hous-

ing shortages were a factor in the February 1990 uprising in Dushanbe. In recent years a vigorous program of urbanization has demolished many of the traditional houses, especially near the center of Dushanbe. The inhabitants are either relocated to new state-built apartments or are compensated with land on which they can build.

Transportation in urban areas, although far better than in the early years after independence, has suffered recently, primarily because supplies of gasoline from Russia and natural gas from Uzbekistan and Turkmenistan have become unreliable and expensive. In addition, roads connecting the residential suburban areas with the city are not designed to handle a large volume of commuter traffic. This leaves the citizens no option but public transportation. Dushanbe has a system of electric trolleys and gas-powered buses, as well as a large number of taxis and *mashrutkas*, small vans that carry 4–5 passengers and larger vans that carry up to about 10 passengers.

Telephone service is also very deficient. International calls must be made through a centralized office, which requires a two-day notice and advance payment. Express mail reaches Dushanbe in 10 days. Now, however, the cell phone, although pricey for the Tajik budget, has become available and calling cards have helped bypass the difficulties of the state service.

The medical infrastructure has deteriorated so significantly that many trained personnel have left the country. There is a general scarcity of medical equipment and medicines and a potential for significant disease outbreaks (such as hepatitis A, diphtheria and polio) due to inadequate immunization and sanitation.

¹⁰FAMILY LIFE

The Tajiks are family oriented. Families are large but do not necessarily live together. Some may live in the city and some may live in the *qishloq* (village). In fact, the more widely the family is spread, the more opportunities it has for drawing on resources for collective use. This kind of orientation allows outsiders to become a part of a family and expand it into a clan. These clans compete for political power, social reform, educational opportunities, and economic initiatives. There are at least four or five major clans in Tajikistan. The most prominent are the Khujand clan in the north and the Kulab clan in the south. During the Soviet period, the Khujand clan was paramount. At present, the Kulab clan is at the helm. The rivalry between the two has long been a major source of discontent, especially in relation to the expenditure of international aid.

¹¹CLOTHING

Traditional Tajik clothing for men consists of a *joma* (a knee-length jacket) tied at the waist with a colorful *mionband* (kerchief), an indicator of status. The paisley design of the Tajik *toqi* (skullcap) distinguishes the Tajiks by region (e.g., four-cornered, tall *toqis* are worn by men from Gharm).

Women wear a *kurta* (blouse), usually made of soft, colorful, bright silk and *shalvor* (long pants) with decorative cuffs (*sheroz*). Women also wear hats with their national costume. Their hats, especially those from Bukhara and Badakhshan, are either embroidered or decorated with precious stones. Village women wear colorful *rusaris* (scarves). This latter is tied in the back and worn in a decorative manner more like a hat than a veil.

Men and women, especially in urban centers, wear European clothes. Rarely are European and traditional styles mixed, except perhaps that a traditional hat might be worn with a European suit. Traditional clothes for both sexes are particularly important in distinguishing ethnic groups—Kulabis, Hissaris, and Badakhshanis. Each region has a particular dance and a special fashion for its male and female dancers. Farmers and herders wear a special heavy boot over their usual shoes. Older Tajik men wear long Islamic cloaks and turbans. They also wear beards.

Students, especially during the Soviet era, wore uniforms with kerchiefs and other distinctive decorations. In recent times, the wearing of uniform and kerchief is being reestablished.

¹²FOOD

The generic word for food is *avqot*. As is the custom elsewhere in the world, various courses are served. *Pish avqot* (appetizer) includes *sanbuse* (meat, squash, or potatoes with onions and spices wrapped in bread and either deep-fried or baked), *yakhni* (cold meats), and salad.

The *avqot* is either *suyuq* (broth based) or *quyuq* (dry). Examples of the former include *shurbo nakhud* (pea soup), *khom shurbo* (vegetable soup), and *qurma shurbo* (meat and vegeta-

bles sautéed in oil and then simmered in water). The main national dish is *osh*, a mixture of rice, meat, carrots, and onions fried and steamed in a deep pot or *deg,* preferably over an open fire. *Pilmeni* (meat and onions in pasta and cooked in water or meat stock), *mantu* (meat and onions in steamed pasta), and *shishlik* are examples of dry *avqot*. Following is a recipe and cooking directions for *osh*:

Osh

1 small onion, diced
200 gr (almost ½ cup) oil
500 gr (just over 1 lb.) meat, cut into medium pieces
500 gr (just over 1 lb.) carrots, julienned
1,000 gr (4 cups, 3 oz.) rice, soaked for 40 minutes before adding
pinch of cumin seeds

Heat oil, then add meat and cook until brown. Add onion, continue cooking until meat is done. Add enough water to cover the meat and simmer until water is gone. Add carrots and sauté for 2 or 3 minutes. Add one cup of water, cumin seeds, and pepper. Add the rice. Add lukewarm water to cover the rice by about 1 cm (nearly ½ inch). Add salt to taste. Increase heat and simmer until all water is evaporated. Turn the rice over so that cooked rice comes to the top. Make 5 or 6 holes or steam vents in the rice, cover, decrease the heat and cook for 15 to 20 minutes. Serve by dishing out the rice onto a platter and then arranging the carrots and meat on top.

Desserts include *tortes*, various types of *murabbo* (jam) and fruits. *Chakka* (drained yogurt) and lamb kabob are favorite treats served on special occasions. Everyday food is less elaborate. Students running to school, for example, might have *shirchoi* (sweetened warm milk and tea poured over bread and butter), *shirberenj* (rice custard), or bread and eggs.

Tea and vodka are common drinks for adults. Black tea is served during winter, green tea during summer. Tea is served ritually in *piyolas* (small cups). Vodka is drunk amid music, dance, and long, cheerful speeches delivered by members of the family and guests. Other drinks include *koumis* (fermented mare's milk) and *kefir* (a thick yogurt drink).

Fruits and vegetables grown in the country form a major subject of conversation. It is important, for instance, to know which part of the country produces the best melon, apple or grapes.

¹³EDUCATION

Until the fall of Bukhara (1920), Bukharan schools taught the *Quran* and the *Shariah.* Attempts by the intellectuals and *jadids* to introduce new-method schools met with severe penalties.

During the Soviet era, Tajik educational establishments became subservient to the educational system of the Soviet Union. Rather than learning about the greats of Tajik culture, Russian literary figures such as Maxim Gorkii and Vladimir Mayakovskii were taught. Sadriddin Aini (d. 1954), the father of Tajik literature, gained his fame by extolling the socialist way at the expense of traditional values. Soviet education transplanted both the Tajiki language and the Tajik culture. In the long run, however, due to the instability of the Soviet system itself, a vacuum was created. By the 1970s, the anti-Russian efforts of the Muslim educators bore fruit and, eventually, ousted the communist regime.

The 1992–97 civil war, devastated southern Tajikistan. In the process, schools were destroyed, many teachers and students were killed, and many non-Tajik educators left the country.

Soviet education had both positive and negative effects on the Tajiks. On the positive side, it essentially eliminated illiteracy by 1960 and acquainted the Tajiks with Russian literature. On the negative side, it alienated most Tajiks from their own cultural heritage. At present, a gradual reversal of that trend is taking shape.

Today, the English language and American culture are finding their way into Tajikistan. English is stressed in schools because many people, including those who intend to emigrate, want to learn English for its role in international business.

Tajik parents expect their children to make steady progress toward a respectable marriage and a good, responsible job. They feel that they owe their children a good education, a respectable wedding *tuy,* and partial expenses for rearing their grandchildren. (They pay for the *gahvorabandon,* a cradling ceremony for a newborn child, for instance.) In return, they expect their children to take care of them in their old age and to see to their needs at the end of their lives.

A painful aspect of Tajik education is a lack of funds for teachers' salaries. This leads, in many cases, to bribery both in finding ones way into schools and in exiting school with an unearned degree.

¹⁴CULTURAL HERITAGE

Tajik music varies by region. In the north, especially in Samarqand and Bukhara, the *shashmaqom* is recognized as the chief musical form normally played on a tanbur. There, the cycle of songs known as *naqsh* plays a prominent role in the festival of the tulips (*sairi guli lola*). In the south, *falak* and *qurughli* predominate. The national *hofiz* (singer) is respected by all.

Various regions have reacted to the new wave from the West differently. The Badakhshanis, for instance, have adopted Western musical innovations; but the Gharmis have not.

Tajik literature covers a wide range of genres over many centuries. Most of the literature, however, is poetry. Rudaki and Firdowsi are prominent classical authors, and Aini and Tursanzadah are well-known Soviet Tajik authors. In the 1990s, a division took place whereby poets such as Layeq Shir'ali and Mu'min Qana'at were distinguished for their affiliation with the communist government, whereas Bozor Sobir and Gulrukhsor Safieva were identified with the Opposition. Bozor Sobir was imprisoned for more than a year (1992–93) for his anti-Uzbek views. Other Tajik writers include the scenarists Saif Rahim and the science fiction author Adash Istad.

A recurring theme in Tajik literature is the exploitative measures of a *bai* (rich man) who "helps" an orphaned boy meet the expenses for his father's funeral. The young man ends up working for the *bai* for the rest of his life to pay the debt.

¹⁵WORK

The makeup and circumstances of the work force in Tajikistan have changed drastically in recent years. Many youth who would traditionally have worked on cotton plantations have migrated to the cities and become involved in trade; they import goods from Pakistan, Japan, and China and sell them in makeshift shops or in stalls alongside the street.

A large number of Tajiks work in the lower echelon of industry—mining, machine-tool factories, canneries, hydroelectric stations—in non-managerial jobs. In general, about 50% of the population is under 20, and over one half of those are not in the labor force. As a result, there are a number of groups in the population that are neither employed nor in school.

In general, work can be divided along agricultural and industrial lines. Work in agriculture revolves around work in kolkhozes and sovkhozes. These collective and state farms produce most of the cotton, fruit, and vegetables consumed in the republic, and some is also exported. Work in the fields entails digging canals, planting, irrigating, and harvesting.

Women's roles vary widely. Sovietized Tajik women participate in all aspects of society and a few are even members of parliament. Muslim wives, on the other hand, stay at home and take care of the children.

Most marriages are arranged. After negotiations, the father of the groom pays most of the expenses for the *tuy* (celebration). Women can initiate divorce procedures and receive half of the family's assets.

Tajik women are fully acquainted with the silk culture, a labor-intensive operation that begins with feeding silkworms mulberry leaves and ends with extracting the silk. The care of orchards and vineyards as well as sheep breeding in the highlands falls on men. Both men and women work in the entertainment business, but mostly women work in textile factories as machinists and administrators.

Alongside the traditional jobs, the growing Tajik bureaucracy employs many youths, as do the burgeoning foreign businesses established in Tajikistan by Turkish and Iranian concerns.

¹⁶SPORTS

The national sport of the Tajiks, *gushtingiri* (wrestling), has a colorful tradition. When the towns were divided into *mahallas* (districts), each district had its own *alufta* (tough) who was also the best wrestler. The position of the *alufta,* usually an upright and respected individual, was often challenged by those of lower rank.

Buzkashi (which means, literally, "dragging the goat") is a sport involving strenuous bodily exertion. In this game, the carcass of a goat is dragged by horsemen who grab it from each other. The aim of the riders is to deposit the carcass in a designated circle in front of the guest of honor. *Buzkashi* is usually performed as part of the *Navruz* celebrations.

In recent years, many European sports have also found their way into Tajikistan. Soccer is so popular that, in the eyes of many, it rivals *buzkashi.*

¹⁷ENTERTAINMENT AND RECREATION

As early as the 9th century, Avicenna compared man's existence on earth with that of a puppet in a puppet show. This tradition, retained over the centuries by the *maskharaboz* (clown), is now expanded by professional troupes.

During the Soviet period, special attention was paid to the arts, both as a means of reducing the Tajiks' demand for jobs in the heavy industry and as compensation for the daily drudgery of the workers on the cotton plantations. Barring the purpose, the result was culturally stimulating. The Tajik cinema, for instance, produced a number of worthy films based on Firdowsi's *Shahname*. They are called *Rustam and Suhrab*, *The Story of Siyavosh*, and *Kaveh the Blacksmith*. Similar advances were made in the production of stunning spectacles on the lives of Rudaki, Umar-i Khayyam, and others.

With the disintegration of the Soviet Union, the arts lost their primary means of support. Producers, directors, actors, and writers either joined the ranks of the jobless or became involved in business. Many left Tajikistan. This fall of the cultural center has not been altogether bad, however. It has given regional groups the opportunity to showcase their talents and abilities. Troupes from Badakhshan, Kulab, and Khujand appear regularly on the national scene.

Not long ago, programs such as *Maria* (a Mexican rags-to-riches soap opera) or the American soap *Santa Barbara* were the only shows that really kept the Tajiks entertained. Local broadcasting was very limited in scope, dealing mostly with regional matters, especially agriculture. Videos allowed Tajik youth a wider choice of programs. The introduction of satellite programming has changed all that.

[18] FOLK ART, CRAFTS, AND HOBBIES

Traditional Tajik crafts include the embroidered Bukhara wall hangings and bedcovers popularized in the 19th century. The Tajik style of the tapestries typically has floral designs on silk or cotton and is made on a tambour frame. Woodcarving and ceramics are also honored Tajik crafts.

[19] SOCIAL PROBLEMS

The social problems of Tajikistan are too numerous to list. Perhaps the most important social problem has to do with authority and control. Since the 10th century, when the Samanid dynasty lost its hegemony over Central Asia, the Tajiks have been ruled by the other peoples of the region, especially the Turks. Since 1868, when the Turks became subservient to the Russians, the Tajiks' situation has become even more precarious. In the 1870s, taxes imposed by Russia drove the Tajiks to revolt a number of times. One such revolt, the Vaase uprising, which was mercilessly put down, is still remembered.

The 1992 Tajik bid for independence was also met with severe reprisals. This time, however, the democratic nature of the age did not allow an open assault on the opposition. The indirect means employed turned into a civil war, crippled the administration in Dushanbe, ruined the economy, and totally destroyed the infrastructure. Russia, on the other hand, achieved its goal. The same set of circumstances that spell out social discontent in Tajikistan gains Russia a steady revenue for defending the Tajik border, places Tajikistan's foreign affairs in Russian hands, and allows Russia to reassert itself forcefully in Tajikistan's internal affairs.

Tajikistan's problems stem from dependence on Russia for military, economic, and foreign policy matters and on the international community for the rest of its needs. This is compounded by a 60% below-poverty-line economy, a high rate of population growth, and a lack of skilled workers. Ethnic tension and regionalism often bring the country to the verge of disintegration.

To remedy this situation, clan wars between the North and South must stop and the mafias of Dushanbe, Khujand, and Kulab must be deactivated. Barring this, Tajikistan cannot achieve its goals of economic and military independence, raising per capita income, decreasing unemployment, stopping population growth, improving transportation to move food and fuel, and introducing meaningful medical and educational reforms.

[20] GENDER ISSUES

Under the Soviet system, women were treated very differently than they are today. They enjoyed equal civil rights, participated in the labor force, and were very active in politics. Most importantly, they had a considerable degree of independence. In Tajikistan, the fall of the Soviet Union was followed by five years of civil war that affected Tajik women the most. In addition to losing sons and husbands to the war and becoming refugees in neighboring lands, the textile factories were closed. That meant loss of livelihood as women were the primary labor force in that industry. Destruction of agriculture and the educational and health services further affected women as they worked in the fields, were teachers, doctors, and nurses. Male chauvinism that prevented women from the decision-making positions also subjected them to harassment and discrimination.

With 60% of the population living below the poverty line, about a million Tajik men seek work in Russia. Women whose men go to Russia stand to lose their husband as he might marry a Russian and stay, as well as their source of income and security, not to mention being burdened with childcare and provision for children.

Men who return from Russia, along with money, bring HIV. This prepares the ground for women to deal with a health system that is virtually nonexistent, fees that are exorbitant, and drugs. Soon, they are engaged in drug trafficking and prostitution to pay their bills.

Instances of domestic violence in Tajikistan are many. Nevertheless, women accept to get married even as a second wife. Those who refuse to be humiliated end up taking their own lives by either self-immolation or drug overdose.

[21] BIBLIOGRAPHY

Abdullaev, Kamaludin and Shahram Akbarzadeh. *Historical Dictionary of Tajikistan*. Lanham, MD: Scarecrow Press, 2002.

Ahmed, Rashid. *The Resurgence of Central Asia: Islam or Nationalism*. Oxford: Oxford University Press, 1994.

Bashiri, Iraj. *Firdowsi's Shahname: 1000 Years After*. Dushanbe, 1994.

_____. *Prominent Tajik Figures of the Twentieth Century*, Academy of Sciences of Tajikistan, 2004.

Bennigsen, Alexandre, and S. Enders Wimbush. *The Muslims of the Soviet Empire*. Bloomington, IN: Indiana University Press, 1986.

Soviet Tajik Encyclopedia (Vols. 1-8) Dushanbe, 1978-88.

Wixman, Ronald. *The Peoples of the USSR: An Ethnographic Handbook*. Armonk NY: M.E. Sharpe, Inc., 1984.

World and its Peoples: Central Asia. Tarrytown, NY: Marshall Cavendish, 2007, pp. 650-671.

—by I. Bashiri

TAMILS

PRONUNCIATION: TAHM-uhls
LOCATION: India (Tamil Nadu region); Sri Lanka
POPULATION: 71 million in India; 4 million in Sri Lanka
LANGUAGES: Tamil
RELIGIONS: Hindu majority; Muslim; Christian

¹INTRODUCTION

The Tamil are a people of southern India, speaking the Tamil language and unified by a common culture. Their name is derived from "Damila," the name of an ancient, warlike non-Aryan people mentioned in early Buddhist and Jain records. The Tamil language is Dravidian in origin, with its roots in western India, Pakistan, and areas farther to the west. The peoples of the Indus Civilization spoke a Dravidian language around 2,500 BC. Dravidian speech and associated cultural traits spread into southern India, especially in the centuries after 1,000 BC. By the early centuries BC, a complex and distinctive culture had developed in what is now *Tamil Nadu*, the "land of the Tamil."

In the following centuries, dynasties, such as the Pandyas, Cheras, and Pallavas, rose to power in Tamil Nadu. An impressive Tamil civilization emerged under the Cholas, who ruled from the 10th to the 13th centuries. Chola sea power allowed them to bring Sri Lanka and even parts of Southeast Asia under their control. The fourteenth century saw virtually the entire region incorporated into the empire of the Telugu-speaking Vijayanagara kings. The region experienced relative peace and prosperity for several centuries under Vijayanagara rule. In the seventeenth century, both the British and the French established themselves in the Tamil region. The British built a trading post at Fort St. George (later Madras, and now called Chennai) in 1639, and the French at Pondicherry in 1674. The British later gained control of all of Tamil Nadu, which became part of the Madras Presidency until India's independence in 1947. In the 1950s, there was a realignment of political boundaries in South India. The French possessions were ceded to India, to be administered as a Union Territory by the national government in New Delhi. Madras was broken up to form the language-based states of Andhra Pradesh (for speakers of Telugu), Kerala (Malayalam), Mysore (Kannada), and Madras (Tamil). The name of Madras State was changed to Tamil Nadu in 1969.

²LOCATION AND HOMELAND

The 2001 census records 62,405,679 persons in Tamil Nadu, of which some 60.8 million belonged to the Tamil people. In addition, there are about one million Tamils in Pondicherry and another 5 million elsewhere in India. Allowing for population growth, there are currently an estimated 71 million Tamils in India. This figure does not include the nearly 4 million Tamils in Sri Lanka and the Tamils found in Asia, Fiji, Africa and the West Indies. The world-population for Tamils is estimated to be around 77 million.

The ancient literature describes the land of the Tamils as stretching from Tirupati, a sacred hill northwest of Madras, to India's southern tip at Cape Comorin. This basically defines the modern Tamil region. In the east, a broad coastal plain runs along the shores of the Bay of Bengal. The basin of the Kaveri (Cauvery) River lies in the center of the state, with the river flowing eastward to enter the ocean in a delta in Thanjavur (Tanjore) District. The Western Ghats (a mountain range) form the western boundary of Tamil Nadu. The Ghats exceed 2,600 m (about 8,500 ft) in elevation in the Nilgiris and the Palni Hills. The climate of the region is tropical, with moderately hot summers and mean winter temperatures that rarely drop below 24°C (about 75°F). Unlike most of India, the Tamil region has its maximum rainfall between October and December, associated with the northeast monsoon. Totals range between 80 and 120 cm (31–47 in) over most of the area. However, around Coimbatore and the southeast coastal section, rainfall dips to 60 cm (about 24 in) or below. Forests, found mainly in the western hills, cover only 15% of the state's area.

³LANGUAGE

Tamil is the language of the Tamil people. It belongs to the Dravidian language family and is considered by Tamils to be the "purest" of the Dravidian tongues. Several regional dialects (e.g., Pandya, Chola, Kangu) are spoken in the area, and the Tamil spoken in northern Sri Lanka may also be considered a dialect of this language. Different forms of Tamil are used by Brahmans and non-Brahmans. There is also a sharp distinction between spoken and literary Tamil. Tamil has two written forms, the modern Vattelluttu ("round script") in everyday use and Grantha, a classical script used in Tamil Nadu for writing in Sanskrit.

Tamil, one of India's 23 official languages, is the official language of Tamil Nadu. It has also recently been designated one of India's two classical languages, the other being Sanskrit.

⁴FOLKLORE

A figure highly venerated in South India is the sage (*rishi*) Agastya. According to legend, all the sages once assembled in the Himalayas. Such was the weight of their wisdom that the earth started to sink. The sages asked Agastya, who was heavier than the rest, to go south so that the earth could rise to its original position. Agastya took with him on his journey some water from the sacred Ganges. One day, after he had arrived in the South, it is said, the sage stopped to bathe. A crow knocked over his water pot, and the water began to flow, forming the Kaveri River. This link with the Ganges helps explain Tamil views toward the Kaveri. The river is regarded as sacred, and it is seen as the duty of every pious Tamil Hindu to bathe in the Kaveri at least once in his or her lifetime.

⁵RELIGION

Tamils are mostly Hindus, although there are some Tamil Muslims and Christians. Hindus follow the rites and practices of the Hindu religion. Devout persons of all castes perform daily prayers (*puja*) at home or in the temple. Shiva is the most important deity, although Vishnu and other Brahmanic gods and their consorts are worshipped. Vinayaka, a form of the god Ganesha, is particularly popular. Brahmans officiate at major temples, although lesser deities may have priests drawn from other castes. One characteristic feature of Tamil religion is the importance given to the Mother Goddess. This tradition predates Hinduism, and most likely has its origins in the Dravidian culture of the Indus Valley Civilization. The Mother Goddess is worshipped as Durga, but also assumes the form of local *ammans,* or goddesses, like Mariamman, who protects against disease. Fire walking is a ritual performed at Mariamman temples. In fact, although Brahmanic Hinduism flourishes in Tamil Nadu, there is also vibrant popular religion based on the worship of village deities. In addition, there is a widespread belief in spirits and ghosts, in the evil eye, and in sorcery and witchcraft. Rituals needed to deal with this spirit world include blood sacrifice, the chanting of sacred *mantras,* and exorcism by sorcerers. People consult mediums, temple soothsayers, and *nadi* leaf readers (fortune tellers who read ancient palm-leaf manuscripts) to predict the future.

⁶MAJOR HOLIDAYS

Although Tamils celebrate the major Hindu festivals, the most important regional festival is Pongal. This three-day celebration falls in mid-January and marks the end of the rice harvest. It also coincides with the end of the northeast monsoon in South India. Newly harvested rice is ceremonially boiled in milk and offered to Surya, the sun god. On the third day of the festival, cattle are decorated and worshipped, and bullfights and bull races take place. The Tamil New Year, in mid-April, is celebrated widely. Temple festivals such as those held at Madurai and in the Srirangam Temple near Tiruchchirappalli (Trichinopoly) are an important aspect of Tamil religious life. The chariot of the Thiruvarur Temple, in which the image of the god is taken in procession around the streets, is reputed to be the largest in the country. It is said that 10,000 people were needed to pull it in days gone by. Numerous shrines in Tamil Nadu are centers of pilgrimage for the pious. Kanchipuram, southwest of Madras, is one of India's seven sacred cities. The island of Rameswaram, between India and Sri Lanka, is the southern *dham,* or shrine, that defines the borders of Hinduism. It is considered almost as sacred as Varanasi.

⁷RITES OF PASSAGE

Tamils have various superstitions that influence the behavior of a pregnant woman. For example, she is not supposed to cross a river or climb a hill during pregnancy. During the fifth or seventh month of her pregnancy, she is given bangles or bracelets, by her husband's family. After the baby is born, the mother and child are kept in seclusion for about two weeks and undergo rituals to remove the pollution believed to accompany childbirth. Then usual naming and hair-shaving ceremonies are performed. A child might be named after the grandparents, some dead relative, or the family deities. Children are brought up in a loving atmosphere, in which they are pampered by their family and adult relatives. As they grow older, girls are expected to help with the housework, and boys are expected to help with the work of farming.

Customs marking the coming of age of children vary. There are no initiation rites for males except for the sacred thread ritual of the higher castes. The Chettiars, however, have ceremonies for both boys and girls reaching adulthood. When a girl reaches puberty, the Tamils mark the occasion with a feast for the family and friends.

Tamil tradition requires people to avoid saying that a person is dead. Instead, the person is said to have reached the world of Lord Shiva, or attained a position in heaven, or reached the world of the dead. A funeral is an occasion when family and caste members come together to mourn the departed. Failure to make a formal visit to console the bereaved family is almost

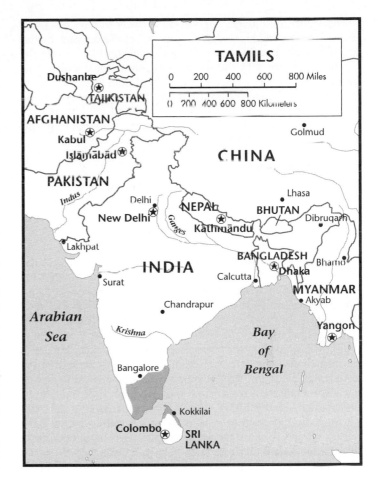

considered a crime. Tamil both cremate and bury the dead, with burial being more common among lower castes. The body is prepared for the funeral by being washed, perfumed, and dressed in new clothes. Funeral music is played as the procession makes its way to the cremation ground or graveyard, except among the Brahmans. A period of mourning is followed by purification rites and a feast for family and caste members. Families observe the anniversary of a death by gathering together of kin, giving gifts to the Brahman priests, and feeding the poor.

⁸INTERPERSONAL RELATIONS

Tamils use the typical Hindu *namaskar,* the joining of the palms of the hands in front of the body, as a sign of greeting and farewell. Expressions such as "please," "thank you," and "excuse me" are rarely used. This is not a sign of rudeness or impoliteness; it is just the custom. A typical welcome on the arrival of a visitor is a straightforward "come in." Every guest is entertained with coffee and snacks. When a visitor leaves, he or she generally says "I'll go and come back," to which the host will respond, "Go and return."

⁹LIVING CONDITIONS

Tamil villages are compact, either square or linear in shape, and often have a tributary hamlet where the untouchable castes live. Each village is built near, or around, a temple, with the priests (usually Brahmans) living close to it in areas known as *agraharam.* Other castes have their own distinct neighborhoods in the village. The village is likely to have a school, shops, shrines to local deities, and a cremation and burial ground. Wells provide water and a nearby "tank" or reservoir, catches and stores rainwater for irrigation. Most villages in Tamil Nadu now have electricity. Individual houses vary from the one-room, thatched mud huts of the lower castes to large two-story brick and tile structures surrounded by their own compounds. Furnishings reflect the economic standing and tastes of a house's owner.

[10] FAMILY LIFE

Tamil family relations are strongly influenced by the Dravidian emphasis on matrilineal ties, that is, links with the wife's relatives. Marriage between cousins is common, and the preferred match is with a man's mother's brother's daughter. In some castes, the marriage of a man to his sister's daughter is customary. Tamils marry within their caste. Only a few Brahmanized castes have clearly defined exogamous clans (*gotras*), that is, those that marry outside their own clan. Marriages are arranged, and the bride's family usually pays for the wedding and a dowry. Details of marriage rituals vary according to caste. Some groups use Brahman priests for the ceremony, while among others marriage is perform by respected community elders. The actual ceremony is usually carried out on a marriage platform with a canopy of thatched coconut leaves. Rituals include walking around the sacred fire, the blowing of conch-shells, and the throwing of rice and colored water. The newlywed couple typically sets up its household in the husband's village. A Tamil family usually consists of parents, children, and elderly or unmarried relatives. Many lower castes permit divorce and the remarriage of widows, but these practices are generally not found among Brahmans and other high-caste communities.

[11] CLOTHING

Traditional dress for Tamils consists of the *dhoti* or loincloth, for men and the *sari* and blouse for women. Women wear their hair long, keeping it oiled and plaited, often with jasmine blossoms braided into it. They also wear various amounts of gold jewelry. College educated or career women may adopt Western styles, and many young men now wear shirts and pants.

Dress is an important indicator of caste in a traditional society, and many groups have their own distinctive manner of wearing clothes. For example, ritual provides for the male Tamil Brahman style of wearing the dhoti with the ends tucked in at five places (*panchakachcham*). Non-Brahmans do not use this style. Similarly, there are differences between Brahman and non-Brahman women in the length of clothes and the way they are worn. Orthodox married Tamil Brahman women wear a sari eighteen cubits long (a cubit is an ancient measure equal to about half a meter, or roughly eighteen in), with the *kachcham* (the ends tucked in various ways). Non-Brahman women wear a shorter sari, without the tuck, but also reaching to the ground as with the Brahmans. Tribal women, the Adi-Dravida, wear a considerably smaller garment that reaches just below the knees, and they often leave the upper body bare.

[12] FOOD

Factors influencing food habits among the Tamil include the local ecology, economic standing, caste, and religion. In drier areas where rice cannot be grown, millet is the main grain.

In other places, rice or a mixture of rice and millet provides the basic starch in the diet. The region around Madras, for instance, is a rice consuming area.

Most people eat three meals a day. Breakfast consists of coffee and items such as *idlis* (steamed rice cakes), *dosas* (pancakes made of rice and lentils), and *vadas* (fried doughnuts made from lentils). Lunch is boiled rice, curried fish or mutton, vegetables, *sambar* (a sauce made with lentils, vegetables, and tamarind) and *rasam* (a thin, peppery soup). The last dish served is usually curds, which is mixed with the rice. The evening meal is a repetition of lunch, but with fewer dishes. People drink both coffee and tea, but coffee is the more popular. Milk is also an important part of the diet. People who are not vegetarians eat poultry, eggs, fish (including prawns), and mutton. Some low castes eat pork, but this is taboo for Muslims. Vegetarian groups among the Tamil include Brahmans, Jains, and devotees of Shiva (the Shaiva Pillai). Some Chettiars (a mercantile caste) and Vellalas (agricultural workers) also avoid meat.

[13] EDUCATION

Tamils have had their own traditional centers of learning that date back to Buddhist times. Modern education, with an emphasis on English, was introduced by the British colonial government and Christian missionaries during the nineteenth century. Education is seen as a step to a better job. The state educational system offers up to 12 years of schooling, beginning with primary school, followed by three years of undergraduate study, and graduate school. In addition to numerous colleges, there are 19 universities, including the University of Madras and numerous other schools, including the Indian Institute of Technology, Madras, in Tamil Nadu state. The literacy rate in the state in 2001 was 73.47% (82.33% for males, 64.55% for females). While this does not approach the literacy rate in Kerala, it is above the national average for India and compares favorably with the literacy rates of other heavily populated states in the country.

[14] CULTURAL HERITAGE

The Tamil have an important literary tradition that dates back to the centuries preceding the Christian era. Three great literary academies, called *sangam,* flourished in the early period, probably between the first and fifth centuries. Writings include epics and secular poetry, but the glory of Tamil literature lies in the religious works of medieval saints and poets. These involve two distinct traditions, one devoted to the worship of Shiva and the other consisting of the Vaishnavite hymns written by poets known as the Alvars. The 10th to 13th centuries mark the Golden Age of Tamil literature.

The Tamil can be proud of major achievements in other areas of the arts. *Bharata-natyam,* one of the four great Hindu classical dance styles, evolved in the Tamil region. Carnatic, or South Indian, music, is also widely practiced. In the field of architecture, Tamils developed a distinctive style of South Indian temple building. The towering *gopurams* (gateways) of Tamil temples are unique to southern India. Covered with elaborately carved, often life-size statues of gods and figures from Hindu mythology, *gopurams* dominate the landscape of Tamil cities. The temples at Madurai, Kanchipuram, and Thanjavur (Tanjore) are classic examples of this architectural style.

Tamil folk culture includes a body of oral literature, ballads, and songs performed or recited by bards and minstrels. Songs

Sri Lankan Tamil refugees line up to enter government-held areas of eastern Sri Lanka. Tamils fled rebel-held areas of the eastern region to escape fighting between the troops and Tamil Tigers. (STRDEL/AFP/Getty Images)

and dances are accompanied by music played on instruments such as the *tharai*, an S-shaped horn, and the *thambattam*, a type of drum. Folk dances include *Kolattam*, performed by young girls with sticks in both hands who rhythmically strike the sticks of the neighbors as they dance. *Kavadi* is a dance form as well as a religious act, in which pilgrims carry a symbolic structure (the *kavadi*) on their shoulders as they dance their way to the shrine of Subrahmanya, Shiva's son. In one dance, the dummy-horse show, the actors don the costume of an elaborately decorated horse and look as if they are actually riding on horseback. Various forms of folk drama and street theater are also performed for the amusement of the people.

¹⁵ WORK

Although cities such as Madras and Coimbatore are manufacturing centers, Tamils work predominantly in agriculture. Agriculture is more commercial in Tamil Nadu than in other parts of the country. Canal irrigation is used in some areas, although most of the region relies on "tanks" or reservoirs,

for its water. Rice and millet are the main food crop, and oilseeds and cotton are the important cash crops. The Vellala are an important group of farming castes. In addition to cultivators, Tamils have a full range of trading, service, and artisan castes that pursue their traditional caste occupations. Fishing is important in coastal areas. As India develops, however, more Tamils are moving into modern sectors of the economy.

¹⁶ SPORTS

Tamil children play games typical of children throughout South Asia. They amuse themselves with games of tag, leapfrog, and hide-and-seek. One particular game requires a player to stand on one leg and try to catch the members of the opposing team within a square playing area marked out on the ground. Another game is something like "Simon Says". An adult, says *Kombari, Kombari* ("They have horns"), and the children repeat this statement. The leader then goes on to list animals with horns. Occasionally a statement such as "elephant has horns" is made, and the children who repeat the incorrect statement are "out". Adult games include stick fighting (*Silambam*), wrestling, and a board game (*Thayam*) similar to chess. The Tamil also engage in modern Western sports.

¹⁷ ENTERTAINMENT AND RECREATION

The movies, and, more recently, television are the leading forms of entertainment for Tamil. Even in rural areas, people tend to prefer them to the more traditional folk dances or street-corner theaters. In the late 1980s, there were 2,364 movie theaters in Tamil Nadu. The Tamil movie industry is centered in Madras, although film studios are located in other cities in Tamil Nadu.

¹⁸ FOLK ARTS, CRAFTS, AND HOBBIES

Every young Tamil girl tries to be fully accomplished in a form of folk art known as *kolam*. This involves using the thumb and the fore-finger to draw intricate geometric designs and floral motifs with a white powder. *Kolam* is drawn on the ground in front of houses, particularly on festive occasions. Among the best known handicrafts of the Tamil region are handmade silk saris from Kanchipuram, pottery figures of various gods, bronze work, and silver inlay on brass and copper. Painted wooden toys and cloth dolls are popular. Tamil artisans are skilled in the art of carving materials such as shell and horn. Woodworkers have made the massive, elaborately carved doors of temples, and they produce furniture such as tables with legs in the form of elephant heads. Stone carving is also highly developed. Soapstone figures of gods and religious items are available in nearly all of the temple towns of the region.

¹⁹ SOCIAL PROBLEMS

Tamils face the usual array of social, economic, and political problems that one finds in India today.

Many of India's social problems are related to population pressure. In Tamil Nadu, however, population growth appears to be slowing. The increase in population between 1981 and 1991 was 14.94%, compared to India's overall rate of 23.5%. The growth rate in Tamil Nadu in 2008 was 1.15% per annum. Obviously, there are differences within the various communities in the region, and some groups still face problems such as poverty, high unemployment, and illiteracy. Agriculture in the state is more commercial than in many other parts of the country, but farmers still rely to a large extent on good monsoons for their harvests. And periodically cyclones from the Bay of Bengal hit the region, bringing widespread destruction.

Although India was by no means the country worst hit by the December 2004 tsunami, in Tamil Nadu, according to estimates from officials in Chennai, 8,031 people are known to have lost their lives and 1,000 disappeared. Almost a million more—around 300,000 families—were affected through bereavement, injury or loss of job or home, and more than 100,000 families ended up in camps. Local industries such as fishing were so disrupted that sought other occupations. Both national and international agencies provided relief in the form of cash aid, and relief supplies, as well as activities such as constructing homes to replace those lost in the disaster.

Corruption in high government circles seems to be endemic in India, and has apparently been a problem in Tamil Nadu. In late 1996, the former Chief Minister (Jayalitha Jayaram, a former film actress turned politician) of the state and several of her cabinet ministers were arrested (and later convicted) on various charges relating to the misuse of public funds. An ongoing problem is Tamil involvement in the ethnic conflict between Tamil and the Sinhalese in nearby Sri Lanka. In addition, a small group of Tamil separatists is campaigning for Tamil independence from India. In 2008, the government, led by Dr. Kalaignar M. Karunanidhi, was formed by the Dravida Munnetra Kazhagam (DMK) (literally "Dravidian Progress Federation"), a regional political party in the state of Tamil Nadu

Tamil Nadu's record with respect to caste discrimination is fairly poor. The state, during the peak of the Dravidian movement, experienced strong anti-Brahmin sentiments. The government's 69% reservation policy in educational institutions for the backward castes is, in general, resented by many for being a policy of reverse discrimination. Tamil Nadu's record of tolerance towards linguistic minorities has, however, been exemplary, despite provocative incidents occurring in other states and despite the state having been the epicenter of anti-Hindi agitations.

In January 2008 the Tamil Nadu government announced its intent to nationalize cement companies in the state, claiming a report following an internal investigation of the Monopolies and Restrictive Trade Practices Commission revealed cartelization leading to "exorbitant" increases in cement prices. It may be noted that the price of cement in Tamil Nadu (perhaps in other states in India, too) is approximately 50% higher than the price of imported cement when it is offloaded at ports. Apparently such a high price differential between the international prices and the domestic prices is prima facie indication that all is not well within the cement industry. Crucially, it highlights the soft underbelly of the Indian economy. Tamil Nadu's economy grew at rate of 12.1% in 2007 and it possessed the fifth largest economy (2005–2006) among states in India. It is also the most industrialized state in the country. The price of cement in Tamil Nadu has declined, but whether a government takeover of the industry is the answer remains to be seen. Neither Tamil Nadu nor its cement industry is an exception in the Indian context. Rather they are the rule and are responsible for many of the ills plaguing the Tamil Nadu economy.

While India ranked 128 in the human development index calculated worldwide with 0.619, Tamil Nadu has performed well with an index of 0.736 in 2006, only 0.041 less than 81st ranked China. HDI is calculated using measures including population, sex ratio, density of population, per capita income, people below the poverty line, infant mortality rate, literacy rate, and women's empowerment. The life expectancy at birth for males is 65.2 years and for females it is 67.6 years. However, Tamil Nadu has a number of challenges. Significantly, poverty is high, especially in the rural areas, though poverty in the state had dropped from 51.7% in 1983 to 21.1% in 2001. For the period 2004–2005, the trend in incidence of poverty in the state was 22.5% as against the national figure of 27.5%. The World Bank is currently assisting the state in reducing poverty. High drop-out rates and low completion of secondary schools continue to hinder the quality of training in the population. Other problems include class, gender, inter-district, and urban-rural disparities.

Despite these problems, Tamils have a strong sense of identity and take great pride in their cultural and historical traditions. Nearly two thousand years ago, Tamils evolved a distinctive regional culture in the southeastern part of the Indian peninsula. Today, Tamils and Tamil culture remain a significant element in the complex of peoples and cultures that make up Indian society.

[20] GENDER ISSUES

Tamils are mainly Hindus, and Tamil women suffer from all the problems of traditional Hindu society. Arranged marriages, child marriages (though technically illegal in India), payment of dowry by the bride's family, and bride burnings and dowry deaths—are all issues faced by women in Tamil society. The traditional preference for male offspring is found and female infanticide (illegal, though rarely prosecuted) and sex selective abortion is not uncommon (in Salem District, the sex ratio in 2006 was 912 females to 1000 males). High castes do not permit divorce or widow remarriage, although this is allowed among some low caste groups.

Cases of domestic violence (though rarely reported) are on the increase, and Tamil women are subject to sexual and physical abuse. Security forces in Sri Lanka, both the Sinhalese and the IPKF, have been accused of rape and murder committed against Tamil women, who are often involved in combat roles in the civil war.

There are, however, women's groups such as the Tamil Nadu Women's Forum which have been formed to fight for women's rights and gender justice and which stand against gender based discrimination, including caste based discrimination, and of course discrimination against Dalit women (low caste or Untouchables). The Tamil Nadu Women's Development Project provides low-cost loans and other financial assistance to women to help them develop a degree of economic independence.

[21] BIBLIOGRAPHY

Béteille, André. *Caste, Class and Power: Changing Patterns of Stratification in a Tanjore Village.* Delhi: Oxford University Press, 1996.

Gunawardane, Prajapala Sri. *Tamil Terrorism and Sinhala Solutions.* Colombo: S. Godage and Brothers, 2001.

Lakshmanan Chettiar, S. M. L. *Folklore of Tamil Nadu.* New Delhi: National Book Trust, 1973.

Mohan, J. *History of Dalit Struggle for Freedom: Dravidian Parties and Dalit Uprise in Tamil Nadu.* Pondicherry: Dhamma Institute of Social Sciences, 2001.

Peyer, Nathalie. *Death and Afterlife in a Tamil Village: Discourses of Low Caste Women.* Munster: Lit, 2004.

Subramanian, P. *Social History of the Tamils 1707-1947.* New Delhi: DK Printworld, 1996.

Subramanian, S. V., and Veerasami, V., eds. *Cultural Heritage of the Tamils.* Madras: International Institute of Tamil Studies, Publication No. 2, 1981.

—by D. O. Lodrick

TAO

PRONUNCIATION: dow-OOII
LOCATION: Island of Lanyu in western Pacific
POPULATION: 3,400 (2007)
LANGUAGE: Bashiic; Mandarin Chinese
RELIGION: Christianity combined with traditional Tao beliefs

¹INTRODUCTION

The Tao are one of the currently 13 officially recognized Indigenous Peoples of Taiwan, but are the only ones not on Taiwan proper. Because of their relative isolation on the island of Lanyu, the Tao have best maintained their Austronesian traditions, language, and culture of all these groups. Named Yami early in the 20th century by Japanese ethnologists, the Tao have now persuaded the state to accept their self appellation as the official name of the group.

Linguistic chronology and oral traditions suggest that the Tao migrated to Lanyu about 800 years ago from the Batanes Archipelago north of Luzon. They maintained communication by boat, trading pigs, goats, and millet for weapons, beads, and gold. These exchanges ceased about three centuries ago, after a fight in which most of the Tao visitors on Batanes were killed. However, the languages spoken by Tao and Batanes are mutually intelligible.

Since 1945 Lanyu has been part of Taiwan (the Republic of China), where it is classified as a township that includes four administrative villages. There is an elected township mayor (who by law must be Tao) and a village head in each village.

²LOCATION AND HOMELAND

Lanyu (known as Orchid Island or Botel Tobago in English, and *Pongso no tao* in Tao) is a small island, 46 sq km, located 40 nautical miles SOUTHEAST of Taiwan. It is hilly, with eight mountains reaching over 400 m (1,312 ft) above sea level. The only flat area is a narrow, uneven belt lying between the mountains and the coast. Because of the lack of level ground, Tao situate their six villages on gentle slopes at the foot of mountains along the alluvial fans of creeks. Most of the island mountain area is covered by rain forests or dense scrub where the islanders obtain lumber to build houses and boats.

Lanyu climate is tropical. Humidity is often over 90%. July temperatures reach 32°C (90°F) and drop below 20°C (68°F) only in January. Rainfall is high, averaging over 2,600 cm (1,024 in) annually, with just over 100 rain-free days per year. It is also quite windy. From October to January or February, the climate is dominated by northeastern monsoons. Days are often cloudy, windy, and rainy, and the sea is rough. The strong winds not only prevent islanders from fishing at sea, but at times blow sea water far ashore, damaging crops. From February to June monsoons gradually dissipate, and the northern tropical current brings flying fish and the larger fish that prey on them near the island where they can be caught. July to early October is typhoon season. When there are no storms, the weather is clear and very warm. Tao take advantage of the good weather to build or repair houses, boats, and irrigation channels and to open new fields. Fishing takes place both day and night. Fruit also ripens in this summer period. Tao are busiest at this time, preparing for the coming winter.

In 2004 the resident population of Lanyu was 3,094, about 90% of whom are Tao. The others are Chinese from Taiwan, among them soldiers, police, civil servants, and shopkeepers. The Tao population has remained relatively stable for most of the 20th century, but grown slowly in recent years. There are several hundred temporary non-Tao residents. About 30% of the Tao population now live and work off the Lanyu in urban Taiwan.

³LANGUAGE

The Tao language is Bashiic, an Austronesian language. It is still spoken by the older generation, those over 50. The younger Tao speak Mandarin Chinese, the official language of Taiwan; many have lost competence to speak their ancestral language. The use and promotion of Bashiic in their churches has been an important factor in the preservation of the language. Bashiic has been put into writing through church initiatives.

Tao naming customs differ greatly from English names. First, Tao distinguish the living from the dead through names. A man named Konpo is *Si*-Konpo while living, *Simina*-Konpo after death. Second, husband and wife keep their own names until they have a child, after which they rename themselves to reflect their offspring. For example, when a child called *Si*-Manowi is born, his parents change their names to *Siaman*-Manowi, father of *Si*-Manowi, and *Sinan*-Manowi, mother of *Si*-Manowi. Later, when *Si*-Manowi marries *Si*-Awan, and later has a child, *Si*-Lotem, he must change his name to *Siaman*-Lotem and his wife to *Sinan*-Lotem. His parents must also take on new names becoming *Siapun*-Lotem or grandparent of Lotem. If Si-Awan is her parents' first child, her parents' names also become *Siapun*-Lotem. When their first great grandchild is born and named, all elders become Siapun-Kotan. This custom of noting parentage is known as teknonymy.

⁴FOLKLORE

Myth has it that the Tao ancestors were sent to earth by the Supreme God in the form of two boys, one in a stone, the other in a bamboo, after a flood that destroyed most of the half-human, half-ghosts who had inhabited Lanyu. When the two emerged from their shells and met, their knees became swollen and eventually split open. Their right knees bore baby boys and the left knees baby girls. When they grew older, brothers married sisters, but their children were crippled, blind, or otherwise handicapped. Later, they married each others' sisters and had many healthy offspring.

Tao gods also bless people—for example, transforming an ugly or deformed individual into a handsome one, presenting a man with a wife from heaven, or showering someone with treasure. They do this only out of sympathy for the person or at the request of a man's ancestors, not because individuals sacrifice or pray to them. Tao believe that the gods are indifferent to direct pleas.

The most important Tao cultural hero is the king of flying fish (flying fish are the most important source of animal protein), and all Tao customs and ceremonies are centered on him. He once appeared to an old man in a dream and arranged to meet next morning on the beach. He then taught him everything proper for a Tao to do, which has since been passed to each generation. Because of this, flying fish are sacred to the Tao. Every year they perform solemn rituals during the flying

fish season, and they observe many taboos when catching and eating flying fish.

⁵RELIGION

The Tao cosmos has eight levels supported by five massive tree trunks on the lowest plane. Humans occupy the middle level, which is Lanyu or *pongso no tao* (island of humans) in the Tao language. Gods of different ranks reside on higher planes, with ghosts and underground people on lower ones.

Tao gods are responsible for natural phenomena, catastrophe, and bounty alike. Tao only have vague images of their gods. They know there are several ranks of deities, but they do not agree on how many ranks there are, on which god dwells where, or on which god is responsible for what.

Tao see their gods as distant, yet they refrain from talking lightly about them. Once a year, on the yearly praying festival, they present offerings to the gods. It is also the only day on which the gods can be freely discussed. Although Tao gods will punish bad individuals such as robbers, they are generally more concerned with an entire village or with all the Lanyu Tao. The gods may favor Tao groups, blessing them with good weather and bountiful harvests (both agricultural and aquatic), or they may inflict disasters upon them.

By contrast, Tao are daily concerned with ghosts who cause such woes as death, injury, sickness, bad harvests, infertility, poor fishing conditions, and so on. The most fearful ghosts are the recently deceased. A dead man in his new condition may feel lonesome and decide to come back to the living to fetch a relative or friend to serve as a companion, thus causing another death or even a chain of deaths. Occasionally a Tao will dream of the spirit of a dead person. If, after a time, the living individual becomes ill, others will believe that the spirit caused it.

Almost all Tao became Christians in the 1960s. There are six Presbyterian and two Catholic churches and an independent Protestant chapel on the island. Tao Presbyterian clergy are important local leaders, having previously been the only educated Tao on the island who were not beholden to the Kuomintang (KMT) party and holding state sponsored jobs. Christian festivals, church events, and church-sponsored social services are an important part of local culture. However, Tao Christianity has not completely replaced their traditional beliefs. Instead, the two systems coexist.

⁶MAJOR HOLIDAYS

Tao mark the year with festivals and ceremonies marking the beginning or end of productive activities. Traditionally most ceremonies centered on group millet-cultivating and catching flying fish, the two most important sources of food. However, this has changed. Millet-cultivating groups no longer exist, and the Tao now celebrate some Chinese and Christian holidays. All Tao holidays, regardless of origin, are celebrated by stopping work for one or two days and serving lunch, a meal that is not generally eaten. Moreover, relatives and friends often visit each other.

The first ceremony of the flying fish season is performed at the landing beach in the tenth Tao month (March on the solar calendar). A chicken or a piglet is killed on the landing beach and its blood collected. Each male must wet his finger with the "magic" blood, smear it on a pebble around the tide line, and pray for a year of health and good harvest. After this ceremony the big boats owned by fishing groups may start nighttime fishing by torchlight.

The second phase of the flying fish season begins in the twelfth Tao month (May). This event includes many rites held beside the fish-drying rack and the small boats, which may be put out to catch migratory fish after the ceremony.

The "good month" ceremony announces the end of the flying fish and millet-growing seasons. Two important activities, exchanging gifts and group millet-pounding, take place on that day. In the morning, families prepare tubers and other food to send to their relatives. The standard gift includes three taro and one dried flying fish.

The millet-pounding ceremony used to be performed separately by individual millet-growing groups, but since such organizations no longer exist, millet pounding has become a village-wide ceremony in which all participate. The sponsor of the millet pounding brings some millet and a wooden mortar to the village plaza. Men who want to participate bring their own pestles. Four or five elders lead the pounding, and then younger people take turns. The participants surround the mortar, bent over at the waist, and pound the millet in turn.

The yearly praying festival is the only occasion on which the Tao make offerings to the gods. The first offering is communal. Several old men represent the village, each bringing a rattan tray to the beach. The offerings include betel nuts, gaud vines (Piper betel), pork, and chicken feathers—every essential Tao food item except fish. They pray to the gods for health, longevity, and a good harvest. Upon returning home, they put similar offerings on the ridge of their roofs, setting out trays on the right side for the gods and on the left side for the ancestors. After praying, they leave the offerings on the roofs.

The ceremony for goats is a two-day festival. On the first, Tao exchange gifts with their relatives and friends. On the second they perform a ritual: a goat herder picks two kinds of abundant wild plants and prays that his goats will be as numerous as the plants.

Finally, Tao celebrate new holidays, including Lunar New Year, Christmas, and Easter. Lunar New Year is the longest holiday, lasting three or more days, and Tao working in Taiwan return for a family reunion. Tao celebrate Christmas and Easter in the same way that other Christians do, adding Tao songs and dances.

7 RITES OF PASSAGE

Tao rites of passage are relatively simple. Tao mark three events: marriage, birth, and death. Tao weddings lack festiveness and the boisterous merriment of the Chinese. Only a few close relatives of the bride and groom attend. The ceremony is simple, private, and exclusive. Couples attracted to each other typically live together for several years before formally marrying. However, the community regards the pair as a couple despite the lack of a wedding. Young Tao may change sexual partners several times before eventually settling down and establishing a family; however, when deciding to live together, by cultural tradition they must be faithful to each other. Because a marriage becomes stable only after a child is born, Tao view the first child's naming ceremony as more significant than a wedding.

The ceremony performed for a newborn is the naming ceremony. On a chosen morning several days after the baby is born, the baby's father carries a knife and a coconut shell bowl to a running spring to collect water. On the way home, he must not speak to or even greet anyone. He must also be very careful not to fall or spill the water, as this would be a very bad omen, foretelling the baby's approaching death. At home, he sprinkles the water onto his baby's hair, touches the top of the baby's head with his moistened finger, and gives it a name and a blessing. This ceremony is especially important to the baby's parents and grandparents if the baby is the first child and if one or both parents is also a first child.

Death and funerals are very private events in Tao society. Only close kin and the most intimate of friends attend a funeral. The corpse is wrapped in cloth and bound into a bundle by the son. If a young man does not know how to wrap a body, he may ask one of his uncles for help. The reward for this service, as well as other funeral services such as pall bearing and grave digging, is a flake of gold or a plot of land. Corpses are buried as soon as possible after death, some within a few hours. The graveyard is a taboo place after sunset; when the death happens in the late afternoon or at night, the burial must wait until dawn. While the body remains at home, men must remain vigilant to prevent ghosts making the body heavy and hard to handle. Some spears and other weapons are placed around the house to keep evil spirits at bay.

Inauguration ceremonies for new houses and new boats are distinctive and important in Tao society and may be viewed as a type of rite of passage. Inaugurations primarily involve the display and distribution of large quantities of pork, goat, and water taro. Because a host family needs about one ton of taro, enough to cover the roof of the new house or bury a new boat, prior to the ceremony they collect water taro for about five days.

Although there are several different kinds of inauguration ceremonies, they follow roughly similar scripts. On the first day, the huge taro pile and domestic animals are displayed. After sunset, guests from other villages gather in the host's house and sing ritual songs to admire his achievement until the sun rises the next morning. Then the taro and butchered pigs and goats are distributed to every guest and every village family.

8 INTERPERSONAL RELATIONS

In daily greetings, the Tao emphasize generation and age differences. The most popular greeting includes a kinship term plus *gon* (be well). On meeting someone, a person has to be aware of his generation relative to that of the other. A younger speaker says *maran* (uncle) *gon* to a male, *kaminan* (aunt) *gon* to a woman. The other responds, *anak* (son or daughter) *gon*. If the other is younger, the greetings and responses are reversed. To an elder peer, he says *kaka* (elder brother or sister) *gon* and to a younger one *wali* (younger brother or sister) *gon*. The kinship terms used here are honorific and do not imply real kinship relations.

There is no need for a Tao to make an appointment before visiting friends or relatives living in other villages. One may arrive at the destination some time before dusk, at which time the host should be on the way or at home. As visits are not expected, the host may not have enough food for guests. Not wanting to inconvenience the host, the visitor brings gifts, usually tubers and dried fish or other meat, eliminating the problem.

Tao tribesmen from Orchid Island row their traditional handmade boat on the Keelung River, in Taipei, Taiwan. (AP Images/Wally Santana)

⁹LIVING CONDITIONS

Since the 1980s a market-based economy has developed in Lanyu, with commercial goods imported and obtainable only with money. However, Tao still have a subsistence economy—that is, they produce most of their food, build their own houses and fishing boats, and make some of their clothing. Many goods they produce do not enter the market. However, the development of tourism from the 1980s, and demand for Tao handicraft has led to significant production of traditional goods for these markets.

Tao have less access to modern medical care than they have to commercial goods. A small public clinic is staffed by two doctors and several nurses, but the limited facilities permit them to treat minor problems only. Islanders afflicted with serious illnesses have to go to a hospital on Taiwan. Although the public clinic is free and Tao have public medical insurance, some live with serious illness because they cannot afford transportation to Taiwan.

Construction of homes is important in Tao culture. The traditional house is a complex consisting of a main residential dwelling, a workshop, and an open, roofed platform each built on separate terraces and descending to the beach. The residential dwelling is built inside a large pit with the roof level with the surface of the terrace. The workshop, on the other hand, is built on top of a somewhat smaller pit so that its floor is level with the terrace ground. The open platform is erected on heavy posts, its floor about 2 m (6.5 ft) above ground. The residence and workshop also rest just off the earth supported by thick posts. Tao residences face the sea, their roofs uniformly parallel to the coastline, while workshops and platforms are perpendicular to the shore.

In the 1960s the local government replaced these traditional houses with small, confining concrete houses. Each family has limited living space. This created many problems and difficulties, and in the hot season these concrete boxes were almost unlivable, so most people built traditional roofed platforms in front of them. Starting in 1995 the government paid for construction of new houses for the whole island. Few people rebuilt traditional houses (unsuited as they are for modern utilities) but chose to design their own versions of modern rural Taiwanese homes.

Tao construct boats almost exclusively for fishing and for carrying harvested millet or taro. Because Lanyu is small, islanders used to get around on foot. Recently, the number of motor vehicles has increased. Many Tao families own motorcycles or even cars. The island has a public bus service. Tao travel to Taiwan is by airplane or steamer.

¹⁰FAMILY LIFE

The family is the most important social unit and the basic economic unit in Tao society. Most Tao families are nuclear, which means that they consist of wife, husband, and unmarried children. Some children may be from previous marriages. Average family size is four persons. In the typical Tao family, relationships between parents and children and spouses are very close. This closeness will endure even after a child marries and establishes his or her own family.

Husband and wife are not only very close emotionally, but also economically reliant on each other, working together to support their families. For religious reasons, Tao women are not permitted aboard fishing boats, so men provide seafood. Women mainly work in their fields, weeding, digging, and hauling heavy loads of tubers back to the village. A man with no wife or with an incapacitated wife will be unable to accumulate enough taro and pigs to hold socially important inauguration ceremonies and unable to reciprocate the gifts of meat received from relatives and other villagers at ceremonies they sponsor. He falls into debt and his status declines.

Although remarrying is both common and easy for the divorced or the widowed, the Tao emphasize monogamy, spiritual loyalty, and sexual fidelity in marriage. Extramarital affairs are unacceptable and rare, and polygyny (multiple wives) is unheard of. As suggested earlier, unstable relationships in the early stages after marriage will result either in separation or, after several children, evolve into more stable unions recognized by the community.

¹¹CLOTHING

Tao clothing is simple. Men wear nothing but a loincloth. Women wear woven skirts tied around the waist with two bands and a breast covering or vest. In summer, older women may wear only skirts, leaving their upper bodies bare.

Men and women traditionally share responsibility for clothing production, but there is a sexual division of labor, with women weaving abaca and other fibers into fabrics from which Tao clothing is made. Men engage in weaving as well, but use different materials such as tree bark, large leaves, bamboo or rattan to create helmets, vests, raincoats and wide-brimmed hats. However, with the recent trend toward the purchase of clothing, Tao weaving skills are slowly disappearing.

Tao women continue to weave certain fabrics to make clothing worn exclusively at ceremonial events. These articles include loincloths, vests, skirts, and lightweight gowns made of white fabric decorated with woven blue stripes. Tao clothing traditionally was simple in construction and style. Women cut and sewed together pieces of fabric from woven sheets 3 m (10 ft) long and 20 cm (8 in) wide. The making of ceremonial vests is a very solemn undertaking. Before Tao can wear these items, they must make offerings of goat or pork to their gods. By these offerings the ceremonial clothing acquires magical powers. Tao wear their ceremonial garments on visits to other villages as a way of showing respect for their hosts, and because they believe that the ritual clothing will protect them from evil spirits to which they are vulnerable whenever they journey outside the safe confines of the village.

¹²FOOD

Tao generally eat two meals a day. They go to work after breakfast but rarely take anything other than tobacco and betel at midday. Dinner is their main meal. They eat lunch only when they stay at home for festivals or because of bad weather.

Tao classify food into two categories: staples and supplements. A regular meal includes both. Ordinarily women are responsible for obtaining staples and men for supplements. The two important staples are sweet potato and water taro. Other basic crops include taro and yams. Millet is also grown but is exchanged as a gift and consumed only on ceremonial occasions. In recent years, rice and noodles have replaced tubers in the daily diet of young Tao.

There are many kinds of supplements, obtained mostly from the ocean. Fish are most important, fresh when available, but otherwise dried and salted. Other types are crab and conch, as well as various kinds of seaweed and an assortment of edible wild plants. Families with little male labor have to depend more on plants.

Pork and goat meat are also supplements, but are generally eaten only on ceremonial occasions; neither is eaten on a daily basis.

Fish is very important in the Tao diet and is classified into good fish that everyone can eat, bad fish (not good for women), and old men's fish, which neither women nor young men are allowed to eat. This classification deeply affects eating etiquette, daily fishing activities, and other aspects of life. Some Tao insist that women will vomit if they eat bad fish or will become ill if they fail to. Every family has two sets of cooking and eating utensils, one for each of these two types of fish.

¹³EDUCATION

There is now an elementary school in every Tao village, and a secondary school, grades 7 through 12, is located in the town. Tao children have compulsory schooling for nine years, and most continue through senior high school. Students board and lodge in the high school five and half days per week, except in winter and summer vacations. Despite special government assistance, few Tao qualify to enter universities.

Prior to the 1980s only poor-quality teachers and public servants were sent to Lanyu, although capable volunteers also went there occasionally. Children learned very little from their teachers, and were often ordered out of their classrooms to gather highly valued wild flora and fauna for their teachers and principals. Most Tao over 60 are hardly able to read. Not surprisingly, when the high school was established, most Tao did not want their children to attend, and soldiers had to pick up students during the first two years. As the generation who began receiving more progressive education beginning in the 1980s become parents, Tao are concerned to invest in education, sometimes sending their children to Taiwan or even moving there to access better schools for their children. There are numerous government and private programs and subsidies for education of Tao children. Computer education in the schools and government provision of computers and Internet linkage for free to each village have made most young Tao computer users, so numerous Internet sites now serve Lanyu and present it to the world.

¹⁴CULTURAL HERITAGE

Tao music consists only of singing; musical instruments are unheard of. There are eight categories of Tao songs, including ritual songs, love songs, lullabies, and work songs. Since most Tao songs use the three-tone or four-tone system, melodies sound more like chanting than singing. However, Tao singers may improvise, adding grace notes or changing the tempo, so that the same song sounds different when sung by different singers. Most well known are ritual songs, sung all night long in inauguration ceremonies.

Most Tao songs, lullabies included, are sung by men, but hand-clapping songs can be performed together by men and women, whereas only women dance in Tao tradition. *Ganam*, a category of songs, is exclusively for females and always accompanies dancing. A famous Tao dance is the hair dance. The dancers swing their hair to and fro while singing and dancing. Since the 1990s men's dances have been created for indigenous cultural festivals and tourism.

¹⁵WORK

Until the 1960s, Tao living on Lanyu relied upon a subsistence economy, consuming primarily, if not exclusively, what they produced. Recently, however, the island population has become increasingly incorporated into Taiwan's market economy. Young people in particular prefer working in Taiwan as wage laborers to staying home and growing tubers or fishing.

Tao youth began to enter the off-island labor market in large numbers during the 1970s. At that time, Taiwan experienced impressive growth in labor-intensive industries that required large numbers of workers. Tao youth worked in construction and factories manufacturing shoes, clothing, electronic goods, etc. On Lanyu, there are not enough good job opportunities; thus at least a third of the Tao population lives and works in Taiwan. Part of the wages earned working in Taiwan comes back to Lanyu to support elderly parents invested in local economic initiatives generally linked to the tourist industry. These include purchase of cars for taxis, investment in a store or upgrading their house to a bed and breakfast. Many people produce traditional artifacts for the tourist industry. In addition there are now job opportunities in government services, schools, or church-operated social services.

¹⁶SPORTS

Lanyu has very few sports facilities, but basketball courts can be found in every village. This sport is popular among young men and children. Although Tao are rarely seen playing softball, there are annual township softball tournaments. Teams organized by villages compete with each other for the prizes. Swimming is the favorite sport of children and teenagers in summer time.

¹⁷ENTERTAINMENT AND RECREATION

There are no theaters on the island, but television and videotapes are popular. In Tao culture reference to sex in the presence of parents, children, or a sibling of the opposite sex is taboo. They feel uneasy when obscene footage appears. Thus, watching television is not "family entertainment" on Lanyu except for sports programs.

¹⁸FOLK ART, CRAFTS, AND HOBBIES

Tao used to make almost everything they used; thus, they were skilled in carpentry, wood sculpture, gold and silver smithery, pottery, and weaving. Recently, they have begun to buy goods they used to make themselves; except for carving miniature

boats and pottery idols sold as souvenirs, the only remaining traditional Tao handicraft is boat construction.

Tao make two sizes of fishing boats, 2–4 m (6.5–13 ft) long for 1 to 3 persons, and 5–8 m (16–26 ft) long for 6 to 10 persons. Boats may be propelled by oars and sails, but sails are rarely used. The typical boat, shaped like a Venetian gondola, requires several grades of wood that are joined together by means of dowels, dovetailing, rattan roping, and glue. The keel must be made of a very hard, abrasion-resistant wood because the shores where Tao beach their boats are strewn with rocks. Many Tao boats are beautifully sculptured and painted in black, white and red. This intricately decorated boat has become a Tao cultural symbol.

¹⁹SOCIAL PROBLEMS

A hundred years ago, Tao did not smoke or drink alcohol. Since the early 1980s, usage of both has skyrocketed. Cigarettes are enjoyed on a daily basis, but alcohol is considered a luxury and is limited to ceremonial occasions or when guests come to visit. Tao families now spend significant proportions of their income on these products. Drinking has brought many problems to Tao society such as marital problems, traffic accidents, and loss of the will to work.

The Tao are a minority people, Lanyu being part of Taiwan (the Republic of China). Their experience with the Taiwan government has often been frustrating. Until the late 1980s human rights were ignored, not just for the Tao but for everyone. Some of the problems have been resolved, but others continue to exist. For example, in the 1950s much land was seized to establish cattle ranches for demobilized Chinese soldiers or for a prison farm. The cattle uprooted Tao crops, and inmates stole Tao property and raped Tao women. Because authorities rarely observed such transgressions first-hand, Tao complaints were seldom taken seriously. In 1982 low level radioactive waste from Taiwan's nuclear power stations began to be stored on the island. The radioactive material is put into drums and stored in concrete trenches. The government neither sought permission from the Tao to establish this facility, nor told them what was being built on their land. The radioactive waste has become the defining issue that shapes Tao relations with the state and the rest of Taiwan since then. Supported by the anti-nuclear and environmental movement, the Tao did obtain a promise from the state that this waste would be removed, but local resistance from other areas in Taiwan chosen for a new site means that the waste is still there (2008). Meanwhile the Taiwan Power Corporation has paid large amounts of subsidies and compensation monies for local infrastructure and welfare, as well as providing free electric power for all Tao on Lanyu. Ironically, it is opposition to the facility that is the strongest basis for island-wide unity in a culture that tends to be highly fragmented by family and village loyalties.

²⁰GENDER ISSUES

Tao only recognize two genders, there being no categories other than male and female. Because the traditional economy depended on close co-operation based on a gendered division of labor, and because affines were often as important in economic and ritual life as kin, there tends to be more basic gender equality in Tao culture than in other Taiwan Indigenous Peoples, or Taiwan as a whole. Nonetheless, the primacy of the male in the household, economic life and ritual life was uncontested. Conversion to Christianity, public education, and development of economic opportunities in the tourist industry have all contributed to problematize gender equality, as well as provide more avenues for women to achieve status as independent social actors. Women now have strong roles in the modern sector as teachers, church leaders, locally elected politicians, small store operators, and cultural performers for tourism and competitive festivals.

[21] BIBLIOGRAPHY

Benedek, Dezso. *The Songs of the Ancestors: A Comparative Study of Bashiic Folklore.* Taipei: SMC Publishing Inc., 1991.

del Re, Arundel. *Creation Myths of the Formosan Natives.* Tokyo: Hokuseido Press, 1951.

Kano, Tadao, and Segawa, Kokichi. *An Illustrated Ethnography of Formosan Aborigines, Vol. 1, the Tao.* Tokyo: Maruzen Company, 1956.

Kim, Uichol, et al, eds. *Indigenous and Cultural Psychology: Understanding People in Context.* New York: Springer, 2006.

Yu, Guang-hong. "Ritual, Society and Culture Among the Tao." Ph.D. diss., University of Michigan, 1991.

—revised by M. Stainton

TAUSUG

PRONUNCIATION: TOW-soog ("-ow" as in "how")
ALTERNATE NAMES: Joloano, Suluk (term in Sabah)
LOCATION: Philippines (Sulu archipelago)
POPULATION: 1.1 million
LANGUAGE: Tausug
RELIGION: Islam
RELATED ARTICLES: Vol. 3: Filipinos

[1] INTRODUCTION

The powerful currents *(sug)* flowing around the Sulu archipelago give the Tausug their name (Sulu itself is from the cognate word *sulog* [used in modern Visayan, for instance]). Beginning in the Song dynasty, an increase in Chinese trade with Southeast Asia attracted the Tausug to their present home in the commercially strategic islands between Mindanao and Borneo. From the 15th to 18th centuries, the Tausug state, the Sulu sultanate (whose hegemony extended to northeastern Borneo, impinging on the sphere of Brunei) maintained close relations with China, sending numerous missions to the imperial capital. Other crucial contacts were with Islam, which the Tausug adopted in the 15th century. The Sulu sultanate relied on slaves taken in wide-ranging raids to harvest marine products (especially, sea cucumber and bird nests) for the Chinese market.

Although the Spanish established a fort early on in Zamboanga at the western tip of Mindanao, they did not take Jolo, the Sulu capital, until 1878 ("Jolo" [hoh-LO] is the Spanish pronunciation of Sulu, the "j" being pronounced as a "sh" in the 16th century). By the late 19th century, the Muslim Tausug and the Christian Spaniards had been engaged in almost continual warfare for 300 years (the Spaniards applied the term "Moro," originally referring to the Muslim Moors of North Africa, to Muslims in the Philippines, a label that continues in use to this day). Tausug aristocrats regularly commissioned fleets to raid for slaves among the Catholicized populations to the north.

The Americans took the Spanish fort at Jolo in 1899 but did not subjugate the entire island until 1913 (Tausug communities fought to the last man, woman, and child in mountain redoubts). In 1915, Sultan Jamal-ul Kiram II abdicated his secular power to the American colonial administration. The relative stability of the following years came to an end with the World War II dissemination of firearms throughout the Philippine countryside, which for Sulu meant a return to the traditional pattern of endemic violence. After the war, the Filipino government exercised minimal control over Sulu, and the population and the Philippine Constabulary, and later military, viewed each other with hostility.

During the 1970s, Sulu became a major center of the Moro separatist movement. Headed by Jolo native Nur Misuari, the leadership of the Moro National Liberation Front (MNLF, a secular movement emphasizing a regional rather than a religious identity) was dominated by Tausug; it came to field a force of 300,000 insurgents, and the conflict ultimately killed 80,000 to 200,000 people. In 1981, the Moro Islamic Liberation Front split off from the MNLF: this was due not only to the break-away faction's commitment to an independent Bangsamoro state under Islamic law (at a time when the MNLF was considering accepting only regional autonomy) but also

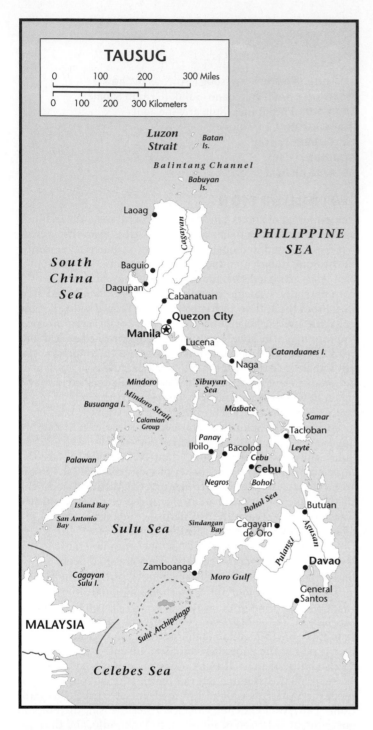

TAUSUG

0   100   200   300 Miles

0   100   200   300 Kilometers

Luzon Strait
Batan Is.

Balintang Channel

Babuyan Is.

Laoag

Cagayan

PHILIPPINE SEA

South China Sea

Baguio

Dagupan

Cabanatuan

Quezon City

Manila

Lucena

Naga

Catanduanes I.

Mindoro

Sibuyan Sea

Busuanga I.

Mindoro Strait

Masbate

Calamian Group

Panay

Iloilo   Bacolod

Cebu

Cebu

Samar

Tacloban

Leyte

Palawan

Negros

Bohol

Island Bay

Bohol Sea

Butuan

San Antonio Bay

Sulu Sea

Sindangan Bay

Cagayan de Oro

Pulangi

Agusan

Cagayan Sulu I.

Zamboanga

Moro Gulf

Davao

MALAYSIA

Sulu Archipelago

General Santos

Celebes Sea

to resentment by Maguindanao of Tausug dominance of the MNLF. The Moro are composed of several distinct ethnicities, of which three equally matched groups, the Tausug, the Maguindanao, and the Maranao, are the most important in size and power. A plebiscite under the Aquino administration led to the establishment of the Autonomous Region in Muslim Mindanao in 1989.

Since then, the MILF has also moved towards compromise with the Philippine government, concluding a peace agreement in 2001, though fighting by (largely non-Tausug) militant groups, including terrorism and kidnappings, the radical Abu Sayyaf continues. Because of some of these groups' links with

Al-Qaeda and the Southeast Asian Jemaah Islamiya militant network, the United States military collaborates with the Philippine military in the region.

Tausug culture (like Moro and non-Christian cultures more generally) has contributed key icons to the national identity of the predominantly Christian and Hispanized Philippines: Tausug dances, for instance, are taught in high schools throughout the country and included in showcases of Philippine national culture abroad (including those staged by Filipino-Americans).

²LOCATION AND HOMELAND

The Tausug dominate the Sulu Archipelago, a chain linking western Mindanao in the southern Philippines to Sabah on Malaysian Borneo. Having totaled 325,000 in 1960, the Tausug numbered around 900,000 in the Philippines and over 120,000 outside the country. More than half of the Tausug (a total of 325,000 people in 1960) reside on Jolo, a rugged island of 950 sq km (367 sq mi). Benefiting from the volcanic soil, agriculture occupies half the land. The rest is mountainous, covered either by rain forest or by the grasslands left behind by slash-and-burn cultivation. Along the coast, mangrove swamps alternate with white sand beaches and coral reefs just off shore. Tausug also occupy the neighboring islands of Pata, Tapul, Lugus, and Siasi, as well as Lahad Datu and Tambisan on the Sabah coast.

In Sulu province itself, 528,000 Tausug constitute 85.3% of the population; in Tawi-Tawi province, they number 114,745 or 35.6% of the population (almost as many as the largest ethnic group, the Sama Dilaya), and in Basilan 76,000 or 23%. There are 98,000 Tausug in Zamboanga City, 38,500 in Zamboanga del Sur province, and 6,700 in Zamboanga del Norte province. Because of the turmoil of the past four decades, a considerable community of Filipino Muslims has grown in northeastern Borneo (a 1981 figure of 12,000 for Indonesian East Kalimantan and a 19821 figure of 110,000 for Malaysian Sabah, where they are called "Suluk").

In addition to the cardinal directions, Tausug orient themselves with reference to direction "towards the interior" (*gimba*) or "towards the sea" (*higad*).

³LANGUAGE

The Tausug language is most closely related to the Visayan languages of the central Philippines, particularly to the speech of Butuan in northeastern Mindanao, which archaeologists have identified as a major trading center in earlier times. Linguists estimate that the ancestors of the Tausug left Butuan and migrated to their present homeland within the last 1,000 years. The Tausug language has long been written in a version of the Arabic script and contains numerous loanwords from Malay (many of which are themselves of Arabic or Sanskrit origin). The language remains a lingua franca for ethnic groups (Sama/Samal, Mapun, Yakan) that were once vassals of the Sulu sultanate.

A newborn child receives a temporary name. If it is sickly, the parents may try out different names until they find a lucky one. Because of Islam, these names are usually Arabic, but Tausug parents have been known to pick the names of famous Americans, such as George Washington, or to select a nonsense string of syllables for their sound alone.

⁴FOLKLORE

Though ubiquitous, spirits tend to congregate at road crossings, rocky shores, large stones, and trees, especially the balete tree, which twines itself around larger trees (white flags mark such magical spots). *Jin Islam* (Muslim spirits) are distinguished from *jin kapil* (infidel spirits): the latter reject God's commandments and cause human illness, whereas the former obey God and fight evil spirits (*saytan*). Malevolent spirits reside in legendary animals, such as a goat with a man's head or in an owl that blinds with its claws. Particularly feared are *barbalan*, which take the form of deformed people by day but which at night turn into flying creatures who eat the livers of fresh corpses. One must resist *Ibiris*, similar to the Christian devil, which is present in each person and is the source of all evil deeds.

Mangubat, traditional healers, deriving their expertise from contact with spirits (including, in some cases, marriage with one), employ herbal medicines and symbolic magic. Tausug often carry amulets that can grant them invulnerability to weapons.

⁵RELIGION

Since its introduction as early as the 15th century by a combination of traders, Arab and Chinese Muslims, and mystics from Malaya and Sumatra, Islam has been the Tausug religion. Religious leaders are careful to distinguish between orthodox Muslim practices and those that derive from a pre-Islamic heritage or represent local innovation; the Tausug pride themselves on being more orthodox in their Islam than the Sama peoples whom they have traditionally dominated. The sultan serves a key function as the sanctifier of mosques and appointer of the *imam muwallam* who preside over them. Other religious officials are, in ascending order of seniority, the *bilal* who intones the call to prayer, the *hatib* who delivers sermons, and the *imam* who leads communal prayer. For the most part, only the elderly engage in pious behavior, such as fasting for the entire month of Ramadan, because young men must display "manly behavior" that often violates Islamic moral standards.

⁶MAJOR HOLIDAYS

On successive Wednesdays in the second Islamic month, communities perform the *pagtulak bala* ritual. All community members gather at the beach to cast a stone into the sea, an act (particularly exciting for children) that ejects the previous year's accumulated evil. In addition, rafts with aromatic food are sent out to sea in hopes of drawing evil spirits away forever.

On *Maulud al-Nabi*, the birthday of Muhammad, each mosque resounds with all-night Arabic chanting. Although the assembled community spends most of the time chatting, smoking, and waiting for the following feast, at certain points in the chant everyone touches special flowers representing the Prophet, a merit-earning act.

On the full moon of the month before the fasting month of Ramadan, people offer prayers and hold a feast for the repose of the dead at the mosque; several days later, they clean the family graves and have a feast there.

Haylaya, marking the end of Ramadan, is an occasion for people to wear their finest clothes and pay visits to each other; the holiday includes gambling, feasting, and watching movies in town.

⁷RITES OF PASSAGE

If his newborn is a girl, a man will let off a few gunshots into the air; he will fire many shots if it is a boy. Placing the placenta in a green coconut shell, the father buries it on the full moon. At the age of one year, the child receives his or her first haircut and is ritually weighed; the equivalent of its weight in uncooked rice is later given to the presiding clergy. Usually at around 10 years of age, boys are circumcised. A slight scraping of the clitoris is also performed on girls.

Men generally marry around the age of 18, women between 16 and 18 years of age. Marriage can be by negotiation between the respective kin-group, elopement, or abduction.

In a negotiated marriage, if the parents approve of a girl suggested by their son, they gather their kin and march to the girl's house to ask for her hand. With the girl's parents, they schedule a formal conference for a few days later when the bride-price (*ungsud*) is set. All the boy's paternal and maternal relatives contribute to the ungsud, and anyone who contributed to raising the girl has the right to ask for a portion of the ungsud.

The wedding takes place only after the bride-price has been gathered and delivered. On the wedding day itself, each side's relatives and allies gather at the respective houses to eat and chat to the sound of *kulintang* music. In the late afternoon, the groom, accompanied by a procession of his guests yelling and shooting off guns, rides or is carried to the bride's house. The groom does not see the bride until after the wedding ceremony itself, which is essentially a contract between him and the bride's father, solemnized by a religious official. Then the bride is brought out, and the groom touches her forehead, declaring his right to touch her. The couple sits motionless and expressionless for the rest of the ensuing party.

Abduction (*pagsaggau*, "capture") and elopement differ only in that theoretically a woman consents to the elopement, while the man's desire alone motivates an abduction. If either set of parents does not permit a match, a man may abduct his bride, who must at least pretend to resist by screaming loudly. Avoiding capture by her relatives, the man takes the woman to the village headman's house. In order to marry, the man must pay an abduction fine set by the sultan to the woman's family, as well as extra money to "cover their shame."

Though grieving in private, a person's loved ones receive his or her death with a public expression of resignation to fate. The family washes and enshrouds the corpse in the Islamic fashion. In the evening, women take turns chanting from the Quran. On the following afternoon, the burial takes place, accompanied by rituals informing the deceased that he or she is dead, otherwise the soul wanders and visits the living in dreams.

⁸INTERPERSONAL RELATIONS

The ideal to which men aspire is being *maisug*, willing to defend his honor without hesitation. In order to erase his shame (*sipug*), a man must take revenge on anyone who has, for example, murdered a kinsman, made advances on his female kin, or insulted him in public. As cowardice is shameful and mercy is only shown by those clearly strong enough to take revenge if they so choose, conflicts tend to escalate to killing. Although arbitration (by a village headman, by the sultan according to Muslim law, or, in the last resort, by a judge under Philippine national law) is available, each man maintains the firepower to obtain his own justice. Thus, firearms take a large chunk of a rural family's budget, though half of ammunition is expended in festive noise-making.

Reciprocity is a key value. One feels rejected (*pangdada*) if a person one has helped does not spontaneously return the favor. One is particularly anxious to reciprocate favors (*buddi*) that the other was not obligated to give. If one cannot pay one's debts, one feels *luman*, the need to maintain a respectful distance from, even defer to, the party whom one owes. Refusal both to pay debts of gratitude and to demand recompense for offenses is described as a grave insult, *way sipug* (shameless).

In traditional society, the sultan, believed to be a descendant of the prophet Muhammad, was the political, judicial, and religious authority of highest appeal. The rival candidates for the sultanate today retain the last type of authority. Although the sultan awarded various ranked titles that could be passed on to sons, actual wealth and power depended on a title-holder's own abilities, particularly in amassing a large following, such as would constitute a slave-raiding party. Ties of alliance remain crucial to winning election campaigns, carrying on feuds, or mounting rites-of-passage celebrations (*paghinang*). In theory, aristocrats (*datu*), forming 2% of the population, were descendants of former sultans. The rest were free or debt-slave commoners. Some 10% of the population consisted of bought or captured non-Tausug slaves. Moreover, various alien groups, such as the Samal or Bajau, acknowledged the sultan's authority and entered into client relationships with Tausug communities. For example, a boat-dwelling group may supply fish to a Tausug group in exchange for protection and agricultural products.

Assumed to be a prelude to sex, touching between the sexes outside of marriage, even as slight as a man touching a woman's arm in the daylight, is subject to fines imposed by the sultan. A young man staying overnight in a house may attempt to grope for (*kap-kap*) the family's daughter in the dark while her parents are asleep (the parents may only care to avoid a public scandal). A young man may have a female relative befriend the girl he wants. On some pretext, the female relative invites the girl to her house or into the forest, where the man can seduce her. Often, the girl desires this, too, as long as they are not publicly discovered.

⁹LIVING CONDITIONS

Consisting of a single rectangular room, a traditional house is raised on 2-m to 2.5-m (6- to 8 ft) piles and has a thatched gable roof. A series of elevated porches leads from the house to a separate kitchen building. On land, a fence may surround the house; animals are kept under the house. In coastal villages, houses are often raised above permanent water and connected to each other by gangplanks. Furniture consists of sleeping mattresses, mosquito nets, reed mats, wooden chests, brassware, and large rice containers that are kept above high beams.

While houses in coastal villages cluster together, in the interior houses are dispersed because farmers choose spots that are most convenient to scattered holdings. Villages encompass from 20 to 100 houses, but proximity does not bond households to each other in the absence of kinship or alliance ties. *Lungan*, hamlets bound by overlapping kinship ties, combine into *kauman*, communities led by the holder of title from the sultan and held together by attendance at a common mosque.

Average family income in the Autonomous Region in Muslim Mindanao, of which Sulu province is a part, amounted to 89,000 pesos (us$1,745) in 2006, the lowest in the country, cf. the national average of ᴘ173,000, the National Capital Region's ᴘ311,000, Southern Tagalog's ᴘ198,000, and those of the neighboring Davao and Zamboanga regions, ᴘ135,000 and ᴘ125,000 respectively. In 2000, Sulu had the lowest Human Development Index, 0.351 (combining measures of health, education, and income) in the country (cf. the Philippines' national HDI of 0.656).

According to the 2000 census, the proportion of houses in Sulu with a roof of galvanized iron/aluminum reached 27% (a great increase over just 9.3% ten years earlier) and with a roof of thatch 56.7% (down from 83.8%); 32.3% of houses had wooden outer walls, and another 53.4% outer walls of bamboo or thatch. In 2000, 12% of households had access to a community faucet and 14.3% to a faucet of their own, while 28.7% obtained their water from a well, and 24.4% from springs, lakes, rivers, or rain. More than half of households (54.6%) disposed of their garbage by burning it, 21.6% by dumping into a household pit, and 7.8% by feeding it to their animals; only 6.4% had it picked up by a collection truck. 64.7% of houses were lit with kerosene lamps, 17.2% with electricity, and 11.7% with firewood. 61.7% possessed a radio, 9.1% a television, 4.8% a refrigerator, 4.5% a VCR, 2.5% a telephone or cell phone, 2.1% a washing machine, and 3.6% a motorized vehicle.

¹⁰FAMILY LIFE

Kinship extends to both the father's side (*usbaq*) and the mother's side (*waris*) and focuses on ties back three generations, i.e., up to and including second cousins. However, children tend to have more contact with their paternal relatives because they usually grow up in the father's community. The bond between brothers and first cousins is the most important in determining support in feuds and political action, only approached by quasi-kin alliances sealed by an oath on the Qur'an.

Tausug address equals by their names but use kin terms with parents (*inaq* and *amaq*) and preferably with uncles (*bapaq*) and aunts (*babu*), although they extend such kin terms to non-kin as well. Children show respect to parents; fathers are more affectionate to children than mothers are. Grandparents and grandchildren have more playful interaction. Siblings are expected to help each other.

Marriage is preferred with kin, especially with a first cousin, in order to preserve landholdings. Taboos prohibit marriage between kin of different generations, however, and between half-siblings. Incest between parent and child was traditionally punished by putting the couple into a fish trap and sinking it at sea. Anonymous notes posted in the mosque accuse grave sexual offenders, such as a man who has made love to his wife's sister. Ritual whipping is the punishment.

A newlywed couple spends one year with the woman's family then moves back to the man's parents' house, from which they will later move to establish a household also in the man's community. Extended households are rare, usually consisting of two married sisters. Adoption of orphaned kin is common.

Divorce is strongly condemned and affects less than 10% of marriages. Village headmen will try to resolve marital conflicts first. A husband's excessive gambling, his proposal to take a second wife, or disagreements on the treatment of children are the usual grounds for divorce.

¹¹CLOTHING

Both men and women wear the *patadyung*, a tube skirt that can also be folded into a headcloth, a sash, a baby sling, a pillow, a blanket, or a flag. While jeans and tee-shirts are common, traditional male apparel, now confined to ceremonial uses, consists of loose, round-necked shirts and loose or tight trousers held up by a waistcloth, completed by a black velvet rimless cap, a palm-leaf conical sun hat, or a head cloth. Women's traditional wear includes blouses (loose for daily wear, form-fitting for formal occasions and *pangalay* dancing), brocaded shawls, and the patadyung. At least one simple piece of jewelry accompanies everyday wear.

¹²FOOD

Rice is the prestige food, served at feasts and to guests. For everyday fare, it is supplemented by maize (fresh, as a gruel, or mixed with rice) and cassava. The simplest meals add dried fish and sautéed vegetables to the starch (*kaunan*). A more elaborate side dish (*lamay*) is fish (fresh or dried) and vegetables stewed with onions, tomatoes, ginger, and lemon grass (*tiula sayul* and *liakbuan*). *Tiula itum* is a broth made from beef ribs spiced with a *pamapa* mixture (onions, lemon grass, garlic, chili, salt, turmeric, and burned coconut). Coconut-milk curry dishes (*kari-kari* and *kurma*) are also popular. Tausug dishes tend to be highly spiced and pungent. Tausug also make several types of sweet cakes from rice flour and eggs. Drunk with coffee (even by children), breakfast consists of anything from boiled or fried sweet potatoes or bananas to fried leftover rice and fish.

¹³EDUCATION

Many children spend seven or eight years learning to read the Arabic script and recite the Qur'an. A ceremony is held to celebrate the completion of this training, where the children in ornate costumes demonstrate their ability in front of guests.

According to the 2000 census, the literacy level in the Autonomous Region of Muslim Mindanao was 68.9%, very low by national standards. In Sulu, only a little over one in three (35%) had completed elementary school, barely one in six (15.38%) high school, and one in thirteen (7.88%) college or university.

¹⁴CULTURAL HERITAGE

Tausug music and dance share many similarities with Javanese, Malay, and Siamese forms. Musical instruments include the *kulintangan* (a series of 8–11 horizontal knobbed gongs), hanging gongs of various sizes, drums, the *gabbang* (a wooden xylophone), the *gitgit* (a two-stringed instrument with a coconut-shell soundbox and a long handle), the violin-like *biula*, a *sawnay* (a high-pitched reed instrument), and the Jew's harp.

Pangalay dance stresses hand movements (in some dances accentuated by *janggay*, metal claws, also worn in Siamese dance) and a reserved facial expression. *Langka* are dances incorporating graceful martial arts moves. Other dances depict work tasks such as catching catfish, or imitate animals, such as flying birds in the *linggisan*, originally sung to *Pagsangbay* ballads. Other dances aim at exorcising evil spirits.

¹⁵WORK

Unirrigated rice on permanent plowed fields is the main crop (only the poorest practice shifting cultivation in forested highlands). Farmers consult an expert on the Islamic calendar to decide when to plant. Tillers of neighboring fields cooperate in harvesting. Maize, millet, sorghum, sesame, cassava, yams, and peanuts are grown. Women tend gardens of tomatoes, onions, and eggplants. The gathering of wild mangos, durian, jackfruit, oranges, and lanzones contribute significantly to the diet. Manila hemp and coconuts are cultivated for cash. A recent shift from rice- to coconut-planting has made many Tausug dependent on unpredictable world market prices and has caused land scarcity (rice-farmers could lay claim to only as much land as they personally could work; coconut-farming, requiring less labor, can take up more land under a single owner). Cattle, water buffalo, chickens, geese, and ducks are kept.

Coastal people fish full-time or as a supplement to agriculture (Samal client groups also supply fish to Tausug). Among other methods, large rattan traps are put into the water and picked up several days later with a full catch. Although officially banned, reef-damaging dynamite has come into vogue as a means to an easy haul.

¹⁶SPORTS

See the article entitled **Filipinos**.

¹⁷ENTERTAINMENT AND RECREATION

See the article entitled **Filipinos**.

¹⁸FOLK ART, CRAFTS, AND HOBBIES

Obtaining both everyday and luxury articles through trade with such peoples as the Samal (mats) and Maranao (brassware), the Tausug are not known as craftspeople. The forging of swords and their decoration (including mother-of-pearl designs on scabbards) are important arts. Weaving is mostly of head cloths.

¹⁹SOCIAL PROBLEMS

See the article entitled **Filipinos**.

²⁰GENDER ISSUES

The sexes keep apart at social gatherings: women and young children stay inside the house while men and older boys sit on the porch. In work, men and women have a clear division of labor; for the former, plowing, fishing, harvesting trees, and tending livestock; for the latter, caring for chickens, gathering fruit, tending vegetable gardens, and preparing food.

In 2000, in Sulu the ratio between men and women was 96.16 men for every 100 women, though women were more numerous in the age group 15 to 39 (which may be partly the result of male insurgent casualties). Literacy levels in the Autonomous Region of Muslim Mindanao, low by national standards, were somewhat higher for men (69.8%) than for women (67.7%). However, in Sulu somewhat more of those completing high school were women than men, and the same was true of those attending or completing tertiary education. In contrast to other parts of the country such as Southern Tagalog, more overseas workers from the ARMM were female (56%) than male; the median age of those female overseas workers was 24 years (there are hiring quotas for Muslim domestic workers employed in Saudi Arabia and other Muslim Middle Eastern states).

[21] BIBLIOGRAPHY

Abdulla, Norma Abubakar. *The Food and Culture of the Tausug.* Manila: Centro Escolar University, 1989.

Fernando-Amilbangsa, Ligaya. *Pangalay: Traditional Dances and Related Folk Artistic Expressions.* Manila: Filipinas Foundation, 1983.

Gordon, Raymond G., Jr. (ed.). *Ethnologue: Languages of the World,* 15th ed. Dallas: Texas: SIL International, 2005. http://www.ethnologue.com (November 21, 2008).

Kiefer, Thomas K. *The Tausug: Violence and Law in a Philippine Moslem Society.* New York: Holt, Rinehart, and Winston, 1972.

LeBar, Frank M., ed. *Ethnic Groups of Insular Southeast Asia.* Vol. 2, *The Philippines and Formosa.* New Haven, CT: Human Relations Area Files Press, 1972.

National Statistics Office: Republic of the Philippines. "Autonomous Region in Muslim Mindanao: Nine Out of Ten Persons Were Muslims." http://www.census.gov.ph/data/pressrelease/2003/pr0301tx.html (November 21, 2008).

_____. "Sulu Had an Average Household Size of Six Persons." http://www.census.gov.ph/data/pressrelease/2002/pr02144tx.html (November 21, 2008).

—revised by A. J. Abalahin

T'BOLI

PRONUNCIATION: tuh-BOH-lee
ALTERNATE NAMES: Tagabili; TauSebu
LOCATION: Philippines
POPULATION: 100,000-120,000 (2000)
LANGUAGE: T'boli
RELIGION: Indigenous beliefs
RELATED ARTICLES: Vol. 3: Filipinos

[1] INTRODUCTION

The T'boli (Tagabili to lowlanders) are an animist ethnic group inhabiting highland areas in southwestern Mindanao, centering on Lake Sebu (*TauSebu* is another of the people's names). Their immediate neighbors are the Manobo and Bilaan, other animist upland peoples (with whom they are often in conflict). The T'boli rely on Muslim traders for contacts with the lowlands and maritime trade.

The Muslim Magindanao (who founded a powerful sultanate) raided for slaves among the T'boli; Muslims appear as villains in T'boli folklore. The resistance of Muslim lowlanders shielded the T'boli from Spanish political and cultural influence. This isolation ended with the imposition of American military control on Mindanao, completed in 1913. Since that time, Christian migrants from the Visayas and elsewhere have greatly increased the local population, pushing the T'boli from much of their traditional territory, a great part of which is also being appropriated by logging companies. Some protection and development aid has been offered by government institutions (such as the controversial PANAMIN) and Catholic missionaries. Adopting as a common designation "Lumad," the Cebuano term for "indigenous," the T'boli and other non-Islamized/non-Christianized ethnic groups in Mindanao are beginning to develop a collective identity and mobilize in their common interests.

[2] LOCATION AND HOMELAND

The T'boli inhabit a 1,940-sq-km (750-sq-mi) territory in southwestern Mindanao, where the coastal mountain range joins the Cotobato Cordillera at an elevation of 915 m or 3,000 ft above sea level. The region has three major lakes, Sebu, Lahit, and Siluton, which drain off through large waterfalls.

Precipitation levels are sufficient for agriculture, the driest period running from December to March.

In 2000, the total number of T'boli stood at 95,000 to 120,000. The T'boli in South Cotabato alone numbered nearly 72,000 (10.4% of the population); this was an increase over the 1978 estimate of over 60,000 T'boli. The province's largest ethnic group, the immigrant Hiligaynon/Ilongo from the Western Visayas, constituted 52.4% of the population.

[3] LANGUAGE

Like the other indigenous languages of Mindanao (such as Maguindanaon and Maranao), the T'boli language is a language of the Southern Philippine sub-branch of the Western Malayo-Polynesian branch of the Austronesian family.

It is taboo to call parents, grandparents, and parents-in-law by their name instead of the kin term; it is also improper to address uncles, aunts, or children-in-law by their name.

The T'boli have an epic, the *Todbulol*, which takes women performers 16 hours to sing. Todbulol is the name of the hero (also Samgulang or Salutan) who has many beautiful, fragrant women and a magical winged horse. In addition, the T'boli tell numerous comic folktales, such as "Bong Busaw ne Tahu Logi" ("The Big Aswang [intestine-sucking demon] and the Old Woman").

5 RELIGION

The T'boli believe in a seven-level upper world inhabited by many gods, foremost of whom are the couple, Kadaw La Sambad and Bulan La Magoaw. They had seven sons and seven daughters who formed couples. Of these, S'fedat and Bong Libun could not have children. Despairing of this, S'fedat asks his wife Bong Libun to kill him; his body becomes the earth and its vegetation. D'wata, another of Kadaw La Sambad and Bulan La Magoaw's offspring, obtains the earth for his children, having agreed to give Bong Libun one of his sons in marriage. This son, however, flees; Bong Libun's children by another husband become the gods of disease. Meanwhile, Hyu We and Sedek We, children of D'wata, create humans from clay, laying them on a banana plant (from this, humans get both their fertility and mortality).

In T'boli belief, a spirit or force lives in all objects, animate and inanimate. The T'boli make offerings (including bracelets) to the spirits of rivers and forests. Parents will place a sword by sleeping to children to protect them from evil spirits. Folktales often feature talking crabs, horses, or other animals. The souls of ancestors are part of everyday reality. The various gods mediate between D'wata and humanity. Of these the most important is L'mugot M'ngay, the god of all food plants. The gods can be vindictive and greedy as well as kind and merciful. They speak to humans through the song of the *l'muhën*, the bird of destiny. When people violate customary norms, they must appease the relevant god by placing a pig, chicken, or goat cooked without salt on an altar where the god resides. A sick person is brought to the altar, and the water that has previously been poured over swords is collected and poured over him or her. Other than this, the T'boli have few set rituals and no religious specialists other than the elders who in general lead the community, though there are *tao d'mangao*, people who can act as spirit mediums.

6 MAJOR HOLIDAYS

There are no holidays as such among the T'boli. Rites of passage ceremonies and ritual celebrations serve as T'boli holidays.

7 RITES OF PASSAGE

Parents arrange their children's marriages as early as just after birth. Taking a child's illness as a sign that he or she needs a partner, parents will ask to borrow a bracelet or other object belonging to a child with whom they wish to match their own; they give this to their sick child. Once their child recovers, the family visits the other child's family to propose marriage. The girl's parents visit the boy's for a feast during which they settle the bride-price (gongs and horses or water buffalo). The two children are made to lie down together on a mat and are covered with a blanket. The girl's parents stay the night. A period of mutual house-visits follows before the formal ceremony. As they are already considered married, the children may sleep together, and the boy helps the girl's family with chores. If one of

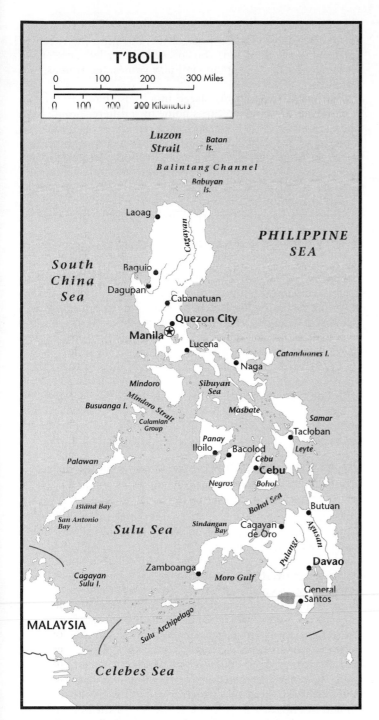

4 FOLKLORE

In the T'boli origin myth, the god D'wata warns humans of a coming deluge. La Bebe, La Lomi, T'mefeles, and La Kagef hide inside a huge bamboo. After the waters recede, the four split their way out of the bamboo. La Bebe and La Lomi married, becoming the ancestors of the Christian Filipinos. La Kagef and T'mfeles also join and go on to produce 10 sons and daughters. Of these, Bou and Umen are the ancestors of the T'boli. The other 8 form couples; their descendants are the other non-Christian peoples of Mindanao, both Muslim and non-Muslim.

the partners dies, a sibling takes his or her place. A child-marriage can be dissolved by returning the bride-price; a *datu* (an elder who is an expert on unwritten customary law) may have to oversee disputes over the exact amount to be handed back.

When the children reach puberty (12 to 13 years of age), a final marriage ceremony is held on a bright moonlit night with no rain (rain symbolizes tears). The bride and groom dress in their own houses amid the sound of music and dancing. An old person sprinkles the bride's face, hands, and feet with water; the same is done for the groom. As soon as the bride's preparations are finished, her family sends a messenger to the groom. Then, to the playing of gongs, the groom and his party proceed to the bride's house.

With a blanket over her head, the bride sits on a cushion in the center of the house. The bride's sister or another female relative escorts the groom into the house and takes off the blanket. Careful not to touch the bride, the groom sits down next to her. The old person who sprinkled her with water before the ceremony feeds the groom, just as the one who sprinkled the groom feeds the bride; the couple give rings, bracelets, and other gifts to these old people. After this, all the assembled kin and guests eat in silence, being careful not to drop anything or sneeze, both of which constitute bad omens. After eating, the bride's kin forms a team to sing poetry *(s'lingon)* in praise of the bride's qualities; the groom's kin do the same for the groom. This is an opportunity to haggle over the final bride-price. After the s'lingon comes the *klakak,* the all-night singing of the *Todbulol* epic; the story enthralls the audience, and some episodes move young women to cry. At daybreak, the groom's family hands over the bride-price. The groom then lives with the bride's family for a time determined by the withering of a branch taken from the forest. Then, another wedding ceremony is held at the groom's house, where the couple stays until they buy their own house.

Important families may choose to hold *mo'minum,* six feasts, alternating between the bride's side and the groom's. All T'boli have the right to attend the mo'minum. The bride's side builds a special house for the hundreds of guests, while the groom's side sets up a house-like structure *(tabule)* for the hanging of gifts (especially antique china plates). The bride's relatives hang gift blankets from a long bamboo frame in front of the guest house. The groom's relatives carry the tabule and pass it under the wall of blankets. The celebration includes mock combat dances depicting rivalry over women. The singing of the *Todbulol* epic occupies the whole night. The following morning, horsefights are held, involving as many as 15 pairs of horses (the horses represent the bride's and groom's respective kin); gambling over the fights is intense.

A person's soul is believed to leave the body during sleep and reenter it upon waking. Evil spirits or divine punishment cause death, the permanent separation of the soul from the body. After a death, family members do not cry for several hours, lest the deceased's spirit return. Small children who died are wrapped in a blanket or mat and hung up high in a tree. Everyone else is put into a boat-shaped coffin made by the *tau mo lungon,* a person specializing in making them. Paintings on the coffin reflect the deceased's specialty, for instance, stars and moon for a poet. The deceased's personal belongings are placed in the coffin. The coffin is left open to give all the bereaved a chance to stroke the body for protection against a similar fate. The coffin of an illustrious *datu* is suspended over

a fire; the grease that trickles out is made into a dipping sauce for sweet potatoes. Those who eat them acquire the excellent qualities of the deceased. The corpse is never left unattended in the house; those keeping vigil play games, tell riddles, and dance.

For burial, the coffin is placed in a house-like structure in a pit. The burial party returns home by a different route than they originally took to get to the burial site. Once home, to ward off evil spirits that may have followed them, they jump over two swords stuck in the ground to form an upright "X." Later, they bathe to purify themselves. All food of the deceased's is consumed, all marketable objects are sold, and the family abandons the house to build another.

The deceased's spirit returns if unhappy in the other world.

⁸INTERPERSONAL RELATIONS

The leaders of T'boli communities are *datu,* elders who are consulted on the unwritten customary law and who settle intertribal disputes. A datu cannot inherit the position but earns it through winning the esteem of others (for instance, through prowess in combat). The datu decides punishment for those who violate custom, imposing fines or requiring the transgressor to do service for the offended party.

T'boli value hospitality so much that they will even kill their last hen to feed a guest. When passing a house, a person calls out; the owners of the house will invite the person to eat. T'boli exchange help with farm work. Families enter friendship pacts, the breaking of which could cause the death of family members.

⁹LIVING CONDITIONS

For defense from enemies, such as neighboring Manobo groups, T'boli houses are built on hillcrests, with slash-and-burn fields covering the slopes below. Houses are only semipermanent because of the need to open new fields and to abandon a house upon the death of a resident. The *gunu bong* ("big house") resembles a roof on 2-m (6-ft) stilts. The low sloping roof of dried cogon grass overhangs the 1-m-high (3-ft high) bamboo side walls (some of which can open out to extend the floor). The interior is spacious (14 by 9 m or 45 by 30 ft) because of the needs of work (looms are long) and entertaining guests. The central space *(lowo)* is where guests sleep. On either side are the *blaba* where family members sit, work, and chat. On one end is the *desyung,* the place of honor, with a Muslim-style *k'labu* canopy at the center, decorated with piles of mats (a status symbol) and cushions. The sleeping quarters *(dofil)* flank the desyung, sometimes raised 1 m (3 ft) above the rest of the house. At the other end of the house is the *döl,* the vestibule floored not with bamboo but with heavy wooden planks. Here is the hearth, a utility area *(fato kohu)* along the wall, and a ladder going down to the ground. Horses are tethered under the house. For a toilet, a low bamboo perch is set up some distance from the house. T'boli bathe in rivers or lakes. Beside the gunu bong stands a granary, a similar structure though smaller.

Average family income in the SOCCSKARGEN (Southern Mindanao) region, of which the T'boli's South Cotabato province is a part, amounted to 114,000 pesos (us$2,235) in 2006, the third lowest in the country (above MIMAROPA [Mindoro-Masbate-Romblon-Palawan] and the Autonomous Region in Muslim Mindanao), cf. the national average of ₽173,000, the National Capital Region's ₽311,000, Southern Tagalog's

P198,000, and those of the neighboring Davao and Northern Mindanao regions, P135,000 and P142,000, respectively.

According to the 2000 census, 15.5% of households in South Cotabato had access to a community faucet, 14.5% to a faucet of their own, 19.4% to a shared deep well, 15.2% to a shallow well, and 14.7% to a household deep well, while 16.4% obtained their water from springs, lakes, rivers, or rain. More than half of households (52.5%) disposed of their garbage by burning it and 21.4% by dumping it into a household pit; only 8.2% had it picked up by a collection truck. 38.7% of houses were lit with kerosene lamps, 57.8% with electricity, and 2.2% with firewood. 68.3% possessed a radio, 37% a television, 25.5% a refrigerator, 10.8% a VCR, 6.4% a telephone or cell phone, 13.7% a washing machine, and 10.6% a motorized vehicle.

10 FAMILY LIFE

Marriages with blood relatives up to and including second cousins are taboo. Those who can afford it may take more than one wife. A household includes from six to eight people, a nuclear family plus other relatives. There are no villages. Houses are scattered, usually an hour's walk from each other, although related families may build houses closer to each other. Weddings and funerals bring together related households who otherwise function independently.

Tao matunga, women versed in abortion techniques, assist women who fear loss of face or the pain of childbirth or who have too many children already. During pregnancy, a woman observes many taboos, including avoiding cooking as this will give the child enormous eyes. Husbands assist midwives.

The orders of a husband or father must be obeyed (but wives have the right to argue their point of view). In the past, parents sold a gravely disrespectful child to non-kin; the parent's siblings or cousins, however, were obliged to buy the child back. The eldest male child inherits the father's rights.

Grounds for divorce are sterility, incompatibility, and infidelity (a husband may kill an unfaithful wife). If the wife is at fault, her family returns the bride-price; otherwise, it is divided between the families.

11 CLOTHING

At five to six years of age, girls begin to use cosmetics like older women, plucking and painting their eyebrows, using lipstick and face powder bought from non-T'boli lowlanders, and arranging their hair into the traditional coiffure with a comb stuck into it horizontally. Beautification for both sexes includes filing and blackening of teeth and tattooing. After death, the tattoos on the forearms and backs of the hands are believed to glow as guides to the dead. As an endurance game, men and boys put hot coals on their arms to make scars.

The T'boli use their traditional clothing for daily wear and not for tourist entertainment, as other groups do. Women wear a *luwek*, a tube sarong, and a long-sleeved, tight-fitting blouse. Blouses for manual labor are black or dark blue; otherwise, heavily embroidered blouses are worn. These may also be worn with lowlander skirts or, less commonly now, Magindanao *malong* (sarongs). The finest blouse is the *k'gal binsiwit*, which is covered with shell spangles.

A woman is not properly dressed without jewelry. These include earrings of shell or glass, necklaces, and beadwork chokers. The *köwöl* or *bëklaw* is a chain that runs from earlobe to earlobe under the chin. Women also wear massive chain-mail girdles, the finest of which include beadwork and have small hawk bells hanging along their lower edge.

Men wear *olew* (turbans) or conical bamboo hats. From a decorative brass belt hangs a sword that may be a long-bladed *sudeng* with a hardwood hilt; a *kafilan*, a large machete; or a 71-cm (28-in) *tok* with incised geometric designs. Narrow shields come to three points at either end. Women also carry knives for work and defense.

12 FOOD

Although an elaborate vocabulary for fruits and other edible plants indicates better nutrition in the past, T'boli meals today are simple, consisting of sweet potatoes, cassava, or maize eaten with vegetables and fish or lake snails. Because of poverty, rice, meat, and eggs are prepared only for feasts or guests.

T'boli prefer dishes that are spicy (using ginger, lemon grass, and onions) as well as pungent (chili, or *male*, is part of every meal). Obtained from Muslim traders, salt and sugar are precious. Wines from palm sap and sugarcane are also bought from lowland traders; the T'boli do not drink to excess. Betelnut-chewing is an integral part of meetings and gatherings.

13 EDUCATION

Parents train their children through cautionary tales. Because of the region's isolation, access to formal education remains limited, though less so than in the past.

According to the 2000 census, of the population over the age of five years in South Cotabato as a whole, 41.1% had completed elementary school, 29% high school, and 8.4% college or university. 2000 literacy levels in Southern Mindanao ranged from over 95% in Davao City to 80.4% in Sarangani province; the percentage for the T'boli's rural South Cotabato province was likely closer to Sarangani's.

14 CULTURAL HERITAGE

According to myth, the T'boli's ancestors fashioned musical instruments to imitate the sound of the souls of those who had perished in the deluge. These are the *d'wegey* (a vertically held bamboo violin), the *hagalong* (a spindle-shaped two-stringed guitar), and the *kubing* (Jew's harp). Other instruments are the *l'nongnong* (a deerskin-headed wooden drum), the *agong* (a large gong struck by the household head to ward off evil spirits), the *k'lintang* (a horizontal set of eight graduated gongs, played with two sticks), the *s'loli* (a 0.6-m or 2-ft bamboo flute), the *s'ludoy* (a bamboo zither), and the *feu* (a small horn). Leisure time is devoted to making music. The most popular song is "Ye Daddang," about a husband who hacks up his unfaithful wife.

15 WORK

Hunting with bow and spears used to be important, but now the T'boli rely more on slash-and-burn agriculture and fishing. The main crops are dry rice, maize, and sweet potatoes. Observation of the stars determines the planting schedule.

16 SPORTS

Children make music, dance, and play tag and *sungka* (a game using beads and a long tray with holes cut into it). Adults gamble on cards and cockfights.

[17] ENTERTAINMENT AND RECREATION

See the article entitled **Filipinos**.

[18] FOLK ART, CRAFTS, AND HOBBIES

Ginton, son of the god D'wata, was the first metalworker and ranks with the gods of life, death, mountains, and forests. His gifts to humanity include the *singkil* (brass anklets), *blonso* (brass bracelets), *hilöt* (women's chain-mail girdles), *t'sing* (rings), and *kafilan* and *tok* (swords). Men are the smiths, though women often operate the capstans. Smiths recycle old gongs and car parts for metal and use no set proportions in making alloys. Swords are made of *balatok,* tempered steel, and are strong enough for cutting down trees. The lost-wax process is employed to make anklets, buckles, betel boxes, hawk bells, and sword hilts.

The ideal maiden is proficient in weaving. A woman uses tie-dying to make designs from memory on handlooms, which are 0.5 m by 3.5 m (1.5 ft by 12 ft). The material is of hemp fiber, and the dyes come from particular leaves and roots. The complex, repetitive, geometric patterns include abstract representations of animals (crabs, birds, frogs, a python's markings). Frogs represent rain, birds the souls of the dead, and a *bangala* (a man in a house) a person's life force (also used as a tattoo design).

[19] SOCIAL PROBLEMS

Lowlanders with money and guns have been pushing the T'boli farther up into the hills. Because T'boli lack a notion of private property, lowlanders can easily stake legal claims to T'boli land.

[20] GENDER ISSUES

Among the T'boli, men slightly (50.7%) outnumbered women. In the South Cotabato population as a whole, more women had a college undergraduate education or higher and received academic degrees than men by a substantial margin; elementary school completion, a measure likely more relevant to the T'boli themselves, was lower for girls than for boys; 53.9% of elementary school graduates were male while only 51% of the population was male.

[21] BIBLIOGRAPHY

Casal, Gabriel S. *T'boli Art in Its Socio-cultural Context.* Makati, Metro Manila: Filipinas Foundation, 1978. Gordon, Raymond G., Jr. (ed.). *Ethnologue: Languages of the World,* 15th edition. Dallas: Texas: SIL International, http://www.ethnologue.com (November 16, 2008).

LeBar, Frank M., ed. *Ethnic Groups of Insular Southeast Asia.* Vol. 2, *The Philippines and Formosa.* New Haven, CT: Human Relations Area Files Press, 1972.

National Statistics Office. "South Cotabato: One Out of Two Persons a Hiligaynon/Ilongo." http://www.census.gov.ph/data/pressrelease/2002/pr0263tx.html (November 21, 2008).

_____. "Southern Mindanao: Ninety Percent of the Population Were Literates." http://www.census.gov.ph/data/pressrelease/2002/pr02188tx.html (November 16, 2008).

—revised by A. J. Abalahin

THAI

PRONUNCIATION: TIE
LOCATION: Thailand
POPULATION: 65 million
LANGUAGE: Thai
RELIGION: Buddhism; mix of Theravada Buddhism, Hinduism, and animism

[1] INTRODUCTION

The Thai in Thailand today are a Thai-speaking group who gradually moved from the north of ancient Southeast Asia or what is now southern China, into the area of the Mekong and Chao Phraya river basins, overcoming Mon and Khmer peoples and mixing with them. The Thai are related culturally and linguistically to other Tai peoples such as the Shan in Burma and the Lao of North and northeast Thailand and Laos. Other Tai-speaking peoples are found in India and Vietnam, but the largest group is in southern China. A Thai kingdom called Siam developed along the lower Chao Phraya River.

Thailand was never directly colonized by Western imperialism. The British and French agreed to leave the country as a buffer zone between the British colonial holdings in Burma and the French colonies in Indochina. However, Thailand suffered many disadvantages from the extraterritorial treaties forced on it by European powers and the United States. A bloodless coup led by Western-educated Thai elites put an end to the absolute monarchy in 1932. A constitutional monarchy and an early attempt at democracy were established, but conflicts within the new government and charges of communism against some political figures who appeared to be "left" led to a successful military coup. Since then, the Thai political scene has oscillated between periods of dictatorship and democracy. Student uprisings in 1973 and 1976 and pro-democracy demonstrations in 1992 tried to halt the power of the military, who have not hesitated to fire on unarmed demonstrators. The right wing used accusations of Communism as an effective tool against their political opponents, especially students and journalists, during the 1960s and 70s, declaring them a threat to the national trilogy—nation, religion, and king. Democracy in Thailand is not yet stable, and the government, both politicians and the bureaucracy, is very corrupt. Although King Phumipol, the present king, is greatly loved and revered and has proved to be very influential in many political crises, the future is difficult to predict. In the late 1990s and into the 2000s, governments were civilian and democratically elected, but in September 2006, the military once again stepped into politics, carrying out a bloodless coup against Prime Minister Thaksin Shinawatra while he was at the United Nations (UN) General Assembly. An interim prime minister was appointed a month later. By December 2007, the military junta had drafted a new constitution and held general elections, marking the beginning of the transition back to civilian rule. The People Power Party (PPP), seen as the reincarnation of Thaksin's Thai Rak Thai (Thais Love Thais) party, was victorious. In January 2008, an elected parliament convened, and Samak Sundaravej was sworn in as prime minister. Thaksin Shinawatra returned from exile.

Thailand has a minority Muslim population, concentrated in its southern ethnic Malay provinces. A decades-old separatist struggle in the region—which abated in the 1980s—emerged again in 2004. The violence has mostly targeted members of Thailand's majority Buddhist population.

²LOCATION AND HOMELAND

Situated in the middle of mainland Southeast Asia with a tropical monsoon climate, Thailand is approximately 514,000 sq km and shares boundaries with Burma (Myanmar), Laos, Cambodia, and Malaysia. There are three main seasons—the hot dry season, the rainy season, and a short, mild cool season. Thailand has four major regions, roughly divided by geographical and cultural characteristics: the central floodplain nurtured by the Chao Phraya River and its tributaries; the mountainous north whose largest forest areas are rapidly being destroyed; the dry northeast on the Khorat Plateau bordering the Mekong River to the east; and the long coastlines of the peninsula south bounded by the Andaman Sea and the Gulf of Thailand. The capital city of Bangkok, called Krungthep by the Thais and once called the "Venice of the East," is divided by the Chao Phraya River. Its location on a floodplain, together with the filling in of the numerous canals to make roads, brings annual flooding and the gradual sinking of the city. The south often suffers catastrophic floods and the northeast often receives insufficient rainfall, or if it does, its poor soils do not hold water. In general, Thailand is a land of abundance, producing and exporting various crops and many varieties of fruit. It suffers relatively few natural calamities.

The Thai population reached 65 million in 2007, with 0.66% annual growth. Around 11 million people are living in Bangkok, the only metropolis. More than 85% of the population speak dialects of Thai, but the Central Thai dialect is the only official language. Life expectancy is 72.5 years.

³LANGUAGE

Many dialects of Thai language are spoken all over the country, and Malay is used in the extreme south. However, because of the government's effort to suppress and marginalize minority ethnic identities, the Central Thai dialect, or Standard Thai, became the only official language taught in schools and used in all official affairs.

Thai is a tonal language and its alphabet is derived from Mon and Khmer scripts. The language has been influenced by Pali and Sanskrit from the Hindu-Buddhist civilization of India. Last names were just introduced to Thailand in the early 20th century, but calling a person by his or her last name is very unusual. Most Thais like to have elaborate names with Pali-Sanskrit roots and one-syllable nicknames, with or without meanings—for example, Suwanna (given name) Rattanasiri (last name) and Lek (nickname.)

"Sawaddee" is used for greeting regardless of time.

"Mai Pen Rai" means "it's O.K., never mind". Women add the polite word "Kha" and men the word "khrab" to phrases and sentences when speaking.

⁴FOLKLORE

The Thais had an indigenous creation myth before the arrival of Buddhism. Than is the Spirit of the Sky, the greatest spirit, who first created everything. In the past, there was nothing on earth, no humans, animals, plants, sun, or moon. Than

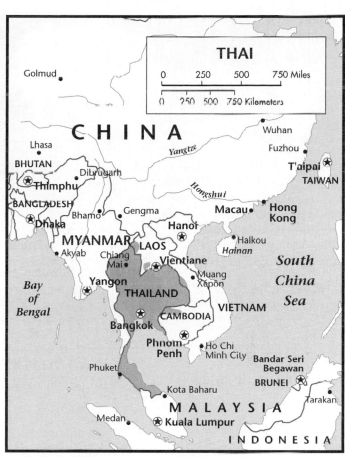

brought a bottle gourd to earth, then pierced it open with an iron. Five types of human beings came out and all were brothers and sisters. Than taught them the way of life and gave them tools to make a living.

Thai society is based on rice culture, so rice myths are very important to agricultural society and rituals. According to legend, the original rice seed was as huge as five times a man's fist. But because humans became more and more greedy, the rice seed became smaller and smaller. Mae Phosop is the Spirit of Rice. The old still teach the young, "Don't leave rice in your dish, Mae Phosop will feel sad."

Si Thanonchai is a very popular local trickster hero whose witty and cunning character many Thais identify with. The adventurous Si Thanonchai always cleverly survived life crises, engaged in deviltry without being caught, and teased and troubled others, including monks and kings, without being seriously punished. The popularity of the story reflects an expression of the suppressed feelings of common people under pressure from a moral and hierarchical society.

⁵RELIGION

Approximately 95% of Thais are Buddhists, and regional people adhere to their own religious traditions of Theravada Buddhism. The mix of Theravada Buddhism, Hinduism, and animism is the core of Thai beliefs, cosmology, and cultures. Hindu beliefs and animism are also seen in popular astrology and fortune-telling. Many southern Thais are Muslims. Most tribal people maintain animistic beliefs and some have con-

A Thai woman works in front of her house in Kalasin province, Thailand. (Charlotte McDonald-Gibson/AFP/Getty Images)

verted to Christianity. Many Chinese Thais follow Mahayana Buddhism, Confucianism, and ancestor worship.

Belief in spirit worship, or animism, is pervasive and intertwined with Buddhism. Spirits are believed to inhabit almost everything—houses, earth, all forms of life, etc.—and can help or harm humans. Large old trees are frequently tied with pieces of colorful cloth and worshipped by local people. Spirit houses are noticed everywhere: in houses, in neighborhood communities, and even in modern office buildings, shopping malls, and hotels.

Because Theravada Buddhism is a scripture-based religion and its teaching rests firmly on wisdom, not faith, it is very difficult for ordinary people to follow. Numerous cults have emerged, especially among the urban middle class, in the increasingly consumerist Thai society to meet the spiritual needs of the people. Some Buddhist sects and temples have become large, politically involved, and business-like organizations.

⁶MAJOR HOLIDAYS

Most holidays are of a religious or royal nature. *Songkran*, the Thai New Year, derived from Hindu astrology, is the longest official holiday of the year, April 13–15. Traditionally, great numbers of people visit their home villages to pay respects

to their parents and elderly relatives. Nowadays, Songkran is mainly celebrated by throwing water on each other like crazy. Some will add white clay or scents to the water for more lasting effect. It is clearly the messiest holiday in Thailand.

The Chinese New Year in mid-February is not an official holiday, but it is a big festival among those who have Chinese ancestors, which includes much of Bangkok and some cities in the South. Some Chinese Thai employers give days off and bonuses to their Thai employees. It is a time for reunion of family members, who gather to worship gods and ancestors. It is also the happiest period for many children, who collect gift money in red or pink envelopes distributed by their elder relatives.

These two grand holidays close down much of Bangkok and empty the roads. Other major holidays are the King's and Queen's birthdays, religious and official holidays.

⁷RITES OF PASSAGE

Thai individual rites, such as birth, ordination into the monkhood, or marriage, are basically associated with *khwan*, the body spirit or life soul. In the past, most young Thai men spent some period in the monkhood. Although the numbers have declined, many Thai men continue this highly valued tradition. Ordination is more common in rural areas and of longer duration than in the cities. At present, ordination ceremonies are occasions for social display and involve lavish expenditures in rural areas as well as among more affluent urban people.

Being a monk means transcending ordinary life and gaining higher status than most people, including one's parents. Women are not allowed to be ordained, but they play a crucial role in supporting Buddhist communities. Becoming a monk is believed to gain great merit, to the person himself and to his parents, while becoming a nun is often viewed as a way to escape life's problems.

⁸ INTERPERSONAL RELATIONS

Although they are a relaxed and fun-loving people, the Thais are relatively concerned about manners. The head is regarded as the most revered part of the body. Improper position or display of the feet is always considered impolite. Gesturing with the feet is terribly rude. Ideally, one should keep one's head lower than that of a superior, such as a teacher. Seniority and authority still play an important role in most social relations.

Greeting with kisses is virtually unknown. The most common way of greeting for all, with regard to seniority and authority, is the *wai* (made by putting the palms together at chest level and bowing). Almost all Thais remove their shoes before entering houses and monasteries. It is inappropriate for lovers to hug or kiss in public. However, holding hands or hugging among the same sex does not have sexual connotation.

In general, the Thais are not very time-conscious for ordinary human affairs but, surprisingly, a minute can't be missed when it comes to supernatural affairs or an auspicious time for ceremonies. Being late because of a traffic jam is the most popular all-occasion excuse in Bangkok. The pace of life in rural areas and villages is usually much slower.

⁹ LIVING CONDITIONS

About 68.5% of the Thai population lives in rural areas, but people are being affected by rapid urbanization. Running water, electricity, and health centers have been extended to most rural areas. Wood or thatch houses built on stilts clustered together in villages or strung out along the rivers or canals are common scenes in the upper country. People often sit under the houses during the heat of the day doing small chores. Some farm animals are also kept there.

Consumerism makes many low-income people struggle to possess basic middle-class property such as televisions, stereos, VCRs, DVDs, etc., while it makes the middle class desire even more luxury in life. For example, changing a Toyota to a BMW would be highly desired. A number of Thai middle- and upper-class people have made a worldwide reputation for being shop-aholics.

Housing and land are increasingly expensive. More working people live in apartments and condominiums. Expensive houses may exist on the same street with slum dwellings. Dining out or buying ready-made food to go is more common than cooking among people living in towns, because of the convenience and affordability. Food hygiene varies from excellent in some restaurants to poor for street peddlers. Many slums in Bangkok have poor housing facilities and living conditions.

Millions of people in Bangkok sacrifice several hours every day in traffic and suffer from extremely high air and noise pollution. Leaving home for workplaces or schools before 5:00 AM and getting home after 8:00 PM is routine for thousands

of people. Waterways attract more people who want to avoid massive road traffic jams. Buses and ferries are always dangerously overcrowded, and rush hours extend almost throughout the day. Elevated train and highway projects to alleviate traffic congestion are under construction.

As an unplanned city, Bangkok sometimes has brief periods of water cutoffs and power shortages. Construction work and repairs of water and sewage systems, roads, or buildings are seen everywhere. Uncollected garbage and accumulated sewage are also major problems in Bangkok and Chiang Mai, the second largest city.

¹⁰ FAMILY LIFE

In villages and rural areas, stem families can still be found, although nuclear families are the norm and urbanization and socio-economic change are breaking family bonds. Children are taught to respect and obey their elders, and elderly people in the family will usually be taken care of with gratitude by younger generations. As people's lives are getting more complicated, care for the elderly is becoming a problem.

Until getting married, most young people do not move out of the family, even if they are already working. Many continue to live with their parents after marriage. In the past, Thai men moved to their wife's household or settled in a new household near the wife's kinsmen and worked for their wife's family. The last daughter usually inherited her parents' property. Now that work and economics are the major concern, people do not necessarily follow the old norms. Having live-in maids for house chores and looking after young children was very common in middle-class households, but it is less and less common now that rural women can find alternative employment in factories.

Dogs and cats are normally kept outside the house and generally are not pampered pets.

¹¹ CLOTHING

The most common traditional lower garment worn by women in the fields or at the markets is *pha sin* or *pha thung*. Pha thung, literally "bag cloth," is a tube of material that looks like a bottomless bag, about one meter wide. The length is typically from the waist to the ankle. When worn, the extra width will be folded in front and the extra top will be tucked into a roll. One size fits all. *Phakhaoma*, a strip of cloth, usually in a checked design, is comfortably worn at knee length by men in villages, both at home and in public. Phakhaoma is a multipurpose favorite garment. It can be worn or just loosely tied around the waist or used as a towel, headwear, belt, sheet, etc.

Jeans, T-shirts, and shirts can be seen everywhere. Western boutique-style attire is preferred by middle- and upper-class people. Because of the hot and humid weather, most Thai wear sandals. Shorts are not generally seen in public, except on young children and as part of schoolboy uniforms.

¹² FOOD

For its great variety and tastiness, Thai cuisine is one of the best in the world—not to mention its delicious tropical fruits. Thai food is a delightful mix of native style and adaptations of Mon, Lao, Chinese, and Indian cooking. Regional foods have their own distinctive characteristics. Foreigners acquire a taste for the chilis and spices that are the salient characteristics of Thai cuisine. Authentic preparation and cooking of many dishes can be very complicated and time consuming.

Rice is usually the main course with side dishes. Glutinous or sticky rice is more identified with the north and northeast. Sticky rice and coconut milk are also used in many wonderful desserts. A spoon and fork are the most common utensils for general food, while the fingers are usually preferred for sticky rice. Chopsticks are also widely used when eating noodles and in Chinese restaurants. In urban areas in Thailand, one can always find something delicious and inexpensive to eat 24 hours a day. Three meals a day is the general idea, but the Thais love to eat whenever they feel like it and have perfected the art of snacking.

The category of *Yum* (mixed hot and sour salads) often fills a page or more in a restaurant's menu. *Yumwunsen,* vermicelli salad usually with cooked minced pork and a choice of chicken, shrimp, squid, or all, is very delicious. Mix boiled vermicelli with minced pork, chicken, shrimp, or squid together with sliced onion in a bowl already prepared with a sauce of fish sauce, lime juice, sugar, and fresh chilis. The real taste of Yum comes from the adding of fresh celery, mint, and basil leaves. Many other Yum follow the same rule and you can vary the ingredients with different meats or vegetables.

13 EDUCATION

Buddhist temples, *wat,* in the past used to be the sole source of most knowledge, both secular and religious. When Western-style education was introduced in the early 20th century, temples rapidly began to lose their educational role. The literacy rate in Thailand is high, about 92.6%, mainly the result of the government's effort to educate people for social and economic development. Education is free and compulsory through the sixth grade, and the government is considering extending it to grade nine.

Choosing good schools at all levels is highly competitive in Bangkok since it is an established value to enter well-known schools. The standards of schools vary and are much lower in rural areas. Even to enter grade one, many private schools set up their own exams for children who are often prepared by their enthusiastic and pushy parents. Other than exams, the most notorious way to enter many famous private schools comes from donations or money under the table.

Many high school students in cities get extra tutoring to prepare for the extremely competitive entrance examination for government universities. About 10% of examinees get seats, and the rest may go to private colleges and universities or make another effort the next year. There are also a number of vocational schools around the country. But because entrance exams are the sole criterion for admission and few rural residents' education is sufficient to pass, an attempt is being made to consider high school performance and other criteria.

At some universities, there is a pervasive practice of upper-classmen taking male college freshmen to prostitutes. Hazing of freshmen has become a popular tradition and is sometimes brutal. Salaries for government civil servants are low, so many university lecturers devote themselves to more well-paid outside jobs and may teach as a hobby. Studying abroad, especially in America, is very popular, and sometimes a fashion among the middle and upper classes.

14 CULTURAL HERITAGE

Masked drama, or *khon* of the royal court tradition, is the most exquisite, stylized, and spectacular of Thai performing arts. Only episodes from the Indian epic, the Ramayana, or *Ramakien* in Thai, are performed in the khon. The masks, dance, and musical accompaniment are considered sacred. However, some clowns and comic actions are added to attract the audience. The main masked characters are demons and monkeys, whereas principal human characters and celestial beings do not wear masks. Folk dances vary from region to region. Many folk performances involve dance, courting poetry, and witty improvised repartee. The shadow-puppet theater, *nang talung,* is a popular entertainment in the south.

There are many different types of Thai traditional music in the various regions. Originally, Thai music's main function was to accompany rituals, ceremonies, and performances. The most important ensemble is *pi phat,* made up of various melodic percussion instruments, Thai oboe, and drums. The gongs have long symbolized sacredness and power. Music is not allowed in Buddhist teaching but a traditional Thai funeral likes to have a boisterous pi phat ensemble to cheer the host and the guests. *Khaen,* a mouth-organ instrument made of tubes of bamboo has a history of more than 3,000 years. This wonderful instrument, which used to be played in the Thai court, later was belittled because of its Lao origins.

The oldest and greatest epic of Thai-Lao literature is a poem of about 20,000 lines called *Thao Hung Khun Cheung,* telling the story of a legendary hero whose deeds were told on both sides of the Mekong River. It was probably written during the 15th century. Thai folk literature is primarily based on oral tradition, so most early literature was written by monks and Thai court elites. Some Thai classics, modern novels, and short stories are also available in English translation.

15 WORK

Approximately 49% of the Thai labor force works in the agricultural sector, but this is changing rapidly. Thai society is in transition from an agricultural to an industrialized and service-oriented society. Because of Thai social structure and its cultural system, Thai women have always played an active role in the social, economic, and household spheres. Rice is the most important crop grown throughout the country, while rubber is extensively produced in the south. Thai farmers are still very poor and suffer from relatively low productivity and low prices. About 10% of the population lives in absolute poverty.

The growing economy, urbanization, and industrialization attract people to city jobs, although labor is cheap. Growing landlessness also pushes people to leave villages and crowd into Bangkok. People with technical skills like engineers and computer or technical specialists are in high demand, while social science and humanities graduates are more likely to be unemployed or underemployed unless they turn to business or service careers. As Thai tourism is booming, large numbers of local people are also involved in the tourist business and services. Bureaucratic occupations that used to be regarded as prestigious are increasingly turned down as the private sector offers much higher pay and a more promising future.

Poor children in urban areas may contribute to family income through various activities such as selling newspapers and small jasmine wreaths on the streets. Some survive by finding sanctuary in Buddhist temples, becoming temple boys who eat and sleep in temples and help with chores. Most middle-class youth, however, are not obliged to take up part-time jobs and are usually supported by their parents all the way through their education.

[16] SPORTS

Thai kick-boxing is a very popular spectator sport and is regularly televised. Traditionally, Thai boxing is usually accompanied by a small Thai ensemble to stimulate the performance. A well-trained boxer can attack his opponent with his feet, knees, or elbows or a combination of them both effectively and gracefully.

Badminton and soccer are widely enjoyed even in the most densely populated areas. Another popular game is called takraw, in which a woven rattan ball is kept in the air by using different parts of the body except the hands. There are two broad types of takraw: one like volleyball with a net, and one like basketball with a suspended hoop.

[17] ENTERTAINMENT AND RECREATION

Traditional entertainments are dying and popular culture is booming. Mohlam, folk singing in Lao, is perhaps the only surviving traditional art, with large numbers of northeastern and Lao fans coming through the commercial tape and music video companies. Televised Thai soap operas and other television programs are closely followed and enjoyed by most Thais of all ages and occupations, from peasants to prime ministers. Popular Thai singers have a huge following among teenagers and also adults. Most Thai movie stars and singers have exclusively local fame, but a few are known in other Asian countries.

Modern-style entertainment like movies, discos, nightclubs and karaoke bars attract the younger generation in the cities. Almost all Thai films are produced for domestic consumption and the standard is low. There are a few good films that capture some international interest. Hollywood action films always make a big hit and lots of money.

[18] FOLK ART, CRAFTS, AND HOBBIES

Exquisite Thai hand-woven silk and cotton, wood carvings, silverwork, basketry and lacquer ware are most well-known in the north, especially in Chiang Mai, the center for crafts. Beautiful hand-woven textiles and basketry can also be found in the northeast. Raising turtledoves and other birds especially for singing competitions, is a popular hobby in the south.

[19] SOCIAL PROBLEMS

Thailand is a rapidly developing nation, with continuously high economic growth. But the costs are enormous and Thailand is confronting numerous social crises. The increasing gap between the poor and the rich is very deep-rooted. Capitalist development and consumerism has led to the collapse of local communities, bringing about many related serious problems. Thailand is notorious for its sex industry and especially its child prostitutes, and has a high prevalence rate of HIV/AIDS. Deforestation and environmental destruction continue to be major problems. Bangkok is one of Asia's most heavily-congested cities, and is plagued by high levels of pollution and traffic.

[20] GENDER ISSUES

There are some 300,000 Buddhist monks in Thailand, but Thailand's Theravada tradition does not permit the full ordination of women. Thai women can take religious vows, shave their heads, and wear white, but they have a fairly servile position compared to monks. Women in rural areas have long maintained an important role in family, community, and work life. Thai women in Bangkok, like other Asian women in urban centers, are quite cosmopolitan. Many Thai women have found work in the growing service sector of the economy. As such, they are demanding new rights and opportunities.

Thailand has an ambivalent attitude toward homosexuality. There are significant numbers of gays, lesbians, and transgenders in Thailand. Thailand has three annual gay pride events in Bangkok, Pattaya, and Phuket. In 1995, the world's first all-gay village, Flower Town, was built in the central mountain area. Cross-dressing and openly gay men are stars in most popular television shows. There are several Bangkok gay neighborhoods and more than 60 gay bars and sex establishments. It is not uncommon to see gay men walking arm in arm in the street. Newspapers carry commitment ceremonies alongside traditional nuptials. However Thai lesbians face far more resistance than their male counterparts. The Thai patriarchal structure has a much more casual attitude toward male sex, regarding experimentation as one way of releasing pent-up energy, while seeing women who do the same as a direct challenge to male control. However tolerant of homosexuality Bangkok seems, there is little public discussion about homosexuality, and the presence of many gay bars has as much to do with maintaining the profits of the tourist industry as with the social acceptance of homosexuals. As such, one expert termed Thailand's ambivalent attitude toward homosexuality as a "curious mixture of tolerance, ignorance, and evasion."

[21] BIBLIOGRAPHY

Costa, LeeRay M. Male Bodies, Women's Souls: Personal Narratives of Thailand's Transgendered Youth. New York: Haworth Press, 2007.

Freedman, Amy L. Political Change and Consolidation: Democracy's Rocky Road in Thailand, Indonesia, South Korea, and Malaysia. New York: Palgrave Macmillan, 2006.

Keyes, Charles F. Thailand: Buddhist Kingdom as Modern Nation-State. Boulder, Co: Westview Press, 1987.

LePoer, Barbara Lietch, ed. Thailand: A Country Study. Washington, DC: Library of Congress, 1989.

McNair, Sylvia. Thailand: Enchantment of the World. Chicago: Children Press, 1987.

Pangsapa, Piya. Textures of Struggle: The Emergence of Resistance among Garment Workers in Thailand. Ithaca: ILR Press/Cornell University Press, 2007.

—revised by J. Hobby

TIBETANS

PRONUNCIATION: tuh-BET-uhns
ALTERNATE NAMES: Bod Qiang
LOCATION: China (Tibet Autonomous Region); India
POPULATION: 5.4 million
LANGUAGE: Tibetan and Chinese
RELIGION: Lamaism
RELATED ARTICLES: Vol. 3: China and Her National Minorities

¹INTRODUCTION

The middle reaches of the Yarlung Zanbo River in present-day Tibet were the cradle of the Tibetan people and of Tibetan civilization. According to literature written in ancient Tibetan language, the "Six Yak Tribes" of Tibet took shape in the mountainous southern area of present-day Tibet. Ancient Chinese books called them "Bod Qiang." In the 6th century, the chieftain of the Yarlung tribe became "Gambo" (king) by unifying the other tribes through political alliance and military force. The new kingdom established direct communications with the Chinese and other nationalities in northwest China. In the early half of the 7th century, Songtsen Gampo ruled the whole Tibetan area. He made Lhasa the capital of all Tibet. Under his leadership, Tibetan writing, calendar, laws, weights and measures, etc., were created and set up. He divided his territory into four provinces and put them under the command of Tubo, establishing a dynasty of his own based in part on the slave system. The Tang Dynasty (618–907) of China and the Kingdom of Nepal agreed to be related to Tibet by marriage. It was these matrimonial relations that led to the coming of Buddhism and of Chinese civilization into Tibet. Princess Wenchen, Songtsen Gampo's Chinese bride, came to Tibet in 641 and exerted a deep cultural influence on the Tibetans. Tibet continued to grow in power, and its armies conquered local chieftains in Yunnan and Qinghai and annexed different tribes in the northwest and southwest Tibetan provinces. On one occasion in 763, they made a breakthrough into Chang'an (present Xi'an). Because of its excessive military activities, internal strife, and slave uprisings, the Tibetan dynasty was weakened and ultimately collapsed in 877. Between the 10th and the 12th centuries, local governments were established in the former provinces, none being able to recreate the political unity. A large part of Tibet submitted to the authority of the Song Dynasty (960–1279). The Emperor of the Mongol Yuan Dynasty (1271–1368) put an end to the state of disunity, subordinating all of Tibet under the command of his central government. The administration of the Ming Dynasty (1368–1644) and the Qing Dynasty (1644–1911) continued the Yuan policy toward Tibet, appointing Tibetan officials in the northwest and southwest Tibetan areas. Furthermore, the Ming recognized the three "Dharma Kings" and "five nobilities" of Tibet. The central government of the Qing Dynasty (1644–1911) set up a special ministry to administer matters relating to the main non-Chinese nationalities of China, in particular Tibet, Mongolia, etc. It recognized formally the two Living Buddha of Gelupa (Yellow Sect of Tibetan Buddhism), the Dalai Lama (1693), and the Panchen Lama (1713); established a local government in Tibet; and appointed a resident minister to Tibet, who handled affairs jointly with the local government. This system continued under the Republic of China until 1949. As for the Tibetans dwelling outside Tibet, they were under the administration of provinces where they lived, namely Qinghai, Gansu, Sichuan, and Yunnan provinces. Following the liberation in 1949, the People's Republic of China established the Tibetan Autonomous Region, covering all of former Tibet. The political power of the former lamas was abolished and transferred to civilian government, whose Tibetan leaders are nominated by the central government in Beijing.

²LOCATION AND HOMELAND

The Tibetans are disseminated on the Qinghai-Tibetan Plateau at an average altitude of 4.8 km (3 mi) above sea level. The Qinghai-Tibetan Plateau extends to the Himalayas, the highest mountain range in the world, where both the Yellow River and the Yangtze River take their source. The plateau contains a great many lakes, including Qinghai Lake, the largest saltwater lake in China. The Tibetans are mainly concentrated in Tibet Autonomous Region, although considerable Tibetan populations are also found in Qinghai, Gansu, Sichuan, and Yunnan provinces. The overall Tibetan population in China was estimated at 5.4 million in 2000. There are about 100,000 Tibetans in India, and tens of thousands living in North America and Europe. The mountain barriers composed by the Himalaya, Gangdise, Kunlun, and Tanggula ranges isolated the Tibetan people for centuries. The Yarlung Zanpo River crosses the length of southern Tibet. Southwest Tibet is called the granary of Tibet because of its damp and mild climate, suitable for growing highland barley, wheat, rice, corn, broad beans, and rape (an herb of the mustard family). Northwest Tibet is rather barren, although some river valleys provide pastureland for nomadic cattle-raising. Tibet abounds with potential hydropower, solar, and geothermal energy.

³LANGUAGE

The Tibetan language belongs to the Sino-Tibetan family, Tibeto-Burman group, Tibetan branch. There are three dialects. Tibetan script, written from left to right, was developed in the beginning of the 7th century. The phonetic alphabet comprises 30 consonants and 4 vowels. Ancient Tibetan script is very important in Buddhist studies, for many sutras originally written in Sanskrit or other languages were lost, and only their Tibetan version is still extant. In urban Tibet, many Tibetans also speak Chinese.

⁴FOLKLORE

According to an important Tibetan myth, a divine monkey married an ogress in Yarlung Valley in remote antiquity. They gave birth to six children who multiplied and spread on the earth. However, their descendants lived on wild fruits of the forest and suffered from their hard life until the divine monkey gave them seven kinds of grain. Thereafter, they learned how to farm and speak. It is said that the first descendant who cultivated land in Tibet established himself near Zetang (Tsetang), where some Tibetans still pay homage to their ancestors every year.

Another myth concerns the youngest prince of Jiangsheng (a descendant of God). Having failed to ascend the divine throne, he escaped to a mountain and descended to the Yarlung Valley. A herdsman asked him where he was from. Unable to answer in the language of the herdsman, he could only

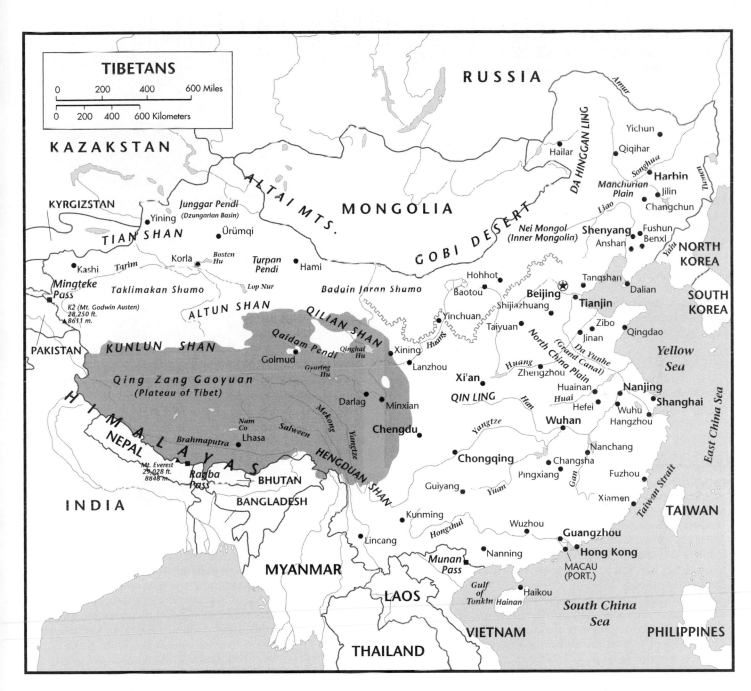

point to the mountain. Misunderstanding what he meant by his gestures, the herdsman thought he had descended from the heaven to be king. The boy was carried on the shoulders, given the title Nyentri Tsenpo (king on the shoulders), and became the first king of Tibet.

⁵RELIGION

Buddhism, originating in northern India, split into two principal schools, *Hinayana* (Small Vehicle) and *Mahayana* (Large Vehicle) after the death of its founder, Sakyamuni. Hinayana was stricter and favored monastic life; Mahayana was more liberal and addressed itself to society in general. It was Mahayana Buddhism that took root in Tibet and interacted with the native Tibetan shamanistic religion, called Bon, to form an original form of Buddhism, namely Lamaism. Many different

lamaist sects arose—the White, the Red, the Flowery, and so on. The Gelupa, or Yellow Sect, which was eventually to dominate Tibet and lead to the establishment of a kind of theocratic state closely allied to the secular nobility, was founded by Tsong Khapa (1357–1419).

Reincarnation was an established Buddhist doctrine. When a high-status lama died, it became the custom to seek his new incarnation (the divine child) among male children who had been born at about the same time. This solved the problem of succession, for monks could not marry and beget heirs.

In western Tibet and pastoral areas in Qinghai and Sichuan, the native religion of Bon still exists. This is a shamanistic faith that worships gods, spirits, and natural phenomena, practicing sacrificial offerings, divination, and shamanistic dance and trance.

⁶MAJOR HOLIDAYS

There are quite a few Tibetan festivals, all established according to the Tibetan calendar (a combination of solar and lunar calendars) and mostly related to their religious traditions. The Tibetan New Year takes place in the first week of January and lasts for three to five days. The Tibetans all dress in their finest clothes. Relatives and friends pay a New Year call to each other and pray for a good year in the monasteries. Tibetan operas are performed. Wearing masks, people disguise themselves as gods; they sing and dance to drive the ghosts away.

The Lantern Festival is held on January 15. Many huge sculptures of birds, animals, and personages made of multi-colored yak butter are paraded in the streets of Lhasa. Various festive lanterns, also made of yak butter, are hung on the trellises. People dance beneath the lanterns all night long.

April 15 marks the double anniversary of the enlightenment of Sakyamuni under the buddhi tree and the date of the Chinese Princess Wenchen's arrival in Tibet. The streets overflow with pilgrims while the monks participate in reciting scriptures and other religious services. People walk round the Potala Palace, go boating on the lake, and then pitch a tent for rest.

⁷RITES OF PASSAGE

Three or four days after a baby's birth, a tiny piece of *zamba* (the Tibetans' main food) is stuck to the infant's forehead. This is regarded as a purification rite. When the baby completes its first month of life, the parents paint the tip of his nose with soot from the bottom of a pan in order to divert the attention of malevolent ghosts. Accompanied by their relatives, the child's parents go the monastery and pray to the Buddha for protection. They may also call on a wealthy household and ask for their blessing so that the baby may be wealthy when it reaches adulthood.

Girls under 12 comb their hair into two braids; three braids when they are 13 or 14; five braids when they are 15 or 16. When a girl reaches 17, expert female hairdressers are invited to comb her hair into tens of braids to indicate that the girl has reached adulthood.

Tibetan funerary rituals are varied and complex, taking into account the social status of the deceased. "Sky burial" is a common practice closely related to Buddhism. The corpse is placed on a platform on a high, lonely place. Family members are not supposed to be present, while friends of the dead burn piles of pine tree branches nearby. Blood, meat, cheese, milk, butter, and zamba are cast over the branches. Heavy smoke rises up to the sky to draw vultures. A professional chops up the body and pounds the bones together with zamba. The remains are exposed to the vultures and leftovers are burned into ashes and scattered over the ground. "Water burial" is reserved for widows, widowers, and people of low economic condition; "fire burial" is for lamas; and "ground burial" for those who died of infectious diseases or who were executed as thugs and murderers. "Stupa burial" is a privilege of the Living Buddhas and other high-ranking lamas. The corpse is rubbed with salty water, dried, coated with spices, and then placed in a *stupa* made of gold, copper, wood, or cement, according to the rank of the dead.

⁸INTERPERSONAL RELATIONS

The Tibetans are courteous. When they meet, they stretch their arms, with palms upward, and bow to each other. To show re-

A Tibetan man in Upper Dharmsala, India. (Alison Wright/ National Geographic/Getty Images)

spect, one nods the head and sticks the tongue out, while the opposite side nods smilingly to return the salute. When people meet for the first time, one must present a *hada*; it is also important on festivals. A *hada* is a long and narrow band of silk (sometimes a cloth), white or light blue, which serves as a symbol of respect. During the presentation, one must hold it on both palms while bowing. If the social position of the two sides is similar, the receiver should take the hada also on both palms and return a hada of his own. If the hada is presented to a Living Buddha, it should be placed before his feet.

Nowadays, young boys and girls are free to meet each other socially. However, some of the restrictions of the past, due to the rigid stratification of society, still influence social behavior between young people of both sexes.

⁹LIVING CONDITIONS

Tibetans build their houses on high ground, facing south, close to water; walls are made by piling up stones or by rammed earth. Houses have two or three stories with a flat roof, many windows, and a courtyard. The living room and bedrooms are located on the second floor, while the first floor is for storage or livestock. Herdsmen dwell in large tents made of canvas or woven yak wool. The tents are easy to set up and to pack for the nomads' many displacements. The traditional means of transport is the yak or donkey, which may serve as mounts or as draught animals. The Tibetans also use a peculiar yak-skin canoe framed with wood and wrapped by a whole yak skin. The yak is an animal only living in the Qinghai Tibetan Plateau, tough and cold-resistant, it is a valuable means of transport. Because of the many rivers criss-crossing the high plateau, bridges are important. The Tibetans have devised different kinds of bridges, such as the chain bridge for walking, the steel cable bridge for sliding, and the simple wooden bridge.

¹⁰ FAMILY LIFE

The Tibetan family is male-centered. The man inherits and monopolizes the property. Women are subordinate to their husbands, even when he lives with the wife's parents. According to custom, women do have a name, but not a surname. The aristocrats put the house or manor name before their own name. In fact, the title is linked to the property of the hereditary manor and has nothing to do with blood ties. The names are different for different sexes. Most of them originate from Buddhist scriptures.

In the past there was a variety of family structures. Today, most families are monogamous. Polygamy appeared only among the rich and is rarely seen in the present. Polyandry (a woman taking more than one husband) also existed, due mainly to economic factors, such as the inheritance and monopoly of property; it was accepted as part of the social structure. Arranged marriage still exists both among nomads and peasants. Lamas and shamans are usually consulted. The Gelupa, or Yellow, sect of Lamaism strictly forbids its monks from marrying, but those belonging to other sects are allowed to have a wife. In these cases, the wedding follows religious rites and is held in the monastery.

¹¹ CLOTHING

Men living in urban areas wear a felt or fur-trimmed hat, a short vest with sleeves, trousers, and a robe with a long waistband. Those who dwell in rural areas wear a very long robe with very long sleeves and loose collars. They put it on from the top and tie it with a long waistband. The robe has a very large pocket inside above the waistband for storing money and personal articles. The herdsmen wear a worn-out sheep fur all year round and a pair of long trousers. They wear different styles of hats: bell-shaped, tube-shaped, single-peaked, or double-peaked. The hat is made of felt for the summer and of fur or padded cotton for the winter. Tibetan men all wear boots. Women usually wear a robe without sleeves, with a shirt inside and a beautifully designed apron around the waist. A long robe with sleeves is worn during the winter. Women living in pastoral areas wear a worn-out fur over a long skirt. Both sexes wear their hair long and combed into braids. Some males, however, cut their hair short, in particular the monks. In their monasteries, monks wear the *kasaya*, a patchwork outer vestment, usually in purplish-red.

¹² FOOD

In rural areas, Tibetans eat highland barley and wheat supplemented by corn and peas. They stir-fry barley and peas and grind them into flour. Then, they mix it with yak butter and tea. This is called zamba. During meals, they knead it with their fingers in a wooden bowl and make it into a ball before eating. They may alternate and cook zamba into a gruel with meat, wild herbs, and water. Their favorite drinks are buttered tea and wine made of barley. The herdsmen take beef, mutton, and milk products as their staple foods. Buttered tea is also their favorite. In rural areas they take five or six meals a day, while in pastoral areas they usually take three or four. Their tableware includes only a knife and a wooden bowl. The bowl is personal. They do not use chopsticks, but eat zamba and meat with their hands. As a rule, lamas recite scriptures before meals. Meat and fish are not taboo to lamas. However, Tibetan lamas in Gansu and Qinghai provinces prohibit fish, shrimp, chicken, and eggs.

¹³ EDUCATION

In the past, education was reserved for the monks in the monasteries. Since 1949, a complete educational system from primary school to university (including medical and technical schools) has been developed in Tibet and Qinghai. Furthermore, an increasing number of young Tibetans go to inland cities for various studies. However, the cultural and educational level of the Tibetans is still below average among the national minorities of China.

¹⁴ CULTURAL HERITAGE

Anyone who has seen a Tibetan dance must remember the peculiar movements of the dancers' limbs, which differ markedly from the dances of other nationalities. Their long sleeves enhance the charm of their postures. Their songs are high-pitched, mostly in the minor mode. Tibetan opera is usually performed in the street without any stage. Accompanied by a band, they sing while dancing. Most of the singers, if not all, are males. When the melody approaches a climax, the musicians of the band participate in the chorus, heightening the sense of participation. Tibetan literature is rich and diversified, including novels, poems, stories, fables, dramas, biographies, etc.; many works have been translated into other languages and published in other countries. Lamaism has influenced every aspect of Tibetan cultural life: writing, music, architecture, sculpture, etc.

¹⁵ WORK

Besides the sheep, goat, yak, horse, and mule, the herdsmen also raise a hybrid ox (from cattle and yak), which is the best draught animal of the plateau as well as a source of milk. The other fine varieties of livestock include the Hequ and Datong horses and the Gongbu mule.

¹⁶ SPORTS

Yak racing, comparable to horse racing, is one of the favorite sports of the Tibetans. On account of the yak's eccentric movements, it takes a highly trained expert to mount a racing yak. Tibetans also excel in mountain climbing.

¹⁷ ENTERTAINMENT AND RECREATION

The Tibetans have developed their own theater company, opera, music ensembles, ballet ensemble, broadcasting station, television station and film studio, thus ensuring the preservation and development of their cultural life. A great number of Tibetan newspapers, magazines, monographs, translated works, and literary masterpieces are published each year.

[18] FOLK ART, CRAFTS, AND HOBBIES

Popular culture has been deeply marked by Lamaism. The figures of Buddha in the monasteries, especially the clay sculptures of the Great Living Buddha (with his "real body" covered by clay) and a great variety of yak buttered figures are all highly skilled sculptures. Gold vessels and silverware include articles for daily use, such as flagons, spoons, chopsticks, bowls, plates, and dishes, as well as ornaments, such as bracelets, rings, and necklaces. *Tangka* is a kind of Tibetan painting for wall hanging, always depicting Buddhist themes.

[19] SOCIAL PROBLEMS

Lack of formal education is one of the most important social problems facing Tibet today; the problem is due, in part, to the scattering of a thin population over vast expanses of land, making communication and concentration very difficult. However, without new advances in education, there can hardly be any further prosperity and development of the Tibetan nationality.

[20] GENDER ISSUES

The Chinese constitution states that women have equal rights with men in all areas of life, and most legislation is gender neutral. However, there are continued reports of discrimination, sexual harassment, wage discrepancies, and other gender related problems. The gap in educational level between women and men is narrowing with women making up 47.1% of college students in 2005, but only 32.6% of doctoral students.

China has strict family planning laws. It is illegal for women to marry before 20 years of age (22 for men), and it is illegal for single women to give birth. The Family Planning Bureau can require women to take periodic pregnancy tests and enforce laws that often leave women with no real options other than abortion or sterilization. Though minority populations were previously exempt from family planning regulations, policy has changed in recent years to limit minority population growth. Today, urban minority couples may have two children while rural couples may have three or four.

Prostitution and the sex trade is a significant problem in China involving between 1.7 and 5 million women. It involved organized crime, businessmen, the police, and government workers, so prosecution against prostitution has limited success. In 2002, the nation removed homosexuality from its official list of mental illnesses, and though it is still a taboo topic, homosexuality is increasingly accepted, especially in large, international cities.

[21] BIBLIOGRAPHY

Chiao, Chien, Nicholas Tapp, and Kam-yin Ho, ed. "Special Issue on Ethnic Groups in China." *New Asia Bulletin* no 8 (1989).

Dreyer, June Teufel. *China's Forty Millions.* Cambridge: Harvard University Press, 1976.

Eberhard, Wolfram. *China's Minorities: Yesterday and Today.* Belmont: Wadsworth Publishing Company, 1982.

Goldstein, Melvyn C. *A History of Modern Tibet, 1913–1951: The Demise of the Lamaist State.* Berkeley: University of California Press, 1989.

Gustafsson, Bjorn A., Shi, Li, and Sicular, Terry, eds. *Inequality and Public Policy in China.* New York: Cambridge University Press, 2008.

Heberer, Thomas. *China and Its National Minorities: Autonomy or Assimilation?* Armonk, NY: M. E. Sharpe, 1989.

Lebar, Frank, et al. *Ethnic Groups of Mainland Southeast Asia.* New Haven: Human Relations Area Files Press, 1964.

Ma Yin, ed. *China's Minority Nationalities.* Beijing: Foreign Languages Press, 1989.

Perrin, Jacques. "Les Sociétés tibétaines." In *Ethnologie régionale II* (Encyclopédie de la Pléiade). Ed. Jacques Lemoine. Paris: Gallimard, 1978.

Ramsey, S. Robert. *The Languages of China.* Princeton: Princeton University Press, 1987.

Shin, Leo Kwok-yueh. *The Making of the Chinese State: Ethnicity and Expansion on the Ming Borderlands.* New York: Cambridge University Press, 2006.

Stein, R. A. *Tibetan Civilization.* Trans. by J. E. Stapleton Driver. Stanford: Stanford University Press, 1972.

Wiens, Harold J. *Han Chinese Expansion in South China.* New Haven: The Shoestring Press, 1967.

—by C. Le Blanc

TIMORESE

LOCATION: East Timor, West Timor (Indonesia)
POPULATION: 2 million
LANGUAGE: Tetum, Portuguese, Indonesian.
RELIGION: Roman Catholic

¹INTRODUCTION

The Timorese people live on the island of Timor in Southeast Asia and also on some nearby islands. Because of their colonial history—the Portuguese occupying the eastern half of the island and several enclaves in the west and the Dutch the remainder—important differences have emerged over time. During the Indonesian Occupation from 1975 until 1999 both West Timor and East Timor were provinces of the Republic of Indonesia, and there were more contacts between the two. However, since 1999 and because of the events that surrounded the move to independence, there has been less contact over the troubled border, with about 1,115,000 living in East Timor, and 1,800,000 in West Timor.

Although there have been archaeological remains dating back to 11,000 BC, the Timorese people are believed to be Austronesians, who arrived on Timor about 5,000 years ago and brought with them new skills in pottery and a tradition of agriculture and domesticated animals. They began to work bronze, and iron and were some of the peoples least influenced, culturally, by Indian and Javanese traders. By about 1,000 BC, the Atoni people arrived. They call themselves the *Atoni Pah Meto* ("the people of the dry land") and they still live in West Timor, with more groups arriving over the next 2,000 years.

Because of the spices grown on Timor and the presence of sandalwood, Chinese merchants started visiting Timor from the 12th century and some of them stayed, with some of these intermarrying with the local Timorese population. The later arrival of the Portuguese and Dutch traders led to some Timorese marrying with Europeans, and this was the origin of the *Topasse*, or Eurasian population, which by 1600 was said to number about 12,000. Another group that also arrived during this time was the Rotinese from the nearby island of Roti, and these people are now culturally similar to the Timorese, although they speak a different language.

From 1566 the Portuguese started to establish bases on East Timor, and they brought missionaries leading to the early conversion of some Timorese to Roman Catholicism. For the most part the Portuguese preferred to operate through Chinese or Topasse middlemen. In the early 17th century the Dutch started taking over parts of West Timor, establishing a fort at Kupang and trading in a similar manner to the Portuguese. It was not until 1913 that the official borders for the Dutch and Portuguese sections of the island were drawn up, leaving the Portuguese with the east, the Oecussi enclave in the northwest, and the Dutch with the rest, which became an integral part of the Netherlands East Indies. This line divided many Timorese tribes in central Timor, but as the border was largely unmarked, people crossed it regularly, often without knowing it. The Timorese attempt to eject the Portuguese in 1887 and again in 1912 had failed, and there were no more major uprisings.

The emergence of Timorese nationalism came in 1933 when some Protestants from West Timor, while studying at the Bandung Institute of Technology in Java, established *De Timorsch Jongeren* ("Timorese Youth"). It led to the formation of the *Perserikatan Kebangsaaan Timor* ("Timor Nationalist Union") four years later. For the Timorese in East Timor, they lacked any central organization, and most of the radicals were exiles from Portugal, who yearned to return to mainland Portugal. However, they did have an important role many years later in educating the Timorese elite.

During World War II the Japanese attacked Dutch West Timor and when the Dutch and Australian forces took East Timor, the Japanese invaded the eastern part of the island. During the Japanese Occupation, the relatively benevolent rule of both the Dutch and Portuguese ended, and the Timorese were persecuted by the Japanese because of their actual and supposed support for the Allies. It is thought that about 70,000 Timorese died under the Japanese, from fighting, retribution, and starvation.

After the war, fighting started between the nationalists and the Dutch in the Netherlands East Indies. It saw the Nationalists under Sukarno triumphant, and his assimilation policies started to take hold throughout Indonesia, as the country had become, with many Timorese in West Timor starting to go to primary and secondary schools and being taught in Bahasa, the new national language of Indonesia. With the rise to power of Suharto in 1965 the assimilation policy and that of *transmigrasi* ("Transmigration"), with migrants from Java being moved to West Timor, saw most west Timorese losing most of their sense of separate identity.

By contrast in East Timor, Portuguese rule had led to a "benign neglect" of the eastern half of the island, with most Timorese customs continuing as they had done for centuries, with little in the way of interference in village life. However, the overthrow of the military government in Portugal in 1974 led to the formation of Timorese political parties, notably the pro-Western UDT (Timor Democratic Union) and the left-wing Fretilin. The latter won the civil war that resulted and took control of East Timor. The extremely anti-Communist government in Indonesia was keen to prevent this and invaded in December 1975. In the following year East Timor became an integral part of Indonesia.

For the Timorese, the standard of living vastly improved under the Indonesians, with schools, hospitals, clinics, and roads. However, they resented the Indonesians and especially the Indonesian migrants who arrived. This did more than anything else to ensure the sense of Timorese identity remained strong. A resistance group run by Fretilin operated from then until 1999 when Indonesia agreed to hold a referendum on independence, and the Timorese voted to reject the autonomy offer by the Indonesian government and move to full independence. Pro-Indonesian militia then wrecked much of the country, destroying large amounts of the infrastructure built by the Indonesians, and many of the Timorese fled. An international force led by Australia then occupied East Timor, and in 2002, East Timor became an independent country and a member of the United Nations. It is believed that up to 200,000 East Timorese died as a result of the Indonesian occupation from 1975 until 1999.

The Timorese people have been heavily politicized by the occupation, and also by political infighting and actual fight-

East Timorese fishermen prepare to catch fish in Dili, East Timor. (Bay Ismoyo/AFP/Getty Images)

ing that followed. This has led to instability in the capital, but many Timorese have now slowly rebuilt their lives.

²LOCATION AND HOMELAND

Most of the Timorese people live on the island of Timor, either on the eastern half and the Oecussi enclave on the northern coast of West Timor or in the Indonesian province of Timur Tengah (West Timor). Because of the links with Indonesia, historical and geographical, there are many Timorese living in Indonesia; because of the historical ties, there are also some in Portugal. The fighting since 1974 has led to large numbers of Timorese refugees escaping to Australia; they live largely in the cities of Darwin, Sydney, and Melbourne.

Within East Timor itself, about 5% of the population (50,800) lives in the capital Dili, with smaller numbers living in the major towns of Liquica, Manatuto, Suai, Baucau, and Viqueque. The vast majority of the Timorese population, both in East Timor and also West Timor, live in villages scattered around the countryside. Many of these are extremely isolated—indeed many Timorese ensured this remained so, to protect their communities from the Japanese and later the Indonesians and the pro-Indonesian militia.

Of the various groups living in East Timor, the Atoni are the most heavily researched. They descend from settlers who arrived in West Timor, and most of them still live in the west of the island, numbering about 300,000 in 1960 and about 600,000 today. The Helong people, related to the Atoni, live in and around the city of Kupang and in the coastal region in the very west of West Timor, as well as on the island of Semau.

In central Timor most of the people are from Bunak (or Bunaq), as are the Mambai who generally occupy the mountains and valleys. The dominant group in East Timor is the Tetum, whose language is now the official language of the country.

They themselves are divided into the Eastern Tetum and the Western Tetum. Mention should also be made of the Cairui and the Waimaka (Uai Ma'a), who live in remote parts of East Timor and whose lifestyles have been least affected by recent history. There are also the Fattaluku, who live around Lorehe. The Rotinese and the Ndaonese, who came from nearby islands in the early modern period, are now also often regarded as Timorese.

³LANGUAGE

For historical reasons, the Timorese in West Timor speakIndonesian, although some older people still speak Dutch. In East Timor, the official language is Tetum, with the second language being Portuguese; however, most young people are interested in speaking English. Those who went to school or who were involved in public life between 1975 and 1999 also speak Indonesian. In addition, there are a large number of other languages spoken by the Timorese, such as Rotinese and Sama Bajau.

⁴FOLKLORE

The folklore of the Timorese varies considerably, depending on the tribe and the part of the island they come from. Traditionally, each tribe had its element of folklore, with the Atoni often talking of their arrival on the island in pre-historic times and the Rotinese talking of their arrival in the early modern period. There are also traditional village stories about rich people, poor people, buffalos, and other elements of morality tales, which are the same all around the world. Some elements of Chinese folklore have also been accommodated in Timorese stories.

In East Timor much of the folklore is concerned with resistance and resistance movements. These include the fighting against the Portuguese in 1887 and again in 1912, during the

Japanese Occupation 1942–1945, the civil war in 1974–1975, and then the fighting against the Indonesians during their occupation from 1975 until 1999.

⁵RELIGION

The vast majority of East Timorese are Roman Catholic, with official figures being 98% of the population (in contrast to about a quarter when Portuguese rule ended in 1975). This growth of Roman Catholicism is said to be attributed to the church's role in working against the Indonesian occupation. Some 1% are Protestant and the remaining 1% are Muslim. In West Timor, because of the Dutch influence, only some 56% are Roman Catholic, but 35% are Protestant, and most of the remainder are Muslim. Most of the small Chinese and Sino-Timorese population of East Timor, who followed Taoism and Buddhism, fled in 1974 and have not returned.

⁶MAJOR HOLIDAYS

The major holidays in East Timor are New Years' Day (January 1), Good Friday, Independence Day (from Indonesia, May 20), the Feast of the Assumption, Consultation Day (August 30), Liberation Day (September 20), All Saints' Day, Santa Cruz Day (November 12), Independence Day (from Portugal, November 28), the Feast of the Immaculate Conception, and Christmas Day (December 25).

In West Timor the major holidays are New Year's Day (January 1), *Lebaran* (the end of Ramadan), Waicak Day (Buddha's birthday, the eighth day of the fourth lunar month), *Muharram* (the start of the Islamic Year), *Maulad Nabi Muhammad* (the birthday of the Prophet Muhammad), Independence Day (August 17), and *Isra Miraj Nabi Muhammad*/Christmas Day (the ascension of the Prophet Muhammad, December 25).

⁷RITES OF PASSAGE

In traditional village life for the Timorese, there were rites of passage ceremonies associated with birth, puberty, marriage, and death. These generally involved ceremonies in the village, with the actual ceremony varying depending on the custom of the tribe. The Atoni had a hereditary nobility, but this has long since died out, although the series of village headmen continues. The Ema people also had a complicated system of social organizations that controlled the ceremonies, most of which worked through community and lineage house structures. The Rotinese had a system of ritual initiation of the youths going through puberty and their method of burial involved people from the village and nearby villages coming for a ceremony that lasted at least three days. Other tribes have similar ceremonies, with one of the major ones for the Eastern Tetum people being "washing the buffalo's leg."

⁸INTERPERSONAL RELATIONS

All village societies of the Timorese have reverence for the elderly, with village elders being respected by all and being used to teach the young in the tribal customs and folklore. In a similar manner, children are brought up to respect their parents and are taught strict rules of behavior, which they also exhibit in schools. Greetings reflect hierarchical terms but are often based on whether a person is elderly, not just whether they are a village headman or not.

Because of the fighting in East Timor for much of the period since 1975, some of this traditional way of life has broken down, and in 1999—and indeed before—the Indonesians were able to recruit young men to serve in their militia where they were involved in harassing locals, either as a part of the government policy, or because they felt they had the power so to do. With so many East Timorese having missed formal schooling from 1999 until 2001, many lack the discipline that their older (and younger) siblings have had.

⁹LIVING CONDITIONS

In villages, most people live in houses raised on stilts and with high thatched roofs, animals being kept under the house at night. These houses were made from wood, and, traditionally, people would build new houses as they moved around the jungle, clearing a new area every few years. However, most people do not move around as much as they have done in the past.

In towns and cities, the best houses resemble small Portuguese or Dutch villas and a very few resemble large ones. The walls are often white-washed rendered brick. Smaller houses in towns and cities are made largely or entirely from wood. In Kupang and other urban areas in West Timor, there are modern prefabricated apartment blocks similar to those elsewhere in Indonesia.

¹⁰FAMILY LIFE

Family life in Timorese society revolves around an extended family. Generally a couple would live with their children and the father's—and possibly sometimes the mother's—elderly relatives, such as their parents and occasionally uncles and aunts. Children might stay in the family house after marriage—sometimes leaving after they start having their own children. Much of this depends on the circumstances of the people concerned, and it is not uncommon for a man in a secure job to have as many as a dozen other people living in his house, surviving off his salary.

¹¹CLOTHING

In East Timor traditional clothing involved wearing, for men, a large cloth similar to the sarong and a large ritual headdress made from feathers, people being ritually bare-chested. Women wear a brightly colored dress. During the Portuguese and Dutch colonial periods men in administrative positions in towns would dress in khaki or white (Dutch) or green (Portuguese), with a bush shirt and shorts. Nowadays, in villages, most men wear a t-shirt or polo shirt and a sarong, with boys often wearing only a pair of shorts. Women and girls wear a blouse and a skirt, often made from bright colors.

¹²FOOD

While wealthier Timorese in towns have access to many types of food, most of the cuisine in the countryside and among poor Timorese is similar to that in Indonesia and Malaysia, with chicken, pork, or beef, and noodles or rice, often with an egg, with root crops, such as cassava and yams, supplemented with fruits, such as pineapples and bananas. Maize was often a part of the diet, and now potatoes are grown in Timor. For drinks, those made from sugar cane are popular, with fruit juices and also fizzy drinks consumed by many people. Much coffee is grown in Timor, but it is largely for export, so few people drink it although drinking of tea is common.

Some tribal groups located near the sea rely heavily on fish for their diet. Among some groups, such as the Bunak, there are a large number of ritual dishes that are prepared only under special conditions. In Ema society there are differences between food that is boiled, which represent main meals, and food that is either grilled or eaten raw, which are regarded as foods for snacks.

13 EDUCATION

During the period of Dutch and Portuguese colonial rule, there was little in the way of formal schooling in the country, with most children being taught at home. Indeed there was only one high school in East Timor when the Indonesians invaded in 1975. Under the Indonesian occupation, large numbers of schools were built throughout East Timor, and, for the first time, schooling was free and compulsory for all Timorese, many of whom were able to go to universities in the rest of Indonesia. However, in 1999, after the East Timorese voted for independence, militia groups destroyed most of the schools, and it took several years before many of these could be rebuilt.

14 CULTURAL HERITAGE

The Timorese, through the wars in the 20th century, have managed to retain much of their cultural heritage. This has been especially important in East Timor where the new government has done much to record and preserve the culture of the Timorese people. This has resulted in work by anthropologists and books and government publications being made available in Tetum, now the official language of the country.

15 WORK

The vast majority of the Timorese are involved in agriculture, living in village societies, with 8.2% of the land being arable and over half of this under permanent cultivation. There are also many people who work on coffee plantations and as laborers on large farms. A very small number have office or administrative jobs. There is high unemployment, estimated at 20% in urban areas, and this has led to much discontent among the youth.

16 SPORTS

Many village games were played in pre-colonial time, and some of these, such as cock-fighting, continued during the period of Dutch and Portuguese colonial rule. However, by the mid-20th century, the most played game on the island was soccer, with children and young men playing it throughout the island. Both the first president of East Timor, Xanana Gusmao, and his successor, José Ramos Horta, were soccer players in their youth, with the former briefly being known as the "goalkeeper" because of the position he played in the game. The presence of Australian soldiers in East Timor since independence has led to attempts to introduce games, such as Australian Rules Football. Other games that are played in East Timor include basketball, volleyball, and badminton. In 2000, for the summer Olympics held in Sydney, a small team from East Timor competed, its first ever involvement in an international sporting event.

17 ENTERTAINMENT AND RECREATION

Because much of the country does not have electricity, the local television station, TV Timor-Leste, founded in 2000 and broadcasting in Tetum and Portuguese, has only a small following. Radio Timor Leste broadcasts are listened to by about 90% of the population, with most villagers having access to transistor radios; this station also broadcasts in Tetum, Portuguese, and English. Three other radio stations also are operating in the country. The highly-politicized nature of the Timorese people has resulted in many newspapers being available, but most of these are only read in Dili and major towns.

Most village entertainment is involved in watching (or taking part in) small sporting activities or cockfighting, as well as hunting and reading.

18 FOLK ART, CRAFTS, AND HOBBIES

Many Timorese have been involved in woodwork and the making of models, especially of human or animal spirits. Some of these are now manufactured for sale to tourists. The making of pottery takes place in all villages, as does weaving and the making of baskets. For children, the large aid effort from Australia and elsewhere has resulted in many plastic toys being distributed throughout the country, augmenting kites, spinning tops, and other toys that have been played for hundreds of years.

19 SOCIAL PROBLEMS

The Timorese are subject to many social problems; this has largely been the effect of history and politics. The Indonesian occupation alienated large numbers of youths, and although the literacy rates improved considerably, many Timorese resented those who managed to get government scholarships or take up places at Indonesian universities. Others were involved in the resistance struggle or were part of the small group of discontented youth hired by the Indonesians to form their militia groups before the 1999 referendum on independence.

The social dislocation of the Indonesian invasion, occupation, and the moves to independence in 1999 led to alienation of many people, and from 1999 until 2001, many children were unable to attend formal schools because the buildings had been destroyed by the militia. Since independence in 2002 there has also been rising unemployment, which by 2008 was estimated at 20% in Dili. There has been anger at the overseas-educated Timorese, some of whom have taken up senior administrative positions and office jobs. Some Timorese want to achieve reconciliation and a lasting peace with Indonesia, and others want to punish those who collaborated with the Indonesians during their brutal occupation of East Timor.

20 GENDER ISSUES

Although most of the tribal societies of the Timorese are patrilineal, following the father, women dominate in religious ceremonies among the Tetum people. In Bunak villages, women have certain specific roles in the agricultural process and in the preparation of food, not just for eating but especially for ritual. A number of Timorese women now have important political roles in East Timor and their position in society has been helped by the work of the wife of Xanana Gusmao, Kirsty Sword. Although she is Australian by birth, she has done much to improve the legal rights of women and promote women's roles in decision making.

21 BIBLIOGRAPHY

Dunn, James. *Timor: A People Betrayed*. Sydney: Australian Broadcasting Corporation, 2001.

Fox, James J., ed. *The Flow of Life: Essays on Eastern Indonesia*. Cambridge, MA: Harvard University Press, 1980.

Gunn, Geoffrey C. *Timor Loro Sae: 500 Years*. Macau: Livros do Oriente, 1999.

Hicks, David. "Timor-Roti." *Ethnic Groups of Insular Southeast Asia*. Frank M. LeBar, ed. New Haven, CT: Human Relations Area Files Press, 1972.

Nordholt, Herman Gerrit Schulte. *The Political System of the Atoni of Timor*. The Hague: Martinus Nijhoff, 1971.

Vondra, J. Gert. *Timor Journey*. Melbourne: Lansdowne, 1968.

—by J Corfield

TODAS

PRONUNCIATION: TOH-duhs
LOCATION: India (primarily Tamil Nadu state)
POPULATION: 1,412 (2000 estimate)
LANGUAGE: Toda
RELIGION: Centered on the sanctity of the buffalo
RELATED ARTICLES: Vol. 3: People of India

¹INTRODUCTION

The Todas are a pastoral tribe inhabiting the higher elevations of the Nilgiri Hills of southern India. It is unlikely that the ancestral homeland of the Todas will ever be identified conclusively, though linguistic evidence suggests a South Indian origin for the group. Other evidence, albeit circumstantial, points to Toda migrations from the Malabar coast region lying to the west of the Nilgiris.

The date of these migrations is uncertain, but most likely it occurred in the years following the 11th century AD. Stone circles enclosing cinerary burial sites (sites where cremated remains are buried), probably erected between the 3rd and 11th centuries, are found throughout the present Toda heartland. These structures, however, are associated with a people whose culture was markedly different from that of the Todas and is quite unlikely to be its precursor. While the Toda may have co-existed with these people, it is more probable they arrived in the high Nilgiris after the disappearance of the circle-builders.

Traditional Toda society was linked to four neighboring groups in the Nilgiris (the Kota, the Kurumba, the Irula, and the Badaga) in a complex of ritual, economic, and social relationships. The opening up of the Nilgiris by the British during the 19th century, along with social and economic development during the present century, have brought about profound changes in traditional Toda society.

²LOCATION AND HOMELAND

The Nilgiri Hills, located in the northwestern part of Tamil Nadu, are a mountainous massif rising from the plains of southern India to over 2,600 m (8,500 ft) above sea level. They lie roughly 11° of latitude north of the equator, where the states of Tamil Nadu, Karnataka, and Kerala meet. Maximum temperatures average between 18°C and 21°C (65°–70°F) throughout the year, but at the higher elevations hard frosts may be experienced during the winter months. Standing full in the path of the southwest monsoon, western locations of the Nilgiris receive up to 500 cm (approximately 200 in) of rain a year. Heavy tropical forests cover the lower slopes of the hills but give way above 1,800–2,000 m (approximately 6,000–6,500 ft) to temperate forest and open savanna grassland. It is here, at the higher elevations, that the Todas live and graze their herds of water buffalo *(Bubalus bubalis)*. Some scholars argue that the Todas themselves created these grasslands through centuries of burning off the vegetation and grazing their buffalo herds.

Historical records show that the Todas have never been a numerous group. European accounts estimated a population of no more than 1,000 people at the beginning of the 17th century, a total that had dropped to 475 by 1952. Successful treatment of venereal diseases and other medical conditions

cred herds. Ön took a rib from the right side of the man's body and from it created the first Toda woman. Ön's wife stood at the other end of the iron bar and brought forth 1,800 buffaloes, from which all the Todas' secular buffaloes are descended.

Toda deities in general seem to be anthropomorphic developments of hill spirits, i.e., they are described or thought of as human. They live very much like the Todas, residing on the high peaks of the Nilgiris and tending their herds of buffalo. Some gods, however, appear to be deified Todas. Legends tell of the exploits of Kwoten, to whom the origins of many Toda practices are ascribed. Kwoten mysteriously disappeared after, so it is believed, intercourse with a female deity. Another Toda, Meilitars, is believed to have tricked the gods into eating buffalo-calf flesh and is credited with originating the ceremonial rituals still used in the calf-sacrifice. Both men are now revered as gods.

⁵RELIGION

The Toda religion centers on the sanctity of the buffalo. Although the Todas have a pantheon of deities, of far greater importance are the buffalo dairies that, along with their contents, pasturage, and water supply, are viewed not only as sacred, but as divine. Toda dairies and their herds are assigned varying degrees of sanctity, each level being subject to more elaborate and complex ritual practices. The most sacred category of dairy is the *Ti* dairy, though the last of these temple-dairies disappeared in the 1950s.

All dairy complexes are served by dairymen who must be ordained, undergoing ceremonies that ritually purify them for their duties. These dairymen-priests are responsible for the care of the dairies, maintaining their ritual purity and the sanctity of the dairying equipment. They also tend the temple herds and, more importantly, milk the temple buffaloes and process the milk into butter, buttermilk, and *ghi* (clarified butter) for distribution to the community. The milk is viewed as sacred, but other milk products have less sanctity attached to them and ghi has none at all. In fact, the entire Toda dairying ritual has been interpreted as a means by which the sanctity of milk is dispelled so that the product may be consumed by the general population.

Temple-dairies and their sacred herds of buffalo form the focus of Toda ritual life. In each Toda settlement, weekly observances are kept to honor its dairy, and special ceremonies are performed when necessary to restore its ritual purity. The naming of a female buffalo, the first milking of a temple buffalo, or the giving of salt to buffaloes all require specific rituals. Historical accounts show that, until recently, male buffalo calves were periodically sacrificed and ritually consumed in a ceremony performed to further the welfare of a kin group and its herds. Buffalo-sacrifice continues to be performed at Toda funerals.

The most important goddess of the Todas is Tökisy *(Tö·kisy)*. Modern Todas believe that she, rather than her brother Ön, created the Todas and their buffaloes. The Todas revere the "gods of the mountains," said to reside on the Niligri peaks, and the gods associated with the sacred dairies. The Toda belief system also encompasses elements of Hinduism, especially Hindu concepts of ritual purity and impurity. Today, many traditional Todas worship Hindu deities, such as Shiva, Marriamman, and Aiyappan, and participate in pilgrimages to Hindu sacred places.

reversed the decline in numbers, and in 2000 the number of Todas stood at 1,412.

Population data regarding the Todas are notoriously inaccurate. The figure given above is the Ethnologue estimate for "ethnic" Toda. However, it is also estimated that only 600 of these speak the Toda language. Murray B. Emeneau, the late Berkeley linguist who did much of his work with the Todas, estimated a population between 700 and 900 during the last century.

³LANGUAGE

The Toda language belongs to the Dravidian linguistic family and is thought to have developed around the 3rd century BC. It has affinities with both Tamil and Malayalam, but it separated from pre-Tamil before these two emerged as independent languages. The Todas traditionally had no written form of language; today, they use the Tamil script for writing purposes.

⁴FOLKLORE

According to the Toda creation myth, humans and their buffaloes were created by the god Ön *(Ö·n)*. One day, so the story goes, Ön and his wife went up to a plateau at the top of the Kundah Range in the Nilgiris. He set up an iron bar stretching from one end of the plateau to the other. Ön stood at one end of the bar and brought out 1,600 buffaloes from the earth. Hanging on to the tail of the last buffalo was a man, who was the first Toda. Ön's buffaloes were the ancestors of the Todas' sa-

Christian missionary efforts among the Todas at the turn of the century have resulted in the emergence of a very small community of Toda Christians. It numbers perhaps 200 persons who follow the Anglican rites of the Church of South India.

⁶MAJOR HOLIDAYS

Toda festivals center around the ritual ceremonies associated with the sacred dairies. For example, in the past clans honored their dairies at the time of the annual clan prayer festival (mod fartyt) in late December or early January. Today, only the Nos clan hold this ceremony, but all Todas try to attend this event. In addition, villages have special days of the week sacred to the settlement and, as noted above, to its dairies. Although they are not marked by any special ceremonies, these sacred days involve restrictions on the normal activities carried out by the village. Many Todas also attend local Hindu festivals, such as that held at the temple of Marriamman in Ootacamund (Udhagamangalam), which is the main center and administrative headquarters of the Nilgiris.

⁷RITES OF PASSAGE

Toda rites of passage vary in their complexity. Birth and death, which are held to be highly polluting and significant threats to the purity of the dairies, are heavily bound by rituals to protect the sanctity of these institutions. Events such as marriage and the attaining of adulthood, on the other hand, do not endanger the ritual status of the dairies and are accompanied by simpler observances.

A woman's first pregnancy is seen as ritually contaminating and, like childbirth, a threat to the dairy or dairies of the woman's settlement. In the past, she had to spend a lunar month (usually around the fifth month of her pregnancy) in a pollution hut constructed outside the bounds of the hamlet. Today, this custom has been abandoned, though the rites associated with the beginning and ending of this period of exile are still followed. In the seventh month of the first pregnancy, the bow-and-arrow ceremony is performed, by which the child-to-be is formally affiliated with the clan of the father (patriclan) and given its place in Toda society. This ceremony, at which the husband prepares and gives his pregnant wife an imitation bow and arrow, is a particularly important communal event and is accompanied by dancing, singing, and feasting.

Childbirth also is considered polluting. In some Toda hamlets, it is not allowed to take place in the settlement, and the soon-to-be mother is sent to a subsidiary hamlet. If a mother is allowed to give birth in her house, she is subject to various restrictions until the appropriate purification rites are held. Between one and three months of age, the face-uncovering and name-giving ceremony is held for the child.

No particular rites mark the attainment of puberty by boys, although they do undergo an ear-piercing ceremony. Traditionally, girls underwent both a symbolic and an actual defloration (loss of virginity) to mark their entry into adulthood, although it is uncertain whether these rites are continued today.

The rites associated with death are among the most significant in Toda society. Friends and relatives gather to pay their respects to the deceased, and a few days after death a "first day funeral" is held. Among the many rituals is the catching of the buffaloes to be sacrificed. For men, both temple and secular buffaloes are killed, whereas only secular animals are sacrificed at the funeral of a woman. Members of every social, kin, and affine (related by marriage) group to which the deceased belonged have specific roles to fulfill in the funeral ceremonies. Following a ritualized mourning and other rites, the corpse is taken to the cremation ground and burned. In the past, a second funeral—complete with buffalo-sacrifice—was held a few months after the first ceremony, but this custom no longer seems to be followed.

⁸INTERPERSONAL RELATIONS

The Todas have different forms of greetings, depending on the person being addressed. When a woman meets her father or mother, for example, she "bows," meaning that she kneels and touches each foot of the parent to her forehead. She accompanies this with a verbal greeting ("etyeya?," "salutations, father") to the father, but not to the mother. A man does not bow to his parents but respectfully says "Salutations, father" or "Salutations, mother." Similarly, the manner in which one greets other relatives is determined by the precise relationship, age, and often sex, of the person being addressed.

⁹LIVING CONDITIONS

The Todas live in small hamlets scattered across the open grasslands of the Nilgiri uplands. A hamlet may have up to five dwellings, its dairy structures, a buffalo pen, and perhaps some calf sheds. The population of the hamlet can vary between 12 and 17 people. Houses and dairy buildings are constructed at some distance from each other and are often surrounded by walls of piled stones. The traditional style of building is a distinctive barrel-vaulted design found nowhere else in India. The rounded roof is made of rattan, supported by crosspieces, and thatched with grass. Heavy wooden planks sunk into the ground form the front and rear walls, with a single opening in the front wall for a door. A raised earthen platform in the one-room hut serves as a sleeping and sitting area. A hearth is placed at the back of the hut, and brass pots and other household utensils are hung along the back wall. A small hole in the center of the hut is used for pounding grain. It also serves the ritual purpose of dividing the hut into "pure" and "impure" areas. The churning of milk, which is a male activity, can only be done in the pure front of the hut; the impure rear half of the structure makes up the women's area.

Traditional Toda housing also includes a front-gabled hut thought to have been adopted from the Badaga. The old-style huts are rapidly being replaced by modern brick or stone housing.

¹⁰FAMILY LIFE

Toda society is divided into two endogamous subcastes (the To·rØas and Töwfily). Each of these has a number of exogamous clans that are patrilineal (patriclans), i.e., descent is traced through the male line. Inheritance of property, rights and duties, ritual obligations—all are determined by one's patriclan. However, all Todas also belong to an exogamous matrilineal clan (matriclan), which is of equal importance in matters of marriage.

The Toda kinship system, which is quite independent of the descent system, follows the basic pattern of Dravidian-speaking peoples. Parents' siblings of the same sex are considered to be parents. Children of these "classificatory" parents are held to be one's siblings and, therefore, marriage with them would be incestuous. One cannot, for instance, marry the child of a mother's sister or of a father's brother. However, parents' siblings of the opposite sex are called "aunts" and "uncles," and belong to a totally different category of kin. Their children are potential and even preferred marriage partners. The ideal union in this system is with the child of a mother's brother or of a father's sister.

Toda marriages are arranged when the partners are mere infants, often less than two or three years of age and sometimes no more than a few months old. The children remain with their parents until maturity, when the girl moves into her husband's family home. The girl's father provides a dowry after the couple begins living together. A girl's family may break off the marriage before this time on payment of an agreed-upon compensation (usually in buffalo) to the husband's family. In time, the couple builds a house of their own nearby and set up a separate household.

In the past, younger brothers became cohusbands to the eldest brother's wife, a custom called fraternal polyandry. This was necessary because of the shortage of women resulting from the now long-abandoned Toda practice of female infanticide. A custom that continues today is that of "wife-capture," by which a Toda may make off with another man's wife and formalize the union by payment of the appropriate compensation.

¹¹CLOTHING

The most distinctive item of traditional Toda clothing is the long cloak (pu·txuly) worn by both men and women. Made of thick cotton, its dimensions are about 2.2 m by 135 cm (roughly 7 ft long by 4 ft wide) and in appearance reminds some of the ancient Greek toga. It is off-white in color, with broad red and black bands woven across one end. Women often add elaborate embroidered designs to these bands. The cloak is wrapped around the body with the striped end thrown over the left shoulder. Underneath the cloak, men wear a cotton waistcloth over a breech cloth. Women wrap the waistcloth under their arms so that their whole body is covered.

Dress habits are changing. Today, Toda men may wear Western-style shirts and pants, with or without the traditional cloak. Shoes are commonly worn, whereas previously Todas went barefoot. Women have taken to wearing the sari and blouse. Children are invariably dressed in South Indian or Western-style clothes.

The Todas have no weaving skills and in the past obtained the cloth for their cloaks from weaving castes living in the surrounding lowlands. Today, materials for making cloaks, as well as ready-made clothes, are purchased in the bazaars of Ootacamund.

Another distinctive aspect of Toda appearance is the hairstyle. Both men and women wear their hair long, women letting their hair fall in ringlets. Older men let their facial hair grow into bushy beards. Jewelry is worn by both men and women. Until recently, it was the custom for girls reaching puberty to be tattooed over extensive areas of the body, although this custom has now fallen out of use.

¹²FOOD

Dairy products, along with cereals and sugar, are the main items of the Toda diet. Buttermilk is used for drinking and for cooking. In the past, millet was the staple cereal, but this has been replaced by rice. A typical meal consists of rice, either boiled in buttermilk and served with butter, or cooked in water and eaten with spiced vegetables. The meal is usually followed by a glass of buttermilk or a glass of coffee, prepared with milk and sweetened with jaggery, a type of brown sugar. The Todas are vegetarians and consume no meat, although in the past the flesh of the sacrificed buffalo calf was ritually consumed.

The Todas usually eat a light meal at about 7:00 AM and a larger one at mid-morning after the buffaloes have been milked. Various snacks and drinks (including buttermilk and coffee) are consumed throughout the day, with another meal being eaten in the late afternoon. Food is served on leaves, or on brass or stainless steel dishes, and is eaten with the right hand. Special foods eaten on festive occasions include millet balls served with honey and ghi (clarified butter) and rice boiled in jaggery water and served with ghi.

The Todas are fond of stimulants. Men smoke bidis, the small brown cigarettes made from rolled tobacco leaves that are common throughout India. Opium is sometimes added to coffee, and both men and women use snuff, placing it inside the lip rather than in the nose. Locally distilled alcohol is consumed in large quantities.

¹³EDUCATION

Though the government school established for Toda children seems to have been well attended, as late as the 1960s few traditionalist Todas advanced beyond an elementary education. The Todas seem open to formal education, however, and their overall literacy rate, according to the 1981 Census, is 43.43% (53% for males and 34.01 for females). Current figures regarding literacy among the Todas are not available, but according to the 2001 census, some 50% of the Scheduled Tribes in the Nilgiris Hill District, where many of the Toda live, were literate. Of course, with a base population of just over a thousand, such figures are virtually meaningless. And literacy among the Toda, for government purposes, essentially means literacy in Tamil.

The Christian Toda community, on the other hand, is highly educated and numbers businessmen, teachers, nurses, and government employees among its ranks. Higher education is favored by parents for both males and females.

¹⁴CULTURAL HERITAGE

Dancing is an important Toda tradition, often occurring at feasts or as part of specific Toda rituals. Only men participate in ceremonial dances, although over the last few decades women have begun dancing for recreation. The men form an inward-facing circle, standing so that their arms are touching. The circle moves in a counterclockwise direction, with each step being taken in unison and accompanied by a shout that marks the beat of the dance. A composer is sometimes invited to the dance. If one is present, he joins the circle and, as it rotates, shouts out standardized phrases appropriate for the festival being celebrated, or perhaps original phrases composed specifically for the occasion.

Singing often accompanies the dancing, and there is a strong tradition of oral poetry among the Todas. All aspects of culture are represented in the songs—milking and dairy rituals, the care of buffaloes, funerals, the sacred names (kwasm) of the Toda world, and even (in modern times) anthropologists studying Toda culture.

[15] WORK

The traditional Toda economy is based on herding water buffaloes. In the past, milk products would be exchanged with the Badaga, Irula, Kota, and Kurumba in return for grains, utensils, forest products, and other items. The Kota, for example, provided articles for Toda funeral rites. Families from the different tribes had hereditary links extending back generations. Such traditional relationships, however, have largely disappeared in the modern cash economy. The Todas sell surplus milk and purchase rice and other goods in the local markets. Few Toda own large enough buffalo herds to subsist entirely on pastoralism, and more and more Todas are becoming involved in agriculture, either leasing their land or cultivating crops, such as potatoes, cabbage, and cereals, themselves. This move towards agriculture has been actively encouraged by the government, though many Todas still show a traditional preference for herding water buffaloes.

[16] SPORTS

Games popular among children include dry-grass "tobogganing" on an old sack or a piece of wood. Children also like to form lines, with their hands on the hips of the person in front of them and weave through the hamlet. Toda girls imitate their mothers, pretending to cook food over imitation fires of twigs and leaves. Young boys play at being buffalo-herders, constructing miniature buffalo pens and making mud figurines of buffaloes and buffalo calves.

Both children and adults play various team games. One, played by males only, resembles tip-cat. A short stick, pointed at both ends, is placed against a stone in the center of the playing area. Teams, composed of 10 to 20 members, take turns batting. The batter takes a stick about a meter in length and strikes the short stick so that it goes straight up in the air. While it is in the air, he hits it towards the fielding team. If the stick is caught by the fielding team, the teams change sides. If the stick falls to the ground, the batter scores three points. If the batter misses the stick altogether, he is replaced by another member of the batting team. Points are scored in sets of 21, and the team with the most number of sets wins the game.

[17] ENTERTAINMENT AND RECREATION

Beyond their ritual functions, singing and dancing are also forms of recreation among the Todas. Riddling is quite popular. Modern forms of entertainment, such as movie theaters where Tamil films are shown, are available in Ootacamund. Men enjoy passing time together in the coffee shops of the town.

[18] FOLK ART, CRAFTS, AND HOBBIES

Toda women are quite expert at embroidery, as seen in the decorative patterns they add to their cloaks. Efforts undertaken in the late 1950s to develop traditional Toda embroidery work as a handicrafts industry met with mixed results, although Toda embroidery is still marketed locally today.

[19] SOCIAL PROBLEMS

For almost two centuries, the Todas have been the focus of efforts at improving their social and economic condition. The British colonial government, Christian missionaries, and Indian government planners have all, according to their own perspectives, initiated reforms. The last several decades, however, have been a period of dramatic change. The Todas have shared in the benefits of modern medicine, education, electrification, modern housing, and other social and economic advances. Following 1947, at the instigation of the local forest department, the Toda grasslands underwent forestation, with a series of collectors ending the annual firing of the grasslands by the Todas and restricting the grazing of buffaloes. Moreover, in 1975, as part of its Hill Area Development Programme, the central government assigned funds for the social and economic development of the Toda community. The Toda Welfare Scheme was organized, under the auspices of the Indo-German Nilgiris Development Project, to introduce the Todas to scientific agriculture, so they would not be so dependent on their buffaloes and pastoralism. Today, most Todas have abandoned pastoralism and are cultivators. Tea now covers more than 50% of the cultivated lands in the Nilgiris.

These changes have brought about tensions within the Toda community. Young Todas have been exposed to broader social currents and many see traditional Toda practices as social "evils" to be eradicated. Buffalo-sacrifice, polyandry, wife-capture, and child marriage, all features of traditional Toda society, are identified as practices to be discarded.

The Todas are thus a people in transition. The challenge that faces them is how Toda society, with its emphasis on its buffalo herds, dairies, and traditional rituals and customs, will move into the social and economic world of India as it enters the 21st century.

[20] GENDER ISSUES

Traditionally, Toda women were prohibited from contact with the buffalo or their milk. Their role in society was to reproduce, cook the food, and clean the house.

However, given the increasing difficulty for Toda men to support a family, more and more Toda women are marrying outside the community. Few Todas own the size of buffalo herd (estimated at 12) necessary to support a family, so they go into agriculture to try and make a living. Increasing debt is a serious problem. Women see education as a way out of their community, so many opt out of arranged marriages at an early age to further their education.

Toda women, like women all over India, are still far from achieving sociopolitical and ritual parity with their men. But much change is in the air. For instance, customs such as female infanticide and polyandry are no longer practiced by the Todas. Moreover, Toda society seems always to have permitted greater liberty to its women than is common in South Asia.

[21] BIBLIOGRAPHY

Chhabra, T. "A Journey to the Toda Afterworld." *The India Magazine of Her People and Culture*. 1993 (September):7–16.

Emeneau, M. B. *Toda Songs*. Oxford: The Clarendon Press, 1971.

Hockings, Paul, ed. *Blue Mountains: The Ethnography and Biogeography of a South Indian Region*. Delhi and New York: Oxford University Press, 1989.

Murdock, G. P. *Our Primitive Contemporaries*. Aliso Viejo: Rimbault Press, 2007.

Noble, William A. "Settlement Patterns and Migrations among Nilgiri Herders." *The Journal of Tropical Geography* 44 (1977): 57–70.

Rivers, W. H. R. *The Todas*. London: Macmillan and Co., 1906.

Walker, Anthony R. "The Truth About the Todas: On the Origins, Customs and Changing Lifestyle of the Tribal Community in the Nilgiris. *Frontline*. Vol. 21, 5 (February 28 -March 12, 2004). .(http://www.hinduonnet.com/fline/fl2105/stories/2004031000206600.htm).

_____. *Between Tradition and Modernity and Other Essays on the Toda of South India*. Delhi: B. R. Pub. Corp. 1998.

_____ *The Toda of South India: A New Look*. Delhi: Hindustan Publishing Corporation, 1986

—by D. O. Lodrick .

TONGANS

PRONUNCIATION: TAHN-guhns
LOCATION: Tonga
POPULATION: 119,000 (July 2008 estimate)
LANGUAGE: Tongan; English (both are official languages of the country)
RELIGION: Christianity (Free Wesleyan Church)

¹INTRODUCTION

The Kingdom of Tonga is an important independent nation located in western Polynesia in the South Pacific. Tonga is one of the world's last remaining constitutional monarchies, currently ruled by His Majesty Taufa'ahau Tupou IV. The current population of Tonga is approximately 119,000 of which 99.9% are Polynesian. Tongans have well-established international family networks that span an entire ocean. Family members often relocate to the United States, Australia, and New Zealand, purchasing property, gaining employment, and, as a result, being able to financially aid their relatives back in Tonga.

²LOCATION AND HOMELAND

Tongans are the indigenous inhabitants of the islands in the Kingdom of Tonga. The Kingdom of Tonga is made up of around 170 small islands with a total land area of 718 sq km (277.2 sq mi). The climate of Tonga is sub-tropical with the warmest months being January, February, and March. Because of its location, Tonga is prone to cyclones.

Tonga has been a constitutional monarchy since 1875, when George Tupou I tried to stave off European colonization in Tonga. Although Tonga was a British protectorate until 1970, when full independence was gained, Tongans are fiercely proud that they belong to one of the few Pacific Island groups that were not a colony of any European nation. Large Tongan immigrant communities are located in the cities of Brisbane and Sydney in Australia and Honolulu, Los Angeles, and San Francisco in the United States. It is estimated that there are as many Tongans living overseas as there are still living in the Kingdom of Tonga.

³LANGUAGE

Tongan is the indigenous language of the islands within the Kingdom of Tonga. Tongan is a Polynesian language very closely related to the Samoan language. The official languages of the kingdom are Tongan and English. English is taught in both elementary school and secondary schools. Most Tongans have some understanding of spoken and written English. The lyrics of the national anthem of the Kingdom of Tonga are in Tongan and the first four lines are reproduced with English translation below:

'E 'Otua mafimafi,
Ko ho mau 'Eimi koe,
Ko koe ko e falala 'anga,
Mo e 'ofa ki Tonga;

Oh Almighty God above,
Thou art our Lord and sure defense,
In our goodness we do trust Thee,
And our Tonga Thou dost love;

⁴FOLKLORE

Tongans have a rich body of folklore, mythology, and oral history. The Tongan creation myth recounts the division of the universe by the offspring of the two original twins. One of the later descendants of the original twins, Maui, is credited with the creation of Tongatapu, the main Tongan island. According to the story, Maui went fishing and hooked something on the bottom of the sea. Thinking he had hooked a very large fish, Maui pulled with all his might and eventually saw that he had brought a large piece of the sea floor to the surface. This was Tongatapu. Maui is also thought to have "created" many of the islands of Samoa and Fiji. There is a large body of stories that recount the various battles of cultural heroes within Tongan history.

⁵RELIGION

Christianity is the dominant religion in the Kingdom of Tonga. The largest church denomination on the islands is that of the Free Wesleyan Church, which claims to have over 30,000 members.

⁶MAJOR HOLIDAYS

The most important secular holiday in Tonga is the King's Birthday on July 4. There are a number of celebrations, competitions, and cultural events that take place during the time around his birthday. Emancipation Day is a national holiday that occurs on June 4. It celebrates Tonga's succession from the Commonwealth and complete independence from Britain.

⁷RITES OF PASSAGE

Birth in traditional Tongan society was an event that men did not participate in. Children were taken care of primarily by their mothers, although soon they were socialized according to sex. Activities and behaviors were learned according to the status of the family. Children formed play and activity groups with other children of a similar social status. They would remain a part of these groups for life. Tattooing was part of the passage into adulthood for both adolescent boys and girls. Young men were more extensively tattooed than women. Men were tattooed in the area that extended from the lower torso, just above the navel, to the lower thighs, just above the knee. Tattooing is no longer practiced in Tonga.

The death of a relative was accompanied by self-abuse by the surviving members of the family. Bruising, burning, beating, stabbing, and other practices were performed by both men and women. Women had patterns of concentric circles burned into their arms. Men would hit themselves in the head with clubs until they bled, knocking out their own teeth, and even stab themselves with their own spears in the thigh and arm. This practice disappeared quickly after European settlement and missionization of Tongatapu.

⁸INTERPERSONAL RELATIONS

A common Tongan greeting is *malo e lelei*, which roughly translates as "a warm welcome to the Friendly Islands." The "Friendly Islands" was the name given to this chain of islands by traders, explorers, and discovers in the Pacific region. Traditional greetings in Tongan society involved a mutual touching of the lips by persons of equal status, and among persons of unequal status the inferior would kiss the hand of the higher-

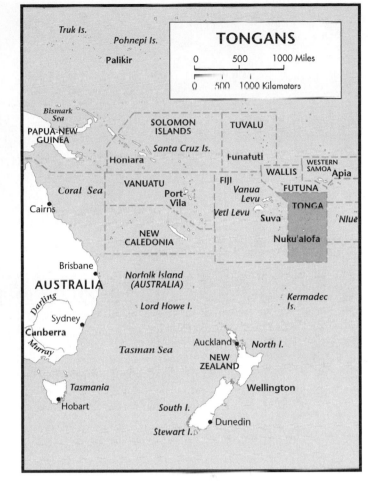

ranking person. In some cases, if the person was of very high status, the inferior person would kiss the feet of the high-ranking person. Western handshakes have replaced traditional greetings except in highly formal ceremonial contexts.

Traditional forms of sitting for men and women of Tonga differ. Men sit cross-legged, while women sit with their legs doubled up and under one side. Mats are the traditional seating items.

Premarital relationships for young men and women in traditional Tongan society did not often lead to marriage, since most marriages were arranged. Courtship did take place and involved an interested young man providing small presents to a young woman. If the woman was of high status, she was expected to remain chaste and refuse his sexual advances. If she was of lower status, then she was less constrained in terms of her response to his advances. The importance of virginity at the time of marriage has been promoted in modern, Christian Tongan society.

⁹LIVING CONDITIONS

Each traditional Tongan village is loosely organized around a central, grassy area for public gatherings. A series of pathways link the households. Household structures vary in shape, size, and decoration depending on social status. Some houses have thatched roofs that come to within 3 or 4 ft of the ground. Some houses have mat walls on some or all sides, while others

Tongans wearing traditional woven bark sarongs line up at a polling booth in Nuku'alofa. (William Nessen/AFP/Getty Images)

have none and are open except for the roof that covers much of the side areas.

Modern Tongan homes of the towns and cities are like most of those in the Pacific area and are made with either block or wood frame with a corrugated iron roof. Affluent Tongans have larger homes with many of the comforts that Americans are accustomed to.

Government-provided medical care is available to all Tongans in the Kingdom of Tonga. Traditional Tongan society viewed illness as being brought about by the acts of supernatural forces. The most common method that Tongans used to propitiate the gods to cure either themselves or a relative of higher status was finger mutilation. Typically, the smallest joint of the little finger was removed. In the cases of chiefs, more severe measures were eventually taken to sway the favor of the gods. The strangulation of small children was reported by early European observers of Tongan life.

There is a road system on the inhabited islands of the Kingdom of Tonga and six airports on the islands, although only one of these has paved runways. Products are transported by trucks to the airports and sea ports. There are no railways on Tonga.

¹⁰FAMILY LIFE

Marriage patterns in traditional Tonga society differed according to social classes. Girls were often betrothed prior to adulthood. Once a premarital agreement was reached between two families, the girl was expected to remain a virgin until she took up residence with her husband. Marriages in almost all

cases were decided by parents. The marriage ceremony itself involved no formal rituals beyond a feast put on by the bride's family. Tongans are now married in Christian ceremonies. In the pre-Christian culture of Tonga, men of the chiefly class often had more than one wife. Although divorce was strictly a male prerogative in precontact Tongan society, both sexes have that option in modern society.

¹¹CLOTHING

Traditional clothing styles are still worn by both Tongan men and women. Tongan males wear a wraparound cloth called *tupenu* on all formal occasions. Tupenu are also worn to work and for leisure. Tongan women wear a long, wraparound skirt that extends to the ankles. In precontact Tongan society this wraparound cloth, called *ngatu*, was the same for men and women and measured around 8 ft in length and 6 ft in width.

¹²FOOD

One of Tonga's major imports is food from New Zealand. Canned fish and meats, flour, sugar, tea, and coffee are some of the more important food imports to the islands. Traditional foods are still prepared and eaten in the Kingdom of Tonga. Traditional feasts involve extensive menus and tremendous amounts of food. Traditional Tongan foods include fish, yams, breadfruit, coconut, arrowroot pudding, bananas, and cooked plantain. Pork and fowl were usually only consumed by the chiefly class or were served if foreign visitors were present. Food was cooked by a variety of methods including the use of pit ovens, boiling, and stewing.

[13] EDUCATION

Overseas education for the children of well-to-do commoners as well as elite families has been taking place within Tongan society since the 1940s. Tonga has a literacy rate of nearly 100% for both men and women. Most Tongans over the age of 15 can read and write basic words and sentences in Tongan and English. Many children, adolescents, and young adults go to New Zealand to pursue their education.

[14] CULTURAL HERITAGE

Music and song are very important in Tongan society today. Tongans hold an annual National Music Festival in June. The Festival is a two-week competition that is open to all Tongans with over 10 different categories of performance. The entire event culminates with the national celebration of the King's Birthday on July 4. Traditional Tongan dance is called *lakalaka;* like other forms of dance in Polynesia, it is group-oriented, with the number of participants ranging from 20 to a few hundred. The gestures of the dancers recount the story that is sung. Traditional dances are never accompanied by musical instruments.

[15] WORK

The Kingdom of Tonga employs Tongans in the range of occupations found in any modern society. Judges, lawyers, doctors, teachers, and other professionals are trained in schools, colleges, and universities overseas. Traditional work was segregated according to sex and social class. Certain occupations were restricted to individuals according to birthright, and this restriction has continued into the present as the norm. Individuals from high-ranking families have more access to opportunities than do those who come from lower ranking families. Nowadays, the majority of rural Tongans are engaged in subsistence farming with a limited production of export crops such as coconuts, bananas, and pumpkin squash.

[16] SPORTS

Basketball, boxing, cricket, rugby, soccer, and volleyball are all popular sports in Tonga. There are a number of traditional children's games that are played in Tonga. One game, *lanita,* is a simplified form of cricket. Other games involve skill in tossing sticks of various sizes. Most children's games are group games in which the participants have to work as a group to win the contest.

[17] ENTERTAINMENT AND RECREATION

Music provides one of the primary forms of entertainment for Tongans. Singing and music are heard at almost every occasion and every venue in Tonga. American musicians and television and film stars are important icons for members of the modern generation of Tongans.

[18] FOLK ART, CRAFTS, AND HOBBIES

Tongans produce more *tapa* cloth than any other Polynesian group. *Tapa* is a decorated textile produced from the inner bark of the paper mulberry and breadfruit trees. In the Tongan language, tapa refers only to unfinished or undecorated pieces of bark cloth. Finished pieces are called *ngatu.* Traditional clothing such as the *tupenu* was made from decorated bark cloth, or ngatu. The bark cloth is an important item for ceremonial occasions. Ngatu is given as gifts at weddings and funerals, used to divide household space at the death of a family member, and has many other important ritual and symbolic functions within the culture.

[19] SOCIAL PROBLEMS

There is a movement among some Tongans that calls for governmental reform and a change from a monarchy to a democracy. Elite rule on Tonga has always been the pattern and has left many of the commoners out of the financial development and financial successes of the island kingdom.

[20] GENDER ISSUES

Rank and gender are important to an understanding of Tongan traditional society. Women always outrank men, and older individuals always outrank younger ones. Females are attributed with a mystical power that provides superior status for them in the rank order system. In the Tongan family, fathers are outranked by their sisters and in particular by their older sisters. Inherited rank is crucial in determining the social roles and rights of specific women. Women of chiefly rank (*hau'eiki*) exerted considerable economic and political power and enjoyed a high degree of individual freedom, while those of commoner rank (*tu'a*) did not.

In precontact Tongan society, women participated in activities that they were prohibited from in other Polynesian societies. For instance, women could drink *kava* in public, eat with men, and go on ocean voyages. Cooking in precontact Tonga was the responsibility of men, except in those cases where a chiefly dish was being prepared. Men were also equally responsible for child rearing in precontact Tongan society. Since the Tongan household was composed of an extended family, grandfathers, uncles, and fathers all participated actively in raising and taking care of children. In modern Tongan society, cooking and child rearing are now within the social domain of women.

Obtaining equal rights and status for women is also seen as a goal by some sectors within modern Tongan society. Women must be 21 years of age and literate to vote. Men must only be taxpayers and literate to vote.

[21] BIBLIOGRAPHY

Ferdon, Edwin N. *Early Tonga*. Tuscon: University of Arizona Press, 1987.

Grijp, Paul van der. *Islanders of the South: Production, Kinship, and Ideology in the Polynesian Kingdom of Tonga*. Leiden: KITLV Press, 1993.

Herda, P., Terrell, J., and N. Gunson, N., eds. *Tongan Culture and History*. Canberra, Australia: Australia National University, 1990.

—by J. Williams

TRADITIONAL ORTHODOX JEWS

ALTERNATE NAMES: Ultra-Orthodox; Hasidic; fundamentalist
LOCATION: Worldwide, particularly Israel, North America, Europe, and Canada
POPULATION: 1.6 to 1.8 million
LANGUAGE: Language of the country in which they live; Hebrew; Yiddish; Aramaic (men)
RELIGION: Orthodox Judaism

¹ INTRODUCTION

Recent decades have seen a worldwide resurgence in Traditional-Orthodox Judaism, variously referred to as "ultra-Orthodox," "Hasidic," or "fundamentalist." Readily recognizable by their Old-World appearance—full-bearded men in black coats and hats; women in long skirts, their heads covered by kerchiefs or wigs—members of this group differ from most modern-day Jews in their rigorous religious observance, in their conservative political views, and, above all, in their refusal to assimilate into mainstream Western culture. Their rejection of the secular world distinguishes them from the large body of Orthodox Jews—referred to here as "Modern-Orthodox"—whose religious beliefs and practices are very similar, but who participate more fully in the cultures of the countries in which they live, dressing in modern Western-style clothing and enjoying many of the same pastimes as their neighbors of other faiths and backgrounds.

Traditional-Orthodox Jews are generally drawn from two segments of the Jewish population: the Hasidic world and the yeshivas (Jewish institutions of higher learning). The most visible—and most numerous—are the Hasidim, composed of various sects belonging to a movement that began in 18th-century Poland. It took its inspiration from the legendary Rabbi Israel ben Eliezer, known as the Baal Shem Tov (literally, "Master of the Good Name"). Hasidism brought new joy and emotional fervor to religious devotion, in sharp contrast to the sober, dry, and often elitist focus on scholarly study that dominated the religious life of Eastern European Jews of the time. Each Hasidic community was led by its own rabbi, or *tzaddik* (holy man), a revered figure whose blessing and advice were sought for virtually all undertakings by members of the community, and whose reputation was spread through tales of his wisdom and holiness. The spiritual leadership of each community was handed down from generation to generation, creating rabbinical dynasties which anchored the numerous Hasidic sects that eventually emerged.

While Hasidism was condemned as heretical and extreme by its opponents (called *Mitnaggedim*), both groups ultimately joined in opposing the greater danger from outside—the growing secularization of Jewry that began with the 18th-century development known as the *Haskalah,* or Enlightenment, that accompanied the growing acceptance of Jews into the mainstream of Western society. The 19th and early 20th centuries saw the growth of Reform and Conservative Judaism, which advocated the adaptation of Jewish tradition to modern life and its reinterpretation in light of contemporary historical scholarship. By the 1950s, only about 10% of Jews in the United States considered themselves Orthodox. A modern secular lifestyle was the norm for the vast majority of Jews worldwide, even in countries such as Israel and Great Britain, where the formal religious leadership remained Orthodox.

The past three decades have seen a revival of Orthodox Judaism of both the more modern, secular kind and the stricter traditional variety. Those remnants of Eastern Europe's Hasidic community that survived the Nazi Holocaust of World War II have served as the catalyst for the growth of Hasidic communities worldwide. Ironically, Hasidism, which started out as a fringe movement condemned by the religious establishment of its day and virulently attacked by its opponents, is today associated with religious conservatism and learned study. Although the strong historical enmity between the Hasidim and the *Mitnaggedim* is now a thing of the past—and the sharp dividing lines between them have even blurred somewhat—they still form two distinct groups within the Traditional-Orthodox community. The non-Hasidic groups are distinguishable by their focus on scholarly study and their allegiance to the head of a yeshiva (institution of higher learning) rather than to a Hasidic spiritual leader or rebbe.

² LOCATION AND HOMELAND

The total number of Traditional-Orthodox Jews worldwide is estimated at between 1.6 and 1.8 million, out of a total Jewish population of about 13.3 million. Over half live in Israel, mostly in Jerusalem and B'nai Barak, and most of the remainder—between 550,000 and 650,000—live in North America. In Europe, London, Manchester, and Antwerp have relatively large Traditional-Orthodox communities.

Brooklyn, New York, has North America's largest concentration of Hasidim, located mainly in the neighborhoods of Boro Park, Williamsburg, and Crown Heights. There are also well-established Hasidic communities elsewhere in New York City and in Rockland County, New York, as well as in such diverse cities as Cleveland, Detroit, Los Angeles, Baltimore, Miami, St. Louis, Philadelphia, and Denver. The largest concentrations of Hasidim in Canada live in Montreal and Toronto.

Hasidic sects take their names from the Eastern European towns in which they originated. Major groups include the Satmar, Lubavitcher, Bobover, Belzer, Vishnitzer, Gerer, Klausenberger, Skverer, and Bratslaver Hasidim. The Satmar are the largest group, followed by the Bobovers and Lubavitchers. The Lubavitchers are known particularly for their spiritual outreach to nonobservant members of the Jewish community through a worldwide network of Habad houses and emissaries called *shlichim.*

³ LANGUAGE

Traditional-Orthodox Jews are multilingual. In addition to the languages of the countries in which they live, they all speak and are literate in Hebrew, the language of the Jewish holy books. A substantial portion (usually more than half) of their formal education is conducted in this language, which they begin to learn at an early age. In addition, the young men also learn to read Aramaic, the language of the Talmud, an authoritative compilation of religious commentary.

While a knowledge of Hebrew is also shared by Modern-Orthodox Jews, the Traditional-Orthodox community is distinguished from other groups by the importance it gives to yet another language—Yiddish, the lingua franca that evolved among European Jews after their expulsion from Germany during the Middle Ages. It combines German syntax with vocabulary from Hebrew, Aramaic, Germanic, Slavic languages, and other languages and it is written in Hebrew characters. Some Traditional-Orthodox children study Yiddish in school, while others pick it up from their parents, and the extent of its use varies among different groups. Other aspects of linguistic practice vary also. For example, members of some Hasidic groups use Hebrew in everyday conversation, while others avoid it, considering it too holy for everyday use.

⁴FOLKLORE

Storytelling combining down-to-earth folk wisdom and sophisticated wit is among the most important Hasidic traditions. A wealth of tales and anecdotes handed down over the generations expresses the Hasidim's faith in God and love of humanity. The Hasidic belief in the efficacy of simple, heartfelt religious devotion is expressed in a typical tale about an uneducated wagon driver. Stopping by the roadside, he calls out the entire Hebrew alphabet letter by letter so that God can help him express his devotion, as he does not know the prayers, only the letters from which to fashion them. Tales based on the wisdom of Hasidic sages have always been an especially important part of the folktale tradition. A favorite pastime, these stories provide spiritual inspiration and moral instruction as well as entertainment. They are especially popular at the *melave malkeh*, a gathering held on Saturday night to mark the end of the Sabbath. A famous collection of these tales is *The Legends of the Baal Shem Tov*.

⁵RELIGION

Founded about 2000 BC by the patriarch Abraham, Judaism is a monotheistic religion based on the belief in one God who is the creator and ruler of the universe. His word is revealed in the books of the Bible known to Christians as the Old Testament, and especially the portion—known as the Torah—that was given to the Jewish people through the prophet Moses on Mt. Sinai (about 1300 BC). Traditional-Orthodox Jews belong to one of the three major groups within the Jewish faith, Orthodox Jewry. This group views the Torah as historically revealed to Moses and therefore absolutely binding on believers (the Conservative and Reform groups allow for varying degrees of adaptation to the changing conditions of the modern world). Orthodox Jews also place special emphasis on the Talmud, a compendium of rabbinical commentaries compiled between the 5th and 7th centuries AD, and the legal tradition, called the halakah, that is based on it.

⁶MAJOR HOLIDAYS

Traditional-Orthodox Jews observe all of the holy days of the Jewish calendar. While their observances are essentially similar to those of the Modern-Orthodox, they may be more elaborate at times. For example, at Passover, when all observant Jews eat unleavened bread, or matzo, some Traditional-Orthodox Jews observe additional prohibitions, such as refraining from wetting the *matzohs*. They may also refuse to eat any processed food at this time, even that which would be considered kosher by less rigorous standards.

⁷RITES OF PASSAGE

For a Traditional-Orthodox Jew, one's birth date on the Hebrew lunar calendar holds a significance equal to or greater than that of the secular Western date. The major rites of passage observed by Traditional-Orthodox Jews are, by and large, those practiced by the larger community of observant Jews. The first in the life cycle is the *bris*, or circumcision ceremony, for a baby boy when he is eight days old, which formally marked him a part of the Jewish community and affirms his relationship with God. The next rite of passage (also for boys) is one that, in the modern West, has been retained primarily by Traditional-Orthodox Jews: the *upsheren*, or first haircut. A boy's hair is allowed to grow until he is three years old, when he undergoes the ritual haircut which is a ceremonial sign that he is ready to begin the study of the Torah. The next major milestone is the coming-of-age ceremony: the bar mitzvah for boys (at age 13) and bat mitzvah for girls (at age 12). (The Hebrew meaning of "bar/bat mitzvah" is "son/daughter of the commandment.") At the age of 13, a boy is traditionally deemed qualified to be counted as part of a *minyan* (the quorum of ten men needed for public prayer) and can begin wearing *tefillin* (phylacteries), small square leather boxes containing slips inscribed with scriptural passages and worn on the forehead and left arm by Orthodox men during weekday-morning prayers. In addition, the child of 12 or 13 is considered ready to participate fully in the ritual fast days of the Jewish calendar.

Traditional-Orthodox weddings are joyous, festive occasions. Among the best-known features of a traditional Jewish wedding are the *ketubah*, or marriage contract; the *hoopah*, or canopy, under which the ceremony is performed; the tradition of having the bride circle the groom seven times just before the ceremony; and the breaking of a glass at the end of it. At weddings, as at all public events, men and women are seated separately, both at the ceremony and at the reception.

A Jewish funeral takes place as soon after death as possible. The *Kaddish*, or memorial prayer, is recited at the funeral, and should also be recited every day by a relative, or a designated substitute, for the first year following death. The mourners observe a formal week-long period of mourning called *shivah*, when they stay home, refrain from ordinary activities, and receive calls from friends, relative, and acquaintances. The gravestone is dedicated in a formal unveiling ceremony held between one month and one year following the person's death.

⁸INTERPERSONAL RELATIONS

Many facets of public (and private) behavior among Traditional-Orthodox Jews are governed by strict conventions regarding modesty, or *tsniut*. Strict separation of the sexes in public places begins at nursery-school age. Many Traditional-Orthodox Jews will not attend even those forms of secular entertainment to which they have no religious objection—such as an orchestra concert—because that would require them to be part of a mixed male and female audience.

A man and woman who are not related to each other are not supposed to be alone together in a room, and even the public behavior of married couples is restricted by a variety of rules, such as a prohibition against either verbal or physical displays of affection in the presence of others. Among some Hasidic sects, husbands and wives are not even supposed to walk together in the street, at least not until they reach middle age.

[9] LIVING CONDITIONS

Traditional-Orthodox Jews have often lived crowded together in aging city neighborhoods because of the importance of proximity to their rabbi and synagogue, which is crucial since they are not allowed to drive on the Sabbath or other Jewish holy days. The presence of a religious school in the neighborhood is also a priority. Given these constraints on location, available housing in desirable areas can be overpriced because of the tight market for it. Increasingly, though, Traditional-Orthodox communities are finding suburbanization an acceptable solution to the problem of overcrowded and deteriorating urban housing, as long as the group that relocates is large enough to maintain its cohesion by providing for the continuation of its religious and cultural institutions.

Many Traditional-Orthodox Jews in the New York City area own or rent summer cottages in upstate New York, where they spend part or all of the summer, with the men commuting to the city or spending weekends with the rest of the family. Members of specific Hasidic sects often cluster together in small "colonies" of cottages or bungalows so that they can spend the summer near their friends and neighbors and have the *minyan*, or quorum of 10 men, that is required for prayer services.

Although they reject many aspects of contemporary Western culture, Traditional-Orthodox Jews enthusiastically embrace modern medicine. Their rabbis routinely advise followers about health problems and monitor their treatment by physicians, and their newspapers devote a relatively large amount of space to health-related stories. Money is often raised within the community to help pay the medical expenses of particular members who require expensive surgery or other forms of treatment. There is also a strong interest in alternative, holistic treatments among certain members of the community, and age-old folk remedies are still practiced as well. Traditional-Orthodox Jews use all forms of transportation available to the general public but will not drive or use other forms of transportation on the Sabbath or on holy days.

[10] FAMILY LIFE

Arranged marriages are the norm among Traditional-Orthodox Jews. Today, however, the participants in a match, or *shiddach*—unlike their Old-World Eastern European counterparts—have the final say in whether or not they choose to marry each other. Although the two people usually spend some time getting to know one another before becoming engaged, this period seldom lasts more than a few weeks. There is no casual dating among people who are not seriously contemplating getting married in the immediate future.

Hasidic weddings are lively, joyous occasions. At both the ceremony and the reception, male and female guests are separated, as men and women are at all public events. Even the bride and groom sit separately at the reception, and both dance only with members of their own sex until the end of the evening, when the bride dances briefly with her male relatives, holding on to one end of a handkerchief or other cloth because she is not allowed to touch any man other than her husband, with whom she dances last.

After marriage, Traditional-Orthodox Jews adhere strictly to the *taharat hamishpacha*, a code of sexual purity that governs a couple's sexual practices, as well as other aspects of their behavior toward each other. As part of this code, a woman is required to frequent a special ritual bath called a *mikvah* at the end of her menstrual period before she can resume sexual relations with her husband. Traditional-Orthodox Jews take the biblical injunction, "Be fruitful and multiply," seriously. Female birth control is frowned upon unless a potential pregnancy poses medical or psychological hazards, and male use of condoms is forbidden entirely. Families generally have at least five children, and it is not uncommon to have eight, ten, or even more.

The women receive a less exacting religious education than their male counterparts, allowing them to devote a proportionately greater amount of their time in school to secular subjects. Thus they are often better educated than the men in secular fields. Although their large families and the rigorous requirements of their observant lifestyle are more than enough to occupy them at home, some Traditional-Orthodox women hold jobs to help meet household expenses that are increased by the cost of private school tuition.

[11] CLOTHING

The most visible way in which Traditional-Orthodox Jews differ from Modern-Orthodox and other Jews is in their clothing, which remains similar to that of their ancestors in Eastern Europe. The men wear a black suit and white shirt and sometimes also a black coat. Both Modern- and Traditional-Orthodox men wear a flat, round skullcap called a yarmulke at all times once they reach the age of 13, removing it only when swimming or showering. However, Traditional-Orthodox men also wear various types of hats over their yarmulkes when they pray or go out-of-doors. Probably the most distinctive is the *streimel*, a round, flat-topped fur hat worn by many Hasidic men. Made from up to 26 sable pelts, a *streimel* can cost over $5,000. Other Hasidim wear the *spodik*, a fur hat that is taller and narrower, while other Traditional-Orthodox Jews, including the Lubavitcher Hasidim, wear ordinary hats. The men also have full beards because the halakah prohibits shaving. Depending on their affiliation, they may wear the hair in front of their ears in earlocks called *peyot*, curly strands that are left to grow long, or, in some cases, tucked behind the ears.

Unlike the men, Traditional-Orthodox women are not restricted to any one style of clothing. They do, however, dress conservatively in keeping with strict religious laws governing female modesty, wearing either dresses or skirts that are long enough to cover their knees when they are standing, sitting, or walking. (In some communities, a stricter length requirement, such as 10 centimeters below the knee, is specified.) They do not wear slacks, jeans, or shorts, and their clothing must have high necklines and long sleeves. Once they are married, they cover their hair with either a kerchief or wig, for only their husband is permitted to see it.

[12] FOOD

The diet of Traditional-Orthodox Jews is distinguished by the strictness with which they observe the laws of Kashrut, kashruth, or kosher, which are derived from Biblical injunctions against eating foods considered to be impure. It is common for Modern-Orthodox and even Conservative Jews to "keep a kosher home." In general, this means separating meat from dairy products in their diet—which includes keeping separate sets of *milchig* (milk) and *fleischig* (meat) dishes and cooking utensils—and eating only meat that has been ritually slaughtered by a qualified Jewish slaughterer, or *shochet*. In addition to these measures, however, Traditional-Orthodox Jews refrain from eating any processed or manufactured food that does not carry a rabbinical *hechsher* (certification) and honor only the *hechshers* of certain rabbis.

13 EDUCATION

Like all Jews, the Traditional-Orthodox place a high value on education. However, they are unique in their concentrated focus on religious studies and in the part that these studies play in daily life. All members of the community—not just scholars or students—regularly spend time studying Jewish religious texts, perpetuating the time-honored tradition of their Eastern European forebears, for whom religious study was the most highly honored of activities. The children attend private religious schools (segregated by sex), which combine the study of religion and the Hebrew language with such secular subjects as English and mathematics. Girls, for whom the religious requirements are less stringent, receive a greater degree of secular education than boys, whose secular studies may or may not meet the minimum required for state certification in some cases, depending upon the school they attend.

The young men attend Jewish colleges called yeshivas, where they pursue advanced religious studies in an atmosphere far different from that of the ordinary academic setting of Western universities. Much of the study is conducted in crowded, noisy public study halls by pairs of students reading and debating together over passages in religious texts. The extracurricular activities of ordinary campus life—team sports, theater productions, mixers—are unknown in the yeshiva. Sports are frowned upon and casual dating is forbidden. There is an additional institution, the *kollel*, for even more advanced study; it is generally attended by married students.

14 CULTURAL HERITAGE

The cultural heritage of Traditional-Orthodox Jews is basically the religious tradition that they have in common with other members of the Jewish faith. However, the Hasidic background shared by many has produced a rich tradition of folktales and music, especially the lyrical, wordless melodies called *niggunim* that create a feeling of spiritual uplift and closeness to God. Traditional-Orthodox Jews also avail themselves of more modern cultural resources to replace the secular culture that they have renounced. These include contemporary literature for both children and adults by Orthodox Jewish writers. Sets of storybooks for girls are especially popular, notably the *Bais Yakov* series, and many adults enjoy the self-help books of authors such as Miriam Adaham and Rabbi Manis Friedman.

15 WORK

Like Modern-Orthodox Jews, the Traditional-Orthodox do not work on the Sabbath (*Shabbos*)—which begins an hour before sundown on Friday night and lasts until sundown on Saturday night—or on a number of other holy days throughout the year. Given these restrictions, many Traditional-Orthodox Jews prefer to be in business for themselves. In Israel, many of the men continue full-time religious study after they are married, while their wives work, often as teachers or secretaries (or, more recently, in such fields as computers, graphics, and bookkeeping). Outside Israel, the men have traditionally gravitated toward the diamond and real estate industries. Electronics re-

tailing is also popular, and a number of Traditional-Orthodox Jews own nursing homes.

16 SPORTS

Sports are generally frowned upon as a form of recreation for adults but considered acceptable for children. Athletic activities are part of the schedule at Traditional Orthodox summer camps although the clothing worn during games varies from ordinary uniforms to Hasidic garb complete with long black coats. The strictest groups, such as the Satmar Hasidim, forbid all sports for children past the age of the bar mitzvah and bat mitzvah (13 for boys and 12 for girls), which traditionally signals the formal beginning of adulthood. Swimming, for all Traditional-Orthodox groups, is strictly segregated by sex: men and women never swim in the presence of members of the opposite gender.

17 ENTERTAINMENT AND RECREATION

Religious considerations play a major role in how Traditional-Orthodox Jews choose to spend their leisure time. They own no televisions, which are seen as a corrupting influence, and most reject virtually all other facets of popular culture, including movies and popular music. Even cultural events such as concerts, to which there is no inherent moral objection, are generally out of bounds, since Traditional-Orthodox Jews are not supposed to mingle with members of the opposite sex in public. For the most part, their recreational needs are met through concerts and other special events organized by the religious community, where they know that the content will not be objectionable and that men and women will be seated separately. It is also considered acceptable to frequent museums and cultural exhibits of other types which do not require mingling at close range with strangers of the opposite sex. Another cultural resource is the variety of recordings of contemporary music by Jewish recording artists such as Mordechai ben David and Avraham Fried, whose songs combine religious content with popular musical styles.

18 FOLK ART, CRAFTS, AND HOBBIES

Centuries of skilled silversmithing has gone into the creation of Jewish ritual objects, many of them for synagogue use, including Torah scroll cases and ornaments, pointers for reading the Torah, and a variety of ceremonial objects such as *esrog* boxes for the Sukkot holiday. Probably the most universal ritual object for home use is the *mezuzah*, a small oblong tube containing a parchment scroll inscribed with a Biblical text and affixed to the doorposts of observant Jewish homes. Mezuzahs may be made of silver, brass, wood, ceramics, or other materials. In the Jewish home, embroidery is found on the tablecloths used at festive Sabbath or holiday meals, and also on such objects as the special cloths used to cover the ceremonial loaf of bread, or *challah*, at Sabbath meals.

A favorite hobby of Traditional-Orthodox Jews is gathering for storytelling sessions at which inspirational tales of rabbinical wisdom and miraculous events are recounted.

19 SOCIAL PROBLEMS

Although Traditional-Orthodox communities are relatively free from crime, suicide, and the high divorce rates common among other segments of society, their members are not immune to some of the same problems that plague the world beyond their neighborhoods. The number of Traditional-Orthodox Jews participating in twelve-step recovery programs for drug and alcohol abuse is rising in spite of deep-seated fears of discovery and subsequent ostracism by others within the community. In 1988 the Lubavitcher Hasidic sect, headquartered in Crown Heights, New York, started a drug and alcohol awareness program—a rarity in the Hasidic world—called Operation Survival, which offers referral services and provides counselors to yeshivas.

Other potential sources of tension inherent in the Traditional-Orthodox lifestyle include the universal custom of arranged marriages (*shiddachs*) and the pressure to produce and support large families. In addition, there is the potential culture clash that can occur between men who continue their full-time religious studies after marriage (a practice particularly common in Israel) and their breadwinner wives, who often find employment in non-Orthodox work environments, where they may enjoy easygoing, informal social contacts with co-workers of a type forbidden them in their role as Orthodox wives. Outside employment also means that a Traditional-Orthodox woman may advance professionally while her husband—if he remains a student—has little hope of advancement to a secure teaching or rabbinical position.

20 GENDER ISSUES

Traditional Orthodox Jewish women are to be helpmates for their husbands. That means that the wife is there for her husband and is loving and supportive, especially in his religious studies. It is the husband's obligation to be the breadwinner of the family. However, sometimes the wife will be the breadwinner, so that her husband can further his Talmudic studies. Women also help raise their children, and play a large role in their religious education.

Traditional Orthodoxy has insulated itself from such evolutions as feminism, the gay rights movement, and laxer sexual norms in the late 20th and early 21st centuries. Allowing changes in women's religious roles is evidence of unacceptable surrender to the broader secular culture. However, for some Orthodox women, Jewish tradition has always engaged and been influenced by prevailing intellectual and cultural norms, strong enough to incorporate them without compromising its core values or laws.

21 BIBLIOGRAPHY

Buxbaum, Yitzhak. *The Light and Fire of the Baal Shem Tov.* New York: Continuum, 2005.

Eisenberg, Robert. *Boychiks in the Hood: Travels in the Chasidic Underground.* New York: HarperCollins, 1995.

Eliach, Yaffa. *Hasidic Tales of the Holocaust.* New York: Avon Books, 1982.

Greenberg, Tsipora. Personal interview, 25 July 1996.

Harris, Lis. *Holy Days: The World of a Hasidic Family.* New York: Summit Books, 1985.

Hass, Nancy. "Hooked Hassidim: The Long and Secret Road to Recovery in Brooklyn's Ultra-Orthodox Communities." *New York.* 28 January, 1991: 32.

Hecht, Eli. *Crossing the Williamsburg Bridge: Memories of an American Youngster Growing Up with Chassidic Survivors of the Holocaust.* Philadelphia, PA: Xlibris, 2004.

Hoffman, Edward. *Despite All Odds: The Story of Lubavitch.* New York: Simon and Schuster, 1991.

Kezwer, Gil. "Shalom, Bonjour: A Flourishing Community of Chassidic Jews Awaits the Messiah in Rural Quebec." *Canadian Geographic.* July-August 1994. Vol. 114:4, p.54.

Landau, David. *Piety and Power: The World of Jewish Fundamentalism.* New York: Hill and Wang, 1993.

Remnick, David. "Waiting for the Apocalypse in Crown Heights." *The New Yorker.* 21 December, 1992: 52–57.

Unterman, Alan. *Dictionary of Jewish Lore and Legend.* London: Thames and Hudson, 1991.

Wertheimer, Jack. *A People Divided: Judaism in Contemporary America.* New York: Basic Books, 1993.

Wiesel, Elie. *Somewhere a Master: Hasidic Portraits and Legends.* New York: Schocken Books, 2005.

Winston, Hella. *Unchosen: The Hidden Lives of Hasidic Rebels.* Boston: Beacon Press, 2005.

—reviewed by J. Hobby

TUJIA

ALTERNATE NAMES: Bizika, Turan, and Tuming
LOCATION: China
POPULATION: 8 million
LANGUAGE: Tujia; Chinese
RELIGION: Polytheism and ancestor worship
RELATED ARTICLES: Vol. 3: China and Her National Minorities

¹INTRODUCTION

The ancestors of the Tujia were descendants of a tribe called Linjun. Early in the Qin Dynasty (221–206 BC), the Linjun migrated from Sichuan and Hubei to the western part of Hunan. The name Tujia reflects the assimilation of many cultural traits of the local aboriginals by the Linjun. From time immemorial, the Tujia lived by hunting, fishing, and slash-and-burn cultivation. Under the leadership of headsmen, they submitted cloth as tribute and tax to the government of successive Chinese dynasties. Uprisings, however, happened frequently. In the 8th century, the Tujia in Xizhou district resisted the rule of the Tang Dynasty (618–907) and set up an independent regime by force of arms. Later on, a Tujia clan called Peng became strong enough to unify the Wushi district in western Hunan and to rule over it for some 800 years. In the 17th century they pledged allegiance to the Qing Dynasty (1644–1911). Tujia headmen were appointed as local officials. Their self-given name was Bizika, which means "native." The historical records from the Song dynasty (960–1276) to the Qing Dynasty called them Turan (natives), Tuming (native people), and Tujia (native household), which expressed the same meaning as their self-given name. The name Tujia is now prevalent.

²LOCATION AND HOMELAND

The Tujia population amounted to over 8 million in 2000. They dwell mainly in a vast area at the juncture of Hunan, Hubei, Sichuan, and Guizhou provinces. It is a hilly country with mild climate and abundant rainfall, traversed by the Wuling Mountains and criss-crossed by three rivers. The famous Zhangjiajie primeval forest is located in this area.

³LANGUAGE

The Tujia language belongs to the Sino-Tibetan family, Tibeto-Burman group; it is as yet unclear whether they form a distinct branch. There are two dialects, one in the north and one in the south, spoken by some 200,000 Tujia. The Tujia have no written language. However, most of the Tujia also speak Chinese and use Chinese characters.

⁴FOLKLORE

Among the ancient songs one finds legends about the origin of human beings, which the Tujia share with other national minorities living in southwest China. In brief, human beings were all drowned in a catastrophic flood, except for a brother and sister. They married and gave birth to a fleshy lump, which was divided into pieces and thrown in all directions. Every piece of the fleshy lump became the ancestor of a particular nationality. Another legend narrates the story of a girl (Shexiangxiang) and an eagle. Since the eagle had saved her life, Shexiangxiang was very grateful. She cultivated the land arduously. Without the help of the eagle, her life would have been even harsher. One night, she dreamed of two small eagles landing in her arms and she became pregnant. She bore a son and a daughter. Years later, Shexiangxiang fell ill and died. Her last words were: "The eagle is your savior, so, never kill the eagle." In fact, the eagle died shortly after her and was buried beside her grave. Time passed swiftly and the children grew up. Unfortunately, there was no one else with whom to marry. According to Heaven's will, they got married. Later, eight sons were born and were given Tan as their surname. They are the ancestors of Tan, an important clan of the Tujia, living in a mountainous area of west Jiangxi Province. Tradition has it that they have never killed an eagle.

A story about creation states that the Heavenly King ordered two gods, Zhang and Li, to produce a sky and an earth respectively. Zhang produced a sky that was orderly, bright, neat, and smooth. Careless in handling things, Li made an earth full of bumps and hollows, mountains and caverns, meandering brooks and zigzagging rivers, an environment that corresponds closely to the geographical features of the land of the Tujia.

⁵RELIGION

The Tujia believe in many gods and worship their ancestors. Their reverence to the white tiger can be traced back thousands of years and is actually related to the name of their ancestor Linjun (meaning "tiger" in ancient times). At ordinary times, they enshrine and worship the White Tiger God and other gods at home. On the first of November (lunar calendar; Western calendar, between November 24 and December 22), they offer sacrifice and pray for the prosperity of their family.

The Tujia narrate a legend about a brave female hunter called Meishan. She was killed in a fight with a group of wild hogs and was transformed into a goddess who protected the hunters. Shortly after the Spring Festival, the Tujia used to organize a hunt in the forest. Before starting off, they always offered sacrifices to the Hunter Goddess Meishan.

An important belief among the Tujia is that the Heavenly King will, in the final instance, settle lawsuits, reversing unjust verdicts and eliminating calamities. Whenever the Tujia fall seriously ill, they pray and make a vow to the Heavenly King in the temple. As soon as they recover from the illness, they offer sacrifices and redeem their vow. When they suffer an injustice, they also go to the King, drink a mixture of cat blood and wine, and ask that the lawsuit be settled by the god. In order to prepare for the celebration of the July Seventh Festival (lunar calendar; Western calendar, between August 1 and 29), butchery, hunting, fishing, music playing, and wearing red are prohibited for a period of two days. Those who violate the ban will be punished by the Heavenly King and will suffer a misfortune.

⁶MAJOR HOLIDAYS

The Spring Festival (lunar calendar; Western calendar, between January 21 and February 20) is the most important of the numerous holidays of the Tujia. It is celebrated one day earlier than the true date. In the 17th century, Tujia soldiers were sent to the frontline to fight against the Japanese invaders. One day, they learned from reliable sources that the invaders planned a sneak attack on the lunar New Year. The Tujia organized their

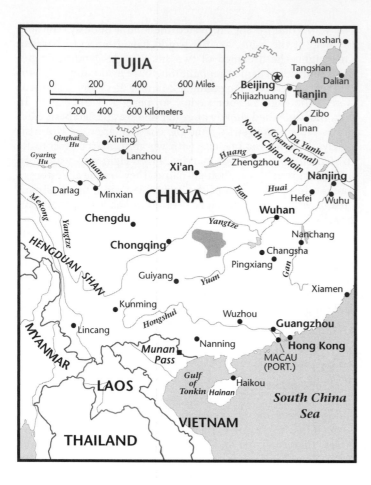

own surprise attack one day before the Spring Festival, which ended in a great victory. Thereafter, the Tujia followed their heroes in celebrating the New Year one day ahead of time. The New Year meal is a casserole of pork, vegetables, carrots, bean starch noodles, deep-fried bean curd, and rice. Early in the morning people scramble to light up firecrackers to "welcome the New Year."

⁷RITES OF PASSAGE

As soon as a baby is born, the father announces the good news to his mother-in-law. Before setting off, he should catch a chicken and bring it there as a gift. Depending on whether the baby is a boy or a girl, he catches a cock or a hen. In the western part of Jiangxi Province, if a girl is born, the father will grow peony in the courtyard. Each year he sells the peony roots and deposits the money in view of the girl's wedding. During the confinement following childbirth, the new mother eats a large number of eggs. A pile of eggshells thus retained will be dumped on the crossroad near the house. It announces to the villagers that the baby is a month old now and that mother and child are all safe and sound. A tile-like embroidered hat is woven for the baby. It means the baby will be rich and will live in a tile-roofed house in the future.

In a family, if a woman does not get pregnant for a long time after the wedding, the couple will go to the temple to pray and make a vow. If a baby (especially a son) is born, they will bring sacrificial offerings to redeem their vow.

The Tujia practiced cremation in the past, but nowadays they bury their dead in the ground. A shaman will be invit-

ed to recite the scriptures, while the funeral procession is led by a Taoist priest. The clansmen sing a mournful song while dancing.

⁸INTERPERSONAL RELATIONS

The Tujia usually receive guests with a gruel of sweetened fried flour. According to custom, they break at least three eggs and drop them, one by one, into the boiling gruel (numbers three and four are regarded as lucky; numbers one, two, five and more are regarded as unlucky). The host will propose three toasts right after the guests' arrival and also before their departure. If a guest does not drink, he should dip his middle finger into the wine three times, each time taking it out and snapping the wine off; this means the guest drank his fill and thanks the host for his kindness. If guests are kept for dinner, the main dish is a bowl of seasoned pork or chops covered by a big piece of fat meat.

On festivals, the host will bake glutinous rice cakes in the firepool for the guests. If a guest takes a cake covered with ash, the host will hasten to help him to pat the ash off the cake; if the guest pats it himself, it might be deemed that he thinks the house is unclean. During the meal, the guest may lay his chopsticks in the form of a cross, indicating he is full.

Singing in antiphonal style is the usual beginning of dating. On a selected day of June, July, or August (lunar calendar; Western calendar, between June 26 and October 21), a "Girls' Meeting" will be held. Singing while dancing, all women of the village participate in the great occasion, wearing their traditional costumes. Dating and lovers' rendezvous are part of this social ritual.

⁹LIVING CONDITIONS

The Tujia usually dwell at the foot or on the slope of a hill or beside a stream. Their houses are shaped like a "sitting tiger." This is probably related to their worship of the white tiger. Whenever they build a house on the slope, they build a platform first. The back side of the platform lies directly on the slope, while the front side is supported by wooden stilts. The living standards of the Tujia, both in urban and rural areas, correspond by and large to those of the Chinese. Only in remote mountainous areas in Hunan do they still live in poverty. Bicycles and tractors provide their main means of transport. Trains and cars are the next. Fully equipped hospitals have been established in counties and townships. There are medical clinics in large villages.

¹⁰FAMILY LIFE

Tujia families are patrilineal, usually small in size, except when two or three generations live under the same roof. Women's position in the family is lower than men's. Monogamy is the rule. Marriages may be arranged by the parents or entered into freely by the couple. Remnants of old customs, such as cousin marriage and levirate (a widow has to marry her husband's brother and the latter also has the duty to marry her) still survive today. "Free marriage" starts with antiphonal singing and dating. If they feel mutual love for each other, boys and girls exchange gifts to symbolize their affection. The girl may give the boy a piece of brocade, and the young man may give her a piece of fur. One week before her wedding, the girl begins her tearful singing. The words in her songs express her grateful feelings to her parents, her unwillingness to leave her family, her trust that her brothers and sister(s)-in-law will take good care of her parents, and her curse for the woman matchmaker, if any. Her parents, relatives, friends, and especially the girls of the same village participate in the tearful chorus. Their feelings are genuine and heartfelt.

On the day of the wedding, a team from the young man's house comes to the bride's house; the bride's family and friends have already placed a table obstructing the entrance. Antiphonal singing or talking begins. If the bridegroom's side wins (which is usually the case), they are welcome and the table will be removed; if they lose, they are allowed to creep beneath the table to enter the house. They then accompany the girl to her fiancé's house. The ritual is lively and humorous.

¹¹ CLOTHING

Tujia daily dress has come to resemble that of the Chinese. Traditionally, however, women wear a short top with loose sleeves and buttons down the left. Two or three layers of lace are edged to the garment. The skirt is made of eight pieces of cloth or silk. These are still used on festivals, as well as silver earrings and bracelets and gold rings. Silver-made small bells, plates, chains, toothpicks, and earpicks are pinned on the front of their upper garment. Tujia women comb their hair into a bun. Men wear short tops with buttons down the front. Both sexes wrap their heads with a blue kerchief.

¹² FOOD

Rice and corn are the staple foods of the Tujia, with urban Tujia eating more rice and rural Tujia eating more corn. Rice is mixed with maize flour and steamed, giving a dry, colored cooked rice, which is taken with vegetable soup. Chicken, duck, goose, and pork, added in varying proportions to the rice-corn vegetable soup, are the principal sources of protein. The Tujia take three meals a day. During the Spring Festival, wild game is added to the regular dishes.

¹³ EDUCATION

The Tujia's cultural and educational level is higher than the average among the national minorities of China. However, education in mountainous areas is still unsatisfactory, illiteracy being widespread. Although 95% of the school-age children do enroll in primary schools, the majority drop out. There is, nonetheless, some progress in the numbers of Tujia students who go through primary and secondary education and continue to college and university. This is possibly due to the fact that the Tujia speak Chinese and write Chinese characters.

¹⁴ CULTURAL HERITAGE

Folk songs are so popular among the Tujia that almost everybody can compose a song and sing it by him- or herself. The traditional "Swing Arm Dance" is also very prevalent. The dance is led by someone who knows well the sequence of the movements. People follow him or her in a circle and continue to move around. The dance movement is mainly the movements of arms, mimicking those of hunting, cultivation, fighting, etc. More than 70 dance movements are performed successively and each movement will be replaced by another during a new circular procession. "Maogusi" is a traditional Tujia drama, usually performed in lunar January (Western calendar, between January 21 and March 18). A lot of straw is bound to the actor's body, indicating the hairy body of the ancestors. It is a play in five acts showing slash-and-burn cultivation, hunting and fishing, spinning and weaving, as well as the marriage ritual.

¹⁵ WORK

The Tujia have a mixed economy, based mainly on agriculture and supplemented by hunting, fishing, handicrafts, and trade. Women share fully in the traditional farming chores with men. Since the Chinese revolution, many new industries have been set up in Tujia territory, with the Tujia participating in a kind of "industrial revolution." These industries include metallurgy, machinery, coal, electric power, textiles, paper mills, winemaking, chemical engineering, architectural engineering, and shipbuilding.

¹⁶ SPORTS

"Hit the flying stick" is the traditional sport of the Tujia. Usually, it is a game between two individuals, but it may also be played by two opposite teams. Each player holds a bat and uses it to hit a stick thrown from the opposite side. The stick hit back should be caught. The structure of the game somewhat reminds one of baseball. Missing or dropping the stick either by the catcher or by another player is recorded.

¹⁷ ENTERTAINMENT AND RECREATION

Movies and television have grown very popular as new forms of entertainment. However, group music with gongs and drums, especially during the off-season of agricultural work, are still prevalent among the peasants. The "Swing Arm Dance" is even more widespread. Sometimes, tens of thousands of people join in group dancing, making it by far the most important recreational activity of the Tujia.

¹⁸ FOLK ART, CRAFTS, AND HOBBIES

The most famous handicraft of the Tujia is a kind of cloth brocade called "Xilankapu." Most girls learn to stitch on cloth some one hundred figures and designs. Girls often stitch it on a blanket and or on a piece of cloth, which they offer as a gift to their boyfriend, to show their superb skill. They usually weave several pieces then sew them together. All the figures and designs of the pieces match each other in a very artistic way.

¹⁹ SOCIAL PROBLEMS

With education and industrialization, a growing number of young people, mainly in the rural areas, have migrated to the new and developing cities in their autonomous prefectures. This kind of social mobility, which tends to increase with the years, has had a destabilizing effect on the small rural villages, which depend on the younger generation to ensure their future—both economic and cultural.

²⁰ GENDER ISSUES

The Chinese constitution states that women have equal rights with men in all areas of life, and most legislation is gender neutral. The gap in educational level between women and men is narrowing with women making up 47.1% of college students in 2005, but only 32.6% of doctoral students. In rural areas, the number of Tujia participating in formal education is small.

Most school-age children drop out of school after just a few years.

China has strict family planning laws. It is illegal for women to marry before 20 years of age (22 for men), and it is illegal for single women to give birth. The Family Planning Bureau can require women to take periodic pregnancy tests and enforce laws that often leave women with no real options other than abortion or sterilization. Though minority populations were previously exempt from family planning regulations, policy has changed in recent years to limit minority population growth. Today, urban minority couples may have two children while rural couples may have three or four.

21 BIBLIOGRAPHY

Chiao, Chien, Nicholas Tapp, and Kam-yin Ho, ed. "Special Issue on Ethnic Groups in China." *New Asia Bulletin* no 8 (1989).

Dreyer, June Teufel. *China's Forty Millions.* Cambridge: Harvard University Press, 1976.

Eberhard, Wolfram. *China's Minorities: Yesterday and Today.* Belmont: Wadsworth Publishing Company, 1982.

Gustafsson, Bjorn A., Shi, Li, and Sicular, Terry, eds. *Inequality and Public Policy in China.* New York: Cambridge University Press, 2008.

Heberer, Thomas. *China and Its National Minorities: Autonomy or Assimilation?* Armonk, NY: M. E. Sharpe, 1989.

Lebar, Frank, et al. *Ethnic Groups of Mainland Southeast Asia.* New Haven: Human Relations Area Files Press, 1964.

Lemoine, Jacques. "Les T'ou Kia." In *Ethnologie régionale II* (Encyclopédie de la Pléiade). Paris: Gallimard, 1978.

Ma Yin, ed. *China's Minority Nationalities.* Beijing: Foreign Languages Press, 1989.

Miller, Lucien, ed. *South of the Clouds: Tales from Yunnan.* Seattle: University of Washington Press, 1994.

Ramsey, S. Robert. *The Languages of China.* Princeton: Princeton University Press, 1987.

Shin, Leo Kwok-yueh. *The Making of the Chinese State: Ethnicity and Expansion on the Ming Borderlands.* New York: Cambridge University Press, 2006.

Wiens, Harold J. *Han Chinese Expansion in South China.* New Haven: The Shoestring Press, 1967.

—by C. Le Blanc

TURKMENS

PRONUNCIATION: TUHRK-mens
LOCATION: Turkmenistan; northern Iran; northern Iraq; northwestern Afghanistan
POPULATION: 7.7 million
LANGUAGES: Turkmen; Russian; Persian
RELIGION: Islam (Sunni Muslim)

¹INTRODUCTION

The ethnic origins of the Turkmens are generally traced to the Oghuz, a loose polity of Turkic tribes that coalesced in and around present-day Mongolia in the 7th and 8th centuries AD. By the 9th century, the Oghuz had migrated west and inhabited steppe areas extending north and west from Central Asia's Aral Sea and Syr Darya river. The term *Turkmen* first appears in the 10th century, and it is believed that it was initially used to designate those Oghuz who adopted Islam and migrated southwest with the leader Seljuk into present-day Turkmenistan and beyond. While the first element of the term *(Turk)* is clear, the original meaning of the second element *(-men)* is unknown. (It has nothing to do with the English word *men*, however.)

By the 12th century, Oghuz and Turkmen tribes had migrated into what are now Iran, Azerbaijan, Turkey, and other parts of the Middle East. In these places, they established dynasties and played an important role in political life. In the case of Turkey and Azerbaijan, Turkmen tribes came to form the ethnic base of the populations. In Turkmenistan, the Turkmens never united into one political force and, until the early 20th century, most of the tribes were at least nominally under the control of the Central Asian khanates Khiva and Bukhara or, in some cases, under Persian suzerainty. The Turkmens gained a reputation as excellent fighters and horsemen whose chief occupation was raiding sedentary peoples for slaves and property. In the 1880s, after bitter fighting, Russia conquered the region and, in 1924, the Turkmen Soviet Socialist Republic became one of the 15 republics of the USSR. Under Soviet rule, the Turkmens endured many drastic changes. Property was collectivized, traditional leaders and (Islamic) religious figures were brutally eliminated, traditional social and political structures were attacked, and the nomadic way of life ceased to exist. Only with the dissolution of the Soviet Union and independence in the early 1990s did the government of Turkmenistan cautiously permit some of the prior traditions. Because most of the political leadership and social and economic institutions are Soviet holdovers, however, genuine and significant change has been slow to materialize.

Between 1990 and 2006, Turkmenistan was governed by Saparmurat Niyazov. Niyazov was known as Turkmenbashy, which means "Leader of the Turkmens." Turkmens living under the rule of Turkmenbashy lacked basic freedoms and were subjected to the watchful eye of the country's secret police force. Most Turkmens lived in poverty, as the government of Turkmenistan spent the profits of state industries on presidential palaces and other massive construction projects. Although Niyazov was replaced by Gurbanguly Berdimuhammedow in 2006, it is unlikely that Turkmenistan will reform its political and economic institutions.

Turkmens maintain a theory of common origin from a mythical ancestor, Oghuz Khan, from whom are supposed to have emerged 22 or 24 original Oghuz tribes—the core of the early Turkmens. Only some of these tribal names are current today, and researchers believe that the present-day Turkmen tribal structure consists of old Oghuz and pre-Oghuz tribes, newer Turkic tribes, and elements of Iranian groups who inhabited the lands taken over by the Turkmens. There are more than two dozen tribal groupings among the Turkmens today, the largest of which are Teke, Yomut, and Ersari. Tribal identity is important among the Turkmens and continues to play a significant role in social relations and politics.

²LOCATION AND HOMELAND

The majority of Turkmens live in Turkmenistan (an estimated 4.4 million) and some 3 million more live in northern Iran, northern Iraq, and northwestern Afghanistan. Because of various ethnic processes that have occurred among the Turkmens, the Turkmens of today may have Indo-European (Iranian) or Mongol-like physical features.

Turkmenistan consists of 488,100 square kilometers (188,450 square miles) and, except for the Balkan and Kopet Dag mountains in the south, the Caspian Sea in the west, and the Amu Darya river in the east, Turkmenistan is a vast arid desert. In fact, Central Asia's two largest deserts—the Garagum (central Turkmenistan) and the Gyzylgum (eastern Turkmenistan into Uzbekistan)—make up from 80–90% of Turkmenistan's territory. The average yearly rainfall in these desert zones does not exceed 150 millimeters (6 inches), and daytime summer temperatures often reach 45°C (113°F). Cold winds from the north bring temperatures well below freezing in the winter, especially in northern Turkmenistan. In spite of the harsh desert environment, the Turkmens have long been known as desert nomads who fully adapted to the environment in their economic pursuits, including sheep, camel, goat, and horse breeding and limited agriculture. They also used the desert to their advantage as an almost impenetrable refuge in time of war and strife.

Because of high rates of poverty and unemployment, thousands of Turkmens have left Turkmenistan to find work. Russia, Kazakhstan and Turkey are the main destinations for Turkmen labor migrants. Thousands of Turkmens have fled Iraq since the 2003 invasion of the country by the United States and its allies.

³LANGUAGE

Turkmen is part of the Oghuz group of Turkic languages. Linguistically, it is close to Azeri (Azerbaijani), Turkish, and Uzbek. Aside from the Turkic words in its vocabulary, there are numerous Persian and Arabic elements as well. The Turkmen language in Turkmenistan borrows many words from Russian. While virtually every Turkmen tribe has its own dialect, all are mutually intelligible. Turkmens also speak the languages of their neighbors. For example, many urban Turkmens in Turkmenistan speak excellent Russian due to decades of Soviet rule, while Turkmens in Iran commonly speak Persian. Prior to Soviet rule, all Turkmens wrote their language in the Arabic script. In Turkmenistan, that script was changed to Latin and then Cyrillic prior to World War II. In 1993, Turkmenbashy decreed that the Latin alphabet be used in place of the Cyrillic.

⁴FOLKLORE

A popular legend among the Turkmen people says that when God made the world, the Turkmens were the first to get a land filled with sunshine, but the last to get any water. Like other Central Asian peoples, the Turkmens have a rich folklore tradition consisting of epic stories, tales, lyric poems, and other genres usually transmitted and performed orally with or without musical accompaniment. Aside from entertaining, the folklore tradition has served to record Turkmen history and genealogy as well as to teach and reinforce Turkmen values, norms, and culture. This oral folklore is replete with heroic deeds performed for the sake of either romantic love or the community or tribe. Each Turkmen tribe and clan has its own series of legends and tales that define tribal genesis and trace genealogy. This folklore continues to play a crucial role in providing the Turkmens with their sense of identity and history and has longed served as a basis for the Turkmen written literary tradition as well.

The folklore tradition also includes various "superstitions" that dictate a wide range of social and familial activity. Knowledge of and belief in amulets, charms, lucky and unlucky omens, lucky and unlucky days of the week, as well as spirits and the evil eye are common to almost every Turkmen. In the traditional setting, virtually every act or type of behavior, no matter how mundane, is governed by a certain set of prescribed rules so that it will not bring on misfortune or bad luck. When activity concerns young children, birth, pregnant women, or other "vulnerable" individuals and critical events, such beliefs are especially apparent. Although outsiders often dismiss this aspect of folklore as mere superstition, many of the beliefs are actually grounded in practical knowledge of the human body, nature, and the environment.

⁵RELIGION

Nearly all Turkmen are Sunni Muslim, and almost every tribe or clan has a legend or account of how it became Muslim. Although Islam has been present in Turkmenistan since the 8th century, a great deal of Islamization took place after the Mongol invasion of the 13th century. Islam in Turkmenistan includes nomadic traditions and shamanist elements. Many Turkmens observe the rituals of Islam, such as daily prayer, pilgrimage to Mecca, and fasting during the month of Ramadan. In addition, the moment or event of conversion to Islam is often the defining element in a tribe's or clan's history, and thus perhaps the most crucial identifying factor for Turkmen society. Each tribe or clan also has its own cemetery and saint's shrine to which members may conduct pilgrimage when the need arises. At the shrine, a pilgrim may appeal to the saint for good fortune, prosperity, the safety of a loved one, a cure for an illness, or the birth of a child. Hundreds of such shrines dot the Turkmen landscape and are important places where Turkmen religious practice is conducted. Years of Soviet rule have lessened the level of religious observance amongst Turkmens, as is evidenced by the popularity of alcohol consumption in Turkmenistan.

In Turkmenistan, the state plays a significant role in religious life. Since the late 1990s, the government has shut down many mosques operating without state approval. The government has also closed foreign-supported *madrasas*—or religious schools—because it fears the spread of Islamic fundamentalism.

⁶MAJOR HOLIDAYS

The most important religious holidays are celebrated according to the lunar calendar and include the *Gurban bairamy* (Sacrifice Holiday), which commemorates God's trial of Abraham in his willingness to sacrifice his son, and the *Oraz bairamy* (Holiday of the Fast), celebrated at the end of the month of fasting (Ramadan). *Nowruz* (New Year's Day) is an ancient holiday celebrated on March 21 (the vernal equinox) and marks the beginning of spring and agriculture. All of these holidays are marked with feasts, family gatherings, and entertainment. National holidays include Independence Day (October 27) and a series of memorial days to commemorate the end of World War II, veterans, and victims of the 1948 earthquake in the capital city, Ashgabat. Turkmenistan also celebrates Neutrality Day on December 12, a reminder of Turkmenistan's "neutrality" in foreign policy.

⁷RITES OF PASSAGE

As Muslims, all Turkmen males are circumcised (usually between the ages of 3 and 7). The ceremony is accompanied by a great deal of celebration and fanfare as it marks a boy's becoming a member of male community. After circumcision, a boy no longer sleeps with his mother, but rather spends more time with adult males, who school him in proper male behavior, etiquette, and so on. Although there is no one analogous ceremony for girls, they too make a conscious (albeit less publicized) passage into womanhood by wearing head scarves, having their ears pierced, and spending more time with women. Wed-

dings too are celebrated with a great deal of festivity and lavish expenditure. From an early age, girls prepare for married life by sewing and crafting a great deal of clothing and household items that are saved until the wedding. Although funerals are also important events, most mourning takes place long after the actual death of an individual. On the third, seventh, and fortieth day after a loved one's death, there are large gatherings dedicated to the deceased's memory. These often continue on a yearly basis as well.

⁸INTERPERSONAL RELATIONS

Much of Turkmen behavior, conduct, etiquette, and other social norms come out of *Adat* (Turkmen customary law), *Sherigat* (Islamic law), and *Edep* (rules of proper etiquette and behavior). Although some aspects of these traditions may have been lost in the Soviet period, their essence (often referred to as *turkmenchilik,* meaning "Turkmenness") provides the Turkmens with a well-grounded corpus of rules and norms that continue to mold social behavior on a daily basis. Some of the more significant aspects of these traditions include elaborate and exact ways of greeting based on age and gender, a heightened sense of hospitality toward guests, a great deal of deference and respect toward elders, and a clear sense of tribal/clan identity.

Turkmenistan's Soviet legacy has left Turkmen society divided. Upper-class Turkmen send their children to Russian schools and live in cities such as Ashgabat. Poorer Turkmen tend to live in rural areas and earn a living from agriculture. Many Russians inhabit the urban working class.

⁹LIVING CONDITIONS

The traditional Turkmen dwelling is the felt tent called a *gara oy* (black house), which is often called a "yurt" in western literature. The felt covering is attached onto a wooden frame, and the dwelling may be assembled or disassembled within an hour. It is usually carried by camel. While some Turkmens in Afghanistan and Iran may still live in the *gara oy* year-round, in Turkmenistan it is no longer a primary residence. Instead it is used in summer pasture areas or constructed for recreation or holidays. In rural Turkmenistan, most people live in one-story homes made from clay and straw. Many times these homes are located within a walled courtyard that also contains a family's agricultural plot and livestock holdings. In the cities of Turkmenistan, high-rise apartment dwellings are also common. Although apartments may have modern plumbing and natural gas capabilities, many Turkmens prefer the courtyard residence as it affords more privacy, and a yard, and it is much cooler in the summer.

Under Soviet rule, living conditions in Turkmenistan were "modernized" in a distinctly Soviet way. Technology and industry were introduced and urban areas developed. Today, Turkmenistan is left with an outdated infrastructure in dire need of technical revamping, and there is a severe shortage of trained personnel and replacement parts. Although modern conveniences (telephones, plumbing, sewers, etc.) do exist in the cities, they usually work only sporadically. Cars, buses, and trains have replaced the horse and camel as the main modes of transportation in Turkmenistan, but the cost of new replacement vehicles and a lack of spare parts make travel difficult and expensive. Neglect of infrastructure has also led to short-

A Turkmen woman throws carnations on a monument erected on the memory of Turkmen soldiers who died during World War II.
(AP Images/Burhan Ozbilici)

ages of clean water and the breakdown of irrigation systems for agriculture.

Since Turkmenistan became independent, the health care system has fallen into disrepair. In 2001 President Niyazov ordered the closing of all hospitals outside Ashgabat. He also replaced 15,000 Turkmen healthcare workers with military conscripts. The rise to power of a new president and high natural gas prices (a boon for Turkmenistan) may lead to improvements in health, education, and infrastructure in Turkmenistan.

10 FAMILY LIFE

As in interpersonal relations, Turkmen custom (*turkmenchilik*) dictates a host of rules and provisions for family life. Most Turkmen families are extended, and elders live with their adult children. Nursing homes are extremely rare in Turkmenistan. The youngest son bears the primary responsibility for his parents' welfare and usually lives with his wife and children in the home of his parents, but other siblings can also share in such duties. Turkmen families are usually large, and families with

six or more children are the norm in rural areas. *Turkmenchilik* also requires that siblings and close relatives assist each other in times of need. It is incumbent on family and clan members to render each other assistance when building homes, organizing weddings and other functions, entering college, getting jobs, and so on.

Many marriages are arranged, and virtually all must be blessed by the parents. Western-style dating is rare. The motivating factor in arranged marriages is finding a suitable match. Such a match will be based on age, social status, education level, tribal affiliation, and other expectations. The young man should be 20–25 years old and have finished his military service. The woman should be 18–22 years old. One common element in the process is the paying of the *galyng* (bride price), which consists of a transfer of either money or goods to the bride's family. In most cases, a couple knows each other and has met at least several times. After the wedding, the bride usually goes to live with the groom in the home of his parents and must work as a member of the household. Because of the poverty of many Turkmen, the practice of "bride kidnapping" has become more common. Grooms who are unable to pay dowries may kidnap their perspective brides, and then try to convince the women to marry them. Often, elopements between a consenting woman and a consenting man are carried out using the tradition of bride kidnapping.

11 CLOTHING

The most prominent feature of traditional Turkmen male clothing is the *telpek*, a high sheepskin hat. Other Central Asian peoples wear sheepskin hats, but only the Turkmen have the large and wide *telpek*, which may be brown, black, or white and is typically very shaggy. Men who wear the *telpek* usually wear a skullcap beneath it and shave their heads. Long, deep-red robes with extended sleeves are also common among men in more traditional settings. In the cities especially, the clothing of the Turkmen male differs little from that of men in the West: no hat, a suit jacket (without a tie), and pants are the norm.

Turkmen women, both urban and rural, typically wear more traditional clothing than men. The main features are a long dress (often made from *ketine*, a silk fabric), a long head scarf, and a cloak-type red robe called a *kurte*, which is worn on top of the head and hangs down off the shoulders. Dresses and skirts above the ankle, sleeveless tops, and other Western-style clothing are considered too immodest by most Turkmen women. Turkmen women also sew a distinct type of embroidery called *keshde*, which adorns the collars and fringes of their clothing.

12 FOOD

Although the Turkmen have adopted some foods from the West, on the whole, Turkmen food is fairly unique and retains its traditional quality. Milk products from camels, cows, goats, and sheep are made into a variety of butters, creams, and yogurts. The meat of these animals is used to make the bulk of Turkmen dishes, with sheep and camel being the most sought after. Most meat dishes are baked (in dough) or boiled and combined with a variety of vegetables and sometimes dough or noodles. Soups and meat pie-type dishes make up the bulk of the dinner fare.

One favorite Turkmen dish is *dograma*, a soup thick with diced bread, lamb, onions, tomatoes, and spices. Hot green tea is part of every meal, even on the hottest days. Round flatbread is a staple throughout Central Asia. It is baked in a *tamdyr*—a round clay oven fired by coals that lie at its bottom. The dough is splashed with water and sticks to the oven's sides. The top of the Turkmen-style *tamdyr* has a large hole, which is covered during baking.

When relatives or guests visit, Turkmen hospitality dictates an all-out feast. The food is spread out on plates and dishes on a large cloth on the floor, and it is around this cloth covered with food (called a *sachak*) that the guests and family members sit and have their meal. A typical Turkmen *sachak* will include a variety of fruits, vegetables, nuts, sweets, tea and other beverages, bread, as well as butters and creams—all this before the main meal!

In Turkmen cities, Russian food is found in many restaurants. Popular Russian dishes include cabbage soup, grilled meat balls, and dumplings.

13 EDUCATION

The government of Turkmenistan reports its literacy rate to be 99%. All children must attend school and receive at least a high school education. Institutes, trade schools, colleges, and a university train those wishing and able to continue training. The economic crisis since Turkmenistan's independence has led to many problems in education. Low teacher pay, meager subsidies, and run-down facilities have resulted in serious problems, especially in rural areas. Children miss many days of school due to a lack of teachers and school space. In some cotton-growing areas, children and teachers are required to work in the fields during school hours for a substantial part of the school year. In addition, the government of Turkmenistan has weakened the national curriculum. The late President Niyazov replaced study of the arts and sciences with the study of a book entitled *The Ruhnama*. The book, written by Niyazov himself, is a mixture of history and pseudo-Islamic theology.

Aside from formal education, Turkmen youth receive a great deal of "practical" schooling at home. Young girls are expected to help out with the household chores, watch over younger children, and learn to cook, sew, and so on. Young boys often take care of livestock and learn basic agricultural and mechanical skills from older males.

14 CULTURAL HERITAGE

The most prominent figure in Turkmen cultural history is the 18th century poet, Magtymguly. The subjects of his poetry include historical events, romantic love, Islam, and a call for Turkmen tribal unity. It is this latter theme especially that is utilized by the government in its nation-building process. Magtymguly's life and works continue to receive much public and scholarly attention, and virtually all Turkmens know his poetry and biography by heart. Numerous pre-20th-century Turkmen poets achieved success by following in the footsteps of Magtymguly. The Turkmens also have a unique musical culture that is tied into the oral tradition (see section on "Folklore"). Turkmen music is characterized by the two-stringed *dutar* and the *gyjak* (a violin-like instrument) accompanied by singing.

Traditional Turkmen cultural traditions were heavily influenced by Soviet cultural policies. Religious and national themes were suppressed, the use of Turkmen language was inhibited, and traditional personal and communal expressions were replaced with propagandistic socialist ideals. Today, in spite of a revival of traditional Turkmen culture, the legacy of the Soviet period is evident, and state control of artistic expression remains tight. For example, the Pushkin Theater in Ashgabat once staged Russian language plays from the Czarist and Soviet era, but now stages productions based on the *Ruhnama*.

15 WORK

In rural areas of Turkmenistan, virtually all work is centered around agricultural and livestock production. As in the Soviet period, the state owns almost all the land and administers all the farms. Because of Turkmenistan's arid climate, irrigation is a critical industry. *Pagta* (cotton) is Turkmenistan's chief crop. It occupies the majority of the irrigated lands and is concentrated in the eastern areas. Fruits, vegetables, and grains are also grown throughout the country, and Turkmenistan's melons are considered some of sweetest in the world. Oil and gas deposits are concentrated along the Caspian coast and in southeastern areas. Turkmenistan is one of the major suppliers of natural gas to Europe, but revenues from natural gas have done little to create jobs in Turkmenistan. In 2007 the unemployment rate in Turkmenistan was estimated at 60%, one of the highest in the world. In some areas of Turkmenistan, there are almost no young men left, because they have all migrated abroad in search of work.

16 SPORTS

Turkmens enjoy numerous traditional and Western-style sports. Soccer is perhaps the most popular sport among young men and is called *futball*. Horse racing is also extremely popular and has become the most celebrated sport in Turkmenistan since independence. The horse has long symbolized the Turkmen spirit and occupies the most prominent spot on the state seal. Equine experts worldwide acknowledge Turkmen thoroughbreds such as the Ahal-teke to be among the swiftest and strongest breeds in the world.

In 2004 Turkmenistan sent eight athletes to the Olympics. They competed in track and field, boxing, weight lifting, shooting, swimming, and Judo.

17 ENTERTAINMENT AND RECREATION

Socializing and visiting friends and relatives are favorite pastimes among Turkmens. Visits usually involve large meals, some sort of entertainment (such as music), and staying overnight. Gatherings are also connected with holidays and may include pilgrimages to local shrines or simple outings to recreation spots in mountain, lake, or stream areas. Many urban Turkmens own summer houses and gardens on the outskirts of town where they spend vacation time. Turkmens also enjoy Russian television, which is only accessible via satellite. In 2008 the government began to curb the use of private satellite dishes.

18 FOLK ART, CRAFTS, AND HOBBIES

Often known as Bukharan carpets or "oriental" carpets, Turkmen carpets are prized as among the world's best by collectors and experts. Many Turkmen tribes have a distinct carpet ornamentation that identifies their carpets. Some carpets have up to 400,000 knots per square meter (37,000 per square foot). Another characteristic of Turkmen carpets is their deep red color. Almost all of the labor connected with carpet weaving and production is carried out by women. In an era of high inflation in Turkmenistan, Turkmens purchase carpets as an investment and hedge against inflation. Unfortunately, traditional carpet weaving is fading in Turkmenistan because of the rise of mechanized production facilities and the difficulties associated with exporting products from Turkmenistan. Aside from carpets, women also weave a variety of items connected with the nomadic life-style. Adornments for the felt tent, such as storage bags and door coverings, as well as items used for horses and camels, are the most common.

19 SOCIAL PROBLEMS

Severe economic problems since the dissolution of the Soviet Union coupled with the legacy of the negative aspects of Soviet rule have contributed to many social problems. High rates of inflation and economic depression has led to a sharp increase in poverty, crime, and unemployment. Corruption is rampant in all government and economic sectors. Another major problem has to do with the fact that some of the wealthiest individuals in Turkmenistan acquired their wealth through questionable or illegal speculation and trade practices. As a result, many people, especially youth, have abandoned attempts to acquire or use education and instead attempt to open small retail businesses. This emphasis on petty retail trade has exacerbated problems connected with Turkmenistan's low industrial and manufacturing production and has led to a high reliance on imported foodstuffs and consumer goods.

Substance abuse is a problem tied to poverty and economic depression. Turkmenistan lies along the transit route by which heroin from Afghanistan makes its way into Russia and Europe. The government of Turkmenistan estimates that 1 in 10 Turkmens is addicted to narcotics. However, the number of addicts is likely much higher. While addiction to alcohol, heroin, and marijuana has traditionally been confined to men, women are increasingly turning to drugs. Drug addiction and the drug trade lead to higher levels of crime, violence, and prostitution in Turkmenistan. Intravenous drug use also puts Turkmens at risk for HIV.

20 GENDER ISSUES

Gender relations in Turkmen society are influenced by Islam and Turkmenistan's Soviet and nomadic past. The veiling of women was never widespread amongst Turkmens, even though it was common amongst other peoples of Central Asia prior to the Russian conquest of the region. During the Soviet period, Turkmen women entered the workforce and gained high positions in the government bureaucracy and all of the major professions. Furthermore, laws in Turkmenistan grant men and women equal inheritance and legal rights.

Despite these areas of equality, Turkmen women do not always enjoy the same rights as Turkmen men. Bride kidnapping is still a common practice among Turkmens. In addition, women are expected to do housework and prepare food, while men are not. Finally, the government of Turkmenistan often carries out policies that discriminate against women. For example, in an attempt to combat sex work, the government of Turkmenistan has forbidden women under the age of 35 from flying to Turkey or the United Arab Emirates.

Homosexuality is illegal in Turkmenistan. The Islamic and Soviet influence on Turkmen society contributes to negative attitudes toward homosexual and transgender people. Sexual minorities are often sent to prison or "re-education" camps, which are designed for political dissidents. Even the gays and lesbians who avoid legal action face job discrimination. Turkmen families often force their homosexual relatives to marry individuals of the opposite sex.

21 BIBLIOGRAPHY

Blackwell, Carole. *Tradition and Society in Turkmenistan: Gender, Oral Culture and Song.* Richmond, Surrey: Curzon Press, 2001.

Blank, Stephen. *Turkmenistan and Central Asia after Niyazov.* Carlisle, PA: Strategic Studies Institute, U.S. Army War College, 2007.

Burghart, Daniel L. and Theresa Sabonis-Helf, eds. *In the Tracks of Tamerlane: Central Asia's Path to the 21st Century.* Washington, D.C.: Center for Technology and National Security Policy, National Defense University, 2004.

Clark, Larry, Mike Thurman, and David Tyson. *Turkmenistan: A Country Study*. Lanham, MD: Federal Research Division, United States Library of Congress, 1997.

Edgar, Adrienne Lynn. *Tribal Nation: The Making of Soviet Turkmenistan*. Princeton, NJ: Princeton University Press, 2004.

O'Bannon, George. *Vanishing Jewels: Central Asian Tribal Weavings*. Rochester, NY: Rochester Museum and Science Center, 1990.

—revised by B. Lazarus

TURKS

PRONUNCIATION: TURKS
LOCATION: Turkey
POPULATION: 70.6 million
LANGUAGE: Turkish
RELIGION: Islam (Sunni Muslim majority, Alevi Muslim minority)

¹INTRODUCTION

The Turks' pride in their country and their nationality is expressed in the popular slogan, first coined by the great Turkish nationalist leader Atatürk: *Ne mutlu Türkum diyene* ("How happy is he who can say he is a Turk"). Turkey is a land of opposites, belonging to both the East and the West. It is a Middle Eastern state and a member of the North Atlantic Treaty Organization (NATO). Historically, it has been a center of both Christianity and Islam. It has been variously regarded as both a first-world economy and a developing nation. In the 2000s, there are many oppositions at the forefront of events in Turkey. One is between the statist-secularist tradition begun by Atatürk in the 1920s and the liberal pro-Islam movement of Justice and Development Party of Prime Minister Erdoğan. Another opposition is between the Turkish state and many of Turkey's Kurds, who seek greater autonomy for the Kurdish-majority provinces of Eastern and Southeastern Turkey.

The land known today as Turkey has only been inhabited by Turkish peoples since the 11th century. Before that, it was home to many different groups, including the ancient Hittites, Greeks, Persians, and Romans. In 330 CE, present-day Istanbul, previously known as Byzantium, was named Constantinople by the Roman Emperor Constantine I and became the seat of the Byzantine Empire (and later of Eastern Orthodox Christianity, when it officially broke from Roman Catholicism). The ancestors of today's Turks, known as the Seljuk Turks, won control of the region from the Byzantines in 1071 CE.

By the 15th century, Turkish culture and the Turkish language had spread throughout Asia Minor (as the region was then called), although the Seljuks themselves had been driven from power in the Mongol invasion of 1243. Turkish power revived under the Ottomans, who conquered Constantinople in 1453, eventually building an empire of some 28 million inhabitants that included not only Asia Minor but stretched as far as North Africa and the Caucasus. The power of the Ottoman Empire reached its height during the reign of Süleyman the Magnificent in the 16th century, when the Ottoman armies made inroads into Europe, and the skylines of the empire's great cities, including Istanbul, Mecca, and Jerusalem, were transformed by the mosques and mausoleums of the architect Sinan under Süleyman's patronage.

Between the 17th and 19th centuries, the Ottoman empire suffered a gradual decline, eclipsed by the great European powers to the west. The defeat of the Turks in World War I, which they entered on the side of the Central Powers, signaled the final dissolution of their empire, by then known as "the sick man of Europe." The harsh conditions imposed on the Turks by the victorious Allied Powers helped instigate a nationalist uprising led by Mustafa Kemal (later known as Atatürk), who presided over the formation of a secular democratic republic in 1923 and, over the 15 years until his death in 1938, implemented many reforms to modernize and secularize the Turkish nation.

Turkey maintained a position of neutrality during most of World War II and became a charter member of the United Nations in 1945. Since the end of World War II, a backlash against Atatürk's secularization measures—known in Turkey as the "Reaction"—has consistently figured to some extent in the country's political life, often exploited by individual politicians for the purpose of gaining votes. Political rule has been marked by coups in 1960 and 1980, neither of which resulted in long-term military rule. In 1974 Turkey invaded Cyprus after a coup that overthrew that country's president, fearing that Greece would annex the island. Turkey's actions resulted in economic and arms embargoes by other nations.

In the wake of the 1991 Gulf War, Kurdish separatists intensified their terrorist activities, resulting in retaliation by the military and international condemnation of human rights abuses. Estimates in 2008 placed the number of Kurds displaced by the conflict at about 1 million. The late 1990s saw the rise of pro-Islam political parties in Turkey. The Welfare Party of Necmettin Erbakan briefly held power in 1997. Its rule was ended by a request from the secularist military that the party step down. Since 2001, the pro-Western, pro-Islam Justice and Development Party (AKP) of Recep Tayyip Erdoğan has held power in Turkey. Although more moderate than its Islamist predecessors, the party is facing closure by the Constitutional Court on the grounds that it seeks to overthrow Turkey's secular system.

²LOCATION AND HOMELAND

Turkey, lying partly in Europe and partly in Asia, has historically served as a bridge between the two continents. With a total area of 779,452 sq km (301,063 sq mi), Turkey is a relatively large country, bounded on the west by Greece, Bulgaria, and the Aegean Sea; on the east by Iran and the former Soviet Union; on the south by Iraq, Syria, and the Mediterranean Sea; and on the north by the Black Sea. It is slightly larger than the state of Texas but has three times the population of the American state. The European portion of Turkey, which is separated from Asian Turkey by the Bosphorus Strait, the Sea of Marmara, and the Dardanelles Strait, is commonly known as Thrace and occupies only 3% of the country's area; the Asian portion, called Anatolia or Asia Minor, accounts for the rest.

At the end of 2007 Turkey had a population of 70.6 million. Between 80% and 90% of the population is composed of ethnic Turks, with Kurds forming the country's largest ethnic minority (estimates of the Kurdish population range from 6 to 12 million). The precise number of Kurds is difficult to determine, as many Kurdish speakers identify as ethnic Turks and many monolingual Turkish speakers identify as ethnically Kurdish. Other minorities include Arabs, Greeks, Armenians, and three other groups who have their origins in the Caucasus Mountains: the Circassians, the Georgians, and the Laz.

³LANGUAGE

More than 90% of Turkey's population speaks Turkish as a first language. In the 1920s the nationalist leader Mustafa Kemal Atatürk instituted two major language reforms, replacing the Arabic script used during the Ottoman era with a modified Latin alphabet and attempting to eradicate loan words from

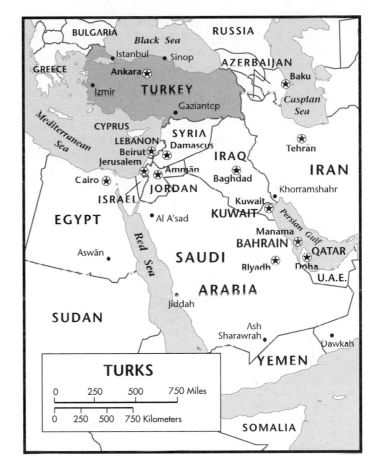

Arabic, Persian, and other languages by substituting Turkish ones. Nevertheless, words with Arabic and Persian origins still remain part of the language. In addition, a number of modern words that had no Turkish equivalents were subsequently borrowed from European languages, such as the English-derived *otomobil*, *tren*, and *taksi*.

Turkish has no gender, so there are no distinct pronouns for *he*, *she*, and *it*, and there are no definite or indefinite articles. Turkish words are formed by adding suffixes denoting action, place, possession, and other qualities to a root that does not change. A root and its suffixes can become comprehensive enough to form an entire sentence, the most famous example being the following, which means "Weren't you one of the people whom we tried without success to make resemble the citizens of Afyonkarahisar?":

Afyonkarahisarlılaturamadıklarımızdanmuymustiniz.

COMMON TURKISH WORDS AND PHRASES

Hello	*merhaba*
Good morning	*günaydin*
Please	*lütfen*
Thank you	*teşekkür ederim*
To your health!	*afiyet olsun* (said at the beginning of a meal)
May your life by spared!	*başiniz sağolsun!* (said when death is mentioned)
May it be in the past!	*geçmiş olsun!* (said in regard to an illness or injury)

There are two forms of "goodbye": *allahaısmarladık*, said by the person who is leaving; and *güle güle*, said by the person who stays behind. There are also two common words for "no": *hayır*, and the more emphatic (and less polite) *yok*, which literally means "there is none" and is often uttered with raised eyebrows and pursed lips.

⁴FOLKLORE

The Turks have a rich tradition of folktales, some of which can take as long as 30 hours to recite. The most popular and numerous involve the legendary Nasrettin Hoca, a comic figure thought to have been a sage and teacher in Akşehir in the 13th century. The following are typical Hoca stories:

One day, the Hoca was sitting in his garden under the shade of a walnut tree. Looking around his garden, he wondered why Allah caused large, heavy watermelons to grow on spindly vines while little walnuts grew on tall trees. He mused that, if he had been the creator, he would have done just the reverse. Just then, a walnut fell from the tree, hitting him on the forehead, and the Hoca thanked Allah for arranging the world just as it was, grateful that he hadn't been struck by a watermelon instead.

When the Hoca lost his donkey, he prayed and thanked God. Asked why he was grateful for losing his donkey, he replied, "I'm fortunate that I wasn't riding him when he got lost, or I would be lost as well."

Other famous folktale heroes include Dedeh Horkut, whose exploits, dating back to the nomadic days of the Turkish people, appear in children's books, and Koroğlu, a Turkish version of Robin Hood. Following are several well-known Turkish proverbs:

On a winter's day, the fireside is a bed of tulips.

The only head free of worries is that of a scarecrow.

Success depends on a man's reputation, not on his soul.

If you dig a grave for your neighbor, measure it for yourself.

Other folktales include stories told using the shadow puppet characters Karagöz and Hacivat. Karagöz, whose name means "Black Eye," entertains the audience with his low-brow humor. Hacivat is the more dignified and educated of the two, but he is always outsmarted by Karagöz. Karagöz and Hacivat shadow plays are often performed during Ramadan.

⁵RELIGION

More than 99% of Turks are Muslims. Most are Hanafi Sunni Muslims. Approximately 15%–25% of Turks subscribe to Allevi Islam, a form of Shia Islam. Allevis pray in prayer houses known as *Cem Evis*. Religious minorities include a small number of Jews whose ancestors fled the Spanish Inquisition in 1492 and found refuge among the Ottomans. There are also small numbers of Armenian, Syrian, and Greek Orthodox Christians. A unique group known as the Dönme are descended from Jews who were followers of the 17th-century false messiah, Shabbatai Zevi, who was ultimately forced to convert to Islam. The religion of the Dönme combines elements of Judaism and Islam.

Although the Turks as a people are Muslims, their country has been a secular state since shortly after World War I, when Atatürk established a democratic republic ruled by codes of law, ending the sovereignty of Islamic law in the country. Nevertheless, Islam is basic to the fabric of everyday life in Turkey. Many Turks interrupt all other activities five times a day for prayer sessions lasting about 10 minutes. The country's religious heritage is also very much in evidence in its legacy of beautiful mosques and minarets that distinguish the Turkish landscape.

Religion is a major point of contention in Turkish society. The leaders of Turkey's judiciary, military, and educational system are highly secularized and suspicious of overt displays of religious piety, such as the wearing of the Muslim headscarf. As of 2008, the popular AK Party of Prime Minister Erdoğan was locked in a struggle with Turkey's secular elite to create more space for the expression of religious beliefs in the public sphere.

⁶MAJOR HOLIDAYS

Turkey observes the following secular holidays: New Year's Day (January 1); Children's Day, also known as National Sovereignty Day, which commemorates the establishment of the country's Grand National Assembly in 1923 (April 23); Atatürk's birthday, also National Youth and Sports Day (May 19); Victory Day, commemorating liberation from Greece in 1922 (August 30); Republic Day (October 28 and 29); and the anniversary of Atatürk's death (November 10), a national day of mourning when all forms of entertainment are shut down and the nation observes a moment of silence at 9:05 PM, the hour of Atatürk's death.

The Turks also observe a number of Islamic holidays dated by the lunar calendar. These include Recep Kandili, commemorating the conception of the prophet Muhammad (first Friday of the month of Recep); Miraç Kandili, marking Muhammad's journey from Mecca to Jerusalem and his subsequent ascension to Heaven (26th day of Recep); Berat Kandili, a nighttime holiday similar to All Hallows' Eve in Christianity (14th and 15th days of Saban); and Kadir Gecesi, commemorating the night when the Quran was revealed to Muhammad and he received his calling as the Messenger of God (27th day of Ramazan).

In addition, the Turks, like Muslims in other countries, observe the holy month of Ramazan (called *Ramadan* in Arab countries), a period of fasting when Muslims do not eat or drink during daylight hours. (Irritability occasioned by this fasting is called *Ramazan kafası*—"Ramazan head.") The end of Ramazan is marked by Şeker Bayramı, a three-day national holiday when families pay social calls and children go from door to door asking for sweets.

⁷RITES OF PASSAGE

A number of popular traditional beliefs and superstitions still surround childbirth, including the use of magical formulas to ensure the birth of a son and the belief that a newborn child is especially vulnerable to evil spirits during the first 40 days of life. All male Turkish Muslims are circumcised, either at the age of seven or later as part of an initiation into adulthood.

For Turkish men, military service is another major rite of passage. All Turkish men are required to serve in the military. Before men leave for military service, they often perform a traditional dance with their families.

Wedding ceremonies are performed in the town or city hall and are followed by a private reception with food, dancing,

Thousands of Turks congregate in front of Mustafa Kemal Ataturk's mausoleum in Ankara in February 2008. They were there to protest against a government plan to lift a ban on the Islamic headscarf in universities. (Adem Altan/AFP/Getty Images)

and music. Dowries are still paid by the bride's family in some rural areas.

Funerals in Turkey, as in other Muslim countries, are attended only by men. Usually a *mevlud* (a poem in honor of the prophet Muhammad's birth) is recited. Like people elsewhere in the Islamic world, the Turks avoid ostentation in connection with death, both in the funeral service and in burial arrangements.

8 INTERPERSONAL RELATIONS

The Turks are an exceptionally polite people, particularly to visitors, and they use many courteous phrases in everyday conversation. They have three different ways of saying "thank you": *sağol*, *teşekkür edermin*, and the French-derived *mersi*. It is considered impolite to hug or kiss members of the opposite sex in public, and a handshake that is too firm is also considered a sign of bad manners. On the other hand, it is acceptable and customary for men to publicly display physical affection toward each other, embracing and kissing when they greet each other and walking down the street arm-in-arm or holding hands. Atatürk introduced the titles of Mr. and Mrs. (*Bey* and *Hanim*) to the country.

A commonly used gesture for "no" consists of raising one's chin and clicking one's tongue, sometimes accompanied by shutting or uplifting one's eyes. ("No" can also be communicated by raising one's eyebrows.) A sharp downward nod means "yes," and shaking one's head sideways means "I don't understand." Waving one's hand up and down with the palm toward the ground is a gesture that means "come here."

Although Turkey is a modern, efficient, secular society, some traditional superstitions and customs persist. For example, charms to ward off the evil eye can be seen in most cars and taxis.

9 LIVING CONDITIONS

Due to its high rate of population growth and the mass migration of the rural poor to cities following World War II, Turkey faces a housing shortage that is among its most serious social problems. Since the 1950s, new urban dwellers unable to afford decent housing have built large numbers of temporary shelters called *gecekondus* on the outskirts of major cities such as Ankara and Istanbul. The squatter communities created by these dwellings have turned into permanent urban slums, often lacking such standard features as running water, sewer systems, electricity, and pavements. By the 1980s, it was estimated that more than half the residents of many urban centers lived in *gecekondus*. The government has taken measures to improve life in these shantytowns, including banning the construction of new *gecekondus* and making provisions to fund the construction of new housing. Between 30% and 40% of Turkey's population still lives in rural areas, where housing types vary by region. Houses in the rural villages of the Black Sea region are made of wood, whereas those on the Anatolian plateau are generally of sun-dried brick. Village houses are generally two stories high with flat roofs. In the eastern part of the country, many lack running water and some have no electricity.

Health care in Turkey is provided by the government through the Ministry of Health. Availability of qualified medical personnel has improved significantly since the 1980s, but it remains better in urban areas than in rural areas, where it is often still inadequate. Persons living in some areas, such as eastern Anatolia, must travel to provincial capitals for medical care. Infant mortality declined from 120 deaths per 1,000 live births in 1980—then one of the highest rates in the world—to 40 per 1,000 in 2008.

By World War I, the Ottoman Empire already had an extensive railway system that included the famous Orient Express line. The country still has excellent rail transportation, although rail service is not available in some parts of southern and southeastern Turkey. There is a modern highway system connected to Europe by the Bosphorus Bridge, and international air service from Istanbul and Ankara. In the 1990s several new highway projects were underway to ease traffic congestion. The main seaports are Istanbul on the Bosphorus and Izmir on the Aegean Sea. In 2008 a new railway linking Turkey with Georgia and Azerbaijan was completed.

¹⁰FAMILY LIFE

Traditionally, Turkish marriages were arranged, and in rural areas some still are. The extended family is still important in rural areas, but less so in cities, although it is not unusual for an urban household to include parents, children, and paternal grandparents. In rural areas, women still marry at young ages, and financial arrangements between the two families are important in making marriage decisions. Massive migrations of rural Turks from the Black Sea and Eastern and Southeastern regions to cities across Turkey has led to a decline in the importance of the extended family. It has also increased the number of women in the labor force.

¹¹CLOTHING

Modern Western-style clothing has been worn in Turkey since the founding of the republic in the 1920s. In urban areas, both adults and teenagers look much the same as those in the cities of the West, with well-dressed businessmen wearing Italian suits, women taking an interest in the latest fashions from Paris, and young people wearing the universal teen uniform of jeans and athletic shoes. In villages and certain tourist areas, one may still see the traditional *salvar*, the baggy, loose-fitting trousers worn by both men and women. Bright colors and flowered prints are favored by village women. Although they do not wear veils, many women in rural areas cover their faces with a scarf or handkerchief when they are in close proximity to men they don't know.

Traditional male dress consisted of the *salvar*, often worn under a long gown with a wide belt in the middle, and the headpiece called a *fez* (outlawed when Atatürk was in power). In recent years, a style of Muslim headscarf known as the *türban* has become popular amongst observant Muslim women

(this is not to be confused with the head covering worn by males that goes by the same name). Between 1998 and 2008 the *türban* was officially prohibited in Turkey's universities. Even though approximately 60% of Turkish women cover their heads, many in Turkey's secular elite view the spread of the *türban* as a worrying sign of increasing religiosity in Turkey.

¹²FOOD

Turkey is famous for its food, which has been called the French cuisine of the East. The most famous dish of Turkish origin is the shish kebab, pieces of lamb grilled on a skewer. Today, the most popular national dish is the *döner kebap*, lamb roasted on a turning vertical spit, from which slices are cut as it cooks. Turkey is also famous for its appetizers, called *meze*, made from meat, fish, and vegetables. The most popular include *böreks*, rolled phyllo dough stuffed with white cheese and parsley; *dolma*, various types of vegetables stuffed with rice and meat; and *imam bayıldı*, eggplant stuffed with ground lamb, onions, and tomatoes. (The name *imam bayıldı*, means "the imam swooned," suggesting that the dish was so delicious it made a religious leader faint when he tried it.)

The Turks are also noted for their desserts, ranging from the well-known *baklava* (small pieces of flaky pastry filled with ground walnuts and dripping in honey) to such exotic creations as "nightingale's nest" and "lady's navel." The basic ingredients of Turkish desserts are milk, honey, eggs, nuts, and phyllo dough. Desserts made with milk include *muhallabi* (rice pudding with cinnamon) and *keşkül* (a milk, almond, and pistachio mixture topped with dried coconut and pistachio).

¹³EDUCATION

In 2004 the adult literacy rate was 87.4% (95.3% for males aged 15 and over, compared with only 79.6% for females of the same age group). Primary education has been available to almost all children between the ages of 6 and 10 since the 1980s. Five levels of education are available: preschool, primary school, middle school, secondary school, and university. Education is not compulsory past middle school, and it is estimated that 89% of children attend primary school. Like medical care in Turkey, the quality of education in rural areas varies significantly. Many rural communities do not have high schools, which sometimes makes it necessary for children to travel great distances if they want to continue their education.

There are several hundred institutions of higher learning in Turkey, including 53 state-supported universities and a number of private universities. In 2005, 2.3 million students were enrolled in Turkish universities, almost double the number that were enrolled 10 years earlier. Students are admitted to Turkey's public universities through a central placement system.

¹⁴CULTURAL HERITAGE

The whirling dervishes, whose white-clad, rapidly turning figures in their swirling skirts are known the world over, are part of a religious tradition that seeks a mystical union with God through music and dance. The Turks also have a centuries-old tradition of folk dancing that varies from one region to the next, each with its own distinctive homemade costumes.

Turkish painting dates back to the court painters of the Ottoman empire who, among other skills, developed the specialty of miniature painting. The contemporary painter Rahmi Pehlivanli is known for his portraits of leading political and diplomatic figures, as well as his landscapes of different regions of the country.

Several of Turkey's leading literary figures in modern times have been involved in political controversies and their works subjected to censorship. The works of Nazim Hikmet, a Marxist-influenced poet who died in the former Soviet Union in 1963, were banned for years but are now gaining belated recognition. The left-wing satirist Aziz Nesin, who published excerpts from Salman Rushdie's controversial *Satanic Verses*, was jailed for much of his life. (Nesin died in 1995.) Yaşar Kemal, a leading novelist, has been harassed in recent years over the content of a newspaper article he authored. Turkey's most famous filmmaker, Yılmaz Güney, was imprisoned for most of his career, writing screenplays in prison and smuggling them out through friends, together with detailed instructions for their direction. Orhan Pamuk, who won the Nobel Prize for literature in 2006, was charged by state prosecutors with "insulting Turkishness," although he was never convicted.

Traditional Turkish music is rich and complex both harmonically and rhythmically, incorporating dozens of tonal modes in addition to the major and minor scales of Western music and containing meters with such irregular rhythms (to Western ears) as 7, 9, 11, or 13 beats per measure. Traditional instruments include the *ud* (which resembles a lute), the *santur* (a Persian version of the dulcimer), and another lute-like instrument, the *tanbur*.

15 WORK

The services sector, including a growing tourist industry, accounts for 41.2% of jobs in the Turkish economy. Agriculture accounts for about 35.9%, while industry accounts for about 22.8% of employment. In rural areas, all family members participate in agricultural work, with women routinely performing tasks such as hoeing vegetables and digging out potatoes. Unemployment is a serious problem in Turkey; in 2007 the country's unemployment rate was 9.7%. Unemployment and underemployment are most widespread in the Black Sea and Eastern and Southeastern regions of the country.

16 SPORTS

The most popular sport in Turkey is soccer, with matches played on weekends between September and May. Like their counterparts in Europe and Latin America, Turkey's soccer fans are wildly enthusiastic, often to the point of violence against each other or against members of losing teams. Large-scale betting is associated with soccer games. Soccer is also played by young people for recreation.

Wrestling is another favorite sport in Turkey, and Turkey has sent many wrestling teams to the Olympic Games. A unique Turkish variety (not represented in the Olympics) is greased wrestling, which makes it harder to hold on to one's opponent. Other sports popular among the Turks include hunting and shooting, skiing (the oldest Turkish ski resort is on Mount Olympus, the legendary home of the gods), and *cirit*, a traditional sport that involves throwing a javelin while mounted on horseback.

17 ENTERTAINMENT AND RECREATION

Among the traditional Turkish forms of relaxation, the best known is the steam bath or *hamam*. Both men and women use the *hamam*, although they use it separately, either going on alternate days or using separate facilities. Wood-burning stoves are used as heat sources, with bathers absorbing the heat by lying on raised slabs directly above the stoves.

The time-honored leisure-time haunt of Turkish men is the coffeehouse (*kiraathane*), where backgammon is often played and one can find customers smoking hookahs. In recent years, hookah bars have become popular amongst young people.

In the large cities of the West, such as Istanbul, Ankara, and Izmir, many young Turks enjoy going to discos and bars. Popular music is also a source of entertainment. Tarkan, Sezan Aksu, and Mustafa Sandal are all famous Turkish pop singers. Turkey has also produced a number of successful rock and rap groups.

18 FOLK ART, CRAFTS, AND HOBBIES

Turkey's most famous handicrafts are its carpets, which sport a dazzling array of designs, many connected with a particular town or region. Most are of the flat-woven *kilim* variety. Tiles and ceramics have been produced in Turkey since the 11th century and can still be seen adorning the walls of mosques and other buildings.

Another craft found in Turkey is tile making. Turkey's most famous tiles come from the town of Iznik in Western Turkey. The first Iznik tiles date back to Ottoman times. The turquoise tiles are now produced mainly for tourists.

19 SOCIAL PROBLEMS

Poverty and unemployment are among Turkey's greatest social problems. In 2003 over 18% of Turks lived on less than $2 per day. Much of the extreme poverty in Turkey is concentrated in the East and Southeast of the country. The conflict with the Kurdistan Workers' Party (PKK), poor infrastructure, and lack of investment have prevented these regions from sharing in the recent prosperity of the rest of the country.

The internal displacement of approximately 1 million Kurdish Turks is another major social problem. Many displaced Kurds live in shantytowns and lack access to educational and employment opportunities. Growing tension between ethnic Turks and ethnic Kurds is also a problem in Turkey. Hundreds of thousands of Kurds have migrated to ethnic Turkish-majority cities, which has contributed to overcrowding. The Kurdistan Workers' Party (PKK) continues to attack the Turkish military. These PKK attacks cause some Turks to view Kurds negatively.

20 GENDER ISSUES

The Turkish constitution grants women the same rights it grants men. Turkey had its first woman prime minister in 1993 and women work in nearly all of Turkey's professions.

However, gender inequality is still present in Turkey, just as it is in nearly every other country around the world. For example, virginity is seen as important for women, but not very important for men. In most Turkish families, women are expected to do the housework and prepare meals for the family. Although women participate in politics, they are underrepresented in parliament and in local governments.

Gender inequality is even more pronounced in the rural areas of Eastern and Southeastern Turkey than in other regions of the country. In the East and Southeast, many girls are prevented by their families from finishing high school. Although uncommon, honor killings of women and girls do occur in conservative areas. Honor killings are murders carried out by male family members against female family members suspected of adultery, pre-marital sex, or other actions perceived to bring dishonor to the family.

Homosexuality is not widely accepted in Turkish culture. Homosexuality is not illegal in Turkey, but gays do not have the right to marry or adopt children. Despite negative attitudes towards Lesbian Gay Bisexual and Transgender (LGBT) people in Turkey, there are a number of well-known gay and transgender artists in Turkey, such as Bülent Ersoy and Zeki Müren.

[21] BIBLIOGRAPHY

Ahmad, Feroz. *The Making of Modern Turkey*. New York: Routledge, 1993.

Arat, Yesim. "Islamic Fundamentalism and Women in Turkey." *Muslim World* (1990,): 17–23.

Balim, Çigdem, Ersin Kalaycioglu, Cevat Karatas, Gareth Winrow, and Feroz Yawamee, eds. *Turkey: Political, Social and Economic Challenges in the 1990s*. New York: E. J. Brill, 1995.

Hale, William. *Turkey, the US, and Iraq*. London: Saqi, 2007.

Kagitcibasi, Cigdem, ed. *Sex Roles, Family, and Community in Turkey*. Bloomington: Indiana University Turkish Studies, 1982.

Mango, Andrew. *The Turks Today*. New York: The Overlook Press, 2004.

Metz, Helen Chapin. *Turkey: A Country Study*. Library of Congress, Federal Research Division. Washington, D.C.: USGPO, 1996.

Onder, Sylvia Wing. *We Have No Microbes Here: Healing Practices in a Turkish Black Sea Village*. Chapel Hill, NC: Carolina Academic Press, 2007.

Tapper, Richard, ed. *Islam in Modern Turkey: Religion, Politics, and Literature in a Secular State*. London: Tauris, 1991.

White, Jenny B. *Money Makes Us Relatives: Women's Labor in Urban Turkey*. Austin: University of Texas Press, 1994.

White, Jenny. *Islamist Mobilization in Turkey: A Study in Vernacular Politics*. Washington: University of Washington Press, 2002.

—revised by B. Lazarus

UIGHURS

PRONUNCIATION: wee-GURS
LOCATION: China (Xinjiang Uighur Autonomous Region)
POPULATION: 8.4 million
LANGUAGE: Uighur
RELIGION: Islam
RELATED ARTICLES: Vol. 3: China and Her National Minorities

[1] INTRODUCTION

The Uighurs are the main body of the population of Xinjiang Uighur Autonomous Region. As far back as 2,000 years ago, the ancestors of the Uighurs lived in an area close to Lake Baikal, to the north of the People's Republic of Mongolia. After the 5th century, a great number of them moved to Xiyu (present-day Xinjiang), which had been governed by the central government of China since 60 BC. Three centuries later, the Uighurs destroyed a country of nomadic Turks and established a dependency under the command of the Tang Dynasty (618–907). Chinese culture was widely disseminated and was accepted. Abandoning their nomadic life, they gradually settled down about 1,000 years ago.

In the 13th and 14th centuries, the Uighurs were ruled by other nationalities, including the Mongols and troops of Chinese soldiers were sent by the descendants of Genghis Khan to cultivate the land. Thereafter, there were long periods of trouble in the history of Xinjiang. Order was finally established by the Manchu government of the Qing Dynasty (1644–1911). Great numbers of Mongols and Chinese living there were assimilated into Uighur society during this chaotic period. However, there was no peace and tranquility until the mid-1940s.

[2] LOCATION AND HOMELAND

The Uighurs live in their own autonomous region of Xinjiang (the largest administrative territory of China) and are mainly concentrated in the oases to the south of the Tianshan Mountains, though they are also found in some counties of Hunan Province in south China. The Tianshan Mountains partition Xinjiang into two parts. The south is warm and dry, while the north is cold with abundant rain and snow. South Xinjiang is characterized by its huge basin (Tarim) and desert (Taklimakan) at the center. Fertilized by rivers, the oases surrounding the basin are the Uighur's land of cotton and fruits. Uighur population amounted to 8.4 million in 2000.

[3] LANGUAGE

The Uighur language belongs to the Altaic family, Turkic group. There are three dialects. The written language, based on Arabic characters, has been used since the 11th century. The name Uighur was self-given; it means "to unite" and "to assist."

[4] FOLKLORE

A Uighur epic narrates how the Queen of Kala Khan gave birth to a son with a blue face and hairy body. His mother breast-fed the infant only once; he then lived on raw meat and wine. He was able to talk right after birth and to walk 40 days later. Before long, he had grown up to be a heroic man. He killed a wild animal with a single horn, saving many lives from death. He was called Wugusi. One day, he hunted in the wilds. At night, he saw a beautiful girl after a flash of blue light. They got married, and she gave birth to three sons called Sun, Moon, and Stars. Wugusi married a second wife who also gave birth to three sons called Heaven, Mountain, and Sea. The six sons had a total of 24 children, who became 24 tribes. Wugusi ascended the throne as Khan and united the neighboring nations to form a large country.

According to another myth, two trees grew intertwined with a chamber between them. Some members of Uighur tribes were greatly surprised to find five infants in the chamber. Uighur women breast-fed them. Later, the children asked about their parents. When they knew the story, they went into the forest. The trees taught them to become pioneers in a great undertaking. The Uighurs elected the youngest boy to be their Khan, and, after ascending the throne, he became a very capable ruler. Reference to the title of "Khan" seems to indicate that these myths took shape rather late in history, after the 11th century.

⁵RELIGION

In the past, the Uighurs believed in Manichaeism, Zoroastrianism, Buddhism, and Nestorian Christianity. Starting with the 11th century, they gradually shifted their beliefs to Islam. Islam in Xinjiang came from central Asia through the land route, the famous Silk Road.

Probably a remnant of their ancient beliefs, the Uighurs traditionally regarded the eagle as a god. They believed that the eagle could see and then peck at the ghost who had made someone sick. If a family member got sick, they placed a falcon in the room and let it clutch and peck at the patient, who was wrapped in a quilt from head to toe.

⁶MAJOR HOLIDAYS

The Uighurs celebrate the two major holidays of Islam, the Corban Festival and the Lesser Bairam. In addition, they have their own traditional holiday, the Naoluzi Festival. The annual Corban Festival is the grandest of all. Each household fries twisted noodles and kills a sheep or an ox. Everybody dresses up and pays visit to the other members of the community. Tradition has it that the Prophet dreamed that Allah wanted him to kill his own son as a sacrificial victim—a trial of his loyalty. Deeply moved by the Prophet's absolute obedience, Allah sent a black head sheep for substitution. This belief gave rise to a major sacrificial ritual held on the tenth of December by Muslims around the world.

The Lesser Bairam (Festival of Fast-Breaking) marks the end of Ramadan. Muslims practice a month of fasting during September (Islamic calendar), which prohibits food and drink in the daytime. At dusk on the twenty-ninth day after the Ramadan, if the new moon is visible in the sky, the next day will be the Lesser Bairam. If the moon is not visible, the festival will be postponed until the following day. On the festival day, Muslims, after bathing, go to the mosque to pray, participate in rituals, and meet each other. The Uighurs visit each other and offer fried twisted noodles and various delicious foods to the guests.

The Naoluzi Festival is similar to the Chinese Spring Festival. A variety of sports and recreation activities are held during that month-long festival.

⁷RITES OF PASSAGE

The Uighur family usually celebrates the birth of a child. The Uighurs have a special reverence for the wolf. They speak of "giving birth to a wolf" if a son is born. The mother-to-be lies on a mat of wolf fur. The ankle bone of a wolf is attached to the infant's neck or hung over its cradle in the hope that the baby will be free from evil and will grow to be a brave man.

Funeral rites follow Islamic regulations. For instance, the body should be cleansed with water, wrapped with white cloth, and then buried underground three days after death. After the funeral, a limited number of sacrificial rites will be performed.

⁸INTERPERSONAL RELATIONS

Meeting after a long separation, Uighur friends often embrace each other. Meeting at ordinary times, they bow slightly or shake hands. The Uighurs are fond of bustle and excitement and love to sing and dance. Accompanied by songs and music, their dance on festivals is so lively and entertaining that everybody feels an impulse to dance together. Participants on those occasions may amount to hundreds. The Uighurs are hospitable. Guests are received with roast lamb and milk tea.

⁹LIVING CONDITIONS

Most Uighur houses are one story, low and small, square in shape, and made of adobes. The door often opens to the north. There are no windows in the side walls, but only a skylight window in the ceiling. Grains, fruits, and melons are piled up on the flat roof, which also serves for drying clothes in the sun

Uighur women sell yoghurt at a Sunday bazaar in Kashgar, China. Many people come to the bazaar that once made Kashgar a major trading post on the legendary Silk Road. (Robert Saiget/AFP/Getty Images)

and enjoying the cool evening air. There is a solid platform inside the house, made of adobes, that is one foot tall and is used both for sitting and for sleeping. One also finds a fireplace, used to cook food and to keep the house warm, and a niche for daily necessities. Tapestry is often hung on the wall as decoration. Almost every household has a courtyard where one grows flowers, fruit trees, and grapes; these form a kind of lattice ceiling of bright colors and offer coolness on warm summer days. Both the courtyard and the house are usually very clean. Some Uighurs have a house for summer and a house for winter.

In the past, transport was done with camels and donkeys. Today, these have been replaced by bicycles and motorcycles. Highways radiate in all directions from the cities; some roads cross wide expanses of desert. Travel by train and by air is not uncommon.

¹⁰FAMILY LIFE

The Uighur family is monogamous. Sons and daughters leave their parents after wedding. Within the family, the man dominates everything; the position of the women is rather low. The name of the child follows the patrilineal line. As in the West (but different from Chinese custom), the personal name comes first and the family (paternal) name comes second. If the child

is a boy, when he grows to be a man and gets married, his name will be the latter half of his child's name.

¹¹CLOTHING

Men usually wear a buttonless cotton robe with two color stripes and a belt at the waist. They may put on a dustcoat over the robe. The women usually wear an overdress with underskirt inside and a black velvet vest covering the top.

The girls plait their hair into braids, usually in odd numbers, as many as 41. The braids symbolize that their hair is thick and dense like the trees of the forest.

Almost all Uighur women like to wear earrings, bracelets, and necklaces. Dressed in their holiday best, they often use makeup and polish their nails. A four-edge small hat, embroidered with multicolored or black-and-white silk threads is the girls' favorite headdress. Both men and women wear boots.

¹²FOOD

Uighur staple foods include flour, corn, and rice. They like a kind of unleavened bread shaped like bagels or pancakes *(nang)*, made with wheat flour or corn maize flour. A popular dish during the festivals is the "rice taken by hand." Raisins are boiled with sliced onions, carrots, and small cubes of fried beef, then put on soaked rice and boiled again. The ingredients are steamed for 20 minutes, then they are served. Before eating, one washes one's hands three times and rubs them dry with handkerchiefs. Sitting cross-legged on cushions, people dish out the rice on the plates and then take the rice with their hand. Roast lamb is a delicacy usually reserved for guests. The Uighurs like butter, tea, and milk tea. Crusty breads (nung) with milk tea is their daily breakfast. They take various dishes and staple foods for lunch. Dinner is similar to breakfast, although some dishes may be added. People wash hands and gargle before and after each meal.

¹³EDUCATION

There are 13 universities and colleges and 2,300 middle (junior and senior) schools in Uighur districts. 95% of children enroll in school when they reach school age. A large number of Uighur scientists and technologists work in various fields of specialization. Generally, the Uighurs strongly support the education of their children.

¹⁴CULTURAL HERITAGE

The Uighurs are well known for their talent for singing and dancing. "The Twelve Great Songs" (some 340 pieces) is an epic narrative whose performance includes both classical and folkloric song, music, and dance. There are dozens of Uighur traditional instruments, including strings, winds, and tambourines. The Uighur violin is played on one knee. The long-necked traditional guitar is played with such celerity by the guitarist that his fingers seem to disappear in a blur.

Uighur dance is famous for its spinning. Besides the basic steps, there are skips with raised arms and quickly rotated wrists. Among the large variety of traditional dances, the most popular one is the impromptu solo dance, *pas de deux,* or group dance in random formations, surrounded by a circle of people who clap and sing in chorus.

Uighur literature includes folk tales, fables, jokes, poems, and proverbs. Some of them have a long history. For example, a narrative poem entitled "Fortune, Happiness and Wisdom" has been handed down since the 11th century. The "Story of Avanti" has been widely known in China for decades.

¹⁵WORK

The Uighurs are mainly engaged in gardening and cotton growing. Their apples, pears, figs, pomegranates, honey peaches, walnuts, almonds, and especially Hami melons, are renowned at home and abroad. The superb skill of the Uighurs in cotton growing has been widely introduced to other provinces of China. The Uighurs are reputed for their know-how as traders. Since ancient times, Uighur caravans penetrated deep into the Mongolian grasslands and into the countries of central Asia and, thus, played an important role in developing the famous Silk Road. Because of internal conflicts and difficult relations with the central government, Uighur trade has declined from the beginning of the 20th century. However, in recent decades, there has been a rapid growth of Uighur domestic and external commerce. Uighurs are now very active in the restaurant, grocery, and clothing businesses not only in Xinjiang, but also in many provinces. They have commercial ties with the Islamic countries of central and west Asia. The trade along the western Chinese border is very active.

¹⁶SPORTS

Ball games like basketball and volleyball are very popular. As a spectator sport, rope walking is the Uighurs' favorite. A pole reaching 120 ft in height is erected on the ground. A 260 ft rope is connected to the top of the pole on one of its ends and hooked solidly in the earth on the other. Holding a rod horizontally, the athlete climbs up the rope and performs jumping, rolling, cross-leg sitting, and other breathtaking movements.

¹⁷ENTERTAINMENT AND RECREATION

In addition to singing and dancing, movies and television are the most popular entertainment of the Uighurs. Most Uighur districts have their own film studio. A number of local musical and theater groups are supported by the Uighurs.

¹⁸FOLK ART, CRAFTS, AND HOBBIES

The Uighurs are skilled in crafts. Hotan jade sculpture is a fine art. Ingisa (Yengisar) knives are famous for their sharpness and precious stone incrustations. Uighur carpets, tapestries, silk embroidered hats, copper teapots, and traditional musical instruments are much sought after not only by the Uighurs, but by foreigners.

¹⁹SOCIAL PROBLEMS

The absence of natural resources and of an industrial infrastructure explains the very low income of the Uighurs, which must be compensated in part by the goods produced directly by the household. Lack of economic opportunities causes more and more Uighurs engaged in trade or in professional venues to leave their homeland to work in other provinces of China. Often, after some time, they return, benefiting their communities by their wealth and expertise.

20 GENDER ISSUES

The Chinese constitution states that women have equal rights with men in all areas of life, and most legislation is gender neutral. However, there are continued reports of discrimination, sexual harassment, wage discrepancies, and other gender related problems. The gap in educational level between women and men is narrowing with women making up 47.1% of college students in 2005, but only 32.6% of doctoral students. China has strict family planning laws. It is illegal for women to marry before 20 years of age (22 for men), and it is illegal for single women to give birth. The Family Planning Bureau can require women to take periodic pregnancy tests and enforce laws that often leave women with no real options other than abortion or sterilization. Though minority populations were previously exempt from family planning regulations, policy has changed in recent years to limit minority population growth. Today, urban minority couples may have two children while rural couples may have three or four.

21 BIBLIOGRAPHY

Chiao, Chien, Nicholas Tapp, and Kam-yin Ho, ed. "Special Issue on Ethnic Groups in China." *New Asia Bulletin* no 8 (1989).

Dreyer, June Teufel. *China's Forty Millions.* Cambridge: Harvard University Press, 1976.

Eberhard, Wolfram. *China's Minorities: Yesterday and Today.* Belmont: Wadsworth Publishing Company, 1982.

Gustafsson, Bjorn A., Shi, Li, and Sicular, Terry, eds. *Inequality and Public Policy in China*. New York: Cambridge University Press, 2008.

Heberer, Thomas. *China and Its National Minorities: Autonomy or Assimilation?* Armonk, NY: M. E. Sharpe, 1989.

Lebar, Frank, et al. *Ethnic Groups of Mainland Southeast Asia*. New Haven: Human Relations Area Files Press, 1964.

Lemoine, Jacques. "Les Ouighour." In *Ethnologie régionale II* (Encyclopédie de la Pléiade). Paris: Gallimard, 1978.

Ma Yin, ed. *China's Minority Nationalities*. Beijing: Foreign Languages Press, 1989.

Miller, Lucien, ed. *South of the Clouds: Tales from Yunnan*. Seattle: University of Washington Press, 1994.

Ramsey, S. Robert. *The Languages of China*. Princeton: Princeton University Press, 1987.

Shin, Leo Kwok-yueh. *The Making of the Chinese State: Ethnicity and Expansion on the Ming Borderlands*. New York: Cambridge University Press, 2006.

Wiens, Harold J. *Han Chinese Expansion in South China*. New Haven: The Shoestring Press, 1967.

—by C. Le Blanc

UZBEKS

PRONUNCIATION: OOZ-beks
LOCATION: Uzbekistan; Afghanistan; China
POPULATION: 27 million
LANGUAGE: Uzbek
RELIGION: Islam (Sunni Muslim)

¹ INTRODUCTION

The modern Uzbeks are believed to have originated from a group of tribes called the Kipchak Khanate, whose domain stretched from the Irtish River valley in the north to the shores of theCaspian Sea and Aral Sea in the south. In the 15th century, a southern migration of one of the tribes began. This tribe captured territory in the Syr Darya and Amu Darya (*darya* means "river" in Persian), as well as the city of Samarkand. The Uzbeks mixed with the earlier settlers of the area, including the Persian peoples of Khorezm and Soghdia. This area became consolidated under three separate khanates (Bukhara, Khiva, and Khokand) that ruled as city-states in the region until the 19th century. Uzbeks accounted for more than 50% of the Khiva khanate population and almost 35% of the Bukhara khanate inhabitants. Although originally nomads, most Uzbeks have been sedentary now for more than 300 years. The mixed heritage of the Uzbeks means that their physical features range from East Asian to European. A small percentage of Uzbeks have light hair and light eyes.

Russian encroachment increased in the mid-1800s. All three khanates fell to the Russians between 1865 and 1873. The imperial Russian government renamed the annexed area Russian Turkistan and allowed Bukhara and Khiva to retain some degree of home rule. After the Bolshevik Revolution, the Autonomous Soviet Socialist Republic of Turkestan was created in 1918. In 1924, the Soviet government began a major revision of Central Asian political boundaries based on ethnic populations. Even though the German army never made it all the way to Central Asia during World War II, that war had a profound effect on Uzbek culture. Entire towns were evacuated from the European part of the Soviet Union to Central Asia (along with their factories and workers). This massive influx of people disturbed the native Uzbek culture and legitimized the imposition of the Russian language and culture into the area that had already started by the turn of the 20th century.

The Soviet era brought tremendous cultural changes to Uzbek society. Perhaps the biggest change was the transformation from informal herding and subsistence agriculture to enormous state-operated farms, the collectivized agriculture imposed in the 1930s. Heavy reliance on irrigation combined with the Soviet cotton monoculture (growing only one crop—cotton—at the expense of others) became prevalent. When Soviet power began crumbling in 1990, leaders in the Uzbek Communist Party hesitated to denounce the Soviet system until it was clear that the Soviet Union had indeed dissolved. Since independence in 1991, the government was slow to institute democratization or market-oriented economic reforms, although commercial development and capitalist property relations were accelerated in the late 1990s. Uzbeks live under a very harsh political regime that has functioned as a self-aggrandizing organization where political and economic liberties are sharply curtailed. Since 2001, thousands of Uzbeks have been jailed and repressed in the name of defense against Islamic extremism, but countless charges against ordinary citizens have been trumped up and prosecuted with little to no evidence of extremist activities. Political oppression is so great today that many Uzbeks claim life was fairer and freer during the late Soviet period.

² LOCATION AND HOMELAND

After the Turks of Turkey, the Uzbeks are the largest ethnic group of Turkic people in the world. The Uzbeks were the third largest ethnic group of the former Soviet Union when it collapsed in 1991, with a population of more than 16.7 million, of which 85% lived in what is now Uzbekistan. The population of Uzbekistan increased by 7 million from 1970 to the mid-1980s. Its current population growth rate rivals that of many sub-Saharan African countries. There are also more than 1 million Uzbeks in Afghanistan, and about 800,000 living in the Sinkiang-Uygur Autonomous Region of China.

The Uzbek homeland is situated on the site of the ancient Bactrian and Sogdianan civilizations. Ancient conquerors who laid claim to the territory included the Persian Empire of Darius the Great and the Greek Empire of Alexander the Great. The region was invaded by Arabs in the 8th century AD, at which time Islam was introduced. In the 13th century, the Mongol Empire controlled the area, and the Empire of Tamerlane gained power thereafter. Around the 15th century, the Uzbeks began to emerge as an organized group of tribes. The modern Uzbek homeland lies much farther south than the region originally inhabited by the Uzbeks centuries ago. Uzbekistan lies between the Aral Sea and the Fergana River valley in the East and includes parts of the Amu Darya River valley and the southern portion of the Kyzyl Kum Desert. The eastern border is in the foothills of the Tien Shan Mountains, which surrounds the Fergana River valley in the lowlands on three sides. Much of the landscape of Uzbekistan consists of three feature types: deserts, dry steppes, and fertile oases near the rivers.

The region of Uzbekistan west of the Aral Sea is called the Ust-Urt Flatland. This area is dry steppe that can only be used for light grazing. The Aral Sea, with an area once larger than Lake Michigan, is an important water resource for much of Central Asia. In the last 30–40 years, however, the area around the Aral Sea has become an environmental disaster as the sea has lost about 60% of its water volume.

³ LANGUAGE

The Uzbek language is considered part of the eastern or Aralo-Caspian branch of the Kipchak group of Turkic languages and is similar to Kazakh and Karakalpak. Contact with the Persian language over the years has influenced the dialect of Uzbeks living near Iran. The Iran-influenced dialect has become the basis of the modern Uzbek literary language. The modern standard for spoken Uzbek is based on the dialects of Tashkent and the Ferghana Valley. The Uzbek language borrowed many words with a Russian or European origin during the early Soviet years but has become more reliant on the incorporation of Turkic and Arabic words into the language since the 1960s.

Names given to Uzbek children, as in other Central Asian cultures, are an important mark of individuality. A person's name was traditionally used to help visitors and residents recognize someone's place of origin. Instead of using a sur-

name, many Central Asian cultures attach the patronymic suffix -oghli (son of) or -qizi (daughter of) onto the father's or grandfather's name. The Russian patronymics—which are transliterated as -aw, -awnä, and -awä became popular during the 1920s but had fallen out of favor by the 1960s. Families who trace their genealogy to Mohammed will often add the title *Sayyid* after their name, and those who are descended from one of the four Imams add the title *Khoja*. Uzbek Muslims who have completed the pilgrimage to Mecca sometimes affix the title *Hajji* before their names.

Everyday terms in the Uzbek language include *salaam aleikhem* ("hello"), *shundei* ("yes"), *yok* ("no"), *markhamat* ("please"), and *rakhmat* ("thank you"). Examples of Uzbek sayings include *Äytkän gäp atqan oq* ("A word said is a shot fired"); *Kob oylä, az soylä* ("Think lots, say little"); *Yamandän yükhshilik kutmä* ("Don't expect good from evil"); and *Yaman yolashän täyaq yäkhshi* ("A beating with a cudgel is better than an evil companion").

⁴ FOLKLORE

Although the Uzbeks have not existed as a nation for very long, they are fascinated with researching their complex ethnic heritage. In the 4th century BC, Alexander of Macedonia came across the Uzbeks during his campaign to conquer India. He stopped in Maracanda, near the ancient city of Samarkand, and married Roxana, the daughter of a local leader. Over the centuries, the local legends surrounding Alexander (called Iskander Zulqornai by the Uzbeks) grew until he became a larger-than-life heroic figure.

Two historical heroes are often the subjects of modern Uzbek historical novels. One of these heroes of Uzbek culture is Tamerlane (1336–1405), a Turko-Mongol who ruled from Samarkand but conquered parts of present-day India, Syria, and southern Russia. His grandson Ulughbek (1394–1449) has become another legendary, semi-sacred figure owing to his monumental contributions to the sciences, especially astronomy.

⁵ RELIGION

The Uzbeks are among the most traditional people in Central Asia, and religion has an important place in traditional Uzbek culture. Most Uzbeks are Sunni Muslims of the Hanafi sect. After the collapse of Communism, religious practices briefly were encouraged, because the new state wanted an antidote to the official Soviet position of atheism. As in other parts of Soviet Central Asia during Soviet rule, the Muslim clergy was persecuted. Since the end of Soviet rule, many new mosques have been built. Tashkent is perhaps the leading Islamic spiritual center in Central Asia, with many Islamic seminaries located there. Sufism (Islamic mysticism) is also practiced by some Uzbeks. A famous Sufi school, the Naqsh-bandi, is located in Bukhara. Today, Namangan in the Ferghana valley is perhaps the most conservatively religious city in all of Central Asia. However, since the late 1990s there has been a steady erosion of religious freedom, both for Muslims and Christians with Muslims bearing the heavier blows. The state claims it opposes religious expression for fear of extremism, but outsiders argue the state's harsh oppression only makes for a self-fulfilling prophecy.

⁶ MAJOR HOLIDAYS

No holiday is more enjoyable to Uzbeks than *Novruz*, and it is rapidly replacing New Year's Eve as the number one holiday. It coincides with the first day of spring and is an ancient Iranic/Turkic holiday dating back at least 2,000 years. Speeches, school skits, dances, and town square celebrations with lots of feasting characterize this time. At home, people prepare *sumalak*, the beloved food of *Novruz*, a sweet pudding that is thick and brown. People cook young, vitamin-rich wheat plants in huge cauldrons overnight until the *sumalak* is done in the morning. All the holidays of the Islamic fast (Ramadan) and various forms of *Haiit* (days to remember one's departed relatives) are now officially recognized in Uzbekistan. Uzbekistani Independence Day is September 1, and people have been celebrating this holiday with great fanfare since 1991. Victory Day is May 9, and all Uzbekistani citizens pay tribute to the Soviet defeat of Nazi Germany in 1945. This holiday has both solemn and joyous sides.

⁷ RITES OF PASSAGE

Births, male circumcision, girls' first menstrual periods, marriage, and death are the primary events around which Uzbeki rites of passage occur. The *sunnat toi* (circumcision party) and the *kelin toi* (wedding) are events for which people spend the most money and celebrate most heartily.

⁸ INTERPERSONAL RELATIONS

Uzbeks take a great deal of time to greet one another. Simply seeing a friend or acquaintance and saying, "Hi" or "What's up?" as one passes by is not acceptable. It is considered far more polite to approach each other, shake hands, and rapidly fire off a number of questions about each other's health, family situation, and work. The elements of sociability are very important. Uzbeks also love to invite "guests" (strangers) into their homes and will signal a passerby in with hand gestures, indicating a cup of tea or something to eat. Once one is invited in, it is absolutely obligatory to serve food and tea, even if the food is just bread or nuts and candies.

Traditionally, Uzbek customs have been oriented toward a reserved patriarchal system. The Uzbeks maintain a strong sense of duty to the elderly and to the community. Children are typically taught that openly confronting adults is wrong, that they should be quiet and composed even if they are upset or angry with their elders. Dignity has an important role in Uzbek society. Someone who talks or laughs too much or is a show-off is considered undignified. In a *gap*, an Uzbek custom that continues today, men meet with friends and former classmates to eat, play games of cards or bingo, and discuss social and intellectual issues while helping one another out with personal problems.

⁹ LIVING CONDITIONS

Uzbek interior design emphasizes the use of traditional themes. Loomed rugs often cover the floors of Uzbek houses, and traditional folk art, emphasizing motifs from the natural world (such as mountains, deer, and peacocks), or scenes painted by local artists from Navoii's (Uzbekistan's Shakespeare) literature, are common wall decorations. Most homes have two or three rooms. Men (and boys) and women (and girls) have separate quarters. Outside the home stands a large eating and resting platform known as the *sura*, and a great deal of time is spent there during the hot weather. It is usually covered by the shade of the grape lattice. A kitchen area is a separate unit of most homes with a large hearth where all the cooking is done.

Medical services in the cities have suffered since the collapse of the centralized Soviet system. Today people turn to mystic healers and herbalists to treat many ailments once cured with modern medicines, which are now often hard to find. In rural areas, people's general knowledge of proper healthcare is poor.

Transportation systems are extensive but unreliable now, especially in the vast countryside. It is easy, convenient, and cheap to travel from city to city in Uzbekistan by bus, rail, or plane. Urban transportation is good overall, but because gasoline and spare parts are in short supply, all forms of mass transit are often very crowded. Tashkent boasts a beautiful and clean subway system.

¹⁰ FAMILY LIFE

The average Uzbek family has five children, but any given home may house two, three, or four generations. Women have a particularly hard time in Uzbekistan because the Soviet era introduced them to the work force, but their duties at home never lessened. The *kelin toi*, or wedding, is the most important joyous celebration in Uzbek social life. Families save for their entire lives to ensure that their children are properly married, and that they themselves enjoy respect among other community members for the wedding party. The bride's family incurs the greatest expense because daughters receive a dowry. A new Uzbek bride will generally move in with her husband's family and do the majority of the work in the home until she has a few children and the next son is ready to marry. If she marries

Uzbeks look at the daily newspapers in Tashkent, Uzbekistan. President Islam Karimov lifted media censorhip in early 2002. (Scott Peterson/Getty Images)

the youngest son, she will probably have to stay in her in-laws' household the rest of her life, because it is customary for the youngest son to stay in his father's home.

Women generally eat in a different room (often the kitchen) from men and guests, and they always eat separately at social gatherings. Family size is usually a joint decision between the couple, although Uzbek society, in general, values large families.

11 CLOTHING

The Uzbeks are among the most traditional peoples in Central Asia, and so conventional and national costumes are still commonly worn. Uzbeks are known for wearing the traditional *doppilar*—small, black, square-shaped skullcaps. Doppilar are embroidered with elaborate abstract swirling patterns that serve to indicate the wearer's family ties, place of birth, social status, or other personal information. Many men wear European-style clothes or mixed outfits of European and traditional Uzbek clothing, which often utilizes bright colors or patterns. Some men wear the traditional *chopan*, originally a long quilted robe used by shepherds. The *chopan* worn today is often ornamented with pastel designs or sequins. Both men and women often wear long tunics and broad trousers with colorful outer robes. Although many women wear European clothes, some wear the atlas pattern (the traditional silk dress).

Atlas is a boldly colored and patterned tie-dyed style. In summer, women wear white head coverings or brightly colored kerchiefs. During winter, they don large woolen shawls that keep their heads and necks warm. Most ethnic Uzbek women have thick black hair traditionally worn in two braids, but Uzbek girls may wear their hair in dozens of small braids.

12 FOOD

Uzbek cuisine includes a huge variety of baked, fried, and steamed dishes that make frequent use of Eastern spices such as cumin, coriander, and spicy dried red pepper. Traditional Uzbek dishes include *lagman* (homemade noodles with mutton, garlic, and vegetables), *d'ighman* (meat with pastry in a rich broth), *dymlama* (a layered vegetable and beef steamed stew), and the all-time favorite, *plov*. *Plov* is rice with beef (or mutton or chicken), cottonseed oil or *dumba* (sheep tail fat), vegetables, spices, garlic, and quinces. Breakfast fare consists of bread, some fruits or nuts, and tea, with occasional servings of *qattiq* (yogurt).

13 EDUCATION

Education in Uzbekistan is universal and mandatory until age 16. City schools are often much better than rural and, historically the Russian-language schools were of higher quality than Uzbek schools. But this is now changing gradually. Turkish *lycees* (European-style high schools) and *medresses* (Muslim schools) have opened in all of the major cities, so education has become much more diversified. Aside from conservative parents, who think daughters need only the minimal schooling, almost all Uzbek parents want a high degree of education for their children, and many hope that their children will be accepted to Tashkent State University or be able to study abroad. Overall, Uzbek people greatly revere study and intellectual life.

¹⁴ CULTURAL HERITAGE

Classical Uzbek music involves instruments such as the *rubob r dutor* accompanying a single singer, whose style is drawn out and plaintive—a kind of wailing. Popular Uzbek music is a mixture of traditional styles with rock and pop. The hand-held *doira*, a tambourine-drum, has a deep, sharp sound, adding very rich beats and rhythms to musical pieces. Some folk singing is accompanied only by the doira.

One of the most famous examples of classic literature revered by the Uzbeks is *Baburname* (the memoirs of Babur), which was originally written in an eastern Turkish variant. Babur (1483–1530) was a descendant of Turko-Mongol warriors who led a military campaign through present-day Afghanistan and India, where he founded the Mogul Empire and became its first emperor. Babur is respected as a soldier and a statesman by modern Uzbeks.

During the 1960s, several prominent Uzbek playwrights produced works that questioned the Soviet policies against the Uzbek cultural and social leadership from the 1930s to the 1950s. The most famous of these dramas are Izzat Sultan's *Iman* ("Faith," 1960) and Rahmatullah A. Uyghun's *Dostlär* ("Friends," 1961), which both show the consequences upon a society when suspicion, malice, and injustice are common in its leadership.

¹⁵ WORK

Most Uzbeks continue to work in the agricultural sector; about 65% remain rural. This work has cyclical patterns. Spring, summer, and fall are periods of great diligence, while winter is a time to rest and relax. In addition to working in the collective fields growing wheat, cotton, fruits, and so on, many also raise silkworms for cocoon production (from which comes silk) and labor very hard on their small household plots, growing the bulk of the nation's fruits and vegetables. Many people sell these crops in the peasant markets of major population centers. The industrial and service sectors of the Uzbek economy cover everything from aircraft manufacturing to gold mining and oil extraction. Today, retail trade in the form of private shops is growing, and private business is bustling. Women have participated in almost all sectors of the economy, but there is a growing trend to have them work primarily in the non-industrial sectors. Uzbek women themselves have mixed feelings about this.

¹⁶ SPORTS

Table tennis became popular during the Soviet era and remains so today. Since the mid-1980s, softball has been a popular women's sport. Soccer is the number one team and spectator sport, and basketball and volleyball are very popular in schools.

Kurash is a unique form of wrestling beloved by Uzbek men and boys. It involves facing and holding an opponent by the back of the neck with one hand while gripping the back of his thigh with the other.

The martial arts have become especially popular over the last decade, and many children train seriously in local clubs. Another sport is a form of polo in which hundreds or even thousands of horsemen participate. The two huge teams attempt to capture the carcass of a goat or sheep and get it to the opponents' goal. The game is incredibly dusty and can be violent as the stakes are often high. This form of polo is a very popular spectator sport, especially in the areas of Samarqand and Tashkent.

¹⁷ ENTERTAINMENT AND RECREATION

A popular and ancient form of entertainment among the Uzbeks is *payr*, an unrehearsed public debate that tests the quick-witted abilities of the opponents. Two competitors stand on a platform and exchange witty and clever comments about each other within the context of a topic chosen before the competition. Each speaker must immediately respond to the other one with a crafty remark. The first one who fails to respond quickly enough is the loser, as determined by the assembled crowd. Sometimes a good payr match will draw thousands of spectators. *Bakka* (tight-rope walking) also draws big crowds during celebrations or parties; it is one of the most common forms of popular entertainment.

Children love to play games such as *top tosh* and *askiia*. Top tosh is equivalent to jacks, except Uzbek children play with rocks or pebbles. Askiia is a word-riddle game where one player makes up questions about a given thing, and the other child must answer to show that he knows what the object of the riddle is.

Movies and television enjoy wide popularity. The most popular genres are martial arts movies, action movies, comedies, and Hindu films, also known as Bombay cinema.

¹⁸ FOLK ART, CRAFTS, AND HOBBIES

Pottery is the oldest craft practiced among the Uzbeks. Archeologists have found ornamental pieces of Uzbek pottery that are nearly 3,000 years old. Folk arts have a rich tradition in Uzbek culture. In addition to internal house paintings, silk weaving, quilt-making, skullcap-making, and *suzama* (cloth embroidery) are well-known elements of Uzbek folk art. *Hunarmandlik* (craftsmanship) shines through in *naqsh* (wood carving) and mosaic tile work in architecture. The best examples of carving are seen in the doors of family homes and in the columns that support buildings. Ceramics (especially fine porcelain tea sets), metalworking (especially urns and pitchers), and boot-making are other examples of traditional crafts in Uzbek culture. Stamp collecting and corresponding with pen-pals are favorite hobbies for young people.

¹⁹ SOCIAL PROBLEMS

The Uzbeks currently face two great problems: the stagnation of the economy and a number of serious environmental problems, including the shrinking of the Aral Sea. The reluctance of the government to renounce the old Soviet ways has caused the standard of living to decline since independence. Heavy reliance on the cotton crop coupled with decades of socialist mismanagement has created ecological problems in the Aral Sea, which has lost much of its area since 1960. This loss has occurred because of the central role of growing *päkhtä* (cotton), which requires copious amounts of water. The irrigation in Uzbekistan (along with Kyrgyzstan and Kazakhstan) needed to grow cotton diverted most of the water from the Amu Darya and Syr Darya, the two main rivers that feed into the Aral Sea. Much of the soil around the Aral Sea is now too salty to grow any crops. Pesticides, herbicides, and chemical fertilizers have also polluted much of the remaining water supply. In the late 1980s, some Soviet scientists indicated that, unless water usage changed, the Aral Sea would completely dry up and disappear within 20 years. With these environmental problems, it may not be possible to grow as much cotton in the future as in the past, which could impede the economy from developing.

The Uzbek human rights record has not been good, especially because of the repression, in the forms of jailings and beatings, of leading opposition figures. However, some improvements were made during 1995–96, as the economy began to stabilize and the state administration relaxed its grip on power ever so slightly. Unfortunately, this all took a decided turn for the worse from the late 1990s and after 2001. Political and economic freedoms in Uzbekistan now appear to be at an all-time low. The state actually makes good profits from cotton, natural gas and oil, and gold mining, but the benefits rarely are shared with ordinary impoverished citizens. After 2005 political repression reached a new high point when the government shot to death hundreds of protesters in the eastern city of Andizhan. Since then the population has been very reluctant to express their myriad grievances in any organized and public forum. Criminal activity, unemployment, homelessness, and child abandonment all have become serious issues in the new millennium.

Alcoholism, drug addiction, and violent crime are the social diseases of present-day Uzbeks, a direct result of rising poverty since the late 1980s and contemporary political, religious, and entrepreneurial repression.

As is true of many other former Soviet territories, labor migration has become a huge social phenomenon today with millions of Uzbeks seeking work in Kazakhstan, Russia, Europe, and the U.S.A. Perhaps 15% of the entire working population lives abroad at least part of the year, and thousands of these people have been subject to myriad forms of abuse including various forms of slavery. It is still hard to determine the overall consequences of these displacements and forms of abuse on the population as a whole.

20 GENDER ISSUES

Uzbeks are among the most inequitable of the Central Asian peoples when it comes to gender. Strict forms of sex segregation are practiced within the domestic sphere as well as in public life. For example, men and women usually do not eat together, and girls are expected to carry out nearly all domestic chores as well as do almost all of the cotton sowing and harvesting work in the rural areas.

While the Soviet period enabled women to perform all kinds of work and receive a higher education, the great gains that Uzbek women made are in danger of being lost. Increasingly, the value of women's education has been lowered, and even though the state guarantees full equality between the sexes before the law, it seems clear that patriarchal values and practices are holding sway.

Traditionally, Uzbek women always marry exogamously—outside of their own patrilineages—and this long has functioned as a gateway to their oppression. With the collapse of Soviet power, Uzbek patriarchal values have become increasingly ascendant, especially with the very trying economic circumstances in which millions find themselves. Thus new available opportunities should go to men not women.

However, labor migration plays havoc with these traditionally discriminatory values as women leave to work abroad, sometimes legally, sometimes not. And when an Uzbek woman is not supervised by her own male kin, then her behavior simply becomes suspect. On the other hand, the labor migration gives women a new economic power, even if the practice may be greatly harming family dynamics. Overall, it is still too early to know the consequences of labor migration in terms of gender relations, but patterns no doubt are taking shape.

21 BIBLIOGRAPHY

Allworth, Edward A. *The Modern Uzbeks: From the Fourteenth Century to the Present*. Stanford, CA: Hoover Institution Press, 1990.

Critchlow, James. *Nationalism in Uzbekistan: A Soviet Republic's Road to Sovereignty*. Boulder, CO: Westview Press, 1991.

Sahadeo, Jeff, and Russell Zanca, eds. *Everyday Life in Central Asia: Past and Present*. Bloomington, IN: Indiana University Press, 2007.

"Uzbeks Prey to Modern Slave Trade," *International War and Peace Reporting: Reporting Central Asia*. http://www.iwpr.net/?p=rca&apc_state=henh&s=f&o=343132 (May 2008).

—revised by R. Zanca

VEDDAS

PRONUNCIATION: VEH-duhz
ALTERNATE NAMES: Veddhas, Veddahs; Vanniyalato,
Vanniyala-Aetto
LOCATION: Sri Lanka
POPULATION: less than 2,000
LANGUAGE: Sinhala; Tamil
RELIGION: Traditional religion with elements of Buddhism and
Hinduism

¹ INTRODUCTION

The Veddas (Veddhas, Veddahs, also Vanniyala-Aetto) are
a small tribal community in Sri Lanka, the island (formerly
called Ceylon) that lies in the Indian Ocean off the southern
tip of India. Physically, the Veddas are of Proto-Australoid
stock, associated with the earliest strata of population identi-
fiable in South Asia. Genetic studies suggest they are related
to the tribes of Malaysia. Modern Veddas are believed to be
descended from the island's earliest aboriginal inhabitants,
though clearly they have been exposed to genetic mixing with
later groups. The name "Vedda" is a Dravidian word meaning "one who uses bows and arrows," and Veddas traditionally lived by hunting and gathering in the forests of Sri Lanka.
However, the Veddas call themselves *Vanniyalato* or "people of
the forest."

² LOCATION AND HOMELAND

At one time, it is likely that the Veddas or their ancestors were
distributed over much of Sri Lanka. Today, however, Veddas
live in three separate areas whose populations have little contact with each other. The largest group is the Anuradhapura Veddas. They are found in Anuradhapura District in the
north-central part of the island. This population was estimated
at over 6,600 people in 1970. A second group, known as the
Coast Veddas, occupies a stretch of the east coast of Sri Lanka
extending south from Trincomalee. The third Vedda group is
identified as the Bintenne Veddas. Their territory extends from
the eastern slopes of the central mountains to the sea, a triangular area roughly defined by the Mahaweli and Gal Oya rivers
and the coast. Estimates of the Bintenne Vedda population are
not available, but it is thought to be considerably less than that
of the other groups.

There is considerable disagreement among scholars concerning the definition of Vedda. There are perhaps 2,000 Veddas remaining in Sri Lanka today. These are people who call
themselves Vedda, are viewed by others as Vedda, but are assimilated to varying degrees into Sinhalese or Tamil society.
They may be Buddhist or Hindu, live in villages, or practice
settled agriculture, but in most ways they closely resemble the
rural populations among whom they live. There are no more
than an estimated 200–300 individuals following the traditional Vedda way of life today. Unless otherwise stated, the
material presented in the following pages is based on the Selig-
manns' study of traditional Vedda culture, undertaken among
the Bintenne Veddas at the beginning of the 20th century.

³ LANGUAGE

Veddas today speak Sinhala or Tamil, depending on whether
they live among Sinhalese or Tamil populations. Evidence exists, however, of what at one time might have been a distinct
Vedda language. This survives today in what some have described as a dialect of Sinhalese but that others see as a creole,
a language that evolved through years of contact between the
original Vedda and Sinhalese tongues.

⁴ FOLKLORE

The Veddas claim royal ancestry through their myth of origin. They trace their descent to Prince Vijaya, the grandson of
a lion and the legendary founder of the Sinhalese nation (*sinha*
means "lion" and *le* is "blood"). Prince Vijaya came to Sri Lanka from North India, so the legend goes. Before sending back
to India for a bride of his own social standing, he had sexual
relations with a local demon princess named Kuveni. Kuveni
gave birth to two children, a boy and a girl. The Veddas, so it is
said, are the result of the incestuous union between this brother and sister. This myth, which is widely known among the
Anuradhapura Veddas and the Sinhalese accomplishes several
objectives. It supports the Veddas' claim to high social status;
it establishes them as the original inhabitants (i.e., owners) of
the land; and it defines the Veddas as a people distinct from,
but having a common origin with, the Sinhalese. In addition,
it creates a link with the supernatural world, which occupies a
significant role in the Vedda belief system.

This particular myth of origin is apparently unknown
among the Bintenne Veddas, whose culture is characterized by
a marked absence of myths. Even myths of origin of the Bintenne Vedda clans are to be found among the Sinhalese, rather
than among the Veddas themselves. One relates that when the
demon princess Kuveni was abandoned by Prince Vijaya, she
returned with her son and daughter to her own people. However, her people killed her and the children fled into the jungle
where they lived on the fruits of the mora tree (*Nephelium lon-
gana*). Some of their descendants gave rise to the Morane clan.

⁵ RELIGION

As far as can be determined, the primitive religion of the Veddas was based on the worship of spirits (*yakku*) rather than of
any gods. Some were the spirits of Veddas who were long dead
and revered almost as heroes. The chief of these, and indeed
the chief of all the yakhu, was Kande Yakka. Kande Yakka and
another spirit, Bilindi Yakka, would be invoked to ensure success in the hunt. And, if they were not offered meat after a successful kill, the hunters would expect bad luck to befall them.
They might even be bitten by snakes or attacked by bears. A
second category of spirits was the *Na Yakku*, the spirits of recently dead ancestors. These are believed to live in hills, caves,
and rocks. The Na Yakku, including the spirits of the deceased,
are invoked on the fifth day after a death. Offerings of coconut
milk and rice are made, and the Vedda shaman becomes possessed by the spirits of the deceased, who promises that yams,
honey, and game shall be plentiful. The Na Yakku must obtain
Kande Yakka's permission to help the living and accept their
offerings.

Over and above this "Cult of the Friendly Dead," as some
have termed it, the Veddas worship foreign spirits who have
become naturalized Vedda yakhu. These are essentially protective of the Veddas and their help is sought in various situations.

The Rahu Yakku, for example, are derived from a Sinhalese demon but have been given their own Vedda identity. They are invoked to cure sickness and to obtain success in hunting and in collecting rock honey. Another class of spirits is foreign spirits who are hostile in nature and who are to be feared. Thus, under Tamil influence, yakhu haunting rocks and hilltops are thought of as dangerous immigrants from beyond the Ocean who bring disease to the Veddas. People tend to avoid rocky mountain tops, and if they venture there, they leave offerings of honey. A less dangerous form of these spirits is the *kiriammas* ("grandmothers"), who are seen more as local deities than as yakhu.

Each Vedda community has a shaman *(kapurale)* who possesses the power and knowledge to intercede with the spirit world. The shaman presides at various ceremonial dances, such as the hunting dance *(kirikoraha)* and the arrow dance. He presents the offerings to the Na Yakku after a death. At such occasions, the shaman becomes possessed by the spirits and acts as their mouthpiece, promising favors and good fortune to the community. The shaman also conducts exorcisms of evil spirits. The shaman trains his own successor, passing on his knowledge to a pupil, usually his son or his sister's son (his actual or potential son-in-law).

Prolonged contact with Tamil and Sinhalese society has resulted in many Vedda groups absorbing elements of Hinduism and, especially, Buddhism. These groups worship gods *(deviyo)* as well as spirits. The Coast Veddas, for example, revere deities that include Hindu gods, such as Shiva, Vishnu, and Bhairava. They have their own temples and shrines where their religious observances and devil-dancing ceremonies take place. Among the Anuradhapura Veddas, the powerful Kataragama is worshipped. The Anuradhapura Veddas are in close contact with the Sinhalese and profess to be Buddhist. They know little of the higher form of the religion, but they have adopted Buddhist rituals. Some invite a Buddhist monk to their burial ceremonies and give alms to Buddhists on behalf of the dead. Such practices fit in well with their own customs relating to death and the spirits of the ancestors.

⁶MAJOR HOLIDAYS

The worship of ancestral spirits among the Veddas is not subject to any fixed festival cycle. Vedda communities that have adopted Hinduism or Buddhism tend to observe the festival calendar of these religions. However, their participation in such festivals may not necessarily indicate a full understanding of the significance of the event. For instance, Veddas take part in the annual festival at the Buddhist temple at Mahiyangana in the southeastern Badulla district. They approach the temple in a procession *(perahera),* bringing offerings of honey, but they do not follow Buddhist observances. They pray at the temple for protection from "elephants and men."

The most important ritual events among the Veddas are the ceremonial dances, in which the shaman becomes possessed by gods or spirits.

⁷RITES OF PASSAGE

There are no particular rituals associated with birth among the Veddas. Birth usually takes place in a cave, with the assistance of a woman of the community. The umbilical cord is cut by an arrow, and the afterbirth is thrown away. Some Vedda groups have food taboos for nursing mothers. For example, the fat of

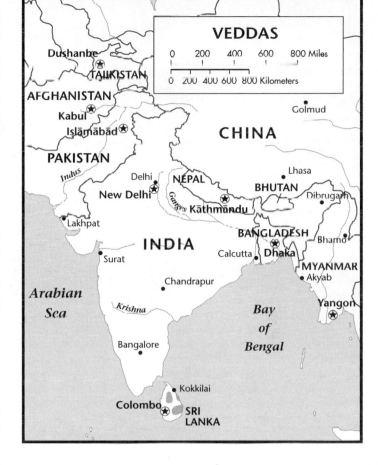

the monitor lizard and of the spotted deer should be avoided as potentially harmful to the infant being suckled. Among village Veddas, a special hut is built for the birth, as is the custom among the rural Sinhalese.

Children are named by their parents, usually within a month of their birth. Among some groups, a child's name is never spoken, apparently to avoid attracting the attention of evil spirits who might harm the infant. Children are called "Tuta" (male) and "Tuti" (female), and in many instances their real names seem to be forgotten. Typical Vedda names are Poromala, Nila, and Badena for males, and Hendi, Selli, and Badani for females.

Veddas are affectionate and indulgent parents, and children have few responsibilities during childhood. There are no puberty rites for either sex, although Vedda groups in contact with the Sinhalese or Tamils have adopted local customs, such as secluding girls for a short time at puberty. Virtually all village Veddas and those who have mixed with Sinhalese society isolate menstruating women in a specially built hut for the duration of their period.

When a Vedda dies, the corpse is left in the cave or rockshelter where the death occurred. The body is not washed or dressed in any way but is covered with leaves and branches. Sometimes a large stone is placed on the chest of the dead person. The cave is then abandoned by the community and avoided for a lengthy period of time (estimated to be around 12 years). Some Veddas claim that if they stayed in the vicinity of the cave, the spirit of the deceased would be displeased, and they

Sri Lankan aboriginals, also known as Veddas, chat in a mud hut at the village Dambana in central Sri Lanka. Veddas preserve a direct line of descent from the island's original Neolithic community dating from at least 16,000 BC. (Sanka Vidanagama/AFP/Getty Images)

would be pelted with stones. Among the more primitive Vedda groups, no particular ceremonies or rituals are performed over the body before it is abandoned. In some instances, however, the person's betel nut bag and its contents would be left with the corpse. On the fifth day after death, ritual offerings are made to the ancestral spirits, including that of the recently deceased.

Among the Anuradhapura and Coast Veddas, beliefs and rituals concerning death have been influenced by Buddhist and Hindu concepts, such as *karma* (belief that one's next life is determined by one's actions in this life), reincarnation, and the transmigration of souls.

8 INTERPERSONAL RELATIONS

Every Vedda helps all other members of his or her community, readily sharing game and honey with them. However, a particularly close relationship exists between father-in-law and son-in-law.

Terms of respect are commonly used when addressing the elderly. Thus, although *siya* or *mutta* actually mean "father" or "grandfather," such words are used in addressing any elderly man. Similarly, elderly women are addressed as *kiriamma* or grandmother.

9 LIVING CONDITIONS

A convenient, though perhaps not totally accurate, distinction has been made by some between "Rock" (or "Jungle") Veddas and "Village" Veddas. The former are held to be closer to the "pure" Vedda culture than are the latter, who are settled cultivators and follow lifestyles resembling those of the Sinhalese or Tamil peasant.

The life of the more primitive Vedda groups is centered on the rock-shelters and caves that are their homes. In the dry season, game gathers around water sources in the lowland forests and so the Veddas are to be found in these locations. However, during the rainy season when the game scatters over the entire countryside, the Veddas move to higher elevations. A single family or several families may occupy a rock-shelter. Veddas sleep on a rock, sometimes lying on a deerskin or piece of cloth, sometimes lying on the bare rock. It is customary for Veddas to keep a small fire burning beside them all night. If living in a communal cave, each family keeps to its own area. Often one woman cooks for the entire group. In communal caves, all the men store their bows and arrows in one place rather than keeping them in their own living space.

The material possessions of people living in this fashion are clearly somewhat limited. The following is a typical list of the objects a Vedda might be expected to own: an axe, a bow and arrows, a deerskin, cooking pots, flints and tinder for making fire, a gourd for carrying water, and a betel pouch, with betel cutters and a small box for holding lime. To this might be added a digging stick, utensils for collecting honey, and the supply of cloth that most Veddas seem to have. In addition, every Vedda owns one or two dogs. The animals are invariably well fed and treated with a great deal of affection by their masters. They are "country" dogs, i.e., of mixed breed, but they are trained in hunting and are clearly of importance to the Veddas. Dogs partake of the sacrificial offerings made at the Na Yukka ceremony, are anointed with milk at the hunting ceremony, and are given as wedding gifts.

Today, few—if any—Veddas live exclusively in rock-shelters. They may construct temporary shelters of wooden frames covered by animal skins, bark, or leaves, or build huts out of wattle and daub. Among the village Veddas, of course, houses are permanent and reflect local styles in materials and construction.

10 FAMILY LIFE

The Veddas are divided into clans (waruge) that some have argued are matrilineal exogamous units (this is a matter of debate among anthropologists). Of greater significance in traditional Vedda society, however, is the community. This consists of one to five families who share the rights of hunting, fishing, and gathering honey over a particular tract of land. The community usually does not remain as a single group but breaks down into smaller units of one or two families living and hunting together.

Each family is made up of parents and unmarried children and married daughters and their husbands. Marriage takes place at an early age, though not much before puberty. The male selects his own partner, though the correct marriage for the Vedda is his father's sister's daughter. The young man goes to his prospective father-in-law with a gift of honey, yams, grain, or dried deer's flesh tied to his unstrung bow. If the proposal is accepted, the girl attaches a string she has made herself around the groom's waist and the marriage ritual is complete. The husband always wears the waist string, and when it wears out he replaces it with a new one made by his wife. Occasionally a charm is placed on the waist string to ensure fidelity. When a girl marries, her father customarily makes over a tract of land, known to be inhabited by the rock bee or bambara, to his new son-in-law. Sometimes the wedding gift is a bow and arrow, or a hunting dog. A custom, now dying out, is the gift to the bride of a lock of hair from the bridegroom.

Traditional marriage customs are less strictly followed among the village Veddas, who have been influenced by the Sinhalese and Tamil societies among whom they live. True cross-cousin marriages are less frequent, although the fiction is often maintained by "finding" kin in distant villages where no one can question the relationship. Marriages with non-Vedda spouses are increasingly common.

11 CLOTHING

No Veddas can remember a time when they could not buy cloth, but they state that at one time their clothing was made from the inner bark of the upas tree (Antiaris toxicaria). Men wear a strip of white cotton some 22–23 cm (9 in) wide. They pass this between their legs and tuck it into their waist string, letting the ends hang down in front and back. This "white" cotton cloth soon becomes discolored to a dull brown, so it is less obvious during the hunt. Strips can be torn off this thin

machine-made cloth to provide tinder for making fire when necessary. On occasion, such as before ceremonial dances, the Veddas put on a sarong-like garment called a hangala. Women wear colored cotton cloth, bought from peddlers, that extends from waist to knee and wraps around like a sarong.

12 FOOD

Traditionally, the Veddas existed by hunting and gathering. Those who continue to do so today gather wild yams, truffles, fruits, and edible flowers from the jungle. This is primarily the work of women. The men hunt for game, mostly deer, monkeys, and iguanas. They will eat fish if it is available. Yams are roasted in the ashes of a fire, and meat may also be cooked this way. The flesh of animals is dried on a rack placed in the sun, but a fire is also built beneath it so it is smoked at the same time. Practically everything else is boiled in a cooking pot over a fire.

Honey plays an important part in the Vedda diet. June and July are the main months for collecting the honey of the rock bee or bambara (Apis indica). Men clamber up rocks or climb creepers or wooden ladders to the hives, smoke out the bees, and cut down the honeycombs using a long stick (masliya). The honey is eaten in large quantities, wax and all, and is considered especially tasty when the comb contains young bees. Honey and meat are used to barter for goods (e.g., cloth, metal axes, etc.) that the Veddas do not produce themselves. In addition to honey, the Veddas are fond of chewing. The betel (areca) nut is their favorite, and every Vedda has a betel bag with a betel cutter and a small box of lime (made from burning the shell of a snail).

The Veddas believe that formerly it was the custom for a man to carry a small piece of dried human liver in his betel bag. The reason for this was not known, but it was thought to be related to increasing a man's valor. The liver had to come from someone personally killed by the Vedda, and it would be eaten to increase the Vedda's strength and resolve.

The Veddas avoid eating certain foods, although the specific reasons for these food taboos are unclear. While they consume the flesh of most animals and birds, the Veddas abstain from eating buffaloes, elephants, leopards, and jackals. This avoidance might stem from the dangers of hunting such animals, but the Veddas also do not eat fowl (wild or domesticated) or pigs. It is particularly important for shamans to avoid fowl and pork before ceremonial dances.

Today, few Veddas survive solely by hunting and gathering, and most groups practice shifting cultivation (chena) or permanent agriculture. The diet of these populations is generally similar to that of the rural communities among whom they live.

13 EDUCATION

Because of their lifestyle, traditional Veddas have no access to formal education. Vedda populations that are settled can avail themselves of state educational facilities. As a group, however, the Veddas can be considered marginal to the social currents of Sri Lankan society.

14 CULTURAL HERITAGE

Ritual dances, accompanied by chanting, music, and possession by spirits, are central to Vedda ceremonial life. These include the arrow dance, the hunting dance, the Na Yakku ceremonies, and the invocation of various yakku (e.g., Bambura Yakka for the hunt, Pata Yakka for aid in pregnancy, or Dola Yakka to ensure successful honey collection). Only the men dance, usually in a circle, and sometimes beating out the rhythm of the dance on their stomachs. The shaman becomes possessed by the spirit of the particular yakka being invoked. The yakka looks over the offerings made to him and, if pleased with what he sees, pronounces success in the hunt, or a normal childbirth, etc.

15 WORK

The Veddas were originally hunters and gatherers, but many subsequently took up shifting agriculture or even permanent cultivation. They grow crops, such as millet, maize, beans, squashes, and eggplants. Some engage in paddy-rice cultivation. Fishing is important among the Coast Veddas who build their own boats and canoes for venturing out onto the ocean. Prawns are an important catch for the Coast Veddas. In addition, many among the Anuradhapura and Coast Veddas resort to casual labor to supplement their incomes.

16 SPORTS

Among traditional Veddas, children play very simply. Babies have toy bows and arrows made for them by their mothers. By about five years of age, young boys make their own small bows and arrows and learn how to use them. They begin to accompany the adults on hunting trips when they are around 10 years old. Children play with clay and sticks, while little girls pretend to cook using broken pots.

17 ENTERTAINMENT AND RECREATION

The Veddas derive their entertainment from their traditional ceremonial dances and the songs that are sung to invoke the spirits. Songs are also sung as charms, as lullabies, and also for amusement. Vedda enjoy pantomime and often enact scenes, such as hunting and honey-gathering for sheer enjoyment.

18 FOLK ART, CRAFTS, AND HOBBIES

The Veddas are not well known for their folk arts and crafts. Formerly, they made their own weapons, but they have now come to rely on trade for metal arrowheads and axes. Crude drawings have been found in rock-shelters, but these appear to have no ritual significance and were probably done for amusement.

19 SOCIAL PROBLEMS

Like all tribals, the Veddas are facing problems of change brought about by contact with more "modern" neighbors. Their traditional means of exploiting natural resources are relatively primitive, and they continue to experience low standards of living. Socially, they remain isolated and often feel they are exploited by the more advanced peoples around them. Numbers of "true" Veddas are declining as a result of disease and scarcity of food. Some Veddas have opted to be resettled under government programs, adopting paddy cultivation and taking advantage of amenities, such as markets, health services, and educational facilities. Many, however, are reluctant to leave their traditional lands, arguing that they will be leaving behind them the spirits of the forests and mountains. Those that have taken to settled agriculture have adopted many cultural features of the rural peasantry around them.

Unfortunately, many Veddas have been uprooted by the pressures of modern economic growth. Development projects along the Gal Oya and Mahaweli rivers have inundated Vedda settlements and forced the relocation of their inhabitants. In 1983, Veddas were evicted from the Maduru Oya National Park in the catchment area of the controversial Mahaweli Development Program. Although they had been demanding rights to their lands since at least 1970, the Veddas had never received secure land tenure that recognized their collective custodianship over traditional hunting and gathering ranges. Neither had they been consulted or represented in any decision-making process that affected their daily lives. The creation of the park forced the Veddas to leave their traditional lands in the semi-evergreen dry monsoon forests, and they were transformed overnight into game poachers and trespassers. Barriers, guards, and outposts were stationed along the park's demarcated borders and the hapless tribals were moved down out of the hill forests to small settlements, where they were provided houses and small irrigated rice paddies. The Vedda—traditionally hunters and gatherers supplementing their subsistence by shifting cultivation—had trouble adapting to a sedentary way of life. Subsequent surveys showed they resented the lack of access to forest produce, game, and land for shifting cultivation and were fast losing their own language. Only one small group, led by the old Vedda chieftain Uru Warige Tissagami (popularly known as Tissahamy) and his kinsfolk of Kotabakinni village refused to be evicted from the land of their ancestors. Officials considered Tissahamy to be very obstinate and stubborn, for he would not budge an inch no matter how many emissaries went to speak to him. Finally the government had to concede that Tissshamy and seven families could remain on their lands as long as the old man lived. However, according to the 1987 Master Plan for Maduru Oya National Park, the day that aged chief Tissahamy expired, the rest of his kinsfolk would have to evacuate the hamlet immediately. Tissahamy finally died in June 1999 at the age of 96.

Under Sri Lanka's Fauna and Flora Protection Ordinance, 1993, all traditional Vedda occupations, including hunting, honey-gathering, and shifting cultivation, were prohibited within national parks but limited human activities were to be permitted within other areas, defined as sanctuaries, of 1,500 acres. There is concern that 1,500 acres may not be able to sustain more than a few families living by hunting, gathering, and shifting cultivation. As of 2008, the creation of these sanctuaries has yet to be achieved.

Some observers have said Veddas are disappearing and have lamented the decline of their distinct culture. Development, government forest reserve restrictions, the movement of settlers into their ancestral lands, and the civil war in Sri Lanka have disrupted traditional Vedda ways of life. However, cultural assimilation of Veddas with other local populations has been going on for a long time. The term Vedda has been used in Sri Lanka to mean not only hunter-gatherers, but also to refer to any people who adopt an unsettled and rural way of life and thus can be a derogatory term not based on ethnic definitions. Over time, it is possible for non-Vedda groups to become Veddas, in this broad cultural sense. Vedda populations of this kind are increasing in some districts of the island of Sri Lanka.

Today, many Sinhalese people and some east coast Tamils claim that they have some trace of Vedda blood. Intermarriage between Veddas and Sinhalese is very frequent. They are not considered outcasts in Sri Lankan society, unlike the untouchables.

[20] GENDER ISSUES

There have been reports alleging that young Vedda women are being tricked into accepting contracts to the Middle East as domestic workers, an attractive proposition for young girls who see no future for themselves in Sri Lanka, when in fact they are trafficked into prostitution or sold as sex slaves.

Given the small size of the Vedda community, gender issues are less significant than the disappearance of Vedda culture and the diminishing size of the group that adhere to it. As with most tribal peoples in South Asia, women in Vedda society are relatively free. However, it is increasingly common for women to marry outside the community.

Change is the inevitable result when a tribal society comes into contact with more advanced cultures and economic systems. In Sri Lanka, this has involved the disruption of Vedda life, the disappearance of traditional Vedda culture, and the loss of Vedda cultural identity.

[21] BIBLIOGRAPHY

Brow, James. *Vedda Villages of Anuradhapura: The Historical Anthropology of a Community in Sri Lanka.* Seattle and London: University of Washington Press, 1978.

Dharmadasa, K. N. O., and S. W. R. de A. Samarasinghe, ed. *The Vanishing Aborigines: Sri Lanka's Veddas in Transition.* New Delhi: Vikas Publishing House, 1990.

Seligmann, C. G., and Brenda Z. Seligmann. *The Veddas.* Cambridge: Cambridge University Press, 1911.

Spittel, R. L. *Vanished Trails: the Last of the Veddas.* Colombo: Associated Newspapers of Ceylon, 1961.

Stegeborn, Wiveca A. "The Disappearing Wanniyala-Aetto ('Veddahs') of Sri Lanka: A Case Study." *Nomadic Peoples.* Vol.8, 1: 43-63, , 2004.

———. "Endangered Wanniyala-Aetto Women as Sex Slaves in the Middle East." *Nomadic Peoples.* Vol. 5, 1:175-78 2001.

———."The Wanniyala-aetta (Veddahs) of Sri Lanka." In Lee, R. B. and Daly, R. H., ed., *The Cambridge Encyclopedia of Hunters and Gatherers.* Cambridge: Cambridge University Press, 1999.

—by D. O. Lodrick

VIETNAMESE

PRONUNCIATION: vee-et-nuh-MEEZ
LOCATION. Vietnam
POPULATION: 70–80 million
LANGUAGE: Vietnamese
RELIGION: Confucianism; Taoism; Buddhism, Roman Catholicism; Cao Daism
RELATED ARTICLES: Vol. 2: Vietnamese Americans

[1] INTRODUCTION

The Socialist Republic of Vietnam, known to most as Vietnam, is located in Southeast Asia. The history of the Socialist Republic of Vietnam has been shaped by its location between China and India. Straddling a crossroads and lines of trade between north and south, east and west, Vietnam has been a center of human trade, interaction, and conflict for centuries.

Archaeological excavations reveal that the first state in Vietnam, known as the Dong-son period, emerged in the Red River delta around 800 BC. The Dong-son people built dikes and canals to control the rivers and irrigate their rice fields and crafted bronze drums, tools, and weapons.

By 250 BC, a Vietnamese ruler created the Au Lac Kingdom by uniting the Dong-son delta people and the neighboring highlanders. Soon after, a Chinese commander subdued the region and demanded that the new kingdom grant allegiance to China. The country was then called Nam Viet, Nam meaning "south" and Viet referring to the people living along China's southern border.

A century later, Nam Viet became a Chinese province and was ruled by China until 900 AD. Despite this history of domination, the Vietnamese were able to retain a certain level of autonomy. An ancient Vietnamese saying held that "The emperor's power stops at the village gate." Only after numerous rebellions by the Vietnamese and their pledge that they would continue to grant loyalty to China did she become an independent country. Vietnam's legacy from China continues to today and includes ideas about government, philosophy, script, education, religion, crafts, and literature.

Over the next centuries as different families ruled the country, the Vietnamese began moving south in search of new areas for rice cultivation. By the late 1400s, Vietnam had conquered the Champa Kingdom in central Vietnam. By the late 1600s, the Vietnamese had migrated deep into southern Vietnam, an area occupied by Cambodian, or Khmer, people.

The first Europeans in Vietnam were Portuguese and French traders. The Portuguese soon left, and the Vietnamese ejected the French. Some Roman Catholic missionaries stayed on. Over the next centuries, sometimes in the favor of Vietnam's rulers, though often not, the missionaries made a number of converts among the Vietnamese.

The French returned to Vietnam in the mid-1800s, ostensibly to protect their missionaries, but in fact to explore economic and trade opportunities. For the next 80 years, France took out many more resources and taxes than it returned in education or wealth. In the mid-1950s the French were forced to abandon their colony by the Vietminh, nationalist Communists led by Ho Chi Minh.

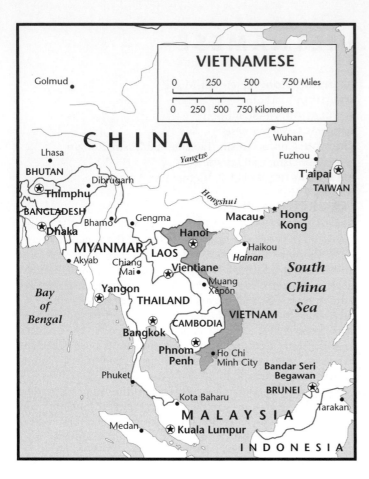

VIETNAMESE

The Geneva Conference of 1954 divided Vietnam into two entities, pending an election to reunify the country, which never took place. The area north of the 17th parallel became North Vietnam, led by Ho Chi Minh and his Communists; south of the line lay South Vietnam, run by a pro-Western prime minister. Fearful that Communism would take over South Vietnam and that other Southeast Asian countries would fall "like dominos," the United States sent advisors to help South Vietnam fight Communism. The United States was soon embroiled in war: the more soldiers the United States sent, the more soldiers and assistance North Vietnam sent to the south.

The war continued until the early 1970s, when the United States Congress ceased military funding for South Vietnam. At a cost of 58,000 soldiers and over $140 billion in military and economic aid, the United States withdrew its last troops in 1973. An estimated 3 million Vietnamese combatants and civilians (North and South) were estimated to have been killed in the war. In 1975, North Vietnam conquered South Vietnam and reunited the country.

In 1975, almost a million Vietnamese left their homeland and were immediately resettled in Western countries. Another million fled Vietnam by sea in 1978. Most eventually were resettled in the United States, France, Canada, and Australia. Vietnamese continued to flee their country for political and economic reasons into the early 1990s.

Peace has been difficult. Isolated by the United States and the international community until the mid-1990s, Vietnam suffered from a stagnant economy and increasing population. In recent years Vietnam has enjoyed strong economic growth

rates and attracted increasing international investment and trade. However, high levels of inflation are threatening Vietnam's status as Asia's newest economic star. The government continues to be run by the Vietnamese Communist Party, with the party chairman being the political leader of the country.

²LOCATION AND HOMELAND

Vietnam has a population of between 70 and 80 million people, making Vietnam one of the most populous countries in the world. Most Vietnamese live in the Red and Mekong river deltas. The population continues to grow at a high rate despite governmental efforts to slow its increase, and, thus, much of the industrial and agricultural advances made in the past years have been consumed by the growing population.

Minorities in Vietnam include highlanders, such as the Jarai and Bahnar of the central highlands, and the Tai and Muong of the northern highlands. Approximately 100,000 Muslim Cham live in the central highlands. Over 700,000 Khmer and 500,000 Chinese live in the southern delta of Vietnam.

Sometimes described as a carrying pole with a rice basket hanging from both ends, Vietnam is in fact long and slender, only 80 km (50 mi) wide at its narrowest point. The "carrying pole" of Vietnam stretches in an S-shape more than 1,000 mi in length from China in the north, curving around to Cambodia in the south. A delta sits at either end of the country, the two "rice baskets," each yielding enormous quantities of rice. In between and along the Western edge of the country are hills and densely forested highlands. Like Cambodia, however, Vietnam is experiencing the impact of changes in the Mekong as more dams are constructed in the upper riparian countries.

Located just north of the equator, Vietnam has a tropical monsoon climate. In northern Vietnam, the rainy season extends from April to October, and Hanoi, the capital, has an annual rainfall of 173 cm (68 in). In mountainous areas, the annual rainfall can exceed 406 cm (160 in). In the southern part of Vietnam, the rainy season extends from May to November with annual rainfall of about 203 cm (80 in) in the lowland regions.

Humidity is high throughout the year, although the climate varies considerably from place to place because of differences in latitude and topographical relief. Summers are generally hot and wet and winters are mild and dry. The typhoon season extends from July through November, often causing serious damage to crops and people especially along the central coast area.

³LANGUAGE

The Vietnamese language has been influenced by classical Chinese more than any other language, although it carries traces of Mon-Khmer, Tai, and other Southeast Asian dialects. Although Chinese was the language used by government officials, scholars, and artists for the thousand years of Chinese domination and following, Vietnamese remained the popular language. More than 1,000 years ago, Vietnamese began devising a script based on Chinese characters in which to write their own literature, and Vietnam adopted the Confucian examination system.

In the 17th century, Portuguese and French missionaries transcribed the Vietnamese language into Roman letters. By the end of the 19th century, this Romanized system, called *quoc ngu*, had replaced the Chinese-based system of writing.

Quoc ngu uses diacritical marks above or below letters to indicate pronunciation and tone. Vietnamese is a tonal language, so that a change in tone alone can change the meaning of a word. The Vietnamese language, with its many tones, sounds strange to many Western ears. To Vietnamese, however, their language has the sound of poetry. In fact, much of Vietnamese literature is in fact poems. Vietnamese is also very difficult for English-speakers to pronounce. Thus, the closest most Westerners can come to saying "Nguyen" is to pronounce it "Win."

Vietnamese carry their father's rather than their mother's family name, as do most Americans. Thus, a child born to Mr. Nguyen will have the name "Nguyen." But, unlike Americans, Vietnamese use the family name first. Their naming patterns reinforce the importance of family over the individual, with the family name first and the individual's name second. If Mr. Nguyen names his son Tai, then the boy will be known as Nguyen Tai. If Mr. Nguyen also gives his son the middle name, Thanh, his son will be called Nguyen Tai Thanh, family name, first name, and finally middle name.

⁴FOLKLORE

In folklore, Vietnamese consider themselves to be the descendants of marriage between a dragon and a fairy and many legends depict the birth of Vietnam in these terms.

The most famous Vietnamese of modern time is Ho Chi Minh. Already a legend in his homeland long before his death in 1969, Ho Chi Minh is considered his country's George Washington. Born in 1880 to a mandarin family, Ho Chi Minh received a good education in Vietnam. After working on a cargo ship and in a restaurant in the United States, he traveled extensively, becoming committed to the goal of freeing his country from French colonialism. After cooperating with the United States to fight the Japanese during World War II, Ho Chi Minh became the president of Vietnam in 1945, before Vietnam was returned to French rule by the Allies. Subsequently, as president of North Vietnam he fought against American troops in an effort to obtain control over southern Vietnam as well. A Communist and a patriot, his prediction that his party would eventually achieve victory in Vietnam came true in April 1975, six years after his death.

Another famous Vietnamese patriot who sought independence for his country was Le Loi, who lived long ago. After leading an elephant-mounted army against Chinese invaders in the 1420s, Le Loi became King of Vietnam. He is remembered as a benevolent ruler, who increased agricultural production and built dams, dikes, and bridges for the Vietnamese people. Over 1,500 years earlier, the Trung sisters also attempted to gain independence from the Chinese. They failed, but they are remembered as great heroines by the Vietnamese people.

⁵RELIGION

The Vietnamese practice a number of different religions, sometimes several at the same time. One philosophy with enormous influence in the country is Confucianism, which came from China over 2,000 years ago. Confucianism emphasizes good behavior, education, and respect for hierarchy. Ancestor worship is an important legacy of the Confucian inheritance. For this reason, the Vietnamese are still deeply bothered by the fact that 300,000 of their people remain unaccounted for from the "American War" and have never received proper burials.

Another religion inherited from China is Taoism, which emphasizes beliefs in the spirit world and ancestor worship. Most homes have an altar to the ancestors holding a small vase of flowers, some incense, a plate or two of food, and candles. Taoism also includes belief in geomancy, which focuses on the importance of aligning human objects and activities with the landscape. Thus, a father's grave must face the proper direction or his son will suffer. Vietnamese go to geomancers in order to tap the earth's energy on their behalf and to determine how the stars or winds will affect them at particular times.

In addition, most Vietnamese call themselves Buddhists. Vietnamese Buddhists believe in reincarnation and karmic destiny, which is the belief that humans reap what they sow. If a man is good in this life, he will have a better life the next time round. If he is bad, however, the opposite will happen. Originally brought from India, Buddhism has undergone significant change during its centuries in Vietnam under Chinese domination. Therefore, in contrast to other Southeast Asian countries, Vietnamese follow Mahayana Buddhism rather than the Theravada strain. Different Buddhist sects exist in the country, including a group called the Hoa Hao, each emphasizing a different aspect of the religion.

There are also several million Catholic Vietnamese, who make up roughly 10% of the population. Most Catholics live in Vietnam's cities, primarily in the south, where the French colonial Catholics had the greatest presence.

A small but important religion called Cao Dai is followed by more than one million people. Cao Daism began in 1919 in southern Vietnam. This religion combines elements of belief and practice from Buddhism, Christianity, and history. Its saints include Jesus Christ, the Buddha, Joan of Arc, and Charlie Chaplin. The importance of the Cao Dai religion has been due in part to its standing army, which was involved in the Vietnam War. While the Cao Dai religion may seem strange to non-believers, its adherents believe they are combining the best beliefs of all the world's religions.

⁶MAJOR HOLIDAYS

The most important Vietnamese holiday is the New Year celebration, which occurs during the full moon that falls in late January or early February. *Tet*, as this holiday is called, is celebrated over a period of three days. The Vietnamese try to return to the home of their parents to unite with family and friends. Tet is a time when Vietnamese honor their ancestors, wrap up the old year, and prepare for a new. People repay their debts and ask for forgiveness from all those whom they have wronged. They put on new clothes, pray for blessings, exchange gifts, and give thanks for being together.

The Vietnamese decorate their homes with peach tree branches and red and gold paper, the colors of happiness. They light firecrackers at night and they spare no expense in preparing the fanciest dishes possible.

Other holidays commemorate important dates in the history of the current government and its victory over South Vietnam. These dates include 27 January, the anniversary of the peace agreement that resulted in America's withdrawal from Vietnam; 29 March, the actual withdrawal of American troops; and 2 September, the establishment of the Democratic Republic of Vietnam.

A motorcycle drives by a pottery market in Bat Trang, Vietnam. Bat Trang is famous for its ceramics, which it ships to many countries. (AP Images/Chitose Suzuki)

⁷RITES OF PASSAGE

In Vietnam, the birth of a child is a welcome occasion, especially if the child is a boy. Most children are born to married couples and join a society in which family is valued and trusted above all other aspects of life. A couple without children is pitied, while a family with several offspring is considered fortunate. Children are cared for not only by their parents, but by an extended family of grandparents and aunts and uncles, especially on the paternal side.

In Vietnam, the primary activity of most children is assisting in the support of their family. In the countryside, boys help their fathers with farm work. In the cities, more boys go to school, help their mothers with house chores or errands, or take part-time jobs on their own.

Girls assist their mothers with housework, caring for younger siblings, and helping with work outside the home. For children in rural areas, that is farming, gardening, and caring for animals. For urban children, it is helping their mothers in the shop or preparing food to sell.

Vietnamese value large families and spend much of their time with other family members. Most Vietnamese see parenthood as the ultimate purpose and pleasure in life and look forward to the day they will wed and have children. However, economic development has brought on intense urbanization in Vietnam, and families are beginning to shrink in the number of children as a result.

After the death of one's parents, Vietnamese honor them by following a traditional period of mourning. Other funeral practices include offering prayers and conducting ceremonies on specific anniversaries of the parent's death.

On all important family occasions, such as the birth of a child, betrothals, marriages, funerals, and the anniversaries of ancestors' deaths, families hold appropriate ceremonies. These include notifying the gods and ancestors of family events by special offerings. The wealth and status of the family determines the elaborateness of the ceremonies.

⁸INTERPERSONAL RELATIONS

Vietnamese have great respect for hierarchy and take care to demonstrate respect to all they consider their superiors and demand respect from those they consider their inferiors. Older people are generally considered superior to younger people, men to women, the wealthy to the poor, and those of higher occupation or status to those of lower.

Vietnamese may greet one another with a slight bow and always with a broad smile. Civility is greatly valued and one's true feelings are concealed beneath smiles and amiability. Vietnamese also honor reserve and modesty, attributing loudness and brashness to immaturity and vulgarity.

Dating is virtually unknown in the countryside, where young people are closely supervised by their elders until marriage. There is little touching in public even by married couples, although young people of the same sex often walk about holding hands to demonstrate their friendship.

⁹LIVING CONDITIONS

The health of the Vietnamese people has suffered from decades of war, upheaval, and population increase. While the infant mortality rate is lower and life expectancy at birth is higher than the average for Southeast Asia, the Vietnamese continue to be plagued by numerous health problems. Malaria and tuberculosis continue to be widespread because many cannot afford medicine to prevent these diseases. Cholera and bubonic plague continue to threaten many Vietnamese. Malnutrition also affects many in the country. An additional legacy of the Vietnam War is a high percentage of birth defects which are linked to chemicals sprayed on Vietnam's forests. Leftover bombs and shells continue to cause injury, especially to children, soldiers, and farmers. Nevertheless, despite its deficiencies in health care, international epidemiologists consider that Vietnam did a good job of handling the SARS crisis, with prompt action and public education campaigns.

Until recently, Vietnam's economy has frustrated many Vietnamese in their desire for consumer goods. While American money was flowing into the country, many South Vietnamese became accustomed to life with televisions, liquors, imported clothes, air conditioning, and other conveniences. When the Americans left and Vietnam was shut off from trade with many Western nations, goods stopped flowing into the country. Many Vietnamese compensated by purchasing goods on the black market. Access to consumer goods is increasing as the country's economy has become incorporated into the global economy. As Vietnam's economy has boomed, luxury goods have become more common. For example, choice—sometimes rare—European wines can be found in hotels in most major cities. Although the Vietnam War and the subsequent economic embargo of Vietnam hurt the economy, in the past decade Vietnam has been able to improve the lives of most citizens. One of the government's proudest achievements is in cutting the poverty rate in half since 1986, when the period of "doi moi" (renovation) began.

Although major cities are growing rapidly, close to 80% of the Vietnamese population still lives in rural areas, primarily in small villages. The housing of northern and southern Vietnam differs due to climatic differences between the two areas. In the cooler north, most rural people live in houses made of wood or bamboo with tile roofs. In the south, which is warmer, most country folk live in houses made of straw, thatch, or palm leaves. Many families now use metal or plastic sheets to roof their houses.

The majority of urban dwellers live in small apartments. Most dwellings are small and cramped, crowding numerous family members into a few small rooms. Building materials are predominately wood, brick, and tile.

In rural areas, few homes have electricity or running water and families carry water to their homes from nearby streams and ponds. Furniture is rare, seldom more than beds on the floor and a low table around which family members gather to eat while sitting on the floor.

Throughout the late 1970s and early 1980s consumer goods remained scarce. While few Vietnamese were starving, most were subsisting on a diet low in protein and calories. In addition, much of a worker's wages went toward buying food. In the early 1990s the situation began to improve with the loosening of international embargoes and increased trade.

American bombing during the Vietnam War destroyed many roads, bridges, rails, and ports, and the country continues to struggle with modern transportation. The major ports are Ho Chi Minh City and Haiphong; other ports for ocean and river travel include Qui Nhon and Nha Trong. Primary rail lines run from Ho Chi Minh City in the south to Hanoi in the north, and between Hanoi and several Chinese cities. The poor condition of the railroads, ports, and roads continue to hamper Vietnam's ability to increase industrial productivity. However, the number of cars, buses, and trucks is increasing in Vietnam, so much so that the country's roads can scarcely handle them. New highways are being built, especially in the south, which contains a greater proportion of the population.

Motorbikes are a popular means of transportation for successful Vietnamese. Most families make do with bicycles and travel any distance at all by bus, ferry, or boat.

¹⁰FAMILY LIFE

Traditionally, Vietnamese families were large. Today, Vietnamese are likely to marry young and have four or five children, although many continue to have as many as possible either out of desire or the inaccessibility of birth control. Children are highly valued, not least for their potential in helping with family chores and supporting their parents in their older years.

Marriage is viewed as a social contract between two people and their families. It is arranged by intermediaries and approved by parents who may or may not allow their children some choice in their spouse.

Vietnamese say that family is the most important element of their lives and the obligations of children to their parents, wives to husbands, and younger people to their elders are constantly emphasized. Individual interests are less important than family interests and each individual is seen as one in a long family line that includes ancestors already dead and current and future family members.

Vietnamese families are patriarchal. Families generally live in nuclear family groups, although grandparents sometimes share the home with a grown child and family. Families also socialize together, gathering with other extended family members for festivals, marriages, funerals, and other important occasions.

Individuals are identified primarily by their patrilineal ties and larger kin groups are defined through men rather than women. While women are generally viewed as resilient and strong-willed and assume extensive responsibilities in supporting and caring for the family, they continue to be defined primarily by their ties to men: as the mother of a male child, the wife of a husband. In Vietnam, women are idealized, romanticized, and serenaded, but men have more rights and opportunities than women. Women join their husbands' families, children belong to their father's family, and male children are preferred over female children. Although the government has attempted to equalize relationships between men and women, most Vietnamese continue to hold traditional views of family, marriage, and childrearing.

Pets are not nearly as common in Vietnam as they are in the United States. While many children are surrounded by animals, including dogs, ducks, chickens, pigs, and cats, few of these animals are considered as pets. Instead, children are required to look after the domestic animals that contribute to the family's income. Animals are primarily for eating, selling, or working. Dogs, for example, may be used for guarding the home, hunting, or food. Cats are kept to keep down rats and mice. In Vietnam, as in many countries where children must help support the family, animals kept as pets are a luxury most families cannot afford.

¹¹CLOTHING

Vietnamese women wear a gown that has been called the most beautiful and flattering garment in the world. This garment, called the *ao dai,* is a dress or long blouse worn over trousers. Usually made of light material, the gown flutters at the slightest movement of the wearer, being both modest and sensuous at the same time.

For everyday wear, most urban Vietnamese wear Western clothes. Men wear short- or long-sleeved and collared shirts, tucked in for a business or more formal look, hanging out for informal activity. Businessmen and students usually wear long trousers, while children and physical laborers often prefer shorts. Shirts are usually light colored, while trousers tend toward dark colors. Because of the heat and humidity of Vietnam, both shirts and trousers are made of much lighter material than most clothing in the West.

In the countryside, farmers often wear baggy pajama-like shirts and pants made of black cotton. Also made of light material, this clothing is the most comfortable for long hours of work in a hot country. Both men and women usually wear sandals. Many Vietnamese, especially in the countryside, wear conical straw hats which are great protection from the sun.

¹²FOOD

Rice is to the Vietnamese what bread, potatoes, and pasta are to Americans. It is served at virtually every meal, including breakfast. Fish is almost as important, since Vietnam is a country that has abundant water with vast resources of fish. In addition to being bound on the east and south by the South China Sea, Vietnam is home to two enormously important rivers, the Red River in the north and the Mekong River in the south. Even more importantly, each of these major rivers has numerous tributaries, for Vietnam is covered with smaller rivers, streams, canals, and channels. The monsoons bring additional waters, all of which yield fish and other edible sealife. Fish and other fresh and salt water life is eaten fresh, but is also frequently dried.

Fowl, such as chicken, ducks, and geese, along with eels and eggs, provide additional protein. Beef and pork are enjoyed only by the wealthy or on special occasions such as at weddings or festivals.

A ubiquitous traditional food of Vietnam is *nuoc mam,* a liquid sauce made from fermented fish. Characterized by an extremely strong smell, especially to many Westerners, nuoc mam is used in much cooking. It is roughly equivalent to Japanese soy sauce in its use and saltiness.

The typical Vietnamese meal consists of a bowl of rice and vegetables cooked in fermented sauce. Vegetables are mainly grown at home and include bamboo shoots, soybeans, sweet potatoes, corn, greens of various kinds, onions, and other root crops. Fruit includes bananas, coconuts, mangos, mangosteens, and pineapple. Noodle dishes are also popular. A distinctive Vietnamese dish is *pho,* a hot soup containing any variety of noodles in sauce with vegetables, onions, and meat or fish.

Vietnamese also love charcoal-broiled filleted fish, fried and battered frog, and *banh chung,* square spiced cakes filled with rice, beans, pork, and scallions that have been wrapped in banana leaves and boiled for a day. Another favorite dish is *cha gio,* thin rice paper rolls filled with noodles, pork, crab, eggs, mushrooms, and onions. These tightly packed rolls are then deep fried.

Many Vietnamese drink tea at every meal and other times throughout the day and evening. On special occasions or when guests are visiting, the Vietnamese serve rice wine, beer, soft drinks, or coffee. Because of the French colonial period, Vietnam is more of a coffee-drinking culture than other Asian nations. The common drink is water.

Vietnamese cooking has a reputation throughout the world for being one of the greatest cuisines in the world. Combining French and Chinese traditions, it is known for its delicacy of taste.

Most women continue to cook their families' daily meals outdoors over wood or charcoal and to purchase food on a daily basis in the absence of refrigeration.

Breakfast is usually eaten shortly after awakening. The large meal of the day is eaten around noon, after the morning's work, before the lighter work of the late afternoon, and during the hottest portion of the day. A lighter meal follows the day's work. Vietnamese also love to snack frequently throughout the day.

The quintessential Vietnamese utensil is chopsticks, with which they eat most meals and many snacks. Vietnamese typically sit on a mat on the floor, each holding a bowl of rice. In the middle are several bowls of vegetables in sauce and maybe a plate of fried vegetables or meat. Using chopsticks, each member of the family takes a bit from the communal dish, alternating with bites from his or her own bowl of rice. Vietnamese are startled when they eat with Westerners, who consider eating quietly to be good manners: Vietnamese eat loudly, slurping, sucking, chomping. Such table noises are not considered bad manners; they are considered evidence that people are enjoying their food.

¹³EDUCATION

Although it is not the richest country in Southeast Asia, Vietnam has one of the highest literacy rates and most Vietnamese are literate. Children begin school at age five and most children spend some years in school, usually completing at least the five elementary years. More city than country children attend school for more than a few years. If children are able to pass the examinations given at the end of an additional four years of secondary school, they can go to three years of high school or a vocational school. Those who cannot pass go into the military or try to find a job. High school graduates are considered fortunate, for they receive better jobs, higher pay, and more respect.

Vietnamese have traditionally valued education and long to send their children to school for as many years as possible. The government offers 12 years of schooling for free, but many parents cannot afford the cost of school books and the loss of earning power that occurs when a child is in the classroom.

¹⁴ CULTURAL HERITAGE

Vietnamese music is very different from Western music in rhythm, sound, and even scale. Classical music is played on instruments that include a two-stringed mandolin, a 16-string zither, a long-necked guitar, a three-stringed guitar, and a four-stringed guitar. Traditional bands include instruments that most closely resemble Western flutes, oboes, xylophones, and drums.

Many traditional tunes are sung without accompaniment, with each region having its own folk melodies. Western love songs, especially slow, sad songs recorded by Asian artists, are also much loved by the Vietnamese. Popular theater combines singing with instruments and has dance, mime, and poetry. Classical theater or opera which came from China in the 13th century is popular, as are puppet shows. A unique Vietnamese form is water puppetry, with the controlling rods and strings handled beneath water so that the puppets appear to be dancing on the water.

Spoken Vietnamese lends itself to poetry and the Vietnamese prefer their literature spoken aloud rather than read silently. Consequently, most literature is poetry. Poems relate love stories, epic tales from long ago, or discuss love of country. One famous poem, *Kim Van Kieu* (The Tale of Kieu), tells how a young girl struggles to preserve her family's honor. This poem is so important to Vietnamese that many have memorized the entire epic.

Poetry in Vietnam is not just for the highly literate or skilled. Common people also value and write poetry. Thus, a young man courts his girlfriend through poetry, young soldiers write in their spare time, and politicians try to sway their public through poems. Poems were found among the effects of soldiers from both sides of the Vietnamese War telling of their hopes, fears, and love of family and country.

French literature is also readily available and popular among high school graduates.

¹⁵ WORK

Work varies enormously in Vietnam, but a basic division can be seen in the work done in the city versus that done in the countryside. In the cities, men work at construction, in government offices, and as teachers, drivers, retailers, and mechanics. Women are primarily trades people or street vendors, selling clothing and a myriad of other items in the marketplace or cooked food on the streets. Women also work in clinics, as teachers, and as factory workers.

In the rural areas, most men are rice farmers and Vietnam is one of the top rice-producing countries in the world. Men's work includes caring for draft animals, fishing, repairing equipment, and helping clear gardens. Other men are full-time fishermen, merchants, traders, drivers, monks, or officials.

¹⁶ SPORTS

Vietnamese children play a variety of games, but the most popular Vietnamese sport by far is soccer. Because most Vietnamese families continue to struggle to make a living, children spend most of their time assisting their parents or going to school. Watching videos or television or hanging around and chatting with their friends are especially valued leisure activities for most Vietnamese youth.

¹⁷ ENTERTAINMENT AND RECREATION

Vietnam is blanketed by a loudspeaker system and music and programs are offered regularly. Many people now own radios and most of the country also receives television, although televisions are much less common than they are in the United States. The Internet has spread rapidly in Vietnam, as a source of communication, education, and entertainment. Although the government promotes it as a development tool, the Internet is also subject to monitoring, especially when political dialogue is concerned.

¹⁸ FOLK ART, CRAFTS, AND HOBBIES

Since the 1400s, Vietnamese artisans have been making lacquer ware. Wooden objects are painted and decorated with pearl, gold, silver, shell, and other objects. The objects are then coated repeatedly with a lacquer obtained from the sap of son trees.

Crafts people make block prints on which scenes have been carved, inked, and then pressed onto paper. The Vietnamese also make porcelain and other ceramics, which they learned from the Chinese many centuries ago.

¹⁹ SOCIAL PROBLEMS

Recently, Vietnam has become less isolated from the international community and is interested in increased contact, trade, and cultural exchange with other countries. The country has consequently made an effort to respond to international concerns about human rights.

Nonetheless, reports of arbitrary arrest, detention, and surveillance over the population continue. Freedom of speech and movement are limited. There is evidence, however, of an increasingly tolerant attitude toward literary and artistic expression. The government has been very concerned with raising the standard of living of the Vietnamese people. A number of political prisoners have been released since the late 1980s and it is generally accepted that all of the prisoners held in postwar "re-education camps" have now been released.

The government of North Vietnam has claimed in the past that its country had no alcohol problem because of the wholesome life experienced by the Vietnamese under Communism. During the same time, however, in the 1960s and 1970s, alcohol and drug abuse were seen as a major problem among South Vietnamese. After 1975, both alcohol and drugs were strictly controlled, and information about substance abuse is severely restricted. Not until the 1980s did the government concede that alcoholism had increased in the cities.

²⁰ GENDER ISSUES

Because Vietnam has often been at war in its history—with the Chinese, French, and Americans— the legend of women warriors has given a particular caché to the female sex in legend.

This was underscored in the Vietnam War when many young women from the North went South to aid the National Liberation Front. Communist mass-based organizations also sought to involve women in all aspects of nation-building and the war. As a result, some women enjoy high-ranking positions in the Party, in the National Assembly, and the executive branch.

However, cultural traditions sometimes mitigated against the rise of women in Vietnam. For example, the Confucian examination system, which enabled bright young men to better their positions in life, depended upon women working in the fields or the shops while their brothers or husbands spent long years studying for the examination. Although the rights of women are guaranteed in Vietnamese law in post-war times, social discrimination has often lagged behind. In addition, trafficking of women has increased as Vietnam has become increasingly involved with the international community.

[21] BIBLIOGRAPHY

Changing Identity: Recent Works by Women Artists from Vietnam. Exhibition curated by Nora Taylor. Washington D.C.: International Arts & Artists, 2007.

Corfield, Justin J. *The History of Vietnam*. Westport, CT: Greenwood Press, 2008.

Crawford, Ann Caddell. *Customs and Culture of Vietnam*. Rutland, VT: Charles E. Tuttle, 1966.

Green, Jen. *Vietnam*. Washington, D.C.: National Geographic, 2008.

Halberstam, David. *The Making of a Quagmire: America and Vietnam During the Kennedy Era*. Lanham, MD: Rowman & Littlefield, 2008.

Hall, D.G. E. *A History of South-East Asia*. New York: St. Martin's Press, 1968.

Kwon, Heonik. *Ghosts of War in Vietnam*. Cambridge: Cambridge University Press, 2008.

Long, Robert Emmet ed. *Vietnam Ten Years After*. New York: H.W. Wilson, 1986.

Osborne, Milton E. *The French Presence in Cochinchina and Cambodia*. Ithaca, NY: Cornell University Press, 1969.

Thayer, Thomas C. *War Without Fronts: The American Experience in Vietnam*. Boulder, CO: Westview Press, 1985.

Woodside, Alexander B. *Vietnam and the Chinese Model*. Cambridge: Harvard University Press, 1971.

—revised by C. Dalpino

VIETNAMESE HIGHLANDERS

PRONUNCIATION: vee-et-nuh-MEEZ HI-land-erz
LOCATION: Vietnam
POPULATION: (Estimated) Tai, 1.4 million; Muong, 1.2 million; Thai, 800,000; Hmong Meo, 800,000; Nung, 700,000; Yao, 500,000; Jarai, 320,000; Rhade, 280,000; Bahnar, 180,000; others from 175,000 to 600 per ethnic group.
LANGUAGE: More than 12 languages
RELIGION: Animism; Christianity
RELATED ARTICLES: Vol. 4: Vietnamese

[1] INTRODUCTION

At least 12% of the population of Vietnam is comprised of over 50 minority groups. Many of these (estimated 7%) are indigenous peoples who live in the highlands of Vietnam. These indigenous people are significantly different from the Vietnamese who occupy the lowlands.

The hill peoples of Vietnam have long been held in contempt by lowland Vietnamese. Their language, culture, and their appearance struck the lowland Vietnamese as strange and barbaric. The hill peoples had a reputation with the Vietnamese of being independent, nomadic, fierce warriors, and potent magicians. They were all so different from the Vietnamese, who viewed themselves as civilized and cultured.

Until the 20th century and even later, the Vietnamese referred to all highland people as "Moi." In the 19th century, French colonizers took over the same term. For both Vietnamese and French, the term "Moi" meant "savage." The ruggedness of the highlands only strengthened the reputation of the indigenous peoples as rough and strange, being a land that to the Vietnamese seemed to be inhabited not only by savages but by wild animals, strange diseases, and mysterious powers. Later, the French began referring to all upland people as Montagnards, meaning "mountaineers." This term was also used by the Americans to refer to the Central Highlands people, who fought alongside them in the 1960s and 70s. Some Central Highlands people refer to themselves collectively as "Degar."

The people of Vietnam's highlands consist of numerous ethnic groups, many with different languages and customs. They differ not only from the lowland Vietnamese but from one another, being distinguished by architecture types, color and design of dress and ornamentation, style of agricultural tools, social organization, and religion.

The origins of Vietnam's hill peoples are not clear. Some, like the Giay, Hmong, Lolo, Nung, San Chay, and Zao are probably descendants of peoples who migrated from southern China many centuries ago. Other groups are probably descendants of Malay lowlanders forced long ago into the Western hills by immigrants from China, or are related to the Thai people of Thailand and Laos, who originated in southern China.

One group, the Muong, believe their people and culture originated in Hoa Binh Province in northern Vietnam. Other groups probably originated in the same area. Over time and with geographical dispersion and cultural isolation, these tribal groups gradually divided and became unique in many cultural and linguistic characteristics. Despite numerous similarities with their neighbors, the Thai to the west and the Vietnamese to the east, the Muong continue to exhibit many unique qualities.

In the 15th century and after, lowland Vietnamese moved south into Cham and Cambodian territory. To separate themselves from the highland peoples, their leaders, or Mandarins, established a military line along the frontier between the highlanders in the mountainous area to the west and the plains to the west and south. Except for some trade and tribute payments paid by the tribes to the Vietnamese, this military boundary restricted contact between the hill people and the Vietnamese lowlanders.

The coming of French colonizers to Vietnam affected the indigenous peoples in a limited way. Although the French administered the highlands separately from the rest of Vietnam, contact between the hill peoples and the Vietnamese increased. Along with French administrators came Christian missionaries to set up schools, hospitals, and sanitariums among the hill groups. Despite various French administrative attempts to govern the highlands, either directly through French officials or indirectly through tribal leaders, the net political effect of French rule was negligible. Most hill people remained isolated from the culture and institutions of lowland Vietnam. Those groups who did have contact with the French and their administrators resented exploitation by French administrators and farmers and wanted them gone.

The economic consequences of French rule were more deeply felt. The highlands of northern Vietnam were seen as a source of coal, while the central and southern highlands were suited to the introduction of cash crops. Entrepreneurs opened rubber plantations on land that had been used previously by the hill people to plant their rotating crops. These plantations of rubber and opium provided employment opportunities to highlanders as well as lowlanders. The French also set up extensive tea and coffee plantations, especially in the area inhabited by the Ede and Jarai. The introduction of new large-scale cash cropping led to increased trade with lowlanders for many hill people.

During the long Vietnamese war of independence against the French, indigenous ethnic minority people fought on both sides. The final defeat of the French at Dien Bien Phu in the Northern Highlands came with the assistance of hill people who fought on the side of the rebelling Vietminh.

After French rule was concluded and Vietnam was divided into North and South Vietnam along the 17th parallel in 1954, administrative handling of the hill peoples changed. In the north, the Communist government recognized the desire of the minorities to be autonomous. To accommodate those sentiments, the government set up two independent zones for the highlanders and allowed them limited self-government. The government did so hoping the minority groups would eventually and without resentment be incorporated into Vietnamese society.

The South Vietnamese government, however, attempted to exert direct control of the minority highlanders, immediately angering them by taking some of their lands for the resettlement of Catholics, who had just migrated from the north. A number of highlanders were also moved from their traditional lands into strategic hamlets, fortified enclaves that were devised to deny food and assistance to the Communist soldiers in the south. Relationships continued with considerable con-

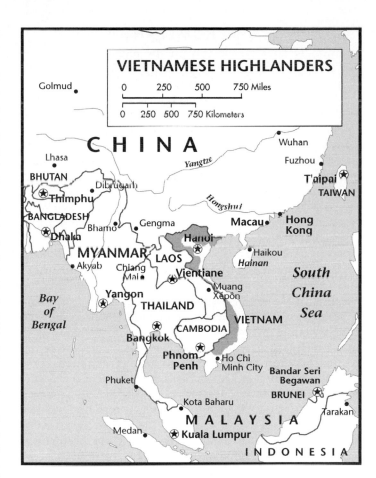

flict, with indigenous ethnic minority soldiers drawn into the war on both sides until the Communist conquest of South Vietnam.

During the Vietnam War, American and Australian Special Forces troops joined with men from the Central Highlands to fight the Vietnamese Communists. These Montagnard troops were valuable allies, although they considered the South Vietnamese their enemies as well. After the Communists gained control of Vietnam in 1975, many indigenous ethnic groups of the Central Highlands suffered retribution for their support of the American war effort.

Since 1975, some highlanders continue their traditional lives, largely isolated from mainstream Vietnamese life. Most, however, are increasingly being incorporated into Vietnamese society. By 1986 over 40% of the hill people had adopted a sedentary lifestyle. That number has increased into the 21st century.

The hill people of the Central Highlands, feeling that their forest land was being encroached on by lowland Vietnamese loggers and plantation interests, held demonstrations in early 2001, calling for land rights protection and religious freedom. This was met with repressive measures by Vietnamese authorities, and in the years since human rights violations against the Central Highlanders, including imprisonment, torture, and executions, have been documented by Amnesty International, Human Rights Watch, and other international organizations.

² LOCATION AND HOMELAND

Many indigenous peoples live in the highlands that cover two-thirds of Vietnam. The landscape in which Vietnam's hill peoples dwell is in startling contrast to the environment of the lowland Vietnamese, which is made up of vast cultivated deltas in the north and south joined by a narrow strip of cultivated flatland along the central coast. The irrigated rice fields, villages, and towns of the lowlanders are replaced by the forests and vegetation of central and northern Vietnam's plateaus and mountains, which stretch from the central coast plain inland to Cambodia and Laos. Here, the rugged hill country is interspersed with narrow deep valleys with luxuriant natural vegetation, many fertile soils, and a subtropical, monsoon climate.

In contrast to the densely populated flatlands of the lowland Vietnamese, the hill people are scattered sparsely through Vietnam's highlands. These highland areas include the Annamite Cordillera, a range of mountains and plateaus, and the Northern Highlands of northwest Vietnam.

In the Northern Highlands of Vietnam, the largest of the minority ethnic groups are the Tai, Thai, Nung, Hmong Meo, and Zao. This area, with a cooler climate than the rest of the country, has the market town of Sapa, which is a cultural center and tourist attraction. One of the larger groups in the Northern Highlands, the Muong, is located along a continuous area of land about 300 kilometers in length, stretching from Yen Bai Province to Nghe An Province. The area is comprised of narrow valleys lying in a mountainous area, with Vietnamese villages to the east and Thai settlements to the west. The area used to be covered with forest, but today much of this wooded cover is gone.

Over a million people live in Vietnam's Central Highlands. The largest number of Central Highlanders are the Jarai, the Ede (including the Rhade), and the Bahnar. Rhade subgroups include the Rhade Kpa, Rhade M'dur, Rhade A'dham, K'tul, Epan, Blo, K'ah, K'drao, and Hwing. The Monom or Bonom and the Hre live in the Central Highlands. The Rengao live in the Gia Lai-Cong Tum Province of the Central Highlands. They may be a sub-group of the Bahnar or Sedang.

Numerous other groups ranging in population from almost 100,000 to less than 100 inhabit either the Northern or Central Highlands. The Chrau are located in Dong Nai Province in Vietnam, and their subgroups include the Ro, Bajieng, Mru, Jre, Buham, Bu-Preng, and Bla. The Katu are located primarily in central Vietnam on the Vietnam-Laos border. The Bru in Vietnam are culturally and linguistically related to the nearby Kalo; in fact, the Kalo may be a sub-group of the Bru. The Ma, also known as the Cau Ma, are located in the highlands of Lam Dong, Dong Mai, and Thuan Hai Provinces in Vietnam. The Stieng are located in Song De Province.

Hill people, particularly those of the Central Highlands, have fled Vietnam as refugees, following the wars. Those who had aided the French were resettled in France. Other hill people who had fought alongside the Americans escaped to Thailand and were then resettled in the United States or other Western countries. Many of those refugees, known as Montagnards or Degar people, live in North Carolina. In the early 20th century, hill people fleeing repression in the Central Highlands were forced back to Vietnam by Cambodia.

³ LANGUAGE

The languages of the hill peoples of Vietnam reflect the complexity of these ethnic groups. The hill ethnic groups speak more than 12 languages and many more dialects, divided into three major language groups. In northern Vietnam, for example, the language of the Tai is similar to the Thai language of Thailand, the Muong language bears resemblance to the Vietnamese language, and the Hmong Meo and Zao languages are dialects of Sino-Tibetan spoken in China. These languages reveal the various origins of the ethnic peoples of the hills.

Rhade subgroups, including the Rhade Kpa, Rhade M'dur, Rhade A'dham, K'tul, Epan, Blo, K'ah, K'drao, and Hwing, speak an Austronesian language. The Muong, on the other hand, speak an unwritten Mon-Khmer Austroasiatic language.

The hill groups were traditionally oral rather than literate societies, in which tradition and knowledge were passed on verbally rather than through writing. The Lahu language, for example, has no traditional script, and the Lahu people once used notched sticks, sometimes with chicken feathers attached, to communicate with one another. In the 20th century Protestant missionaries, Catholic missionaries, and Chinese linguists romanized the Lahu language, and the exposure of Lahu children to education has consequently increased.

⁴ FOLKLORE

The heroes and myths of the hill peoples are religious and familial in nature. Heroes are actual or fictional ancestors whose deeds and characteristics are passed down from generation to generation. Many of these heroes are considered to have originated particular clans and are respected, even worshipped, by their descendants not only as great people, but also as the founders of their tribal or descent group. The myths of particular groups relate to these founding ancestors. Other oral traditions relate stories of the spirits, landscape, animals, and plants of a group's environment and explain their surroundings, forming part of their traditional religious beliefs.

⁵ RELIGION

Most members of the highland peoples of Vietnam practice traditional beliefs, which they have followed for many centuries. These animist beliefs and practices, which vary significantly from group to group, center on worshipping natural phenomena. Highlanders believe that trees, lakes, storm clouds, forests, and thunder, among numerous other physical elements, have souls. They must be respected and appeased because, upset or irritated, they can cause enormous damage to human beings.

Most highland groups believe that spirits are basically capricious. Spirits are quick to take offense and to punish humans for the slights they perceive. Human beings must therefore take great care to propitiate the spirits, informing them of human activities, sharing with them information, food, and drink in the hope that the spirits will not take revenge on them, and quickly giving apologies and offerings if the spirits appear to have been upset. Other spirits, especially those of people who died unnaturally, are thought to be malicious. These spirits must be protected against, usually by purchasing the preventive or curative services of a shaman.

Among the Mnong, for instance, spirits rule everything in the world, including all domestic and wild animals, plants, and even inanimate objects. There are also the spirits of ancestors, heroes, and other legendary characters to be honored. An altar to the ancestors stands in the central living room of a Muong house. Shamans and other spirit-guides who preside over rituals and ceremonies that often include buffalo sacrifice, are extremely influential, acting as intermediaries between the multitude of spirits and human beings.

Many hill people have become Catholic or Protestant during their contact with Westerners. Catholic missionaries came to minister to the hill peoples of Vietnam in the 19th century and were quite successful in converting entire villages to Christianity. Catholic communities were known not only by their religious practices and the heath centers and schools established by the missionaries but by their prosperity. Evangelical Protestantism spread through the Central Highlands in the late 20th century. This was viewed as potentially subversive by the Vietnamese government and repression of the Christian churches in the hills took place in the early years of the 21st century.

6 MAJOR HOLIDAYS

Virtually all the holidays of hill people are religious celebrations. Rice-growing tribes celebrate annual agricultural rituals, especially the Festival of New Rice. Festivals are held to propitiate the spirits and exorcise evil spirits. The beginning of the lunar New Year is always an important festival. For hill people who have converted to Christianity, Christmas and Easter are major holidays.

Life-cycle events, such as birth, puberty, marriage, and death, are celebrated by families and villages. These are often major festivals involving multiple families and villages and considerable money and preparation.

7 RITES OF PASSAGE

Among most hill groups, infants and small children are greatly desired and are treated with great indulgence. Seldom reprimanded or hit, they are carried constantly by parents, siblings, or extended family members.

The children of most hill groups are socialized primarily by the immediate family, with assistance from extended family members and fellow villagers. By the time girls are five or six years of age, they are assisting their mother in the home and with younger siblings, and boys are assisting with garden duties and caring for the family's livestock. Among the Muong, for example, children often pasture the buffalo, spending their days with the buffalo and one another, returning with their animals to the village at night. By the age of eight or nine, both boys and girls are helping in the fields.

Many youth marry while they are still teenagers. Among the Lahu, for example, girls generally marry after puberty, when they reach 13 or 14. Boys marry a little later, at 16 or 17. This is the case because by the time most hill people have reached their early teens, they are fully socialized into adult life. By 13 and 14 years of age, boys and girls are acting as adults. After marriage, then, they have the skills to support their new family. The lives of adult hill people center on family, making a living, and dealing with the spirits or gods who rule the earth.

At death, ceremonies are held to help the soul of the deceased go to the afterlife. These consist for most people of prayers and ritual offerings held at regular intervals. For people who die unnatural deaths, special ceremonies must be conducted to exorcise their spirit to prevent it from doing similar harm to living relatives. Some tribal groups bury their dead, others cremate them.

8 INTERPERSONAL RELATIONS

For Vietnam's indigenous peoples, interpersonal relations are based on fairly strict rules of etiquette. Since most villagers have known one another since birth and will continue living with one another for years to come, people treat one another as extended family and try to avoid conflict in their everyday relations.

Greetings are important, for they assist villagers in acknowledging one another, keeping harmony, and preventing conflict. With strangers, most hill people are modest and reserved. With family and fellow villagers, they are more demonstrative. Always, however, there is an emphasis on getting along with one another. Men and women, even closely related, seldom display affection openly. Women, especially, must be respectful and cautious, particularly with strangers.

Visiting among hill peoples is a major activity and form of entertainment. Visiting between families within a village appears casual, but is less so than it appears. While neighbors go to one another's homes often and apparently without announcement, they are careful to go only at acceptable times. Visiting between villages is even more formal. While relatives may visit from one village to another fairly casually, visits by larger groups of people for ceremonies or festivals are arranged ahead of time as to place, time, and the obligations of both hosts and guests.

Young people usually do not date. Courtship may be brief and involve little contact between the future bride and groom in some groups, with parents or matchmakers doing most of the visiting and arranging. In other tribes, courtship may occur over years and involve relatively frequent contact between the couple. Usually, contact between young men and women is careful, supervised, and understood to be leading to marriage. In Christian villages, young couples may meet each other through church groups or activities.

9 LIVING CONDITIONS

Most hill groups live in areas remote from the lowland cities and towns and dense population of Vietnam. Their distance from the centers of Vietnamese life has isolated them also from many governmental services, including health and education. Tourism has brought more outside contact for the indigenous people of the Northern Highlands, but the Central Highlands are off-limits to foreign visitors, including most journalists and human rights investigators.

Health facilities remain much less available to hill people than to lowland Vietnamese and life expectancy is lower than among fellow countrymen. Most hill groups attribute illness and physical and mental misfortune to supernatural causes, especially spirits, and much health care centers on seeking to prevent and cure spirit action. Most illness and accidents continue to be dealt with through local healers rather than medical clinics. Most of the indigenous people have extensive knowledge of traditional medicinal plants and herbs, which are grown in backyard gardens or gathered in the nearby forest. Among some groups, in addition, community specialists are available to treat serious illness.

Highland villages have been traditionally the basic political unit of social life, autonomous and self governing. Although the French installed an administrative system of districts and provinces, villages continued to be run as they had been. Today, Bahnar villages are governed by a headman, and neighboring villages are tied together into one administrative unit. Scholars speculate that traditional Bahnar village society may have displayed a class structure consisting of freemen, debtors, foreigners, and slaves. Other groups, such as the Stieng, traditionally have been more egalitarian. Each family constitutes the basic social and political unit, and there is no political organization at a higher level.

Everyday arrangements of space and activity reflected traditional hierarchy and continues to be the case for many groups. Among the Muong, the higher one's status, the closer he sits to the window and the portion of the house that looks to the upper valley. Lower status people sit on the opposite side, where the windows overlook the lower portion of the valley. Hierarchy is maintained even when eating, with men, elders, and those with higher status sitting in favored spots.

Many highlanders continue to live in housing modeled on the traditional and ancient styles of their ancestors. Most highlanders live in stilt houses. Muong houses, for example, stand on posts approximately 6 feet in height. A typical house is 5 to 15 yards in length, and 4 to 7 yards in width. The roof is thatched with elephant grass and the floor is made of wood and bamboo. The house is divided into two rooms by a shoulder-high bamboo screen. The larger room is a guest room, kitchen, and dining area. The smaller room is a bedroom and storage area where women spend much of their time. The rooms are reached by separate stairs. The front of the house is used by men, the back part by women.

The housing of the hill peoples reflects their social structure. Some groups live in longhouses with nuclear families each occupying a section with their own hearth. Rhade live in longhouses arranged along paths. Each nuclear family has its own apartment within the long house. In addition there are apartments also for older people and for women and their guests. Bahnar villages have large communal men's houses, well-built, and located in the center of the village.

In contrast, other hill groups live in single-family dwellings. The housing of the Lahu, a small group in northwest Vietnam, more closely reflects their emphasis on hunting and gathering. Their houses are temporary huts, sometimes just shelters from the wind, made of bamboo or wood and covered with wild banana or bamboo leaves. These huts must be rebuilt monthly.

Most hill people have few consumer items and live much as their ancestors did without the electricity, running water, cell phones, and appliances available to most lowland Vietnamese. The degree of contact with lowland Vietnamese determines the kind of transportation: the more contact, the greater the reliance of hill people on motor vehicles, motorbikes, and bicycles. For many groups still living in isolated villages, transportation is primarily by foot.

10 FAMILY LIFE

Families tend to be large, for most hill people continue to rely on their children to assist with household and subsistence activities. As their contacts with the lowland Vietnamese increases, along with the expense of educating their children and the availability of family planning and contraceptives, some highlanders are choosing to have smaller families.

Marriages tend to remain traditional. In many Muong marriages, for instance, the choice of a mate and wedding arrangements are made by parents, often before the youth reach puberty. The family of the groom gives large quantities of pork and alcohol and a few silver coins to the bride's family. Most Muong are monogamous, with second marriages allowed only if the first wife is unable to bear children. In the past, Muong nobles and headsmen often had more than one wife. As contact with lowlanders continues so does change in marriage and other patterns of family life. Intermarriage between the Muong and neighboring Vietnamese, Thai, and other ethnic groups is increasing, and more Muong parents today allow their children to decide on their choice of a husband or wife.

Many highlanders keep domesticated animals, such as buffalo, pigs, and chickens, but these are kept to trade, eat, or sacrifice on special ritual occasions. Dogs are kept by some for protection both from other humans and from wild animals. Some families keep cats as a countermeasure to rats.

11 CLOTHING

The highland peoples of Vietnam weave their traditional clothing on homemade looms and often add colorful embroidery or appliqué work to the textiles. Each ethnic group has a different style of clothing and jewelry. Clothing is made of cotton woven with thousands of tiny patterns, with decorations such as silver hoops added. Just one outfit can take weeks to make. Some highland groups file their front teeth and practice tattooing just as their ancestors did. Men and women wear handmade jewelry of silver and brass, including bracelets, necklaces, and earrings.

The decrease in isolation from lowland Vietnam has resulted in the use of imported clothing, so that highlanders increasingly wear a combination of traditional and modern clothing. It is not unusual today to see a hill resident wearing a traditional loincloth, a European-style shirt, a Vietnamese conical hat, and a towel slung over his shoulders, or some other combination of the ancient and the new.

12 FOOD

Some hill groups are primarily rice cultivators. Other groups primarily raise root crops, such as cassava, taro, and yams. Other important food crops include maize, eggplant, beans, sugar cane, and bananas. Rice and vegetable crops are supplemented by greatly valued meat either from domestic animals, such as pigs and poultry, or game and birds from the neighboring forests. Additional valued foods include fish and eggs. Every group has a method for making beer or rice wine from the products close to home. Rice wine and cassava beer are common and are consumed primarily on ritual or life-cycle occasions.

Because modern appliances are few and packaged goods a rarity, much time and energy goes into the growing, preservation, and preparing of a family's daily meals. Women are primarily responsible for everyday food preparation, while men often bear the responsibility for making alcoholic beverages and cooking ritual foods.

Food is vital among hill peoples, not only for sustenance but for ritual. Virtually every ritual includes an offering of food and drink to the spirits and a communal feast by the participants. A sacrifice of a valued animal, such as a buffalo or pig, marks an important ceremony. Buffalo are kept primarily for ritual sacrifices and become the central food at religious festivals.

Food taboos are common among the hill ethnic groups and vary considerably according to group, age, gender, and situation. Pregnant women, women after childbirth, or hunters may be required to consume or refrain from consuming particular foods for specific periods of time.

13 EDUCATION

Schools and teachers from the lowlands are increasingly available for highland children. Government schools usually teach children in Vietnamese, rather than local languages. Few people from the highlands have gone on to university education.

14 CULTURAL HERITAGE

The hill people play music for religious purposes, on life-cycle occasions, such as marriage and funerals, and for popular entertainment. Among the Mnong Gar, for instance, the people gather on the first day of the new year to assure the spirits that they will fulfill the promises they have made by sacrificing buffalo and pigs to honor the spirits of the soil. After blessing the musical instruments, an older man leads the young men playing instruments in and out of each village house, playing, praying, and conducting rituals to protect the villagers in the future. Music is a major form of entertainment. Instruments include flutes, mouth organs and harps, and percussion instruments, most made from bamboo, as well as modern guitars. Traditional bronze drums are not only musical instruments but a symbol of wealth and status used in important community ceremonies. Some of the old songs feature elaborate poetic verses.

The literature of the hill peoples has traditionally been oral, consisting of the myths, legends, stories, and entire body of group knowledge passed on from generation to generation. In the absence of writing and modern entertainment, youth learned the beliefs and events of their past from their elders, in turn passing them on to their children.

15 WORK

The hill people of Vietnam are either sedentary or nomadic. Sedentary groups, which are more populous, are primarily wet rice cultivators. Some are engaged in growing crops for outside sale.

Nomadic groups, on the other hand, are farmers growing their own crops with the swidden method of cultivation. After finding a good garden area, the men cut the trees down or cut them severely enough so that they die. They then set the fallen trees on fire until the trees and brush cover have been reduced to ash. The ashes help enrich the soil in which sticky rice, root crops, and other crops are then sown. The hill men tend their crops and harvest them over the next two to four years using hand implements. When the soil loses its nutrients, the group moves on to establish new garden areas, following the same slash-and-burn techniques. After a few decades, the original plot of soil has regained its nutrients and can again support crops. In that way, the hill people move through the forest over the years, stopping to build a village in which they live for several years, and moving on when the soils are exhausted to reestablish a village some miles away near their new gardens. Because of the small population groups this has usually had little impact on the forests. However, in recent years forest cover has decreased greatly in Vietnam, due to timber cutting and conversion of forest to large-scale agricultural use. Central Highlands groups have accused the lowland Vietnamese of forcing them off their ancestral lands in order to log the forests and convert the hills to massive coffee plantations for international export.

The Rhade primarily raise rice, which they cultivate in highland swidden gardens or rice fields. When they are fortunate enough to cultivate rice fields, the Rhade usually obtain two harvests each year. Among the Rhade, kitchen gardens are placed behind the house. There, Rhade women cultivate vegetables, spices, and medicinal plants. Their most important kitchen crop is corn. Each village has its own bamboo patch, which is considered sacred. The Mnong also have upland rice as their staple crop. In addition, they cultivate maize, eggplant, taro, yams, beans, sugar cane, bananas, and other fruits, vegetables, and tobacco.

In addition to horticulture, hill people also raise a few domestic animals, including pigs, poultry, and buffalo. Among the Lahu, for example, pigs are the most important domesticated animal, but chickens are everywhere. They also raise ducks and geese. The Mnong are noted for trading pigs and poultry for buffalo.

Men hunt game and birds in the surrounding forests. Muong men hunt with guns, crossbows, traps, snares, and nets. Men organize communal hunts on festival days. A successful hunt is seen as a good omen for the rice harvest. In addition, Muong men fish with scoop nets, lines, bows, and knives.

Women do most of the vegetable and herb gathering. Muong women collect edible tubers, leaves, mushrooms, bamboo shoots, vegetables, berries, and fruit. When food is scarce, they gather breadfruit and eat it as bread. They also collect wood for fuel, materials for building houses, medicinal plants, and other products such as feathers and skins for trade. As the forests decrease under pressure from plantations and timber cutting, these resources are decreasing for the highland peoples.

16 SPORTS

Children who attend school may also play competitive games, such as soccer or volleyball. This is increasingly the situation, as more and more children of the highlands are sent to Vietnamese public schools.

17 ENTERTAINMENT AND RECREATION

Children still spend many nighttime hours listening to the stories and legends of their people. As they sit around their homes in the evening, they may listen to a story from a grandmother, an ancient tale from an older man, or hear the hunters relate their hunting experiences.

The highland peoples rely on singing, dancing, and instrument playing for much of their entertainment, but radios and CD players now bring Vietnamese pop music to the hills, and market towns have movies to watch on disc, as well as Vietnamese television. Some highland folk music has been recorded to be sold in Vietnam and overseas.

18 FOLK ART, CRAFTS, AND HOBBIES

Hill women weave clothing such as skirts and blouses for themselves, loincloths and jackets for their men, and blankets, and embroider or appliqué these items. Men weave mats and baskets and make jewelry, as well as agricultural, hunting, and gathering tools. Hill people make a number of musical instruments which include gourd flutes, mouth harps, guitars, and banjos. They buy most other domestic items, such as pottery and metal objects, from lowlanders. Textiles and baskets may be traded for such goods, or sold directly to tourists in northern market towns like Sapa.

19 SOCIAL PROBLEMS

The indigenous ethnic groups of the highlands continue to struggle for more autonomy from the lowland Vietnamese. They continue to be viewed by many lowlanders as inferior, with strange customs that are best abolished. The Vietnamese government remains suspicious of the loyalty of the Central Highlanders and their religious beliefs, which the government associates with efforts by exiles and dissidents to undermine the Communist state. Land rights remain tenuous for many of Vietnam's indigenous people and their forested mountains are being taken over by powerful economic interests, as Vietnam joins the global marketplace. Indigenous people in the Northern Highlands interact with the tourism industry, causing cultural changes, while those in the Central Highlands are isolated and have suffered persecution.

20 GENDER ISSUES

Hill people in Vietnam tend to observe a strict gender division of labor. Women have the primary responsibility for domestic chores, child care, carrying water, and looking after the domestic animals. They also gather food and weave. In agricultural villages, they are also involved in some rice cultivation chores such as transplantation, irrigating, weeding, harvesting, and husking. Men normally do the hunting and the heavy agricultural tasks. They clear the ground, plow, and thresh. They also make and repair tools and build and repair houses. Village leadership tends to be male, although women, especially elders, participate in decision making.

Among many groups, descent is matrilineal and by clans. While political power is held by men, women control family property and inheritance is passed through females. Residence patterns after marriage reflect kinship arrangements. For instance, among the Rhade in the Central Highlands, young couples live with the wife's family, reflecting a matrilineal emphasis.

The children spend much of their time assisting their parents in hunting, gathering, and cultivation. They follow traditional gender roles in those ways. Boys learn from an early age to help their fathers and their play centers on learning to do what their fathers do. Village boys practice with tiny bows, shooting small animals, trying to catch birds and fish, and in numerous ways imitating the activities of their elders. Girls, also, learn from their elders, assisting their mothers and other village women in caring for smaller children, looking after the house, and preparing food.

The indigenous cultures and pervasive Christian religious beliefs emphasize male/female marriage and tend to disapprove of gay, lesbian, or transgender relations and identities.

21 BIBLIOGRAPHY

American University, Cultural Information Analysis Center. *Minority Groups in the Republic of Vietnam*. Ethnographic Study Series. Washington D.C.: U.S. Government Printing Office, 1966.

Amnesty International. *Socialist Republic of Vietnam / Kingdom of Cambodia—No Sanctuary: The Plight of the Montagnard Minority*. London: Amnesty International, 2002.

Amnesty International. *Socialist Republic of Viet Nam: Renewed Concern for the Montagnard Minority*. London: Amnesty International, 2004.

Brocheux, Pierre. "Vietnamiens et minorites en Cochinchine pendant la periode coloniale." *Modern Asian Studies* 6, no. 4 (1972):443-457

Cima, Ronald J., ed. *Vietnam. A County Study*. Washington D.C.: U.S. Government Printing Office, 1989.

Condominas, Georges. *We Have Eaten the Forest. The Story of a Montagnard Village in the Central Highlands of Vietnam*. New York: Hill and Wang, 1977.

Hickey, Gerald C. "Ma." In *Ethnic Groups of Mainland Southeast Asia*. Frank M. LeBar, G. C. Hickey, and J. K. Musgrave, ed. New Haven, CT: Human Relations Area Files, 1964.

———. "Rhade." In *Ethnic Groups of Mainland Southeast Asia*. Frank M. LeBar, G. C. Hickey, and J. K. Musgrave, ed. New Haven, CT: Human Relations Area Files, 1964.

———. *Free in the Forest: Ethnohistory of the Vietnamese Central Highlands, 1954–1976*. New Haven, CT: Yale University Press, 1982.

———. *Sons of the Mountains: Ethnohistory of the Vietnamese Central Highlands to 1954*. New Haven, CT: Yale University Press, 1982.

———. *Shattered Worlds: Adaptation and Survival among Vietnam's Highland Peoples during the Vietnam War*. Philadelphia: University of Pennsylvania Press, 1993.

Howard, Michael C., and Kim Be Howard. *Textiles of the Central Highlands of Vietnam*. Bangkok, Thailand: White Lotus Press, 2002.

Human Rights Watch. *Repression of Montagnards: Conflicts over Land and Religion in Vietnam's Central Highlands*. New York: Human Rights Watch, 2002. http://www.hrw.org/reports/2002/vietnam/ (5 July 2008).

LeBar, Frank M., Gerald D. Hickey, and John K. Musgrave. *Ethnic Groups of Mainland Southeast Asia*. New Haven, CT: Human Relations Area Files, 1964.

Mole, Robert L. *The Montagnards of South Vietnam: A Study of Nine Tribes*. Rutland, VT. Charles E. Tuttle, 1970.

Montagnard Foundation. http://www.montagnard-foundation.org/homepage.html (5 July 2008).

Petersen, Barry. *Tiger Men: A Young Australian Soldier Among the Rhade Montagnards of Vietnam*. Bangkok: Orchid Press, 1998.

Schrock, Joann L, et al. *Minority Groups in North Vietnam*. Department of the Army Pamphlet 50–110 Ethnographic Study Series). Washington D.C.: U.S. Government Printing Office, 1972.

U.S. Department of State. "International Religious Freedom Report 2007." Washington D.C.: Bureau of Democracy, Human Rights, and Labor, U.S. Department of State, 2007 http://www.state.gov/g/drl/rls/irf/2007/90131.htm (5 July 2008).

— revised by E. Mirante

YAO

PRONUNCIATION: YOW
ALTERNATE NAMES: Mian, Jinmen, Bunu, Bingduoyou,
Lajia, Pangu Yao, Shanzi Yao, Dingban Yao, Hualan Yao,
Guoshan Yao, White Pants Yao, Red Yao, Indigo Yao, Plain
Yao, Col Yao, Chashan Yao, etc.
LOCATION: China
POPULATION: 2.6 million
LANGUAGE: Yao, Miao, Dong-Shui
RELIGION: Polytheism; ancestor worship
RELATED ARTICLES: Vol. 3: China and Her National Minorities

¹INTRODUCTION

The Yao are historically linked with the ancient "Jingman" and "Changsha Wulingman." Their ancestors were called Muoyao in ancient books of the Northern and Southern Dynasties (420–589) and Yaoren during the Tang Dynasty (618–907). Actually, it seems the Yao and the Miao had common ancestors. From the Tang onward, the name of Yao appeared separately in ancient Chinese books. It seems the Yao were the result of the assimilation of neighboring tribes by one main group.

For a long period of time, the Yao practiced the double system of *yaolao* and *shipai*. The former was practiced inside a village and the latter among the villages. *Yaolao* (Elders of Yao) was an administrative organization consisting of six powerful men. The "number one man" took charge of matters of his village (basically a clan), both inside and outside, including the refereeing of clan quarrels and the command of armed troops to fight against other clans. The "number two man" was his assistant. A third man was responsible for deciding the dates of agricultural activities. Another man took charge of religious affairs. The last man was responsible for water administration for irrigation and drinking. The number one man was chosen among the aged, changed annually, and could hold office only once. The number two man was elected every two years.

Shipai (Stone Tablet) was a union of villages. A small *shipai* consisted of several villages; a large shipai consisted of several small ones. Each shipai made a joint pledge according to customary laws and asked all members of the clan to follow the agreement to ensure order. The joint pledge was carved on a stone tablet, which was erected at the village gate. The executing person was called shipai head, and had the power to punish anyone violating the pledge. Up to the present, the remnants of these two systems still exist, especially in remote areas.

²LOCATION AND HOMELAND

Yao population amounted to 2.6 million in 2000. They are mainly scattered in Guangxi, Hunan, Yunnan, Guangdong, and Guizhou provinces. The feature of their inhabitation is "wide distribution and tiny colonies." They dwell in mountainous areas, most of which are forested and picturesque.

³LANGUAGE

Yao language is classified as belonging to the Sino-Tibetan family, Miao-Yao group, Yao branch. In fact, only about half of the population use the Yao language, while about 40% of the Yao speak Miao. Some use another language, classified as Dong-Shui branch. There is no Yao writing. Most of the Yao use Chinese characters.

On account of their dispersion, the Yao call themselves by different names, such as Mian, Jinmen, Bunu, Bingduoyou, and Lajia. According to their different styles of clothing, totems, economic activities, and dwellings, the ancient Chinese books called them Pangu Yao, Shanzi Yao, Dingban Yao, Hualan Yao, Guoshan Yao, White Pants Yao, Red Yao, Indigo Yao, Plain Yao, Col Yao, Chashan Yao, and so on. The Chinese, not always realizing that they were dealing with a single ethnic group, traditionally used more than 30 names to designate the various groups. Since 1956, the unified name for all of these groups is Yao.

⁴FOLKLORE

The Yao have a rich mythology. One of their origin myths relates that a long, long time ago, King Ping received a dragon-dog called Panhu. It was about 3 ft in length. Its hair was multicolored. At that time, King Ping's kingdom was frequently invaded by King Gao, and nobody was able to stop him. The dragon-dog told King Ping that he could kill King Gao. King Ping promised that he would give Panhu his princess daughter in marriage if he killed King Gao. The dragon-dog went to King Gao; the king was very happy to have such an exceptional dog and let him stay by his side. One day, King Gao got drunk and the dog seized this opportunity to bite him to death. Holding King Gao's head in his mouth, Panhu came back to King Ping's kingdom. Although appointing Panhu to a high position, the king did not redeem his obligation of marriage. On the contrary, he put the dog under a big golden bell. Six days later, King Ping regretted what he did. As the bell was removed, he found the dog had turned into a man. Panhu and the princess married. They gave birth to six sons and six daughters. King Ping was so happy that he appointed Panhu as King Pan, the earliest ancestor of the Yao.

⁵RELIGION

The Yao are polytheistic. They worship their ancestors, especially their first ancestor, Panhu. Taoist priests and shamans are in charge of religious activities and play the role of intermediary between man and the world of ghosts and gods. Yao beliefs were deeply influenced by the Chinese religious traditions, in particular Taoism. Those who live around Nandan (in northwest Guangxi) revere Pangu (the god who created the world, according to Chinese mythology; there is obviously a connection between Panhu, the first ancestor, and Pangu, the Creator God) and the Jade Emperor (the Supreme Deity of Taoism). They also believe in the god of witchery. In a Pangu temple (actually a straw mat shed) set up in many villages of the Yao, three stones evoking human forms are erected. The stone in the center is Pangu. The Jade Emperor is on the right and the witchery god on the left. This is an illustration of Yao polytheistic beliefs. On March 30 (lunar calendar; Western calendar, between March 20 and May 19), a chicken is sacrificed to the three gods. Three months later, a pig or a buffalo is killed and offered in sacrifice for the purpose of obtaining from the gods good weather for the crops and well-being for the villagers and their livestock.

Those dwelling in the Great Yao Mountains (in west Guangxi) sacrifice to King Panhu (originally a dog). The temple of Panhu is actually a pavilion with four high posts and a

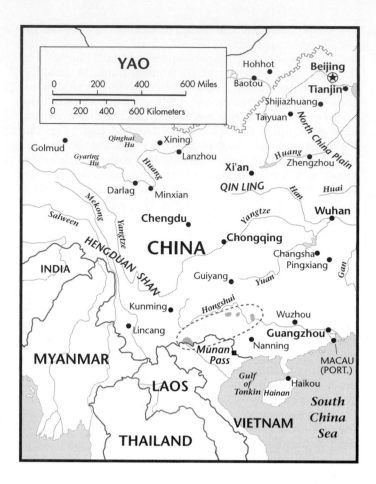

roof made of the bark of the China fir tree. There is a tablet on a small platform, but no statue. Community sacrifice is held every year or every other year. Members of the community make a dozen rice cakes beforehand and place them on a dustpan. Then a small cock is killed. Its trunk is cut into pieces and put on the cakes. The head, tail, wings, and legs are then disposed around the cakes so as to reproduce the figure of a live chicken. The head must point toward the tablet. Three shamans dance around the platform while playing drums. The sacrifice may be offered by an individual family faced with particularly difficult problems.

6 MAJOR HOLIDAYS

The Yao celebrate a large number of festivals, almost one each month. The festivals often differ from district to district. On lunar New Year's Eve (Western calendar, between January 21 and February 20), the whole family reunites around the dinner table. Firecrackers are kindled. Spring Festival pictures are pasted on the walls of their houses. The next day, arrow shooting, dramatic performances, or sometimes buffalo fighting will be held. The youngsters gather on a lawn beside the village. They sing and dance, accompanied by the *lüsheng* (a reed-pipe wind instrument) and the *yueqin* (a four-stringed plucked instrument, similar to the mandolin). Newly married couples pay a New Year's call to the wife's family. At the dinner party, her father sings, wishing his daughter and son-in-law conjugal love and harmony.

The Danu ("keep in mind") Festival is held on May 29 (lunar calendar; Western calendar, between June 21 and July 21).

Depending on local economic conditions, it may not be held every year, but put off one or more years. It is a commemorative day for one of their famous ancestors, Milotuo, but has turned into a grand popular festival. People dress up and bring their own dishes and wine to dine together. They play hide-and-seek, dance to the rhythms of the bronze drum, and fire the blunderbuss.

Some festivals are for recreation after a good harvest, such as the Harvest Festival around Jianghua in Hunan; some are for social intercourse of the youngsters, such as the Singing Festival in many areas.

7 RITES OF PASSAGE

An adulthood ceremony is held for Yao young men from 16 to 22. The rite is organized by five or seven Taoist priests. The young man has to live at the priest's house. He is not allowed to go outdoors, neither to have a view of the sky, nor to talk with anybody except the priests. In the evening, he is instructed in various religious rites. On the day of the ceremony, he is led to a platform on a lawn. He should swear that he will never commit murder or set fires, never steal or rob, never abduct or rape a woman, never mistreat his parents or wrongly accuse an innocent person, and so on. The priest throws a firebrand into a bowl of water, indicating the misfortune of violating one's vows. Then the young man curls up his body, holds his knees in his arms, and rolls down from the platform. Thereafter, he is allowed to participate in adult society and get married. Moreover, it is believed that only after the adulthood ceremony may a man go to Heaven after death. This rite is considered so important for a young man that a grand feast will be organized by his family in the following days. Since the adulthood ceremonies consumed too much time, they have been recently reformed and simplified to various degrees in different districts.

The burial rite of the Yao has been deeply influenced by Chinese Taoism. The funeral is performed according to Taoist rites. The deceased is not allowed to be put into a coffin until his sins have been expiated by the reciting of scriptures by the priest. Native Yao beliefs are often combined with the Taoist ritual. For example, if an infant dies, it should be wrapped with used clothes or palm leaves, then put inside a bamboo basket and hung on a tree in the forest. The Yao believe that the soul of the infant will go back to its patron saint, Huapo (Flower Woman), and wait for reincarnation. The quick decay of the infant's body will result, they believe, in an earlier reincarnation; here, one also sees the influence of Buddhism on Yao beliefs.

It is a custom to announce a death in the family to the uncle (mother's brother) and to the uncle's uncle.

8 INTERPERSONAL RELATIONS

When calling on a family, the guest should offer greetings to the lady of the house first; otherwise, the host may deem the guest arrogant. In traditional Yao homes, the guest is offered salted meat and oil tea.

Yao youngsters are free to date. Antiphonal singing is the usual way to get acquainted and to fall in love. Around Libo in Guizhou, there is a unique way to talk about love. When a girl reaches 16 or 17 years of age, she is allowed to live alone in a room with a small hole in a wall. A young man may come to her side of the house in the middle of the night, wake her up, and express his affection. She may give a positive answer.

When both of them fall deeply in love, they ask their parents to confirm their will to get married. Around Jianghua in Hunan, there is also a unique way of dating. During fairs and festivals, each girl carries an empty basket (covered by a new towel) in her hand. If a young man likes her, he will take the basket from her and put inside some refreshments. If the girl accepts, they go to the forest and take the refreshments while singing in antiphonal style. Next time, the girl puts nine pairs of cloth shoes in the basket, indicating her lasting love. The third time, he carries the basket and accompanies her to the market where the dowry is selected. If they are satisfied with each other through the three dates, the young man makes an appointment with her parents and proposes.

⁹LIVING CONDITIONS

Yao houses come in different styles, often depending on the physical environment: thatched cottages, bamboo and wooden houses, and, less frequent, tile-roofed adobe houses. Most houses have three rooms. The main room is the central one; one of the side rooms is for sleeping, the other for the firepool and kitchen. The livestock pen is in the rear. Some houses are built on mountain slopes; these are usually two-story stilt dwellings. People occupy the second floor, livestock the ground floor. In some two-story houses, people live downstairs while grain and other commodities are stored upstairs.

Taking advantage of the abundance of water and the availability of bamboo, they often connect long "bamboo pipes" to channel the water from springs to a barrel in their house.

¹⁰FAMILY LIFE

The Yao live in small patrilineal families. After marriage the son moves out. Parents live with their youngest son. Most of the villagers are of the same clan and same surname. The position of women in families is equal to that of their husbands. The Yao pay much attention to the power of the maternal uncle, who not only is respected, but also takes the responsibility of deciding important affairs.

In Chashan (in south Guangdong), the wedding ceremony is simple and frugal. The bridegroom's side sends several cousins to the bride's family in the middle of the night. They congratulate and thank the girl's parents, then accompany the bride on foot to her husband. The wedding ceremony takes place at his house and lasts all night long. The bride and the bridegroom take a nap at dawn and then resume their work in the fields in the morning.

In some areas, the son of a girl's maternal uncle has priority in offering to marry her. If the uncle has no son, she is allowed to marry somebody else. A son-in-law may be allowed to live with his bride's family, usually when her parents do not have a son. Divorce is always a serious matter and the couple is first encouraged by the aged to reconcile. If the couple has no choice but to separate, they go to the mountain, break a bamboo tube into two, each taking one half, depart in opposite directions, and never repent. There is no discrimination against a remarried widow.

¹¹CLOTHING

Yao clothing varies according to region. Men's garments include edge-to-edge, collarless tops and another type with buttons down the left. A waistband is generally used. They wear trousers or shorts covering their knees. All are made of hand-woven cloth in blue or dark blue. Men around Nandan like to wear white, trimmed, knee-covering knickerbockers. Men around Liannan in Guangdong comb their hair into a bun plucked with pheasant feathers for decoration. There is also a great variety of women's dress. In some areas they wear collarless tops with buttons down the right side and a waistband. Their skirts come in different lengths. Some of them wear an edge-to-edge long garment with a waistband and long trousers or shorts. Their collars, cuffs, fronts of garments, waistbands, bottoms of trouser legs, and edges of skirts are all decorated with cross-stitches and embroideries. They wear few silver ornaments in daily life, but quite a number of them during festivals, including hair clasps, flowers, strings of beads, curved hairpins (maybe the largest silver ornament among minorities, reaching 1 lb in weight), plates, bracelets, rings, necklaces, and earrings. Young girls are also fond of earrings, hairpins, necklaces, bracelets, and so on. The Yao hang the teeth or claws of wild hogs, leopards, or tigers on children's waists, with a view to protecting them from evil.

¹²FOOD

The Yao take three meals a day. Their staple foods include rice, millet, corn, yams, and taro. Hot pepper, pumpkin, and soybean are their main vegetables. The proteins in their diet come from livestock and domestic fowl. Their favorite all-season dishes are salted meat and fish. In some districts, dog meat is taboo, being related to totem worship. They drink wine and oil tea. The latter is made of fried tea leaves, cooked in water, and seasoned with ginger, hot pepper, and salt.

¹³EDUCATION

There are now primary schools in large villages and middle schools (junior and senior) in small towns. The majority of children reaching school age are enrolled. Nevertheless, their cultural and educational level is lower than average among minorities. Illiteracy still predominates in remote rural areas. Some mountainous areas have very little contact with the outside world.

¹⁴CULTURAL HERITAGE

The Yao love to sing. Antiphonal singing parties usually last all night long. The lyrics are all-encompassing, from astronomy to geography, from ancient legends about creation to production work and daily life. Ironic or comical songs are well received by the community.

Yao dances comprise two main types: the Bronze Drum Dance and the Long Drum Dance. The long drum is made of wood, about 32 inches long, more slender toward the middle, with animal skin over its ends. It is held over the waist of a dancer, who plays while dancing. The bronze drum is bottomless, with carved figures on its surface and sides. The Bronze Drum Dance is rather unique. It is performed by two men and a woman. One man dances while playing the bronze drum; the other man, standing still, accompanies him with a skin drum; the woman, dancing behind the drummer, cools him with a fan.

Most Yao literature has been handed down orally. Only a small number of poems or mythical tales were recorded in Chinese; among these the "Songs of King Panhu," thousands of lines long, is a unique literary treasure of the Yao.

[15] WORK

Yao economy is based principally on agriculture, mainly on rice. Forestry and hunting provide important dietary and economic supplements. Hunting also aims at protecting farmers and domestic animals from the wild animals. The hunting bag is divided evenly among all participants; even a baby on one's back has his own share. However, the hunter who hit or caught the animal receives a double share.

[16] SPORTS

Whipping a top is a traditional sport of the Yao. The top is made of hard wood, 1 to 3 lbs in weight. Two teams participate in the game. One team sets all the tops rotating within a circle. Then the members of the opposing team throw successively their tops from a distance of 5–10 yds, trying to hit the rotating tops and stop them. If no rotating top is hit, the hitting side loses. If one or several tops are hit, the rotating time of the tops of both teams is recorded and compared to decide the winner.

[17] ENTERTAINMENT AND RECREATION

Quite a number of television stations have been set up in Yao territory. Guangxi, Guangdong, Guizhou, Hunan, and Yunnan provinces are all provided with television broadcasting stations and film studios. These are available for Yao programs. Movie theaters now thrive even in small towns. In addition, various recreational activities are held on traditional festivals. The Spring Buffalo Dance may be compared to the Chinese Lion Dance. Yao artisans build a frame with thin bamboo strips, then cover it with black paper in the shape of a buffalo head. The trunk is made of dark gray cloth painted with black whirlpool-shaped hairs. Two young men prop it up for performance, accompanied by a team of musicians (gongs and drums) and a team of dancers. They make a circuit through the villages. Wherever they go, the villagers dress up and line both sides of the street to welcome the parade. They are escorted by crowds in front and behind. The "buffalo" walks around the performing place, then stamps its hoofs, sways its horns, swings its tail, and rolls on the ground. All the "buffalo" movements are remarkably true to life. That is why it is well received by the villagers, who have had an intimate knowledge of the animal since childhood.

[18] FOLK ART, CRAFTS, AND HOBBIES

Cross-stitch work, embroidery, brocade, and batik are the better known traditional handicrafts of the Yao. The apron and satchel made of Yao brocade are much sought after by connoisseurs and tourists.

[19] SOCIAL PROBLEMS

The Yao inhabit a rugged mountainous environment, which does not allow significant increases of their traditional crop yields. Physical environment is the major obstacle to the economic development of Yao society. To change their current socio-economic situation would require major decisions about their present territorial settlement.

[20] GENDER ISSUES

The Chinese constitution states that women have equal rights with men in all areas of life, and most legislation is gender neutral. However, there are continued reports of discrimination,

sexual harassment, wage discrepancies, and other gender related problems. The gap in educational level between women and men is narrowing with women making up 47.1% of college students in 2005, but only 32.6% of doctoral students.

China has strict family planning laws. It is illegal for women to marry before 20 years of age (22 for men), and it is illegal for single women to give birth. The Family Planning Bureau can require women to take periodic pregnancy tests and enforce laws that often leave women with no real options other than abortion or sterilization. Though minority populations were previously exempt from family planning regulations, policy has changed in recent years to limit minority population growth. Today, urban minority couples may have two children while rural couples may have three or four.

Prostitution and the sex trade is a significant problem in China involving between 1.7 and 5 million women. It involved organized crime, businessmen, the police, and government workers, so prosecution against prostitution has limited success. In 2002, the nation removed homosexuality from its official list of mental illnesses, and though it is still a taboo topic, homosexuality is increasingly accepted, especially in large, international cities.

[21] BIBLIOGRAPHY

Bai Ziran, ed. *Mœurs et coutumes des Miao.* Beijing: Éditions en langues étrangères, 1988.

Chiao, Chien, Nicholas Tapp, and Kam-yin Ho, ed. "Special Issue on Ethnic Groups in China." *New Asia Bulletin* no 8 (1989).

Dreyer, June Teufel. *China's Forty Millions.* Cambridge: Harvard University Press, 1976.

Eberhard, Wolfram. *China's Minorities: Yesterday and Today.* Belmont: Wadsworth Publishing Company, 1982.

Gustafsson, Bjorn A., Shi, Li, and Sicular, Terry, eds. *Inequality and Public Policy in China.* New York: Cambridge University Press, 2008.

Heberer, Thomas. *China and Its National Minorities: Autonomy or Assimilation?* Armonk, NY: M. E. Sharpe, 1989.

Lebar, Frank, et al. *Ethnic Groups of Mainland Southeast Asia.* New Haven: Human Relations Area Files Press, 1964.

Lemoine, Jacques. "Les Miao-Yao." In *Ethnologie régionale II* (Encyclopédie de la Pléiade). Paris: Gallimard, 1978.

Litzinger, Ralph A. "Making Histories: Contending Contentions of the Yao Past." In *Cultural Encounters on China's Ethnic Frontiers,* edited by Stevan Harrell, 117–139. Seattle: University of Washington Press, 1994.

Ma Yin, ed. *China's Minority Nationalities.* Beijing: Foreign Languages Press, 1989.

Miller, Lucien, ed. *South of the Clouds: Tales from Yunnan.* Seattle: University of Washington Press, 1994.

Ramsey, S. Robert. *The Languages of China.* Princeton: Princeton University Press, 1987.

Shin, Leo Kwok-yueh. *The Making of the Chinese State: Ethnicity and Expansion on the Ming Borderlands.* New York: Cambridge University Press, 2006.

Wiens, Harold J. *Han Chinese Expansion in South China.* New Haven: The Shoestring Press, 1967.

—by C. Le Blanc

YAZIDIS

PRONUNCIATION: YAH-zuh-deez
LOCATION: Armenia, Iran, Syria, and Iraq (Zagros Mountains)
POPULATION: 100,000–200,000 (some estimates are as high as 500,000)
LANGUAGE: Yazidi; Kourmanji; Armenian
RELIGION: Yazidi

OVERVIEW

The Yazidis are members of a religious sect who think of themselves as a totally separate people from the rest of humanity. According to their beliefs, they were created independently; they are not descended from Adam and Eve, as other human beings are believed to be. Because of this belief, they keep themselves isolated from the rest of human society. For this reason, not much is known about them. The Yazidis live in the Zagros Mountains in Armenia, Iran, Syria, and Iraq, with a few scattered settlements elsewhere and small diaspora communities in Europe, particularly Germany. Their religion combines elements from a variety of faiths, including Islam, Buddhism, Judaism, Manichaeism, Zoroastrianism, and Nestorian Christianity. Muslims consider the Yazidis infidels and have persecuted them over the centuries. The Yazidis have fought back, often successfully, leading to a great deal of bloodshed on both sides.

The Yazidis originated as separate groups of people who migrated at different times to the mountains of Iraq from other parts of the Middle East. The first migration may have occurred as early as the 6th century BC. These diverse peoples lived together in isolated mountain valleys, practicing their different religions, until Islam arrived in AD 750. At that time, they added Islam to their mix of religious beliefs and came together as one people, keeping elements of their former religions as well. Shaikh Adi (AD 1072–1161) became their leader, and the Yazidis worshiped him as a god. In 1830–40, a number of Yazidis migrated north to Armenia. Since then, the Yazidis have settled in other places as well, but the largest group outside Iraq can be found Armenia. The Yazidis and Kurds [see **Kurds**] were lumped together in Armenia as one ethnic group beginning in 1931. Many Kurds and Yazidis speak the same Kourmanji dialect. However, the Yazidis continue to think of themselves as a separate people, and in 1988, the official census takers in Armenia agreed, listing Kurds and Yazidis separately once again. "Yazidi" is the name given to the group by others. They call themselves the *Dasin*.

Location and homeland. Most Yazidis live in the Zagros mountain range, which runs north to south from Armenia through Iran and Syria to Iraq. The mountains reach heights of up to 1,500 m (5,000 ft). The Yazidis live in the valleys. Annual rainfall in the valleys is 65–100 cm (25–40 in), most of which falls in December and January. Temperatures in the summer are mild. In the winter, temperatures often drop well below freezing.

Population estimates for the Yazidis vary widely. A 1992 estimate put their population at 200,000, though more recent estimates suggest 100,000 or fewer; some Yazidis insist that they number close to half a million. A 1989 census taken in Armenia counted 5,190 Yazidis in that country; in 2002, censuses in

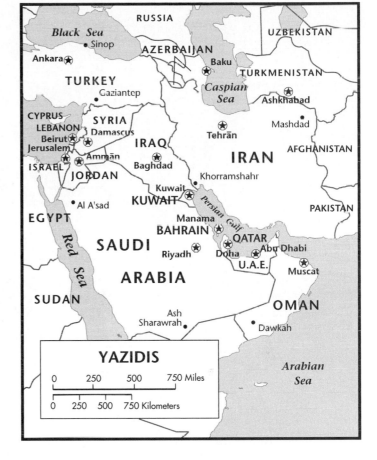

Russia, Georgia, and Iran counted roughly 31,000 altogether. The difficulty of arriving at a consistent number derives from the persecution the group has endured in many countries, which makes them reluctant to accurately report their numbers to government census takers.

Language. Yazidis speak Yazidi, a language with an alphabet of 33 letters. In Armenia, Yazidis speak the Kourmanji dialect of Kurdish. Some Yazidis in Armenia speak Armenian so well that it is difficult to tell them from native Armenians. Some have even adopted the typically Armenian -*ian* suffix at the end of their names.

Religion. The origins of the Yazidi religion are unclear. Mistakenly called "devil worshipers," the Yazidis believe that Satan was once the chief angel in heaven. Because of his pride, he fell (or was banished) from that position. This belief accords with that of other religious groups, such as Christians and Jews. However, the Yazidis go further, believing that Satan repented and was restored to his position as chief angel and now oversees the running of the universe. The supreme God created the universe and then turned it over to Satan (or Melek-Tavous, as the Yazidis call him) and six other angels. The creator God, they believe, has no direct interest in the universe.

The name "Melek-Tavous" means King Peacock, or Peacock Angel. In much of the East, peacocks are revered as symbols of beauty and majesty. Melek-Tavous and the six angels are thought to rule the universe, and they are worshiped in the form of peacocks, represented by seven bronze peacock figures called *sanjaq*. The largest of the sanjaq weighs about 320 kg (700 lbs). These seven figures are kept at Lalesh in Iraq. Each

A Yazidi boy tends to sheep on Mount Sinjar, Iraq The Yazidis originated as a separate group of people who migrated at different times to the mountains of Iraq and elsewhere. (AP Images/Jacob Silberberg)

year they are taken out and paraded around Yazidi neighborhoods to bring wealth and good fortune to all believers. Lalesh is the Yazidis' holy land. The tomb of their principal saint, Shaikh Adi, is located there, as are the sanjaq. Shaikh Adi was a 12th-century Muslim mystic who became the leader of the Yazidis. The Yazidis believe that he achieved divinity through reincarnation, and they worship him as a god. His tomb is the site of an annual pilgrimage.

Each morning, the Yazidis pray to the sun, the source of life, so that there will be health and well-being in the world. Yazidis pray five times a day, facing the holy city of Lalesh at the noon prayer. Each Yazidi is obliged to make a pilgrimage to Lalesh at least once during his or her life.

The holy scriptures of the Yazidi religion consist of two short books in Arabic: the *Kitab al-jilwah* (Book of Revelation) and the *Mashaf rash* (Black Writing). An Arabic hymn in praise of Shaikh Adi is also recited.

The Yazidis deny the existence of evil, sin, the devil as an evil force (they believe that Satan, or Melek-Tavous, was restored to heaven), and hell. What other religions call sin—the breaking of divine laws—is mended, according to the Yazidis, through reincarnation and the progressive purification of the spirit or soul.

Shaikh Adi excused his followers from saying the five daily prayers, as well as from other Muslim practices. Wednesday is the Yazidis' holy day, and Saturday is their day of rest.

Rites of passage. Boys are generally circumcised. They are baptized on their first birthday by a *shaikh* (leader of the tribe). The shaikh takes a handful of the boy's hair, recites some prayers, and then cuts the hair.

Interpersonal relations. The Yazidis are a very isolated people, choosing to remain separate from their non-Yazidi neighbors. It is traditionally forbidden for a Yazidi to enter any public place where he or she might hear words that are contrary to the Yazidi faith, including schools, theaters, and so on. This restriction has been relaxed as more Yazidis have moved out of their isolated mountain valleys and into towns and cities, where they must interact with nonbelievers.

Family life. Yazidi society is organized according to a strict division of castes. Rulers make up the three highest castes. At the top is the prince, or emir, who is a descendent of Shaikh Adi and serves as his sole representative on earth. Next are the *Pesmrreyyah,* cousins of the prince, who act as his advisors. The next caste is made up of the shaikhs of the Yazidi tribes and the elders from the house of Shaikh Adi. Religious leaders make up the next set of three castes: the *faqirs,* who are ascetics (those who deny their bodily needs in order to attain a higher spirituality); the chanters, who recite religious songs and poems for the people; and the *kochaks,* who serve as spiritual advisors to the people. The kochaks also prepare the dead for burial and foretell the fate of the dead person's soul. At the bottom of the caste system are the *Merides,* or believers—the everyday Yazidis—and the commoners, who work as serfs for those in the higher castes. Commoners are either sold to or inherited by higher-caste families.

Yazidis may not marry outside their caste, and marriage to non-Yazidis is forbidden as well. Marriages are arranged by the tribe's shaikh. A young man tells the shaikh which young woman he wishes to marry. The shaikh talks with the young man's father and settles on the bride price, or dowry, to be paid to the young woman's father. Polygamy is legal, and Shaikh Adi's teachings allow adultery. Each Yazidi also has a special relationship with another person who is chosen to be a brother or sister in the afterlife. This brother or sister is with the person in times of sickness or need in this life.

Clothing. Unmarried women and girls wear flowers in their hair; necklaces made of grain, coins, or small pearls; and colorful clothing, with a red or black cloth on the head and a white veil that hangs down from the chin. Married women wear white, with a white turban on the head. Women's traditional dress consists of a long dress, ankle-length cotton pants, and a heavy coat in winter. Men traditionally wear a coat and broadcloth pants with a woolen belt and a white cloth with red polka dots on the head. Some men wear a high, brown, cone-shaped hat covered by a black or red turban. In the winter, men add a cloak and furs to their other clothing. Yazidi men must wear mustaches—they are forbidden to shave them. Young Yazidis are beginning to wear Western-style clothing.

Food. A staple food of the Yazidis is a dried cream formed into round pieces, which are ground into a sort of meal that is mixed with butter and garlic. Yazidis are permitted to drink alcohol, unlike Muslims.

Education. Education was once the sole privilege of descendants of one Yazidi family headed by Shaikh Hasan al-Basri. However, others have begun attending government schools. Traditional Yazidis still live only according to the teachings of their holy books.

Work. Most Yazidis are rural farmers, although some nomadic tribes exist. Those who farm and raise livestock do so on communal land. The main crops are wheat, barley, chickpeas, lentils, olives, and corn. Livestock animals include mules,

Social Problems. Yazidis have been subject to much persecution, particularly by the Muslims who live around them. The Yazidis have fought back, resulting in a great deal of bloodshed on both sides. In Iraq, persecution has been relatively rare, but in August 2007, significant violence was directed against the community in the northwestern Iraqi region of Jabal Sinjar, Ninawa Governate. News reports vary as to the number of people who were killed in the attack. Four separate car bombs were detonated in different parts of the traditional Yazidi area, killing at least 500 and injuring 1,000.

In Armenia, the Yazidis also face conflicts with the Kurds, the largest ethnic minority in that country. The Kurds oppose the Yazidis' separateness and refuse to recognize them as a separate people. Instead, they want the Yazidis to consider themselves Muslim Kurds. The Yazidis, however, insist on maintaining their separate identity. This has led to significant tensions between the two groups. The group has also faced persecution by Persian Turks .

Because of religious persecution, many Yazidis have fled the Kurdish areas of their traditional homelands and now reside in Germany and in the United States, where their largest settlement is located in the small Midwestern town of Lincoln, Nebraska.

Gender issues. Gender roles are highly prescribed among the Yazidis. Polygamy is allowed, although it is restricted to the higher castes. Marriages are typically arranged. In April 2007, a Yazidi girl was videotaped being stoned to death by a Yazidi crowd who believed that she had converted to Islam and married a Sunni Muslim she had been seen with in Nineveh Province of Kurdistan, Iraq. (The truth of the matter is in dispute, and no definitive judgment exists.) Two weeks later, Sunni extremists murdered 24 Yazidis in what some considered a warning to the Yazidi community not to mix with Muslims. In the twentieth century, the Yazidis were ruled by Mayan Khatun, a woman regarded by most historians of the area as a remarkable and astute ruler. She assumed power in 1913 after the murder of her husband, Mir Ali Beg. She held power, along with her son and then her grandson, until 1957.

BIBLIOGRAPHY

Guest, John. Review of *The Yazidis: A Study in Survival.* American Historical Review 95, no. 4 (October 1990): 1260.

Johannes, Armineh, and Ani Kltchian. "Mosaic: Devil's Advocates; Yazidis and Kurds; The Two Faces of Armenia's Largest Ethnic Minority." *Armenian International Magazine* 3, no. 5 (May 1992): 30.

Kabasakal Arat, Zehra F. Human Rights in Turkey. Philadelphia: University of Pennsylvania Press, 2007.

Kjeilen, Tore. "Yazidism." Encyclopedia of the Orient. http://lexicorient.com/e.o/uyazidism.htm (accessed March 7, 2008).

Louay Bahry. "Iraq." *Britannica Book of the Year, 2008.* http://0-search.eb.com.lib.aucegypt.edu:80/eb/article-9437865 (accessed March 7, 2008).

Moss, Joyce, and George Wilson. *Peoples of the World: The Middle East and North Africa.* Detroit: Gale Research, 1992

"When Murder Is Just Plain Murder." *The Economist,* August 8, 2007, 38.

—by D. K. D. de Mott

YEMENIS

PRONUNCIATION: YEM-uh-neez
LOCATION: Republic of Yemen
POPULATION: 22.3 million (2007)
LANGUAGE: Arabic
RELIGION: Islam; Judaism

¹INTRODUCTION

Ancient Yemen was known as "Arabia Felix," or "Happy (or Fortunate) Arabia," because of its great wealth from its location on the most important trade routes of the time—both over land and sea—and its lucrative trade in frankincense and myrrh. Made from resins derived from trees growing only in that area, frankincense and myrrh were greatly desired throughout the ancient world to make perfumes and incense used for religious purposes. Today, Yemen is one of the poorest countries in the world. When the emperor Constantine declared Christianity the official religion of the Roman Empire in AD 323 and banned the use of "pagan" incense in Christian rituals, the demand for frankincense and myrrh dropped off sharply. Improvements in sea travel eliminated much of the need for the overland trade route across the Arabian Peninsula. Later innovations (such as air travel) and changes in trading patterns around the world led to Yemen's economic decline and the poverty it experiences today.

Inhabited for at least 40,000 years, Yemen has seen many rulers come and go. The first-known advanced civilization in the region was that of the Sabeans, who called their land Saba (or Sheba). They occupied the land in the centuries around 1000 BC. The famed Queen of Sheba was a legendary Sabean ruler. The Sabeans were large-scale farmers who lived in close-knit family clans who fiercely protected their lands from other clans. This protective clannish attitude still prevails among Yemenis today. Around AD 300, a series of battles with invaders from Ethiopia, Egypt, and Turkey began that continued on and off for the next 1,300 years. During this time, the Islamic revolution also swept through the Middle East, and the Yemenis converted in large numbers in the early days of the movement, during Muhammad's lifetime (AD 570–632). Jewish and Christian missionaries had won many southern Arabians to their respective faiths during the 4th and 5th centuries AD, but when the Persian governor of Yemen converted to Islam in 628, most other Yemenis followed suit. This began an era of conflicts between different Islamic caliphates and imamates (religious dynasties) that lasted for several hundred years. The Ottoman Turks eventually took over Egypt in 1517, and had most of Yemen under their control by 1548. Yemen remained under Ottoman rule for more than a century, during which time the Turks developed an extensive trade of superior coffee beans from the Red Sea port of Mocha in Yemen. Although the trade has since suffered from international competition, the *arabica* coffee beans are still considered among the best in the world.

The Zaydi imams overthrew the Turks in 1636, but the Turks regained control of northwestern Yemen by the mid-1800s. Britain had taken over southern Yemen in the early 1800s. The Ottoman Turks and the British drew a borderline between north and south Yemen by 1905, and the region remained di-

vided into North Yemen and South Yemen throughout most of the 20th century. After the Turks were defeated in World War I (1914–18) the Zaydi imamate once again took control of North Yemen, under the rulership of Imam Yahya. The British retained control of South Yemen. In 1962, a military coup in North Yemen led to the establishment of the Yemen Arab Republic (YAR). Five years later, in 1967, nationalist fighters ousted the British from South Yemen and established the communist People's Republic of South Yemen, or as it came to be called two years later, the People's Democratic Republic of Yemen (PDRY). Finally, after two more decades of skirmishes and near-unifications, North and South Yemen united on 22 May 1990 to become the Republic of Yemen, a constitutional democracy. The motivating factor for unification was the discovery of oil along their mutual border in 1988. Rather than fight for exclusive rights to the oil, or split the desperately needed income, the two countries decide to join forces, once and for all.

The Republic of Yemen was threatened by secessionists in the south who triggered a brief civil war in 1994. The secessionists were defeated, however, and all but a small number of instigators were given amnesty. The country has been led by President Ali Abdullah Saleh since reunification in 1990. He was reelected to the post in 2006.

²LOCATION AND HOMELAND

Yemen is located in the Middle East, on the southern tip of the Arabian Peninsula. It is bordered by Oman to the northeast and Saudi Arabia to the north. The boundary with Saudi Arabia has never been clearly defined, but the countries have been negotiating a final marking since 2002. Much of the border lies in the Empty Quarter of the Arabian Desert—a land of shifting sands where it is difficult to mark definitive borders. The Gulf of Aden (part of the Indian Ocean) lies to the south of Yemen, and the Red Sea to the west. The strait of Bab al-Mandab connects the Red Sea to the Gulf of Aden, and separates Yemen from the African continent. Across this narrow strait are the African countries of Djibouti, Ethiopia, and Somalia. Since there is no definite boundary with Saudi Arabia, it is impossible to get a definite total area measurement for Yemen. The Yemeni government claims about 80,000 sq km (207,000 sq mi), just slightly less than the area of the U.S. state of Texas. Yemen's territory also includes the Hanish Islands and the islands of Kamaran and Perim in the Red Sea, and the island of Socotra in the Indian Ocean.

Yemen's terrain is made up of mountains and highlands, deserts, and plains. It is cut off from the northern countries of the Arabian Peninsula by vast stretches of desert (the Empty Quarter), so it has always been somewhat isolated. (With the advent of modern communications and transportation, this is beginning to change, but Yemen has centuries of isolated independence to overcome.) Western Yemen has flat coastal plains extending from the south and west coasts inward to fertile highlands surrounded by mountains. Eastern Yemen is a hilly plateau in the south and desert in the north (the southern edge of the Empty Quarter). Some of Yemen's mountains are volcanically active, and earthquakes occur on occasion. The climate varies with the terrain, from hot and dry in the desert, to hot and humid on the coasts, to mild in the highlands. Rainfall amounts also vary with the terrain, from monsoons (heavy downpours) in the western highlands, to none at all in

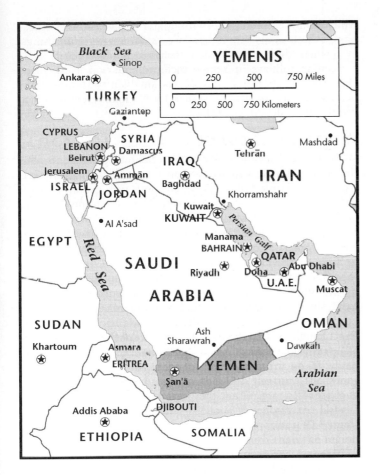

as 500 km (300 mi) apart may not be able to understand one another. Even in the small country of Yemen, different dialects are spoken. The written form of Arabic is called Classical Arabic or Modern Standard Arabic. It is the same for all literate Arabs, regardless of how different their spoken forms are. Arabic is written from right to left in a unique alphabet that has no distinction between upper and lower cases. It is not necessary for the letters to be written on a straight line, as English letters must be. Punctuation conventions are also quite different from English.

Arabic speakers are very interested in the poetry of the language. "Hello" in Arabic is *marhaba* or *ahlan*, to which one replies, *marhabtayn* or *ahlayn*. Other common greetings are *As-salam alaykum*, "Peace be with you," with the reply of *Wa-laykum as salam*, "and to you peace." *Ma'assalama* means "Goodbye." "Thank you" is *Shukran*, and "You're welcome" is *Afwan*. "Yes" is *na'am* and "no" is *la'a*. The numbers one to ten in Arabic are *wahad, itnin, taluta, arbu'a, khamsa, sitta, saba'a, tamania, tisa'a,* and *ashara*.

Arabs traditionally have long names, consisting of their given name, their father's name, their paternal grandfather's name, and finally their family name. Women do not take their husband's name when they marry, but rather keep their mother's family name as a show of respect for their family of origin. Given names usually indicate an Arab's religious affiliation. Muslims use names with Islamic religious significance, such as Muhammad and Fatima.

⁴FOLKLORE

Yemeni tradition is that Shem, the son of the biblical character Noah, founded the city of Sanaa. Another legendary figure of the land of Yemen is the Sabean queen Bilqis, better known as the Queen of Sheba. Legend has it that she visited King Solomon of Israel (who ruled from 965–925 BC) to establish friendly relations, since she and Solomon controlled either end of the trans-Arabian trade route. Her visit with Solomon is mentioned in both the Hebrew and Christian Bibles (the Old and New Testaments), and in the Islamic holy book, the Koran. According to some traditions, the Queen of Sheba is the subject of the love poem the *Song of Solomon*, supposedly written by King Solomon. Ethiopians believe themselves to be descended from a child born to King Solomon and Queen Bilqis. It is unknown whether or not the Queen of Sheba of legendary fame was actually an historical figure, but queens did rule in Arabia at that time. The Queen of Sheba as a character of legend has taken on many of the attributes and story lines of pre-Islamic pagan folk tales. She has also become a symbol of Yemen for the poets of Islamic Yemen, particularly those of the 20th century, representing a former highly developed civilization that once existed in the much poorer land of today.

⁵RELIGION

The ancient Yemenis were polytheistic, worshipping many different goddesses and gods. During the 4th and 5th centuries AD, Jewish and Christian missionaries converted numbers of Yemenis to their respective faiths. Then, in the 7th century AD, the Islamic revolution swept through the Middle East. The Persian governor of Yemen at that time converted to Islam, while the Prophet Muhammad (570–632) was still alive. Most Yemenis followed suit. About 50% of the population now belongs to the Shafai sect of Sunni Islam. Some 33% belong to the Za

the desert. Plant life ranges from desert cacti to tropical palms, depending on the region. The highland forests have nearly all been cut down, and the government cannot currently afford a wide-scale reforestation program. With the lack of forests, wildlife is reduced to small animals, some baboons in the mountains, and a variety of birds.

Traditionally, most Yemenis have lived on farms and in small villages. Urbanization—driven by a long drought, high population growth (Yemen has one of highest rates of population growth in the world, 3.2% annually in 2007), and lack of employment opportunities—began increasing in the 1990s. The largest cities are Sanaa, the political capital, with about 1,750,000 people; Aden, the economic capital, with 600,000 people; Taizz, with over 400,000 people; and Hodeida, with just around 340,000 people. The modern city of Marib is built on the ruins of the famous ancient Sabean city of Marib, dating to 1000 BC. The ruins are still visible, existing right alongside the modern city structures. Yemen's rapidly increasing population is causing significant economic, environmental and social strains. UN projections anticipate Yemen's population to reach 55 million by 2050. Currently, 47% of the population is under the age of 15.

³LANGUAGE

The official language of Yemen is Arabic. Some Yemenis learn English, and links with the former Soviet Union during the days of the PDRY prompted some Yemenis to learn Russian.

Arabic, spoken by 100 million people worldwide, has many dialects that are very distinctive, so that people living as little

Yemenis chew qat leaves in the capital of San'a, Yemen. Chewing qat is a centuries-old social custom in this tribal-dominated nation. (AP Images/Paul Garwood)

ydi sect of Shia Islam. The Zaydis once ruled the country (during the 17th and 18th centuries AD). Although they are now a minority numerically, they still have a great deal of influence in the country. The Zaydis have since reunification occasionally staged revolts in the country's north, seeking autonomy and a more religious government. The revolts have all been successfully put down. Some 2% of the population belongs to the Ismaili Shia sect, a sect that is similar to the Zaydis. The largest non-Muslim group in Yemen today is Jewish, although the majority of Yemeni Jews moved to Israel when it became an independent Jewish state in 1948 (see "Israelis"). There are small Christian and Hindu communities in southern Yemen.

Shafai Sunnis believe the Quran is the word of God as dictated directly by God to the Prophet Muhammad. Zaydi Shias, on the other hand, believe the Koran was created by Muhammad himself; it is his interpretation, or translation, of the word of God.

6 MAJOR HOLIDAYS

Since the majority of Yemenis are Muslim, Muslim holidays are the official ones. Perhaps the most significant holiday is *Eid al-Fitr,* which comes at the end of the month of fasting, *Ramadan.* During Ramadan, Muslims refrain from eating, drinking, or having sex during daylight hours, in order to reflect on God and on the plight of the unfortunate who do not have enough food. At the end of the month, Muslims celebrate *Eid al-Fitr* for three days. The other major Muslim holiday is *Eid al-Adha,*

which commemorates the willingness of the Prophet Abraham, as well as his son, to obey God's command in all things, even when Abraham was told to sacrifice his son.

Secular holidays in Yemen include January 1, New Year's Day; May 1, Labor Day; May 22, National Unity Day; September 26, Revolution Day; October 14, National Day; and November 30, Independence Day.

7 RITES OF PASSAGE

Weddings are occasions for much celebrating. First, there is the betrothal feast, usually held on a Thursday or Friday (Friday is the Islamic holy day), when the future groom and his father visit the bride's father to settle on a wedding date and bride-price. The groom and his father give the bride's father the engagement ring, as well as other gifts (such as clothes and jewelry for the bride and her mother). The bride-price is used to buy fine clothes and jewelry and other valuable items for the bride. These things are hers for the rest of her life, so that if anything happens, such as divorce or the death of her husband, she has some property that is definitely hers.

The wedding itself lasts for three days, usually from Wednesday through Friday. The most public part of the wedding takes place on Friday and is called the *laylat az-Zaffa.* Butchers arrive early in the morning to prepare the meat for the feast, where up to 100 or more guests will be fed. Men have a *qat* party in the afternoon, where they sit together and chew *qat* leaves (a mild narcotic) and smoke the *narghile,* or water-pipe. The women help prepare the food. In the evening, the men go to the mosque, and then return for dancing and singing around the groom, who is carrying a golden sword. Drummers keep the beat. The feast is eaten, more qat is chewed, the narghile is smoked once again, incense is passed around with blessings, poems are recited, a lute is played, and songs are sung. Some of the women go to the bride's home to help her dress. A special make-up artist paints delicate designs on her hands and feet, and the palms of her hands and soles of her feet are reddened with henna. Eventually, the men line up outside the groom's house, and he walks with them toward the door, leaping over the threshold when he reaches it. The men are singing all the while, and the women have climbed up on the roofs and started making a high-pitched trilling sound called the *zaghrada.* The bride will come to the house later; the guests may or may not wait for her arrival. Once the bride enters the groom's house, she becomes part of his family.

8 INTERPERSONAL RELATIONS

Arab hospitality reigns in Yemen. An Arab will never ask personal questions, as that is considered rude. It is expected that a person will say what he or she wishes, without being asked. Food and drink are always taken with the right hand because the left hand is used for "unclean" purposes, such as cleaning oneself. When speaking, Arabs touch each other much more often and stand much closer together than Westerners do. People of the same sex will often hold hands while talking, even if they are virtual strangers. (Members of the opposite sex, even married couples, never touch in public.) Arabs talk a lot, talk loudly, repeat themselves often, and interrupt each other constantly. Conversations are highly emotional and full of gestures. In Yemen, the Western "o.k." sign—touching the thumb to the tip of the forefinger in a circle—is considered obscene. Common acceptable Yemeni gestures are the thumbs-up "victory" sign (as in the West); raised eyebrows indicating "no"; and both eyes closed at once, indicating "yes." It is also common in Yemen, and many Arab cultures, to indicate "no" by making a clicking noise with the mouth.

The Arab sense of time is also quite different from that of the West. Schedules are loose and fluid, with the day divided not into hours and minutes but into "morning," "lunchtime," and "evening." There are no clocks in public places. The Western obsession with punctuality does not exist in Yemen.

Yemeni society is strictly structured according to certain divisions of people. *Sayyids* are direct descendants of the Prophet Muhammad and members of the formerly ruling Zaydi sect—a privileged and influential wealthy class. The *qadhis* are descendants of pre-Islamic Yemeni rulers who are traditionally scholars and judges. They are considered wise—a well-educated and well-respected class. The *sheikhs* (leaders) of each clan or tribe are also quite influential. Craftspeople and merchants are divided into guilds: the *manasib* are skilled artisans, such as goldsmiths; *muzayyin* are less-skilled workers, such as bricklayers; and the *akhdam* are unskilled laborers, such as street-cleaners. In recent times, as the economic situation of the country changes, the social structure is changing as well. Previously low-status jobs that now pay well are becoming more respectable.

⁹LIVING CONDITIONS

Since unification, Yemen has been attempting to improve living conditions for its people. However, as one of the poorest countries in the world, it lacks the resources to make many improvements very quickly. Therefore, living conditions remain fairly difficult in most areas of the country. In rural areas, where most of the population continues to live, running water has been made available but sewer systems have yet to be installed. The water is often polluted, and diseases such as dysentery are common. Medical care is limited, if available at all, although the government has begun to establish some rural medical clinics. Few children are vaccinated, thus diseases like measles and tuberculosis spread quickly. Malnutrition is widespread. Buses and cars only recently replaced camels and donkeys as the primary mode of transportation, and few paved roads exist outside cities and large towns. The government has made new road construction a priority. Telephone services are very rare in rural villages, and there is no door-to-door postal delivery anywhere in the country. Yemenis must pick up their mail from post office boxes.

Although life in the cities and larger towns is better than in the rural areas, conditions are still far below modern Western standards. The average life expectancy for Yemenis in 2004 was 59 years for men and 62 years for women. The infant mortality rate in the same year was 75 per 1,000 births. In an attempt to improve health care, the government has built new hospitals in the cities (as well as the rural medical clinics), and has opened a new school of medicine at the University of Sanaa.

In 2007 there were 2.8 million houses in Yemen, 16% of which had access to some kind of sewage network. Homes in Yemen differ by region. In eastern Yemen, they are made of sun-dried clay bricks. People of the Tihama (the western coastal plain) live in round or rectangular huts made of mud-covered reeds and sticks. Each one-room hut serves a specific purpose, such as the cooking hut, sleeping hut, storage hut, the hut where guests are received, etc. The interior walls of the reed huts have colorful scenes painted on them. In the highlands, houses are six to seven stories high. Stables and storage rooms are on the lower floors, while several generations of a family share the living quarters upstairs, with kitchens, living rooms, bedrooms, and other rooms. Every house has one large room called a *diwan*, used for celebrations, and an attic room called a *mafraj* where guests are entertained. In the capital city of Sanaa, many of the houses are more than 400 years old. The original walled city built in the 1st century AD still stands. The old houses are six to seven stories high, made of stone, brick, and mud. The exterior walls are ornately decorated with white plaster. Ancient Yemenis used colored alabaster, a soft stone, for windows. Modern Yemenis use stained glass to achieve the ancient look. The old city homes are being divided up for renters, as wealthier Yemenis move to the suburbs. The rental units are poorly maintained, and many of these historic homes have suffered water damage from leaky pipes. The UN has funded restoration and preservation projects in the old city to protect these fine examples of a unique architecture. As tourism increased in Yemen in the late 1990s and early 2000s, many of these old buildings were converted into hotels.

¹⁰FAMILY LIFE

The nuclear family, called *'ayla* in Arabic, is the basic social unit of Yemeni society. Most families are large, with 8 to 10 members not uncommon. A Yemeni woman gives birth to an average of 7.7 children in her lifetime—many women bear more than 10. The average age for marriage is 22 for men and 18 for women, although it is not unknown for girls younger than 14 years old to marry. (In rural areas, girls as young as 12 or even 10 may marry.) Parents usually arrange marriages for their children. The groom's family pays a bride-price to the bride's family, which is then used to buy fine clothes and jewelry that the bride will own outright for the rest of her life. These valuables serve as insurance in case of divorce or widowhood. Divorce is fairly simple for both men and women and happens relatively often. Some 15–20% of Yemeni women have been divorced and remarried at least once in their lifetimes.

Several generations of an extended family, or *bayt* (meaning "house") in Arabic, live together in one home. Several bayts together make up a clan, or tribe. Each tribe elects a *sheikh* (a leader) within the community to solve local disputes. Men and women are segregated in public, and women keep themselves veiled and fully covered when anyone but family is present. Most Yemeni women will not eat in public restaurants. More women are going to school and getting jobs outside the home today, but Islamic traditions of segregation for women make this difficult. Yemeni universities now accept women as students, but men are still given priority for admission.

¹¹CLOTHING

Clothing styles in Yemen, particularly for women, vary greatly by region. Men generally wear one of two styles. In hot coastal regions, men wear a lightweight shirt with an embroidered skirt called a *futa*, with a straw hat or other head covering. In the cooler highlands, they wear a calf-length shirt called a *zanna*, with a jacket. Many men wear a belt with a *jambiyya*, or ceremonial dagger, thrust beneath it. A man's jambiyya identifies his clan and is a symbol of manhood. Boys start wearing them at about the age of 14.

Women's styles are much harder to classify, as they are so varied. Yemeni women like bright colors and lots of jewelry, particularly silver. In Sanaa, many women wrap themselves in brilliant cloths imported from India called *sitaras*. In the highlands, they wear baggy embroidered trousers called *sirwals* under their dresses. Women wear black robes and pointed straw hats to work in the fields in eastern Yemen. Many Yemeni women across the country wear the traditional Islamic covering, the *abaya*—a loose black robe that covers the woman from head to toe—when in public. The *sharshaf*—a black skirt, cape, veil, and head covering—is also worn by women throughout Yemen. In line with much of the Islamic world, women's clothing has become much more conservative and traditional in Yemen toward the end of the 20th and into the 21st century. In cities and towns across the country, virtually all women cover their faces either completely or with a scarf that reveals only their eyes. Most women also wear gloves in public so that no part of their body can be seen. In rural areas, women working in fields will often go without face coverings.

12 FOOD

The Yemeni diet is quite simple. Staple foods are rice, bread, vegetables, and lamb, with fish in the coastal regions. Breakfast is a light meal consisting of scrambled eggs with tomatoes, or a bean dish called *ful,* served with flatbread. Supper in the evening is very similar. Lunch is the heavy meal for Yemenis. Eaten at midday, it generally consists of chicken, lamb, or beef, with cooked vegetables, and rice mixed with raisins and almonds. Flatbread soaked in buttermilk and covered with tomatoes, onions, and spices is served at almost every meal, as is a spicy green stew called *salta*. Salta could perhaps be called the national dish of Yemen. It is made with meat broth, onions, tomatoes, mincemeat, eggs, and *hulba*—a mixture of fenugreek and grated leeks. Sweet custards with either tea or coffee are usually served for dessert.

Coffee originated in Mocha, a port town on the Red Sea in Yemen, and made its way to Europe on trading vessels during the 16th and 17th centuries. By the end of the 17th century, the Dutch had smuggled some young coffee plants out of Yemen and planted them in Ceylon and Java. Other European countries soon followed suit, planting the smuggled coffee in their colonial territories where the climate was suitable for growing. Until the end of the 18th century, Yemen continued to export some 22,000 tons of coffee each year. But during the 19th century, trade declined sharply due to competition from cheaper coffee sources, and the population of Mocha fell from 20,000 people to 400. Yemeni coffee is still exported and is still considered one of the finest coffees of the world. It is known as *coffee arabica*. In Yemen, both the husks and beans are used to make drinks, as opposed to just the beans (as in Western countries). Traditional Arab coffee, called *bun* in Yemen, is made from the beans. A drink called *qishr* is made from steeping the husks in hot water, then adding ginger, cinnamon, and cardamom for flavor. Qishr is milder than bean-coffee and is actually preferred in Yemen. The price of husks is higher than the price of beans in Yemen.

Meals are served on a cloth or plastic sheet spread on the floor. Yemenis eat with their fingers, not utensils. A soup that is popular in Yemen is *shourba bilsen*, made with lentils.

Shourba Bilsen
(Thick Lentil Soup)

1 pound soup bones, beef or lamb
8 cups water
2 cups brown lentils
2 onions, finely chopped
3 cloves garlic, finely chopped
2 cups stewed tomatoes
¼ cup finely chopped fresh cilantro, or 3 tablespoons dried cilantro
salt and pepper to taste

Rinse soup bones and put in large saucepan with water. Bring to a boil over high heat, then reduce heat to simmer. Add lentils, onions, garlic, tomatoes, cilantro, and salt and pepper to taste. Cover and cook for 1½ hours, stirring every few minutes to prevent sticking. Makes 6 servings.

(adapted from Albyn and Webb, p. 72)

13 EDUCATION

For much of Yemen's history, education was only available to the wealthy. The constitution guarantees the right of all citizens to education, and the government has opened a number of public schools in large cities and towns. Rural areas are still limited to Muslim religious schools. In 2004 it was estimated that 80% of boys and 50% of girls attended primary school. At the secondary level, 55% of boys and 22% of girls attend school. The literacy rate has doubled since the mid-1990s; in 2004, it was about 50%. That year, among men literacy was 70%; among women, 30%.

14 CULTURAL HERITAGE

There is a strong rural tradition in Yemen of oral literature, poetry, and song. Arab music is much like the Arab language—rich, repetitive, and exaggerated. The *oud*, or *kabanj*, is a popular instrument; it is an ancient stringed instrument that is the ancestor of the European lute. Another traditional instrument is the *rebaba*, a one-stringed instrument. A traditional Arab dance is the *ardha,* or men's sword dance. Men carrying swords stand shoulder to shoulder and dance, and from among them a poet sings verses while drummers beat out a rhythm. A popular Yemeni singer, Badwi Zubayr, is known all over the Arabian Peninsula. Iskandar Thabit (b. 1924) wrote popular songs for the Yemeni revolutions during the 1960s. The most-respected living Yemeni writer is 'Abdallah al-Baraduni, a poet.

Islam forbids the depiction of the human form, so Yemeni art focuses on geometric and abstract shapes. Yemen is famous for its silver jewelry. Stained glass and pottery are also popular art forms. Calligraphy is a sacred art, with the Quran being the primary subject matter. Muslim art finds its greatest expression in mosques.

15 WORK

More than half of all Yemenis are small farmers. In cities and towns, there is a staggeringly high unemployment rate. This was made worse in 1990 when Saudi Arabia expelled all Yemeni workers there, after Yemen refused to support the stationing of foreign troops in Saudi Arabia during the Gulf War (1990–91). Over 700,000 workers lost their jobs in Saudi Arabia and returned home to Yemen, looking for work. In 1992, thousands of refugees from Somalia arrived in Yemen, also looking for work. Yemen is attempting to expand its industrial base, but poor transportation systems make that difficult.

The industry that exists consists of oil and oil processing; natural gas; salt, limestone, and marble mining; fishing and fish-processing plants; and coffee. The oil and gas sectors are the most profitable sectors of the Yemeni economy. In 2005 the country exported oil worth $3.1 billion. The government derives 70% of its earnings from the oil sector.

Rural women have very heavy workloads. Not only do they do 70–75% of the work in the fields, but they are also responsible for fetching all the wood and water (which means carrying 20- to 25-kg or 44- to 55-lb loads on their heads for long distances, often uphill); cutting alfalfa to feed the cow (one cow requires six to eight hours per day of labor to care for it); all the cooking and housekeeping; and caring for the children. In addition to this, many women also sell dairy produce, dried cow or sheep dung, animal products, and/or crafts for extra family income. Only 1.5% of Yemeni women are employed in wage earning jobs.

16 SPORTS

Football (or soccer, as it is known in the United States) is the national pastime of Yemenis. Organized sports are rare, and Yemen has few athletes who are skilled enough to compete at an international level. In 2008 the Yemen national football team was ranked 141st by FIFA (International Federation of Association Football), the world governing body of international football. Yemen has sent athletes to the Olympic Games since 1992, but the country has yet to win a medal. The Yemeni Cricket League finished its first season in 1995 and cricket is played primarily by expatriate workers from South Asia.

17 ENTERTAINMENT AND RECREATION

The favorite form of entertainment in Yemen is chewing *qat* leaves, a mild narcotic. Men gather every afternoon for qat parties that last until sunset. Women chew qat as well, but not nearly as much as men. Women's afternoon gatherings are known as *tafritas;* here, marriages are arranged, goods sold, and information and experiences shared.

18 FOLK ART, CRAFTS, AND HOBBIES

Silver jewelry is one of the most important forms of art in Yemen, and also a traditional folk art. Other crafts include textiles, leather, baskets, and stained glass. Because the *jambiya* men wear is so significant a social marker, many craftspeople specialize in making elaborately decorated knives, leather belts, and jeweled knife covers.

19 SOCIAL PROBLEMS

The use of the narcotic *qat* is a significant problem in Yemen, although most Yemenis would disagree. Farmers are growing qat on land where they used to grow food crops, because qat brings in a much higher price. But then they spend their profits on qat to chew, so they cannot buy food to replace what they did not grow in the fields. Malnutrition is an increasing problem in Yemen. Also, men spend so much time chewing qat that the women are left to do most of the work to provide for their families. This creates much stress for the women and, consequently, for their families. Qat is legal in Yemen, but it is con-

sidered an illegal drug in international markets so it cannot be exported for profit. The national addiction to this drug has also caused severe environmental problems. Yemen is fairly arid and a significant portion of the country's supply of water is being used in inefficient irrigation of qat plantations.

The extremely high rate of unemployment is a tremendous problem in Yemen. The sluggish economy is improving very slowly, so it does not appear there will be any significant increase in jobs in the near future. Population growth is so rapid and economic growth so low that many economists predict a bleak future for the country. Oil revenues, while increasing, are not significant enough to help in a substantive way, as they do in all the other countries that make up the Arabian peninsula.

Since 2004 there has been violence in the north of Yemen, where the Zaydi sect has been fighting the government for autonomy and to establish a religious state. Violence has been intermittent with long periods of relative peace followed by uprisings, which the government is generally successful at putting down. Gun ownership is widespread, particularly in the countryside where even boys as young as 11 and 12 are armed. They can be seeing carrying military assault rifles as well as the ubiquitous *jambiya*. Because of Yemen's tribal tradition and weak government, many disputes are settled with violence. Small armed skirmishes are relatively common in the countryside.

Yemen is a close military and political ally of the United States, particularly in its War on Terror. Al Qaeda has a fairly strong presence in Yemen and in the early 2000s there were several violent terrorist incidents, mainly targeting western tourists. In early 2008 there were frequent bombings of Western and particularly U.S. housing compounds and embassies.

20 GENDER ISSUES

Women in Yemen face many difficulties, including lack of educational opportunities, forced early marriages, water shortages, and qat addiction among male members of the family, which often leaves the women as the only workers in a family. In fact, in 2007 the World Economic Forum's Gender Gap Report ranked Yemen last (128th out of 128 countries surveyed) in terms of political and economic empowerment of women. In the same year, the international charity organization Save the Children ranked Yemen 138th out of 140 countries studied in its annual Mothers Index, which considers the best and worst countries for mothers and children (1 being the best, 140 the worst) when taking into account maternal mortality, access to contraception, and the percentage of women in national government, among other factors. Yemen has been near the bottom of the list in other years as well.

Although women have the right to vote in Yemen and also have equal access to education by law, the reality is that women in Yemen generally lead difficult lives. The nation is deeply religious, tribal, and traditional. Islamic and Arab customs dictate that women should be covered in public, and in Yemen women are generally completely covered, often simply wearing a traditional sheet pulled over themselves rather than a fitted *abaya* as women do in most other countries on the Arabian peninsula. In the larger cities, younger Yemeni women will sometimes wear the traditional black abaya with gloves and a *niqab*, a veil that completely covers their face.

Virtually all marriages in Yemen are arranged by family members. There is a strong historical and cultural preference for marriages within the clan or tribe, and often between first cousins. Yemeni men are allowed to have as many as four wives at any one time, but because of Islamic rules requiring that all wives be treated equally, few men in Yemen can afford to have more than one wife. Female genital mutilation was outlawed in 2001, but the effectiveness of the law on the practice in Yemeni society is not known.

About 25% of Yemeni women work outside the home, primarily in crafts industries and as domestic help. Although Yemen is culturally very traditional, the government does promote the idea of equality between the genders and there are usually a few women serving in parliament.

²¹ BIBLIOGRAPHY

Albyn, Carole Lisa, and Lois Sinaiko Webb. *The Multicultural Cookbook for Students.* Phoenix, AZ: Oryx Press, 1993.

Chwaszcza, Joachim, ed. *Insight Guides: Yemen.* Singapore: APA Publications (HK) Ltd., 1992.

Hämäläinen, Pertii. *Yemen: A Lonely Planet Travel Survival Kit.* Hawthorn, Australia: Lonely Planet Publications, 1996.

Hansen, Eric. *Motoring with Mohammed: Journeys to Yemen and the Red Sea.* New York. Vintage, 1992.

Macintosh-Smith, Tim. *Yemen: The Unknown Arabia.* New York. Overlook TP, 2001.

Schwedler, Jillian. *Faith in Moderation: Islamist Parties in Jordan and Yemen.* Cambridge: Cambridge University Press, 2006.

Vom Bruck, Gabriele. *Islam, Memory, and Morality in Yemen: Ruling Families in Transition.* New York: Palgrave Macmillan, 2005.

—revised by J. Henry

YI

PRONUNCIATION: YEE
ALTERNATE NAMES: Nosu, Nasu, Luowu, Misapo, Sani, and Axi
LOCATION: China
POPULATION: 7.76 million
LANGUAGE: Yi
RELIGION: Ancestor worship
RELATED ARTICLES: Vol. 3: China and Her National Minorities

¹ INTRODUCTION

The ancestors of the Yi were called the Qiang, one of the more ancient national minorities in China. The Qiang originally lived in the north and northwest of present-day China (Shanxi, Gansu, and Qinghai) and raised stock. Some 4,000–5,000 years ago, a part of the Qiang population migrated in successive waves toward southwest China, mixed with the native peoples, and finally settled in Sichuan, Yunnan, Guizhou, and Guangxi. After settling, the Yi transformed from being nomads engaged in stockraising to farmers. It seems this process was completed under the Western Han Dynasty (206 BC–AD 8). It was from this time that they were known under the name of Yi. However, they kept until the 18th century a slave-owning system and resisted any attempt by the imperial government to interfere in their social structure. It was only under the Qing Dynasty (1644–1911) that their leaders, who formed a kind of aristocracy, were replaced by Manchu or Chinese officers appointed by the central government. This marked the decline of the slavery system.

² LOCATION AND HOMELAND

As we have seen, the Yi are distributed in Yunnan, Sichuan, Guizhou, and Guangxi provinces. They live in compact communities, sharing their territory with other nationalities. Except for a small number living in river valleys, they reside on high plateaus. Most of them live in mountainous areas as high as 10,000–11,000 ft above sea level, with a varied topography and a changeable climate. They have a saying: "Different skies every five miles." The Yi population was 7.76 million in 2000.

³ LANGUAGE

Yi language belongs to the Sino-Tibetan family, Tibeto-Burman group, Yi branch. There are 6 dialects, 5 subdialects, and 25 regional idioms. The Yi invented an ideographic writing system, called *chuan wen* ("traditional script") in ancient Chinese books. Yi script, which is no longer used today, seems to have derived from Chinese characters. The Yi have many self-given names, such as Nosu, Nasu, Luowu, Misapo, Sani, Axi, etc. However, Yi has now become the most common designation.

⁴ FOLKLORE

Yi mythology, like that of many other national minorities of China, centers around the flood and the origin of human beings. However, many aspects of the myths reflect Yi customs and political conceptions. For example, in "The Story of the Flood," the god Entiguzi and his family live in Heaven and ruthlessly rule the people on earth, who are too poor to pay their taxes. Following a dispute, three brothers beat a tax collector to death. Thereafter, when they ploughed their field, the next day the field reverted to untilled soil. They worked hard for three days, but all their efforts were in vain. One night they discovered that it was an old man who restored the ploughed field to virgin land. The two elder brothers wanted to kill him, but the younger brother asked the old man why he was doing this. The old man told them it was useless to plough any more, because Entiguzi in Heaven had decided to flood the earth. They were to build three ships made of iron, copper, and wood, respectively. However, when the flood came, only the youngest brother, Wuwu, escaped death by sheer luck. As the only survivor on earth, Wuwu told Entiguzi that he hoped to marry his daughter. Entiguzi refused. Since Wuwu rescued a great many animals from the flood, they helped him to go to Heaven. He met Entiguzi's youngest daughter. They fell in love at first sight. Entiguzi had no alternative but to agree to their marriage. Later on, she gave birth to three sons. The eldest was the ancestor of the Tibetans, the second of the Chinese, and the third of the Yi.

Another Yi myth of origins, centering on the "Tiger Clan," spread in Yunnan Province. It also begins with a god opening the doors of Heaven to flood the earth. Later, the god opened a calabash and found a brother and a sister inside. Yielding to the god's will, they married. The woman gave birth to seven daughters. One day, a tiger came and asked to marry one of the girls. Only the youngest daughter was willing to marry to ensure the continuation of mankind. The tiger took her away to the mountains. After entering a cave, the tiger was transformed into a good-looking young man. The woman gave birth to nine sons and four daughters. Her nine sons were the ancestors of nine nationalities, among them the Yi. The Yi are described as living in the mountains, as being hunters and pastors, and as being fond of buckwheat and corn. The burial customs of the Yi are linked to the Tiger myth. The Yi still believe that the dead should be cremated, for only cremation will transform the dead into tigers. In some Yi districts, the corpse should be covered with tiger fur to recall that the deceased was the descendent of a tiger and will revert to being a tiger after death. The myth of the "Tiger Clan" is probably the remnant of totemic worship of the tiger in the remote past.

⁵RELIGION

The Yi believe that everything that moves or grows has its own spirit. They worship their ancestors and revere ghosts and gods. Moreover, the Yi borrowed many beliefs and practices from religious Taoism and Buddhism. The religious rites are performed by the shaman Bimuo and the sorcerer Suye. These two kinds of priests are literate, know the ancient Yi script, and are capable of divination. Beating sheepskin drums, they recite the scriptures, expel the ghosts, offer sacrifices, and perform sacred dances while in a state of trance. It is believed that things left behind by the deceased possess their own spirits and the power to protect the people.

The Yi worship the Buddha of Peace and Tranquillity (*Taiping*), considered the God of Grain, three times a year. What is called the "Heavenly Buddha" is simply a braid on the forehead of a man. The braid, about 8 inches long and 1.5 inches around, is wrapped tightly in a piece of cloth and made to stand out. In the eyes of the Yi, this braid is the lord of fortune and misfortune, so sacred and inviolable that anybody who touches it will

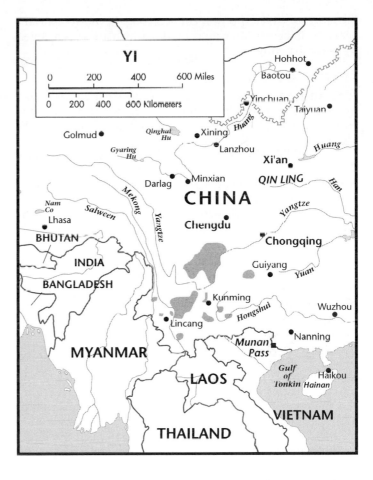

be looked upon as an enemy. A man will fight desperately to protect his braid.

In some districts, the Yi worship Asailazi, the god who created the ideographic script of the Yi. There is also a cult to the God of Wind.

Since the 18th century, a considerable number of Yi have converted to Catholicism and Protestantism as a result of missionary work.

⁶MAJOR HOLIDAYS

The Yi celebrate three main festivals: the Spring Festival, the Yi New Year Festival, and the Torch Festival. As the Yi inhabit areas where there are many Chinese, they fully participate in the festivities surrounding the Chinese Spring Festival. Families kill pigs and sheep to prepare special meals and visit each other. On the first of January (lunar calendar; Western calendar, between January 21 and February 20), the first thing is to carry on a shoulder pole two buckets of water. The family members may use it for cooking or washing, but not for laundry. They go to the countryside for picnicking, singing, dancing, wrestling, and horse racing. The date of the Yi New Year is not fixed (usually in October or November, lunar calendar; Western calendar, between October 24 and January 18) but decided through divination by the shaman. The activities are similar as those of the Spring Festival. The Torch Festival is prevalent in all Yi districts. It is held on June 24 or 25 (lunar calendar; Western calendar, between July 22 and August 20). Holding a torch, everybody runs in the fields for fun. Buffalo fighting, sheep fighting, wrestling, arrow-shooting, dancing, singing, swinging,

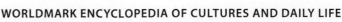

horse racing, and tug-of-war count among the most important sporting and entertainment activities, which are accompanied by heavy drinking.

⁷RITES OF PASSAGE

Right after the birth of a girl, her parents will wind a red thread around her head and change it with a new one frequently. It is treasured as a symbol of purity and happiness until the girl's wedding.

A rite of "skirt changing" is held for teenage girls in their odd years of age. The parents prepare lace, a black kerchief, a new skirt, multicolored beads, and silver collar plate beforehand. Old folks will be invited to reckon the lucky day. When it is decided, the household will entertain many guests at a dinner party. During the rite, males must leave the house, while women and girls happily surround the girl, tease her, and express their good wishes. She is combed, helped to wear the new kerchief overhead, and change to a new skirt. Only then are men and boys allowed to come in the house to admire the enhanced beauty of the girl.

The bodies of the dead are usually cremated. The ashes are buried underground or put in a cavern. Because of Chinese influence, some practice burial of the dead in the ground. The funeral rites include "calling back the spirit of the dead." A wooden cross is made, half a foot in length, with wool on the top, plant leaves on the sides, and some grass at the bottom. It is the symbol of the spirit. The shaman recites the scripture and the family offers a sacrifice. For underground burial, a man will dress up like a ghost and lead the way before the coffin while beating a drum. The shaman also walks before the coffin. After the burial, the family should prepare a "mourning plate," which is hung on a wall in the home. The plate, according to ritual prescriptions, should be "sent off" two or more years later. In accordance with the position of the dead, a send-off team consisting of five to seven persons is arranged. They take the mourning plate down from the wall, place it in front of the house, kill livestock for sacrificial offerings, put the plate on a family member's back, then follow the shaman to send it off. They put the mourning plate in the cavern of their ancestors. Moreover, a ceremony is performed to save the souls of the dead.

⁸INTERPERSONAL RELATIONS

When receiving guests, the host will prepare a special meal of oxen, pig, sheep, or chicken, according to the position and familiarity of the guests. Before the meal, the host will present the animal or poultry to the guests, to show that it is live and healthy. After being killed, the animal or poultry will be cooked entirely, including the head, the tail, and the internal organs. These will all be shown after cooking, one by one, to the guests. The meal is very copious, the host inviting the guests to eat and drink without reserve. The host usually asks the guests to take home the head or upper arm of the animal.

The Yi are known for their hospitality. Refusing a toast offered by the host is looked upon as most impolite behavior. The Yi pay much attention to courtesy shown older generations, not on the basis of age, but of seniority in the family or clan.

Young people have full freedom in dating. They take advantage of recreational group activities, such as singing and dancing, as well as country fairs, to meet partners and develop courtship relations. The eighth of February (lunar calendar;

Western calendar, between March 1 and 30) is a special festival for youngsters; one of the rituals is for boys to stick an azalea flower in the hair of one's sweetheart.

⁹LIVING CONDITIONS

Because of rigid social stratification in the past, there are imposing dwellings and spacious courtyards, even with watchtowers. These were the living quarters of the nobles. For the common people, houses are low and damp, made of wood and adobes, without windows. The master's room is usually on the left. The room on the right is for livestock and groceries, usually with a loft for the children or for storage of grain. The central piece is the living room and serves for many functions. Furniture and utensils are mostly made of wood.

¹⁰FAMILY LIFE

The Yi family is patrilineal. Sons and daughters leave their parents after wedding. Parents usually live with their youngest son. Males inherit family property. Since ancient times, the Yi have practiced a joint naming system of father and son. The last one or two syllables of the father's name should be put in front of the son's name. A man of noble origin could recite the names of his ancestors up to tens of generations. In the family, the women find themselves in a subordinate position, without the right of inheritance. The Yi lay stress on the power of their mother's brother. Arranged marriage is common. In principle, the Yi family is monogamous. However, there are still polygamy problems left over by history. For older generations that practiced polygamy, the relation between the wife and the concubines is distinct: the wife's sons have the right of succession and inheritance, while the concubines' sons have not.

Cross-cousin marriage (Dravidian marriage) is common among the Yi. The woman, after wedding, will live in her parents' house until she gets pregnant.

¹¹CLOTHING

Men's clothes vary according to regions. In some districts, men wear multi-pleated loose pants; in others, they wear tight ones. The above-mentioned braid enclosed by cloth on the men's foreheads is their most peculiar symbol of identity. They usually wear a large earring of red or yellow on their left ear. Women wear garments embroidered or trimmed at the edge with cotton lace. They wear multi-pleated long skirts; below the knee, the skirt is made of cloths of different colors. Teenage girls cover their head with a black kerchief; young and middle-aged women usually wear an embroidered square kerchief. Women are fond of wearing ornaments, particularly earrings and a hand-sized, finely carved silver plate attached right below the collar. When they leave home, men and women all wear black wool cloaks, which are decorated by a long fringe at the bottom.

¹²FOOD

The staple food of the Yi includes corn, buckwheat, oats, and potatoes. Rice is rare. They raise and grow their own livestock, poultry, and vegetables. Few vegetables grow on the high plateaus, but some of the wild herbs are edible. They like spicy and sour food; this is probably related to insufficient salt intake in the past. They make wine from corn and buckwheat and like baked tea.

[13]EDUCATION

Illiteracy is still widespread among the Yi, especially among women. Although primary schooling is, by law, compulsory and free of charge, many students in rural areas drop out each year. Few reach middle school (junior and senior) and even fewer go through college.

[14]CULTURAL HERITAGE

Dancing is one of the major art forms developed by the Yi. The Moon Dance of Axi is probably their most famous dance and has been performed frequently on stage, at home, and abroad. There are many other dance styles and scenarios. Performers usually sing while dancing.

As we have seen, the Yi invented an original writing system. Hundreds of manuscripts in Yi writing have been published. The Yi also have their own calendar, which divides the year into 10 months of 36 days.

[15]WORK

The Yi are mainly engaged in farming and raising livestock, which is mostly men's work. Men are also trained as hunters, carpenters, and lacquer workers. Spinning, weaving, dyeing, sewing, designing and making clothes, and embroidering all are done by women at home.

[16]SPORTS

Wrestling, arrow-shooting, top-whipping, horse racing, tug-of-war, and a variety of ball games are popular sports with the Yi.

[17]ENTERTAINMENT AND RECREATION

Despite the growing popularity of movies and television, the Yi treasure and often prefer their traditional recreation activities. Besides gamecock and buffalo fighting, which the whole community attends, there are two favorite pastimes for the young people, namely *Ganhuachang* (Rushing to the flower place) and *Paohuashan* (Running around the flower mountain). Ganhuachang is actually a form of dating. As soon as a young fellow knows that a girl is now visiting a certain family, he arrives there at once and sings a tune accompanied by his traditional full moon-shaped mandolin outside the door. If the girl agrees to go dating, he will invite her to sing and dance at the flower place (a place for outdoor activities). Even married persons might add to the fun on occasion, especially when the dating couple becomes more serious. Paohuashan is a group activity organized by the village. Each household invites a guest from outside their village. The young men and girls line up and move round the mountains. They sing as they walk along. Whenever they arrive on a hilltop, they dance. When they return to the village in the evening, they meet the old folks waiting at the gate. Singing in antiphonal style with the old folks, they are allowed to enter the village only after they have won the singing contest.

[18]FOLK ART, CRAFTS, AND HOBBIES

Yi lacquerwares are renowned internationally. Many domestic utensils, such as wooden dishes, plates, bowls, cups, spoons, and flagons, are painted vividly with decorative figures and patterns in black, red, and yellow. They have become collector's items and are sought eagerly by tourists.

[19]SOCIAL PROBLEMS

On account of their environment (high plateaus) and of their mode of production based on artisanal farming, it is very difficult for the Yi to develop a prosperous economy. They face a real dilemma: if they move out of their mountainous terrain, they have to change their traditional professions and risk losing their identity; if they stay, they may retain their traditional ways, but remain relatively poor as China develops economically.

[20]GENDER ISSUES

The Chinese constitution states that women have equal rights with men in all areas of life, and most legislation is gender neutral. While the gap in educational levels between women and men is narrowing with women making up 47.1% of all college students in 2005, illiteracy is still widespread among Yi women.

China has strict family planning laws. It is illegal for women to marry before 20 years of age (22 for men), and it is illegal for single women to give birth. Though minority populations were previously exempt from family planning regulations, policy has changed in recent years to limit minority population growth. Today, urban minority couples may have two children while rural couples may have three or four.

[21]BIBLIOGRAPHY

Chiao, Chien, Nicholas Tapp, and Kam-yin Ho, ed. "Special Issue on Ethnic Groups in China." *New Asia Bulletin*, no. 8, 1989.

Dreyer, June Teufel. *China's Forty Millions*. Cambridge: Harvard University Press, 1976.

Eberhard, Wolfram. *China's Minorities: Yesterday and Today*. Belmont: Wadsworth Publishing Company, 1982.

Gustafsson, Bjorn A., Shi, Li, and Sicular, Terry, eds. *Inequality and Public Policy in China*. New York: Cambridge University Press, 2008.

Harrell, Stevan. "The History of the History of the Yi." In *Cultural Encounters on China's Ethnic Frontiers*, edited by Stevan Harrell, 63–91. Seattle: University of Washington Press, 1994.

Heberer, Thomas. *China and Its National Minorities: Autonomy or Assimilation?* Armonk, NY: M. E. Sharpe, 1989.

Lebar, Frank, et al. *Ethnic Groups of Mainland Southeast Asia*. New Haven: Human Relations Area Files Press, 1964.

Lemoine, Jacques. "Les Yi." In *Ethnologie régionale II* (Encyclopédie de la Pléiade). Paris: Gallimard, 1978.

Ma Yin, ed. *China's Minority Nationalities*. Beijing: Foreign Languages Press, 1989.

Miller, Lucien, ed. *South of the Clouds: Tales from Yunnan*. Seattle: University of Washington Press, 1994.

Ramsey, S. Robert. *The Languages of China*. Princeton: Princeton University Press, 1987.

Shin, Leo Kwok-yueh. *The Making of the Chinese State: Ethnicity and Expansion on the Ming Borderlands*. New York: Cambridge University Press, 2006.

Wiens, Harold J. *Han Chinese Expansion in South China*. New Haven: The Shoestring Press, 1967.

—by C. Le Blanc

ZHUANG

ALTERNATE NAMES: Buzhuang, Bunong, Buyang, Butu, Buyue, Buman, Gaolan
LOCATION: China
POPULATION: 16.2 million
LANGUAGE: Zhuang
RELIGION: Polytheistic; ancestor worship, Christianity
RELATED ARTICLES: Vol. 3: China and Her National Minorities

¹INTRODUCTION

The Zhuang developed as a branch of the ancient Baiyue people. They are historically linked with the Xi'ou and Luoyue people of the Spring and Autumn Period (770–476 bc) and the Warring States (475–221 bc) during the Zhou Dynasty (1121–221 bc); with the Liao, Li, and Wuhu of the Han (206 bc–ad 220) and Tang dynasties (618–907); and with the Zhuang, Liang, and Tu of the Song Dynasty (960–1279), as recorded in ancient Chinese books. After unifying China, the First Emperor of Qin (221–207 bc) sent an army half a million strong to Lingnan (present Guangxi and Guangdong). Having conquered the Xi'ou, he set up three command posts and ordered the local population to dig a canal connecting the Xiangjiang and Lijiang rivers, thus linking the Yangzi River system with the Zhujiang River system. A great number of Chinese moved from the middle and lower reaches of the Yellow River to the south to live together with the Xi'ou and the Luoyue. After the fall of the imperial Qin in 207 bc, Zhao Tuo, an ex-general of Qin, proclaimed himself King of South Yue. The rebellion was put down by Emperor Wu of the Western Han Dynasty (206 bc–ad 7). After the fall of the Han Dynasty in ad 220, there appeared in present Guangxi large clans, such as Lu, Xian, Ning, etc., each of whom had large numbers of slaves, extensive property and great political power. The imperial Tang Dynasty appointed local hereditary chieftains as its officials. Thereafter, the ancestors of the Zhuang, despite sporadic restlessness and rebellions, submitted to the rule of the central government.

²LOCATION AND HOMELAND

Zhuang is the largest national minority of China. Their population was 16.2 million in 2000. More than 90% of them live in Guangxi Zhuang Autonomous Region. There are also compact Zhuang communities in Wenshan Zhuang and Miao Autonomous Prefecture (in southeast Yunnan) and smaller groups in Guangdong, Hunan, Guizhou, and Sichuan provinces. The Guangxi landscape is typical of southern China. In its central portion, a chain of undulating hills formed by eroded limestone of an ancient uplifted seabed casts a spell on Chinese and foreigners alike. Strings of jadeite-green peaks seem suspended from the blue sky. A number of grottoes have been found inside those hills. Some of them are large enough to accommodate thousands of people. It is also in those hills that one finds the famous "gorge paintings"; there are more than 60 gorges stretching over some 125 mi. The largest one is 130 ft high and more than 325 ft long. In all, more than 1,300 images can be seen. The largest drawings exceed 10 ft, while the small ones are only 12 in.

³LANGUAGE

Zhuang is classified as belonging to the Sino-Tibetan linguistic family, Zhuang-Dong group, Zhuang-Dai branch. A writing system was created on the basis of the Chinese script as early as the Southern Song Dynasty (1127–1279) but had only a limited use, recording genealogies, contracts, scriptures, and popular stories; it nevertheless contributed greatly to the knowledge of traditional Zhuang society and culture. A new alphabetical system based on Latin was put in use in 1955 and revised in 1982.

The Zhuang call themselves Buzhuang. "Bu" means "man." Other self-given names include Bunong, Buyang, Butu, Buyue, Buman, Gaolan, etc., as many as 20 and more. Zhuang has now become the unified name of all these groups.

⁴FOLKLORE

The Zhuang have a rich mythology, revolving in good part around the question of origins. In one story, it is said that there were no seeds of grains in ancient times, so people had to allay their hunger with wild herbs. Because of the multiplication of mankind, their demand far exceeded supply. Actually, there were seeds of grains in the heavens, but people living there were not willing to give them to people living on earth. The latter had no choice but to send a dog to look for seeds in Heaven. In those days, a dog had nine tails. On arriving on the threshing ground, the dog put its tails on the floor so that many seeds stuck themselves onto the hairs. Unfortunately, the dog was discovered by a guard, who chopped off eight out of its nine tails; but, the dog was able run away. The seeds stuck on the remaining tail of the dog brought great benefits to mankind. For this reason, dogs are kept at home and fed with rice. Today, dogs have only one tail, but the grains have nine spikes reminding people that dogs formerly had nine tails.

Another story concerning the origins of the Zhuang relates that human beings were few in ancient times. A Carpenter God came to a large forest and made men and women from wood; they were able to talk and move, like real people. There were three groups: the "wooden" Yao were located beside a stream; the "wooden" Zhuang, halfway up the hill; and the "wooden" Miao, on the hilltop. The Carpenter God's wife did the cooking and his son took the meal to his father in the forest. One day, the Carpenter God wanted to know which of the two sexes was cleverer. When the son called his father to lunch in the forest, the wooden men all responded. The child could not tell who his father was. When he went back, his mother taught him to find the man with sweat on his nose due to manual labor. The child returned to the forest and found his father easily without calling. When the Carpenter God realized that his wife had outwitted him, he made a wooden stick of even thickness for his wife, which was delivered by the child. His wife had to guess which end was the original root and which was the tip. His wife hung the stick by the middle. The weighty end was marked as the root. The Carpenter God was astonished by her wisdom and became so angry that he burned the wooden people on the spot. The wooden Yao were charred and became black. That is why the Yao wear black clothes. The wooden Zhuang halfway up the hill were not seriously burnt, so they wear blue clothes. The wooden Miao were caught unawares by the fire and fled in turmoil. Some of them escaped; some had burns over different parts of the body. Therefore, there are Flowery Miao, White Miao, and Black Miao today.

⁵RELIGION

The Zhuang are polytheistic. They worship their ancestors and revere big stones, large trees, snakes, birds, and the earth. There are part-time shamans (*daogong*) in the rural areas, frequently solicited by Zhuang people to chase ghosts away. The Zhuang offer sacrifices to the Mountain God, the Water God, the Kitchen God, the Sun God, and so on. For example, they offer glutinous rice and colored boiled eggs to the Crop God beside the fields prior to sowing grain. The third day of lunar March (Western calendar, between March 26 and April 24) is regarded as the birthday of Shennong (Divine Farmer), who is said to have invented agriculture; on that occasion, pigs are butchered for sacrificial offerings. The second day of lunar June (Western calendar, between June 23 and July 23) is the birthday of the great King Muyi, who saved the Zhuang from disasters; not only do they offer a sacrifice every year, but they also hold a grand ceremony in his honor every six years. The numerous sacrifices offered by the Zhuang all aim at receiving the blessings of the gods: well-being of the family, healthy livestock, and abundant crops. The Zhuang were influenced by organized Buddhism and Taoism since the Tang Dynasty (618–907). Since the beginning of this century, a small number have adopted Christian beliefs and practices.

⁶MAJOR HOLIDAYS

There are dozens of holidays among the Zhuang, all according to the lunar calendar. On the Lunar New Year's Eve (Western calendar, between January 21 and February 20), the whole family reunites at the dinner table. They talk cheerfully all night long. On the first day of the New Year, a lot of things will be done. They all dress up. Firecrackers are kindled. The women draw water from the wells or rivers and then boil it with brown sugar, bamboo leaves, shallot, and ginger to concoct a beverage for the family. In some areas, the sacrificial rites to the ancestors are performed in the morning. Then, the children should study seriously for a while, for the day is believed to be propitious for rapid advance in their studies. The lady of the house will place a little fertilizer and seeds in the field and drop some chicken feathers on the village road to beckon a flourishing year for the crops and the livestock. In other areas, the Zhuang offer a sacrifice in a tiny temple housing the Village God. Wooden swords and spears included among the offerings are expected to be used by the god to protect the village. In small towns, sporting and recreational events, such as "tossing an embroidered ball" (a kind of ball game for children), Lion Dance, Dragon Dance, and Zhuang drama will be held. The same festive activities will be repeated on January 30 (lunar calendar; Western calendar, between February 19 and March 18), the "Late New Year." It is said that a long time ago the local people had to fight against an invading army on a lunar New Year and during the whole month of January, obtaining victory only on January 30.

The eighth of April (lunar calendar; Western calendar, between May 2 and May 30) is the birthday of Buffalo God. People clean the pen, wash and brush the buffalo at the riverside, feed it with multicolored glutinous rice, and give it a day off.

⁷RITES OF PASSAGE

Huapo (flower woman) is the goddess of reproduction and also the patron saint of babies. Right after childbirth, a holy tablet dedicated to Huapo and a bouquet of wild flowers are placed by the wall along the bedside. It is said that all babies are flowers cultivated by the goddess. If the baby falls ill, the mother makes offerings to Huapo and abundantly waters the wild flowers, which symbolize her baby.

The Zhuang's funerary rites are unique. The coffin is made of thin plank and buried about 2 ft from the surface to hasten the decaying of the corpse. Three to five years later (never even-numbered years), the coffin is opened, the bones are cleansed of any remnants of soft tissue; the skeleton is then placed in a sitting posture inside an earthen jar, sprinkled with cinnabar. The name of the deceased and his or her dates of birth and death are written on the inside of the lid, and the sealed jar is finally buried in the clan graveyard.

⁸INTERPERSONAL RELATIONS

A straw hat hung on a door is a warning that there is a lying-in woman inside and that no entrance is allowed unless authorized. The guest should pay attention to this warning. This custom is quite common among the national minorities.

Zhuang youngsters enjoy full freedom in dating. Antiphonal singing parties are a popular way to choose partners of the opposite sex; they are held on all festivals. The lyrics include astronomy, geography, history, social life, productive labor, ethics, and, of course, passions. Someone adept in antiphonal singing is much admired and will be the "target" of the opposite sex.

[9] LIVING CONDITIONS

Most of the Zhuang houses are now similar to those of the local Chinese. Some areas, however, still retain traditional "stilt dwelling" housing. The house is built on stilts, keeping the family above the damp earth and away from animals. This type of house is not much different from that of the ancient Baiyue more than 1,000 years ago. It is well adapted to the climate and environment of south China. In Guangxi the house and stilts are made of bamboo and wood. The size of the house may vary from three to seven rooms. Livestock and stored goods are placed on the ground floor.

A number of infectious diseases prevalent in bygone days, including schistosomiasis (a parasitic disease), are now completely eradicated.

[10] FAMILY LIFE

The Zhuang family is patrilineal, monogamous, and relatively small in size. The women's position is somewhat lower than that of men. The custom of "not living in the husband's house" has been prevalent since remote antiquity. Right after the wedding ceremony, the bride, accompanied by her bridesmaids, goes back to her own family. She will only return to her husband during festivals; in the busy agricultural seasons, she will only visit her husband when invited by him. If she gets pregnant, she will then move to her husband's house; otherwise, she will move three to five years after the wedding.

Among the Zhuang living in compact communities in north Guangdong, the bride and her bridesmaids all wear black. They hold black umbrellas while accompanying the bride from her home family to her husband's house. The dresses are prepared by the bridegroom's side and delivered to the bride's family by the matchmaker. According to tradition black costumes are joyous and auspicious.

[11] CLOTHING

Nowadays, the Zhuang's clothes are, by and large, the same as those of the local Chinese. In some rural areas, however, they preserve ancient traditions. For example, in northwest Guangxi, the aged women still wear a collarless, trimmed garment with buttons down the left side and trimmed loose trousers, with an embroidered apron on their waist. Some of them wear wax-printed straight skirts in dark navy, with embroidered shoes and an embroidered kerchief wrapped around the head. Zhuang peasants put on dark navy blue cloth pants and upper garments.

Zhuang women are fond of wearing gold or silver hair clasps, earrings, bracelets, and necklaces. Most of them have abandoned the tradition of tattooing their faces.

[12] FOOD

The staple foods of the Zhuang are rice and corn. They like salted and sour dishes. Raw fish fillets are one of their delicacies. On festivals, they make various dishes from glutinous rice, such as cakes, rice-flour noodles, and pyramid-shaped dumplings wrapped in bamboo or reed leaves. Women like to chew areca, especially those in Longzhou near the Vietnam border. In some districts, they do not eat beef because they follow the old custom handed down from their ancestors, who regarded the buffalo as their savior.

[13] EDUCATION

About 95% of school-age children are registered in state schools. There are 17 universities in Guangxi. One-quarter of the college students are from the national minorities, the vast majority being from the Zhuang people. The cultural and educational level of the Zhuang is higher than the average for the national minorities but still lower than the average for China as a whole.

[14] CULTURAL HERITAGE

A large part of Zhuang popular culture revolves around singing. For instance, singing is the main activity during festivals. Singing parties are organized on different scales. A grand gathering during a major festival may attract more than 10,000 participants. They form small groups of boys and girls within the larger gathering and engage in antiphonal singing. Song, thus, has a very important social function. Dance is also important but is performed independently from singing. There are a variety of dances, such as the Bronze Drum Dance, the Tea-Leaves Collecting Dance, the Shoulder Pole Dance, the Buffalo Dance, and so on.

Studies of the Zhuang nationality have developed rapidly since the 1960s. The researchers, mainly Zhuang, collected 1,000 ancient Zhuang books concerning ancient writings, literature, art, history, and religions. A dictionary of ancient Zhuang language, an epic relating the origin of the Zhuang, a collection of their folk songs and love songs, a general history of the Zhuang, an encyclopedia on the Zhuang, and books concerning Zhuang culture were published in the past decade.

[15] WORK

The Zhuang have traditionally engaged in agriculture and in forestry. The land is fertile and the climate propitious both for wet crops and dry crops. Besides the labor-intensive cultivation of rice and other grains, the Zhuang of Guangxi produce commercial quantities of sugarcane, banana, longan, litchi, pineapple, shaddock, and mango. The coastal area they inhabit abounds in quality pearls.

[16] SPORTS

The Zhuang are renowned as outstanding athletes in different fields of gymnastics. Intensive training for young boys and girls is provided on a voluntary basis after school hours.

"Tossing the embroidered ball" is a traditional game. The ball is a cloth bag padded with rice husks or cottonseed, about 1 lb in weight and variable in size. A colored string is attached to it. In a match, youngsters are divided into two teams of opposing sex. They are separated by a paling. The method of tossing the ball is to hold the string in one hand, swing the ball in circles, then release it; it resembles the hammer throw. The opposite side should catch the ball; if not, one member of the opposite team is captured. Whenever the commander (usually the last team member) is captured, the game is over.

[17] ENTERTAINMENT AND RECREATION

Television has become a very popular pastime for the urban Zhuang. Most of the small towns are now provided with television broadcasting stations; rural families with a television set are thus able to watch a wide variety of television programs at home. Guangxi set up its own film studio decades ago.

There are many recreational festivals during the year. A grand fair is held annually in the spring; in addition to the interflow of commodities, a number of recreational activities are held. Commemorative feasts for the ancestors are celebrated twice a year, in spring and autumn; they now contain many recreational elements, such as singing parties, dancing performances, and Zhuang opera.

18 FOLK ART, CRAFTS, AND HOBBIES

The Zhuang are internationally famous for the antiquity and beauty of their bronze drums. The size of the drums varies considerably. The drums are hollow and bottomless with a flat surface. Artistic figures and designs decorate the drums. They were used as percussion instruments, both in religious and governmental rituals. They became a sign of power and wealth. They are considered as a national treasure by the Zhuang.

Brocade is also a well-known traditional art form of the Zhuang. The brocade is woven with cotton and multicolored silk to form beautiful, sophisticated, and durable designs. Wall hangings, table cloth, cushions, and curtains made of Zhuang brocade are highly appreciated both in China and abroad. Zhuang girls are particularly fond of brocaded knapsacks.

19 SOCIAL PROBLEMS

Although Guangxi is an area of fertile soil, warm climate and abundant rainfall, the Zhuang are far from wealthy. The rich mineral resources, coastal areas, and tourism potential of Guangxi are not yet fully tapped. For this reason, large numbers of surplus rural labor of the Zhuang and other nationalities move from Guangxi to its neighboring province Guangdong, which is more developed economically. This population movement poses serious problems both to Guangdong and to Guangxi.

20 GENDER ISSUES

The Chinese constitution states that women have equal rights with men in all areas of life, and most legislation is gender neutral. However, Zhuang women's status is regarded as somewhat lower than that of Zhuang men. A wife does not live with her husband until the couple has been married at least three years. For the first three years of marriage, the wife only visits the husband when he invites her. However, if the wife becomes pregnant, she moves into her husband's house.

China has strict family planning laws, and it is illegal for women to marry before 20 years of age, 22 for men, and it is illegal for single women to give birth. The Family Planning Bureau can require women to take periodic pregnancy tests, and enforce laws that often leave women with no real options other than abortion or sterilization. Though minority populations were previously exempt from family planning regulations, policy has changed in recent years to limit minority population growth. Today, urban minority couples may have two children while rural couples may have three or four.

Prostitution and the sex trade is a significant problem in China involving between 1.7 and five million women. It involved organized crime, businessmen, the police and government workers, so prosecution against prostitution has limited success. In 2002, the nation removed homosexuality from its official list of mental illnesses, and though it is still a taboo topic, homosexuality is increasingly accepted, especially in large, international cities.

21 BIBLIOGRAPHY

Chiao, Chien, Nicholas Tapp, and Kam-yin Ho, ed. "Special Issue on Ethnic Groups in China." *New Asia Bulletin* no 8 (1989).

Dreyer, June Teufel. *China's Forty Millions.* Cambridge: Harvard University Press, 1976.

Eberhard, Wolfram. *China's Minorities: Yesterday and Today.* Belmont: Wadsworth Publishing Company, 1982.

Heberer, Thomas. *China and Its National Minorities: Autonomy or Assimilation?* Armonk, NY: M. E. Sharpe, 1989.

Lebar, Frank, et al. *Ethnic Groups of Mainland Southeast Asia.* New Haven: Human Relations Area Files Press, 1964.

Lemoine, Jacques. "Les Chouang." In *Ethnologie régionale II* (Encyclopédie de la Pléiade). Paris: Gallimard, 1978.

Ma Yin, ed. *China's Minority Nationalities.* Beijing: Foreign Languages Press, 1989.

Miller, Lucien, ed. *South of the Clouds: Tales from Yunnan.* Seattle: University of Washington Press, 1994.

Ramsey, S. Robert. *The Languages of China.* Princeton: Princeton University Press, 1987.

Wiens, Harold J. *Han Chinese Expansion in South China.* New Haven: The Shoestring Press, 1967.

—by C. Le Blanc

GLOSSARY

a capella: singing without musical accompaniment.

aboriginal: the first inhabitants of a country. A species of animals or plants which originated within a given area.

acupuncture: ancient practice of treating disease or relieving pain by inserting needles into pressure points on the body. The Chinese are associated with this medical treatment.

adobe: a clay from which bricks are made for use in making houses.

adult literacy: the capacity of adults to read and write.

agglutinative tongue: a language in which the suffixes and prefixes to words retain a certain independence of one another and of the stem to which they are added. Turkish is an example of an agglutinative tongue.

agrarian economy: an economy where agriculture is the dominant form of economic activity.

active volcano: a large rock mass formed by the expulsion of molten rock, or lava, which periodically erupts.

acute accent: a mark (') used to denote accentual stress of a single sound.

agglutinative tongue: a language in which the suffixes and prefixes to words retain a certain independence of one another and of the stem to which they are added. Turkish is an example of an agglutinative tongue.

agrarian economy: an economy where agriculture is the dominant form of economic activity.

agrarian society: a society where agriculture dominates the day-to-day activities of the population.

All Saints' Day: a Christian holiday on 1 November (a public holiday in many countries). Saints and martyrs who have no special festival are commemorated. In the Middle Ages, it was known as All Hallows' Day; the evening of the previous day, October 31, was called All Hallow Even, from which the secular holiday Halloween is derived.

All Souls' Day: a Christian holiday. This day, 2 November, is dedicated to prayer for the repose of the souls of the dead.

allies: groups or persons who are united in a common purpose. Typically used to describe nations that have joined together to fight a common enemy in war.

Altaic language family: a family of languages spoken by people in portions of northern and eastern Europe, and nearly the whole of northern and central Asia, together with some other regions, and divided into five branches, the Ugrian or Finno-Hungarian, Samoyed, Turkish, Mongolian, and Tungus.

altoplano: refers to the high plains of South American mountain ranges on the Pacific coast.

Amerindian: a contraction of the two words, American Indian. It describes native peoples of North, South, or Central America.

Amerindian language group: the language groups of the American Indians.

Amish: Anabaptist Protestants originally from Germany. Settled in Pennsylvania and the American Midwest.

Anabaptist: Christian sect that was founded in Switzerland during the 16th century. Rejected infant baptism as invalid.

ancestor worship: the worship of one's ancestors.

Anglican: pertaining to or connected with the Church of England.

animism: the belief that natural objects and phenomena have souls or innate spiritual powers.

anthropologist: one who studies the characteristics, customs, and development of mankind.

anti-miscegenation laws: prohibition of marriage or sexual relations between men and women of different races.

anti-Semitism: agitation, persecution, or discrimination (physical, emotional, economic, political, or otherwise) directed against the Jews.

apartheid: the past governmental policy in the Republic of South Africa of separating the races in society.

appliqué: a trimming made from one cloth and sewn onto another cloth.

aquaculture: the culture or "farming" of aquatic plants or animals.

arable land: land which can be cultivated by plowing, as distinguished from grassland, woodland, common pasture, and wasteland.

archipelago: any body of water having many islands, or the islands themselves collectively.

arctic climate: cold, frigid weather similar to that experienced at or near the North Pole.

arid: dry; without moisture; parched with heat.

aristocracy: a small minority that controls the government of a nation, typically on the basis of inherited wealth. Political power is restricted to its members. Also may referred to any privileged elite of a country.

artifacts: objects or tools that date back to an ancient period of human history.

Ash Wednesday: a Christian holiday. The first day of Lent, observed 46 days before Easter, is so called from the practice of placing ashes on the forehead of the worshipper as a sign of penitence. In the Roman Catholic Church, these ashes are obtained from burning palm branches used in the previous year's Palm Sunday observation. (Palm Sunday commemorates the entry of Jesus into Jerusalem a week before Easter Sunday, and it begins Holy Week.) On Ash Wednesday, the ashes are placed on the forehead of the communicant during Mass. The recipient is told, "Remember that you are dust, and unto dust you shall return" or "Turn away from sin and be faithful to the Gospel."

Ashura: a Muslim holiday. This fast day was instituted by Muhammad as the equivalent of the Jewish Yom Kippur but later became voluntary when Ramadan replaced it as a holiday of penance. It also commemorates Noah's leaving the ark on Mt. Ararat after the waters of the Great Flood had subsided. In Iran, the martyrdom of Husayn, grandson of Muhammad, is commemorated with passion plays on this day.

assembly: in government, a body of legislators that meets together regularly.

Assumption: a Christian holiday. This holiday, observed on 15 August in many countries, celebrates the Roman Catholic and Eastern Orthodox dogma that, following Mary's death, her body was taken into heaven and reunited with her soul.

atheist: a person who denies the existence of God, or of a supreme intelligent being.

atherosclerosis: a disease of the arteries. Characterized by blockages that prevent blood flow from the heart to the brain and other parts of the body.

atoll: a coral island, consisting of a strip or ring of coral surrounding a central lagoon. Such islands are common in the Pacific Ocean and are often very picturesque.

aurora borealis: the northern lights, consisting of bands of light across the night sky seen in northern geographical locations.

Australoid: pertains to the type of aborigines of Australia.

Austronesian language: a family of languages which includes Indonesian, Melanesian, Polynesian, and Micronesian sub-families.

B

Babushka: a head scarf worn by women.

Baltic States: the three formerly communist countries of Estonia, Latvia, and Lithuania that border on the Baltic Sea.

Bantu language group: a name applied to the south African family of tongues. The most marked peculiarity of these languages is their prevailing use of prefixes instead of suffixes in derivation and inflection. Some employ clicks and clucks as alphabetic elements.

baptism: any ceremonial bathing intended as a sign of purification, dedication, etc. Baptisms are performed by immersion of the person in water, or by sprinkling the water on the person.

Baptist: a member of a Protestant denomination which practices adult baptism by immersion.

barren land: unproductive land, partly or entirely treeless.

barter: Trade in which merchandise is exchanged directly for other merchandise or services without use of money.

bilingual: able to speak two languages. Also used to describe anything that contains or is expressed in two languages, such as directions written in both English and Spanish.

boat people: a term used to describe individuals (refugees) who attempt to flee their country by boat.

Bolshevik Revolution: pertaining to the Russian revolution of 1917. Russian communists overthrew Tsar Nicholas II and ended the feudal Russian empire.

borscht: cold beet soup, topped with sour cream.

Brahman: a member of the sacred caste among the Hindus. There are many subdivisions of the caste, often remaining in isolation from one another.

bratwurst: seasoned fresh German sausage. Made from pork or veal.

bride price: the price paid to the family of the bride by the young man who seeks to marry her.

bride wealth: the money or property or livestock a bride brings to her marriage. *See* **dowry.**

Buddhism: the religious system common in India and eastern Asia. Founded by and based upon the teachings of Gautama Buddha, Buddhism asserts that suffering is an inescapable part of life. Deliverance can only be achieved through the practice of charity, temperance, justice, honesty, and truth.

bureaucracy: a system of government which is characterized by division into bureaus of administration with their own divisional heads. Also refers to the institutional inflexibility and red tape of such a system.

bush country: a large area of land which is wild with low, bushlike vegetation.

Byzantine Empire: an empire centered in the city of Byzantium, now Istanbul in present-day Turkey.

C

Cajun: name given to Canadians who emigrated to Louisiana from Acadia, the old name for Nova Scotia. Contraction of the name Accadian.

Calvinist: a follower of the theological system of John Calvin.

Candlemas: a Christian holiday. A national holiday on 2 February in Liechtenstein, this observation is now called the Presentation of the Lord, commemorating the presentation of the infant Jesus in the Temple at Jerusalem. Before a 1969 Vatican reform, it commemorated the Purification of Mary 40 days after giving birth to a male child in accordance with a Jewish practice of the time.

capital punishment: the ultimate act of punishment for a crime; the death penalty.

capitalism: an economic system in which goods and services and the means to produce and sell them are privately owned, and prices and wages are determined by market forces.

cash crop: a crop that is grown to be sold, rather than kept for private use.

caste system: one of the artificial divisions or social classes into which the Hindus are rigidly separated according to the religious law of Brahmanism. The privileges and disabilities of a caste are passed on to each succeeding generation.

Caucasian: the "white" race of human beings, as determined by genealogy and physical features.

Caucasoid: belonging to the racial group characterized by light skin pigmentation. Commonly called the "white race," although it can refer to peoples of darker skin color.

celibate: a person who voluntarily abstains from marriage. In some religious practices, the person will often take a vow of abstention from sexual intercourse as well.

censorship: the practice of withholding certain items of news that may cast a country in an unfavorable light or give away secrets to the enemy.

census: an official counting of the inhabitants of a state or country with details of sex and age, family, occupation, possessions, etc.

Central Powers: in World War I, Germany and Austria-Hungary, and their allies, Turkey and Bulgaria.

centrally planned economy: an economic system in which all aspects are supervised and regulated by the government.

cerebrovascular: pertains to the brain and the blood vessels leading to and from the brain.

chancellery: the office of an embassy or consulate.

chaperone: an older married person, usually female, who supervises the activities of young, unmarried couples.

chattel: refers to the movable personal property of an individual or group. It cannot refer to real estate or buildings.

cholera: an acute infectious disease characterized by severe diarrhea, vomiting, and often, death.

Christianity: the religion founded by Jesus Christ.

Christmas: a Christian holiday. The annual commemoration of the nativity of Jesus is held on 25 December. A midnight Mass ushers in this joyous celebration in many Roman

Catholic churches. The custom of distributing gifts to children on Christmas Eve derives from a Dutch custom originally observed on the evening before St. Nicholas' Day (6 December). The day after Christmas—often called Boxing Day, for the boxed gifts customarily given—is a public holiday in many countries.

Church of England: the national and established church in England. The Church of England claims continuity with the branch of the Catholic Church which existed in England before the Reformation. Under Henry VIII, the spiritual supremacy and jurisdiction of the Pope were abolished, and the sovereign was declared head of the church.

chaplet: a wreath or garland of flowers placed on a woman's head.

cistern: a natural or artificial receptacle or reservoir for holding water or other fluids.

city-state: an independent state consisting of a city and its surrounding territory.

civil law: the law developed by a nation or state for the conduct of daily life of its own people.

civil rights: the privileges of all individuals to be treated as equals under the laws of their country; specifically, the rights given by certain amendments to the U.S. Constitution.

civil unrest: the feeling of uneasiness due to an unstable political climate or actions taken as a result of it.

civil war: a war between groups of citizens of the same country who have different opinions or agendas. The Civil War of the United States was the conflict between the states of the North and South from 1861 to 1865.

coca: a shrub native to South America, the leaves of which produce alkaloids which are used in the production of cocaine.

cohabitation: living together as husband and wife without being legally married.

cold war: refers to conflict over ideological differences that is carried on by words and diplomatic actions, not by military action. The term is usually used to refer to the tension that existed between the United States and the USSR from the 1950s until the breakup of the USSR in 1991.

collard greens: a hearty, leafy green vegetable. Popular part of southern American and West Indian cuisine.

collective farm: a large farm formed from many small farms and supervised by the government; usually found in communist countries.

collective farming: the system of farming on a collective where all workers share in the income of the farm.

colloquial: belonging to the language of common or familiar conversation, or ordinary, everyday speech; often especially applied to common words and phrases which are not used in formal speech.

colonial period: in the United States, the period of time when the original thirteen colonies were being formed.

colonist: any member of a colony or one who helps settle a new colony.

colony: a group of people who settle in a new area far from their original country, but still under the jurisdiction of that country. Also refers to the newly settled area itself.

commerce: the trading of goods (buying and selling), especially on a large scale, between cities, states, and countries.

commodity: any items, such as goods or services, that are bought or sold, or agricultural products that are traded or marketed.

common law: a legal system based on custom and legal precedent. The basic system of law of the United States.

common law spouse: a husband or wife in a marriage that, although not legally formalized through a religious or state-sanctioned ceremony, is legally acknowledged based on the agreement of the two people to consider themselves married.

communicable disease: referring to infectious or contagious diseases.

communion: 1. The act of partaking of the sacrament of the Eucharist; the celebration of the Lord's Supper. 2. A body of Christians who have one common faith, but not necessarily ecclesiastical union; a religious denomination. 3. Union in religious worship, or in doctrine and discipline.

communism: a form of government whose system requires common ownership of property for the use of all citizens. All profits are to be equally distributed and prices on goods and services are usually set by the state. Also, communism refers directly to the official doctrine of the former USSR.

compulsory education: the mandatory requirement for children to attend school until they have reached a certain age or grade level.

condolence: expression of sympathy.

Condomblé: American name for the Yoruba pantheon of 401 gods and goddesses.

Confucianism: the ethical system taught by the Chinese philosopher Confucius. It was enlarged upon by his contemporary Mencius so that political systems would be tested with the same ethical standards. (*See* **Taoism**)

constitution: the written laws and basic rights of citizens of a country or members of an organized group.

consumer goods: items that are bought to satisfy personal needs or wants of individuals.

Coptic Christians: members of the Coptic Church of Egypt, formerly of Ethiopia.

Corpus Christi: a Christian holiday. This holiday in honor of the Eucharist is observed on the Thursday or Sunday after Trinity Sunday, which is the Sunday after Pentecost. In the Roman Catholic and Eastern Orthodox Churches, the Eucharist is a sacrament in which the consecrated bread and wine become the body and blood of Jesus Christ, a belief stemming from New Testament accounts of the Last Supper.

corrugated steel: galvanized metal with furrows that give added strength. This metal is often used as roofing materials on houses in tropical countries because of its strength.

coup d'état: a sudden, violent overthrow of a government or its leader.

covert action: secret, concealed activities carried out without public knowledge.

cricket (sport): a game played by two teams with a ball and bat, with two wickets being defended by a batsman.

criminal law: the branch of law that deals primarily with crimes and their punishments.

crown colony: a colony established by a commonwealth over which the monarch has some control, as in colonies established by the British Commonwealth.

Crowning of Our Lady of Altagracia: a Christian holiday in honor of Mary, this day is celebrated in the Dominican Republic on 15 August with a pilgrimage to her shrine. (Altagracia Day, 21 January, is also a holiday in the Dominican Republic.)

Crusades: military expeditions by European Christian armies in the 11th, 12th, and 13th centuries to win land controlled by the Muslims in the Middle East.

cuisine: a particular style of preparing food, especially when referring to the cooking of a particular country or ethnic group.

cultivable land: land that can be prepared for the production of crops.

cursive script: a style of writing in which the letters are joined together in a flowing manner.

Cushitic language group: a group of Hamitic languages which are spoken in Ethiopia and other areas of eastern Africa.

cyclone: any atmospheric movement, general or local, in which the wind blows spirally around and in towards a center. In the northern hemisphere, the cyclonic movement is usually counter-clockwise, and in the southern hemisphere, it is clockwise.

Cyrillic alphabet: an alphabet adopted by the Slavic people and invented by Cyril and Methodius in the 9th century as an alphabet that was easier for the copyist to write. The Russian alphabet is a slight modification of it.

D

Day of Our Lady of Mercy (Las Mercedes): a Christian holiday in honor of Mary, this observance on 24 September is a holiday in the Dominican Republic.

Day of Santa Rosa of Lima: a Christian holiday. The feast day in honor of the first native-born saint of the New World, declared patron saint of South America by Pope Clement X in 1671, is 23 August, but in Peru, she is commemorated by a national holiday on 30 August.

Day of St. Peter and St. Paul: a Christian holiday. This observance, on 29 June, commemorates the martyrdom of the two apostles traditionally believed to have been executed in Rome on the same day (c. AD 67) during the persecution of Christians ordered by Emperor Nero.

deforestation: the removal of a forest ecosystem.

deity: a being with the attributes, nature, and essence of a god; a divinity.

delta: triangular-shaped deposits of soil formed at the mouths of large rivers.

democracy: a form of government in which the power lies in the hands of the people, who can govern directly, or indirectly by electing representatives.

demography: that department of anthropology which relates to vital and social statistics and their application to the comparative study of races and nations.

desegregation: the act of removing restrictions on people of a particular race that keep them separate from other groups, socially, economically, and, sometimes, physically.

détente: the official lessening of tension between countries in conflict.

developed countries: countries which have a high standard of living and a well-developed industrial base.

diacritics: as in diacritical marks, a dot, line, or other mark added or put adjacent to a letter or sign in order to give it a different sound or to indicate some particular accent, tone, stress, or emphasis. An example of diacritical marks would be those used in dictionaries to aid in pronunciation of words.

dialect: One of a number of related forms of speech regarded as descending from a common origin. The speech pattern of a locality or social class as distinguished from the generally accepted literary language.

dictatorship: a form of government in which all the power is retained by an absolute leader or tyrant. There are no rights granted to the people to elect their own representatives.

direct descendant: the offspring in an unbroken line of ancestors.

divine origin: having originated directly, or by direct descendant, from a divine being.

dogma: a principle, maxim, or tenet held as being firmly established.

domicile: a place of residence of an individual or family; a place of habitual abode.

dowry: the sum of the property or money that a bride brings to her groom at their marriage.

druid: a member of a Celtic religion practiced in ancient Britain, Ireland, and France.

Druze: a member of a religious sect of Syria, living chiefly in the mountain regions of Lebanon.

ducal: Referring to a duke or a dukedom.

dysentery: painful inflammation of the large intestine.

E

Easter: the chief Christian holiday is Easter, the annual celebration of the resurrection of Jesus Christ. Like Passover, the Jewish feast from which it is derived, the date of observation is linked to the phases of the moon. Since the Christian calendar is a solar one rather than a lunar one, the date of Easter changes from year to year. Easter is celebrated on the first Sunday after the first full moon following the spring equinox; in the Gregorian calendar, it can occur as early as 22 March or as late as 25 April. The Easter date determines the date of many other Roman Catholic holidays, such as Ash Wednesday, Ascension, and Pentecost.

Easter Monday: a Christian holiday. The day after Easter is a public holiday in many countries.

empire: a group of territories ruled by one sovereign, or supreme ruler.

Epiphany of Our Lord: a Christian holiday. Traditionally observed on 6 January but now observable on the Sunday falling between 2 January and 7 January, this feast commemorates the adoration of the Magi, who journeyed to the place of Jesus' birth. In the Orthodox churches, however, it is the feast celebrating Jesus' baptism.

episcopal: belonging to or vested in bishops or prelates; characteristic of or pertaining to a bishop or bishops.

equestrian culture: a culture that depends on horses for its livelihood. Mastery of the horse is an essential part of the culture's identity.

escarpment: a steep cliff formed from a geological fault or erosion.

ethnographic: referring to the division of anthropology which studies primitive cultures.

ethnolinguistic group: a classification of related languages based on common ethnic origin.

exodus: the departure or migration of a large body of people or animals from one country or region to another.

extinction: dying out of a species of animals or a culture of people.

F

fauna: referring to species of animals found in a specific region.

Feast of Our Lady of Angels: a Christian holiday. This feast, on 2 August, is celebrated as a national holiday in Costa Rica in honor of the Virgin Mary. Pilgrimage is made to the basilica in Cartago, which houses a black stone statue of the Virgin.

fetishism: the practice of worshipping a material object which one believes has mysterious powers residing in it or is the representation of a deity to which worship may be paid and from which supernatural aid is expected.

feudal society: In medieval times, an economic and social structure in which persons could hold land given to them by a lord (nobleman) in return for service to that lord.

Finno-Ugric language group: a subfamily of languages spoken in northeastern Europe, including Finnish, Hungarian (Ugric, Magyar), Estonian, Lapp, and others.

flora: referring to native plant life in a specific region.

folk religion: a religion with origins and traditions among the common people of a nation or region; relevant to their particular lifestyle.

folk tale: an oral story that is passed from generation to generation. Folktales are cultural records of the history and progress of different ethnic groups.

free-market economy: an economic system that relies on the market, as opposed to government planners, to set the prices for wages and products.

fundamentalist: a person who holds religious beliefs based on the complete acceptance of the words of the Bible or other holy scripture as the truth. For instance, a fundamentalist would believe the story of creation exactly as it is told in the Bible and would reject the idea of evolution.

G

gastroenteritis: inflammation of the stomach and small intestines.

geometric pattern: a design of circles, triangles, or lines on cloth.

geriatrics: the study and treatment of diseases of old age.

Germanic language group: a large branch of the Indo-European family of languages including German itself, the Scandinavian languages, Dutch, Yiddish, Modern English, Modern Scottish, Afrikaans and others. The group also includes extinct languages such as Gothic, Old High German, Old Saxon, Old English, Middle English and the like.

glottal stop: a sound formed in speech by a brief but complete closure of the glottis, the opening between the vocal cords. It is a typical sound in certain British dialects.

godparent: a male or female adult who is asked by the parents of a newborn child to assume responsibility for the care and rearing of the child in the event of the death of the parents. Godparents sometimes contribute school tuition, gifts on birthdays and holidays, as well as take an active part in the child's life.

Good Friday: a Christian holiday. The day after Holy Thursday, it is devoted to remembrance of the crucifixion of Jesus and is given to penance and prayer.

Greek Catholic: a person who is a member of an Orthodox Eastern Church.

Greek Orthodox: the official church of Greece, a self-governing branch of the Orthodox Eastern Church.

H

haiku: a form of Japanese poetry, consisting of three lines. Each line has a specific measurement of syllables.

Hanukkah: a Jewish holiday. The Festival of Lights, corresponding roughly to the winter solstice, is celebrated over an eight-day period beginning on 25 Kislev, the third month. Also known as the Feast of Dedication and Feast of the Maccabees, Hanukkah commemorates the rededication of the Temple at Jerusalem in 164 BC. According to tradition, the one ritually pure container of olive oil, sufficient to illuminate the Temple for one day, miraculously burned for eight days, until new oil could be prepared. A feature of the Hanukkah celebration is the lighting in each Jewish home of an eight-branched candelabrum, the menorah. This festival, though not a public holiday in Israel, is widely observed with the lighting of giant menorahs in public places.

harem: in a Muslim household, refers to the women (wives, concubines, and servants in ancient times) who live there and also to the area of the home they live in.

harmattan: an intensely dry, dusty wind felt along the coast of Africa between Cape Verde and Cape Lopez. It prevails at intervals during the months of December, January, and February.

Hinduism: the religion professed by a large part of the inhabitants of India. It is a development of the ancient Brahmanism, influenced by Buddhistic and other elements. Its forms are varied and numerous.

Holi: a Hindu holiday. A festival lasting 3 to 10 days, Holi closes the old year with processions and merriment. It terminates on the full moon of Phalguna, the last month, corresponding to February or March.

Holocaust: the mass slaughter of European civilians, the vast majority Jews, by the Nazis during World War II.

Holy (Maundy) Thursday: a Christian holiday. The Thursday preceding Easter commemorates the Last Supper, the betrayal of Jesus by Judas Iscariot, and the arrest and arraignment of Jesus. In Rome, the pope customarily performs a ceremony in remembrance of Jesus' washing of his apostles' feet (John 13:5–20).

Holy Roman Empire: a kingdom consisting of a loose union of German and Italian territories that existed from around the ninth century until 1806.

Holy Saturday: a Christian holiday. This day commemorates the time during which Jesus was buried and, like Good Friday, is given to solemn prayer.

homeland: a region or area set aside to be a state for a people of a particular national, cultural, or racial origin.

homogeneous: of the same kind or nature, often used in reference to a whole.

homophonic: music that has a single part with no harmonies.

Horn of Africa: the Horn of Africa comprises Djibouti, Eritrea, Ethiopia, Somalia, and Sudan.

human rights issues: any matters involving people's basic rights which are in question or thought to be abused.

humanist: a person who centers on human needs and values, and stresses dignity of the individual.

hydrology: the science of dealing with the earth's waters and their distribution above and below ground.

I

Id al-Adha: a Muslim holiday. The Great Festival, or Sacrificial Feast, celebrates the end of the special pilgrimage season, or Hajj, to Mecca and Medina, an obligation for Muslims once in their lifetime if physically and economically feasible. The slaughter of animals pays tribute to Abraham's obedience to God in offering his son to the Lord for sacrifice; a portion of the meat is supposed to be donated to the poor. The feast begins on 10 Dhu'l-Hijja and continues to 13 Dhu'l-Hijja (14 Dhu'l-Hijja in a leap year). In Malaysia and Singapore, this festival is celebrated as Hari Raya Haji; in Indonesia, Lebaran Haji; in Turkey, Kurban Bayrami.

Id al-Fitr: a Muslim holiday. The Little Festival, or Breaking-Fast-Festival, which begins just after Ramadan, on 1 Shawwal, the 10th month, is the occasion for three or four days of feasting. In Malaysia and Singapore, this festival is called Hari Raya Puasa; in Turkey, Seker Bayrami.

Iemanja: Brazilian name for Yoruba river goddess, Yemoja. Represented as a mermaid.

Immaculate Conception: a Christian holiday. This day, 8 December, celebrates the Roman Catholic dogma asserting that Mary's conception, as the future mother of God, was uniquely free from original sin. In Paraguay, it is observed as the Day of Our Lady of Caacupé.

incursion: a sudden or brief invasion or raid.

indigenous: born or originating in a particular place or country; native to a particular region or area.

indigent: person without any means of economic support.

indigo: a blue dye that is extracted from plants.

Indo-Aryan language group: the group that includes the languages of India; within a branch of the Indo-European language family.

Indo-European language family: the large family of languages that includes those of India, much of Europe, and southwestern Asia.

indulgence: a Catholic blessing given for a person's soul after death.

infant mortality: infant deaths.

infant mortality rate: the number of deaths of children less than one year old per 1,000 live births in a given year.

infanticide: the act of murdering a baby.

infidel: one who is without faith, or unbelieving; particularly, one who rejects the distinctive doctrines of a particular religion, while perhaps remaining an adherent to another religion.

inflective: refers to a language in which differences in tone and pitch give meaning to words and indicate grammatical constructions.

interferon: a drug used in the treatment of cancer in Mexico.

Inuit: an indigenous people of northwestern Canada. They are sometimes mistakenly called Eskimos.

Islam: the religious system of Mohammed, practiced by Muslims and based on a belief in Allah as the supreme being and Mohammed as his prophet. The term also refers to those nations in which it is the primary religion.

isthmus: a narrow strip of land with connecting large bodies of water on either side.

J

Jehovah's Witness: a member of a Christian sect that believes that the end of the world is near and that God should establish a theocracy on earth.

Judaism: the religious system of the Jews, based on the Old Testament as revealed to Moses and characterized by a belief in one God and adherence to the laws of scripture and rabbinic traditions.

Judeo-Christian: the dominant traditional religious makeup of the United States and other countries based on the worship of the Old and New Testaments of the Bible.

Juneteenth: an African American holiday that celebrates the freeing of slaves in America. It is thought to coincide with the surrender of the Confederacy to the Union armies.

Junkanoo: a holiday celebrated around December in the Caribbean and South America. It also has been observed in the United States in Alabama. The holiday has West African origins. Also known as John Canoe and Yancanu.

K

kale: Another hearty, green leafy vegetable that is sometimes mixed with spinach and collard greens to vary the flavor of these vegetables.

khan: a title given Genghis Khan and his successors who ruled over Turkey and Mongolia in the Middle Ages.

kielbasa: seasoned Polish sausage. Made from beef or pork.

L

lagoon: a shallow body of water connected to a larger body of water. It is sometimes separated from the larger body by reefs.

lama: a celebrated priest or ecclesiastic belonging to that variety of Buddhism known as Lamaism. The Dalai-Lama and the tesho or bogdo-lama are regarded as supreme pontiffs.

land reforms: steps taken to create a fair distribution of farm land, especially by governmental action.

latke: potato pancake.

Leeward Islands: northern islands of the Lesser Antilles in the Caribbean that stretch from Puerto Rico southward.

leprosy: an infectious disease of the skin or nerves which can cause ulcers of the skin, loss of feeling, or loss of fingers and toes.

life expectancy: an individual's expected lifespan, calculated as an average.

lingua franca: Originally, a mixed language or jargon of Mediterranean ports, consisting of Italian mixed with Arabic, Turkish, Greek, French, and Spanish. Nowadays, the phrase is used to denote any hybrid tongue used similarly in other parts of the world; an international dialect.

linguist: a person skilled in the use of languages.

linguistic group: a group of related languages.

literacy: the ability to read and write.

lox: kosher smoked salmon.

Lutheran: of or pertaining to Martin Luther (1483–1546), the reformer, to the Evangelical Protestant Church of Germany which bears his name, or to the doctrines taught by Luther or held by the Evangelical Lutheran Church.

M

macron: a horizontal mark placed over a vowel to indicate its pronunciation as long.

maize: another name (Spanish or British) for corn or the color of ripe corn.

Malayo-Polynesian language group: also referred to as the Austronesian language group, which includes the Indonesian, Polynesian, Melanesian, and Micronesian subfamilies.

mangrove: a kind of evergreen shrub growing along tropical coasts.

marimba: a type of xylophone found in Central and South America.

massif: a central mountain-mass or the dominant part of a range of mountains. A part of a range which appears, from the position of the depression by which it is more or less isolated, to form an independent whole.

matriarchy: a society in which women are recognized as the leaders of the family or tribe.

matrifocal: a society in which women are the focus of activity or attention.

matrilineal (descent): descending from, or tracing descent through, the maternal line.

Mayan language family: the languages of the Central American Indians, further divided into two subgroups: the Maya and the Huastek.

Mecca (Mekkah): a city in Saudi Arabia; a destination of pilgrims in the Islamic world.

Mennonite: a member of the Christian denomination which originated in Friesland, Holland in the early part of the 16th century and upholds the doctrine of which Menno Simons (1492–1559) was the chief exponent.

mestizo: the offspring of a person of mixed blood; especially, a person of mixed Spanish and American Indian parentage.

metamorphosis: referring to the shamanic practice of changing from a person to an animal.

Methodist: a member of the Christian denomination founded by John Wesley (1703–1791). The name was first applied to Wesley and his companions on account of their methodical habits in study and in religious life.

millennium: any one-thousand-year period, but also refers to a real or imagined period of peace and happiness.

missionary: a person sent by ecclesiastical authority to work to spread his religious faith in a community where his church has no self-supporting organization.

Mohammed (or Muhammed or Mahomet): an Arabian prophet, known as the "Prophet of Allah" who founded the religion of Islam in 622, and wrote The Koran, the scripture of Islam. Also commonly spelled Muhammed, especially by Islamic people.

Mongol: one of an Asiatic race chiefly resident in Mongolia, a region north of China proper and south of Siberia.

Mongoloid: having physical characteristics like those of the typical Mongols (Chinese, Japanese, Turks, Eskimos, etc.).

monogamy: the practice of marrying one spouse.

monolingual: speaking one language only.

monsoon: a wind occurring in the alternation of the trade-winds in India and the north Indian Ocean. They occur between April and October when the regular northeast trade-winds are reversed and, with occasional interruptions, the wind blows at almost a steady gale from the southwest. In some areas, as in China, the change of the monsoons is followed with storms and much rain.

Moors: one of the Arab tribes that conquered Spain in the 8th century.

Mormon: an adherent of the religious body the Church of Jesus Christ of Latter-day Saints founded in 1830 by Joseph Smith.

Moslem: a follower of Mohammed (spelled Muhammed by many Islamic people), in the religion of Islam.

mosque: a Mohammedan place of worship and the ecclesiastical organization with which it is connected.

mother tongue: a tongue or language to which other languages owe their origin. One's native language.

Motown: nickname for Detroit. A contraction of Motor City Town.

mujahideen or **mujahedeen:** *see* **mujahidin.**

mujahidin: rebel fighters in Islamic countries, especially those supporting the cause of Islam.

mulatto: one who is the offspring of parents of whom one is white and the other is black.

multicultural: awareness of the effect and existence of more than one cultural viewpoint within one's value system and world view.

multilingual: having the ability to speak several languages. Also used to describe anything that contains or is expressed in several languages, such as directions written in English, Spanish, and French.

mummify: ancient method used to preserve the dead. Associated with ancient Egyptian culture.

Muslim: same as Moslem.

Muslim New Year: a Muslim holiday. Although in some countries 1 Muharram, which is the first month of the Islamic year, is observed as a holiday, in other places the new year is observed on Sha'ban, the eighth month of the year. This practice apparently stems from pagan Arab times. Shab-i-Bharat, a national holiday in Bangladesh on this day, is held by many to be the occasion when God ordains all actions in the coming year.

N

native tongue: one's natural language. The language that is indigenous to an area.

Nobel Laureate: a person awarded a prize for lifetime achievement in literature, sciences, economics, or peace. Prize founded by Swedish industrialist Alfred Nobel, inventor of dynamite.

nomad: a wanderer; member of a tribe of people who have no fixed place or abode, but move about from place to place depending on the availability of food sources.

novena: a series of prayers in honor of a saint for a specific reason.

O

obsidian: a black, shiny volcanic rock, resembling glass.

official language: the language in which the business of a country and its government is conducted.

Ottoman Empire: a Turkish empire founded by Osman I in about 1603, that variously controlled large areas of land around the Mediterranean, Black, and Caspian Seas until it was dissolved in 1918.

outback region: the rural interior region of the continent of Australia. It is sparsely populated, mainly by aboriginal peoples.

overgrazing: allowing animals to graze in an area to the point that the ground vegetation is damaged or destroyed.

P

pagan: a person who worships more than one diety. Sometimes refers to non-Christians.

pagoda: in the Far East, a sacred tower, usually pyramidal in outline, richly carved, painted, or otherwise adorned, and of several stories. They can be, but are not always, connected to a temple.

Paleoasiatic languages: languages that date back to a prehistoric or unwritten era in linguistic history.

parochial: an institution supported by a church or parish.

parody: dance or song ridiculing a serious subject in a silly manner. Usually focuses on the person or people who dominate another cultural group.

Parsi: one of the descendants of those Persians who settled in India about the end of the seventh century in order to escape Mohammedan persecution, and who still retain their ancient religion. Also Parsee.

Passover (Pesach): a Jewish holiday. Pesach, lasting seven days in Israel and eight outside it, begins on 15 Nisan, at roughly the spring equinox, and recalls the exodus of the Hebrews from Egypt and their delivery from bondage. The chief festival of Judaism, Pesach begins with a ceremonial family meal, or seder, at which special foods (including unleavened bread, or matzoh) are eaten and the Passover story (Haggadah) is read.

pastoralist: a nomadic people who move with their herds of sheep or cattle, searching for pasture and water.

patois: a dialect peculiar to a district or locality, in use especially among the peasantry or uneducated classes; hence, a rustic, provincial, or barbarous form of speech.

patriarchal system: a social system in which the head of the family or tribe is the father or oldest male. Kinship is determined and traced through the male members of the tribe.

patrilineal (descent): Descending from, or tracing descent through, the paternal line.

patrilocal: a society in which men take the larger role in activities and receive greater attention.

peccary: a pig-like animal native to North and South America and the Caribbean Islands. Noted for its musky smell, sharp tusks, and gray color.

pentatonic: music consisting of a five tone scale.

Pentecost Monday (Whitmonday): a Christian holiday. This public holiday observed in many countries occurs the day after Pentecost (derived from the ancient Greek pentekostos, "fiftieth"), or Whitsunday, which commemorates the descent of the Holy Spirit upon Jesus' apostles on the seventh Sunday after Easter and is derived from the Jewish feast of Shavuot. It was an important occasion for baptism in the early church, and the name "Whitsunday" originated from the white robes worn by the newly baptized.

Pentecostal: having to do with Pentecost, a Christian holiday celebrated the seventh Sunday after Easter, marking the day that the Holy Spirit descended upon the Apostles.

peyote: the tops of the small spineless mescal cactus. Native to the southwestern United States and northern Mexico.

phoneme: slightly different sounds in a language that are heard as the same by a native speaker.

pierogie: a Polish dumpling made from pastry dough. It contains various fillings, such as meat and potatoes.

pilgrimage: a journey to a sacred place in order to perform some religious vow or duty, or to obtain some spiritual or miraculous benefit.

polygamy: the practice of having two or more spouses at the same time.

polygyny: the practice of having two or more wives and/or mistresses.

polyphonic: combining a number of harmonic sounds. Music that has more than one sound.

polytheism: belief and worship of many gods.

post traumatic stress disorder: psychological disorder that accompanies violent or tragic experiences. Known as shell-shock during World War I.

Prayer Day: a Christian holiday. This Danish public holiday is observed on the fourth Friday after Easter.

Presbyterian: of or pertaining to ecclesiastical government by elders or by presbyteries.

Prophet Muhammed: *see* **Mohammed**.

proselytizing: inducing or persuading someone to become the adherent of some religion, doctrine, sect, or party. To convert.

Protestant: a member or an adherent of one of those Christian bodies which descended from the Reformation of the sixteenth century. Originally applied to those who opposed or protested the Roman Catholic Church.

province: an administrative territory of a country.

Purim: a Jewish holiday. This holiday, celebrated on 14 Adar (Adar Sheni in a leap year), commemorates the delivery of the Jews from potential annihilation at the hands of Haman, viceroy of Persia, as described in the Book of Esther, which is read from a scroll (megillah). The day, though not a public holiday in Israel, is widely marked by charity, exchange of edible gifts, and feasting.

R

rabbi: a Jewish religious leader; head of a congregation.

racial integration: to remove all restrictions and barriers preventing complete access to society to persons of all races.

racially homogeneous: composed of persons all of the same race.

rain forest: a tropical vegetation in the equatorial region of the world which consists of a dense growth of a wide variety of broadleaf evergreen trees and vines.

Raksha Bandhan: a Hindu holiday. During this festival, which usually falls in August, bracelets of colored thread and tinsel are tied by women to the wrists of their menfolk, thus binding the men to guard and protect them during the year. It is celebrated on the full moon of Sravana.

Ramadan: a Muslim holiday. The first day of Ramadan (the ninth month) is a public holiday in many countries, although the religious festival does not officially begin until the new moon is sighted from the Naval Observatory in Cairo, Egypt. The entire month commemorates the period in which the Prophet received divine revelation and is observed by a strict fast from sunrise to sundown. This observance is one of Islam's five main duties for believers.

Rastafarian: a member of a Jamaican cult begun in 1930 as a semi-religious, semi-political movement. Rastafarians are usually lower class men who are anti-white and advocate the return of blacks to Africa.

refugee: one who flees to a refuge, shelter or place of safety. One who in times of persecution or political commotion flees to a foreign country for safety.

respiratory: pertaining to the lungs and other breathing passages.

Roman alphabet: the alphabet of the ancient Romans from which the alphabets of most modern western European languages, including English, are derived.

Roman Catholic Church: the designation of the church of which the pope or bishop of Rome is the head, and which holds him, as the successor of St. Peter and heir of his spiritual authority, privileges, and gifts, as its supreme ruler, pastor, and teacher.

Romance language: the group of languages derived from Latin: French, Spanish, Italian, Portuguese and other related languages.

Rosh Hashanah: a Jewish holiday. The Jewish New Year is celebrated on 1 Tishri, the first month. In synagogues, the sounding of the shofar (ram's horn) heralds the new year. Rosh Hashanah begins the observance of the Ten Penitential Days, which culminate in Yom Kippur. Orthodox and Conservative Jews outside Israel celebrate 2 Tishri, the next day, as well.

runic music: music that is ancient, obscure, and mystical.

Russian Orthodox: the arm of the Orthodox Eastern Church which was the official church of czarist Russia.

S

Sacred Heart: a Christian holiday. The Friday of the week after Corpus Christi is a holiday in Colombia. The object of devotion is the divine person of Jesus, whose heart is the symbol of his love for mankind.

Samaritans: a native or an inhabitant of Samaria; specifically, one of a race settled in the cities of Samaria by the king of Assyria after the removal of the Israelites from the country.

samba: a Brazilian dance and musical tradition based on two beats to the measure.

sambo: indicates a person of visible African ancestry. Familiar form of address for an uncle from the Foulah language of West Africa.

Santer'a: Christian religion with West African origins. It merges Christian saints with Yoruban dieties.

savanna: a treeless or near treeless plain of a tropical or subtropical region dominated by drought-resistant grasses.

schistosomiasis: a tropical disease that is chronic and characterized by disorders of the liver, urinary bladder, lungs, or central nervous system.

sect: a religious denomination or group, often a dissenting one with extreme views.

self-determination: the desire of a culture to control its economic and social development.

Semitic tongue: an important family of languages distinguished by triliteral verbal roots and vowel inflections.

Seventh-day Adventist: one who believes in the second coming of Christ to establish a personal reign upon the earth. They observe the seventh day of the week as the Sabbath and believe in the existence of the spirit of prophecy among them.

shaman: holy man or woman said to have the power to heal diseases. Also thought to have magical powers.

shamanism: a religion centered on a belief in good and evil spirits that can be influenced only by shamans.

Shavuot: a Jewish holiday. This festival, on 6 Sivan, celebrates the presentation of the Ten Commandments to Moses on Mt. Sinai and the offering of the first harvest fruits at the temple in Jerusalem. The precursor of the Christian Pentecost, Shavuot takes place on the 50th day after the first day of Passover.

Shia Muslim: member of one of two great sects of Islam. Shia Muslims believe that Ali and the Imams are the rightful successors of Mohammed (also commonly spelled Muhammed). They also believe that the last recognized Imam will return as a messiah. Also known as Shiites. (*Also see* **Sunni Muslim.**)

Shiites: *see* **Shia Muslim.**

Shintoism: the system of nature- and hero-worship which forms the indigenous religion of Japan.

Shivarati (Mahashivarati): a Hindu holiday. Dedicated to the god Shiva, this holiday is observed on the 13th day of the dark half of Magha, corresponding to January or February.

Shrove Monday and Shrove Tuesday: a Christian holiday. These two days occur just prior to the beginning of Lent (a term which derives from the Middle English lente, "spring"), the Christian season of penitence that ends with Easter Sunday. These are days of Carnival, public holidays of feasting, and merriment in many lands. Shrove Tuesday is also known as Mardi Gras.

shunning: Amish practice of not interacting in any way with a person who has been cast out by the church and the community.

sierra: a chain of hills or mountains.

Sikh: a member of a politico-religious community of India, founded as a sect around 1500 and based on the principles of monotheism and human brotherhood.

Sino-Tibetan language family: the family of languages spoken in Eastern Asia, including China, Thailand, Tibet, and Burma.

slash-and-burn agriculture: a hasty and sometimes temporary way of clearing land to make it available for agriculture by cutting down trees and burning them.

slave trade: the transportation of black Africans beginning in the 1700s to other countries to be sold as slaves-people owned as property and compelled to work for their owners at no pay.

Slavic languages: a major subgroup of the Indo-European language family. It is further subdivided into West Slavic (including Polish, Czech, Slovak and Sorbian), South Slavic (including Bulgarian, Serbo-Croatian, Slovene, and Old Church Slavonic), and East Slavic (including Russian Ukrainian and Byelorussian).

Society of Friends: a religious sect founded about 1650 whose members shun military service and believe in plain dress, behavior and worship. Also referred to as the Quaker religion by those outside it.

Solemnity of Mary, Mother of God: a Christian holiday. Observed on 1 January, this celebration was, before a 1969 Vatican reform, the Feast of the Circumcision of Our Lord Jesus Christ.

sorghum: a type of tropical grass that is grown for grain, syrup, and livestock feed.

St. Agatha's Day: a Christian holiday. Celebrated on 5 February, it is the feast day of the patron saint of San Marino. St. Agatha is also the patron saint of nurses, firefighters, and jewelers.

St. Dévôte Day: a Christian holiday. Observed on 27 January in Monaco in honor of the principality's patron saint, this day celebrates her safe landing after a perilous voyage, thanks to a dove who directed her ship to the Monaco shore.

St. James's Day: a Christian holiday. Observed on 25 July, this day commemorates St. James the Greater, one of Jesus' 12 apostles. St. James is the patron saint of Spain.

St. Joseph's Day: a Christian holiday. The feast day in honor of Mary's husband is observed on 19 March as a public holiday in several countries.

St. Patrick's Day: a Christian holiday. This holiday, observed on 17 March, is celebrated in Ireland to honor its patron saint.

St. Stephen's Day: a Christian holiday. The feast day in honor of the first martyred Christian saint is 26 December, the day after Christmas. St. Stephen is the patron saint of Hungary.

steppe: a level tract of land more or less devoid of trees. It is a name given to certain parts of European and Asiatic Russia, of which the most characteristic feature is the absence of forests.

stigmatize: branding someone as a disgrace because of his or her behavior.

straits: a narrow passage of water connecting two bodies of water.

stroganoff: Russian beef stew. Sauce made from sour cream and wine.

subcontinent: a landmass of great size, but smaller than any of the continents; a large subdivision of a continent.

subsistence farming: farming that provides the minimum food goods necessary for the continuation of the farm family.

Sudanic language group: a related group of languages spoken in various areas of northern Africa, including Yoruba, Mandingo and Tshi.

Sufi: a Mohammedan mystic who believes (a) that God alone exists, and all visible and invisible beings are mere emanations from Him; (b) that, as God is the real author of all the acts of mankind, man is not a free agent, and there can be no real difference between good and evil; (c) that, as the soul existed before the body, and is confined within the latter as in a cage, death should be the chief object of desire, for only then does the soul return to the bosom of the divinity; and (d) that religions are matters of indifference, though some are more advantageous than others, and Sufism is the only true philosophy.

Sukkot: a Jewish holiday. This ancient Jewish harvest festival, which begins on 15 Tishri, recalls the period in which harvesters left their homes to dwell in the fields in sukkot, or booths—small outdoor shelters of boards, leaves, and branches—in order to facilitate gathering the crops before the seasonal rains began. In religious terms, it commemorates the 40 years of wandering in the desert by the ancient Hebrews after their exodus from Egypt. The 8th day of Sukkot (and the 22d day of Tishri) is Shmini Azeret/Simhat Torah, a joyous holiday in which the annual cycle of reading the Torah (the Five Books of Moses) is completed and begun anew. Outside of Israel, Simhat Torah and the beginning of a new reading cycle are celebrated on the next day, 23 Tishri.

sultan: a king of a Muslim state.

Sunni Muslim: Member of one of two major sects of the religion of Islam. Sunni Muslims adhere to strict orthodox traditions and believe that the four caliphs are the rightful successors to Mohammed, founder of Islam. (Mohammed is commonly spelled Muhammed, especially by Islamic people.) (*Also see* **Shia Muslim.**)

surname: a person's last name. Generally different from his or her first name.

T

taboo: a system, practice, or act whereby persons, things, places, actions, or words are placed under ban, curse, or prohibition, or set apart as sacred or privileged in some specific manner.

taiga: a coniferous forest in the far northern areas of Canada, Alaska, and Eurasia.

Taoism: the doctrine of Lao-Tzu, an ancient Chinese philosopher (about 500 BC) as laid down by him in the Tao-te-ching.

Thaipusam: a Hindu holiday. A holiday in Malaysia, Thaipusam honors Subrimaya, son of Shiva and an important deity in southern India. The three-day festival is held in the month of Magha according to when Pusam, a section of the lunar zodiac, is on the ascendant.

Tibeto-Burman language group: a subgroup of the Sino-Tibetan language family which includes Tibetan and Burmese.

Tishah b'Av: a Jewish holiday. This holiday, which takes place on 9 Av, commemorates the destruction of the First Temple by the Babylonians (Chaldeans) in 586 BC and of the Second Temple by the Romans in AD 70. It is observed by fasting.

toboggan: a kind of sled without runners or a steering mechanism.

topography: an accurate drawing representing the surface of a region on maps and charts.

toucan: a brightly colored, fruit-eating bird of tropical America with a distinctive beak.

trachoma: contagious, viral infection of the cornea. Causes scarring in the eye.

tribal society: a society based on tribal consciousness and loyalties.

tribal system: a social community in which people are organized into groups or clans descended from common ancestors and sharing customs and languages.

tsetse fly: any of the several African insects which can transmit a variety of parasitic organisms through its bite. Some of these organisms can prove fatal to both human and animal victims.

tundra: a nearly level treeless area whose climate and vegetation are more characteristically arctic due to its northern position. Although the region attains seasonal temperatures warm enough to allow a thin layer of soil on the surface to unthaw enough to support the growth of various species of plants, the subsoil is permanently frozen.

tutelary: a god or spirit who acts a guardian that watches over a person or group of people.

typhoon: a violent hurricane occurring in the China Sea or Philippine region, principally between the months of July and October.

U

unemployment rate: the overall unemployment rate is the percentage of the work force (both employed and unemployed) who claim to be unemployed. The natural unemployment rate is the lowest level at which unemployment in an economy can be maintained and still reflect a balance of the labor market and the product market.

untouchables: in 19th century India, members of the lowest caste in the caste system, a hereditary social class system.

They were considered unworthy to touch members of higher castes.

urban center: a city.

USSR: an abbreviation of Union of Soviet Socialist Republics.

V

veldt: in South Africa, an unforested or thinly forested tract of land or region, a grassland.

Vesak: this last full moon day of Visakha highlights a three-day celebration of the birth, enlightenment, and death of the Buddha. It falls in April or May.

voodoo: a belief system which is based on sorcery and other primitive rites and the power of charms and fetishes, originating in Africa.

W

wadi(s): the channel of a watercourse which is dry except in the rainy season. Also called wady.

Windward Islands: a southern group of islands stretching south to Trinidad. Part of the Lesser Antilles, but does not include Barbados.

Y

Yom Kippur: a Jewish holiday. The Day of Atonement, spent in fasting, penitence, and prayer, is the most solemn day in Judaism. It takes place on 10 Tishri.

yucca: a plant native to Mexico, Central and South America, and the southwestern United States. Can grow to the 12 feet in height.

yurt: a framework tent of stretched felt or skins. Associated with Siberia and Mongolia.

Z

Zoroastrianism: the system of religious doctrine taught by Zoroaster and his followers in the Avesta; the religion prevalent in Persia until its overthrow by the Muslims in the 7th century.

INDEX

The "v" accompanied by a numeral that precedes the colon in these index citations designates the volume number for *Worldmark Encyclopedia of Cultures and Daily Life, Second Edition*. Thus, v1 references are found in the Africa volume; v2 in Americas, v3 in Asia & Oceania, v4 in Asia and Oceania continued, and v5 in Europe. Page numbers follow the colon.

A

Ababukusu v1:337
Abagusii. *See* Gusii
Abaidakho v1:337
Abaisukha v1:337
Abakisa v1:337
Abaluhya. *See* Luhya
Abamarachi v1:337
Abamarama v1:337
Abanyala v1:337
Abasamia v1:337
Abashidze, Aslan v5:21
Abatachoni v1:337
Abatiriki v1:337
Abbasids v1:23
Abaza language v5:376
    Karachai v5:250
Abdallah, Ahmed v1:134
Abdoulkarim, Mohammed Taki v1:134
Abelard, Peter v5:90
Abkhazians v5:15–19
Abkhazian language
    Abkhazians v5:15
    Peoples of the Caucasus v5:376
Aborigines of Australia v 4:898
Abyssinia v1:30, 210
Abyssinian Plateau v1:205
Acadians. *See* Cajuns
Acehnese v3:11–15
Acehnese language
    Acehnese v3:11
    Indonesians v3:374
Aconcagua River v2:345
Adal. *See* Afar
Adamawa dialect v1:222
Adamōs Bridge v4:898
Adare v1:450
Adja. *See* Beninese
Adjarians v5:19–23
Adriatic Sea v5:137, 238, 325, 435, 460
Adunis. *See* Said, Ahmad
Adyges. *See* Circassians
Adygheia v5:130
Adygheians. *See* Circassians
Adzharians. *See* Adjarians
Aeschylus v5:223
Aesops Fables v3:164
Afaan Oromoo language, Oromoo v1:450
Afar v1:7–11, 163, 203, 205
Afar language v1:8
Afghanis v3:16–23
    Pakistanis v4:770
    See also Pashtun
Afghanistan
    Afghanis v3:16
    Baluchi v3:97
    Brahui v3:151

Hazaras v3:311
Pashtun v4:795
Turkmens v4:998
Uzbeks v4:1014
African Americans v2:11–15, 38
African Brazilians v2:16–20
African languages
    African Americans v2:11
    African Brazilians v2:16
    Antiguans and Barbudans v2:56
    Cameroonians v1:96
    Chadians v1:111
    Guineans v1:257
    See also specific languages
Afrikaans language v1:193
    Afrikaners v1:12
    Colored People of South Africa v1:129
    Karretjie People v1:310
    Namibians v1:409
    Ndebele v1:415
Afrikaners v1:12–16
Afro-Brazilians. *See* African Brazilians
Agau language
    Amhara v1:30
Agha Khan v4:940
Aghamov, M. v5:487
Aguaruna v2:323
Agul language
    Dagestan v5:368
Ahirs v3:24–27
Ahmadu Bello University v1:275
Ahmed Shah Durrani v3:16
Aini, Sadriddin v4:943
Ainu v3:27–31
Air Mountain v1:548
Aizo/Houjda. *See* Beninese
Aka v1:17–22
Akan language v1:295
    Ghanaians v1:240
    Ivoirians v1:294
Akhas v4:866
Alabama River v2:155
Alava region, Spain
    Basques v5:65
'Alawis v3:32–34
al-Asad, Hafiz v3:34
Alaska v2:20
Alawite. *See* Alawis
Albanian language
    Albanians v5:23
    Bosnians v5:82
    Kosovars v5:266
Albanians v5:23–29
Albéniz, Isaac v5:470
Aleixandre, Vicente v5:470
Alemannic German
    Alsatians v5:30

Liechtensteiners v5:276
Aleut language v2:20
Aleutian Islands v2:20; v5:259
Aleuts v2:20
Aleuts v2:20–24
Alexander II v5:414
Alexander the Great v3:24, 276, 390; v4:1015; v5:221, 27, 291
Alexandrescu, Grigorie v5:411
Alexandri, Vasile v5:411
Algeria
    Algerians v1:23
    Berbers v1:78
    Tuaregs v1:548
Algerians v1:23–29
Alice Springs v3:66
All Saints' Day v5:56
Almohads v1:554
Almoravid Empire v1:382
Almoravids v1:554
Alps v5:238, 477
    Austrians v5:55
Alsace v5:29
Alsatian language v5:29–30
Alsatians v5:29–37
Altai Mountains v3:482; v5:243
Altaic languages
    Buriat v5:96
    Balkar v5:375
    China v3:209
Altamira cave paintings v5:470
Altays v5:37–41
Amahuacas v2:25–28
Amandebele. *See* Ndebele
Amazon River v2:25, 71, 103
Ambedkar, Dr. B. R. v3:166, 199
Ambonese v3:35–40; v4:1025
Amei. *See* Gaoshan
American Immigrants v2:29–38
    See also Arab Americans, Armenian Americans, Asian Indian Americans, Cajuns, Cambodian Americans, Central Americans in the US, Chinese Americans, Cuban Americans, Dominican Americans, Dutch Americans, English Americans, Filipino Americans, French Americans, Garifuna, German Americans, Greek Americans, Haitian Americans, Hmong Americans, Hungarian Americans, Irish Americans, Italian Americans, Japanese Americans, Jewish Americans, Korean Americans, Laotian Americans, Lebanese Americans, Mexican Americans, Norwegian

Americans, Polish Americans, Russian Americans, Scottish and Scotch-Irish Americans, Swedish Americans, Ukrainian Americans, and Vietnamese Americans

American Indians. *See* Native North Americans

Americans v2:38–47

Amerindian languages
  Amahuacas v2:25
  Venezuelans v2:535

Amhara v1:30–34

Amharic language
  Amhara v1:30
  Ethiopians v1:210
  Tigray v1:536

Amin, Idi v1:50, 67, 574

Amis. *See* Taiwan Indigenous People

Amish v2:48–54

Amu Darya River v4:999, 1015

Amu River v3:460; v4:940

Amur River v3:27; v5:170, 334, 351

Anandpur Resolution v4:881

Anatolian Highlands, Armenians v5:50

Andaluca v5:467

Andalusians v5:42–45

Andaman Islands, Andamanese v3:40

Andaman Sea v4:670, 967

Andamanese v3:40–44, 163, 361; v4:710, 742

Andes Mountains v2:79, 99
  Jivaro v2:323
  Páez v2:418

Andhras v3:44–48

Andorran National Day v5:47

Andorrans v5:46–49

Andreanof Islands:Aleuts v2:20

Angad v4:877

Angelou, Maya v2:14

Anglo Australians v3:49–54

Anglo-Indians v3:54–58

Angolans v1:35–40

Anishinabe. *See* Ojibwa

Anjouan (Nzwani) v1:134, 135

Ankalit. *See* Chukchi

Ankobra River v1:240

Ankole v1:61

Annamite Cordillera v4:1034

Annuak v1:450

Antakarana v1:357

Antambahoako v1:357

Antandrona v1:356

Antandroy v1:356

Antanosy v1:356

Anteifsy v1:356

Anteimoro v1:356

Antigua and Barbuda v2:54

Antiguans and Barbudans v2:54–58

Antonescu, General Ion v5:405

Anuradhapura Veddas. *See* Veddas

Apennines Mountains v5:435

Aquino, Corazon v3:250; v4:710

Arab Americans v2:59–62
  See also American Immigrants

Arabian Desert v4:1046

Arabian Gulf v4:864

Arabian Peninsula v4:859

Arabian Sea v3:97, 285, 361; v4:628, 772, 775, 882

Arabic langauge
  'Alawis v3:32
  Algerians v1:23
  Bedu v3:122
  Chadians v1:116
  Comorians v1:134
  Congolese v1:139, 140
  Congolese (DROC) v1:144
  Djiboutis v1:163
  Dyula v1:167
  Eritreans v1:203
  Ethiopians v1:210
  French v5:191
  Frisians v5:196
  Fulani v1:222
  Gabonese v1:227
  Guineans v1:257, 263
  Hausa v1:272
  Israelis v3:397
  Ivoirians v1:294, 295
  Lebanese v4:553, 554
  Luxembourgers v5:287
  Malagasy v1:355
  Malians v1:371
  Maronites v4:632, 633
  Mauritanians v1:382
  Moroccans v1:388
  New Caledonians v4:721
  Nigeriens v1:425
  Ni-Vanuatu v4:747
  Polynesians v4:803
  Rwandans v1:456
  Senegalese v1:473
  Seychellois v1:479
  Songhay v1:501
  Sri Lankans v4:899
  Syrians v4:920
  Tahitians v4:930
  Tunisians v1:553
  Tutsi v1:277, 562, 564
  Walloons v5:517

Arakan Yoma Mountains v4:832

Aral Sea v3:460, 465, 482; v4:940, 1014, 1015, 1018

Aramaic language
  Iraqis v3:390
  Orthodox Jews v4:990
  Syrians v4:921
  Traditional-Orthodox Jews v4:990

Ararat Valley, Armenians v5:50

Araucanians. *See* Mapuches

Aravalli Mountains v4:818

Aravalli Range v4:660

Arawak v2:89

Araz River v3:71

Arctic Circle v5:153, 229, 259, 358, 430, 472

Ardennes Mountains v5:287

Arecuna. *See* Pemon

Argentina
  Argentines v2:62
  Galicians v5:200
  Mapuches v2:345

Argentine native languages, Argentines v2:62

Argentines v2:62–66

Aristophanes. v5:223

Aristotle v5:223

Arkansas River v2:155

Armani, Giorgio v5:240

Armenia
  Armenians v5:50
  Georgia v5:373
  Kurds v3:518
  Yazidis v4:1043

Armenian Americans v2:67–70
  See also American Immigrants

Armenian language v5:51
  Armenian Americans v2:67
  Bulgarians v5:92
  Iraqis v3:390
  Yazidis v4:1043

Armenians v5:50–55

Armstrong, Louis v2:14

Arunachal Pradesh state, India, Naga v4:699

Asháninka v2:70–75

Asháninka language
  Asháninka v2:70
  Matsigenka v2:350

Asho. *See* Chin

Ashoka v3:163

Asian Indian Americans v2:75–78
  See also American Immigrants

Asmat v3:58–62

Assamese v3:62–66
  Bhutanese v3:137

Atatürk v4:1004

Atbara River v1:512

Athapaskan languages, Canadians v2:117

Atilla the Hun v5:483

Atlas Mountains v1:556
  Berbers v1:78

Atoni. *See* Timorese

Atwood, Margaret v2:119

Aushi v1:68

Australia and Oceania
  Anglo Australians v3:49
  Australian Aborigines v3:66
  Roma v5:395

Australian Aborigines v3:66–70

Australians. *See* Anglo Australians

Austria
  Austrians v5:55
  Slovenes v5:459
  Tyrolese v5:495

Austrians v5:55–60

Austro-Hungarian Empire v5:81, 459

Austronesian dialects
  Minahasans v4:650
  Mountain Mon-Khmer Groups (Cambodian Tribespeople) v4:682

Austronesian people. *See* Taiwan Indigenous People

Autumnal Equinox v3:413

Avalogoli v1:337

Avestan language, Parsis v4:790

Axi. *See* Yi

Aymara v2:79–83, 98

Aymara language v2:79

Azande v1:40–44

Azayr, Mauritanians v1:382

Azerbaijan
  Armenians in v5:50

Azerbaijanis v3:70
  People of Dagestan v5:367
Azerbaijanis v3:70–75
Azeri language
  Azerbaijanis v3:71
  Peoples of the Caucasus v5:376

B

Babuende v1:52
Babur v3:16; v4:1018
Badaga v4:981
Badakhshan Mountains v4:940
Badjao. *See* Bajau
Baffin Island v2:116
Bafour v1:382
Baganda v1:44–51, 574, 580
Bagdanovich, Maksim v5:75
Bagobo. *See* Manuvu' (Upland Bagobo)
Bahamians v2:84–89
Bahasa Indonesia language
  Batak v3:118
  Dani v3:224
  Indonesians v3:371, 373
  Manggarai v4:606
  Melanesians v4:635
  Minahasans v4:650
Bahasa Melayu Ambon language, Ambonese v3:36
Bahasa Tae' language, Sa'dan Toraja v4:840, 841
Bahrainis v3:76–82
Bai v3:208–85
Bai language, Bai v3:82
Baiyi. *See* Dai
Baiyue people v4:1056
Bajans. *See* Barbadians
Bajau v3:86–90
Baka. *See* Twa
Bakongo v1:51–55
Bakuba people v1:148
Baldwin, James v2:14
Balearic Islands v5:467
Balengue v1:198
Baler Bay v3:356
Balese language, Twa v1:569
Bali v3:90, 112, 170, 373; v4:606, 738
Balinese v3:90–96
  See also Sasak
Balkan Mountains v4:999; v5:91
Balkan Peninsula v5:221, 325, 443
  Serbs v5:444
Balkar language
  Peoples of the Caucasus v5:375
Ballesteros, Seve v5:470
Baloch. *See* Baluchi
Balti language, Pakistanis v4:773
Baltic Sea v3:70; v5:147, 164, 282, 384, 413
Baltic States v5:281, 472
Baluch. *See* Jats
Baluchi 3:97–102
Baluchi language
  Baluchi v3:97
  Hazaras v3:311
  Pakistanis v4:770, 773
Bamana v1:56–60
Bambara. *See* Bamana
Bambatha v1:612

Bambuti. *See* Efe and Mbuti Pygmies of the Ituri Forest
Bamiléké v1:96–100
Bamum v1:96
Banas River v4:660
Banat v5:405
Banda v1:106
Bandama River v1:295
Bangalis. *See* Bengalis
Bangladesh
  Bangladeshis v3:102
  Bengalis v3:127
  Chakmas v3:185
  Hindus v3:319
  Muslims v4:693
  Santals v4:848
Bangladeshis v3:102–107
Bangxi. *See* Naxi
Banias v3:108–111
Banjarese v3:116–181
Banjarese language
  Banjarese v3:112
  Indonesians v3:374
Bantu v1:227, 519, 543
  See also Shambaa
Bantu language v1:607
  Aka v1:18
  Angolans v1:35
  Baganda v1:45
  Banyankole v1:61
  Bemba v1:68
  Cameroonians v1:96
  Kiembu v1:187
  Luhya v1:337
  Nigerians v1:420
  Tutsi v1:277, 562
  Xhosa v1:587
  See also specific languages
Banyankole v1:61–67, 580
Baoulé (Akan) language v1:295
  Ivoirians v1:294
Bara v1:356
Bara-Antevondro v1:356
Bara-Be v1:356
Baradulin, Ryhor v5:75
Bara-Iantsantsa v1:356
Baram River v3:487; v4:799
Bara-Vinda v1:356
Barbadians v2:89–93
Barbuda v2:54
Bariba. *See* Beninese
Barito River v3:112
Barlavento islands v1:101
Barrakunda Falls v1:234
Barre, General Muhammad Siad v1:500
Barrie, J. M. v5:441
Basa v1:96
Bashiic v4:952
Bashiic language, Tao v4:951
Bashkirs v5:61–65
Bashkir language, Bashkirs v5:61
Bashkirtista v5:483
Bashkortostan v5:501
Basolongo v1:52
Basque language,
  Basques v5:65–69
  French v5:191

Basques v5:65–69, 467
Basquiat, Jean-Michel v2:14
Basse-Navarre region, France. Basques v5:65
Basundi v1:52
Batak v3:117–122
Batan Archipelago v4:951
Batchelor, John v3:28
Bateke language, Congolese v1:139
Bateke Plateau v1:227
Batu Islands v4:738
Batwa. *See* Twa
Bay of Bengal v3:40, 44, 48, 104, 130, 491; v4:689, 710, 742, 766, 832, 836, 848, 946
Bay of Biscay v5:65, 67
Bearden, Romare v2:14
Beas River v4:807, 877
Beatles v5:161
Beatrice, Dona v1:52
Beckett, Samuel v5:237
Bedouin. *See* Bedu
Bedu v3:122–126
Beethoven, Ludwig van v5:59
Begin, Menachem v1:177
Beinan. *See* Gaoshan
Beja v1:205
Belarusan language v5:72
Belarusans v5:70–76
Belau, Republic of v4:647
Belgians v5:77–81
Belgium
  Belgians v5:77–81
  Flemish v5:187
  Walloons v5:517
Belize
  Belizeans v2:94–98
  Garifuna v2:226
  Maya v2:355
Belizeans v2:94–98
Bell, Douala Manga v1:96
Bemba v1:68–72
  Tonga v1:543
Bemba language
  Bemba v1:68–72
  Zambians v1:600, 602
Benetton v5:240
Bengali language
  Asian Indian Americans v2:76
  Bengalis v3:127
  Chakmas v3:187
  Indians v3:360
  Muslims in South Asia v4:694
  People of India v3:362
  Rohingyas v4:836
  Santals v4:848
Bengalis v3:127–131
Beni Amirs v1:205
Benin
  Beninese v1:73–77
  Ewe v1:217
  Songhay v1:501
  Yoruba v1:593
Beninese v1:73–77
Benti, Brigadier General Teferi v1:203
Benue River v1:222
Ber, Sonni Ali v1:501, 502
Berber language v1:78, 79

Algerians v1:25
Bahrainis v3:76, 77
Chadians v1:111
Circassians v5:130
Comorians v1:134
Druze v3:232
Dyula v1:167
Egyptians v1:177, 178
Emirians v3:236
Eritreans v1:203, 205
Ethiopians v1:210
Fulani v1:222
Hausa v1:272
Iraqis v3:390, 392
Israelis v3:399
Jordanians v3:436
Kuwaitis v3:523, 524
Lebanese v4:553, 554
Libyans v1:329, 332
Madan v4:571
Maronites v4:632, 633
Moroccans v1:388
Moroccans v1:388
Muslims v4:693
Muslims in South Asia v4:694
Omanis v4:750, 751
Qataris v4:813, 814
Saudis v4:859
Somalis v1:495
Sudanese v1:512, 513
Syrians v4:920
Tanzanians v1:530
Tunisians v1:553, 556
Yemenis v4:1046
Berbers v1:78–84, 329, 382, 548
Bergman, Ingmar v5:475
Bergman, Ingrid v5:475
Bering Sea v5:259
Bering Straits v2:116
Berta v1:450
Bessarabia. See Moldovans
Betsileo v1:355
Betsimisaraka v1:355
Bezanozano v1:356
Bhaca v1:587
Bhandar Plateau v3:506
Bhils v3:131–136
Bhima River v4:567
Bhot. See Bhutia
Bhotia. See Bhutia
Bhundu Boys v1:610
Bhutan
  Bhutanese v3:137–142
  Bhutia v3:142
  Hindus v3:319
  Lepchas v4:559
  Muslims v4:693
Bhutanese v3:137–142
Bhute. See Bhutia
Bhutia v3:142–146
Bhutia language
  Bhutia v3:142–146
  Buddhists v3:163
  Nepalis v4:716
Biacometti, Alberto v5:480
Bicolano language, Filipinos v3:249, 251
Bié Plateau v1:35

Bihar state, India
  Ahirs v3:24
  Mundas v4:688
  Oraons v4:760
Bilbao, Spain v5:67
Bilen Agew v1:205
Bimini v2:84, 85
Bingduoyou. See Yao
Bintenne Veddas. See Veddas
Bío Bío River v2:345
Bioko Island v1:198
Biqila, Ababa v1:453
Bira language, Twa v1:569
Biratu, Wami v1:453
Bird, Lester B. v2:55
Bird, Vere Cornwall v2:55
Bisa v1:68, 85
Bislama language
  Melanesians v4:635
  Ni-Vanuatu v4:747
Bizika. See Tujia
Bjørnson, Bjørnstjerne v5:360
Black and White Volta v1:240
Black English Vernacular (BEV) v2:11
Black Sea v3:70; v4:1005; v5:91, 384, 406, 413
  Abkhazians v5:15
  Adjarians v5:20
Blacks. See African Americans
Black Teeth. See Dai
Bo. See Bai
Bobo v1:85
Bobo language, Malians v1:371
Bobo-Dioulasso language, Burkinabe v1:85
Bod Qiang. See Tibetans
Boers v1:12
Boganda, Barthelemy v1:105
Bogdania. See Moldovans
Boggy Peak v2:55
Bohemian plateau, Austrians v5:56
Bohol v3:251
Bol, Manute v2:496
Bolivar, Simon v2:98
Bolivia
  Aymara v2:79
  Bolivians v2:98–103
  Quechua v2:462
Bolivians v2:98–103
Bolshevik v5:414
Bombay, India, Parsis v4:789
Bomvana v1:587
Bon Festival v3:412
Borneo v3:112, 117, 447; v4:580, 595, 733
  Bruneians v3:156
Bosnia and Herzegovina
  Bosnians v5:81–86
  Serbs v5:443
Bosnians v5:81–86
Bosphorus Strait v4:1005
Botany Bay v3:66
Botev, Hristo v5:94
Boulkhou v1:549
Bourbon Dynasty v5:102
Bourguiba, Habib v1:555
Bozo language, Malians v1:371
Brahmans v3:146–151
Brahmaputra River v3:103, 127, 361
Brahmaputra Valley v3:62, 137, 491

Brahmins. See Brahmans
Brahms, Johannes v5:59
Brahui v3:151–155
Brahui language
  Brahui v3:152–155
  Pakistanis v4:773
Braithwaite, Edward Kamau v2:92
Brao language v4:684
Brazil
  African Brazilians v2:16
  Asháninka v2:70
  Brazilians v2:103–108
  Guaranis v2:245
  Kayapos v2:327
  Tenetehara v2:507
  Xavante v2:543
Brazilians v2:103–108
Breton langauge
  Bretons v5:87–91
  French v5:191
  Léonard v5:87
  Trégorrois v5:87
Bretons v5:87–91
Breugel, Pieter the Elder v5:80
Brink, Andre v1:196
British South African Company v1:68
Brittany, Bretons v5:87
Britten, Benjamin v5:161
Brohi. See Brahui
Brown, Andy v1:610
Broz, Josip v5:81
Bruneians v3:155–162
Bry, Janka v5:75
Bubi v1:198
Bubi language, Equatorial Guineans v1:198
Bucovina v5:405
Buddha, Gautama v3:163
Buddhists v3:163–169
Buganda v1:574
Bugis, Makassarese, and Mandarese
    v3:169–174
Bugkalut. See Ilongot
Bujeba v1:198
Bulgar realm v5:483
Bulgaria
  Armenians in v5:50
  Bulgrarians v5:91–96
Bulgarians v5:91–96
Bulgars v5:123
Bullfighting v5:467
Buman
  Buyi v3:181
  Zhuang v4:1056
Bunong
  Buyi v3:181
  Gaoshan v3:260
  Zhuang v4:1056
Bunu. See Yao
Bunun. See Taiwan Indigenous People
Bunyankole v1:574
Bunyon, Paul v2:39
Bunyoro v1:574
Burao. See Buyi
Buriaad. See Buriats
Buriats v5:96–102
Burkina Faso
  Dyula v1:167

Mossi v1:395
  Tuaregs v1:548
Burkinabe v1:85–90
Burma. See Myanmar
Burman v3:174–180
Burmese
  Karens v3:467
  Rakhines v4:832
Burmese language
  Mons v4:669
  Rakhines v4:832
  Shans v4:866
Burns, Robert v5:441
Burundi
  Burundians v1:90–95
  Hutu v1:277
  Tutsi v1:562
Burundians v1:90–95
Burushaski language, Pakistanis v4:773
Buryats. See Buriats
Bushmen v4:898
Busoga v1:574
Butoro v1:574
Butu. See Zhuang
Buyai. See Buyi
Buyang. See Zhuang
Buyi v3:181–184
Buyue
  Buyi v3:181–184
  Zhuang v4:1056
Buzhang. See Buyi
Buzhuang. See Zhuang
Bykau, Vasil v5:75
Byrd, William v5:161
Byzantine Empire v4:1004; v5:23, 27, 91, 135,
  221

C

Caballé, Montserrat v5:110
Cádiz province, Spain, Andalusians v5:42
Caesar, Julius v5:77
Cagayan River v3:345
Cairui. See Timorese
Cajuns v2:109–112
  Creoles of Louisiana v2:161
  French Canadians v2:217
  See also American Immigrants
Calamian Islands v4:926, 928
Cales. See Roma
Calvin, John v5:478
Cambodia
  Cham v3:191
  Khmer v3:495
  Mountain Mon-Khmer Groups
    (Cambodian Tribespeople) v4:682
Cambodian Americans v2:113–115
  See also American Immigrants
Cambodian language
  Cambodians v3:497
  Cham v3:192
  Khmer v3:495
Cambodian tribespeople. See Mountain
  Mon-Khmer Groups
Cambodians. See Khmer
Cameroon
  Cameroonians v1:95–100
  Twa v1:569

Cameroonians v1:95–100
Campa (derogatory). See Ashaninka
Canada
  Amish v2:48
  Canadians v2:116–121
  Dakota and Lakhota v2:179
  French Canadians v2:217
  Inuit v2:296
  Iroquois v2:304
  Native North Americans v2:384
  Ojibwa v2:412
Canadian River v2:155
Canadians v2:116–121
Canary Islands v5:467
Cang Mountain v3:82, 84
Cao, Diego v1:51
Cape of Good Hope v1:587
Cape Verdeans v1:101–105
Capone, Al v2:39
CAR. See Central Africans
Caraballo Range v3:355
Cardamom Hills v4:916
Cardamom Mountains v4:683
Carib Indians v2:89
Carib, Guatemalans v2:250
Carlyle, Thomas v5:441
Carol of Hohenzollern, Prince v5:405
Carpathian foothills, Austrians v5:56
Carpathian Mountains v5:312, 406, 506
Carreras, Josep v5:110
Carter, Jimmy v3:383
Carthaginians, Maltese v5:298
Casals, Pablo v5:110, 470
Casely-Hayford, author v1:244
Caspian Sea v3:70, 384, 482; v4:999, 1014;
  v5:368, 483
Castilian Spanish language
  Andalusians v5:42
  Castilians v5:102–106
  Catalans v5:107
  Galicians v5:200
  Spaniards v5:467
Castilians v5:102–106
Catalan language
  Catalans v5:106–111
  Andorrans v5:46
  French v5:191
Catalans v5:106–111
Catherine II v5:414
Caucasus Mountains v3:73; v4:1005; v5:111,
  112, 206, 250, 361, 362, 367, 368, 373
Caucasus region
  Abkhazians v5:15
  Adjarians v5:20
  Circassians v5:130
  Peoples of the Caucasus v5:376
Cavally River v1:295
Cebu v3:251
Cebuano language, Filipinos v3:249, 251
Cela, Camilo José v5:470
Celtic influence
  Bretons v5:87
  Castilians v5:102
Celtic tribes
  Scots v5:439
  Swiss v5:477
Celts v5:157

Central African Republic
  Aka v1:17
  Central Africans v1:105–111
Central Africans v1:105–111
Central Americans in the U.S. v2:122–160
  See also American Immigrants
Central Brahui Range v3:151
Cerruti, Nino v5:240
Cervantes, Miguel de v5:470
Ceylon. See Sri Lanka
Chad
  Chadians v1:111–117
  Fulani v1:222
Chadians v1:111–117
Chadic languages
  Cameroonians v1:96
  Nigeria v1:420
  See also specific languages
Chaga. See Chagga
Chagga v1:117–122
Chakmas v3:185–190
Cham v3:191–196
Chamârs v3:197–201
Chambal River v4:660
Champa Kingdom v4:848
Chang, Michael v2:133
Changbai Mountains v3:514
Changhua River v4:564
Changma. See Chakmas
Chao Phraya River v4:966
Chari-Nile v1:205
  Eritreans v1:203
Chashan Yao. See Yao v4:1039
Chattahoochee River v2:155
Chavacano language, Moro v4:675
Chavchu. See Chukchi and Koriak
Chavchyvav. See Koriak
Chechcno-Ingushetia v5:113
Chechens v5:111–118
Chekov, Anton v5:421
Chelkans v5:37
Chen, Steve v2:133
Chenab River v4:807, 877
Cher v2:68
Cheremis. See Maris
Cherkess language v5:131
Cherkess. See Circassians
Cherkessian language, Karachai v5:250
Chewa v1:123–128
  See also Bemba, Tonga, Zambians
Chibchan languages, Cuna v2:175
Chico River v3:450
Childrens Day v3:412
Chile
  Aymara v2:79
  Chileans v2:124–129
  Mapuches v2:345
Chileans v2:124–129
Chillida, Eduardo v5:68
Chiluba, Frederick v1:68
Chin v3:202–207
Chin, Frank v2:132
Chin, Tiffany v2:133
China
  Bai v3:82
  Buyi v3:181
  China and Her National Minorities v3:208

Dai v3:217
Derong v3:225
Dong v3:228
Ewenki v3:241
Gaoshan v3:260
Hakka v3:297
Han v3:302
Hani v3:307
Hmong v3:327
Hui v3:332
Kachins v3:442
Kazakh Chinese v3:479
Korean Chinese v3:514
Kyrgyz v4:543
Li v4:564
Man (Manchus) v4:602
Miao v4:642
Mongols v4:664
Naxi v4:705
Shans v4:866
Tibetans v4:972
Tujia v4:995
Uighurs v4:1010
Uzbeks v4:1014
Yao v4:1039
Yi v4:1052
Zhuang v4:1056
Chindwin Valley v3:202
Chinese Americans v2:130–134
    See also American Immigrants
Chinese langauge
    Americans v2:39
    Bai v3:82
    Canadians v2:117
    Ewenki v3:241
    Gaoshan v3:260
    Hui v3:332
    Malaysian Chinese v4:585
    Malaysian Indians v4:590
    Malaysian Malays v4:595
    Man (Manchus) v4:602
    Naxi v4:705
    Seychellois v1:479
    Shans v4:866
    Tibetans v4:972
    Tujia v4:995
    Yunnanese dialect v4:866
Chinese, Mandarin. *See* Mandarin Chinese
Chippendale, Thomas v5:162
ChiShona language, Zimbabweans v1:606
Chitimukulu v1:68
Chitonga language, Tonga v1:543
Chittagong-Bandarban Hills v3:202
Chittagong Hills v3:103
Choctaw v2:134–138
Choctaw language v2:134
Chokwe language, Angolans v1:35
Cholas v4:946
Chopin, Frederic v5:388
Chota Nagpur Plateau v4:688, 848
Christians, Syrian. *See* Syrian Christians
Chu River v4:543
Chuka v1:185
Chukchee. *See* Chukchi
Chukchi v5:118–123
Chukchi language
    Uelen dialect v5:119

    Pevek dialect v5:119
Chuuk v4:648
Chuvash v5:123–129
Ciluba language, Congolese (DROC) v1:144
Circassian language v5:130
    Karachai v5:250
Circassians v4:1005; v5:130–134
    See also Abkhazians
CIS. *See* Commonwealth of Independent
        States
Coast Veddas. *See* Veddas
Cochin, Jews of v3:431–435
Codrington, Sir Christopher v2:54
Coetzee, J. M. v1:196
Col Yao. *See* Yao
Colombia
    Colombians v2:139
    Guajiros v2:241
    Páez v2:418
    Vaupés v2:530
Colombians v2:144
Colored People of South Africa v1:129–133
Columbians v2:138
Columbus, Christopher v1:101; v2:54, 84
Comanche language v2:144
Comanches v2:144–149
Coming of Age Day v3:412
Commonwealth of Independent States (CIS)
        v5:70
Comoé River v1:295
Comorians v1:134–139
Congo, Democratic Republic of
    Azande v1:40
    Bakongo v1:51
    Efe and Mbuti Pygmies of the Ituri Forest
        v1:171
    Tutsi v1:562
    Twa v1:569
Congo, Republic of the
    Bakongo v1:51
    Congolese v1:139–143
Congolese v1:139–143
Congolese (Zairians) v1:144–149
Congo River v1:35, 51, 139, 144, 172
    Congolese v1:139
    Congolese (DROC) v1:144
Conrad, Joseph v1:139
Constable, John Bacon, v5:161
Constantine v4:1004, 1046
Constantinescu, Emil v5:405
Constitution Day v3:412
Cook Islands v4:804
Cook, Captain James v3:66
Coosa River v2:155
Coptic Christians v1:149–154
Coptic language v1:149, 150
Coptic Orthodox Church v1:149, 150
Copts. *See* Coptic Christians
Córdoba province, Spain, Andalusians v5:42
Cossacks v5:118
Costa del Sol, Spain, Andalusians v5:42
Costa Ricans v2:149–154
Cosxbuc, George v5:411
Côte d'Ivoire (Ivory Coast)
    Dyula v1:167
    Malinke v1:375
    Mossi v1:395

Cotobato Cordillera v4:962
Creek language, Creeks v2:156
Creeks v2:154–160
Creole language
    Belizeans v2:94
    Creoles of Louisiana v2:161
    Guyanans v2:255
    Seychellois v1:479
Creoles of Louisiana v2:161–165
Creoles of Sierra Leone v1:154–158
Crimean peninsula v5:488
Crimean War, v5:313
Crioulo language
    Cape Verdeans v1:101
    Guineans of Guinea-Bissau v1:263
Crixá. *See* Xavante
Croatia
    Croats v5:135–142
    Serbs v5:443
Croatian language v5:137
    Austrians v5:55
    Croats v5:135
Croats v5:82, 83, 135–142, 142
Cruixá. *See* Xavante
Cuban Americans v2:166–169
    See also American Immigrants
Cubans v2:170–174
Cujar River v2:28
Cullen, Countee v2:14
Cuna-Cueva. *See* Cunas
Cunas v2:175–178
Cunene River v1:35
Cuza, Alexandr John v5:405
Cyrenaica v1:329
Cyrillic alphabet v5:82
    Bulgarian v5:92
    Chukchi v5:119
    Chuvash v5:125
    Moldovan v5:314
Cyrus the Great v3:382; v4:750
Czech language v5:143
    Austrians v5:56
    Czechs v5:143
    Even v5:177
Czechs v5:143–147

D

da Gama, Vasco v1:101; v3:54
da Vinci, Leonardo v5:241
Dacians. *See* Moldovans
Dacko, David v1:110
Daddah, Moktar Ould v1:382
Dadu-Panth v4:819
Dadu River v3:307
Dagari v1:85
Dai v3:221–225
Dai language v3:217, 220
Daibeng. *See* Dai
Daile. *See* Dai
Daina. *See* Dai
Daiya. *See* Dai
Dakota and Lakhota v2:179–186
Dal v5:109
Dalai Lama v3:140, 166
Dali, Salvador v5:467, 470
Dalmatia, Croats v5:137
Damodar River v4:848

Damodar River Valley v4:689
Dan. *See* Dai
Danakil Desert v1:7, 163
    Afar v1:7
Dance
    Acehnese v3:14
    Ahirs v3:26
    Ambonese v3:38
    Andamanese v3:42
    Andhras v3:47
    Assamese v3:64
    Australian Aborigines v3:69
    Bajau v3:89
    Balinese v3:95
    Baluchi v3:100
    Bangladeshis v3:106
    Banjarese v3:116
    Batak v3:121
    Bhils v3:135
    Bugis, Makassarese, and Mandarese v3:172
    Buyi v3:183
    Cambodians v3:500
    Dai v3:220
    Derong v3:227
    Dong v3:231
    Ewenki v3:243
    Fijians v3:248
    Filipinos v3:258
    Gaoshan v3:263
    Gonds v3:274
    Greek Cypriots v3:281
    Gujaratis v3:288
    Gurungs v3:294
    Hani v3:309
    Iban v3:343
    Japanese v3:416
    Javanese v3:429
    Khasi v3:494
    Konds v3:512
    Lepchas v4:562
    Li v4:566
    Malaysian Chinese v4:589
    Malaysian Malays v4:600
    Man v4:604
    Maoris v4:621
    Maranao v4:626
    Melanesians v4:638
    Micronesians v4:649
    Minahasans v4:653
    Minangkabau v4:657
    Mongols in China v4:668
    Mons v4:672
    Motu v4:681
    Naxi v4:708
    Pamiri v4:788
    Peoples of the Caucasus v5:381
    Polynesians v4:806
    Romanians v5:411
    Santals v4:852
    Sinhalese v4:892, 902
    Slovaks v5:456
    Slovenes v5:465
    South Koreans v4:896
    Spaniards v5:467
    Syrians v4:925
    Tahitians v4:933
    Tamils v4:949

Tausug v4:961
Thai v4:970
Tibetan v4:975
Toda v4:984
Tujia v4:997
Uighurs v4:1013
Veddas v4:1023
Yao v4:1042
Yi v4:1055
Zhuang v4:1058
Dandangli Mountains v3:225
Dande River v1:52
Danes v5:147–152
Dani v3:224
Danube River v5:312, 406, 453
Danube Valley, Austrians v5:56
Dardanelles Strait v4:1005
Dari v3:16
Dari language
    Afghanis v3:17, 21
    Hazaras v3:311
    Pamiri v4:785
Darius the Great v4:1015
Darwin, Charles v1:101
Dasht-e-Kavir (Great Salt Desert) v3:384
Davao River v4:615
Davies, Robertson v2:119
Davis, Miles v2:14
de Abreu, Antonio v3:35
De Falla, Manuel v5:470
De Gaulle, Charles v1:24, 139
de Lima, Jorge v2:18
de Soto, Hernando v2:154
de Valdivia, Pedro v2:125
Dead Sea v3:398
DeAlmagro, Diego v2:98
Deane, Seamus v5:237
Debelyanov, Dimcho v5:94
Deccan Plateau v3:45, 361; v4:567, 766
Decebalus, King v5:404
Dekker, Edouard Douwes v5:349
Delaney, Benford v2:14
Delft pottery v5:350
Delvaux, Paul v5:519
Democratic Republic of Congo. *See* Congo,
    Democratic Republic of
Dendi v1:73
Deng Xiaoping v3:297
Deng, Simon v2:496
Denmark
    Danes v5:147
    Frisians v5:196
Der Seropian, Christopher v2:68
Derong v3:225–228
Derong River v3:225
Devanagari script, Sindhi language v4:883
Dholuo language, Luo v1:342, 343
di Lasso, Orlando v5:80
Diaka dialect, Aka v1:18
Dialect of Bengali, Chakmas v3:185
Dianyue. *See* Dai
Dinaric Karst v5:460
Diné. *See* Navajos
Dinesen, Isak v1:326
Dingban Yao. *See* Yao
Dinka v1:158–162
Dinka language

Dinka v1:158
Nuer v1:431
Diola. *See* Jola
Diop, Djibril Mambeti v1:585
Dir clan v1:163
Djibouti
    Afar v1:7
    Djiboutians v1:162–167
    Eritreans v1:203
Djiboutians v1:162–167
Dnestr River v5:312
Dogon language, Malians v1:371
Dolgan language v5:153
Dolgany v5:152–156
Domiciled Europeans. *See* Anglo Indians
Dominica
    Dominicans v2:190
Dominican Americans v2:187–189
    See also American Immigrants
Dominicans (Dominica) v2:190–194
Dominicans (Dominican Republic)
    v2:195–199
Donatello v5:241
Donelaitis, Kristijonas v5:285
Dong v3:228–231
Dong-Shui language, Yao v4:1039
Doric dialect v5:439
Dorobo v1:248
Dorsale Mountains v1:556
Dostoevsky, Fyodor v5:421
Douglas, Aaron v2:14
Douglas, Jacok v2:14
Dovbush, Oleksa v5:506
Dove, Rita v2:14
Dowland, John v5:161
Doyel, Arthur Conan v5:441
Drake, Sir Francis v1:101
Drakensberg Mountains v1:506
Dravidian v3:45, 102, 152, 265, 270, 362, 510;
    v4:568, 580, 659, 760, 773, 946
Druze v3:232–235
Dschagga. *See* Chagga
Duala v1:96
Dubcek, Alexander v5:452
Dudaev, Dzhokhar v5:112
Dudh Kosi River v4:871
Dulgaan. *See* Dolgany
Dutch
    Belgians v5:77
    Netherlanders v5:346
    Surinamese v2:501
Dutch Americans v2:200–202
    See also American Immigrants
Dutch language
    Belgians v5:77–81
    Frisians v5:196
    Netherlanders v5:346
    Surinamese v2:501
Dvina River v3:70
Dvorak, Antonin v5:145
Dyribal language, Australian Aborigines
    v3:67
Dürrenmatt, Friedrich v5:480
Dyula v1:167–171
Dzongkha, Bhutanese v3:137
Dzongkha language, Bhutanese v3:138

E

East Timor v4:977
Easter Island v4:803
Eastern Ghats v3:361, 510; v4:766
Ebonics v2:11
EC. *See* European Community
Echegaray, José v5:470
Ecuador
  Ecuadorians v2:203
  Jivaro v2:323
  Quechua v2:462
Ecuadorans v2:203–207
Efate Island v4:747
Efe and Mbuti v1:171–176
Egypt
  Coptic Christians v1:149, 150
  Egyptians v1:177
Egyptian Americans. *See* Arab Americans
Egyptians v1:177–185
Ekegusii language v1:267
Ekegusii. *See* Gusii
El Cid v5:102, 103
El Grec v5:470
El Hadj Oumar v1:258
El Salvador
  Maya v2:355
  Salvadorans v2:481
Elburz Mountains v3:384
Elgeyo. *See* Keiyo
Elgeyo Escarpment v1:316
Ellington, Duke v2:14
Ellis Island: American immigrants v2:30
Ellison, Ralph v2:14
Embu v1:185–193
Emi Koussi v1:112
Emirians (United Arab Emirates) v3:236–241
England v5:157–224
English v5:157–224
English Americans v2:207–210
English in South Africa v1:193–197
English language
  African Americans v2:11
  Americans v2:39
  Amish v2:48
  Andorrans v5:46
  Anglo Australians v3:49
  Antiguans and Barbudans v2:56
  Arab Americans v2:59
  Argentines v2:62
  Armenian Americans v2:67
  Asian Indian Americans v2:76
  Australian Aborigines v3:66, 67
  Austrians v5:55
  Azande v1:41
  Bahamians v2:84
  Bahrainis v3:76, 77
  Banyankole v1:61
  Barbadians v2:90
  Belizeans v2:94
  Bemba v1:68
  Beninese v1:73
  Cajuns v2:109
  Cameroonians v1:95
  Canadians v2:116
  Chagga v1:118
  Chewa v1:123, 124

Choctaw v2:134
Circassians v5:130
Colored People of South Africa v1:129
Comanches v2:144
Costa Ricans v2:149
Creeks v2:154
Dakota and Lakhota v2:179
Danes v5:147
Dominicans v2:190
English v5:157
Eritreans v1:203
Ethiopians v1:210
Fijians v3:245
French v5:191
Frisians v5:196
Fulani v1:222
Garifuna v2:226
Ghanaians v1:240
Greek Cypriots v3:276
Guyanans v2:255
Hausa v1:272
Hawaiians v2:271
Hindus of Guyana v2:276
Hondurans v2:282
Hopi v2:287
Ijo v1:289
Indians v3:360
Indo-Fijians v3:369
Irish v5:234
Iroquois v2:304
Israelis v3:397, 399
Jamaicans v2:314
Jordanians v3:436
Kalenjin v1:305
Keiyo v1:316
Kenyans v1:321
Kittitians and Nevisians v2:331
Kosovars v5:266
Kuwaitis v3:523
Kyrgyz v4:543
Lebanese v4:553, 554
Luo v1:342
Malaysian Chinese v4:585
Malaysian Malays v4:595
Maltese v5:300
Maori v4:619
Maronites v4:632, 633
Melanesians v4:635
Micronesians v4:647
Miskito v2:373
Monégasques v5:318
Mormons v2:378
Moroccans v1:388
Motu v4:679
Namibians v1:409
Navajos v2:397
Ndebele v1:415
New Zealanders v4:724
Nicaraguans v2:402
Nigerians v1:420
Ni-Vanuatu v4:747
Nyamwezi v1:439
Ojibwa v2:412
Omanis v4:750
Paiutes v2:424
Pakistanis v4:770
Panamanians v2:432

Parsis v4:789, 790
Polynesians v4:803
Puerto Ricans v2:458
Qataris v4:813
Rwandans v1:456
Samoans v4:844
Seminoles and Miccosukees v2:488
Seychellois v1:479
Sri Lankans v4:899
St. Lucians v2:471
St. Vincentians v2:477
Sudanese v1:512, 513
Surinamese v2:501
Swedes v5:472
Syrian Christians v4:917
Syrians v4:920
Tahitians v4:930
Tanzanians v1:530
Tlingit v2:512
Tongans v4:986
Trinidadians and Tobagonians v2:517
Tutsi v1:277, 562
Ugandans v1:574
Welsh v5:521
Zambians v1:600, 602
Zimbabweans v1:606
Zulu v1:612
English with West African dialect influences:
  Barbadians v2:89
Ensor, James v5:80
Equatoguineans. *See* Equatorial Guineans
Equatorial Guineans v1:198–202
Erasmus, Desiderius v5:349
Eritrea
  Afar v1:7
  Eritreans v1:203–209
  See also Djiboutians
  Tigray v1:536
Eritreans v1:203–209
Er'hai Lake v3:82
Ertra. *See* Eritreans
Erzias. *See* Mordvins
Eskimo. *See* Inuit
Espirtu Santo Island v4:747
Espriu, Salvador v5:109
Estonians v5:163–169
Estonian language v5:163, 165
  Estonians v5:163–169
Ethiopia
  Afar v1:7, 10
  Amhara v1:30
  Ethiopians v1:210
  Fulani v1:222
  Oromos v1:449
  Tigray v1:536
Ethiopian empire v1:536
Ethiopians v1:210–216
Euphrates River v3:390
  Armenians v5:50
  Madan v4:571
Euripides v5:223
European Americans v2:38
European Community (EC) v5:77
Europeans v1:91
Euskadi
  Basques v5:66
Euskal-Herria

Basques v5:66
Euskera
    Basques v5:65
Euskera language
    Basques v5:66
Evans-Pritchard, E. E. v1:40, 431
Even language v5:177
    Evens v5:176
Evenki v5:170-175
Evenki language v5:170
    Evenki v5:170
    Kalmyk v5:244
    Karachai v5:250
Evens v5:176-182
Ewe v1:217-221
Ewe language v1:217
Ewen. See Evens
Ewenki v3:241-245
Ewenki language
    Ewenki v3:241

F

Faizullin, R. v5:487
Falaika Island v3:523
Falkland Islands v2:63
Fang v1:96, 231
Fang language v1:227
    Equatorial Guineans v1:198
Fang peoples v1:198
Faroe Islands v5:147
Faroese language
    Danes v5:147
Farsi language
    Bahrainis v3:77
    Iranians v3:385
    See Parsis
Fatimid Dynasty v1:553
Fattaluku. See Timorese
Feast of the Assumption v5:56
Feast of the Immaculate Conception v5:56
Ferdinand of Arago v5:102
Ferdinand, King v5:405
Fergana River v4:1015
Fergana River Valley v4:543, 544
Ferlo Desert v1:582
Fernandino v1:198
Fezzan v1:329
Fiji Islands v4:803
    Banias v3:108
    Fijians v3:245
    Indo-Fijians v3:369
Fiji Hindi language
    Indo-Fijians v3:369
Fijian language
    Fijians v3:245
Fijians v3:245-249
Filipino Americans v2:211 214
    See also American Immigrants
Filipinos v3:249-260
    Ifugao v3:345
    Ilocanos v3:351
    Ilongot v3:355
    Kalinga v3:450
    Mangyan (Hanuno'o Group) v4:610
    Manuvu' (Upland Bagobo) v4:615
    Maranao v4:623
    Negrito (Pinatubo Aeta Group) v4:710

T'boli v4:962
Tagbanua v4:926
Tausug v4:957
Finland
    Finns v5:182
    Sami v5:430
Finnish language
    Finns v5:182
    Sami v5:430
    Swedes v5:472
Finno-Ugric language
    Sami v5:431
Finno-Ugric people v5:501
Finns v5:182-186
Fish River v1:587
Fitzgerald, Ella v2:14
Fjellner, Anders v5:432
Flanders, Flemings v5:187
Flemings v5:187-191
Flemish
    Belgians v5:77
    See also Flemings
Flemish language
    Belgians v5:77
    Flemish v5:187
    French v5:191
Flint River v2:155
Flores v3:373; v4:606
    Manggarai v4:606
Folk dances
    Basque v5:69
    Belarusan v5:75
    Bosnian v5:85
    Breton v5:90
    Bulgarian v5:94
    Catalan v5:110
Fon language
    Beninese v1:73
Forrester, Maureen v2:119
Forster, E. M. v3:57
Fouta Djallon v1:262
Fox Islands v2:20
France
    Alsatians v5:29, 30
    Armenians v5:50
    Basques v5:65
    Bretons v5:87
    French v5:191
Francis v5:161
Franck, César v5:80, v5:519
Franco, Francisco v5:102, 106, 107
Franco, General v5:470
Frank, Anne v5:346
Frankish dialects
    Alsatians v5:30
Franko, Ivan v5:510
French v5:191-196
French Americans v2:214-217
French Canadians v2:217-222
French Creole, Creoles of Louisiana v2:161
French Guiana, French Guianans v2:222
French Guianans v2:222-22
French language v1:91
    Algerians v1:23
    Alsatians v5:29, 30
    Americans v2:39
    Andorrans v5:46

Azande v1:41
Bamana v1:56
Basques v5:65
Belgians v5:77
Beninese v1:73
Bretons v5:87
Burkinabe v1:85
Cajuns v2:109
Cameroonians v1:95
Canadians v2:116
Canadians v2:117
Central Africans v1:105
Chadians v1:111
Comorians v1:135
Creoles of Louisiana v2:161
French Canadians v2:217
French Guianans v2:222
Haitians v2:262
Italians v5:238
Liechtensteiners v5:276
Malagasy v1:358
Seychellois v1:479
Swiss v5:477
Syrians v4:921
Wolof v1:582
French Polynesia, Polynesians v4:803
French Somaliland. See Djibouti
Friesland, Frisians v5:196
Frisch, Max v5:480
Frisian language v5:197
Frisians v5:196-200
Fruilian language, Italians v5:238
Fugard, Athol v1:196
Fula language, Gambians v1:232
Fulani v1:73, 96, 222-226
    See also Nigeriens
Fulani language, Beninese v1:73
Fulbe. See Fulani
Fulfulde language
    Chadians v1:112
    Fulani v1:222
    Guineans v1:257
    Malians v1:371
    Mauritanians v1:382
    Nigeriens v1:425
Fundamentalist Jew. See Traditional-
    Orthodox Jews
Futa Jallon dialect v1:222
Futa Toro dialect v1:222

G

Ga language v1:241
Gabes, Gulf of v1:555
Gabon
    Gabonese v1:227
    Twa v1:569
Gabonese v1:227-232
Gaelic, Irish v5:234
Gaelic language
    Scots v5:438
Gaer, Evdokiia v5:339
Gal Oya River v4:1020
Galicia v5:200
Galicians v5:200-205, 467
Gallego language, Galicians v5:200
Gallegos. See Galicians
Galtieri, General Leopoldi v2:63

Gambia, The
  Gambians v1:232
  Jola v1:299, 300
  Malinke v1:375
Gambians v1:232–240
Gan v3:208
Gandhi, Indira v3:362
Gandhi, Mahatma v3:286, 362
Gangdise Mountains v4:972
Ganges River v3:40, 103, 127, 148, 163, 197,
    506; v4:693, 729, 760, 825–826, 848
Gaolan. *See* Zhuang
Gaoligong Mountains v3:225
Gaoshan v3:260–265
Gaoshan language, Gaoshan v3:261
Garagum Desert v4:999
Gäray, R. v5:487
Garcia Lorca, Federico v5:470
Garibaldi, Giuseppe v5:240
Garifuna v2:226–229
Garifuna language v2:226
Gaspé Peninsula v2:116
Gaudí, Antoni v5:109
Gaura. *See* Ahirs
Gaza Strip v4:777, 778
  Palestinians v4:777
Gbaya v1:106
Gê language, Xavante v2:543
Ge tribes v2:327
Ge'ez language, Eritreans v1:205
Gee, Yung v2:133
Gei. *See* Li
Gekoyo. *See* Gikuyu
Geling. *See* Dong
Geluolo. *See* Kazakh Chinese
Genghis Khan v3:16, 382, 460, 479; v4:664,
    667, 1010; v5:483
Georgia
  Abkhazians v5:15
  Adjarians v5:19
  Georgians v5:205
  Karachai v5:250
  Ossetians v5:361
  People of Dagestan v5:367
Georgians v4:1005; v5:205–213
German Americans v2:230–232
  See American Immigrants
German language
  Americans v2:39
  Amish v2:48
  Austrians v5:55
  Belgians v5:77
  Canadians v2:116
  Danes v5:147
  Frisians v5:196
  Germans v5:214
  Hungarians v5:225
  Italians v5:238
  Liechtensteiners v5:276
  Luxembourgers v5:287
  Tyrolese v5:495
German, Alemannic, Liechtensteiners v5:276
Germanic tribes
  Swedes v5:472
  Swiss v5:477
Germans v5:214–221
Germany

Frisians v5:196
  Germans v5:214
Ghana
  Ewe v1:217
  Ghanaians v1:240
Ghanaians v1:240–247
Gharategin Mountains v4:940
Ghat Mountains (Western Ghats) v4:946
Ghaznavid Empire v5:394
Ghegs, Albanians v5:24
Gikuyu v1:186, 248–256
Gikuyu language v1:248, 249
Gikuyuland v1:248
Gillespie, Dizzy v2:14
Gir Range v3:285
Girnar Hills v3:284
Goa state, Goans v3:265
Goala. *See* Ahirs
Goans v3: 55, 265, 270
  Anglo-Indians v3:54
Gobi Desert v3:467
Godavari River v3:44; v4:628
Golan Heights v3:398
Gold Teeth. *See* Dai
Goldsmith, Oliver v5:237
Gomal River v4:795
Gomo River v4:739
Goncalves, Olga v5:392
Gondi language, Gonds v3: 270–276
Gonds v3:270–276
Gopal. *See* Ahirs
Gorbachev, Mikhail v5:112, 122, 250
Gordimer, Nadine v1:196
Gorkhali (Nepali) language, Nepalis v4:714
Gorkii, Maxim v4:943
Gould, Glenn v2:119
Gourmantche v1:85
Gourmantche language, Nigeriens v1:425
Gourounsi v1:85
Grabar. *See* Armenian language
Granada province, Spain, Andalusians v5:42
Granados, Enrique v5:470
Grande Comore (Njazdja) v1:134, 135
Great Dividing Range v3:49
Great Hun Empire v5:483
Great Migration. *See* American Immigrants
Great Rift Valley v1:210, 316
Great Yao Mountains v4:1039
Greater Xingan Mountains v3:241
Greece
  Albanians v5:23
  Greeks v5:221
Greek Americans v2:233–236
Greek Cypriots v3:276–284
Greek Empire v4:1015
Greek language v5:222
  Bulgarians v5:92
  Greek Cypriots v3:276
  Greeks v5:221
  Syrians v4:921
Greeks v5:221–224
Greenery Day v3:412
Greenlandic language, Danes v5:147
Gregory the Illuminator v5:51
Grenada, Grenadians v2:237
Grenadians v2:237–241
Grieg, Edvard v5:360

Gruyère region, Switzerland v5:480
Guajajara. *See* Tenetehara
Guajajara language, Tenetehara v2:508
Guajiro language, Guajiros v2:241
Guajiros v2:241–245
Guam, Micronesians v4:647
Guan language v1:241
Guaran language v2:246
  Guaranis v2:245
Guarani, Paraguayans v2:437
Guaranis v2:245–250
Guatemala
  Guatemalans v2:250
  Maya v2:355
Guatemalans v2:250–255
Guden River v5:147
Guinea
  Fulani v1:222
  Guineans v1:257
  Malinke v1:375
Guinea Bissau
  Guineans of Guinea Bissau v1:262–266
  Jola v1:299, 300
  Malinke v1:375
Guineans v1:257–261
Guineans of Guinea Bissau v1:262–266
Guineans, Equatorial. *See* Equatorial
    Guineans
Guipúzcoa region, Spain, Basques v5:65
Gujarat state, India
  Banias v3:108
  Kolis v3:502
  Gujaratis v3:284
Gujarati dialects, Kolis v3:502
Gujarati language
  Ahirs v3:24
  Gujaratis v3:284, 285
  Kenyans v1:321
  Kolis v3:502–503
  Parsis v4:789, 790
Gujaratis v3:284–290, 290
Gulf of Aden v4:859, 1046
Gulf of Cambay v3:285
Gulf of Guinea v1:294
Gulf of Kachch v3:285
Gulf of Lingayen v3:351
Gulf of Oman v3:97; v4:751, 859
Gulf of Saleh v4:908
Gulf of Thailand v4:967
Guoshan Yao. *See* Yao
Gur language v1:295
  Burkinabe v1:86
  Ghanaians v1:240
  Ivoirians v1:294
  Seychellois v1:479
Guraghe v1:450
Gurian dialect (Georgian), Adjarians v5:19
Gurjara region v5:394
Gurji. *See* Georgians
Gurkhas v4:714
Gurmukhi script, Punjabi language v4:877
Gurung language
  Bhutanese v3:137
  Gurungs v3:291
Gurungs v3:291–296
Gusii v1:267–272
Guyana

Guyanans v2:255
Hindus of Guyana v2:276
Guyanans v2:255–258
Guérzé people v1:257
Gwembe Valley v1:543
Gypsies. See Roma
Gyzylgum Desert v4:999

H

Ha. See Li
Haba Mountains v4:705
Habsburg Empire v5:81, 143, 225, 478, 55, 56, 59
Hafsids v1:554
Hageners. See Melpa
Haile Selassie v1:542
Haile Sellassie I v1:33
Hainan Island v4:564
Haiti v2:262
Haitian Americans v2:259–262
See also American Immigrants
Haitian Creole v2:262
Haitians v2:262–270
Hakka v3:208, 297–301
Hambartsumian, Victor v5:54
Hammamet, Gulf of v1:555
Hammurabi v3:390
Hamun-i-Mashkel Desert v3:97
Han v3: 35, 302–306; v4:894, 1056
See also China and Her National Minorities; Hakka
Han language
China v3:208
Han v3:302
Han'gul, Korean language v4:894
Hani v3:307–310
Hanish Islands v4:1046
Hanunoʾo. See Mangyan
Hapsburg Empire. See Habsburg Empire
Harappans v4:882
Haring, Keith v2:14
Hasidic. See Traditional-Orthodox Jews
Hassaniyya Arabic language v1:382
Hattic v5:131
Hausa v1:272–276
See also Nigeriens
Hausa language
Ghanaians v1:240–241
Hausa v1:272
Nigeriens v1:425
Hausaland (West Africa) v1:272
Havel, Vaclav v5:143, 145, 452
Hawaiian language
Hawaiians v2:271
Japanese v3:409
Polynesians v4:803
Samoans v4:844
Polynesians v4:804
Hawaiians v2:271–275
Hawar Islands v3:76; v4:814
Hay. See Armenians
Haydn, Franz Joseph v5:59
Haymanot, Tekle v1:537
Hazaras v3:311–314
Heaney, Seamus v5:237
Hebraeus, Bar v4:924
Hebrew language

Circassians v5:130
Israelis v3:397, 399
Jews of Cochin v3:431
Traditional-Orthodox Jews v4:990
Hebrides v5:439
Heilongjiang River v3:241
Helong. See Timorese
Henry, John v2:39
Hepplewhite, George v5:162
Herzegovina v5:81
Hidaka Mountains v3:27
High Tatras v5:453
Hiligaynon v3:315–318
Hiligaynon language
Filipinos v3:249, 251
Hiligaynon v3:315, 316
Hill tribespeople. See Mountain Mon-Khmer Groups
Hillary, Sir Edmund v4:719, 875
Hima v1:574
Himalaya Mountains v3:127, 138, 142, 186, 291, 361, 442; v4:559, 714, 716, 729, 760, 807, 825, 871, 882, 972
Hina Matsuri v3:412
Hindi and Urdu
Asian Indian Americans v2:76
Bhutanese v3:137
Bhutia v3:142–146
Guyanans v2:255
Kenyans v1:321
Kols v3:506
Surinamese v2:501
Trinidadians and Tobagonians v2:516–521
Hindi language
Bahrainis v3:76, 77
Chamârs v3:198
Hindus of Guyana v2:276
Indians v3:360
Indo-Fijians v3:369
Minas v4:660
Nicobarese v4:742
Oraons v4:760
People of India v3:362
Rajasthanis v4:819
Rajputs v4:826
Hindu Kush v3:16–17
Hindus v3:319–327
Guyanans v2:255
Rajasthanis v4:819
Hindus of Guyana v2:276–279
Hiri Motu language
Melanesians v4:635
Motu v4:679
Hirohito, Showa Emperor v3:410
Hissar Mountains v4:940
Hitler, Adolph v5:55, 70, 281
Hkakabo Razi (mountain) v3:442
Hmong v3:327–332
See also Miao
Hmong Americans v2:279–282
See also American Immigrants
Hmong language v3:327
Ho Chi Minh v4:1025
Hochdeutsch (High German)
Mennonites of Paraguay v2:360
German v5:214
Hockney, David v5:161

Hofmansthal, Hugo von v5:59
Hoggar Mountains v1:548, 549
Hokkaidò, Japan v3:27, 410
Holchu. See Nicobarese
Holland. See Netherlands
Homer v5:223
Hondurans v2:282–286
Honduras
Hondurans v2:282
Maya v2:355
Miskito v2:373
Sumu v2:497
Hong Kong v3:108
Honshu v3:410
Hooghly River v3:130
Hopi v2:287–292
Hopi language v2:287
Hor hopon ko. See Santals
Hor ko. See Santals
Houphouët-Boigny, Félix v1:294
Hualan Yao. See Yao
Huelva province, Spain v5:42
Hughes, Langston v2:14
Hui v3:332–336
See also China and Her National Minorities
Huihu. See Hui; Kazakh Chinese
Hui v3:332
Huma v1:574
Hume, David v5:441
Hungarian Americans v2:292–295
See also American Immigrants
Hungarian language
Austrians v5:56
Hungarians v5:225
Slovenes v5:459
Hungarians v5:225–229
Huoyi. See Hani
Hurston, Zora Neale v2:14
Husayn, Taha v1:183
Hussein, King v3:436
Hussein, Saddam v3:391, 523
Hut v1:574
Hutu v1:277–281, 456, 562
Huxley, Elspeth v1:326
Hwang, David Henry v2:132

I

Iatmul v3:336–339
Iban v3:340–344
Kelabit v3:487
Malaysian Chinese v4:585
Orang Asli v4:756
Penan v4:799
Iberia. See Andalusians; Spaniards; Portuguese
Ibo language, Equatorial Guineans v1:198
Ibsen, Henrik v5:360
Iceland v5:229
Icelanders v5:229–233
Ifugao v3:345–351
Ilongot v3:355
Kalinga v3:450
Igbo v1:282–288
Igboland v1:282
Ignatius Loyola v5:67
Igorots. See Ifugao
Ijaw. See Ijo

Ijo v1:289–293
Ili River Valley v3:479
Illegal immigrants. *See* American Immigrants
Ilocano language
    Filipinos v3:249, 251
    Ilocanos v3:351
Ilocanos v3:351–355
Ilocos Mountains v4:710
Ilongo language v3:249
Ilongot v3:355–359
Imazighen. *See* Berbers
Imerina v1:355
Immigrants, American. *See* American
        Immigrants
Incas v2:124
India
    Ahirs v3:24
    Andamanese v3:40
    Andhras v3:44
    Anglo-Indians v3:54
    Assamese v3:62
    Banias v3:108
    Bengalis v3:127
    Bhils v3:131
    Bhutia v3:142–146
    Brahmans v3:146
    Buddhists v3:163
    Chakmas v3:185–190
    Chamârs v3:197
    Chin v3:202
    Goans v3:265
    Gujaratis v3:284
    Hindus v3:319
    Indians v3:360
    Jains v3:404
    Jats v3:418
    Jews of Cochin v3:431
    Kachins v3:442
    Khasi v3:491
    Kolis v3:502
    Kols v3:506
    Konds v3:510
    Lingayats v4:567
    Marathas v4:627
    Minas v4:659
    Mundas v4:688
    Muslims v4:693
    Naga v4:699
    Nicobarese v4:742
    Oraons v4:760
    Oriya v4:766
    Punjabis v4:807
    Rajasthanis v4:818
    Rajputs v4:825
    Roma v5:394
    Santals v4:848
    Shans v4:866
    Sikhs v4:877
    Syrian Christians v4:916
    Tamils v4:946
    Tibetans v4:972
    Todas v4:981
Indian Americans. *See* Asian Indian
        Americans
Indian Desert v4:883
Indian Ocean v1:210, 531, 612; v3:225, 424;
        v4:855, 898, 1046

Indians (Asian) v3:360, 360–368, 368
    See Asian Indian Americans
Indigo Yao. *See* Yao
Indo-Fijians v3:369–371, 371
Indonesia
    Acehnese v3:11
    Ambonese v3:35–40; v4:1025
    Bajau v3:86
    Balinese v3:90
    Banjarese v3:112
    Batak v3:117
    Bugis, Makassarese, and Mandarese v3:169
    Indonesians v3:371
    Javanese v3:423
    Madurese v4:575
    Malays v4:580
    Manggarai v4:606
    Minahasans v4:650
    Minangkabau v4:654
    Ngaju Dayak v4:733
    Niasans v4:738
    Sa'dan Toraja v4:840
    Sasak v4:854
    Sumbanese v4:903
    Sumbawans v4:908
    Sundanese v4:911
    Timorese v4:977, 978
Indonesians v3:371–381
Induráin, Miguel v5:470
Indus River v4:770, 795, 807, 877, 882, 883,
        884; v5:394
Industrial Revolution v5:413
Inga Dam v1:144
Inner Mongolia Autonomous Region, China
        v4:664
International Women's Day v5:52
Inuit v2:296–299
Inuktitut language v2:117
Iran
    Armenians in v5:50
    Azerbaijanis v3:70
    Baluchi v3:97
    Brahui v3:151
    China and Her National Minorities v3:208
    Iranians v3:382
    Kurds v3:518
    Pamiri v4:785
    Turkmens v4:998
Iranian Plateau v3:97
Iranians v3:382–390
Iraq
    Bedu v3:122–126
    Iraqis v3:390
    Kurds v3:518
    Ma'dan v4:571
    Yazidis v4:1043
Iraqis v3:390–396
Ireland
    Irish v5:234–238
Irian Jaya v3:221, 373
Irish v5:234–238
Irish Americans v2:300–303
    See also American Immigrants
Irish Gaelic v5:234
Irish Sea v5:234
Iroquois v2:304–310
Irrawaddy River v3:442

Irtysh River v3:460
Iru v1:574
Irula v4:981
Isabella of Castile v5:102
Ishkashims. *See* Tajiks
IsiNdebele language
    Ndebele v1:415–420
    Xhosa v1:587
    Zimbabweans v1:607
IsiZulu language v1:612
Isle of Afallon v5:522
Israel
    Bedu v3:122
    Circassians v5:130
    Druze v3:232
    Israelis v3:397
    Palestinians v4:777
    Traditional-Orthodox Jews v4:990–994
Israelis v3:397–404
Issa clan v1:163
Italian Americans v2:310–313
    See also American Immigrants
Italian language
    Americans v2:39
    Argentines v2:62
    Austrians v5:55–56
    Canadians v2:116–117
    Eritreans v1:203, 205
    Ethiopians v1:210
    Italians v5:238
    Monégasques v5:318
    Sammarinese v5:435
    Somali v1:495
    Swiss v5:477
    Tyrolese v5:495
Italians v5:238–242
Italy v5:435
    Italians v5:238
    Slovenes v5:459
    Tyrolese v5:495
Itelmen (Kamchadal) language v5:119
Iteso v1:574
Ituri forest
    Efe and Mbuti Pygmies of the Ituri Forest
        v1:171
Ivan IV, Tsar v5:483
Ivanov, Konstantin v5:127
Ivasiuk, Volodymyr v5:510
Ivoirians v1:294–299
Ivory Coast. *See* Côte d'Ivoire
Izo. *See* Ijo

J

Jabal an Nusayriyah Mountains v3:32
Jacob of Edessa v4:924
Jad Bhutia v3:143
Jaen province, Spain v5:42
Jagga. *See* Chagga
Jains v3:404–408
Jamaicans v2:314–317
James VI v5:438
Jamhuri Day v1:520
Japan
    Ainu v3:27
    Japanese v3:409
Japanese v3:409–418
    See also Ainu

Japanese Americans v2:317–320
    See also American Immigrants
Japanese language
    Ainu v3:27
    Japanese v3:409
Jarawas. *See* Andamanese
Jaruzelski, General Wojciech v5:384
Jats v3:418–423
Java v3:91, 112, 170, 373; v4:575, 911
    Javanese v3:423
    Madurese v4:575
    Sundanese v4:911
Java Sea v3:424; v4:734
Javanese v3:423–431
Javanese language
    Indonesians v3:374
    Javanese v3:423
    New Caledonians v4:721
Jawara, D. K. v1:233
Jejawan script v4:855
Jen, Gish v2:132
Jerusalem, Armenians in v5:50
Jewish Americans v2:320–322
    See also American Immigrants
Jews of Cochin v3:431–435
Jhelum River v4:807, 877
Jibouti. *See* Djibouti
Jilin province, China v3:514
Jinmen. *See* Yao
Jinsha River v4:705
Jivaro v2:323–326
Jola v1:299–303
Jola language
    Gambians v1:232
    Jola v1:300
Jola-Foni. *See* Jola
Jordan
    Bedu v3:122
    Circassians v5:130
    Druze v3:232
    Jordanians v3:436
Jordan River v3:436; v4:780
Jordanian Americans. *See* Arab Americans
Jordanians v3:436–442
Joyce, James v5:234, 237
Jung, Carl v5:480
Jura Mountains v5:477
Jurchens. *See* Man (Manchus)
Juula language v1:371

K

Ka v3:260
Kaale. *See* Roma
Kaale dialect v5:396
Kabardino-Balkaria v5:130
Kabardins. *See* Circassians
Kabila, Laurent v1:144
Kaboré, Gaston v1:89
Kabul River v3:18
Kachin language v3:442
Kachins v3:442–446
Kadare, Ismail v5:27
Kadavu v3:246
Kadazan v3:446–450
Kaficho v1:450
Kafka, Franz v5:59, 145
Kafue River v1:543, 601

Kahayan River v4:734
Kaimur Rang v3:506
Kakongo v1:52
Kakum National Park v1:245
Kaladan River v4:832, 836
Kalahari desert v1:12
Kalat Plateau v3:151
Kalenjin v1:304–310, 337
    See also Keiyo
Kalenjin language v1:305
    Kalenjin v1:304
    Keiyo v1:316
Kali Gandaki River v3:291
Kalimantan v3:86, 112, 173, 340, 373, 423;
    v4:580, 733
Kalimantan, Indonesia v4:733
Kalinga v3:450–454
    See also Ifugao
Kalmykia v5:243
Kalmyks v5:243–249
    See also Altays
Kamarakoto. *See* Pemon
Kamaran v4:1046
Kamba v1:185
Kamba River v1:53
Kambera language v4:903
Kamchatka v3:27
Kammu v3:455–459
    See also Lao
Kamonikan. *See* Ewenki
Kampuchea, Miao v4:642
Kamruguru v4:848
Kanaks. *See* New Caledonians
Kandha. *See* Konds
Kannada language
    Indians (Asian) v3:360
    Lingayats v4:567, 568
    People of India v3:360
Kaousan v1:549
Kapwepwe, Simon v1:546
Kara Kum Desert v3:482
Karacha language v5:375
Karachaevo-Cherkessian Republic
    Karachai v5:130, 250
Karachai v5:250–254
Karakalpaks v3:460–466
Karakalpakistan v3:460
Karakoram Mountains v3:361; v4:773
Karamojong v1:574, 580
Karane (Indo-Pakistan) v1:355
Karens v3:467–471
Karnataka state, India v4:567
Karo-Dairi dialect v3:118
Karoo v1:310
Karretjie People v1:310–315
Kartvelebi. *See* Georgians
Kasavubu, Joseph v1:51
Kashmir v3:163, 472
Kashmiri language
    Indians (Asian) v3:360
    Kashmiris v3:472
    Pakistanis v4:773
    People of India v3:360
Kashmiris v3:472–478
Kastrioti, Gjergh v5:27
Kathmandu Valley v4:714, 716, 729
Kaunda, Kenneth v1:546, 68, 601

Kaveri (Cauvery) River v4:946
Kawle. *See* Roma
Kayapos v2:327–330
Kazakh Chinese v3:479–481
Kazakh language
    Altay v5:38
    Kazakh Chinese v3:479
    Kazakhs v3:482
Kazakhs v3:482–486
Kazakhstan
    Karakalpaks v3:460
    Kazakh Chinese v3:479
    Kazakhs v3:482
Kazanka River. v5:485
Keating, Paul v3:49
Keita, Modibo v1:371
Keiyo v1:304, 316–320
    See also Kalenjin
Kelabit v3:487–491; v4:543–547
    Orang Asli v4:756
    Penan v4:799
Keller, Gottfried v5:480
Kemal, Mustafa v4:1004
Kente Mountains v4:664
Kenya
    Embu v1:185
    Gikuyu v1:248
    Gusii v1:267
    Kalenjin v1:304
    Keiyo v1:316
    Kenyans v1:321
    Luhya v1:337
    Maasai v1:350
    Oromos v1:449
    Swahili v1:519
Kenya, Mount v1:186
Kenyans v1:321–328
Kenyatta, Jomo v1:248, 321
Kenzaburo, Oe v3:416
Kerala state, India
    Jews of Cochin v3:431
    Syrian Christians v4:916
Kerei. *See* Kazakh Chinese
Kerulen River v4:664
Khachaturian, Aram v5:54
Khakasia, Republic of v5:255
Khakass v5:255–259
Khalili, Khalilullah v3:21
Khalmg. *See* Kalmyks
Khamu. *See* Kammu
Khan, General Yahya v3:103
Khan, Genghis. *See* Genghis Khan
Khanate v5:483
Kharijites v1:23, 553
Kharisov, R. v5:487
Khasi v3:491–495
Khassonke language v1:371
Khmer v3:495–502
Khmer language
    Cambodian Americans v2:113
    Khmer v3:495
Khmu. *See* Kammu
Khoisan dialect
    Karretjie v1:311
    Namibians v1:409
Khomeini, Ayatollah Ruhollah v3:382
Khond. *See* Konds

Khorasan Mountains v3:384
Khorasani Persian v3:311
Khrushchev, Nikita v5:112
Khyber Pass v4:773, 795
Ki Khasi. *See* Khasi
Kiangan. *See* Ifugao
Kichagga langauge v1:118
Kiembu language v1:185, 187
Kikongo language v1:52
Kikuyu language v1:321
   See also Gikuyu
Kilimanjaro, Mount v1:185
Kiluyia language v1:321
Kimbangu, Simon v1:53
Kimbanguisim v1:51
King, Dr. Martin Luther, Jr. v2:15
King's Men, The. *See* Baganda
Kingman, Dong v2:133
Kingston, Maxine Hong v2:132
Kinyamwezi language v1:441
   Nyamwezi v1:439
Kinyarwanda language v1:278
   Rwandans v1:456
   Tutsi v1:563
   Twa v1:569
Kipchak dialects (Turkic) v5:38
Kipkorir, Benjamin v1:304
Kipling, Rudyard v3:57
Kipsigis v1:304
Kiribati v4:647
Kirthar Range v3:97; v4:883
Kirundi language v1:278, 91
   Burundians v1:90
   Tutsi v1:563
   Twa v1:569
Kisii. *See* Gusii
Kiskito Coast v2:498
Kissi people v1:257
Kistna River v3:44, 48
Kisukuma v1:441
Kiswahili language v1:248, 441, 519
   Banyankole v1:61
   Kenyans v1:321
   Luo v1:342
   Nyamwezi v1:439
   Swahili v1:519
   Ugandans v1:575
Kitami Mountains v3:27
Kittitians and Nevisians v2:331–335
Kiwi. *See* New Zealanders
Klee, Paul v5:480
Klima, Ivan v5:145
Kmhmu. *See* Kammu
Knights Hospitaller v5:299
Knox, John v5:439
Kobar Depression v1:205
Kodály, Zoltán v5:228
Koi. *See* Gonds
Koitur. *See* Gonds
Kokang Chinese v4:866
Kol language v3:506
Kolas, Jakub v5:75
Kolis v3:502–506
Kols v3:506–510
Koma v1:450
Kombe v1:198
Kondh. *See* Konds

Konds v3:510–514
Kongo language v1:35–36
   See also Bakongo
Konkani language
   Goans v3:266
Konstantinov, Aleko v5:92
Kony dialect v1:305
Kopet Dag Mountains v4:999
Korat Plateau v3:153
Korea, Republic of
   South Koreans v4:893
Korea, South. *See* Korea, Republic of
Korean alphabet v4:894
Korean Americans v2:335–338
   See also American Immigrants
Korean Chinese v3:514–517
   China and Her National Minorities v3:208
Korean language
   Korean Chinese v3:514
   South Koreans v4:893
Koreans, South v4:893–897
Koriak v5:118, 259–264
Koriak language v5:119, 260
   Koriak v5:259
   Macedonian v5:292
   Nanais v5:335
   Nenets v5:341
Korogwe dialect v1:485
Koryak. *See* Koriak
Kosova. *See* Gusii
Kosovars v5:265–270
Kosovo
   Serbs v5:443
   Kosovars v5:265
Kota v4:981
Kotliarevsky, Ivan v5:510
Kotokoli v1:73
Kotuba, Mono language v1:52
Kourmanji language v4:1043
Kozhumiaka, Kyrylo v5:506
Krio language v1:154, 155
Krishna River v4:567, 628
Kru language v1:295
   Ivoirians v1:294
Ksatriya caste. *See* Rajputs
Ku. *See* Konds
Ku Klux Klan v2:36
Kuanza River v1:35
Kuchma, Leonid D. v5:505
Kui language v3:510, 511
Kulo v1:450
Kulubali, Biton v1:56
Kumandins v5:37
Kumzar language v4:751
Kunama v1:203–205
Kundera, Milan v5:145
Kunlun Mountains v4:972
Kupala, Janka v5:75
Kura River v3:71
Kurdish language
   Iraqis v3:390, 392
   Kurds v3:518
   Peoples of the Caucasus v5:375
Kurds v3:518–522
Kuril Islands v3:27
Kurram River v4:795
Kurukh. *See* Oraons

Kurukh language v4:760
Kurumba v4:981
Kutter, Joseph v5:289
Kuvi language v3:510, 511
Kuwait
   Bedu v3:122
   Kuwaitis v3:523
Kuwaitis v3:523–530
Kwa language v1:282
Kwabena Nketia, J. H. v1:244
Kwan, Michelle v2:133
Kwango River v1:35, 52
KwaZulu-Natal Province, South Africa
   Zulu v1:612
Kwéyòl dialect v2:190
Kwilu River v1:52
Kyôsuke, Kindaichi v3:28
Kyrenia Range v3:277
Kyrgyz v4:543–547
   See also Altay
Kyrgyzstan
   Kazakh Chinese v3:479
   Kyrgyz v4:543
Kysyl Kum Desert v4:1015
Kyushu v3:410

L

La. *See* Chin
Labourd region, France v5:65
Lac Sale v1:136
Ladakh v3:167
Ladakh region of Kashmir v3:142
Ladin language v5:495
Lagerlof, Selma v5:475
Lahit Lake v4:962
Lahus v4:866
Lajia. *See* Yao
Lake Alaotra v1:356
Lake Baikal v4:543; v5:424
Lake Balaton v5:225
Lake Bangweulu v1:68
Lake Chad v1:95, 111
Lake Edward v1:61
Lake Fianga v1:112
Lake Issyk v3:479; v4:543
Lake Lanao v4:623
Lake Mweru v1:68
Lake Sebu v4:962
Lake Tanganyika v1:92, 93, 531
Lake Titicaca v2:79, 98
Lake Toba v3:118, 121
Lake Tondano v4:651
Lake Victoria v1:45, 61, 321, 347, 349, 350,
      439, 442, 532, 574
Lal Shabhaz Qalande v4:884
Lallans dialect v5:439
Lamming, George v2:92
Lancang River v3:82
Lanchang Jiang River v3:307
Lango v1:574
Lanyu v4:951
Lanyu Island v3:261
   See also Taiwan Indigenous People
Lao v4:548–553
Lao language v4:548
Laos
   Hmong v3:327

Kammu v3:455
Lao v4:548
Miao v4:642
Shans v4:866
Laotian Americans v2:339–341
See also American Immigrants
Lapland v5:430
Lapps. See Sami
Lari dialect v4:883
Latter-day Saints. See Mormons
Latvians v5:270–275
Lau, Alan Chong v2:132
Laurence, Margaret v2:119
Lavvo v5:432
Lawangan language v4:734
Laz v4:1005
Laz language v5:376
Le Corbusier v5:480
Lebanese v4:553–559
Lebanese Americans v2:342–344
See also American Immigrant; Arab
Americans
Lebanon
Armenians in v5:50
Bedu v3:122
Druze v3:232
Kurds v3:518
Maronites v4:632
Lee, Gus v2:132
Lee Kwan Yew v3:297
Lee Teng-hui v3:297
Leeward Islands v2:331
Lemro River v4:832
Lenin, Nikolai v5:414
Lepcha language
Buddhists v3:163
Lepchas v4:559
Lepchas v4:559–563
Lesage, Alain-René v5:90
Lesotho
Sotho v1:506
Lesser Sunda island chain v4:903
Lettish v5:270
Letts. See Latvians
Letzebürgesch v5:287
Levante, Moslem v5:467
Leyte v3:251
Lezgin language v5:368
Li v4:564–567
Li language v4:564
Liao. See Dai; Dong
Liberia v1:375
Libya
Berbers v1:78
Libyans v1:329
Tuaregs v1:548
Libyans v1:329 337
Liechtensteiners v5:276–280
Lightfoot, Gordon v2:119
Limbang River v3:487
Limbu language v4:716
Lin, Maya v2:133
Lincoln, Abraham v2:11, 15
Lindgren, Astrid v5:475
Lingala language
Congolese v1:139
Congolese (DROC) v1:144

Lingayats v4:567–570
Lion Mountains v1:155
Lithuania
Lithuanians v5:280
Roma v5:394
Lithuanians v5:280–286
Liuqiu. See Gaoshan
Livingstone, David v1:68, 543
Llorenç v5:109
Lobi v1:85
Lombok v3:91, 112, 170, 373; v4:854
Lomwe v1:123
Longfellow, Henry Wadwsorth v2:109
Lord, Betty Bao v2:132
Lord Byron v5:441
Louie, David Wong v2:132
Luanda v1:96
Luangwa River v1:601
Luapula River v1:601
Luba peoples v1:68
Luganda language
Baganda v1:44–45
Ugandans v1:574
Luhya v1:337–342
Luimbe-Nganguel v1:36
Lukai. See Gaoshan
Luo v1:337, 342–350
Luo language v1:321
Luowu. See Yi
Lushoto dialect v1:485
Luther, Martin v5:478
Luxembourgers v5:286–290
Luyia. See Luhya
Luzon, Philippines v3:251, 345, 351, 450;
v4:710
Ifugao v3:345
Ilocanos v3:351
Ilongot v3:355
Kalinga v3:450
Negrito (Pinatubo Aeta Group) v4:710
Lyatoshynsky, Borys v5:510
Lygoraveltlat. See Chukchi
Lysenko, Mykola v5:510

M

M'ranao. See Maranao
Ma, Yo Yo v2:133
Ma'anyan language
Ngaju Dayak v4:734
Ma'dan v4:571–574
Maa language v1:351
Maasai v1:186, 337, 350–355
MacArthur, Douglas v4:710
MacCarthy Island v1:234
Macedonia
Albanians v5:23
Macedonians v5:291
Macedonians v5:291–297
Madagascar v1:355
Madaraka Day v1:520
Made-related language v1:86
Madhya Pradesh region, India
Kols v3:506
Oraons v4:760
Madriu-Perafita-Claror Valley v5:46
Madura v4:575
Madurese v4:575–579

Maeterlinck, Maurice v5:80
Magar language v4:716
Magat River v3:345
Magellan, Ferdinand v2:124; v3:249; v4:926
Maghrib
Algerians v1:23
Tunisians v1:553
Magritte, René v5:80, 519
Magtymguly v4:1002
Maguindanao language v4:673, 675
Magyar language. See Hungarian
Magyars. See Hungarians
Mahabharat Lekh Mountains v4:729
Mahafaly v1:356
Mahanadi River v3:510; v4:766
Maharashtra state, India
Banias v3:108
Kolis v3:502
Marathas v4:627
Mahaweli River v4:1020
Mahé v1:479
Mahfouz, Naguib v1:183
Mahler, Gustav v5:59
Mahrattas. See Marathas
Maikala Range v3:271
Majaivana, Lovemore v1:610
Maka or Masombiky v1:356
Makassarese. See Bugis, Makassarese, and
Mandarese; Makassarese
Makonnen, Ababa v1:453
Mala River v3:38
Malabar Christians. See Syrian Christians
Malabar coast v4:916, 981
Málaga province, Spain v5:42
Malagasy v1:355–363
Malakula Island v4:747
Malawi v1:123
Malay language
Ambonese v3:35
Bruneians v3:155, 157
Iban v3:340
Malays v4:580
Malays in Indonesia v4:580
Malaysian Chinese v4:585
Malaysian Indians v4:590
Malaysian Malays v4:595, 596
Minahasans v4:650
Orang Asli v4:756
Malay Peninsula v3:11; v4:596
Malayalam language
Indians v3:360
Jews of Cochin v3:431
Muslims in South Asia v4:694
People of India v3:362
Syrian Christians v4:916
Malays 580–584, 799
See also Banjarese, Javanese, Malaysian
Indians, Orang Asli
Malaysia
Banias v3:108
Hakka v3:297
Iban v3:340
Kadazan v3:446
Kelabit v3:487
Malaysian Chinese v4:585
Malaysian Indians v4:590
Malaysian Malays v4:595

Orang Asli v4:756
Penan v4:799
Malaysian Chinese v4:585–589
Malaysian Indians v4:590–595
Malaysian Malays v4:595–4:601
Maldivians v1:364–370
Mali, Republic of
Bamana v1:56
Berbers v1:78
Dyula v1:167
Malians v1:371
Malinke v1:375
Songhay v1:501
Tuaregs v1:548
Mali Empire v1:167, 294, 371, 376
Malians v1:371–375
Malimasha. *See* Naxi
Malinke v1:375–381
Malta v5:298, 299
Maltese v5:298–308
Mamikonian, Vartan v5:51
Man (Manchus) v4:602–605
Man Mountains v1:294
Manala. *See* Ndebele
Manchu language v4:602
Manchus. *See* Man (Manchus)
Mandarese v3:169
Mandarin Chinese language
China and Her National Minorities v3:208
Han v3:302
Taiwan Indigenous People v4:934
Tao v4:951
Mandchus. *See* China and Her National
Minorities
Mandé language v1:295
Dyula v1:167
Ivoirians v1:294
Malinke v1:375
Mandé. *See* Malinke
Mande-kan v1:382
Mandin (Manding, Mandingo). *See* Malinke
Mandinka. *See* Malinke v1:375
Mandinka language v1:232
Mang'anja v1:123
Mang'anja v1:124
See also Chewa
Manga language v1:425
Mangbetu v1:569
Manggarai v4:606–610
Mangyan (Hanuno'o group) v4:614–610
Maninka. *See* Malinke
Manipur state, India v4:699
Manjhi. *See* Santals
Mano people v1:257
Manueline architectural style v5:392
Manuvu' (Upland Bagobo) v4:615–618
See also Kalinga
Manzhou. *See* Man (Manchus)
Mao Zedong v3:208, 213
Maori v4:619–622
See also New Zealanders
Maori language
Maori v4:619
Polynesians v4:803, 804
Mapfumo, Thomas v1:610
Mapuches v2:345–349
Mapuche language v2:345

Maradona, Diego v2:66
Marakwet v1:304
Maranao v4:623–627, 678
Maranao language
Maranao v4:623
Moro v4:673, 675
Marathas v4:627–631
Marathi language
Goans v3:265–266
Indians v3:360
Kolis v3:503
People of India v3:362
Christians v4:916
Maravi v1:123
Marcos, Ferdinand v3:250, 351
Mari langauge v5:308
Mari Republic v5:501
Mariam, Lt. Colonel Mengistu Haile v1:203
Mariana Islands, Northern v4:647
Maris v5:308–312
Maromainty v1:356
Maromena v1:356
Maronites v4: 553, 632–635
Marsh Arabs. *See* Ma'dan
Marshall Islands v4:647
Martapura River v3:112
Marthi language v4:627, 628
Marwaris. *See* Rajasthanis
Masbate v3:251
Mashio, Chiri v3:28
Mashtots, Mesrop v5:51
Masina dialect v1:222
Masters, John v3:57
Masuka, Dorothy v1:610
Matsigenka v2:349–354
Maure language v1:382
Mauritania
Berbers v1:78
Mauritanians v1:382
Mauritanians v1:382–387
Mauryan Empire v3:44, 164, 284, 360
Maxaad tiri language v1:495
May Day v5:52
Maya v2:355–359
Mayakovskii, Vladimir v4:943
Mayan languages v2:355
Guatemalans v2:250
Mayotte (Mahore) v1:134, 135
Mayu River v4:836
Mayumbe v1:52
Mbaye v1:113
Mbeere v1:185
Mbini v1:198
Mboya, Tom v1:349
Mbundu v1:35–36
Mbuti v1:171
See also Twa
McGillivray, Alexander v2:154
Meciar, Vladimir v5:453
Mediterranean Sea v1:184, 331, 555; v4:1005;
v5:42, 299, 318, 467
Medlpa. *See* Melpa
Meghalaya state, India v3:491
Meghna River v3:103, 187
Mejerda River v1:556
Mekong River v3:192, 455; v4:548, 866, 966,
970, 1026

Melanesians v4:635–639
Melanesians, indigenous. *See* New
Caledonians
Melpa v4:639–642
Melville, Herman v4:804
Mengistu v1:542
Mengwushiwei. *See* Mongols
Mennonites of Paraguay v2:360–363
Meo. *See* Hmong
Meos. *See* Minas
Meranao. *See* Maranao
Merina language v1:355
Meru v1:186
Meskhetian language v5:375
Mesopotamia v4:882
Meuse River v5:519
Mewati. *See* Minas
Mexican Americans v2:364–367
See also American Immigrants
Mexicans v2:367–373
Mexico
Maya v2:355
Mexicans v2:367
Meymaneh v3:22
Mfengu v1:587
Mian. *See* Yao
Miao (Hmong) v4:642–646
See also China and Her National
Minorities; Hmong
Miao language
Miao v4:642
Yao v4:1039
Miccosukees v2:488–405
Michael the Brave v5:405
Michelangelo v5:241
Michener, James v4:747
Mickiewicz, Adam v5:388
Micmac language v2:117
Micronesia, Federated States of v4:647
Micronesians v4:647–650
Middle Ages v5:56
Mikasuki (Hitchiti) v2:488
Milev, Geo v5:94
Milin. *See* Gaoshan
Milles, Carl v5:475
Milosz, Czeslaw v5:388
Min v3:208
Minahasans v4:650–653
Minang language v4:654
Minangkabau v4:654–658
Minas v4:659–664
Mindanao v3:251; v4:623
Mindoro v3:251; v4:611
Mangyan (Hanuno'o Group) v4:610
Mingalimov, R. v5:487
Mingrelian language v5:376
Minianka language v1:371
Minoan civilization v5:221
Miró, Joan v5:109, 470
Mirambo v1:442
Misapo. *See* Yi
Miskito v2:373–378, 378
Mississippi River v2:109
Mitchell, Joni v2:119
Mittelland, Switzerland v5:477
Mizo. *See* Chin
Mkara, Benjamin v1:530

Mlalo dialect v1:485
Mogul (Moghal) Empire v4:1018
Mogul. See Mughal v3:284
Moi-Fau. See Li
Moksha River v5:330
Mokshas. See Mordvins
Moldavia. See Moldovans
Moldova River v5:312
Moldovan language (Romanian) v5:312
Moldovans v5:312 317
Molucca Islands v3:373; v4:653
Mõmbugu-Schelling, Flora v1:534
Mon language v4:669
Monaco v5:318
Monastel, Alejandro v2:153
Monégasques v5:318–324
Mongol language
    Kalmyk v5:244
    Mongols v4:664
    Mongols in China v4:665
    Tuvans v5:489
Mongolia v5:489
    China and Her National Minorities v3:208
    Ewenki v3:241
Mongols in China v4:664–669
    See also China and Her National Minorities
Mon-Khmer language
    Mountain Mon-Khmer v4:684
    Mountain Mon-Khmer Groups v4:682
Mono River v1:76
Mons v4:669–673
Montenegrins v5:324–329
Montenegro v5:324
    Albanians v5:24
    Serbs v5:443, 444
Monteverdi v5:241
Montgomery, Lucy Maud v2:119
Moore, Henry v5:161
Moors v5:102, 106
Mordvins v5:330–333
Moré language v1:395–396
Mormons v2:378–383
Moro v4:673–679
Moroccans v1:388–395
Morocco
    Berbers v1:78
    Moroccans v1:388
Morrison, Toni v2:14
Moselle River v5:29, 287
Moshu. See Naxi
Mosquito. See Miskito
Mossi v1:395–403
Motu v4:679–682
Moundang v1:112–113
Mount Abu v3:406; v4:660
Mount Aliwliwan v4:612
Mount Annapurna v4:716
Mount Ararat v5:51
Mount Bagzan v1:548
Mount Cameroon v1:95
Mount Chionistra v3:277
Mount Cook v4:724
Mount Damavand v3:384
Mount Dhaulagiri v4:716
Mount Elbruz v5:373
Mount Elgo v1:304
Mount Everest v3:361; v4:716, 718, 719, 871

Mount Hagen v4:639
Mount Kanchenjunga v4:559, 560, 716
Mount Kazbek v5:373
Mount Khartala v1:135, 136
Mount Kilimanjaro v1:117, 350, 531
Mount Klabat v4:651
Mount Moco v1:35
Mount Nimba v1:257
Mount Olympus v3:277
Mount Pinatubo v4:710
Mount Sescan v4:840
Mount Shatrunjaya v3:406
Mount Soputa v4:651
Mount Titano v5:435
Mountain Mon-Khmer Groups (Cambodian
        tribespeople) v4:682–688
Mountain Tajiks. See Pamiri
Moxieman. See Naxi
Mozambicans v1:404–409
Mozambique
    Chewa v1:123
    Mozambicans v1:404
    Swahili v1:519
Mozart, Wolfgang Amadeus v5:59
Mpondo v1:587
Mpondomise v1:587
Mpumalanga Province (South Africa) v1:415
Mubarak, Husni v1:177
Mughals v4:877
Mukongo. See Bakongo
Muller Mountain v4:734
Muller, Daniel v5:289
Muluzu, Bakili v1:127
Munch, Edvard v5:360
Mundari language v4:688, 689
Mundas v4:688 692
Munkácsy, Mihály v5:228
Muong language v4:1034
Muoshayi. See Naxi
Muoxie. See Naxi
Museveni, Gen. Yoweri Kaguta v1:67, 574
Musical instruments
    Ainu v3:31
    Albanian v5:27
    Ambonese v3:38
    Angolans v1:38
    Araucanians v2:348
    Australian Aborigines v3:68
    Azerbaijanis v3:75
    Bahrainis v3:80
    Bajau v3:89
    Balinese v3:95
    Baluchi v3:100
    Basque v5:69
    Batak v3:121
    Bolivian v2:101
    Bosnian v5:85
    Brahui v3:154
    Bugis, Makassarese, and Mandarese v3:172
    Burundians v1:94
    Buyi v3:183
    Catalan v5:110
    Celtic v5:90
    Chad v1:116
    Chagga v1:120
    Châkmâs v3:188
    China v3:214

    Chuvash v5:128
    Cifteli v5:27
    Dong v3:231
    Emirians v3:239
    Ghanaians v1:244
    Greek v5:224
    Hani v3:309
    Iban v3:343
    Ifugao v3:350
    Irish v5:237
    Japanese v3:416
    Kadazan v3:449
    Kalmyks v5:248
    Kammu v3:458
    Kazakh Chinese v3:480
    Kazaks v3:485
    Kelabit v3:490
    Konds v3:512
    Lao v4:552
    Li v4:566
    Luhya v1:341
    Madurese v4:578
    Maranao v4:626
    Melanesians v4:638
    Minahasans v4:653
    Minangkabau v4:657
    Moro v4:677
    Mountain Mon-Khmer v4:686
    Nivkh v5:356
    Orang Asli v4:758
    Peoples of the Caucasus v5:381
    Polish v5:388
    Polynesians v4:806
    Senegal v1:476
    Sindhi v4:886
    Slovaks v5:456
    South Koreans v4:896
    Spaniards v5:467, 470
    Sundanese v4:914
    Syrians v4:924
    Tahitians v4:933
    Tamils v4:949
    Tausug v4:961
    Thai v4:970
    Turkmen v4:1002
    Uighurs v4:1013
    Wolof v1:585
Muskogee
    Creeks v2:154
    Seminoles and Miccosukees v2:488
Muslims v4:693–699
Mussolini, Benito v5:240
Mutesa, Sir Edward v1:50, 574
Myanmar (Burma)
    Burman v3:174–180
    Chin v3:202
    Kachins v3:442
    Karens v3:467
    Miao v4:642
    Mons v4:669
    Rakhines v4:832
    Rohingyas v4:836
    Shans v4:866
Myene language v1:227
Mysore Plateau v4:567

N

Naaf River v4:836
Naga v4:699–704
Nagaland state, India v4:699
Nagamese language
    Naga v4:700
Nagavali River v3:510
Naheng. *See* Naxi
Naiman. *See* Kazakh Chinese
Nam Viet. *See* Viet Nam
Namibians v1:409–414
Namsaraev, Khotsa v5:100
Nanais v5:334–340
Nanda Devi v3:143
Nandi v1:304
Nandu River v4:564
Napoleon Bonaparte v5:77, 414
Nari. *See* Naxi
Narmada River v3:271, 506; v4:825
Nasa. *See* Páez
Nasu. *See* Yi
National Foundation Day v3:412
Native North Americans v2:384–396
    Aleuts v2:20
    Amahuacas v2:25
    Choctaw v2:134
    Comanches v2:144
    Creeks v2:154
    Creoles of Louisiana v2:161
    Dakota and Lakhota v2:179
    Hawaiians v2:271
    Hopi v2:287
    Inuit v2:296
    Iroquois v2:304
    North Americans v2:384
    Navajos v2:397
    Ojibwa v2:412
    Paiutes v2:424
    Seminoles and Miccosukees v2:488
    Tlingit v2:512
NATO v5:77
Nauru, Republic of v4:647
Navajos v2:397–402
Naxi v4:705–709
Naylor, Gloria v2:14
Ndaonese. *See* Timorese
Ndebele v1:415–420
    Xhosa v1:587
    See also Zimbabweans
Ndebele, Njabulo v1:196
Ndzundza. *See* Ndebele
Near Islands: Aleuts v2:20
Nebuchadnezzar II v3:390
Negev Desert v3:398
Negrito (Pinatubo Aeta group) v4:710–714
Negros (island) v3:251, 316
Negruzzi, Costache v5:411
Nehru, Jawaharlal v3:362
Nemunas River v5:282
Nen River v3:241
Nentsy v5:341–346
Nepal
    Buddhists v3:163
    Gurungs v3:291
    Hindus v3:319
    Lepchas v4:559
    Muslims v4:693

Nepalis v4:714
Newars v4:729
Nepalese. *See* Nepalis
Nepali language
    Bhutanese v3:137
    Gurungs v3:291
    Lepchas v4:559
    Nepalis v4:714
    Newars v4:729
    Sherpas v4:871
Nepalis v4:714–720
Nera v1:203, 205
Netherlanders v5:346–350
Netherlands v5:346
    Frisians v5:196
    Netherlanders v5:346
New Caledonia v4:635
    Melanesians v4:635
    New Caledonians v4:721
New Caledonians v4:721–723
New Guinea v3:221; v4:635, 639, 679
New Hebrides. *See* Vanuatu
New immigrants. *See* American immigrants
New Zealand
    Maori v4:619
    New Zealanders v4:724
    Polynesians v4:803
    Roma v5:395
New Zealanders v4:724–728
Newari language
    Nepalis v4:716
    Newar v4:729
Newars v4:729–733
Ngaju Dayak v4:733–737
Ngaju language v4:733, 734
Ngbaka v1:106
Ngbandi v1:106
Ngoni v1:123
Nguni-speaking people v1:612
Niasans v4:738–742
Nicaragua
    Miskito v2:373
    Nicaraguans v2:402
    Sumu v2:497
Nicaraguans v2:402–407
Nicas. *See* Nicaraguans
Nicholas II v5:414
Nicobar Islands, India v3:163, 361; v4:742
Nicobarese v4:742–747
Nielsen, Carl v5:151
Niger
    Berbers v1:78
    Hausa v1:272
    Nigeriens v1:425
    Songhay v1:501
    Tuaregs v1:548
Niger River v1:56, 257, 222, 282, 289, 343, 371, 501, 548
Niger-Congo (Kongo) language family v3:295
    Azande v1:40
    Burkinabe v1:85
    Central Africans v1:105
    Gabonese v1:227
    Ghanaians v1:241
    Igbo v1:282
    Malinke v1:376

Nigeria
    Fulani v1:222
    Hausa v1:272
    Igbo v1:282
    Ijo v1:289
    Nigerians v1:420
    Yoruba v1:593
Nigerians v1:420–425
Nigeriens v1:425–431
Nile River v1:40, 45, 111, 158, 178, 431, 490, 512, 562
Nilgiris Hills v4:946, 981
Nilotic peoples v1:158
Ni-Vanuatu v4:747–750
Nivkh language v5:353
    Nivkhs v5:351
    Sakha v5:425
Nivkhs v5:351–357
Nkisi River v1:52
Nkrumah, Kwame v1:240
Nkumbula, Harry v1:546
Noah v3:122, 311
Nobel, Alfred v5:475
Nõdour, Youssou v1:585
Noghay language
    Peoples of the Caucasus v5:375
Norgay, Tenzing v4:875
Norsemen v5:439
North Atlantic Treaty Organization (NATO) v5:77
North Island v4:619, 724
North Sea v3:70; v5:346, 147, 519
Northern Province (South Africa) v1:415
Norway
    Norwegians v5:358
    Sami v5:430
Norwegian Americans v2:408–411
    See also American Immigrants
Norwegian language
    Bokmål v5:358
    Norwegians v5:358–361
    Nynorsk v5:358
Norwegians v5:358–361
Nosu. *See* Yi
Ntumu Fang v1:198
Nu River v3:82, 226
Nuer v1:431–438
Nuristan v3:18
Nyamwezi v1:439–449
Nyanja language
    Chewa v1:124
    Zambians v1:600, 602
Nyanza Province (Kenya) v1:342
Nyara. *See* Iatmul
Nyaneka-Humbe v1:36
Nyasaland. *See* Malawi
Nyerere, Julius v1:531
Nymylgu. *See* Koriak
Nzebi language v1:227

O

Obambe/Teke language v1:227
Obeng, R. E. v1:244
Obote, Milton v1:50, 67
Obrecht, Jacob v5:349
Ocmulgee River v2:154
Odinga, Oginga v1:349

Odobescu, Alexandru v5:411
Oecussi v4:978
Ofin River v1:240
Ogelbeng Plai v4:639
Oghuz v4:998
Ogooue River v1:227
Ogot, Grace v1:326
O'Higgins, Bernardo v2:124
Ojibwa v2:412–417
Oka River v5:330
Okak Fang v1:198
Okinawa v3:410
Olchiki script v4:848
Olentzero v5:66
Oman
  Baluchi v3:97
  Bedu v3:122
  Omanis v4:750
Omanis v4:750–755
Onge. See Andamanese
Onon River v4:664
Orang Asli v4:756–759
Orang Ulu v4:596
Oraons v4:760–765
Orissa v3:147
Orissa state, India
  Ahirs v3:24
  Konds v3:510
  Oraons v4:760
  Oriya v4:766
Oriya v4:766–770
Oromia (Ethiopia) v1:449
Oromos v1:449–455
Ossetians v5:361–367
Ot Danum language v4:734
Ottoman Empire v1:23, 177, 490; v2:67;
        v3:278, 391, 518; v4:777, 859, 1046;
        v5:27, 91, 135, 265, 443
Oubanguian language v1:18
Ouédraogo, Idrissa v1:89
Ovimbundu language v1:35–36
Oxus River v3:418

P

Pacific-Chibchan language: Cuna v2:175
Pacil River v3:450
Paderewski, Ignacy Jan v5:388
Páez v2:418–441
Pahari language v4:826
Paiutes v2:424–432
Paiwan
  Gaoshan v3:260
  Taiwan Indigenous People v4:935
Pakhtun. See Pashtun
Pakistan
  Baluchi v3:97
  Brahui v3:151
  Hindus v3:319
  Jats v3:418
  Muslims v4:693
  Pakistanis v4:770
  Parsis v4:789
  Pashtun v4:795
  Punjabis v4:807
Pakistanis v1:91; v4:770–777
Palaungs v4:866
Palawan v3:251

Palawan Island v4: 673, 926
Paleoasiatic languages v5:119
Palestinians v4:777–784
Palestinian Americans. See Arab Americans
Palgen, Paul v5:289
Palme, Olaf v5:472
Palni Hills v4:940
Pamiri v4:785–789
Pampango language v3:249, 251
Panamanians v2:432–437
Panay v3:251, 316
Pancha Dravida v3:147
Pancha Gauda v3:147
Pangasinan language v3:249
Pangu Yao. See Yao
Panj River v4:940
Panoan language v2:25
Pa-Os v4:866
Papua New Guinea
  Iatmul v3:336
  Melanesians v4:635
  Melpa v4:639
  Motu v4:679
Papuans. See Melanesians
Paraguay
  Guaranis v2:245
  Mennonites of Paraguay v2:360
  Paraguayans v2:437
Paraguayans v2:437–441
Parker, Charlie v2:14
Parsees. See Parsis
Parsis v4:789–794
Pashkevich (Ciotka), Alojza v5:75
Pashto language
  Afghanis v3:17
  Muslims in South Asia v4:694
Pashtoon. See Pashtun
Pashtu language v4:795
Pashtun v4:795–798
Passarella, Daniel v2:66
Pastu language v3:311
Patagonia
  Argentines v2:63
  Mapuches v2:345
Pathan
  Jats v3:418
  Pashtun v4:795
Pathet Lao v3:327, 455; v4:548
Patois, Jamaicans v2:314
Paton, Alan v1:196
Pedi language v1:193
Pei, I. M. v2:133
Pele v2:19
Pemon v2:442–447
Penan v4:799–803
Pennsylvania Dutch language v2:48
People of India v3:360–368
Peoples of Dagestan v5:367–373
Peoples of the Caucasus v5:373–384
Perim v4:1046
Perry, Matthew v3:409
Persian
  Empire v4:1015
  Gulf v3:384, 523; v4:751, 789, 859
  Iranians v3:382
  Turkmens v4:998
Persian language

Bahrainis v3:76
Iraqis v3:390
Pamiri v4:785
Persson, Sigurd v5:475
Peru
  Amahuacas v2:25
  Asháninka v2:70
  Aymara v2:79
  Jivaro v2:323
  Matsigenka v2:349
  Peruvians v2:447
  Quechua v2:462
Peruvians v2:447–452
Pessoa, Fernando v5:392
Peter the Great v5:414
Peters, Lenrie v1:238
Petofi, Sándor v5:228
Peulh v1:85
Peuls. See Fulani
Philippines
  Filipinos v3:249
  Hiligaynon v3:315
  Ifugao v3:345
  Ilocanos v3:351
  Ilongot v3:355
  Kalinga v3:450
  Mangyan (Hanuno'o Group) v4:610
  Manuvu' (Upland Bagobo) v4:615
  Maranao v4:623
  Moro v4:673, 674
  Negrito (Pinatubo Aeta Group) v4:710
  Tagbanua v4:926
  Tausug v4:957
Phoenicians v1:329
Piaget, Jean v5:480
Picasso, Pablo v5:109, 470, 467
Pico de Aneto v5:106
Picunche. See Araucanians
Pidgin, English language
  Cameroonians v1:97
  Equatorial Guineans v1:198
Pidurutala Peak v4:888, 898
Piedras River v2:28
Pilsudski, Marshal Jozef v5:384
Pinatubo Aeta group. See Negrito (Pinatubo
        Aeta Group)
Pingpu. See Gaoshan
Pinzón, Vicente Yánez v2:25
Pippin, Horace v2:14
Pires, Tomé v3:249
Pizarro, Francisco v2:98
Plain Yao. See Yao
Plato v5:223
Plattdeutsch (Low German dialect):
        Mennonites of Paraguay v2:360
Po River v5:238
Pokot v1:304
Pol Pot v4:683
Poland
  Poles v5:384
  Roma v5:394
Poles v5:384–389
Polish Americans v2:453–455
  See also American Immigrants
Polo, Marco v3:40, 70
Polynesia v4:844
  Polynesians v4:803

Samoans v4:844
Tahitians v4:930
Polynesians v4:803–807
Portuguese v5:390–394
  Goans v3:265
  Timorese v4:978
Portuguese language
  African Brazilians v2:16
  Angolans v1:35
  Brazilians v2:103
  Cape Verdeans v1:101
  Equatorial Guineans v1:198
  Guineans of Guinea-Bissau v1:263
  Mozambicans v1:404
  Portuguese v5:390
  São Toméans v1:469
  Timorese v4:977
Pra River v1:240
Pribilof Islands v2:20
Prince Edward Island v2:116
Príncipense v1:469
Provençal French v5:191
Prut River v5:313
Przybos, Julian v5:388
Ptolemies v3:276
Ptolemy v3:40
Puerto Rican Americans v2:456–458
Puerto Ricans v2:458–462
Pulaar language v1:257
Pulangi River v4:615
Punjab v4:877
Punjabi language
  Chamârs v3:198
  Jats v3:419
  Muslims in South Asia v4:694
  Pakistanis v4:770, 773
  People of India v3:362
  Punjabis v4:807, 808
  Sikhs v4:877
Punjabis v4:807–813
Punu language v1:227
Purcell, Henry v5:161
Puritans v2:29
Pushkin, Alexander v5:421
Pushto v3:16
Pushto language v4:770, 773
Pushtun. See Pashtun
Puxití. See Xavante
Puyuma. See Taiwan Indigenous People
Pwo dialect (Karen) v3:467–468
Pygmies v1:227
  See also Aka, Efe, Mbuti
Pyrenees Mountains v5:46, 106, 467

Q
Qadhafi, Muammar v1:331, 335
Qafar Af langauge v1:7
Qalmg. See Kalmyks
Qatar v4:813
Qataris v4:813–817
Qiao. See Derong
Qin Dynasty v4:995
Qing Dynasty v4:972, 1010, 1052
Qinghai-Tibetan Plateau v4:972
Qiu men. See Derong
Qoraqolpoqlar. See Karakalpaks
Qudus, Gebre Memfis v1:537

Quechua v2:462–467
  Argentines v2:62
  Bolivians v2:98
  Ecuadorans v2:203
  Jivaro v2:323
  Peruvians v2:447

R
Rahmanov, Imamali v4:940
Rai language v4:716
Rajasthan state, India
  Banias v3:108
  Chamârs v3:198
  Minas v4:659
  Rjputs v4:825
Rajasthanis v4:818–825
Rajputs v4:825–831
  See also Jats
Rakhines v4:832–835
Ramadhan v1:520
Ramdas v4:878
Ramos, Fidel v3:250
Ranchi Plateau v4:689
Raphael v5:241
Rat Islands v2:20
Ravel, Maurice v5:68
Ravi River v4:807, 877
Rawat. See Ahirs
Ray, Satyajit v3:130
Reagan, Ronald v2:11; v3:383
Red River v4:1025, v4:1026
Red Sea v1:178, 210; v4:859, 864, 1046
Red Yao. See Yao
Reformation v5:413
Rembrandt van Rijn v5:348
Renaissance v5:413
Reymont, Wladyslaw v5:388
Rhaeto-Roman dialect v5:477
Rhine River v5:30, 276
Rhodes, Cecil v1:68
Rhodesia. See Zambia
Rhodesians. See Zimbabweans
Ri Lum. See Khasi
Richard I v3:276
Richler, Mordecai v2:119
Rift Valley v1:321, 337
Rilke, Rainer Maria v5:59
Rio Muni v1:198
River Gambia v1:232
Roba, Fatuma v1:453
Robbe-Grillet, Alain v5:90
Roberts, Gabriel v1:238
Roca, General Julio Argentine v2:345
Rockefeller, Nelson v3:58
Rocky Mountains v2:116
Rodrigo, Joaquín v5:470
Rohingyas v4:836–839
Rolwaling River v4:871
Rom. See Roma
Roma v5:394–404
Roma language v5:396
Romagna, Sammarinese v5:435
Roman Empire v1:23; v3:35; v4:1046; v5:46,
    81, 106, 135, 157, 191, 312
Romani
  Bosnians v5:82
  Roma v5:394

Romania
  Armenians in v5:50
  Roma v5:394
  Romanians v5:404, 514
Romanian language
  Bulgarians v5:92
  Romanians v5:404, 514
  Moldovan v5:314
Romanians v5:404–413, 514–517
Romanichals. See Roma
Romanov dynasty v5:414
Romany. See Roma
Romnimus dialect v5:396
Rong. See Lepchas
Rongring language v4:560
Roshans. See Tajiks
Roti v3:373
Rotinese. See Timorese
Rousseau, Jean-Jacques v5:480
Rubens, Peter Paul v5:80
Rubinstein, Artur v5:388
Rukai. See Taiwan Indigenous People v4:935
Rukiga language v1:569
Runyankole language v1:61
Rus, Kievan v5:510
Russia
  Altays v5:37
  Armenians in v5:50
  Bashkirs v5:61
  Buriats v5:96
  Chukchi v5:118
  Chuvash v5:123
  Circassians v5:130
  Dolgany v5:152
  Evenki v5:170
  Evens v5:176
  Inuit v2:296
  Kalmyks v5:243
  Karachai v5:250
  Karakalpaks v3:460
  Khakass v5:255
  Koriak v5:259
  Mordvins v5:330
  Nanais v5:334
  Nentsy v5:341
  Nivkhs v5:351
  Ossetians v5:361
  People of Dagestan v5:367
  Russians v5:413
  Sakha v5:424
  Tatars v5:483
  Tuvans v5:489
  Udmurts v5:501
Russian Americans v2:467–470
  See also American Immigrants
Russian Empire v5:484
Russian langauge
  Altays v5:37
  Armenians v5:51
  Bashkirs v5:61
  Belarusans v5:72
  Chechens v5:116
  China and Her National Minorities v3:208
  Circassians v5:130
  Czechs v5:143
  Dagestan v5:368
  Dolgany v5:152–153

Evens v5:176
Karachai v5:250
Karakalpaks v3:460
Kazakhs v3:482
Khakass v5:255
Koriak v5:259
Kyrgyz v4:543
Maris v5:308
Mordvins v5:330
Ossetians v5:361–362
Pamiri v4:785
People of Dagestan v5:367
Peoples of the Caucasus v5:377
Russians v5:413
Tajiks v4:940
Turkmens v4:998
Tuvans v5:489
Udmurts v5:501
Russians v5:413–424
Rutli Oath v5:478
Ruwenzori Mountains v1:144
Rwanda
  Hutu v1:277
  Rwandans v1:456
  Tutsi v1:562
  Twa v1:569
Rwandans v1:456–463
Rytkheu, Yuri v5:122
Ryukyu Islands v3:410

S

Sabah state, Malaysia v3:446
Sabaot v1:304–305
Sabatini, Gabriela v2:66
Sabean language v1:30
Sabeans v4:1046
Sa'dan River v4:840
Sa'dan Toraja v4:840–844
Sadat, Anwar v1:177
Sahara Desert v1:167, 329, 383, 548, 556
  Berbers v1:78
  Cameroonians v1:96
  Coptic Christians v1:150
Sahel region v1:112, 114, 503, 505
Sahelia v1:383
Sahelian region v1:548
Saho v1:203, 205
Sahyadri Hills v3:266
Said, Ahmad v4:924
Saide v3:260
St. Kitts and Nevis v2:331
St. Lawrence River v2:116
St. Lucians v2:470–475
St. Vincent and the Grenadines v2:475
St. Vincentians v2:475–480, 485
Saisiat. See Taiwan Indigenous People
Saixia. See Gaoshan
Saixiate v3:260
Sakalava v1:356
Sakha v5:424–430
Sakhalin v3:27
Sakhalin River v5:351
Sakha-tyla. See Sakha
Saladin v3:519
Salazar, Antnio v5:390
Salvador v5:109
Salvadorans v2:481–485

Salween River v4:866
Samal language v3:86
Samanids v4:940
Samar v3:251
Samba music v2:18, 107
Sambal dialects v4:710
Samel. See Saml
Sami v5:430–434
Sami language
  Sami v5:430
  Swedes v5:472
Sammarinese v5:435–438
Samoa, American v4:844
Samoan language v4:844
Samoa, Western v4:844
Samoans v4:844–847
Samosir Island v3:118
Samoyed language v5:489
San v1:463–468
San Blas Islands:Cunas v2:175
San, General Aung v3:174
San Marino v5:435
San Martin, General José de v2:62
Sangha language v1:139
Sango language v1:105
Sani. See Yi
Sanmarinese v5:435–438
Sanmei. See Gaoshan
Sanskrit v3:24, 44, 64, 91, 108, 127, 131, 167,
    197, 285, 321, 324, 366, 431, 497, 502;
    v4:548, 568, 660, 729, 760, 766
Santali language v4:848
Santals v4:848–854
Sao people v1:112
São Tomé & Principe v1:469
São Toméans v1:469–472
  Angolares v1:469
  Forros v1:469
  Mestico v1:469
  Servicais v1:469
  Tongas v1:469
Sao. See Taiwan Indigenous People
Sarakolle language v1:371
Sarawak v3:340
Sarawak state, Malaysia
  Iban v3:340
  Kelabit v3:487
  Penan v4:799
Sariyan, Martiros v5:54
Saroyan, William v5:54
Saru basin v3:27
Sasak v4:854–858
Sassandra River v1:295
Satpura Hills v3:271
Satpura Mountains v3:132
Saudi Arabia v4:859
Saudis v4:859–865
Savai'i v4:844
Sawngma. See Chakmas
Saxons v5:406
Scandinavia v5:358
  Danes v5:147
  Finns v5:182
  Icelanders v5:232
  Sami v5:430
  Swedes v5:472

Scandinavian Americans. See American
    Immigrants
Scheduled Caste. See Chamârs
Schnitzler, Arthur v5:59
Schöenberg, Arnold v5:59
Schubert, Franz v5:59
Schwaner Mountains v4:734
Schweitzer, Albert v1:227
Schwyzerdütsch (Swiss-German dialect)
    v5:477
Scots v5:438–442
Scots language v5:438
Scott, Paul v3:57
Scott, Sir Walter v5:441
Scottish and Scotch-Irish Americans
    v2:485–488
  See also American Immigrants
Sea Gypsies. See Bajau
Sea of Azov v5:373
Sea of Marmar v4:1005
Sea of Okhotsk v5:170, 176, 259
Sebei dialect v1:305
Sebu Lake v4:962
Second-wave immigrants. See American
    immigrants
Segovia, Andrés v5:470
Segu v1:56
Seindaung River v4:836
Seminoles and Miccosukees v2:488–495
Senegal
  Fulani v1:222
  Jola v1:299, 300
  Malinke v1:375
  Senegalese v1:473
  Wolof v1:582
Senegal River v1:383, 582
Senegalese v1:473–478
Senghor, Leopold v1:473
Senoufo v1:85
Sénoufo (Voltaic) language
  Ivoirians v1:294–295
  Malians v1:371
Sentinelese. See Andamanese
Sepedi language v1:415
Sepik River v3:336, 339
Serbia
  Albanians v5:24
  Kosovars v5:265
  Serbs v5:443, 444
Serbian language v5:444
  Kosovars v5:266
  Montenegrins v5:324, 326
  Serbs v5:443
  Tajiks v4:940
  Turkmens v4:999
  Tuvans v5:489
  Ukrainian v5:506
Serbo-Croatian v5:81, 82
  Serbs v5:82–83, 443–452
Serendib. See Sri Lanka
Serra Xilengue v1:35
Sesotho language v1:506
Seville province, Spain v5:42
Seychelle Islands v1:479
Seychellois v1:479–484
Sgaw dialect (Karen) v3:467–468
Sha v3:260

Shadri language v4:760
Shafigullin, F. v5:487
Shah, Nadir v4:877
Shaikh Adi v4:1043
Shambaa v1:485–490
Shambala language v1:485
Shambala. See Shambaa
Shan language v4:866
Shan Plateau, Myanmar (Burma) v4:866
Shans v4:866–870
Shanzi Yao. See Yao
Shao v3:260
Shaw, George Bernard v5:237
Sherpa language v4:871
Sherpas v4:871–876
Shevchenko, Taras v5:510
Shigeru, Kayano v3:28, 30, 31
Shikoku v3:410
Shikomori language v1:134, 135
Shilluk v1:490–494
Shining Path v2:74
Sho. See Chin
Shqiptar. See Albanians
Shughnans. See Tajiks
Siberia v5:489
    Altays v5:37
    Buriats v5:96
    Chukchi v5:118
    Estonians v5:164
    Evenki v5:170
    Evens v5:176
    Koriak v5:259
    Lithuanians v5:280
Sidama v1:450
Sienkiewicz, Henryk v5:388
Sierra Leone v1:154, 375
Sierra Morena Mountains v5:42
Sigmarsson, Jon Pall v5:231
Sihanaka v1:356
Sihanouk, Norodom v3:495, 497
Sikhs v4:877–882
Silat River v4:799
Silk Road v3:70
Siluton Lake v4:962
Silver Teeth. See Dai
Simalungun dialect v3:118
Simenon, Georges v5:80, 519
Sindhi language
    Brahui v3:151
    Indians v3:360
    Jats v3:419
    Muslims in South Asia v4:694
    Pakistanis v4:770, 773
    People of India v3:362
    Sindhis v4:882
Sindhis v4:882–888
Singapore
    Banias v3:108
    Hakka v3:297
Singh, Gobind v4:877
Singh, Ranjit v4:877
Sinhala language
    Buddhists v3:163
    Sinhalese v4:888
    Sri Lankans v4:898
    Veddas v4:1020
Sinhalese v4:888–893, 898

Sinti/Manouches. See Roma
Sioux. See Dakota and Lakhota v2:179
Siraiki dialect v4:883
Siretul River v5:312
SiSwati language v1:525
Skåne v5:472
Skaryna, Dr. Francishak v5:75
Skorecky, Josef v5:145
Sky Palace pyramid v2:94
Slavic languages
    Russian v5:415
    Bulgarians v5:92
    Czech v5:143
    Slovak v5:452
Slipyj, Yosyf v5:507
Slovakia v5:452
Slovaks v5:452–459
Slovenci. See Slovenes
Slovene (Slovenian) language
    Austrians v5:56
    Italians v5:238
    Slovenes v5:459
Slovenes v5:459–466
Slovenians. See Slovenes
Småland v5:472
Smith, Adam v5:441
Snakes. See Paiutes
Society Islands v4:619, 804, 930
Socotra v4:1046
Socrates v5:223
Soglo, Nicéphore v1:73
Sokoto dialect v1:222
Solomon Islands v4:635, 638
Solomon, King v3:431; v4:751
Somali v1:163
Somalia
    Afar v1:7
    Djiboutians v1:162
    Oromos v1:449
    Somalis v1:495
    Swahili v1:519
    See also Djiboutians
Somalians. See Somalis
Somalis v1:495–500
Son River v3:271, 506
Song Dynasty v4: 957, 972, 1056
Songhai. v1:371, 425
    See also Nigeriens
Songhay v1:501–505
Songhay language
    Nigeriens v1:425
    Songhay v1:501
Soninke language v1:371
Sonrai language v1:371
Sophocles v5:223
Sotavento islands v1:101
Sotho v1:506–511
Soule region, France v5:65
South Africa, Republic of
    Afrikaners v1:12
    Colored People of South Africa v1:129
    English in v1:193
    Karretjie People v1:310
    Ndebele v1:415
    Roma v5:395
    Sotho v1:506
    Xhosa v1:587

Zulu v1:612
South Island v4:619, 724
South Koreans. See Koreans, South
South Pentecost Island v4:748
Southern Alps v4:724
Soyots. See Tuvans
Spain
    Andalusians v5:42
    Basques v5:65
    Castilians v5:102
    Catalans v5:106
    Galicians v5:200
    Roma v5:394
    Spaniards v5:467
Spaniards v5:467–471
    American Immigrants v2:29
    Americans v2: 38–39
    Andalusians v5:42
    Belizeans v2:94
    Bolivians v2:98
    Canadians v2:116
    Castilians v5:102
    Chileans v2:124
    Colombians v2:139
    Cubans v2:170
    Dominicans v2:195
    Galicians v5:200
    Garifuna v2:226
    Guatemalans v2:250
    Hondurans v2:282
    Maya v2:355
    Mennonites of Paraguay v2:360
    Mexicans v2:367
    Miskito v2:373
    Nicaraguans v2:402
    Panamanians v2:432
    Paraguayans v2:437
    Peruvians v2:447
    Puerto Ricans v2:458
    Salvadorans v2:481
    Sumu v2:497
    Surinamese v2:501
    Trinidadians and Tobagonians v2:516
    Uruguayans v2:525
    Vaupés v2:530
    Venezuelans v2:535
Spanish language
    Andalusians v5:42
    Andorrans v5:46
    Argentines v2:62
    Asháninka v2:70–71
    Aymara v2:79
    Basques v5:65
    Canadians v2:117
    Colombians v2:139
    Cunas v2:175
    Ecuadorans v2:203
    Equatorial Guineans v1:198
    Filipinos v3:249
    French v5:191
    Galicians v5:200
    Maya v2:355
    Moroccans v1:388
    Spaniards v5:467
Spinoza, Baruch v5:349
Spode, Josiah v5:162
Sports Day v3:413

Spyri, Johanna v5:478
Sranan Tongo (Taki-Taki) v2:501
Sri Lanka
   Buddhists v3:163
   Hindus v3:319
   Muslims v4:693
   Sinhalese v4:888
   Sri Lankans v4:898
   Tamils v4:946
   Veddas v4:1020
Sri Lankans v4:898–903
Stalin, Joseph v3:71; v4:543; v5:70, 82, 101,
     112, 119, 122, 281
Stevens, Dr. Siaka v1:154
Stevenson, Robert Louis v5:441
Stradivarius v5:241
Strait of Hormuz v4:751
Strindberg, August v5:475
Sudan
   Azande v1:40
   Dinka v1:158
   Fulani v1:222
   Nuer v1:431
   Shilluk v1:490
   Sudanese v1:512
Sudanese v1:512–518
Sudanese Americans v2:495–497
   See also American Immigrants
Sudanic language v1:491
Suez Canal v1:177
Suharto v3:170, 372; v4:911
Sukarno v3:372; v4:651
Sulaiman Range v3:97; v4:808
Sulawesi v3:86, 169, 173, 373; v4:651, 840
Sultan, Izzat v4:1018
Sulu Archipelago, Philippines v3:86; v4: 673,
    957
Sumatra v3:86, 117, 373; v4:580
   Acehnese v3:11
   Minangkabau v4:654
Sumba, Indonesia v4:903
Sumbanese v4:903–907
Sumbawa v3:373; v4:908
Sumbawan language v4:908
Sumbawans v4:908–910
Sumerians v3:77, 390
Sumu v2:497–500
Sun Yatsen v3:208
Sundanese v4:911–915
Suolun. See Ewenki
Suriname v2:501
Surinamese v2:501–504
Susu language, Guineans v1:257
Sutherland, Graham v5:161
Sutlej River v4:807, 877
Suu Kyi, Aung San v3:444
Sviyaga River v5:124
Swabians v5:406
Swahili v1:519–524
Swahili language v1:91, 519
   Burundians v1:90
   Chagga v1:117
   Congolese (DROC) v1:144
   Kalenjin v1:304
   Keiyo v1:316
   Rwandans v1:456
   Shambaa v1:485

Tanzanians v1:530
Swazi language v1:193
Swaziland v1:525
Swazis v1:525–530
Sweden
   Finns v5:182
   Sami v5:130
   Swedes v5:472
Swedes v5:472–476
Swedish Americans v2:505–507
   See also American Immigrants
Swedish language
   Finns v5:182
   Swedes v5:472
Sweelinck, Jan v5:349
Swift, Jonathan v5:237
Swiss v5:477–483
Swiss-German dialect v5:477
Switzerland v5:477
Syr River v3:460
Syria
   'Alawis v3:32
   Armenians in v5:50
   Bedu v3:122
   Circassians v5:130
   Druze v3:232
   Kurds v3:518
   Syrians v4:920
   Yazidis v4:1043
Syriac language
   Iraqis v3:390
   Maronites v4:633
   Syrian Christians v4:916
   Syrians v4:921
Syrian Americans. See Arab Americans
Syrian Christians v4:916–920
Syrians v4:920–926

T

Tabwa v1:68
Tacitus v5:270, 472
Tagabili. See T'boli
Tagalog/Filipino language
   Filipinos v3:249, 251
   Tagbanua v4:926, 927
Tagbanua v4:926–930
Tagore, Rabrindanath v3:130
Tahitian language
   New Caledonians v4:721
   Polynesians v4:803, 804
   Tahitians v4:930
Tahitians v4:930–934
Tai. See Shans
Taiwan
   Gaoshan v3:260
   Hakka v3:297
   Han v3:302
   Tao v4:951
   Taiwan Indigenous People v4:934
Taiwan Indigenous People v4:934–939
Taiyer v3:260
Tajik language
   Pamiri v4:785
   Tajiks v4:940
Tajikistan
   Kazakh Chinese v3:479
   Pamiri v4:785

Tajiks v4:940
Tajiks v4:940–945
Tajiks, Mountain. See Pamiri
Taki-Taki v2:222
Taklimakan Desert v4:1010
Talas River v3:479, v4:543
Talev, Dimitur v5:94
Talish Mountains v3:71
Tallapoosa River v2:155
Talysh language v5:375
Tamacheq (Tamasheq) language
   Malians v1:371
   Nigeriens v1:425
   Tuaregs v1:548
Tamang language v4:716
Tamazight language v1:79
Tambora volcano v4:908
Tamerlane v3:382
Tamil v4:1020
Tamil language
   Malaysian Chinese v4:585
   Malaysian Indians v4:590
   Malaysian Malays v4:595
   Muslims in South Asia v4:694
   Sri Lankans v4:898
   Tamils v4:946
   Veddas v4:1020
Tamil Nadu state, India
   Tamils v4:946
   Todas v4:981
Tamils v4:946–951
   See also Malaysian Indians
Tamu. See Gurungs
Tan, Amy v2:132
Tanala v1:356
T'ang Dynasty v4:972, 1010, 1056
Tanggula Mountains v4:972
Tannu-Uriankhaitsy. See Tuvans
Tano River v1:240
Tanzania
   Chagga v1:117
   Luo v1:342
   Maasai v1:350
   Nyamwezi v1:439
   Shambaa v1:485
   Swahili v1:519
   Tanzanians v1:530
   Twa v1:569
Tanzanians v1:530–536
Tao v4:951–957
Tapacua. See Xavante
Tápies, Antoni v5:109
Taprobane. See Sri Lanka
Tapti River v4:628
Taroko. See Taiwan Indigenous People
Tasman, Abel v4:724
Tasmania v3:49
Tat language v5:375
Tatar language
   Maris v5:308
   Tatars v5:483
Tatars v5:483, 483–488, 501
Tatarstan v5:483, 501
Taufa'ahau Tupou IV v4:986
Taukei. See Fijians
Taurepan. See Pemon
TauSebu. See T'boli

Tausug v4:676, 678, 957–962
Tausug language
    Moro v4:673
    Tausug v4:957
Tayal. See Taiwan Indigenous People
T'boli v4:962–966
Tell, William v5:478, 482
Telengits v5:37
Telesy v5:37
Teleuts v5:37
Telugu. See Andhras
Telugu language v3:44, 45
Tembe. See Tenetehara
Tenetehara v2:507–511
Tenzing, Norgay v4:719
Teresa, Mother v3:365
Terik v1:304
Tetum. See Timorese
Tetum language v4:977, 978
Thai v4:966–971
Thai language
    Orang Asli v4:756
    Thai v4:966
    Viet Nam v4:1034
Thaike, Sao Shwe v4:866
Thailand
    Hmong v3:327
    Kachins v3:442
    Karens v3:467
    Lao v4:548
    Miao v4:642
    Shans v4:866
    Thai v4:966
Thal Desert v4:795
Thar Desert v3:361; v4:660, 807, 818, 883
Thareli dialect v4:883
Thema of Illyricum v5:23
Thembu v1:587
Thirty Years' War v1:382
Tianshan Mountains v4:1010
Tibet Autonomous Region, China v4:972
Tibetan language v4:972
    Sherpas v4:871–872
    Tibetans v4:972
    Tuvans v5:490
Tibetans v4:972–976
    See also China and Her National Minorities
Ticos. See Costa Ricans
Tien Shan Mountains v3:482, 485; v4:543,
        1015; v5:243
Tierradentro v2:418
Tifinagh language v1:548
Tigrai. See Tigray
Tigray v1:536–542
Tigray province (Ethiopia) v1:536
Tigre. See Tigray
Tigriñña language v1:536
Tigrinya See Tigray
Tigris River v3:390; v4:571
Timor v3:373; v4:606, 977
Timorese v4:977–981
Timur Tengah v4:978
Tinguely, Jean v5:480
Titian v5:241
Tito, Marshal v5:81
Tlingit v2:512–516
Toba-Angkola-Mandailing dialect v3:118

Toda language v4:981
Todas v4:981–986
Togo
    Ewe v1:217
    Yoruba v1:593
Tok Pisin language
    Iatmul v3:336
    Melanesians v4:635
    Melpa v4:639
    Motu v4:679, 680
Tola River v4:664
Tolstoy, Leo v5:421
Toma people v1:257
Tonga v1:543–547
    Bemba v1:68
    Polynesians v4:803
    Tongans v4:986
Tongans v4:986–989
Tongusi. See Ewenki
Tonle Sap River v3:192, 496
Tontemboan. See Minahasans
Toraja. See Sa'dan Toraja
Tosks v5:24
Toupouri language v1:112
Traditional-Orthodox Jews v4:990–994
    Canada v4:990
    Europe v4:990
    North America v4:990
Transvaal v1:525
Transylvania v5:405
Treaty of Lausanne v3:276
Trinidadians and Tobagonians v2:516–521
Tripolitania v1:329
Trobriand Islands v4:638
Troodos Mountains v3:277
Tropical forest foragers. See Aka
Tsangla v3:137
Tsimihety v1:356
Tsivil River v5:124
Tsonga language v1:193
Tsou. See Taiwan Indigenous People
Tswana language v1:193
Tuareg language v1:371
Tuaregs v1:548–552
    See also Nigeriens
Tubalars v5:37
Tubu language v1:425
Tudai-Menghe v5:485
Tugen v1:304
Tujia v4:995–998
Tukano language v2:530
Tullu, Daraartu v1:453
Tuming. See Tujia
Tungabhadra River v4:567
Tungus v3:208
Tunis, Gulf of v1:555
Tunisians v1:553–562
Tupi language v2:104
Turan. See Tujia
Turgenev, Ivan v5:421
Turkey
    Adjarians in v5:20
    Circassians v5:130
    Kurds v3:518
    Turks v4:1004
Turkic kingdoms v5:483
Turkic language

Altays v5:37, 38
Azeri v5:375
Bashkir v5:61
Chuvash v5:124
Hazaras v3:311
Meskhetian v5:375
Tuvans v5:489
Turkic peoples
    Altay v5:37
    Bashkirs v5:61
Turkish language
    Afghanis v3:16, 17
    Bulgarians v5:92
    Circassians v5:130
    Germans v5:214
    Greek Cypriots v3:281
    Iraqis v3:390
    Turks v4:1004
Turkmenistan
    Baluchi v3:97
    Karakalpaks v3:460
    Kazakh Chinese v3:479
    Turkmens v4:998
Turkmens v4:1004–998
Turks v4:1004–1010
    See also Kazakh Chinese
Turner, Joseph v5:161
Tutsi v1:456, 562, 562–568, 574
Tutu, Desmond v1:195
Tuva. See Russia
Tuvan Republic v5:489
Tuvans v5:489–494
Tuwaiq Mountains v3:77
Tuwin, Julian v5:388
Twa v1:91, 456, 568–573
Twahka. See Sumu
Tyroleans. See Tyrolese
Tyrolese v5:495–500
Tyva. See Tuvans

U
Ubangian language group v1:105
Ubangi-Shari v1:106
Udmurts v5:501–504
Uganda
    Baganda v1:44
    Banyankole v1:61
    Twa v1:569
    Ugandans v1:574
Ugandans v1:574–582
Ugarit alphabet v4:921
Uighurs v4:1010–1014
Ukraine v5:505
Ukrainian Americans v2:522–525
    See also American Immigrants
Ukrainian language
    Bosnians v5:82
    Peoples of the Caucasus v5:375
    Ukrainians v5:505, 506
Ukrainians v5:505–513
Ukrainka, Lesia v5:510
Ultra-Orthodox. See Traditional-Orthodox
    Jews
Ulwa. See Sumu
Unamuno y Jugo, Miguel de v5:68
Unangan. See Aleuts
Undset, Sigrid v5:360

United Arab Emirates (UAE)
    Bedu v3:122
    Emirians v3:236
United Kingdom
    English v5:157
    Scots v5:438
    Welsh v5:521
United Nations v3:302, 497, 526; v4:778, 781
United States
    African Americans v2:11
    Aleuts v2:20
    Americans v2:38
    Amish v2:48
    Arab Americans v2:59
    Armenian Americans v2:67
    Armenians v5:50
    Asian Indian Americans v2:75
    Cajuns v2:109
    Cambodian Americans v2:113
    Cape Verdeans v1:101
    Central Americans in the U.S. v2:122
    Chinese Americans v2:130
    Choctaw v2:134
    Comanches v2:144
    Creeks v2:154
    Creoles of Louisiana v2:161
    Cricassians v5:130
    Cuban Americans v2:166
    Dakota and Lakhota v2:179
    Dominican Americans v2:187
    Dutch Americans v2:200
    English Americans v2:38, 207
    Filipino Americans v2:211
    French Americans v2:214
    French Canadians v2:217
    German Americans v2:230
    Greek Americans v2:233
    Haitian Americans v2:259
    Hawaiians v2:271
    Hmong Americans v2:279
    Hopi v2:287
    Hungarian Americans v2:292
    Inuit v2:296
    Irish Americans v2:300
    Iroquois v2:304
    Italian Americans v2:310
    Japanese Americans v2:317
    Jewish Americans v2:320
    Korean Americans v2:335
    Laotian Americans v2:339
    Lebanese Americans v2:342
    Mexican Americans v2:364
    Mormons v2:378
    Native North Americans v2:384
    Navajos v2:397
    Norwegian Americans v2:408
    Ojibwa v2:412
    Paiutes v2:424
    Polish Americans v2:453
    Puerto Rican Americans v2:456
    Russian Americans v2:467
    Salvadorans v2:481
    Samoans v4:844
    Scottish and Scotch-Irish Americans
        v2:485
    Seminoles and Miccosukees v2:488
    Sudanese Americans v2:495

Swedish Americans v2:505
Tlingit v2:512
Ukrainian Americans v2:522
Vietnamese Americans v2:539
Untouchables. See Chamârs
Unyamwezi (Tanzania) v1:439
Upland Bagobo. See Manuvu' (Upland
    Bagobo)
Upolo v4:844
Upper Volta
    Burkina Faso v1:85
    Burkinabe v1:85
Ural Mountains v5:61, 414
Uraons. See Oraons
Urdu language
    Asian Indian Americans v2:76
    Bahrainis v3:76–77
    Guyanans v2:255
    Hindus of Guyana v2:276
    Muslims v4:693–694
    Pakistanis v4:770
    Parsis v4:790
    People of India v3:362
Urianghais. See Tuvans
Uru islands v2:79
Uruguay v2:525
Uruguayans v2:525–529
Ussuri River v5:334
Ust-Urt Flatland v4:1015
Uttar Pradesh, India v3:24
Uttarakhand v3:143, 144
Uyghun, Rahmatullah A. v4:1018
Uzbek language
    Tajiks v4:940
    Uzbeks v4:1014
Uzbekistan
    Karakalpaks v3:460
    Kazakh Chinese v3:479
    Uzbeks v4:1014
Uzbeks v4:1014–1019

V

Valkeapää, Nils-Aslak v5:431
van Eyck, Jan v5:80
van Gogh, Vincent v5:348
Vandals v1:23, 553
Vania. See Bania
Vanua Levu v3:245, 369
Vanuatu v4:635
    Melanesians v4:635
    Ni-Vanuatu v4:747
Varangians. See Vikings
Vattelluttu script v4:946
Vaughn Williams, Ralph v5:161
Vaupés v2:530–535, 535
Vaupés River v2:530
Vazimba. See Malagasy
Vazov, Ivan v5:94
Vedda language v4:1020
Veddahs. See Veddas
Veddas v1:617; v4:898, 1025–1020
    See also Sri Lankans
Velázquez, Diego v5:470
Venda language v1:193
Venezuela
    Guajiros v2:241
    Pemon v2:442

Venezuclans v2:535
Venezuelans v2:535–539
Verdaguer, Jacint v5:109
Vermeer, Jan v5:348
Vernal Equinox v3:412
Verne, Jules v5:90
Versace, Gianni v5:240
Vezo v1:357
Vicario, Arancha Sánchez v5:470
Vicholi dialect v4:883
Vickers, Jon v2:119
Victoria Falls v1:35, 606
Vienna Boys' Choir v5:59
Vietnam
    Cham v3:191
    Hmong v3:327
    Jarai v4:1034
    Miao v4:642
    Muong v4:1034
    Shans v4:866
    Vietnamese v4:1025
    Vietnamese Highlanders v4:1032
Vietnamese v4:1025–1032
Vietnamese Americans v2:539–549
    See also American Immigrants
Vietnamese Highlanders v4:1032–1038
Vietnamese language
    New Caledonians v4:721
    Vietnamese v4:1025
Vikings v5:147, 157, 358, 413
Vilas, Guillermo v2:66
Vindhya Mountains v3:131
Vindhya Range v3:506
Virashaivas. See Lingayats
Viti Levu v3:245, 247, 369
Vivaldi v5:241
Vizcaya region, Spain v5:65
Vlaams. See Flemish
Vlach Roma. See Roma
Vlachs v5:517
Volga River v3:70; v5:123, 243, 308, 330, 483,
    484
Volta, Upper. See Burkinabe
Voltaic language v1:295
    Ivoirians v1:294
von Sydow, Max v5:475
Vosges Mountains v5:30
Votyaks. See Udmurts
Vridi Canal v1:294

W

Wadden Sea v5:197
Wahgi Valley v4:639
Waldjewa language v4:903
Waiganga Valley v3:271
Waimaka. See Timorese
Wakhis. See Tajiks
Wales v5:521
Walker, Alice v2:14
Wallace, Susan v2:87
Wallachia v5:405
Wallis and Futuna islands v4:721, 723
Wallisian language v4:721
Wallonia v5:518
Walloons v5:77, 80, 190, 517–521
Walpiri language v3:66
Wanyamwezi. See Nyamwezi

Waray-Waray language v3:249, 251
Was v4:866
Waschagga. *See* Chagga
Wedgwood, Josiah v5:162
Welsh v5:521–526
Wergeland, Henrik v5:360
West Bank v3:436; v4:777–778
West Indies v2:517
West Java v4:911
Western Desert language v3:66, 67
Western Ghat Mountains v3:132, 266, 361;
    v4:567, 916, 946
Western Pamir Mountains v4:785
Western Province (Kenya) v1:342
White Pants Yao. *See* Yao
White Russians. *See* Belarusans
White Ruthenians. *See* Belarusans
Wickham, John v2:92
Wilde, Oscar v5:237
Windward islands v2:471, 476
Wolcott, Derek v2:92
Wolof language
    Gambians v1:232
    Mauritanians v1:382
    Senegalese v1:473
    Wolof v1:582
Wong, Nellie v2:132
Woods, Tiger v2:133
Wright, Richard v2:14
Wu v3:208
Wuling Mountains v4:995
Wuman. *See* Naxi
Wusun. *See* Kazakh Chinese

X

Xavante v2:543–549
Xavier, St. Francis v3:35, 266, 412; v5:67
Xesibe v1:587
Xhosa v1:587–592
Xhosa language v1:193, 587
Xiang v3:208
Xinjiang Uighur Autonomous Region, China
    v4:1010

Y

Yacouba (south Mandé) language v1:295
Yacouba language v1:294
Yakovlev, I. Y. v5:125, 127
Yakut language
    Dolgan language v5:153
    Evens v5:176
    Sakha v5:424
Yakut. *See* Sakha
Yakute. *See* Ewenki
Yakutia v5:424
Yamei. *See* Gaoshan
Yami. *See* Taiwan Indigenous People; Tao
Yangtze River v3:302; v4:642, 699, 1056
Yao v1:123; v4:1039–1042
Yap v4:648
Yarlung Zanbo River v4:972
Yasunari, Kawabata v3:416
Yaw. *See* Chin
Yazidis v4:1043–1045
Yeats, William Butler v5:237, 234
Yellow River v3:302; v4:699
Yeltsin, Boris v5:112
Yemen
    Bedu v3:122
    Yemenis v4:1046
Yemenis v4:1046–1052
Yenisei River v4:543; v5:153, 170, 255
Yi v4:1052–1055
Yiddish v4:990
Yoruba v1:73, 289, 593–600
Young, Neil v2:119
Ysaye, Eugène v5:519
Yuan Dynasty v4:972
Yuan Jiang River v3:307
Yuanke. *See* Naxi
Yuanzhuminzu, Taiwan. *See* Taiwan
    Indigenous People
Yue v3:208
Yugoslavia. *See* Bosnians and Hercegovinans
Yukagirs v5:118
Yulong Mountains v4:705
Yunnan-Guizhou Plateau v3:82
Yurt v5:491

Z

Zagros Mountains v3:384, 391; v4:1043
Zaire. *See* Congo, Democratic Republic of
Zairians. *See* Congolese (DROC)
Zambales Mountains v4:710
Zambezi River v1:35, 543, 601
Zambia
    Bemba v1:68
    Chewa v1:123
    Tonga v1:543
    Twa v1:569
    Zambians v1:600
Zambians v1:600–606
Zamboanga Bay v3:86
Zande *see* Azande
Zarafshan Mountains v4:940
Zargun Mountain v3:97
Zarma language, Nigeriens v1:425
Zayanids v1:554
Zenobia v4:921
Zhangjiajie Forest v4:995
Zhele, Zhelyu v5:91
Zhivkov, Todor v5:91
Zhou Dynasty v4:1056
Zhuang v3:208, v4:1056–1059
Zhuang language v4:1056
Zhujiang River v4:1056
Zimbabweans v1:606–611
Zo. *See* Chin
Zog, President and King v5:26
Zöl'fat v5:487
Zomi. *See* Chin
Zou. *See* Gaoshan
Zuider Zee v5:197
Zulu v1: 193, 612–617
Zumbi v2:16
Zun. *See* Li
Zweig, Stefan v5:59
Zwingli, Huldrych v5:478